Law and Violence Against Women
Cases and Materials on Systems of Oppression

ZEKE GIORGI LEGAL CLINIC
NORTHERN ILLINOIS UNIVERSITY

Law and Violence Against Women
Cases and Materials on Systems of Oppression

Beverly Balos

&

Mary Louise Fellows

CAROLINA
ACADEMIC
PRESS

700 KENT ST.
DURHAM, NC
27701

ISBN: 0–89089–567–8
LCCN: 93–74421

Carolina Academic Press
700 Kent Street
Durham, North Carolina 27701
(919) 489-7486
FAX (919) 493-5668

Printed in the United States of America

Contents

Table of Cases

The principal cases are in italic type. Other cases are in roman type. References are to pages.

Table of Constitutions, Statutes, and Regulations

The principal statutes and regulations are in italic type. Constitutional provisions and other statutes and regulations are in roman type. References are to pages.

Constitutions

Statutes

Federal

State

English

Federal Regulations

Table of Secondary Authorities

Principal authorities are in italic type. Other authorities are in roman type. References are to pages.

________, Feminist Jurisprudence: Grounding the Theories, 4 Berkeley Women's L.J. 191 (1989), 63, 150

John O. Calmore, Critical Race Theory, Archie Shepp, and Fire Music: Securing an Authentic Intellectual Life in a Multicultural World, 65 S. Cal. L. Rev. 2129 (1992), 105

Jane Caputi, Advertising Femicide: Lethal Violence Against Women in Pornography and Gorenography, in Femicide: The Politics of Woman Killing 203 (Jill Radford & Diana E.H. Russell eds., 1992), 593

________, The Sexual Politics of Murder, 3 Gender & Soc'y 437 (1989), 579

________, The Age of Sex Crime (1987), 612

Martha Chamallas, Feminist Constructions of Objectivity: Multiple Perspectives in Sexual and Racial Harassment Litigation, 1 Tex. J. Women & L. 95 (1992), 354

Lucie C. Cheng, Free, Indentured, Enslaved: Chinese Prostitutes in Nineteenth-Century America, 5 Signs 3 (1979), 524

Phyllis Chesler, A Woman's Right to Self-Defense: The Case of Aileen Carol Wuornos, 66 St. John's L. Rev. 933 (1993), 579

Chi. Defender, Dec. 18, 1915, quoted in Ralph Ginzburg, One Hundred Years of Lynchings 96 (1969), 390

Marvin A. Chirelstein, Federal Income Taxation (6th ed., 1991), 319

Ella E. Clark & Margot Evans, Sacagawea of the Lewis and Clark Expedition (1979), 36 n.12

Francis X. Clines, When Black Soldiers Were Hanged: A War's Footnote, N.Y. Times, Feb. 7, 1993, at 14, 392

Jean L. Cohen, Strategy or Identity: New Theoretical Paradigms and Contemporary Social Movements, 52 Soc. Res. 663 (1985), 114 n.11

Ruth Colker, Pornography and Privacy: Towards the Development of a Group Based Theory for Sex Based Intrusions of Privacy, 1 Law & Ineq. J. 191 (1983), 596

Patricia Hill Collins, Reply, 6 Gender & Soc'y 517 (1992), 64

________, *Black Feminist Thought: Knowledge, Consciousness, and the Politics of Empowerment (1990)*, 43, 55, 59 nn.3-4, 60 nn.5-6, 161 n.35, 162, 375, 485, 486, 597

Convention on The Elimination of All Forms of Sexual Exploitation of Women, Art. 6 (Revised Draft Mar. 1, 1993), 537, 561, 604

Madeleine Pelner Cosman, Christine de Pizan's Well-Tempered Feminism, in Christine de Pizan, A Medieval Woman's Mirror of Honor: The Treasury of the City of Ladies 11 (Madeleine Pelner Cosman ed. & Charity Cannon Willard trans., 1989), 9

Carrie G. Costello, Legitimate Bonds and Unnatural Unions: Race, Sexual Orientation, and Control of the American Family, 15 Harv. Women's L.J. 79 (1992), 159

Kimberlé Crenshaw, Whose Story Is It, Anyway? Feminist and Antiracist Appropriations of Anita Hill, in Race-ing Justice, En-gendering Power: Essays on Anita Hill, Clarence Thomas, and the Construction of Social Reality 402 (Toni Morrison ed., 1992), 315, 374

Phyllis Crocker, The Meaning of Equality for Battered Women Who Kill Men in Self-Defense, 8 Harv. Women's L.J. 121 (1985), 269, 279, 280

Angela Y. Davis, Women, Race and Class (1983), 10, 21 n.6, 104, 373, 374, 376, 391, 392

Richard Delgado, When a Story is Just a Story: Does Voice Really Matter?, 76 Va. L. Rev. 95 (1990), 106 n.3

Richard Delgado, Storytelling for Oppositionists and Others: A Plea for Narrative, 87 Mich. L. Rev. 2411 (1989), 108 n.5

John D'Emilio, Capitalism and Gay Identity, in Powers of Desire: The Politics of Sexuality 100 (Ann Snitow, Christine Stansell & Sharon Thompson eds., 1983), 82

Christine de Pizan, The Book of the City of Ladies, Part II, (Earl Jeffrey Richards trans., 1982), 6

Bonnie Thornton Dill, The Dialectics of Black Womanhood, 4 Signs 543 (1979), 485

Dorothy Dinnerstein, The Mermaid and the Minotaur: Sexual Arrangements and the Human Malaise (1976), 74 n.8

R. Emerson Dobash & Russell P. Dobash, Women, Violence and Social Change (1992), 183, 184, *223*

__________, *Wives: The 'Appropriate' Victims of Marital Violence, 2 Victimology 426 (1978), 185*

Andrea Dworkin, Living in Terror, Pain: Being a Battered Wife, in Violence Against Women: The Bloody Footprints 237 (Pauline B. Bart & Eileen Geil Moran eds., 1993), 216

__________, Women in the Public Domain: Sexual Harassment and Date Rape, in Sexual Harassment: Women Speak Out 1 (Amber Coverdale Sumrall & Dena Taylor eds., 1992), 303

__________, *Pornography: Men Possessing Women (1979), 596*

Julie K. Ehrhart & Bernice R. Sandler, Campus Gang Rape: Party Games? (Project on the Status and Education of Women, Assoc. of Am. Coll. 1985), 414

Susan Estrich, Palm Beach Stories, 11 Law & Phil. 5 (1992), 456, 460, 471

__________, *Sex at Work, 43 Stan. L. Rev. 813 (1991)*, 316, 317, 338, *339*

__________, *Rape, 95 Yale L.J. 1087 (1986), 421*

Lin Farley, Sexual Shakedown, The Sexual Harassment of Women on the Job (1978), 281

I. Elena Featherston, On Becoming a Dangerous Woman, in Sexual Harassment: Women Speak Out 71 (Amber Coverdale Sumrall & Dena Taylor eds., 1992), 285

Feminist Discourse, Moral Values, and the Law—A Conversation, 34 Buff. L. Rev. 11 (1984), 124

Kathleen J. Ferraro, Cops, Courts, and Woman Battering, in Violence Against Women: The Bloody Footprints 165 (Pauline B. Bart & Eileen Geil Moran eds., 1993), 244

Lucinda Finley, Breaking Women's Silence in Law: The Dilemma of the Gendered Nature of Legal Reasoning, 64 Notre Dame L. Rev. 886 (1989), 115

__________, A Break in the Silence: Including Women's Issues in a Torts Course, 41 Yale J.L. & Feminism 41 (1989), 320

Owen M. Fiss, Freedom and Feminism, 80 Geo. L.J. 2041 (1992), 630

Louise F. Fitzgerald, Science v. Myth: The Failure of Reason in the Clarence Thomas Hearings, 65 S. Cal. L. Rev. 1399 (1992), 282

Michel Foucault, The History of Sexuality (1976-84), 91 n.10, 407 n.15

Elizabeth V. Spelman, Inessential Woman: Problems of Exclusion in Feminist Thought (1988), 45

Elizabeth Cady Stanton, "Our Girls," 1872, in Beth M. Waggenspack, The Search for Self-Sovereignty: The Oratory of Elizabeth Cady Stanton 141 (1989), 25

Evan Stark & Anne Flitcraft, Woman-battering, Child Abuse and Social Heredity: What is the Relationship?, in Marital Violence (Norman Johnson ed., 1985), 221

Maria W. Stewart, Mrs. Stewart's Farewell Address To Her Friends In The City Of Boston, in Maria W. Stewart, America's First Black Woman Political Writer, Essays and Speeches 67 (Marilyn Richardson ed., 1987), 22

__________, America's First Black Woman Political Writer: Essays and Speeches (Marilyn Richardson ed., 1987), 18 n.3, 21 nn.5-6 & 8, 22 n.9, 24 n.10, 25

Saundra Sturdevant & Brenda Stoltzfus, Disparate Threads of the Whole: An Interpretive Essay, in Let the Good Times Roll: Prostitution and the U.S. Military in Asia 300 (1992), 522, 537

Carl F. Stychin, Exploring the Limits: Feminism and the Legal Regulation of Gay Male Pornography, 16 Vt. L. Rev. 857 (1992), 595

Fran Sugar & Lana Fox, Nistum Peyako Séht'wawin Iskwewak: Breaking Chains, 3 Can. J. Women & L. 465 (1989), 394 nn.5-6

Harriet Taylor & John Stuart Mill, The Subjection of Women (1869), 143 n.21

__________, Enfranchisement of Women (1851), 143 n.21

__________, Early Essays on Marriage and Divorce (1832), 143 n.21

Thelma and Louise, Metro-Goldwyn-Mayer 1991, written by Callie Khouri; directed by Ridley Scott, 457 n.34

Thirty Years of Lynching in the United States: 1889-1918 (NAACP 1919), 390

George C. Thomas, III, A Critique of the Anti-Pornography Syllogism, 52 Md. L. Rev. 122 (1993), 610

Kendall Thomas, Beyond the Privacy Principle, 92 Colum. L. Rev. 1431 (1992), 81, 181

Barrie Thorne, Book Review (reviewing Patricia Hill Collins, Black Feminist Thought: Knowledge, Consciousness, and the Politics of Empowerment (1991)), 6 Gender & Soc'y 515 (1992), 63

Thunder Bay: Ontario Native Women's Ass'n, Breaking Free: A Proposal for Change to Aboriginal Family Violence (Thunder Bay: Ontario Native Women's Ass'n), 398 n.9

Rosemarie Tong, Feminist Thought (1989), 143 n.21

Morrison Torrey, When Will We Be Believed? Rape Myths and the Idea of a Fair Trial in Rape Prosecutions, 24 U.C. Davis L. Rev. 1013 (1991), 444

Carla Trujillo, Chicana Lesbians: Fear and Loathing in the Chicano Community, in Chicana Lesbians: The Girls Our Mothers Warned Us About 186 (Carla Trujillo ed., 1991), 92

Mary Ann Tucker & Sharon Young, Dimensions (Dignity/San Diego Newsletter), 79

Mary Ellen Turpel, Aboriginal Peoples and the Canadian Charter: Interpretative Monopolies, Cultural Differences, 6 Can. Hum. Rts. Y.B. 3 (1989-90), 399 nn.10-11

U.S. Dep't of Labor, Office of Policy Planning and Research, The Negro Family: The Case for National Action (1965), 485

Venny Villapando, The Business of Selling Mail-Order Brides, in Making Waves,

Preface

This book grew out of our experience co-teaching a seminar on gender and the law in Fall 1990. As the seminar evolved in subsequent years and expanded from a weekly two-hour seminar to a three-hour course, we came to realize that concentrating on violence against women brings into sharp focus how violence operates on a continuum to inflict harm and constrain women's lives. Isolating women's experiences into separate categories of battering, sexual harassment, rape, prostitution, and pornography tends to obscure the pervasiveness of violence—or the threat of violence—in women's lives. Centering wholly on violence uncovers the interrelationships between harms that traditionally are viewed as separate and distinct phenomena. We can see how one form of violence supports other forms and how all forms share the same social dynamics. We also see how legal and social responses to one form of violence against women may influence, negatively and positively, behavior and attitudes about other forms. In this book we bring together materials that provide a context for extended thought and discussion about the operation of the continuum, the interconnections among the various forms of violence, and the particular forces functioning within each form.

We base our approach to issues of violence against women on three principles. First, although each act of violence takes place in a particularized context and involves the individual responsibility of the perpetrator, each act also is part of interlocking social and legal systems that support violence against women. Second, violence against women is a product of abilism, classism, heterosexism, racism/ethnocentrism, and sexism and can be addressed only by identifying how all the forms of oppression operate simultaneously. Third, it is worthwhile to work toward reform of the legal system to address issues of violence against women, even though looking to an institution that reflects the dominant segments of our society for solutions is problematic.

These principles are embodied in the organization of the book and in each of the chapters. The first three chapters provide historical background and a critical analytical framework to apply to the substantive areas of battering, sexual harassment, rape, prostitution, and pornography. In Chapter 1, we elaborate on the principles through historical essays and analysis. In Chapter 2 we explore the systems of oppression from a multi-disciplinary perspective. In Chapter 3 we complete the foundational structure upon which the succeeding chapters are built by presenting critiques of dominant legal discourse.

Chapters 4 through 8 are structured around the traditional categories of violence against women: battering, sexual harassment, rape, prostitution, and pornography. We planned each chapter to meet two goals: first, to present materials—including narratives, historical analysis, and social science and legal critiques—that present issues that are particular to that category of violence while at the same time challenging the categories themselves; second, to show the development of the law and the possible directions for legal reform.

The book concentrates on violence against adults. Child abuse, although clearly related, raises a unique set of concerns requiring different areas of concentration and analysis. Moreover, attention to children can sometimes lead to the minimization of the harm that women suffer. Children are viewed as always deserving of sympathy and protection while adult women often are not. To avoid the risk that women's harm would become invisible, issues about child abuse are discussed in this book only when they are relevant to an understanding of violence against adult women.

Editorial Conventions. Except for cases, we use ellipses to indicate omission of substantive material in the extracted sources. We delete footnotes and references without indicating the omission. For cases, we use ellipses to indicate deletions of footnotes and citations as well as of substantive material. Any footnotes that we include in cases or other materials are renumbered in order of appearance in the chapter. *Eds.* is used at the end of a footnote that we have added. The readings come from a variety of sources, all having a unique set of citation rules. For the most part, we have rearranged the information to conform to *The Bluebook: A Uniform System of Citation* (15th ed. 1991). The typeset recommended by *The Bluebook* is not followed.

Acknowledgments

We are grateful to the many students who have provided helpful comments and suggestions during our work on this book. We especially want to thank Jill Bergquist, Johanna Bond, Renee Cogdell, Charlene D'Cruz, Jessica Hughes, and Kari Nordstrom who as University of Minnesota law students provided research assistance and gave generously of their time to meet our schedule. Our special thanks go to Susan Gibel who, during the last year, was always willing to do one more research project right away. In addition, we are indebted to the staff of the University of Minnesota law library for their exceptional work assisting us with this project. Tami Gierloff, Marci Hoffman, George Jackson, Suzanne Thorpe, and Julia Wentz were tireless in their efforts in obtaining research materials and pursuing the answers to obscure questions. Special thanks also are due to Linda Shimmin for her extraordinary administrative and secretarial support over the period of the writing of this book. We also acknowledge the generous research support provided by the University of Minnesota Law School.

We also thank Margaret Baldwin, Martha Chamallas, Adrienne Davis, Evelina Giobbe, and Stephanie Wildman for reading early drafts of chapters and providing us encouragement for this project. We also benefited greatly from the thoughtful editing provided by Katherine Tyler. While appreciating the complexity of the material, she helped us convey that complexity with greater clarity and directness.

Further, we want to recognize the support and patience of our dear friends, Jo Isgro, Kristin Lockhart, Toni McNaron, Eugenia Smith, and Katherine Tyler. Throughout the writing of this book they gave us words of encouragement and the sustaining diversion of long dinners and great conversation.

We also thank the following authors and copyright holders for permission to use their works:

Sharon Angella Allard, Rethinking Battered Woman Syndrome: A Black Feminist Perspective, 1 UCLA Women's L.J. 191. Copyright © 1991 by The Regents of the University of California. Originally published in 1 UCLA Women's Law Journal 191, Copyright 1991, The Regents of the University of California. All Rights Reserved. Reprinted by permission of the author and The Regents of the University of California.

Paula Gunn Allen, Who Is Your Mother? Red Roots of White Feminism, in The Sacred Hoop: Recovering the Feminine in American Indian Traditions (1986). Copyright © 1986, 1992 by Paula Gunn Allen. Reprinted by permission of Beacon Press.

Ann Althouse, Beyond King Solomon's Harlots: Women in Evidence, 65 S. Cal. L. Rev. 1265-77 (1992). Reprinted by permission of the author and the Southern California Law Review.

Ann Althouse, *Thelma and Louise* and the Law: Do Rape Shield Rules Matter? 25 Loyola L.A. L. Rev. 757 (1992). Copyright © 1992 by the Loyola of Los Angeles Law Review, all rights reserved. Reprinted by permission of the author and Loyola of Los Angeles Law Review.

Teresa L. Amott & Julie A. Matthaei, Race, Gender and Work: A Multicultural Economic History of Women in the United States (1991). Copyright © 1991 by Teresa Amott and Julie Matthaei. Reprinted by permission of South End Press, 116 S. Botolph Street, Boston, MA 02115.

Yvon Appleby, Disability and 'Compulsory Heterosexuality,' in Heterosexuality: A Feminism & Psychology Reader (Sue Wilkinson & Celia Kitzinger eds., 1993). Copyright © 1993 by Sage Publications Ltd.: London and Newbury Park. Reprinted by permission of the author, the editors, and Sage Publications.

Elvia R. Arriola, "What's the Big Deal?" Women in the New York City Construction Industry and Sexual Harassment Law, 1970-1985, 22 Colum. Hum. Rts. L. Rev. 21 (1990). Reprinted by permission of the author and Columbia Human Rights Law Review.

Jo-Ellen Asbury, African-American Women in Violent Relationships: An Exploration of Cultural Differences, in Violence in the Black Family: Correlates and Consequences 89 (Robert L. Hampton ed. 1987). Copyright © 1987 by Lexington Books. Reprinted by permission of Lexington Books, an imprint of Macmillan Publishing Company.

Margaret A. Baldwin, Split at the Root: Prostitution and Feminist Discourses of Law Reform, 5 Yale J.L. & Feminism 47 (1992). Reprinted by permission of the author.

Jacqueline Baker Barnhart, The Fair But Frail: Prostitution in San Francisco 1849-1900 (1986). Copyright © 1986 by Jacqueline Baker Barnhart. Reprinted by permission of the author and University of Nevada Press.

Kathleen Barry, Social Etiology of Crimes Against Women, 10 Victimology 164 (1985). Copyright © 1985 by Victimology Inc., all rights reserved. Reprinted by permission of the author and Victimology: An International Journal.

Marlene D. Beckman, Note, The White Slave Traffic Act: The Historical Impact of a Criminal Law Policy on Women, 72 Geo. L.J. 1111 (1984). Copyright © 1984 by The Georgetown Law Journal Association and Georgetown University. Reprinted by permission of the publisher.

Nasa Begum, Disabled Women and the Feminist Agenda, Originally published in Vol. 40 Feminist Rev. 70 (Spring 1992). Reprinted by permission of the author and Feminist Review.

Cynthia Grant Bowman, Street Harrassment and the Informal Ghettoization of Women, 106 Harv. L. Rev. 517 (1993). Reprinted by permission of the author and Harvard Law Review.

Cynthia Grant Bowman, The Arrest Experiments: A Feminist Critique, J. Crim. L. & Criminology, Volume 83, Issue #1, 201-208 (1992). Reprinted by permission of the author and special permission of Northwestern University School of Law.

Arthur Brittan & Mary Maynard, Sexism, Racism and Oppression (1984).

Copyright © 1984 by Arthur Brittan and Mary Maynard. Reprinted by permission of Blackwell Publishers.

Victoria Byerly, Hard Times Cotton Mill Girls: Personal Histories of Womanhood and Poverty in the South (1986). Copyright © 1986 by Cornell University. Reprinted by permission of the publisher, ILR Press, School of Industrial and Labor Relations, Cornell University, Ithaca, NY 14853-3901.

Patricia Cain, Feminism and the Limits of Equality. Originally published at 24 Ga. L. Rev. 803 (1990). Reprinted by permission of the author and Georgia Law Review.

Patricia Cain, Feminist Jurisprudence: Grounding the Theories, Vol.4 No.2, Berkeley Women's L.J. 191-214 (1989). Reprinted by permission of the author and Berkeley Women's Law Journal.

John O. Calmore, Critical Race Theory, Archie Shepp, and Fire Music: Securing an Authentic Intellectual Life in a Multicultural World, 65 S. Cal. L. Rev. 2129 (1992). Reprinted by permission of the author.

Jane Caputi, The Age of Sex Crime. Copyright © 1987 by Bowling Green University Popular Press. Reprinted by permission of the author and Bowling Green State University Popular Press.

Martha Chamallas, Feminist Constructions of Objectivity: Multiple Perspectives in Sexual and Racial Harassment Litigation, 1 Tex. J. Women & L. 95 (1992). Reprinted by permission of the author and Texas Journal of Women and the Law.

Lucie C. Cheng, Free, Indentured, Enslaved: Chinese Prostitutes in Nineteenth-Century America, 5 Signs 3 (1979). Copyright © 1979 by The University of Chicago. Reprinted by permission of the author and publisher, The University of Chicago Press.

Ruth Colker, Pornography and Privacy: Towards the Development of a Group Based Theory for Sex Based Intrusions of Privacy, 1 Law & Ineq. J. 191 (1983). Reprinted by permission of the author and Law & Inequality Journal.

Patricia Hill Collins, Reply, 6 Gender & Soc'y 517 (1992). Reprinted by permission of the author and Sage Publications.

Patricia Hill Collins, Black Feminist Thought: Knowledge, Consciousness, and the Politics of Empowerment (1990). Copyright © 1990. Reprinted by permission of the author and the publisher, Routledge, Chapman and Hall, Inc.

Madeleine Pelner Cosman, Christine de Pizan's Well-Tempered Feminism, in Christine de Pizan, A Medieval Woman's Mirror of Honor: The Treasury of the City of Ladies 11 (translated by Charity Cannon Willard, and edited by Madeleine Pelner Cosman, 1989). Copyright © 1989 by Madeleine Pelner Cosman. Reprinted by permission of Persea Books.

Carrie G. Costello, Legitimate Bonds and Unnatural Unions: Race, Sexual Orientation, and Control of the American Family, 15 Harv. Women's L.J. 79 (1992). Copyright © 1992 by the President and Fellows of Harvard College. Reprinted by permission of the author and Harvard Women's Law Journal.

Angela Y. Davis, Women, Race and Class (1983). Copyright © 1981 by Angela Y. Davis. Reprinted by permission of Random House, Inc.

John D'Emilio, Capitalism and Gay Identity, in Powers of Desire: The Politics of Sexuality 100 (Ann Snitow, Christine Stansell, & Sharon Thompson eds., 1983). Copyright © 1983 by Ann Snitow, Christine Stansell, and Sharon Thompson. Reprinted by permission of Monthly Review Foundation.

Christine de Pizan, The Book of the City of Ladies, Part II (translated by Earl Jeffrey Richards 1982). Copyright © 1982 by Persea Books, Inc. Reprinted by permission of Persea Books, Inc.

R. Emerson Dobash & Russell P. Dobash, Women, Violence, and Social Change (1992). Copyright © 1992. Reprinted by permission of the authors and Routledge.

R. Emerson Dobash & Russell P. Dobash, Wives: The 'Appropriate' Victims of Marital Violence. Copyright © 1978 Victimology Inc., all rights reserved. Reprinted by permission from the authors and Victimology: An International Journal, Volume 2, Numbers 3-4, 426-36.

Andrea Dworkin, Living in Terror, Pain: Being a Battered Wife, in Violence Against Women: The Bloody Footprints 237 (Pauline B. Bart & Eileen Geil Moran eds., 1993). Copyright © 1993 by Sociologists for Women in Society. Reprinted by permission of the author. The unabridged version of this essay, What Battery Really Is, appears in Letters from a War Zone by Andrea Dworkin (Lawrence Hill Books, 1993).

Andrea Dworkin, Women in the Public Domain: Sexual Harassment and Date Rape, in Sexual Harassment: Women Speak Out 1 (Amber Coverdale Sumrall & Dena Taylor eds., 1992). Copyright © 1992 by Andrea Dworkin. Reprinted by permission of the author.

Andrea Dworkin, Pornography: Men Possessing Women (1979). Copyright © 1979, 1980, 1981 by Andrea Dworkin. Reprinted by permission of Andrea Dworkin.

Susan Estrich, Palm Beach Stories, 11 Law & Phil. 5 (1992). Copyright © 1992 by Kluwer Academic Publishers. Reprinted by permission of the author and Kluwer Academic Publishers.

Susan Estrich, Sex at Work, 43 Stan. L. Rev. 813 (1991). Copyright © 1992 by the Board of Trustees of the Leland Stanford Junior University. Reprinted by permission of the author, Stanford Law Review, and Fred B. Rothman & Company.

Susan Estrich, Rape, 95 Yale L.J. 1087-1184 (1986). Reprinted by permission of the author, The Yale Law Journal Company, and Fred B. Rothman & Company.

I. Elena Featherston, On Becoming a Dangerous Woman, in Sexual Harassment: Women Speak Out 71 (Amber Coverdale Sumrall & Dena Taylor eds., 1992). Copyright © 1992 by Amber Coverdale Sumrall & Dena Taylor. Reprinted by permission of the author and The Crossing Press.

Feminist Discourse, Moral Values, and the Law—A Conversation, 34 Buff. L. Rev. 11 (1984). Reprinted by permission of Buffalo Law Review.

Kathleen J. Ferraro, Cops, Courts, and Woman Battering, in Violence Against Women: The Bloody Footprints 165 (Pauline B. Bart & Eileen Geil Moran eds., 1993). Copyright © 1993 by Sociologists for Women in Society. Reprinted by permission of the author, Pauline B. Bart, and Sage Publications.

Lucinda Finley, Breaking Women's Silence in Law: The Dilemma of the Gendered Nature of Legal Reasoning, 64 Notre Dame L. Rev. Issue 5, 886-910 (1989). Copyright © by Notre Dame Law Review, University of Notre Dame. Reprinted by permission of the author and Notre Dame Law Review. Carolina Academic Press bears responsibility for any errors that may have occurred in reprinting or editing.

Owen M. Fiss, Freedom and Feminism, 80 Geo. L.J. 2041 (1992). Copyright © 1992 by The Georgetown Law Journal Association and Georgetown University. Reprinted by permission of the author and the publisher.

Louise F. Fitzgerald, Science v. Myth: The Failure of Reason in the Clarence Thomas Hearings, 65 S. Cal. L. Rev. 1399-1409 (1992). Reprinted by permission of the author and Southern California Law Review.

Jody Freeman, The Feminist Debate Over Prostitution Reform: Prostitutes' Rights Groups, Radical Feminists, and the (Im)Possibility of Consent, 5 Berkeley Women's L.J. 75-105. Copyright © 1990 by Berkeley Women's Law Journal. Reprinted by permission of the author and Berkeley Women's Law Journal.

Mary Joe Frug, Progressive Feminist Legal Scholarship: Can We Claim "A Different Voice"?, from Postmodern Legal Feminism Copyright © 1992 by Routledge, Chapman & Hall, Inc. Reprinted by permission of publisher, Routledge, Chapman and Hall, Inc.

Marilyn Frye, Oppression, in The Politics of Reality: Essays in Feminist Theory. Copyright © 1983 by Marilyn Frye. Reprinted by permission of The Crossing Press, Freedom, CA.

Marilyn Frye, To Be and Be Seen, The Politics of Reality: Essays in Feminist Theory, Copyright © 1983 by Marilyn Frye. Reprinted by permission of The Crossing Press, Freedom, CA.

Diana Fuss, Essentially Speaking: Feminism, Nature and Difference (1989). Copyright © 1989 by Routledge, Chapman and Hall, Inc. Reprinted by permission of the publisher, Routledge, Chapman and Hall, Inc.

Tracey Gardner, Racism in Pornography in the Women's Movement, in Take Back the Night: Women on Pornography 105 (Laura Lederer ed., 1980). Reprinted by permission of William Morrow & Co. Inc.

B. Glenn George, The Back Door: Legitimizing Sexual Harassment Claims, 73 B.U.L. Rev. 1 (1993). Reprinted by permission of the author and Boston University Law Review.

Paula Giddings, When and Where I Enter: The Impact of Black Women on Race and Sex in America (1984). Copyright © 1984 by Paula Giddings. Reprinted by permission of the author and William Morrow & Co., Inc.

Angela Ginorio & Jane Reno, "Violence in the Lives of Latina Women," in "The Speaking Profits Us: Violence in the Lives of Women of Color" 13 (Maryviolet Burns, ed., Center for the Prevention of Sexual & Domestic Violence, Seattle, WA 1986). Copyright © 1986 by Center for the Prevention of Sexual and

Domestic Violence, Seattle, WA. Reprinted by permission of the authors and publisher.

Evelina Giobbe, Prostitution: Buying the Right to Rape in Rape and Sexual Assault III: A Research Handbook 143 (Ann Wolbert Burgess ed. 1991). Reprinted by permission of the author and editor.

Evelina Giobbe, Confronting the Liberal Lies About Prostitution, in The Sexual Liberals and the Attack on Feminism 67 (Dorchen Leidholdt & Janice G. Raymond eds., 1990). Reprinted by permission of the author, D. Leidholdt, J. Raymond, eds., The Sexual Liberals and the Attack on Feminism, Teacher's College Press, 1234 Amsterdam Ave., New York, NY 10027.

Susan Griffin, Pornography and Silence: Culture's Revenge Against Nature. Copyright © 1981 by Susan Griffin. Reprinted by permission of HarperCollins Publishers, Inc.

Nora E. Groce, Special Groups at Risk of Abuse: The Disabled in Abuse and Victimization Across the Life Span 223 (Martha B. Straus ed., 1988). Reprinted by permission of the editor and The John Hopkins University Press, Baltimore/London.

Jane Gross, Abused Women Who Kill Seek a Way Out of Cells, N.Y. Times, Sept. 15, 1992. Copyright © 1992 by The New York Times Company. Reprinted by permission.

Jacquelyn Dowd Hall, Revolt Against Chivalry: Jessie Daniel Ames and the Women's Campaign Agsinst Lynching. Copyright © 1979 by Columbia University Press, New York. Reprinted by permission of the author and Columbia University Press.

Nancy Hammond, Lesbian Victims and the Reluctance to Identify Abuse, in Naming the Violence: Speaking Out About Lesbian Battering 190 (Kerry Lobel ed., 1986). Copyright © 1986 by National Coalition Against Domestic Violence. Reprinted by permission of the author and Seal Press.

Cheryl I. Harris, Whiteness as Property, 106 Harv. L. Rev. 1707 (1993). Reprinted by permission of the author and Harvard Law Review.

Lynne N. Henderson, Review Essay: What Makes Rape a Crime?, 3 Berkeley Women's L.J. 193 (1987-88). Reprinted by permission of the author.

bell hooks, Ain't I a Woman: Black Women and Feminism (1981). Copyright © 1981 by Gloria Watkins. Reprinted by permission of the author and South End Press.

bell hooks & Cornel West, Breaking Bread: Insurgent Black Intellectual Life. Copyright © 1991 by Gloria Watkins and Cornel West. Reprinted by permission of South End Press.

Diane Hugs, Mandatory Doctor's Visit, in Sexual Harassment: Women Speak Out (Amber Coverdale Sumrall & Dena Taylor eds., 1992). Copyright © 1992 by Amber Coverdale Sumrall & Dena Taylor. Reprinted by permission of the author and The Crossing Press.

Sheila Jeffreys, Eroticizing Women's Subordination, in The Sexual Liberals and the Attack on Feminism 132 (Dorchen Leidholdt & Janice G. Raymond eds., 1990). Reprinted by permission of D. Leidholdt, J. Raymond, eds., The Sexual

Liberals and the Attack on Feminism, Teacher's College Press, 1234 Amsterdam Ave., N.Y. N.Y. 10027.

Jean Johnston, Out in the Cold in Sex Work: Writings by Women in the Sex Industry 29 (Frédérique Delacoste & Priscilla Alexander eds. 1988). Reprinted by permission of Cleis Press.

James T. R. Jones, Battered Spouses' State Law Damage Actions Against the Unresponsive Police, 23 Rutgers L.J. 1 (1991). Reprinted by permission of the author and Rutgers Law Journal.

Jenny Kitzinger, Sexual Violence and Compulsory Heterosexuality, 2 Feminism & Psychol. 399 (1992). Reprinted by permission of the author, Sage Publications Limited, and Feminism and Psychology.

Andrew Koppelman, Note, The Miscegenation Analogy: Sodomy Law as Sex Discrimination, Yale L.J. Vol.98, 145-64 (1988). Reprinted by permission of the author, The Yale Law Journal Company, and Fred B. Rothman & Company.

Laura Lederer, Then and Now: An Interview with a Former Pornography Model, in Take Back the Night: Women on Pornography 57 (Laura Lederer ed., 1980). Copyright © 1980 by Laura Lederer. Reprinted by permission of William Morrow & Co. Inc.

Christine Littleton, Women's Experience and the Problem of Transition: Perspectives on Male Battering of Women, 1989 U. Chi. Legal F. 23. Reprinted by permission of the author and University of Chicago Legal Forum.

Gloria Lockett, What Happens When You Are Arrested, in Sex Work: Writings by Women in the Sex Industry 39 (Frédérique Delacoste & Priscilla Alexander eds., 1988). Reprinted by permission of Cleis Press.

Paul A. Lombardo, Miscegenation, Eugenics, and Racism: Historical Footnotes to *Loving v. Virginia*, 21 U.C. Davis L. Rev. 421 (1988). Copyright © 1988 by the Regents of the University of California. Reprinted with permission of the author and the University of California Davis Law Review.

María C. Lugones and Elizabeth V. Spelman, Have We Got a Theory For You! Feminist Theory, Cultural Imperialism and the Demand for "The Woman's Voice," 6 Women's Stud. F. 573 (1983). Reprinted by permission of the authors.

Catharine A. MacKinnon, Pornography as Defamation and Discrimination, 71 Bost. U.L. Rev. 793 (1991). Reprinted by permission of the author and Boston University Law Review.

Catharine A. MacKinnon, Reflections on Sex Equality Under Law, 100 Yale L.J. 1281-1328 (1991). Reprinted by permission of the author, The Yale Law Journal Company, and Fred B. Rothman & Company.

Catharine A. MacKinnon, Toward a Feminist Theory of the State (1989). Copyright © 1989 by Catharine A. Mackinnon. Reprinted by permission of the author and Harvard University Press, Cambridge, Mass.

Catharine A. MacKinnon, Feminism Unmodified: Discourses on Life and Law (1987). Copyright © 1987 by the President and Fellows of Harvard College. Reprinted by permission of the author and Harvard University Press, Cambridge, MA.

Catharine A. MacKinnon, Sexual Harassment of Working Women: A Case of

Sex Discrimination (1979). Copyright © 1979 by Yale University. Reprinted by permission of the author and Yale University Press, publisher.

Melton A. McLauin, Celia, A Slave (1991). Copyright © 1991 by The University of Georgia Press. Reprinted by permission.

Cathy McPherson, Violence Against Women with Disabilities, 11 Canadian Woman Studies 49 (1991). Originally appeared in Canadian Woman Studies/les cahiers de la femme "Violence Against Women," vol.11, no.4 (Summer 1991). Reprinted by permission of the author and Canadian Woman Studies.

Kathleen Mahoney, The Canadian Consitutional Approach to Freedom of Expression in Hate Propaganda and Pornography, 55 Law & Contemp. Probs. 77 (Winter 1992). Copyright © 1993 by Law and Contemporary Problems, Duke University. Reprinted by permission of the author and Law and Contemporary Problems.

Martha Mahoney, Exit: Power and the Idea of Leaving in Love, Work, and the Confirmation Hearings, 65 S. Cal. L. Rev. 1283 (1991). Reprinted by permission of the author.

Martha Mahoney, Legal Images of Battered Women: Redefining the Issue of Separation, 90 Mich. L. Rev. 1 (1991). Reprinted by permission of the author and Michigan Law Review.

Samuel Marcosson, Harassment on the Basis of Sexual Orientation: A Claim of Sex Discrimination Under Title VII, 81 Geo. L.J. 1 (1992). Copyright © 1992 by The Georgetown Law Journal Association and Georgetown University. Reprinted by permission of the author and the publisher.

David Margolick, "A Mixed Marriage's 25th Anniversary of Legality," June 12, 1992. Copyright © 1992/1993 by The New York Times Company. Reprinted by permission.

Michigan Compiled Laws §§ 750.520 a-e, g-j, 1 (1991). Copyright ©by West Publishing Company. Reprinted by permission of Michigan Compiled Laws Annotated.

Minnesota Supreme Court Task Force for Gender Fairness in the Courts, Final Report, first published in 15 Wm. Mitchell L. Rev. 826 (1989). Reprinted by permission of William Mitchell Law Review and the Minnesota Supreme Court.

Toni Morrison, Introduction: Friday on the Potomac, in Race-ing Justice, Engendering Power: Essays on Anita Hill, Clarence Thomas, and the Construction of Social Reality vii (Toni Morrison ed., 1992). Copyright © 1992 by Toni Morrison. Reprinted by permission of International Creative Management, Inc.

Margo L. Nightingale, Judicial Attitudes and Differential Treatment: Native Women in Sexual Assault Cases, 23 Ottawa L. Rev. 71 (1991). Reprinted by permission of the author.

Donna Marie Niles, Confessions of a Priestesstute, in Sex Work: Writings by Women in the Sex Industry 148 (Frédérique Delacoste & Priscilla Alexander eds., 1988). Reprinted by permission of Cleis Press.

Frances E. Olsen, Statutory Rape: A Feminist Critique of Rights Analysis. Published originally in 63 Tex. L. Rev. 387 (1984). Copyright © 1984 Texas Law

Review Association. Reprinted by permission of the author and Texas Law Review.

Gail Pheterson, The Consequences of Unchastity, in Sex Work: Writings by Women in the Sex Industry 215 (Frédérique Delacoste & Priscilla Alexander eds., 1988). Reprinted by permission of Cleis Press.

Arthur F. Raper, The Tragedy of Lynching (1969). Copyright © 1933 by The University of North Carolina Press. Reprinted by permission.

Laura Reanda, Prostitution as a Human Rights Question: Problems and Prospects of United Nations Action, 13 Hum. Rts. Q. 202 (1991). Reprinted by permission of John Hopkins University Press.

Report of the Florida Supreme Court Gender Bias Study Commission, March 1990, in 42 Fla. L. Rev. 803 (1990). Reprinted by permission of Florida Law Review.

Adrienne Rich, Compulsory Hetereosexuality and Lesbian Existence, Blood, Bread, and Poetry: Selected Prose 1979-1985, at 23 (1986). Copyright © 1986 by Adrienne Rich. Reprinted by permission of the author and W.W. Norton & Company, Inc.

Mardi Richmond, Just Trying to Have Some Fun, in Sexual Harassment: Women Speak Out 208 (Amber Coverdale Sumrall & Dena Taylor eds., 1992). Copyright © 1992 by Amber Coverdale Sumrall & Dena Taylor. Reprinted by permission of the author and The Crossing Press.

Stephanie Riger, Gender Dilemmas in Sexual Harassment Policies and Procedures, 46 Am. Psychologist 497 (1991). Copyright © 1991 by the American Psychological Association. Reprinted by permission of the author and the American Psychological Association.

Nilda Rimonte, Domestic Violence Among Pacific Asians, in Making Waves: An Anthology of Writings by and About Asian American Women 327 (Asian Women United of California ed., 1989). Copyright ©1989 by Asian Women United. Reprinted by permission of the author and Beacon Press.

Kim Romenesko and Eleanor M. Miller, The Second Step in Double Jeopardy: Appropriating the Labor of Female Street Hustlers, 35 Crime & Delinq. 109 (1989). Reprinted by permission of Sage Publications.

Diana E.H. Russell, Pornography and Rape: A Causal Model, 9 Pol. Psychol. 41 (1988). Reprinted by permission of the author and Plenum Publishing Corporation.

Peggy Reeves Sanday, Fraternity Gang Rape: Sex, Brotherhood, and Privilege on Campus (1990). Copyright © 1990 by New York University. Reprinted by permission of New York University Press.

Susan Schechter, Women and Male Violence: The Visions and Struggles of the Battered Women's Movement (1982). Copyright ©1992 by Susan Schechter. Reprinted by permission of South End Press.

Neil Larry Shumsky, Tacit Acceptance: Respectable Americans and Segregated Prostitution, 1870-1910, 19 J. Soc. Hist. 665 (1985/1986). Reprinted by permission of Journal of Social History.

Mimi H. Silbert & Ayala M. Pines, Pornography and Sexual Abuse of Women, 10 Sex Roles 857 (1984). Reprinted by permission of Mimi Silbert and Plenum Publishing Corporation.

Carol Smart, Feminism and the Power of Law (1989). Copyright ©1989 by Routledge. Reprinted by permission of the author and Routledge.

Melissa Spatz, A "Lesser" Crime: A Comparative Study of Legal Defenses for Men Who Kill Their Wives, 24 Colum. J.L. & Soc. Probs. 597 (1991). Reprinted by permission of Columbia Journal of Law & Social Problems.

Elizabeth Cady Stanton, "Our Girls," 1872, in Beth M. Waggenspack, The Search for Self-Sovereignty: The Oratory of Elizabeth Cady Stanton 141 (1989). Copyright © 1989 by Beth M. Waggenspack, Greenwood Publishing Group, Inc., Westport, CT, an imprint of Greenwood Publishing Group, Inc., Westport, CT. Reprinted with permission.

Maria W. Stewart, Mrs. Stewart's Farewell Address To Her Friends In The City of Boston, in Maria W. Stewart, America's First Black Woman Political Writer: Essays and Speeches 67 (Marilyn Richardson ed., 1987). Copyright © 1987 by Marilyn Richardson. Reprinted by permission of Indiana University Press.

Saundra Sturdevant & Brenda Stoltzfus, Disparate Threads of the Whole: An Interpretive Essay in Let the Good Times Roll: Prostitution and the U.S. Military in Asia 300 (1992). Copyright © 1992 by The New Press. Reprinted by permission.

Kendall Thomas, Beyond the Privacy Principle. This article originally appeared at 92 Colum. L. Rev. 1431 (1992). Reprinted by permission of the author and Columbia Law Review.

Carla Trujillo, Chicana Lesbians: Fear and Loathing in the Chicano Community, in Chicana Lesbians: The Girls Our Mothers Warned Us About (Carla Trujillo ed., 1991). Copyright © 1991 by Third Woman Press. Reprinted by permission of the author and Third Women Press.

Venny Villapando, The Business of Selling Mail-Order Brides, 318 in Making Waves, An Anthology of Writings By and About Asian American Women 318 (Asian Women United of California ed., 1989). Copyright © 1989 by Asian Women United. Reprinted by permission of Beacon Press.

Judith Walkowitz, Prostitution and Victorian Society: Women, Class, and the State (1980). Copyright © 1980 by Cambridge University Press. Reprinted by permission of the author and Cambridge University Press.

Barbara Faye Waxman, Hatred: The Unacknowledged Dimension in Violence Against Disabled People, 9 Sexuality & Disability 185 (1991). Reprinted by permission of the author and Human Sciences Press, Inc.

Robin L. West, The Feminist-Conservative Anti-Pornography Alliance and the 1986 Attorney General's Commission on Pornography Report, 4 Am. B. Found. Res. J. 681 (1987). Reprinted by permission of the author.

Charity Cannon Willard, The Franco-Italian Professional Writer: Christine de Pizan, in Medieval Women Writers 333 (Katharina M. Wilson ed., 1984). Copyright © 1984 by the University of Georgia Press. Reprinted by permission of The University of Georgia Press.

Joan Williams, Dissolving the Sameness/Difference Debate: A Post-Modern Path Beyond Essentialism in Feminist and Critical Race Theory, 1991 Duke L.J. 296. Reprinted by permission of the author and Duke Law Journal.

Sarah Winnemucca, The Way Agents Get Rich, in Native American Testimony: A Chronicle of Indian-White Relations From Prophecy to the Present 1492-1992, at 198 (Peter Nabokov ed., 1991). Copyright © Peter Nabokov 1978, 1991. Published by Penguin Group, New York in 1991 by Viking Penguin, a division of Penguin Books USA, Inc. Reprinted by permission of Susan Bergholz Literary Services, New York.

Gail Elizabeth Wyatt, The Sociocultural Context of African-American and White American Women's Rape, 48 J. Soc. Issues 77 (1992). Reprinted by permission of the author.

LAW AND VIOLENCE AGAINST WOMEN

Chapter 1

Glimpses of the Past/ Signposts for the Future

The aim of this chapter is to recover the words of past women thinkers and activists, not only to reestablish connections to prior generations but also to establish a historical background for the consideration of an analysis of violence against women. These selective writings provide a glimpse into the intellectual thought that is the foundation for the modern-day understanding in the United States of women, gender, sexuality, and the role of law in women's lives.

Our choice of authors here has been guided by our understanding of violence against women as related simultaneously to abilities, class, gender, race/ethnicity, and sexual orientation. The four authors we have chosen are Christine de Pizan, a fourteenth-century Franco-Italian writer; Maria Stewart, a free African-American woman who in 1832 became the first native-born woman in the United States to make a public speech; Elizabeth Cady Stanton, a white middle-class woman who was viewed by women within the nineteenth-century suffrage movement as one of its radical leaders; and Sarah Winnemucca, a Paiute woman who became a leading critic of U.S. Indian policy in the late nineteenth century. We introduce each woman's writings by including historical and biographical materials that place her ideas and observations in a political context so that each author and her work can be considered in a multi-dimensional way.

The excerpts from Pizan's *The Book of the City of Ladies* and from Stanton's speech "Our Girls" are clear about how men through their social, religious, and political institutions constrain women from achieving their potential. Neither writer accounts for the constraints experienced by women because of racism and classism; they focus on describing the lives of women like themselves who enjoyed race and class privilege. In contrast, the excerpt from Stewart's "Farewell Address to Her Friends In the City of Boston" focuses on racism and classism as well as on sexism in the United States during the antebellum period. Winnemucca's chronicle *Life Among the Paiutes* describes the constraints she and her tribe experience because of U.S. imperialism, made manifest especially in forced removal of her tribe from its lands. A common theme found in each of the authors' works is how legal and social institutions support and reinforce the control of those who are in a position to exercise power. Each author, however, observes and understands the exercise of that power and its consequences in a particular way that derives from her experiences and societal position.

The selections found in this chapter are not representative of women thinkers throughout history. We should remember that we have available the words only of those women who had access to public forums because of their social, political, or economic status. The historical essays and analysis read together, however, introduce us to the interlocking social and legal systems that support violence against women.

Charity Cannon Willard, The Franco-Italian Professional Writer: Christine de Pizan, in *Medieval Women Writers* 333–40 (Katharina M. Wilson ed., 1984)

[Christine de Pizan's] writings were far from unappreciated in her own lifetime and even during the century after her death. She was forgotten for a time because of the change in taste which threw nearly all medieval French literature into eclipse. Rediscovered toward the end of the eighteenth century, she was then alternately praised to the skies and denigrated by a prejudiced literary criticism which preferred to regard her as a woman rather than a remarkably innovative writer. She has been enthusiastically adopted by latter-day feminists, sometimes for reasons that would undoubtedly have astonished her, and she has been disdained because she was an intellectual woman . . . .Both sorts of judgment were too often based on an inadequate knowledge of what Christine wrote, due in many cases to the lack of modern editions. It is only in the last half century that a serious effort has been made to improve this situation, and only recently has there been a solid basis for judging her works as a whole and her true contribution as a writer.

It is now becoming clear that Christine de Pizan should be viewed as one of the writers who marked the transition in France between the so-called later Middle Ages and the Renaissance. Her role was predestined by the circumstances of her life, for born in Venice but spending most of her years in Paris, she was able to combine her Italian heritage with her knowledge of French life and thought as she experienced them.

Christine was born around 1365 into a somewhat unusual family. Both her father and [her maternal] grandfather belonged to the limited circle of university-educated men of their day, and both were public officials of the Venetian Republic. They had originally known each other as fellow students at the University of Bologna, where Christine's father. . .received a medical degree in 1343 and held a chair of astrology from then until 1356. . . .Less is known of Christine's grandfather, Tommaso Mondini of Forli, except that it was through his influence that [Christine's father]. . .went to Venice and subsequently married his daughter.

Soon after Christine's birth, her father returned to Bologna to look after some property he owned there. He was then. . .[offered the opportunity] to go to Paris to the court of Charles V . . . .It was an era when kings thought it advantageous to have official astrologers to advise them on medical, scientific, and even political matters . . . .He agreed to go for one year, but having been persuaded by the king to remain, in 1368 he sent for his family to join him.

So it was that Christine grew to maturity in the shadow of the court of Charles V, one of the most intellectual and forward-looking monarchs of his day. . . .To judge from Christine's recollections of her father, along with being an astrologer he was an accomplished mathematician with an interest in speculative natural philosophy (the ancestor of modern physics), all of which had a profound influence on her intellectual development—even though she was denied anything more than the elementary education which was then permitted to young girls.

By the time she was fifteen, a husband was chosen for her—a young notary, Etienne de Castel, who must also have had a certain amount of university training, for he is often given the title of Maître de Castel in official records. In 1380, the year of their marriage, he received an appointment as royal secretary which not only opened the way to a promising career but, in his attachment to the royal chancellery, assured his contact with the young men destined to become France's first humanists. These men cultivated their Latin prose, read Petrarch and Boccaccio, and, in certain cases, exchanged letters with. . .Italian counterparts . . . .Therefore, if Christine herself was denied the education she longed for, she at least spent her early years in the company of educated men.

The marriage, which was a happy one, resulted in the birth of two sons and a daughter. Problems arose in the household all too soon, however, because with the untimely death of Charles V and the minority of the pleasure-loving Charles VI, the studious, middle-class courtiers of the earlier reign were no longer held in high regard. Furthermore, Tommaso's health began to fail, and he died in relative poverty around 1387. Far more devastating was the death of Etienne de Castel some three years later . . . .Christine's sorrow was profound and nothing in her previous life had prepared her for the responsibilities she was now obliged to assume, but it was out of these misfortunes that her career as a writer developed.

Although Christine herself explains that during her early years of widowhood she turned to writing poetry in search of consolation for and distraction from the problems which beset her, this does not explain how she dealt with her serious financial problems during the ten years between the death of her husband and the beginning of her career as a writer. On the basis of manuscript copies of her works which have been identified in recent years as autographs, it now seems possible to suggest that she probably occupied herself as a copyist, employed in the book trade which was beginning to flourish in Paris at the end of the fourteenth century. This was one of the few profitable occupations open to women, and Christine's connections with the professional notaries at the royal court and with Giles Malet, the librarian of the royal library in the Louvre, as well as her subsequent close association with certain illustrators of manuscripts would all lend support to such an idea. . . .

Eventually, as her poetry began to meet with a certain success, she wrote on other themes—mythology, events at the royal court, and so-called courtly love—for in the final years of the fourteenth century the court of Charles VI was enjoying a somewhat artificial revival of earlier chivalric customs. . . .By 1402, the date of the first collection of her poetry, she had put together the *Cent balades* as well as cycles of the other forms. Both in the *Cent balades* and in a series of *rondeaux* she told the story of love affairs which ended in deception for the lovers, especially the woman. Disillusionment resulting from the false perceptions bred by the conventions of courtly love was to become one of her principal themes, along with the highly original theme of the sorrows of widowhood.

In the meantime, as she explained in her most autobiographical work, the *Avision-Christine*, her attention had turned to more serious matters; she read ancient history, Boethius' *The Consolation of Philosophy*, . . .and the lengthy medieval commentary on Ovid's *Metamorphoses*, the *Ovide moralisé*. The most significant result of her studies was the allegorical, mythological work entitled the *Epître d'Othea, la deesse, que elle envoya a Hector de Troye, quant il estoit en l'aage de quinze ans*. This took the form of a letter from the goddess of wisdom to a young man on the formation of a perfect knight, consisting of one hundred quatrains inspired by mythology or Trojan history, with moral and theological commentaries based on an astonishing variety of sources. Although little to the taste of modern readers, it proved to be one of her most popular works among her contemporaries.

Christine's new interests were further encouraged, around 1402, by a debate over the merits of Jean de Meung's part of the *Roman de la rose* in which she became engaged with several young Parisian humanists. Christine considered the poem much overrated by certain of her contemporaries. . . .

[In this debate she attacked the poem], especially the slander heaped on women not only by Jean de Meung but by the whole tradition of misogynistic literature. Some of the reactions of the Parisian intellectuals were far from courteous, illustrating the attitudes about which Christine was complaining, but she did not hesitate to answer the attacks with eloquence and considerable wit. . . .The whole discussion, in spite of the heat it apparently generated, is best understood as a sort of intellectual exercise inspired by debates among Italian humanists. Its greatest importance for Christine was that it gave her considerable publicity as a defender of her sex and encouraged her to undertake even more ambitious objectives.

She next turned her attention to two more long allegorical works. The first of these was a poem entitled the *Livre du chemin de long estude*, . . . [whose] basic inspiration was undoubtedly drawn from Dante's *Divine Comedy* . . . .The second allegory, the *Mutacion de fortune*, is also a long poem . . . .This rather diffuse work had the merit of attracting the duke of Burgundy's attention; he immediately commissioned Christine to write an official, and humanistic, biography of his brother, the late Charles V. . . .[After his death] his heir, John the Fearless, continued to interest himself in Christine's writings, procuring copies of them for the ducal library and making use of her talents for his own purposes. The court of Burgundy's marked taste for didactic literature further encouraged her interests in that direction.

Having become involved in the problem of women's role in society, Christine devoted two more long works to the subject. The first, the *Cité des dames*, described an allegorical city devoted to outstanding women. Inspired in large measure by Saint Augustine's *Civitate Dei* and Boccaccio's *De claris mulieribus*, translated into French for the first time in 1401, she described the foundation of this city under the direction of three goddesses, Justice, Reason, and Discretion, who appeared to her in a vision. The city was to be set aside for women who had made important contributions to society. Christine made use of famous women taken from Boccaccio, adapting his accounts to her own purposes; she also added examples from French history and even from contemporary society. More interesting than the biographies, however, are the discussions of women's problems in society carried on by Christine with her mentors as the city is being built. [The excerpts from de Pizan's writing that follow this biographical sketch are from this book. They involve an exchange between Rectitude (Discretion) and Christine regarding men's myths about the rape of women and the unreliability and untrustworthiness of women.]

The concept of the city once established, it seemed necessary to provide some guidelines for women who aspired to be worthy of it. This inspired Christine to write a companion volume, the *Livre des trois vertus*, dedicated to Marguerite of Burgundy on the occasion of her marriage to the French dauphin, Louis of Guienne. The book was intended, however, for women on all levels of society, suggesting how they could make the most of such opportunities as they might have. For the modern reader, it provides interesting glimpses of the life of women from different walks of life in fifteenth-century France. . . .

[Christine wrote educational treatises including] the *Livre de la paix*, dedicated to the duke of Guienne, the official head of the French government due to Charles VI's increasing insanity. The immediate inspiration was a Parisian revolution known as the Cabochien revolt, which created a crisis in the rapidly deteriorating political situation in the country. Not only was there a mortal struggle between two French factions, the Burgundians and the Armagnacs, but an excuse was provided for English intervention, leading eventually to Henry V's overwhelming victory at Agincourt in November 1415. After the failure of the Cabochien uprising, the duke of Burgundy was exiled from Paris and the young duke died unexpectedly, leaving the Armagnacs to institute a veritable reign of terror in Paris.

It was in these troubled times that Christine wrote her *Epître de la prison de vie humaine* to console Frenchwomen who had suffered so much already; worse was in store for them all. Christine's son, Jean de Castel, was by now one of the royal secretaries attached to the new dauphin, the future Charles VII. When, in May 1418, Paris was betrayed to Burgundian troops, Jean was obliged to flee from the city. Christine likewise sought refuge outside the city, probably in the royal convent at Poissy, where her daughter had been a nun for many years. It was from behind convent walls that she wrote her last two works. In the *Heures de contemplacion sur la Passion de nostre Seigneur*, the evocation of Mary grieving for her Son at the foot of the cross suggests that the work might have been written around 1425, after her own son's death in exile.

Christine's final poem is more joyous, written to celebrate the victory of Joan of Arc at Orléans and the coronation of Charles VII at Reims. Dated July 31, 1429, it was the first poem to celebrate the events which seemed miraculously to have brought about a change in France's fortunes. The fact that a young woman had brought this about seemed to crown Christine's efforts on behalf of womankind. Thus her long career ended on a note of triumph. Her voice was not heard again—a description of Paris written by Guillebert de Mets in 1434 refers to her in the past tense. . . .

Among those who owned and read her works were the leaders of the next generation of women, among others Marguerite of Austria and Mary of Hungary, both of them governors of the Netherlands for the Holy Roman

Emperor Charles V, and Louise of Savoy, the regent of France during the minority of Francis I. Anne of Brittany, twice queen of France, encouraged the printing of the *Livre des trois vertus*, as did Queen Leonora of Portugal. The multiplicity of paper copies which exist along with the handsome illuminated manuscripts, as well as the repeated printings, attest to the fact that these works were also read by more ordinary women.

From the beginning of her literary career, Christine had been preoccupied by renown, although she never seemed to doubt seriously that she would enjoy her share of it or that her name would be remembered after her death. . . .Perhaps the time has finally come when she can be appreciated for her true merits and contributions, for the record she left of her evolution from sorrowful young widow to defender of the worthiness of all women, would-be reformer of France, and educator of its future rulers. All this is truly remarkable and would not be paralleled for many years to come.

Christine de Pizan, *The Book of the City of Ladies, Part II*, 160–62, 164–66 (Earl Jeffrey Richards trans., 1982)

Refuting Those Men Who Claim Women Want to be Raped, Rectitude Gives Several Examples, and First of All, Lucretia.

Then I, Christine, spoke as follows, "My lady, I truly believe what you are saying, and I am certain that there are plenty of beautiful women who are virtuous and chaste and who know how to protect themselves well from the entrapments of deceitful men. I am therefore troubled and grieved when men argue that many women want to be raped and that it does not bother them at all to be raped by men even when they verbally protest. It would be hard to believe that such great villainy is actually pleasant for them."

She answered, "Rest assured, dear friend, chaste ladies who live honestly take absolutely no pleasure in being raped. Indeed, rape is the greatest possible sorrow for them. Many upright women have demonstrated that this is true with their own credible examples, just like Lucretia, the noblest Roman woman, supreme in chastity among Roman women, wife of a nobleman named Tarquin Collatinus. Now, when another man, Tarquin the Proud, son of King Tarquin, was greatly taken with love for this noble Lucretia, he did not dare to tell her because of the great chastity he saw in her, and, despairing of achieving his goal with presents or entreaties, he considered how he could have her through ruse. Claiming to be a close friend of her husband, he managed to gain entrance into her house whenever he wished, and once, knowing her husband was not at home, he went there and the noble lady received him with the honors due to someone whom she thought to be a close friend of her husband. However, Tarquin, who had something altogether different on his mind, succeeded in entering Lucretia's bedroom and frightened her terribly. Put briefly, after trying to coax her for a long time with promises, gifts, and favors, he saw that entreaties were getting him nowhere. He drew his sword and threatened to kill her if she made a sound and did not submit to his will. She answered that he should go ahead and kill her, for she would rather die than consent. Tarquin, realizing that nothing would help him, concocted a great malice, saying that he would publicly declare that he had found her with one of his sergeants. In brief, he so scared her with this threat (for she thought that people would believe him) that finally she suffered his rape. Lucretia, however, could not patiently endure this great pain, so that when daylight came she sent for her husband, her father, and her close relatives who were among the most powerful people in Rome, and, weeping and sobbing, confessed to them what had happened to her. Then, as her husband and relatives, who saw that she was overwhelmed with grief, were comforting her, she drew a knife from under her robe and said, 'This is how I absolve myself of sin and show my innocence. Yet I cannot free myself from the torment nor extricate myself from the pain. From now on no woman will ever live shamed and disgraced by Lucretia's example.' Having said this, she forcibly plunged the knife into her breast and collapsed dead before her husband and friends. They rushed like madmen to attack Tarquin. All Rome was moved to this cause, and they drove out the king and would have killed his son if they had found him. Never again was there a king in Rome. And because of this outrage perpetrated on Lucretia, so some claim, a law was enacted whereby a man would be executed for raping a woman, a law which is fitting, just, and holy." . . .

Refutation of the Inconstancy of Women. Christine Speaks, and Then Rectitude Answers Her Regarding the Inconstancy and Weakness of Certain Emperors.

"My lady, you have given me a remarkable account of the marvelous constancy, strength, endurance, and virtue of women. What more could one say about the strongest men who have lived? Men, especially writing in books, vociferously and unanimously claim that women in particular are fickle and inconstant, changeable and flighty, weak-hearted, compliant like children, and lacking all stamina. Are the men who accuse women of so much changeableness and inconstancy themselves so unwavering that change for them lies outside the realm of custom or common occurrence? Of course, if they themselves are not that firm, then it is truly despicable for them to accuse others of their own vice or to demand a virtue which they do not themselves know how to practice."

She replied, "Fair sweet friend, have you not heard the saying that the fool can clearly see the mote in his neighbor's eye but pays no attention to the beam hanging out of his own eye? Let me point out to you the contradiction in what these men say concerning the variability and inconstancy of women: since they all generally accuse women of being delicate and frail by nature, you would assume that they think that they are constant, or, at the very least, that women are less constant than they are. Yet they demand more constancy from women than they themselves can muster, for these men who claim to be so strong and of such noble condition are unable to prevent themselves from falling into many, even graver faults and sins, not all of them out of ignorance, but rather out of pure malice, knowing well that they are in the wrong. All the same, they excuse themselves for this by claiming it is human nature to sin. When a few women lapse (and when these men themselves, through their own strivings and their own power, are the cause), then as far as these men are concerned, it is completely a matter of fragility and inconstancy. It seems to me right, nevertheless, to conclude—since they claim women are so fragile—that these men should be somewhat more tolerant of women's weaknesses and not hold something to be a crime for women which they consider only a peccadillo for themselves. For the law does not maintain, nor can any such written opinion be found that permits them and not women to sin, that their vice is more excusable. In fact these men allow themselves liberties which they are unwilling to tolerate in women and thus they—and they are many—perpetrate many insults and outrages in word and deed. Nor do they deign to repute women strong and constant for having endured such men's harsh outrages. In this way men try in every question to have the right on their side—they want to have it both ways! You yourself have quite adequately discussed this problem in your *Epistre au Dieu d'Amour*.

"But as for your question whether men are so strong and so constant that they are justified in accusing others of inconstancy, if you consider, starting with wise men in Antiquity up to the present, I can tell you that, from books and from what you have seen in your own time and what you can see every day with your own eyes, not in simple men nor in those of low estate but in the most prominent, indeed, generally in the majority of them, you will be able to observe their perfection, strength, and constancy and to see how many wise, constant, and strong men there are and how great the need for them is.

"And if you want me to give you proof, from the past and present, of why they accuse women so often of this vice, as well as whether inconstancy or fickleness are found in men's hearts, you need only consider whether the behavior of the most powerful princes and greatest men is more shameless than that of emperors which I can tell you about. Let me ask you where there was ever a woman's heart so frail, so fearful, so utterly vulgar, and so inconstant as that of Emperor Claudius? He was so changeable that he would countermand orders which he had given an hour before, nor was he consistent in his pronouncements. He could agree to every bit of advice. In his madness and cruelty he had his wife killed, and that same evening asked why she had not come to bed. And he would summon retainers whom he had had beheaded to come and entertain him. He was so weakhearted that he constantly shook with fear and he trusted no one. What more can I tell you about him? Every misfortune of mores and emotions were combined in this servile emperor.

Note and Questions

1. *Medieval Literary Conventions.* The following excerpt explains the function that allegory played in Christine de Pizan's writing.

> An international cultural force, Christine affected the attitudes of both women and men in France, Portugal, and England by arguing cogently and convincingly, as well as by utilizing the literary conventions her audience loved. Daughter of her time, she wrote allegories. She pleased her market with those precious "mind battles," the *psychomachias*, which personified abstract ideas. Today, out of context, allegory seems slightly ludicrous. Yet, it is simply out of conscious fashion, but remains potent in the modern subconscious. In modern language we allegorize constantly, and it is not difficult to

train ourselves to enjoy allegories in the medieval manner. For example: my colleague looked at an exquisite, rich chocolate cake for dessert, salivated, and said, "My desire for this is tremendously powerful, but my discretion is holding me back." We need only capitalize the initials of those abstractions; clothe, arm, and horse Desire in flaming red while similarly garbing Discretion as a warrior in sedate royal blue; then allow them to lunge and fight furiously on the battlefield of the Undecided Mind. If Desire emerges victorious, the prize cake is sensually devoured. If Discretion prevails, caloric temptation is overthrown and the cake is untouched.

Imaginative medieval battles between opposites, questions of conscience, or choices between extremes routinely were personified within medieval literature and literate conversation. The more cleverly detailed the transference of qualities from level to level of meaning, the more the audience praised. Modern readers will have to make a greater effort than Christine's contemporaries, who were more experienced at this, literally to see her *Vision*, in which Truth, Justice, and Chivalry languish in prison, while Voluptuousness, Fraud, and Avarice frolic at court. Modern readers expecting character development will be surprised that the best medieval allegories have only linear consistency with each upper or lower parallel stratum. The educated medieval mind perceived the literal, the allegorical, and other implied levels of meaning (such as the anagogical or inspirational; tropological or dogmatic; and the historical) simultaneously, allowing for the intellectual delight of discovering hidden meanings and. . .dark conceits.

Madeleine Pelner Cosman, Christine de Pizan's Well-Tempered Feminism, in Christine de Pizan, A Medieval Woman's Mirror of Honor: The Treasury of the City of Ladies 11, 15–16 (Madeleine Pelner Cosman ed. & Charity Cannon Willard trans., 1989).

2. *Chasteness*. According to de Pizan, what kind of woman deserves protection against rape? What is the consequence of creating a class of "chaste woman?" How did the category of "chaste woman" serve to reinforce Tarquin the Proud's power and how did it affect Lucretia's view of herself during and after the rape? What connection does de Pizan make between social and economic status and chasteness? Does the division of women into chaste and unchaste categories have continuing social and legal vitality?

3. *Love and Violence*. De Pizan describes Tarquin the Proud as having "love for this noble Lucretia." What are we to make of her understanding of love when she goes on to describe how Tarquin the Proud obtained sexual access?

4. *Defining Rape*. Is rape defined in Lucretia's story by the acts of Tarquin the Proud or by the behavior and status of Lucretia?

5. *Stereotyping*. According to de Pizan, how do men use the stereotype of women's fragility and inconstancy? Could she have made a similar critique of how men use the stereotype of the chaste woman?

6. *Class*. How does de Pizan use class status to prove the worthiness of women and the duplicity of men?

Angela Y. Davis, *Women, Race and Class* 37–44, 46–59, 64–65, 70–71, 73–74, 80–84 (1983)

The Anti-Slavery Movement and the Birth of Women's Rights

. . .Only four women were invited to attend the 1833 founding convention of the American Anti-Slavery Society. The male organizers of this Philadelphia meeting stipulated, moreover, that they were to be "listeners and spectators" rather than full-fledged participants. This did not deter Lucretia Mott—one of the four women—from audaciously addressing the men at the convention on at least two occasions. . . .

A practicing Quaker minister, Lucretia Mott undoubtedly astounded the all-male audience, for in those days women never spoke out at public gatherings.[1]. . .[The male leaders'] sexist attitudes prevented them from grasping the vast potential of women's involvement in the anti-slavery movement. Lucretia Mott, who was not so short-sighted, organized the founding meeting of the Philadelphia Female Anti-Slavery Society in the immediate aftermath of the men's convention. She was destined to become a leading public figure in the anti-slavery movement, a woman who would be extensively admired for her overall courage and for her steadfastness in the face of raging racist mobs. . . .

Like Lucretia Mott, many other white women with no previous political experience joined the abolitionist movement and literally received their baptism in fire. A pro-slavery mob burst into a meeting chaired by Maria Chapman Weston and dragged its speaker—William Lloyd Garrison—through the streets of Boston. A leader of the Boston Female Anti-Slavery Society, Weston realized that the white mob sought to isolate and perhaps violently attack the Black women in attendance, and thus insisted that each white woman leave the building with a Black woman at her side. The Boston Female Anti-Slavery Society was one of the numerous women's groups that sprang up in New England immediately after Lucretia Mott founded the Philadelphia society. If the number of women who were subsequently assaulted by racist mobs or who otherwise risked their lives could actually be determined, the figures would no doubt be astoundingly large.

As they worked within the abolitionist movement, white women learned about the nature of human oppression—and in the process, also learned important lessons about their own subjugation. In asserting their right to oppose slavery, they protested—sometimes overtly, sometimes implicitly—their own exclusion from the political arena. If they did not yet know how to present their own grievances collectively, at least they could plead the cause of a people who were also oppressed.

The anti-slavery movement offered women of the middle class the opportunity to prove their worth according to standards that were not tied to their

---

1. The first woman to speak publicly in the United States was the Scottish-born lecturer and writer Frances Wright. . . .When the Black woman Maria W. Stewart delivered four lectures in Boston in 1832, she became the first native-born woman to speak publicly. . . .

role as wives and mothers. In this sense, the abolitionist campaign was a home where they could be valued for their concrete *works*. . . .They discovered that sexism, which seemed unalterable inside their marriages, could be questioned and fought in the arena of political struggle. . . .

Of all the pioneering women abolitionists, it was the Grimke sisters from South Carolina—Sarah and Angelina—who most consistently linked the issue of slavery to the oppression of women. From the beginning of their tumultuous lecturing career, they were compelled to defend their rights as women to be public advocates of abolition—and by implication to defend the rights of all women to register publicly their opposition to slavery.

Born into a South Carolina slaveholding family, the Grimke sisters developed a passionate abhorrence of the "peculiar institution" and decided, as adults, to move North. Joining the abolitionist effort in 1836, they began to lecture in New England about their own lives and their daily encounters with the untold evils of slavery. Although the gatherings were sponsored by the female anti-slavery societies, increasing numbers of men began to attend. . . .These assemblies were unprecedented, for no other women had ever addressed mixed audiences on such a regular basis without facing derogatory cries and disruptive jeers hurled by men who felt that public speaking should be an exclusively male activity.

While the men attending the Grimkes' meetings were undoubtedly eager to learn from the women's experiences, the sisters were vengefully attacked by other male forces. The most devastating attack came from religious quarters: on July 28, 1837, the Council of Congregationalist Ministers of Massachusetts issued a pastoral letter severely chastising them for engaging in activities which subverted women's divinely ordained role . . . .Framed by the largest Protestant domination in Massachusetts, this pastoral letter had immense repercussions. If the ministers were correct, then Sarah and Angelina Grimke were committing the worst of all possible sins: they were challenging God's will. The echoes of this assault did not begin to fade until the Grimkes finally decided to terminate their lecturing career.

Neither Sarah nor Angelina had originally been concerned—at least not expressly—about questioning the social inequality of women. Their main priority had been to expose the inhuman and immoral essence of the slave system and the special responsibility women bore for its perpetuation. But once the male supremacist attacks against them were unleashed, they realized that unless they defended themselves as women—and the rights of women in general—they would be forever barred from the campaign to free the slaves. . . .

An entire decade before white women's mass opposition to the ideology of male supremacy received its organizational expression, the Grimke sisters urged women to resist the destiny of passivity and dependence which society had imposed upon them—in order to take their rightful place in the struggle for justice and human rights. . . .

Because the Grimke sisters had such a profound consciousness of the inseparability of the fight for Black Liberation and the fight for Women's Liberation, they were never caught in the ideological snare of insisting that one struggle was absolutely more important than the other. They recognized the dialectical character of the relationship between the two causes. . . .

Class and Race in the Early Women's Rights Campaign

> As Lucretia Mott and Elizabeth Cady Stanton wended their way arm in arm down great Queen Street that night, reviewing the exciting scenes of the day, they agreed to hold a woman's rights convention on their return to America, as the men to whom they had just listened had manifested their great need of some education on that question. . . .

This conversation, which took place in London on the opening day of the 1840 World Anti-Slavery Convention, is frequently assumed to contain the real story behind the birth of the organized women's movement in the United States. . . .This anecdote and its surrounding circumstances have been made the basis of a popular interpretation of the women's rights movement as having been primarily inspired—or rather provoked—by the insufferable male supremacy within the anti-slavery campaign. . . .

Yet for. . .[Lucretia Mott] who had been excluded from membership in the Society some seven years previously, this was no new experience. . . .

Unlike Lucretia Mott, Elizabeth Cady Stanton was not an experienced political activist when the London convention took place. Accompanying her husband of only several weeks on what she called their "wedding journey," she was attending her first anti-slavery meeting not as a delegate but, rather, as the wife of an abolitionist leader. . . .When she wrote (along with Susan B. Anthony, in their *History of Woman Suffrage*) that during her conversation in 1840 with Lucretia Mott, "a missionary work for the emancipation of women. . .was then and there inaugurated," her remarks did not account for the accumulated lessons wrought by almost a decade during which abolitionist women had battled for their political emancipation as women. . . .

Whereas Elizabeth Cady Stanton's interest in abolitionism was quite recent, she had conducted a personal fight against sexism throughout her youth. Encouraged by her father—a wealthy and unabashedly conservative judge—she had defied orthodoxy in her studies as well as in her leisure activities. She studied Greek and mathematics and learned horseback riding, all of which were generally barred to girls. At age sixteen, Elizabeth was the only girl in her high school graduating class. Before her marriage, the young Stanton passed much of her time with her father and had even begun to study the law seriously under his guidance.

By 1848 Stanton was a full-time housewife and mother. Living with her husband in Seneca Falls, New York, she was often unable to hire servants because they were so scarce in that area. Her own anticlimactic and frustrating life made her especially sensitive to the middle-class white woman's predicament. . . .

As the Seneca Falls Convention was being planned, Elizabeth Cady Stanton proposed a resolution which appeared too radical even to her co-conventioner Lucretia Mott. . . .[S]he opposed the introduction of a resolution on woman suffrage. Such a move would be interpreted as absurd and outrageous, she thought, and would consequently undermine the importance of the meeting. Stanton's husband also opposed the raising of the suffrage issue—and kept his promise to leave town if she insisted on presenting the resolution. Frederick Douglass was the only prominent figure who agreed that the convention should call for women's right to vote. . . .

Among the approximately three hundred women and men attending the Seneca Falls Convention, the issue of electoral power for women was the only major point of contention: the suffrage resolution alone was not unanimously endorsed. That the controversial proposal was presented at all, however, was due to Frederick Douglass' willingness to second Stanton's motion and to employ his oratorical abilities in defense of women's right to vote.

During those early days when women's rights was not yet a legitimate cause, when woman suffrage was unfamiliar and unpopular as a demand, Frederick Douglass publicly agitated for the political equality of women. . . .Frederick Douglass was also responsible for officially introducing the issue of women's rights to the Black Liberation movement, where it was enthusiastically welcomed. . . .

The advocacy of women's rights could not be forbidden. Not yet acceptable to the makers of public opinion, the issue of women's equality, now embodied in an embryonic movement, supported by Black people who were fighting for their own freedom, established itself as an indelible element of public life in the United States. . . .

The inestimable importance of the Seneca Falls Declaration was its role as the *articulated consciousness of women's rights* at midcentury. It was the theoretical culmination of years of unsure, often silent, challenges aimed at a political, social, domestic and religious condition which was contradictory, frustrating and downright oppressive for women of the bourgeoisie and the rising middle classes. However, as a rigorous consummation of the consciousness of white middle-class women's dilemma, the Declaration all but ignored the predicament of white working-class women, as it ignored the condition of Black women in the South and North alike. In other words, the Seneca Falls Declaration proposed an analysis of the female condition which disregarded the circumstances of women outside the social class of the document's framers.

But what about those women who *worked* for a living—the white women, for example, who operated the textile mills in the Northeast?. . .

Beginning in the late 1820s. . .working women staged "turn-outs" and strikes, militantly protesting the double oppression they suffered as women and as industrial workers. In Dover, New Hampshire, for example, the mill women walked off the job in 1828 to dramatize their opposition to newly instituted restrictions. . . .

Judging from the struggles conducted by white working women—their relentless defense of their dignity as workers and as women, their conscious as well as implicit challenges to the sexist ideology of womanhood—they had more than earned the right to be lauded as pioneers of the women's movement. But their trailblazing role was all but ignored by the leading initiators of the new movement, who did not comprehend that women workers experienced and challenged male supremacy in their own special way. . . .

At the last session of the convention, Lucretia Mott proposed a final resolution calling both for the overthrow of the pulpit and "for the securing to women *an equal participation with men in the various trades*, professions and commerce." [my emphasis] Was this a mere afterthought? A charitable gesture toward Charlotte Woodward [a glovemaker and labor activist] and her working-class sisters? Or did the small contingent of working-class women protest the exclusion of their interests from the original resolutions, causing Lucretia Mott, the long-time anti-slavery activist, to stand up on their behalf?. . .

If the recognition accorded working women at the Seneca Falls meeting was all but negligible, there was not even a cursory mention of the rights of another group of women who also "rebelled against the lives into which they were born." In the South they rebelled against slavery and in the North against a dubious condition of freedom called racism. While at least one Black man was present among the Seneca Falls conferees, there was not a single Black woman in attendance. Nor did the convention's documents make even a passing reference to Black women. In light of the organizers' abolitionist involvement, it would seem puzzling that slave women were entirely disregarded.

But this problem was not a new one. The Grimke sisters had previously criticized a number of female anti-slavery societies for ignoring the condition of Black women and for sometimes manifesting blatantly racist prejudices. During the preparations for the founding convention of the National Female Anti-Slavery Society, Angelina Grimke had to take the initiative to guarantee more than a token presence of Black women. Moreover, she suggested that a special address be delivered at that convention to the free Black people of the North. Since no one—not even Lucretia Mott—would prepare the address, Angelina's sister Sarah had to deliver the speech. As early as 1837 the Grimke sisters chastised the New York Female Anti-Slavery Society for failing to involve Black women in their work. . . .

The absence of Black women at the Seneca Falls Convention was all the more conspicuous in light of their previous contributions to the fight for women's rights. More than a decade before this meeting, Maria Stewart had responded to attacks on her right to deliver public lectures by emphatically asking, "What if I am a woman?". . .

The failure to recognize the potential for an integrated women's movement—particularly against sexism in education—was dramatically revealed in an episode occurring during the crucial summer of 1848. Ironically, it involved the daughter of Frederick Douglass. After her official admission to a girls' seminary in Rochester, New York, Douglass' daughter was formally prohibited from attending classes with the white girls. The principal who issued the order was an abolitionist woman! When Douglass and his wife protested this segregationist policy, the principal asked each white girl to vote on the issue, indicating that one objection would suffice to continue the exclusion. After the white girls voted in favor of integrating the classroom, the principal approached the girls' parents, using the one resulting objection as an excuse to exclude Douglass' daughter.

That a white woman associated with the anti-slavery movement could assume a racist posture toward a Black girl in the North reflected a major weakness in the abolitionist campaign—its failure to promote a broad anti-racist consciousness. This serious shortcoming, abundantly criticized by the Grimke sisters and others, was unfortunately carried over into the organized movement for women's rights. . . .

Meanwhile, large numbers of Black women were manifesting their commitment to freedom and equality in ways that were less closely connected with the newly organized women's movement. The Underground Railroad claimed the energies of numerous Northern Black women. Jane Lewis, for example, a resident of New Lebanon, Ohio, regularly rowed her boat across the Ohio River, rescuing many a fugitive slave. Frances E. W. Harper, a dedicated feminist and the most popular Black poet at midcentury, was one of the most active lecturers associated with the anti-slavery movement. Charlotte Forten, who became a leading Black educator during the post-Civil War period, was likewise an active abolitionist. Sarah Remond, who lectured against slavery in England, Ireland and Scotland, exercised a vast influence on public opinion, and according to one historian, "kept the Tories from intervening on the side of the Confederacy."

Even the most radical white abolitionists, basing their opposition to slavery on moral and humanitarian grounds, failed to understand that the rapidly developing capitalism of the North was also an oppressive system. They viewed slavery as a detestable and inhuman institution, an archaic transgression of justice. But they did not recognize that the white worker in the North, his or her status as "free" laborer notwithstanding, was no different from the enslaved "worker" in the South: both were victims of economic exploitation. . . .

Racism in the Woman Suffrage Movement

> Although this may remain a question for politicians to wrangle over for five or ten years, the black man is still, in a political point of view, far above the educated white women of the country. The representative women of the nation have done their uttermost for the last thirty years to secure freedom for the negro; and as long as he was lowest in the scale of being, we were willing to press his claims; but now, as the celestial gate to civil rights is slowly moving on its hinges, it becomes a serious question whether we had better stand aside and see "Sambo" walk into the kingdom first. . . .
>
> "This is the negro's hour." Are we sure that he, once entrenched in all his inalienable rights, may not be an added power to hold us at bay? Have not "black male citizens" been heard to say they doubted the wisdom of extending the right of suffrage to women?. . .If the two millions of Southern black women are not to be secured the rights of person, property, wages and children, their emancipation is but another form of slavery. In fact, it is better to be the slave of an educated white man, than of a degraded, ignorant black one. . . .

This letter to the editor of the *New York Standard*, dated December 26, 1865, was authored by Elizabeth Cady Stanton. Its indisputably racist ideas indicate that Stanton's understanding of the relationship between the battle for Black Liberation and the struggle for women's rights was, at best, superficial. . . .

At the outbreak of the Civil War, Elizabeth Cady Stanton had urged her feminist colleagues to devote all their energies during the war years to the anti-slavery campaign. Later she argued that women's rights advocates had committed a strategic error in subordinating themselves to the cause of abolitionism. . . .

As soon as the Union Army triumphed over their Confederate opponents, she [Stanton] and her co-workers insisted that the Republican party reward them for their wartime efforts. The reward they demanded was woman suffrage . . . .

Of course the Republicans did not lend their support to woman suffrage after the Union victory was won. But it was not so much because they were *men*, it was rather because, as politicians, they were beholden to the dominant economic interests of the period. . . .

If woman suffrage was not to be included in the postwar agenda of the Republican party, neither were the innate political rights of Black people of any real concern to these triumphant politicians. That they conceded the necessity of extending the vote to newly emancipated Black men in the South did not imply that they favored Black males over white females. Black male suffrage. . .was a tactical move designed to ensure the political hegemony of the Republican party in the chaotic postwar South. . . .

The women's rights leaders of the post-Civil War era tended to view the vote as an end in itself. Already in 1866, it seemed that whoever furthered the cause of woman suffrage, however racist their motives, was a worthwhile recruit for the women's campaign. Even Susan B. Anthony detected no apparent contradiction in the advocacy of woman suffrage by a congressman who was a self-avowed white supremacist. . . .

In representing the interests of the former slaveholding class, the Democratic party sought to prevent the enfranchisement of the Black male population in the South. Thus many Democratic leaders defended woman suffrage as a calculated measure against their Republican opponents. Expediency was the watchword of these Democrats, whose concern for women's equality was imbued with the same dishonesty as the Republicans' announced support for Black male suffrage. If Elizabeth Cady Stanton and Susan B. Anthony had more carefully analyzed the political situation of the post-Civil War period, they might have been less willing to associate their suffrage campaign with the notorious George Francis Train. . .[an] unabashedly racist Democrat. . . .

But Stanton and Anthony were hurting for support, and since Train was willing to assist them, they welcomed him with open arms. With his financial backing, they founded a journal which—at his insistence—was called *Revolution*. . . .

By the time the Equal Rights Association held its 1869 convention, the Fourteenth Amendment—with its implication that only male citizens were unconditionally entitled to the ballot—had already been passed. The Fifteenth Amendment—prohibiting disenfranchisement on the grounds of race, color or previous condition of servitude (but not sex!)—was on the verge of becoming law. On the agenda of this ERA convention was the endorsement of the Fifteenth Amendment. Since the leading proponents of woman suffrage passionately opposed this position, it was clear that an open schism was inevitable. Although the delegates recognized that this would probably be the Association's final meeting, Frederick Douglass made a last-minute appeal to his white sisters:

> When women, because they are women, are dragged from their homes and hung upon lamp-posts; when their children are torn from their arms and their brains dashed upon the pavement; when they are objects of insult and out-

> rage at every turn; when they are in danger of having their homes burnt down over their heads; when their children are not allowed to enter schools; then they will have [the same] urgency to obtain the ballot.

As blunt and polemical as this argument may have been, there was a lucidity about it that was unmistakable. Its vivid visual imagery demonstrated that the former Black slaves suffered an oppression that was qualitatively and brutally different from the predicament of white middle-class women. . . .

Two years earlier Sojourner Truth might possibly have opposed the position of Frederick Douglass. . . .By the final meeting of the Equal Rights Association in 1869, Sojourner Truth had recognized the dangerous racism underlying the feminists' opposition to Black male suffrage. . . .When Sojourner Truth insisted that "if you bait the suffrage-hook with a woman, you will certainly catch a black man,"[2] she issued yet another profound warning about the menacing influence of racist ideology. . . .

As women, Frances E. W. Harper and Sojourner Truth were outnumbered by those who were not persuaded by Frederick Douglass' appeal for unity. Elizabeth Cady Stanton and Susan B. Anthony were among those who successfully argued for the dissolution of the Equal Rights Association. Shortly thereafter they formed the National Woman Suffrage Association. As supporters within the ERA of the ratification of the Fifteenth Amendment, Lucy Stone and her husband were joined by Julia Ward Howe as founders of the American Woman Suffrage Association.

The dissolution of the Equal Rights Association brought to an end the tenuous, though potentially powerful, alliance between Black Liberation and Women's Liberation.

Questions

1. *Nineteenth-Century Anti-Slavery and Women's Rights Movements.* Based on the excerpt from Angela Davis' book, how would you describe how racism functioned in the women's rights movement and how sexism functioned in the anti-slavery movement?

2. *The Fifteenth Amendment.* Is it possible to have opposed the Fifteenth Amendment with nonracist arguments?

3. *Economic Interests.* Davis' account of post-Civil War party politics is focused primarily on class and economic issues. What role do you think sexism and racism might have played in the Republican party's pursuit of economic and political interests?

4. *Coalition Building.* Do you see parallels in your experiences working with political or community groups and the problematic relationship described by Davis between the anti-slavery and women's rights movements? What factors inhibit coalition building?

---

2. Sojourner Truth was criticizing Henry Ward Beecher's approach to the suffrage question. . . .

Paula Giddings, *When and Where I Enter: The Impact of Black Women on Race and Sex in America* 48–54 (1984)

"Victorian morality," as Gerda Lerner observed "applied to the 'better' classes only. It was taken for granted during the period and well into the 20th century that working-class women—and especially Black women—were freely available for sexual use by upper-class males." The assumption had less to do with real circumstances than with the idea of immutable natural laws that governed morality and femininity. These laws stated that women who worked outside the home, or whose race had a history of sexual exploitation, were outside the realm of "womanhood" and its prerogatives.

Black women activists traversed a tricky and sometimes contradictory path in responding to the challenge. On the one hand they agreed with the fundamental premises of the Victorian ethic. On the other, they opposed its racist and classist implications. At the same time they were conscious of the pressure on free Blacks to prove they could be acculturated into American society. Because of their alleged inability to do so, organizations like the American Colonization Society, which included some of the most influential White liberals in the country, were stepping up efforts to repatriate free Blacks to Africa. For Black women, *acculturation* was translated as their ability to be "ladies"—a burden of proof that carried an inherent class-consciousness.

In part, the proliferation of Black ladies' literary, intelligence, temperance, and moral improvement societies in this period was a reaction to that pressure. But despite their titles, these organizations did more than pursue cultural activities. The Ohio Literary Ladies Society, for example, "probably did more towards the establishment of schools for Black children than any other group of the time in the state," noted the Howard University archivist Dorothy Porter in her study of the Black women's literary societies organized between 1828 and 1846. The societies also helped needy Black women, gave financial aid to Black newspapers, and provided forums for discussion of relevant issues.

In the latter capacity, the Afric-American Female Intelligence Society of Boston did a daring thing. It sponsored a young abolitionist's speech before a mixed audience of men and women in Boston's Franklin Hall. The act was a daring one because the abolitionist was a woman, and a Black woman at that. In 1832 women didn't speak in public, especially on serious issues like civil rights and, most especially, feminism. In June, just four months before her appearance, the most progressive of the abolitionist newspapers, *The Liberator*, counseled: "The voice of woman should not be heard in public debates, but there are other ways in which her influence would be beneficial." But the speaker, Maria Stewart, who had been born free in Connecticut twenty-nine years earlier, would hear none of that.[3] Not only did she speak, thus becom-

---

3. At the age of twenty-three she married James Stewart, a veteran of the War of 1812 and a shipping agent. The couple were a part of Boston's African-American middle class for three years until James Stewart's death. *See* Maria W. Stewart, America's First Black Woman Political Writer: Essays and Speeches 3, 7 (Marilyn Richardson ed., 1987) [hereinafter Richardson]. Eds.

ing the first American-born woman to give public speeches and leave extant texts of her addresses, but in speaking about civil and women's rights, she used a chastening tongue. Although her public career was short-lived, lasting barely a year, Stewart articulated the precepts upon which the future activism of Black women would be based. Her ideas reflected both the fundamentals of the Victorian ethic and criticism of its inherent biases. Out of that mix emerged a distinct ethos which underlined Black women's activism for generations to come. And as is evident in Stewart's words, it was an ethos that had its contradictions.

Naturally, Stewart railed against the racism toward Blacks that fueled discrimination in the North and provided a rationale for slavery in the South. Although Stewart had a rudimentary education, her rhetoric often demonstrated knowledge of ancient history. Though "we are looked upon as *things*," she said, "we sprang from a scientific people." Stewart also spoke of the relegation of Blacks to menial jobs. Continual hard labor "deadens the energies of the soul, and benumbs the faculties of the mind," she said. Orphaned at the age of five and "bound out" to work thereafter, Stewart told her audiences that she had learned the consequences of constant drudgery by bitter experience.

Nevertheless, Stewart castigated free Blacks for not doing enough for their own uplift. She believed they were politically lethargic and ultimately responsible for the continuance of slavery. "Were the American free people of color to turn their attention more assiduously to moral worth and intellectual improvement, this would be the result," she said: "Prejudice would gradually diminish, and the whites would be compelled to say, unloose those fetters!"

In keeping with the Victorian ethic, Stewart believed that Black women had an important part to play in the race's moral and intellectual development. She counseled that Black women excel in "good house-wifery, knowing that prudence and economy are the road to wealth." The role of mothers was essential. "O ye mothers," Stewart implored, "what a responsibility rests on you! It is you that must create in the minds of your little girls and boys a thirst for knowledge, the love of virtue, the abhorrence of vice, and the cultivation of the pure heart." Like most women of the period, Stewart also seemed to subscribe to the doctrine of submissiveness. "My beloved brethren. . .it is upon you that woman depends; she can do little besides using her influence," she concluded.

But in Stewart's view, that influence was undermined by uncultivated women who, in her words, "did not blush at vulgarity." As a woman of her times, Maria Stewart believed in the "cult" notion that only "true women" could exercise the proper moral influence on the family.[4] "Did the daughters of our land [Africa] possess a delicacy of manners, combined with gentleness and dignity; did their pure minds hold vice in abhorrence and contempt, did they frown when their ears were polluted with its vile accents, would not their influence become powerful? Would not our brethren fall in love with their virtues?" she asked. However, Stewart and other Black woman activists

---

4. *See* Note 1, at p. 300 for discussion of the "cult of the lady," to which Paula Giddings is referring in the text. Eds.

challenged the cult idea in a very fundamental way. Though they may have agreed with many of its precepts, they fought against the idea that morality and worth were inherent to a particular class or race. On the contrary, it was external circumstance rather than natural law that determined character, morality, and, in the case of women, "true womanhood." Stewart revealed this perspective in remarks directed toward White women who believed differently:

> O ye fairer sisters whose hands are never soiled, whose nerves and muscles are never strained, go learn by experience! Had we the opportunity that you have had, to improve our moral and mental faculties, what would have hindered our intellects from being as bright, and our manners from being as dignified as yours? Had it been our lot to have been nursed in the lap of affluence and ease, and have basked beneath the smiles and sunshine of fortune, should we not have naturally supposed that we were never made to toil?

Although she felt Blacks could do more on their own behalf, she understood that Whites, including White women, conspired to keep Blacks from "rising above the condition of servants." She had once asked White women "who transact business for themselves" to hire Black girls to work for them, she told her audience, but the women had refused for fear of "losing the public patronage."

Most significantly, Stewart opposed the idea that women, including Black women, were responsible for their own degradation—an attitude which was perhaps the most destructive (and controlling) of any of the cult ideas. Although Stewart criticized the dearth of Black women "who will blush at vulgarity," the primary responsibility lay on America, "who caused the daughters of Africa to commit whoredoms and fornications;. . .upon thee be their curse."

Stewart's assumptions—what would later become known as modernist thinking—gave Black women a freer rein to express and act upon ideas that liberated them from the oppression of both sex and race. The moral urgency of their being Black and female—heightened especially in times when Black men were politically lethargic ("It is of no use for us to wait any longer for a generation of well educated men to arise," Stewart said scornfully)—suffused Black women with a tenacious feminism, which was articulated before that of Whites like Sarah Grimke, who is credited with providing the first rationale for American women's political activism.

For Black women no such rationale was necessary. In their world view, many of the obstacles that White women faced simply didn't apply to their circumstances or beliefs. For example, Black women saw no contradiction between domesticity and political action. So Stewart could talk about dependence on men and excelling in good house-wifery, and at the same time make an unmistakably feminist appeal to Black women.

> Do you ask what we can do? Unite and build a store of your own. . . .Do you ask where is the money? We have spent more than enough for nonsense. . . .We have never had an opportunity of displaying our talents; therefore the world thinks we know nothing. . . .Possess the spirit of men, bold and enterprising, fearless and undaunted. Sue for your rights and privileges. Know the reason that you cannot attain them. Weary them [men] with your importunities.

Black women also bypassed the barrier of religious thought that circumscribed even radical White activists until the late 1830s, when abolitionist William Lloyd Garrison introduced a rationale for criticizing organized religion. Again, Black women had been able to justify their activism even earlier. "What if I am a woman?" Stewart declared. "Did [God] not raise up Deborah to be mother, and a judge in Israel? Did not Queen Esther save the lives of the Jews? And Mary Magdalene first declare the resurrection of Christ from the dead?"[5]. . .

Their perspective also enabled Black women to see a world not of fixed proportions, but of change. Speaking of a past which was bound to become a present again, Stewart talked of women in history who had had a voice in moral, political, and religious affairs. She spoke of women in the pre-Renaissance days who occupied chairs of philosophy and justice, who "harangued" in Latin before the Pope, who were poets as well as nuns. . . .[6]

Stewart had little doubt that Black women's prospects were "fair and bright." However, a year after her debut, she announced that her own immediate future in Boston was dim. Citing prejudice among her own people, she announced that she was going to leave the city, perhaps never to return. Her parting thoughts, sanctioned in her mind by God, history, and the need for racial progress, showed that she left undaunted. . . .[7] Maria Stewart left Boston and ended her public career.[8]

---

5. Maria Stewart's writings, speeches, and activism can be understood only through her religion. A year after her husband's death, she underwent a "born again" experience.

> [M]oved by "holy indignation," she began to write and to speak out publicly against tyranny, victimization, and injustice as she felt them affecting her life, her community and her nation. "In 1831 [I] made a public profession of my faith in Christ," she declared in the document which stands as the first political manifesto written by a black American woman, and pronounced herself willing to place her faith at the service of social activism, as a "strong advocate for the cause of God and for the cause of freedom.". . .
>
> An opponent not only of slavery, but also of political and economic exploitation, she invoked both the Bible and the Constitution of the United States as documents proclaiming the universal birthright to justice and freedom. Resistance to oppression was, for Stewart, the highest form of obedience to God.

Richardson, *supra* note 3, at 8–9. Eds.

6. Maria Stewart fought tirelessly for the education of African-American women. *See id.* at 20–22. It is noteworthy that Stewart's farewell address was delivered in the same year that Prudence Crandall, a young white woman, suffered terrorist attacks and arrest for recruiting and enrolling African-American girls in her school. *See* Angela Y. Davis, Women, Race and Class 34–36 (1983) (describing this case and its role in forging the connection between the anti-slavery movement and the women's rights movement). Eds.

7. *See* p. 22 for excerpt from this farewell address. Eds.

8. She later pursued a teaching career in New York and finally moved to Washington, D.C., where she became the Matron of the Freedmen's Hospital, which at the end of the Civil War became a refugee camp for former slaves and which ultimately included an industrial school. She continued to do this work until her death in 1879. *See* Richardson, *supra* note 3, at xiv, 84–85. Eds.

Mrs. Stewart's Farewell Address To Her Friends In The City Of Boston, in Maria W. Stewart, *America's First Black Woman Political Writer: Essays and Speeches* 67–72 (Marilyn Richardson ed., 1987)

Delivered September 21, 1833

[T]o begin my subject: "Ye have heard that it hath been said, whoso is angry with his brother without a cause, shall be in danger of the judgment; and whoso shall say to his brother, Raca, shall be in danger of the council. But whosoever shall say, thou fool, shall be in danger of hell-fire [Matthew 5:22]." For several years my heart was in continual sorrow. And I believe that the Almighty beheld from his holy habitation, the affliction wherewith I was afflicted, and heard the false misrepresentations wherewith I was misrepresented, and there was none to help. Then I cried unto the Lord in my troubles. And thus for wise and holy purposes, best known to himself, he has raised me in the midst of my enemies, to vindicate my wrongs before this people; and to reprove them for sin, as I have reasoned to them of righteousness and judgment to come. . . .I believe, that for wise and holy purposes, best known to himself, he hath unloosed my tongue, and put his word into my mouth, in order to confound and put all those to shame that have rose up against me. For he hath clothed my face with steel, and lined my forehead with brass. He hath put his testimony within me, and engraven his seal on my forehead [Revelation 9:4]. And with these weapons I have indeed set the fiends of earth and hell at defiance.

What if I am a woman; is not the God of ancient times the God of these modern days? Did he not raise up Deborah, to be a mother, and a judge in Israel [Judges 4:4]? Did not queen Esther save the lives of the Jews? And Mary Magdalene first declare the resurrection of Christ from the dead? Come, said the woman of Samaria, and see a man that hath told me all things that ever I did, is not this the Christ? St. Paul declared that it was a shame for a woman to speak in public, yet our great High Priest and Advocate did not condemn the woman for a more notorious offence than this; neither will he condemn this worthless worm. The bruised reed he will not break, and the smoking flax he will not quench, till he send forth judgment unto victory. Did St. Paul but know of our wrongs and deprivations, I presume he would make no objections to our pleading in public for our rights. Again; holy women ministered unto Christ and the apostles; and women of refinement in all ages, more or less, have had a voice in moral, religious and political subjects. Again; why the Almighty hath imparted unto me the power of speaking thus, I cannot tell. . . .

But to convince you of the high opinion that was formed of the capacity and ability of woman by the ancients, I would refer you to "Sketches of the Fair Sex."[9] Read to the 51st page, and you will find that several of the Northern

9. The full title of this book is *Woman, Sketches of the History, Genius, Disposition, Accomplishments, Employments, Customs and Importance of the Fair Sex in All Parts of the World Interspersed with Many Singular and Entertaining Anecdotes by a Friend of the Sex* published by John Adams in 1790. *See* Maria W. Stewart, America's First Black Woman Political

nations imagined that women could look into futurity, and that they had about them, an inconceivable something, approaching to divinity. Perhaps that idea was only the effect of the sagacity common to the sex, and the advantages which their natural address gave them over rough and simple warriors. Perhaps, also, those barbarians, surprised at the influence which beauty has over force, were led to ascribe to the supernatural attraction, a charm which they could not comprehend. . . .Among the Greeks, women delivered the Oracles; the respect the Romans paid to the Sibyls is well known. . . .And in the most barbarous nations, all things that have the appearance of being supernatural, the mysteries of religion, the secrets of physic, and the rites of magic, were in the possession of women.

If such women as are here described have once existed, be no longer astonished then, my brethren and friends, that God at this eventful period should raise up your own females to strive, by their example both in public and private, to assist those who are endeavoring to stop the strong current of prejudice that flows so profusely against us at present. No longer ridicule their efforts, it will be counted for sin. For God makes use of feeble means sometimes, to bring about his most exalted purposes. . . .

Why cannot a religious spirit animate us now? Why cannot we become divines and scholars? Although learning is somewhat requisite, yet recollect that those great apostles, Peter and James, were ignorant and unlearned. They were taken from the fishing boat, and made fishers of men.

In the 13th century, a young lady of Bologne devoted herself to the study of the Latin language, and of the laws. At the age of twenty-three she pronounced a funeral oration in Latin, in the great church of Bologne. And to be admitted as an orator, she had neither need of indulgence on account of her youth or of her sex. At the age of twenty-six, she took the degree of Doctor of Laws, and began publicly to expound the Institutions of Justinian. At the age of thirty, her great reputation raised her to a chair, where she taught the law to a prodigious concourse of scholars from all nations. She joined the charms and accomplishments of a woman to all the knowledge of a man. And such was the power of her eloquence, that her beauty was only admired when her tongue was silent.

What if such women as are here described should rise among our sable race? And it is not impossible. For it is not the color of the skin that makes the man or the woman, but the principle formed in the soul. Brilliant wit will shine, come from whence it will; and genius and talent will not hide the brightness of its lustre.

But, to return to my subject; the mighty work of reformation has begun among this people. The dark clouds of ignorance are dispersing. The light of science is bursting forth. Knowledge is beginning to flow, nor will its moral influence be extinguished till its refulgent rays have spread over us from East to West, and from North to South. Thus far is this mighty work begun, but not as yet accomplished. Christians must awake from their slumbers. Religion must flourish among them before the church will be built up in its purity, or immorality be suppressed.

Writer: Essays and Speeches 24 (Marilyn Richardson ed., 1987) [hereinafter Richardson]. Eds.

Yet, notwithstanding your prospects are thus fair and bright, I am about to leave you, perhaps never more to return. For I find it is no use for me as an individual to try to make myself useful among my color in this city. It was contempt for my moral and religious opinions in private that drove me thus before a public. Had experience more plainly shown me that it was the nature of man to crush his fellow, I should not have thought it so hard. Wherefore, my respected friends, let us no longer talk of prejudice, till prejudice becomes extinct at home. Let us no longer talk of opposition, till we cease to oppose our own. For while these evils exist, to talk is like giving breath to the air, and labor to the wind. Though wealth is far more highly prized than humble merit, yet none of these things move me. Having God for my friend and portion, what have I to fear? Promotion cometh neither from the East or West, and as long as it is the will of God, I rejoice that I am as I am; for man in his best estate is altogether vanity. Men of eminence have mostly risen from obscurity; nor will I, although a female of a darker hue, and far more obscure than they, bend my head or hang my harp upon willows [Psalm 137:2]; for though poor, I will virtuous prove. And if it is the will of my heavenly Father to reduce me to penury and want, I am ready to say, amen, even so be it. . . .

But some of you have said, "do not talk so much about religion, the people do not wish to hear you. We know these things, tell us something we do not know." If you know these things, my dear friends, and have performed them, far happier, and more prosperous would you now have been. . . .Religion is the most glorious theme that mortals can converse upon. . . .

Again, those ideas of greatness which are held forth to us, are vain delusions, are airy visions which we shall never realize. All that man can say or do can never elevate us, it is a work that must be effected between God and ourselves. And how? By dropping all political discussions in our behalf, for these, in my opinion, sow the seed of discord, and strengthen the cord of prejudice.[10] . . .

Finally, my brethren, let us follow after godliness, and the things which make for peace. Cultivate your own minds and morals; real merit will elevate you. Pure religion will burst your fetters. Turn your attention to industry. Strive to please your employers. Lay up what you can. And remember, that in the grave, distinction withers, and the high and low are alike renowned. . . .

Notes and Questions

1. *Hidden in Plain Sight.* Maria Stewart's life and work has been generally ignored, but there is some indication that she may finally gain recognition.

> In recent years, following the pathbreaking work of Dorothy B. Porter, who as early as 1936 described Stewart as "probably the earliest Negro woman

10. Here Stewart espouses the Garrisonian view opposing a political solution to the question of slavery. Garrison vowed that he would never hold office or exercise the franchise in a government that included slave-holders. The Constitution, as he saw it, was a proslavery instrument and hence not to be supported by a true abolitionist. . . .[William Lloyd Garrison established an abolitionist newspaper, *The Liberator*, in the early 1830s. It became a major voice and chronicle of the anti-slavery movement. Much of what Stewart wrote was published first in *The Liberator* in the "Ladies' Department" and later by Garrison and his partner Isaac Knapp as pamphlets and volumes for sale to earn money for the anti-slavery cause. *See* Richardson, *supra* note 9, at 10–11.]

lecturer and writer and one who has been neglected by historians and bibliographers," selections from Maria W. Stewart's speeches and essays have begun to appear in publications in Black Studies and Women's Studies. Still, she remains a significant historical figure hidden in plain sight, one might say, in that she has not been singled out for critical scholarly attention.

Maria W. Stewart, America's First Black Woman Political Writer: Essays and Speeches xv (Marilyn Richardson ed., 1987).

How does the hiding of Maria Stewart in plain sight contribute to the contemporary stereotype of African-American women?

2. *Religion.* Stewart's understanding of the world and call for action arise out of her religious devoutness, which cannot be disconnected from her experience as an African-American woman in the United States during the antebellum era. A contemporary explanation of the importance of religion to two African-American intellectuals, bell hooks and Cornell West, may be helpful in placing Stewart's words in context.

> bh: Let us say a little bit about ourselves. Both Cornel and I come to you as individuals who believe in God. That belief informs our message.
>
> cw: One of the reasons we believe in God is due to the long tradition of religious faith in the Black community. I think, that as a people who have had to deal with the absurdity of being Black in America, for many of us it is a question of God and sanity, or God and suicide. And, if you are serious about Black struggle, you know that in many instances you will be stepping out on nothing, hoping to land on something. That is the history of Black folks in the past and present, and it continually concerns those of us who are willing to speak out with boldness and a sense of the importance of history and struggle. You speak, knowing that you won't be able to do that for too long because America is such a violent culture. Given those conditions, you have to ask yourself what links to a tradition will sustain you, given the absurdity and insanity we are bombarded with daily. And so the belief in God itself is not to be understood in a noncontextual manner. It is understood in relation to a particular context, to specific circumstances.

bell hooks & Cornel West, Breaking Bread: Insurgent Black Intellectual Life 8–9 (1991).

3. *Audience.* Did Stewart have a different message for the African-American women in her audience than she had for the African-American men? Did Stewart avoid the problem experienced by the participants in the anti-slavery and women's rights movements of having to choose between fighting against racism and fighting against sexism?

4. *Plea for Justice.* What solution was Stewart proposing for remedying prejudice against African-American women?

Elizabeth Cady Stanton, "Our Girls," 1872, in Beth M. Waggenspack, *The Search for Self-Sovereignty: The Oratory of Elizabeth Cady Stanton* 141–57 (1989)

They are the music, the flowers, the sunshine of our social life. How beautiful they make our homes, churches, schools and festive scenes; how glad and gay they make our streets with their scarlet plumes, bright shawls and tartan plaids. Who can see a bevy of girls tripping home from school without pausing to watch their graceful motions, pretty faces, feet and legs, to listen to their merry words and peals of laughter. See how they romp and play with hoops and balls, with sleds and skates, wash their brothers' faces in the snow and beat them in a race on yonder pond. These boys and girls are one today in school, at play, at home, never dreaming that one sex was foreordained to clutch the stars, the other but to kiss the dust. But watch a while and you will see these dashing, noisy, happy, healthy girls grow calm, pale, and sad and even though lodged in palace homes mid luxury and ease, with all the gorgeous trappings wealth can give, with silks, bright jewels, gilded equippage, music, dancing, books, flowers, they still are listless and unsatisfied. And why? They have awakened to the fact that they belong to a subject, degraded, ostracized class: that to fill their man-appointed sphere, they can have no individual character, no life purpose, personal freedom, aim or ambition. They are simply to revolve around some man, to live only for him, in him, with him; to be fed, clothed, housed, guarded and controlled by him, today by Father or Brother, tomorrow by Husband or Son, no matter how wise or mature they are, never to know the freedom and dignity that are secured in self-dependence and self-support. Girls feel all this though they may never utter it, far more keenly than kind fathers imagine.

Walking in Madison Park one day with my little boy, reading the signs hung in the trees, "No dogs admitted here," he remarked, "It's a good thing, Mother, that dogs cannot read. It would hurt their feelings so to know that they were forbidden to walk in the parks." Yes, we said, the dogs are like the girls seem to be, shut out of the green pastures of life; while both alike are ignorant of the statutes by which it is done. Bruno sleeps on his master's rug in some dark street, pining for the sunshine and the grass and a frolic through the field or forest, without knowing his degradation published in that one invidious announcement, "No dogs admitted here," but if he should try to enter the park, a smart rap on the nose would remind him that he was a dog and not a boy. So our young girls pine and perish for lack of freedom, for the stimulus of work and wages, something to widen their ambitions and love of distinction. They are clothed in purple and fine linen and in their gilded cages fare sumptuously every day, but if by chance, with some new inspiration they awake to life and go forth to claim the place in the world that is by birthright theirs, they find at the very gates of life, at the entrance to every winding path leading to the Temple of Knowledge, wealth, or fame, there self-same little signs hung out, "No girls admitted here." While the dogs and the girls suffer alike the penalty of the law, the degradation of the latter is greatly aggravated by the fact that they can read the signs and what adds to the girl's humiliation is the fact that the boy by her side reads them also and finds out that to him alone the universe is free. The universe of matter and mind is his domain, no constitutions, customs, creeds or codes block his onward way, but all combine to urge him on, his triumphs in science, literature, and art are hailed with loud huzzas. He accepts the homage of the multitude as his sole right and looks with jealous eye at any girl that dares to tread upon his heels. In these artificial distinctions, boys learn their first lessons of contempt for all womankind. They naturally infer that they are endowed with some superior powers to match their superior privileges. But what avails it, that here and there some proud girl repudiates these invidious distinctions, laughs at the supercilious airs these boys affect and braces up her mind to resist this tyranny of sex. She feels she is the peer of any boy she knows. She has measured many a lance on the playground and in the school and now shall custom make her bow to sex, to those inferior to herself. She scorns the thought, but what can one brave girl do against the world. Custom has made this type of boy and soon these grow to perpetuate the custom. Man makes the creeds and the constitutions and codes, while woman is not but a lay figure in the world, a mere appendage to lordly man, a something on which to hang his titles, name and fame. With blighted girlhood, wasted youth and vacant age, the ambition of most women we meet today is simply to be distinguished as the daughter, wife, or mother of General, Honorable, or Judge So-and-so, to shine in their reflected light, to wear their deeds and words of valor and of eloquence as their own bracelet, necklace, or coronal. This should not be. Every girl should be something in and of herself, have an individual aim and purpose in life. As the boy approaches manhood, he gathers up his forces and concentrates them in some definitive work, trade, or profession, as a wish, a will, or way of his own everyone respects.

Hence, he begins life with enthusiasm, early learns the pleasure of self-dependence, growing stronger, braver every day he lives. But alas for the girl; she leaves school with her ambition at white heat; perchance she has outstripped the foremost in sciences and languages, she has her heart ready to carve her way to distinction. She too has a will of her own and desires the dignity of independence and self-support. But any career for a woman is tabooed by the world, and nothing she proposes to do is acceptable to family and friends. If in spite of opposition a woman does step outside all conventional trammels to do something her grandmother did not do, she meets a dozen obstacles where a man does one. Surely the battle of life without any artificial trammels is hard enough, for multitudes of young men even perish in the struggle. But the girl who earns her bread or makes for herself a name has all the boy has to surmount and these artificial barriers of law and custom in addition.

Do you wonder that so few are ready to take their rights? Oh! Men of the Republic! Strike off these chains! The distinctions that God has made he will maintain, he needs none of your puny legislation to vindicate his wisdom or carry out his will. Multitudes of our noblest girls are perishing for want of something to do. The hope of marriage, all we offer girls, is not enough to feed an immortal mind, and if that goal is never reached, what then? The more fiery genius a girl has with no outlets for her powers, the more complete is her misery when all these forces are turned back upon herself. The pent-up fires that might have glowed with living words of eloquence in courts of justice, in the pulpit, or on the stage are today consuming their victims in lunatic asylums, in domestic discontent and disgust, in peevish wailings about trifles and in the vain pursuit of pleasure and fashion longing for that peace that is found only in action. Thus multitudes of girls live and die, unloving and loved, who might have stood high in the shining walks of life as a blessing to themselves and others. . . .

The cunning girl is to be healthy, wealthy and wise. She is to hold one equal place with her brothers in the world of work, in the colleges, in the state, in the church and in the home. Her sphere is to be no longer bound by the prejudices of a dead past, but by her capacity to go wherever she can stand. The cunning girl is to be an independent, self-supporting being, not as today a helpless victim of fashion, superstition, and absurd conventionalisms.

Let us consider then the reforms in her education necessary to realize the grand result. First, she is to be healthy. As by law of Nature, women mold themselves to man's ideal, she must educate our young men to demand something better than they have yet subsidized. All our customs and fashions, however, trivial and transient, are based on the theory that woman was made simply to please man, and to do this not by meeting him on the higher plain of spiritual and intellectual attraction in the world of thought, where, through ages of culture, he is supposed to dwell, and where she, through ignorance and inferiority, is supposed to be unable to go, but by a mere physical (?)[11] such as beauty, manners, and duty can give. Hence, she amuses man by an endless variety in her costume and calls out his chivalry by her seeming helplessness and dependence.

When there is a demand for healthy, happy, vigorous, self-reliant women, they will make their appearance. But with our feeble type of manhood the present supply of vanity and vacuity meets their wants. Woman, as she is today, is men's handiwork. With iron shoes, steel-ribbed corsets, hoops, trains, high heels, chignons, paniers, limping gait, feeble muscles, with her cultivated fears of everything seen and unseen, of snakes, spiders, mice and millers, cows, caterpillars, dogs and drunken men, firecrackers and cannon, thunder and lightning, ghosts and gentlemen, women die ten thousand deaths, when if educated to be brave and self-dependent, they would die but one. This sheer affectation of fear and feebleness men too have become so depraved in their taste as to admire and they really suppose that woman as she is is Nature's work, and when they see a woman with brains and two hands in practical life, capable of standing alone, earning her own bread and thinking her own thoughts, conscious of the true dignity and glory of womanhood, they call her "unsexed." The real facts of life show that man's chivalry and devotion is not manifested in proportion to a girl's need of them, but just the opposite. The beautiful, highly educated, wealthy heiress, who is in no hurry to marry either for a master or a house, calls out ten times the more chivalry than the friendless orphan girl or the penniless widow with half a dozen children. Man's devotion is always in exact proportion to woman's actual independence!. . .

It is a great truth to impress on the mind of every girl that she is an independent, creative wildflower, made primarily for her own happiness, making self-development and self-support and the highest good of the race the end of her being. I would have girls regard themselves not as adjectives but nouns, not mere appendages made to qualify somebody else, but independent, responsible workers in carrying forward the grand, eternal plans in the redemption of mankind. There is a very pretty theory extant that every woman has a strong right arm on which to lean until she is safe on the other side of Jordan, but the facts of life conflict with the theory. We see on all sides multitudes of

11. The editor of the collection of Stanton's speeches uses a question mark to indicate uncertainty concerning the original text. Eds.

girls and women, maids and maidens, alike, thrown on their own resources for their daily bread; hence the importance of educating women for these positions that will secure pecuniary independence. I do not wish to undervalue domestic avocations, but the tasks of women vary as much as the tasks of men, and to educate all women for teachers and seamstresses, cooks and chambermaids is to make the supply in the home sphere greater than the demand, thus permanently to keep down wages and degrade all these branches of labor. . . .

The cunning girl is to have health. One of the first needs for every girl is to be trained for some life work, some trade or profession, is good health. As a sound body is the first step towards a sound mind, food, clothes, exercise, all the conditions of daily life are important in training girls either for high scholarship or practical work. Hence, girls, in all your getting of good health, it is the foundation in every undertaking. Sick men and women always take sickly views of everything and fail in the very hour they are needed. One of the essential elements of health is freedom of thought and action. A right to individual life, opinion, ambition. The problems of body and mind so universal in women may be attributed mainly to their being forever in a condition of tutelage and minority. I am sure, gentlemen, you will all be glad to hear that the millennium is close at hand when you are to hear no more of headaches, earaches, sideaches, and backaches, that your homes are to be changed from the gloomy hospitals of today to abodes of health and happiness, when nerves are to be superseded by muscles. It is as one of the conditions of health that the question of dress becomes one of importance. "There was a time in the history of man," says Carlyle, "when man was primary and his rags secondary, but times have sadly changed, clothes now make the man." I hope we are fast coming to that period in the history of woman when in her dress, health and freedom are to be the first considerations. As women are now rapidly asserting themselves in the world of work, an entire revolution in this respect is inevitable. A physiological need, but look at the forms of all our young girls to appreciate the violence done Nature in the small waists and constrained gait and manners of all we meet. Ordinarily a girl of fourteen is a healthy, happy being in short hair, short dress, in clothes hung loosely on her shoulders. But as soon as her skirts trail and her dressmakers lace and tighten her clothes "to form the waist" as they say, a change takes place at once in her whole manner and appearance. She is moody, listless, weary, strolls when she should run, cries when she should laugh, and this at the very age when she should manifest newfound vigor and enthusiasm. Much of this may be attributed to the many unnatural restraints placed on all girls, the indoor life and sedentary habits, but more to her dress than any one cause. The tight waist prevents a free circulation of the blood and action of the heart and lungs, contracts the ribs and paralyzes a belt of the nerves and muscles at least six inches in width round that part of the body. The long dress prevents all freedom of motion. When we remember that deep breathing has much to do with deep thinking, we see the relation between scholarship and clothes. Girls by the style and material of their dress are practically debarred from outdoor exercise, and yet they need it as much as boys do, and if well trained would enjoy it equally with them. . . .

I urge upon the consideration of all parents, guardians, and teachers the necessity of educating girls under their care to some profitable life work, some trade or profession. There cannot be too much said on the helpless condition in which a girl is left when thrown alone on the world without money, without friends, without skill or place in the world of work. One half the stimulus to a girl's education is lost in the fact that she has no aim or ambition in the future. Boys may be doctors, clergymen, lawyers, editors, poets, painters, presidents, congressmen, senators, anything and everything, be what they can, go where they can stand; but girls must be wives and nothing more, or if they are not wives, most people consider their lives failures. Now I want to secure the standard for old maids and teach girls two things, that marriage as a profession nine cases in ten times ends a failure because the wife is pecuniarily dependent. To be independent she must have some trade or profession beside that of the wife, mother, or housekeeper, as only in the happiest and most lasting relations are these offices honored and renumerated. Beside in the most fortunate marriages, women are not secure against want, for good husbands sometimes die bankrupt, leaving a young wife with half a dozen little children to provide for, helpless, friendless, alone, with no trade or profession by which she can gain a livelihood and worse than all with the feeling that labor is a degradation, that it is more honorable for a woman to live on the bounty of another, buy bread or sell herself for a home either in marriage or out of it, than it is to work side by side with her brother anywhere and maintain a lofty independence. A mighty multitude of women find themselves in this position in all our large cities. Over fifty thousand in New York alone earn their daily bread by the needle and below these are deeper depths, where dwell the daughters of vice and folly and want. God only knows how many over whom society draws the veil of forgetfulness or before that sad problem stands hardened or appalled. Full three fourths the girls before me will be called on some period of their lives to support themselves. Shall we prepare them for the facts of life, its real emergencies, or sacrifice them to a theory? Today, perchance, your daughters rest at ease in your palace homes clothed in purple and fine linen or living comfortably. Tomorrow, unfortunate seems as it may to all, your bonds, deeds, mortgages change hands. Your home, furniture, books, pictures, all your household goods are put up at auction to the highest bidder. Sick, sorrowful, disappointed, weary of life, the grave welcomes you to rest, but leaves your helpless wife and daughter to begin alone the hard struggle of life. Go to the departments of Washington and what do you find there, a large majority of the female clerks from the first families in the land. Go to the mercantile establishments, the garrets and cellars of our metropolis, the sinks of iniquity and vice, the busy marts of trade in your own city, and there are the daughters and sisters of Supreme Court judges, presidents, senators, congressmen, priests and bishops.

Remember, vice recruits its ranks not from the children of lust but from the gay, the fashionable, the helpless, those who know not how to work, but yet must eat. The stern question presses itself on our consideration: what can these soft white hands and listless brains do for an honorable support? Make shirts at twelve cents a piece in a New York garret? Teach school at $30 a month and pay $6 a week for board? Go out to service as a waitress or chambermaid at $12 a month and be on the jump 16 hours out of the 24? Or marry a millionaire who drives fast horses, drinks good whiskey, puffs tobacco smoke in her face, and reminds her every day that he married a pauper and expects her to act with becoming humility. "Give a man," says Alexander Hamilton, "a right over any subsistence and he has a power over my whole moral being." When a woman marries a man for a home, for silks, jewels, equippage, she not only degrades herself, but sacrifices him. The sweet incense of love never rises from such attars, and the fruit of such union is blighted ere it blooms. . . .

Encourage your daughters, sisters, wives to enter into all honest and profitable employment, not only for their own first hand happiness, but for the safety of public morals, for thus only can you strike a blow at licentiousness and excess that shall be seen and felt throughout the land. Girls see all this more readily than their parents. I am in daily receipt of letters from them from all parts of the country expressing the strongest desire for education and profitable work, but unfortunately, these are the very girls who have no means to carry out their desires. Those who have rich parents and who could be thoroughly educated are so enervated by ease and luxury and the firm faith that hardship and trial can never come to them, that they have no motive stimulating them to effort.

But, say some, would not all this conflict with what seems to be the special destiny of girls, marriage and maternity? When women are independent and self-supporting, fewer will enter the marriage relation with the present gross conceptions of its rights and duties, for the cunning girl is to be wise as well as healthy and self-supporting. In the higher civilization now dawning upon us, the love element of pure, refined women guided and controlled by conscience, science, and religion, will find higher, purer outlets for its forces, giving us that glorious period when old maids will be honored and revered. The world has always had its Marys as well as Marthas, women who preferred to sit at the feet of wisdom, to learn science and philosophy rather than to be busy housewives; mothers of ideas, music, poetry and painting rather than of men. All honor to the Mary Carpenters, Florence Nightingales, Maria Mitchells, Harriet Hossners, Louisa Alcotts, Anna Dickensons, Susan B. Anthonys, and the long line of Grimkes, saints and philanthropists, who have directed themselves to act, religion, and reform. It is as absurd to educate all girls for wives and nothing more as it would be to educate all boys for husbands and nothing more.

Again, no girl should marry until she is at least 25 years of age, as she does not reach physical maturity before that time. Thus, many years could be devoted to reading, thought, and study, to a preparation for that higher companioned life of the spirit and intellect with pure, cultivated, scholarly men.

If husbands found this companionship in their wives in science, philosophy, and government, our whole social life would be refined and educated and marriage would be a far more happy and permanent relation than it is today. But marriage has thus far been based wholly on the mass idea, a condition of subjection for women. The Methodist Church has taken the initiative step to the higher idea. I understand by an act in their ecclesiastical councils, they have dropped the word "obey" from their marriage ceremony. All praise to the Methodist Church! When sinners have a proper self-respect, a laudable pride of sex, they will (?) all their old barbarisms of the past that point in any way to the subject condition of woman in either the state, the church, or the home.

Until all others follow her example, I hope all girls will insist on being married by the Methodist ceremony and clergymen. . . .

Questions

1. *Abilities, Class, Gender, Race/Ethnicity, and Sexual Orientation.* Do Elizabeth Cady Stanton's arguments for change in the rearing of girls reinforce dominant societal views about abilities, class, gender, race/ethnicity, and sexual orientation?

2. *Common Themes.* What common themes are found in the Stewart and Stanton speeches?

Paula Gunn Allen, Who Is Your Mother? Red Roots of White Feminism, in *The Sacred Hoop: Recovering the Feminine in American Indian Traditions* 209, 209–21 (1986)

At Laguna Pueblo in New Mexico, "Who is your mother?" is an important question. At Laguna, one of several of the ancient Keres gynocratic societies of the region, your mother's identity is the key to your own identity. Among the Keres, every individual has a place within the universe—human and nonhuman—and that place is defined by clan membership. In turn, clan membership is dependent on matrilineal descent. Of course, your mother is not only that woman whose womb formed and released you—the term refers in every individual case to an entire generation of women whose psychic, and consequently physical, "shape" made the psychic existence of the following generation possible. But naming your own mother (or her equivalent) enables people to place you precisely within the universal web of your life, in each of its dimensions: cultural, spiritual, personal, and historical.

Among the Keres, "context" and "matrix" are equivalent terms, and both refer to approximately the same thing as knowing your derivation and place. Failure to know your mother, that is, your position and its attendant traditions, history, and place in the scheme of things, is failure to remember your significance, your reality, your right relationship to earth and society. It is the same as being lost—isolated, abandoned, self-estranged, and alienated from your own life. This importance of tradition in the life of every member of the community is not confined to Keres Indians; all American Indian Nations place great value on traditionalism.

The Native American sense of the importance of continuity with one's cultural origins runs counter to contemporary American ideas: in many instances, the immigrants to America have been eager to cast off cultural ties, often seeing their antecedents as backward, restrictive, even shameful. Rejection of tradition constitutes one of the major features of American life, an attitude that reaches far back into American colonial history and that now is validated by virtually every cultural institution in the country. Feminist practice, at least in the cultural artifacts the community values most, follows this cultural trend as well. . . .

Contemporary Indian communities value individual members who are deeply connected to the traditional ways of their people, even after centuries of concerted and brutal effort on the part of the American government, the churches, and the corporate system to break the connections between individuals and their tribal world. In fact, in the view of the traditionals, rejection of one's culture—one's traditions, language, people—is the result of colonial oppression and is hardly to be applauded. They believe that the roots of oppression are to be found in the loss of tradition and memory because that loss is always accompanied by a loss of a positive sense of self. In short, Indians think it is important to remember, while Americans believe it is important to forget.

The traditional Indians' view can have a significant impact if it is expanded to mean that the sources of social, political, and philosophical thought in the Americas not only should be recognized and honored by Native Americans but should be embraced by American society. If American society judiciously modeled the traditions of the various Native Nations, the place of women in society could become central, the distribution of goods and power would be egalitarian, the elderly would be respected, honored, and protected as a primary social and cultural resource, the ideals of physical beauty would be considerably enlarged (to include "fat," strong-featured women, gray-haired, and wrinkled individuals, and others who in contemporary American culture are viewed as "ugly"). Additionally, the destruction of the biota, the life sphere, and the natural resources of the planet would be curtailed, and the spiritual nature of human and nonhuman life would become a primary organizing principle of human society. And if the traditional tribal systems that are emulated included pacifist ones, war would cease to be a major method of human problem solving.

Re-membering Connections and Histories

The belief that rejection of tradition and of history is a useful response to life is reflected in America's amazing loss of memory concerning its origins in the matrix and context of Native America. America does not seem to remember that it derived its wealth, its values, its food, much of its medicine, and a large part of its "dream" from Native America. It is ignorant of the genesis of its culture in this Native American land, and that ignorance helps to perpetuate the longstanding European and Middle Eastern monotheistic, hierarchical, patriarchal cultures' oppression of women, gays, and lesbians, people of color, working class, unemployed people, and the elderly. Hardly anyone in America speculates that the constitutional system of government might be as much a product of American Indian ideas and practices as of colonial American and Anglo-European revolutionary fervor.

Even though Indians are officially and informally ignored as intellectual movers and shapers in the United States, Britain, and Europe, they are peoples with ancient tenure on this soil. During the ages when tribal societies existed in the Americas largely untouched by patriarchal oppression, they developed elaborate systems of thought that included science, philosophy, and government based on a belief in the central importance of female energies, autonomy of individuals, cooperation, human dignity, human freedom, and egalitarian distribution of status, goods, and services. Respect for others, reverence for life, and, as a by-product, pacifism as a way of life; importance of kinship ties in the customary ordering of social interaction; a sense of the sacredness and mystery of existence; balance and harmony in relationships both sacred and secular were all features of life among the tribal confederacies and nations. And in those that lived by the largest number of these principles, gynarchy was the norm rather than the exception. Those systems are as yet unmatched in any contemporary industrial, agrarian, or postindustrial society on earth.

[T]here are many female gods recognized and honored by the tribes and Nations. Femaleness was highly valued, both respected and feared, and all social institutions reflected this attitude. Even modern sayings, such as the Cheyenne statement that a people is not conquered until the hearts of the women are on the ground, express the Indians' understanding that without the power of woman the people will not live, but with it, they will endure and prosper.

Indians did not confine this belief in the central importance of female energy to matters of worship. Among many of the tribes (perhaps as many as 70 percent of them in North America alone), this belief was reflected in all of their social institutions. The Iroquois Constitution or White Roots of Peace, also called the Great Law of the Iroquois, codified the Matrons' decision-making and economic power:

> The lineal descent of the people of the Five Fires [the Iroquois Nations] shall run in the female line. Women shall be considered the progenitors of the Nation. They shall own the land and the soil. Men and women shall follow the status of their mothers. (Article 44)
>
> The women heirs of the chieftainship titles of the League shall be called Oiner or Otinner [Noble] for all time to come. (Article 45)
>
> If a disobedient chief persists in his disobedience after three warnings [by his female relatives, by his male relatives, and by one of his fellow council members, in that order], the matter shall go to the council of War Chiefs. The Chiefs shall then take away the title of the erring chief *by order of the women in whom the title is vested.* When the chief is deposed, the women shall notify the chiefs of the League. . .and the chiefs of the League shall sanction the act. The women will then select another of their sons as a candidate and the chiefs shall elect him. (Article 19) (Emphasis mine)

The Matrons held so much policy-making power traditionally that once, when their position was threatened they demanded its return, and consequently the power of women was fundamental in shaping the Iroquois Confederation sometime in the sixteenth or early seventeenth century. It was women

> who fought what may have been the first successful feminist rebellion in the New World. The year was 1600, or thereabouts, when these tribal feminists decided that they had had enough of unregulated warfare by their men. Lysistratas among the Indian women proclaimed a boycott on lovemaking and childbearing. Until the men conceded to them the power to decide upon war and peace, there would be no more warriors. Since the men believed that the women alone knew the secret of childbirth, the rebellion was instantly successful.
>
> In the Constitution of Deganawidah the founder of the Iroquois Confederation of Nations had said: "He caused the body of our mother,

> the woman, to be of great worth and honor. He purposed that she shall be endowed and entrusted with the birth and upbringing of men, and that she shall have the care of all that is planted by which life is sustained and supported and the power to breathe is fortified: *and moreover that the warriors shall be her assistants.*"
>
> The footnote of history was curiously supplied when Susan B. Anthony began her "Votes for Women" movement two and a half centuries later. Unknowingly the feminists chose to hold their founding convention of latter-day suffragettes in the town of Seneca [Falls], New York. The site was just a stone's throw from the old council house where the Iroquois women had plotted their feminist rebellion. (Emphasis mine)

Beliefs, attitudes, and laws such as these became part of the vision of American feminists and of other human liberation movements around the world. Yet feminists too often believe that no one has ever experienced the kind of society that empowered women and made that empowerment the basis of its rules of civilization. The price the feminist community must pay because it is not aware of the recent presence of gynarchical societies on this continent is unnecessary confusion, division, and much lost time.

The Root of Oppression Is Loss of Memory

An odd thing occurs in the minds of Americans when Indian civilization is mentioned: little or nothing. As I write this, I am aware of how far removed my version of the roots of American feminism must seem to those steeped in either mainstream or radical versions of feminism's history. I am keenly aware of the lack of image Americans have about our continent's recent past. I am intensely conscious of popular notions of Indian women as beasts of burden, squaws, traitors, or, at best, vanished denizens of a long-lost wilderness. How odd, then, must my contention seem that the gynocratic tribes of the American continent provided the basis for all the dreams of liberation that characterize the modern world.

We as feminists must be aware of our history on this continent. We need to recognize that the same forces that devastated the gynarchies of Britain and the Continent also devastated the ancient African civilizations, and we must know that those same materialistic, antispiritual forces are presently engaged in wiping out the same gynarchical values, along with the peoples who adhere to them, in Latin America. I am convinced that those wars were and continue to be about the imposition of patriarchal civilization over the holistic, pacifist, and spirit-based gynarchies they supplant. To that end the wars of imperial conquest have not been solely or even mostly waged over the land and its resources, but they have been fought within the bodies, minds, and hearts of the people of the earth for dominion over them. I think this is the reason traditionals say we must remember our origins, our cultures, our histories, our mothers and grandmothers, for without that memory, which implies continuance rather than nostalgia, we are doomed to engulfment by a paradigm that is fundamentally inimical to the vitality, autonomy, and self-empowerment essential for satisfying, high-quality life. . . .

A Feminist Heroine

Early in the women's suffrage movement, Eva Emery Dye, an Oregon suffragette, went looking for a heroine to embody her vision of feminism. She wanted a historical figure whose life would symbolize the strengthened power of women. She found Sacagawea (or Sacajawea) buried in the journals of Lewis and Clark. The Shoshoni teenager had traveled with the Lewis and Clark expedition, carrying her infant son, and on a small number of occasions acted as translator.[12]

Dye declared that Sacagawea, whose name is thought to mean Bird Woman, had been the guide to the historic expedition, and through Dye's work Sacagawea became enshrined in American memory as a moving force and friend of the whites, leading them in the settlement of western North America.[13]

But Native American roots of white feminism reach back beyond Sacagawea. The earliest white women on this continent were well acquainted with tribal women. They were neighbors to a number of tribes and often shared food, information, child care, and health care. Of course, little is made of these encounters in official histories of colonial America, the period from the Revolution to the Civil War, or on the ever-moving frontier. Nor, to my knowledge, has either the significance or incidence of intermarriage between Indian and white or between Indian and Black been explored. By and large, the study of Indian-white relations has been focused on government and treaty relations, warfare, missionization, and education. It has been almost entirely documented in terms of formal white Christian patriarchal impacts and assaults on Native Americans, though they are not often characterized as assaults but as "civilizing the savages." Particularly in organs of popular culture and miseducation, the focus has been on what whites imagine to be degradation of

12. Ella E. Clark & Margot Evans, Sacagawea of the Lewis and Clark Expedition 93–98 (1979). Clark details the fascinating, infuriating, and very funny scholarly escapade of how our suffragette foremothers created a feminist hero from the scant references to the teenage Shoshoni wife of the expedition's official translator, Pierre Charbonneau.

13. The implications of this maneuver did not go unnoticed by either whites or Indians, for the statues of the idealized Shoshoni woman, the Native American matron Sacagawea, suggest that American tenure on American land, indeed, the right to be on this land, is given to whites by her. While that implication is not overt, it certainly is suggested in the image of her that the sculptor chose: a tall, heavy woman, standing erect, nobly pointing the way westward with upraised hand. The impression is furthered by the habit of media and scholar of referring to her as "the guide." Largely because of the popularization of the circumstances of Sacagawea's participation in the famed Lewis and Clark expedition, Indian people have viewed her as a traitor to her people, likening her to Malinalli (La Malinche, who acted as interpreter for Cortés and bore him a son) and Pocahontas, that unhappy girl who married John Rolfe (not John Smith) and died in England after bearing him a son. Actually none of these women engaged in traitorous behavior. Sacagawea led a long life, was called Porivo (Chief Woman) by the Commanches, among whom she lived for more than twenty years, and in her old age engaged her considerable skill at speaking and manipulating white bureaucracy to help in assuring her Shoshoni people decent reservation holdings.

A full discussion is impossible here but an examination of American child-rearing practices, societal attitudes toward women and exhibited by women (when compared to the same in Old World cultures) as well as the foodstuffs, medicinal materials, countercultural and alternative cultural systems, and the deeply Indian values these reflect should demonstrate the truth about informal acculturation and cross-cultural connections in the Americas.

Indian women ("squaws"), their equally imagined love of white government and white conquest ("princesses"), and the horrifyingly misleading, fanciful tales of "bloodthirsty, backward primitives" assaulting white Christian settlers who were looking for life, liberty, and happiness in their chosen land.

But, regardless of official versions of relations between Indians and whites or other segments of the American population, the fact remains that great numbers of apparently "white" or "Black" Americans carry notable degrees of Indian blood. With that blood has come the culture of the Indian, informing the lifestyles, attitudes, and values of their descendents. Somewhere along the line—and often quite recently—an Indian woman was giving birth to and raising the children of a family both officially and informally designated as white or Black—not Indian. In view of this, it should be evident that one of the major enterprises of Indian women in America has been the transfer of Indian values and culture to as large and influential a segment of American immigrant populations as possible. Their success in this endeavor is amply demonstrated in the Indian values and social styles that increasingly characterize American life. Among these must be included "permissive" childrearing practices . . . .Native Americans did not believe that physical or psychological abuse of children would result in their edification. They did not believe that children are born in sin, are congenitally predisposed to evil, or that a good parent who wishes the child to gain salvation, achieve success, or earn the respect of her or his fellows can be helped to those ends by physical or emotional torture.

The early Americans saw the strongly protective attitude of the Indian people as a mark of the "savagery"—as they saw the Indian's habit of bathing frequently, their sexual openness, their liking for scant clothing, their raucous laughter at most things, their suspicion and derision of authoritarian structures, their quick pride, their genuine courtesy, their willingness to share what they had with others less fortunate than they, their egalitarianism, their ability to act as if various lifestyles were a normal part of living, and their granting that women were of equal or, in individual cases, of greater value than men.

Yet the very qualities that marked Indian life in the sixteenth century have, over the centuries since contact between the two worlds occurred, come to mark much of contemporary American life. And those qualities, which I believe have passed into white culture from Indian culture, are the very ones that fundamentalists, immigrants from Europe, the Middle East, and Asia often find the most reprehensible. Third-and fourth-generation Americans indulge in growing nudity, informality in social relations, egalitarianism, and the rearing of women who value autonomy, strength, freedom, and personal dignity—and who are often derided by European, Asian, and Middle Eastern men for those qualities. Contemporary Americans value leisure almost as much as tribal people do. They find themselves increasingly unable to accept child abuse as a reasonable way to nurture. They bathe more than any other industrial people on earth—much to the scorn of their white cousins across the Atlantic, and they sometimes enjoy a good laugh even at their own expense (though they still have a less developed sense of the ridiculous than one might wish).

Contemporary Americans find themselves more and more likely to adopt a "live and let live" attitude in matters of personal sexual and social styles. Two-thirds of their diet and a large share of their medications and medical treatments mirror or are directly derived from Native American sources. Indianization is not a simple concept, to be sure, and it is one that Americans often find themselves resisting; but it is a process that has taken place, regardless of American resistance to recognizing the source of many if not most of American's vaunted freedoms in our personal, family, social, and political arenas.

This is not to say that Americans have become Indian in every attitude, value, or social institution. Unfortunately, Americans have a way to go in learning how to live in the world in ways that improve the quality of life for each individual while doing minimal damage to the biota, but they have adopted certain basic qualities of perception and certain attitudes that are moving them in that direction.

An Indian-Focused Version of American History

American colonial ideas of self-government came as much from the colonists' observations of tribal governments as from their Protestant or Greco-Roman heritage. Neither Greece nor Rome had the kind of pluralistic democracy as that concept has been understood in the United States since Andrew Jackson, but the tribes, particularly the gynarchical tribal confederacies, did. It is true that the *oligarchic* form of government that colonial Americans established was originally based on Greco-Roman systems in a number of important ways, such as its restriction of citizenship to propertied white males over twenty-one years of age, but it was never a form that Americans as a whole have been entirely comfortable with. Politics and government in the United States during the Federalist period also reflected the English common law system as it had evolved under patriarchal feudalism and monarchy—hence the United States' retention of slavery and restriction of citizenship to propertied white males.

The Federalists did make one notable change in the feudal system from which their political system derived on its Anglo side. They rejected blooded aristocracy and monarchy. This idea came from the Protestant Revolt to be sure, but it was at least reinforced by colonial America's proximity to American Indian nonfeudal confederacies and their concourse with those confederacies over the two hundred years of the colonial era. It was this proximity and concourse that enabled the revolutionary theorists to "dream up" a system in which all local polities would contribute to and be protected by a central governing body responsible for implementing policies that bore on the common interest of all. It should also be noted that the Reformation followed Columbus's contact with the Americas and that his and [the sixteenth-century explorer Peter] Martyr's reports concerning Native Americans' free and easy egalitarianism were in circulation by the time the Reformation took hold.

The Iroquois federal system, like that of several in the vicinity of the American colonies, is remarkably similar to the organization of the federal system of the United States. It was made up of local, "state," and federal bodies composed of executive, legislative, and judicial branches. The Council of Matrons was the executive: it instituted and determined general policy. The village, tribal (several villages), and Confederate councils determined and implemented policies when they did not conflict with the broader Council's decisions or with theological precepts that ultimately determined policy at all levels. The judicial was composed of the men's councils and the Matron's council, who sat together to make decisions. Because the matrons were the ceremonial center of the system, they were also the prime policymakers.

Obviously, there are major differences between the structure of the contemporary American government and that of the Iroquois. Two of those differences were and are crucial to the process of just government. The Iroquois system is spirit-based, while that of the United States is secular, and the Iroquois Clan Matrons formed the executive. The female executive function was directly tied to the ritual nature of the Iroquois politic, for the executive was lodged in the hands of the Matrons of particular clans across village, tribe, and national lines. The executive office was hereditary, and only sons of eligible clans could serve, at the behest of the Matrons of their clans, on the councils at the three levels. Certain daughters inherited the office of Clan Matron through their clan affiliations. No one could impeach or disempower a Matron, though her violation of certain laws could result in her ineligibility for the Matron's council. For example, a woman who married *and took her husband's name* could not hold the title Matron.

American ideas of social justice came into sharp focus through the commentaries of Iroquois observers who traveled in France in the colonial period. These observers expressed horror at the great gap between the lifestyles of the wealthy and poor, remarking to the French philosopher Montaigne, who would heavily influence the radical communities of Europe, England, and America, that "they had noticed that in Europe there seemed to be two moities, consisting of the rich 'full gorged' with wealth, and the poor, starving 'and bare with need and povertie.' The Indian tourists not only marveled at the division, but marveled that the poor endured 'such an injustice, and that they took not the others by the throte, or set fire on their house.' " It must be noted that the urban poor eventually did just that in the French Revolution. The writings of Montaigne and of those he influenced provided the theoretical framework and the vision that propelled the struggle for liberty, justice, and equality on the Continent and later throughout the British empire.

The feminist idea of power as it ideally accrues to women stems from tribal sources. The central importance of the clan Matrons in the formulation and determination of domestic and foreign policy as well as in their primary role in the ritual and ceremonial life of their respective Nations was the single most important attribute of the Iroquois, as of the Cherokee and Muskogee, who traditionally inhabited the southern Atlantic region. The latter peoples were removed to what is now Oklahoma during the Jackson administration, but prior to the American Revolution they had regular and frequent communication with and impact on both the British colonizers and later the American people, including the African peoples brought here as slaves.

Ethnographer Lewis Henry Morgan wrote an account of Iroquoian matriarchal culture, published in 1877, that heavily influenced Marx and the development of communism, particularly lending it the idea of the liberation of women from patriarchal dominance. The early socialists in Europe, especially in Russia, saw women's liberation as a central aspect of the socialist revolution. Indeed, the basic ideas of socialism, the egalitarian distribution of goods and power, the peaceful ordering of society, and the right of every member of society to participate in the work and benefits of that society, are ideas that pervade American Indian political thought and action. And it is through various channels—the informal but deeply effective Indianization of Europeans, and christianizing Africans, the social and political theory of the confederacies feuding and then intertwining with European dreams of liberty and justice, and, more recently, the work of Morgan and the writings of Marx and Engels—that the age-old gynarchical systems of egalitarian government found their way into contemporary feminist theory.

When Eva Emery Dye discovered Sacagawea and honored her as the guiding spirit of American womanhood, she may have been wrong in bare historical fact, but she was quite accurate in terms of deeper truth. The statues that been erected depicting Sacagawea as a Matron in her prime signify an understanding in the American mind, however unconscious, that the source of just government, of right ordering of social relationships, the dream of "liberty and justice for all" can be gained only by following the Indian Matrons' guidance. For, as Dr. Anna Howard Shaw said of Sacagawea at the National American Woman's Suffrage Association in 1905:

> Forerunner of civilization, great leader of men, patient and motherly woman, we bow our hearts to do you honor!. . .May we the daughters of an alien race. . .learn the lessons of calm endurance, of patient persistence and unfaltering courage exemplified in your life, in our efforts to lead men through the Pass of justice, which goes over the mountains of prejudice and conservatism to the broad land of the perfect freedom of a true republic; one in which men and women together shall in perfect equality solve the problems of a nation that knows no caste, no race, no sex in opportunity, in responsibility or in justice! May 'the eternal womanly' ever lead us on!

Sarah Winnemucca, The Way Agents Get Rich, in *Native American Testimony: A Chronicle of Indian-White Relations From Prophecy to the Present, 1492–1992*, at 198–202 (Peter Nabokov ed., 1991)

Sarah Winnemucca always spoke her mind. A nationally known Paiute Indian critic of reservation policy in the late nineteenth century, she had been born in 1844 in present-day Nevada. Although her father, Chief Winnemucca, had guided Captain John C. Fremont to California, her childhood was relatively free from white influence.

After the Paiute War of 1860, however, tensions rose between her tribe and encroaching settlers. Sarah's own mother, sister, and brother died at white hands. In 1872 she experienced the removal of her tribe to a temporary reservation in Oregon, and then another forced move to a second reservation in Washington State, before they were allowed back to Nevada.

Sarah was scarred by these experiences. Her bitter chronicle, Life Among the Paiutes, *published in 1883, described her eviction from a Catholic convent school because she was Indian, and a series of personal feuds with*

Indian agents in Oregon and Nevada. This selection opens with Paiute experiences on their earliest Nevada reservation. It ends with the story of her brother, a leader named Natchez, whose defiance of the Indian agent's power led to imprisonment at Alcatraz Island in California.

In 1864–65 there was a governor by the name of Nye. There were no whites living on the reservation at that time, and there was not any agent as yet. My people were living there and fishing, as they had always done. Some white men came down from Virginia City to fish. My people went up to Carson City to tell Governor Nye that some white men were fishing on their reservation. He sent down some soldiers to drive them away. Mr. Nye is the only governor who ever helped my people,—I mean that protected them when they called on him in this way.

In 1865 we had another trouble with our white brothers. It was early in the spring, and we were then living at Dayton, Nevada, when a company of soldiers came through the place and stopped and spoke to some of my people, and said, "You have been stealing cattle from the white people at Harney Lake." They said also that they would kill everything that came in their way, men, women and children. . . .

After the soldiers had killed all but some little children and babies still tied up in their baskets, the soldiers took them also, and set the camp on fire and threw them into the flames to see them burn alive. I had one baby brother killed there. My sister jumped on father's best horse and ran away. As she ran, the soldiers ran after her; but, thanks be to the Good Father in the Spirit-land, my dear sister got away. This almost killed my poor papa. Yet my people kept peaceful. . . .

I will tell you the doings of the agents in [that]agency. The first six who came I did not know. In 1866, after my poor mother and sister Mary died, I came down from Virginia City to live with my brother Natchez, while there were some white men living on the agency. They had a great many cattle on the reservation at the time. My people did not know how to work as yet.

The agent was living there, and had a store of dry goods which he sold to my people. I staid [*sic*] with my brother all winter, and got along very poorly, for we had nothing to eat half of the time. Sometimes we would go to the agent's house and he would get my sister-in-law to wash some clothes, and then he would give us some flour to take home.

In the month of May the agent sold an Indian man some powder. He crossed the river, when he was met by one of the agent's men, who shot him dead on the spot, because he had the powder. My brother and I did not know what to do. All our people were wild with excitement. Brother and I thought he did wrong to sell the powder to one of our men, knowing it was against the law. . . .this is the way all the Indian agents get rich. The first thing they do is to start a store; the next thing is to take in cattle men, and cattle men pay the agent one dollar a head. In this way they get rich very soon, so that they can have their gold-headed canes, with their names engraved on them. . . .

Then came another agent by the name of Spencer. He was a better one than we had ever had. He issued some blankets to some old men and women and blind people, and gave brother some pieces of land to work upon. He then gave my people wagons,—about ten altogether; and he had his daughter brought as a teacher, at the rate of fifty dollars a month. But he soon died, and then came our present agent.

He was not married at the time, but he very soon learned that there was money to be made, so he went back and got married. Of course he put his wife in as teacher. Mr. MacMasters, for that is his name, has his own method of making my people divide the produce. If they raise five sacks of grain, they give one sack for the Big Father in Washington; if they have only three sacks, they still have to send one. Every fourth load of hay goes to the Big Father at Washington, yet he does not give my people the seed.

The head-farmer, who is called Mushrush, never shows my people how to work. This is why they said, "Why does the Big Father want us to pay him when he does not give us the seed? We have to pay for the seed ourselves." Both the agent and farmer told my people they would have to pay it or the Big Father would take away their wagons. So my people talked it over and said, "We will pay it."

Later they got up a paper, which the agent and the farmer wanted my people to sign. The subchief would not put his hand to the pen. He said to the agent,—"I have been working for so many years, and I have never received anything as yet. You say it is supplies you are sending me and my people; but I am sick and tired of lies, and I won't sign any paper."

Of course our agent, Mr. MacMasters, told him to leave the reservation. His wagon was taken from him. At this my people sent me down to San Francisco to tell the commanding officer. I did so. I gave Gen. McDowell a full account of the doings, and he reported him to the authorities.

The following spring my poor brother Natchez went to the agent and asked him to help him to a plough, and to give him a set of harness. He told my brother to go away. "You and your sister," he said, "talk about me all the time. I don't want you and your sister here."

At this my poor brother got angry and said to him, "This is my reservation, not yours. I am going to stay here just as long as I like. My poor father and I never got so much as an old rag from any agent that ever came here." At this our minister got angry, and telegraphed to the soldiers to come and take brother and carry him to the Acotrass [Alcatraz] Islands.

He wrote a letter, saying all my people wanted him to send my brother away where they could never see him any more. After he had written it, he called up all the head men of our people, and told them he had written to their father in Washington for good clothing for them, and wished them to sign the paper. Of course, they did not know any better; they put their names to the paper, and signed their chief away! So the soldiers came and took brother to San Francisco, Cal.

Questions

1. *Hidden in Plain Sight Redux*. Paula Gunn Allen discusses the ways in which Native American thought and culture inform values, practices, and social institutions in the contemporary United States. What purposes are served by the dominant society failing to acknowledge these contributions?

2. *Difference without Domination*. Allen explains that Native American cul-

ture celebrates differences, recognizing that they contribute to balance in nature and in society. In Western European thought, however, differences are often viewed not as complementary but as oppositional, with one of the opposites more favored by the dominant society. For example, reason is frequently understood as the opposite of emotion. Rather than appreciating that reason and emotion together provide balance in intellectual thought, identifying the difference between reason and emotion leads to assigning reason a higher value. Explain how the excerpt from the Iroquois Constitution as it applied to the Iroquois Confederation of Nations creates differences that are complementary rather than oppositional and hierarchical. *See* Patricia Hill Collins, Black Feminist Thought: Knowledge, Consciousness, and the Politics of Empowerment, at p.55, for further discussion of hierarchical differences.

3. *Sacagawea*. How does Eva Emery Dye's story of Sacagawea reinforce racial and gender stereotypes? How do those stereotypes contribute to the widespread acceptance of the story in the dominant culture?

4. *Under Color of Law*. From Sarah Winnemucca's description of life on the reservation, how was the law used to legitimate exploitation of Native Americans?

Chapter 2

Systems of Oppression

The writings of Christine de Pizan and Paula Gunn Allen in Chapter 1 introduced us to the use of stereotypes and dichotomous, hierarchical thinking and how both are used to support and reinforce domination. The writings of Maria Stewart and Elizabeth Cady Stanton were helpful to us in understanding how abilism, classism, heterosexism, racism/ethnocentrism, and sexism operate simultaneously to perpetuate violence against women. The material found in this chapter will explore further these themes. An additional, related, theme in this chapter is how women act as agents even as they are subjected to victimization.

We are focusing on the social categories of abilities, class, gender, race/ethnicity, and sexual orientation in developing these themes because Western society is constructed around and attaches value to these categories. It is not, however, just that these categories have value, but that they have value in a particular way. Within each category one group is identified as "more important or more human or in some sense better than the others." Elizabeth V. Spelman, Inessential Woman: Problems of Exclusion in Feminist Thought 11-12 (1988).

Each person is unique; therefore, we can identify a great many differences between any two people. Western society, however, has not attached the same significance to all differences. The corollary to the observation that Western society has not attached significance to all differences is that differences based on abilities, class, gender, race/ethnicity, and sexual orientation are significant only because society has made them so. That is to say, the categories themselves as well as the consequences that flow from them are not innate or natural but are constructed by society. Teresa Amott and Julie Matthaei elaborate on the historical specificity of social categories:

> The concepts of gender, race-ethnicity, and class are neither trans-historical nor independent. Hence, it is artificial to discuss them outside of historical time and place, and separately from one another. At the same time, without such a set of concepts, it is impossible to make sense of women's disparate economic experiences.
>
> Gender, race-ethnicity, and class are not natural or biological categories which are unchanging over time and across cultures. Rather, these categories are socially constructed: they arise and are transformed in history, and themselves transform history. Although societies rationalize them as natural or god-given, ideas of appropriate feminine and masculine behavior vary widely across history and culture. Concepts and practices of race-ethnicity usually justified by religion or biology, also vary over time, reflecting the politics, economics, and ideology of a particular time and, in turn, reinforcing or transforming politics, economics, and ideology. For example,

> nineteenth-century European biologists Louis Agassiz and Count Arthur de Gobineau developed a taxonomy of race which divided humanity into separate and unequal racial species; this taxonomy was used to rationalize European colonization of Africa and Asia, and slavery in the United States. Class is perhaps the most historically specific category of all, clearly dependent upon the particular economic and social constellation of a society at a point in time. Still, notions of class as inherited or genetic continue to haunt us, harkening back to earlier eras in which lowly birth was thought to cause low intelligence and a predisposition to criminal activity.

Teresa L. Amott & Julie A. Matthaei, Race, Gender, and Work: A Multicultural Economic History of Women in the United States 12 (1991).

Marilyn Frye examines the oppression of women by identifying, through the metaphor of the bird cage, the systemic and pervasive constraints placed on women. A systemic analysis provides important insights for developing a framework for understanding and redressing violence against women. The metaphor of the bird cage directs us to focus on social and cultural institutions rather than on isolated, individual acts. The remaining excerpts in this chapter will serve to expand the bird cage metaphor, which Frye designs around gender domination, to take into account the interlocking oppressions of abilities, class, gender, race/ethnicity, and sexual orientation.

The excerpt taken from Patricia Hill Collins' book uses the framework of a matrix of domination consisting of interlocking systems of oppression. The matrix analysis allows for the consideration of multiple subordinated social categories as well as of a person's simultaneous experience of being an oppressor and oppressed. Collins also explores the entrenchment in Western European thought of dichotomous thinking and its concomitant dominant and subordinate hierarchies. Another important theme found in Collins' excerpt is the simultaneous interplay in women's lives of being victim/object and being agent/subject. All of these themes are critical to understanding the context in which violence against women occurs and all will be referenced frequently throughout the text.

Collins suggests that if we acknowledge the matrix of domination with regard to class, gender, and race, that will cause a paradigmatic shift of our thinking to include other oppressions such as sexual orientation. The last four essays in this chapter focus on issues of sexual orientation; heterosexism and homophobia contribute, along with abilism, classism, racism/ethnocentrism, and sexism, to violence against women. By *heterosexism* we mean the privileging of male-female sexual relationships, or as Gary Kinsman states "the practices of heterosexual hegemony to institutional and social settings and to sex and gender relations." Gary Kinsman, The Regulation of Desire: Sexuality in Canada 29 (1987). By *homophobia* we mean the fear of female-female or male-male sexual relationships as well as the fear of lesbians and gay men.[1]

The four essays consider the meaning of the social construction of homo-

---

1. The term *homophobia* might suggest that discrimination against lesbians and gay men is a psychological and individualized reaction. To understand homophobia in this way, however, ignores the political and social institutions that support it.

sexuality and heterosexuality. Adrienne Rich explores the invisibility of the assumption of heterosexuality that pervades our society. She exposes some of the underlying political forces supporting heterosexism that belie the claims that heterosexuality is "natural." Although Rich is clear about the social and economic forces supporting heterosexuality, her analysis suggests that both the "lesbian continuum" and the "lesbian existence" are part of a range of "woman-identified experience[s]" that are psychologically and biologically based. Yvon Appleby offers a critique of Rich that examines the meaning of sexuality, violence, compulsory heterosexuality, and the lesbian culture for women who are disabled.

John D'Emilio argues that a lesbian/gay identity was made possible by the development of the capitalist system of free labor that transformed the structure and function of the nuclear family. The essay's central contention is that the lesbian/gay identity is neither innate nor constant over history. A comparison of Rich's and D'Emilio's view of homosexuality is difficult because of the primacy that Rich places on gender differences, which are all but ignored by D'Emilio.

Finally, Carla Trujillo describes how homophobia and heterosexism operate in the Chicana/o community where women's sexuality is invisible, women are defined in terms of their relationship to men, womanhood is achieved through motherhood, and the Catholic religion exercises strong patriarchal control. Her account of the constraints on her life as a Chicana lesbian starkly delineates the axes of class, ethnicity, gender, and sexual orientation within the matrix of domination and demonstrates how oppressions interact to define her as an outsider.

Marilyn Frye, Oppression, in *The Politics of Reality: Essays in Feminist Theory* 1, 2–14 (1983)

The root of the word 'oppression' is the element 'press'. *The press of the crowd; pressed into military service; to press a pair of pants; printing press; press the button.* Presses are used to mold things or flatten them or reduce them in bulk, sometimes to reduce them by squeezing out the gasses or liquids in them. Something pressed is something caught between or among forces and barriers which are so related to each other that jointly they restrain, restrict or prevent the thing's motion or mobility. Mold. Immobilize. Reduce.

The mundane experience of the oppressed provides another clue. One of the most characteristic and ubiquitous features of the world as experienced by oppressed people is the double bind—situations in which options are reduced to a very few and all of them expose one to penalty, censure or deprivation. For example, it is often a requirement upon oppressed people that we smile and be cheerful. If we comply, we signal our docility and our acquiescence in our situation. We need not, then, be taken note of. We acquiesce in being made invisible, in our occupying no space. We participate in our own erasure. On the other hand, anything but the sunniest countenance exposes us to being perceived as mean, bitter, angry or dangerous. This means, at the least, that we may be found "difficult" or unpleasant to work with, which is enough to cost one one's livelihood; at worst, being seen as mean, bitter, angry or dangerous has been known to result in rape, arrest, beating and murder. One can only choose to risk one's preferred form and rate of annihilation.

Another example: It is common in the United States that women, especially younger women, are in a bind where neither sexual activity nor sexual inactivity is all right. If she is heterosexually active, a woman is open to censure and punishment for being loose, unprincipled or a whore. The "punishment" comes in the form of criticism, snide and embarrassing remarks, being treated as an easy lay by men, scorn from her more restrained female friends. She may have to lie and hide her behavior from her parents. She must juggle the risks of unwanted pregnancy and dangerous contraceptives. On the other hand, if she refrains from heterosexual activity, she is fairly constantly harassed by men who try to persuade her into it and pressure her to "relax" and "let her hair down"; she is threatened with labels like "frigid," "uptight," "man-hater," "bitch" and "cocktease." The same parents who would be disapproving of her sexual activity may be worried by her inactivity because it suggests she is not or will not be popular, or is not sexually normal. She may be charged with lesbianism. If a woman is raped, then if she has been heterosexually active she is subject to the presumption that she liked it (since her activity is presumed to show that she likes sex), and if she has not been heterosexually active, she is subject to the presumption that she liked it (since she is supposedly "repressed and frustrated"). Both heterosexual activity and heterosexual nonactivity are likely to be taken as proof that you wanted to be raped, and hence, of course, weren't *really* raped at all. You can't win. You are caught in a bind, caught between systematically related pressures.

Women are caught like this, too, by networks of forces and barriers that expose one to penalty, loss or contempt whether one works outside the home or not, is on welfare or not, bears children or not, raises children or not, marries or not, stays married or not, is heterosexual, lesbian, both or neither. Economic necessity; confinement to racial and/or sexual job ghettos; sexual harassment; sex discrimination; pressures of competing expectations and judgments about *women, wives* and *mothers* (in the society at large, in racial and ethnic subcultures and in one's own mind); dependence (full or partial) on husbands, parents or the state; commitment to political ideas; loyalties to racial or ethnic or other "minority" groups; the demands of self-respect and responsibilities to others. Each of these factors exists in complex tension with every other, penalizing or prohibiting all of the apparently available options. And nipping at one's heels, always, is the endless pack of little things. If one dresses one way, one is subject to the assumption that one is advertising one's sexual availability; if one dresses another way, one appears to "not care about oneself" or to be "unfeminine." If one uses "strong language," one invites categorization as a whore or slut; if one does not, one invites categorization as a "lady"—one too delicately constituted to cope with robust speech or the realities to which it presumably refers.

The experience of oppressed people is that the living of one's life is confined and shaped by forces and barriers which are not accidental or occasional and hence avoidable, but are systematically related to each other in such a way as to catch one between and among them and restrict or penalize motion in any direction. It is the experience of being caged in: all avenues, in every direction, are blocked or booby trapped.

Cages. Consider a birdcage. If you look very closely at just one wire in the cage, you cannot see the other wires. If your conception of what is before you is determined by this myopic focus, you could look at that one wire, up and down the length of it, and be unable to see why a bird would not just fly around the wire any time it wanted to go somewhere. Furthermore, even if, one day at a time, you myopically inspected each wire, you still could not see why a bird would have trouble going past the wires to get anywhere. There is no physical property of any one wire, *nothing* that the closest scrutiny could discover, that will reveal how a bird could be inhibited or harmed by it except in the most accidental way. It is only when you step back, stop looking at the wires one by one, microscopically, and take a macroscopic view of the whole cage, that you can see why the bird does not go anywhere; and then you will see it in a moment. It will require no great subtlety of mental powers. It is perfectly *obvious* that the bird is surrounded by a network of systematically related barriers, no one of which would be the least hinderance to its flight, but which, by their relations to each other, are as confining as the solid walls of a dungeon.

It is now possible to grasp one of the reasons why oppression can be hard to see and recognize: one can study the elements of an oppressive structure with great care and some good will without seeing the structure as a whole, and hence without seeing or being able to understand that one is looking at a cage and that there are people there who are caged, whose motion and mobility are restricted, whose lives are shaped and reduced.

The arresting of vision at a microscopic level yields such common confusion as that about the male door-opening ritual. This ritual, which is remarkably widespread across classes and races, puzzles many people, some of whom do and some of whom do not find it offensive. Look at the scene of the two people approaching a door. The male steps slightly ahead and opens the door. The male holds the door open while the female glides through. Then the male goes through. The door closes after them. "Now how," one innocently asks, "can those crazy womenslibbers say that is oppressive? The guy *removed* a barrier to the lady's smooth and unruffled progress." But each repetition of this ritual has a place in a pattern, in fact in several patterns. One has to shift the level of one's perception in order to see the whole picture.

The door-opening pretends to be a helpful service, but the helpfulness is false. This can be seen by noting that it will be done whether or not it makes any practical sense. Infirm men and men burdened with packages will open doors for able-bodied women who are free of physical burdens. Men will impose themselves awkwardly and jostle everyone in order to get to the door first. The act is not determined by convenience or grace. Furthermore, these very numerous acts of unneeded or even noisome "help" occur in counterpoint to a pattern of men not being helpful in many practical ways in which women might welcome help. What *women* experience is a world in which gallant princes charming commonly make a fuss about being helpful and providing small services when help and services are of little or no use, but in which there are rarely ingenious and adroit princes at hand when substantial assistance is really wanted either in mundane affairs or in situations of threat, assault or terror. There is no help with the (his) laundry; no help typing a report at 4:00 a.m.; no help in mediating disputes among relatives or children. There is nothing but advice that women should stay indoors after dark, be chaperoned by a man, or when it comes down to it "lie back and enjoy it."

The gallant gestures have no practical meaning. Their meaning is symbolic. The door-opening and similar services provided are services which really are needed by people who are for one reason or another incapacitated—unwell, burdened with parcels, etc. So the message is that women are incapable. The detachment of the acts from the concrete realities of what women need and do not need is a vehicle for the message that women's actual needs and interests are unimportant or irrelevant. Finally, these gestures imitate the behavior of servants toward masters and thus mock women, who are in most respects the servants and caretakers of men. The message of the false helpfulness of male gallantry is female dependence, the invisibility or insignificance of women, and contempt for women.

One cannot see the meanings of these rituals if one's focus is riveted upon the individual event in all its particularity, including the particularity of the individual man's present conscious intentions and motives and the individual woman's conscious perception of the event in the moment. It seems sometimes that people take a deliberately myopic view and fill their eyes with things seen microscopically in order not to see macroscopically. At any rate, whether it is deliberate or not, people can and do fail to see the oppression of women because they fail to see macroscopically and hence fail to see the various elements of the situation as systematically related in larger schemes.

As the cageness of the birdcage is a macroscopic phenomenon, the oppressiveness of the situations in which women live our various and different lives is a macroscopic phenomenon. Neither can be *seen* from a microscopic perspective. But when you look macroscopically you can see it—a network of forces and barriers which are systematically related and which conspire to the immobilization, reduction and molding of women and the lives we live. . . .

The image of the cage helps convey one aspect of the systematic nature of oppression. Another is the selection of occupants of the cages, and analysis of this aspect also helps account for the invisibility of the oppression of women.

It is as a woman (or as a Chicana/o or as a Black or Asian or lesbian) that one is entrapped.

> "Why can't I go to the park; you let Jimmy go!"
> "Because it's not safe for girls."
>
> "I want to be a secretary, not a seamstress; I don't want to learn to make dresses."
> "There's no work for negroes in that line; learn a skill where you can earn your living."

When you question why you are being blocked, why this barrier is in your path, the answer has not to do with individual talent or merit, handicap or failure; it has to do with your membership in some category understood as a "natural" or "physical" category. The "inhabitant" of the "cage" is not an individual but a group, all those of a certain category. If an individual is oppressed, it is in virtue of being a member of a group or category of people that is systematically reduced, molded, immobilized. Thus, to recognize a person as oppressed, one has to see that individual *as* belonging to a group of a certain sort.

There are many things which can encourage or inhibit perception of someone's membership in the sort of group or category in question here. In particular, it seems reasonable to suppose that if one of the devices of restriction and definition of the group is that of physical confinement or segregation, the confinement and separation would encourage recognition of the group as a group. This in turn would encourage the macroscopic focus which enables one to recognize oppression and encourages the individuals' identification and solidarity with other individuals of the group or category. But physical confinement and segregation of the group as a group is not common to all oppressive structures, and when an oppressed group is geographically and demographically dispersed the perception of it as a group is inhibited. There may be little or nothing in the situations of the individuals encouraging the macroscopic focus which would reveal the unity of the structure bearing down on all members of that group.*

A great many people, female and male and of every race and class, simply do not believe that *woman* is a category of oppressed people, and I think that this is in part because they have been fooled by the dispersal and assimilation of women throughout and into the systems of class and race which organize men. Our simply being dispersed makes it difficult for women to have knowledge of each other and hence difficult to recognize the shape of our common cage. The dispersal and assimilation of women throughout economic classes and races also divides us against each other practically and economically and thus attaches *interest* to the inability to see: for some, jealousy of their benefits, and for some, resentment of the others' advantages.

To get past this, it helps to notice that in fact women of all races and classes *are* together in a ghetto of sorts. There is a women's place, a sector, which is inhabited by women of all classes and races, and it is not defined by geographical boundaries but by function. The function is the service of men and men's interests as men define them, which includes the bearing and rearing of children. The details of the service and the working conditions vary by race and class, for men of different races and classes have different interests, perceive their interests differently, and express their needs and demands in different rhetorics, dialects and languages. But there are also some constants.

Whether in lower, middle or upper-class home or work situations, women's service work always includes personal service (the work of maids, butlers, cooks, personal secretaries),* sexual service (including provision for his genital sexual needs and bearing his children, but also including "being nice," "being attractive for him," etc.), and ego service (encouragement, support, praise, attention). Women's service work also is characterized everywhere by the fatal combination of responsibility and powerlessness: we are held responsible and we hold ourselves responsible for good outcomes for men and children in almost every respect though we have in almost no case power adequate

---

* Coerced assimilation is in fact one of the *policies* available to an oppressing group in its effort to reduce and/or annihilate another group. This tactic is used by the U.S. government, for instance, on the American Indians.

* At higher class levels women may not *do* all these kinds of work, but are generally still responsible for hiring and supervising those who do it. These services are still, in these cases, women's responsibility.

to that project. The details of the subjective experience of this servitude are local. They vary with economic class and race and ethnic tradition as well as the personalities of the men in question. So also are the details of the forces which coerce our tolerance of this servitude particular to the different situations in which different women live and work.

All this is not to say that women do not have, assert and manage sometimes to satisfy our own interests, nor to deny that in some cases and in some respects women's independent interests do overlap with men's. But at every race/class level and even across race/class lines men do not serve women as women serve men. "Women's sphere" may be understood as the "service sector," taking the latter expression much more widely and deeply than is usual in discussions of the economy. . . .

It seems to be the human condition that in one degree or another we all suffer frustration and limitation, all encounter unwelcome barriers, and all are damaged and hurt in various ways. Since we are a social species, almost all of our behavior and activities are structured by more than individual inclination and the conditions of the planet and its atmosphere. No human is free of social structures, nor (perhaps) would happiness consist in such freedom. Structure consists of boundaries, limits and barriers; in a structured whole, some motions and changes are possible, and others are not. If one is looking for an excuse to dilute the word 'oppression', one can use the fact of social structure as an excuse and say that everyone is oppressed. But if one would rather get clear about what oppression is and is not, one needs to sort out the sufferings, harms and limitations and figure out which are elements of oppression and which are not.

From what I have already said here, it is clear that if one wants to determine whether a particular suffering, harm or limitation is part of someone's being oppressed, one has to look at it *in context* in order to tell whether it is an element in an oppressive structure: one has to see if it is part of an enclosing structure of forces and barriers which tends to the immobilization and reduction of a group or category of people. One has to look at how the barrier or force fits with others and to whose benefit or detriment it works. As soon as one looks at examples, it becomes obvious that not everything which frustrates or limits a person is oppressive, and not every harm or damage is due to or contributes to oppression. . . .

The boundaries of a racial ghetto in an American city serve to some extent to keep white people from going in, as well as to keep ghetto dwellers from going out. A particular white citizen may be frustrated or feel deprived because s/he cannot stroll around there and enjoy the "exotic" aura of a "foreign" culture, or shop for bargains in the ghetto swap shops. In fact, the existence of the ghetto, of racial segregation, does deprive the white person of knowledge and harm her/his character by nurturing unwarranted feelings of superiority. But this does not make the white person in this situation a member of an oppressed race or a person oppressed because of her/his race. One must look at the barrier. It limits the activities and the access of those on both sides of it (though to different degrees). But it is a product of the intention, planning and action of whites for the benefit of whites, to secure and maintain privileges that are available to whites generally, as members of the dominant and privileged group. Though the existence of the barrier has some bad consequences for whites, the barrier does not exist in systematic relationship with other barriers and forces forming a structure oppressive to whites; quite the contrary. It is part of a structure which oppresses the ghetto dwellers and thereby (and by white intention) protects and furthers white interests as dominant white culture understands them. This barrier is not oppressive to whites, even though it is a barrier to whites.

Barriers have different meanings to those on opposite sides of them, even though they are barriers to both. The physical walls of a prison no more dissolve to let an outsider in than to let an insider out, but for the insider they are confining and limiting while to the outsider they may mean protection from what s/he takes to be threats posed by insiders—freedom from harm or anxiety. A set of social and economic barriers and forces separating two groups may be felt, even painfully, by members of both groups and yet may mean confinement to one and liberty and enlargement of opportunity to the other.

The service sector of the wives/mommas/assistants/girls is almost exclusively a woman-only sector; its boundaries not only enclose women but to a very great extent keep men out. Some men sometimes encounter this barrier and experience it as a restriction on their movements, their activities, their control or their choices of "lifestyle." Thinking they might like the simple nurturant life (which they may imagine to be quite free of stress, alienation and hard work), and feeling deprived since it seems closed to them, they thereupon announce the discovery that they are oppressed, too, by "sex roles." But that barrier is erected and maintained by men, for the benefit of men. It consists of cultural and economic forces and pressures in a culture and economy controlled by men in which, at every economic level and in all racial and ethnic subcultures, economy, tradition—and even ideologies of liberation—work to keep at least local culture and economy in male control.*

The boundary that sets apart women's sphere is maintained and promoted by men generally for the benefit of men generally, and men generally do benefit from its existence, even the man who bumps into it and complains of the inconvenience. That barrier is protecting his classification and status as a male, as superior, as having a right to sexual access to a female or females. It protects a kind of citizenship which is superior to that of females of his class and race, his access to a wider range of better paying and higher status work, and his right to prefer unemployment to the degradation of doing lower status or "women's" work.

If a person's life or activity is affected by some force or barrier that person encounters, one may not conclude that the person is oppressed simply because the person encounters that barrier or force; nor simply because the encounter is unpleasant, frustrating or painful to that person at that time; nor simply because the existence of the barrier or force, or the processes which maintain or apply it, serve to deprive that person of something of value. One must look at the barrier or force and answer certain questions about it. Who constructs and maintains it? Whose interests are served by its existence? Is it

---

* Of course this is complicated by race and class. Machismo and "Black manhood" politics seem to help keep Latin or Black men in control of more cash than Latin or Black women control; but these politics seem to me also to ultimately help keep the larger economy in *white* male control.

part of a structure which tends to confine, reduce and immobilize some group? Is the individual a member of the confined group? Various forces, barriers and limitations a person may encounter or live with may be part of an oppressive structure or not, and if they are, that person may be on either the oppressed or the oppressor side of it. One cannot tell which by how loudly or how little the person complains.

Note and Questions

1. *Double Bind and the Bird Cage.* According to Marilyn Frye, how does the metaphor of the bird cage illustrate how the double binds experienced by women are a product of systemic oppression? How does Frye use the bird cage metaphor to help us understand that women are offered inadequate (bad) choices and why those choices are inadequate?

2. *Victim/Agent and the Bird Cage.* Does the bird cage metaphor necessarily portray women only as victims?

3. *Door Opening and the Bird Cage.* How does the metaphor of the bird cage help us to understand how a seemingly insignificant gesture, such as a man opening the door for a woman, represents and reinforces sexism? How does the interpretation of the gesture of opening the door change depending on the abilities, class, race/ethnicity, and sexual orientation of the man and the woman?

4. *Builders of the Bird Cage.* Although implicit in Frye's theory is that men are the builders of the bird cage and the beneficiaries of women's entrapment within it, her occasional use of the passive voice to explain the operation of the bird cage blunts a fundamental point that "human actors in specific social contexts can and do oppress each other." Arthur Brittan and Mary Maynard, Sexism, Racism and Oppression 213 (1984). A benefit to identifying the active agents of oppression is that we are more likely to be clear about the interactive dynamics of abilism, classism, heterosexism, racism/ethnocentrism, and sexism. Arthur Brittan and Mary Maynard in their examination of oppression through the lens of feminism and anti-racism explain the importance of continually acknowledging human intentionality.

> Most accounts of domination deny the existence of active agents who 'do' the oppressing. It is not men who oppress women, rather it is the 'mode of production', a 'programmed genetic trait', or the 'system of patriarchy' which is responsible. Similarly, racism is explained in terms of the 'logic of capitalism' or the inevitability of 'kin altruism'. Reductionist theories, therefore, treat those who oppress as though they are clockwork oppressors, wound up by some inexorable determining mechanism which resides in the 'system'. Whites do not oppress Blacks, it is the 'system', the logic and laws of historical development which force them to do so. Clockwork oppression thus assumes a world without agency or purpose, where both oppressors and oppressed are engaged in a continuous round of stimulus-response relationships in which sexism and racism are seen as simple reflexes or preprogrammed responses to objective situations. Whites and men are thereby absolved from involvement in, and accountability for, oppressive acts. In addition, because racism

> and sexism are always attributed to other forces for which men and whites are the mediators, racial and sexual oppression disappear as forms of domination in their own right. They become mere manifestations of some hidden, underlying base. . . .
>
> Our purpose here is not to claim that single individuals are necessarily responsible for their racist or sexist practices, (although we would not want to completely deny such a claim), but to establish the obviousness of the fact that human actors in specific social contexts can and do oppress each other, not roles, genes, or modes of production. The obviousness of this fact may seem to be unproblematic. Yet it is almost impossible to unpack its implications. To say that individuals oppress each other is to imply that oppression is the result of human agency. . . .Hence, at one level oppression is extremely personal, and at another level the personal is political. All racist and sexist practice involves a power relationship in which the subjectivity of personal experience is intertwined with the objectivity of collective and political relationships. By this we mean that oppression is simultaneously an individual and collective phenomenon. But because of this collective dimension, we find it impossible to argue that expressions of anti-fascist or anti-sexist sentiments or attempts to structure personal relations in a non-dominating way can acquit either men or whites from responsibility for oppression, however genuine and sincere their views may be. To the extent that society is constructed on racist and sexist lines, men and whites accrue advantages, however unintentionally, which are denied to others.

Id. at 211–13.

Patricia Hill Collins, *Black Feminist Thought: Knowledge, Consciousness, and the Politics of Empowerment* 67–70, 93, 222–27 (1990)

> Called Matriarch, Emasculator and Hot Momma. Sometimes Sister, Pretty Baby, Auntie, Mammy and Girl. Called Unwed Mother, Welfare Recipient and Inner City Consumer. The Black American Woman has had to admit that while nobody knew the troubles she saw, everybody, his brother and his dog, felt qualified to explain her, even to herself.

Race, class, and gender oppression could not continue without powerful ideological justifications for their existence. As Cheryl Gilkes contends, "Black women's assertiveness and their use of every expression of racism to launch multiple assaults against the entire fabric of inequality have been a consistent, multifaceted threat to the status quo. As punishment, Black women have been assaulted with a variety of negative images." Portraying African-American women as stereotypical mammies, matriarchs, welfare recipients, and hot mommas has been essential to the political economy of domination fostering Black women's oppression. Challenging these controlling images has long been a core theme in Black feminist thought.

As part of a generalized ideology of domination, these controlling images of Black womanhood take on special meaning because the authority to define these symbols is a major instrument of power. In order to exercise power, elite white men and their representatives must be in a position to manipulate appropriate symbols concerning Black women. They may do so by exploiting already existing symbols, or they may create new ones relevant to their needs. Hazel Carby suggests that the objective of stereotypes is "not to reflect or represent a reality but to function as a disguise, or mystification, of objective social relations." These controlling images are designed to make racism, sexism, and poverty appear to be natural, normal, and an inevitable part of everyday life.

Even when the political and economic conditions that originally generated controlling images disappear, such images prove remarkably tenacious because they not only keep Black women oppressed but are key in maintaining interlocking systems of race, class, and gender oppression. The status of African-American women as outsiders or strangers becomes the point from which other groups define their normality. Ruth Shays, a Black inner-city resident, describes how the standpoint of a subordinate group is discredited: "It will not kill people to hear the truth, but they don't like it and they would much rather hear it from one of their own than from a stranger. Now, to white people your colored person is always a stranger. Not only that, we are supposed to be dumb strangers, so we can't tell them anything!" As the "Others" of society who can never really belong, strangers threaten the moral and social order. But they are simultaneously essential for its survival because those individuals who stand at the margins of society clarify its boundaries. African-American women, by not belonging, emphasize the significance of belonging.

The Objectification of Black Women as the Other

Black feminist critic Barbara Christian asserts that in America, "the enslaved African woman became the basis for the definition of our society's *Other*." Maintaining images of Black women as the Other provides ideological justification for race, gender, and class oppression.

Certain basic ideas crosscut all three systems. Claimed by Black feminist theorist bell hooks to be "the central ideological component of all systems of domination in Western society," one such idea is either/or dichotomous thinking. Either/or dichotomous thinking categorizes people, things, and ideas in terms of their difference from one another. For example, the terms in the dichotomies black/white, male/female, reason/emotion, culture/nature, fact/opinion, mind/body, and subject/object gain meaning only in *relation* to their counterparts.

Another basic idea concerns the relationship between notions of differences in either/or dichotomous thinking and objectification. In either/or dichotomous thinking, difference is defined in oppositional terms. One part is not simply different from its counterpart; it is inherently opposed to its "other." Whites and Blacks, males and females, thought and feeling are not complementary counterparts—they are fundamentally different entities related only through their definition as opposites. Feeling cannot be incorporated into thought or even function in conjunction with it because in either/or dichotomous thinking, feeling retards thought, values obscure facts, and judgment clouds knowledge.

Objectification is central to this process of oppositional difference. In either/or dichotomous thinking, one element is objectified as the Other, and is viewed as an object to be manipulated and controlled. Social theorist Dona Richards suggests that Western thought requires objectification, a process she describes as the "separation of the 'knowing self' from the 'known object.' " Intense objectification is a "prerequisite for the despiritualization of the universe," notes Richards, "and through it the Western cosmos was made ready for ever increasing materialization." A Marxist assessment of the culture/nature dichotomy argues that history can be seen as one in which human beings constantly objectify the natural world in order to control and exploit it. Culture is defined as the opposite of an objectified nature that, if left alone, would destroy culture. Feminist scholars point to the identification of women with nature as being central to women's subsequent objectification by men as sex objects. Black scholars contend that defining people of color as less human, animalistic, or more "natural" denies African and Asian people's subjectivity and supports a political economy of domination.

Domination always involves attempts to objectify the subordinate group. "As subjects, people have the right to define their own reality, establish their own identities, name their history," asserts bell hooks. "As objects, one's reality is defined by others, one's identity created by others, one's history named only in ways that define one's relationship to those who are subject." The treatment afforded Black women domestic workers exemplifies the many forms that objectification can take. Making Black women work as if they were animals or "mules uh de world" represents one form of objectification.[2]. . .

Finally, because oppositional dichotomies rarely represent different but equal relationships, they are inherently unstable. Tension is resolved by subordinating one half of the dichotomy to the other. Thus whites rule Blacks, men dominate women, reason is thought superior to emotion in ascertaining truth, facts supersede opinion in evaluating knowledge, and subjects rule objects. The foundations of a complex social hierarchy become grounded in the interwoven concepts of either/or dichotomous thinking, oppositional difference, and objectification. With domination based on difference forming an essential underpinning for this entire system of thought, these concepts invariably imply relationships of superiority and inferiority, hierarchical bonds that mesh with political economies of race, gender, and class oppression.

African-American women occupy a position whereby the inferior half of a series of these dichotomies converge, and this placement has been central to our subordination. The allegedly emotional, passionate nature of Black women

---

2. The phrase "mules uh de world" is found in Zora Neale Hurston's *Their Eyes Were Watching God* (1937). Nanny uses it to explain a Black women's place to her granddaughter in the following passage:

> Honey, de white man is de ruler of everything as fur as Ah been able tuh find out. Maybe it's some place way off in de ocean where de black man is in power, but we don't know nothin' but what we see. So de white man throw down de load and tell de nigger man tuh pick it up. He pick it up because he have to, but he don't tote it. He hand it to his womenfolks. De nigger woman is de mule uh de world so fur as Ah can see.

Id. at 16. Eds.

has long been used to justify Black women's sexual exploitation. Similarly, restricting black women's literacy, then claiming that we lack the facts for sound judgment, relegates African-American women to the inferior side of the fact/opinion dichotomy. Denying Black women status as fully human subjects by treating us as the objectified Other in a range of such dichotomies demonstrates the power that dichotomous either/or thinking, oppositional difference, and objectification wield in maintaining interlocking systems of oppression. Analyzing the specific, externally defined, controlling images applied to African-American women both reveals the specific contours of Black women's objectification and offers a clearer view of how systems of race, gender, and class oppression actually interlock.

Controlling Images and Black Women's Oppression

. . ."A system of oppression," claims Black feminist activist Pauli Murray, "draws much of its strength from the acquiescence of its victims, who have accepted the dominant image of themselves and are paralyzed by a sense of helplessness." Black women's ideas and actions force a rethinking of the concept of hegemony, the notion that Black women's objectification as the Other is so complete that we become willing participants in our own oppression. Most African-American women simply do not define ourselves as mammies, matriarchs, welfare mothers, mules, or sexually denigrated women. The ideology of domination in which these controlling images are embedded is much less cohesive or uniform than imagined.

African-American women encounter these controlling images, not as disembodied symbolic messages but as ideas that should provide meaning in our daily lives. Black women's work and family experiences create the conditions whereby the contradictions between everyday experiences and the controlling images of Black womanhood become visible. Seeing the contradictions in the ideologies opens them up for demystification. Just as Sojourner Truth deconstructed the term *woman* by using her own concrete experiences to challenge it, so in a variety of ways do everyday African-American women do the same thing.[3] That fewer Maria Stewarts, Sojourner Truths, Ella Surreys,

---

3. Earlier in her book, Collins looks to Sojourner Truth's 1851 speech at an Akron, Ohio, women's rights convention as she reclaims the Black feminist intellectual tradition. At the convention Truth said:

> That man over there says women need to be helped into carriages, and lifted over ditches, and to have the best place everywhere. Nobody ever helps me into carriages, or over mud-puddles, or gives me any best place! And ain't I a woman? Look at me! Look at my arm! I have ploughed, and planted, and gathered into barns, and no man could head me! And ain't I a woman? I could work as much and eat as much as a man—when I could get it—and bear the lash as well! And ain't I a woman? I have borne thirteen children, and seen them most all sold off to slavery, and when I cried out with my mother's grief, none but Jesus heard me! And ain't I a woman?

Black Women in Nineteenth-Century American Life: Their Words, Their Thoughts, Their Feelings 235 (Bert J. Loewenberg & Ruth Bogin eds., 1976). Collins says the following about Sojourner Truth's speech:

> Sojourner Truth exposes the concept of woman as being culturally constructed by

or Johnny Mae Fieldses are heard from is less a statement about the existence of Black women's ideas than it is a reflection of the suppression of ideas that do exist. . . .

Paradigmatic Shifts: Domination and Resistance

Reconceptualizing Race, Class, and Gender as Interlocking Systems of Oppression

"What *I* really feel is radical is trying to make coalitions with people who are different from you," maintains Barbara Smith. "I feel it is radical to be dealing with race and sex and class and sexual identity all at one time. I think *that* is really radical because it has never been done before." Black feminist thought fosters a fundamental paradigmatic shift that rejects additive approaches to oppression. Instead of starting with gender and then adding in other variables such as age, sexual orientation, race, social class, and religion, Black feminist thought sees these distinctive systems of oppression as being part of one overarching structure of domination. Viewing relations of domination for Black women for any given sociohistorical context as being structured via a system of interlocking race, class, and gender oppression expands the focus of analysis from merely describing the similarities and differences distinguishing these systems of oppression and focuses greater attention on how they interconnect. Assuming that each system needs the others in order to function creates a distinct theoretical stance that stimulates the rethinking of basic social science concepts.

Afrocentric feminist notions of family reflect this reconceptualization process. Black women's experiences as bloodmothers, othermothers,[4] and community othermothers[5] reveal that the mythical norm of a heterosexual, mar-

---

using the contradictions between her life as an African-American woman and the qualities ascribed to women. Her life as a second-class citizen has been filled with hard physical labor, with no assistance from men. Her question, "and ain't I a woman?" points to the contradictions inherent in blanket use of the term *woman*. For those who question Truth's femininity, she invokes her status as a mother of thirteen children all sold off into slavery, and asks again, "and ain't I a woman?" Rather than accepting the existing assumptions about what a woman was and then trying to prove that she fit the standards, Truth challenged the very standards themselves. Her actions demonstrate the process of deconstruction—namely, exposing a concept as ideological or culturally constructed rather than as natural or a simple reflection of reality.

Patricia Hill Collins, Black Feminist Thought: Knowledge, Consciousness, and the Politics of Empowerment 14 (1990) (emphasis in original). Eds.

4. In African-American communities, fluid and changing boundaries often distinguish biological mothers from other women who care for children. Biological mothers, or bloodmothers, are expected to care for their children. But African and African-American communities have also recognized that vesting one person with full responsibility for mothering a child may not be wise or possible. As a result, othermothers—women who assist bloodmothers by sharing mothering responsibilities—traditionally have been central to the institution of Black motherhood.

Id. at 119. Eds.

5. Black women's experiences as othermothers provide a foundation for Black women's political activism. Nurturing children in Black extended family networks stimulates a more generalized ethic of caring and personal accountability among African-American women who often feel accountable to all the Black community's children.

ried couple, nuclear family with a nonworking spouse and a husband earning a "family wage" is far from being natural, universal, and preferred but instead is deeply embedded in specific race and class formations. Placing African-American women in the center of analysis not only reveals much-needed information about Black women's experiences but also questions Eurocentric masculinist perspectives on family.

Black women's experiences and the Afrocentric feminist thought rearticulating them also challenge prevailing definitions of community. Black women's actions in the struggle for group survival suggest a vision of community that stands in opposition to that extant in the dominant culture. The definition of community implicit in the market model sees community as arbitrary and fragile, structured fundamentally by competition and domination. In contrast, Afrocentric models of community stress connections, caring, and personal accountability. As cultural workers, African-American women have rejected the generalized ideology of domination advanced by the dominant group in order to conserve Afrocentric conceptualizations of community. Denied access to the podium, Black women have been unable to spend time theorizing about alternative conceptualizations of community. Instead, through daily actions African-American women have *created* alternative communities that empower.

This vision of community sustained by African-American women in conjunction with African-American men addresses the larger issue of reconceptualizing power. The type of Black women's power discussed here does resemble feminist theories of power which emphasize energy and community. However, in contrast to this body of literature whose celebration of women's power is often accompanied by a lack of attention to the importance of power as domination, Black women's experiences as mothers, community othermothers, educators, church leaders, labor union centerwomen,[6] and commu-

---

This notion of Black women as community othermothers for all Black children traditionally allowed African-American women to treat biologically unrelated children as if they were members of their own families. . . .

Community othermothers have made important contributions in building a different type of community in often hostile political and economic surroundings. Community othermothers' actions demonstrate a clear rejection of separateness and individual interest as the basis of either community organization or individual self-actualization. Instead, the connectedness with others and common interest expressed by community othermothers models a very different value system, one whereby Afrocentric feminist ethics of caring and personal accountability move communities forward.

Id. at 129, 131-32. Eds.

6. Certain women in these overlapping community and workplace networks became "centerwomen." The skills centerwomen gained from their centrality in their families enabled them to keep people together, ensure that obligations were fulfilled, and maintain group consensus. Thus the Black women's mothering tradition emerged in the union-organizing drive as a powerful foundation for this particular effort at institutional transformation. The drive was successful because of the existence of two equally important dimensions of leadership: that offered by spokesmen or spokespersons who engaged in direct negotiations with management, and that provided by centerwomen or centerpersons who fostered group solidarity among the workers. While men and women are capable of exercising both types, in this particular case the functions were divided by gender. Men were spokespersons and women were centerpersons.

Id. at 158. Eds.

nity leaders seem to suggest that power as energy can be fostered by creative acts of resistance.

The spheres of influence created and sustained by African-American women are not meant solely to provide a respite from oppressive situations or a retreat from their effects. Rather, these Black female spheres of influence constitute potential sanctuaries where individual Black women and men are nurtured in order to confront oppressive social institutions. Power from this perspective is a creative power used for the good of the community, whether that community is conceptualized as one's family, church community, or the next generation of the community's children. By making the community stronger, African-American women become empowered, and that same community can serve as a source of support when Black women encounter race, gender, and class oppression.

Rethinking Black women's activism uncovers a new vision of Black women's empowerment that is distinct from existing models of power as domination. Black women have not conceptualized our quest for empowerment as one of replacing elite white male authorities with ourselves as benevolent Black female ones. Instead, African-American women have overtly rejected theories of power based on domination in order to embrace an alternative vision of power based on a humanist vision of self-actualization, self-definition, and self-determination.

It is important to develop analyses of contemporary social phenomena that explore the connections among race, class, and gender oppression and use new reconceptualizations of family, community, and power in doing so. Such analyses must retain the creative tension between the specificity needed to study the workings of race, class, and gender in Black women's lives and generalizations about these systems created by cross-cultural and transhistorical research. . . .

The Matrix of Domination

. . .Replacing additive models of oppression with interlocking ones creates possibilities for new paradigms. The significance of seeing race, class, and gender as interlocking systems of oppression is that such an approach fosters a paradigmatic shift of thinking inclusively about other oppressions, such as age, sexual orientation, religion, and ethnicity. Race, class, and gender represent the three systems of oppression that most heavily affect African-American women. But these systems and the economic, political, and ideological conditions that support them may not be the most fundamental oppressions, and they certainly affect many more groups than Black women. Other people of color, Jews, the poor, white women, and gays and lesbians have all had similar ideological justifications offered for their subordination. All categories of humans labeled Others have been equated to one another, to animals, and to nature.

Placing African-American women and other excluded groups in the center of analysis opens up possibilities for a both/and conceptual stance, one in which all groups possess varying amounts of penalty and privilege in one historically created system. In this system, for example, white women are penalized by their gender but privileged by their race. Depending on the context, an individual may be an oppressor, a member of an oppressed group, or simultaneously oppressor and oppressed.

Adhering to a both/and conceptual stance does not mean that race, class, and gender oppression are interchangeable. For example, whereas race, class, and gender oppression operate on the social structural level of institutions, gender oppression seems better able to annex the basic power of the erotic and intrude in personal relationships via family dynamics and within individual consciousness. This may be because racial oppression has fostered historically concrete communities among African-Americans and other racial/ethnic groups. These communities have stimulated cultures of resistance. While these communities segregate Blacks from whites, they simultaneously provide counter-institutional buffers that subordinate groups such as African-Americans use to resist the ideas and institutions of dominant groups. Social class may be similarly structured. Traditionally conceptualized as a relationship of *individual* employees to their employers, social class might be better viewed as a relationship of *communities* to capitalist political economies. Moreover, significant overlap exists between racial and social class oppression when viewing them through the collective lens of family and community. Existing community structures provide a primary line of resistance against racial and class oppression. But because gender cross-cuts these structures, it finds fewer comparable institutional bases to foster resistance.

Embracing a both/and conceptual stance moves us from additive, separate systems approaches to oppression and toward what I now see as the more fundamental issue of the social relations of domination. Race, class, and gender constitute axes of oppression that characterize Black women's experiences within a more generalized matrix of domination. Other groups may encounter different dimensions of the matrix, such as sexual orientation, religion, and age, but the overarching relationship is one of domination and the types of activism it generates.

bell hooks labels this matrix a "politic of domination" and describes how it operates along interlocking axes of race, class, and gender oppression. This politic of domination

> refers to the ideological ground that they share, which is a belief in domination, and a belief in the notions of superior and inferior, which are components of all of those systems. For me it's like a house, they share the foundation, but the foundation is the ideological beliefs around which notions of domination are constructed.

Johnella Butler claims that new methodologies growing from this new paradigm would be "non-hierarchical" and would "refuse primacy to either race, class, gender, or ethnicity, demanding instead a recognition of their matrix-like interaction." Race, class, and gender may not be the most fundamental or important systems of oppression, but they have most profoundly affected African-American women. One significant dimension of Black feminist thought is its potential to reveal insights about the social relations of domination organized along other axes such as religion, ethnicity, sexual orientation, and age. Investigating Black women's particular experiences thus promises to reveal much about the more universal process of domination.

Notes and Questions

1. *Both/And.* Patricia Cain describes the following classroom exercise and her experiences using it:

> First I ask each student to write down three self-descriptive nouns or adjectives, to name three aspects of her (or his) personal self. When they have finished writing, we go around the room and each student reads the three choices aloud. For my women students, the list almost always includes either the word woman or female. . . .
>
> As to the rest of the list, there are important differences. For example, no white woman ever mentions race, whereas every woman of color does. Similarly, straight women do not include "heterosexual" as one of the adjectives on their lists, whereas lesbians, who are open, always include "lesbian" as one of the words on their lists.

Patricia Cain, Feminist Jurisprudence: Grounding the Theories, 4 Berkeley Women's L.J. 191, 208 (1989). How is the "matrix of domination" operating in the students' self-descriptions?

2. *Victim/Agent.* How are the interests of the dominant groups served by viewing the "Other" as victim? How are they served by viewing the "Other" as agent? Why is it important to view the "Other" as simultaneously both victim and agent?

3. *Audience.* María Lugones offers another theory about the cause of the self-descriptions that took place in Cain's classroom.

> [Y]ou do not see me because you do not see yourself and you do not see yourself because you declare yourself outside of culture. But declaring yourself outside of culture is self-deceiving. The deception hides your seeing only through the eyes of your culture. So disengagement is a radical form of passivity toward the ideology of the ethnocentric racial state which privileges the dominant culture as the only culture to "see with" and conceives this seeing as to be done non-self-consciously.

María Lugones, Hablando cara a cara/Speaking Face to Face: An Exploration of Ethnocentric Racism, in Making Face, Making Soul Haciendo Caras: Creative and Critical Perspectives by Women of Color 51 (Gloria Anzaldúa ed., 1990). Taking into account Lugones' analysis of how ethnocentrism functions, who is Patricia Hill Collins writing about and who is her intended audience?

4. *Standpoint.* In her review of Collins' book, Barrie Thorne explores both the strength and the weakness of Collins' analysis as built on a unitary standpoint held by all African-American women. Barrie Thorne, Book Review, 6 Gender & Soc'y 515, 516 (1992). Collins responded to this review as follows:

> While writing *Black Feminist Thought*, I deliberately decided to minimize the obvious heterogeneity among African-American women created by differences in experience because I had to attend to the political context in which I was writing. I decided not to focus on diversity, although I was and am well aware that it exists. My goal was to delineate the contours of Black feminist

thought, so that it would be taken seriously as an area of intellectual inquiry. . . .

[I]n order to get Black feminist thought accepted as a legitimate discourse that can quite rightfully take its place among discourses created by those with much more power, it was necessary to present the group itself as being overly homogeneous. Prematurely claiming heterogeneity among African-American women could have easily become a "divide-and-conquer" tool, allowing the differences among Black women to be used to discredit the notion that any worthwhile community of Black women existed at all.

Patricia Hill Collins, Reply, 6 Gender & Soc'y 517, 518 (1992).

Adrienne Rich, Compulsory Heterosexuality and Lesbian Existence, in *Blood, Bread, and Poetry: Selected Prose 1979–1985*, at 23, 26–27, 35–43, 47, 49–57, 59–60, 63–68 (1980)

The bias of compulsory heterosexuality, through which lesbian experience is perceived on a scale ranging from deviant to abhorrent or simply rendered invisible, could be illustrated from many texts . . . .The assumption[s]. . .that women are "innately" sexually oriented only toward men, [or]. . .that the lesbian is simply acting out of her bitterness toward men, are. . .widely current in literature and in the social sciences.

I am concerned here with two other matters as well: first, how and why women's choice of women as passionate comrades, life partners, co-workers, lovers, community has been crushed, invalidated, forced into hiding and disguise; and second, the virtual or total neglect of lesbian existence in a wide range of writings, including feminist scholarship. Obviously there is a connection here. I believe that much feminist theory and criticism is stranded on this shoal.

My organizing impulse is the belief that it is not enough for feminist thought that specifically lesbian texts exist. Any theory or cultural/political creation that treats lesbian existence as a marginal or less "natural" phenomenon, as mere "sexual preference," or as the mirror image of either heterosexual or male homosexual relations is profoundly weakened thereby, whatever its other contributions. Feminist theory can no longer afford merely to voice a toleration of "lesbianism" as an "alternative life style" or make token allusion to lesbians. A feminist critique of compulsory heterosexual orientation for women is long overdue. In this exploratory paper, I shall try to show why. . . .

If women are the earliest sources of emotional caring and physical nurture for both female and male children, it would seem logical, from a feminist perspective at least, to pose the following questions: whether the search for love and tenderness in both sexes does not originally lead toward women; *why in fact women would ever redirect that search*; why species survival, the means of impregnation, and emotional/erotic relationships should ever have become so rigidly identified with each other; and why such violent strictures should be found necessary to enforce women's total emotional, erotic loyalty and subservience to men. I doubt that enough feminist scholars and theorists have taken the pains to acknowledge the societal forces which wrench women's emotional and erotic energies away from themselves and other women and from woman-identified values. These forces, as I shall try to show, range from literal physical enslavement to the disguising and distorting of possible options.

I do not assume that mothering by women is a "sufficient cause" of lesbian existence. But the issue of mothering by women has been much in the air of late, usually accompanied by the view that increased parenting by men would minimize antagonism between the sexes and equalize the sexual imbalance of power of males over females. These discussions are carried on without reference to compulsory heterosexuality as a phenomenon, let alone as an ideology. I do not wish to psychologize here, but rather to identify sources of male power. I believe large numbers of men could, in fact, undertake child care on a large scale without radically altering the balance of male power in a male-identified society.

In her essay "The Origin of the Family," Kathleen Gough lists eight characteristics of male power in archaic and contemporary societies which I would like to use as a framework: "men's ability to deny women sexuality or to force it upon them; to command or exploit their labor to control their produce; to control or rob them of their children; to confine them physically and prevent their movement; to use them as objects in male transactions; to cramp their creativeness; or to withhold from them large areas of the society's knowledge and cultural attainments." (Gough does not perceive these power characteristics as specifically enforcing heterosexuality; only as producing sexual inequality.) Below, Gough's words appear in italics; the elaboration of each of her categories, in brackets, is my own.

Characteristics of male power include:
the power of men

1. *to deny women* [their own] *sexuality*
   [by means of clitoridectomy and infibulation; chastity belts; punishment, including death, for female adultery; punishment, including death, for lesbian sexuality; psychoanalytic denial of the clitoris; strictures against masturbation; denial of maternal and postmenopausal sensuality; unnecessary hysterectomy; pseudolesbian images in the media and literature; closing of archives and destruction of documents relating to lesbian existence]

2. *or to force it* [male sexuality] *upon them*
   [by means of rape (including marital rape) and wife beating; father-daughter, brother-sister incest; the socialization of women to feel that male sexual "drive" amounts to a right; idealization of heterosexual romance in art, literature, the media, advertising, etc.; child marriage; arranged marriage; prostitution; the harem; psychoanalytic doctrines of frigidity and vaginal orgasm; pornographic depictions of women responding pleasurably to sexual violence and humiliation (a subliminal message being that sadistic heterosexuality is more "normal" than sensuality between women)]

3. *to command or exploit their labor to control their produce*
   [by means of the institutions of marriage and motherhood as unpaid production; the horizontal segregation of women in paid employment; the decoy of the upwardly mobile token woman; male control of

abortion, contraception, sterilization, and childbirth; pimping; female infanticide, which robs mothers of daughters and contributes to generalized devaluation of women]

4. *to control or rob them of their children*
   [by means of father right and "legal kidnapping"; enforced sterilization; systematized infanticide; seizure of children from lesbian mothers by the courts; the malpractice of male obstetrics; use of the mother as "token torturer" in genital mutilation or in binding the daughter's feet (or mind) to fit her for marriage]
5. *to confine them physically and prevent their movement*
   [by means of rape as terrorism, keeping women off the streets; purdah; foot binding; atrophying of women's athletic capabilities; high heels and "feminine" dress codes in fashion; the veil; sexual harassment on the streets; horizontal segregation of women in employment; prescriptions for "full-time" mothering at home; enforced economic dependence of wives]
6. *to use them as objects in male transactions*
   [use of women as "gifts"; bride price; pimping; arranged marriage; use of women as entertainers to facilitate male deals—e.g., wife-hostess, cocktail waitress required to dress for male sexual titillation, call girls, "bunnies," geisha, *kisaeng* prostitutes, secretaries]
7. *to cramp their creativeness*
   [witch persecutions as campaigns against midwives and female healers, and as pogrom against independent, "unassimilated" women; definition of male pursuits as more valuable than female within any culture, so that cultural values become the embodiment of male subjectivity; restriction of female self-fulfillment to marriage and motherhood; sexual exploitation of women by male artists and teachers; the social and economic disruption of women's creative aspirations; erasure of female tradition]
8. *to withhold from them large areas of the society's knowledge and cultural attainments*
   [by means of noneducation of females; the "Great Silence" regarding women and particularly lesbian existence in history and culture; sex-role tracking which deflects women from science, technology, and other "masculine" pursuits; male social/professional bonding which excludes women; discrimination against women in the professions]

These are some of the methods by which male power is manifested and maintained. Looking at the schema, what surely impresses itself is the fact that we are confronting not a simple maintenance of inequality and property possession, but a pervasive cluster of forces, ranging from physical brutality to control of consciousness, which suggests that an enormous potential counterforce is having to be restrained.

Some of the forms by which male power manifests itself are more easily recognizable as enforcing heterosexuality on women than are others. Yet each one I have listed adds to the cluster of forces within which women have been convinced that marriage and sexual orientation toward men are inevitable—

even if unsatisfying or oppressive—components of their lives. The chastity belt; child marriage; erasure of lesbian existence (except as exotic and perverse) in art, literature, film; idealization of heterosexual romance and marriage—these are some fairly obvious forms of compulsion, the first two exemplifying physical force, the second two control of consciousness. While clitoridectomy has been assailed by feminists as a form of woman torture, Kathleen Barry first pointed out that it is not simply a way of turning the young girl into a "marriageable" woman through brutal surgery. It intends that women in the intimate proximity of polygynous marriage will not form sexual relationships with each other, that—from a male, genital-fetishist perspective—female erotic connections, even in a sex-segregated situation, will be literally excised. . . .

In her brilliant study *Sexual Harassment of Working Women: A Case of Sex Discrimination*, Catharine A. MacKinnon delineates the intersection of compulsory heterosexuality and economics. Under capitalism, women are horizontally segregated by gender and occupy a structurally inferior position in the workplace. This is hardly news, but MacKinnon raises the question why, even if capitalism "requires some collection of individuals to occupy low-status, low-paying positions. . .such persons must be biologically female," and goes on to point out that "the fact that male employers often do not hire qualified women, *even when they could pay them less than men* suggests that more than the profit motive is implicated" [emphasis added]. She cites a wealth of material documenting the fact that women are not only segregated in low-paying service jobs (as secretaries, domestics, nurses, typists, telephone operators, child-care workers, waitresses), but that "sexualization of the woman" is part of the job. Central and intrinsic to the economic realities of women's lives is the requirement that women will "market sexual attractiveness to men, who tend to hold the economic power and position to enforce their predilections." And MacKinnon documents that "sexual harassment perpetuates the interlocked structure by which women have been kept sexually in thrall to men at the bottom of the labor market. Two forces of American society converge: men's control over women's sexuality and capital's control over employees' work lives." Thus, women in the workplace are at the mercy of sex as power in a vicious circle. Economically disadvantaged, women—whether waitresses or professors—endure sexual harassment to keep their jobs and learn to behave in a complaisantly and ingratiatingly heterosexual manner because they discover this is their true qualification for employment, whatever the job description. And, MacKinnon notes, the woman who too decisively resists sexual overtures in the workplace is accused of being "dried up" and sexless, or lesbian. This raises a specific difference between the experiences of lesbians and homosexual men. A lesbian, closeted on her job because of heterosexist prejudice, is not simply forced into denying the truth of her outside relationships or private life. Her job depends on her pretending to be not merely heterosexual, but a heterosexual *woman* in terms of dressing and playing the feminine, deferential role required of "real" women.

MacKinnon raises radical questions as to the qualitative differences between sexual harassment, rape, and ordinary heterosexual intercourse. ("As one accused rapist put it, he hadn't used 'any more force than is usual for males during the preliminaries.' ") She criticizes Susan Brownmiller for separating rape from the mainstream of daily life and for her unexamined premise that "rape is violence, intercourse is sexuality," removing rape from the sexual sphere altogether. Most crucially she argues that "taking rape from the realm of 'the sexual,' placing it in the realm of 'the violent,' allows one to be against it without raising any questions about the extent to which the institution of heterosexuality has defined force as a normal part of 'the preliminaries.'" "Never is it asked whether, under conditions of male supremacy, the notion of 'consent' has any meaning."

The fact is that the workplace, among other social institutions, is a place where women have learned to accept male violation of their psychic and physical boundaries as the price of survival; where women have been educated—no less than by romantic literature or by pornography—to perceive themselves as sexual prey. A woman seeking to escape such casual violations along with economic disadvantage may well turn to marriage as a form of hoped-for protection, while bringing into marriage neither social nor economic power, thus entering that institution also from a disadvantaged position. MacKinnon finally asks:

> What if inequality is built into the social conceptions of male and female sexuality, of masculinity and femininity, of sexiness and heterosexual attractiveness? Incidents of sexual harassment suggest that male sexual desire itself may be aroused by female vulnerability. . . .Men feel they can take advantage, so they want to, so they do. Examination of sexual harassment, precisely because the episodes appear commonplace, forces one to confront the fact that sexual intercourse normally occurs between economic (as well as physical) unequals. . .the apparent legal requirement that violations of women's sexuality appear out of the ordinary before they will be punished helps prevent women from defining the ordinary conditions of their own consent.

Given the nature and extent of heterosexual pressures—the daily "eroticization of women's subordination" as MacKinnon phrases it—I question the more or less psychoanalytic perspective (suggested by such writers as Karen Horney, H. R. Hayes, Wolfgang Lederer, and, most recently, Dorothy Dinnerstein) that the male need to control women sexually results from some primal male "fear of women" and of women's sexual insatiability. It seems more probable that men really fear not that they will have women's sexual appetites forced on them or that women want to smother and devour them, but that women could be indifferent to them altogether, that men could be allowed sexual and emotional—therefore economic—access to women *only* on women's terms, otherwise being left on the periphery of the matrix. . . .

We still need to ask why some women never, even temporarily, turn away from "heretofore primary relationships" with other females. And why does male identification—the casting of one's social, political, and intellectual allegiances with men—exist among lifelong sexual lesbians?. . .In the mystique of the overpowering, all-conquering male sex drive, the penis-with-a-life-of-its own, is rooted the law of male sex right to women, which justifies prostitution as a universal cultural assumption on the one hand, while defending sexual slavery within the family on the basis of "family privacy and cultural uniqueness" on the other. The adolescent male sex drive, which, as both young women and men are taught, once triggered cannot take responsibility for itself or take no for an answer, becomes. . .the norm and rationale for adult male sexual behavior: a condition of *arrested sexual development.* Women learn to accept as natural the inevitability of this "drive" because they receive it as dogma. Hence, marital rape; hence, the Japanese wife resignedly packing her husband's suitcase for a weekend in the *kisaeng* brothels of Taiwan; hence, the psychological as well as economic imbalance of power between husband and wife, male employer and female worker, father and daughter, male professor and female student. . . .

[W]hatever its origins, when we look hard and clearly at the extent and elaboration of measures designed to keep women within a male sexual purlieu, it becomes an inescapable question whether the issue feminists have to address is not simple "gender inequality" nor the domination of culture by males nor mere "taboos against homosexuality," but the enforcement of heterosexuality for women as a means of assuring male right of physical, economic, and emotional access. One of many means of enforcement is, of course, the rendering invisible of the lesbian possibility, an engulfed continent which rises fragmentedly into view from time to time only to become submerged again. Feminist research and theory that contribute to lesbian invisibility or marginality are actually working against the liberation and empowerment of woman as a group.[7]

The assumption that "most women are innately heterosexual" stands as a theoretical and political stumbling block for feminism. It remains a tenable assumption partly because lesbian existence has been written out of history or catalogued under disease, partly because it has been treated as exceptional rather than intrinsic, partly because to acknowledge that for women heterosexuality may not be a "preference" at all but something that has had to be imposed, managed, organized, propagandized, and maintained by force is an immense step to take if you consider yourself freely and "innately" heterosexual. Yet the failure to examine heterosexuality as an institution is like failing to admit that the economic system called capitalism or the caste system of racism is maintained by a variety of forces, including both physical violence and false consciousness. To take the step of questioning heterosexuality as a "preference" or "choice" for women—and to do the intellectual and emotional work that follows—will call for a special quality of courage in heterosexually identified feminists, but I think the rewards will be great: a freeing-up of thinking, the exploring of new paths, the shattering of another great silence, new clarity in personal relationships. . . .

I have chosen to use the terms *lesbian existence* and *lesbian continuum* because the word *lesbianism* has a clinical and limiting ring. *Lesbian existence* suggests both the fact of the historical presence of lesbians and our continuing creation of the meaning of that existence. I mean the term *lesbian con-*

7. I would suggest that lesbian existence has been most recognized and tolerated where it has resembled a "deviant" version of heterosexuality—e.g., where lesbians have, like Stein and Toklas, played heterosexual roles (or seemed to in public) and have been chiefly identified with male culture. . . . Lesbian existence has also been relegated to an upper-class phenomenon, an elite decadence (as in the fascination with Paris salon lesbians such as Renée Vivien and Natalie Clifford Barney), to the obscuring of such "common women" as Judy Grahn depicts in her *The Work of a Common Woman* (1978) and *True to Life Adventure Stories* (1978).

tinuum to include a range—through each woman's life and throughout history—of woman-identified experience, not simply the fact that a woman has had or consciously desired genital sexual experience with another woman. If we expand it to embrace many more forms of primary intensity between and among women, including the sharing of a rich inner life, the bonding against male tyranny, the giving and receiving of practical and political support, if we can also hear in it such associations as *marriage resistance* and the "haggard" behavior identified by Mary Daly (obsolete meanings: "intractable," "willful," "wanton," and "unchaste," "a woman reluctant to yield to wooing"), we begin to grasp breadths of female history and psychology which have lain out of reach as a consequence of limited, mostly clinical, definitions of *lesbianism*.

Lesbian existence comprises both the breaking of a taboo and the rejection of a compulsory way of life. It is also a direct or indirect attack on male right of access to women. But it is more than these, although we may first begin to perceive it as a form of naysaying to patriarchy, an act of resistance. It has, of course, included isolation, self-hatred, breakdown, alcoholism, suicide, and intrawoman violence; we romanticize at our peril what it means to love and act against the grain, and under heavy penalties; and lesbian existence has been lived (unlike, say, Jewish or Catholic existence) without access to any knowledge of a tradition, a continuity, a social underpinning. The destruction of records and memorabilia and letters documenting the realities of lesbian existence must be taken very seriously as a means of keeping heterosexuality compulsory for women, since what has been kept from our knowledge is joy, sensuality, courage, and community, as well as guilt, self-betrayal, and pain.

Lesbians have historically been deprived of a political existence through "inclusion" as female versions of male homosexuality. To equate lesbian existence with male homosexuality because each is stigmatized is to erase female reality once again. Part of the history of lesbian existence is, obviously, to be found where lesbians, lacking a coherent female community, have shared a kind of social life and common cause with homosexual men. But there are differences: women's lack of economic and cultural privilege relative to men; qualitative differences in female and male relationships—for example, the patterns of anonymous sex among male homosexuals, and the pronounced ageism in male homosexual standards of sexual attractiveness. I perceive the lesbian experience as being, like motherhood, a profoundly *female* experience, with particular oppressions, meanings, and potentialities we cannot comprehend as long as we simply bracket it with other sexually stigmatized existences. Just as the term *parenting* serves to conceal the particular and significant reality of being a parent who is actually a mother, the term *gay* may serve the purpose of blurring the very outlines we need to discern, which are of crucial value for feminism and for the freedom of women as a group.

As the term *lesbian* has been held to limiting, clinical associations in its patriarchal definition, female friendship and comradeship have been set apart from the erotic, thus limiting the erotic itself. But as we deepen and broaden the range of what we define as lesbian existence, as we delineate a lesbian continuum, we begin to discover the erotic in female terms: as that which is unconfined to any single part of the body or solely to the body itself; as an energy not only diffuse but, as Audre Lorde has described it, omnipresent in "the sharing of joy, whether physical, emotional, psychic," and in the sharing of work; as the empowering joy which "makes us less willing to accept powerlessness, or those other supplied states of being which are not native to me, such as resignation, despair, self-effacement, depression, self-denial."...

If we consider the possibility that all women—from the infant suckling at her mother's breast, to the grown woman experiencing orgasmic sensations while suckling her own child, perhaps recalling her mother's milk smell in her own, to two women, like Virginia Woolf's Chloe and Olivia, who share a laboratory, to the woman dying at ninety, touched and handled by women—exist on a lesbian continuum, we can see ourselves as moving in and out of this continuum, whether we identify ourselves as lesbian or not.

We can then connect aspects of woman identification as diverse as the impudent, intimate girl friendships of eight or nine year olds and the banding together of those women of the twelfth and fifteenth centuries known as Beguines who "shared houses, rented to one another, bequeathed houses to their room-mates. . .in cheap subdivided houses in the artisans' area of town," who "practiced Christian virtue on their own, dressing and living simply and not associating with men," who earned their livings as spinsters, bakers, nurses, or ran schools for young girls, and who managed—until the Church forced them to disperse—to live independent both of marriage and of conventual restrictions. It allows us to connect these women with the more celebrated "Lesbians" of the women's school around Sappho of the seventh century B.C., with the secret sororities and economic networks reported among African women, and with the Chinese marriage-resistance sisterhoods—communities of women who refused marriage or who, if married, often refused to consummate their marriages and soon left their husbands, the only women in China who were not footbound and who, Agnes Smedley tells us, welcomed the births of daughters and organized successful women's strikes in the silk mills. It allows us to connect and compare disparate individual instances of marriage resistance: for example, the strategies available to Emily Dickinson, a nineteenth-century white woman genius, with the strategies available to Zora Neale Hurston, a twentieth-century black woman genius. Dickinson never married, had tenuous intellectual friendships with men, lived self-convented in her genteel father's house in Amherst, and wrote a lifetime of passionate letters to her sister-in-law Sue Gilbert and a smaller group of such letters to her friend Kate Scott Anthon. Hurston married twice but soon left each husband, scrambled her way from Florida to Harlem to Columbia University to Haiti and finally back to Florida, moved in and out of white patronage and poverty, professional success, and failure; her survival relationships were all with women, beginning with her mother. Both of these women in their vastly different circumstances were marriage resisters, committed to their own work and selfhood, and were later characterized as "apolitical." Both were drawn to men of intellectual quality; for both of them women provided the ongoing fascination and sustenance of life.

If we think of heterosexuality as *the* natural emotional and sensual inclination for women, lives such as these are seen as deviant, as pathological, or as emotionally and sensually deprived. Or, in more recent and permissive jargon, they are banalized as "life styles." And the work of such women, whether merely the daily work of individual or collective survival and resistance or the work of the writer, the activist, the reformer, the anthropologist, or the artist—the work of self-creation—is undervalued, or seen as the bitter fruit of "penis envy" or the sublimation of repressed eroticism or the meaningless rant of a "man-hater." But when we turn the lens of vision and consider the degree to which and the methods whereby heterosexual "preference" has actually been imposed on women, not only can we understand differently the meaning of individual lives and work, but we can begin to recognize a central fact of women's history: that women have always resisted male tyranny. A feminism of action, often though not always without a theory, has constantly re-emerged in every culture in every period. We can then begin to study women's struggle against powerlessness, women's radical rebellion, not just in male-defined "concrete revolutionary situations" but in all the situations male ideologies have not perceived as revolutionary—for example, the refusal of some women to produce children, aided at great risk by other women; the refusal to produce a higher standard of living and leisure for men . . . .We begin to observe behavior, both in history and in individual biography, that has hitherto been invisible or misnamed, behavior which often constitutes, given the limits of the counterforce exerted in a given time and place, radical rebellion. And we can connect these rebellions and the necessity for them with the physical passion of woman for woman which is central to lesbian existence: the erotic sensuality which has been, precisely, the most violently erased fact of female experience.

Heterosexuality has been both forcibly and subliminally imposed on women. Yet everywhere women have resisted it, often at the cost of physical torture, imprisonment, psychosurgery, social ostracism, and extreme poverty. "Compulsory heterosexuality" was named as one of the "crimes against women" by the Brussels International Tribunal on Crimes against Women in 1976. . . .

Nor can it be assumed that women like those in Carroll Smith-Rosenberg's study, who married, stayed married, yet dwelt in a profoundly female emotional and passional world, "preferred" or "chose" heterosexuality. Women have married because it was necessary, in order to survive economically, in order to have children who would not suffer economic deprivation or social ostracism, in order to remain respectable, in order to do what was expected of women, because coming out of "abnormal" childhoods they wanted to feel "normal" and because heterosexual romance has been represented as the great female adventure, duty, and fulfillment. We may faithfully or ambivalently have obeyed the institution, but our feelings—and our sensuality—have not been tamed or contained within it. There is no statistical documentation of the numbers of lesbians who have remained in heterosexual marriages for most of their lives. But in a letter to the early lesbian publication *Ladder*, the playwright Lorraine Hansberry had this to say:

> I suspect that the problem of the married woman who would prefer emotional-physical relationships with other women is proportionally much higher than a similar statistic for men. (A statistic surely no one will ever really have.) This because the estate of woman being what it is, how could we ever begin to guess the numbers of women who are not prepared to risk a life alien to what they have been taught all their lives to believe was their "natural" destiny—AND—their only expectation for ECONOMIC security. It

> seems to be that this is why the question has an immensity that it does not have for male homosexuals. . . .A woman of strength and honesty may, if she chooses, sever her marriage and marry a new male mate and society will be upset that the divorce rate is rising so—but there are few places in the United States, in any event, where she will be anything remotely akin to an "outcast." Obviously this is not true for a woman who would end her marriage to take up life with another woman.

This *double life*—this apparent acquiescence to an institution founded on male interest and prerogative—has been characteristic of female experience: in motherhood and in many kinds of heterosexual behavior, including the rituals of courtship; the pretense of asexuality by the nineteenth-century wife; the simulation of orgasm by the prostitute, the courtesan, the twentieth-century "sexually liberated" woman. . . .

Woman identification is a source of energy, a potential springhead of female power, curtailed and contained under the institution of heterosexuality. The denial of reality and visibility to women's passion for women, women's choice of women as allies, life companions, and community, the forcing of such relationships into dissimulation and their disintegration under intense pressure have meant an incalculable loss to the power of all women *to change the social relations of the sexes, to liberate ourselves and each other*. The lie of compulsory female heterosexuality today afflicts not just feminist scholarship, but every profession, every reference work, every curriculum, every organizing attempt, every relationship or conversation over which it hovers. It creates, specifically, a profound falseness, hypocrisy, and hysteria in the heterosexual dialogue, for every heterosexual relationship is lived in the queasy strobe light of that lie. However we chose to identify ourselves, however we find ourselves labeled, it flickers across and distorts our lives.

The lie keeps numberless women psychologically trapped, trying to fit mind, spirit, and sexuality into a prescribed script because they cannot look beyond the parameters of the acceptable. It pulls on the energy of such women even as it drains the energy of "closeted" lesbians—the energy exhausted in the double life. The lesbian trapped in the "closet," the woman imprisoned in prescriptive ideas of the "normal" share the pain of blocked options, broken connections, lost access to self-definition freely and powerfully assumed.

The lie is many-layered. In Western tradition, one layer—the romantic—asserts that women are inevitably, even if rashly and tragically, drawn to men; that even when that attraction is suicidal (e.g., *Tristan and Isolde*, Kate Chopin's *The Awakening*), it is still an organic imperative. In the tradition of the social sciences it asserts that primary love between the sexes is "normal" that women *need* men as social and economic protectors, for adult sexuality, and for psychological completion; that the heterosexually constituted family is the basic social unit; that women who do not attach their primary intensity to men must be, in functional terms, condemned to an even more devastating outsiderhood than their outsiderhood as women. Small wonder that lesbians are reported to be a more hidden population than male homosexuals. The Black lesbian-feminist critic, Lorraine Bethel, writing on Zora Neale Hurston, remarks that for a Black woman—already twice an outsider—to choose to assume still another "hated identity" is problematic indeed. Yet the lesbian continuum has been a lifeline for black women both in Africa and the United States.

> Black women have a long tradition of bonding together. . .in a Black/women's community that has been a source of vital survival information, psychic and emotional support for us. We have a distinct Black woman-identified folk culture based on our experiences as Black women in this society; symbols, language and modes of expression that are specific to the realities of our lives. . . . Because Black women were rarely among those Blacks and females who gained access to literary and other acknowledged forms of artistic expression, this Black female bonding and Black woman-identification has often been hidden and unrecorded except in the individual lives of Black women through our own memories of our particular Black female tradition.

Another layer of the lie is the frequently encountered implication that women turn to women out of hatred for men. Profound skepticism, caution, and righteous paranoia about men may indeed be part of any healthy woman's response to the misogyny of male-dominated culture, to the forms assumed by "normal" male sexuality, and to *the failure even of "sensitive" or "political" men to perceive or find these troubling*. Lesbian existence is also represented as mere refuge from male abuses, rather than as an electric and empowering charge between women. One of the most frequently quoted literary passages on lesbian relationship is that in which Colette's Renée, in *The Vagabond*, describes "the melancholy and touching image of two weak creatures who have perhaps found shelter in each other's arms, there to sleep and weep, safe from man who is often cruel, and there to taste *better than any pleasure, the bitter happiness of feeling themselves akin, frail and forgotten* [emphasis added]."[8] Colette is often considered a lesbian writer. Her popular reputation has, I think, much to do with the fact that she writes about lesbian existence as if for a male audience; her earliest "lesbian" novels, the Claudine series, were written under compulsion for her husband and published under both their names. At all events, except for her writings on her mother, Colette is a less reliable source on the lesbian continuum than, I would think, Charlotte Brontë, who understood that while women may, indeed must, be one another's allies, mentors, and comforters in the female struggle for survival, there is quite extraneous delight in each other's company and attraction to each others' minds and character, which attend a recognition of each others' strengths.

By the same token, we can say that there is a *nascent* feminist political content in the act of choosing a woman lover or life partner in the face of institutionalized heterosexuality. But for lesbian existence to realize this political

8. Dinnerstein, the most recent writer to quote this passage, adds ominously: "But what has to be added to her account is that these 'women enlaced' are sheltering each other not just from what men want to do to them, but also from what they want to do to each other." Dorothy Dinnerstein, The Mermaid and the Minotaur: Sexual Arrangements and the Human Malaise 103 (1976). The fact is, however, that woman-to-woman violence is a minute grain in the universe of male-against-female violence perpetrated and rationalized in every social institution.

content in an ultimately liberating form, the erotic choice must deepen and expand into conscious woman identification—into lesbian feminism.

The work that lies ahead, of unearthing and describing what I call here "lesbian existence," is potentially liberating for all women. It is work that must assuredly move beyond the limits of white and middle-class Western women's studies to examine women's lives, work, and groupings within every racial, ethnic, and political structure. There are differences, moreover, between "lesbian existence" and the "lesbian continuum," differences we can discern even in the movement of our own lives. The lesbian continuum, I suggest, needs delineation in light of the "double life" of women, not only women self-described as heterosexual but also of self-described lesbians. We need a far more exhaustive account of the forms the double life has assumed. Historians need to ask at every point how heterosexuality as institution has been organized and maintained through the female wage scale, the enforcement of middle-class women's "leisure," the glamorization of so-called sexual liberation, the withholding of education from women, the imagery of "high art" and popular culture, the mystification of the "personal" sphere, and much else. We need an economics which comprehends the institution of heterosexuality, with its doubled workload for women and its sexual divisions of labor, as the most idealized of economic relations.

The question inevitably will arise: Are we then to condemn all heterosexual relationships, including those which are least oppressive? I believe this question, though often heartfelt, is the wrong question here. We have been stalled in a maze of false dichotomies which prevents our apprehending the institution as a whole: "good" versus "bad" marriages; "marriage for love" versus arranged marriage; "liberated" sex versus prostitution; heterosexual intercourse versus rape; *Liebeschmerz* versus humiliation and dependency. Within the institution exist, of course, qualitative differences of experience; but the absence of choice remains the great unacknowledged reality, and in the absence of choice, women will remain dependent upon the chance or luck of particular relationships and will have no collective power to determine the meaning and place of sexuality in their lives. As we address the institution itself, moreover, we begin to perceive a history of female resistance which has never fully understood itself because it has been so fragmented, miscalled, erased. It will require a courageous grasp of the politics and economics, as well as the cultural propaganda, of heterosexuality to carry us beyond individual cases or diversified group situations into the complex kind of overview needed to undo the power men everywhere wield over women, power which has become a model for every other form of exploitation and illegitimate control.

Yvon Appleby, Disability and 'Compulsory Heterosexuality,' in *Heterosexuality: A Feminism & Psychology Reader* 266 (Sue Wilkinson & Celia Kitzinger eds., 1993)

In suggesting that heterosexual feminists need to examine 'compulsory heterosexuality' as an institution, Adrienne Rich omits to include the different experiences of disabled women, whose reality is in many ways external to that of 'compulsory heterosexuality'. I use the term 'disabled' to describe the fact that some people are disabled by a society which organizes to exclude, separate and disempower some of its members. Being disabled, then, is a statement about a power relationship that is socially constructed and socially maintained. It is a form of apartheid. This segregation is maintained by the organization of space and transport solely around the needs of ablebodied people; the lack of understanding and acceptance of mental illness or learning difficulties; and the general social invisibility that is a result of being excluded from the major dialogues that take place within society.

Ablebodied feminists have a responsibility actively to ensure that they do not block or prevent the access of disabled women's experience within feminist theory and practice. This responsibility should be undertaken with vigour, courage and honesty—questioning, perhaps painfully, our ablebodied assumptions and privileges. Simply leaving a space for disabled women to fill themselves is not facing up to this responsibility and places all the responsibility and work upon disabled women themselves. This actively ignores the real differences in power, access and income that exist between disabled and ablebodied women. It is also essential that ablebodied feminists do not speak on 'behalf' of disabled women as this would further the power imbalance that exists and in any case disabled women are more than 'able' to speak with knowledge and clarity on their own behalf and construct their own agenda for us to follow. Jenny Morris writes about the importance of integrating disabled women's experience into feminist theory:

> This does not mean that the experience of disability and old age should be 'added on' to existing feminist theory. Integrating these two aspects of identity into feminist thought will be just as revolutionary as feminism's political and theoretical challenge to the way that the experience of the white male was taken as representative of general human experience. Indeed feminism's challenge must remain incomplete while it excludes two such important aspects of human experience and modes of social and economic oppression.

Here I point to the exclusion of disabled women from Adrienne Rich's theory of 'compulsory heterosexuality'.

Adrienne Rich argues that heterosexuality is heavily promoted. The pressures on disabled women to engage in heterosexual practice operate differently from those to which ablebodied women are subjected. Disabled women are particularly at risk of (hetero)sexual abuse and rape, while they are generally not considered to have any sexual feelings or functions (motherhood) and are therefore considered to be less than female. Indeed for many disabled women the right to bear and raise their children is denied them and if they do then it is monitored and controlled by external forces. It is therefore inappropriate for Rich to suggest that disabled women have the same option to 'escape such causal violations along with economic disadvantages [and] may well turn to marriage as a hoped for protection. . .' In reality this does not appear to be a 'choice' that many disabled women feel that they have. Rich also talks of women responding to the New Right's oppression of difference by using a strategy of 'assimilation' and 'retreat into the sameness'. Again, these are perhaps not 'choices' that disabled women have as their reality is of invisibility and exclusion. The assumption of asexuality, and the *denial* of disabled women's sexuality means that heterosexuality can seem far less 'compulsory', and this can facilitate the acceptance of a lesbian identity, as in Kate's experience:

> I have a strong sense of my accident having liberated me when it comes to relationships. I was 19 when I had my accident and I'd grown up with an unthinking expectation of getting married and having numerous children. My immediate reaction in hospital, and for months and years afterwards, was of feeling neutered and completely rejected as a sexual being by men. But I also remember the glimmers of feeling real freedom from Society's expectations of me. Society had rejected me, but that also meant it didn't have any power over me, either. I didn't have to achieve the role of wife and mother any more. . . .Eventually I was able to have my first relationship with a woman without any of the traumas that many of my gay women friends have gone through. I haven't had to face family reactions of 'Why haven't you got married?' or Society's reaction of 'Why haven't you got a man?' because I'm not expected to have one!

In my own research into the invisibility of disabled lesbians within the lesbian community many of the women I interviewed described similar experiences. 'Lucy' came out at the age of 22 and found her sexuality easier to accept than her identity as a disabled woman: 'There was no model of sexuality pushed at me'. At that time she says that she found it hard to look at her own reflection as her visible difference from the ablebodied norm was more difficult for her to accept than the invisible difference of being a lesbian, as she was considered to be asexual. For some women, though, exclusion from heterosexuality can make the choice of a lesbian identity or celibacy seem less positive a choice because of the implication that they could not get a man anyway. Moreover, the assumed asexuality of disabled women means that a *lesbian* sexuality is equally denied. The father of Sharon Kowalski, disabled in a car crash, is reported to have said 'What the hell difference does it make if she's gay or lesbian or straight because she's laying there in diapers?. . . Let the poor kid rest in peace'. In this case, Sharon Kowalski's expressed wish to continue her chosen relationship with her lesbian lover Karen Thompson was for many years denied her.

Adrienne Rich also points to the oppression and denial of lesbianism as a feature of *all* women's lives. This is especially the case for disabled women. Although freer from heterosexual surveillance and control, many obstacles prevent free entry into lesbian community and lesbian culture. Lack of access to information, ramps, signers and braille material, together with a lack of awareness of the needs of women deemed to have mental illness or learning difficulties are some of the factors that work to exclude disabled lesbians. Unfortunately ablebodied lesbians are not free from the prevailing dominant ideas that disabled women are somehow 'other' and nothing to do with them. Organizations 'for' disabled people tend to provide insufficient information about lesbianism, and lesbian groups are ill prepared to deal with disability issues.

I contacted a range of charitable organizations which maintain a high profile on disability issues to ask what they offered lesbians. Some were able to reference useful material (e.g. The Disabled Living Foundation) while others expressed a broad support for an individual's right to choose her own sexuality (Campaign for Valued Futures for People Who Have a Learning Difficulty). Mencap (Royal Society for Mentally Handicapped Children and Adults) replied that if the issue of lesbianism arose their first obligation would be 'to ensure that this was not environmental or other pressures that was leading someone to misinterpret their own situation'. SPOD (Association to Aid Sexual and Personal Relationships of Disabled People) showed a more vigorous and active response and anticipates publishing a booklet on disability and homosexuality. The lack of access to information can make contact with the lesbian community very difficult. 'Pat' describes the process:

> I heard a public announcement for [a lesbian and gay befriending service] on the television. I couldn't ask anyone to tape it for me so for months I sat with my tape recorder at 10.39 each evening when I thought that it might be on. Sure enough it was, literally months later that I was able to tape the telephone number.

Access to information does not guarantee entry into the lesbian community. I contacted six lesbian lines to find out what was wheelchair accessible in their area. Wheelchair accessibility is only one area of access that would prevent a disabled woman's entry into the lesbian community but I used this as a comparison as most people have some understanding of physical access. Of the six lines that were contacted only one was able to offer a partially accessible venue. All the women I spoke to were concerned and explained that it was very difficult to find somewhere that accepted lesbian bookings at affordable prices and those that did were often in basement or in upstairs rooms and not accessible.

Adrienne Rich's analysis of compulsory heterosexuality is both an important milestone in the development of feminist theory and provides a clear example of where the experiences of disabled women are external to the analysis of 'all women'. This is perhaps a reflection of its time of writing, where disabled women were at best 'added on' and at worst totally ignored. Rich speaks of the 'special quality of courage' which is necessary when we question the shaping of identity, power, preference and desire. As feminists we must use this courage to question our collusion with 'ablebodiedism' and must seek continually to develop feminist theories and practice which integrate the experiences of disabled women from the outset.

Notes

1. *Compulsory Heterosexuality*. Adrienne Rich's essay shows the dominant role that heterosexuality plays in our society. The following questions supplement her essay by illustrating traditionally unexamined assumptions resulting from the compulsory nature of heterosexuality. These questions are seldom asked of a heterosexual person, but that they are often asked of openly bisexual, lesbian, and gay persons is evidence of homophobia and of stereotypical thinking.

a. What do you think caused your heterosexuality?

b. When and how did you decide you were a heterosexual?

c. To whom have you disclosed your heterosexual tendencies? How did they react?

d. Why do heterosexuals feel compelled to seduce others into their lifestyle?

e. Why do you insist on flaunting your heterosexuality?

f. A disproportionate majority of child molesters are heterosexuals. Do you feel it is safe to expose your children to heterosexual teachers?

g. With all the societal support marriage receives, the divorce rate is spiraling. Why are there so few stable relationships among heterosexuals?

Mary Ann Tucker & Sharon Young, Dimensions (Dignity/San Diego Newsletter) (questions were selected from a questionnaire titled "How Do You Know You're Straight?").

2. *Invisibility of Lesbians.* A corollary to Rich's observation about the pervasiveness of heterosexuality is that lesbians are invisible within our society. Marilyn Frye analyzes that invisibility in her essay, which examines standard dictionary definitions of the word *lesbian* and how those definitions erase the possibility of a lesbian existence.

> If you look up the word 'lesbian' in *The Oxford English Dictionary*, you find an entry that says it is an adjective that means *of or pertaining to the island of Lesbos*, and an entry describing at length and favorably an implement called a lesbian rule, which is a flexible measuring device used by carpenters. Period. . . .
>
> A recent edition of *Webster's Collegiate Dictionary* tells us that a lesbian is a woman who has sex, or sexual relations, with other women. Such a definition would be accepted by many speakers of the language and at least seems to be coherent, even if too narrow. But the appearance is deceptive, for this account collapses into nonsense, too. The key word in this definition is 'sex': having sex or having sexual relations. But what is having sex? It is worthwhile to follow this up because the pertinent dictionary entries obscure an important point about the logic of sex. . . .
>
> Dictionaries generally agree that 'sexual' means something on the order of *pertaining to the genital union of a female and a male animal*, and that "having sex" is having intercourse—intercourse being defined as the penetration of a vagina by a penis, with ejaculation. . . .
>
> When one first considers the dictionary definitions of 'sex' and 'sexual', it seems that all sexuality is heterosexuality, by definition, and that the term 'homosexual' would be internally contradictory. There are uses of the term according to which this is exactly so. But in the usual and standard use, there is nothing semantically odd in describing two men as having sex with each other. According to that usage, any situation in which one or more penises are present is one in which something could happen which could be called having sex. But on this apparently "broader" definition there is noth-

> ing women could do in the absence of men that could, without semantic oddity, be called "having sex.". . .
>
> Flinging the net wider, one can look up the more Victorian words, like sapphism and sapphist. . . .*The Oxford English Dictionary* introduces another twist. Under the heading of 'sapphism' is an entry for 'sapphist' according to which sapphists are those addicted to unnatural sexual relations between women. The fact that these relations are characterized as unnatural is revealing. For what is unnatural is contrary to the laws of nature . . . .But what is contrary to the laws of nature cannot happen: that is what it means to call these laws the laws of nature. And I cannot do what is contrary to my nature, for if I could do it, it would be in my nature to do it. . . .This definition defines sapphists, that is lesbians, as *naturally* impossible as well as *logically* impossible. . . .
>
> Lesbian.
>
> One of the people of the Isle of Lesbos.
>
> It is bizarre that when I try to name myself and explain myself, my native tongue provides me with a word that is so foreign, so false, so hopelessly inappropriate. Why am I referred to by a term which means *one of the people of Lesbos?*
>
> The use of the word 'lesbian' to name us is a quadrifold evasion, a laminated euphemism. To name us, one goes by way of a reference to the island of Lesbos, which in turn is an indirect reference to the poet Sappho (who used to live there, they say), which in turn is itself an indirect reference to what fragments of her poetry have survived a few millenia of patriarchy, and this in turn (if we have not lost you by now) is a prophylactic avoidance of direct mention of the sort of creature who would write such poems or to whom such poems would be written. . .assuming you happen to know what is in those poems written in a dialect of Greek over two thousand five hundred years ago on some small island somewhere in the wine dark Aegean Sea.
>
> This is a truly remarkable feat of silence.

Marilyn Frye, To Be and Be Seen: The Politics of Reality, in The Politics of Reality: Essays in Feminist Theory 152, 156–60 (1983).

3. *Violence and Heterosexuality.* The systems of oppressions represented by the matrix of domination produce two related forms of violence against women. First, the oppressive behavior of dominant groups constrains and limits the possibilities for a woman so that she becomes what others demand of her rather than what she demands of herself. The compulsory nature of heterosexuality creates significant barriers for a woman to exercise choice about her sexuality. Even if she is able to choose she may be forced to keep her lesbian or bisexual identity secret. The denial of one's identity is another form of spiritual violence.

For women who are disabled, Yvon Appleby explains how the spiritual violence occurs in multiple and simultaneous ways. Abilism, inside and outside the lesbian community, leads to women who are disabled being treated as asexual. Denying a woman's sexuality violates her spirit by making her invisible.

The second form of violence produced by systems of oppression is domination, which frequently manifests itself in physical violence against members of subordinated groups. Kendall Thomas, discussing violence and heterosexuality, explains that the aim of homophobic violence is "to regulate the erotic economy of contemporary American society, or more specifically, to enforce the institutional and ideological imperatives of what Adrienne Rich has termed 'compulsory heterosexuality.' Insofar as homophobic violence functions to prevent and punish actual or imagined deviations from heterosexual acts and identities, it carries a determinate political valence and value." Kendall Thomas, Beyond the Privacy Principle, 92 Colum. L. Rev. 1431, 1467 (1992).

Compulsory heterosexuality not only places lesbians and gay men in danger, but it also places heterosexual women at risk. Heterosexuality is constructed around the myth of romantic love. Two aspects of that romantic love are the right to be jealous and the right to possess one's beloved. When a man is or imagines that he is at risk of losing control over a woman, he takes action to try to regain the control he feels he is losing. Frequently, that action is physical violence, including assault, harassment, and rape. The role of compulsory heterosexuality in violence will be a recurring theme in the chapters that follow.

4. *Violence and Disability*. Appleby indicates that disabled women are particularly at risk of violence (p. 76). Cathy McPherson explains the dynamics of that risk.

> The reasons women with disabilities are more likely to be assaulted and sexually assaulted have less to do with their actual disability than with the large number of people who have contact with them in their intimate circle as assistants. That, coupled with a learned passivity that is reinforced in institutional settings, makes them more vulnerable to abuse. There is no doubt, however, that women with multiple handicaps or who are profoundly disabled, are less able to speak out when someone abuses them and are often not taken seriously either in reporting the abuse or by the justice system itself.
>
> Many women with disabilities miss out on sex education. When abuse occurs, they know something is wrong but are not sure what it is.
>
> What makes it even more difficult for a woman with disabilities to leave a violent situation is that she is often dependent on the very person abusing her for support care and for financial support. . . .
>
> If a woman in a wheelchair manages to get out of an abusive situation, in spite of the fact that there is likely no accessible transportation and her abuser might have taken the chair away from her, she may find herself in an institution because no attendant care is available in the community; an institution where she may be *more* likely to be abused. The withdrawal of support care services is a threat that *all* disabled women run the risk of when they complain, particularly if the abuser is support care staff. The removal of her children from her, should she leave an abusive situation, is also a risk.

Cathy McPherson, Violence Against Women with Disabilities, 11 Canadian Women Stud. 49, 49–50 (1991) (emphasis in original).

John D'Emilio, Capitalism and Gay Identity, in *Powers of Desire: The Politics of Sexuality* 100 (Ann Snitow, Christine Stansell, & Sharon Thompson eds., 1983)

For gay men and lesbians, the 1970s were years of significant achievement. Gay liberation and women's liberation changed the sexual landscape of the nation. Hundreds of thousands of gay women and men came out and openly affirmed same-sex eroticism. We won repeal of sodomy laws in half the states, a partial lifting of the exclusion of lesbians and gay men from federal employment, civil rights protection in a few dozen cities, the inclusion of gay rights in the platform of the Democratic Party, and the elimination of homosexuality from the psychiatric profession's list of mental illnesses. The gay male subculture expanded and became increasingly visible in large cities, and lesbian feminists pioneered in building alternative institutions and an alternative culture that attempted to embody a liberatory vision of the future.

In the 1980s, however, with the resurgence of an active right wing, gay men and lesbians face the future warily. Our victories appear tenuous and fragile; the relative freedom of the past few years seems too recent to be permanent. In some parts of the lesbian and gay male community, a feeling of doom is growing: analogies with McCarthy's America, when "sexual perverts" were a special target of the Right, and with Nazi Germany, where gays were shipped to concentration camps, surface with increasing frequency. Everywhere there is the sense that new strategies are in order if we want to preserve our gains and move ahead.

I believe that a new, more accurate theory of gay history must be part of this political enterprise. When the gay liberation movement began at the end of the 1960s, gay men and lesbians had no history that we could use to fashion our goals and strategy. In the ensuing years, in building a movement without a knowledge of our history, we instead invented a mythology. This mythical history drew on personal experience, which we read backward in time. For instance, most lesbians and gay men in the 1960s first discovered their homosexual desires in isolation, unaware of others, and without resources for naming and understanding what they felt. From this experience, we constructed a myth of silence, invisibility, and isolation as the essential characteristics of gay life in the past as well as the present. Moreover, because we faced so many oppressive laws, public policies, and cultural beliefs, we projected this into an image of the abysmal past: until gay liberation, lesbians and gay men were always the victims of systematic, undifferentiated, terrible oppression.

These myths have limited our political perspective. They have contributed, for instance, to an overreliance on a strategy of coming out—if every gay man and lesbian in America came out, gay oppression would end—and have allowed us to ignore the institutionalized ways in which homophobia and heterosexism are reproduced. They have encouraged, at times, an incapacitating despair, especially at moments like the present: How can we unravel a gay oppression so pervasive and unchanging?

There is another historical myth that enjoys nearly universal acceptance in the gay movement, the myth of the "eternal homosexual." The argument runs something like this: gay men and lesbians always were and always will be. We are everywhere; not just now, but throughout history, in all societies and all periods. This myth served a positive political function in the first years of gay liberation. In the early 1970s, when we battled an ideology that either denied our existence or defined us as psychopathic individuals or freaks of nature, it was empowering to assert that "we are everywhere." But in recent years it has confined us as surely as the most homophobic medical theories, and locked our movement in place.

Here I wish to challenge this myth. I want to argue that gay men and lesbians have *not* always existed. Instead, they are a product of history, and have come into existence in a specific historical era. Their emergence is associated with the relations of capitalism; it has been the historical development of capitalism—more specifically, its free labor system—that has allowed large numbers of men and women in the late twentieth century to call themselves gay, to see themselves as part of a community of similar men and women, and to organize politically on the basis of that identity.[9] Finally, I want to suggest some political lessons we can draw from this view of history.

What, then, are the relationships between the free labor system of capitalism and homosexuality? First, let me review some features of capitalism. Under capitalism, workers are "free" laborers in two ways. We have the freedom to look for a job. We own our ability to work and have the freedom to sell our labor power for wages to anyone willing to buy it. We are also freed from the ownership of anything except our labor power. Most of us do not own the land or the tools that produce what we need, but rather have to work for a living in order to survive. So, if we are free to sell our labor power in the positive sense, we are also freed, in the negative sense, from any other alternative. This dialectic—the constant interplay between exploitation and some measure of autonomy—informs all of the history of those who have lived under capitalism.

As capital—money used to make more money—expands, so does this system of free labor. Capital expands in several ways. Usually it expands in the same place, transforming small firms into larger ones, but it also expands by taking over new areas of production: the weaving of cloth, for instance, or the baking of bread. Finally, capital expands geographically. In the United States, capitalism initially took root in the Northeast, at a time when slavery was the dominant system in the South and when noncapitalist Native American societies occupied the western half of the continent. During the nineteenth century, capital spread from the Atlantic to the Pacific, and in the twentieth, U.S. capital has penetrated almost every part of the world.

The expansion of capital and the spread of wage labor have effected a profound transformation in the structure and functions of the nuclear family, the ideology of family life, and the meaning of heterosexual relations. It is these

9. I do not mean to suggest that no one has ever proposed that gay identity is a product of historical change. See, for instance, Jeffrey Weeks, *Coming Out: Homosexual Politics in Britain* (1977); Mary McIntosh, The Homosexual Role, 16 Soc. Probls. 182 (1968). . . . However, this does represent a minority viewpoint and the works cited above have not specified how it is that capitalism as a system of production has allowed for the emergence of a gay male and lesbian identity. As an example of the "eternal homosexual" thesis, see John Boswell, *Christianity, Social Tolerance, and Homosexuality* (1980), where "gay people" remains an unchanging social category through fifteen centuries of Mediterranean and Western European history.

changes in the family that are most directly linked to the appearance of a collective gay life.

The white colonists in the seventeenth-century New England established villages structured around a household economy, composed of family units that were basically self-sufficient, independent, and patriarchal. Men, women, and children farmed land owned by the male head of household. Although there was a division of labor between men and women, the family was truly an interdependent unit of production: the survival of each member depended on the cooperation of all. The home was a workplace where women processed raw farm products into food for daily consumption, where they made clothing, soap, and candles, and where husbands, wives, and children worked together to produce the goods they consumed.

By the nineteenth century, this system of household production was in decline. In the Northeast, as merchant capitalists invested the money accumulated through trade in the production of goods, wage labor became more common. Men and women were drawn out of the largely self-sufficient household economy of the colonial era into a capitalist system of free labor. For women in the nineteenth century, working for wages rarely lasted beyond marriage; for men, it became a permanent condition.

The family was thus no longer an independent unit of production. But although no longer independent, the family was still interdependent. Because capitalism had not expanded very far, because it had not yet taken over—or socialized—the production of consumer goods, women still performed necessary productive labor in the home. Many families no longer produced grain, but wives still baked into bread the flour they bought with their husband's wages; or, when they purchased yarn or cloth, they still made clothing for their families. By the mid-1800s, capitalism had destroyed the economic self-sufficiency of many families, but not the mutual dependence of the members.

This transition away from the household family-based economy to a fully developed capitalist free labor economy occurred very slowly, over almost two centuries. As late as 1920, 50 percent of the U.S. population lived in communities of fewer than 2,500 people. The vast majority of blacks in the early twentieth century lived outside the free labor economy, in a system of sharecropping and tenancy that rested on the family. Not only did independent farming as a way of life still exist for millions of Americans, but even in towns and small cities women continued to grow and process food, make clothing, and engage in other kinds of domestic production.

But for those people who felt the brunt of these changes, the family took on new significance as an affective unit, an institution that produced not goods but emotional satisfaction and happiness. By the 1920s among the white middle class, the ideology surrounding the family described it as the means through which men and women formed satisfying, mutually enhancing relationships and created an environment that nurtured children. The family became the setting for a "personal life," sharply distinguished and disconnected from the public world of work and production.

The meaning of heterosexual relations also changed. In colonial New England, the birthrate averaged over seven children per woman of childbearing age. Men and women needed the labor of children. Producing offspring was as necessary for survival as producing grain. Sex was harnessed to procreation. The

Puritans did not celebrate *hetero*sexuality but rather marriage; they condemned *all* sexual expression outside the marriage bond and did not differentiate sharply between sodomy and heterosexual fornication.

By the 1970s, however, the birthrate had dropped to under two. With the exception of the post-World War II baby boom, the decline has been continuous for two centuries, paralleling the spread of capitalist relations of production. It occurred even when access to contraceptive devices and abortion was systematically curtailed. The decline has included every segment of the population—urban and rural families, blacks and whites, ethnics and WASPs, the middle class and the working class.

As wage labor spread and production became socialized, then, it became possible to release sexuality from the "imperative" to procreate. Ideologically, heterosexual expression came to be a means of establishing intimacy, promoting happiness, and experiencing pleasure. In divesting the household of its economic independence and fostering the separation of sexuality from procreation, capitalism has created conditions that allow some men and women to organize a personal life around their erotic/emotional attraction to their own sex. It has made possible the formation of urban communities of lesbians and gay men and, more recently, of a politics based on a sexual identity.

Evidence from colonial New England court records and church sermons indicates that male and female homosexual behavior existed in the seventeenth century. Homosexual *behavior*, however, is different from homosexual *identity*. There was, quite simply, no "social space" in the colonial system of production that allowed men and women to be gay. Survival was structured around participation in a nuclear family. There were certain homosexual acts—sodomy among men, "lewdness" among women—in which individuals engaged, but family was so pervasive that colonial society lacked even the category of homosexual or lesbian to describe a person. It is quite possible that some men and women experienced a stronger attraction to their own sex than to the opposite sex—in fact, some colonial court cases refer to men who persisted in their "unnatural" attractions—but one could not fashion out of that preference a way of life. Colonial Massachusetts even had laws prohibiting unmarried adults from living outside family units.

By the second half of the nineteenth century, this situation was noticeably changing as the capitalist system of free labor took hold. Only when *individuals* began to make their living through wage labor, instead of as parts of an interdependent family unit, was it possible for homosexual desire to coalesce into a personal identity—an identity based on the ability to remain outside the heterosexual family and to construct a personal life based on attraction to one's own sex. By the end of the century, a class of men and women existed who recognized their erotic interest in their own sex, saw it as a trait that set them apart from the majority, and sought others like themselves. These early gay lives came from a wide social spectrum: civil servants and business executives, department store clerks and college professors, factory operatives, ministers, lawyers, cooks, domestics, hoboes, and the idle rich: men and women, black and white, immigrant and native born.

In this period, gay men and lesbians began to invent ways of meeting each other and sustaining a group life. Already, in the early twentieth century, large cities contained male homosexual bars. Gay men staked out cruising areas, such as Riverside Drive in New York City and Lafayette Park in Washington. In St. Louis and the nation's capital, annual drag balls brought together large numbers of black gay men. Public bathhouses and YMCAs became gathering spots for male homosexuals. Lesbians formed literary societies and private social clubs. Some working-class women "passed" as men to obtain better paying jobs and lived with other women—lesbian couples who appeared to the world as husband and wife. Among the faculties of women's colleges, in the settlement houses, and in the professional associations and clubs that women formed one could find lifelong intimate relationships supported by a web of lesbian friends. By the 1920s and 1930s, large cities such as New York and Chicago contained lesbian bars. These patterns of living could evolve because capitalism allowed individuals to survive beyond the confines of the family.

Simultaneously, ideological definitions of homosexual behavior changed. Doctors developed theories about homosexual*ity*, describing it as a condition, something that was inherent in a person, a part of his or her "nature." These theories did not represent scientific breakthroughs, elucidations of previously undiscovered areas of knowledge; rather, they were an ideological response to a new way of organizing one's personal life. The popularization of the medical model, in turn, affected the consciousness of the women and men who experienced homosexual desire, so that they came to define themselves through their erotic life.

These new forms of gay identity and patterns of group life also reflected the differentiation of people according to gender, race, and class that is so pervasive in capitalist societies. Among whites, for instance, gay men have traditionally been more visible than lesbians. This partly stems from the division between the public male sphere and the private female sphere. Streets, parks, and bars, especially at night, were "male space." Yet the greater visibility of white gay men also reflected their larger numbers. The Kinsey studies of the 1940s and 1950s found significantly more men than women with predominantly homosexual histories, a situation caused, I would argue, by the fact that capitalism had drawn far more men than women into the labor force, and at higher wages. Men could more easily construct a personal life independent of attachments to the opposite sex, whereas women were more likely to remain economically dependent on men. Kinsey also found a strong positive correlation between years of schooling and lesbian activity. College-educated white women, far more able than their working-class sisters to support themselves, could survive more easily without intimate relationships with men.

Among working-class immigrants in the early twentieth century, closely knit kin networks and an ethic of family solidarity placed constraints on individual autonomy that made gayness a difficult option to pursue. In contrast, for reasons not altogether clear, urban black communities appeared relatively tolerant of homosexuality. The popularity in the 1920s and 1930s of songs with lesbian and gay male themes—"B. D. Woman," "Prove It on Me," "Sissy Man," "Fairey Blues"—suggests an openness about homosexual expression at odds with the mores of whites. Among men in the rural West in the 1940s, Kinsey found extensive incidence of homosexual behavior, but, in contrast with the men in large cities, little consciousness of gay identity. Thus even as capitalism exerted a homogenizing influence by gradually transforming more individuals into wage laborers and separating them from traditional communities, different groups of people were also affected in different ways.

The decisions of particular men and women to act on their erotic/emotional preference for the same sex, along with the new consciousness that this preference made them different, led to the formation of an urban subculture of gay men and lesbians. Yet at least through the 1930s this subculture remained rudimentary, unstable, and difficult to find. How, then, did the complex, well-developed gay community emerge that existed by the time the gay liberation movement exploded? The answer is to be found during World War II, a time when the cumulative changes of several decades coalesced into a qualitatively new shape.

The war severely disrupted traditional patterns of gender relations and sexuality, and temporarily created a new erotic situation conducive to homosexual expression. It plucked millions of young men and women, whose sexual identities were just forming, out of their homes, out of towns and small cities, out of the heterosexual environment of the family, and dropped them into sex-segregated situations—as GIs, as WACs and WAVEs, in same-sex rooming houses for women workers who relocated to seek employment. The war freed millions of men and women from the settings where heterosexuality was normally imposed. For men and women already gay, it provided an opportunity to meet people like themselves. Others could become gay because of the temporary freedom to explore sexuality that the war provided.

Lisa Ben, for instance, came out during the war. She left the small California town where she was raised, came to Los Angeles to find work, and lived in a women's boarding house. There she met for the first time lesbians who took her to gay bars and introduced her to other gay women. Donald Vining was a young man with lots of homosexual desire and few gay experiences. He moved to New York City during the war and worked at a large YMCA. His diary reveals numerous erotic adventures with soldiers, sailors, marines, and civilians at the Y where he worked, as well as at the men's residence club where he lived, and in parks, bars, and movie theaters. Many GIs stayed in port cities like New York, at YMCAs like the one where Vining worked. In his oral histories of gay men in San Francisco, focusing on the 1940s, Allan Bérubé has found that the war years were critical in the formation of a gay male *community* in the city. Places as different as San Jose, Denver, and Kansas City had their first gay bars in the 1940s. Even severe repression could have positive side effects. Pat Bond, a lesbian from Davenport, Iowa, joined the WACs during the 1940s. Caught in a purge of hundreds of lesbians from the WACs in the Pacific, she did not return to Iowa. She stayed in San Francisco and became part of a community of lesbians. How many other women and men had comparable experiences? How many other cities saw a rapid growth of lesbian and gay male communities?

The gay men and women of the 1940s were pioneers. Their decisions to act on their desires formed the underpinnings of an urban subculture of gay men and lesbians. Throughout the 1950s and 1960s, the gay subculture grew and stabilized so that people coming out then could more easily find other gay women and men than in the past. Newspapers and magazines published articles describing gay male life. Literally hundreds of novels with lesbian themes were published. Psychoanalysts complained about the new ease with which their gay male patients found sexual partners. And the gay subculture was not just to be found in the largest cities. Lesbian and gay male bars existed in places like Worcester, Massachusetts, and Buffalo, New York; in Columbia, South Carolina, and Des Moines, Iowa. Gay life in the 1950s and 1960s became a nationwide phenomenon. By the time of the Stonewall Riots in New York City in 1969—the event that ignited the gay liberation movement—our situation was hardly one of silence, invisibility, and isolation. A massive, grass-roots liberation movement could form almost overnight precisely because communities of lesbians and gay men existed.

Although gay community was a precondition for a mass movement, the oppression of lesbians and gay men was the force that propelled the movement into existence. As the subculture expanded and grew more visible in the post-World War II era, oppression by the state intensified, becoming more systematic and inclusive. The Right scapegoated "sexual perverts" during the McCarthy era. Eisenhower imposed a total ban on the employment of gay women and men by the federal government and government contractors. Purges of lesbians and homosexuals from the military rose sharply. The FBI instituted widespread surveillance of gay meeting places and of lesbian and gay organizations, such as the Daughters of Bilitis and the Mattachine Society. The Post Office placed tracers on the correspondence of gay men and passed evidence of homosexual activity on to employers. Urban vice squads invaded private homes, made sweeps of lesbian and gay male bars, entrapped gay men in public places, and fomented local witch hunts. The danger involved in being gay rose even as the possibilities of being gay were enhanced. Gay liberation was a response to this contradiction.

Although lesbians and gay men won significant victories in the 1970s and opened up some safe social space in which to exist, we can hardly claim to have dealt a fatal blow to heterosexism and homophobia. One could even argue that the enforcement of gay oppression has merely changed locales, shifting somewhat from the state to the arena of extralegal violence in the form of increasingly open physical attacks on lesbians and gay men. And, as our movements have grown, they have generated a backlash that threatens to wipe out our gains. Significantly, this New Right opposition has taken shape as a "pro-family" movement. How is it that capitalism, whose structure made possible the emergence of a gay identity and the creation of urban gay communities, appears unable to accept gay men and lesbians in its midst? Why do heterosexism and homophobia appear so resistant to assault?

The answers, I think, can be found in the contradictory relationship of capitalism to the family. On the one hand, as I argued earlier, capitalism has gradually undermined the material basis of the nuclear family by taking away the economic functions that cemented the ties between family members. As more adults have been drawn into the free labor system, and as capital has expanded its sphere until it produces as commodities most goods and services we need for our survival, the forces that propelled men and women into families and kept them there have weakened. On the other hand, the ideology of capitalist society has enshrined the family as the source of love, affection, and emotional security, the place where our need for stable, intimate human relationships is satisfied.

This elevation of the nuclear family to preeminence in the sphere of personal life is not accidental. Every society needs structures for reproduction and childrearing, but the possibilities are not limited to the nuclear family. Yet the privatized family fits well with capitalist relations of production. Capitalism has socialized production while maintaining that the products of socialized labor belong to the owners of private property. In many ways, childrearing has also been progressively socialized over the last two centuries, with schools, the media, peer groups, and employers taking over functions that once belonged to parents. Nevertheless, capitalist society maintains that reproduction and childrearing are private tasks, that children "belong" to parents, who exercise the rights of ownership. Ideologically, capitalism drives people into heterosexual families: each generation comes of age having internalized a heterosexist model of intimacy and personal relationships. Materially, capitalism weakens the bonds that once kept families together so that their members experience a growing instability in the place they have come to expect happiness and emotional security. Thus, while capitalism has knocked the material foundation away from family life, lesbians, gay men, and heterosexual feminists have become the scapegoats for the social instability of the system.

This analysis, if persuasive, has implications for us today. It can affect our perception of our identity, our formulation of political goals, and our decisions about strategy.

I have argued that lesbian and gay identity and communities are historically created, the result of a process of capitalist development that has spanned many generations. A corollary of this argument is that we are *not* a fixed social minority composed for all time of a certain percentage of the population. *There are more of us* than one hundred years ago, more of us than forty years ago. And there may very well be more gay men and lesbians in the future. Claims made by gays and nongays that sexual orientation is fixed at an early age, that large numbers of visible gay men and lesbians in society, the media, and the schools will have no influence on the sexual identities of the young, are wrong. Capitalism has created the material conditions for homosexual desire to express itself as a central component of some individuals' lives; now, our political movements are changing consciousness, creating the ideological conditions that make it easier for people to make that choice.

To be sure, this argument confirms the worse fears and most rabid rhetoric of our political opponents. But our response must be to challenge the underlying belief that homosexual relations are bad, a poor second choice. We must not slip into the opportunistic defense that society need not worry about tolerating us, since only homosexuals become homosexuals. At best, a minority group analysis and a civil rights strategy pertain to those of us who already are gay. It leaves today's youth—tomorrow's lesbians and gay men—to internalize heterosexist models that it can take a lifetime to expunge.

I have also argued that capitalism has led to the separation of sexuality from procreation. Human sexual desire need no longer be harnessed to reproductive imperatives, to procreation; its expression has increasingly entered the realm of choice. Lesbians and homosexuals most clearly embody the potential of this split, since our gay relationships stand entirely outside a procreative framework. The acceptance of our erotic choices ultimately depends on the degree to which society is willing to affirm sexual expression as a form of play, positive and life-enhancing. Our movement may have begun as the struggle of a "minority," but what we should now be trying to "liberate" is an aspect of the personal lives of all people—sexual expression.

Finally, I have suggested that the relationship between capitalism and the family is fundamentally contradictory. On the one hand, capitalism continually weakens the material foundation of family life, making it possible for individuals to live outside the family, and for a lesbian and gay male identity to develop. On the other, it needs to push men and women into families, at least long enough to reproduce the next generation of workers. The elevation of the family to ideological preeminence guarantees that capitalist society will reproduce not just children, but heterosexism and homophobia. In the most profound sense, capitalism is the problem.

How do we avoid remaining the scapegoats, the political victims of the social instability that capitalism generates? How can we take this contradictory relationship and use it to move toward liberation?

Gay men and lesbians exist on social terrain beyond the boundaries of the heterosexual nuclear family. Our communities have formed in that social space. Our survival and liberation depend on our ability to defend and expand that terrain, not just for ourselves but for everyone. That means, in part, support for issues that broaden the opportunities for living outside traditional heterosexual family units: issues like the availability of abortion and the ratification of the Equal Rights Amendment, affirmative action for people of color and for women, publicly funded daycare and other essential social services, decent welfare payments, full employment, the rights of young people—in other words, programs and issues that provide a material basis for personal autonomy.

The rights of young people are especially critical. The acceptance of children as dependents, as belonging to parents, is so deeply ingrained that we can scarcely imagine what it would mean to treat them as autonomous human beings, particularly in the realm of sexual expression and choice. Yet until that happens, gay liberation will remain out of our reach.

But personal autonomy is only half the story. The instability of families and the sense of impermanence and insecurity that people are now experiencing in their personal relationships are real social problems that need to be addressed. We need political solutions for these difficulties of personal life. These solutions should not come in the form of a radical version of the pro-family position, of some left-wing proposals to strengthen the family. Socialists do not generally respond to the exploitation and economic inequality of industrial capitalism by calling for a return to the family farm and handicraft production. We recognize that the vastly increased productivity that capitalism has made possible by socializing production is one of its progressive features. Similarly, we should not be trying to turn back the clock to some mythic age of the happy family.

We do need, however, structures and programs that will help to dissolve the boundaries that isolate the family, particularly those that privatize childrearing. We need community-or worker-controlled daycare, housing where privacy and community coexist, neighborhood institutions—from medical clinics to performance centers—that enlarge the social unit where each of us has a secure place. As we create structures beyond the nuclear family that provide a sense of belonging, the family will wane in significance. Less and less will it seem to make or break our emotional security.

In this respect gay men and lesbians are well situated to play a special role. Already excluded from families as most of us are, we have had to create, for our survival, networks of support that do not depend on the bonds of blood or the license of the state, but that are freely chosen and nurtured. The building of an "affectional community" must be as much a part of our political movement as are campaigns for civil rights. In this way we may prefigure the shape of personal relationships in a society grounded in equality and justice rather than exploitation and oppression, a society where autonomy and security do not preclude each other but coexist.

Notes and Questions

1. *Social Construction/Essentialism.* John D'Emilio argues "lesbian and gay identity and communities are historically created" (p. 89) and refers to a claim that lesbianism and gay identity is innate as the "myth of the 'eternal homosexual' " (p. 82). Julia Penelope challenges his argument by refusing to choose sides between the "'essentialists'. . .who maintain that our identities are innate, and the 'social constructionists,'. . .who claim that our identities are the result of social forces peculiar to the time and place we are born into. . . .[B]oth accounts of Lesbian identity are accurate. It's not an either/or situation. I was born a Lesbian in a specific social and historical context." Julia Penelope, Call Me Lesbian: Lesbian Lives, Lesbian Theory 17, 20 (1992).

Diana Fuss, in exploring the question of identity politics, suggests the debate may have gendered underpinnings.

> In general, current lesbian theory is less willing to question or to part with the idea of a "lesbian essence" and an identity politics based on this shared essence. Gay male theorists, on the other hand, following the lead of Foucault,[10] have been quick to endorse the social constructionist hypothesis and to develop more detailed analyses of the historical construction of sexualities. . . .[This suggests] that if the adherence to essentialism is a measure of the degree to which a particular political group has been culturally oppressed. . ., then the stronger lesbian endorsement of identity and identity politics may well indicate that lesbians inhabit a more precarious and less secure subject position than gay men.

Diana Fuss, Essentially Speaking: Feminism, Nature & Difference 98 (1989). Fuss continues her discussion of the debate by identifying the strengths of a constructionist approach and its vulnerabilities and in so doing provides a deeper understanding of homosexuality, heterosexuality, and bisexuality in our society.

> First, invention theories, by rejecting the view of homosexuality as an

10. Michel Foucault was a leading French structuralist philosopher who examined the history of Western attitudes toward sexuality in an influential three-volume treatise titled *The History of Sexuality* (1976-84). Eds.

> eternal, culturally uniform "condition," work against the tendency to produce ethnocentric analyses of sexuality. Although the temptation to take the white, male, middle-class homosexual as the prototype for the homosexual role still persists in some constructionist work, invention theories have the theoretical capabilities to explore the variations *among* and *within* sexual subcultures. Second, a constructionist view of homosexual identity opens the door to studies of the production of *all* sexual identities, including (and crucially) heterosexuality; for the constructionist, heterosexuality is not "natural" or "given," any more than non-hegemonic sexual classifications. Third, constructionism permits us to investigate "homosexuality," "heterosexuality," "bisexuality," and all other sexual roles precisely *as classifications*, as historically contingent categories and not transhistorical phenomena. Fourth, in addition to favoring more sophisticated analyses of how homosexual identities are socially produced, invention theories allow us to make important distinctions between male homosexuals and lesbians, two groups which are frequently conflated in the research on sexual minorities. . .but which, in fact, are not constructed in precisely the same ways. And finally, related to all of the above strengths, invention theories are marked by an impulse to historicize and to contextualize; such studies move us out of the realm of ontology (what the homosexual *is*) and into the realm of social and discursive formations (how the homosexual role is *produced*). . . .
>
> But the social constructionist position is not without its vulnerabilities. The most serious problem with most constructionist studies is a tendency to elide altogether the category of the psychic. . . .
>
> The problem with most emergence [invention] theory is that while it rightly insists that identities are constructions, it sees them as *social* constructions only. But to hold that there is no such thing as a natural or innate sexuality is not to abjure necessarily the category of the psychic. . . .In other words, it is to disregard the importance of the psychoanalytic insight which holds that homosexuality is not opposed to heterosexuality but lies within it—as its very precondition since all identity is based on exclusion.

Id. at 108–10.

2. *Boundaries/Dichotomies*. Adrienne Rich focuses on the construction of heterosexuality and its constraining effect on women. D'Emilio focuses on the construction of homosexuality and how it could produce a shift in the meaning of sexuality for everyone. How does Patricia Hill Collins help us to understand and reconcile Rich's and D'Emilio's viewpoints?

Carla Trujillo, Chicana Lesbians: Fear and Loathing in the Chicano Community, in *Chicana Lesbians: The Girls Our Mothers Warned Us About* 186 (Carla Trujillo ed., 1991)

The vast majority of Chicano heterosexuals perceive Chicana lesbians as a threat to the community. Homophobia, that is, irrational fear of gay or lesbian people and/or behaviors, accounts, in part, for the heterosexist response to the lesbian community. However, I argue that Chicana lesbians are perceived as a greater threat to the Chicano community because their existence disrupts the established order of male dominance, and raises the consciousness of many Chicana women regarding their own independence and control. Some writers have addressed these topics, however an analysis of the complexities of lesbian existence alongside this perceived threat has not been undertaken. While this essay is by no means complete, it attempts to elucidate the underlying basis of these fears which, in the very act of the lesbian existence, disrupt the established norm of patriarchal oppression.

Sexuality

As lesbians, our sexuality becomes the focal issue of dissent. The majority of Chicanas, both lesbian and heterosexual, are taught that our sexuality must conform to certain modes of behavior. Our culture voices shame upon us if we go beyond the criteria of passivity and repression, or doubts in our virtue if we refuse. We, as women, are taught to suppress our sexual desires and needs by conceding all pleasure to the male. As Chicanas, we are commonly led to believe that even talking about our participation and satisfaction in sex is taboo. Moreover, we (as well as most women in the United States) learn to hate our bodies, and usually possess little knowledge of them. Lourdes Arguelles did a survey on the sexuality of 373 immigrant Latina women and found that over half of the women possessed little knowledge of their reproductive systems or their own physiology. Most remarked they "just didn't look down there."

Not loving our bodies affects how we perceive ourselves as sexual beings. As lesbians, however, we have no choice but to confront our sexuality before we can confront our lesbianism. Thus the commonly held viewpoint among heterosexuals that we are "defined by our sexuality" is, in a way, partially true. If we did not bring our sexuality into consciousness, we would not be able to confront ourselves and come out.

After confronting and then acknowledging our attraction, we must, in turn, learn to reclaim that what we're told is bad, wrong, dirty, and taboo—namely our bodies, and our freedom to express ourselves in them. Too often we internalize the homophobia and sexism of the larger society, as well as that of our own culture, which attempts to keep us from loving ourselves. As Norma Alarcón states, "[Chicana lesbians] must act to negate the negation." A Chicana lesbian must learn to love herself, both as a woman and a sexual being, before she can love another. Loving another woman not only validates one's own sexuality, but also that of the other woman, by the very act of loving. Understanding this, a student in a workshop Cherríe Moraga and I conducted on lesbian sexuality stated, "Now I get it. Not only do you have to learn to love your own vagina, but someone else's too." It is only then that the subsequent experiences of love and commitment, passion and remorse can also become our dilemmas, much like those of everyone else. The effort to consciously reclaim our sexual selves forces Chicanas to either confront their own sexuality or, in refusing, castigate lesbians as *vendidas* to the race, blasphemers to the church, atrocities against nature, or some combination.

Identification

For many Chicanas, our identification as women, that is, as complete women, comes from the belief that we need to be connected to a man. Ridding ourselves of this parasitic identification is not always easy, for we grow up, as my Chicana students have pointed out, defined in a male context: daddy's girl, some guy's girlfriend, wife, or mother. Vying for a man's attention compromises our own personal and intellectual development. We exist in a patriarchal society that undervalues women. We are socialized to undervalue ourselves, as well as anything associated with the concept of self. Our voice is considered less significant, our needs and desires secondary. As the Chicanas in the MALCS workshop indicated, our toleration of unjust behavior from men, the church, the established order, is considered an attribute. How much pain can we bear in the here-and-now so that we may be better served in the afterlife? Martyrdom, the cloth of denial, transposes itself into a gown of cultural beauty.

Yet, an alliance with a man grants a woman heterosexual privileges, many of which are reified by the law, the church, our families and, of course, "la causa." Women who partake in the privileges of male sexual alliance may often do so at the cost of their own sense of self, since they must often subvert their needs, voice, intellect, and personal development in these alliances. These are the conditional contradictions commonly prescribed for women by the patriarchy in our culture and in the larger society. Historically, women have been viewed as property. Though some laws may have changed, ideologically little else has. Upon marriage, a father feels he can relinquish "ownership" and "responsibility" of his daughter to her husband. The Chicana feminist who confronts this subversion, and critiques the sexism of the Chicano community, will be called *vendida* if she finds the "male defined and often anti-feminist" values of the community difficult to accept.

The behaviors necessary in the "act of pursuing a man" often generate competition among women, leading to betrayal of one another. When a woman's sense of identity is tied to that of a man, she is dependent on this relationship for her own self-worth. Thus, she must compete with other women for his attention. When the attention is then acknowledged and returned, she must work to ensure that it is maintained. Ensuring the protection of this precious commodity generates suspicion among women, particularly single, unattached women. Since we're all taught to vie for a man's attention, we become, in a sense, sexual suspects to one another. The responsibility is placed entirely upon the woman with little thought given to the suspected infidelity of the man.

We should ask what role the man places himself in regarding his support of these behaviors. After all, the woman is commonly viewed as his possession. Hence, in the typical heterosexual relationship both parties are abetting the other, each in a quest that does not improve the status of the woman (nor, in my view, that of the man), nor the consciousness of either of them.

How does the Chicana lesbian fit into this picture? Realistically, she doesn't. As a lesbian she does many things simultaneously: she rejects "compulsory heterosexuality"; she refuses to partake in the "game" of competition for men; she confronts her own sexuality; and she challenges the norms placed upon her by culture and society, whose desire is to subvert her into proper roles and places. This is done, whether consciously or unconsciously, by the very aspect of her existence. In the course of conducting many workshops on lesbian sexuality, Chicana heterosexuals have often indicated to me that they do not associate with lesbians, since it could be assumed that either (1) they too, must be lesbians, or (2) if they're not, they must be selling out to Anglo culture, since it is implied that Chicana lesbians do and thus any association with lesbians implicates them as well. This equivocation of sexual practice and cultural alliance is a retrograde ideology, quite possibly originating from the point of view that the only way to uplift the species is to propagate it. Thus, homosexuality is seen as "counter-revolutionary."

Heterosexual Chicanas need not be passive victims of the cultural onslaught of social control. If anything, Chicanas are usually the backbone of every familia, for it their strength and self-sacrifice which often keeps the family going. While heterosexual Chicanas have a choice about how they want to live their lives (read: how they choose to form their identities), Chicana lesbians have very little choice, because their quest for self-identification comes with the territory. This is why "coming out" can be a major source of pain for Chicana lesbians, since the basic fear of rejection by family and community is paramount.[11] For our own survival, Chicana lesbians must continually embark on the creation or modification of our own familia, since this institution, as traditionally constructed, may be non-supportive of the Chicana lesbian existence.[12]

Motherhood

The point of view that we are not complete human beings unless we are attached to a male is further promoted by the attitude that we are incomplete as women unless we become mothers. Many Chicanas are socialized to believe that our chief purpose in life is raising children. Not denying the fact that motherhood can be a beautiful experience, it becomes rather, one of the few experiences not only supported, but expected in a traditional Chicano community. Historically, in dual-headed households, Chicanas (as well as other women) were relegated to the tasks of home care and child rearing, while the men took on the task of earning the family's income. Economic need, rather than feminist consciousness, has been the primary reason for the change to two-income households. Nevertheless, for many Chicanas, motherhood is still seen by our culture as the final act in establishing our "womanhood."

Motherhood among Chicana lesbians does exist. Many lesbians are mothers as by-products of divorce, earlier liaisons with men, or through artificial insemination. Anecdotal evidence I have obtained from many Chicana lesbians in the community indicates that lesbians who choose to become mothers in our culture are seen as aberrations of the traditional concept of motherhood, which stresses male-female partnership. Choosing to become a mother via alter-

---

11. Rejection by family and community is also an issue for gay men, however, their situation is muddied by the concomitant loss of power.

12. Cherríe Moraga attests to the necessity of Chicanas needing to "make familia from scratch" in *Giving Up the Ghost* 58 (1986).

native methods of insemination, or even adopting children, radically departs from society's view that lesbians and gay men cannot "successfully" raise children. Therefore, this poses another threat to the Chicano community, since Chicana lesbians are perceived as failing to partake in one of their chief obligations in life.

Religion

Religion, based on the tradition of patriarchal control and sexual, emotional, and psychological repression, has historically been a dual means of hope for a better afterlife and social control in the present one. Personified by the Virgen de Guadalupe, the concept of motherhood and martyrdom go hand in hand in the Catholic religion. Nevertheless, as we are all aware, religion powerfully affects our belief systems concerning life and living. Since the Pope does not advocate a homosexual lifestyle, lesbians and gay men are not given sanction by the largely Catholic Chicano community—hence, fulfilling our final threat to the established order. Chicana lesbians who confront their homosexuality must, in turn, confront (for those raised in religious households) religion, bringing to resolution some compromise of religious doctrine and personal lifestyle. Many choose to alter, modify, or abandon religion, since it is difficult to advocate something which condemns our existence. This exacerbates a sense of alienation for Chicana lesbians who feel they cannot wholly participate in a traditional religion.

In sum, Chicana lesbians pose a threat to the Chicano community for a variety of reasons, primarily because they threaten the established social hierarchy of patriarchal control. In order to "come-out," Chicana lesbians must confront their sexuality, therefore bringing a taboo subject to consciousness. By necessity, they must learn to love their bodies, for it is also another woman's body which becomes the object of love. Their identities as people alter and become independent of men, hence there is no need to submit to, or perform the necessary behaviors that cater to wooing the male ego. Lesbians (and other feminist women) would expect to treat and be treated by men as equals. Men who have traditionally interacted with women on the basis of their gender (read femininity) first, and their brains second, are commonly left confused when the lesbian (or feminist) fails to respond to the established pecking order.

Motherhood, seen as exemplifying the final act of our existence as women, is practiced by lesbians, but usually without societal or cultural permission. Not only is it believed that lesbians cannot become mothers (hence, not fulfilling our established purpose as women), but if we do, we morally threaten the concept of motherhood as a sanctified entity, since lesbianism doesn't fit into its religious or cultural confines. Lastly, religion, which does not support the homosexual lifestyle, seeks to repudiate us as sinners if we are "practicing," and only tolerable if not. For her personal and psychological survival, the Chicana lesbian must confront and bring to resolution these established cultural and societal conflicts. These "confrontations" go against many of the values of the Chicano community, since they pose a threat to the established order of male control. Our very existence challenges this order, and in some cases challenges the oftentimes ideologically oppressive attitudes toward women.

It is widely assumed that lesbians and heterosexual women are in two completely different enclaves in regard to the type and manner of the oppression they must contend with. As illustrated earlier in this essay, this indeed, may be true. There do exist, however, different levels of patriarchal oppression which affect all of us as women, and when combined inhibit our collective liberation. If we, as lesbian and heterosexual Chicana women, can open our eyes and look at all that we share as women, we might find commonalities even among our differences. First and foremost among them is the status of *woman*. Uttered under any breath, it implies subservience; cast to a lower position not only in society, but in our own culture as well.

Secondly, the universal of the body. We are all female and subject to the same violations as any woman in society. We must contend with the daily threat of rape, molestation, and harassment—violations which affect all of us as women, lesbian or not.

As indicated earlier, our sexuality is suppressed by our culture—relegated to secrecy or embarrassment, implicating us as wrongful women if we profess to fulfill ourselves sexually. Most of us still grow up inculcated with the dichotomy of the "good girl-bad girl" syndrome. With virtue considered as the most admirable quality, it's easy to understand which we choose to partake. This generates a cloud of secrecy around any sexual activity, and leads, I am convinced, to our extremely high teenage pregnancy rate, simply because our families refuse to acknowledge the possibility that young women may be sexually active before marriage.

We are taught to undervalue our needs and voices. Our opinions, viewpoints, and expertise are considered secondary to those of males—even if we are more highly trained. Time and again, I have seen otherwise sensible men insult the character of a woman when they are unable to belittle her intellectual capacities.[13] Character assassinations are commonly disguised in the familiar "*vendida* to the race" format. Common it seems, because it functions as the ultimate insult to any conscientious *política*. Because many of us are taught that our opinions matter little, we have difficulty at times, raising them. We don't trust what we think, or believe in our merits. Unless we are encouraged to do so, we have difficulty thinking independently of male opinion. Chicanas must be constantly encouraged to speak up, to voice their opinions, particularly in areas where no encouragement has ever been provided.

As Chicanas (and Chicanos), most of us are subject to the effects of growing up in a culture besieged by poverty and all the consequences of it: lack of education, insufficient political power and health care, disease and drugs. We are all subject to the effects of a society that is racist, classist and homophobic, as well as sexist, and patriarchally dominant. Colonization has imposed itself and affected the disbursement of status and the collective rights of us as individuals. Chicana women are placed in this order at a lower position, ensconsed [sic] within a tight boundary which limits our voices, our bodies, and our brains. In classic dissonant fashion, many of us become complicit in this

---

13. This occurred often to the women MeChA (Movimiento Estudiantil Chicano de Aztlán) leaders who were on the Berkeley campus between 1985-1989. It also occurred to a Chicana panel member during a 1990 National Association for Chicano Studies presentation, when a Chicano discussant disagreed with the recommendations based on her research.

(since our survival often depends on it) and end up rationalizing our very own limitations.

The collective liberation of people begins with the collective liberation of half its constituency—namely women. The view that our hierarchical society places Chicanos at a lower point, and they in turn must place Chicanas lower still, is outmoded and politically destructive. Women can no longer be relegated to supporting roles. Assuaging delicate male egos as a means of establishing our identities is retrograde and subversive to our own identities as women. Chicanas, both lesbian and heterosexual, have a dual purpose ahead of us. We must fight for our own voices as women, since this will ultimately serve to uplift us as a people.

Question

Privileged Position. Based on the excerpts you read by Adrienne Rich, Yvon Appleby, John D'Emilio, and Carla Trujillo, how do you think each of these writers would describe herself or himself if asked to participate in Patricia Cain's classroom exercise (Note 1, at p. 63)?

Chapter 3

The Complaint: Legal Discourse

Chapter 2 identified the interlocking systems of oppression and how they produce violence against women. The readings in this chapter apply a critical analysis to the law to expose how it participates in and reflects those systems of oppression. The analytical tools presented in these readings are necessary to evaluate the statutes and court opinions included in this book to represent the law's response to violence against women.

The first reading is an excerpt of an article by Cheryl Harris. She examines the law by using an historical and economic framework and shows how race is deeply embedded in the legal concepts of property and rights. Her analysis saliently establishes the gendered and racial nature of traditional legal discourse. By showing how seemingly neutral and objective legal principles protect and preserve the privileges of whiteness, Harris reveals the substantial role the law has played and continues to play in maintaining white supremacy.

Harris further reveals the contradiction the law represents for those oppressed by the dominant society. Implicitly her analysis raises the question that recurs throughout the book: How can the law, which has been an agent of domination, be used as an agent of social change? This is a central tension in an analysis of the law and violence against women: expecting the legal system to protect women from violence while exposing how the law traditionally has sustained and reinforced that violence. We cannot avoid the contradiction, but we can be more attentive to how legal reforms can be distorted to support the violence rather than to ameliorate or eliminate it.

The dualistic approach is further explored by John Calmore, who explains the approach and purposes of critical race theory. Calmore resists the narrow confines of legal doctrines and challenges what the law counts as an appropriate action or claim. His critique shows how the law's failure to use race as a central principle of analysis leads to its creating and recreating racially subordinating rules.

The next two pieces continue the critique of traditional legal discourse through a feminist lens. Lucinda Finley analyzes how legal language excludes women. The panel conversation on feminist discourse involving Mary Dunlap, Carol Gilligan, and Catharine MacKinnon exhibits differing feminist theories and approaches to the law. Together the two excerpts show how the law's failure to use gender as a central principle of analysis leads to its creating and recreating gender subordinating rules. Along with Calmore's and Harris' articles, these two pieces destabilize the concept of neutral law and expose to whose benefit the claim of neutrality operates.

To help readers appreciate the implications of the critiques, the chapter ends with two U.S. Supreme Court cases: *Loving v. Virginia* and *Bowers v. Hardwick*. Both cases present issues involving gender, race, and sexual orientation. The Court's opinions provide the opportunity to analyze traditional legal discourse and consider its limitations and to reflect on how critical race and feminist theories might change the Court's approach to the issues.

Cheryl I. Harris, Whiteness as Property 106 Harv. L. Rev. 1707, 1710–11, 1713–14, 1721–25, 1737–41, 1745, 1757–59, 1760–61, 1766, 1768, 1778–80, 1784-85 (1993)

In the 1930s, some years after my mother's family became part of the great river of Black migration that flowed north, my Mississippi-born grandmother was confronted with the harsh matter of economic survival for herself and her two daughters. Having separated from my grandfather, who himself was trapped on the fringes of economic marginality, she took one long hard look at her choices and presented herself for employment at a major retail store in Chicago's central business district. This decision would have been unremarkable for a white woman in similar circumstances, but for my grandmother, it was an act of both great daring and self-denial, for in so doing she was presenting herself as a white woman. In the parlance of racist America, she was "passing."...

[I]n the burgeoning landscape of urban America, anonymity was possible for a Black person with "white" features. She was transgressing boundaries, crossing borders, spinning on margins, traveling between dualities of Manichean space, rigidly bifurcated into light/dark, good/bad, white/Black. No longer immediately identifiable as "Lula's daughter," she could thus enter the white world, albeit on a false passport, not merely passing, but *tres*passing. . . .

The persistence of passing is related to the historical and continuing pattern of white racial domination and economic exploitation that has given passing a certain economic logic. It was a given to my grandmother that being white automatically ensured higher economic returns in the short term, as well as greater economic, political, and social security in the long run. Becoming white meant gaining access to a whole set of public and private privileges that materially and permanently guaranteed basic subsistence needs and, therefore, survival. Becoming white increased the possibility of controlling critical aspects of one's life rather than being the object of others' domination.

My grandmother's story illustrates the valorization of whiteness as treasured property in a society structured on racial caste. In ways so embedded that it is rarely apparent, the set of assumptions, privileges, and benefits that accompany the status of being white have become a valuable asset that whites sought to protect and that those who passed sought to attain—by fraud if necessary. Whites have come to expect and rely on these benefits, and over time these expectations have been affirmed, legitimated, and protected by the law. Even though the law is neither uniform nor explicit in all instances, in protecting settled expectations based on white privilege, American law has recognized a property interest in whiteness that, although unacknowledged, now forms the background against which legal disputes are framed, argued, and adjudicated. . . .

Slavery linked the privilege of whites to the subordination of Blacks through a legal regime that attempted the conversion of Blacks into objects of property. Similarly, the settlement and seizure of Native American land supported white privilege through a system of property rights in land in which the "race" of the Native Americans rendered their first possession rights invisible and justified conquest. This racist formulation embedded the fact of white privilege into the very definition of property, marking another stage in the evolution of the property interest in whiteness. Possession—the act necessary to lay the basis for rights in property—was defined to include only the cultural practices of whites. This definition laid the foundation for the idea that whiteness—that which whites alone possess—is valuable and is property.

Although the Indians were the first occupants and possessors of the land of the New World, their racial and cultural otherness allowed this fact to be reinterpreted and ultimately erased as a basis for asserting rights in land. Because the land had been left in its natural state, untilled and unmarked by human hands, it was "waste" and, therefore, the appropriate object of settlement and appropriation. Thus, the possession maintained by the Indians was not "true" possession and could safely be ignored. This interpretation of the rule of first possession effectively rendered the rights of first possessors contingent on the race of the possessor. . . .

The conquest and occupation of Indian land was wrapped in the rule of law. The law provided not only a defense of conquest and colonization, but also a naturalized regime of rights and disabilities, power and disadvantage that flowed from it, so that no further justifications or rationalizations were required. A key decision defending the right of conquest was *Johnson and Graham's Lessee v. M'Intosh*,[1] in which both parties to the action claimed the same land through title descendant from different Indian tribes. The issue specifically presented was not merely whether Indians had the power to convey title, but to whom the conveyance could be made—to individuals or to the government that "discovered" land. In holding that Indians could only convey to the latter, the Court reasoned that Indian title was subordinate to the absolute title of the sovereign that was achieved by conquest because "[c]onquest gives a title which the Courts of the conqueror cannot deny. . . ." If property is understood as a delegation of sovereign power—the product of the power of the state—then a fair reading of history reveals the racial oppression of Indians inherent in the American regime of property.

In *Johnson* and similar cases, courts established whiteness as a prerequisite to the exercise of enforceable property rights. Not all first possession or labor gave rise to property rights; rather, the rules of first possession and labor as a basis for property rights were qualified by race. This fact infused whiteness with significance and value because it was solely through being white that property could be acquired and secured under law. Only whites possessed whiteness, a highly valued and exclusive form of property. . . .

The legal legacy of slavery and of the seizure of land from Native American peoples is not merely a regime of property law that is (mis)informed by racist and ethnocentric themes. Rather, the law has established and protected an actual property interest in whiteness itself, which shares the critical characteristics

1. 21 U.S. (8 Wheat.) 543 (1823).

of property and accords with the many and varied theoretical descriptions of property.

Although by popular usage property describes "things" owned by persons, or the rights of persons with respect to a thing, the concept of property prevalent among most theorists, even prior to the twentieth century, is that property may "consist[] of rights in 'things' that are intangible, or whose existence is a matter of legal definition." Property is thus said to be a right, not a thing, characterized as metaphysical, not physical. . .Thus, the fact that whiteness is not a "physical" entity does not remove it from the realm of property. . . .

The law assumed the crucial task of racial classification, and accepted and embraced the then-current theories of race as biological fact. This core precept of race as a physically defined reality allowed the law to fulfill an essential function—to "parcel out social standing according to race" and to facilitate systematic discrimination by articulating "seemingly precise definitions of racial group membership." This allocation of race and rights continued a century after the abolition of slavery.

The law relied on bounded, objective, and scientific definitions of race. . .to construct whiteness as not merely race, but race plus privilege. By making race determinant and the product of rationality and science, dominant and subordinate positions within the racial hierarchy were disguised as the product of natural law and biology rather than as naked preferences. Whiteness as racialized privilege was then legitimated by science and was embraced in legal doctrine as "objective fact.". . .

In adjudicating who was "white," courts sometimes noted that, by physical characteristics, the individual whose racial identity was at issue appeared to be white and, in fact, had been regarded as white in the community. Yet if an individual's blood was tainted, she could not claim to be "white" as the law understood, regardless of the fact that phenotypically she may have been completely indistinguishable from a white person, may have lived as a white person, and have descended from a family that lived as whites. Although socially accepted as white, she could not *legally* be white. Blood as "objective fact" dominated over appearance and social acceptance, which were socially fluid and subjective measures.

But, in fact, "blood" was no more objective than that which the law dismissed as subjective and unreliable. The acceptance of the fiction that the racial ancestry could be determined with the degree of precision called for by the relevant standards or definitions rested on false assumptions that racial categories of prior ancestors had been accurately reported, that those reporting in the past shared the definitions currently in use, and that racial purity actually existed in the United States. Ignoring these considerations, the law established rules that extended equal treatment to those of the "same blood," albeit of different complexions, because it was acknowledged that, "[t]here are white men as dark as mulattoes, and there are pure-blooded albino Africans as white as the whitest Saxons."

The standards were designed to accomplish what mere observation could not: "That even Blacks who did not look Black were kept in their place." Although the line of demarcation between Black and white varied from rules that classified as Black a person containing "any drop of Black blood," to more liberal rules that defined persons with a preponderance of white blood to be white, the courts universally accepted the notion that white status was something of value that could be accorded only to those persons whose proofs established their whiteness as defined by the law. . . .In effect, the courts erected legal "No Trespassing" signs.

In the realm of *social* relations, racial recognition in the United States is thus an act of race subordination. In the realm of *legal* relations, judicial definition of racial identity based on white supremacy reproduced that race subordination at the institutional level. In transforming white to whiteness, the law masked the ideological content of racial definition and the exercise of power required to maintain it: "It convert[ed] [an] abstract concept into [an] entity.". . .

The inherent contradiction between the bondage of Blacks and republican rhetoric that championed the freedom of all men was resolved by positing that Blacks were different. The laws did not mandate that Blacks be accorded equality under the law because nature—not man, not power, not violence—had determined their degraded status. Rights were for those who had the capacity to exercise them, a capacity denoted by racial identity. This conception of rights was contingent on race—on whether one could claim whiteness—a form of property. This articulation of rights that were contingent on property ownership was a familiar paradigm, as similar requirements had been imposed on the franchise in the early part of the republic. For the first two hundred years of the country's existence, the system of racialized privilege in both the public and private spheres carried through this linkage of rights and inequality, and rights and property. Whiteness as property was the critical core of a system that affirmed the hierarchical relations between white and Black. . . .

In the modern period, neither the problems attendant to assigning racial identities nor those accompanying the recognition of whiteness have disappeared. Nor has whiteness as property. Whiteness as property continues to perpetuate racial subordination through the courts' definitions of group identity and through the courts' discourse and doctrine on affirmative action. The exclusion of subordinated "others" was and remains a central part of the property interest in whiteness and, indeed, is part of the protection that the court extends to whites' settled expectations of continued privilege. . . .

Even as the capacity of whiteness to deliver is arguably diminished by the elimination of rigid racial stratifications, whiteness continues to be perceived as materially significant. Because real power and wealth never have been accessible to more than a narrowly defined ruling elite, for many whites the benefits of whiteness as property, in the absence of legislated privilege, may have been reduced to a claim of relative privilege only in comparison to people of color. Nevertheless, whiteness retains its value as a "consolation prize": it does not mean that all whites will win, but simply that they will not lose, if losing is defined as being on the bottom of the social and economic hierarchy—the position to which Blacks have been consigned. . . .

Although dominant societal norms have embraced the idea of fairness and nondiscrimination, removal of privilege and antisubordination principles are actively rejected or at best ambiguously received because expectations of white privilege are bound up with what is considered essential for self-realization. Among whites, the idea persists that their whiteness is meaningful. Whiteness is an aspect of racial identity surely, but it is much more; it remains a concept based on relations of power, a social construct predicated on white dominance and Black subordination. . . .

The assumption that whiteness is a property interest entitled to protection is an idea born of systematic white supremacy and nurtured over the years, not only by the law of slavery and "Jim Crow," but also by the more recent decisions and rationales of the Supreme Court concerning affirmative action. . . .

Current legal definitions interpret race as a factor disconnected from social identity and compel abandonment of race-consciousness. Thus, at the very historical moment that race is infused with a perspective that reshapes it, through race-conscious remediation, into a potential weapon *against* subordination, official rules articulated in law deny that race matters. Simultaneously, the law upholds race as immutable and biological. The assertion that race is color and color does not matter is, of course, essential to the norm of colorblindness. To define race reductively as simply color, and therefore meaningless, however, is as subordinating as defining race to be scientifically determinative of inherent deficiency. The old definition creates a false linkage between race and inferiority; the new definition denies the real linkage between race and oppression under systematic white supremacy. Distorting and denying reality, both definitions support race subordination. . . .

The property interest in whiteness has proven to be resilient and adaptive to new conditions. Over time it has changed in form, but it has retained its essential exclusionary character and continued to distort outcomes of legal disputes by favoring and protecting settled expectations of white privilege. The law expresses the dominant conception of "rights," "equality," "property," "neutrality," and "power": rights mean shields from interference; equality means formal equality; property means the settled expectations that are to be protected; neutrality means the existing distribution, which is natural; and, power is the mechanism for guarding all of this.

One reason then for the court's hostility toward affirmative action is that it seeks to de-legitimate the assumptions surrounding existing inequality. It exposes the illusion that the original or current distribution of power, property, and resources is the result of "right" and "merit." It places in tension the settled expectations of whites, based on both the ideology of white supremacy and the structure of the U.S. economy, that have operated to subordinate and hyper-exploit groups identified as the "other." It opens to critique the idea that individualized and discrete claims to remedy identified discrimination will achieve the promise of equality contained in the Fourteenth Amendment. It conceives of equality in transgenerational terms, and demands a new and different sense of social responsibility in a society that defines individualism as the highest good, and the "market value" of the individual as the just and true assessment. It unmasks the limited character of rights granted by those who dominate. In a word, it is destabilizing. . . .

Rereading affirmative action to de-legitimate the property interest in whiteness suggests that if, historically, the law has legitimated and protected the settled expectations of whites in white privilege, de-legitimation should be accomplished not merely by implementing equal treatment, but by *equalizing* treatment among the groups that have been illegitimately privileged or unfairly subordinated by racial stratification. Obviously, the meaning of equalizing treatment would vary, because the extent of privilege and subordination is not constant with reference to all societal goods. In some instances, the advantage of race privilege to poorer whites may be materially insignificant when compared to their class disadvantage against more privileged whites. But exposing the critical core of whiteness as property as the unconstrained right to exclude directs attention toward questions of redistribution and property that are crucial under both race and class analysis. . . .

If whiteness as property is the reification, in law, of expectations of white privilege, then according privilege to Blacks through systems of affirmative action might be challenged as performing the same ideological function, only on the other side of the racial line. . . .Equating affirmative action with whiteness as property, however, is false and can only be maintained if history is ignored or inverted and the premises inherent in the existing racial hierarchy are retained. . . .

Fundamentally, affirmative action does not reestablish a property interest in Blackness because Black identity is not the functional opposite of whiteness. . . .Acknowledging Black identity does not involve the systematic subordination of whites, nor does it even set up a danger of doing so. Affirmative action is based on principles of antisubordination, not principles of Black superiority.

Question

The Law as an Instrument of Oppression. How does Cheryl Harris' analysis of the law assist in understanding how the systems of oppression discussed in Chapter 2 are established and maintained?

John O. Calmore, Critical Race Theory, Archie Shepp, and Fire Music: Securing an Authentic Intellectual Life in a Multicultural World, 65 S. Cal. L. Rev. 2129, 2160–72, 2178, 2180–82, 2210–16 (1992)

Critical Race Theory Themes, Perspectives, and Directions

An Overview of Critical Race Theory

Critical race theory begins with a recognition that "race" is not a fixed term. Instead, "race" is a fluctuating, decentered complex of social meanings that are formed and transformed under the constant pressures of political struggle. The challenge thus presented is to examine how individual and group identities, under broadly disparate circumstances, as well as the racial institutions and social practices that are linked to those identities, are formed and transformed historically by actors who politically contest the social meanings of race.[2]

---

2. Michael Omi & Howard Winant, Racial Formation in the United States: From the 1960s to the 1980s, at 68–69 (1986). Omi and Winant emphasize "race formation" and "racialization" to elaborate on this political struggle. The former refers to the process whereby social, political, and economic forces shape the content and salience of racial categories,

As a form of oppositional scholarship, critical race theory challenges the universality of white experience/judgment as the authoritative standard that binds people of color and normatively measures, directs, controls, and regulates the terms of proper thought, expression, presentment, and behavior. As represented by legal scholars, critical race theory challenges the dominant discourses on race and racism as they relate to law. The task is to identify values and norms that have been disguised and subordinated in the law. As critical race scholars, we thus seek to demonstrate that our experiences as people of color are legitimate, appropriate, and effective bases for analyzing the legal system and racial subordination. This process is vital to our transformative vision. This theory-practice approach, a praxis, if you will, finds a variety of emphases among those who follow it, and the concepts are now rather open and still being explored.[3]

From this vantage, consider for a moment how law, society, and culture are texts—not so much like a literary work, but rather like the traditional black minister's citation of text as a verse or scripture that would lend authoritative support to the sermon he is about to deliver. Here, texts are not merely random stories; like scripture, they are expressions of authority, preemption, and sanction. People of color increasingly claim that these large texts of law, society, and culture must be subjected to fundamental criticism and reinterpretation. . . .

On one hand, we challenge the forms of domination that structure not only culture's production but also its reception. On the other hand, we try to identify and clarify progressive social changes whose needs arise from the symbolic world of culture and whose realization lies in political self-organization and action. Moreover, to advance such a project, we discover the required interpretive procedures. . .at the point where cultural heritages and social critique converge.

In sum, as critical race theorists confront the texts of America's dominant legal, social, and cultural strata, we are critical, fundamentally so, because we engage these texts in a manner that counters their oppressive and subordinating

---

which, in turn, determine racial meanings: "Crucial to this formulation is the treatment of race as a *central axis* of social relations which cannot be subsumed under or reduced to some broader category or conception." *Id.* at 61-62. "Racialization" signifies the spread of racial meanings to a relationship, social practice, or group that was previously unclassified in racial terms. *Id.* at 64. Much of today's racialization is coded and covert. Ironically, we have now a policy of what I call "racialized color blindness," which never explicitly refers to race in talking about cultures of poverty, welfare cheats, inner-city poor or underclass poor, etc. In such instances, the unstated reference is to blacks.

3. My discussion of critical race theory presents my understanding, incorporation, and emphasis. Richard Delgado refers to critical race scholars in these terms:

> Whatever label is applied to this loose coalition, its scholarship is characterized by the following themes: (1) an insistence on "naming our own reality"; (2) the belief that knowledge and ideas are powerful; (3) a readiness to question basic premises of moderate/incremental civil rights law; (4) the borrowing of insights from social science on race and racism; (5) critical examination of the myths and stories powerful groups use to justify racial subordination; (6) a more contextualized treatment of doctrine; (7) criticism of liberal legalisms; and (8) an interest in structural determinism—the ways in which legal tools and thought-structures can impede law reform.

Richard Delgado, When a Story is Just a Story: Does Voice Really Matter?, 76 Va. L. Rev. 95, 95 n.4 (1990). . . .

features. In this endeavor we are not simply in opposition; we are not rebels without a cause. We are the "new interpreters," who demand of the dominant institutions a new validity . . . .

[C]ritical race theory presents not only a different methodology and grounding, but also a message different from traditional race scholarship, now euphemistically known as "civil rights" or "antidiscrimination" scholarship. Critical race theory recombines and extends existing means of legal redress. Hence, critical race theory is necessarily eclectic, incorporating what appears to be helpful from various disciplines, doctrines, styles, and methods. The theory attempts to extend the narrow world of traditional legal scholarship without indulging in dysfunctional deviance, instead establishing intellectual credibility on one hand and reconciling the elements of effective theory and practice on the other. Explanation arises from the particular and the personal. In contrast to traditional scholarship, the focus is much more extralegal and contextual, less restricted by doctrinal analysis as a controlling center. It is concerned with redressing conditions of oppression and subordination that exist beyond their narrow translation into judicially recognizable claims and relief. Historical discrimination and its legacy merge more definitively and symbiotically with the present to provide the temporal context.[4] While not abandoning a faith in rights strategy, critical race theory recognizes that such a strategy cannot be divorced from the larger economics and politics of things. It recognizes that whatever the specific issues of legal cases and controversies are, the overriding issues of social justice and institutional legitimacy always lurk nearby.

Critical race theory recognizes the inadequacy of disaggregating individual plaintiffs and causes of action from the larger context of social conflict that lies at the heart of a racist regime. Hence, formal, individualized equality of opportunity and objective norms of meritocracy can hardly serve as viable opposition to group inequality and subjective bias. Moreover, societal fault and accountability cannot be reduced to actionable claims only when evidenced by individual responsibility for intentional wrong. Finally, many adherents of critical race theory see an interlocking set of oppressions that extend beyond the singular base of race and include the bases of gender, economic class, and sexual orientation.

Critical race theory attempts to construct a social reality and direct operation within it. It is a way of finding meaning within legal scholarship through combining language, thought, and experience. Voice is important: how voice

---

4. . . .In discussing the U.S. Supreme Court decision City of Richmond v. J.A. Croson Co., 488 U.S. 469 (1989) (holding unconstitutional the city's minority-business set-aside program), Michael Rosenfeld criticizes it as follows:

> *Croson* achieves its superficial order through a process of decontextualization. As we shall see, such decontextualization takes many forms, including lifting race relations out of their historical setting; treating process as though it were unrelated to any content; "disaggregating" evidence so as to produce the impression that tightly linked and mutually reinforcing facts actually stand apart; and dealing with key conceptual constructs as though they were self-sustaining when actually they are dependent on particular theoretical assumptions and on the existence of certain specified sets of facts.

Michael Rosenfeld, Decoding Richmond: Affirmative Action and the Elusive Meaning of Constitutional Equality, 87 Mich. L. Rev. 1729, 1732 (1989) (citations omitted). . . .

is expressed, how voice is informed, how our voice differs from the dominant voice. Hence, critical race theory's linguistics is experiential and pragmatic, focusing on "the nature of language as a social instrument, an instrument through which human beings create or constitute or stipulate a (social) world they may share, and then. . .'get things done with words' in that world."[5] Our voice, as heard in legal scholarship, recounts our perception, experience, and understanding of law in ways that are primarily colored, if you will, by our own unique biography and history. As people of color, we recognize the centrality of race in a social order that is maintained and perpetuated in significant ways by the rule of law. As scholars, our writing acknowledges this centrality that contextualizes our work.

Authenticity and the Existential Grounding of Critical Race Theory

The power to define ourselves and our world is radical per se. But critical race theory also helps to erect and maintain a sense of authenticity, without which our work will probably fail to connect significantly with our community's agenda of social action. Authenticity implies trustworthiness and good faith in presentment. I associate it quite closely with integrity. According to Robert Terry, by guiding our actions, authenticity characterizes a force in our lives that allows us not only to make sense of our world, but also to act purposefully within it. In this way, authenticity connotes being true to both oneself and one's world. Terry explains further:

---

5. Jerome Brunner, Pragmatics of Language and Language of Pragmatics, 51 Soc. Res. 969 (1984) (quoting John Austin, How to do Things with Words (1962)). . . .Patricia Williams characterizes "critical interpretation" as "that part of interpretive discourse that explores the limits of meaning, that gives meaning by knowing its bounds." Patricia J. Williams, The Obliging Shell: An Informal Essay on Formal Equal Opportunity, 87 Mich. L. Rev. 2128, 2132 (1989). Thus, Angela Harris asserts, "[I]n order to energize legal theory, we need to subvert it with narratives and stories, accounts of the particular, the different, and the hitherto silenced." Angela Harris, Race and Essentialism in Feminist Legal Theory, 42 Stan. L. Rev. 581, 615 (1990). Richard Delgado eloquently examines how using stories and counterstories can affect the struggle for racial justice. He explains how outgroups, "whose marginality defines the boundaries of the mainstream, whose voice and perspective—whose consciousness—has been suppressed, devalued, and abnormalized," use stories to subvert the reality of dominant, ingroup reality. Richard Delgado, Storytelling for Oppositionists and Others: A Plea for Narrative, 87 Mich. L. Rev. 2411, 2412 (1989). The outsider/marginalized counterstory is aimed at destroying the prevailing mind-set that enables the dominant group to justify the status quo arrangements of whites on top and people of color at the bottom. *Id.* at 2413. Delgado contends:

> Stories, parables, chronicles, and narratives are powerful means for destroying mindset—the bundle of presuppositions, received wisdoms, and shared understandings against a background of which legal and political discourse takes place. These matters are rarely focused on. They are like eyeglasses we have worn a long time. They are nearly invisible; we use them to scan and interpret the world and only rarely examine them for themselves. Ideology—the received wisdom—makes current social arrangements seem fair and natural. Those in power sleep well at night—their conduct does not seem to them like oppression.

Id. at 2413–14. For Delgado stories and counterstories can "stir imagination in ways in which more conventional discourse cannot," in hope of quickening and engaging conscience. *Id.* at 2415.

> Inauthenticity destroys our groundedness. It substitutes a false foundation for a solid one, and guarantees a false understanding of the world. Thus if I am untrue to myself, I say one thing and do another. Not only do I cease to be trusted by others, but eventually, if not immediately, I cease to know myself as well. I become unrooted, subject to external pressures, and unsure of my direction and my ability to act on my deepest insights about life and myself. . . .
>
> If I am untrue to the world, I lose my grasp on what is happening around and to me and thus make judgments that lead to behaviors that are inappropriate to situations in which I find myself. I distort what is happening to me and, because of this false diagnosis of my situation, continually make erroneous judgments.

Terry is analyzing racism as a source of inauthenticity in white people, their organizations, and their institutions. He distinguishes the inauthenticity of whites from the alienation of people of color. But racism, particularly in integrated settings (however minimal or token), tends to move people of color from the alienated to the inauthentic. Etzioni's distinction is helpful here. He observes that an inauthentic relation, institution, or society presents the appearance of responsiveness against the backdrop of an underlying alienating condition. While both inauthentic and alienating conditions exclude, inauthentic structures more than alienating ones operate to conceal their contours and to generate a feigned flexibility, or mere appearance of responsiveness. Etzioni aptly describes the inauthenticity that so many professors of color must feel:

> Subjectively, to be alienated is to experience a sense of not belonging and to feel that one's efforts are without meaning. To be involved inauthentically is to feel cheated and manipulated. The alienated feel that they have no power; the inauthentic feel that they have pulled a disconnected lever, without quite knowing where and how, so that shadows are confused with reality. The alienated are imprisoned; the inauthentic work at Sisyphean labor.
>
> Authenticity exists where responsiveness exists and is experienced as such. The world responds to the actor's efforts, and its dynamics are comprehensible. . . .[A]uthenticity requires not only that the actor be conscious, committed, and hold a share of the societal power, but also that the three components of the active orientation be balanced and connected. It is the fate of the inauthentic man that what he knows does not fit what he feels, and what he affects is not what he knows or is committed to do. His world has come apart.

Hence, a major theme of critical race theory reflects the colored intellectual's persistent battle to avoid being rendered inauthentic by the pressures of adapting to the white world and to take instead an oppositional stance by relying on one's true existential life, which is rooted in a world of color even though not stuck there. As Leslie Espinoza points out: "Critical Race Scholarship is one vehicle through which minorities in law understand and reconcile the world as predicted, the world as experienced, and the world as dreamed." Relatedly, critical race theory calls upon one to adopt a "multiple consciousness," as Mari Matsuda terms it. The consciousness that she describes is not the random, ambidextrous perspective that enables us to incorporate all points of view, but rather the consciousness that involves deliberate attempts to view the world through the eyes of the oppressed. Such a view forces us to focus on the concrete particulars of their lives. . . .[I]t counters the abstraction and detachment that remove us from the discomfort of direct confrontation with the offensive and shocking reality—in a word, the ugliness—of oppression.

In Matsuda's view, abstraction allows theorists to discuss the liberal aspirations of liberty, property, and rights by first severing them from what those concepts mean in real people's lives. Mainstream intellectual training values abstraction at the expense of detail. However, if scholars of color hold onto a multiple consciousness, we will be able to operate "within the abstractions of standard jurisprudential discourse," but without abandoning or discounting the "details of our own special knowledge." Although scholars reflecting critical race theory are for the most part on faculties at mainstream white law schools, there is a certain "pedagogy of the oppressed" at work here. . . .

As a reflection of authenticity, critical race scholarship also rejects the traditional dictates that implore one to write and study as a detached observer whose work is purportedly objective, neutral, and balanced. In the classic sense of "professing," critical race scholars advocate and defend positions. Fran Olsen points out that traditional scholarship's appearance of balance presupposes a status quo baseline that hinders both understanding and social change. Critical race theory tends, in response, toward very personal expression that allows our experiences and lessons, learned *as people of color*, to convey the knowledge that we possess in a way that is empowering to us and, it is hoped, ultimately empowering to those on whose behalf we act. Those of us who profess critical race theory are, in simplest terms, trying to be true to ourselves. And in so doing, we quest more for social transformation and self-respect than for social acceptance, scholarly citation, or, in some cases, even tenure. Critical race theory, at bottom, is a matter of existential voice. As people of color we recognize the centrality of race and write about law—its operation, its social ordering, its history, its values, and its ideological vectors—in a way that reflects our different experience, insight, and views. . . .

Linking Separate African-American Class Interests

[T]he experiential basis of our writing need not defeat our own intragroup diversities; it need not collapse into an absurd essentialism. Professor [Regina] Austin warns of the dangers of purporting to represent the views of all African-Americans in our writings:

> It is imperative that our writing acknowledge and patently reflect that we are *not* the voices of a monolithic racial/sexual community that does not know class divisions or social and cultural diversity. This recognition should check the basically conservative impulse to rely on generalizations about racism and sexism that are the product of our own experiences. It should also make us vigilant about lapsing into outrageous themes which suggest that black people are united by biological essences that produce in all of us a refined instinctive sense of justice.

While Professor Austin's point about "biological essences" is valid, I believe she overstates the danger in allowing our experiences to prompt generalizations about racism. Stereotypes must not be reinforced, but valid generalizations, while tricky, must be set forth. In Gordon Allport's classic study of prejudice, he defines a stereotype, whether positive or negative, as "an exaggerated belief associated with a category. Its function is to justify (rationalize) our conduct in relation to that category." Essentialism and stereotyping are complementary. As suggested by Professor [Randall] Kennedy's critique of critical race scholarship for its tendency to reinforce stereotypes and Professor Austin's warning to avoid essentialism, people of color who adopt critical race theory walk a thin line between these concepts and valid generalization. Allport points out that distinguishing between a valid generalization and a stereotype is possible "only if we have solid data concerning the existence of (probability of) true group differences." *Generally*, the life chances, experiences, and styles of blacks and whites, however, are distinctively separate, sufficiently so—indeed extremely so—to provide very different "data" that support certain generalizations.

Although antiessentialist, critical race theory nonetheless emphasizes the commonalities developed from a race consciousness that recognizes, in Patricia Williams' words, that "the simple matter of color of one's skin so profoundly affects the way one is treated, so radically shapes what one is allowed to think and feel about this society, that the decision to generalize from this division is valid." What critical race theory expresses in this way is not a matter of essence, but certainly one of prevalence. It is not a matter of necessary, inevitable expression, but one of deliberate identification and incorporation of data available from colored histories and subjugated narratives, from colored biographies and group identities.

The distinctiveness of colored voices often traces back to an oppositional cultural frame of reference that is shaped by our experiences of racial stratification rather than benign race relations. Of course, African-American culture is rich and extends far beyond reacting to this stratification. However, because of the long history and starkness of black-white stratification, the oppositional cultural frame of reference is a key factor that generates a distinctive voice orientation.

When people of color deemphasize an individuality that tries to transcend color—when we attempt, in other words, to express valid generalizations generated out of race consciousness—we challenge the underlying inadequacy of dominant legal discourse, that which Kimberlé Crenshaw has labeled "perspectivelessness." This position of perspectivelessness holds that legal analysis is possible without taking into account various conflicts of individual values, experiences, and world views. According to Crenshaw, by stripping away the analysis of any particular cultural, political, or class characteristic, this perspectivelessness is presented as the objective, neutral legal discourse, with a corollary of "color blindness," used to reduce conflict and devalue the relevance of our particular perspectives. . . .

Critical Race Theory and Future-Society Rights

The Utility of Rights

. . .Scholars of color use rights in two related but very different ways. First, we employ the language of rights to facilitate our access to a variety of legal norms and enforcement mechanisms by which we try to vindicate, in a particular case or controversy, important claims. Second, we invoke the ideology of rights to mobilize people in support of a particular agenda. Until the subjugated group feels a sense of moral outrage, the group will almost certainly fail to resist the injustice that is oppressing it. The group must obtain justice for itself. The language of rights is used to provoke within the oppressed group the sense of outrage necessary to mobilize the group in a just cause. It is in this fashion that a right can most effectively be utilized. Accordingly, Morton Deutsch has emphasized that in awakening the sense of injustice in the victim

> the process basically entails falsifying and delegitimizing the officially sanctioned ideologies and myths that justify the injustices; exposing the victim to new ideologies, new models, and new reference groups that justify and give life to the possibilities of a change in his status; stimulating hope by successful efforts to improve his situation; and reducing fear by increasing his relative bargaining strength.

This describes critical race theory's basic rights strategies.

Viewed rhetorically, a fundamental role of linguistic construction is to create paradigms through which our experiences become significant in establishing a new mode of public discourse. In a sense, then, much of our world, particularly as people of color, is not merely observed individually but is also audited collectively. Rhetoric in this sense is more than a mere tool of persuasion. Indeed, as Barry Burmmet observes, "it is in the deepest and most fundamental sense the advocacy of realities." The advocacy of reality is absolutely crucial to redirecting rights strategies. In the following subsection, I develop the role of such advocacy in constructing a rights strategy toward relieving oppression.

The Oppressed and the Strategy of Rights

Beyond the realms of constitutional and legislative enactment, administrative regulation, and judicial declaration, the rights namer is *sui juris*. While often philosophical or theoretical, rights imagining by and for the oppressed is nonetheless justified in instrumental terms: Will utilization of the right as imagined lead to improvement in the life conditions plaguing the oppressed?[6]

Rights discourse is both principled and expedient, both technical and rhetorical. The technical is the attribute of the right that compels recognition as a legal claim. The claimant relies on a constitution, statute, code, or judicial precedent to impose a duty or obligation on an individual, group, or the state. All rights, though, potentially carry rhetorical force. Indeed, as with the civil rights movement, the rhetorical force of rights can inspire people on their own behalf to counter injustice, deprivation, inequality, and restricted freedom.[7] Rights assertion can involve the technical and the rhetorical at once, one

---

6. This of course is Alan Freeman's ultimate question associated with the victim perspective. . . .Kimberlé Crenshaw argues that an expansive view of civil rights law directs antidiscrimination law toward eradicating the substantive conditions of African-American subordination and seeks to employ the courts' institutional power to erase the effects of racial oppression. . . .

7. Today, some characterize the crucial issues facing civil rights proponents in terms of the

at the expense of the other, or vacillate between the two. For the oppressed, rights assertion tends to travel a continuum from the rhetorical to the technical. That continuum is dynamic and often dialectically so.[8]

Because established rights must correlate with obligations, the oppressed find that the early stages of rights assertion are quite adversarial as interpretations of needs, interests, and duties are contested. As with any strategy of rights, the tricky part is to move from a social ideal to an institutional program. Cultural themes and world views are implicated. Moral and ethical values are posited. At bottom, however, are issues of politics and power. Thus, while the contestants will call upon various legitimating references, the oppressed should almost never strive for a consensus of shared values or rely on "neutral principles" because too much of the struggle will be shaped and directed, indeed validated and legitimated, in terms of the status quo's dominant power holdings.

In the beginning, the social psychology of rights assertion suggests a *self-directed* evaluation and orientation with an eye to consequences, to fixing things up. Because this process is played out as a power struggle, the rights of the oppressed are seldom effectively asserted and exercised within the dominant institutionalized channels of the social order, at least as these channels are constituted in the early going. Residing outside the beneficent reach of these channels, the oppressed must use rights as *attention grabbers* and *wedges*. Here, "wedge" is defined as "an action, procedure, or idea constituting the earliest stage in a division of unity, change of policy, intrusive action, etc."[9] Rights in

---

need to "define the image, agenda and relevance of the civil rights movement itself" and to again present a compelling moral message that can mobilize minorities without alienating whites. . . .

8. . . .Antonie Peters characterizes law as "a polarity between finality and provisionality, closedness and openness." Antonie A.G. Peters, Law as Critical Discussion, in Dilemmas of Law in the Welfare State 250 (Gunther Teubner ed., 1988). Peters describes these views of law as follows:

> In one view, probably the dominant one among jurists and laymen, law is associated with order, unequivocal meaning, settlement of disputes *lites finiri oportet*, enforcement of rules. It is a view which emphasizes the decisive role of statements by authorities: legislators, courts, expecially [sic], especially [sic] supreme legislators and supreme courts; but also prevailing doctrines and official opinions, which congeal normative options as positive facts by placing them in an established context of government, power, interests and ideology. This conception appeals to a traditional mentality of deference to the status quo; it feeds on man's inclination towards regularity, his need of certainty, his complacence. As is often said, law is a form of social control.
>
> In the other contrasting view law is associated with liberation from existing restrictions, with the possibility of improvement, critique of authority. Emphasis is on justification, not only of deviations from established norms and opinions but, in the case of deviance or contestation, of these norms and opinions as well. The distinctive feature of a "legal" order is not its official confirmation of a *status quo* but its recognition that things can be changed, that there is always a multiplicity of meanings [and] that law lends itself to quite different interpretations and uses. In this view, legal life embodies the belief that social reality is faulty but that it can be reformed.

Id. Of necessity, the oppressed are motivated by the latter view.

9. . . .As a form of antisubordination advocacy, the wedge use of rights will generally challenge issues of legitimacy, probably in the sense Foucault characterized as "dispersed and discontinuous offensives" against official truths in the "insurrection of subjugated knowledges." Michael Foucault, Power/Knowledge: Selected Interviews and Other Writings 80

these senses express demands for the reformulation of institutional norms, structures, and functions. Rights here call for a reevaluation of basic legitimating notions and cultural orientations—for societal themes to be rewritten. In short, the rights holders claim a new social order. The new social order will entail a new recognition of the claimant as a rights holder, and new notions of citizenship or personhood will pertain.[10] In the context of collective conflict, the assertion of rights must be seen as claims to *power*, *privileges*, and *resources*. These claims, in turn, further *collective identity* and *solidarity*.[11]

In both the metalegal and legal senses, then, rights are seen by the oppressed and their advocates as the means to achieve the ends to which they feel they are *entitled*. These ends are thought of in terms of human well-being, dignity, and personhood. The material prerequisites to these ends are accompanying objectives sought in the process of asserting rights and establishing the circumstances for their effective exercise.[12]

(1980). This requires legal advocates, especially lawyers, to cross traditional boundaries where "the practice of law primarily consists of the hermeneutic reproduction of that which already exists." Thomas C. Heller, Legal Discourse in the Positive State: A Post-Structuralist Account, in Dilemmas of Law in the Welfare State 173, 186 (Gunther Teubner ed., 1988). . . .The theory-practice nexus is joined by adopting a litigation style that supplements a command of the craft with an orientation of border crossing and fundamental criticism directed at challenging legitimation or simply mitigating the judiciary's pluralistic ignorance.

10. As Patricia Williams observes:

> For blacks, then, the battle is not deconstructing rights, in a world of no rights; nor of constructing statements of need, in a world of abundantly apparent need. Rather the goal is to find a political mechanism that can confront the *denial* of need. The argument that rights are disutile, even harmful, trivializes this aspect of black experience specifically, as well as that of any person or group whose vulnerability has been truly protected by rights.

Patricia J. Williams, The Alchemy of Race and Rights 152 (1991).

11. As Jean Cohen explains:

> Contemporary collective actors consciously struggle over the power to socially construct new identities, to create democratic spaces for autonomous social action, and to reinterpret norms and reshape institutions. It thus becomes incumbent on the theorist (a) to look into the processes by which collective actors create the identities and solidarities they defend, (b) to assess the relations between adversaries and the stakes of their conflicts, and (c) to analyze the structural and cultural developments that contribute to such heightened reflexivity.

Jean L. Cohen, Strategy or Identity: New Theoretical Paradigms and Contemporary Social Movements, 52 Soc. Res. 663, 690 (1985). As Catharine MacKinnon asserts, "[T]he first task of a movement for social change is to face one's situation and name it." Catharine A. MacKinnon, Toward A Feminist Theory of the State 241 (1989). Drawing upon the work of Alain Touraine, Cohen elaborates:

> . . .[T]he cultural orientations of a particular society (its pattern of knowledge, type of investment, and image of the relation of man to nature) are not seen as incontestable givens, seamlessly transposed into social norms and institutions. Rather, the way a society produces its cultural orientations involves both social conflict and social relations of domination. Society itself is understood as "the changing, unstable, loosely coherent product of social relations, cultural innovation and political processes."

Cohen, *supra*, at 699 (quoting Alain Touraine, Triumph or Downfall of Evil Society?, in Humanities in Review 220 (1982)).

12. Iredell Jenkins, Social Order and the Limits of Law 243 (1980). The early career of rights assertion is described by Jenkins as follows:

We now see in the post-civil-rights era, for example, that after the effective use of rights as a wedge is achieved, the basic rights articulated are never completely delineated and stabilized. As the judicial decisions interpreting certain rights develop, a body of doctrine emerges that reflects a process of legalization. This process whereby rights are defined by law, however, is substantially isolated from the very needs that generated those rights and the values they envisaged. As Professor Iredell Jenkins explains further:

> When it is held that the meaning of a particular right is exhaustively given by the relevant body of legal doctrine, then argument is confined to this doctrinal apparatus, while the decisions that are reached are strongly influenced by. . . extrinsic and unacknowledged considerations. . . .
>
> When this attitude prevails—and it may do so in some fields of law and not in others during the same period of time—law loses touch with the needs and aspirations of people. . . .To the extent that law is responsive only to its own inner logic and the individual consciences of judges, it ceases to be sensitive to the conditions and the mood of the time. I do not mean to denigrate the quality of this logic and these consciences, but there is no guarantee that they will be contemporary or representative. When they are not, legal doctrine moves at a tangent to social reality.

Questions

1. *Stereotypes*. John Calmore suggests the possibilities of positive as well as negative stereotypes. Is a positive stereotype as much a product of objectification as a negative one and as likely to contribute to domination in the form of violence?

2. *Law and Social Change*. How does Calmore's critique help us to understand why accomplishing social change in the law is difficult? How does he help us to understand why accomplishing social change in the law is possible?

Lucinda Finley, Breaking Women's Silence in Law: The Dilemma of the Gendered Nature of Legal Reasoning, 64 Notre Dame L. Rev. 886, 895–900, 903–10 (1989)

Analysis of the way the law structures thought and talk about social prob-

---

> In their original occurrence and long before there is any machinery for their enforcement or even recognition of their legitimacy, rights already carry the double weight of *need* and *title*. It is exactly this that gives the assertion of a right its emotional force and its practical urgency. When men declare that they have a right to something, they are voicing the conviction that what they are demanding is both legitimate and necessary: it belongs to them as human beings, and it is requisite to their human well-being. . . .
>
> The primary locus of rights might thus be said to lie in the sense of injustice. Rights have their origin in the effort to redress what is experienced as an undeserved harm; that is, as a wrong. The purpose of a right is thus to right a wrong. As with everything else that men pursue, rights are felt and fought for well before they are enunciated and catalogued, much less justified.

Id. at 243–44.

lems is necessary to understand how the law can limit our understandings of the nature of problems and can confine our visions for change. The analysis can also be instructive for suggesting strategies for change. . . .[A] male-gendered way of thinking about social problems is to speak in terms of objectivity, of universal abstractions, of dichotomy, and of conflict. These are essentially the ways law talks about social problems.

Modern Anglo-American law talks about social problems within the individualistic framework of patriarchal Western liberalism, a theory that itself has been challenged by feminists as resting on a fundamentally male world view. This framework sees humans as self-interested, fundamentally set-apart from other people, and threatened by interactions with others. To control the threat of those who would dominate you or gain at your expense, you must strive to gain power over them. This power can easily become domination because the point of its exercise is to protect yourself by molding another to your will.

As part of this individualistic framework, law is conceptualized as a rule-bound system for adjudicating the competing rights of self-interested, autonomous, essentially equal individuals capable of making unconstrained choices. Because of the law's individualistic focus, it sees one of the central problems that it must address to be enforcing the agreements made by free autonomous individuals, as well as enforcing a few social norms to keep the battle of human life from getting out of hand. It envisions another central task to be eliminating obvious constraints on individual choice and opportunity. The constraints are thought to emanate primarily from the state or from the bad motivations of other individuals. An individualistic focus on choice does not perceive constraints as coming from history, from the operation of power and domination, from socialization, or from class, race and gender. A final key task for individualistic liberal law is to keep the state from making irrational distinctions between people, because such distinctions can frustrate individual autonomy. It is not an appropriate task to alter structures and institutions, to help the disempowered overcome subordination, to eliminate fear and pain that may result from encounters masquerading as "freely chosen," to value nurturing connections, or to promote care and compassion for other people.

To keep its operation fair in appearance, which it must if people are to trust resorting to the legal method for resolving competing claims, the law strives for rules that are universal, objective, and neutral. The language of individuality and neutrality keeps law from talking about values, structures, and institutions, and about how they construct knowledge, choice, and apparent possibilities for conducting the world. Also submerged is a critical awareness of systematic, systemic, or institutional power and domination. There are few ways to express within the language of law and legal reasoning the complex relationship between power, gender, and knowledge.[13] Yet in order for fem-

13. *Cf.* Sandra Harding, The Science Question in Feminism (1986), in which Professor Harding suggests that science may be particularly resistent to theorizing about gender because it is an empirical, positivistic discipline and consequently without a tradition of critical inquiry into the social origins of conceptual systems and patterns of behavior, including the concepts and behaviors of scientific inquirers. *Id.* at 33. Law and science share many characteristics in this

inists to use the law to help effectuate change, we must be able to talk about the connection between power and knowledge. This connection must be acknowledged in order to demystify the "neutrality" of the law, to make the law comprehend that women's definitions have been excluded and marginalized, and to show that the language of neutrality itself is one of the devices for this silencing.

The language of neutrality and objectivity can silence the voices of those who did not participate in its creation because it takes a distanced, decontextualized stance. Within this language and reasoning system, alternative voices to the one labeled objective are suspect as biased. An explicit acknowledgement of history and the multiplicity of experiences—which might help explode the perception of objectivity—is discouraged. To talk openly about the interaction between historical events, political change, and legal change is to violate neutral principles, such as adherence to precedent—and precedents themselves are rarely talked about as products of historical and social contingencies. For example, in the recent U.S. Supreme Court decision declaring a municipal affirmative action plan unconstitutional, *City of Richmond v. Croson*, the majority talks in the language of neutrality, of color-blindness, and of blind justice—and it is the more classicly legal voice. The dissent, which cries out in anguish about the lessons of history, power, and domination, is open to the accusation that it speaks in the language of politics and passions, not law.

In legal language, experience and perspective are translated as bias, as something that makes the achievement of neutrality more difficult. Having no experience with or prior knowledge of something is equated with perfect neutrality. This way of thinking is evident in jury selection. A woman who has been raped would almost certainly be excluded as a juror in a rape trial—it is assumed that her lived experience of rape makes her unable to judge it objectively. Legal language cannot imagine that her experience might give her a nuanced, critical understanding capable of challenging the male-constructed vision of the crime. Yet someone with no experience of rape, either as victim, perpetrator, or solacer/supporter of victim, is deemed objective, even though it may be just their lack of experience that leaves them prone to accept the biased myths about women's behavior that surround this crime.

Because it is embedded in a patriarchal framework that equates abstraction and universalization from only one group's experiences as neutrality, legal reasoning views male experiences and perspectives as the universal norm around which terms and entire areas of the law are defined. Examples of this phenomenon abound, and exposing them has been a central project of feminist jurisprudence. Thus, for example, my previous work, as well as that of several others, has examined how talk about equality, couched in comparative language of sameness/difference, requires a norm or standard for comparison—and that norm becomes white males. The more a non-white person can be talked about as the same as a white male, the more deserving she or he is to be treated equally to, or the same as, white males. This language not only uses white males as the reference-point, but it also exalts them. To be the same as

---

regard. Despite some tradition of normative theorizing, law is essentially an empirical, positivistic discipline, dedicated, as is science, to objective truth, rather than destabilizing critical inquiry.

white males is the desired end. To be different from them is undesirable and justifies disadvantage.

Many doctrinal areas of the law are also fundamentally structured around men's perspectives and experiences. The field of labor law uses a gendered meaning of work—as that which is done for wages outside your own home—as its focus. Thus, any talk about reforming labor law, or regulating work, will always leave unspoken, and thus unaffected, much of what women do, even women who also "work" in the legal conventional sense. Legal intervention in work—or the perception that no intervention is needed—assumes that workers are men with wives at home who tend to the necessities of life. It is only in this framework that we can even think of work and family as separate and conflicting spheres.[14]

Tort law defines injuries and measures compensation primarily in relation to what keeps people out of work and what their work is worth. It is in this framework that noneconomic damages, such as pain and suffering or compensation for emotional injuries, which are often crucial founts of recovery for women, are deemed suspect and expendable. In the language of criminal law, the paradigmatic criminal is a male, and women criminals are often viewed as doubly deviant. Another example of the manifestation of the male reference-points is how self-defense law looks to male notions of threat and response to assess what is reasonable. Contract law is built around the form of transactions that predominates in the male-dominated marketplace, and doctrines that are regarded as necessary to assist the weak (*i.e.*, helpless women), such as reliance and restitution, are subtly demeaned by the language as "exceptions," as deviations from the normal rules of contract. All of this suggests that for feminist law reformers, even using the terms "equality," "work," "injury," "damages," "market," and "contract" can involve buying into, and leaving unquestioned, the male frames of reference. It also leaves unspoken, and unrecognized, the kinds of work women do, or the kinds of injuries women suffer.

The language of law is also a language of dichotomies, oppositions, and conflict. No doubt this is partly attributable to the fact that law so frequently is invoked in situations of conflict—it is called on to resolve disputes, to respond to problems that are deemed to arise out of conflicting interests. Another reason legal language is put in terms of opposing interests is due to its place within an intellectual tradition—Western liberal thought—that orders the world in dualisms: culture/nature, mind/body, reason/emotion, public/private. Law is associated with the "male" and higher valued side of each of these dualisms. This means that law adopts the values of the privileged side of the dualisms, such as the self-interested, "rational" exchange values of the marketplace, or the shunning of emotion. It also means that legal language has few terms for comprehending in a positive, valuable way the content of the devalued sides of the dualisms—or those, such as women, who are associated with

14. The paradigm of the male worker is also evident in the structure of the social security system. . . . It is also evident in the structure of unemployment insurance, which regards family or reproductive reasons for disengaging from employment as voluntary quits or as rendering a worker unavailable for work, as reasons to disqualify a worker from unemployment compensation. . . .

the devalued sides. For example, law's operation within a perceived dichotomy of public/private, and its preference for the public as the proper area for its concern, leaves law largely ignorant of and unresponsive to what happens to women within the private realm. Thus the "public" language of law contributes to the silencing of women.

The conflict aspect of legal language—the way it talks about situations and social problems as matters of conflicting rights or interests—fosters polarized understandings of issues and limits the ability to understand the other side. It also squeezes out of view other ways of seeing things, nonoppositional possibilities for dealing with social problems. Since a language of conflict means that one side has to be preferred, there will always be winners and losers. In a polarized language of hierarchical dualisms set within a patriarchal system, it will often be women, and their concerns, that will lose, be devalued, or be overlooked in the race to set priorities and choose sides.

The special treatment/equal treatment debate over pregnancy leave is one example of conflict-talk that has proved troublesome for women—they face the danger of losing either way. To insist that women must be treated equally with men when there is a fundamental way in which they differ—they become pregnant—can mean that needs associated with pregnancy are not addressed in the workplace. And to have one's needs labeled "special" simply because they are not men's needs, in a society where men's needs are the unstated reference-point for equality, means any effort to address "special" needs is suspect for violating equality. Round and round, tugging back and forth go the debaters. Feminists are forced to choose sides, only to be denounced by the other side. Meanwhile, both labels, equal treatment and special treatment, prop up the assumption that men are the norm. Both views keep the needs of workers who also have children mired in polarized sameness/difference equality talk. This talk precludes discussing the needs of pregnant workers as an important human issue of concern to both parents, and as a matter of social responsibility on the part of employers. . . .

One of the other languages that the law does not easily hear is that associated with the emotions, with expression of bursting human passion and aspirations. Law is a language firmly committed to the "reason" side of the reason/emotion dichotomy. Indeed, the law distrusts injuries deemed emotional in character; it suspects them as fraudulent, as feigned, as not important. The inability to hear the voice of emotion, to respond to thinking from the emotions, is one of the limitations of the legal voice. There are some things that just cannot be said by using the legal voice. Its terms depoliticize, decharge, and dampen. Rage, pain, elation, the aching, thirsting, hungering for freedom on one's own terms, love and its joys and terrors, fear, utter frustration at being contained and constrained by legal language—all are diffused by legal language. Thus, Derrick Bell resorts to fantasy to express far more powerfully than reasoned legal analytic language ever could the hope-frustration-tension-push-gain-get contained relationship between African-Americans and white american law. Alice Walker speaks about the ways in which the term "civil rights" is a bureaucratic, placating term, how the translation of it by the tongues of some blacks to "silver writes" so much better expresses the desire to break all boundaries, the desire of a black man "to run naked on a beach. . .in Alabama." Patricia Williams resorts to the allegorical and metaphorical signifying language of literature to express her reality of being a black woman in America, and to express her relation to the legal system that once saw her family members as the object of property law. And Audre Lord [sic] reminds us that, especially for women of color, who have been most invisible to and silenced by legal, analytic and reasoned language, "poetry is not a luxury" but an essential means of expression, of self-articulation and definition, of survival. . . .

Legal language frames the issues, it defines the terms in which speech in the legal world must occur, it tells us how we should understand a problem and which explanations are acceptable and which are not. Since this language has been crafted primarily by white men, the way it frames issues, the way it defines problems, and the speakers and speech it credits, do not readily include women. Legal language commands: abstract a situation from historical, social, and political context; be "objective" and avoid the lens of nonmale experience; invoke universal principles such as "equality" and "free choice;" speak with the voice of dispassionate reason; be simple, direct, and certain; avoid the complexity of varying, interacting perspectives and overlapping multi-textured explanations; and most of all, tell it and see it "like a man"—put it in terms that relate to men and to which men can relate.

Feminist theory, on the other hand, which is not derived from looking first to law, but rather to the multiple experiences and voices of women as the frame of reference, tells us to look at things in their historical, social, and political context, including power and gender; distrust abstractions and universal rules, because "objectivity" is really perspectived and abstractions just hide the biases; question everything, especially the norms or assumptions implicit in received doctrine, question the content and try to redefine the boundaries; distrust attributions of essential difference and acknowledge that experiences of both men and women are multiple, diverse, overlapping and thus difference itself may not be a relevant legal criterion; break down hierarchies of race, gender, or power; embrace diversity, complexity, and contradiction—give up on the need to tell "one true story" because it is too likely that that story will be the story of the dominant group;[15] listen to the voice of "emotion" as well as the voice of reason and learn to value and legitimate what has been denigrated as "mere emotion.". . .

So, what's a woman do? Give up on law, on legal language entirely? Disengage from the legal arena of the struggle? Neither of these strategies is really an available option. We cannot get away from law, even if that is what we would like to do. As Sandra Harding has said, "[w]e do not imagine giving up speaking or writing just because our language is deeply androcentric; nor do we propose an end to theorizing about social life once we realize that thoroughly androcentric perspectives inform even our feminist revisions of the social theories we inherit." Because law is such a powerful, authoritative language, one that insists that to be heard you try to speak its language, we cannot pursue the strategy suggested by theorists from other disciplines such

15. For example, white feminists tend to tell a story of women's true situation that excludes the differing situations of poor women and women of color and women of different ethnic backgrounds. . . .

as the French feminists, of devising a new woman's language that rejects "phallologocentric" discourse.

Nor can we abandon caring whether law hears us. Whether or not activists for women look to law as one means for pursuing change, the law will still operate on and affect women's situations. Law will be present through direct regulation, through nonintervention when intervention is needed, and through helping to keep something invisible when visibility and validation are needed. Law will continue to reflect and shape prevailing social and individual understandings of problems, and thus will continue to play a role in silencing and discrediting women.

Since law inevitably will be one of the important discourses affecting the status of women, we must engage it. We must pursue trying to bring more of women's experiences, perspectives, and voices into law in order to empower women and help legitimate these experiences. But this is not as easy as it sounds, because there is no "one truth" of women's experiences, and women's own understandings of their experiences are themselves affected by legal categorizations.

To the extent that the law's authoritative definitions are based on male perspectives, much of women's own understandings of things whose meaning is greatly influenced by legal definitions—such as rape or equality—will be constructed with reference to the male meanings. So the feminist project of incorporating "women's experience" into legal definitions is not as simple as "one, figure out who or what is 'women'; two, consult women's experience; and three, add it to law and stir." Women's experiences are diverse and often contradictory; and there is no true women's experience unaffected by social construction, which includes legal construction, which includes male defined understandings. How many women have thought of themselves as not having been "raped," when they know that what happened to them did not match the legal definition of rape which informs the social understanding of rape? How many women have thought of themselves as not victims of discrimination when the law says they are different because they are pregnant or capable of becoming pregnant, or subject to greater health risks, or too short, or not strong enough, or working in jobs and at rates of pay they have freely chosen to accept, or not reacting to workplace "horseplay" (manplay) the way a reasonable "person" would?

The answer to both questions is many, some, but not all, and not the many or some totally. There may be instances of dissonance, of resistance, and of wondering if the legal definition is really right. A woman may still feel violated and coerced even though she was not "raped," and she may begin to wonder if maybe feeling violated and coerced is so much like being raped that she was raped even though she knew the man and agreed to go to his room. A woman may still feel that she was treated unfairly or was not really given any choice or was expected to accept something that really disturbed her or hurt her, and that all this was because she had no power. She may then begin to suspect that the lack of power, and thus the way she was treated has something to do with the fact that she is a woman, and she may wonder whether maybe this is what discrimination is really all about anyway. The dissonances, resistances, and wonderings are also part of women's experiences. Once they are articulated and shared with other women, understandings often begin to change. Legal activists can explore these voices of dissonance, these barely audible questions. They can embrace the fact that women have many very different experiences and can start working into the law the questions raised by women's challenges to the prevailing legal constructions of situations. For example, as women themselves started to talk to each other about experiences of violently coerced sex on dates, and these women talked to other women who had been raped in the conventional sense, the similarities between the way their experience made them feel and the recognized rape became apparent. And so they began to question whether maybe they, too, had been "raped." This opening in women's understandings is now being used to change the legal understanding of rape as something that only happens between strangers.

In engaging the law over the meaning of women's experiences, people representing women must remain constantly critically aware of the dilemma of legal language, of its simultaneous power and limitations. While its power can help women by validating and affecting societal consciousness about women's situations, its power also has a negative aspect. Precisely because it is an authoritative discourse, it demands that we try to speak within its confines—it threatens us with not being heard or credited if we do not. The patriarchal bias in legal language, and its limited way of framing and envisioning situations, can easily distort what women have to say. It can put women on the defensive, because of their "difference" from men. It can force women to respond to sameness/difference arguments, public/private arguments, or free speech arguments, not on women's own terms, but on the terms of the traditional arguments. This creates a stark dilemma: in light of the power of existing meanings, can we change the meanings of terms while still using those terms?

By talking about family/work conflicts, are we helping to reinforce the view of these two worlds as separate spheres? Are we continuing to privilege the existing definition of work, and are we shoring up the notion of family as two opposite sex parents, with some number of children? By using the term "equality," are we helping to keep the focus on women and their differences from men, thus reinforcing the male norm? Or is it possible to use this term in a way that makes women's experiences the reference point, and shifts attention to structures and values of the workplace? Even if we modify "rape" with "date" or "acquaintance," are we leaving unchallenged the baggage that comes along with the "r" word—that this is a crime of sex, in which women's consent is the main issue, rather than a crime of violence in which the violator's conduct is the issue? If we capitulate to the language of private choice in the abortion debate, are we losing sight of the reasons why, beyond privacy and choice, control over one's reproductive destiny is so essential to women's position in a society of male domination? Are we leaving ourselves wide-open to the moral high ground of the term "pro-life" when all we can juxtapose against it is "choice," rather than freedom and equality? The word "choice" can seem as trivial as the color of one's clothes or one's preferred brand of car, when it is life that some say they are fighting for.

There have been examples of promising word changes and consequent meaning changes in legal discourse. Consider the now widespread use of the term "sexual harassment," for what used to be considered a tort of invading individual dignity or sensibilities; the term "battering" for domestic violence.

But even these language changes get confined by the legal frameworks into which they are placed. For example, the individualistic and comparative discrimination framework now applied to sexual harassment leaves some judges wondering about bisexual supervisors as a means to deny that discrimination is what is occurring. The contract model of damages in discrimination law means that the dignity and personal identity values that tort law once recognized often go undercompensated. And the use of the term "sexual assault" in place of "rape" in some rape reform statutes has not obviated the problems of "objective" male-perspectived judgments of female sexuality and consent.

It is not my purpose to offer a simple, neat, for all times solution to the dilemma of legal language. Indeed, to even think that is possible would be contradictory to my message—it would be a capitulation to the legal ways of thinking that I seek to destabilize in order to expand. But I am not without solutions to the dilemma of the gendered nature of legal reasoning. The message of this Article presents one solution: critical awareness of the dilemma is itself important. Awareness encourages thinking critically about whose perspective has informed a term or doctrine, and about the norms or assumptions upon which the term may rest. This leads to self-conscious strategic thinking about the philosophical and political implications of the meanings and programs we do endorse. For example, just what are the implications of arguing either sameness or difference? If both have negative implications, then this should suggest the need to reframe the issue, to ask previously unasked questions about the relevance or stability of differences, or about the role of unexamined players such as employers and workplace structures and norms. Critical thinking about norms and what they leave unexamined opens up conversations about altering the norms and thus the vision of the problem. This leads to thinking about new ways of reasoning and talking. It leads to offering new definitions of existing terms; definitions justified by explorations of context and the experiences of previously excluded voices. Or, it leads to thinking about offering wholly new terms.

In addition to critical engagement with the nature of legal language, another promising strategy is to sow the mutant seeds that do exist within legal reasoning. My previous description of legal reasoning is obviously overly general. It highlights tendencies or widely held assumptions about the nature of law. But this description, too, can be deconstructed. For example, while law is generally ahistorical and abstract in its highest pronouncements of doctrine, it is also a fact-driven system, one that works with and exploits variations between situations. Because legal reasoning can be sensitive to context, we can work to expand the context that it deems relevant. By pulling the contextual threads of legal language, we can work towards making law more comfortable with diversity and complexity, less wedded to the felt need for universalizing, reductive principles.

The law's oft-proclaimed values of equity and fairness can also work as mutating agents. The equity side of law counsels taking individual variations and needs into account. Arguments about when this should be done in order to achieve fairness must proceed with reference to context, to differing perspectives, and to differing power positions. The more we can find openings to argue from the perspective of those often overlooked by legal language, such as the people upon whom the legal power is being exercised, or those disempowered or silenced or rendered invisible by the traditional discourse, the more the opportunities to use the engine of fairness and equity to expand the comprehension of legal language.

Note and Questions

1. *Language of Law/Language of Dichotomies.* Lucinda Finley analyzes the language of the law as the language of dichotomies and conflicts (p. 118). How might we use this insight to understand how the language of the law contributes to violence?

2. *Process of Awareness.* In her discussion of feminist legal methodology, Finley describes a process by which a woman's understanding of her experiences is influenced by legal definitions that are "constructed with reference to male meanings" (p. 121). At some point, according to Finley, the woman begins "to suspect that. . .the way she was treated has something to do with the fact that she is a woman. . ." (p. 121). Compare this description of women coming to terms with sexism with Patricia Hill Collins' description of African-American women's understandings of their experiences. Collins rejects the notion that the dominant society's "controlling images" are embedded in African-American women's view of themselves. "Black women's work and family experiences create the conditions whereby the contradictions between everyday experiences and the controlling images of black womanhood become visible" (p. 58).

The differences between the process of awareness described by Finley and that by Collins reflect differences of class and race. In their conversation about class and race differences among feminists, Barbara Smith and Beverly Smith provide some insight into why the process of awareness described by Finley might differ from that described by Collins.

> [Barbara]: There is a political savvyness, I don't know what word to use, canniness—some difference in attitude I think between Black and white feminists. I think what it is, is like the surprise factor. There is virtually no Black person in this country who is surprised about oppression. Virtually not one. Because the thing is we have had it meted out to us from infancy on. . . .
>
> [Beverly]:. . .My perception about racial oppression and class oppression is that it's something that starts from Day One. . . .

Barbara Smith & Beverly Smith, Across the Kitchen Table: A Sister-to-Sister Dialogue, in This Bridge Called My Back: Writings by Radical Women of Color 113, 114 (Cherríe Moraga & Gloria Anzaldúa eds., 1981).

3. *Critiques of Legal Discourse.* What common themes are found in the Calmore and Finley excerpts?

Feminist Discourse, Moral Values, and the Law—A Conversation, 34 Buff. L. Rev. 11, 12, 18–28, 30, 36–42, 44–49, 73–76, 84–85 (1984)

[*Mary*] *Dunlap* [Member, California Bar. Founder, Equal Rights Advocates]: . . .The title of this morning's conversation, "Feminist Discourse, Moral Values, and the Law," raises a sundry set of definitional problems which I am going to completely skip over. . . .

What I want to say is that when we consider redistributing the power and the resources and the strength (materially, physically, spiritually, and every other way you can redistribute resources), there are several options. One is the option of erring in favor of equality over other approaches. One (and a very common option it is) is keeping the status quo, because changing it seems all too hard. Underlying that is the belief which is, if not widespread, at least common enough that it rears its ugly head with some regularity: the belief that men are better. "Tough luck, honey. That's the way it is, because men are better. Men are stronger, men are smarter, men are this, men are that. Yes, women are this, and let's say some nice compensatory things about the girls, but society is the way it is because men are better." That is another response to the question of redistribution of resources. It is very real, and I suggest to you that, although we do not like to think so, it has a lot of adherents, both casual and die-hard.

So there is the equality approach to redistribution and there is the "men-are-better" approach. Let me suggest to you that there is the "women-are-better" approach. The "women-are-better" approach commends itself to those of us who want to believe that we are better. This is something we want to think when we look at the stuff that we identify as being correlated with men—and I can talk from cruise missiles on up and down. But people tune us out if we say: "Everything we see tells us women are better. We do not want equal distribution of the resources, we want to be in charge. We merely want our turf. O.K.?"

Now, it's crucial to remember that whether or not one is loyal to the principle of equality does not necessarily depend on one's beliefs. Lots of men buy the status quo because they believe they're better. Other men say in the backs or fronts of their minds: "Well, she is really not going to do that well, but we will give her a chance." What I am saying is that when all else fails, we should try at least to equalize opportunity. Let us see if we can reduce those instances of wrong that are correlated with gender. This, I suggest, is an integral part of the equality model. And that process is not necessarily precluded by one's belief that one gender or another is "better."

I want to offer an illustration. A very popular stereotype is that women are compassionate healers, that we are the ones to fix things and nurture. Now the temptation is to discard the stereotypes. How sad. Some of those very same values—nurturing and compassion and healing—are precisely what is making feminism have its best and greatest impact in a long time. We cannot afford to defy the patriarchy in the same way that one defies an abusive parent—"*everything* you say or do is wrong," and "everything we have said and done that makes you think we are a certain way is wrong." We cannot permit this. As to the operation of moral values through feminism, I suggest that we, those of us who are feminists, men and women alike, are challenged to choose, from all of the imagery, that which is closest to what we believe, care about, and can move forward through our minds and hearts and everything we have to offer. It is terribly important not to get caught in the categorizations in either direction. Categorizations are whipsaws. "Oh, women are more emotional than men." This one I always love. The last time I heard somebody say that seriously, the person was a male law professor ripping the microphone cord out of the wall while it was malfunctioning. The problem with that is, if you get offended by it, you are getting offended by emotions. Do not get offended by emotions—we need them all. We need the full range of emotion. In court we need anger (wow, do we need it). We need compassion. We need tenderness. We need all the things that make the legal system, or could make the legal system, more of a healer and less of a slayer. And those values I suggest are feminist. They are not necessarily female, but they are feminist—and I think that the challenge is not to live up or down to anybody's stereotypes. That is a very real challenge.

So I have taken my position on that. I am in favor of equality; I do not favor supremacy even as sweet as the vengeance would seem. No! I confess that. I favor equality because I think it's going to move us all toward a better place for people—for women, who are my first priority, and for men, who are my other priority.

[*Catharine*] *MacKinnon* [Associate Professor of Law, University of Minnesota]: I am really glad to be here to have what is openly billed as a dialogue within feminism, particularly as it is clearly premised on a rather unusual assumption: All women are not the same.

I want to talk about the terrain of feminism, which has to do with relations between the sexes. I want to speak in particular about this principle of equality that Mary alluded to, and make reference to some particular legal applications in the doctrinal area of sex discrimination, which is (supposedly, at least) one area of law where the equality principle is fielded.

One question that feminism poses is: "What is the gender question a question of?" I see two answers. The first answer has historically been the politically dominant, legally and conceptually: The gender question is a question of difference. There are two options under it. The first option I call the "male standard": Women can be the *same* as men. In law, it is called gender neutrality. The other option I call the "female standard": You can be *different* from men. In law, it is called special protection. These bear a remarkable parallel resemblance to the masculine and the feminine.

The other answer to the question, a dissident view from the dominant mainstream legal and political position and discourse, is that gender is a question of dominance. In this answer, the issue of discrimination or inequality is not centrally one of accurate categorization, as it is in the first. It is one of hierarchy, the top and the bottom of a hierarchy are different all right, but that is hardly all. One part of the distinction is dominant, and the other part of the distinction is subordinate.

From this second standpoint—which is my answer to the gender question—we see that the two standards in the first answer are two different versions of the male standard. If you see gender as a hierarchy—in which some people have power and some people are powerless, relatively speaking—you realize that the options of either being the same as men or being different from men are just two ways of having men as your standard. Men are set up as a standard for women by saying either: "You can be the same as men, and *then* you will be equal," or, "You can be different from men, and then you will be *women*."...

In my opinion, to take the differences approach is to take a moral approach, whereas to criticize hierarchy is to take a political approach. To take a differences view is also to take a liberal view (although that view, of course, includes conservatism as well), and to take the view that we are dealing with a hierarchy is to take a radical approach. I also think that to make issues of gender turn on the so-called gender difference is, ultimately, to take a male perspective. I therefore call the differences approach masculinist. The position that gender is first a political hierarchy of power is, in my opinion, a feminist position. . . .

The first drawback of. . .[the sameness approach] has been that it does not deal with what are taken to be real differences. There *are* some. For instance, pregnancy, an ability which some women have and all men do not. They lack it. What this means is that if one enters a world in which the standard is already constructed according to an implicit but suppressed male referent, you have a marketplace structured according to a male biography, a male-based series of social expectations, wherein only those women who are the most like that are the same as that, and therefore have a right to be treated equally by this definition of equality. There is no critique of the standard itself as gender based. Only women who are most *like* the male norm are advanced or advantaged by this notion of equality—as women of the right have tried to point out to those who have been willing to listen. Another disadvantage of the sameness approach, which I will articulate in expressly feminist terms, is that what we get in these cases—the athletic cases, the academic cases, and so on—is the right to pay the price of admission that men are supposed to pay but often do not, simply because they are benefited by that affirmative action plan for white men otherwise known as American society.

There is, however, a deeper critique of this standard: we can play with the boys but we cannot question competition as a measure of merit. We can think but we are not allowed to question objectivity as the measure of what we know. We are allowed to compete but we are not allowed to question competition as the test of accomplishment. Nor do we get to criticize conflict as a peculiarly ejaculatory means of conflict resolution.

I have talked about the sameness standard—what it gets us, what it does not, what we (or I, anyway) feel moved by in it, where it lets us down. When I read women's accounts of struggling with the decision of whether or not to have an abortion, I see how the sameness standard has let women down because there is no moral equivalent to abortion in the life of a man. The sameness standard has also let women down with regard to comparable worth. That is why we are having such trouble with it: There are no men around to compare with. They have other alternatives. How do we determine what equal treatment is if there are no men around to be made equal with? In the comparable worth cases, the struggle is to find men to be comparable with, when, because of sex segregation, men do other things, better things.

The other alternative the differences approach gives you is to ground equality claims *in* difference: "We are different from you." We want this difference equally accommodated. Legally, this has been codified as the special protection rule in sex discrimination law. It does not have to be limited to that. That is what it has meant, however, in men's hands. Women say: "We want to be taken on our own terms." Male-supremacist logic transforms that to: "You want to be treated as a woman," and men define what a woman is.

Having said what the single standard does for us, I would like to say a couple of things about what the double standard has done for us. Well, there were those protective laws that said all those things we could not do and all those stools we had to have to sit on, and how our reproductive organs would be abused if we were to work X number of hours. . . .

The double standard is rather beautifully articulated in Carol Gilligan's book, *In a Different Voice*. Again, I do not mean that the only way one can accommodate the perspective that women have something distinctive to offer social life is by a double standard under discrimination law. The importance of the recognition that women are different has had to do with valuing women's experience—not only the experience of relatedness, responsibility, and care virtues, but also the experience reflected in the following insight, which is the impulse behind the discipline of women's history in many respects: "Wait a second. You may have defined history as wars, empires, governments, and so on, but we were there, too." This insight is effective only if you count what we were there *for* and what we were *doing* there, and only if you can see that other things are going on in society besides those things that men have measured as valuable. Women make history. Quilts are art. Those gardens are expression and creativity. A shorthand way of saying this is that, men notwithstanding, man is *not* "the measure of all things."

Up to now I've been talking about one answer to the equality question—the "difference" answer. I have not talked about who has power over whom, although there has been a sensitivity as to who sets the standards. In the view I have just characterized, we saw gender as a *difference* first and as an *inequality* second. In this second view I am suggesting, gender is a question of inequality first. The question is not so much how to make rules fit reality, but rather how to change reality. This perspective, this dissident view, criticizes the empirical world and the standards that are part of it. It criticizes the standards that set us up to be either the same as men or different from men; it criticizes the requirement that we have to define ourselves in terms of men. Its agenda is one of explaining and criticizing what women have had little choice to become, in order to change it.

Here I should quickly supply some facts. Consider that thirty-eight percent of young girls are sexually abused as children by older men in their dominant family unit with whom they are close. That is true for ten percent of boys. (Gender comparisons of little kids are about the only ones that make sense.) About forty to forty-four percent of women are either raped—in the usual legal sense of the word, not including marital rape—or are victims of an attempted rape. Around eighty-five percent of all women are, or have been, sexually harassed in the workforce at some point. . . .Diana Russell. . .found that thirty-eight percent of all girls are victims of child sexual abuse. The battery figure for women is between one-fourth and one-third. As for prostitution—as far as we can tell (statistics are hard to get a hold of, for reasons that are obvious)—apparently about twelve to fifteen percent of all American women are, or have been, prostitutes, by which is meant they make or have made their living more-or-less exclusively through the sale of their sexuality. The data on economics is also well known: a woman makes fifty-nine cents for every dollar a man makes, and that gap is widening. The segregation on jobs, too, is well known. And, the pornography industry, an excellent example of the dominance model, makes the sex difference sexy to the tune of $8 billion a year in entertainment. One manifestation of being a member of a degraded group must be that people call your torture and humiliation entertainment and pay a lot of money to enjoy it.

Few people, I have found, even Phyllis Schlafly, are interested in calling this picture the sex difference. Is it the sex difference to be targeted for rape, to be sexually molested, to be set up to be bought and sold, and then to be trivialized and humiliated, passed around, patted, put in place, and told to smile about it? None of these issues are traditionally seen as equality issues. Isn't that interesting? I think that is partly because, when these issues are seen at all, they are seen as issues of force, and sex inequality is *not* seen as an issue of force. Racial inequality, by contrast, *is* seen as a question of force, not just as a question of racial differences.

What this all means is that women are a subordinate group. And nothing is being done about it. Really, nothing. This abuse is passing unacknowledged as the sex difference, while the issues that are litigated as sex discrimination issues are seen as differentiation problems against a reality which is fundamentally equal. The practices I just described are that reality. Dominance and submission made into sex, made into the gender difference, constitute the suppressed social content of the gender definitions of men and women.

When you look at that, it makes a lot of sense that women might have a somewhat distinctive perspective on social life. We may or may not speak in a different voice—I think that the voice that we have been said to speak in is in fact in large part the "feminine" voice, the voice of the victim speaking without consciousness. But when we understand that women are forced into this situation of inequality, it makes a lot of sense that we should want to negotiate, since we lose conflicts. It makes a lot of sense that we should want to urge values of care, because it is what we have been valued for. We have had little choice but to be valued this way. It sure would be nice if somebody would care for *us*. Women of the right speak particularly strongly about values of responsibility. They are responsible; it would be nice if men would live up to their end of the bargain. It makes a lot of sense that women should claim our identity in relationships because we have not been allowed to have a social identity on our own terms. As to whether these values are women's, possessive, voice, I think that women's silence—and, for the same reasons, the damage to women's sexuality—goes deeper than the absence of words; it is the absence of life, of the ability to live in security or wholeness—hence, the inability to articulate or to express. This prior absence does affect questions of morality. If the first problem of inequality is the problem of the subordination of women and not the inaccurate differentiation between people on the basis of sex, it is inappropriate to discuss the reality or proposition of treating women as subhuman as a matter of good versus evil. Appropriate, instead, is an argument and a discussion about empowerment, about power. Gender then becomes a question of how people who do not have power are going to get some, and how people who do not have a voice are going to be able to speak in anything other than a male voice in a higher register. It is about how this romance with gender, elaborately played out as either sameness or difference, is going to be turned into something that is *not* going to look like our freedom to be feminine, which keeps us where we have been placed, but rather like something which values us for what we are without keeping us there; *not* our freedom to be masculine, but our right to have access to everything men have always kept for themselves whether we do with it what they have done with it, or not.

The freedom we have is so small compared to the kind of freedom that we could have if we transformed this society, if we were able to get this foot off our necks. If somebody has got their foot on your neck, what do you do? I don't think you negotiate. I don't think you compromise. I don't think you even address the foot on your neck in your own voice, such as it is, and attempt to persuade it to move off. You try to figure out how to get it up off of you so that you can, among other things, have something to say. . . .

Dunlap:. . .I have never taken the position that men should define merit and that we then should equal it. Pardon me, but that's crap. I take the position that the values that we are conveying and pursuing are related to gender and at the same time deeper than gender.

Let me see if I can give you an example. One that comes to mind is our relationships with children. Kitty MacKinnon's statistics on child abuse are interesting. Thirty-eight percent of female children are abused and ten percent of males. That by itself ought to tell us that sexist violence does not necessarily focus upon women. Men are raped (I can speak to this, coming from San Francisco and being close to a gay male community that has a facet of violence that goes well beyond rape), men are beaten in the street, called "fags," and killed. This is frequent all over the country. If that is not sexist violence, then I am not quite sure what it is. If the bond among women is based primarily upon opposition to men and a belief that it is only women who can be raped, then, I think, we have missed the boat. . . .

[*Carol*] *Gilligan* [Associate Professor of Education, Harvard University]: [I]n 1973, the Supreme Court legalized abortion. The last thing on my mind at the time was the fact that this would bring me into contact with a population of women. Though that question was not at the center of my work at the time, I am certain that my own thinking was very influenced by the resurgence of the women's movement. I began to interview women who were pregnant and for one reason or another were deciding whether or not to have abortions. I did not make any assumptions about whether this was a moral problem or about what the moral problem was, and this was absolutely key to the findings of my work. I did not say, "Well, here you are facing a decision between liberty and life—how do you resolve it?" or, "When do you think life begins and how does that affect your thinking about the morality of your decision?" I simply asked the women: "How did you get pregnant and how have you been thinking about it so far?" As women began to talk about their decision, I picked up moral language. Spontaneously, words appeared like "should," "ought," "right," "wrong," "good," and "bad." And I asked: "When you say, 'This would be the better thing to do,' or when you say, 'This would be wrong,' what do you mean?" As I began to follow the moral language which spontaneously appeared in women's narratives about decisions that they were actually making, I began to trace the construction of morality implied in this use of moral language. I ended up (I'm shortcutting several steps) calling this "a different voice." I deliberately called it a different voice; I did not call it a woman's voice. I am going to talk later about the whole issue of gender difference as it came into my work and as it appears in the current analysis of findings that my research group has done.

I called the construction of morality I heard a different voice because I was not comparing women with men. Rather, as indicated by my book's subtitle—"Psychological Theory and Women's Development"—I was comparing women with theory. I said this voice is different from the voice that has been described in the psychology of moral development, in moral philosophy, and in the legal and political system which was sitting all around my work. The way in which women were talking about the moral problem in abortion did not fit the public discussion of abortion in this country. In other words, it was *not* construed as an adversary fight between the mother and the fetus. In fact, the whole dilemma arose from the very connection between them. Women perceived that there were two lives that were in fact interconnected. Women who were pregnant talked about the fact that if they took drugs they would hurt the fetus. Here, therefore, were two lives which were by definition interdependent, and connected physically for about nine months. You might ask how long the lives were connected *psychically*. The women sometimes said eighteen years, sometimes twenty years, sometimes forever. They asked, in effect, whether it is responsible or irresponsible, moral or immoral, to sustain and deepen an attachment under circumstances in which you cannot be, for whatever reason, responsible, and in which you cannot exercise care? Where they decided it was not, they sometimes then concluded that abortion might be the better thing to do—it would not necessarily be a good thing to do, nor the right thing to do. There was seen no "right" thing to do in this situation. It might be, however—and I quote from women just picked at random—"the lesser of two evils," "the better of two things," "the more responsible thing." If you are interested in all the kinds of ways in which that has meaning, I provide a lot of examples in my book of how that construction was worked out and how it changed over time, and of the various things that women meant when they said "care" and "responsibility." But the main point was that the assumptions that underlie the "justice" approach or the "rights" approach were not being made, and in fact were being seen as a distortion and a deformation of the situation. Women realized that to say that they thought pregnancy meant a life, developing through time—if nothing intervened, accident or biology—into a child, meant that you could not bring the issue into the legal system. To enter the legal system, therefore, women had to act as though they did not know things that they felt they knew, and that they did not in a sense understand issues of connection which could not be represented within the adversarial-rights model which pitted one life against the other. I was therefore talking about a voice literally different from the voice represented in psychology, from the voice represented in moral philosophy (that psychology was wedding itself to), and from the voice that was represented in the legal system. I began to say: "Let us explore this difference.". . .

I once interviewed a woman in her early twenties about a moral dilemma. She said: "Would you like to know what I think, or would you like to know what I *really* think?" I thought that this was very interesting; she had learned to "think" in a way that was very different from the way that she "really thought." I thought about that when I talked about secondary education and the failure of interpretative schemes to reflect women's experiences. I thought I would tell you about Amy and Jake, whom I wrote about in my book when they were eleven. When they were interviewed again at the age of fifteen, the interview caught Amy at the moment where you could see the erosion of self-confidence starting to happen. During the re-interview, she was again asked about the Heinz dilemma, which is one of Kohlberg's standard dilemmas and one of the most frequently used instruments for assessing moral maturity.

In the Heinz dilemma there is a man, Heinz, who cannot afford to buy a drug that will save the life of his wife. The question is: Should he steal the drug? Amy said, "I hated these dilemmas last time as much as I do now," and she elaborated the same reasoning that she had given at eleven: "It all depends. What if the husband got caught? It would not help his wife. And anyway, from everything I know about cancer, it cannot be cured by a single treatment. And, where would this drug be, sitting out on the shelf of a drugstore? The whole situation is unreal." She then said: "Like I had said last time [actually she had not], life comes before property. He should steal the drug."

That, by the way, is the "right" answer. She jumps a full stage in moral development, as measured by Kohlberg's scale—from eleven to fifteen years. But look what she has done now: She is learning that if she enters into a construction of reality which she has identified as unreal and problematic, she will advance in "moral development." In other words, if you equate moral development with justice reasoning, then, in a sense you render her more deeply uncertain, more susceptible to the tension between what she thinks and what she really thinks, less convinced that her voice will be heard.

I wanted to tell you about the re-interview of Jake at fifteen because that is very interesting, too. It tells us how psychological systems of assessment distort male as well as female thinking. Jake is the one who said at age eleven, that moral dilemmas are like "math problems with humans." Anyone who can do math can solve these problems and agree on what the right answer is: that is, that life comes before property. At fifteen, he says (beginning the same way he did at eleven): "Money comes and goes but human life only comes once, so therefore the wife's claim to her life takes precedence over the druggist's claim to his property." But then Jake is asked to comment about the fact that the druggist feels strongly about his profit. Jake responds: "He's got the wrong set of priorities." That's the approach that says there is one logical way to answer and that if you disagree it is because you do not understand or because you have the wrong set of priorities. We say in psychology that it is because you are at a lower stage. But then Jake says something else which is extremely interesting. He starts to consider the situation and the feelings that would be evoked both by theft and by death and he says: "I think that what the druggist is going to experience is some sorrow and some anger over losing his money, and it is a shame that he has to feel that." Look what Jake is doing now: he is not detaching himself from the druggist. Instead he is moving very close to the druggist to consider how a druggist would feel in that situation. But, he says: "It is not as deplorable a thing as the idea of Heinz—with his wife dying and him having to deal with his wife's dying."

The point I want to make is that, when measured by Kohlberg's scale of moral development, Jake does not show any evidence of moral development between eleven and fifteen because his justice reasoning has not changed.

Thus, these interpretative schemes encourage Amy to become more deeply uncertain and Jake to become more simply dogmatic—to take the position that anyone who does not agree with him has "the wrong set of priorities."...

You see two modes of thinking that are not just "different," that are not just alternative, but are in fundamental tension. . . .

This is what I mean by two voices, two ways of speaking. One voice speaks about equality, reciprocity, fairness, rights; one voice speaks about connection, not hurting, care, and response. My point is that these voices are in tension with each other. In my work I have attempted to ask, "What does it mean to include both voices in defining the domain of morality, of humanity, and so forth?" I want to give one example that illustrates well what I think it means, and what this inclusion implies. I do not think it implies a simple addition, a kind of separate-but-equal thing or an androgynous solution. I think it implies a transformation in thinking.

The best way I can illustrate this is through an example provided by two four-year-olds who were playing together and wanted to play different games. The girl said: "Let's play next-door neighbors." The boy said: "I want to play pirates." "Okay," said the girl, "then you can be the pirate who lives next door." She has reached what I would call *an inclusive solution* rather than *a fair solution*—the fair solution would be to take turns and play each game for an equal period. "First we will play pirates for ten minutes and then we will play neighbors for ten minutes." Each child would enter the other's imaginative world. The girl would learn about the world of pirates and the boy would learn about the world of neighbors. It is a kind of tourism on a four-year-old's level. Really, it's simple. But the interesting thing is that neither game would change—the pirate game would stay the pirate game, and the neighbor game would stay the neighbor game. Both children would learn both games, hopefully for an equal period of time. It is what is called "androgyny."

Now look what happens in the other solution, what I would call *the inclusive solution*. By bringing a pirate into the neighborhood, both the pirate game and neighbor game change. In addition, the pirate-neighbor game, the combined game, is a game that *neither* child had separately imagined. In other words, a new game arises through the relationship.

That is basically my point: The inclusion of two voices in moral discourse, in thinking about conflicts, and in making choices, transforms the discourse. It is no longer either simply about justice or simply about caring; rather, it is about bringing them together to transform the domain. We are into a new game whose parameters have not been spelled out, whose values are not very well known. We are at the beginning of a process of inquiry, in which the methods themselves will have to be re-examined because the old methods are from the old game. . . .

Now I will go back to the question of gender differences. A student working with me found that you could systematically differentiate the two voices and the way in which people—(this is absolutely crucial)—*defined* a "moral" problem. In other words, the voices were manifest in the very definition of the problem, because the definition of the problem sets the answer. (We all say that, but we do not actually think about what it means.) We asked people to describe an experience of moral conflict, a situation in which they had to make a decision when they were not sure what was the "right" thing to do.

They would describe the situation and then we asked: "What was the conflict for you in that situation?" We could thus see how the person constructed the conflict. Finally, we asked: "In thinking about what to do, what did you consider? What did you do? Do you think it was the right thing to do? Right just for you, or for anyone?"

You can identify the presence of justice reasoning and care reasoning in the construction, resolution, and evaluation of the problem. What did we find from this analysis? Across six studies, most people, male and female, represent both voices in defining and resolving moral problems. This was true with regard to an average of sixty-five percent, and in no sample less than fifty percent, of the approximately two hundred people in the study, including medical students, college students, high school students, and adults across the life cycle. Of the two hundred people, seventy percent were women, a percentage we thought to be appropriate, given our focus on women's experience. Nevertheless, most people, both men and women (the percentages were not different) represent both voices in defining moral problems.

The unexpected finding of the study was that there is a very strong tendency to focus on one voice or the other. Let me make this very clear. The presence of both voices suggests that most people know about both inequality and detachment as moral problems. Most people use both voices. As a developmental psychologist, I would argue that this results from the fact that inequality is not just a social event but rather is a life cycle phenomenon. Everyone has been a child, everyone has experienced inequality, everyone knows what it's like to be less powerful than someone who is more powerful. Since inequality is a fact in the human life cycle, the idea of justice will recur over and over again across every generation. But there is another fact in the human life cycle: that no human child survives unless an adult attaches to that child. What characterizes the human species is its long period of dependence. And attachment has a different dynamic and different set of moral implications. By virtue of making an attachment to someone, we become vulnerable to him or her. And not only the parent but also the child is powerful: she or he is able to have an effect on others through the attachment. One is not powerless in a situation of attachment, but the nature of the power is different from the power one holds by virtue of inequality. It has nothing to do with domination. Rather, it has to do with efficacy, the ability to move, to have an effect on another person, to elicit a response from others and to respond to them.

Everybody knows about attachment and everybody knows about inequality; my findings basically represent that fact. Everybody thinks that inequality and detachment are moral problems. That notion is built into the life cycle and then of course is constructed in the social context.

The next finding is that most people who use both orientations focus on one orientation and minimally represent the other. About seventy percent of people who use both orientations focus on one, and this finding holds across orientation and gender. This is very key for people in the law. The adversarial system can not [*sic*] easily accommodate two perspectives which are in a fundamental tension with each other. There is a wish to resolve or reduce ambiguity, to arrive at certainty, and that is done by eliminating one perspective or the other.

What is the nature of the focus phenomenon? There is in these samples of advantaged Americans an overwhelming tendency in men to focus on justice and only minimally to represent caring. Only three men from a total of sixty demonstrated a care focus. Among these advantaged American women, some focused on justice, and some on care (about sixty percent). Look at what happens if you start, as psychology did, with samples of men. You will come empirically to the position that moral reasoning is justice reasoning. In a sense you can now hear through these findings the empirical basis for such statements of psychologists as Freud's observations that women have less sense of justice than men and that women have less tendency to focus on justice issues in resolving moral problems or Piaget's observation that girls are less concerned with the elaboration of rules and are "deficient in the legal sense." If you start with all male samples, the inclusion of women becomes problematic because it challenges the very definition of the problem. You have this group that focuses on care and cannot be accounted for by a theory that equates morality with justice reasoning. The question shifts by virtue of the observation that *both* men and women in fact represent both justice and care considerations in defining moral problems. The question shifts from, "Why are women confusing morality with care or interpersonal relationships?" to, "Why are men not representing in their formal decision-making procedures what in fact is present in their thinking—the realization that there is another dimension to moral problems, a dimension which has to do with issues of care, responsibility, and interdependence?" The question thus really shifts in some ways away from women and toward men, toward a phenomenon within male psychology which permits what is known, seen, and present to be lost or unrepresented. This work (which initially started with taking seriously the discrepant data on women) thus leads to a change in the question. . . .

Question from audience: What do you think about the discovery and elaboration of the women's voice as a different voice (as articulated by Carol Gilligan in psychology) as a political development? She seems to imply that we are going to start to talk to each other differently now that we understand this voice, and that this will force a change.

MacKinnon: I didn't think she predicted that that would happen. Rather, I thought she said that *if* the voice were listened to, the discourse would be transformed. I am—it will shock you to hear—ambivalent about it. On the one hand, I feel excited by the strong and elegant sensitivity in the work. There is something deeply feminist there: the impulse to listen to women. I also think the data is right. I don't think the attributes she advanced are biological but I do think that accurate social regularities were found—and for me gender is a social regularity. On the other hand, what is infuriating about it (which is a very heavy thing to say about a book that is so cool and graceful and gentle in its emotional touch), and this is a political infuriation, is that it neglects the explanatory level. *Why* do women become these people, more than men, who represent *these* values? This is really very important. For me, the answer is clear: the answer is the subordination of women. That does not mean that I throw out those values. Those are nice values; everyone should have them. I'm not saying that taking these values seriously would not transform discourse, which would be a good thing under any circumstance of gender. She also has found the voice of the victim—yes, women are a victimized group. The articulation of the voice of the victim is crucial because laws about victimization typically are made by people with power, and come from the perspective with power. I think the interjection of that perspective has important possibilities. What bothers me is identifying women with it. I'm not saying that Carol does this expressly in her book. But I am troubled by the possibility of women identifying with what is a positively valued feminine stereotype. It is "the feminine." It is actually called "the feminine" in the middle chapter of the book. Given existing male dominance, those values amount to a set-up to be shafted. I am particularly worried about the legal impact of this. . . .If Jake and Amy converse, what happens? Well, we heard if Jake does not listen to Amy, he wins. There is something gendered about that. What happens if Amy doesn't listen to Jake? She loses. You see what I mean? The reason I put it out like that is because I think the power issues are crucial and unignorable. If it is male dominance which has created people in these images, then *recognizing that* really matters for the applications. So I think the explanation part is crucial on its own, but also for the applications. Power is socially constructed such that if Jake simply chooses not to listen to Amy, he wins; but if Amy simply chooses not to listen to Jake, she loses. In other words, Jake still wins because that is the system. And I am trying to work out how to change that system, not just how to make people be more fully human within it.

Gilligan: Your definition of power is his definition.

MacKinnon: That is because the society *is* that way, it operates on his definition, and I am trying to change it.

Gilligan: To have her definition come in?

MacKinnon: That would be part of it, but more to have a definition that she would articulate that she cannot now, because his foot is on her throat.

Gilligan: She's saying it.

MacKinnon: I know, but she is articulating the feminine. And you are calling it hers. That's what I find infuriating.

Gilligan: No, I am saying she is articulating a set of values which are very positive.

MacKinnon: Right, and I am saying they are feminine. And calling them hers is infuriating to me because we have never had the power to develop what ours really would be.

Dunlap: I am speaking out of turn. I am also standing, which I am told by some is a male thing to do. But I am still a woman—standing.

I am not subordinate to any man! I find myself very often contesting efforts at my subordination—both standing and lying down and sitting and in various other positions—but I am not subordinate to any man! And I have been told by Kitty MacKinnon that women have never *not* been subordinate to men. So I stand here an exception and invite all other women here to be an exception and stand.

Everyone who believes it is true that we have never *not* been subordinate to men, remain seated. Everyone who believes that you do not have to be subordinate to men, stand if you can.

Today we have been subordinated to a definition of who is radical, who is feminist, what sex is good, and who gets to talk. I think all those things are very subordinating and also very male. I also think such things happen in these kinds of environments and I'm not going to make a big deal out of it. . . .[16] . . .

Gilligan: I just want to say one thing: I held up the androgyny solution in using the pirate-and-the-neighbor game as the solution that I rejected—the implication that we can have two games that can fit happily alongside each other. When I gave the example, using that as the shorthand illustration of the combination of the games, it was not an illustration of androgyny. It was precisely the opposite. It was an illustration of how to listen seriously and take seriously women's experience. It implied a transformation, a change, in both old games, in both the old masculine game and the old feminine game. I then illustrated exactly what I meant because the old masculine game had said "equality" for (you can correct me about how many years) a hundred years while sustaining inequality. The old feminine game had said "attachment and care" while silencing women. I was really suggesting that the androgyny model sustains both that definition of equality and that definition of attachment or care, both of which I reject. It also suggested that, in fact, if you include women's experience (my definition of feminism is to see in women's experience human experience) if you take it seriously, attend to it, explore it, that would be transformative.

Question from audience: I guess that I did not hear the example of what you described as being transformative.

Gilligan: You do not think that is a new notion of care—a notion that is not destructive to women? Or a new notion of equality that does not co-exist with, as Kitty said, fifty-nine cents to the dollar? What does the word "equality" mean?

Comment from audience: Getting back to the point on androgyny: I interpreted the resolution which the children arrived at as more a recognition that even at the age of four years, the young woman in the scenario knew quite well that she would not be able to influence the pirate's game and had decided instead to settle for as much of her own space as possible. This was to simply say: "Well, let's be neighbors."

Gilligan: That is very interesting and very illuminating because you assume there are two choices: either she dominates or she is subordinate. I say that her solution is transformative because it creates a game that is neither the neighbor game nor the pirate game but a new game—the pirate-neighbor game—which is different from the one that either imagined. How it works out in practice is one thing. But one sees this, as a matter of fact, in studies of small children. They do not resort to aggression as their first means of resolving conflict. Contrary to the image psychologists have created, they in fact play out solutions that are creative and cooperative, like the solution of a pirate-neighbor game. She says, basically: "Instead of my losing and your winning, let's invent a new game." I identify that as the creative solution.

16. Catharine A. MacKinnon had to leave at this point, by pre-arrangement, to catch a plane.

Comment from audience: I guess I would be interested in the cultural content in the game of the four-year-old girl.

Gilligan: That's a very good question. If you observe the pirate-neighbor game, is it a concealed form of domination and subordination or is it in fact a kind of creative adventure for both kids?. . .

Notes and Questions

1. *MacKinnon's Response*. As noted in the Feminist Discourse conversation, Catharine MacKinnon had to leave for the airport as Mary Dunlap was challenging MacKinnon's dominance/subordination analysis (p. 137 n. 16). MacKinnon did respond later in print as follows:

> A stunning example of the denial of gender occurred in a dialogue in which I participated at Buffalo Law School. . . .[Mary Dunlap's] statement turns a critique of a structural condition into a statement of individual inevitability, an indictment of oppression into a reason for passivity and despair. An empirical indictment of what is becomes opposed by a rallying cry of what does not have to be—surely a misplaced opposition. And any woman's victory over sexism becomes a source of proud disidentification from the rest of her sex and proud denial of the rest of her life. If subordination had to be, it would surely be a waste of time to fight for women's rights. But under existing conditions, asking women to single themselves out as exceptions to the condition of women amounts to saying, "all women who are exempt from the condition of women, all women who are not women, stand with me." I was encouraged that only about a quarter of an audience of predominately female law students fell for it. And I understood with new clarity what conservative women have been trying to tell us about feminists.

Catharine A. MacKinnon, Feminism Unmodified: Discourses on Life and Law 305 n.6 (1987). Note 6 from *Feminism Unmodified* assists us in understanding MacKinnon's comments in the Discourse regarding the victimization of women. How can we use MacKinnon's dominance/subordination analysis in considering issues regarding violence against women while simultaneously recognizing that women have agency and operate in our society as subjects as well as objects?

2. *A Different Voice*? Carol Gilligan's 1982 book *In a Different Voice* has had significant influence on the direction of feminist scholarship. It has been a source of controversy both as to its meaning and its use, as Mary Joe Frug explains:[17]

> For conservative readers, the sex differences Gilligan discusses in the book *validate gender differences*. Pursuant to this reading of Gilligan, her book constitutes evidence that women are contextually focused, relationship-oriented, and care-giving, whereas men are abstract, individualistic, and dom-

---

17. Mary Joe Frug, who was a professor at the New England School of Law, was murdered in Cambridge, Massachusetts, on April 4, 1991. This article was in draft form at the time of her death and only minor editorial changes have been made. Eds.

inating. Gilligan's sympathetic presentation of women and her generalizations about the sexes are important to the conservative conclusion that, although Gilligan draws the cluster of sex-linked traits she discusses from the discourse of moral choice, these traits are universal characteristics of the sexes. . . .

In contrast to the conservative position, a progressive reading would interpret Gilligan's use of sex differences as a methodology for challenging gender, as an example of how contingently-formed gender differences can be strategically deployed to unsettle existing inequities between the sexes.[18] Sex differences, pursuant to a progressive reading, are context-bound. They are associated with language, more than individual identity, so that to the extent language can be changed, gender identity can also be transformed. Progressive readers ground the sex differences Gilligan identifies in the context of the moral development theory she sought to change, overlooking the many instances where Gilligan seems to speak of sex differences as if they are universal. . . .

[T]he most significant problem. . .with reading Gilligan conservatively is that a static interpretation of gender stereotypes drawn from Gilligan's book excludes alternative stances and postures of women who do not conform to the conservative reading of Gilligan's book. Those excluded are likely to be different from the subjects of Gilligan's research projects, which means they are likely to be women of color, non-middle-class, lesbian, non-Western, or aged. There is harm caused to these women by neglecting their interests, and there is harm caused to all women by privileging differences between the sexes, as the conservative interpretation does, to differences within the sexes.

Under a progressive reading of Gilligan, sex-linked differences in discourse function as a clue, as a "logic of identification" to the location of silenced, marginalized, or subordinated groups for whom legal assistance may be helpful. This use of sex-linked differences is cautious, nondualistic, partial, contingent, and sensitive to many constituencies of women. These characteristics make it a decided improvement over a conservative use of *In a Different Voice*. Nevertheless, to the extent sex differences are deployed at all, they are likely to have some effect on the construction and protection of gender.

Mary Joe Frug, Progressive Feminist Legal Scholarship: Can We Claim "A Different Voice"?, in Postmodern Legal Feminism 30, 39-40, 48-49 (1992). When Gilligan describes the four-year-olds at play (p. 133), does her analysis of the pirate-neighbor game reinforce gender stereotypes and support the conservative reading of her work? Do you think that the inclusive solution of "the pirate who lives next door" is transformative?

3. *Sameness/Difference*. The sameness/difference controversy has been a central tension in feminist theory; that tension was demonstrated in the debate

18. The conservative reading of Gilligan has been so persuasive, and alternative sources informing the danger of the difference strategy are so intriguing that, like me, progressive feminist legal scholars have tended to give Gilligan's book short shrift in their work. The progressive interpretation I offer here is therefore more dependent on my own reading of Gilligan than the conservative interpretation.

among the participants in the Feminist Discourse. Joan Williams detects a similar controversy in debates by scholars and activists who are working toward racial justice. Her analysis of these two controversies is useful in understanding what happened in the Discourse and appreciating the difficulties of trying to transform existing legal frameworks.

> What is it about the "sameness/difference" framework that causes scholars concerned with racial and gender injustice to turn that concern into arguments that the relative absence of women and minorities in desirable jobs results not from discrimination but from the "choice" or the failings of women and minorities themselves? What is the dynamic by which the sameness/difference approach causes advocacy of structural change to degenerate into a "blame the victim" argument that reinforces the status quo?. . .
>
> Post-modern reformulations of sameness and difference can transform the controversy over whether blacks and whites, men and women are "essentially" the same, into quite a different set of debates. The first centers around how to proceed in the face of a standard loaded against outsiders: If a frontal attack on "male" or "white" standards is impractical, should outsiders ask for "special" treatment, or should they avoid doing so? A second source of disagreement is over divergent descriptions of difference. One need not adopt the essentialist notion that gender, or race, or some other single quality defines "the" one stable category of difference to acknowledge the existence of shared patterns of experience (often linked to oppression). Yet we need to describe difference in ways that avoid essentialism and stereotypes. . . .
>
> [B]oth sameness and difference can function as arguments that veil the structural disadvantages of women in the workplace, and for the same reason: both take that disadvantage as a given. Sameness arguments do so by asking only that women be allowed to participate in the current discriminatory system in which males have access to gender privilege that women lack; difference arguments do so when they turn evidence of structural disadvantage into evidence of women's "choice.". . .
>
> Scholars who argue from a sameness position, as well as those who argue from difference, ultimately concede the legitimacy of such structural disadvantage by arguing that outsiders can do as well as "anyone else" if only given the chance (the sameness position), or that they should be given special treatment because they can't live up to societal standards designed without them in mind (the difference position).
>
> Both sameness and difference advocates act at times as if the opposite strategy will inevitably backfire. In fact, both sameness and difference are equally vulnerable to being used to reinforce the status quo, and for the same reason: neither formulates a direct challenge to the structures that disadvantage outsiders. . . .To join our society on anything like equal terms, minorities and women must demand neither mere entry nor special accommodation. Instead, they must demand transformation. . . .[B]oth sameness and difference arguments will be used to reinforce the status quo to the extent they are not used to challenge it.[19]. . .

---

19. I suspect MacKinnon overestimates the possibility of getting women to adopt a language of dominance formed in the Marxist tradition. That language can jolt women to defensiveness

[A] post-modern approach starts from the notion of a fragmented and shifting self. Sometimes I feel like a white, sometimes a heterosexual, sometimes a Jew, sometimes a lawyer, sometimes an Episcopalian. Often I feel simply like my mother's daughter. A post-modern approach to difference highlights that each person is embedded in a matrix of social and psychological factors that interact in different contexts. Essentialism dissolves before the notion of a shifting, constantly reconfigured self, shaped but not determined by membership in sets of social categories that crystallize power relations in America. . . .

The basic problem with sameness arguments is the claim that people who are as "obviously" different as men and women or blacks and whites are actually the same. This embarrassment is easy to solve if we stress not sameness but equal dignity. . . .

Once reformulated in this way, "sameness" entails not a claim that A and B are the same; instead, it entails the assertion that the differences that exist should be irrelevant in this particular context. This approach links equality with questions of policy rather than biology. Ultimately, one is left with disagreements not about who is similar to whom, but about which differences should matter in which contexts.

This approach to sameness reflects a post-modern sensitivity to the constructedness of categories. After all, no two people are truly "the same." Thus, when we call Person A the same as Person B we are constructing a category of "sameness" that ignores a whole series of differences for strategic reasons. . . .

Post-modern sameness makes explicit outsiders' demand not to be disadvantaged by physical (or social) characteristics that should be irrelevant when it comes to distributing societal benefits. . . .

[For difference, w]e begin once again with a post-modern sensitivity to the constructedness of categories. Traditional epistemology assumed the existence of a firm foundation, a "God's eye point of view," a truth not dependent upon human strivings. Non-foundationalists since the late nineteenth century have stressed the inevitability of different perspectives and different truths, starting from the axiom that things look different from different points of view. Non-foundationalists argue that because every interpretation entails a viewpoint, no interpretation is final or objective. Different interpretations serve different purposes.

This outlook offers a way to dissolve difference in much the same way that it dissolved sameness. Post-modern sameness translated arguments about physical or cultural *similarity* into arguments about which differences are rel-

---

about their intimate relationships and life choices as often as it moves them to agree. . . .MacKinnon's highly confrontational style can play a vital role, but it needs to be linked with a more approachable language that meets women on their own terms: on the sameness/difference territory that they feel "naturally" captures their experience of gender.

MacKinnon also underestimates the extent to which sameness and difference arguments are inevitable to the extent that women or other outsiders choose to operate within the liberal tradition. Immediate deconstruction of the male standard is often not a possibility in litigation and a wide variety of other contexts. . . .Consequently, we are forced to claim either sameness or difference. Indeed, this is true of MacKinnon herself. The test she has advocated (allowing special treatment of women to the extent that such treatment challenges women's traditional subordination) is in a very real sense a difference position. . . .

evant in which contexts. Post-modern difference dissolves claims about *difference* into arguments about which differences should matter in which contexts. Once reformulated, difference dissolves into sameness and vice versa. . . .

Relational feminists use the different voice to express caring and communal values in counterpoint with the individualistic, self-interested focus of liberalism. In so doing, they mobilize a gendered critique of possessive individualism integral to domesticity since its inception. Nancy Cott has called domesticity a "cri-de-coeur against modern work relations" . . . .Domesticity from the beginning has linked gender ideology to political discourse, and has offered a native American language to critique the ceaseless pursuit of self-interest in "that bank note world.". . .

This native language of critique presents two interlocking problems. One is its essentialism. Its description of men and women assumes that gender alone determines the way men and women feel about a very broad sweep of issues. The second problem is that its tracking of traditional stereotypes operates to marginalize women . . . .By linking rejection of mainstream values of competition and self-interest with a description of women's personality, Gilligan's modern reformulation of domesticity opened the way to the argument that women. . .were too "different" to succeed in the competitive, "bank note world". . . .[20]

[I]t is worth noting what outsider-scholars do not do. They do not seek to resuscitate existing cultural stereotypes, as do relational feminists. This is hardly surprising: The traditional stereotypes of African-Americans are so unambiguously insulting that they hold little conceivable attraction. Although this is an important distinction between outsider-scholars and relational feminists, the second difference goes even deeper. Unlike relational feminists, outsider-scholars do not generally posit a comprehensive set of perfectly-matched differences that parallel different political traditions. Instead, the bulk of their work explores in conscientious detail the ways that the experience of discrimination has shaped the outlook of its victims. . . .

We can distinguish in outsider-scholarship two quite distinct sorts of claims. One is that minorities' personal experience of discrimination yields a different perspective on rights talk, civil rights law, and other law that addresses issues of discrimination. . . .

Outsider-scholars do not argue (as relational feminists often seem to do) that the "different perspective" yields an "outsider answer" on virtually any topic. Their claim is much more limited. They claim that blacks react *as blacks* when they see themselves being discriminated against *because they are black*. This proposition does not require a claim that race washes out less easily than class . . . .

[T]he scope of commonality. . .[outsider-scholars] posit is much narrower than that posited by relational feminists. Outsider-scholars claim for

20. Joan Williams in this article focuses on EEOC v. Sears, Roebuck & Co., 628 F. Supp. 1264 (N.D. Ill. 1986), *aff'd*, 839 F.2d 302 (7th Cir. 1988), to demonstrate how "relational feminism failed to change existing stereotypes enough to avoid the traditional pitfalls of domesticity." Joan Williams, Dissolving the Sameness/Difference Debate: A Post-Modern Path Beyond Essentialism in Feminist and Critical Race Theory, 1991 Duke L.J. 296, 314. Eds.

minorities a special insight into the dynamics and the effects of discrimination; relational feminists claim for women a critique of mainstream institutions that many women do not share. . . .

[O]utsider-scholars suggest ways that we can begin to explore difference without falling into old stereotypes or essentialist thinking. One key is to remain thoughtful about the threshold issue of what is the relevant category of analysis in a given situation. Another is to be wary that our descriptions of difference do not posit commonality of too sweeping a scope. A third is to ask especially searching questions when we see descriptions of difference resonant of the traditional stereotypes of the moral mother or the witch, the mammy or the jezebel.

Joan Williams, Dissolving the Sameness/Difference Debate: A Post-Modern Path Beyond Essentialism in Feminist and Critical Race Theory, 1991 Duke L.J. 296, 298-99, 303-05, 307-09, 313-14, 317-19, 322.

4. *Schools of Feminist Thought.* The views of Dunlap, MacKinnon, and Gilligan, as well as those of Frug and Williams, reflect the differing approaches to legal analysis feminists have adopted. The following comparison of these approaches by Patricia Cain may help you to appreciate the controversies found in the Discourse and to analyze the writings by feminists found in future chapters.

1. *Liberal Feminism.* Liberal feminism is rooted in the belief that women, as well as men, are rights-bearing, autonomous human-beings. Rationality, individual choice, equal rights and equal opportunity are central concepts for liberal political theory. Liberal feminism, building on these concepts, argues that women are just as rational as men and that women should have equal opportunity with men to exercise their right to make rational, self-interested choices. Early liberal feminists include Mary Wollstonecraft (1759–1799) and Harriet Taylor.[21]. . .

Liberal feminists have been criticized by more radical feminists for being concerned only with equal pay in the public sphere. Litigators. . .have been charged as being short-sighted because they adopted an assimilationist theory of equality that would benefit women only if they acted like men.[22]

Let me spell out the critique a bit further. Remember that equality theory, as applied to gender, has been conceptually limited by the "similarly situated" requirement. If members of the dominant gender (men) enjoy rights that members of the nondominant gender (women) want, then the only way for women to obtain these rights under existing equal protection doctrine is to argue that, as to the right in question, women are similarly situated to men. If men are being paid X dollars for performing a job in the public sphere, then

21. Harriet Taylor co-authored a number of important works with John Stuart Mill. *See* Harriet Taylor & John Stuart Mill, The Subjection of Women (1869); Harriet Taylor & John Stuart Mill, Enfranchisement of Women (1851); Harriet Taylor & John Stuart Mill, Early Essays on Marriage and Divorce (1832). Taylor and Mill eventually married each other after the death of Taylor's husband. *See* Rosemarie Tong, Feminist Thought 13–22 (1989).

22. Some feminists additionally criticize this early equality litigation because it included cases like Craig v. Boren, 429 U.S. 190 (1976), in which men successfully argued for rights held by women: in *Craig*, the right to buy 3.2% beer. . . .

women should be entitled to the same pay for performing the same job. The equality argument is that women are workers just like men. It is this argument of similarity that makes it possible to expand women's rights. Radical feminists complain, however, that to argue on the basis of women's similarity to men merely assimilates women into an unchanged male sphere. In a sense, the result is to make women into men.

The liberal feminist response to this is that early feminist litigation was concerned with breaking down male-created categories. The point was not to make women into men, but to expand the possibilities for female life-experience by freeing women from the limitations of the male-constructed category "woman." "Woman" was to be freed from the private domestic sphere, if she so chose.

The radical feminist rejoinder is: Yes, but on whose terms? The workplace remains male-constructed. The category "worker" is male-constructed. To force women from one male-constructed category to another is not a real victory, especially if the newly constructed female worker adopts the existing patriarchal view of the world.

Wherever one comes out on this particular debate between liberal and radical feminists, it is important to understand both sides. Both sides agree that women should not be limited by male-constructed categories. Their disagreement is over which categories are most worthy of challenge. At this level, the disagreement is political and instrumental. The disagreement becomes substantive, however, when we shift the focus to the question of what should take the place of the male-constructed category "woman." Radical feminists fear that arguments couched in equal protection terms alleging the similarity between women and men may ultimately be harmful because such arguments endorse entrenched patriarchal values. The new category "woman" that emerges from such arguments is still male-constructed. This concern is valid. But if radical feminists think that liberal feminist legal scholars do not share this concern, they are mistaken. . . .

2. *Radical Feminism.* Radical feminism is not easily defined because it takes many forms. For my purposes, it will be sufficient to contrast radical feminist thought with liberal feminist thought. First, whereas liberal feminists emphasize the individual (men and women as individual human beings), radical feminists focus on women as a class, typically as a class that is dominated by another class known as men. Second, whereas liberal feminist equality arguments are based primarily on the similarities between men and women, radical feminists tend to build arguments that focus on the differences between men and women. These differences, argue radical feminists, have been constructed in such a way as to contribute to women's inequality.

Radical feminists in the legal academy include Catharine MacKinnon . . . .Consider the current dilemma over pregnancy in the workplace. If women had participated equally in designing the workplace from the beginning, employers would not be asked to make accommodations for pregnancy. Instead, the workplace would have been structured so that pregnant workers were not viewed as different from the norm. To move from the male-modeled workplace that currently exists to one that fully accepts women will require some fundamental changes in the model itself. We will have achieved "equality as acceptance" only when woman's difference from man is costless.

Catharine MacKinnon argues that because men have defined women as different, equality arguments cannot succeed.

> Put another way, gender is socially constructed as difference epistemologically; sex discrimination law bounds gender equality by difference doctrinally. A built-in tension exists between this concept of equality, which presupposes sameness, and this concept of sex, which presupposes difference. Sex equality thus becomes a contradiction in terms, something of an oxymoron, which may suggest why we are having such a difficult time getting it.

Recognizing that women as a class are different from men as the two sexes have been socially constructed, MacKinnon would abandon liberal equality arguments. In MacKinnon's view, "an equality question is a question of the distribution of power." The most important difference between women and men is the difference in power. Men dominate women. Men take from women. Furthermore, men have been in control for so long that legal discourse completely ignores the reality of women's lives. Thus, equality theory, as a legal discourse, has focused on public sphere issues like pregnancy in the workplace—issues of import in male lives—rather than focusing on those long-silenced parts of female experience such as rape and other forms of sexual assault.[23]

Using the rhetoric of domination and sexual subordination instead of equality, radical feminists in the MacKinnon camp argue for changes in laws that will end the inequality in power. Sex equality, in this view, affirmatively requires protecting women from such things as sexual harassment, rape and battering by men. An extension of this theory is used to justify a ban on pornography because pornography is thought to contribute to women's sexual subordination.

Some liberal feminists question parts of the radical feminist agenda on grounds that special protections for women often lead to inequality. The most serious disagreement between liberal and radical feminists is over pornography. Radical feminists, especially MacKinnon, support laws that will suppress pornography. Pornography, in their view, is male-created, and defines "woman" as a sexual object. Liberal feminists agree that most pornography is male-created and that male-created pornography defines "woman" as a sexual object.[24] But, argue liberal feminists, to allow the state to ban pornography is to give the state power to define acceptable sex. Since

23. "These experiences have been silenced out of the difference definition of sex equality largely because they happen almost exclusively to women. Understand: for this reason, they are considered *not* to raise sex equality issues." Catharine A. MacKinnon, Difference and Dominance: On Sex Discrimination, in Catharine A. MacKinnon, Feminism Unmodified: Discourses on Life and Law 41 (1987).

24. Some liberal feminists worry, however, that laws used to suppress pornography will be used first against the less powerful members of society who produce pornography, specifically lesbians, who are attempting to create erotic images of women free from male-defined "woman-as-sexual-object" imagery.

the current state is a creature of male power, there is no reason to believe the state will define acceptable sex in a way that is consistent with an individual woman's own definition of her sexual self. In the pornography debate, the radical feminists' reliance on equality theory as a class-based theory (pornography contributes to woman's inequality) clashes with the liberal feminists' commitment to individual liberty.

Some liberal feminists (as well as postmodern feminists) also challenge the radical feminists' emphasis on "woman" as a class. They argue that radical feminists fail to take account of the many differences among women, focusing only on how all women are different from men. To focus on "woman" as a unitary category is to define her in some essential way, to claim that all women are alike in some essential way.

Radical feminists respond to this challenge by denying the existence of a female essence. Radical feminists embrace totally the claim that women are socially constructed. They do not believe that by deconstructing her we will find some underlying true essence. Rather they believe that by challenging the male construction of the category "woman," we can begin to construct our own category. We may not be able to free ourselves from socially constructed categories, but a woman-defined "woman" is at least an improvement over the present state of affairs.

3. *Cultural Feminism.* Cultural feminists,[25] like radical feminists, focus on woman's difference from man. Cultural feminists, however, unlike their radical sisters, embrace woman's difference. Carol Gilligan, for example, argues that women, because of their different life experiences, speak in a "different voice" from their male counterparts. Gilligan identifies the female voice with caring and relationships. Woman's moral vision encompasses this different voice. Woman's difference is good.

Feminists in the Gilligan camp are interested in changing institutions to give equal weight to woman's moral voice. They argue that the category "woman" has not been so much misdefined by men, as it has been ignored and undervalued. Yes, women are nurturing. Yes, women value personal relationships. These attributes are to be valued. Using equality rhetoric, cultural feminists argue for material changes in present conditions that would support woman-valued relationships. . . .

I have defined cultural feminism to include feminists who ascribe fully to the social construction thesis. In such cases, the only difference between radical and cultural feminists is that radical feminists have chosen to emphasize in their theory a negative aspect of "woman"—her sexual objectification—whereas, cultural feminists emphasize a positive aspect—her special bond to others. Because their emphasis is different, radical and cultural feminists may contribute differently to the project of self-definition.[26]

---

25. Although I am carving out cultural feminists as a separate category from radical feminists, the categories are not so easily divided as my taxonomy may suggest. Cultural feminism, as I use the phrase, is often described as relational feminism; that is, feminists who focus on women's relationships. . . .

26. Radical feminists can fight against the sexual objectification of woman without intentionally creating a positive concept of woman as sexual subject. And cultural feminists can fight to protect woman's special bond to others without intentionally adopting the definition of

Some cultural feminists, however, can be understood to support the concept that "woman," although currently constructed in a certain way, has a discoverable natural essence. Whether viewed as natural or socially constructed, woman's capacity for caring and connection has provided substance for an interesting debate between radical feminist MacKinnon and cultural feminist Gilligan. Gilligan's work encourages us to value woman's view of herself and the world around her. MacKinnon, however, is suspicious of this "different voice." This voice, after all, has been constructed in response to the patriarchy. For those who subscribe to the social construction thesis, the voice is just another voice of the patriarchy. Alternatively, if there is such a thing as a natural or authentic "woman," how can we know that this is her voice? MacKinnon argues that until women cease to be victims of subordination they cannot speak for themselves.

This argument has a certain Catch-22 effect. Woman-identified values, such as caring and connection to others, are suspect because they are values that women have created in response to the patriarchy. We value caring because that is what our oppressors have caused us to value (because we define ourselves in relation to our oppressors, we aren't really engaging in self-definition). But if all women are victims of the patriarchy, how can any woman ever claim knowledge of what is truly in woman's best interest? How can we know that any equality arguments will further the best interests of women?

There must be some way to free ourselves sufficiently from the patriarchy to engage in the project of self-definition. Feminist theorists outside the field of law have argued in favor of separatism at least as an interim step in creating a woman-defined "woman." But legal theorists have been obsessed with equality, a concept which is inconsistent with separatism.

4. Postmodern Feminism. Postmodern feminists eschew the idea of unitary truth, of objective reality. They readily admit that categories, especially gender categories, are mere social constructs. Equality, too, is a social construct. It is true that these constructs, as products of the patriarchy, are in need of a feminist reconstruction. But postmodern feminism tells us to beware of searching for a new truth to replace the old. There simply is no such thing as the essential "woman." There is no such thing as the woman's point of view. There is no single theory of equality that will work for the benefit of all women. Indeed, there is probably no single change or goal that is in the best interest of all women.

Some would argue that the concept "postmodern feminism" is an oxymoron. It is a phrase that combines two concepts—postmodernism and feminism—that cannot logically coexist. For if postmodernism views the category "woman" as being so multifarious that it denies unitariness, how can it ever ascribe to be feminist, since feminism is a theory that focuses on the unitary category "woman"? My own answer to this supposed conundrum is that postmodern feminism does not focus on the category "woman." Rather, it focuses on the situated realities of women, plural. Postmodern feminists ques-

"woman" as archetypical nurturer. Yet, in both cases, legal arguments produce rhetoric that shape our future reality. Some forms of feminist argument may reshape our concept of men more than our concept of "woman." I have in mind MacKinnon's arguments that men have all the power and that men abuse women.

tion earlier feminist attempts to redefine the category "woman." Any definition, even one articulated by feminists, is limiting and serves to "tie the individual to her identity as a woman." Furthermore, feminists who support any single definition of "woman" are viewed by postmodernists as tending toward essentialism.

One need not embrace postmodernism completely to criticize the tendency toward essentialism found in radical and cultural feminist writings. Wendy Williams, usually viewed as a liberal feminist, has raised concerns about the homogeneity of certain feminist concepts of "woman." Similarly, Angela Harris has argued that the meta-theories of gender constructed by Catharine MacKinnon and Robin West rely on a concept of "woman" that has been abstracted from the experience of white women. I have made a similar claim that the "woman" constructed by these theorists also appears to be heterosexual. If feminists are fighting for maximum liberation, then equality arguments and theories aimed primarily at white heterosexual women will not accomplish that task.

At the same time, postmodern thought poses a certain dilemma. Any theory requires some degree of abstraction and generalization. Thus, if feminists embrace the particular situated realities of all individual women, plural, we will find it difficult to build a theory, singular, to combat oppression.

Patricia Cain, Feminism and the Limits of Equality, 24 Ga. L. Rev. 803, 829-39 (1990).

5. *The Complaint: Feminist Theory.* Most of the analyses developed by the differing schools of feminist thought focus on issues of gender, leaving the implication that the other social categories are unnecessary for analyzing women's lives and experiences. The following three excerpts show why an analysis that fails to address the interlocking systems of oppression is incomplete.

(a) *The Silencing of Racial and Ethnic Differences.*

(In the voice of a white/Anglo woman who has been teaching and writing about feminist theory)[27]

[W]hat more exactly is the feminist demand that the woman's voice be heard? There are several crucial notes to make about it. First of all, the demand grows out of a complaint, and in order to understand the scope and focus of the demand we have to look at the scope and focus of the complaint. The complaint does not specify *which* women have been silenced, and in one way this is appropriate to the conditions it is a complaint about: virtually no women have had a voice, whatever their race, class, ethnicity, religion, sexual alliance, whatever place and period in history they lived. And if it is as women that women have been silenced, then of course the demand

27. The authors describe the process of thinking, talking and writing together. They stated that "[i]n the process of our talking and writing together, we saw that the differences between us did not permit our speaking in one voice. . . .Thus the use of two voices is central both to the process of constructing this paper and to the substance of it." María C. Lugones & Elizabeth V. Spelman, Have We Got a Theory for You! Feminist Theory, Cultural Imperialism and the Demand for "The Woman's Voice," 6 Women's Stud. F. 573, 573 (1983). Eds.

must be that women as women have a voice. But in another way the complaint is very misleading, insofar as it suggests that it is women as women who have been silenced, and that whether a woman is rich or poor, Black, brown or white, etc. is irrelevant to what it means for her to be a woman. For the demand thus simply made ignores at least two related points: (1) it is only possible for a woman who does not feel highly vulnerable with respect to other parts of her identity, e.g. race, class, ethnicity, religion, sexual alliance, etc., to conceive of her voice simply or essentially as a 'woman's voice'; (2) just because not all women are equally vulnerable with respect to race, class, etc., some women's voices are more likely to be heard than others by those who have heretofore been giving—or silencing—the accounts of women's lives. For all these reasons, the women's voices most likely to come forth and the women's voices most likely to be heard are, in the U.S. anyway, those of white, middle-class, heterosexual Christian (or anyway not self-identified non-Christian) women. Indeed, many Hispanas, Black women, Jewish women—to name a few groups—have felt it an invitation to silence rather than speech to be requested—if they are requested at all—to speak about being 'women' (with the plain wrapper—as if there were one) in distinction from speaking about being Hispana, Black, Jewish, working-class, etc., women. . . .

(In an Hispana voice)

I think it necessary to explain why in so many cases when women of color appear in front of white/Anglo women to talk about feminism and women of color, we mainly raise a complaint: the complaint of exclusion, of silencing, of being included in a universe we have not chosen. We usually raise the complaint with a certain amount of disguised or undisguised anger. I can only attempt to explain this phenomenon from a Hispanic viewpoint and a fairly narrow one at that: the viewpoint of an Argentinian woman who has lived in the US for 16 yr. who has attempted to come to terms with the devaluation of things Hispanic and Hispanic people in 'America' and who is most familiar with Hispano life in the Southwest of the US. I am quite unfamiliar with daily Hispano life in the urban centers, though not with some of the themes and some of the salient experiences of urban Hispano life. . . .

We and you do not talk the same language. When we talk to you we use your language: the language of your experience and of your theories. We try to use it to communicate our world of experience. But since your language and your theories are inadequate in expressing our experiences, we only succeed in communicating our experience of exclusion. We cannot talk to you in our language because you do not understand it. So the brute facts that we understand your language and that the place where most theorizing about women is taking place is your place, both combine to require that we either use your language and distort our experience not just in the speaking about it, but in the living of it, or that we remain silent. . . .

[Y]ou theorize about women and we are women, so you understand yourselves to be theorizing about us and we understand you to be theorizing about us. Yet none of the feminist theories developed so far seem to me to help Hispanas in the articulation of our experience. We have a sense that in using them we are distorting our experiences. Most Hispanas cannot even understand the language used in these theories—and only in some cases the reason is that the Hispana cannot understand English. We do not recognize ourselves in these theories. They create in us a schizophrenic split between our concern for ourselves as women and ourselves as Hispanas, one that we do not feel otherwise. Thus they seem to us to force us to assimilate to some version of Anglo culture, however revised that version may be. They seem to ask that we leave our communities or that we become alienated so completely in them that we feel hollow. When we see that you feel alienated in your own communities, this confuses us because we think that maybe every feminist has to suffer this alienation. But we see that recognition of your alienation leads many of you to be empowered into the remaking of your culture, while we are paralyzed into a state of displacement with no place to go.

María C. Lugones & Elizabeth V. Spelman, Have We Got a Theory for You! Feminist Theory, Cultural Imperialism and the Demand for "The Woman's Voice," 6 Women's Stud. F. 573, 573–76 (1983).

(b) *The Silencing of Lesbians.*

If feminist legal theory is derived from a feminist method uninformed by critical lesbian experience, the theory will be incomplete. Lesbian experience is essential to the formation of feminist theory because it stands in opposition to the institution of heterosexuality, which is a core element of male-centered reality. To the extent feminist legal theory seeks to challenge the male view of reality, it cannot afford to ignore lesbian experience. . . .

It is not enough to name the differences of race, class, and sexuality. The differences need to be understood. Much recent feminist legal scholarship includes the perfunctory footnote, dropped the first time the essential category "woman" is mentioned, which acknowledges the differences of race and class, and sometimes of sexual preference. Such politically correct footnotes name the differences, but I see no evidence in the accompanying texts that the differences matter. Scholarship that nominally recognizes differences, but still categorizes "woman" from a single perspective is stuck in the assimilationist/essentialist trap. . . .

My "lesbian standpoint" enables me to see two versions of reality. The dominant reality, which I experience as "theirs," includes the following: lesbians are not mothers, all women are dominated by men, male relationships are valuable and female relationships are not, lesbian is a dirty word, lesbians are sick, women who live alone desire men, women who live together desire men, no one knows a lesbian, lesbians don't have families, all feminist legal theorists are heterosexual, all women in this room are heterosexual, lesbians are sex, most women are heterosexual and not lesbian.

By contrast, the reality that I live, the reality I call "mine," includes the following: some mothers are lesbian, many women are lesbian, many lesbian women are not dominated by men, many women do not desire men, lesbian is a beautiful word, lesbians are love, love is intimacy, the heterosexual/lesbian dichotomy is false, all lesbians are born into families, lesbians are family, some feminist legal theorists are lesbian, lesbians are brave.

Patricia Cain, Feminist Jurisprudence: Grounding the Theories, 4 Berkeley Women's L.J. 191, 191-92, 206, 213-14 (1989).

(c) *The Silencing of Disabled Women.*

There are essentially two theoretical frameworks for understanding the concept of disability. The first may be described as the individualistic perspective, in which disability is interpreted as a deviation from accepted or expected notions of normality, the differentness is regarded as a personal tragedy which the individual must seek to 'come to terms with'. Stereotypes of passivity and childlike dependency are created for members of the 'disabled' and, at the same time, roles are prescribed which render us powerless. To avoid embarrassment and inconvenience to the nondisabled world, an emphasis is placed on accepting the goal of normality. . . .The individual perspective of disability makes no attempt to examine the social, economic and political perspectives which influence the lives of disabled people. Therefore an alternative framework re-defining disability as a form of social oppression has been put forward by disabled people: disability is a form of social oppression which is articulated through prevailing ideological, social and political determinants and, as a consequence of these, disabled people are socially excluded and handicapism is constructed. . . .

Although disability may be the predominant characteristic by which a disabled person is labelled, it is essential to recognize that gender influences play an important role in determining how that person's disability is perceived and reacted to. . . .Both disability and gender are understood as socially constructed classifications, the impact of each may be mitigated or exacerbated according to whether the individual can be identified with an alternative social group which is perceived to be inferior. . . .Both roles available to disabled women label us as inferior, passive and weak. . . .Disabled women have become perennial outsiders, our powerless position has not been seriously addressed by either the disability rights or the women's movement. This simultaneous neglect is unforgivable; the exclusion on the basis of gender or disability cannot be defended by groups which purport to express the demands of all those who are ascribed membership to them by virtue of a particular biological criterion. . . .

There are certain aspects of women's oppression which highlight the parallels and the differences between disabled women and nondisabled women. The basic issues may be the same for both groups but the impact of disability means that the implications or effects may differ.

Nasa Begum, Disabled Women and the Feminist Agenda, 40 Feminist Rev. 70, 71-73 (1992).

Loving v. Virginia,

388 U.S. 1 (1967)

Chief Justice Warren delivered the opinion of the Court. This case presents a constitutional question never addressed by this Court: whether a statutory scheme adopted by the State of Virginia to prevent marriages between persons solely on the basis of racial classifications violates the Equal Protection and Due Process Clauses of the Fourteenth Amendment. . . .

In June 1958, two residents of Virginia, Mildred Jeter, a Negro woman, and

Richard Loving, a white man, were married in the District of Columbia pursuant to its laws. Shortly after their marriage, the Lovings returned to Virginia and established their marital abode in Caroline County. At the October Term, 1958, of the Circuit Court of Caroline County, a grand jury issued an indictment charging the Lovings with violating Virginia's ban on interracial marriages. On January 6, 1959, the Lovings pleaded guilty to the charge and were sentenced to one year in jail; however, the trial judge suspended the sentence for a period of 25 years on the condition that the Lovings leave the State and not return to Virginia together for 25 years. He stated in an opinion that:

> "Almighty God created the races white, black, yellow, malay and red, and he placed them on separate continents. And but for the interference with his arrangement there would be no cause for such marriages. The fact that he separated the races shows that he did not intend for the races to mix."

After their convictions, the Lovings took up residence in the District of Columbia. On November 6, 1963, they filed a motion in the state trial court to vacate the judgment and set aside the sentence on the ground that the statutes which they had violated were repugnant to the Fourteenth Amendment. The motion not having been decided by October 28, 1964, the Lovings instituted a class action in the United States District Court for the Eastern District of Virginia requesting that a three-judge court be convened to declare the Virginia antimiscegenation statutes unconstitutional and to enjoin state officials from enforcing their convictions. On January 22, 1965, the state trial judge denied the motion to vacate the sentences, and the Lovings perfected an appeal to the Supreme Court of Appeals of Virginia. On February 11, 1965, the three-judge District Court continued the case to allow the Lovings to present their constitutional claims to the highest state court.

The Supreme Court of Appeals upheld the constitutionality of the antimiscegenation statutes and, after modifying the sentence, affirmed the convictions.[28] The Lovings appealed this decision. . . .

The two statutes under which appellants were convicted and sentenced are part of a comprehensive statutory scheme aimed at prohibiting and punishing interracial marriages. The Lovings were convicted of violating § 20-58 of the Virginia Code:

> "*Leaving State to evade law.* If any white person and colored person shall go out of this State, for the purpose of being married, and with the intention of returning, and be married out of it, and afterwards return to and reside in it, cohabiting as man and wife, they shall be punished as provided in § 20-59, and the marriage shall be governed by the same law as if it had been solemnized in this State. The fact of their cohabitation here as man and wife shall be evidence of their marriage."

Section 20-59, which defines the penalty for miscegenation, provides:

> "*Punishment for marriage.* If any white person intermarry with a colored person, or any colored person intermarry with a white person, he shall be guilty

28. 206 Va. 924, 147 S.E.2d 78 (1966).

> of a felony and shall be punished by confinement in the penitentiary for not less than one nor more than five years."

Other central provisions in the Virginia statutory scheme are § 20-57, which automatically voids all marriages between "a white person and a colored person" without any judicial proceeding,[29] and §§ 20-54 and 1-14 which, respectively, define "white persons" and "colored persons and Indians" for purposes of the statutory prohibitions.[30] The Lovings have never disputed in the course of this litigation that Mrs. Loving is a "colored person" or that Mr. Loving is a "white person" within the meanings given those terms by the Virginia statutes.

Virginia is now one of 16 States which prohibit and punish marriages on the basis of racial classifications. . . .Penalties for miscegenation arose as an incident to slavery and have been common in Virginia since the colonial period. . . .The present statutory scheme dates from the adoption of the Racial Integrity Act of 1924, passed during the period of extreme nativism which followed the end of the First World War. The central features of this Act, and current Virginia law, are the absolute prohibition of a "white person" marrying other than another "white person,". . .a prohibition against issuing marriage licenses until the issuing official is satisfied that the applicants' statements as to their race are correct,. . .certificates of "racial composition" to be kept by both local and state registrars,. . .and the carrying forward of earlier prohibitions against racial intermarriage. . . .

[T]he State argues that the meaning of the Equal Protection Clause, as

---

29. Section 20-57 of the Virginia Code provides: "*Marriages void without decree.* All marriages between a white person and a colored person shall be absolutely void without any decree of divorce or other legal process." Va. Code Ann. § 20-57 (1960 Repl. Vol.).

30. Section 20-54 of the Virginia Code provides:

"*Intermarriage prohibited; meaning of term 'white persons.'* It shall hereafter be unlawful for any white person in this State to marry any save a white person, or a person with no other admixture of blood than white and American Indian. For the purpose of this chapter, the term 'white person' shall apply only to such person as has no trace whatever of any blood other than Caucasian; but persons who have one-sixteenth or less of the blood of the American Indian and have no other non-Caucasic blood shall be deemed to be white persons. All laws heretofore passed and now in effect regarding the intermarriage of white and colored persons shall apply to marriages prohibited by this chapter." Va. Code Ann. § 20-54 (1960 Repl. Vol.).

The exception for persons with less than one-sixteenth "of the blood of the American-Indian" is apparently accounted for, in the words of a tract issued by the Registrar of the State Bureau of Vital Statistics, by "the desire of all to recognize as an integral and honored part of the white race the descendants of John Rolfe and Pocahontas. . . ." Walter Ashby Plecker, The New Family and Race Improvement, 17 Va. Health Bull., Extra No. 12, at 25-26 (New Family Series No. 5, 1925), cited in Walter Wadlington, The *Loving* Case: Virginia's Anti-Miscegenation Statute in Historical Perspective, 52 Va. L. Rev. 1189, 1202, n.93 (1966).

Section 1-14 of the Virginia Code provides:

"*Colored persons and Indians defined.* Every person in whom there is ascertainable any Negro blood shall be deemed and taken to be a colored person, and every person not a colored person having one fourth or more of American Indian blood shall be deemed an American Indian; except that members of Indian tribes existing in this Commonwealth having one fourth or more of Indian blood and less than one sixteenth of Negro blood shall be deemed tribal Indians." Va. Code Ann. § 1-14 (1960 Repl. Vol.).

illuminated by the statements of the Framers, is only that state penal laws containing an interracial element as part of the definition of the offense must apply equally to whites and Negroes in the sense that members of each race are punished to the same degree. Thus, the State contends that, because its miscegenation statutes punish equally both the white and the Negro participants in an interracial marriage, these statutes, despite their reliance on racial classifications, do not constitute an invidious discrimination based upon race. The second argument advanced by the State assumes the validity of its equal application theory. The argument is that, if the Equal Protection Clause does not outlaw miscegenation statutes because of their reliance on racial classifications, the question of constitutionality would thus become whether there was any rational basis for a State to treat interracial marriages differently from other marriages. On this question, the State argues, the scientific evidence is substantially in doubt and, consequently, this Court should defer to the wisdom of the state legislature in adopting its policy of discouraging interracial marriages.

Because we reject the notion that the mere "equal application" of a statute containing racial classifications is enough to remove the classifications from the Fourteenth Amendment's proscription of all invidious racial discriminations, we do not accept the State's contention that these statutes should be upheld if there is any possible basis for concluding that they serve a rational purpose. The mere fact of equal application does not mean that our analysis of these statutes should follow the approach we have taken in cases involving no racial discrimination. . . .In the case at bar. . .we deal with statutes containing racial classifications, and the fact of equal application does not immunize the statute from the very heavy burden of justification which the Fourteenth Amendment has traditionally required of state statutes drawn according to race.

The State argues that statements in the Thirty-ninth Congress about the time of the passage of the Fourteenth Amendment indicate that the Framers did not intend the Amendment to make unconstitutional state miscegenation laws. Many of the statements alluded to by the State concern the debates over the Freedmen's Bureau Bill, which President Johnson vetoed, and the Civil Rights Act of 1866, 14 Stat. 27, enacted over his veto. While these statements have some relevance to the intention of Congress in submitting the Fourteenth Amendment, it must be understood that they pertained to the passage of specific statutes and not to the broader, organic purpose of a constitutional amendment. As for the various statements directly concerning the Fourteenth Amendment, we have said in connection with a related problem, that although these historical sources "cast some light" they are not sufficient to resolve the problem; "[a]t best, they are inconclusive. The most avid proponents of the post-War Amendments undoubtedly intended them to remove all legal distinctions among 'all persons born or naturalized in the United States.' Their opponents, just as certainly, were antagonistic to both the letter and the spirit of the Amendments and wished them to have the most limited effect." *Brown v. Board of Education*, 347 U.S. 483, 489 (1954). . . .We have rejected the proposition that the debates in the Thirty-ninth Congress or in the state legislatures which ratified the Fourteenth Amendment supported the theory advanced by the State, that the requirement of equal protection of the laws is satisfied by penal laws defining offenses based on racial classifications so long as white and Negro participants in the offense were similarly punished. *McLaughlin v. Florida*, 379 U.S. 184 (1964).

The State finds support for its "equal application" theory in the decision of the Court in *Pace v. Alabama*, 106 U.S. 583 (1883). In that case, the Court upheld a conviction under an Alabama statute forbidding adultery or fornication between a white person and a Negro which imposed a greater penalty than that of a statute proscribing similar conduct by members of the same race. The Court reasoned that the statute could not be said to discriminate against Negroes because the punishment for each participant in the offense was the same. However, as recently as the 1964 Term, in rejecting the reasoning of that case, we stated "*Pace* represents a limited view of the Equal Protection Clause which has not withstood analysis in the subsequent decisions of this Court." *McLaughlin v. Florida*, *supra*, at 188. As we there demonstrated, the Equal Protection Clause requires the consideration of whether the classifications drawn by any statute constitute an arbitrary and invidious discrimination. The clear and central purpose of the Fourteenth Amendment was to eliminate all official state sources of invidious racial discrimination in the States. *Slaughter-House Cases*, 16 Wall. 36, 71 (1873) . . . .

There can be no question but that Virginia's miscegenation statutes rest solely upon distinctions drawn according to race. The statutes proscribe generally accepted conduct if engaged in by members of different races. Over the years, this Court has consistently repudiated "[d]istinctions between citizens solely because of their ancestry" as being "odious to a free people whose institutions are founded upon the doctrine of equality." *Hirabayashi v. United States*, 320 U.S. 81, 100 (1943). At the very least, the Equal Protection Clause demands that racial classifications, especially suspect in criminal statutes, be subjected to the "most rigid scrutiny," *Korematsu v. United States*, 323 U.S. 214, 216 (1944), and, if they are ever to be upheld, they must be shown to be necessary to the accomplishment of some permissible state objective, independent of the racial discrimination which it was the object of the Fourteenth Amendment to eliminate. Indeed, two members of this Court have already stated that they "cannot conceive of a valid legislative purpose. . .which makes the color of a person's skin the test of whether his conduct is a criminal offense." *McLaughlin v. Florida*, *supra*, at 198 (Stewart, J., joined by Douglas, J., concurring).

There is patently no legitimate overriding purpose independent of invidious racial discrimination which justifies this classification. The fact that Virginia prohibits only interracial marriages involving white persons demonstrates that the racial classifications must stand on their own justification, as measures designed to maintain White Supremacy.[31] We have consistently denied the

---

31. Appellants point out that the State's concern in these statutes, as expressed in the words of the 1924 Act's title, "An Act to Preserve Racial Integrity," extends only to the integrity of the white race. While Virginia prohibits whites from marrying any nonwhite (subject to the exception for the descendants of Pocahontas), Negroes, Orientals, and any other racial class may intermarry without statutory interference. Appellants contend that this distinction renders Virginia's miscegenation statutes arbitrary and unreasonable even assuming the constitutional validity of an official purpose to preserve "racial integrity." We need not reach this contention because we find the racial classifications in these statutes repugnant to the Fourteenth Amendment, even assuming an even-handed state purpose to protect the "integrity" of all races.

constitutionality of measures which restrict the rights of citizens on account of race. There can be no doubt that restricting the freedom to marry solely because of racial classifications violates the central meaning of the Equal Protection Clause. . . .

These statutes also deprive the Lovings of liberty without due process of law in violation of the Due Process Clause of the Fourteenth Amendment. The freedom to marry has long been recognized as one of the vital personal rights essential to the orderly pursuit of happiness by free men.

Marriage is one of the "basic civil rights of man," fundamental to our very existence and survival. *Skinner v. Oklahoma*, 316 U.S. 535, 541 (1942). . . .To deny this fundamental freedom on so unsupportable a basis as the racial classifications embodied in these statutes, classifications so directly subversive of the principle of equality at the heart of the Fourteenth Amendment, is surely to deprive all the State's citizens of liberty without due process of law. The Fourteenth Amendment requires that the freedom of choice to marry not be restricted by invidious racial discriminations. Under our Constitution, the freedom to marry or not marry, a person of another race resides with the individual and cannot be infringed by the State.

These convictions must be reversed. *It is so ordered.*

Justice Stewart, concurring. I have previously expressed the belief that "it is simply not possible for a state law to be valid under our Constitution which makes the criminality of an act depend upon the race of the actor." *McLaughlin v. Florida*, 379 U.S. 184, 198 (concurring opinion). Because I adhere to that belief, I concur in the judgment of the Court.

Notes and Questions

1. *Twenty-Five Years after Loving.*

> Mildred Jeter Loving is now a widow, the marriage that made her famous having ended in tragedy. But she remains the same intensely private woman she was a quarter-century ago, when her name entered the lawbooks, and she is as reluctant to acknowledge her contribution to the civil rights movement as she once was to participate in it.
>
> In the wee hours of one morning in July 1958, the quiet life that Mrs. Loving and her husband, Richard, enjoyed in this remote hamlet was shattered when three law officers opened the unlocked door of their home, walked into their bedroom and shined a flashlight on the couple. What they saw confirmed what they had been told: Mrs. Loving was black and Mr. Loving white, making their marriage illegal in Virginia.
>
> "What are you doing in bed with this lady?" Sheriff R. Garnett Brooks of Caroline County asked Mr. Loving, who was 24 years old at the time. Mr. Loving pointed to the wall where the couple had hung their marriage certificate, from the District of Columbia. "That's no good here," Sheriff Brooks replied. He charged the couple with unlawful cohabitation, carted them into nearby Bowling Green and threw them into the county jail. . . .
>
> The county circuit judge, Leon M. Bazile, sentenced the Lovings to a year in prison. . . .But the judge offered the Lovings a deal: they could go free as

long as they promised to steer clear of Virginia, at least as man and wife, for the next 25 years. . . .

[F]or Mrs. Loving, whose husband was killed in an automobile accident in 1975, the blazing legal trails was an experience she would gladly have forgone. The ordeal—which included five days in jail and banishment to a place where she could no longer walk down a country lane to pick up her mail—is one she revisits only reluctantly.

"It was thrown in my lap," she said about the case. "What choice did I have?"

Mrs. Loving, fingering a crumpled paper napkin at her kitchen table, continued, "We weren't bothering anyone, and if we were hurting somebody's feelings, too bad.". . .

The High Court's decision, which Mrs. Loving said she never read, allowed her, her husband and their three young children, who were considered illegitimate under the law, to live in Virginia in peace and to begin building the simple white cinderblock house in which Mrs. Loving still lives, a mile and a half from where the sheriff and his deputies rousted them. . . .

But while laws can be changed by judicial fiat or the stroke of a pen, attitudes cannot, particularly racial attitudes among some people in an area where storied names from the Confederate past—A. P. Hill and Stonewall Jackson, Spottsylvania Court House and Chancellorsville—pop up alongside Golden Arches and Texaco stars.

In the 34 years since the raid, Mr. Brooks and Mrs. Loving have not exchanged a single word. Mrs. Loving said she sees him occasionally, including once last week while he was cutting his grass, but steers clear of him. Mr. Brooks said he would not know Mrs. Loving if he saw her. But he made clear he had no qualms about his actions.

"I was acting according to the law at the time, and I still think it should be on the books," said Sheriff Brooks, sitting with his wife on the porch of his home in Bowling Green. "I don't think a white person should marry a black person. I'm from the old school. The Lord made sparrows and robins, not to mix with one another."

Mr. Brooks said he had rarely pondered the case in the last 35 years. "If they'd been outstanding people, I would have thought something about it," he said. "But with the caliber of those people, it didn't matter. They were both low-class."

Robert D. McIlawin 3d of Petersburg, Va., who as an assistant State Attorney General argued before the Supreme Court that Virginia's anti-miscegenation law served the same public health interests as laws barring polygamy, incest and marriages between retarded people, also said he has thought little about the case since it was handed down. "Nobody even remembers it," he said. "It's a footnote to history."

Even in Caroline County, an area known for relatively benign race relations and a high degree of racial commingling, Richard Loving and Mildred Jeter, who grew up seven miles apart, attended different churches and schools. But their families were friendly, and when he was 17 and she was 11, they began courting. But when thoughts turned to marriage, the statute stood in the way. . . .

Thus, when the Lovings decided to marry in June 1958, they went to Washington. After the raid, the two lived separately with their parents until January 1959, when Judge Bazile offered them exile as an alternative to incarceration.

"Each one of them can come to Caroline separately to visit his or her people as often as they please," he ruled. The couple moved to Washington.

It was in that time that Mr. Loving's cousin suggested she write the Attorney General of the United States. "I was crying the blues all the time, so she said, 'Why don't you write Robert Kennedy?'" she recalled. "She said that's what he's there for."

Mr. Kennedy told the Lovings to contact the American Civil Liberties Union, she said, and the group placed two lawyers from Alexandria, Va., Philip J. Hirschkop and Bernard S. Cohen, on the case.

The two men paid a price for their part in legal history. There were cold shoulders from some disapproving bar colleagues, nasty anonymous telephone calls, disparaging references to "two Jew lawyers" in the Ku Klux Klan newspaper and sugar dumped into the gasoline tanks of family cars.

From 1963 until 1967 the case bounced around the courts. . . .

Mr. Cohen, now a member of Virginia's House of Delegates, recalled how, before oral arguments, he explained various constitutional doctrines to Mr. Loving. "That stuff don't mean nothing to me," Mr. Loving told him. "Mr. Cohen, tell the Court I love my wife, and it is just unfair that I can't live with her in Virginia."

Peggy Loving Fortune, at 32 the youngest of the Lovings' three children, is married to a man of mixed parentage. By challenging the law, she said, her parents had made things "a whole lot easier" for people of such backgrounds.

"I'm very proud of them," she said. "To me, they set the world free to be with whomever they want. I feel it's what they were put on this earth for, that God used them to do what they did."

Mrs. Loving makes no such claims about her role, but agrees that things have improved. "A few are still very hostile, but attitudes toward people have really changed," she said. "The Old South is going away."

David Margolick, A Mixed Marriage's 25th Anniversary of Legality, N.Y. Times, June 12, 1992, at B20.

2. *Social Construction of Race*. In an essay exploring the legislative history surrounding the passage of the Virginia Racial Integrity Act of 1924, the act that was struck down in *Loving*, Paul Lombardo describes a change in the bill's definition of the white race:

> The Bill originally included a provision exempting persons with less than one sixty-fourth of American Indian blood from the prohibition of marriage with whites. This fractional exception was increased to one-sixteenth as a means of honoring the descendants of John Rolfe and Pocahontas. Apparently some of the "first families" of Virginia took exception to the use of their distant Indian heritage to exclude them from the white race.

Paul A. Lombardo, Miscegenation, Eugenics, and Racism: Historical Footnotes to *Loving v. Virginia*, 21 U.C. Davis L. Rev. 421, 434 (1988). This statutory change demonstrates that race is "not a naturally given and naturally maintained grouping of human individuals with naturally determined sets of traits." Marilyn Frye, White Woman Feminist, in Willful Virgin: Essays in Feminism 1976-1992, at 147, 150 (1992). It provides a clear example of how whites construct race through the law to serve their interests.

3. *Historical Context of Miscegenation.* As Carrie Costello shows, science and politics combined to fuel "antimiscegenist fervor" after the Civil War.

> The term "miscegenation" first appeared in a counterfeit Republican pamphlet in 1864.[32] The spurious pamphlet, which was widely circulated, purported to advocate miscegenation as a means of eliminating racial problems.[33]. . .
>
> Antimiscegenist fervor was born soon after the abolitionist movement and became terribly potent. . . .
>
> After the Civil War. . .[a]ntimiscegenationist sentiment moved from being the province of firebrands to permeating the respectable institutions employed. . .to define social reality. . . .In the early twentieth century, biologists, sociologists, anthropologists, and other scientists made scientific racism an urgently developed field of "rational" study.[34] Politicians were equally active, passing dozens of antimiscegenation statutes on the local and state level both inside and outside of the South, with a peak in the amount of legislation in 1913. Bills banning interracial marriage in Washington, D.C. passed the U.S. House in 1913 and 1915, and continued to be introduced periodically until 1927. . . .
>
> In 1930, thirty American states had antimiscegenation laws on their books. In 1967,. . .sixteen states had intermarriage bans in force.

Carrie G. Costello, Legitimate Bonds and Unnatural Unions: Race, Sexual Orientation, and Control of the American Family, 15 Harv. Women's L.J. 79, 109-11, 119 (1992).

How do antimiscegenation laws contribute to violence against women?

4. *Racial and Sexual Politics.* Patricia Hill Collins examines the relationships of African-American women with African-American men, with whites, and with one another. Her analysis provides an important perspective for

---

32. The pamphlet was entitled "Miscegenation, the Theory of the Blending of the Races, Applied to the American White Man and Negro," and was published in New York by David Croly and George Wakeman, an editor and a reporter for the New York World. David H. Fowler, Northern Attitudes Towards Interracial Marriage: Legislation and Public Opinion in the Middle Atlantic and the States of the Old Northwest 1780-1930, at 204-05 (1987).

33. *Id.* The pamphlet was intended to stir antiabolitionist sentiment by exploiting racism in order to damage the Republican party.

34. In the late nineteenth and early twentieth centuries, the eugenics movement became influential in the United States. Based on a distorted application of genetic theory, eugenicists promoted the reproduction of the "highly developed" Western European races and discouraged reproduction among those seen as less fit. The eugenics movement attempted to promote its theory of social engineering through various legal enactments, *i.e.*, restrictive immigration laws as well as sterilization statutes. Eds.

thinking about antimiscegenation laws historically and the links between race, sexuality, and power in contemporary thought and culture.

One key issue for Black feminist thought is the need to examine the processes by which power as domination on the social structural level—namely, institutional structures of racism, sexism, and social class privilege—annexes this basic power of the erotic on the personal level—that is, the construct of power as energy, for its own ends. . . .

"White men use different forms of enforcing oppression of white women and of women of Color," argues Chicana scholar Aida Hurtado. "As a consequence, these groups of women have different political responses and skills, and at times these differences cause the two groups to clash." For Black women the historical relationship with white men has been one of rejection: white men have exploited, objectified, and rejected African-American women. Because white male power is largely predicated on Black female subordination, few delusions of sharing that power and enjoying the privileges attached to white male power have existed among Black women. In contrast, white women have been offered a share of white male power, but only if they agree to be subordinate. "Sometimes I really feel more sorrier for the white woman than I feel for ourselves because she been caught up in this thing, caught up feeling very special," observes Fannie Lou Hamer. Thus "white women, as a group, are subordinated through seduction, women of Color, as a group, through rejection."

This historical legacy of rejection and seduction frames relationships among Black and white women. Black women often express anger and bitterness against white women for their history of excusing the transgressions of their sons, husbands, and fathers. In her diary a slaveholder described white women's widespread predilection to ignore white men's actions:

> Under slavery, we live surrounded by prostitutes. . . .Who thinks any worse of a negro or mulatto woman for being a thing we can't name? God forgive us, but ours is a monstrous system. . . .Like the patriarchs of old, our men live all in one house with their wives and their concubines; and the mulattoes one sees in every family partly resemble the white children. Any lady is ready to tell you who is the father of all the mulatto children in everybody's household but her own. Those, she seems to think drop from the clouds.

If white women under slavery could ignore actions of this magnitude, grappling with the subtleties of contemporary racism must present even more of a challenge for many white women.

For many African-American women, far too few white women are willing to acknowledge—let alone challenge—the actions of white men because they have benefited from them. Fannie Lou Hamer analyzes white women's culpability in Black women's subordination: "You've been caught up in this thing because, you know, you worked my grandmother, and after that you worked my mother, and then finally you got hold of me. And you really thought. . .you thought that you was *more* because you was a woman, and especially a white woman, you had this kind of angel feeling that you were untouchable."

White women's inability to acknowledge their own racism, especially how it privileges them, is another outcome of the differential relationship that white and Black women have to white male power. "I think whites are carefully taught not to recognize white privilege," argues white feminist scholar Peggy McIntosh, "just as males are taught not to recognize male privilege.". . .

Relationships among Black and white women are framed by the web of sexual politics that seduce white women with an artificial sense of specialness and vest them with the power to sustain that illusion. When white women come to accept Fannie Lou Hamer's analysis of the interlocking nature of race, class, and gender oppression, groundwork might be laid for better relationships:

> In the past, I don't care how poor this white woman was, in the South she still felt like she was more than us. In the North, I don't care how poor or how rich this white woman has been, she still felt like she was more than us. But coming to the realization of the thing, her freedom is shackled in chains to mine, and she realizes for the first time that she is not free until I am free.

The relationships among Black women and white men have long been constrained by the legacy of Black women's sexual abuse by white men and the unresolved tensions this creates. Traditionally, freedom for Black women has meant freedom *from* white men, not the freedom to choose white men as lovers and friends. Black women who have willingly chosen white male friends and lovers have been severely chastized in African-American communities for selling out the "race," or they are accused of being like prostitutes, demeaning themselves by willingly using white men for their own financial or social gain. . . .

In spite of the powerful restrictions imposed by the sex/gender hierarchy on interpersonal relationships, many African-American women refuse to "protect themselves and love small,"[35] and manage to form close, loving

35. This phrase refers to a scene between Sethe and Paul D in Toni Morrison's *Beloved* (1987), which Collins discussed earlier:

Sethe tells her friend Paul D how she felt after escaping from slavery:

> It was a kind of selfishness I never knew nothing about before. It felt good. Good and right. I was big, Paul D, and deep and wide and when I stretched out my arms all my children could get in between. I was *that* wide. Look like I loved em more after I got here. Or maybe I couldn't love em proper in Kentucky because they wasn't mine to love. But when I got here, when I jumped down off that wagon—there wasn't nobody in the world I couldn't love if I wanted to. You know what I mean? [Toni Morrison, Beloved 162 (1987).]

By distorting Sethe's ability to love her children "proper," slavery annexed Sethe's power as energy for its own ends. Her words touch a deep chord in Paul D, for he too remembers how slavery felt. His mental response to Sethe expresses the mechanisms used by systems of domination such as slavery in harnessing potential sources of power in a subordinated group:

> So you protected yourself and loved small. Picked the tiniest stars out of the sky to own; lay down with head twisted in order to see the loved one over the rim of the trench before you slept. Stole shy glances at her between the trees at chain-up. Grass blades, salamanders, spiders, woodpeckers, beetles, a kingdom of ants. Anything bigger wouldn't do. A woman, a child, a brother—a big love like that would split you wide open in Alfred, Georgia. He knew exactly what she meant: to get to a place where you could love anything you chose—not to need permission for desire—well, now, *that* was freedom. [*Id.*]

Patricia Hill Collins, Black Feminist Thought: Knowledge, Consciousness, and the Politics of Empowerment 181-82 (1991). Eds.

relationships with whites. But given the legacy of the sexual politics of Black womanhood, for large numbers of African-Americans, full human relationships with whites remain out of reach. . . .

"In order to perpetuate itself, every oppression must corrupt or distort those various sources of power within the culture of the oppressed that can provide energy for change."[36] The ability of social institutions such as pornography, prostitution, and rape to infuse the private domain of Black women's love relationships with Black men, with whites, and with one another typifies this process. The parallels between distortions of deep human feelings in racial oppression and of the distortions of the erotic in gender oppression are striking. Analysts of the interpersonal dynamics of racism point out that whites fear in Blacks those qualities they project onto Blacks that they most fear in themselves. By labeling Blacks as sexually animalistic and by dominating Blacks, whites in actuality aim to repress these dimensions of their own inner being. When men dominate women and accuse them of being sexually passive, the act of domination, from pressured sexual intercourse to rape, reduces male anxiety about male impotence, the ultimate sexual passivity. Similarly, the suppression of gays and lesbians symbolizes the repression of strong feelings for members of one's own gender, feelings this culture has sexualized and stigmatized in the overarching sex/gender hierarchy. All of these emotions—the fact that whites know that Blacks are human, the fact that men love women, and the fact that women have deep feelings for one another—must be distorted on the emotional level of the erotic in order for oppressive systems to endure. Sexuality and power on the personal level become wedded to the sex/gender hierarchy on the social structural level in order to ensure the smooth operation of race, gender, and class oppression.

Recognizing that corrupting and distorting basic feelings human beings have for one another lies at the heart of multiple systems of oppression opens up new possibilities for transformation and change.

Patricia Hill Collins, Black Feminist Thought: Knowledge, Consciousness, and the Politics of Empowerment 166, 189-92, 196-97 (1990).

5. *Rewriting Loving*. How would critical race and feminist theorists critique the *Loving* decision? How would the analysis of antimiscegenation laws change if the central focus of the inquiry were African-American women?

Bowers v. Hardwick,

478 U.S. 186 (1986)

Justice White delivered the opinion of the Court. In August 1982, respondent Hardwick (hereafter respondent) was charged with violating the Georgia statute criminalizing sodomy[37] by committing that act with another adult

---

36. Audre Lorde, Sister Outsider 53 (1984).

37. Georgia Code Ann. § 16-6-2 (1984) provides, in pertinent part, as follows:

"(a) A person commits the offense of sodomy when he performs or submits to any sexual act involving the sex organs of one person and the mouth or anus of another. . . ."

(b) A person convicted of the offense of sodomy shall be punished by imprisonment for not less than one nor more than 20 years. . . ."

male in the bedroom of respondent's home. After a preliminary hearing, the District Attorney decided not to present the matter to the grand jury unless further evidence developed.

Respondent then brought suit in the Federal District Court, challenging the constitutionality of the statute insofar as it criminalized consensual sodomy.[38] He asserted that he was a practicing homosexual, that the Georgia sodomy statute, as administered by the defendants, placed him in imminent danger of arrest, and that the statute for several reasons violates the Federal Constitution. The District Court granted the defendants' motion to dismiss for failure to state a claim. . . .

A divided panel of the Court of Appeals for the Eleventh Circuit reversed. . . .hold[ing] that the Georgia statute violated respondent's fundamental rights because his homosexual activity is a private and intimate association that is beyond the reach of state regulation by reason of the Ninth Amendment and the Due Process Clause of the Fourteenth Amendment. . . .

We agree with petitioner that the Court of Appeals erred, and hence reverse its judgment. . . .

This case does not require a judgment on whether laws against sodomy between consenting adults in general, or between homosexuals in particular, are wise or desirable. . . .The issue presented is whether the Federal Constitution confers a fundamental right upon homosexuals to engage in sodomy and hence invalidates the laws of the many States that still make such conduct illegal and have done so for a very long time. The case also calls for some judgment about the limits of the Court's role in carrying out its constitutional mandate.

We first register our disagreement with the Court of Appeals and with respondent that the Court's prior cases have construed the Constitution to confer a right of privacy that extends to homosexual sodomy and for all intents and purposes have decided this case. The reach of this line of cases was sketched in *Carey v. Population Services International*, 431 U.S. 678, 685 (1977). *Pierce v. Society of Sisters*, 268 U.S. 510 (1925), and *Meyer v. Nebraska*, 262 U.S. 390 (1923), were described as dealing with child rearing and education; *Prince v. Massachusetts*, 321 U.S. 158 (1944), with family relationships; *Skinner v. Oklahoma ex rel. Williamson*, 316 U.S. 535 (1942), with procreation; *Loving v. Virginia*, 388 U.S. 1 (1967), with marriage; *Griswold v. Connecticut*, 381 U.S. 479 (1965) and *Eisenstadt v. Baird*, 405 U.S. 438 (1972) with contraception; and *Roe v. Wade*, 410 U.S. 113 (1973), with abortion. The latter three cases were interpreted as construing the Due Process Clause of the

---

38. John and Mary Doe were also plaintiffs in the action. They alleged that they wished to engage in sexual activity proscribed by § 16-6-2 in the privacy of their home,. . .and that they had been "chilled and deterred" from engaging in such activity by both the existence of the statute and Hardwick's arrest. . . .The District Court held, however, that because they had neither sustained, nor were in immediate danger of sustaining, any direct injury from the enforcement of the statute, they did not have proper standing to maintain the action. . . .The Court of Appeals affirmed the District Court's judgment dismissing the Does' claim for lack of standing,. . .and the Does do not challenge that holding in this Court.

The only claim properly before the Court, therefore, is Hardwick's challenge to the Georgia statute as applied to consensual homosexual sodomy. We express no opinion on the constitutionality of the Georgia statute as applied to other acts of sodomy.

Fourteenth Amendment to confer a fundamental individual right to decide whether or not to beget or bear a child. . . .

Accepting the decisions in these cases and the above description of them, we think it evident that none of the rights announced in those cases bears any resemblance to the claimed constitutional right of homosexuals to engage in acts of sodomy that is asserted in this case. No connection between family, marriage, or procreation on the one hand and homosexual activity on the other has been demonstrated, either by the Court of Appeals or by respondent. Moreover, any claim that these cases nevertheless stand for the proposition that any kind of private sexual conduct between consenting adults is constitutionally insulated from state proscription is unsupportable. Indeed, the Court's opinion in *Carey* twice asserted that the privacy right, which the *Griswold* line of cases found to be one of the protections provided by the Due Process Clause, did not reach so far. . . .

Precedent aside, however, respondent would have us announce, as the Court of Appeals did, a fundamental right to engage in homosexual sodomy. This we are quite unwilling to do. It is true that despite the language of the Due Process Clauses of the Fifth and Fourteenth Amendments, which appears to focus only on the processes by which life, liberty, or property is taken, the cases are legion in which those Clauses have been interpreted to have substantive content, subsuming rights that to a great extent are immune from federal or state regulation or proscription. Among such cases are those recognizing rights that have little or no textual support in the constitutional language. *Meyer*, *Prince*, and *Pierce* fall in this category, as do the privacy cases from *Griswold* to *Carey*.

Striving to assure itself and the public that announcing rights not readily identifiable in the Constitution's text involves much more than the imposition of the Justices' own choice of values on the States and the Federal Government, the Court has sought to identify the nature of the rights qualifying for heightened judicial protection. In *Palko v. Connecticut*, 302 U.S. 319, 325, 326 (1937), it was said that this category includes those fundamental liberties that are "implicit in the concept of ordered liberty," such that "neither liberty nor justice would exist if [they] were sacrificed." A different description of fundamental liberties appeared in *Moore v. East Cleveland*, 431 U.S. 494, 503 (1977) (opinion of Powell, J.), where they are characterized as those liberties that are "deeply rooted in this Nation's history and tradition." *Id.* at 503 (Powell, J.). See also *Griswold v. Connecticut*, 381 U.S. at 506.

It is obvious to us that neither of these formulations would extend a fundamental right to homosexuals to engage in acts of consensual sodomy. Proscriptions against that conduct have ancient roots. . . .Sodomy was a criminal offense at common law and was forbidden by the laws of the original 13 States when they ratified the Bill of Rights. . . .In 1868, when the Fourteenth Amendment was ratified, all but 5 of the 37 States in the Union had criminal sodomy laws. . . .In fact, until 1961,. . .all 50 States outlawed sodomy, and today, 24 States and the District of Columbia continue to provide criminal penalties for sodomy performed in private and between consenting adults. . . .Against this background, to claim that a right to engage in such conduct is "deeply rooted in this Nation's history and tradition" or "implicit in the concept of ordered liberty" is, at best, facetious.

Nor are we inclined to take a more expansive view of our authority to discover new fundamental rights imbedded in the Due Process Clause. The Court is most vulnerable and comes nearest to illegitimacy when it deals with judge-made constitutional law having little or no cognizable roots in the language or design of the Constitution. That this is so was painfully demonstrated by the face-off between the Executive and the Court in the 1930's, which resulted in the repudiation of much of the substantive gloss that the Court had placed on the Due Process Clauses of the Fifth and Fourteenth Amendments. There should be, therefore, great resistance to expand the substantive reach of those Clauses, particularly if it requires redefining the category of rights deemed to be fundamental. Otherwise, the Judiciary necessarily takes to itself further authority to govern the country without express constitutional authority. The claimed right pressed on us today falls far short of overcoming this resistance.

Respondent, however, asserts that the result should be different where the homosexual conduct occurs in the privacy of the home. He relies on *Stanley v. Georgia*, 394 U.S. 557 (1969), where the Court held that the First Amendment prevents conviction for possessing and reading obscene material in the privacy of one's home: "If the First Amendment means anything, it means that a State has no business telling a man, sitting alone in his house, what books he may read or what films he may watch." *Id.*, at 565.

Stanley did protect conduct that would not have been protected outside the home, and it partially prevented the enforcement of state obscenity laws; but the decision was firmly grounded in the First Amendment. The right pressed upon us here has no similar support in the text of the Constitution, and it does not qualify for recognition under the prevailing principles for construing the Fourteenth Amendment. Its limits are also difficult to discern. Plainly enough, otherwise illegal conduct is not always immunized whenever it occurs in the home. Victimless crimes, such as the possession and use of illegal drugs, do not escape the law where they are committed at home. *Stanley* itself recognized that its holding offered no protection for the possession in the home of drugs, firearms, or stolen goods. . . .And if respondent's submission is limited to the voluntary sexual conduct between consenting adults, it would be difficult, except by fiat, to limit the claimed right to homosexual conduct while leaving exposed to prosecution adultery, incest, and other sexual crimes even though they are committed in the home. We are unwilling to start down that road.

Even if the conduct at issue here is not a fundamental right, respondent asserts that there must be a rational basis for the law and that there is none in this case other than the presumed belief of a majority of the electorate in Georgia that homosexual sodomy is immoral and unacceptable. This is said to be an inadequate rationale to support the law. The law, however, is constantly based on notions of morality, and if all laws representing essentially moral choices are to be invalidated under the Due Process Clause, the courts will be very busy indeed. Even respondent makes no such claim, but insists that majority sentiments about the morality of homosexuality should be declared inadequate. We do not agree, and are unpersuaded that the sodomy laws of some 25 States should be invalidated on this basis.[39]

---

39. Respondent does not defend the judgment below based on the Ninth Amendment, the Equal Protection Clause, or the Eighth Amendment.

Accordingly, the judgment of the Court of Appeals is *Reversed*.

Chief Justice Burger, concurring. I join the Court's opinion, but I write separately to underscore my view that in constitutional terms there is no such thing as a fundamental right to commit homosexual sodomy.

As the Court notes,. . .the proscriptions against sodomy have very "ancient roots." Decisions of individuals relating to homosexual conduct have been subject to state intervention throughout the history of Western civilization. Condemnation of those practices is firmly rooted in Judeao-Christian [*sic*] moral and ethical standards. Homosexual sodomy was a capital crime under Roman law. . . .During the English Reformation when powers of the ecclesiastical courts were transferred to the King's Courts, the first English statute criminalizing sodomy was passed. . . .Blackstone described "the infamous *crime against nature*" as an offense of "deeper malignity" than rape, a heinous act "the very mention of which is a disgrace to human nature," and "a crime not fit to be named." 4 W. Blackstone, Commentaries *215. The common law of England, including its prohibition of sodomy, became the received law of Georgia and the other Colonies. In 1816 the Georgia Legislature passed the statute at issue here, and that statute has been continuously in force in one form or another since that time. To hold that the act of homosexual sodomy is somehow protected as a fundamental right would be to cast aside millennia of moral teaching.

This is essentially not a question of personal "preferences" but rather of the legislative authority of the State. I find nothing in the Constitution depriving a State of the power to enact the statute challenged here.

Justice Powell, concurring. . . .I agree with the Court that there is no fundamental right—*i.e.*, no substantive right under the Due Process Clause—such as that claimed by respondent. . . .This is not to suggest, however, that respondent may not be protected by the Eighth Amendment of the Constitution. The Georgia statute at issue in this case. . .authorizes a court to imprison a person for up to 20 years for a single private, consensual act of sodomy. In my view, a prison sentence for such conduct—certainly a sentence of long duration—would create a serious Eighth Amendment issue. . . .

In this case, however, respondent has not been tried, much less convicted and sentenced.[40] Moreover, respondent has not raised the Eighth Amendment issue below. For these reasons this constitutional argument is not before us.[41]

40. It was conceded at oral argument that, prior to the complaint against respondent Hardwick, there had been no reported decision involving prosecution for private homosexual sodomy under this statute for several decades. See Thompson v. Aldredge, 187 Ga. 467, 200 S.E. 799 (1939). Moreover, the State has declined to present the criminal charge against Hardwick to a grand jury, and this is a suit for declaratory judgment brought by respondents challenging the validity of the statute. The history of nonenforcement suggests the moribund character today of laws criminalizing this type of private, consensual conduct. Some 26 States have repealed similar statutes. But the constitutional validity of the Georgia statute was put in issue by respondents, and for the reasons stated by the Court, I cannot say that conduct condemned for hundreds of years has now become a fundamental right.

41. A number of years after the decision in *Bowers* and after Justice Powell had retired, he publicly stated that he "probably made a mistake" in this case, adding that he regarded the decision as "one of little or no importance" because no one actually had been prosecuted. N.Y. Times, Nov. 5, 1990, at A14. Eds.

Justice Blackmun, with whom Justice Brennan, Justice Marshall, and Justice Stevens join, dissenting. This case is no more about "a fundamental right to engage in homosexual sodomy," as the Court purports to declare. . .than *Stanley v. Georgia*, 394 U.S. 557 (1969), was about a fundamental right to watch obscene movies. . . .Rather, this case is about "the most comprehensive of rights and the right most valued by civilized men," namely, "the right to be let alone." *Olmstead v. United States*, 277 U.S. 438, 478 (1928) (Brandeis, J., dissenting). . . .

I believe that "[i]t is revolting to have no better reason for a rule of law than that so it was laid down in the time of Henry IV. It is still more revolting if the grounds upon which it was laid down have vanished long since, and the rule simply persists from blind imitation of the past." Holmes, The Path of the Law, 10 Harv. L. Rev. 457, 469 (1897). I believe we must analyze respondent Hardwick's claim in the light of the values that underlie the constitutional right to privacy. If that right means anything, it means that, before Georgia can prosecute its citizens for making choices about the most intimate aspects of their lives, it must do more than assert that the choice they have made is an " 'abominable crime not fit to be named among Christians.'" *Herring v. State*, 119 Ga. 709, 721, 46 S.E. 876, 882 (1904). . . .

In its haste to reverse the Court of Appeals and hold that the Constitution does not "confe[r] a fundamental right upon homosexuals to engage in sodomy,". . .the Court relegates the actual statute being challenged to a footnote and ignores the procedural posture of the case before it. A fair reading of the statute and of the complaint clearly reveals that the majority has distorted the question this case presents.

First, the Court's almost obsessive focus on homosexual activity is particularly hard to justify in light of the broad language Georgia has used. Unlike the Court, the Georgia Legislature has not proceeded on the assumption that homosexuals are so different from other citizens that their lives may be controlled in a way that would not be tolerated if it limited the choices of those other citizens. . . .Rather, Georgia has provided that "[a] person commits the offense of sodomy when he performs or submits to any sexual act involving the sex organs of one person and the mouth or anus of another." Ga. Code Ann. § 16-6-2(a) (1984). The sex or status of the persons who engage in the act is irrelevant as a matter of state law. In fact, to the extent I can discern a legislative purpose for Georgia's 1968 enactment of § 16-6-2, that purpose seems to have been to broaden the coverage of the law to reach heterosexual as well as homosexual activity.[42] I therefore see no basis for the Court's decision to treat this case as an "as applied" challenge to § 16-6-2. . .or for Georgia's attempt, both in its brief and at oral argument, to defend § 16-6-2 solely on the grounds that it prohibits homosexual activity. Michael Hardwick's

42. Until 1968, Georgia defined sodomy as "the carnal knowledge and connection against the order of nature, by man with man, or in the same unnatural manner with woman." Ga. Crim. Code § 26-5901 (1933). In *Thompson v. Aldredge*, 187 Ga. 467, 200 S.E. 799 (1939), the Georgia Supreme Court held that § 26-5901 did not prohibit lesbian activity. And in *Riley v. Garrett*, 219 Ga. 345, 133 S.E.2d 367 (1963), the Georgia Supreme Court held that § 26-5901 did not prohibit heterosexual cunnilingus. Georgia passed the actspecific statute currently in force "perhaps in response to the restrictive court decisions such as *Riley*" . . . .

standing may rest in significant part on Georgia's apparent willingness to enforce against homosexuals a law it seems not to have any desire to enforce against heterosexuals. . . .But his claim that § 16–6–2 involves an unconstitutional intrusion into his privacy and his right of intimate association does not depend in any way on his sexual orientation.

Second, I disagree with the Court's refusal to consider whether § 16-6-2 runs afoul of the Eighth or Ninth Amendments or the Equal Protection Clause of the Fourteenth Amendment. . . .Respondent's complaint expressly invoked the Ninth Amendment. . .and he relied heavily before this Court on *Griswold v. Connecticut*, 381 U.S. 479, 484 (1965), which identifies that Amendment as one of the specific constitutional provisions giving "life and substance" to our understanding of privacy. . . .More importantly, the procedural posture of the case requires that we affirm the Court of Appeals' judgment if there is *any* ground on which respondent may be entitled to relief. . . .Thus, even if respondent did not advance claims based on the Eighth or Ninth Amendments, or on the Equal Protection Clause, his complaint should not be dismissed if any of those provisions could entitle him to relief. I need not reach either the Eighth Amendment or the Equal Protection Clause issues because I believe that Hardwick has stated a cognizable claim that § 16-6-2 interferes with constitutionally protected interests in privacy and freedom of intimate association. But neither the Eighth Amendment nor the Equal Protection Clause is so clearly irrelevant that a claim resting on either provision should be peremptorily dismissed. . . .The Court's cramped reading of the issue before it makes for a short opinion, but it does little to make for a persuasive one. . . .

In construing the right to privacy, the Court has proceeded along two somewhat distinct, albeit complementary, lines. First, it has recognized a privacy interest with reference to certain *decisions* that are properly for the individual to make. . . .Second, it has recognized a privacy interest with reference to certain *places* without regard for the particular activities in which the individuals who occupy them are engaged. . . .The case before us implicates both the decisional and the spatial aspects of the right to privacy. . . .

The Court concludes today that none of our prior cases dealing with various decisions that individuals are entitled to make free of governmental interference "bears any resemblance to the claimed constitutional right of homosexuals to engage in acts of sodomy that is asserted in this case.". . .While it is true that these cases may be characterized by their connection to protection of the family. . .the Court's conclusion that they extend no further than this boundary ignores the warning in *Moore v. East Cleveland*, 431 U.S. 494, 501 (1977) (plurality opinion), against "clos[ing] our eyes to the basic reasons why certain rights associated with the family have been accorded shelter under the Fourteenth Amendment's Due Process Clause." We protect those rights not because they contribute, in some direct and material way, to the general public welfare, but because they form so central a part of an individual's life. . . .And so we protect the decision whether to marry precisely because marriage "is an association that promotes a way of life, not causes; a harmony in living, not political faiths; a bilateral loyalty, not commercial or social projects." *Griswold v. Connecticut*, 381 U.S. at 486. We protect the decision whether to have a child because parenthood alters so dramatically an individual's self-definition, not because of demographic considerations or the

Bible's command to be fruitful and multiply. . . .And we protect the family because it contributes so powerfully to the happiness of individuals, not because of a preference for stereotypical households. . . .

Only the most willful blindness could obscure the fact that sexual intimacy is "a sensitive, key relationship of human existence, central to family life, community welfare, and the development of human personality," *Paris Adult Theatre I v. Slaton*, 413 U.S. 49, 63 (1973). . . .The fact that individuals define themselves in a significant way through their intimate sexual relationships with others suggests, in a Nation as diverse as ours, that there may be many "right" ways of conducting those relationships, and that much of the richness of a relationship will come from the freedom an individual has to *choose* the form and nature of these intensely personal bonds. . . .

In a variety of circumstances we have recognized that a necessary corollary of giving individuals freedom to choose how to conduct their lives is acceptance of the fact that different individuals will make different choices. For example, in holding that the clearly important state interest in public education should give way to a competing claim by the Amish to the effect that extended formal schooling threatened their way of life, the Court declared: "There can be no assumption that today's majority is 'right' and the Amish and others like them are 'wrong.' A way of life that is odd or even erratic but interferes with no rights or interests of others is not to be condemned because it is different." *Wisconsin v. Yoder*, 406 U.S. 205, 223-224 (1972). The Court claims that its decision today merely refuses to recognize a fundamental right to engage in homosexual sodomy; what the Court really has refused to recognize is the fundamental interest all individuals have in controlling the nature of their intimate associations with others. . . .

The behavior for which Hardwick faces prosecution occurred in his own home, a place to which the Fourth Amendment attaches special significance. The Court's treatment of this aspect of the case is symptomatic of its overall refusal to consider the broad principles that have informed our treatment of privacy in specific cases. Just as the right to privacy is more than the mere aggregation of a number of entitlements to engage in specific behavior, so too, protecting the physical integrity of the home is more than merely a means of protecting specific activities that often take place there. . . .

The Court's interpretation of the pivotal case of *Stanley v. Georgia*, 394 U.S. 557 (1969), is entirely unconvincing. *Stanley* held that Georgia's undoubted power to punish the public distribution of constitutionally unprotected, obscene material did not permit the State to punish the private possession of such material. According to the majority here, *Stanley* relied entirely on the First Amendment, and thus, it is claimed, sheds no light on cases not involving printed materials. . . .But that is not what *Stanley* said. Rather, the *Stanley* Court anchored its holding in the Fourth Amendment's special protection for the individual in his home. . . .

Indeed, the right of an individual to conduct intimate relationships in the intimacy of his or her own home seems to me to be the heart of the Constitution's protection of privacy. . . .

The Court's failure to comprehend the magnitude of the liberty interests at stake in this case leads it to slight the question whether petitioner, on behalf of the State, has justified Georgia's infringement on these interests. I believe that neither of the two general justifications for § 16-6-2 that petitioner has advanced warrants dismissing respondent's challenge for failure to state a claim.

First, petitioner asserts that the acts made criminal by the statute may have serious adverse consequences for "the general public health and welfare," such as spreading communicable diseases or fostering other criminal activity. . . .Inasmuch as this case was dismissed by the District Court on the pleadings, it is not surprising that the record before us is barren of any evidence to support petitioner's claim. . . .In light of the state of the record, I see no justification for the Court's attempt to equate the private, consensual sexual activity at issue here with the "possession in the home of drugs, firearms, or stolen goods,". . .to which *Stanley* refused to extend its protection. . . .Nothing in the record before the Court provides any justification for finding the activity forbidden by § 16-6-2 to be physically dangerous, either to the persons engaged in it or to others.[43]

The core of petitioner's defense of § 16-6-2, however, is that respondent and others who engage in the conduct prohibited by § 16-6-2 interfere with Georgia's exercise of the " 'right of the Nation and of the States to maintain a decent society' ". . . .Essentially, petitioner argues, and the Court agrees, that the fact that the acts described in § 16-6-2 "for hundreds of years, if not thousands, have been uniformly condemned as immoral" is a sufficient reason to permit a State to ban them today. . . .

I cannot agree that either the length of time a majority has held its convictions or the passions with which it defends them can withdraw legislation from this Court's scrutiny. See, *e.g.*, *Roe v. Wade*, 410 U.S. 113 (1973); *Loving v. Virginia*, 388 U.S. 1 (1967); *Brown v. Board of Education*, 347 U.S. 483 (1954).[44]. . .It is precisely because the issue raised by this case touches the

---

43. Although I do not think it necessary to decide today issues that are not even remotely before us, it does seem to me that a court could find simple, analytically sound distinctions between certain private, consensual sexual conduct, on the one hand, and adultery and incest (the only two vaguely specific "sexual crimes" to which the majority points. . .), on the other. For example, marriage, in addition to its spiritual aspects, is a civil contract that entitles the contracting parties to a variety of governmentally provided benefits. A State might define the contractual commitment necessary to become eligible for these benefits to include a commitment of fidelity and then punish individuals for breaching that contract. Moreover, a State might conclude that adultery is likely to injure third persons, in particular, spouses and children of persons who engage in extramarital affairs. With respect to incest, a court might well agree with respondent that the nature of familial relationships renders true consent to incestuous activity sufficiently problematical that a blanket prohibition of such activity is warranted. . . .Notably, the Court makes no effort to explain why it has chosen to group private, consensual homosexual activity with adultery and incest rather than with private, consensual heterosexual activity by unmarried persons or, indeed, with oral or anal sex within marriage.

44. The parallel between *Loving* and this case is almost uncanny. There, too, the State relied on a religious justification for its law. Compare 388 U.S. at 3 (quoting trial court's statement that "Almighty God created the races white, black, yellow, malay and red, and he placed them on separate continents. . . .The fact that he separated the races shows that he did not intend for the races to mix"), with Brief for Petitioner. . .(relying on the Old and New Testaments and the writings of St. Thomas Aquinas to show that "traditional Judeo-Christian values proscribe such conduct"). There, too, defenders of the challenged statute relied heavily on the fact that when the Fourteenth Amendment was ratified, most of the States had similar prohibitions. Compare Brief for Appellee in *Loving v. Virginia*. . .with *ante* . . . .There, too, at the time the

heart of what makes individuals what they are that we should be especially sensitive to the rights of those whose choices upset the majority.

The assertion that "traditional Judeo-Christian values proscribe" the conduct involved. . .cannot provide an adequate justification for § 16-6-2. That certain, but by no means all, religious groups condemn the behavior at issue gives the State no license to impose their judgments on the entire citizenry. The legitimacy of secular legislation depends instead on whether the State can advance some justification for its law beyond its conformity to religious doctrine. . . .Thus, far from buttressing his case, petitioner's invocation of Leviticus, Romans, St. Thomas Aquinas, and sodomy's heretical status during the Middle Ages undermines his suggestion that § 16-6-2 represents a legitimate use of secular coercive power.[45] A State can no more punish private behavior because of religious intolerance than it can punish such behavior because of racial animus. "The Constitution cannot control such prejudices, but neither can it tolerate them. Private biases may be outside the reach of the law, but the law cannot, directly or indirectly, give them effect." *Palmore v. Sidoti*, 466 U.S. 429, 433 (1984). No matter how uncomfortable a certain group may make the majority of this Court, we have held that "[m]ere public intolerance or animosity cannot constitutionally justify the deprivation of a person's physical liberty." *O'Connor v. Donaldson*, 422 U.S. 563, 575 (1975). . . .

Nor can § 16-6-2 be justified as a "morally neutral" exercise of Georgia's power to "protect the public environment," *Paris Adult Theatre I*, 413 U.S. at 68–69. Certainly, some private behavior can affect the fabric of society as a whole. Reasonable people may differ about whether particular sexual acts are moral or immoral, but "we have ample evidence for believing that people will not abandon morality, will not think any better of murder, cruelty and dishonesty, merely because some private sexual practice which they abominate is not punished by the law." H. L. A. Hart, Immorality and Treason, reprinted in The Law as Literature 220, 225 (Louis Jacques Blom-Cooper ed., 1961). Petitioner and the Court fail to see the difference between laws that protect public sensibilities and those that enforce private morality. Statutes banning public sexual activity are entirely consistent with protecting the individual's liberty interest in decisions concerning sexual relations: the same recognition that those decisions are intensely private which justifies protecting them from governmental interference can justify protecting individuals from unwilling

case came before the Court, many of the States still had criminal statutes concerning the conduct at issue. Compare 388 U.S. at 6, n.5 (noting that 16 States still outlawed interracial marriage), with *ante*. . . (noting that 24 States and the District of Columbia have sodomy statutes). Yet the Court held, not only that the invidious racism of Virginia's law violated the Equal Protection Clause. . .but also that the law deprived the Lovings of due process by denying them the "freedom of choice to marry" that had "long been recognized as one of the vital personal rights essential to the orderly pursuit of happiness by free men.". . .

45. The theological nature of the origin of Anglo-American antisodomy statutes is patent. It was not until 1533 that sodomy was made a secular offense in England. 25 Hen. VIII, ch. 6. Until that time, the offense was, in Sir James Stephen's words, "merely ecclesiastical." 2 James Stephen, A History of the Criminal Law of England 429-30 (1883). . . .The transfer of jurisdiction over prosecutions for sodomy to the secular courts seems primarily due to the alteration of ecclesiastical jurisdiction attendant on England's break with the Roman Catholic Church, rather than to any new understanding of the sovereign's interest in preventing or punishing the behavior involved. . . .

exposure to the sexual activities of others. But the mere fact that intimate behavior may be punished when it takes place in public cannot dictate how States can regulate intimate behavior that occurs in intimate places. . . .[46]

This case involves no real interference with the rights of others, for the mere knowledge that other individuals do not adhere to one's value system cannot be a legally cognizable interest. . .let alone an interest that can justify invading the houses, hearts, and minds of citizens who choose to live their lives differently. . . .

I can only hope that here, too, the Court soon will reconsider its analysis and conclude that depriving individuals of the right to choose for themselves how to conduct their intimate relationships poses a far greater threat to the values most deeply rooted in our Nation's history than tolerance of nonconformity could ever do. Because I think the Court today betrays those values, I dissent.

Justice Stevens, with whom Justice Brennan and Justice Marshall join, dissenting. Like the statute that is challenged in this case,. . .the rationale of the Court's opinion applies equally to the prohibited conduct regardless of whether the parties who engage in it are married or unmarried, or are of the same or different sexes. . . .Sodomy was condemned as an odious and sinful type of behavior during the formative period of the common law. . . .That condemnation was equally damning for heterosexual and homosexual sodomy. . . .Moreover, it provided no special exemption for married couples. . . .The license to cohabit and to produce legitimate offspring simply did not include any permission to engage in sexual conduct that was considered a "crime against nature."

The history of the Georgia statute before us clearly reveals this traditional prohibition of heterosexual, as well as homosexual, sodomy. . . .Indeed, at one point in the 20th century, Georgia's law was construed to permit certain sexual conduct between homosexual women even though such conduct was prohibited between heterosexuals. . . .The history of the statutes cited by the majority as proof for the proposition that sodomy is not constitutionally protected. . .similarly reveals a prohibition on heterosexual, as well as homosexual, sodomy. . . .

Because the Georgia statute expresses the traditional view that sodomy is an immoral kind of conduct regardless of the identity of the persons who engage in it, I believe that a proper analysis of its constitutionality requires consideration of two questions: First, may a State totally prohibit the described conduct by means of a neutral law applying without exception to all persons subject to its jurisdiction? If not, may the State save the statute by announc-

---

46. At oral argument a suggestion appeared that, while the Fourth Amendment's special protection of the home might prevent the State from enforcing § 16-6-2 against individuals who engage in consensual sexual activity there, that protection would not make the statute invalid. . . .The suggestion misses the point entirely. If the law is not invalid, then the police *can* invade the home to enforce it, provided, of course, that they obtain a determination of probable cause from a neutral magistrate. One of the reasons for the Court's holding in *Griswold v. Connecticut*, 381 U.S. 479 (1965), was precisely the possibility, and repugnancy, of permitting searches to obtain evidence regarding the use of contra-ceptives. . . .Permitting the kinds of searches that might be necessary to obtain evidence of the sexual activity banned by § 16-6-2 seems no less intrusive, or repugnant. . . .

ing that it will only enforce the law against homosexuals? The two questions merit separate discussion. . . .

Our prior cases make two propositions abundantly clear. First, the fact that the governing majority in a State has traditionally viewed a particular practice as immoral is not a sufficient reason for upholding a law prohibiting the practice; neither history nor tradition could save a law prohibiting miscegenation from constitutional attack.[47] Second, individual decisions by married persons, concerning the intimacies of their physical relationship, even when not intended to produce offspring, are a form of "liberty" protected by the Due Process Clause of the Fourteenth Amendment. *Griswold v. Connecticut*, 381 U.S. 479 (1965). Moreover, this protection extends to intimate choices by unmarried as well as married persons. *Carey v. Population Services International*, 431 U.S. 678 (1977); *Eisenstadt v. Baird*, 405 U.S. 438 (1972). . . .[48]

The essential "liberty" that animated the development of the law in cases like *Griswold*, *Eisenstadt*, and *Carey* surely embraces the right to engage in nonreproductive, sexual conduct that others may consider offensive or immoral.

Paradoxical as it may seem, our prior cases thus establish that a State may not prohibit sodomy within "the sacred precincts of marital bedrooms," *Griswold*, 381 U.S. at 485, or, indeed, between unmarried heterosexual adults. *Eisenstadt*, 405 U.S. at 453. . . .

If the Georgia statute cannot be enforced as it is written—if the conduct it seeks to prohibit is a protected form of liberty for the vast majority of Georgia's citizens—the State must assume the burden of justifying a selective application of its law. Either the persons to whom Georgia seeks to apply its statute do not have the same interest in "liberty" that others have, or there must be a reason why the State may be permitted to apply a generally applicable law to certain persons that it does not apply to others.

The first possibility is plainly unacceptable. Although the meaning of the principle that "all men are created equal" is not always clear, it surely must mean that every free citizen has the same interest in "liberty" that the members of the majority share. From the standpoint of the individual, the homosexual and the heterosexual have the same interest in deciding how he will live his own life, and, more narrowly, how he will conduct himself in his personal and voluntary associations with his companions. State intrusion into the private conduct of either is equally burdensome.

The second possibility is similarly unacceptable. A policy of selective application must be supported by a neutral and legitimate interest—something more substantial than a habitual dislike for, or ignorance about, the disfavored group. Neither the State nor the Court has identified any such interest in this case. The Court has posited as a justification for the Georgia statute "the presumed belief of a majority of the electorate in Georgia that homosexual

47. See Loving v. Virginia, 388 U.S. 1 (1967). Interestingly, miscegenation was once treated as a crime similar to sodomy. . . .

48. Indeed, the Georgia Attorney General concedes that Georgia's statute would be unconstitutional if applied to a married couple. See Tr. of Oral Argument at 8 (stating that application of the statute to a married couple "would be unconstitutional" because of the "right of marital privacy as identified by the Court in *Griswold*"). Significantly, Georgia passed the current statute three years after the Court's decision in *Griswold*.

sodomy is immoral and unacceptable." . . .But the Georgia electorate has expressed no such belief—instead, its representatives enacted a law that presumably reflects the belief that *all sodomy* is immoral and unacceptable. Unless the Court is prepared to conclude that such a law is constitutional, it may not rely on the work product of the Georgia Legislature to support its holding. For the Georgia statute does not single out homosexuals as a separate class meriting special disfavored treatment.

Nor, indeed, does the Georgia prosecutor even believe that all homosexuals who violate this statute should be punished. This conclusion is evident from the fact that the respondent in this very case has formally acknowledged in his complaint and in court that he has engaged, and intends to continue to engage, in the prohibited conduct, yet the State has elected not to process criminal charges against him. As Justice Powell points out, moreover, Georgia's prohibition on private, consensual sodomy has not been enforced for decades. . . .The record of nonenforcement, in this case and in the last several decades, belies the Attorney General's representations about the importance of the State's selective application of its generally applicable law. . . .

Both the Georgia statute and the Georgia prosecutor thus completely fail to provide the Court with any support for the conclusion that homosexual sodomy, *simpliciter*, is considered unacceptable conduct in that State, and that the burden of justifying a selective application of the generally applicable law has been met. . . .

The Court orders the dismissal of respondent's complaint even though the State's statute prohibits all sodomy; even though that prohibition is concededly unconstitutional with respect to heterosexuals; and even though the State's *post hoc* explanations for selective application are belied by the State's own actions. At the very least, I think it clear at this early stage of the litigation that respondent has alleged a constitutional claim sufficient to withstand a motion to dismiss.[49]

I respectfully dissent.

Notes and Question

1. *Loving and Bowers: Gender Implications. Bowers* uses history as a reason for continuing the subordination of lesbians and gay men. *But see* Anne B. Goldstein, History, Homosexuality, and Political Values: Searching for the Hidden Determinants of *Bowers v. Hardwick*, 97 Yale L.J. 1073 (1988) (showing that the historical accounts by Justice White and Chief Justice Burger are misleading and in some instances inaccurate). This approach contrasts sharply with *Loving*, which found that maintenance of the tradition of white

---

49. Indeed, at this stage, it appears that the statute indiscriminately authorizes a policy of selective prosecution that is neither limited to the class of homosexual persons nor embraces all persons in that class, but rather applies to those who may be arbitrarily selected by the prosecutor for reasons that are not revealed either in the record of this case or in the text of the statute. If that is true, although the text of the statute is clear enough, its true meaning may be "so intolerably vague that evenhanded enforcement of the law is a virtual impossibility." Marks v. United States, 430 U.S. 188, 198 (1977) (Stevens, J., concurring in part and dissenting in part).

supremacy was a reason for invalidating the state statute. In neither case, however, was a historical analysis used to reveal the gender implications of the state laws. In *Bowers* that probably would not have made a difference because, unlike in *Loving*, the Court was not committed to a constitutional interpretation that would promote equality regardless of whether the issue was discrimination against lesbians, gay men, heterosexual women, or all three. Although the *Loving* Court did not analyze the antimiscegenation laws in terms of gender, its anti-discrimination/supremacy approach to race does provide a framework for analyzing the sodomy laws in terms of gender, as demonstrated by Andrew Koppelman. In a Note, Koppelman explores an analogy between the sodomy statutes and the miscegenation laws. He concludes that miscegenation laws and sodomy statutes violate the Equal Protection Clause because their purpose is to support a hierarchical caste system that imposes a subordinate position on some people at birth. Miscegenation laws discriminate on the basis of race to maintain white supremacy and sodomy laws discriminate on the basis of sex to impose traditional sex roles. Koppelman asks the following question:

> Do statutes that outlaw homosexual sex impose traditional sex roles?. . .
>
> Begin by considering the familiar conservative defense of the sodomy laws, which is that the traditional prohibition of homosexual acts is necessary in order to protect the family.[50] It is. . .a curious notion. Most heterosexual family members do not appear to be so eager to become homosexual that only the fear of externally imposed sanctions prevents them from doing so. . . .Moreover, there have been cultures in which homosexuality has been openly tolerated, and in them families do not appear to have been less common or enduring than they are in contemporary America. How, then, can homosexuals be said to threaten the family?. . .
>
> Hostility to homosexuals is linked to other traditional, restrictive attitudes about sex roles.[51]. . .Homosexuality threatens not the family as such, but a certain traditional ideology of the family. That ideology is one in which men, but not women, belong in the public world of work and are not so much members as owners of their families, while women, but not men, should rear children, manage homes, and obey their husbands. It has been under stress for a long time. Intolerance of homosexuality may have ancient roots, but its basis is no more historically invariant than that of

50. This theme appears repeatedly in the briefs in *Bowers*, both by the state and by the amici supporting its position. Thus the state argued that "homosexual sodomy is the anathema of the basic units of our society—marriage and the family. To decriminalize or artificially withdraw the public's expression of its disdain for this conduct does not uplift sodomy, but rather demotes these sacred institutions to merely other alternative lifestyles." Brief for Petitioner at 37-38, Bowers v. Hardwick, 478 U.S. 186 (1986) (No. 85-140). Similar arguments appear in Brief of Amicus Catholic League for Religious and Civil Rights at 1, Brief of Amicus Concerned Women for America Education and Legal Defense Foundation at 2, and Brief of Amicus The Rutherford Institute at 26.

51. Numerous studies by social psychologists support this conclusion. For example, one study found that "a major determinant of negative attitudes toward homosexuality is the need to keep males masculine and females feminine, that is, to avoid sex-role confusion. . . ." . . .Even if such studies did not exist, a court might reasonably draw the same conclusion from ordinary experience. . . .

> racism or anti-semitism. Today that basis is anxiety about the boundaries of gender.
>
> Just as the central tenet of White Supremacy was the extreme differentiation of the races—so extreme that intercourse between them could be deemed "miscegenation," meaning literally the mixing of different species—so the central tenet of the subordination of women is the extreme differentiation of the sexes. The element of both differentiations that promotes hierarchy is the idea that certain anatomical features *necessarily* entail certain social roles: One's status in society is obviously and unproblematically determined by the color of one's skin or the shape of one's reproductive organs. Homosexuality threatens the hierarchy of the sexes because its existence suggests that even in that realm where a person's sex has been regarded as absolutely determinative, anatomy has less to do with destiny than one might have supposed.
>
> Just as miscegenation was threatening because it called into question the distinctive and superior status of being white, homosexuality is threatening because it calls into question the distinctive and superior status of being male. "[M]en cannot simultaneously be used 'as women' and stay powerful because they are men." Lesbianism also challenges male privilege, but in a different way: It denies that female sexuality exists, or should exist, only for the sake of male gratification.

Andrew Koppelman, Note, The Miscegenation Analogy: Sodomy Law as Sex Discrimination, 98 Yale L.J. 145, 158-60 (1988).

2. *Same-Sex Marriage and Gender Implications*. *Loving*'s anti-discrimination/supremacy approach to race also provides a framework for analyzing the prohibition against same-sex marriage in terms of sex discrimination. The prohibition against same-sex marriage has been defended on the basis that the prohibition applies equally to both sexes. This is the same rationale used by the state of Virginia in defending the state's antimiscegenation statute, *i.e.*, the statute equally punished whites and African Americans for entering into inter-racial marriages. As we saw in *Loving*, however, this reasoning was expressly rejected by the Supreme Court. Even if, arguably, these prohibitions apply equally, they are based on, in the case of antimiscegenation laws, racial classifications and, in the case of same-sex marriage, gender classifications.

The Hawaii Supreme Court recently considered the constitutionality of the prohibition against same-sex marriage in *Baehr v. Lewin*, 852 P.2d 44 (Haw. 1993). A divided court held that the state's Equal Protection Clause found in its constitution requires strict scrutiny of laws that discriminate on the basis of sex and that the prohibition against same-sex marriage must be reviewed under the strict scrutiny standard. Two of the justices relied on the *Loving* rationale. A third justice agreed that the prohibition against same-sex marriage is subject to the strict scrutiny standard because it is based on a sex classification, but only "[i]f heterosexuality, homosexuality, bisexuality, and asexuality are 'biologically fated'" and, therefore, included in the classification of sex found in Hawaii's Equal Protection Clause.

3. *Legitimating Homophobic Violence*. Most of the critique on *Bowers*

proceeds within the framework of the privacy and/or the equal protection doctrines. Kendall Thomas, however, argues that the privacy doctrine has limited potential because of its lack of attention to the actual human beings whose bodies are touched by laws like that challenged in *Bowers*. Thomas asserts that when viewed against the violent backdrop of homophobia, the claim in *Bowers* is best seen as a right to "corporal integrity," whose textual grounding is the Eighth Amendment prohibition against "cruel and unusual" punishment. The thesis of his article is that homosexual sodomy statutes work to legitimate homophobic violence and thus violate the right to be free from state-legitimated violence at the hands of private and public actors. The article begins by describing certain facts about *Bowers* that were not part of the record before the Supreme Court:

> Michael Hardwick's first encounter with the police power of the state of Georgia took place one morning a block away from the gay bar in Atlanta where he worked. An Atlanta police officer named K.R. Torick stopped Hardwick after seeing him throw a beer bottle into a trashcan outside the bar. As Hardwick recounts the story, the officer "made me get in the car and asked me what I was doing. I told him that I worked there, which immediately identified me as homosexual, because he knew it was a homosexual bar." Torick then issued Hardwick a ticket for drinking in public. Because of a discrepancy on the ticket between the day and the date he was to appear in court, Hardwick failed to appear. Within two hours of Hardwick's scheduled appearance, Torick went to Hardwick's house with a warrant for his arrest, only to find that he was not at home. When Hardwick returned to his apartment, his roommate told him of the police officer's visit. Hardwick then went to the Fulton County courthouse, where he paid a $50 fine. In Hardwick's words:
>
>> I told the county clerk the cop had already been at my house with a warrant and he said that was impossible. He said it takes forty-eight hours to process a warrant. He wrote me a receipt just in case I had any problems with it further down the road. That was that, and I thought I had taken care of it and everything was finished, and I didn't give it much thought.
>
> Three weeks later, Hardwick arrived home from work to find three men whom he did not know outside his house. In his account of the incident, Hardwick admits that he has no proof that these men were police officers, "but they were very straight, middle thirties, civilian clothes."
>
>> I got out of the car, turned around, and they said 'Michael' and I said yes, and they proceeded to beat the hell out of me. Tore all the cartilage out of my nose, kicked me in the face, cracked about six of my ribs. I passed out. I don't know how long I was unconscious. . . .I managed to crawl up the stairs into the house, into the back bedroom. What I didn't realize was that I'd left a trail of blood all the way back.
>
> A few days after this incident, and nearly a month after his first visit, Officer Torick again appeared at Hardwick's home. Torick found Hardwick in his bedroom having sex with another man.
>
>> He said, My name is Officer Torick. Michael Hardwick, you are under arrest. I said, For what? What are you doing in my bedroom? He said, I

have a warrant for your arrest. I told him the warrant isn't any good. He said, It doesn't matter, because I was acting under good faith.

Torick handcuffed Hardwick and his partner and took them to jail, where they were booked, fingerprinted, and photographed. As the two men were taken to a holding tank, Hardwick recalls that the arresting officer "made sure everyone in the holding cells and guards and people who were processing us knew I was in there for 'cocksucking' and that I should be able to get what I was looking for. The guards were having a *real* good time with that." Some hours later, Hardwick and his partner were transferred to another part of the building in which he was being held, in the course of which the jail officers made it clear to the other inmates that the men were gay, remarking "Wait until we put [him] into the bullpen. Well, fags shouldn't mind—after all, that's why they are here." Hardwick and his partner remained in jail for the greater part of the day, when friends were permitted to post bail for their release. . . .

Thomas goes on to assert that the fundamental interest at stake with regard to the constitutionality of homosexual sodomy statutes is the interest in corporal integrity.

[I]t would be a mistake to view *Hardwick* as raising only the question whether the State of Georgia could prohibit and punish Michael Hardwick for engaging in sexual acts with another consenting adult male in the privacy of his own home. Close attention to its factual background indicates that an even more fundamental issue presented in *Hardwick* was whether the State of Georgia could constitutionally permit its police power, specifically, its criminalization of homosexual sodomy, to serve as a justification for threatened and actual violence toward one of its citizens. . . .We would do well here to remember that the road that led Michael Hardwick to the bar of the Supreme Court was, in his words, "a trail of blood"—his own. . . .*Hardwick* ought to be understood as a case about Michael Hardwick's right to be protected from state-sanctioned invasion of his corporal integrity, that is, of his very bodily existence. . . .

Even if we were able to document every instance of homophobic violence in America, our understanding of its effects would still be incomplete. To be sure, many men and women in the gay and lesbian communities have escaped direct physical attack by perpetrators of homophobic violence. However, the horror and sinister efficacy of homophobic violence are in many ways like those of racist violence. Like people of color, gay men and lesbians always and everywhere have to live their lives on guard, knowing that they are vulnerable to attack at any time. As one observer has noted, "being gay means living with the reality that although you may not personally be the victim of outright homophobic attacks every day, at any moment you *could* be attacked—walking down the street, going to work, on the job, shopping, or in a restaurant." Indeed, much of the efficacy of homophobic violence lies in the message it conveys to those who are not its immediate victims.

In this respect, homophobic violence bears many of the characteristics associated with terrorism. As in the case of terrorism, much of the force of violence against gay men and lesbians lies in its randomness: individuals may know that the assertion or ascription of gay or lesbian identity marks them as potential targets of homophobic violence, but they cannot know until too late whether or when they will actually be hit. Like the terrorist, the perpetrator of homophobic violence strikes without giving warning. A second characteristic common to terrorism and homophobic violence is its utter impersonality. Like perpetrators of terrorist acts, those who attack gays and lesbians do not know, and are most often unknown to, their victims.

Another feature that homophobic violence shares with terrorism is its "communicative" thrust. Although attacks on gays and lesbians might be random and impersonal, such attacks are far from meaningless. The communicative dimensions of homophobic violence may be seen on a number of levels. Survivors of homophobic violence have reported that their attackers verbally expressed hatred of homosexuality, boasted of heterosexuality, or otherwise taunted them. However, in most instances, perpetrators of violence against gays and lesbians have no need to resort to language to communicate: the expressive force of the violence itself makes verbal communication unnecessary. One of the most salient features of homophobic violence is its excessive brutality. . . .The characteristic "overkill and excessive mutilation" of attacks on gay men and lesbians suggest that this is a species of violence whose form conveys its expressive content: the medium *is* the message.

The terroristic dimensions of homophobic violence compel us to understand it as a mode of power. To put the point in slightly different terms, homophobic violence is a form of "institution," in the sense that John Rawls elaborates that concept.[52]. . .Viewed systemically, the objective and outcome of violence against lesbians and gays is the social control of human sexuality. . . .

For gay men and lesbians, the state has honored this fundamental obligation [to protect citizens from random violence by other citizens or government officials] more in the breach than in the observance. . . .This violence takes two forms. One form is violence at the hand of state officials such as the police. . . .The second form of homophobic violence is that perpetrated by private individuals. Although this type of violence is of lower visibility than that committed by public officials, the available evidence suggests that it is even more extensive. Both involve the unlawful use of state power as a tool of law enforcement. . . .

I would argue that violence against gays and lesbians perpetrated by other citizens represents the states' *constructive delegation* of governmental power to these citizens. . . .[T]he fact that homophobic violence occurs within the context of "private" relations by no means implies that such violence is without "public" origins or consequence. The apparently private character of homophobic violence should not blind us to the reality of the state power that enables and underwrites it. . . .

In order to see why the private lawlessness of homophobic violence is very much a problem for constitutional law, we must turn from considering *who* perpetrates this violence to considering *how* the state responds to the fact

52. *See* John Rawls, A Theory of Justice 55 (1971) (defining "institution" as "a public system of rules which defines officers and positions with their rights and duties, powers and immunities and the like").

of its occurrence. . . .To paraphrase Justice Brandeis, the most important thing state governments do with respect to homophobic violence is to do nothing.

State officials seem unwilling or unable to use the criminal justice system to reach crimes of homophobic violence.[53]. . .

When political pressures or the persistence of victims have forced state officials to prosecute perpetrators of homophobic violence, those accused have very often been acquitted. The relatively few individuals who have been convicted of criminal violence against gay men or lesbians have often received reduced sentences or been granted a mitigation in the degree of criminal offense. These outcomes result from the emergence of two curious defenses, which are termed "homosexual panic" and "homosexual advance." The "homosexual panic" defense permits individuals accused of attacking or murdering a gay man or lesbian to assert that their acts stemmed from a violent reaction to their own "latent" homosexual tendencies, triggered after the accused was homosexually propositioned. The "homosexual advance" defense allows the accused to claim that he was the subject of a homosexual overture. The "homosexual advance" defense differs from the "homosexual panic" defense insofar as it does not require the defendant to introduce evidence about his "latent homosexual tendencies." The critical point is that the effect of both of these defenses is to create a doctrinal space within the criminal justice system that permits the perpetrators of violent crimes against gay men and lesbians to lay the blame for their brutality at the feet of their victims.[54]. . .Because gay men and lesbians are seen as members of a criminal class,[55] it is almost as though state governments view prosecution of those who commit crimes of homophobic violence as an invasion of the perpetrator's rights.[56]. . .

---

53. A Texas judge justified his leniency in sentencing the convicted murderer of two men on the grounds that "I put prostitutes and queers on the same level. . . .And I'd be hard put to give somebody life for killing a prostitute.". . .In another case involving the murder of a gay man, the presiding judge asked the prosecuting attorney whether it was "a crime now, to beat up a homosexual." The prosecutor responded, "Yes, sir. And it's also a crime to kill them." The judge rejoined, "Times have really changed.". . . In addition to the forms of inaction internal to the criminal justice system it should be observed that the overwhelming majority of state legislatures have resolutely refused to define homophobic violence as a species of "hate crime." This legislative resistance is telling when one considers that these proposals simply seek to include homophobic violence within already existing laws providing increased penalties for persons convicted of crimes motivated by gender, racial or religious bias. . . .

54. In the words of a staff attorney with the National Gay Rights Advocates, the fundamental injustice of the "homosexual advance" and "homosexual panic" defenses becomes clear when we realize that variations on these doctrines would almost certainly not be available to defendants accused of bias-motivated violence against women or people of color: "Just as our society will not allow a defendant to use racial or gender-based prejudices as an excuse for his [sic] violent acts, a defendant's homophobia is no defense to a violent crime.". . .

55. I believe that the perception of gay men and lesbians as a criminal class holds true even in those jurisdictions that have judicially invalidated or legislatively repealed the laws against homosexual crime. . . .Thus, the sodomy statutes that remain on criminal calendars in some states might be said to carry a symbolic dimension of a different order than instrumental legal force, a symbolic dimension whose effects are not confined within state borders. . . .

56. This last feature of state response to the phenomenon of homophobic violence shares a strong ideological resemblance to the administration of rape law: like rape, "queer bashing" belongs to the system of male, heterosexual privilege. . . .

Broadly speaking, homosexual sodomy statutes express the official "theory" of homophobia; private acts of violence against gay men and lesbians "translate" that theory into brutal "practice." In other words, private homophobic violence punishes what homosexual sodomy statutes prohibit.[57] When situated within this framework, the terms and target of my Eighth Amendment-based account of the criminal laws against homosexual sodomy become clear: one might call it an "anti-terrorist" case for judicial invalidation of homosexual sodomy laws, whose textual grounding is a *functional*, rather than *formal* interpretation of the prohibition against the infliction of cruel and unusual punishments.[58]

Kendall Thomas, Beyond the Privacy Principle, 92 Colum. L. Rev. 1431, 1437-39, 1459-60, 1465-67, 1477, 1481-86 (1992).

Considering Koppelman's gender-role analysis, Note 1, *supra*, along with Thomas' homophobic-violence analysis, can you explain how traditional gender roles are maintained through violence directed at women?

---

57. I have been careful to avoid asserting a direct causal connection between homosexual sodomy laws and homophobic violence. . . .Nonetheless, when one looks at the issue from a broader systemic perspective, it is hard to avoid the conclusion that homosexual sodomy laws do not simply passively reflect, but rather actively produce and perpetuate the homophobia that motivates the perpetrators of violence against persons who are (or are thought to be) gay or lesbian. That is, I believe that homosexual sodomy laws have a "constitutive" effect. . . .

58. Thus, I reject the notion that the term "punishment" may properly be used to refer only to statutorily authorized sanctions imposed by official state actors following an official adjudicative determination of guilt. This definition of punishment possesses a certain conceptual neatness, but it has little value in understanding the actual infliction of pain with which I am concerned. Moreover, given the structural tendency toward privatization of penal power, one may wonder whether traditional formalist conceptions of punishment have not run their course. . . .

Chapter 4

Battering

This chapter focuses on battering, which is one of the five traditional categories of violence against women. While presenting issues that are particular to battering, we also identify the interrelationship between battering and other forms of violence against women. The interrelationships of battering, sexual harassment, rape, prostitution, and pornography are one part of what we mean throughout the book by *continuum of violence.* The interrelationships challenge the traditional categories of violence; cause each form of violence to support the others; and cause the legal and social responses to one form of violence to have implications for other categories.

We also use continuum of violence to mean a continuum along which the law tolerates some forms and levels of violence. Rather than developing effective deterrents to any violence, the law focuses on distinguishing between acceptable and unacceptable levels of violence to determine when state intervention is appropriate. In doing so, the law trivializes much of the harm done to women by "domestic" and other forms of violence and also implicitly supports the perpetuation of a culture of violence against women.

Battering is a pervasive problem, faced by millions of women every day. "Studies have shown that more women are abused by their husbands or boyfriends than are injured in car accidents, muggings, or rape, and that 3 to 4 million households live with this violence every day." Nat'l Center on Women and Family Law, The Effect of Woman Abuse on Children: Psychological and Legal Authority i (1991). While this figure is alarming, criminal justice experts acknowledge that battering is a severely under reported crime. The overwhelming majority of the victims/survivors are women who have been abused by men. Studies from the United States and Canada show that 90 to 95 percent of the victims of domestic assaults are women. *See* R. Emerson Dobash & Russell P. Dobash, Women, Violence and Social Change 265 (1992).

The issue of battering seemed to come out of nowhere in the 1970s. In fact, it grew out of the emerging feminist movement, which had its antecedents in the civil rights, anti-war, and black liberation movements of the 1950s and 1960s. *See* Susan Schechter, Women and Male Violence 29-30 (1982).

The lack of meaningful response by social, religious, medical, and legal institutions led women in the 1970s to organize grassroots services: first telephone hotlines, then networks of safehomes, and eventually shelters. Women soon realized the need to exchange information among their localities.

> Discussions about forming a national organization began among activists attending several different conferences . . . .They culminated at the United States Civil Rights Commission Consultation on Battered Women in Wash-

> ington DC (January, 1978) where The National Coalition Against Domestic Violence (NCADV) was formed. Previous discussions were translated into action over the few days of the Washington meeting as sixty women worked to create regional caucuses, an interim structure and a statement of purpose. . . .The initial goals emphasized gaining financial aid for shelters and grassroots services, sharing information and supporting research beneficial to the movement. . . .
>
> The simple fact of American geography served as a major impediment to forming a national organization, particularly for groups without sufficient funding to run their local shelter, much less travel. . .to meet even on an infrequent basis . . . .Work continued, but the first national conference was not held until two years later, in 1980. Meanwhile, the steering committee decided on the goals:
>
> 1 To monitor and impact legislation relating to domestic violence and family policy.
> 2 To aid in the develoment [sic] of state and regional coalitions.
> 3 To develop a national network of shelters.
> 4 To educate the public to a non-acceptance of violence and to strive towards the complete elimination of violence in our society.
> 5 To support and initiate change in traditional sex-role expectations for women and men.
>
> . . .State coalitions began to form in the USA after the formation of the National Coalition. Combining shelter groups into larger state-wide organizations required local groups, already greatly overworked opening and running shelters, to take on yet another task of developing a state-wide organization. Many, however, saw this as crucial in gaining greater political influence, particularly in working for legislation and funding, and in solidifying the grassroots, feminist base of the movement. . . .Some, no doubt, felt less need to form larger groups oriented to wider social change than to expand the number of smaller groups working directly on the issue at the local level.

Dobash & Dobash, *supra*, at 36-37.

The number of women seeking shelter services in the seventies consistently overwhelmed the capacity of the shelters. Advocates and survivors began to question the burden placed on the victim/survivor by requiring her to move out of her home and neighborhood. In response, they developed a model of advocacy services that attempted to empower battering survivors by making the legal system more accessible and responsive.

The growth of shelter and advocacy programs presents new challenges and dilemmas for contemporary women activists. What began as grassroots resistance organizations have evolved into agencies that are economically dependent on dominant social institutions, including governmental bodies and charities. From this position, will advocates' and survivors' demands for a more effective response to battering be tempered for fear of losing what has been gained? Similar challenges and dilemmas face all those who work to transform the legal system into a system that does not harm, but rather protects, women. This chapter is organized around those challenges and dilemmas.

Part A uses a variety of sources to show how social, religious, medical, and legal institutions traditionally either have supported battering or provided an inadequate response to it. The article by R. Emerson Dobash and Russell Dobash presents the fundamental analysis of the dynamics of domestic violence. They argue that social, economic, and religious institutions historically have supported men's control of women through violence. The article is followed by four cases that span one hundred years and that offer proof of Dobash and Dobash's thesis. The critique of the law developed in Chapter 3 provides a framework for analyzing these cases. We then consider essays by Nora Groce, Nancy Hammond, Jo-Ellen Asbury, Nilda Rimonte, and Angela Ginorio and Jane Reno. Each describes how institutions that grow out of the dominant culture, including those designed to provide support services to women, fail to meet the specific needs of women who are viewed as outside of the dominant culture with regard to physical and mental abilities, sexual orientation, race, and ethnicity. These essays also examine the specific ways that stereotyping operates against members of a nondominant group and how the stereotyping contributes to violence. Part A concludes with an essay by Andrea Dworkin in which she describes having been battered when she was married.

Part B primarily focuses on the legal reforms of the last twenty years that have been the product of grassroots advocacy. Dobash and Dobash detail the evolution of legal changes during the twentieth century. This is followed by two examples of modern statutory reform in Minnesota. The first has to do with orders for protection and the second deals with probable cause arrest. Also included is a report of the Minnesota Supreme Court Task Force for Gender Fairness in the Courts that examines the efficacy of civil and criminal remedies available to victims/survivors of domestic violence. The last selection in Part B is an excerpt from an article by Martha Mahoney, in which she looks at women attempting to separate from their abusers. Through the stories told by victims/survivors of battering and court opinions, Mahoney shifts the perspective away from the inevitable question "why didn't she leave?" to the recognition of how violent abusers exercise control over women who are attempting to or have separated from their abusers. She identifies this aspect of domestic violence as separation assault.

Part C considers law's response to women who kill their abusers. Through the case of *State v. Norman* and an excerpt from an article by Sharon Angella Allard, expert testimony about the battered woman syndrome and its use in self-defense claims is explored.

A. Systems Supporting Battering

R. Emerson Dobash & Russell P. Dobash, Wives: The 'Appropriate' Victims of Marital Violence, 2 Victimology 426, 426–32, 434–35, 438–39 (1978)

It has only been a hundred years since men were denied the legal right to beat their wives in Britain and the United States. Prior to the late 19th century it was considered a necessary aspect of a husband's marital obligation to control and chastise his wife through the use of physical force. The legal prescriptions which once supported this practice no longer exist yet the behaviour continues unabated. Behaviour which was once legally condoned is now proscribed by law, yet cultural and normative prescriptions still support such practice and it is only mildly condemned, if at all, by law enforcement and judicial institutions.

We will elucidate the historical processes which aid in the understanding and explanation of this form of violence and provide evidence from diverse sources to document the prevalence and predominance of violence directed at wives[1] in contemporary western societies. Our understanding will not, however, be increased by merely documenting the prior existence of wifebeating [*sic*]. What is required is a form of historical analysis which illustrates the interrelationship between this form of violence and other social processes and institutions. This will provide a better understanding of the social meaning of wife beating, of its acceptability throughout society and of the institutional mechanisms by which it was supported and maintained. Placing violence against women in this wider socio-historical context, leads to a more complete understanding of its manifestations in contemporary society. This methodology enables one to go beyond a myopic empiricism which focuses solely upon individuals or couples, and provides a framework for placing such couples in a wider social context from which more meaningful explanations can be drawn.

When this methodology is applied to the problem of violence against women in the home, it leads to the indisputable conclusion that wifebeating [*sic*] is not, in the strictest sense of the words, a 'deviant', 'aberrant', or 'pathological' act. Rather, it is a form of behaviour which has existed for centuries as an acceptable, and, indeed, a desirable part of a patriarchal family system within a patriarchical society, and much of the ideology and many of the institutional arrangements which supported the patriarchy through the subordination, domination and control of women are still reflected in our culture and our social institutions. The following sketch of the historical roots of this violence and the reinterpretation and deciphering of a wide variety of contemporary research provides overwhelming evidence that it is women in their position as wives who become the 'appropriate' victims of violence in the home. Before proceeding, it is vital that we make explicit the type of violence we intend to explore. Although we do not discount the cruelty nor the coerciveness of psychological forms of violence, it is not our intention to consider this form of violence. Our intent is to focus explicitly upon violence which involves the use of physical force. However, to define the domain of inquiry in such gross and all inclusive terms as physical violence or physical force would be both imprecise and misleading. A lack of specificity concerning the term 'physical violence' leaves the reader uncertain about the nature of the phenomenon being studied and thus unclear about the generalizations being made. There is considerable variation in the social meaning and the physical consequences of the acts involving force which occur between husbands and wives. This includes periodic slapping or pushing and shoving,

1. The term wives is used to refer to the social relationship between cohabitees and is not meant to imply legality.

which rarely if ever escalates and is not intended to result in serious injury or intimidation; repeated punching and kicking which is intended to do injury and to severely intimidate the victim but not to kill them (although this sometimes happens); and violence with the intention to kill. These behaviours differ in terms of motivations, purposes and coerciveness and should not be seen as necessarily cumulative or progressive. In this paper, we are not concentrating upon the least serious category, slapping and shoving, but upon homicides and especially upon the more severe and systematic assaults involving kicking and punching intended to injure and seriously intimidate. . . .

Reputedly, the first law of marriage was proclaimed by the Roman, Romulus, in 753 B.C. It proclaimed that married women were "to conform themselves entirely to the temper of their husbands and the husbands to rule their wives as necessary and inseparable possessions." There was no place in Roman society for detached persons, and a woman had no alternative except to marry and become a 'necessary and inseparable possession.' By marriage a woman 'came into the hand,' or under the control, of her husband. The man was the absolute patriarch who owned and controlled all properties and people within the family. A wife was obligated to obey her husband and he was given the legal right and the moral obligation to control and punish her for any 'misbehaviour,' including adultery, drinking wine, attending public games without his permission or appearing unveiled in public. The husband was given full powers to judge and censor his wife and there was a definite standard which protected the rights and authority of husbands and legitimized the subjugation of wives through force. This was most clearly put in a speech delivered by Cato the Censor during the fifth century B.C. Speaking about the appropriate response to marital infidelity, he said, "If you catch your wife in adultery, you could put her to death with impunity, she, on her part would not dare to touch you with her finger; and it is not right that she should."

There were numerous Roman laws about adultery, infidelity and sexual jealousy; they all reflected a double standard and punishments for such offenses were very severe. The reasons were not related to thwarted love, but to property. The husband's authority had to remain inviolate in order that there would be no question about the pedigree of the male children who were to inherit the family name and possessions. Any indication that a wife was not under the complete control of her husband was deemed sufficient grounds for beating her, even to excess. There was the case of a husband:

> who beat his wife to death because she had drunk some wine; and this murder, far from leading to his being denounced was not even blamed. People considered that her exemplary punishment had properly expiated her offense. . .for any woman who drinks wine immoderately closes her heart to every virtue and opens it to every vice.

There were many changes in the Roman family in the later stages of the Empire. The Punic Wars meant that men were absent for long periods and during that time women had taken on more responsibility, gained more independence, and some of them inherited property, were educated, and engaged in traditional male pursuits such as politics and philosophy. The severe sexual code was modified and, relative to the earlier period, women were greatly emancipated. Although a man could still beat his wife, greater limits and restrictions were placed upon him, and it was made illegal to beat a woman of the upper classes.

The changes in the independence of women and the dilution of the absolute patriarch were looked upon with particular horror among the poorer sections of society. In terms of family structures and relations, an obscure, small sect known as the Christians was not struggling for revolutionary change but for the maintenance of the power and authority of the patriarch. Christianity embraced the hierarchical family structure and celebrated the subordination of wives to their husbands. Their scriptures were teaching:

> ". . .wives be in subjection to your own husbands." (Peter, 3:1)
> ". . .the head of the woman is the man." (I Corinthians, 11:3)
> "But I suffer not a woman to teach or to usurp authority of man, but to be in silence." (I Timothy, 3:12)
> (Women) "are commanded to be under obedience." (I Corinthians, 14:34)

Wives were to obey and be in subjection but the Christian attitude was that this should not be achieved through force but through an adherence to a moral order which made obedience sacred. "The law of marriage (I Corinthians, 7) and the prescriptions for conjugal duties" (Ephesians, 5; Titus, 2:4-5) stated that love and obedience constituted the proper role for a wife. A husband was also expected to love his spouse, but in addition he was to rule his household well and to keep everyone in subjection (I Timothy, 3).

Continuing from these very early periods, both the Church and the State supported the subordination of women in marriage and the husband's control over his wife; the Church through a moral order and the State through actively propagandizing for the authority of husbands and legitimizing their use of violence against their wives. This can be seen in the writings of Martin Luther, John Knox, and Calvin, each of whom reiterated ideas similar to those in the Homily on Marriage, which was ordered by the Crown to be read in Church every Sunday from 1562 onward, and in the very popular marriage manuals of the day . . . .

Accompanying these moral imperatives were the many laws of chastisement. During the Middle Ages women throughout Spain, Italy, France and England could be flogged through the city streets, exiled for years or killed if they committed adultery or numerous 'lesser' offenses. In France a man could beat his wife, "when she contradicts or abuses him, or when she refuses, like a decent woman, to obey his reasonable commands." Even the French code of chivalry specified that the husband of a scolding wife could knock her to the earth, strike her in the face with his fist and break her nose so that she would always be blemished and ashamed. Thus, "the wife ought to suffer and let the husband have the word, and be the master."

Under English Common Law a married woman lost all of her civil rights, had no separate legal status and became the chattel of her husband. The right of the husband to chastise his wife was considered a natural part of his responsibilities. In 1763, Blackstone wrote, "The husband also, by the old law might give his wife moderate correction. For, as he is to answer for her misbehaviours, the law thought it reasonable to entrust him with his power of restraining her by domestic chastisement. . . ." This was considered to be a reasonable part of the marital relationship and was thought to be for the benefit of both husband and wife. Blackstone stated emphatically that, "the female sex was a great favourite of the Laws of England." As the old common law was changed to the new civil law, this 'favouritism' was continued in statutes which allowed the husband, "for some misdemeanors to give his wife a severe beating with whips and clubs; for others, only to apply moderate correction."

All of the legal systems of Europe, England and early America supported a husband's rights to beat his wife and so did the community norms. In 18th Century France, for example, it was considered appropriate for a husband to chastise his wife for reasons such as assertion of her independence, wanting to retain control of her property after marriage, adultery, or even suspected infidelity, but the beatings were supposed to conform to the rules of legitimate punishment. The chastisement of wives like that of children, was to be restricted to "blows, thumps, kicks or punches on the back. . . which did not leave any marks. . . ." Men were to control their wives because, "The man who is not master of his wife is not worthy of being a man," but he should restrict his attacks to the tacit limits set by the community. During that time, as today, physical violence against wives provoked little disapprobation unless it was extremely severe. Only if the attack was public and went beyond the tacit limits set by the community was the husband likely to be rebuked or subject to moral sanctions. Upon observing a man severely attacking his wife a neighbour exclaimed, "Oh, that's a bit much. We all know that wives need beating but you must be reasonable all the same.". . .

It was not until the eighteenth century that the husband's power of correction even began to be doubted, and a woman could gain security of peace from her spouse. Yet, it was not until the nineteenth century that the struggle for reform began in Britain and America and laws against wife beating were actually passed.

The American colonies had, as would be expected, adopted much of English law and incorporated it into their own legal structure. The husband's right to chastise his wife had a curious legal history, since it was not formally written into law until 1824 when the Supreme Court of Mississippi was the first U.S. Court to acknowledge this right. The principles stated were the same as Blackstone's, and other States soon followed Mississippi's lead. In 1864 a court in North Carolina ruled that the State should not interfere in cases of domestic chastisement unless "permanent injury or excessive violence" was involved. They preferred to "leave the parties to themselves as the best mode of inducing them to make the matter up and live together as a man and wife should." The neutral terminology of this ruling ignored the fact that leaving the 'parties to themselves' meant leaving the husband to beat his wife.

Within fifty years of the legal recognition of wife beating in Mississippi, it was made illegal in Alabama and Massachusetts. In 1871 it was declared that, "the privilege, ancient though it be, to beat her with a stick, to pull her hair, choke her, spit in her face or kick her about the floor, or to inflict upon her other indignities, is not now acknowledged by our law." The rejection of this legal right was not complete in America until 1891 when in the case of Reg. v. Jackson the courts declared that, "the moral sense of the community revolts at the ideas that the husband may inflict personal chastisement upon his wife, even for the most outrageous conduct." The courts had declared that this offense was morally revolting and that no nonviolent behaviour on the part of wives could be defined as warranting such abuse. The idea of provocation had clearly been rejected in judicial statements, and by 1910 all but eleven States allowed absolute divorce for cruelty.

At about this same time, there was a struggle to change the English laws. Speeches were made in the House of Commons to the effect that, "the country should treat its married women no worse than it treated its domestic animals." The Act for Better Prevention and Punishment of Aggravated Assaults upon Women and Children (1853) was passed but later repealed, and it is not surprising that in 1856 the members of a Protestant sect in Whitehaven "defended the practice of wife-beating as an article of faith." The practice was still quite legal, but there was considerable confusion about the legal limits which were being placed upon it. In the History of the Rod (1860's) the Reverend Cooper writes:

> Authorities are not agreed as to what constituted a 'moderate castigation', and the instrument wherewith it was to be inflicted. . .though a husband might not by law beat his spouse with a stick of a certain size, he might safely do so with a switch of a certain size or with his hand. Some men, not inclined to be severe, used to restrict the size of the thickness of the rod to the little finger.

When the public and parliamentary debate became more heated, Disraeli set up a special Parliamentary Committee to investigate the frequency of this practice and to consider the adequacy of fines and imprisonment, and the possible introduction of flogging as a punishment for those who *brutally* assaulted their wives. Fifty-two counties from England and Wales reported hundreds of cases of brutal assault against wives which occurred between 1870-1875. The comments of the constables revealed a high level of intolerance of *brutal* assaults against wives but a high level of acceptance of what they called *ordinary* assaults against them.

By 1878 women were allowed to use cruelty as a grounds for divorce, but the law and its implementation were merely oriented toward setting limits on assaults against wives and not toward making it truly illegal. In the late 1800's there were at least four cases of aggravated assaults against wives in litigation each day, and thousands of women were "perambulating punching-bags, who knew this and who only wanted to get through life with as few bruises as possible." So little was done to bring about any meaningful change in the daily lives of women that by 1910 the Suffragettes made assaults on wives one of their platforms. Women were no longer the legitimate victims of marital violence, but were they still the 'appropriate' victims?. . .

In this century research reports have consistently indicated that it is in a marital setting that women are most likely to be involved in violence, and this is usually as victims not attackers. It is in the institution of the family that the patriarchal legacy persists through the continuation of the hierarchical relationship between men and women. Male authority is still, regardless of the so-called liberation of women, revered and protected by social institutions and reinforced and perpetuated through the socialization of children.

Research findings relating to interpersonal violence consistently establish the association between intimate relationships and homicides and assaults, but social scientists have been just as consistent in their failure to note the direction of these attacks. In order to establish the direction and recurring patterns of violence in the family it is necessary to tease out findings and implications from existing research reports, and when this task is carried out it clearly indicates that it is women in their position as wives who are the most likely victims of systematic and persistent violent attacks in the family. . . .

The research relating to violence occurring within the home points in an unequivocal manner to the differential nature of this violence. Men are usually violent toward their wives (common-law or legal) and this violence is often of a persistent nature. . . .Men are more likely to be taught to be aggressive and dominant, to be sensitive to affronts to their authority and attempt to preserve such authority and dominance through the use of force. They are more likely to be taught the skills related to physical force and to be inculcated with the willingness to use them in circumstances which "warrant" their use. One of these circumstances is systematically structured within the family in which women are to be subordinate to their husbands.

Social scientists have primarily conceptualized violence as a breakdown in social order in which either individuals or social structures are thought to be deviant or aberrant. We prefer to see violence used by men against women in the family as attempts to establish or maintain a patriarchal social order. Violence is used by men to chastise their wives for real or perceived transgressions of his authority and as attempts to reaffirm and maintain a hierarchical and moral order within the family. This conception of violence against wives is irrefutable in the light of the evidence sketched above and takes us beyond the sociological reductionism that permeates most of the work relating to interpersonal violence; research which is primarily oriented to determining the background characteristics of offenders and/or victims. We must go beyond the individuals or couples involved in violent marriages and episodes and seek explanations that are firmly embedded in a wider socio-historical context. . . .

In-depth interviews were conducted with 109 women who had been systematically and violently beaten on numerous occasions by their husband or paramour. These interviews lasted from two to six hours and covered a wide variety of topics from the childhood of the man and woman through the early stages of courtship and family life. Both the violent and nonviolent aspects of their relationship were examined in terms of factors associated with the emergence of violence and its continuation.

The early stages of the couple's relationship were not unlike those of any couple going out together. Most of the couples saw each other quite frequently and went out to movies, dancing and pubs several times a week. Once the relationship became somewhat serious both the men and women began to restrict their activities with their same sex friends in order to spend more time together. Although more women were likely to restrict their social lives completely to their partner (61 percent), there was nevertheless a large percentage of men (41 percent) who did the same. During this period most of the men were very attentive and the women felt loved and satisfied with the relationship.

As the relationship continued there was a growing sense of exclusivity and possession. As would be expected, this was especially true among the males who were less likely to give up the 'nights out with the boys' but were more likely to expect that their girlfriend would go out exclusively with them. The man's increasing possessiveness and periodic displays of sexual jealousy served as signs of commitment to the relationship. Although, in retrospect, many of the women saw these as early warning signs, the behaviour was not uncharacteristic for courting couples and did not cause concern at the time. Some of the men did hit their future wives prior to marriage. Those who did (23 percent), usually did so because of sexual jealousy, usually unfounded, or as a protest against the women's threats to terminate the relationship. An analysis of these few cases indicates that the men came to consider it their right to question their future wife's activities and object through the use of physical force.

For most couples, however, violence did not occur until after they were married, but it usually occurred very soon after marriage. Fifty nine percent of the women had experienced violence by the end of their first year of marriage, and 92 percent within the first five years. After marriage, the authority relationships between men and women become more explicit. Husbands came to feel that their wives should meet their demands immediately and without question no matter how reasonable or unreasonable. The major sources of contention centered on what might be called "wifely obligations" and the husband's authority. The obligations of a wife to care for her husband, to serve his needs and remain his exclusive sexual partner are all expectations which are supported to some degree by most social institutions and have very heavy moral overtones. In western society, a man feels that marriage gives him the right to expect domestic service and sexual exclusivity from his wife. The fulfillment of these behaviours is not only personally pleasant for him; it also becomes an outward sign of his 'rightful' possession of her, authority over her and ability to control her.

In our research, it was the real or perceived challenges to the man's possession, authority and control which most often resulted in the use of violence. A late meal, an unironed shirt, a conversation with any man no matter how old or young all served as 'justifications' for beatings. Many of the precipitating factors were exceedingly innocuous and would appear inexplicable without an understanding of the context of authority, subordination and control in which they occurred.

The historical and contemporary documents presented in this article elucidate the legal, religious and cultural legacies which have supported a marital hierarchy, subordinated women in marriage and legalized violence against them. The husband's right to control his wife by force extended far beyond slaps and shoves and into systematic beatings and brutalizing which sometimes resulted in death. Although domestic chastisement of wives is no longer legal, most of the ideologies and social arrangements which formed the underpinnings of this violence still exist and are inextricably intertwined in our present legal, religious, political and economic practices. Wives may no longer be the legitimate victims of marital violence, but in social terms they are still the 'appropriate' victims. Thus, it would be truly ironic if in the current climate, some magical twist of egalitarian terminology were to be used to deny centuries of oppression and to further repress contemporary women by obscuring the undeniable fact that spousal violence is to all extents and purposes wife beating.

Notes and Question

1. *Euro-American Institutions Supporting Battering*. R. Emerson Dobash and Russell Dobash illustrate that social, economic, and religious institutions historically have supported violence against women in marriage. It is important for us to recognize that the analysis presented by Dobash and Dobash arises out of a Euro-American perspective of society. Paula Gunn Allen helps us to understand how this perspective dominates our views about violence and justice.

> In the beginning the continent and sub-continent were populated largely by peaceful tribes, nations, and confederacies. Early travelers reported that the native people were open, friendly, warm, and innocent. Travelers also reported that these very traits made them vulnerable and easily exploited. The conquest of the tribes and nations by Anglo-Europeans was accompanied by its analog, the conquest and degradation of Indian women by men, Indian and otherwise. At every stage of conquest the disempowerment of women progressed. . .from an egalitarian, gynocratic social structure to a christianized, patriarchal hierarchical one. . . .
>
> I do not justify the abuse that Indian women suffer at the hands of Indian men. I will not excuse the claim that some of the abuse is actually traditional religious practice. But I also will not ignore the historical realities which are relevant to that abuse. For the abuse of Indian women and children by Indian men can be traced to the introduction into Indian culture of alcohol and Christianity. The message of the conquerors was that female subservience was the will of God.

Paula Gunn Allen, Violence and the American Indian Woman, in The Speaking Profits Us: Violence in the Lives of Women of Color 5, 6 (Center for the Prevention of Sexual & Domestic Violence, Seattle, Wash., Maryviolet Burns ed., 1986).

2. *Bird Cage*. How does the metaphor of the bird cage presented in Marilyn Frye's article "Oppression," at p. 49, help to explain Dobash and Dobash's analysis of battering?

3. *A Critique of Psychological Theories of Battering*. As Dobash and Dobash suggest, one approach to battering has been to view it as deviant and pathological behavior that has psychological causes and therapeutic solutions. Susan Schechter analyzes a number of psychological theories of why men batter women and demonstrates why each of them inadequately explains battering.

> Such men are pictured as weak, insecure, inadequate, or dependent. They suffer from poor impulse control, poorly developed egos, and deprived childhoods. Some theorists suggest that they abuse because they are unable to express feelings. . . .It is true that batterers often *feel* powerless and that they bluster, bully, and threaten to cover up their sense of impotence and their inability to express their feelings. While psychiatric descriptions and per-

sonal experiences make us sympathetic toward individual abusers, they cannot erase the fact that batterers are dangerous and that they beat women and escalate their intimidating tactics as a way to regain what they believe is their rightful control of the situation.

In "Psychological Aspects of Wife-Beating," Natalie Shainess, a psychiatrist, maintains that men who batter may be under great stress and have no tools for handling it. Some of them are infantile, unable to tolerate frustration and therefore lash out. Although the descriptions may accurately portray some violent men, they still fail to explain why these men choose their wives as targets. It is easy to read backward into deprived childhoods to find the cause of violence, but many "deprived" people are not violent. Indeed, men who were loved as children also learn to dominate and abuse women.

Stress is a totally inadequate concept to explain abuse. Under enormous stress, many men do not batter. Insecure women under stress do not beat up men in large numbers. . . .[S]tress does not "cause" abuse; men choose to deal with stress in specific ways. The belief in one's right to use violence, batter, and dominate women is what causes a man to relieve his stress by beating his wife. . . .

Personality theories suggest that battering is about illness and poor impulse control rather than power. Poor impulse control is a grossly misleading term; many men are only violent with their wives in the privacy of their homes. Sometimes, they carefully select which area of a woman's body to abuse. They usually do not kill. Some exercise substantial control and stop their abuse when they are threatened with jail sentences. Although they act "out of control," most batterers know what they are doing.

Many [therapists] place the source of violence within conflictual couples or families. . . .

Many family therapists lose sight of the power differential available to the man to invoke violence as he sees fit. For these theorists, there is not a power dynamic in marriage; there are equals with problems. Or there are those therapists who define power as a symptom of illness, rather than a reality of domination, by saying, "some people are more powerful because their partners let them be." Although the argument contains a grain of truth, it denies the intimidating quality of violence, and the superior material resources men can withhold from women, like money for food. These therapists incorrectly place the source of the problem within the family system, not within the person who beats, the traditions that maintain abuse, or the institutions that support male domination.

An equally misleading and attractive theory suggests that an intergenerational cycle of violence creates battering. Violence is learned in one's family of origin, either by watching father hit mother or by being hit oneself. Again, this theory must be recognized as an attempt to understand social causation by describing influences in individuals' lives. Even in this context, however, some of the conclusions of those who support such a theory appear suspect. . . .

Childhood experiences do profoundly influence adult behavior and may be one factor in explaining why some men batter and why some women have difficulty leaving abusive men. For example, activists working in shelters report that a significant number of women who use the shelters were victims of incest. Incest victims learn a variety of "lessons," one of which is to keep family secrets. Often they feel intensely guilty and fear destroying the family. Some activists suggest that incest, a compelling "lesson" about male dominance and abuse, heightens women's later vulnerability to further violence.

However, the influence of childhood experiences of abuse on adult behavior is not mechanistic. While some men may learn that violence is a useful tool to get one's way and that women and children are acceptable targets, others may be repelled by violence. Many men who saw their fathers beat their mothers do not beat their wives. And one wonders if the fact that shelter residents experienced incest signifies a correlation between incest and battering or whether it may instead be one indication that incest is much more widespread than anyone has previously recognized. . . .

When feminists suggest that violence is about neither sick psyches nor sick relationships, the reader should not conclude that they are dismissing psychology or ignoring violent individuals. They are stressing the need for a psychology that analyzes wife beating in its proper contexts, accounts for power differentials, and asks why women have been brutalized. Rather than label battering as pathology or a family systems failure, it is more conceptually accurate to assume that violence against women, like that directed toward children, is behavior approved of and sanctioned in many parts of the culture. . . .

Individual men who abuse have varied personalities. Clearly, their family histories, intimacy problems, stress levels, and alcohol intake will affect their behavior. In individual cases, such factors may contribute to abuse or heighten the likelihood of its occurrence, but they do not explain the consistent target—women.

Susan Schechter, Women and Male Violence: The Visions and Struggles of the Battered Women's Movement 210-13, 215-16 (1982).

State v. Black,

60 N.C. 262 (Win. 1864)

The defendant was indicted for an assault on Tamsey Black, his wife. The evidence showed, that the defendant and his wife lived separate from one other. The defendant was passing by the house of one Koonce, where his wife then resided, when she called to him in an angry manner and asked him, if he had patched Sal Daly's bonnet, (Sal Daly being a woman of ill-fame.) She then went into the house, and defendant followed her and asked her what she wanted, when she repeated her question about the bonnet. Angry words then passed between them. He accused her of connection with a negro man, and she called him a hog thief, whereupon the defendant seized her by her hair, and pulled her down upon the floor, and held her there for some time. He gave her no blows, but she stated on the trial, that her head was considerably hurt, and that her throat was injured, and continued sore for several months, but that he did not choke her, nor attempt to do so. At the trial she was entirely recovered. After she got up from the floor, she continued her abuse of him. . . .

Pearson, C.J. A husband is responsible for the acts of his wife, and he is required to govern his household, and for that purpose, the law permits him to use towards his wife such a degree of force, as is necessary to control an unruly temper, and make her behave herself; and unless some permanent injury be inflicted, or there be an excess of violence, or such a degree of cruelty as shows that it is inflicted to gratify his own bad passions, the law will not invade the domestic forum, or go behind the curtain. It prefers to leave the parties to themselves, as the best mode of inducing them to make the matter up and live together as man and wife should.

Certainly, the exposure of a scene like that set out in this case, can do no good. In respect to the parties, a public exhibition in the Court House of such quarrels and fights between man and wife, widens the breach, makes a reconciliation almost impossible, and encourages insubordination; and in respect to the public, it has a pernicious tendency: so, *pro bono publico,* such matters are excluded from the Courts, unless there is a permanent injury or excessive violence or cruelty indicating malignity and vindictiveness.

In this case the wife commenced the quarrel. The husband, in a passion provoked by excessive abuse, pulled her upon the floor by the hair, but restrained himself, did not strike a blow, and she admits he did not choke her, and she continued to abuse him after she got up. Upon this state of facts the jury ought to have been charged in favor of the defendant. . . .

It was insisted by Mr. Winston [counsel for the state] that, admitting such to be the law when the husband and wife lived together, it did not apply when, as in this case, they were living apart. That may be so when there is a divorce "from bed and board," because the law then recognizes and allows the separation, but it can take no notice of a private agreement to live separate. The husband is still responsible for her acts, and the marriage relation and its incidents remain unaffected. . . .

State v. Rhodes,

61 N.C. 453 (Phil. Law 1868)

The defendant was indicted for an assault and battery upon his wife, Elizabeth Rhodes. Upon the evidence submitted to them the jury returned the following special verdict:

"We find that the defendant struck Elizabeth Rhodes, his wife, three licks, with a switch about the size of one of his fingers (but not as large as a man's thumb) without any provocation except some words uttered by her and not recollected by the witness."

His Honor was of opinion that the defendant had a right to whip his wife with a switch no larger than his thumb, and that upon the facts found in the special verdict he was not guilty in law. Judgment in favor of the defendant was accordingly entered and the State appealed.

Reade, J. The violence complained of would without question have constituted a battery if the subject of it had not been the defendant's wife. The question is how far that fact affects the case.

The courts have been loth to take cognizance of trivial complaints arising out of the domestic relations—such as master and apprentice, teacher and pupil, parent and child, husband and wife. Not because those relations are not subject to the law, but because the evil of publicity would be greater than the evil involved in the trifles complained of; and because they ought to be left to family government. On the civil side of this court, under our divorce laws, such cases have been unavoidable, and not unfrequent. On the criminal side there are but two cases reported. In one the question was, whether the wife was a competent witness to prove a battery by the husband upon her, which inflicted no great or permanent injury. It was decided that she was not. In discussing the subject the court said, that the abstract question of the husband's right to whip his wife did not arise. . . .The other case was one of a slight battery by the husband upon the wife after gross provocation. He was held not to be punishable. In that case the court said, that unless some permanent injury be inflicted, or there be an excess of violence, or such a degree of cruelty as shows that it is inflicted to gratify his own bad passions, the law will not invade the domestic forum, or go behind the curtain. *State v. Black*, 1 Winst., 266. Neither of those cases is like the one before us. The first case turned upon the competency of the wife as a witness, and in the second there was a slight battery upon a strong provocation.

In this case no provocation worth the name was proved. The fact found was that it was "without any provocation except some words which were not recollected by the witness." The words must have been of the slightest import to have made no impression on the memory. We must therefore, consider the violence as unprovoked. The question is therefore plainly presented, whether the court will allow a conviction of the husband for moderate correction of the wife without provocation.

Our divorce laws do not compel a separation of husband and wife, unless the conduct of the husband be so cruel as to render the wife's condition intolerable, or her life burdensome. What sort of conduct on the part of the husband, would be allowed to have that effect, has been repeatedly considered. And it has not been found easy to lay down any iron rule upon the subject. In some cases it has been held that actual and repeated violence to the person, was not sufficient. In others that insults, indignities and neglect without any actual violence, were quite sufficient. So much does each case depend upon its peculiar surroundings.

We have sought the aid of the experience and wisdom of other times, and of other countries.

Blackstone says "that the husband, by the old law, might give the wife moderate correction, for as he was to answer for her misbehavior, he ought to have the power to control her; but that in the polite reign of Charles the Second, this power of correction began to be doubted.". . .Wharton says, that by the ancient common law the husband possessed the power to chastise his wife; but that the tendency of criminal courts in the present day, is to regard the marital relation as no defense to a battery. . . .Chancellor Walworth says of such correction, that it is not authorized by the law of any civilized country; not indeed meaning that England is not civilized, but referring to the anomalous relics of barbarism which cleave to her jurisprudence. . . .The old law of moderate correction has been questioned even in England, and has been repudiated in Ireland and Scotland. The old rule is approved in Mississippi, but it has met with but little favor elsewhere in the United States. . . .In looking into the discussions of the other States we find but little uniformity.

From what has been said it will be seen how much the subject is at sea. And, probably, it will ever be so: for it will always be influenced by the habits, manners and condition of every community. Yet it is necessary that we should lay down something as precise and practical as the nature of the subject will admit of, for the guidance of our courts.

Our conclusion is that family government is recognized by law as being as complete in itself as the State government is in itself, and yet subordinate to it; and that we will not interfere with or attempt to control it, in favor of either husband or wife, unless in cases where permanent or malicious injury is inflicted or threatened, or the condition of the party is intolerable. For, however great are the evils of ill temper, quarrels, and even personal conflicts inflicting only temporary pain, they are not comparable with the evils which would result from raising the curtain, and exposing to public curiosity and criticism, the nursery and the bed chamber. Every household has and must have, a government of its own, modelled to suit the temper, disposition and condition of its inmates. Mere ebullitions of passion, impulsive violence, and temporary pain, affection will soon forget and forgive; and each member will find excuse for the other in his own frailties. But when trifles are taken hold of by the public, and the parties are exposed and disgraced, and each endeavors to justify himself or herself by criminating the other, that which ought to be forgotten in a day, will be remembered for life.

It is urged in this case, that as there was no provocation the violence was of course excessive and malicious; that every one in whatever relation of life should be able to purchase immunity from pain, by obedience to authority and faithfulness in duty. And it is insisted, that in the *State v. Pendegrass*, 2 D. & B., 365, which was the case of a school-mistress whipping a child, that doctrine is laid down. It is true that it is there said, that the master may be punishable even when he does not transcend the powers granted; *i.e.*, when he does not inflict permanent injury, if he grossly abuse his powers, and use them as a cover for his malice. But observe, the language is, if he *grossly* abuse his powers. So that every one would say at once, there was no cause for it, and it was purely malicious and cruel. If this be not the rule then every violence which would amount to an assault upon a stranger, would have to be investigated to see whether there was any provocation. And that would contravene what we have said, that we will punish no case of trifling importance. If in every such case we are to hunt for the provocation, how will the proof be supplied? Take the case before us. The witness said, there was no provocation except some slight words. But then who can tell what significance the trifling words may have had to the husband? Who can tell what had happened an hour before, and every hour for a week? To him they may have been sharper than a sword. And so in every case, it might be impossible for the court to appreciate what might be offered as an excuse, or no excuse might appear at all, when a complete justification exists. Or, suppose the provocation could in every case be known, and the court should undertake to weigh the provocation in every trifling family broil, what would be the standard? Suppose a case coming up to us from a hovel, where neither delicacy of sentiment nor refinement of manners is appreciated or known. The parties themselves would be amazed, if they were to be held responsible for rudeness or trifling violence. What do they care for insults and indignities? In such cases what end would be gained by investigation or punishment? Take a case from the middle class, where modesty and purity have their abode but nevertheless have not immunity from the frailties of nature, and are sometimes moved by the mysteries of passion. What could be more harassing to them, or injurious to society, than to draw a crowd around their seclusion. Or take a case from the higher ranks, where education and culture have so refined nature, that a look cuts like a knife, and a word strikes like a hammer; where the most delicate attention gives pleasure, and the slightest neglect pain; where an indignity is disgrace and exposure is ruin. Bring all these cases into court side by side, with the same offense charged and the same proof made; and what conceivable charge of the court to the jury would be alike appropriate to all the cases, except, That they all have domestic government, which they have formed for themselves, suited to their own peculiar conditions, and that those governments are supreme, and from them there is no appeal except in cases of great importance requiring the strong arm of the law, and that to those governments they must submit themselves.

It will be observed that the ground upon which we have put this decision, is not, that the husband has the *right* to whip his wife much or little; but that we will not interfere with family government in trifling cases. We will no more interfere where the husband whips the wife, than where the wife whips the husband; and yet we would hardly be supposed to hold, that a wife has a *right* to whip her husband. We will not inflict upon society the greater evil of raising the curtain upon domestic privacy, to punish the lesser evil of trifling violence. Two boys under fourteen years of age fight upon the playground, and yet the courts will take no notice of it, not for the reason that boys have the *right* to fight, but because the interests of society require that they should be left to the more appropriate discipline of the school room and of home. It is not true that boys have a right to fight; nor is it true that a husband has a right to whip his wife. And if he had, it is not easily seen how *the thumb* is the standard of size for the instrument which he may use, as some of the old authorities have said; and in deference to which was his Honor's charge. A light blow, or many light blows, with a stick larger than the thumb, might produce no injury; but a switch half the size might be so used as to produce death. The standard is the *effect produced*, and not the manner of producing it, or the instrument used.

Because our opinion is not in unison with the decisions of some of the sister States, or with the philosophy of some very respectable law writers, and could not be in unison with all because of their contrariety,—a decent respect for the opinions of others has induced us to be very full in stating the reasons for our conclusion. There is no error. . . .Per curiam.

State v. Mabrey,
64 N.C. 592 (1870)

The jury found, by a special verdict, that on the 7th day of June 1869, at the house of the defendant, &c., the latter and his wife had some words and he threatened to leave her; after some very improper language by him, she started off, when he caught her by the left arm, and said he would kill her, and drew his knife and struck at her with it, but did not strike her; that he drew back as if to strike again, and his arm was caught by a bystander, whereupon the wife got away and ran about fifteen steps; that the defendant did not pursue her, but told her not to return, if she did he would kill her; that he did not strike her, or inflict any personal injury, and that he was a man of violent character . . . .

His Honor thereupon being of opinion that the defendant was not guilty, there was a Verdict and Judgment accordingly; and the Solicitor for the State appealed.

Reade, J. The facts present a case of savage and dangerous outrage, not to be tolerated in a country of laws and Christianity. We rigidly adhere to the doctrine, in *State v. Rhodes*, Phil. 453, and precedent cases in our reports, that the Courts will not invade the domestic forum, to take cognizance of trifling cases of violence in family government; but there is no relation which can shield a party who is guilty of malicious outrage or dangerous violence committed or threatened. In *State v. Rhodes*, the jury had been charged that "the husband had the right to whip his wife with a switch no larger than his thumb." In combatting that error, the Court said: "A light blow, or many light blows with a stick larger than the thumb, might produce no injury; but a switch half the size might be so used as to produce death. The standard is the *effect produced*, and not the manner of producing it, or the instrument used." Those words were used as applicable to the facts in that case. But on the argument at the bar in this case, they were perverted to mean that in any case, no matter what weapon was used or from what motive or intent, unless permanent injury were inflicted, the Court would not interfere therefore, *here,* although death was threatened a deadly knife used, yet as it was averted by a bystander, the Court will not interfere. We repudiate any such construction of *State v. Rhodes*.

Upon the special verdict there ought to have been judgment against the defendant. . . .There is error. Per curiam.

People v. Berry,
18 Cal. 3d 509, 556 P.2d 777, 134 Cal. Rptr. 415 (1976)

Sullivan, J. Defendant Albert Joseph Berry was charged by indictment with one count of murder. . .and one count of assault by means of force likely to produce great bodily injury . . . .The indictment was amended to allege one prior felony conviction which defendant admitted. . . .The assault was allegedly committed on July 23, 1974, and the murder on July 26, 1974. In each count, the alleged victim was defendant's wife, Rachel Pessah Berry. A jury found defendant guilty as charged and determined that the murder was of the first degree. . . .Defendant was sentenced to state prison for the term prescribed by law. He appeals from the judgment of conviction.

Defendant contends that there is sufficient evidence in the record to show that he committed the homicide while in a state of uncontrollable rage caused by provocation and flowing from a condition of diminished capacity and therefore that it was error for the trial court to fail to instruct the jury on voluntary manslaughter as indeed he had requested. He claims: (1) that he was entitled to an instruction on voluntary manslaughter. . . since the killing was done upon a sudden quarrel or heat of passion; and (2) that he was also entitled to an instruction on voluntary manslaughter in the context of a diminished capacity defense. . .since malice was negatived by mental defect or disease. . . .We agree with defendant as to the first instruction, but not as to the second.

Defendant, a cook, 46 years old, and Rachel Pessah, a 20-year-old girl from Israel, were married on May 27, 1974. Three days later Rachel went to Israel by herself, returning on July 13, 1974. On July 23, 1974, defendant choked Rachel into unconsciousness. She was treated at a hospital where she reported her strangulation by defendant to an officer of the San Francisco Police Department. On July 25, Inspector Sammon, who had been assigned to the case, met with Rachel and as a result of the interview a warrant was issued for defendant's arrest.

While Rachel was at the hospital, defendant removed his clothes from their apartment and stored them in a Greyhound Bus Depot locker. He stayed overnight at the home of a friend, Mrs. Jean Berk, admitting to her that he had choked his wife. On July 26, he telephoned Mrs. Berk and informed her that he had killed Rachel with a telephone cord on that morning at their apartment. The next day Mrs. Berk and two others telephoned the police to report a possible homicide and met Officer Kelleher at defendant's apartment. They gained entry and found Rachel on the bathroom floor. A pathologist from the coroner's office concluded that the cause of Rachel's death was strangulation. Defendant was arrested on August 1, 1974, and confessed to the killing.

At trial defendant did not deny strangling his wife, but claimed through his own testimony and the testimony of a psychiatrist, Dr. Martin Blinder, that he was provoked into killing her because of a sudden and uncontrollable rage so as to reduce the offense to one of voluntary manslaughter. He testified that upon her return from Israel, Rachel announced to him that while there she had fallen in love with another man, one Yako, and had enjoyed his sexual favors, that he was coming to this country to claim her and that she wished a divorce. Thus commenced a tormenting two weeks in which Rachel alternately taunted defendant with her involvement with Yako and at the same time sexually excited defendant, indicating her desire to remain with him. Defendant's detailed testimony, summarized below, chronicles this strange course of events.

After their marriage, Rachel lived with defendant for only three days and then left for Israel. Immediately upon her return to San Francisco she told defendant about her relationship with and love for Yako. This brought about further argument and a brawl that evening in which defendant choked Rachel and she responded by scratching him deeply many times. Nonetheless they continued to live together. Rachel kept taunting defendant with Yako and demanding a divorce. She claimed she thought she might be pregnant by Yako. She showed defendant pictures of herself with Yako. Nevertheless, during a return trip from Santa Rosa, Rachel demanded immediate sexual intercourse with defendant in the car, which was achieved; however upon reaching their apartment, she again stated that she loved Yako and that she would not have intercourse with defendant in the future.

On the evening of July 22d defendant and Rachel went to a movie where they engaged in heavy petting. When they returned home and got into bed, Rachel announced that she had intended to make love with defendant, "But I am saving myself for this man Yako, so I don't think I will." Defendant got out of bed and prepared to leave the apartment whereupon Rachel screamed and yelled at him. Defendant choked her into unconsciousness.

Two hours later defendant called a taxi for his wife to take her to the hospital. He put his clothes in the Greyhound bus station and went to the home of his friend Mrs. Berk for the night. The next day he went to Reno and returned the day after. Rachel informed him by telephone that there was a warrant for his arrest as a result of her report to the police about the choking incident. On July 25th defendant returned to the apartment to talk to Rachel, but she was out. He slept there overnight. Rachel returned around 11 a.m. the next day. Upon seeing defendant there, she said, "I suppose you have come here to kill me." Defendant responded, "yes," changed his response to "no," and then again to "yes," and finally stated "I have really come to talk to you." Rachel began screaming. Defendant grabbed her by the shoulder and tried to stop her screaming. She continued. They struggled and finally defendant strangled her with a telephone cord.

Dr. Martin Blinder, a physician and psychiatrist, called by the defense. . ., testified that Rachel was a depressed, suicidally inclined girl and that this suicidal impulse led her to involve herself ever more deeply in a dangerous situation with defendant. She did this by sexually arousing him and taunting him into jealous rages in an unconscious desire to provoke him into killing her and thus consummating her desire for suicide. Throughout the period commencing with her return from Israel until her death, that is from July 13 to July 26, Rachel continually provoked defendant with sexual taunts and incitements, alternating acceptance and rejection of him. This conduct was accompanied by repeated references to her involvement with another man; it led defendant to choke her on two occasions, until finally she achieved her unconscious desire and was strangled. Dr. Blinder testified that as a result of this cumulative series of provocations, defendant at the time he fatally strangled Rachel, was in a state of uncontrollable rage, completely under the sway of passion.

We first take up defendant's claim that on the basis of the foregoing evidence he was entitled to an instruction on voluntary manslaughter as defined by statute which is "the unlawful killing of a human being, without malice. . .upon a sudden quarrel or heat of passion.". . .In *People v. Valentine*, 28 Cal. 2d 121, 169 P.2d 1 (1946), this court, in an extensive review of the law of manslaughter, specifically approved the following quotation from *People v. Logan*, 175 Cal. 45, 48-49, 164 P. 1121 (1917), as a correct statement of the law: "In the present condition of our law *it is left to the jurors* to say whether or not the facts and circumstances in evidence are sufficient to lead them to believe that the defendant did, or to create a reasonable doubt in their minds as to whether or not he did, commit his offense under a heat of passion. The jury is further to be admonished and advised by the court that this heat of passion must be such a passion as would naturally be aroused in the mind of an ordinarily reasonable person under the given facts and circumstances, and that, consequently, no defendant may set up his own standard of conduct and justify or excuse himself because in fact his passions were aroused, unless further the jury believe that the facts and circumstances were sufficient to arouse the passions of the ordinarily reasonable man. . . .For the fundamental of the inquiry is whether or not the defendant's reason was, at the time of his act, so disturbed or obscured by some passion—not necessarily fear and never, of course, the passion for revenge—to such an extent as would render ordinary men of average disposition liable to act rashly or without due deliberation and reflection, and from this passion rather than from judgment." (. . .italics in original.)

We further held in *Valentine* that there is no specific type of provocation required. . .and that verbal provocation may be sufficient. [In later cases] we. . .declared that evidence of admissions of infidelity by the defendant's paramour, taunts directed to him and other conduct, "supports a finding that defendant killed in wild desperation induced by [the woman's] long continued provocatory conduct.". . .We find this reasoning persuasive in the case now before us. Defendant's testimony chronicles a two-week period of provocatory conduct by his wife Rachel that could arouse a passion of jealousy, pain and sexual rage in an ordinary man of average disposition such as to cause him to act rashly from this passion. It is significant that both defendant and Dr. Blinder testified that the former was in the heat of passion under an uncontrollable rage when he killed Rachel.

The Attorney General contends that the killing could not have been done in the heat of passion because there was a cooling period, defendant having waited in the apartment for 20 hours. However, the long course of provocatory conduct, which had resulted in intermittent outbreaks of rage under specific provocation in the past, reached its final culmination in the apartment when Rachel began screaming. Both defendant and Dr. Blinder testified that defendant killed in a state of uncontrollable rage, of passion, and there is ample evidence in the record to support the conclusion that this passion was the result of the long course of provocatory conduct by Rachel . . . .

[The court set out the state of the law regarding defendant's second contention that under the evidence in the record he was entitled to an instruction on voluntary manslaughter in the context of a diminished capacity defense.] Dr. Blinder specifically testified that defendant was sane and that he was neither schizophrenic nor psychotic. He at no time testified that defendant was suffering from a mental illness or mental defect. Rather he stated that at the time of the killing, defendant was in an "altered mental state," which the doctor identified as one of uncontrollable rage and he further explained that this state was "a product of having to contend with what seems to me an incredibly provocative situation, an incredibly provocative young woman, and that this immediate situation was superimposed upon Mr. Berry having encountered the situation time and time again." In sum, Dr. Blinder testified to a heat of passion aroused in defendant by a course of provocatory conduct on the part of Rachel, but never testified to any mental illness or mental defect on the part of defendant. Therefore, defendant was not entitled to an instruction on voluntary manslaughter in the context of diminished capacity and the trial court did not err in refusing such instruction. . . .

[The conviction for murder in the first degree is reversed. The conviction for assault by means of force likely to produce great bodily injury is modified to strike reference to a prior felony conviction, but as modified is affirmed.]

Chief Justice Wright and Justices McComb, Tobriner, Mosk, Clark, and Richardson concur.

Nora E. Groce, Special Groups at Risk of Abuse: The Disabled, in *Abuse and Victimization Across the Life Span* 223, 232–33 (Martha B. Straus ed., 1988)

The term "the disabled" includes persons with a number of physical and psychological conditions ranging from hyperactivity to mental retardation and including cerebral palsy, epilepsy, autism, deafness, blindness, paraplegia, quadriplegia, and many others. What the disabled in our society have most in common is not their specific physical or mental limitations, which may vary widely, but the fact that they must all deal with a larger nondisabled population that dictates the norms.

Although our definitions of what constitutes a disability and who is included within the disabled group are at times imprecise, nevertheless the literature on domestic violence indicates that disabled individuals appear statistically to be at a substantially greater risk for abuse and neglect than other members of society. Disabled children, disabled adults, and disabled adults who are themselves parents constitute three subgroups within this population. . . .

Almost all the literature on violence and disability deals with the abuse or neglect of disabled children. In keeping with a general cultural perception of disabled individuals as being "childlike," issues such as sexuality, marriage, and childbearing, and parenting, and by extension domestic violence, and sexual abuse, are rarely addressed. But disabled adults, particularly those whose condition makes them dependent on others for some or all of their care, are also at risk for physical and sexual abuse in the home, in the hospital, in nursing homes, and in institutions. Again the body of carefully collected data is minimal, but all who have worked in the field, as well as many disabled individuals and groups in the disability rights movement, increasingly have called attention to this widespread and disturbing situation.

Violence is a very real presence in many American homes, and the homes of disabled adults are no exception. Violence in the deaf community, for example, has become an acknowledged "hot" topic in recent years. Disabled spouses often find themselves in a situation where they not only are victims of violence in their homes, but are also unable to apply for even the few community programs designed for the nondisabled. Without a TTY (teletype machine) for example, a hotline is of little help to a deaf woman. A shelter without ramps is inaccessible to a wheelchair user who has been repeatedly beaten and needs to leave home. A general prejudice against the disabled that in part tells them they are "lucky to find anyone" further militates against their even considering a request for help.

Those who must relegate part or all of their physical care to others often rely on individuals or staff who are frequently undertrained, undersupervised, underpaid and overworked. Staff members' anger may build, and often the victims are the very people they have been hired to care for. The most vulnerable are often the easiest targets. For example, abuse is known to be most widespread among elderly women with multiple physical and mental disabilities.

Sexual abuse of the disabled is also known to exist, though it has rarely been discussed until recently. Again statistics are few, but they do suggest that victimization is as prevalent among the disabled as among others. Although the National Rape Information Center does not keep separate statistics on the disabled, [a study has]. . . estimated that between ten thousand and one hundred thousand disabled women were victims of rape in 1981. [It is noted]. . .that these figures do not include incest or other types of sexual assault by individuals well known to the victim, which are more prevalent than rape. Similarly, the Seattle Rape Relief and Sexual Assault Center provided services to nearly seven hundred rape victims who had some form of disability between 1977 and 1983, and project administrators estimate that this figure represents perhaps 20 percent of the total number of sexually abused disabled. The high percentage of abuse by known assailants reflects the more isolated and protected lives of many disabled, who are likely to live in more restricted and intimate environments. As disabled men and women increasingly move into the mainstream, they may well become more frequent targets of stranger assaults.

Nancy Hammond, Lesbian Victims and the Reluctance to Identify Abuse, in *Naming the Violence: Speaking Out About Lesbian Battering* 190, 193–96 (Kerry Lobel ed., 1986)

It is critical, as we expand and explore our strengths as women and lesbians, that we continue to turn to other women for emotional support and constructive feedback. This process has been a very difficult one for the lesbian abuse victim. In addition to the traditional socialization messages about her role as a relationship nurturer, she has added conflicts and commitments as a lesbian (and often as a feminist) that support her reluctance to identify and acknowledge the extent of her abuse.

Lesbians often draw their emotional support from the lesbian subculture, and the number of women participating in a lesbian community often seems limited even in large cities. Many lesbian couples share close friends. When battering occurs, the battered lesbian is presented with a conflict about whom she can talk to. She may fear shaming her partner before the women who are the partner's friends, as well as hers. She may fear that mutual friends will take her lover's side, and minimize the significance of the violence because the perpetrator is a friend, and another lesbian. The lesbian victim who is isolated from other lesbians—because of geographical location, fear of coming out, or lack of knowledge about how to find other lesbians—is faced with far greater loneliness in her victimization. She may see her current partner as her only support system or her only available choice if she wishes to have a lover. She may perceive confronting the violence as a choice to live alone, with no other lesbian contact, for years into her future.

For most of us, it is relatively easy to spot male victimization of women, and to see the need for women to leave those situations where they are being abused by men. It is far more difficult for us to sort out our victimization of each other, both as women and as lesbians. We may believe that it is our responsibility, even as victims of abuse, to support our partners and to help them to change their violent behavior. We may fear that, as the truth of the violence is realized, mutual friends will totally reject us or our violent partner. We may hold ourselves responsible for labeling the ones we have loved as batterers, with this label following them, and isolating them from other women, far into the future. If we would prefer to remain with a partner who had been violent, and to work on those issues, we may fear that friends will tell us to leave the relationship, that it will never work out.

Ironically, we may be more tempted as lesbians to hold victims responsible for the physical violence they suffer. As members of a lesbian feminist culture, we support women's assumption of power. We take pride in our strength and fortitude as individuals, and in our ability to survive and grow even stronger. It is hard for our friends to see us, strong and tough-minded women that we are, as victims of abuse from partners who may be physically smaller. Paradoxically, even our friends might buy into the old stereotype that somehow, women aren't big enough or strong enough to really do each other damage in a physical fight. It is hard for us to acknowledge that a woman we love is capable of being cruel, violent, and brutal. We may fear to defend ourselves, believing that we are capable of inflicting far greater damage on our lovers than they are inflicting on us. If we do fight back to defend ourselves, our guilt may cause us to feel equally to blame, leading us to label ourselves as abusive. The shame from this may lead us to further secret-keeping and isolation. . . .

Homophobia clearly plays a role in the reluctance of lesbian victims to seek help. The controversies within the shelter movement about lesbian issues are now well known. Although many shelter workers are lesbians, they are often under pressure to stay in the closet to protect funding possibilities controlled by the straight community. Shelter programs have been designed for straight women, and shelter residents may be homophobic themselves. It is often difficult for those shelter workers who might reach out to the lesbian victim to do so because of the homophobia around them. Many lesbians would be horrified at the thought of calling for police protection, or arrest of their partner, an option increasingly more available to white heterosexual women. And lesbians are less likely than heterosexual women to turn to family members for emotional support in the aftermath of violence. Those who are not out to family members would have a hard time talking around the issue. Those who are out may fear reinforcing stereotypes of the "sickness" of lesbian relationships and lifestyles.

Jo-Ellen Asbury, African-American Women in Violent Relationships: An Exploration of Cultural Differences, in *Violence in the Black Family: Correlates and Consequences* 89, 100–02 (Robert L. Hampton ed., 1987)

One resource that typically has been available to African-American women, perhaps to a greater extent than to women of other cultures, is the extended family. . . .[B]attered women, regardless of culture, are likely to seek support and guidance from family and friends. This predilection is likely to be even stronger among African-American women, given the longstanding tradition of extended families and social support in African-American communities . . . .This option may not be advantageous, however, because most family members and friends lack the professional training necessary to handle such crises. Certainly they lack the objectivity that someone outside the family network is likely to possess.

Beyond questions of whether appropriate help is available, the women must choose to take advantage of the help. The African-American woman's special experience results in different considerations in making that choice. . . .[Research] suggests a greater feeling of social isolation among African-American women, which may influence their decision to seek out domestic violence shelters. Because they are African-Americans in a society dominated by European-Americans, they may feel that they will not be understood or even welcomed at shelters outside their immediate community.

An African-American woman's decision to seek help may also be influenced by her feelings about her abuser. Although studies have shown that battered women of all ethnic backgrounds may be reluctant to reveal their abuse out of concern for their abusers, this may be an even greater consideration among African-American women. . . .African-American males are in a more vulnerable position than other males relative to the dominant culture. Being aware of this suppression,. . .may make African-American women reluctant to expose them to more ridicule.

An African-American woman may also be more reluctant to bring attention to her situation if she has internalized common stereotypes about African-American women. In the media and in popular literature these women are portrayed as everything from sexual temptresses to ugly mammies, from the sturdy bridges who hold together the race (and therefore the community) to emasculating matriarchs who are responsible for the instability of the family (and therefore the community) because they drive away their men with their domination. Of particular interest to the present discussion is the image of African-American women as a source of strength and independence. To gain this impression, one has only to survey the titles of some recent publications about African-American women, such as *Sturdy Black Bridges* and *. . .But Some of Us Are Brave.*

An African-American woman's decision to seek help may also depend on whether she has internalized some of these stereotypes. While many African-American women have had to exhibit strength and independence for their own survival, this image may be problematic for those women who find themselves in violent relationships. When an abused woman believes that strength and independence are expected of her, she may be more reluctant to call attention to her situation, feeling that she should be able to handle it on her own; she may deny the seriousness of her situation. Thus she may remain immobile, hampered by her belief in inner resources she may not possess.

Confronted continually with European-American standards of beauty and femininity, an African-American woman might well conclude that she is unattractive. This possibility, combined with recent estimates that there are four African-American women for every African-American male, may make her less likely to risk endangering the relationship by exposing the batterer. . . .

Finally, we must consider unique aspects of the African-American experience in attempts to change the battered woman's situation. Most of the mainstream literature on this question focuses on ways of inducing the woman to end the relationship. Certainly this is often the only alternative. The African-American woman, however, has typically been led to believe that it is her responsibility to maintain the family, regardless of the costs to herself; thus she may be likely to remain and do nothing. She may also be more interested than women of other ethnic groups in working with a professional toward modifying her abuser's behavior. These differences must be considered in designing a therapeutic approach in working with African-American women.

Other factors, however, suggest that it may be less difficult for an African-American woman to walk away from an abusive relationship. Though typically they occupy the lowest-paying positions, African-American women have historically participated in the paid labor force in greater proportions than European-American women. Combined with the image of strength and independence, this concrete indicator of her ability to support herself and her children may facilitate her leaving. Obviously this hypothesis contradicts the notion that the image of strength and independence is debilitating and raises yet another question for future study. Does the internalization of these images immobilize the African-American woman or empower her? Because it is likely that both possibilities occur, what are the differentiating variables or conditions? Counseling African-American women without this knowledge is not likely to be appropriate or effective.

Nilda Rimonte, Domestic Violence Among Pacific Asians, in *Making Waves: An Anthology of Writings by and about Asian American Women* 327, 327–32, 334–35, 337 (Asian Women United of California ed., 1989)

The typical Pacific Asian battered woman exhibits a wide range of characteristics. She may be a first-generation immigrant or a refugee. She may speak fluent English or any of the forty different Pacific Asian languages and dialects that are represented in Los Angeles County. She may be highly educated or preliterate, have an income of $22,050 or make less than the legal minimum hourly wage. She may have arrived here legally or "creatively"; lived in the United States for years or be an imported bride of barely three months. Such a woman will in time also exhibit the characteristics of someone so badly abused that she feels helpless; so diminished in self-esteem that she feels she deserves nothing more; and so lacking in a sense of self that she is almost invisible to herself as well as to her family and community.

Of the approximately three thousand Pacific Asian clients served by the Center for the Pacific Asian Family in Los Angeles between 1978 and 1985, one-third were Korean, one-third Southeast Asians (mostly Vietnamese), and the last third distributed among Chinese, Filipinos, Japanese, South Asians, Thais, Samoans, and others. It should be noted that this breakdown reflects to some degree the presence of staff from, and their outreach to, specific ethnic groups. For instance, having Korean-speaking workers at the center from the start has resulted in more response from that community. . . .

Domestic violence, or wife abuse, occurs among Pacific Asians as often as it does in the dominant community, in approximately one out of every two marital relationships. Factors contributing to this fact include the Pacific Asian family's traditionally patriarchal system and the attendant belief in the supremacy of the male; the socialization goals and processes which favor the family and community over the individual; the cultural emphasis on silent suffering versus open communication of needs and feelings; and the enormous adjustment pressures which test the limits of immigrants' and refugees' survival skills. Cultural norms and values directly or indirectly sanction abuse against women and tend to minimize it as a problem in the community.

Traditionally Pacific Asians conceal and deny problems that threaten group pride and may bring on shame. Because of the strong emphasis on obligations to the family, a Pacific Asian woman will often remain silent rather than admit to a problem that might disgrace her family. If domestic violence is made public, the topic is given short shrift. . . .

[M]any Pacific Asian families can survive only on the combined incomes of husband and wife . . . .This need for both spouses to work creates changes in the family and sex role system. These changes are perceived as liberating by the woman, but extremely threatening by the man. Often he will describe these changes as the Americanization of his Asian wife. . . .

[T]he Pacific Asian man resists the change. He insists on his accustomed privileges and esteemed place: she mustn't change; she mustn't turn her back on her ethnic culture; she mustn't become Americanized. She mustn't, that is, abandon him.

Such dependency is made clear in the desperate efforts of abusive husbands to retrieve women whom they have abused and who have fled for their lives. . . .

Thus a woman is first brutalized, and then pressured to conceal her victimization. Fear, guilt, and shame are the means by which pressure is applied. Hence the community shelters the inequality between women and men and nurtures the ancient patriarchal family structure. . . .

The Pacific Asian family has been the traditional source of support and nurturance to its members. The emotional and economic security that the individual finds within the bosom of her family are seen to compensate for the harsh restrictions and de-emphasis on individuality. Even the achievements of individual Asians are generally laid at the doorstep of a highly supportive family which throws the full weight of all its resources behind the aspiring individual—albeit for the glory and future economic well-being of the family itself.

Nevertheless, this system, which is propped up by traditional sex roles, that is, male dominance, results in a power imbalance. Wherever that imbalance exists—especially without the mediating presence of elders—there is always at least the potential for violence. . . .

[T]he Pacific Asian woman faces betrayal. First, her attacker comes from the very group to which she has been taught to turn. Second, when relatives are available, they often discourage her from taking steps toward safety and rescue because they too believe in the traditional role of women. Even when they recognize her need to risk family disapproval for the sake of survival, they often are in no position economically to provide significant assistance. Third, community gatekeepers are interested in maintaining the status quo in order to preserve the culture. Church leaders, for example, preach the acceptance of private suffering for the sake of peace. In any case, the Pacific Asian woman is often ineluctably alone. . . .

If a woman does leave, she must face the possible loss of control over her children. . . .

The woman who chooses to leave suffers from intense conflicts. . . .[S]he feels guilt about having chosen herself and her goals over those of her family; she feels she has betrayed her ethnic values. She also experiences shame about her failure to live up to community-prescribed roles and behaviors; she is deeply concerned about what the community might think of her. Finally, her children—depending on their ages and on their relationship with their father—bring pressures to bear on her decision to stay away or return. . . .

Immigrants and refugees all confront loss. What is lost is the security which comes from the familiar . . . .

In order to cope in the new country, immigrants are forced to accept change, but the change involves still another kind of loss. This time the loss is of traditional beliefs, attitudes, roles, and lifestyles. . . .

Asian Pacific cultures allow a certain amount of violence as a behavior-shaping tool and a way of venting frustrations. Nonetheless such violence seems acceptable only when directed at women and children and other social inferiors.

Acknowledging that the use of violence as a form of power and control is rooted in and sanctioned by a culture does not mean, however, that the culture is itself the problem. The problem is still the battering. Shifting responsibility for battering from the abuser to the cultural system means that the individual is not held responsible. If this is true, then there is no victimizer and consequently no victim. Without a victim, no law has been broken, and therefore there is no crime. An additional problem results from blaming the culture: Because the system of beliefs, values, and norms is difficult to alter, those working for the abolition of violence against women and children could feel paralyzed by the enormity of their task. . . .

It would be ironic if the cultural concept of a strong family should become the very force that would cause the family to disintegrate. . . .In articulating the mission and philosophy of the Center for the Pacific Asian Family I wrote in 1979 that "adaptability is the hallmark of the survivor species." I believe this to be true of the Pacific Asian.

Angela Ginorio & Jane Reno, Violence in the Lives of Latina Women, in *The Speaking Profits Us: Violence in the Lives of Women of Color* 13 (Center for the Prevention of Sexual & Domestic Violence, Seattle, Wash., Maryviolet Burns ed., 1986)[2]

Published facts and statistics about violence in the lives of Latina[3] women are difficult to find. An examination of standard professional literature, government reports, and recent publications confirms this opinion. A recent literature search of publications in psychology and sociology for the past three years yielded only three references on Hispanics and violence. [O]nly one was directly related to violence in women's lives. With the exception of rape, official government reports provide little information that includes Latinas and most publications that address the issue of violence in women's lives do not mention women of color beyond the perfunctory disclaimer that results discussed may not apply to them. . . .

This absence of information about Latina women reflects the triple burden of discrimination under which we function in this society: ignored by men because we are women, ignored by white women because we are women of color, and ignored by the English-speaking because so often we can only speak in Spanish or Portuguese. As social scientists and practitioners we have experienced this lack of written information before and have made the study of Latina women's issues a main focus of concern. At such times our own experiences become facts—limited, individualized, incomplete, but still facts; facts rooted in our experiences as Latina women, as women of color in a racist society, as social researchers and counselors working with women. These facts are also shaped by the collective and individual cumulative adaptions that Latina women in the U.S. have made to the culture of origin (the impact of Spanish/Portuguese colonization) and to the U.S. society.

Before we could begin to tackle the enormous task before us we had to rid ourselves of the universal burden that comes from the desire not to see that which is painful or that for which there is no framework outside of 'that's the way things are'. In 1971 two Puerto Rican women lawyers wrote a 500 page report about women's rights in Puerto Rico in which the only aspect of violence in women's lives mentioned is compulsory sterilization—and that only in the bibliography. There are also the many *students* of the Hispanic family who speak at length about the authoritarianism of the husband/father, timidly alluding to the potential abusive manifestations of this trait with regard to the children while carefully avoiding any mention of the most logical result of that with regard to the wife.

---

2. Authors names appear in alphabetical order thus a result not of our efforts which are equal but of the fortune of birth.

3. Throughout this paper Latina and Hispanic will be used interchangeably, Latina/o encompassing all people born south of the border with Mexico and Hispanics limited to those whose language is Spanish. The awkwardness of some phrase constructions with the word Latina precludes its usage throughout. Although these terms are used as a self-referent when speaking in global terms the authors prefer for themselves the more specific terms Chicana and Puerto Rican.

Helen Keller once said "The worst thing is to be born sighted but to lack vision". We were not born with the vision to see the violence around us; and once we saw it—there was always the inconsiderate neighbor or uncle who beat his wife publicly or too brutally—we did not have a framework that allowed us to place those instances within the realm of the right of women to live without violence. "She must have done something to deserve it". "He's a difficult man but she's too strongheaded/independent for her own good". "After a woman gets married her only choice is to obey/tolerate/understand/please"—you choose your own ending, for these were all acceptable explanations offered by family and society for wife abuse. And even today Mexican battered women living in the United States offer these as reasons to explain other women's abuse—although not their own. Even women such as my mother (Angela's) who was unwilling to accept the societal norm (and who threatened to maim the hand which my father was raising against her), judged other women harshly if they did not fit some prescribed norm of wifely behavior. This lack of support from family and friends often placed women in positions of total dependence upon their abusive husbands.

Women who were outspoken in the defense of other women's rights were the exception in an environment where women—in spite of the biblical injunction, "*Esposa te doy y no esclava*" ("A wife I give you and not a slave")—were seen as responsible for fulfilling all of men's wishes.

Our inability to place the abuse of women within the realm of violence stems from the patriarchal system under which we live. As in other traditional agricultural societies, family solidarity, subordination of women and respect for elders created a structure where large and extended families lived under patriarchal authority. Under the pattern which is prevalent, older family members order the younger and the men the women. This establishes interpersonal patterns in the family around the dimensions of respect and obedience to elders and male dominance. Paternalism was the prevailing attitude towards women. Women were regarded as irrational creatures who needed the strong discipline of more rational man ". . .who being born before woman was consequently more noble than she". Women's subordination was believed to be confirmed by natural and biblical law.

After decades of mixture of indigenous, Spanish/Portuguese, and in some regions African cultures, a prescriptive set of roles developed for each gender coded under the terms *machismo* and *marianismo*. Machismo is found in all cultures populated by Iberians and their descendants and refers to that constellation of behaviors that defined a man. The *machismo* concept has been given prominence in the literature as an almost exclusively Mexican phenomenon largely through the writings of Octavio Paz and the Mexican psychiatrist, Diaz Guerrero and as mainly a sexual phenomenon due to the misunderstanding of those researchers who brought the concept to the attention of U.S. readers. . . .

While the male role was defined in secular terms, the female role was more closely tied to the values and traditions of the Catholic Church. As females, the models presented to us were accepting, silent and constantly responsive to others' needs. We were told we were morally superior to and spiritually stronger than the male. Thus we must be mediators for him and represent him by our presence in the church and by our exemplary behavior. Any misbehavior by any family members reflects on the honor, pride and prestige of the male.

While the sexual component of the masculine sex role encouraged sexual experiences as part of any normal man's entitlement, the sexual component of the feminine counterpart discouraged it and limited it to an adjunct of maternity. Given the emphasis on the Virgin Mary, mother of God, as a model, the only acceptable reason for non-virginity was motherhood with no mention of sexual enjoyment. Childless non-virgins were objects of pity if married and of scorn if unmarried. Within this context, the violence of a woman's rape is compounded by the guilt and shame she experiences: in the case of unmarried women because she is no longer a virgin and in the case of married women because she has been "used" by a man other than her husband. The forms of address used for women emphasize virginity rather than marital status; if it is known that an unmarried woman is not a virgin she will be denied the title of *senorita* and she will not be granted that of *senora*. The set of beliefs that make the ideal of *marianismo* possible flow directly from the traditional doctrine of the Catholic Church. Because for so many women the Church has been the only avenue for participation and expression outside of the family, we have looked to the Church for leadership and support to help in establishing our identity as women. However, our moral and religious beliefs have often been a powerful impediment to change. Sexism in the Church has often reinforced passivity and acceptance of male domination. The religious stance on sexuality, rape, abortion and birth control has not made it possible to openly and frankly confront these issues so central to women's lives—neither in the privacy of the family nor in the public forum of society.

Although at least nominally, the vast majority of the population in Latin America (80-90 percent) is baptized Catholic, there is a long tradition of anticlericalism among men and a diversity of other religious practices. Those practices include traditional Protestantism, revivalist Protestant churches, spiritualism centers, *santería* (especially among the people from the Caribbean Basin), *curanderismo* (mostly among Mexicans), and other indigenous belief systems. The prescribed role for women in Protestant churches followed closely the cultural prescriptions although women were common among the clergy of the revivalist Protestant churches (often associated with lower class membership). About 90 percent of the 'mediums' in spiritualist centers are women, but not enough is known by the authors about their practices beyond the realm of belief to ascertain the impact this has on the prescriptions for women's roles. The impact of religion in the lives of Hispanics is probably as affected as language, food preference and other important aspects of their lives by their residence in the U.S. There is some evidence that practice diminishes and religious affiliation often changes. . . .

The following observations are made in reference to our experience with Hispanic women.

1. Violence is a term that carries many definitions. The question of how the Latina woman has experienced violence may be answered in several ways:
   a. As members of an ethnic minority Latina women suffer a triple

oppression: sexism as women, racism as Latinas, and often classism as poor. Violence often stems from the hopelessness and desperation of the poor and can be seen as symptomatic of our society. The conditions of poverty result in stress and crises associated with abuse.

b. Within the culture, marriage is often motivated by economic need. (Marriage then becomes a form of abuse in which a woman sells her body for food and shelter). A little publicized factor related to this is the incidence of majority males married to Latina women. Women lacking English language skills may be placed in virtual slavery and exploitation if they are in the U.S. alone.

c. Institutional violence is socially accepted. Latina women are used as subjects for birth control devices and medication. This type of violence must be recognized and eradicated.

2. In the move towards dealing with the problem of abuse, reference is made to the cultural aspects of abuse. If this is not merely an euphemism for race, it is imperative to modify our present systems to be more responsive to those who differ from the mainstream. The application of models foreign to the Latin America reality (such as undiluted psychoanalysis) results in explanations of personality, gender roles (*marianismo* and *machismo*), and family dynamics in pathological terms that equate difference to inferiority, irresponsibility and ineptitude.

3. A primary concern is that of under-reporting. Failure to report to majority agencies has resulted in limitations of statistical data. Gathering factual data must be a priority if the true extent of the problem of violence is to be addressed. Hispanics do not turn to majority services for many reasons, many of these not culturally related. The ambivalence toward "the system" is partly due to a belief that reporting abuse may be more harmful than the abuse itself. This harm may stem not only from the negative or indifferent response that has been reported for the police but also because of styles of interaction that find the standard modes of intervention offensive or intrusive. Explicit questions by the police or advocates may be considered too forward. For fear of bringing shame upon the family, private violence is often treated as an internal problem to be dealt with in the confines of the family. But the cultural values of modesty, respect and indirectness in communication discourage women from openly raising their concerns even in that intimate circle. Therefore, assessments of needs should not be based solely on official reports. Although data consistently show that majority women seek shelter with greater frequency than Hispanics, Consejo, a Seattle local agency serving Hispanics, received an average of five to seven requests for assistance per month during a pilot period. Referrals came from ethnic networks or by word of mouth rather than from professional sources. A similar observation has been made by service providers in Hartford, Connecticut among a population of Puerto Ricans and Dominicans where in cases of rape Hispanics were more likely to report to informal, community-based agencies rather than to a city-wide rape service or the police.

4. Existing shelters evolved in a manner that excluded a sensitivity to the needs of women of color. Historically, minority women played no role in the establishment of existing facilities. This precludes a high rate of minority participation, since few directors, volunteers or staff are either ethnic or familiar with the language, customs and culture of Hispanic women.

5. The role and concept of mental health professional or counselor has no counterpart in the Hispanic culture. Close interpersonal relationships are reserved for family members, or *comadres* (or *compadres* (co-parents)[)]. Mediums or *curanderas* (traditional healers) have sometimes filled the role of counselor. Within the context of illness or spiritual discomfort people will admit to problems that would not be acknowledged if individual responsibility and directness of communication are prerequisites.

6. A very important aspect of culture that must be considered when interacting with Latin Americans is the language and the communication style. Despite proficiency in English in oral communication there may be differences in expressive style in voice, intonation, gesture and the unspoken body language that is unique to each region. Likewise, it must not be assumed that speaking English necessarily means proficiency in reading or the reverse. Explaining the concepts of advocacy, victim assistance, the law and court processes may be a difficult task even for the Spanish speaker if there is no understanding of the subtleties of the culture.

   While the use of interpreters is commendable it must not be forgotten that the introduction of a third party into a sensitive conversation will influence the communication process beyond the practical impact of technical concerns such as competency levels of the translator. The message will be diluted three times before a response is attained. Equally important when dealing with issues of victimization, a woman may be reluctant to expose intimate and shameful details via a second party. Mere translations to English make no adaptation for the diverse regional difference in expression represented within the Spanish speaking groups—in other words Spanish is not necessarily just Spanish.

There is one last point we would like to make. Although many Anglos see us as one unified group, Latinos in the United States are as diverse as the color of their skins, the countries they come from, the accents of their language, their political affiliations, their socioeconomic classes and their gender. To that native diversity must be added the diversity that comes from their situation in the United States. First-, second- or nth-generation, bilingual/bicultural or monolingual, assimilated or ethnically identified, living in the large Latino metropolis of Miami, New York City, or Los Angeles or in the relative isolation of Dubuque, Iowa.

We speak out of our own experience as Latina women but we do not speak *for* (all) Latina women because to paraphrase Adenauer, although we all live under the same sky we do not all have the same horizon.

Andrea Dworkin, Living in Terror, Pain: Being a Battered Wife, in *Violence Against Women: The Bloody Footprints* 237, 237–39 (Pauline B. Bart & Eileen Geil Moran eds., 1993)

On November 1, 1987, Joel Steinberg, a criminal defense lawyer, beat his illegally adopted daughter, Lisa, into a coma. She died November 5. Hedda Nussbaum, who had lived with Steinberg since 1976, was also in the apartment. Her face and body were deformed from his assaults, she had a gangrenous leg from his beatings. With 6-year-old Lisa lying on the bathroom floor, Steinberg went out for dinner and drinks. Nussbaum stayed behind. When Steinberg came home, he and Nussbaum freebased cocaine. Early the next day, Lisa stopped breathing and Nussbaum called 911. She was arrested with Steinberg, then given immunity for testifying against him.

Steinberg had started beating Nussbaum in 1978. In that year alone, she reportedly suffered at least 10 black eyes. In 1981, he ruptured her spleen. During this time, she worked as a children's book editor at Random House. She was fired in 1982 for missing too much work. Socially speaking, she was "disappeared."

Many say Lisa's death is Nussbaum's fault. They mourn Lisa, they blame Nussbaum. A perception is growing that Nussbaum is responsible legally and morally for the death of Lisa Steinberg.

I don't think Nussbaum is "innocent." I don't know any innocent adult women; life is harder than that for everyone. But adult women who have been battered are especially not innocent. Battery is a forced descent into hell and you don't get by in hell by moral goodness. You disintegrate. You don't survive as a discrete personality with a sense of right and wrong. You live in a world of pain, in isolation, on the verge of death, in terror; and when you get numb enough not to care whether you live or die you are experiencing the only grace God is going to send your way. Drugs help.

I was battered when I was married and there are some things I wish people would understand. I thought things had changed but it is clear from the story of Hedda Nussbaum that nothing has.

Your neighbors hear you screaming. They do nothing. The next day they look through you. If you scream for years they will look through you for years. Your neighbors, friends, and family see the bruises and injuries—and do nothing. They will not intercede. They send you back. They say it's your fault or you like it or they deny it is happening. Your family believes you belong with your husband.

If you scream and no one helps and no one acknowledges it and people look right through you, you begin to feel you don't exist. If you existed and you screamed, someone would help you. If you existed and were visibly injured, someone would help you. If you existed and asked for help in escaping, someone would help you.

When you go to the doctor or to the hospital because you are injured and they don't listen or help you or they give you tranquilizers or threaten to commit you because they say you are disoriented, paranoid, you begin to believe that he can hurt you as much as he wants and no one will help you. When the police refuse to help you, you begin to believe that he can hurt you or kill you and it will not matter because you do not exist.

You become unable to use language because it stops meaning anything. If you try to say you have been hurt and by whom and you point to visible injuries and are treated as if you made it up or as if it doesn't matter or as if it is your fault or as if you are worthless, you become afraid to say anything. You cannot talk to anyone because they will not help you and if you do talk, the man who is battering you will hurt you more. Once you lose language, your isolation is absolute.

Eventually I waited to die. I wanted to die. I hoped the next beating would kill me. When I would come to after being beaten unconscious, the first feeling I had was a sorrow that I was alive.

I would ask God to let me die now. My breasts were burned with lit cigarettes. My husband beat my legs with a wood beam so that I couldn't walk. I was present when he did immoral things to other people. When he hurt other people, I didn't help them. Nussbaum's guilt is not foreign to me.

A junkie said he would give me a ticket to far away and $1,000 if I would carry a briefcase through customs. I said I would. I knew it had heroin in it. I kept hoping I would be caught and sent to jail because in jail he couldn't beat me.

I had been sexually abused in the Woman's House of Detention in New York City (arrested for an anti-Vietnam War demonstration) so I didn't have the idea that jail was a friendly place. I just hoped I would get 5 years and for 5 years I could sit in a jail cell and not be hit by him. In the end the junkie didn't give me the briefcase to carry, so I didn't get the $1,000. He did kindly give me the ticket. I stole the money I needed. Escape is heroic, isn't it?

I've been living with a kind and gentle man I love for the last 15 years. For 8 of those years, I would wake up screaming in blind terror, not knowing who I was, where I was, who he was, cowering and shaking. I'm more at peace now, but I've refused until recently to have my books published in the country where my former husband lives, and I've refused important professional invitations to go there. Once I went there in secret for 4 days to try to face it down. I couldn't stop trembling and sweating. I could barely breathe. There still isn't a day when I don't feel fear that I will see him and he will hurt me.

Death looks different to a woman who has been battered. It seems not nearly so cruel as life. I'm upset by the phony mourning for Lisa Steinberg—the hypocritical sentimentality of a society that would not really mind her being beaten to death once she was an adult.

If Lisa hadn't died, she would be on West 10th Street being tortured—now. Why was it that we wanted her to live? So that when the child became a woman and then was raped or beaten or prostituted we could look right through her? It's bad to hit a girl before she's of age. It's bad to torture a girl before she's of age. Then she's of age and, well, it isn't so bad, because she wants it, she likes it, she chose it.

Why is it all right to hurt adult women? Those who love children but don't think adult women deserve much precisely because we are not innocent—we are used and compromised and culpable—should try to remember this: The only way to have helped Lisa Steinberg was to have helped Nussbaum. But to do it, you would have had to care that an adult woman was being hurt—care enough to rescue her.

There was a little boy there too, Mitchell, 17 months old, tied up and covered in feces. And the only way to have spared him was to rescue Hedda. Now he has been tortured and he did not die. What kind of man will he grow up to be? I wish there was a way to take the hurt from him. There isn't. Is there a way to stop him from becoming a batterer? Is there?

Notes and Questions

1. *Law's Neutrality*? What explanations are used in the opinions in *Black*, *Rhodes*, *Mabrey*, and *Berry* to justify the violence by husbands against their wives? In thinking about this question, consider the analytical frameworks suggested by John Calmore in "Critical Race Theory, Archie Shepp,and Fire Music: Securing an Authentic Intellectual Life in a Multicultural World," at p. 105, Patricia Hill Collins in *Black Feminist Thought: Knowledge, Consciousness, and the Politics of Empowerment*, at p. 55, and Lucinda Finley, in "Breaking Women's Silence in Law: The Dilemma of the Gendered Nature of Legal Reasoning," at p. 115.

A recent legislative response to the type of judicial reasoning found in *Berry* is Minn. Stat. § 609.185(6) (1992). The statute provides that a person is guilty of murder in the first degree if she or he "causes the death of a human being. . .while committing domestic abuse, when the perpetrator has engaged in a past pattern of domestic abuse upon the victim and the death occurs under circumstances manifesting an extreme indifference to human life."

2. *The Cultural Defense*. Courts have invoked racial, ethnic, and religious factors as a basis for reducing a defendant's responsibility for a crime. The defense is often invoked in cases involving violence against women. The reasoning by some of the courts parallels the provocation excuse found in *Berry*.

> The defense rests on the theory that someone raised in a foreign culture should not be held fully accountable for conduct that violates United States law but would be acceptable in his or her native culture.
>
> Courts have used the cultural defense to assess the defendant's mental state, incorporating cultural factors into traditional defenses. . . .Courts thus invoke cultural characteristics and beliefs to negate the possibility that the defendant possessed the intent necessary to commit the crime in question. . . .
>
> An examination of the types of cases in which defendants have successfully employed the cultural defense suggests that it will increasingly be invoked by men who kill their wives. Because it is used to establish the defendant's innocent state of mind, the defense is most often employed—and most often accepted by judges—in prosecutions for serious crimes, particularly murder. The defense is also commonly employed in cases involving family matters, such as child abuse. Japanese women who have responded to marital infidelity by attempting to kill themselves and their children have also invoked the cultural defense to explain their motivations. . . .Courts also have been most willing to accept the logic of the cultural defense when the crime is violent and the victim is a woman. Thus, courts have accepted the defense in cases of rape and kidnapping. . . .The cultural defense, then, is most widely invoked in murder cases, family matters and in cases involving female victims of violence. The defense is obviously appealing to defense attorneys and judges in cases of men who murder their wives.

Melissa Spatz, A "Lesser" Crime: A Comparative Study of Legal Defenses for Men Who Kill Their Wives, 24 Colum. J.L. & Soc. Probs. 597, 620, 624-26 (1991).

3. *"Raising the Curtain."* The courts in the North Carolina cases expressed an unwillingness to subject family conduct to public scrutiny. The essays by Nora Groce, Nancy Hammond, Jo-Ellen Asbury, Nilda Rimonte, Angela Ginorio and Jane Reno, and Andrea Dworkin demonstrate that the curtain remains lowered on domestic violence for many women. The essays identify the societal forces that keep the curtain lowered and show how these forces operate differently depending on the victim's/survivor's and batterer's respective abilities, classes, races/ethnicities, and sexual orientations. What are the forces in the dominant culture that keep the curtain lowered on domestic violence by obstructing a woman seeking to end the violence she is experiencing? What forces in the dominant culture contribute to unresponsiveness in programs ostensibly established to raise the curtain?

4. *Heterosexism.* The North Carolina cases along with the history described by R. Emerson Dobash and Russell Dobash make clear that within the Euro-American culture women are defined through their relationships with men. Viewing women's connection with men as an inevitable and natural phenomenon is part of what constitutes compulsory heterosexuality. *See* Adrienne Rich, Compulsory Heterosexuality and Lesbian Existence, at p. 64. Compulsory heterosexuality contributes to violence by creating an environment that limits women's choices and encourages them to maintain their relationships with men even though those relationships may include violent episodes. It also contributes to violence when a husband becomes jealous of his wife's female friends. Consider the following excerpt from a case history of a woman who was repeatedly assaulted by her husband.

> Tracy explained [to the police] that she had met her husband in a bar after work as they had planned. He was there first, and she found him in a bad mood. Tracy arrived with one of the girls from her office, and they were both laughing and acting silly. Her husband was nasty and insulting. He made a remark about her "queer" friend that she let pass. Tracy had a drink with Tom [her husband], and they left. While driving home, Tom accused her of having a homosexual affair with the girl from the office.
>
> "At first I thought he was making a bad joke, but he said it several times, and I knew he was serious. I tried to laugh it off, but he called me a lesbian again, so I slapped his face. We didn't say anything more all the way home, and I thought that was the end of it. When we got into the apartment, he punched me and sent me flying over the coffee table.
>
> "He punched me in the face and breast and stomach, and I started to scream. He kept calling me a lesbian and punching me. I screamed and the guy next door kept banging on the wall yelling at me to shut up. He yelled he was going to call the cops, and I screamed back, 'Please do!' All the while, Tom kept punching me and calling me names. I don't know what made him stop. . .I guess he got tired. . . ."

Tracy's Story—A Case History in Battering, in *Wife Beating: The Silent Crisis* 140, 141-42 (Roger Langley & Richard C. Levy eds., 1977).

The husband's remarks made manifest heterosexism and homophobia. How are we to understand the wife's response to the accusation that she was a lesbian? How are we to understand the verbal exchange between the defendant and his wife in *State v. Black*, at p. 195? Do you see a relationship between the spouses' interchange in "Tracy's Story" and the spouses' interchange in *Black*?

5. *Medicine's Responsibility*. Andrea Dworkin raised the question about the reluctance of the medical profession to become actively involved in cases of battering (p. 216). *See also* Carole Warshaw, Limitations of the Medical Model in the Care of Battered Women, in Violence Against Women: The Bloody Footprints 134-44 (Pauline B. Bart & Eileen Geil Moran eds., 1993). Recognizing the pervasiveness of domestic violence and the reluctance of doctors to acknowledge the violence experienced by their women patients, the American Medical Association [A.M.A.] issued guidelines suggesting that doctors should routinely screen their female patients for abuse and violence:

> Because some women may not initially recognize themselves as "battered," the physician should routinely ask all women direct, specific questions about abuse. . . .
>
> [P]hysicians must be willing to ask all women patients about abuse and should know how to diagnose it. . . . Physicians also should be aware of certain "red flags" that can signal particularly dangerous situations for the woman: stalking behavior by the abuser; substance abuse by the abuser; and threatened suicide by the abuser (increased risk for a murder/suicide).

American Medical Association Diagnostic and Treatment Guidelines on Domestic Violence, 1 Archives Fam. Med. 39, 41, 46 (1992).

6. *Children*. (a) *Battering the Mother/Harming the Child*. When a mother is abused, children typically witness the violence by actually viewing the battering; by hearing the mother's screams and crying, the abuser's threats, or other violent sounds; or by seeing the results of the abuse, such as blood, bruises, or broken furniture. The harm to the children who witness their mother's abuse is well documented.

> Infants exposed to violence are often characterized by "poor health, poor sleeping habits, and excessive screaming" (all of which could contribute to further abuse of the mother). Studies have found that preschoolers showed signs of "terror, as evidenced by the children's yelling, irritable behavior, hiding, shaking, and stuttering.". . .
>
> By the time children in violent homes reach adolescence, the violence typically becomes more commonplace, yet children in this age groups are often more guarded and secretive about the circumstances at home, and often deny it. These children often use aggression as a predominate form of problem solving, projecting blame on others and exhibit a high correlation of anxiety behaviors . . . .

Nat'l Center on Women & Family Law, The Effect of Woman Abuse on Children 32-34 (1991) [hereinafter Center on Women & Family Law].

> In the vast majority of families, women are the primary caretakers of children. Therefore the devastation of their lives caused by their partner's

> abuse and coercion affects the children . . . .Battered women are physically and emotionally worn down by the abuse. This may interfere with a woman's capacity to meet her children's needs. The partner's efforts to isolate the woman may result in the children being denied access to other family members who could offer support and nurturance to the child.
>
> Battering is a major cause of homelessness. Children suffer physical and emotional consequences when they are forced to leave their home . . . .
>
> Children are also damaged when used as a pawn in the abuser's attempt to hurt his partner. Attempts to undermine the woman's authority as a parent, convince the child that the mother is worthless, initiating custody battles or violating visitation agreements are common tactics that harm children.

Jann Jackson, Intervention With Children Who Have Witnessed Abuse 3 (Published by House of Ruth, Baltimore, Maryland).

(b) *Custody Issues.* (1) *Charging the Mother with Abuse or Failure to Protect.* A woman in a violent home who seeks outside intervention may risk losing custody of her children temporarily or permanently. Child protection services may determine either that she has abused her children or that she has not protected her children from abuse by her partner. The medical professions, social service agencies, and women's advocates are working together to develop alternative intervention protocols in recognition of the correlation between incidences of abuse of children and of abuse of their mothers. One hospital study reported that 45 percent of the mothers of abused children also were battered and that when children of battered women were abused, the perpetrator of the child abuse was most often the man who battered the mother. *See* Evan Stark & Anne Flitcraft, Woman-battering, Child Abuse and Social Heredity: What is the Relationship?, in Marital Violence (Norman Johnson ed., 1985). The goal of these intervention programs is to "unite the services that are often offered separately and conflictually to women and their children." Susan Schechter, Health Care Services for Battered Women and Their Abused Children: A Manual About Advocacy for Women and Kids in Emergencies [AWAKE] 11. These coordinated services are based on the assumption that, in many cases, "the best way to protect the child is to protect the mother from an assaultive partner." *Id.* at 20. This is likely to be true even when the mother has abused the child. Studies show that as the mother's safety increases, the likelihood of her abusing her child significantly decreases. *See* Jackson, *supra*, at 4.

(2) *Custody Disputes Upon Separation.* The legal system's acknowledgment of the detrimental effects battering of a mother has on her children has prompted many states to adopt laws that require courts to consider a batterer's violence in deciding child custody cases. *See* Center on Women & Family Law, *supra*, at 49-87 for review of state laws. It also has led to the passage of the following concurrent resolution by the U. S. Congress in 1990.

> Expressing the sense of the Congress that, for purposes of determining child custody, credible evidence of physical abuse of one's spouse should create a statutory presumption that it is detrimental to the child to be placed in the custody of the abusive spouse.
>
> Whereas State courts have often failed to recognize the detrimental effects

> of having as a custodial parent an individual who physically abuses his or her spouse, insofar as the courts do not hear or weigh evidence of domestic violence in child custody litigation;
>
> Whereas there is an alarming bias against battered spouses in contemporary child custody trends such as joint custody and mandatory mediation;
>
> Whereas joint custody guarantees the batterer continued access and control over the battered spouse's life through their children;. . .
>
> Whereas a batterer's violence toward an estranged spouse often escalates during or after a divorce, placing both the abused spouse and children at risk through shared custody arrangements and unsupervised visitation;
>
> Whereas physical abuse of a spouse is relevant to child abuse in child custody disputes;. . .
>
> Whereas few States have recognized the interrelated nature of child custody and battering and have enacted legislation that allows or requires courts to consider evidence of physical abuse of a spouse in child custody cases: Now, therefore, be it
>
> *Resolved by the House of Representatives (the Senate concurring),*
>
> Section 1. It is the sense of the Congress that, for purposes of determining child custody, credible evidence of physical abuse of a spouse should create a statutory presumption that it is detrimental to the child to be placed in the custody of the abusive spouse.
>
> Sec. 2. This resolution is not intended to encourage States to prohibit supervised visitation.

H.R. Con. Res. 172, 101st Cong., 2d Sess. (1990) (unanimously passed House on Sept. 27, 1990 and the Senate on Oct. 25, 1990).

Women's fears of losing their children in a custody dispute sometimes cause them to stay with an abusive spouse or, if they decide to separate, to make concessions about financial support and statutory protections. Martha Mahoney explains why these fears are realistic:

> The past two decades have seen major changes in child custody litigation. . . .[T]he advent of gender-neutral rules in custody decisionmaking create[s] a situation that actually disfavors women, since factors that would favor women, such as nurturing, are defined as gender-biased. In devaluing past caregiving and seeking decisionmaking factors that would not inherently prefer women, courts have wound up relying on factors such as financial resources that usually favor men.
>
> With the advent of no-fault divorce, fault became relevant only in custody proceedings. This contributes to a critical evaluation of mothering and holds particular problems for women leaving violent marriages. Violence against women is less likely to be raised at all in a no-fault action. It may be dangerous for women to raise the issue of domestic violence, since it invokes stereotypes that judges or social workers may hold. . . .
>
> Indeed, by making violence against women less visible at divorce, no-fault divorce laws may have indirectly contributed to cultural stereotypes of battered women by removing public blame of the perpetrator of the violence. Once the man as bad actor disappears, it is easy to shift the focus to the woman. Rather than asserting his harm to her from the beginning, the

woman must raise battering as an issue defensively, while she is being clinically evaluated, with greater attendant risk of stereotyping. . . .

No-fault divorce and the widespread adoption of the "best interest of the child" standard for resolving custody disputes also put more power in the hands of professionals such as social workers. Judges follow the recommendations in evaluations ninety percent of the time. The increased reliance on these professionals created problems for battered women with children. Even before separation, it may be dangerous to place much trust in a counselor who may later be called on to testify regarding the qualities of the parents . . . .

Finally, battered women with children face an image problem. We need to be strong, resourceful, effective as a parent, meeting the needs of the children when we appear in court. On the other hand, if we do that too well, the court may disbelieve our stories because of stereotypes held by judges or psychologists. If the court will consider violence as a factor at all in custody decisions, we may be seen as—or in effect be *required* to appear as—having been weak, helpless, and economically dependent to have "stayed" with the man all these years.

Martha Mahoney, Legal Images of Battered Women: Redefining the Issue of Separation, 90 Mich. L. Rev. 1, 45-49 (1992) (emphasis in original).

7. *Immigration Laws*. The Immigration Act of 1990 includes a provision that waives the joint petition requirement for conditional residence for battered women and children in immigration cases. *See* 8 U.S.C. § 1186a (1988 & Supp. II. 1990). The purpose of the statute is to limit the control that abusers have over immigrant women and children they are sponsoring. The rules implementing the act, however, have limited the usefulness of this provision to immigrant women and their children because they require that the abused immigrant women document their battering. *See* 8 C.F.R. § 216.5 (1993). *See also* Maxine Yi Hwa Lee, A Life Preserver for Battered Immigrant Women: The 1990 Amendments to the Immigration Marriage Fraud Amendments, 41 Buff. L. Rev. 779 (1993).

B. Legal Reforms

R. Emerson Dobash & Russell P. Dobash, *Women, Violence and Social Change* 156–69, 199, 206–07, 209 (1992)

By the last half of the nineteenth century, the problem of violence against women in the home was being placed on the public agenda in the United States and Britain. . .by women who raised their voices outside of the institutions of the state. Early feminists, such as Frances Power Cobbe in England and Lucy Stone in the United States condemned such violence and championed reform in legal responses. . . .

The campaigns for battered women in the late nineteenth century emerged in the context of the concerns of social purity leagues and temperance groups (such as the US Women's Christian Temperance Union) and a growing middle-class fear of the public violence of the 'dangerous classes'. In Britain and the United States there emerged a growing antagonism towards working people and a near 'panic' about crime and the criminal classes. Public concern for assaulted and murdered wives was never as strong or as vehement. However, a few campaigns were waged in both countries to introduce flogging as a punishment for wife beaters. . . .These laws had little impact; only a few men were ever whipped for the offence of wife assault.

Moral panics, subsequent debates and legislation were not so much about protecting women as they were about concern for public order. Assaults on wives were incidental to the more general debate and concern. With this background of growing concern for the immorality and violence of the working classes, individual women and women's groups were able to raise the issue of wife beating, to argue that it affected many working-class women and successfully to pressure male parliamentarians and state legislators to enact legislation aimed at providing greater protection for married women. . . .Most of the campaigners focused their concern on the 'lower orders'. . . .The lessons of the late nineteenth century in both countries point to how the demands of activists may be shaped, co-opted and/or absorbed within an existing legal system. . . .

If legislators and judges often ignored or slighted the problems of women, new professional groups emerging in the late nineteenth century would make these problems one of their primary concerns. Psychiatry, psychoanalysis and criminology were emerging disciplines during the late nineteenth and early twentieth centuries. These new professions offered explanations of victims, crime and criminals . . . .

Freud's conception of incest as an expression of unconscious female desire is probably the best known example of the transformation of female experiences into fantasies. Female victims of crimes such as sexual assault, rape and violence in the home, who had in the past been characterized as prone to exaggeration, were now 'confirmed' in these perceptions. Psychiatric discourse identified them as suffering from delusions, hysteria and sexual fantasies. Women were conceived of as the cause of the violence against them. 'Nagging' wives precipitated beatings and 'seductive' daughters provoked their fathers into incestuous acts. . . .By the 1930s psychoanalysis had enshrined the myth of masochism into its conceptions of normal female psychology. Based on these speculations presented as scientific truths, it was argued that women derived sexual gratification from the violence they experienced. These professional discourses filtered into judicial thinking of the time both in Britain and in the United States, reinforcing and legitimating conventional perceptions of female victims.

As a result of their inclusion in new institutions in the United States, such as juvenile and family courts, therapeutic professionals and their views began to have an important impact on the conceptions and treatment of female victims. This happened at the turn of the century, when US cities embarked upon new social experiments combining social welfare and justice. . . .By 1920, over ten major cities had juvenile, family or domestic relations courts. Fuelled by the advent of the new behavioural sciences and its allied professions, clinical psychology and social work, reformers set about creating mechanisms for aiding children and families. . . .These US courts and their allied professionals were extraordinarily ambitious. A few embraced radical ideals and sought to apply new techniques to social problems. One of their major ambitions was to make immigrant and working-class families 'respectable', 'moral' and 'industrious'; free from violence like 'normal' American families. To create this healthier society, they urged both state and private social service intervention in families through institutions such as family courts.

Family courts held out the promise of solving marital problems through timely intervention, patient concern, and social investigation, followed by the application of psychological and social remedies. Judicial experts agreed that domestic disputes, troubles regarding children and other contentious matters should not be solved through the antagonistic procedures of criminal courts. Domestic relations courts would be able to solve family problems in a setting which emphasized discussion and reconciliation engineered by social service intervention. Legal procedures and solutions were intended to play only a minor role. . . .

Nineteenth-century justice had often ignored violence against women in the home, excused and sometimes tacitly supported men who beat their wives based on the idea that they were merely following an established patriarchal right. In the twentieth century, new rationales would emerge and intermingle with the old. . . .Social workers and judges usually recommended reconciliation, advised women to improve their housekeeping, cooking and child care and to cope with their husbands' violence. . . .

Domestic relations and family courts are still thriving in the United States, attempting to settle family problems through social or psychological means. In the 1960s the ideals of the mental health movement penetrated these courts, further expanding the therapeutic conceptions of the problem of violence against women. Long-term psychotherapy was considered the ideal, followed by short-term couple counseling emphasizing problems of family interaction. Despite this promise, the usual response of such courts was an avoidance of intervention. One of the most common responses was a summary dismissal, a 'go home' order. Sometimes such decisions were preceded by judicial admonitions addressed to the husband and wife, involving directions for the husband to refrain from violence and for the woman to be a better wife and mother. . . .By the time of the rediscovery of the problems of battered women in the early 1970s, family courts and psychiatric and social work approaches had reduced these criminal assaults to problems of individual or social pathology. The CJS [Criminal Justice System] was not considered the appropriate institution for dealing with violence against women within the home; it was now defined as a family and personal problem best dealt with through social and psychological solutions. . . .

In the late 1960s these ideals were extended into police work in the United States through the introduction of programmes of crisis intervention and mediation. The criminal justice establishment conceived of crisis intervention as a humane programme that would aid the police and courts and assist victims. Psychologists and criminologists working in conjunction with the police urged the introduction of new behaviourally based intervention techniques into police responses to problems in the family. Police officers were overburdened and court calenders and city jails were bulging at the seams. Using crisis intervention to deal with 'family disputes' was one method for dealing with these problems. Family crisis intervention was another strand in the growing web of psychiatric interventions into the community. . . .

According to the therapeutic professionals who urged crisis intervention, domestic disturbances rarely involved violence. Arrest was inappropriate for solving the complex social and psychological problems evident in these non-violent 'family squabbles'. 'Family fights', they argued, were dangerous events, apparently not for women, but for police officers. Police officers, they pointed out, often inflamed these conflicts and increased the risks of injury to themselves by 'forming protective-seductive alliances' with women and thus 'contributing to the emasculation of male disputants'. Instead of arrest, which they incorrectly argued was frequently used, police officers should become counsellors and mediators, trained in the skills of crisis intervention. Once intervention had occurred couples could be referred to the appropriate social or psychiatric agency.

In order to demonstrate the efficacy of these approaches, Law Enforcement and Assistance Administration (LEAA) created 'model projects' in six cities. . . .

The New York evaluation conducted in the late 1960s which was used to justify the introduction of most innovations was surprisingly modest. Eighteen officers initially trained in crisis intervention techniques carried out the programme in selected areas. Bard's [the researcher] initial reports on the results of this evaluation research are glowing. . . .With these early results, Bard and others became even more committed to crisis intervention and strongly supported its introduction through the publication of papers in police journals and the presentation of talks to criminal justice audiences. . . .

By 1977, over 70 percent of police departments with over 100 staff were training police officers in crisis intervention. . . .

Subsequent assessments of the initial studies and additional research reveal that in most respects these programmes were dismal failures in dealing with violence and disputes in families. . . .

Probably the most important impact of these programmes was not radically to change police perceptions and practices but to reinforce established ones. LEAA training materials taught police officers that most family disputes were *not* violent and therefore not crimes. Training Manuals sometimes depicted the women and men involved in such disputes in a manner which reinforces sexist and racist attitudes. Women are presented as depressed, menopausal, dominating and 'likely to resort to physical violence' and it is claimed that 'physical force is the common response among certain ethnic groups'. . . .

The successful introduction of crisis intervention into so many U.S. police forces must be understood against a backdrop of traditional police response stressing non-intervention, a need to reduce pressure on courts and police, a history of the entrance of psychological orientations and professionals into the criminal justice system and a political need to appear to deal with problems of violence and conflict within the family. In crisis intervention we have what is an apparent success story for criminal justice administrators and policy makers. They successfully introduced a new, 'radical' programme into the police, notoriously conservative and resistant to change. The reason for success is that crisis intervention did not urge new action but basically reinforced and legitimized existing police practices of nonarrest, diversion and minimal response to the problem. Historical evidence suggests that the police have usually treated the problem as a private matter requiring personal and civil solutions. Here was a new 'professional' response which legitimated these practices, providing a novel language and ideological justification. Crisis intervention and mediation served the purpose of negotiating the offender away from the CJS and appeasing the growing moral concerns for protection of the victim by providing a supposedly effective means of stopping or reducing future violence. The fact that it did not work was conveniently ignored by all except, of course, the repeat victims and their abusers, and, somewhat later, by activists in the battered-women's movement. . . .

One of the early catalysts for change in the CJS response to battering in the United States was the class action lawsuits brought on behalf of battered women against police departments in New York City and Oakland, California for failure to protect women from physical abuse. With the growing awareness of abuse and the outcry coming from the movement, feminist lawyers joined the effort to ensure provisions for legal safety, which had so frequently been neglected. Legal action was necessary because law enforcement agencies were extremely reluctant to change policy and practice. . . .Within this context of resistance, lawsuits were extremely important; they raised public awareness of the problem, publicized institutional forms of injustice, led to changes in State laws and set a precedent for police response all over the country.

In October 1976, the case of Scott vs. Hart was filed against the Oakland Police; two months later the case of Bruno vs. Codd was filed against the New York City police. In New York, the Litigation Coalition for Battered Women charged police and courts with gross failure to comply with the New York State laws. The case was brought on behalf of twelve women all of whom had received no action from police when called to respond to a physical attack upon them by their male partners. . . .

On 26 June 1978, nearly two years after the case was filed, the New York City Police Department settled out of court. Without admission of guilt, they agreed to change their practice by: arresting men who commit felonious assaults, misdemeanours and for violations of family court protection orders; sending officers to every call from a battered woman; assisting women in receiving medical help and pursuing men who have left the scene of the assault. The Oakland Police Department also capitulated with a similar settlement. With successes on both the East and West Coasts, the precedent was set and could be used in any city or state as a model of action and, more importantly, as a lever against police resistance to local pressure for change. Leverage provided by these lawsuits was very important to other groups who sought to persuade their local police to enforce the law and assist women. . . .The era of crisis intervention, family court diversion and police inaction appeared to be ending.

Following the successful New York and Oakland class actions against police, there was a flurry of activity. New legislation was introduced, increasing pressure was brought on local police departments and innovative experiments appeared to spread throughout the CJS. The initial period of reform from 1976 to the early 1980s, witnessed the creation of research and demonstration projects in law enforcement and police training in several states, often under the auspices of the LEAA. Innovative criminal justice programmes and new law enforcement legislation were often the result of local and national pressure by activists.

As the movement began to pressure for changes it was confronted in each state with a seemingly bewildering variety of laws, procedures and practices. Yet there was considerable commonality across jurisdictions: orders of protection (injunctions) were often useless and only available to women who filed for divorce; crisis intervention, mediation and diversion were widespread; few men were being arrested for wife abuse and even fewer cases ended in court. Keeping the peace and keeping the family together, even a violent one, took precedence over arresting violent offenders and protecting victims. Legal changes required the introduction of criminal justice legislation in each of the fifty state legislatures; these efforts were often aided by the publication of model legislation in movement publications. The acts proposed new laws and new directions for all segments of the CJS. One of the most important areas of concentration was on the introduction of new or improved protection orders. Two of the first model forms of legislation focusing on protection orders were successfully introduced in Pennsylvania and Massachusetts.

The provisions of the 1976 Pennsylvania Protection from Abuse Act defined abuse as bodily injury, serious bodily injury, fear of serious bodily injury and sexual abuse of minor children. The definition of the family included spouses and people living as spouses as well as others related by marriage or consanguinity, thus providing protection for cohabitants. Protection is provided after filing a petition with the court alleging abuse, and attempts to overcome the usual causes of delay and ineffective enforcement include: allowing justices to act when the court is closed, immediately notifying police of the issuance of an injunction, and permitting emergency injunctions prior to a full hearing which must be held within ten days of the issuance of the order. At the hearing, abuse must be proved based on a 'preponderance of evidence' rather than beyond a reasonable doubt. The forms of relief can include issuing protection orders or consent agreements directed at cessation of the violence, granting possession of the residence to the victim and/or excluding the abuser and decisions regarding custody and visitation rights pertaining to children. If the husband breaches these provisions he may be judged to be in contempt of court, arrested and subjected to a $1,000 fine and six months in jail.

In 1983 only seventeen states provided protection orders, but by 1990 forty-eight had enacted or revamped injunctions that enabled courts to refrain men from abusing, harassing and assaulting the women with whom they live. In many states these statutes only apply to married couples while others also include cohabitees. Forty-eight of the fifty states also provide powers to exclude the man from the household for a specified period of time. As a means of reducing harassment and intimidation, other provisions allow for exclusion of the man from the woman's business or place of employment or the children's school. Orders may require men to make temporary support payments to the family, to pay restitution for lost earnings, moving expenses associated with abuse and to compensate women for medical and legal expenses arising from violent attacks. . . .

Approximately forty states now consider a breach of injunction either a misdemeanour, criminal offence or criminal contempt and therefore include the power of arrest in their enforcement. . . .

One of the most significant developments is a change in the requirements of arrest. In twenty-three states, police officers are now able to arrest on 'probable cause' in cases of simple or minor assault within the home. In many states similar provisions apply to the violation of a protection order. Probable cause refers to a situation where a police officer observes conditions—injuries, a frightened dishevelled woman, damaged property—that leads to the conclusion that a crime has been committed. Prior to the enactment of new laws police officers were unable to arrest without a warrant in instances of simple assault unless they actually witnessed the attack. Probable cause arrests were only possible in serious or felony assaults. Further criminal justice action was possible, though apparently not very probable, if women themselves sought redress directly from the courts. If judges accepted their accounts they might issue a warrant for the arrest of her attacker. In the past, such procedures rarely resulted in the issuance of a warrant or an arrest, nor did they bring relief to the victim.

In addition to expanding the authority of the police to make probable cause arrests, a few of the new state and city statutes go even further by imposing a *mandatory* duty to arrest the violent offender. Connecticut, Maine, New Jersey, North Carolina, Oregon, Utah and Wisconsin now 'mandate' arrest for domestic assault usually by extending the concept of probable cause. . . .

States have also enacted legislation mandating police and courts to provide greater assistance to victims. Massachusetts law requires officers to stay until imminent danger has passed, to help the victim obtain medical treatment and to advise her of her rights. Officers are also required to carry and dispense cards providing women with information about their rights and possible avenues for gaining assistance and telephone numbers of hot-lines, shelters and social services. Some states mandate legal counsel for women seeking protection orders and provide legal advocates to assist women in their attempts to seek such orders. . . .

Mandatory arrest policies have also resulted in some unintended consequences, with women being arrested as a consequence of these policies. In Connecticut, women have been arrested for 'technical violations' of the law when, for example, they defended themselves or used minimal forms of violence in the process of being attacked. In the first few months after the introduction of mandatory arrest in the state of Washington there were 'wholesale arrests of battered women. . .[and] large numbers of double arrests for mutual assault'. One woman was arrested when she revealed, while seeking treatment for injuries sustained from her boyfriend, that she had spat at him. Another woman was arrested for throwing yoghurt at her partner after an attack. In some instances police officers informed victims and assailants that both parties must be arrested under the mandatory arrest laws. Indiscriminate and over-enforcement of mandatory arrest laws has been used by police officers to express their rejection of the law and to protest the loss of their discretion in family violence cases. Their actions are also aimed at convincing those who created these laws that they are inappropriate and ill-founded.

According to legal advocates, there are various methods for overcoming these attempts to undermine the intent of mandatory arrest legislation. In Washington, efforts were directed at clarifying legislation by providing training regarding the intent of the laws. In Connecticut subsequent legal clarification emphasized that arrest should be for a predominance of violence associated with the primary aggressor. Informal discussions and training are directed at convincing police that they should speak separately to the victim and aggressor to determine the nature of the violence and not arrest women who are responding in self-defence. Discussions, persuasion and training are important, but some advocates believe that 'the most powerful tool to [changing] police behavior would be individual and class action lawsuits claiming damages and injunctive relief against false arrest'. . . .

Successes in changing the CJS raise important questions about the politics and pragmatics associated with working against and within the justice system. It is possible to identify a number of problematic issues. There are dangers of overestimating the depth and spread of new practices. There are a host of concerns regarding the potential political costs associated with these developments, and the limits of progressive change within what many believe to be a repressive system. We have already highlighted one of the problems associated with a policy of pro-arrest, that of women being arrested for reacting to male violence. An allied problem is women being arrested and prosecuted for failing to appear in court as witnesses under aggressive prosecution practices.

Another potential problem is that new arrest laws and greater police reactions may amplify discriminatory practices within criminal justice by increasing arrests of men from the working-class and ethnic minorities. . . .In the United States. . ., women of colour working within and outside of the movement have articulated the political and personal dilemmas they face concerning the use of the criminal justice system. On a political level, co-operating with the justice system may mean support for racist state repression leaving individual women to choose between continued violence or the risk of racist treatment to themselves and their partners by police and courts. . . .Contradictorily, while men of colour may be discriminated against by more frequent arrest and harsh treatment, women of colour seeking legal protection are discriminated against by failures to assist. . . .

The problem faced by women of colour should be a problem faced by all, that is, how to provide assistance without reinforcing racist tendencies within criminal justice. In Duluth [Minnesota]. . .pro-arrest strategy minimizing police discretion appears to have reduced discriminatory patterns of arrest. . . .

We must also consider the potential political costs to the movement of working with criminal justice. . . .

The politics of the movement in the United States may now be truncated to the immediate concerns of improving criminal justice. Entering criminal justice machinery may mean yielding to the exigencies of that system. Once encapsulated within criminal justice, reform movements must inevitably serve the needs of that system and potentially assist its expansion into more areas of civil society. The CJS may embrace the movement and yet subvert its demands, particularly within a law and order agenda, as a means of gaining greater resources and of widening the net of its response.

Minnesota Domestic Abuse Act,

Minn. Stat. § 518B.01 (1992)

Subd. 2. Definitions. As used in this section, the following terms shall have the meanings given them:

(a) "Domestic abuse" means: (i) physical harm, bodily injury, assault, or the infliction of fear of imminent physical harm, bodily injury or assault, between family or household members; or (ii) criminal sexual conduct. . . committed against a minor family or household member by an adult family or household member.

(b) "Family or household members" means spouses, former spouses, parents and children, persons related by blood, and persons who are presently residing together or who have resided together in the past, and persons who have a child in common regardless of whether they have been married or have lived together at any time. "Family or household member" also includes a man and woman if the woman is pregnant and the man is alleged to be the father, regardless of whether they have been married or have lived together at any time. Issuance of an order for protection on this ground does not affect a determination of paternity . . . .

Subd. 3a. Filing fee. The filing fees for an order for protection under this section are waived for the petitioner. The court administrator and the sheriff of any county in this state shall perform their duties relating to service of process without charge to the petitioner. . . .

Subd. 4. Order for Protection. There shall exist an action known as a petition for an order for protection in cases of domestic abuse.

(a) A petition for relief under this section may be made by any family or household member personally or on behalf of minor family or household members.

(b) A petition for relief shall allege the existence of domestic abuse, and shall be accompanied by an affidavit made under oath stating the specific facts and circumstances from which relief is sought. . . .

(d) The court shall provide simplified forms and clerical assistance to help with the writing and filing of a petition under this section. . . .

Subd. 5. Hearing on application; notice. (a) Upon receipt of the petition, the court shall order a hearing which shall be held not later than 14 days from the date of the order. Personal service shall be made upon the respondent not less than five days prior to the hearing. In the event that personal service cannot be completed in time to give the respondent the minimum notice required under this paragraph, the court may set a new hearing date. . . .

Subd. 6. Relief by the court. (a) Upon notice and hearing, the court may provide relief as follows:

(1) restrain the abusing party from committing acts of domestic abuse;

(2) exclude the abusing party from the dwelling which the parties share or from the residence of the petitioner;

(3) award temporary custody or establish temporary visitation with regard to minor children of the parties on a basis which gives primary consideration

to the safety of the victim and the children. . . .If the court finds that the safety of the victim or the children will be jeopardized by unsupervised or unrestricted visitation, the court shall condition or restrict visitation as to time, place, duration, or supervision, or deny visitation entirely, as needed to guard the safety of the victim and the children. The court's decision on custody and visitation shall in no way delay the issuance of an order for protection granting other reliefs provided for in this section;

(4). . .establish temporary support for minor children or a spouse, and order the withholding of support from the income of the person obligated to pay the support. . .;

(5) provide upon request of the petitioner counseling or other social services for the parties, if married, or if there are minor children;

(6) order the abusing party to participate in treatment or counseling services;

(7) award temporary use and possession of property and restrain one or both parties from transferring, encumbering, concealing, or disposing of property except in the usual course of business or for the necessities of life, and to account to the court for all such transfers, encumbrances, dispositions, and expenditures made after the order is served or communicated to the party restrained in open court;

(8) exclude the abusing party from the place of employment of the petitioner, or otherwise limit access to the petitioner by the abusing party at the petitioner's place of employment;

(9) order the abusing party to pay restitution to the petitioner; and

(10) order, in its discretion, other relief as it deems necessary for the protection of a family or household member, including orders or directives to the sheriff or constable, as provided by this section.

(b) Any relief granted by the order for protection shall be for a fixed period not to exceed one year, except when the court determines a longer fixed period is appropriate. . . .

(d) An order granting the relief authorized in paragraph (a), clause (2), is not voided by the admittance of the abusing party into the dwelling from which the abusing party is excluded. . . .

Subd. 7. Temporary order. (a) Where an application under this section alleges an immediate and present danger of domestic abuse, the court may grant an ex parte temporary order for protection, pending a full hearing, and granting relief as the court deems proper, including an order:

(1) restraining the abusing party from committing acts of domestic abuse;

(2) excluding any party from the dwelling they share or from the residence of the other except by further order of the court; and

(3) excluding the abusing party from the place of employment of the petitioner or otherwise limiting access to the petitioner by the abusing party at the petitioner's place of employment.

(b) A finding by the court that there is a basis for issuing an ex parte temporary order for protection constitutes a finding that sufficient reasons exist not to require notice under applicable court rules governing applications for ex parte temporary relief.

(c) An ex parte temporary order for protection shall be effective for a fixed period not to exceed 14 days . . . .A full hearing, as provided by this section, shall be set for not later than seven days from the issuance of the temporary order. The respondent shall be served forthwith a copy of the ex parte order along with a copy of the petition and notice of the date set for the hearing. . . .

Subd. 8. Service of order. Any order issued under this section shall be personally served upon the respondent.

Subd. 9. Assistance of sheriff in service or execution. When an order is issued under this section upon request of the petitioner, the court shall order the sheriff. . .to accompany the petitioner and assist in placing the petitioner in possession of the dwelling or residence, or otherwise assist in execution of service of the order of protection.

Subd. 10. Right to apply for relief. (a) A person's right to apply for relief shall not be affected by the person's leaving the residence or household to avoid abuse.

(b) The court shall not require security or bond of any party unless it deems necessary in exceptional cases. . . .

Subd. 14. Violation of an order for protection. (a) Whenever an order for protection is granted pursuant to this section, and the respondent or person to be restrained knows of the order, violation of the order for protection is a misdemeanor. Upon conviction, the defendant must be sentenced to a minimum of three days imprisonment and must be ordered to participate in counseling or other appropriate programs selected by the court. If the court stays imposition or execution of the jail sentence and the defendant refuses or fails to comply with the court's treatment order, the court must impose and execute the stayed jail sentence. A person who violates this paragraph within two years after a previous conviction under this paragraph or within two years after a previous conviction under a similar law of another state, is guilty of a gross misdemeanor. Upon conviction, the defendant must be sentenced to a minimum of ten days imprisonment and must be ordered to participate in counseling or other appropriate programs selected by the court. . . .

(b) A peace officer shall arrest without a warrant and take into custody a person whom the peace officer has probable cause to believe has violated an order granted pursuant to this section restraining the person or excluding the person from the residence or the petitioner's place of employment, even if the violation of the order did not take place in the presence of the peace officer, if the existence of the order can be verified by the officer. The person shall be held in custody for at least 36 hours, excluding the day of arrest, Sundays, and holidays, unless the person is released earlier by a judge or judicial officer. . . .

(c) A violation of an order for protection shall also constitute contempt of court and be subject to the penalties therefor.

(d) If the court finds that the respondent has violated an order for protection and that there is reason to believe that the respondent will commit a further violation of the provisions of the order restraining the respondent from committing acts of domestic abuse or excluding the respondent from the petitioner's residence, the court may require the respondent to acknowledge an obligation to comply with the order on the record. The court may require a bond sufficient to deter the respondent from committing further violations of the order for protection . . . .If the respondent refuses to comply with an order to acknowledge the obligation or post a bond under this paragraph, the court shall commit the respondent to the county jail during the term of the order for protection or until the respondent complies with the order under this paragraph. . . .

(g) The admittance into petitioner's dwelling of an abusing party excluded from the dwelling under an order for protection is not a violation by the petitioner of the order for protection.

A peace officer is not liable. . .for a failure to perform a duty required by paragraph (b). . . .

Subd. 17. Effect on custody proceedings. In a subsequent custody proceeding the court may consider, but is not bound by, a finding in a proceeding under this chapter that domestic abuse has occurred between the parties. . . .

Subd. 21. Order for protection forms. The state court administrator, in consultation with the advisory council on battered women, city and county attorneys, and legal advocates who work with victims, shall develop a uniform order for protection form that will facilitate the consistent enforcement of orders for protection throughout the state.

Allowing Probable Cause Arrests for Domestic Violence; Immunity From Liability,

Minn. Stat. § 629.341 (1992)

Subdivision 1. Arrest. [A] peace officer may arrest a person anywhere without a warrant, including at the person's residence if the peace officer has probable cause to believe that the person within the preceding four hours has assaulted, threatened with a dangerous weapon, or placed in fear of immediate bodily harm the person's spouse, former spouse, or other person with whom the person resides or has formerly resided. The arrest may be made even though the assault did not take place in the presence of the peace officer.

Subd. 2. Immunity. A peace officer acting in good faith and exercising due care in making an arrest pursuant to subdivision 1 is immune from civil liability that might result from the officer's action.

Subd. 3. Notice of rights. The peace officer shall tell the victim whether a shelter or other services are available in the community and give the victim immediate notice of the legal rights and remedies available. The notice must include furnishing the victim a copy of the following statement:

"IF YOU ARE THE VICTIM OF DOMESTIC VIOLENCE, you can ask the city or county attorney to file a criminal complaint. You also have the right to go to court and file a petition requesting an order for protection from domestic abuse. . . .The notice must include the resource listing, including telephone number, for the area battered women's shelter, to be designated by the department of corrections.

Subd. 4. Report required. Whenever a peace officer investigates an allegation that an incident described in subdivision 1 has occurred, whether or not an arrest is made, the officer shall make a written police report of the alleged incident. The officer shall submit the report to the officer's supervisor or other person to whom the employer's rules or policies require reports of similar allegations of criminal activity to be made.

Subd. 5. Training. The board of peace officer standards and training shall provide a copy of this section to every law enforcement agency in this state . . . .

Upon request of the board of peace officer standards and training to the bureau of criminal apprehension, at least one training course must include instruction about domestic abuse. A basic skills course required for initial licensure as a peace officer must. . .include at least three hours of training in handling domestic violence cases.

Minnesota Supreme Court Task Force for Gender Fairness in the Courts, Final Report, in 15 Wm. Mitchell L. Rev. 826, 871–72, 874–880, 882–91 (1989)

Domestic Violence

Introduction

Sixty-three thousand incidents of domestic abuse were reported in Minnesota in 1984. Ninety percent of the victims were women. To address this problem, our state has some of the nation's most progressive domestic abuse statutes. It has, along with that, longstanding and knowledgeable advocates—both in the public and private sectors—of enforcement of the domestic abuse laws. In spite of these assets, the Task Force found compelling evidence to conclude that domestic abuse victims do not receive the relief, either civil or criminal, that our legislature intended to provide.

Although civil Orders for Protection (OFPs) are frequently issued and are relatively easy to obtain, they are rarely enforced. Although numerous criminal arrests are made and domestic assault charges brought, discretionary dismissal by prosecutors prevent [sic] final resolution of the cases in criminal court. The evidence reveals an enormous problem, much of which is occurring outside the reach of judicial intervention. . . .

Context of the Problem

. . .[The] evidence leaves little doubt that thousands of Minnesota women suffer seriously from domestic abuse. The Task Force heard numerous accounts of domestic abuse cases in which the victim's efforts to invoke the judicial process resulted in greater victimization. The following two accounts, provided by the victims, reflect that reality in both the civil and criminal contexts. They are representative of a disturbing number of such accounts provided to the Task Force, not only by victims but by judges, domestic abuse advocates, prosecutors, and defense lawyers.

In the civil case, a middle-aged, middle-class homemaker with a twenty-five year history of abuse wrote to the Task Force of her attempt to use the court system for the first time after her husband threw a golf ball at her twelve-year old son. Her petition for an OFP was denied. She said the judge told her that she was "the type who requested an order one day and asked to have it rescinded the next." The judge suggested that she provoke a more serious incident in order to make sure that her case was strong enough to support the OFP. She said, "I guess I need a knife in my back or at least to be bleeding profusely from the head and shoulders to get an OFP." The judge told her, "That's just about it."

In the criminal case, the victim of the domestic assault testified at a public hearing. She stated that the police were present when she was brought to a hospital emergency room by the man with whom she was living. She was bleeding profusely from all ten fingers and required five hours of surgery and forty stitches. According to the police report, [her other injuries included]. . .a cut in excess of six inches on her back and bruises on her body. The man reported that she had attacked him and then self-inflicted the wounds. The woman testified at the public hearing that he had cut the inside flesh of each of her fingers with a pair of scissors in the course of a beating. The case was charged as a third-degree felony assault.

This woman testified that she had called police repeatedly over a four-year period, reporting instances of abuse. Each time no charges were filed. The county attorney's office dismissed this felony case one week before trial, over her vigorous objection.

Frustration over the failure of the court system to provide relief in cases such as these was echoed by members of Minnesota's judiciary. A metro judge commented, "Domestic violence is an outrage. Our system of justice does a very poor job of dealing with this problem.". . .

Stereotyping and Sensitivity. Gender bias results when men or women are perceived as conforming to a single personality profile or a small range of behaviors deemed typical of their gender. The Task Force identified several kinds of stereotypical thinking. . .that have a negative effect on the administration of justice in domestic abuse proceedings.

Many of the examples of stereotypes described to the Task Force involved victim-blaming. The "nagging female" stereotype, suggesting that the woman asks for abuse, is evidenced by the police officer's comment, related by a women's advocate, that "the problem with battered women is that their alligator mouths can't keep up with their hummingbird brains." Women who live with men outside of marriage are seen to be asking for trouble by getting into unsanctioned relationships. A number of attorneys, primarily male, responding to the lawyers' survey suggested that women are crafty schemers who use the OFP proceeding to punish men or gain advantage in a dissolution proceeding. Some male attorneys also suggested that sometimes paternalistic judges grant unwarranted OFPs and encourage women to use the victim image to unfair advantage. . . .

"If you'd have supper on the table this wouldn't happen," was one judicial comment relayed at the Marshall public hearing. "You've been married for ten years, you must like being hit," was a judge's comment reported at the Moorhead public hearing.

A judge's insensitivity to the circumstances of abuse can result in the denial of badly needed relief. A male lawyer wrote to the Task Force about a client who sought an OFP after her husband struck her in the head, threw her to the floor, threatened her life and the lives of her children, and then forced her into his truck while he drove around for an hour while continuing to threaten her. The woman lost consciousness for a short time after her husband hit her. The judge found that the husband had committed domestic abuse and ordered him to move out of the home, but allowed him to return to the property whenever he "deemed it appropriate," in order to feed his dog. Another attorney commented on the lawyers' survey:

> A sitting district court judge once told me in chambers while both sides were trying to reach a stipulation in a final hearing for an OFP that "if my wife slept around I'd kick her butt too." The judge went on to deny the woman's petition. (Male attorney, Greater Minnesota)

Yet another lawyer, a participant at the lawyers' meeting in St. Cloud, told the Task Force of a woman whose boyfriend threatened to kill her if she didn't leave the house. The judge said, "Well, he gave you a choice," and refused to issue a protective order.

The Civil Process: Orders for Protection

. . .The Minnesota Domestic Abuse Act requires court personnel to assist petitioners in preparing and filing the forms necessary for an OFP. This is an area in which the Task Force found that circumstances vary a great deal from county to county. A number of witnesses made a point of crediting helpful court personnel for their supportive role. In some areas, however, the attitudes of court employees actively discourage petitioners from attempting to use the system.

An advocate testified at the Moorhead public hearing about a battered woman who was told "this county doesn't do OFPs." In other counties court employees will notify the respondent that the petitioner is seeking an order. . . .A lawyer from rural Minnesota commented. . .about the practice in one county:

> The Director of Court Services tells [abused women], "OFPs are a pain in the ass. . . ." A petitioner cannot see the judge. She must first see the Director of Court Services who goes over the petition and then on some occasions he will call the abusing party and ask to hear how he feels about the OFP and get his side of what happened. (Female attorney, Greater Minnesota)

. . .

Issuance of Mutual OFPs. . . .The practice of issuing mutual OFPs appears to vary greatly by county. [A 1987 Minnesota Court of Appeals decision makes it clear that the issuance of mutual OFPs when only one person has petitioned and there is no evidence of mutual abuse is improper]. . .[A]dvocates reported that, in their county at least, mutual OFPs are still routinely issued. . . .[An] advocate noted that judges will frequently initiate discussion about a mutual OFP by asking the petitioner if she objects. Very few petitioners do so, because they don't want to antagonize the judge. . . .

The harmful consequences of mutual OFPs were illustrated by testimony . . . .When police officers are called out to enforce the order and learn that it is a mutual OFP they often arrest both parties, "just to be safe," even if there isn't any evidence of mutual abuse. . . .[I]ssuance of mutual OFPs gives abusers the wrong message. Mutual OFPs suggest that the court is not serious about holding the abuser accountable for the violent behavior. Mutual orders also reinforce the notion that the victim is to blame for the abuse.

Denial of Supervised Visitation. The Minnesota Domestic Abuse Act explicitly authorizes the judge in an OFP proceeding to restrict or condition the time, place, or manner of a non-custodial parent's visitation. . .if the court finds that the safety of the victim or the parties' children would be jeopardized by an order that does not provide for supervision. . . .

Witnesses at several of the public hearings told of judges who refused to order supervised visitation in cases with long histories of violence. . . .

Other witnesses told the Task Force of judges who will issue an OFP excluding the abuser from the petitioner's residence and then order unsupervised visitation to take place at that residence. The witnesses emphasized that this kind of order defeats the purpose of an OFP. . . .

Recommendations. 1. Judges, attorneys, court personnel and law enforcement officers should be sensitized to the problems of individuals who have been victims of domestic abuse.

2. The topic of domestic abuse and Orders for Protection—including information about the abuse dynamic and the dangers of victim blaming—should be addressed in judicial education programs.

3. The practice of issuing mutual Orders for Protection in cases without cross-petitions must cease.

4. Continuing legal education programs should address domestic abuse issues.

5. The topic of domestic abuse should become part of the curriculum in family law courses in the state's law schools.

6. Domestic abuse issues should be addressed at local bar association meetings. The Minnesota State Bar Association could prepare a videotape presentation for use by local bar associations.

7. Court administrators and their deputies should have training in the area of domestic abuse as well as a good understanding of Minnesota's Domestic Abuse Act.

8. The state's courts should set a uniform standard regarding the role of the domestic abuse advocate at OFP hearings. The advocate should be allowed to attend the hearing, be present at counsel table and address the court. The courts should also take action to ensure that the advocates are allowed to assist in the preparation of OFP petitions.

9. State funding for the hiring and training of advocates should be increased.

10. The forms used to petition the court for an Order for Protection

should be simplified. For example, proposed orders could contain more sections which would be checked off by the judge.

Criminal Enforcement: Dismissals

At the heart of criminal enforcement of domestic violence complaints is the phenomenon of discretionary dismissal by the prosecutor, before the charge can be determined on the merits either by guilty plea or by trial. . . .The essential prosecutorial issues are the handling of what is commonly referred to as the "victim cooperation" question and the devotion of energy to use of evidentiary tools. The most basic factor may be dedication of adequate prosecutorial resources, especially in the misdemeanor prosecution area. . . .

The dismissal problem is real. Prosecutors stated in narrative comments . . .:

> Our dismissal rates for these types of cases run 80 to 90% in a jurisdiction that bills itself as being in the forefront of domestic abuse. . .I believe . . .Prosecution is, largely, a waste of time. (Male attorney, Twin Cities). . . .
>
> In all 15 cases, the victims demanded we dismiss. I have never tried any of the cases because of these witness problems. . . .[T]he victims demand dismissals. I dismiss. These are all misdemeanor charges. (Male attorney, Greater Minnesota)

These comments indicate not only a pervasive dismissal practice, but a related issue of prosecutorial attitudes which contribute to the problem. . . .

"Victim Cooperation". . . .The term ["victim cooperation"] is used in quotations because it connotes a responsibility on the victim for the survival of the case. . . .[T]hat responsibility is misplaced . . . .

[A] female attorney from the Twin Cities reported:

> I have had a judge tell me, in chambers, perhaps my female client deserved to be beaten up by her husband; maybe she said or did something that really angered him.

This victim-blaming. . .focus[es]. . .on the victim's characteristics rather than on the defendant's conduct. In addition, witnesses and survey comments described incidents of intimidation—threatened or actual reprisals and further battery—by criminal domestic assault defendants attempting to force dismissals. The combination of victim-blaming in the legal system and victim intimidation outside of the system can effectively deter prosecution of criminal domestic assault.

The prosecutor's willingness to dismiss criminal domestic assault charges in this milieu is a contributory factor to cycles of violence and the inability of the criminal process to deal with domestic violence. It is, further, a *de facto* delegation of the prosecutorial responsibility to enforce the domestic violence laws to the victims of the crime. . . .

[I]t may be necessary for the prosecutor to subpoena the victim to appear in court. . . .In a prosecutor-victim relationship where the victim comes to know and trust the prosecutor at the outset of the case. . .[a] subpoena could. . .serve as a means of taking the pressure off the victim, making it clear that the government, rather than the victim, is responsible for the pending prosecution. . . .

Consistent, sensitive use of subpoena power, coupled with the uniform involvement of domestic abuse intervention projects would make a stark difference in dismissal rates. . . .

Evidentiary Tools. [A number of evidentiary tools are available or can be developed, which may help the prosecutor go forward with the case.]

Medical Evidence. . . .The police report in all. . .cases [where there is physical injury] can be required to contain a photograph of all physical injuries. A protocol can be developed with the medical care providers for the gathering of photographic and physical evidence. . . .

"Prompt Complaint" Evidence. . . .A concerted effort to document the original complaint of the domestic violence victim in the victim's own words, whether by videotape or audio record, would make such evidence available to the prosecuting lawyer. . . .

Same Prosecutor. Effective use of these suggested evidentiary tools, including close interaction with the victim, requires that a single attorney be assigned to handle a case from the initial charge through trial. Testimony of victims and intervention project personnel indicates that in some jurisdictions, the identity of the trial prosecutor is unknown until the assigned day of trial. To that end, establishment of special domestic assault prosecutors has been recommended.

Prosecutor Resources. Each of the preceding parts of the discussion. . .entails the commitment of prosecutorial resources beyond those normally allotted. . . .If the domestic violence problem is serious, and if misdemeanor courts are where the most commonly enforceable remedy is available, the Task Force concludes that these resource allocations must be made. The physical trauma to thousands of victims, the familial upheaval, and the secondary consequences in the workplace, the schools, and the cultural environment may well be a greater cost to society than the cost of judicial and prosecutorial resources necessary to deal comprehensively with the problem of domestic abuse.

Addressing Enforcement Issues. . . .Many of the obstacles to effective enforcement of both civil and criminal domestic abuse laws parallel those that, until recently, prevented effective enforcement of drunken driving laws:

- cultural reluctance to intervene in what was seen as essentially a private matter;
- inconsistent attitudes toward enforcement from prosecutor to prosecutor and judge to judge; and
- insufficient commitment of law enforcement and judicial resources.

. . .As it now stands, disturbing numbers of Minnesota women suffer physical injury within their homes and family settings, without adequate recourse in the courts. Such systemic inability to consider the merits of domestic violence cases in our courts should cause serious thinking and action by the bench, the bar, and the public. . . .

Recommendations. 1. Legislation should be enacted that mandates funds and makes available domestic abuse advocacy programs in each county of the state.

2. The state should create a statewide computerized data base on domestic violence, available to law enforcement, prosecutors, courts, and probation, to be accessed under both victim and abuser names, to include: (a) existing OFPs and their conditions; (b) existing conditions of bond or probation; (c) pending criminal charges; (d) past domestic violence criminal history; and (e) past OFPs.

3. Police reporting requirements regarding domestic violence should be expanded to require law enforcement officers, prosecutors, courts and probation officers to report the items above into the statewide data base.

4. Legislation should require medical care providers to report incidents of domestic violence to law enforcement authorities, and to preserve and make available physical evidence of injury to the victim.

5. Legislation should mandate presentence investigations in all cases of conviction for domestic violence, without ability to waive the requirement.

6. Legislation should require all county and city prosecuting authorities to have a plan for the effective prosecution of domestic violence cases.

7. A policy commitment should be implemented to end discretionary dismissals on account of "victim cooperation" reasons, and to develop effective means of reversing this phenomenon.

8. A single prosecutor should be responsible for each case from initial charge to disposition.

9. Early contact between prosecutor and victim, with earliest possible domestic abuse advocate intervention, should be used to explain the use of subpoenas, and the role of victim as a witness.

10. The use of subpoenas should become standard procedure in all domestic violence prosecutions necessitating appearance of the victim.

11. Coordination should be established with law enforcement authorities to preserve prompt complaint evidence by means of videotape or audio recording.

12. Adequate resources must be allocated to permit prosecutors to execute the foregoing.

13. The Supreme Court should promulgate a rule which provides that domestic abuse advocates do not commit the unauthorized practice of law when appearing with or assisting victims of domestic violence in criminal proceedings.

14. The prosecutor's statutory obligation to notify domestic violence victims in advance of case dismissals should be uniformly enforced and coupled with a requirement that prosecutors state the reason for dismissal in open court.

15. Courts should require supervision of conditions of release by court services pending trial in criminal actions and of probationary conditions following sentence.

16. Courts should create uniform forms for statewide use in bail matters for criminal domestic violence proceedings.

17. Courts should enforce the statutory mandatory fine requirement in instances of conviction for domestic violence, except in cases of sworn indigency.

18. Police and sheriff's departments should be encouraged to present in-service training programs concerning domestic abuse. . . .

Notes and Questions

1. *Arrest, Deterrence, and Discretion.* R. Emerson Dobash and Russell Dobash detail how battered women's advocates in the early eighties sought to increase the frequency of arrests in cases of domestic assault. Lawrence Sherman designed and directed an experimental study between 1980 and 1983 to test the effects of arrest for domestic assault.

> The Minneapolis experiment found that arrest and a night in jail for the suspect cut in half the risk of repeat violence against the same victim over a six-month follow-up period, from about 20% to 10%. The comparison treatments were police either ordering the suspect out of the home for eight hours, or for the police to leave the home after advising the couple to calm down. Both official records and interviews of victims showed that "arrest worked best." On the strength of these results, the report recommended that police in all 50 states be allowed to make warrantless [probable cause] arrests in misdemeanor domestic violence cases.

Lawrence W. Sherman, Policing Domestic Violence: Experiments and Dilemmas 2-3 (1992).

While Sherman recommended a policy that arrest be preferred, he was against mandatory arrest laws. *See id.* at 3. Subsequent to the Minneapolis experiment, five other jurisdictions instituted studies in an attempt to replicate the Minneapolis experiment. According to Sherman, the results of those studies are "complex, but they clearly challenge the central premise of mandatory arrest laws: that arrest always works best. The replications in [three of the cities] even produced evidence that arrest *increased* the frequency of domestic violence by the suspects." *Id.* (emphasis in original).

The methodologies and results of these studies and Sherman's position against mandatory arrest have generated controversy. A number of commentators have offered feminist critiques of the research conducted regarding arrest. Cynthia Grant Bowman argues that the studies

> distort. . .our understanding of the effect of different police responses to domestic violence (1) by isolating one factor—arrest—from the larger context of domestic violence and the response of the criminal justice system to it; (2) by reducing the subjects of the study to statistics and thus losing the important information which could be provided by the voices of the victims themselves; and (3) by analysing both the problem under study and the potential policy implications solely in individualistic, non-relational terms. . . .
>
> Arrest is only one stage of response to any crime. It is preceded by the act of calling the police; it is followed, at least in theory, by charging and prosecution. In the domestic relations context, there is evidence that the mere fact of calling the police, without more, has some deterrent impact. In addition, . . .abusers and their victims cannot fail to notice that ninety-five percent of domestic violence cases are not subsequently prosecuted. Finally, even if convicted, very few abusers ever serve any time in prison. These other factors may well be more important than arrest. By simply correlating arrest with subsequent reports of abuse, there is no way of knowing which of the factors actually caused or deterred recidivism. . . .

> The quantitative approach not only misses the voice of the victim; it loses her perspective as well. Even amidst the seeming neutrality of statistics, the authors of these reports appear automatically to assume the male perspective from which to explain data. The unquestioned assumption is that arrest produces certain results either by deterring or failing to deter the abuser. . . .
>
> If statistics are truly neutral, however, why is it to be assumed that the effects of arrest result from its impact on the abuser rather than on his victim? Arrest may empower the victim, both because it affirms her rights and because it allows her time to make arrangements to ensure her own safety, assuming she is psychologically ready to do so. . . .
>
> [T]he balance of benefits from an arrest must be assessed not only from the point of view of deterring continued abuse within one couple but also, and perhaps more importantly, from the point of view of the community's critical interest in addressing the problem of domestic violence on a societal and long-term basis. Arresting and removing the abuser may thus be important, quite apart from any specific deterrent effect, because arrest delivers an empowering message to the victim and communicates society's condemnation of the abusive behavior to children or other witnesses.

Cynthia Grant Bowman, The Arrest Experiments: A Feminist Critique, 83 J. Crim. L. & Criminology 201, 201-04, 206 (1992).

Lisa Frisch, in exploring the goal of deterrence in the criminal justice system in relation to the arrest studies, observes that:

> [d]eterrence is but one goal of the justice system, and it is largely a hypothetical one. . . .[T]he studies' findings that unemployed, socially "marginal" batterers are not deterred by arrest is no more surprising than the fact that our entire justice system fails to deter the majority of socially marginal criminals from committing *any* crime. Our criminal justice system chooses to continue to respond to burglars, armed robbers, drug dealers and muggers even though deterrence is rarely achieved. . . .
>
> When these batterers assaulted their victims subsequent to an arrest, the researchers presumed that the assault was the direct result of the *arrest*, rather than the responsibility and choice of the offender. Should we then believe that when a burglar burglarizes again when released from jail, he did so *because* he was incarcerated?

Lisa A. Frisch, Research That Succeeds, Policies That Fail, 83 J. Crim. L. & Criminology 209, 212-13 (1992) (emphasis in original).

Dobash and Dobash suggest that reducing police discretion through a pro-arrest policy reduces discriminatory patterns of arrest (p. 230). What are the risks and benefits of a reform strategy that seeks to reduce the discretion of police, prosecutors, and judges?

2. *Victims'/Survivors' Cooperation.* The Minnesota Supreme Court Task Force Report expresses concern about the role of the victim/survivor in the prosecution of domestic assaults (p. 239). Kathleen Ferraro reviewed prosecutors' records in Maricopa County, Arizona, for 1987 and 1988 to examine victims'/survivors' participation in the prosecution process. She made the following observations regarding case dismissals:

> Intimate victims were less likely to follow through with prosecution than

> strangers, but victim cooperation was only one of the factors determining case outcome.
>
> Of all intimate victims, 39 percent wanted charges dropped, whereas only 6 percent of nonintimate victims made this request. But other responses to prosecution diminish differences in cooperation between the two groups: Over one quarter (27 percent) of nonintimate victims were missing at the time of trial, whereas only 7 percent of intimate victims were missing. Another 16 percent of intimate victims cooperated with the prosecution, but specifically stated that they desired help for their abusers rather than prison. This response was entirely absent in the nonintimate group. Of the cases where women victims of intimate assault requested that charges be dropped, 65 percent resulted in guilty pleas. So, even if women do not want to follow through with prosecution, it is likely that there is enough evidence to obtain a plea of guilt if the case is serious enough to warrant felony prosecution. At the same time, 16 percent of cases where victims fully cooperated with and desired prosecution resulted in dismissals. The prevalent belief that prosecuting battering is a waste of time because of victim noncooperation overlooks the importance of other legal and extralegal factors in case dismissal.
>
> There are many factors that influence a woman's request to drop charges against an abuser. Many women are dependent on men's economic contributions for support of children. Imprisonment eliminates current employment and endangers future opportunities. Several months usually pass between the violent incident and court hearings. Most offenders are released from custody during this period and find ways to intimidate and manipulate women into dropping charges against them. Some battered women have other legal problems, such as immigration status or outstanding traffic warrants, which lead them to be wary of involvement with the courts. Women who ask for help for their abusers rather than incarceration may believe that prison will lead to an increase in violence upon the abuser's release.
>
> Most large cities now have victim witness assistance programs to provide advocacy services to victims of crime. Those programs that assist battered women with the prosecution process have had dramatic success in improving victim cooperation. . . .When battered women are provided with information about the legal process and support for testifying, successful prosecution is the norm.

Kathleen J. Ferraro, Cops, Courts, and Woman Battering, in Violence Against Women: The Bloody Footprints 165, 171-72 (Pauline B. Bart & Eileen Geil Moran eds., 1993).

The Minnesota Supreme Court Task Force Report recommends that prosecutors routinely issue subpoenas to victims in abuse cases (p. 241). The Report, however, made no recommendation about whether prosecutors should charge victims with contempt for failing to appear or refusing to testify. Use of the subpoena and contempt power may deter lesbians and women of color, in particular, from seeking legal help because they already encounter a range of obstacles in the criminal justice system and have reasons to have less confidence in it. Susan Schechter sets forth feminist arguments on both sides of this issue:

> Some argue that such strategies force prosecutors to do their jobs by removing victim "non-cooperation" from their list of rationalizations for not proceeding with cases. Moreover, such actions demonstrate that the state is on the woman's side, eager to punish abusers while it protects her from intimidation. These activists argue that battered women do not really have a choice when they drop charges; because violent men control their wives with repeated threats and brutality, women are not free to decide if they will prosecute. In this situation, some advocates insist that the victim alone should not decide how to proceed. Rather, they suggest that police should arrest, attorneys should prosecute vigorously, and the victim should be treated as a witness rather than a complainant. They argue that when a woman fears for her safety, she should not appear in court; the prosecutor should find others who have witnessed her husband's brutality. Underlying these suggestions is the belief that it cannot be the woman's role to control her husband's violence. Instead, institutions must take responsibility for stopping the violence, using their power to declare that men cannot beat their wives.
>
> These arguments, however, are in conflict with those that insist on women's rights to self-determination. Advocates for this position believe that battered women must decide how to proceed. The essence of victimization is to strip women of control, and the criminal justice system cannot be given powers to further deny women control. Additionally, many believe that prosecutors will abuse their increased privileges by ignoring their clients' concerns for safety. A dangerous precedent can be set as prosecutors gain the power to shape women's futures. Many argue that battered women would not use community institutions, like the courts, if prosecution is automatically the result. Because of the narrowness of the solutions available in this society to stop violence, women's rights to free themselves from violent men may conflict with their rights to self-determination.

Susan Schechter, Women and Male Violence: The Visions and Struggles of the Battered Women's Movement 175 (1982).

3. *Continuum of Violence.* Consider the definition of domestic abuse in Minn. Stat. § 518B.01 (p. 231) and the standard of conduct allowing an officer to make a probable-cause arrest in Minn. Stat. § 629.341 (p. 234). Compare Minnesota's approach to determine when state intervention is appropriate with the approach taken in *State v. Black*, at p. 195, *State v. Rhodes*, at p. 196, and *State v. Mabrey*, at p. 200.

4. *Tort Remedies.* In addition to criminal sanctions and civil orders for protection, victims/survivors of domestic abuse may be able to bring civil actions for damages against their abusers. Actions for battery, assault, and intentional infliction of emotional distress are available for victims/survivors who seek monetary damages. As Douglas Scherer noted in an article exploring tort remedies for victims of domestic abuse:

> Public policy favors a vigorous response by the legal system to the widespread problem of domestic abuse. Interspousal tort immunity does not bar the great majority of potential actions. Moreover, most jurisdictions prefer independent litigation of tort and divorce actions. Tort actions for battery and assault, based upon physical injury and threats of imminent physical injury, are as appropriate in domestic abuse cases as they would be in a nondo-

> mestic setting. The tort of intentional infliction of emotional distress permits recovery for nonimminent threats and verbal abuse intended to cause severe emotional distress.

Douglas D. Scherer, Tort Remedies for Victims of Domestic Abuse, 3 S.C. L. Rev. 543, 573 (1992).

Victims/survivors of domestic violence also may have a cause of action against police officers and police departments that do not protect them. James Jones examines damage claims against unresponsive police comparing possible federal and state remedies:

> The best way to guarantee that law enforcement officials will assist battered spouses is to hold police departments and their employees civilly liable when proper police action would have prevented the harm.
>
> Scores of abused spouses and children use federal constitutional law, through Section 1983 of Title 42 of the United States Code in suits for damages against both the police who do not protect them and the municipalities and public officials which employ the nonresponsive officers. . . .[However,] Section 1983 is not the ideal remedy for several major reasons.
>
> First, battered spouses cannot always use Section 1983 against unresponsive authorities. Neither state officers acting in their official capacities nor the states themselves are liable under Section 1983. While domestic violence victims theoretically can prevail under Section 1983 against the state (or municipal) representatives they sue as individuals, the doctrine of qualified immunity under Section 1983 often shields government officials. . . .
>
> To recover under Section 1983 for violations of their federal right to due process of law, victims must show that the police demonstrated gross negligence, recklessness, or actual wrongful intent. By comparison, actions grounded in state law seldom require the victim to carry such a heavy burden.
>
> Finally, and perhaps most significantly, the Supreme Court, in 1989. . .[i]n *DeShaney v. Winnebago County Department of Social Services*, the Court all but abolished the substantive due process cause of action domestic violence victims had frequently invoked. . . .
>
> An abused spouses's most effective weapon is likely to be common law negligence. However, such actions have substantial pitfalls because of defenses derived from principles of sovereign or official immunity. . . .
>
> Some battered spouses may also profit from a[n]. . .implied statutory tort claim. . . .Under a statutory tort claim, plaintiffs need only convince a court that they are the beneficiaries of focused pieces of legislation which impose a duty upon government officials, the violation of which is impliedly a tort. The spouse abuse victims who are most likely to win in such cases are those who have obtained orders of protection and/or related mandatory arrest orders under state law.
>
> State constitutional law provides the final major type of state damage action. Among the state constitution-based approaches, equal protection claims are the most promising. . . .[I]n states which adopt a[n]. . .enlightened approach to their charters, . . .courts may readily hold that the special treatment of domestic violence victims by police constitutes a form of sex discrimination which only rarely will withstand judicial scrutiny. Courts in states which have enacted equal rights provisions are most likely to hold this way.

> Battered spouses may also invoke state due process protections. . . .As in negligence and statutory tort cases, state procedural due process law will help the beneficiaries of judicial protection decrees the most.

James T. R. Jones, Battered Spouses' State Law Damage Actions Against the Unresponsive Police, 23 Rutgers L.J. 1, 4-8, 10, 77-78 (1991).

5. *Transition.* The readings and notes identify some unresolved issues facing victims/survivors including mutual arrests, mutual orders for protection, and use and enforcement of subpoenas against victims/survivors. Common to each of these issues is that state intervention has led to the use of coercive state power against victims/survivors. As demonstrated in Section A, historically victims/survivors suffered from the state's failure to intervene in domestic violence. It is ironic that legal reform has caused some victims/survivors to suffer from too much state intervention. The tension of using the legal system for reform and the risk that reform will be distorted is characterized by Christine Littleton as the problem of transition.

> It is. . .necessary to ask two. . .questions. First, what would this legal landscape look like if women had constructed it for ourselves? This question may be unanswerable, at least in a complete form. Nevertheless, the effort of thinking about a woman-centered ideal is both necessary and desirable. . . .The second question is. . .: What strategies might move us in the direction of the tentative ideal while minimizing the dangers of partial reform? In this endeavor lies the problem of transition.

Christine Littleton, Women's Experience and the Problem of Transition: Perspectives on Male Battering of Women, 1989 U. Chi. Legal F. 23, 30-31.

Martha Mahoney, Legal Images of Battered Women: Redefining the Issue of Separation, 90 Mich. L. Rev. 1, 5–6, 65–76, 78–79 (1991)

As one example of a strategic effort to change both law and culture, this article proposes that we seek to redefine in both law and popular culture the issue of women's separation from violent relationships.[4] The question "why didn't she leave?" shapes both social and legal inquiry on battering; much of the legal reliance on academic expertise on battered women has developed in order to address this question. At the moment of separation or attempted separation—for many women, the first encounter with the authority of law—the batterer's quest for control often becomes most acutely violent and potentially lethal. Ironically, although the proliferation of shelters and the elaboration of statutory structures facilitating the grant of protective orders vividly demonstrate both socially and legally the dangers attendant on separation, a woman's "failure" to permanently separate from a violent relationship is still widely held

4. Redefining separation must include rethinking many assumptions—that it is the woman's job to separate from a battering relationship, that separation is the appropriate choice for all women when violence first occurs within a relationship, that appropriate separation is an immediate and final break rather than the process of repeated temporary separations made by many women—as well as identifying the violent assault on women's attempts to separate.

to be mysterious and in need of explanation, an indicator of *her* pathology rather than her batterer's. We have had neither cultural names nor legal doctrines specifically tailored to the particular assault on a woman's body and volition that seeks to block her from leaving, retaliate for her departure, or forcibly end the separation. I propose that we name this attack "separation assault."...

Defining Separation Assault

. . .*Separation assault* is the attack on the woman's body and volition in which her partner seeks to prevent her from leaving, retaliate for the separation, or force her to return. It aims at overbearing her will as to where and with whom she will live, and coercing her in order to enforce connection in a relationship. It is an attempt to gain, retain, or regain power in a relationship, or to punish the woman for ending the relationship. It often takes place over time.

Attacks on separation pervaded the stories of the women who spoke with me. The announcement of intent to separate may be fraught with grave danger:

> He was on strike for the second time in a year. I was pregnant with the second baby in a row. There was absolutely no money. Every day, he yelled at me for a long time—an hour, two hours—about how awful I was. . . .I remember how desperate I felt and how much I needed it to stop.
>
> [One day, when he seemed receptive, she told him it had to stop.] He wouldn't listen. *I said I couldn't live like that anymore and would leave if he didn't stop. He kept saying I couldn't leave because we didn't have enough money to support two households. I said that only his failure to listen could make me leave—I couldn't live like that anymore. . . .*
>
> Suddenly he lost his temper. . . .He stormed upstairs, and I heard him pushing around in the closet. I thought, "That's funny. It sounds like he's getting the gun." And I didn't sit down or move—I stood in the middle of the living room floor and waited. He came down the stairs shouting and I saw that he really did have the shotgun. I knew it was fully loaded. I remember making the conscious decision that this was different than waiting through other outbursts, and that any argument would be deadly.
>
> I turned around and ran out the front door screaming that I was pregnant and ran up the landlady's front steps. I was going to call the police. But I realized that I had heard the baby crying upstairs. All the noise had wakened her from her nap. I couldn't believe he would shoot his child, but I didn't know why he'd gotten the gun, how well he actually knew what he was doing. . .how irritating her crying might be. I turned around and went back into the house. I could hear him putting the gun away in the closet. We got to the baby at the same moment.
>
> I dressed her, put on my own clothes, and left. I had $1.60 and no more money coming for several days. I took the better car. I drove away without knowing where I was going to go. (Emphasis added.)

Although women's stories recount many attacks triggered by separation, the nature of the attack *on separation itself* generally goes unrecognized. Similarly, women describe coercive violence escalating after separation—violence clearly aimed at denying their autonomy—in terms that show they may internalize self-blame rather than clearly identifying the man's attempt at control:

> We had been separated nine months. I came home late one night with a date. I was sitting in the living room playing backgammon with this man, when I saw the car drive up. I thought of sending [my date] home, but I didn't, maybe because I knew I needed help. Maybe I was just defiant.
>
> He knocked. I kept the chain lock on the door, and I told him to go home. He wouldn't leave. He rang the bell for fifteen minutes without stopping. I woke up my roommate, and she disconnected the doorbell.
>
> He started pounding on the door. He broke it in and started a fight with this man. I'm sitting there in horror, watching it—the door broken down, them crashing around the living room. . . .The kids woke up. I sat them on the couch with me.
>
> Then—he was very *drunk*—the fighting stopped. It was pretty short. But it took two hours to try to get him to leave. He ran around with a butcher knife. . .he left the house with it. Finally, I could call the police. Then I don't know if he came back in with the knife—I think he came back after the police were called. The kids were on the couch screaming and crying, I was trying to take care of them.
>
> The police saw the door leaning in the middle of the room, the room trashed and crashed. [They refused to arrest him because "his name is still on the lease."] They told me to get a TRO the next day.
>
> I was left to put the pieces back together. And you know what I did? I went and made love to that guy who was there. I had to—anything to not think. I feel kind of whorish about that—I hardly knew him. I didn't even want to, it was 6 a.m., my whole body hurt, I was just exhausted. It seems bizarre.
>
> So I went and got the TRO. Now when I talk about it, I feel like I should be more upset about it.
>
> No, nobody in the building heard anything. They're afraid to. They didn't hear him break down the door, or even ring the doorbell for fifteen minutes in the middle of the night. . . .None of them heard anything!

This woman's sexual choice seems at least partly explicable as a reassertion of control over her body, over her choice in men, and as a specific denial of power to the ex-husband who had put her through so much pain. Her husband might break down the door, but she could affirm her separation again.

Women describe protracted and inventive attacks on their moves to separate:

> Well, leaving took months. When I first left, I really didn't even know I was leaving the marriage. I was just going to California to get the car that he had left there. But being on my own again, and away from him, I began to regain some of my self-confidence, and I liked it. And people liked me.
>
> But then he came out to California to reclaim me. And totally humiliated me in front of my friends. ["Humiliation" including forcing her to have sex—essentially committing marital rape—in the back of a Volkswagen van while two other men were in the vehicle.] I was scared of him, I was still scared of his violence. As strong as I had been when he wasn't around, as soon as

he came around, I would fall back into the baby talk, I would fall back into the patterns.

Then we got back to Michigan, and I left again and went to stay with my friends. I was in Ann Arbor, and I had a fever. And he came to check on me. . . .He got my heirloom ring off my finger that night. The ring that all my life I felt separated me from poor white trash. The ring that my great-great-grandmother brought over from Germany when she fled the failed revolution of 1848. I never saw that ring again. He threatened to burn down the house I was staying in, but he was satisfied when I gave him the ring because he knew I would come back for it.

I went back again [because he promised to return the ring]. I never got it. And then when it was time for my friends to leave town, they came to our house in Detroit, en masse, and said it was time to go. And I picked up, and I walked out. "Well, it's time to go, we're leaving." And I went.

Some of these attacks on separation will go unnoticed until we begin identifying them specifically:

I felt guilty, so I went back. That lasted a month, until Valentine's Day. . . .Finally, on Valentine's Day, he was throwing things. He was throwing glass—I was barefoot—it was totally absurd. I was being held prisoner in my bed by glass!

I picked the kids up, scrunched my feet so they were under the glass, dragged my feet over the floor so they weren't getting cut too much, and made it out of the house.

One of the best-known battered women in America is Francine Hughes, whose story was told in The Burning Bed. The trial and movie brought the atrocities against her to public attention, but there was little cultural attention to the lessons of her search for autonomy:

Hughes' entire marriage—and her life after divorce—was a search for the exit. [Family], in-laws, friends, social services, police, sheriff's office, county prosecutor—she tried them all. And even when Mickey Hughes came within moments of choking her to death or cutting her throat, no one helped.

We already recognize the danger of the attack on separation pragmatically and intuitively. This is a major reason for the existence of shelters, which protect women against attacks while giving them a place to live. It is the main reason that shelter numbers and addresses are not listed in telephone directories. It is the main reason women seek protective orders. It fills the pages of our newspapers with accounts of attacks on women by their separated husbands. Although we see this attack everywhere, we cannot analyze it until it has a name.

Naming Separation Assault and Understanding Battering

Naming women's experience is an important component of feminist struggle for social and legal change. Naming separation assault has the potential to change consciousness in a manner comparable to the concept of "date rape." "Date rape" and "separation assault" name phenomena women know from our own experience, but which remain invisible without names. These terms do more, however, than merely identify hitherto unnamed experience. Each term identifies one aspect of a common attack on women in a way that illuminates the whole picture. Date rape is not all rape; separation assault is not the whole story of battering. Yet in each case, the act of identifying and describing the formerly invisible part transforms our understanding of the formerly misunderstood whole.

"Date rape" was a term women recognized when we heard it. It helped popularize a redefinition of the concept of rape: "Acquaintance rape is forced, manipulated or coerced sexual intercourse by a friend or an acquaintance. It is an act of violence, aggression and power." Naming date rape helped move discussion of rape past its old starting point, an image of sexual violence committed by a stranger. The concept of date rape thereby allowed women to recognize that the assault they had experienced was, in fact, rape.

Naming and recognizing separation assault will make women's experience more comprehensible to ourselves as well as to the legal system: We know it when we hear it. Attacks on our autonomy are one point at which women can—without stereotyping or invoking the likelihood of denial—locate our own experiences and those of our sisters and friends on a continuum of control attempts that includes those extremes of violence that become known through the sensational cases covered by the press. Women may find the current terminology of battering stigmatizing or alienating, yet be willing to admit that they have experienced inappropriate control attempts by their partners, including assaults on their capacity to separate from "bad" marriages. Exposing control attempts reveals the woman's struggle, rather than defining her according to the behavior of her assailant.

The name "separation assault" also helps women understand our own long-term reactions to violence or to the threats accompanying the end of relationships. Shelters and counseling provide short-term separation assistance, but the impact of separation assault goes on: Fear of an ex-husband becomes part of a woman's life.

> The first year I was at Stanford, I saw *The Burning Bed.* I couldn't *not* watch it, and I couldn't stop watching. I was so scared when it finished. I started calling my ex-husband. It was the middle of the night there. I kept calling him frantically for over an hour. He wasn't home. I became convinced he was on his way there with a gun on a plane. I was sure he would kill me.
>
> I locked the door and got in bed with the kids and shook all night, waiting for him. It was two and a half years later. I was two thousand miles away.

This woman had withstood physical attacks before and after separation, as well as poverty, the indignities inflicted by welfare workers, and the threat of a custody suit. Naming the phenomenon that renewed her fear will allow her to recognize her experience and weigh the dangers of her particular situation. When women blame ourselves for the difficulties we face, this internalized fear becomes part of the culture of women, part of advice mothers give to daughters and friends give each other, as marriages fray and when women are threatened. Naming the assault on separation may begin to pull loose the threads of intimidation from the fabric of feminine wisdom, and to legitimate women's perception of danger while directing our attention toward the resources and support we will need, rather than to our own deficiencies or inadequacies.[5]

Popularizing the concept of separation assault is not without hidden dangers, however. Separation assault is effective in part because, rather than *directly* confronting existing stereotypes of battered women, it provides a partial explanation of women's actions that redirects attention toward the batterer. It works in part through its very resonance with existing stereotypes that ask why the woman didn't leave. Therefore, this concept alone cannot remake our understanding of domestic violence; by itself, separation assault becomes merely another explanation of the woman's apparent "failure" to separate—at worst, subtle reinforcement of existing stereotypes. Without further cultural redefinition of battering as a process of power and control, naming separation assault may not deeply challenge oppressive ideology regarding women and domestic violence. However, on a broader scale, separation assault should help the larger goal of shifting cultural perception because it helps change "objective" judgment—that is, shared cultural perceptions and wisdom—about what is normal in relationships. . . .

Naming separation assault is an attempt to use a social definition, a cultural concept, to resolve doctrinal problems in law. It should not articulate a new test for women's behavior ("did this woman in fact leave and how shall we judge the energy with which she attempted separation?") but rather promote a new understanding of violence against women. As it intervenes in cultural consciousness, separation assault allows legal actors (including attorneys, prosecutors, judges, jurors, social workers, and legal scholars) to reconceive many legal questions that depend on an understanding of women's lives and experiences. Our understanding of "objective" reasonableness depends on our cultural intuitions about normal experience and normal response. By reflecting a consciousness of power and control, and by emphasizing the dangers attendant on separation, separation assault helps make women's experience comprehensible in law. . . .

A. Recognizing Separation Assault in the Cases: The Problem of the Dead Woman's Voice

. . .There is a two-layered problem in seeing through the criminal cases involving abuse of women. First, these cases appear in various doctrinal guises, and few explicitly acknowledge that they concern domestic violence at all. Second, on closer examination, many of the "wife-murder" cases turn out to be "ex-wife murder," the most extreme violence turned against women at separation. Many of the women killed by their husbands are killed after they have separated. Ironically, since those women are not alive to tell their stories,

5. Women often blame themselves and internalize responsibility for the violence. . . . Gondolf and Fisher report studies showing women most likely to blame themselves for the first incident; after that, they increasingly blame the batterer and seek to change him. Edward Gondolf & Ellen Fisher, Battered Women as Survivors: An Alternative to Treating Learned Helplessness 1, 16 (1988).

their voices disappear into the narrative voices of the courts, where the women are not usually identified as battered:

> On a day in early September in 1977, the petitioner and his wife of 28 years had a heated argument in their home. During the course of this altercation, the petitioner, who had consumed several cans of beer, threatened his wife with a knife and damaged some of her clothing. At this point, the petitioner's wife declared that she was going to leave him, and departed to stay with relatives. [This was not the first time that he and his wife had been separated as a result of his violent behavior.] That afternoon she went to a Justice of the Peace and secured a warrant charging the petitioner with aggravated assault. A few days later, while still living away from home, she filed suit for divorce. [A court hearing date was set and several efforts to persuade the wife to return home were rebuffed.] At some point during this period, his wife moved in with her mother. . . .[Several angry phone calls were exchanged, while she refused to reconcile.]
>
> At this juncture, the petitioner got out his shotgun and walked with it down the hill from his home to the trailer where his mother-in-law lived. Peering through a window, he observed his wife, his mother-in-law, and his 11-year-old daughter playing a card game. He pointed the shotgun at his wife through the window and pulled the trigger. The charge from the gun struck his wife in the forehead and killed her instantly. He proceeded into the trailer, striking and injuring his fleeing daughter with the barrel of the gun. He then fired the gun at his mother-in-law, striking her in the head and killing her instantly.[6]

Godfrey v. Georgia presents an almost perfect picture of the dangers for women at separation: Mrs. Godfrey had resolutely separated from her husband and energetically sought the protection of the law. However, her story does not enter the criminal law casebook as a domestic violence case. Rather, *Godfrey* is a death penalty case presenting the issue of whether this murder was unambiguously "outrageously or wantonly vile, horrible or inhuman," or whether the case revealed ambiguity and vagueness in the death penalty statute. The Supreme Court essentially found Mrs. Godfrey's death to be quite an ordinary murder. I believe the majority was correct—this *was* an ordinary murder—but the facts were even more ordinary than the majority realized. . . .

The California case of *People v. Berry*, doctrinally significant for its holding on cooling off periods when killers claim provocation by their victims, also concerns a hidden separation assault. The only account of the marriage is the one Berry gave the police and at trial. According to Berry's story, his wife, Rachel Pessah, had gone to Israel within days of their marriage; on her return, she taunted him about her love for another man and her plans to leave Berry. After repeated arguments and threats or attempts to separate, he tried to strangle her. He called a cab to take her to a hospital, and she later filed a police report that resulted in a warrant for his arrest. He told her he was leaving their home and going to stay with a friend. Two days later, he returned to the

6. Godfrey v. Georgia, 446 U.S. 420, 424-25 (1980).

apartment and waited overnight. She returned the next day and said she supposed he had come to kill her. He was indecisive, but said he had. She screamed. He strangled her.

Even feminist literature on battering may overlook the particularity of attacks on women's autonomy. For example, the feminist newsletter *Response* cites the 1988 case of *Balistreri v. Pacifica Police Department*[7] in a short article entitled "Court Rules in Favor of Abused Wife." The one-paragraph article describes Balistreri as

> an abused wife who sued police for not protecting her. . . .Police had refused to arrest the batterer when summoned following a beating, failed to offer medical assistance, and did not protect the woman over a 3-year period during which she reported incidents to police and obtained a restraining order.

Most of the facts of *Balistreri* concern attacks after separation. When Balistreri's husband beat her severely in February 1982, officers failed to help her. She divorced her husband—apparently promptly, because "throughout 1982" she complained to police of vandalism and harassing phone calls by the husband "from whom she was now divorced." In November that year, her "former husband" crashed his car into her garage, and in March 1983, a firebomb was thrown through the window of her house. From 1983 to 1985, telephone harassment and vandalism continued. Balistreri emerges as a woman of great strength—resisting her ex-husband's repeated attacks and pursuing her complaint within the legal system when her lawyer would go no further.[8] "Abused wife," the term used by *Response*, captures neither her determined resistance nor her separation as the keys to the repeated violence she suffered.

B. Recognizing the Danger to Women at Separation

Recognizing the assault on separation can help disentangle a number of complex legal issues in cases in which women have been killed or harmed. In some areas of substantive law, identifying separation assault will change the questions posed by the court in its decisionmaking process. In other doctrinal areas, the shift in time frame made possible by highlighting the assault on separation can change judicial comprehension of the assault on the woman or of the probability that more assaults may occur. Separation assault may also, as in contested custody actions, help reveal underlying motivations in the legal action itself.

Restraining Orders

In some jurisdictions, when women seek orders of protection against violent men, courts routinely grant mutual orders of protection rather than

7. 855 F.2d 1421 (9th Cir. 1988), *amended on other grounds*, 901 F.2d 696 (9th Cir. 1990).

8. Balistreri won her appeal pro se; her lawyer had refused to continue working on the case after the initial dismissal for failure to state a claim. 855 F.2d at 1423.

orders specifically protecting the women. Mutual orders of protection direct each party not to assault, endanger, or threaten the other. If mutual orders are violated, police officers believe they must either arrest both parties or do nothing. The New York Task Force on Women in the Courts concluded that a woman with a mutual order of protection is in a worse position than a woman with no order at all, since the mutual order makes her look equally violent in the eyes of the courts, and the husband may not be held responsible if there is another violent incident. Also, it may be harder for her to obtain a more restrictive order if the violence recurs. The Task Force concluded that this was particularly dangerous if the mutual order was granted when the woman had requested protection for herself at the same time she filed an action to end the marriage—an especially dangerous period. Even in jurisdictions that do not routinely grant mutual orders, battering men may make cross-accusations of violence against battered women. While many battered women do fight back against their husbands, their violence is largely defensive and less severe than the men's violence—yet since it is also described as "violence," these allegations can prove troubling and confusing to judges.

If we understood better the particular attacks women face at separation, courts could sort both cross-accusations of violence and requests for mutual orders of protection by examining the nature of current threats and the history of violence in relation to the issue of separation. The question then becomes: "Which of these people needs her [or his] capacity to separate protected?" Answering this question will help sort the dangers and should result in the grant of appropriate protective orders. . . .

Custody Determinations: Understanding Dominance and Time-Framing Assault

The concept of separation assault provides insight into the difficult bargains women strike during custody determinations. Women may accept mutual orders of protection, rather than orders that specifically protect them against their batterers, in exchange for the husband's agreement not to contest custody. Courts often award joint custody to batterers, and some courts that do not perceive violence against the mother as an aspect of the custody determination may even award them sole custody.[9] The problem is exacerbated for battered women by the professional analyses of the social workers in whom the court vests the power to evaluate women, and by the possibility that the judge will share a stereotypical, stigmatizing image of battered women.

Separation assault provides a link between past violence and current legal disputes by illuminating the custody action as *part of* an ongoing attempt, through physical violence and legal manipulation, to force the woman to make concessions or return to the violent partner. It reveals the potential for continuing danger from a batterer who may not have struck out physically in the recent past. Threats against the woman's separation attempts may reveal

9. . . .Advisory Comm. on Gender Bias in the Courts, California Judicial Council, Achieving Equal Justice for Women and Men in the Courts pt. 6, at 37 (draft Mar. 23 1990) (less than half of judges surveyed viewed spousal abuse as a reason not to award joint custody).

that the "domestic" violence has outlasted the marriage. Recognizing separation assault can therefore help judges understand the relevance of past violence and threats, and the relevance of the nature of present attacks, to custody cases. Also, when there is evidence of violent separation assault, a judge could give more intense scrutiny to the motives behind custody disputes and reconsider the appropriateness of joint custody awards or liberal visitation decrees. This would help diminish "legal separation assault" in custody cases. Finally, by remaking the cultural concept of separation, we may hope to affect positively the evaluation of women by the social workers in whom the legal system places so much power.

Judging the Wife-Killer: Time-Framing, Provocation, and the Nature of the Assault

In *Berry*, the defendant's arguments for a jury instruction on provocation depended entirely upon his statements that his wife had taunted him sexually and provoked her own murder. In fact, he did not kill her when she taunted him, but when she left him. Recognizing separation assault expands the relevant time frame to show his behavior was consistent with numerous prior assaults that seem at least as responsive to her departure as to sexual provocation. He had violently assaulted his first wife as well.[10] *Berry* is cited for its holding that twenty hours of waiting in the apartment—some days after his wife's last "provocative" conduct—was not as a matter of law too long a period to permit an instruction on provocation. The court might have viewed the case differently had the assault on separation been as cognizable as his response to her alleged sexual taunts: it is difficult to find "heat-of-passion" in a repeatedly attempted assault carried out over a period of time.

A short time frame favors men in these cases, as it does in many types of cases, by removing violence from a context of power and struggle. Prior attacks on the woman's attempts to separate may essentially be rehearsals for the final killing. Alternatively, the long-term assault on her separation may be perceived as one ongoing attack. If only the final, deadly assault is cognizable, the nature of the assault as an attack on separation, rather than on the woman's sexual provocation, may remain disguised. Separation assault can therefore change the time frame within which the man's mental state is to be evaluated by changing the perception of the ways in which the woman's autonomy is under attack.

Questions

1. *Transition Revisited.* How does Christine Littleton's understanding of the problem of transition help us to evaluate the naming of separation assault? *See* Note 5, at p. 247.

2. *Provocation and Separation.* Compare the effect of the traditional legal

---

10. He stabbed her with a kitchen knife. Berry's account of his assault on his first wife shows that both sexual jealousy and fear of separation were present in that relationship as well. Reporter's Transcript, at 252-53 (on file with author).

and cultural focus on provocation as exemplified in *State v. Black*, at p. 195, *State v. Rhodes*, at p. 196, and *People v. Berry*, at p. 200, with the effect of the current legal and cultural focus on the question "why didn't she leave?".

C. Self-defense

State v. Norman,
324 N.C. 253, 378 S.E.2d 8 (1989)

Mitchell, J. The defendant was tried [for]. . .the first degree murder of her husband. The jury found the defendant guilty of voluntary manslaughter. The defendant appealed from the trial court's judgment sentencing her to six years imprisonment.

The Court of Appeals granted a new trial, citing as error the trial court's refusal to submit a possible verdict of acquittal by reason of perfect self-defense. Notwithstanding the uncontroverted evidence that the defendant shot her husband three times in the back of the head as he lay sleeping in his bed, the Court of Appeals held that the defendant's evidence that she exhibited what has come to be called "the battered wife syndrome" entitled her to have the jury consider whether the homicide was an act of perfect self-defense and, thus, not a legal wrong.

We conclude that the evidence introduced in this case would not support a finding that the defendant killed her husband due to a reasonable fear of imminent death or great bodily harm, as is required before a defendant is entitled to jury instructions concerning either perfect or imperfect self-defense. Therefore, the trial court properly declined to instruct the jury on the law relating to self-defense. Accordingly, we reverse the Court of Appeals.

At trial, the State presented the testimony of Deputy Sheriff R.H. Epley of the Rutherford County Sheriff's Department, who was called to the Norman residence on the night of 12 June 1985. Inside the home, Epley found the defendant's husband, John Thomas Norman, lying on a bed in a rear bedroom with his face toward the wall and his back toward the middle of the room. He was dead, but blood was still coming from wounds to the back of his head. A later autopsy revealed three gunshot wounds to the head, two of which caused fatal brain injury. The autopsy also revealed a .12 percent blood alcohol level in the victim's body.

Later that night, the defendant related an account of the events leading to the killing, after Epley had advised her of her constitutional rights and she had waived her right to remain silent. The defendant told Epley that her husband had been beating her all day and had made her lie down on the floor while he slept on the bed. After her husband fell asleep, the defendant carried her grandchild to the defendant's mother's house. The defendant took a pistol from her mother's purse and walked the short distance back to her home. She pointed the pistol at the back of her sleeping husband's head, but it jammed the first time she tried to shoot him. She fixed the gun and then shot her husband in the back of the head as he lay sleeping. After one shot, she felt her husband's chest and determined that he was still breathing and making sounds. She then shot him twice more in the back of the head. The defendant told Epley that she killed her husband because "she took all she was going to take from him so she shot him."

The defendant presented evidence tending to show a long history of physical and mental abuse by her husband due to his alcoholism. At the time of the killing, the thirty-nine-year-old defendant and her husband had been married almost twenty-five years and had several children. The defendant testified that her husband had started drinking and abusing her about five years after they were married. His physical abuse of her consisted of frequent assaults that included slapping, punching and kicking her, striking her with various objects, and throwing glasses, beer bottles and other objects at her. The defendant described other specific incidents of abuse, such as her husband putting her cigarettes out on her, throwing hot coffee on her, breaking glass against her face and crushing food on her face. Although the defendant did not present evidence of ever having received medical treatment for any physical injuries inflicted by her husband, she displayed several scars about her face which she attributed to her husband's assaults.

The defendant's evidence also tended to show other indignities inflicted upon her by her husband. Her evidence tended to show that her husband did not work and forced her to make money by prostitution, and that he made humor of that fact to family and friends. He would beat her if she resisted going out to prostitute herself or if he was unsatisfied with the amounts of money she made. He routinely called the defendant "dog," "bitch" and "whore," and on a few occasions made her eat pet food out of the pets' bowls and bark like a dog. He often made her sleep on the floor. At times, he deprived her of food and refused to let her get food for the family. During those years of abuse, the defendant's husband threatened numerous times to kill her and to maim her in various ways.

The defendant said her husband's abuse occurred only when he was intoxicated, but that he would not give up drinking. She said she and her husband "got along very well when he was sober," and that he was "a good guy" when he was not drunk. She had accompanied her husband to the local mental health center for sporadic counseling sessions for his problem, but he continued to drink.

In the early morning hours on the day before his death, the defendant's husband, who was intoxicated, went to a rest area off I-85 near Kings Mountain where the defendant was engaging in prostitution and assaulted her. While driving home, he was stopped by a patrolman and jailed on a charge of driving while impaired. After the defendant's mother got him out of jail at the defendant's request later that morning, he resumed his drinking and abuse of the defendant.

The defendant's evidence also tended to show that her husband seemed angrier than ever after he was released from jail and that his abuse of the defendant was more frequent. That evening, sheriff's deputies were called to the Norman residence, and the defendant complained that her husband had been beating her all day and she could not take it anymore. The defendant was advised to file a complaint, but she said she was afraid her husband would kill her if she had him arrested. The deputies told her they needed a warrant before they could arrest her husband, and they left the scene.

The deputies were called back less than an hour later after the defendant had taken a bottle of pills. The defendant's husband cursed her and called her names as she was attended by paramedics, and he told them to let her die. A sheriff's deputy finally chased him back into his house as the defendant was put into an ambulance. The defendant's stomach was pumped at the local hospital, and she was sent home with her mother.

While in the hospital, the defendant was visited by a therapist with whom she discussed filing charges against her husband and having him committed for treatment. Before the therapist left, the defendant agreed to go to the mental health center the next day to discuss those possibilities. The therapist testified at trial that the defendant seemed depressed in the hospital, and that she expressed considerable anger toward her husband. He testified that the defendant threatened a number of times that night to kill her husband and that she said she should kill him "because of the things he had done to her."

The next day, the day she shot her husband, the defendant went to the mental health center to talk about charges and possible commitment, and she confronted her husband with that possibility. She testified that she told her husband later that day: "J.T., straighten up. Quit drinking. I'm going to have you committed to help you." She said her husband then told her he would "see them coming" and would cut her throat before they got to him.

The defendant also went to the social services office that day to seek welfare benefits, but her husband followed her there, interrupted her interview and made her go home with him. He continued his abuse of her, threatening to kill and to maim her, slapping her, kicking her, and throwing objects at her. At one point, he took her cigarette and put it out on her, causing a small burn on her upper torso. He would not let her eat or bring food into the house for their children.

That evening, the defendant and her husband went into their bedroom to lie down, and he called her a "dog" and made her lie on the floor when he lay down on the bed. Their daughter brought in her baby to leave with the defendant, and the defendant's husband agreed to let her baby-sit. After the defendant's husband fell asleep, the baby started crying and the defendant took it to her mother's house so it would not wake up her husband. She returned shortly with the pistol and killed her husband.

The defendant testified at trial that she was too afraid of her husband to press charges against him or to leave him. She said that she had temporarily left their home on several previous occasions, but he had always found her, brought her home and beaten her. Asked why she killed her husband, the defendant replied: "Because I was scared of him and I knowed when he woke up, it was going to be the same thing, and I was scared when he took me to the truck stop that night it was going to be worse than he had ever been. I just couldn't take it no more. There ain't no way, even if it means going to prison. It's better than living in that. That's worse hell than anything."

The defendant and other witnesses testified that for years her husband had frequently threatened to kill her and to maim her. When asked if she believed those threats, the defendant replied: "Yes. I believed him; he would, he would kill me if he got a chance. If he thought he wouldn't a had to went to jail, he would a done it."

Two expert witnesses in forensic psychology and psychiatry who examined the defendant after the shooting, Dr. William Tyson and Dr. Robert Rollins, testified that the defendant fit the profile of battered wife syndrome. This condition, they testified, is characterized by such abuse and degradation that the battered wife comes to believe she is unable to help herself and cannot expect help from anyone else. She believes that she cannot escape the complete control of her husband and that he is invulnerable to law enforcement and other sources of help.

Dr. Tyson, a psychologist, was asked his opinion as to whether, on 12 June 1985, "it appeared reasonably necessary for Judy Norman to shoot J.T. Norman?" He replied: "I believe that. . .Mrs. Norman believed herself to be doomed. . .to a life of the worst kind of torture and abuse, degradation that she had experienced over the years in a progressive way; that it would only get worse, and that death was inevitable. . . ." Dr. Tyson later added: "I think Judy Norman felt that she had no choice, both in the protection of herself and her family, but to engage, exhibit deadly force against Mr. Norman, and that in so doing, she was sacrificing herself, both for herself and for her family."

Dr. Rollins, who was the defendant's attending physician at Dorothea Dix Hospital when she was sent there for evaluation, testified that in his opinion the defendant was a typical abused spouse and that "[s]he saw herself as powerless to deal with the situation, that there was no alternative, no way she could escape it." Dr. Rollins was asked his opinion as to whether "on June 12th, 1985, it appeared reasonably necessary that Judy Norman would take the life of J.T. Norman?" Dr. Rollins replied that in his opinion, "that course of action did appear necessary to Mrs. Norman."

Based on the evidence that the defendant exhibited battered wife syndrome, that she believed she could not escape her husband nor expect help from others, that her husband had threatened her, and that her husband's abuse of her had worsened in the two days preceding his death, the Court of Appeals concluded that a jury reasonably could have found that her killing of her husband was justified as an act of perfect self-defense. The Court of Appeals reasoned that the nature of battered wife syndrome is such that a jury could not be precluded from finding the defendant killed her husband lawfully in perfect self-defense, even though he was asleep when she killed him. We disagree.

The right to kill in self-defense is based on the necessity, real or reasonably apparent, of killing an unlawful aggressor to save oneself from *imminent* death or great bodily harm at his hands. . . .Our law has recognized that self-preservation under such circumstances springs from a primal impulse and is an inherent right of natural law. . . .

In North Carolina, a defendant is entitled to have the jury consider acquittal by reason of *perfect* self-defense when the evidence, viewed in the light most favorable to the defendant, tends to show that at the time of the killing it appeared to the defendant and she believed it to be necessary to kill the decedent to save herself from imminent death or great bodily harm. . . .That belief must be reasonable, however, in that the circumstances as they appeared to the defendant would create such a belief in the mind of a person of ordinary firmness. . . .Further, the defendant must not have been the initial aggressor provoking the fatal confrontation. . . .A killing in the proper exercise of the right of *perfect* self-defense is always completely justified in law and constitutes no legal wrong.

Our law also recognizes an *imperfect* right of self-defense in certain circumstances, including, for example, when the defendant is the initial aggressor, but without intent to kill or to seriously injure the decedent, and the decedent escalates the confrontation to a point where it reasonably appears to the defendant to be necessary to kill the decedent to save herself from imminent death or great bodily harm. . . .Although the culpability of a defendant who kills in the exercise of *imperfect* self-defense is reduced, such a defendant is *not justified* in the killing so as to be entitled to acquittal, but is guilty at least of voluntary manslaughter. . . .

The defendant in the present case was not entitled to a jury instruction on either perfect or imperfect self-defense. The trial court was not required to instruct on *either* form of self-defense unless evidence was introduced tending to show that at the time of the killing the defendant reasonably believed herself to be confronted by circumstances which necessitated her killing her husband to save herself from *imminent* death or great bodily harm. . . .No such evidence was introduced in this case, and it would have been error for the trial court to instruct the jury on *either* perfect or imperfect self-defense. . . .

The jury found the defendant guilty only of voluntary manslaughter in the present case. As we have indicated, an instruction on imperfect self-defense would have entitled the defendant to nothing more, since one who kills in the exercise of imperfect self-defense is guilty at least of voluntary manslaughter. Therefore, even if it is assumed arguendo that the defendant was entitled to an instruction on imperfect self-defense—a notion we have specifically rejected—the failure to give such an instruction was harmless in this case. Accordingly, although we recognize that the imminence requirement applies to both types of self-defense for almost identical reasons, we limit our consideration in the remainder of this opinion to the issue of whether the trial court erred in failing to instruct the jury to consider acquittal on the ground that the killing was justified and, thus, lawful as an act of *perfect* self-defense.

The killing of another human being is the most extreme recourse to our inherent right of self-preservation and can be justified in law only by the utmost real or apparent necessity brought about by the decedent. For that reason, our law of self-defense has required that a defendant claiming that a homicide was justified and, as a result, inherently lawful by reason of perfect self-defense must establish that she reasonably believed at the time of the killing she otherwise would have immediately suffered death or great bodily harm. Only if defendants are required to show that they killed due to a reasonable belief that death or great bodily harm was imminent can the justification for homicide remain clearly and firmly rooted in necessity. The imminence requirement ensures that deadly force will be used only where it is necessary as a last resort in the exercise of the inherent right of self-preservation. It also ensures that before a homicide is justified and, as a result, not a legal wrong, it will be reliably determined that the defendant reasonably believed that absent the use of deadly force, not only would an unlawful attack have occurred, but also that the attack would have caused death or great bodily harm. The law does not sanction the use of deadly force to repel simple assaults. . . .

The term "imminent," as used to describe such perceived threats of death or great bodily harm as will justify a homicide by reason of perfect self-defense, has been defined as "immediate danger, such as must be instantly met, such as cannot be guarded against by calling for the assistance of others or the protection of the law.". . .Our cases have sometimes used the phrase "about to suffer" interchangeably with "imminent" to describe the immediacy of threat that is required to justify killing in self-defense.

The evidence in this case did not tend to show that the defendant reasonably believed that she was confronted by a threat of imminent death or great bodily harm. The evidence tended to show that no harm was "imminent" or about to happen to the defendant when she shot her husband. The uncontroverted evidence was that her husband had been asleep for some time when she walked to her mother's house, returned with the pistol, fixed the pistol after it jammed and then shot her husband three times in the back of the head. The defendant was not faced with an instantaneous choice between killing her husband or being killed or seriously injured. Instead, *all* of the evidence tended to show that the defendant had ample time and opportunity to resort to other means of preventing further abuse by her husband. There was no action underway by the decedent from which the jury could have found that the defendant had reasonable grounds to believe either that a felonious assault was imminent or that it might result in her death or great bodily injury. Additionally, no such action by the decedent had been underway immediately prior to his falling asleep.

Faced with somewhat similar facts, we have previously held that a defendant who believed himself to be threatened by the decedent was not entitled to a jury instruction on either perfect or imperfect self-defense when it was the defendant who went to the decedent and initiated the final, fatal confrontation. . . .

Additionally, the lack of any belief by the defendant—reasonable or otherwise—that she faced a threat of imminent death or great bodily harm from the drunk and sleeping victim in the present case was illustrated by the defendant and her own expert witnesses when testifying about her subjective assessment of her situation at the time of the killing. The psychologist and psychiatrist replied affirmatively when asked their opinions of whether killing her husband "appeared reasonably necessary" to the defendant at the time of the homicide. That testimony spoke of no *imminent* threat nor of any fear by the defendant of death or great bodily harm, imminent or otherwise. Testimony in the form of a conclusion that a killing "appeared reasonably necessary" to a defendant does not tend to show all that must be shown to establish self-defense. More specifically, for a killing to be in self-defense, the perceived necessity must arise from a reasonable fear of imminent death or great bodily harm.

Dr. Tyson additionally testified that the defendant "believed herself to be doomed. . .to a life of the worst kind of torture and abuse, degradation that she had experienced over the years in a progressive way; that it would only get worse, and that death was inevitable." Such evidence of the defendant's speculative beliefs concerning her remote and indefinite future, while indicating she had felt generally threatened, did not tend to show that she killed in the belief—reasonable or otherwise—that her husband presented a threat of *imminent* death or great bodily harm. Under our law of self-defense, a defendant's subjective belief of what might be "inevitable" at some indefinite point in the future does not equate to what she believes to be "imminent." Dr.

Tyson's opinion that the defendant believed it was necessary to kill her husband for "the protection of herself and her family" was similarly indefinite and devoid of time frame and did not tend to show a threat or fear of *imminent* harm.

The defendant testified that, "I knowed when he woke up, it was going to be the same thing, and I was scared when he took me to the truck stop that night it was going to be worse than he had ever been." She also testified, when asked if she believed her husband's threats: "Yes. . . .[H]e would kill me if he got a chance. If he thought he wouldn't a had to went to jail, he would a done it." Testimony about such indefinite fears concerning what her sleeping husband might do at some time in the future did not tend to establish a fear—reasonable or otherwise—of *imminent death or great bodily harm* at the time of the killing.

We are not persuaded by the reasoning of our Court of Appeals in this case that when there is evidence of battered wife syndrome, neither an actual attack nor threat of attack by the husband at the moment the wife uses deadly force is required to justify the wife's killing of him in perfect self-defense. The Court of Appeals concluded that to impose such requirements would ignore the "learned helplessness," meekness and other realities of battered wife syndrome and would effectively preclude such women from exercising their right of self-defense. . . .Other jurisdictions which have addressed this question under similar facts are divided in their views, and we can discern no clear majority position on facts closely similar to those of this case. . . .

The reasoning of our Court of Appeals in this case proposes to change the established law of self-defense by giving the term "imminent" a meaning substantially more indefinite and all-encompassing than its present meaning. This would result in a substantial relaxation of the requirement of real or apparent necessity to justify homicide. Such reasoning proposes justifying the taking of human life not upon the reasonable belief it is necessary to prevent death or great bodily harm—which the imminence requirement ensures—but upon purely subjective speculation that the decedent probably would present a threat to life at a future time and that the defendant would not be able to avoid the predicted threat.

The Court of Appeals suggests that such speculation would have been particularly reliable in the present case because the jury, based on the evidence of the decedent's intensified abuse during the thirty-six hours preceding his death, could have found that the decedent's passive state at the time of his death was "but a momentary hiatus in a continuous reign of terror by the decedent [and] the defendant merely took advantage of her first opportunity to protect herself.". . .Requiring jury instructions on perfect self-defense in such situations, however, would still tend to make opportune homicide lawful as a result of mere subjective predictions of indefinite future assaults and circumstances. Such predictions of future assaults to justify the defendant's use of deadly force in this case would be entirely speculative, because there was no evidence that her husband had ever inflicted any harm upon her that approached life-threatening injury, even during the "reign of terror." It is far from clear in the defendant's poignant evidence that any abuse by the decedent had ever involved the degree of physical threat required to justify the defendant in using deadly force, even when those threats were imminent.

The use of deadly force in self-defense to prevent harm other than death or great bodily harm is excessive as a matter of law. . . .

As we have stated, stretching the law of self-defense to fit the facts of this case would require changing the "imminent death or great bodily harm" requirement to something substantially more indefinite than previously required and would weaken our assurances that justification for the taking of human life remains firmly rooted in real or apparent necessity. That result in principle could not be limited to a few cases decided on evidence as poignant as this. The relaxed requirements for perfect self-defense proposed by our Court of Appeals would tend to categorically legalize the opportune killing of abusive husbands by their wives solely on the basis of the wives' testimony concerning their subjective speculation as to the probability of future felonious assaults by their husbands. Homicidal self-help would then become a lawful solution, and perhaps the easiest and most effective solution, to this problem. . . .It has even been suggested that the relaxed requirements of self-defense found in what is often called the "battered woman's defense" could be extended in principle to *any type of case* in which a defendant testified that he or she subjectively believed that killing was necessary and proportionate to any perceived threat. . . .

In conclusion, we decline to expand our law of self-defense beyond the limits of immediacy and necessity which have heretofore provided an appropriately narrow but firm basis upon which homicide may be justified and, thus, lawful by reason of perfect self-defense or upon which a defendant's culpability may be reduced by reason of imperfect self-defense. As we have shown, the evidence in this case did not entitle the defendant to jury instructions on either perfect or imperfect self-defense.

For the foregoing reasons, we conclude that the defendant's conviction for voluntary manslaughter and the trial court's judgment sentencing her to a six-year term of imprisonment were without error. Therefore, we must reverse the decision of the Court of Appeals which awarded the defendant a new trial.

Reversed.

Martin, J., dissenting. At the outset it is to be noted that the peril of fabricated evidence is not unique to the trials of battered wives who kill. The possibility of invented evidence arises in all cases in which a party is seeking the benefit of self-defense. Moreover, in this case there were a number of witnesses other than defendant who testified as to the actual presence of circumstances supporting a claim of self-defense. This record contains no reasonable basis to attack the credibility of evidence for the defendant.

Likewise, the difficulty of rebutting defendant's evidence because the only other witness to many of the events is deceased is not unique to this type of case. This situation is also commonplace in cases in which self-defense is raised, although, again, in the case sub judice there was more than one surviving witness to such events. In considering the argument that the state is faced with a difficult burden in attempting to rebut evidence of which defendant is the only surviving witness, one must not overlook the law: the burden is always on the state to prove that the killing was intentional beyond a reasonable doubt. "Defendant may always rest ultimately on the weakness of the state's case and the state's failure to carry its burden of proof.". . .

At the heart of the majority's reasoning is its unsubstantiated concern that to find that the evidence presented by defendant would support an instruction on self-defense would "expand our law of self-defense beyond the limits of immediacy and necessity." Defendant does not seek to expand or relax the requirements of self-defense and thereby "legalize the opportune killing of allegedly abusive husbands by their wives," as the majority overstates. Rather, defendant contends that the evidence as gauged by the existing laws of self-defense is sufficient to require the submission of a self-defense instruction to the jury. The proper issue for this Court is to determine whether the evidence, viewed in the light most favorable to the defendant, was sufficient to require the trial court to instruct on the law of self-defense. I conclude that it was.

In every jury trial, it is the duty of the court to charge the jury on all substantial features of the case arising on the evidence, whether or not such instructions have been requested. . . .All defenses presented by the defendant's evidence are substantial features of the case, even if that evidence contains discrepancies or is contradicted by evidence from the state. . . .This rule reflects the principle in our jurisprudence that it is the jury, not the judge, that weighs the evidence.

A defendant is entitled to an instruction on self-defense when there is evidence, viewed in the light most favorable to the defendant, that these four elements existed at the time of the killing:

(1) it appeared to defendant and he believed it to be necessary to kill the deceased in order to save himself from death or great bodily harm; and

(2) defendant's belief was reasonable in that the circumstances as they appeared to him at the time were sufficient to create such a belief in the mind of a person of ordinary firmness; and

(3) defendant was not the aggressor in bringing on the affray, i.e., he did not aggressively and willingly enter into the fight without legal excuse or provocation; and

(4) defendant did not use excessive force, i.e., did not use more force than was necessary or reasonably appeared to him to be necessary under the circumstances to protect himself from death or great bodily harm.

. . .The first element requires that there be evidence that the defendant believed it was necessary to kill in order to protect herself from serious bodily harm or death; the second requires that the circumstances as defendant perceived them were sufficient to create such a belief in the mind of a person of ordinary firmness. Both elements were supported by evidence at defendant's trial.

Evidence presented by defendant described a twenty-year history of beatings and other dehumanizing and degrading treatment by her husband. In his expert testimony a clinical psychologist concluded that defendant fit "and exceed[ed]" the profile of an abused or battered spouse, analogizing this treatment to the dehumanization process suffered by prisoners of war under the Nazis during the Second World War and the brainwashing techniques of the Korean War. The psychologist described the defendant as a woman incarcerated by abuse, by fear, and by her conviction that her husband was invincible and inescapable:

> Mrs. Norman didn't leave because she believed, fully believed that escape was

> totally impossible. There was no place to go. He, she had left before; he had come and gotten her. She had gone to the Department of Social Services. He had come and gotten her. The law, she believed the law could not protect her; no one could protect her, and I must admit, looking over the records, that there was nothing done that would contradict that belief. She fully believed that he was invulnerable to the law and to all social agencies that were available; that nobody could withstand his power. As a result, there was no such thing as escape.

When asked if he had an opinion whether it appeared reasonably necessary for Judy Norman to shoot her husband, this witness responded:

> Yes. . . .I believe that in examining the facts of this case and examining the psychological data, that Mrs. Norman believed herself to be doomed. . .to a life of the worst kind of torture and abuse, degradation that she had experienced over the years in a progressive way; that it would only get worse, and that death was inevitable; death of herself, which was not such, I don't think was such an issue for her, as she had attempted to commit suicide, and in her continuing conviction of J.T. Norman's power over her, and even failed at that form of escape. I believe she also came to the point of beginning to fear for family members and her children, that were she to commit suicide that the abuse and the treatment that was heaped on her would be transferred onto them.

This testimony describes defendant's perception of circumstances in which she was held hostage to her husband's abuse for two decades and which ultimately compelled her to kill him. This testimony alone is evidence amply indicating the first two elements required for entitlement to an instruction on self-defense.

In addition to the testimony of the clinical psychologist, defendant presented the testimony of witnesses who had actually seen defendant's husband abuse her. These witnesses described circumstances that caused not only defendant to believe escape was impossible, but that also convinced *them* of its impossibility. Defendant's isolation and helplessness were evident in testimony that her family was intimidated by her husband into acquiescing in his torture of her. Witnesses also described defendant's experience with social service agencies and the law, which had contributed to her sense of futility and abandonment through the inefficacy of their protection and the strength of her husband's wrath when they failed. Where torture appears interminable and escape impossible, the belief that only the death of the oppressor can provide relief is reasonable in the mind of a person of ordinary firmness, let alone in the mind of the defendant, who, like a prisoner of war of some years, has been deprived of her humanity and is held hostage by fear. . . .

In the context of the doctrine of self-defense, the definition of "imminent" must be informed by the defendant's perceptions. It is not bounded merely by measurable time, but by all of the facts and circumstances. Its meaning depends upon the assessment of the facts by one of "ordinary firmness" with regard to whether the defendant's perception of impending death or injury was so pressing as to render reasonable her belief that it was necessary to kill.

Evidence presented in the case sub judice revealed no letup of tension or fear, no moment in which the defendant felt released from impending serious harm, even while the decedent slept. This, in fact, is a state of mind common to the battered spouse . . . .Psychologists have observed and commentators have described a "constant state of fear" brought on by the cyclical nature of battering as well as the battered spouse's perception that her abuser is both "omnipotent and unstoppable.". . .Constant fear means a perpetual anticipation of the next blow, a perpetual expectation that the next blow will kill. "[T]he battered wife is constantly in a heightened state of terror because she is certain that one day her husband will kill her during the course of a beating. . . .Thus from the perspective of the battered wife, the danger is constantly 'immediate.' " Eber, *The Battered Wife's Dilemma: To Kill or To Be Killed*, 32 Hastings L.J. 895, 928-29 (1981). For the battered wife, if there is no escape, if there is no window of relief or momentary sense of safety, then the next attack, which could be the fatal one, is imminent. In the context of the doctrine of self-defense, "imminent" is a term the meaning of which must be grasped from the defendant's point of view. Properly stated, the second prong of the question is not whether the threat was *in fact* imminent, but whether defendant's belief in the impending nature of the threat, given the circumstances as she saw them, was reasonable in the mind of a person of ordinary firmness. . . .

Defendant's intense fear, based on her belief that her husband intended not only to maim or deface her, as he had in the past, but to kill her, was evident in the testimony of witnesses who recounted events of the last three days of the decedent's life. This testimony could have led a juror to conclude that defendant reasonably perceived a threat to her life as "imminent," even while her husband slept. . . .

The third element for entitlement to an instruction on self-defense requires that there be evidence that the defendant was not the aggressor in bringing on the affray. If the defendant was the aggressor and killed with murderous intent, that is, the intent to kill or inflict serious bodily harm, then she is not entitled to an instruction on self-defense. . . .A hiatus between provocation by the decedent and the killing can mark the initiation of a new confrontation between the defendant and the decedent, such that the defendant's earlier perception of imminent danger no longer appears reasonable and the defendant becomes the aggressor. . . .

Where the defendant is a battered wife, there is no analogue to the victim-turned-aggressor, who. . .turns the tables on the decedent in a fresh confrontation. Where the defendant is a battered wife, the affray out of which the killing arises can be a continuing assault. There was evidence before the jury that it had not been defendant but her husband who had initiated "the affray," which the jury could have regarded as lasting twenty years, three days, or any number of hours preceding his death. And there was evidence from which the jury could infer that in defendant's mind the affray reached beyond the moment at which her husband fell asleep. Like the ongoing threats of death or great bodily harm, which she might reasonably have perceived as imminent, her husband continued to be the aggressor and she the victim.

Finally, the fourth element of self-defense poses the question of whether there was any evidence tending to show that the force used by defendant to repel her husband was not excessive, that is, more than reasonably appeared to be necessary under the circumstances. This question is answered in part by abundant testimony describing defendant's immobilization by fear caused by abuse by her husband. Three witnesses, including the decedent's best friend, all recounted incidents in which defendant passively accepted beating, kicks, commands, or humiliating affronts without striking back. From such evidence that she was paralyzed by her husband's presence, a jury could infer that it reasonably appeared to defendant to be necessary to kill her husband in order ultimately to protect herself from the death he had threatened and from severe bodily injury, a foretaste of which she had already experienced. . . .

By his barbaric conduct over the course of twenty years, J.T. Norman reduced the quality of the defendant's life to such an abysmal state that, given the opportunity to do so, the jury might well have found that she was justified in acting in self-defense for the preservation of her tragic life.

It is to be remembered that defendant does not have the burden of persuasion as to self-defense; the burden remains with the state to prove beyond a reasonable doubt that defendant intentionally killed decedent without excuse or justification. . . .If the evidence in support of self-defense is sufficient to create a reasonable doubt in the mind of a rational juror whether the state has proved an intentional killing without justification or excuse, self-defense must be submitted to the jury. This is such a case.

Notes and Questions

1. *Self-defense and the Battered Woman Syndrome.* The central issue before the court in *Norman* was whether the "defendant reasonably believed herself to be confronted by circumstances which necessitated her killing her husband to save herself from *imminent* death or great bodily harm" (p. 261). If the answer to this question was yes, then the law would treat the killing as justified because it was done in self-defense. The defense offered expert testimony in *Norman* to provide the jury with background information by which to judge the reasonableness of her actions. This approach is based on the work of Lenore Walker that identified the battered woman syndrome. Walker documented a three-stage battering cycle and applied the concept of learned helplessness as a way of understanding the victim's/survivor's responses and actions. *See* Lenore Walker, Battered Women [*sic*] Syndrome and Self-Defense, 6 Notre Dame J.L. Ethics & Pub. Pol'y 321 (1992). The battering cycle consists of phase one, a period of tension-building; phase two, an acute battering incident; and phase three, the period of loving-contrition. *See id.* at 330. According to Walker, battered women learn that they cannot control their abuser's violence and they begin to believe that they cannot influence or escape it. "Once the women are operating from a belief of helplessness, the perception becomes reality and they become passive, submissive, 'helpless.'" Lenore Walker, The Battered Woman 47 (1979).

The expert testimony based on the battered woman syndrome focuses on three distinct aspects of self-defense. First, it provides information useful in judging the defendant's reasonable belief that she is at risk of imminent harm. The expert explains the testimony of the defendant and other witnesses to the recurrent cycle of violence and shows why the defendant is reasonable in believing that another attack was impending. Second, the expert's testimony provides information useful in assessing the defendant's belief that she is at risk of death or serious bodily harm. The expert can explain that a battered woman becomes attuned to her abuser's behavior, which allows her to interpret his conduct and to predict whether an attack is likely to be severe and imminent. Third, the expert's testimony provides information useful in judging the defendant's belief that the only way to protect herself is to kill her abuser.

As Phyllis Crocker explains, testimony on the battered woman syndrome can be understood as a challenge to traditional self-defense law and as an effort to eliminate its sexual bias.

> The goal is to make the jury see that the woman's actions are reasonable rather than hysterical, inappropriate, or insane, and that the differences between men's and women's perceptions are a legitimate basis for differentiation. . . .
>
> To implement this strategy, the feminist theory starts with the premise that battered women's acts of self-defense are justifiable rather than merely excusable. Although both excusable and justifiable self-defense fully pardon the defendant from criminal liability, an important ideological distinction separates the two. Society holds an excusable act to be wrong, but tolerates it because of the actor's state of mind. . . .Society perceives a justified act of self-defense as correct and even laudable behavior. . . .
>
> By focusing on the actor as wrong but pardonable, excusable self-defense would imply that her response was typically and idiosyncratically emotional. The doctrine would perpetuate the views that the woman could not have been rational in assessing the danger and that the legal system must compensate for her mental and physical weaknesses.
>
> Justification, on the other hand, would assume that society values a woman's and a man's lives equally, and thus considers women's lives worthy of self-defense.

Phyllis Crocker, The Meaning of Equality for Battered Women Who Kill Men in Self-Defense, 8 Harv. Women's L.J. 121, 130-31 (1985).

2. *Battered Woman Syndrome and Separation Assault*. Separation assault, as explained by Martha Mahoney in "Legal Images of Battered Women: Redefining the Issue of Separation," at p. 247, emphasizes the woman's reasonableness and supports her rational perception of danger if she tries to escape. The concept of separation assault should not be viewed as inconsistent with the battered woman syndrome and learned helplessness but as providing a means of more fully explaining the battered woman's experience to the jury.

> Learned helplessness is in essence a theory of deficiency at perceiving exit. Separation assault confirms the difficulties of exit. Separation assault does not contradict the possibility of developing learned helplessness; the woman's subjective belief could still overestimate the difficulties of leaving. . . .Rather, by supporting the woman's rational perception of danger, the concept of separation assault supports that aspect of battered woman's syndrome which emphasizes the woman's reasonableness and the normal character of her reaction to violence. . . .

> Since separation assault appears in the cases where women are killed or harmed as well as the self-defense cases, the concept of separation assault helps reveal the real and deadly constraints within which learned helplessness develops. . . .
>
> [N]aming separation assault cannot end the need for expert testimony on the subject of battered woman's syndrome and learned helplessness. Collectively, the jury can only "know" what it is possible for them to discuss. Women will still find it impossible to incorporate our own experience in the jury room unless the lens through which we perceive battered women has been entirely transformed.

Martha Mahoney, Legal Images of Battered Women: Redefining the Issue of Separation, 90 Mich. L. Rev. 1, 81-82 (1991).

3. *Berry Revisited.* The issues presented in *Berry* and *Norman* were similar to the extent that time was a central element in the legal defense claimed by each defendant. The *Berry* court held that the defendant was entitled to an instruction on voluntary manslaughter based on his defense that he killed his wife in the "heat of passion" notwithstanding that twenty hours had passed between the time of his wife's last provocatory act and the killing (p. 203). The *Norman* court held that the defendant was not entitled to an instruction regarding perfect self-defense because no evidence was presented that the threat of death or great bodily injury was imminent. The two courts evaluated the issues regarding time quite differently. What facts in *Berry* influenced the court in coming to its conclusion that twenty hours was not too long a period so as to negate the heat of passion defense? What facts in *Norman* influenced the court in coming to its conclusion that the threat of death or great bodily injury was not imminent? What facts in *Berry* did the court ignore or minimize? What facts in *Norman* did the court ignore or minimize?

4. *Continuum of Violence.* In what two ways does the continuum of violence operate in *Norman*?

5. *Clemency for Battered Women.* In recent years, advocates have focused their attention on battered women and other survivors of abuse who are in prison for protecting themselves and their children against their abuser's violence. Studies show that only a small percentage of women accused of killing their abusive partners are acquitted at trials. Rather, the vast majority (72-80 percent) are convicted or accept a plea bargain, and many receive long, harsh sentences.

> [T]wo Governors have recognized the plight of many incarcerated women. . . .Governor Richard F. Celeste [of Ohio] granted executive clemency to 26 battered women who were incarcerated at the state prison . . . .Celeste announced his decision. . .just weeks before he left office. . . .Governor William Donald Schaefer of Maryland granted clemency to 8 imprisoned battered women convicted of killing or assaulting their abusive husbands or boyfriends.
>
> Most of the battered women reviewed by Celeste and Schaefer had not been able to introduce essential testimony about being abused, nor had they been allowed to have an expert witness testify at trial on their behalf.
>
> [T]here are now organizing activities [to encourage other governors to fol-

low the lead of Governors Celeste and Schaefer] in Arizona, California, Colorado, Connecticut, Delaware, Florida, Illinois, Kansas, Massachusetts, Michigan, New York, Pennsylvania, Texas, and Washington State.

Sue Osthoff, Clemency for Battered Women, Double-Time, (Nat'l Clearinghouse for Def. Battered Women, Phila., Pa.), Oct. 1991, at 1, 3.

A description of the clemency effort in California was reported as follows:

When Brenda Clubine arrived in prison 7 years ago to serve 15 years to life for killing a husband more than twice her size, she was beginning to ask herself questions about the violence she had suffered and in turn had meted out, about the Gordian knot that ties the abuser and the abused.

"I had two choices," said Ms. Clubine, a tiny, 41-year-old former nurse who said she had endured years of savage beatings by her husband. "I could commit suicide, or I could try to understand what was going on in my life."

At the California Institution for Women here, a gentle-looking place except for the perimeter of coiled razor wire, she asked other women why they were imprisoned, and heard stories that matched her own.

But when she asked if there was a group for battered women who had killed their mates, she was told there was not. So Ms. Clubine set about organizing one, a three-year battle with the prison bureaucracy that ended in 1988 with the first weekly meeting of Convicted Women Against Abuse. It began with 10 members and has grown to 45.

Today, in her 8-foot-by-6-foot cell, in the prison mail room where she works as a clerk, and in the classroom where she leads the support group, Ms. Clubine carries pressed to her chest a copy of a commutation petition she hopes will win her release. . . .

The original document and 21 others like it sit on the desk of Gov. Pete Wilson. Each pleads the case of a woman convicted of first-or second-degree murder in California before last year's passage of a state law that made admissible testimony about battered women's syndrome, in which prolonged abuse can convince a victim that violence is the only way out.

About 20 more petitions are expected to be filed next month, all the outgrowth of the group Ms Clubine started here after she was convicted of the 1983 killing of her husband, a retired Los Angeles police detective, who she says broke her ribs and jaw, stabbed her and tore the skin off her face during a stormy marriage that ended when she shattered his skull with an empty wine bottle. . . .

Here as in other states, the primary opponents of clemency for such women have been prosecutors, who are divided about whether battered women's syndrome is a valid defense or an exaggerated claim by someone grasping for a way out of a murder conviction. . . .

Here the women themselves initiated the clemency drive, writing Governor Wilson last year, imploring him to consider commutation of their sentences and inviting him to one of their meetings so he could better understand what brought them to this place.

The invitation to visit drew a polite "no thank you" from Mr. Wilson. But the letter attracted the attention of lawyers and advocates from throughout the state who banded together and offered free representation.

At about the same time, Jackie Spier, a state assemblywoman, held legislative hearings at Frontera at which Ms. Clubine, who has a parole hearing on Sept. 16, and seven other women in her group told their stories.

Among those testifying was Frances Caccavale, a 78-year-old Italian immigrant who described snatching a knife from the kitchen drain board and stabbing her elderly husband as he threatened her with a gun. Mrs. Caccavale said she had earlier wept to her priest about a half-century of beatings. 'Go home and try harder,' she said the priest told her. . . .

If there is anything striking about the women it is how ordinary they seem. Ranging in age from 25 to 78, some with sheets of long hair like graduate students, others with age spots on their hands, they wear bluejeans and T-shirts or state-issued muumuus, make-up, nail polish and perfume. Alternating between devilish humor and sodden tears, they sound like women gathered anywhere to talk about their men.

In this prison classroom, unlike the police stations where they filed complaints against their husbands and the courtrooms where they were tried, nobody asks: Why did you put up with it?

At this week's meeting, many talked of loving and hating their abusers at the same time. They said they once believed they were to blame for the violence they suffered and could stop it if they only figured out how to behave. They recalled the terror of facing a beating if they came home 10 minutes late or served a lukewarm dinner.

Many of them said they had been turned away from overcrowded women's shelters and had been treated dismissively by police officers. They said they had tried to flee their husbands, only to stalked and beaten worse.

Most said they had been threatened with death if they left and had been told, "If I can't have you, nobody else can." Glenda Virgil observed dryly that those words should be the "password into this club and the motto on our T-shirts."

Most of the women said they had grown up in families where violence was common, and that the events they had witnessed as children later had been duplicated with uncanny precision in their relationships with men.

Ms. Virgil remembers her father throwing her mother out of a moving car on Highway 101 near the California coast, and she said that years later, at that very spot, her husband did the same to her. Now, Ms. Virgil says, her 22-year-old daughter is being beaten by her mate. "She's making the same excuses I made," Ms. Virgil said. "She's saying, 'If I stick this out I can make it work.' "

Rosemary Dyer once lay in bed with her mother after church, moments after the older woman had been beaten. "Mama, can we run away now?" she asked. Her mother said no, they would have to stay, because, "I love him, and anyway, he wouldn't let us."

Years later, when she was black-and-blue herself, Ms. Dyer's mother pleaded with her, "Honey, come home. I'll come get you." Her answer echoed the past: "I can't, mama. I love him, and he won't let me go."

Ms. Dyer, like others in the group, said that prison sometimes feels like a sanctuary. "We may be locked up," she said, "but we can look in the mirror without seeing black eyes and knocked-out teeth. We don't have to be afraid to flush the toilet or cough at the wrong time. We can like ourselves and know who we are for the first time."

> And it is that knowledge that the women hope to carry outside the fences. "To leave here with the information we have in our heads," Ms. Virgil said. "If we can get outside and talk to other women, I know we can make a difference."

Jane Gross, Abused Women Who Kill Seek a Way Out of Cells, N.Y. Times, Sept. 15, 1992, at A16. The New York Times reported that on May 29, 1993, the Governor of California denied the clemency petitions of fourteen women including the petition by Brenda Clubine. Frances Caccavale received clemency on the basis of her advanced years and deteriorated medical condition. One woman, Brenda Aris, received a reduced sentence based on the record of her husband's extreme abuse and threats to kill her and other family members. *See* N.Y. Times, May 30, 1993, at 14.

6. *Prosecution of Domestic Assaults and the Battered Woman Syndrome.* How might a prosecutor use expert testimony regarding the battered woman syndrome in the prosecution of a domestic assault of a woman by her male partner?

Sharon Angella Allard, Rethinking Battered Woman Syndrome: A Black Feminist Perspective, 1 UCLA Women's L.J. 191, 195–202, 204–07 (1991)

The Need for an Intersectional Analysis of Battered Woman Syndrome

An intersectional approach—one which incorporates a gender and race analysis—of battered woman syndrome is needed if the law is to address adequately the needs of all battered women. Existing studies on the sexual biases in the law of self-defense and battered woman syndrome include little, if any, analysis as to how race and gender shape women's experiences of violence. Ideally, theories about battered woman syndrome should not marginalize any group of women, but should incorporate those experiences shaped by race and gender.[11] Racism alone does not cause the disproportionate conviction of Black women who kill their batterers. We must expose why stories about battered Black women are less credible to a jury than stories about battered white women.

---

11. *See* bell hooks, Ain't I a Woman: Black Women and Feminism (1981); Paula Giddings, When and Where I Enter: The Impact of Black Women on Race and Sex in America (1984). Both works offer an historical analysis of the impact of Black women on race and gender in American society. Hooks's introduction presents the problem:

> No other group in America has so had their identity socialized out of existence as have black women. . . . When black people are talked about, sexism militates against the acknowledgement of the interests of black women; when women are talked about, racism militates against a recognition of black female interests. When black people are talked about the focus tends to be on black *men*; and when women are talked about the focus tends to be on *white* women.

bell hooks, *supra*, at 7.

Battered woman syndrome relies on prevailing gender characterizations of dominant, white society. A recent study identified forty-one sex role stereotypes. A number of these stereotypes about women can be found in the battered woman syndrome characterization of women: very emotional, very submissive, very excitable in a minor crisis, very passive, very uncomfortable about being aggressive, very dependent, very gentle. Each of these characterizations reflects traditional notions of what society considers appropriate behavior for "normal" women.

In contrast to these stereotypes, both the stereotypical images and the historical reality of Black women's experiences in the United States are interpreted by the dominant society as a manifestation of Black women's deviance from "normal" women. This deviance is reflected in the omnipresent images of the hostile Sapphire,[12] the wanton Jezebel,[13] and the strong and assertive Sojourner Truth.[14] The characterizations of the antagonistic yet subordinated Sapphire and the promiscuous Jezebel reaffirm society's belief that Blacks are less human and less individualistic than whites, while the strength found in the characterization of Sojourner is a direct challenge to the prevailing definitions of "passive" womanhood. Consequently, Black women must overcome the demeaning stereotypes of both race and gender.

To the extent that battered woman syndrome theory is based on stereotypes of white women, the theory is inapplicable to women of color. For instance, Black women's exclusion is evident in Lenore Walker's discussion of battered women and anger. Walker stresses that for a battered woman to present a successful defense to a charge of killing her batterer, the woman must not appear angry. If the jury perceives that a woman killed out of anger, rather than fear, the jury is likely to give her a harsher penalty. This has disturbing implications for Black women, who Walker acknowledges are subject to the stereotype that all Black women are "angry."[15] Given that the legal system legitimizes

---

12. Sapphire is the name of the Black female character in the television comedy *Amos 'n' Andy* about two Black males. Sapphire was the loud and sassy wife of one of the men. She regularly fought with her husband about his annoying behavior. The show was eventually discontinued after civil rights organizations complained about the stereotypical and derogatory depiction of Blacks. Today the term "Sapphire" conjures up images of a shrill, nagging, hostile, and aggressive Black woman. . . .

13. Jezebel is defined as a woman who is "impudent, shameless, or abandoned." Webster's New Collegiate Dictionary 616 (150th ed. 1981). "Jezebel was the wanton, libidinous black woman whose easy ways excused white men's abuse of their slaves as sexual partners." Regina Austin, Sapphire Bound!, 1989 Wis. L. Rev. 539, 570. . . .

14. Sojourner Truth freed herself from slavery to become an active abolitionist and suffragist. Her bold spirit and unswaying convictions became a touchstone within the 1970s women's rights movement. Truth is widely known for her response to a heckler at a women's rights convention in 1871:

> Truth asserted that women were not inherently weak and helpless. Raising herself to her full height of six feet, flexing a muscled arm, and bellowing with a voice one observer likened to the apocalyptic thunders, Truth informed the audience that she could outwork, outeat, and outlast any man. Then she challenged: "Ain't I a woman?"

Giddings, *supra* note 11, at 54. . . .

15. The ratio of Black women to white women convicted of killing their abusive husbands is nearly two to one in one of my studies. My feeling is that this is the result of

these perceptions, there is a greater likelihood that a jury would believe a prosecutor's story that a battered Black woman acted out of revenge and anger, as opposed to fear, in taking the life of her batterer. . . .

The Historical Legal View of "Women" Is Race-Based

The Anglo-American legal tradition initially viewed women as property. This view was based on the patriarchal gender stereotypes of active, masculine, powerful, and authoritative men and passive, feminine, powerless, and deferential women. In 1897, British jurist William Blackstone held that men were responsible for the actions of their wives and therefore authorized to control them.[16] Included within men's responsibility was a duty to protect their wives. Therefore, "good" women were not expected to have to defend themselves in any fashion. Women were certainly not permitted to kill their protectors for any reason.

Feminist theorists criticize these traditional laws as reflecting the "origin of law as a form of male authority and power." These theorists argue that the adoption of sexist images results in paternalistic laws designed to protect women. But such critiques ignore the distinct impact of race in the assignment of gender definitions. Sexist as these protectionist images may have been, they were not meant for Black women. Throughout history, Black women's experiences with patriarchy differed from those of white women.[17]

Black women's historical and social experiences under slavery and thereafter resulted in images which define Black women as deviant. While the Victorian notion of "true womanhood" defined white women as possessing unquestionable moral character, Black women were defined as immoral. This race-based difference in stereotypes made it easier for white men to justify the sexual exploitation of Black women. Such stereotypes also made it easier for white women to accept the exploitation of Black women. Because exploita-

---

> our society's misperceptions of Black people in general, of women in general, and of Black women in particular. The "angry Black woman" is a common stereotype in many white minds; subtly, but no less powerfully, white society in America fears "Black anger."

Lenore Walker, Terrifying Love: Why Battered Women Kill and How Society Responds 206 (1989).

16. Husband and wife, in the language of the law, are styled *baron* and *feme*. . . .

> [I]f the baron kills his feme it is the same as if he had killed a stranger, or any other person; but if the feme kills her baron, it is regarded by the laws as a much more atrocious crime, as she not only breaks through the restraints of humanity and conjugal affection, but throws off all subjection to the authority of her husband. And therefore the law denominates her crime a species of treason, and condemns her to the same punishment as if she had killed the king. And for every species of treason. . .the sentence of women was to be drawn and burnt alive.

Elizabeth Schneider, Equal Rights to Trial For Women: Sex Bias in the Law of Self-Defense, 15 Harv. C.R.-C.L. L. Rev. 623, 629 (1980) (quoting 1 W. Blackstone, Commentaries on the Laws of England 418 n.103 (R. Welsh & Co. ed., 1897)).

17. Family life during slavery presents but one example of this difference. While white women's experiences were marked by a paternalistic protection in the domestic sphere, Black women were subjected to the sexual and economic desires of their captors.

tion was ignored or justified, Black women were not perceived as deserving of male protection. For example, the law historically denied that Black slave women could be raped because they were regarded as immoral. This perception continues to influence the investigation and prosecution of rape charges brought by Black women today.

The difference between how Black and white women are treated and perceived also stems from the fact that Blacks as a group have not received the protection of the law and have historically been denied all rights.[18] While laws formally changed, recent statistics continue to reflect that crimes committed against whites have higher prosecution rates and result in longer sentences than crimes committed against Blacks.[19] Again, Black women are saddled with dual stereotypes of race and gender. As women, they have to overcome the presumption that the law provides sufficient protection for them. As Black women, they must further prove that they are deserving of such protection. . . .

Media Images and Social Perceptions of Black Women: The Impact of Race and Gender in the Law of Self-Defense and Battered Woman Syndrome

Black women generally fall outside the dominant gender definitions upon which battered woman syndrome and feminist analyses of self-defense rely. The media provides much of the information about persons outside of the majority population.[20] Deviant images of Black women abound in society. Images which accurately represent the experiences of Black women exist, but nonetheless remain outside the dominant view of who is a "real" woman.

One image of the Black woman is that of an immoral, promiscuous being. This image arose from a perverted reversal of the historical sexual exploitation of Black women. Current media images perpetuate this perversion. For example, in a commercial for an automobile, Tina Turner appears in shorn clothing while her counterpart, Lindsay Wagner, appears in long, light, and airy ensembles. Actress/singer Grace Jones will never run out of material to continue her public persona as strange yet enticing and seemingly masochistic.[21]

---

18. Both during and after slavery, Blacks were subjected to white discipline and control as a matter of law; first through the use of slavery codes and then through "Black" codes. For a more expansive treatment of these issues, see Derrick Bell, Race, Racism and American Law 85 (1980); A. Leon Higginbotham, Jr., In the Matter of Color (1978).

19. *See* McCleskey v. Kemp, 481 U.S. 279, 312 (1987) (statistics show that the race of the defendant and the victim are often factors which lead to disparities in death penalty sentencing); Bureau of Justice Statistics, U.S. Dep't of Justice, Sourcebook of Criminal Justice Statistics 692 table 6.70 (1984) (data indicates that a larger number of nonwhites than whites are executed).

20. Mass media contributes to the "public's conceptions of reality, the 'facts', concepts, and definitions from which people construct their beliefs about the world in general and about social reality in particular." Discourse and Discrimination 24 (Geneva Smitherman-Donaldson & Teun Van Dijk eds., 1988).

21. Grace Jones is a Jamaican-born Black woman who is a singer, model, and actress. Her hairstyle, attire, and performance style have earned her a myriad of images including: "jungle cat," Rosenberg, Guillotines, Sheep Chopped From French Revolution Parade, Reuters,

These commercial images do not exactly replicate the extreme degradation of Black women found in the Black exploitation films[22] of the 1970s. Many contemporary images of Black women, however, may be derived from these films. Black exploitation films portrayed Black women as mindless sex objects "to be used and abused without rationale by white and black males in films." Black women's sexuality continues to be portrayed as deviant. Black women are represented as sex objects and as comparatively more sexually aggressive and available than white women. . . .

Because battered woman syndrome is based on the traditional view of the "normal," passive woman, the theory does little to help Black women who are excluded from this stereotype. The dominant images of Black women as domineering, assertive, hostile, and immoral may hinder a judge's or juror's ability to comprehend a Black woman's act of self-defense as based on "learned helplessness" in much the same way that gender definitions of white women serve as an obstacle in the law of self-defense. While a white woman's conduct in killing may be viewed as inapposite to traditional gender roles, the same conduct by a Black woman may be viewed as typical of her character.

The historical acceptance of wife beating also makes it less likely that a jury will perceive any present or prior beating as indicative of bodily harm sufficient to justify the use of deadly harm by any woman. This is particularly likely to be the case for Black women who are considered "strong and suffering."[23] The perception that Black women possess more physical strength than white women may decrease the likelihood that a Black woman reasonably believed that she was in danger of serious bodily harm.[24] This perception of Black women is further perpetuated today in theories which assert either implicit-

---

Feb. 11, 1989 (LEXIS, Nexis); "androgynous," Wrong, French Impresario Plans Surrealist Bastille Day Parade, Reuters, Feb. 11, 1989 (LEXIS, Nexis); "erotic menace—she once appeared in a tiger cage gnawing raw meat," The Stars, The Sounds, The Screens of June, Life, June 1985, at 139; "an image either sexless or voraciously sexy, depending on your point of view," Jungle Fever; by Jean-Paul Goude, People, Oct. 25, 1982, at 12. Grace Jones "once wore a dress so tight she had to be carried up the stairs to the stage by a bodyguard," O'Malley & Gratteau, No Biz Like Show Biz, Chi. Tribune, Mar. 11, 1987, § 1, at 16, col. 1.

The purpose of sketching this contrast is simply to identify the fact that the public images which we observe reflect a historical construction which labels Black women as "other."

22. The term refers to a genre of film from the 70s which depicted streetwise Black men (and sometimes women) as the central characters in action adventure stories. The films were widely criticized as derogatory for their portrayal of Blacks as pimps, drug dealers, hustlers, or other criminal types. *See* David Mills, Blaxploitation 101: A Brief Film History of Sticking It to the Man, Wash. Post, Nov. 4, 1990, at G1, col. 2.

23. Gloria Naylor in an essay on the myth of the strong Black woman also traces the roots of this imagery to the role of Black women during slavery: "They were stronger creatures; they didn't feel pain in childbirth; they didn't have tear ducts."

Gloria Naylor, The Myth of the Matriarch, Life, Spring 1988, at 65. Naylor also points out that Black women themselves may have adopted this perception at great cost to their personal well-being by feeling that if they are not able to withstand all things they are somehow inadequate. This observation provides an interesting perspective from which to evaluate the experiences of Black women who are battered. *Id.*

24. The image of the strong Black woman arose during slavery to justify the disparate treatment of Black women and white women with regard to labor. "To explain the black-female's ability to survive without the direct aid of a male and her ability to perform tasks that were culturally defined as 'male' work, white males argued that black slave women were not 'real' women but were masculinized sub-human creatures." hooks, *supra* note 11, at 71.

ly or explicitly that Black women are emasculating or matriarchal. For example, the current policy debate concerning the status of the "underclass" tends to focus on the plight of Black men, which implies that Black female-headed households are the real problem for the underclass.[25] Moreover, the moralistic overtones of this debate contributes to the perception that Black women are sexually immoral.

The relevance of the differences in the normative definitions of Black women and white women may not be significant with regard to self-defense if neither woman's behavior is considered reasonable. The distinction is significant, however, in the context of battered woman syndrome theory. The theory's use of characterizations which reflect traditional gender role stereotypes appears to be an attempt to restore the battered woman's image to reflect society's normative definition of a normal woman. But this definition does not apply to women who are considered "other." "Black men and women live in a society that creates sex-based norms and expectations which racism operates simultaneously to deny; Black men are not viewed as powerful, nor are Black women seen as passive." Thus, battered woman syndrome essentially excludes Black women. . . .

Battered woman syndrome presents a troubling paradox. For some battered women, the theory is a viable tool for satisfying the legal standard of self-defense and for explaining their behavior as reasonable. For others, the theory's use of standard gender definitions may not only exclude some battered women but may actually impose an additional obstacle. To the extent that battered woman syndrome restores a battered woman's image to that of a "good" woman, the theory implicitly embraces the notion that there are "good" women and "bad" women. This dichotomy necessarily implies there is an "other" who can be pointed to as lacking in the characteristics of "true womanhood." Therefore, to assert battered woman syndrome successfully, a woman must avoid association with any of the images of "other."[26] Such avoidance is especially difficult for a Black woman, who is viewed as "other" simply by virtue of her skin color. Thus, battered woman syndrome fails as a viable theory for *all* battered women. . . .

Measures must be taken to isolate and redefine established gender norms. . . .This is not to suggest that the existing studies and theories are without merit. Rather, it is a call to recognize the harm which will continue in the absence of an intersectional analysis of feminist legal principles.

Notes

1. *Expert Testimony*. The use of expert testimony about the battered

---

25. "Anti-feminists argue that changing sex role patterns have threatened males so that they are demonstrating their anger by domestic brutality. As supporters of male dominance they assert that violent acts against women will continue until society returns to the good old-fashioned days of sharply delineated sex roles." *Id.* at 105. *See also* William J. Wilson, The Truly Disadvantaged: The Inner City, The Underclass and Public Policy (1987); Daniel Moynihan, The Tangle of Pathology in The Negro Family: A Case for National Action (1965) (This controversial report asserted the existence of a matriarchal family structure among Black households was the reason for the low socio-economic progress of Blacks in America).

26. Such images include those based on ethnicity, class, and sexual orientation as well as race.

woman syndrome worries legal feminists who, while acknowledging the syndrome's benefits, fear that it reinforces the notion that women's actions are not understandable.

> [In *Smith v. State*[27] t]he Georgia Supreme Court. . .[held] that "[e]xpert opinion testimony. . .is admissible where the conclusion of the expert is one which jurors would not ordinarily be able to draw for themselves; i.e., the conclusion is beyond the ken of the average layman." The "average layman," the court reasoned, might think that the "'logical reaction' of a battered woman would be to call the police or leave her husband (boyfriend)." Only through use of expert testimony on the "battered woman syndrome" could a jury learn that "typically victims of battered woman syndrome believe that their husbands are capable of killing them, that there is no escape, and that if they leave they will be found and hurt even more." Without such expert testimony, a jury probably would not suspect that battered women believe "that they themselves are somehow responsible for their husbands' violent behavior, and that they are low in self-esteem and feel powerless." Nor would they know that the primary emotion of a battered woman is fear. . . .
>
> [T]he sub-text of the opinion is deeply troubling.
>
> First, battered women were viewed by the *Smith* court as alien, their reasoning and actions "beyond the ken of the average layman." This view is indeed plausible: Not only battered women, but all women, may appear alien from a male perspective. In this sense, the court's characterization may be even truer than the court itself imagined. Second, whether accurate or not, the truth of an expert's assertion that the battered woman's "primary emotion is fear" is largely irrelevant. Unless she can convince the jury that she was afraid in a way they understand, she will go to jail. *That* is a powerful truth. Third, battered women are said to *believe* that there is no escape. This statement seems consistent with women's accounts, but it is also incomplete in a particularly insidious way. That is, not only is the objective accuracy of the belief deemed irrelevant, but so is its very reasonableness. It is precisely because the belief appears so incredible that expert testimony is introduced.

Christine Littleton, Women's Experience and the Problem of Transition: Perspectives on Male Battering of Women, 1989 U. Chi. Legal F. 23, 35-36 (emphasis in original).

2. *Inherent Contradiction.* The stereotype of the passive woman, which is a part of the battered woman syndrome, creates a contradiction for a woman on trial for killing her abuser.

> On the one hand, the defendant is a woman who has been battered by her husband. She typically has a history of passive socialization, heightened and reinforced by the beatings. On the other hand, she is on trial for defending her life and killing her husband, a very atypical act for a woman, especially a battered one. Accordingly, the defendant may be seen as an exception to the group of which she is a part.

Phyllis L. Crocker, The Meaning of Equality for Battered Women Who Kill Men in Self-Defense, 8 Harv. Women's L.J. 121, 136 (1985).

---

27. 247 Ga. 612, 277 S.E.2d 678 (1981).

In addition to its inherently contradictory depiction of a passive killer, the battered woman syndrome poses other problems for defendants. In some courts it has become

> a standard to which all battered women must conform rather than as evidence that illuminates the defendant's behavior and perceptions. As a result, a defendant may be considered a battered woman only if she never left her husband, never sought assistance, and never fought back. Unless she fits this rigidly-defined and narrowly-applied definition, she is prevented from benefiting from battered woman syndrome testimony.

Id. at 144.

As Sharon Angella Allard demonstrates, the stereotypical images of an African-American woman as domineering and hostile only heighten the passive killer contradiction, making it less likely that an African-American woman can benefit from battered woman syndrome testimony. Use of the testimony to date suggests that any woman who is viewed as deviating from dominant society's norms, whether by reason of abilities, class, race/ethnicity, or sexual orientation, may have a difficult time meeting the standard of the battered woman syndrome and overcoming its central contradiction.

Chapter 5

Sexual Harassment

Catharine MacKinnon writes in her foreword to her pathbreaking book that "[s]exual harassment of working women has been one of the most pervasive but carefully ignored features of our national life." Catharine A. MacKinnon, Sexual Harassment of Working Women: A Case of Sex Discrimination vii (1979). The presence of sexual harassment in the workplace and in educational institutions cannot be underestimated. Surveys of sexual harassment in the federal government conducted by the U.S. Merit Systems Protection Board in 1981 and in 1988 found that 42 percent of the women had experienced sexual harassment. A 1990 study of military personnel indicated that two-thirds of the women said that they had experienced some form of sexual harassment. *See* Claudia A. Withers, Guidelines for the Victim of Sexual Harassment 1 (Practicing Law Institute 1992). *See also* Lin Farley, Sexual Shakedown, The Sexual Harassment of Women on the Job (1978) (tracing the history of sexual harassment). The reason why this ugly aspect of the workplace and of educational institutions remains so well concealed is that women are faced with many obstacles in attempting to stop the harassment through formal or informal complaints.

> Despite the widespread nature of sexual harassment, most victims do not report it, and, in fact, the modal response of women when harassed is simply to endure the situation and hope that it will cease. . . .
>
> The Merit Systems investigation. . .reported that the majority of the victims in their 1987 study either ignored the behavior or did nothing, even though they noted that this strategy was ineffective in that the harassment generally did not cease.
>
> Other studies confirm this finding. [One study]. . .interviewed a subset of [the]. . .sample of woman harassment victims and noted that fewer than one in five ever complained to management or reported it to anyone in authority. Thirty percent of the victims said that reporting the matter would just hurt them, and another twenty-four percent said that they did not want to hurt the man involved. . . .
>
> In [a] student study, only three percent of the victims studied had attempted to report the situation; when those who had not done so were asked why they had not, they most commonly noted that (1) they felt they would not be believed; and (2) they had not wanted to cause trouble or be labeled as troublemakers. In still another study of professional women employed at a large public university, more than twenty-five percent had received unwanted sexual attention, one in ten had been touched, fondled, kissed or grabbed; and one in twenty received a direct sexual proposition—yet, almost none of them ever reported it, mainly because they did not think it was a problem with

> which the institution could or would help them. Over one-third feared retaliation, and an equal number were concerned about the effect such reporting would have on their careers.

Louise F. Fitzgerald, Science v. Myth: The Failure of Reason in the Clarence Thomas Hearings, 65 S. Cal. L. Rev. 1399, 1402-03 (1992).

Like women who are battered in the home, women who are sexually harassed at work or school struggle with limited choices in trying to minimize their risk of further physical and emotional harm while preserving their work life and economic security. Like battering in the home, sexual harassment cannot be defined without consideration of the abilities, class, race/ethnicity, and sexual orientation of the harasser and of the victim.

One purpose of this chapter is to familiarize readers with the kinds of abusive conduct endured by women when they work or study outside their homes. The narratives in Part A provide useful historical and contemporary perspectives on the daily lives of women when they leave their homes. The stories of women who suffered sexual harassment provide essential background for evaluating the legal reforms that are described in Part B.

A second purpose is to provide cases and materials to examine the development of sexual harassment law and to consider future reform strategies. Part B begins with the EEOC Regulations to Title VII of the 1964 Civil Rights Act, which were first promulgated in 1980 and which provide primary guidance in defining sexual harassment and determining employer liability. The Supreme Court case of *Meritor Savings Bank, FSB v. Vinson* follows. It represents an important milestone in sexual harassment law because it established that the creation of a hostile environment through sexual harassment is a form of sex discrimination under Title VII. It also is important for what it said and did not say regarding employer liability for the conduct of supervisors.

Vinson is followed by an excerpt from an article by Stephanie Riger, which details the endemic problems faced by women who use the formal and informal procedures established by educational institutions in response to the EEOC Regulations and *Vinson* to address issues of sexual harassment. The Ninth Circuit opinion in *Ellison v. Brady* then explores the question of objective and subjective standards for determining whether a hostile environment exists in the workplace. The question of what degree of harm the plaintiff must show for the conduct to be actionable as hostile environment harassment is further explored by the Supreme Court in *Harris v. Forklift Systems, Inc.* The Court found that a plaintiff need not show that the conduct caused tangible psychological injury to have an actionable claim under Title VII. An excerpt of an article by Susan Estrich and of another by B. Glenn George follow *Harris*. They both critique the current sexual harassment law and propose reforms in interpreting Title VII to improve its effectiveness in providing a remedy for sexual harassment. The chapter ends with *Dillon v. Frank*, which was decided by the Sixth Circuit Court of Appeals. This case raises the question about whether harassment of a man perceived by his coworkers to be gay constitutes sex discrimination under Title VII.

Parts A and B of this chapter taken together reveal underlying social and institutional structures that support and even encourage abilism, classism, heterosexism, racism/ethnocentrism, and sexism and how sexual harassment is one of the means used to support the power and perspectives of dominant groups. Our aim is to make clear that sexual harassment is not a new phenomenon between coworkers, between supervisors and subordinates, between students, or between faculty and students. What is new is that, since the late 1970s, some types of sexual harassment have been made illegal, workers and students have been provided limited remedies against their employers and schools for failure to establish rules, and employers and schools have developed procedures designed to prevent harassment and to respond to it when it occurs.

A. No Safe Place: Then and Now

Black Women in White America: A Documentary History 155-58 (Gerda Lerner ed., 1973)

We Are Little More Than Slaves—Anonymous

I remember very well the first and last work place from which I was dismissed. I lost my place because I refused to let the madam's husband kiss me. He must have been accustomed to undue familiarity with his servants, or else he took it as a matter of course, because without any love-making at all, soon after I was installed as cook, he walked up to me, threw his arms around me, and was in the act of kissing me, when I demanded to know what he meant, and shoved him away. I was young then, and newly married, and didn't know then what has been a burden to my mind and heart ever since; that a colored woman's virtue in this part of the country has no protection. I at once went home, and told my husband about it. When my husband went to the man who had insulted me, the man cursed him, and slapped him, and—had him arrested! The police judge fined my husband $25. I was present at the hearing, and testified on oath to the insult offered me. The white man, of course, denied the charge. The old judge looked up and said: "This court will never take the word of a nigger against the word of a white man.". . .I believe nearly all white men take, and expect to take, undue liberties with their colored female servants—not only the fathers, but in many cases the sons also. Those servants who rebel against such familiarity must either leave or expect a mighty hard time, if they stay. By comparison, those who tamely submit to these improper relations live in clover. They always have a little "spending change," wear better clothes, and are able to get off from work at least once a week—and sometimes oftener. This moral debasement is not at all times unknown to the white women in these homes. I know of more than one colored woman who was openly importuned by white women to become the mistresses of their white husbands, on the ground that they, the white wives, were afraid that, if their husbands did not associate with colored women, they would certainly do so with outside white women, and the white wives, for reasons which ought to be perfectly obvious, preferred to have their husbands do wrong with colored women in order to keep their husbands *straight*! And again, I know at least fifty places in my small town where white men are positively raising two families—a white family in the "Big House" in front, and a colored family in a "Little House" in the backyard. In most cases, to be sure, the colored women involved are the cooks or chambermaids or seamstresses, but it cannot be true that their real connection with the white men of the families is unknown to the white women of the families. . . .

I have already told you that my youngest girl was a nurse. With scores of other colored girls who are nurses, she can be seen almost any afternoon, when the weather is fair, rolling the baby carriage or lolling about on some one of the chief boulevards of our town. The very first week that she started out on her work she was insulted by a white man, and many times since has been improperly approached by other white men. It is a favorite practice of young white sports about town—and they are not always young, either—to stop some colored nurse, inquire the name of the "sweet little baby," talk baby talk to the child, fondle it, kiss it, make love to it, etc., etc., and in nine of ten cases every such white man will wind up by making love to the colored nurse and seeking an appointment with her.

I confess that I believe it to be true that many of our colored girls are as eager as the white men are to encourage and maintain these improper relations; but where the girl is not willing, she has only herself to depend upon for protection. If their fathers, brothers or husbands seek to redress their wrongs, under our peculiar conditions, the guiltless negroes will be severely punished, if not killed, and the white blackleg will go scot-free!

We poor colored women wage-earners in the South are fighting a terrible battle. . . .On the one hand, we are assailed by white men, and, on the other hand, we are assailed by black men, who should be our natural protectors; and, whether in the cook kitchen, at the washtub, over the sewing machine, behind the baby carriage, or at the ironing board, we are but little more than pack horses, beasts of burden, slaves! In the distant future, it may be, centuries and centuries hence, a monument of brass or stone will be erected to the Old Black Mammies of the South, but what we need is present help, present sympathy, better wages, better hours, more protection, and a chance to breathe for once while alive as free women.

[From] "More Slavery at the South," by a Negro nurse, *The Independent*, Vol. 72, No. 3295 (Jan. 25, 1912), at 197-200.

Victoria Byerly, Hard Times Cotton Mill Girls: Personal Histories of Womanhood and Poverty in the South 120-22 (1986)

[This book contains a collection of the oral histories of twenty women from the textile mill villages of the Carolina Piedmont area of the country. The excerpt that follows is an oral history by Clara Thrift of Thomasville, North Carolina and tells about her life during the 1950s and 1960s. She was a single parent of two children who had survived severe beatings by her husband. After she left him, she started working two mill jobs to get the money to make a down payment on a home for her and her children.]

One time this supervisor put me on this bad set of machines and I complained because my threads kept breaking and that was the whole idea, tying up ends. The threads kept breaking and I was running to keep them tied up.

I kept complaining to him that I couldn't make any money and he wouldn't do anything about it, so I just started tying them up the best I could to make the money. There are different kinds of knots and with this particular kind of job you weren't suppose to tie chicken-head knots, which was the fastest kind. But I said the heck with him, I'm going to tie chicken-heads because I got to make the money. Then he come and complained to me and we got into it about that. Well, there was more to the story than that. This particular boss man was going out with some of his workers. He had said something to me about going out with him and I had said no. He was married and I knew his wife. I used to work with her. Well after I had said no, he put me on this bad set of machines. One thing led to another and I quit.

When you have a grievance in the mill, you can do one of two things. You can go to your boss man and argue with him until he fires you, or you can go to another mill worker and complain to her and then forget it. However, the boss man favored some women over the others. He'd give the ones he liked the best set of machines. It was supposed to go according to seniority, but we all knew that it didn't always work that way. Management liked competition between us women because they wanted to get the most work done for the least amount of money. . . . Favoritism meant like, you go out with me and I'll see that you get a good set of machines and make good money. I never was a part of this. That was why I quit that time. Me and my boss had a big fight about it. I quit my job at four o'clock in the morning and went home. I was so mad I didn't realize what I had done until I got home. Then I decided that I wasn't going to let him get away with this, so I waited until after nine o'clock and went back to the mill to talk to someone in the personnel office, who, as it turned out, was also involved with going out with the women. I know that now, but at the time, when he told me, "I'll help you," I believed him. Well, he got me on at another plant and even got me first shift. I had been working third. Then the whole thing died down. His transferring me was just a cover-up, a hush-hush, because he was afraid I was going to tell the whole story.

Now that stuff is still going on today because I talk to the women still in there today and that's what they say. The boss men had a lot of control over your life. The ones they respected the least was the ones that didn't stand up for their rights. If you kept your mouth shut and just went on and did your job, then they'd do you around. But if you told them, "Listen, I'm not going to do this," then they'd give you a better job. Men were always superior over women. I guess that's the best way of describing it. The women had a choice; they could speak up for themselves and risk getting fired or play the game—the dating game.

I. Elena Featherston, On Becoming a Dangerous Woman, in *Sexual Harassment: Women Speak Out* 71 (Amber Coverdale Sumrall & Dena Taylor eds., 1992)

I speak with a very specific voice, that of a dark-skinned African-American (Black) woman. I speak against more than individual occurrences of sexual harassment in my life. My voice is lifted against the systematic harassment of women of color—Black women in particular and dark-skinned women—that permeates American culture. Speaking defies the conspiracy of racist and sexist pressure to keep Black women silent and under sexual siege.

The most consistent, overt sexual violation, in my life, comes from white men: on the street, in the workplace, on the telephone, applying for a job, dining out, driving my car, checking into hotels, traveling on business. Anytime, anyplace. Perhaps my experience would be different if I lived in a predominantly Black community. These white sons and fathers behave as if they have a right to act like boors, if the boorish behavior is directed at Black women. Many are genuinely surprised and offended when their sexual approaches are repelled. They assume the color of their skin guarantees our being flattered by their "attention."

Their acts of harassment, which are both racist and sexist, began quite early in my life. A white, middle-aged merchant closed his store, guided me to a secluded aisle and offered me "whatever I wanted" to let him touch me. Saying I was beautiful, he promised what he did would make me feel good. I was seven years old.

This sweet-tempered gentleman had exchanged pleasantries with my mother almost daily for as long as I could remember. We purchased our food and household necessities from him. In his store my mother had taught me the importance of honesty, forcing me to return and pay for a stolen Snickers bar. A few days after the Snickers incident, he had me cornered between the paper towels and the bathroom cleanser trying to molest me. I was convinced my stealing led him to think he could say and do nasty things to me. But, I knew what he wanted to do was wrong. There was no way I was going to let him touch me. I didn't have sense enough to be afraid. At seven, I was a force to be reckoned with—a small, skinny-legged force, but, a force nonetheless. I declined his offer and left the store.

Being abandoned by my father had taught me a cold fierceness, disguised as self-reliance. I felt capable of taking care of myself. Mine was a fortuitous admixture of mother's love, father's absence and innate stubbornness, an alchemy which gave the inner strength necessary to enforce my will with a potentially abusive adult.

In the weeks and months that followed, I rebuffed all his friendly gestures and efforts to re-establish his usual patterns of behavior. Secretly, I savored what I supposed to be his fear of my family's anger. But I never told anyone and for very good reason. I felt guilty.

Only seven years old, yet insidious social messages were already clear: the burden of proper sexual conduct rested with the female, even a female child. How this knowledge was transmitted, or when, I don't know. With hindsight I could point to fairy tales, movies, jokes, or constant reminders to be "ladylike." Any one, or a combination of a thousand things, might have been the reason, but my responsibility for this man's behavior seemed clear. From this first instance of harassment, I learned to take care of my self and to keep my mouth shut, and it was only the beginning.

Four years later, as I walked home from school with several friends one sunny, Spring afternoon, another white man invaded my life. Suddenly, everyone was shrieking, laughing, or muttering nervously, "Look at that." Nearsighted, unable to see what had them so agitated, I stepped closer to the green Buick with silver ports glistening in the sun and the big, well-dressed, blond stranger leaning on it. The giggling and shouting grew louder as a result of my approach. The man smiled an invitation, and vigorously jiggled what appeared to be a set of car keys. My friends' carrying on seemed unwarranted, but they wouldn't stop snickering, pointing and backing away. Stepping a bit closer, I realized what he shook were not keys, but his penis. I was stunned. His eyes, concealed by sunglasses, were not visible, but his smile was unforgettable.

For him this behavior had some bizarre justification. Parked five minutes from our homes, he basked in the sunlight and his power to make us scream, his power to intimidate. I was furious. Not about his pathetic penis, but his supercilious smile. It suggested we deserved his filthy, degrading attention. I wanted to claw that smirk off his face, but I was unsure how. Force was not the best option, the guy was six feet tall. Then it came to me. Being a "tomboy" had its advantages. I knew boys were as insecure about their penises as girls about their breasts.

Peering analytically at his crotch, I advised him to put the "itty-bitty thing" in his pocket because it looked like a key chain. Part bravado, part truth. Staring at him, real hard, I asked my now-tittering friends if they were amused because his "weenie" was so small, or because it was so white. Our insolent flasher wilted and blushed deep maroon. As he climbed into his fancy car, he hollered, "Niggers." Once. Viciously. Face contorted. The air was charged with his impotent rage, our laughter and my churning desire to do murder. Stony-eyed I watched his car until it was out of sight. If he looked in his rear-view mirror, it was important that he see my fearless, smiling face. It was imperative he never know how vulnerable he had made me feel.

My mother called the police. Though two white officers came to our home, they didn't take the complaint seriously. Quite the contrary, they questioned *my* ability to remember so much so clearly. One asked if my mother had coached me. He then told her, sounding a bit skeptical, that I was very smart. The way it was said, instead of lending credibility to my allegations, implied that intelligence made me less believable. Nothing was done.

I didn't realize that hundreds of such men stalked the Black community, safe from prosecution and conviction. But, only eleven, I was getting the message that if you were Black no one really cared what happened to you. The flasher's disrespect, coupled with the cops' indifference, made me want to go to war. For weeks I had fantasies about kicking him in the balls, spitting in his face, watching police cars careen into trees, beating them with a bat—assorted childish revenges.

It was clear to me that white men—walking-down-the-street-store-owning-police-officer-car-driving-everyday white men—were dangerous to me. Sick sexual aberration, the need to thrust themselves at young girls, was obviously a white man's disease. This behavior, like their racism, like their belief that Blacks should be unintelligent, and their unwillingness (or inability) to be fair in their dealings with people, especially people of color, seemed genetic. My experiences and conversations with other Black girls demonstrated the truth of that analysis. (The treatment to which their own white daughters, mothers or sisters might be subjected was never considered.) But, white men were not the only culprits, as I discovered all too soon.

It was not an unduly obscene experience, and the male involved was only 18. It did not break my spirit, but it did hurt my heart. It still does.

Six of us were watching American Bandstand—three girlfriends, my "play sister," her older brother and me. He suggested that we "dance." It was a game we had played before. One at a time we sat on his lap, and were bounced up and down while he undulated playfully to the music. We "danced," we laughed, ate popcorn and were having an all-American afternoon. But this time something felt strange. His face was "funny," it looked odd. On my third turn, I noticed he had an extra "knee." The truth is, I didn't want to understand what was happening. He was Black. I thought: There is a mistake, I must be confused.

He was my friend, a protector. He had carried me on his shoulders when I was younger, bought ice cream, told stories, helped fix my bike, taught me to box. He never once made fun of me for being a tomboy. He was my surrogate big brother, my comrade. He was a good person, I loved him. Most important, he was BLACK! Black men definitely did not act like crazy, white men. I had to be wrong.

As the other girls continued to take turns "dancing," I watched his face, his body. When we finally made direct eye contact, what passed between us was ghastly. I wasn't wrong. He knew what he was doing and now he knew I knew. He was apprehensive, but composed. He pretended nothing was amiss. I can still see him seated, reaching out his hand, beckoning me to take my turn. The spasm of distrust and resentment which rippled briefly across his face when I said I didn't want a turn, reverberated deep inside me.

Heavy-hearted, wounded by an undefined sense of loss, I went home. Black men were my men—my brothers, my cousins, my godfather, my minister, my friends, even my father. I had always felt safe with them. Until that moment my battle had been with the occasional demented white man who invaded community and serenity without warning or reason. It had not been necessary to be on guard with Black men. This was a betrayal. My safety zone was gone. In truth it never existed. I began to realize that being Black and female meant there were no safe places, unless we created them ourselves.

This time I would not be silent. I sat in the window waiting for his father to come home, plotting my revenge. This time I was talking and someone was going to listen. Unlike white men who ravished minds and bodies with anonymity and impunity, this young man was going to learn he had to respect me. His father, after hearing my story, did a brutal thing. He invited his son outside and whipped him publicly with a garden hose. Curious neighbors looked on. It is only brutal in retrospect; at the time it seemed quite fair. No one ever mentioned the incident to me again. I never forgot it. It changed my life.

That evening, lying in bed, I made a decision. As a Black woman, considered fair game by everyone, having respect meant demanding it. Hell, fighting for it, when necessary. It meant refusing to spend time with men who did not respect me. I consciously crossed a line—the one defining male and female sexual behavior—into a grey zone. I would not be exploited. I would not be silent. I would not be afraid. I would choose if, when and with whom I had sex. I would discover what it meant to be me and how to express what I found. This betrayal gave me access to a part of myself unnamed until then. Rebel, fighter, outspoken, "womanish" child. I was a 13-year-old virgin.

The most recent—and hopefully last—instance of harassment occurred at an Alameda computer company in 1988. For three months, I was systematically badgered, racially and sexually, by a white manager. Let's call him Mike.

Mike and my boss, "Steve," were friendly rivals. Both had their eyes on the same Vice Presidency. Both had many women working in their departments. Mike demanded fawning loyalty from the women in his group and underpaid them. Steve, though paternalistic, treated us with respect and paid us well. Perhaps this was his downfall; he was eventually ousted. Mike gained control of both departments.

In Steve's office, on the day he told me the bad news, Mike, flushed with victory, casually placed his arm around my shoulders, hand lightly (and deliberately) brushing my left breast. Smiling into my eyes, he told me Steve's dismissal meant I would become his sex slave. Maybe it was his smile that pushed me over the top. It didn't matter, he had "torn his drawers." No corporate code of conduct was keeping me under control, or forcing me to submit to his crap. I reached down, hefted his balls speculatively, and smiling back into his face, disdainfully answered, "No, I really don't think so." The inference was that he was not well-endowed enough to carry out his "sex master" mission. Men are still very sensitive about their weenies. Turning a deeply gratifying crimson, he rushed from the office and never said anything suggestive to me again. Instead, he became the enemy and launched a campaign to have me dismissed.

For more than a year, a powerless woman held corporate honchos at bay. I would not bend. I would not betray other Black women as they wanted and I knew how to use the law to my advantage—a powerful combination. The corporate powerbrokers were at a loss. I finally left the company, when I wanted to. If Black women refuse to play the game, have integrity and bond with other Black women, we have more power than the system likes to acknowledge.

Sexual harassment is so subtle, so pervasive. Women are asked to betray themselves and their children, especially their daughters, to the power of male domination. This means placing power in the hands of men and allowing them to decide whether or not to abuse it. Oh, please !! I don't think so, boyz.

When my daughter was young, I made it clear to every man I knew that touching her inappropriately would result in serious bodily injury. Graphic details were supplied concerning my women friends who would help me castrate them if the need arose. Some men left and never came back, good riddance. Those who stayed treated me and my children with respect. My experiences taught me to champion my children until they could champion themselves. My responsibility was to them, not the male ego.

Recently a friend, a sensitive soul and lover of children, tried guilt-tripping my two-year-old granddaughter into letting him pick her up. She didn't want to be held. His autocratic behavior suggested she had no right to choose. He wanted contact, so she must comply. She was told to be "a good girl." Instead, she held her ground, firing back a perky little "no." He changed tactics. Pulling himself to his full height—six feet two inches—he talked down to her in a "playful" gruff voice, saying, "I said come here." She became apprehensive. Her voice faded to a whisper. This was to be her first lesson in male domination. One she would never "consciously" recall, but might react to for the rest of her life. It was imperative she feel empowered.

Suddenly, I was prepared to kill or die in that hallway, if necessary, so she could choose. I told her so. Louder and firmer, she said: no. Astounded by my "saying such a violent thing to a child," he backed off. He never admitted that his behavior was unacceptable. Instead he decided I was becoming a rabid feminist. Rabid because he recognized a "violent thing" said to him in response. My granddaughter sensed my intensity and knew she had an ally. Allies are important to a Black woman, at any age, in a racist, sexist culture. The sooner we have them the stronger we become.

These are overt examples of sexual harassment; they, like overt examples of racism, make it possible for the subtler indignities to be ignored. Men are not the only offenders; women are often covert harassers.

My humanity has been as much negated by other women as any man of any color. Often these women are white. Often they are not. This is a reality with which we must grapple if significant changes are to be made in the unjust behavior which victimizes all women.

In the circle of misconception which surrounds and protects the rights of others to invade women's lives, only Black women are systematically subjected to this invasion by other women: The women who assume Black women are as exotic and "sexual" as do their men. The women who stare when we enter a restaurant with a man not of our own race, their assumption of prostitution vibrating in the air between us.

Perhaps sexual harassment begins immediately after birth as one is wrapped in blankets of pink or blue. From that moment on we are shaped by oppressive expectations, manipulations, "shoulds," "ought tos" and "musts" which can cripple for a lifetime. In every culture there are stereotypes of what male and female behavior should be and the differences between genders are artificially exaggerated. Our culture is empowered to twist our spirits and create a mental environment which allows sexual harassment, misuses and abuse to flourish.

As Black women we must love, respect and defend ourselves. We have to combat, nay negate, the hatred and contempt that bombards us daily. Forget the night, my sisters, take back your minds.

I feel like a dangerous woman much of the time; dangerous to those who would curtail or overthrow my freedoms. I question their assumptions about themselves, and certainly those they have about me. Sexual harassment is too often seen as an issue of men and their attitudes about women. Of more importance are women and our attitudes and assumptions about ourselves. Always be vigilant. Given choices among resistance, compromise and compliance—when possible choose resistance.

Elena Featherston is a 44-year-old lecturer, filmmaker and writer who produced and directed Alice Walker's "Visions of the Spirit."

Diane Hugs, Mandatory Doctor's Visit, in *Sexual Harassment: Women Speak Out* 114 (Amber Coverdale Sumrall & Dena Taylor eds., 1992)

Being a disabled woman with a progressive disability requires that I document some of that disability through social security. Knowing that my primary physician documented what she saw on my visits, it surprised me a little when Social Security sent me a letter stating that I must see their doctor or I might no longer be considered disabled. This was funny because the small progression of my disability was not even the reason I was on Social Security and could no longer work. But they set up an appointment for me with a doctor I had never heard of and assigned the day and time of this appointment, and they stipulated that I had to go to that appointment.

As usual I took along a friend to the doctor's office; I've found it useful to have someone with me as a patient advocate and to help me remember what I wanted to ask. The doctor's office was in an old building with many rooms in his suite. When we got there it was unusually quiet for an office. We checked around and could not find anyone there. So we picked out what we thought might be the waiting room and waited for the doctor to show up.

The exam was routine and did not require that I remove my clothing. During the exam the doctor started by stroking my thigh as he looked over my chart sent by Social Security. He then asked me about my level of sensation since I am a paraplegic and cannot feel below the point of my paralysis. I held out my hands in front of me indicating that my sensation ended about the same level as my breasts. The doctor stroked my breast and asked me if I could feel that. Since he was below where I can feel I told him no, biting my lip so I wouldn't scream at him. Then he moved up to my level of sensation and touched my breast again with a stroking motion. I said, "Yes I can feel that. But is this necessary?" The reason I wondered was because he was checking neurological data and he was not a neurologist. He answered, "Actually it isn't, I was just curious."

During the exam he rubbed my shoulders and even kissed me; in fact he tried to kiss me on the lips but I turned away. There was no safe way I could think of to stop him; after all, his report would affect my Social Security status, and that is all the income I have in the world. Even though he could not deny I was disabled, he could have messed with my case to stop my checks at least temporarily. This was a psychological weapon which I felt was held over me the entire time I was there. So I kept my mouth shut and held myself back from hitting him during the exam.

As soon as I made it out of the office I burst into tears. My friend felt terrible for not having stood up for me but she was afraid of making more trouble for me. I was numb as I waited for the accessible van to pick me up and drive me home. Once inside the van I broke into tears again and told the driver what had happened. She was furious and told me to call the Center for Independent Living to get some advice. That was very helpful because at that time I could barely think at all.

Upon returning home I called the Center and the first person I talked to told me to call the rape crisis line. At first I was surprised at this suggestion; I had not been raped, just molested. But then I remembered that the local rape crisis center did more than counsel women who had been raped. They also gave information about what you can do or who you can contact in situations like this. So I called the crisis line and talked to one of their counselors. She told me to file a complaint with the police, that this was a crime and I should prosecute. It took me by surprise to have my feelings validated so strongly. Keeping the momentum up I called the police immediately after speaking with the counselor. During the hour and a half that it took before the officer arrived I went through a tornado of feelings. Was I taking this all too seriously? Would the officer think I was paranoid to be making such a charge? Were my perceptions accurate or was I blowing this out of proportion?

While the officer was not the most understanding or sensitive person, he did take what I was saying seriously. He wrote out the complaint and told me they would be back in touch with me for more information and that the medical ethics board would be notified. A few days later my friend was asked to meet with the police and an investigator from the Board of Medical Quality Assurance. She told me the investigator was a really nice guy who seemed seriously interested in seeing this case prosecuted. The next day the investigator came by to take my statement. He was disgusted by the story and hoped they would be able to do something to stop this doctor. It made me feel stronger to be taken so seriously and the investigator thanked me for filing the charges. He had two similar cases with physicians he was working on but it had taken the women years to come forward, making it a lot more difficult to prosecute. Because I had reported the event so quickly, there was a better chance of the investigator being able to prosecute. He first contacted Social Security to obtain a list of others who had been sent to this particular doctor. He needed to know if there were other women who had been similarly mistreated but who had not had the courage to report it. Although he went through every channel including the police, Social Security would not release any information. They claimed it would violate rights to privacy of Social Security recipients. He even asked if they would have their own people contact other patients they had sent to this doctor to see if anyone else had been abused, but they simply refused his requests. I was so angry—it was a lame excuse for Social Security to say it was a violation of our rights to privacy when they were the ones that made me (and how many other women) go to see this doctor.

Finally the investigator came up with a plan that Social Security would go along with. An undercover policewoman was to be sent in to see the doctor as if she were a disabled woman being sent in by Social Security. She sat in a wheelchair and had all the same forms as I had from Social Security. The exam went the same, the doctor did almost exactly the same things to her. When I learned of this, I realized this must be routine for him to mistreat and abuse Social Security or disabled patients during the exam. And although the undercover policewoman felt horrible and powerless when he kissed her and fondled her breasts, she wrote in her report that she wasn't sure if his actions were criminal. What I think she and the system did not understand was that he had power over my life through what he could do to my Social Security payments. I know it wasn't a weapon he could hold over the undercover policewoman, but I wished she had understood that he had no way of stopping her income. She could have fought back without risking her livelihood.

The district attorney did not see grounds to prosecute. This same D.A. was known for not prosecuting sex-related crimes; in fact later that year he was required by the City Council to prosecute over seventy rape cases he had passed by. Knowing that he did not take sex crimes very seriously, I checked to see if there was any other way to get this into court. But the sad fact is that the D.A. has the final call on whether or not to prosecute a case, and nothing I could do or say could change that fact. My next hope was the Board of Medical Quality Assurance. They brought him up before the discipline board and asked him to explain himself. The doctor admitted to everything that had happened; he just didn't think there was anything wrong with it. The Board warned him to keep his hands to himself and left it at that. Even though I wrote the Board an impassioned plea to reconsider on the grounds that his position of working for Social Security was a weapon against disabled women, they would not hear me.

This was more than I could take. On one hand I was told that I was right, that he had no right to fondle and kiss me, that in fact it was criminal; on the other hand no one would do anything to stop him from doing it to every woman he came into contact with. It really bothered me that he was not only going to get away with what he had done, but there was also no way for my testimony to keep other women safe. I told Social Security that his report on me was invalid since I was a victim, not a client; they told me they didn't want to hear about my personal problems. No way could I make them stop sending people to this doctor. It was driving me crazy to feel so helpless.

Having exhausted all means of legal prosecution, I decided to take him into civil court. There was a lawyer, Leslie Levy, with an outstanding reputation, so I decided to call her. She took the case even though I didn't have a dime and went right to work on it. The malpractice insurance company jumped into defending him even though they said they were in no way liable, because there is an exclusion for the insurance companies for any act that may be deemed criminal rather than a malpractice claim. So we had to battle these high-priced lawyers even though their company assumed no responsibility. There were two years of foot dragging and legal manipulation which my lawyer had to fight while the doctor continued to practice. He said he would settle for five hundred dollars. I rejected this because I could see no indication that he had the slightest clue that he had done something wrong.

Two years after filing this case and having every legal trick in the book thrown at us, we finally got around to doing court depositions. I was unable to sit upright at the time so not only was I unable to go to his deposition, I had to give mine from my bed. Instead of having all these strangers in my bedroom I used the bed in the living room. That was a very good thing because the doctor decided to show up and listen to my statement. A deposition requires the presence of lawyers from both sides along with a court reporter, and that felt like a huge invasion in itself. The deposition lasted about three hours and I was very lucky to have such a brilliant lawyer on my side. She did not let them get away with asking anything that was not relevant. She jumped up and down a lot, screaming at the other lawyer to back off. Since Leslie was familiar with abusive lawyers and litigants, she protected me from unnecessary harassment and abuse, for which I am eternally grateful to her.

That deposition did the job. The doctor seemed to realize I had been hurt. For the first time he understood that he had done damage, though he was not willing to pay for it. So onwards towards court we went. It was finished four months later and while I cannot divulge the outcome, I can say that the judge was understanding and resolved the case so I didn't have to go before a whole courtroom with it. The terms of the settlement prohibit me from saying anything.

I am still left with feelings of rage and sadness about what he did to me and how the system let him get away with it. If it had not been for the interest of Leslie Levy I would have been left out in the cold. There are not enough lawyers like her.

The legal system is still predominately male and does not take women seriously. It is not a lucrative business for lawyers to take on such cases since there's not that much money in these cases even if you get the court system to see the damage done. For me that was the hardest part, being asked, "Describe how this hurt you" in front of strangers who were not sensitive to my feelings. How to explain what having this uncaring authority figure run his hands all over me did to me, how he made me feel like a whore.

I used to trust doctors, but not anymore. I lost trust not only in the system which ignored my pain, but also I lost trust in people in general. It took over four years for me to let a stranger touch me at all. I had to explain to the doctor's lawyer that this lack of trust, not wanting to be touched, was damage in itself. He tried to downplay it by asking me if I would ever let anyone touch me again. I told him I had every intention of healing from this and hoped to be able to regain my trust. I fought hard. I fought long. It was worth the effort. The doctor knows he was wrong now. I just wish I had been able to stop him from continuing to practice. But I did everything I could and I can live with that.

What I would like to say to other women, disabled or not, is that a doctor does not have the right to touch you in any inappropriate way. We all have the right to fight back. More women need to fight the doctors who don't know the limits of conduct. If you are not sure whether your doctor went too far, but you do not feel good about what happened, follow it through. Contact the Board of Medical Quality Assurance, rape crisis centers and please, if you think there is even a possibility of a criminal case, call the police. The more women who call doctors on misconduct, the fewer doctors will continue to do harm to their women patients. If you cannot do this for yourself, please consider doing it for the next woman. Even though your doctor may not have taken you seriously, having to answer to all the different authorities will make him think twice before he treats another patient the same way again.

Diane Hugs is a working-class woman with severe multiple sclerosis who is a writer and disabled activist.

Mardi Richmond, Just Trying to Have Some Fun, in *Sexual Harassment: Women Speak Out* 208 (Amber Coverdale Sumrall & Dena Taylor eds., 1992)

Jack sometimes worked in the shop. He was big and tough and strong and rumored to be about the best carpenter in this county. One thing for sure, he always seemed to know what he was doing. He was about as confident as they come, cocky in a way.

Jack reminded me of two boys that I lived next door to when I was a kid. They were big and tough and strong, like Jack, and they wore their hair in a short, almost crew-cut style, like Jack.

When I was eight years old, the two boys next door paid me a nickel to come into their house when nobody was home. I didn't want to go in because their house was dark and always smelled like their dad's cigars. But they said, Come on in, we just want to have some fun. So I went inside. They shut and locked the door behind me and one of them grabbed my arms and the other pulled my pants down. They took turns holding me and touching me in ways I did not want to be touched. Then the oldest boy, he must have been fifteen or sixteen, tried to stick a broom handle up inside of me. I started crying so hard that they let me go, but not before they made me promise that I would never, never tell anyone what they did. Then they gave me another nickel and said, Stop crying, we were just trying to have a little fun. I ran straight home to my room and made myself sit in the corner. When my mom came in and asked me what was wrong I told her nothing. I never, never told, but I knew that what they had done was not fun.

Fourteen years later, at work, Jack took a stick—it could have been the handle of a broom—and stuck it between my legs when I was bent over nailing off a toe board on a cabinet. I turned around furious and told him to cut it out. He said, Hey, I'm just having a little fun, and walked off laughing.

The next day, Jack did it again. This time he grabbed my breasts and started making remarks about how I liked it and wanted it, in front of all men I worked with. They all started laughing. I pushed Jack's hands off my breasts and walked away, mad and scared. That time, I could not even find the words to tell him to stop. A feeling of terror filled my heart and the words would not come out. Later the same afternoon, when I was carrying one end of a one-foot by one-foot by eighteen-foot fir beam, he grabbed my ass as I walked by. I jumped, startled, started to drop the huge beam, and felt a twinge of pain in the small of my back as I caught it. Three of the other men I worked with laughed, one frowned. Later the man who had frowned, carefully out of ear shot of the other men, told me he did not think it was right for Jack to treat me that way.

I went home from work that day scared, not knowing what to do. I was afraid to tell anybody. I heard the voices of those boys in my childhood memory saying never never tell. And I felt, much as I had when I was eight, that it was my fault. When I was eight, it was my fault because I went into their house for a nickel; now it was my fault because I had lost my voice. I was not able to tell him to stop.

I tried to tell my husband about it. He was furious and threatened to find Jack and punch him in the face. My husband could make him stop temporarily, but could I feel like I was strong enough to take care of myself if he did? And how could I keep working with men who thought this was funny, who were likely to do it again, if I couldn't take care of myself? I knew I had to find my own power to make him stop, and I knew that that had to start with finding a voice with which to say no.

I found that power and that voice through the anger of another woman. I visited a friend, and told her about the harassment. I told her about Jack grabbing me and touching me. I told her about his constant words, threatening and loud. I told her about the laughter of the other men. We were walking down the street when I told her and she began yelling at the top of her lungs.

She yelled how fucked what he did had been and she yelled how fucked the other men were for laughing. When she stopped yelling and when the people driving down the street stopped staring, I felt my own surge of anger, and of energy. I realized how his words had stolen my energy and when I felt it coming back, I felt my voice coming back. My friend and I talked for hours that night about how to make him stop. I knew that shrugging it off would not work, and I knew that in a non-union shop I had very little political recourse; there was no one to complain to. What I realized I had to do was to confront him directly and loudly, the very next time it happened, before he had a chance to steal my dignity and energy again.

The next day, Jack took the nozzle from the pneumatic hose and blew air down my shirt. I grabbed the hose out of his hand, stood as tall and firm as I knew how, and told him loudly but calmly that it was not OK with me for him to do this and he had to stop right now. And he was never to touch me again. This time when he said he was trying to have a little fun, I told him it was not funny and he was never to do it again. And he never did.

About a year later, another man I had worked with for several years approached me outside the building, saying he wanted to talk to me about something. I went over to the doorway where he was standing, and he grabbed me, pushing me into the doorway. He stood with his arms on either side of me, blocking my way out, and leaned his tall frame over me, to kiss me, trying to force his tongue in my mouth. I did not even hesitate, I pushed him away with all of my strength yelling NO. My yell startled him enough that he staggered backwards, just as several faces looked out of a nearby shop. Hey, I wasn't going to rape you or anything, he said. I was just trying to have some fun.

Mardi Richmond spent the first twelve years of her adult life working as a cabinetmaker and finish carpenter; today she is a freelance writer.

Nomination of Judge Clarence Thomas to be Associate Justice of the Supreme Court of the United States: Hearings before the Senate Committee on the Judiciary, 102nd Cong., 1st Sess.

36-40 (1991) (testimony of Anita F. Hill, Professor of Law, University of Oklahoma)

Ms. Hill. Mr. Chairman, Senator Thurmond, members of the committee, my name is Anita F. Hill, and I am a professor of law at the University of Oklahoma.

I was born on a farm in Okmulgee County, OK, in 1956. I am the youngest of 13 children. I had my early education in Okmulgee County. My father, Albert Hill, is a farmer in that area. My mother's name is Erma Hill. She is also a farmer and a housewife.

My childhood was one of a lot of hard work and not much money, but it was one of solid family affection as represented by my parents. I was reared in a religious atmosphere in the Baptist faith, and I have been a member of the Antioch Baptist Church, in Tulsa, OK, since 1983. It is a very warm part of my life at the present time.

For my undergraduate work, I went to Oklahoma State University, and graduated from there in 1977. I am attaching to the statement a copy of my résumé for further details of my education.

The Chairman. It will be included in the record.

Ms. Hill. Thank you.

I graduated from the university with academic honors and proceeded to the Yale Law School, where I received my J.D. degree in 1980.

Upon graduation from law school, I became a practicing lawyer with the Washington, DC, firm of Ward, Harkrader & Ross. In 1981, I was introduced to now Judge Thomas by a mutual friend. Judge Thomas told me that he was anticipating a political appointment and asked if I would be interested in working with him. He was, in fact, appointed as Assistant Secretary of Education for Civil Rights. After he had taken that post, he asked if I would become his assistant, and I accepted that position.

In my early period there, I had two major projects. First was an article I wrote for Judge Thomas' signature on the education of minority students. The second was the organization of a seminar on high-risk students, which was abandoned, because Judge Thomas transferred to the EEOC, where he became the Chairman of that office.

During this period at the Department of Education, my working relationship with Judge Thomas was positive. I had a good deal of responsibility and independence. I thought he respected my work and that he trusted my judgment.

After approximately 3 months of working there, he asked me to go out socially with him. What happened next and telling the world about it are the two most difficult things, experiences of my life. It is only after a great deal of agonizing consideration and a number of sleepless nights that I am able to talk of these unpleasant matters to anyone but my close friends.

I declined the invitation to go out socially with him, and explained to him that I thought it would jeopardize what at the time I considered to be a very good working relationship. I had a normal social life with other men outside of the office. I believed then, as now, that having a social relationship with a person who was supervising my work would be ill advised. I was very uncomfortable with the idea and told him so.

I thought that by saying "no" and explaining my reasons, my employer would abandon his social suggestions. However, to my regret, in the following few weeks he continued to ask me out on several occasions. He pressed me to justify my reasons for saying "no" to him. These incidents took place in his office or mine. They were in the form of private conversations which would not have been overheard by anyone else.

My working relationship became even more strained when Judge Thomas began to use work situations to discuss sex. On these occasions, he would call me into his office for reports on education issues and projects or he might suggest that because of the time pressures of his schedule, we go to lunch to a government cafeteria. After a brief discussion of work, he would turn the conversation to a discussion of sexual matters. His conversations were very vivid.

He spoke about acts that he had seen in pornographic films involving such matters as women having sex with animals, and films showing group sex or rape scenes. He talked about pornographic materials depicting individuals with large penises, or large breasts involved in various sex acts.

On several occasions Thomas told me graphically of his own sexual prowess. Because I was extremely uncomfortable talking about sex with him at all, and particularly in such a graphic way, I told him that I did not want to talk about these subjects. I would also try to change the subject to education matters or to nonsexual personal matters, such as his background or his beliefs. My efforts to change the subject were rarely successful.

Throughout the period of these conversations, he also from time to time asked me for social engagements. My reactions to these conversations was to avoid them by limiting opportunities for us to engage in extended conversations. This was difficult because at the time, I was his only assistant at the Office of Education or Office for Civil Rights.

During the latter part of my time at the Department of Education, the social pressures and any conversation of his offensive behavior ended. I began both to believe and hope that our working relationship could be a proper, cordial, and professional one.

When Judge Thomas was made chair of the EEOC, I needed to face the question of whether to go with him. I was asked to do so and I did. The work itself, was interesting, and at that time, it appeared that the sexual overtures, which had so troubled me, had ended.

I also faced the realistic fact that I had no alternative job. While I might have gone back to private practice, perhaps in my old firm, or at another, I was dedicated to civil rights work and my first choice was to be in that field. Moreover, at that time the Department of Education, itself, was a dubious venture. President Reagan was seeking to abolish the entire department.

For my first months at the EEOC, where I continued to be an assistant to Judge Thomas, there were no sexual conversations or overtures. However, during the fall and winter of 1982, these began again. The comments were random, and ranged from pressing me about why I didn't go out with him, to remarks about my personal appearance. I remember his saying that "some day I would have to tell him the real reason that I wouldn't go out with him."

He began to show displeasure in his tone and voice and his demeanor and his continued pressure for an explanation. He commented on what I was wearing in terms of whether it made me more or less sexually attractive. The incidents occurred in his inner office at the EEOC.

One of the oddest episodes I remember was an occasion in which Thomas was drinking a Coke in his office, he got up from the table, at which we were working, went over to his desk to get the Coke, looked at the can and asked, "Who has put pubic hair on my Coke?"

On other occasions he referred to the size of his own penis as being larger than normal and he also spoke on some occasions of the pleasures he had given to women with oral sex. At this point, late 1982, I began to feel severe stress on the job. I began to be concerned that Clarence Thomas might take out his anger with me by degrading me or not giving me important assignments. I also thought that he might find an excuse for dismissing me.

In January 1983, I began looking for another job. I was handicapped because I feared that if he found out he might make it difficult for me to find other employment, and I might be dismissed from the job I had.

Another factor that made my search more difficult was that this was during a period of a hiring freeze in the Government. In February 1983, I was hospitalized for 5 days on an emergency basis for acute stomach pain which I attributed to stress on the job. Once out of the hospital. [sic] I became more committed to find other employment and sought further to minimize my contact with Thomas.

This became easier when Allyson Duncan became office director because most of my work was then funneled through her and I had contact with Clarence Thomas mostly in staff meetings.

In the spring of l983, an opportunity to teach at Oral Roberts University opened up. I participated in a seminar, taught an afternoon session in a seminar at Oral Roberts University. The dean of the university saw me teaching and inquired as to whether I would be interested in pursuing a career in teaching, beginning at Oral Roberts University. I agreed to take the job, in large part, because of my desire to escape the pressures I felt at the EEOC due to Judge Thomas.

When I informed him that I was leaving in July, I recall that his response was that now, I would no longer have an excuse for not going out with him. I told him that I still preferred not to do so. At some time after that meeting, he asked if he could take me to dinner at the end of the term. When I declined, he assured me that the dinner was a professional courtesy only and not a social invitation. I reluctantly agreed to accept that invitation but only if it was at the very end of a working day.

On, as I recall, the last day of my employment at the EEOC in the summer of 1983, I did have dinner with Clarence Thomas. We went directly from work to a restaurant near the office. We talked about the work that I had done both at education and at the EEOC. He told me that he was pleased with all of it except for an article and speech that I had done for him while we were at the Office for Civil Rights. Finally he made a comment that I will vividly remember. He said, that if I ever told anyone of his behavior that it would ruin his career. This was not an apology, nor was it an explanation. That was his last remark about the possibility of our going out, or reference to his behavior.

In July 1983, I left the Washington, DC, area and have had minimal contacts with Judge Clarence Thomas since. I am, of course, aware from the press that some questions have been raised about conversations I had with Judge Clarence Thomas after I left the EEOC.

From 1983 until today I have seen Judge Thomas only twice. On one occasion I needed to get a reference from him and on another, he made a public appearance in Tulsa. On one occasion he called me at home and we had an inconsequential conversation. On one occasion he called me without reaching me and I returned the call without reaching him and nothing came of it. I have, at least on three occasions been asked to act as a conduit to him for others.

I knew his secretary, Diane Holt. We had worked together both at EEOC and Education. There were occasions on which I spoke to her and on some of these occasions, undoubtedly, I passed on some casual comment to then, Chairman Thomas. There were a series of calls in the first 3 months of 1985, occasioned by a group in Tulsa which wished to have a civil rights conference. They wanted Judge Thomas to be the speaker and enlisted my assistance for this purpose.

I did call in January and February to no effect and finally suggested to the person directly involved, Susan Cahall, that she put the matter into her own hands and call directly. She did so in March 1985.

In connection with that March invitation, Ms. Cahall wanted conference materials for the seminar, and some research was needed. I was asked to try and get the information and did attempt to do so. There was another call about another possible conference in July 1985.

In August 1987, I was in Washington, DC, and I did call Diane Holt. In the course of this conversation she asked me how long I was going to be in town and I told her. It is recorded in the messages as August 15, it was, in fact, August 20. She told me about Judge Thomas' marriage and I did say, congratulations.

It is only after a great deal of agonizing consideration that I am able to talk of these unpleasant matters to anyone, except my closest friends as I have said before. These last few days have been very trying and very hard for me, and it hasn't just been the last few days this week. It has actually been over a month now that I have been under the strain of this issue. Telling the world is the most difficult experience of my life, but it is very close to have to live through the experience that occasioned this meeting. I may have used poor judgment early on in my relationship with this issue. I was aware, however, that telling at any point in my career could adversely affect my future career. And I did not want, early on, to build [*sic*] all the bridges to the EEOC.

As I said, I may have used poor judgment. Perhaps I should have taken angry or even militant steps, both when I was in the agency or after I had left it, but I must confess to the world that the course that I took seemed the better, as well as the easier approach.

I declined any comment to newspapers, but later when Senate staff asked me about these matters, I felt that I had a duty to report. I have no personal vendetta against Clarence Thomas. I seek only to provide the committee with information which it may regard as relevant.

It would have been more comfortable to remain silent. It [*sic*] took no initiative to inform anyone. [*sic*] I took no initiative to inform anyone. But when I was asked by a representative of this committee to report my experience I felt that I had to tell the truth. I could not keep silent.

Notes and Questions

1. *Women Laborers Lacked Virtue*. In the mid-1800s industrialization "created a new middle class striving for upper-class status. For women, the vehicle for these aspirations was what became known as the 'cult of the lady. . . .' " Paula Giddings, When and Where I Enter: The Impact of Black Women on Race and Sex in America 47 (1984). Paula Giddings elaborates on the "cult of the lady," suggesting how it categorizes women as those who are deemed deserving of protection and those who are not. Any women in the

public workplace is not viewed as being in the protected category; she therefore is an appropriate target of harassment. Statistics support the conclusion that harassment is prevalent in the workplace (p. 281) and belie the societal myth of sexual harassment as isolated and aberrational conduct. From Giddings' analysis, we see not only that the construction of a group of women who are not "ladies" is one means of rationalizing sexual harassment in the workplace but also that class, race/ethnicity, and sexual orientation figure in sexual harassment: Working-class women, women of color, and lesbians are denied the status of "lady" and thereby denied social protections from sexual harassment.

> Domesticity had a central position in the cult idea. The true woman's exclusive role was as homemaker, mother, housewife, and family tutor of the social and moral graces. Isolated within the home, women "raised" men above lusty temptation while keeping themselves beyond its rapacious grasp. Women's imprisonment in the home virtually guaranteed piety and purity. . . .
>
> For White men, the cult was convenient. In an increasingly industrial economy, more of them were forced to leave the farms for occupations that middle-class women had enjoyed. Factory owners benefited from the new status symbol as well. During the early rise of the factory system, the main source of labor was proud—if needy—Puritan girls who saw their work as a stopgap until they married. Although the work was strenuous and the wages low, such employment still carried a certain status—and the women showed themselves willing to organize in order to better working conditions and pay. With the coming of the cult idea, however, work outside the home lost its prestige, and women like the Puritan girls were no longer expected to be *in* the labor force but to stay home and *reproduce* the labor force. So when the cult of the lady took hold, they were replaced by poorer immigrant women, a cheaper, more permanent, and more exploitable source of workers. Therefore it was no coincidence, Lerner observed, that "the slogan 'a woman's place is in the home' took on a certain aggressiveness and shrillness precisely at the time when increasing numbers of poorer women *left* their homes to become factory workers." It was also no coincidence, she could have added, that it occurred at a time when the abolition of slavery brought Black women into the wage-labor force. They, however, were excluded from the factories, which for white women had afforded, in the words of the nineteenth-century writer Harriet Martineau, "a most welcome resource to some thousands of young women, unwilling to give themselves to domestic service." The exclusion of Black women from the industrial labor force created a legacy that continued for more than a century. . . .
>
> As the women's magazines and romance literature of the period suggested, madness, sometimes death, and always tragedy were the fate of a woman who could not fulfill the "attributes" of true womanhood. To be lacking in any of those qualities meant a woman was unnatural, unfeminine, and thus a species of a different—if not lower—female order. Since only women of leisure could even hope to join the pantheon of ladyhood, true women, with all the attendant moral implications, became virtually synonymous with the upper class. . . .[A]s Gerda Lerner observed ". . .[i]t was taken for granted during the period and well into the 20th century that working-class women—

> and especially Black women—were freely available for sexual use by upper-class males." The assumption had less to do with real circumstances than with the idea of immutable natural laws that governed morality and femininity. These laws stated that women who worked outside the home, or whose race had a history of sexual exploitation, were outside the realm of "womanhood" and its prerogatives.

Id. at 47-49 (emphasis in original). For a discussion of the connections between sexual harassment and prostitution and how the law of sexual harassment inappropriately "seeks to disidentify. . .[the] victim from the status of 'prostitute' by distinguishing her behavior from at least one of the legal elements of prostitution," see Margaret A. Baldwin, Split at the Root: Prostitution and Feminist Discourses of Law Reform, at p. 571.

Given the readings on battering in Chapter 4, do you believe that the "cult of the lady" served to protect any woman from male abuse? What is the connection between the prevalence of battering in the home and the prevalence of sexual harassment in the workplace?

2. *Inside/Outside*. The preceding narratives show that sexual harassment is not limited to the workplace, but occurs in grocery stores, doctors' offices, and on the streets. Andrea Dworkin extends the analysis of the effects of the cult of the lady to show how restrictions on women in both the public and private spheres are related to the harassment women risk by venturing outside.

> In the European tradition, men have tried to keep women from working for money except as prostitutes. . . .The most protected woman was the married woman, a prisoner in her own home, except, of course, that it was not hers, any more than the cage belongs to the bird. . . .She was physically confined to the house to guarantee the husband that his legal children were his biological issue.
>
> Any women less isolated was more collectively owned. . . .
>
> The wife was the private woman in the private (domestic) sphere, protected inside, legally bound there. *Inside* meant confinement, captivity, isolation; high value; a reproductive as well as a sexual function; a privatized ownership. The prostitute was the public woman—publicly owned. She lived outside the home. *Outside* meant the breaching of one's body by more than one, how many and under which circumstances depending on one's closeness to or distance from the male elite—the small, wealthy ruling class. . . .*Outside*, money paid for acts and access. *Outside*, women were for sale. *Inside* meant that a woman was protected from the commerce in her kind; the value of a woman was high only when she was immune from the contamination of a money exchange. . . .In the public domain by virtue of the male use of her, she became venal by male definition and design, according to male power and perception.
>
> These zones—private and public, inside and outside—continue to suggest a real geography of female experience under the rule of men. The insularity of the domestic sphere for women has been treasured or honored or valued even in poor or working-class families; a man's honor is compromised or contaminated when his wife works outside the home for money. The gender-specific exclusiveness of housework creates a literal and symbolic

synthesis between woman and house. . . .Her association with the home is nativist and in the wider world, which is his real domain, she is an unwanted alien, at best a guest worker with a short-term visa, a stigmatized immigrant.

In the workplace, her money is seen to supplement his. He is first, she is second. She is paid less than men are paid for the same work, if men do the same work; she may be segregated into female-only work, menial and low-paid. . . .

So, outside, the woman is public in male territory, a hands-on zone; her presence there is taken to be a declaration of availability—for sex and sexual insult. . . .The verbal assaults and some physical assault are endemic in the environment . . . .None of us can stand up to all of it; we are incredulous as each new aggression occurs. We hurry to forget. It can't have happened, we say; or it happens all the time, we say—it is too rare to be credible or too common to matter. We won't be believed or no one will care; or both.

Andrea Dworkin, Women in the Public Domain: Sexual Harassment and Date Rape, in Sexual Harassment: Women Speak Out 1-5 (Amber Coverdale Sumrall & Dena Taylor eds., 1992) (emphasis in original).

Cynthia Grant Bowman addresses the street harassment women commonly experience in an effort to make its harm more visible:

First, street harassment both increases women's dependence on men and contributes to distrust and hostility between the sexes. For example, street harassment, and the related danger of sexual assault, encourage women to seek male escorts in public—men to protect them from harassment by other men . . . .Moreover, it is difficult for a man, however well-intentioned, to address an unfamiliar woman on the street without evoking some suspicion or fear in her, unless he goes to some lengths to assure her that he—unlike other unfamiliar males—is indeed trustworthy. Thus, the possibility of harassment complicates casual communication and impedes solidarity among unacquainted men and women.

Second, contrary to the folk wisdom that "sticks and stones may break my bones but words will never hurt me," language is instrumental in the construction of reality; language locates individuals within that reality and thus constructs their gender identities. Women learn to associate their bodies with shame, fear, and humiliation. Women also learn their place in society from language, and they learn that this place is not a public one. The remarks women hear from harassers on the street carry the implicit (and sometimes explicit) message that women do not belong in public, where they draw attention by their mere appearance, but rather in the private sphere, at home. . . .

In sum, the continuation and near-general tolerance of street harassment has serious consequences both for women and for society at large. It inflicts the most direct costs upon women, in the form of fear, emotional distress, feelings of disempowerment, and significant limitations upon their liberty, mobility, and hopes for equality. It also increases distrust between men and women and reinforces rigid gender roles, hierarchy, and the confinement of women to the private sphere. Street harassment thus performs a function as a social

> institution that is antithetical to the acceptance of women into American public life on terms equal to men.

Cynthia Grant Bowman, Street Harassment and the Informal Ghettoization of Women, 106 Harv. L. Rev. 517, 540-42 (1993).

3. *Racialized Hearings*. Much has been said and written about the value of having the citizenry focus on the issues of sexual harassment in October 1991—*i.e.*, Justice Clarence Thomas' confirmation hearings. Toni Morrison asks us to go further and consider the racialized meaning of the public airing of sexual harassment charges in this forum.

> An accusation of such weight as sexual misconduct would probably have disqualified a white candidate on its face. . . .But in a racialized and race-conscious society, standards are changed, facts marginalized, repressed, and the willingness to air such charges, actually to debate them, outweighed the seemliness of a substantive hearing because the actors were black. . . .[I]t seems blazingly clear that with this unprecedented opportunity to hover over and to cluck at, to meditate and ponder the limits and excesses of black bodies, no other strategies were going to be entertained. . . .The participants were black and therefore "known," serviceable, expendable in the interests of limning out one or the other of two mutually antagonistic fabulations. Under the pressure of voyeuristic desire, fueled by mythologies that render blacks publicly serviceable instruments of private dread and longing, extraordinary behavior on the part of the state could take place. . . .Under the pressure of racist mythologies, . . .the chairman of the committee could apply criminal court procedure to a confirmation hearing and assure the candidate that the assumption of innocence lay with the nominee. . . .
>
> Would such accusations have elicited such outsize defense mechanisms if the candidate had been white? Would the committee and many interest groups have considered the suitability of a white candidate untainted by these accusations? Hardly, but with a black candidate, already stained by the figurations of blackness as sexual aggressiveness or rapaciousness or impotence, the stain need only be proved reasonably doubted, which is to say, if he is black, how can you tell if that really is a stain? Which is also to say, blackness is itself a stain, and therefore unstainable. Which is also to say, if he is black and about to ascend to the Supreme Court bench, if the bench is to become stain-free, this newest judge must be bleached, race-free, as his speeches and opinions illustrated. Allegations of sexual misconduct re-raced him, which, in this administration, meant, restained him, dirtied him. Therefore the "dirt" that clung to him following those allegations, "dirt" he spoke of repeatedly, must be shown to have originated elsewhere. In this case the search for the racial stain turned on Anita Hill. Her character. Her motives. Not his.

Toni Morrison, Introduction: Friday on the Potomac, in Race-ing Justice, En-gendering Power: Essays on Anita Hill, Clarence Thomas, and the Construction of Social Reality vii, xvii-xix (Toni Morrison ed., 1992).

4. *Capitalism and Sexual Harassment*. The Thrift story suggests that women were placed in positions of competing with one another and that

their supervisors used sexual harassment to goad on that competition. Did that competition serve management's profit goals?

B. Legal Developments

E.E.O.C. Regulations to Title VII of the Civil Rights Act of 1964,
29 C.F.R. § 1604.11 (1992)

§ *1604.11* Sexual harassment.

(a) Harassment on the basis of sex is a violation of section 703 of title VII.[1] Unwelcome sexual advances, requests for sexual favors, and other verbal or physical conduct of a sexual nature constitute sexual harassment when (1) submission to such conduct is made either explicitly or implicitly a term or condition of an individual's employment, (2) submission to or rejection of such conduct by an individual is used as the basis for employment decisions affecting such individual, or (3) such conduct has the purpose or effect of unreasonably interfering with an individual's work performance or creating an intimidating, hostile, or offensive working environment.

(b) In determining whether alleged conduct constitutes sexual harassment, the Commission will look at the record as a whole and at the totality of the circumstances, such as the nature of the sexual advances and the context in which the alleged incidents occurred. The determination of the legality of a particular action will be made from the facts, on a case by case basis.

(c) Applying general title VII principles, an employer, employment agency, joint apprenticeship committee or labor organization (hereinafter collectively referred to as "employer") is responsible for its acts and those of its agents and supervisory employees with respect to sexual harassment regardless of whether the specific acts complained of were authorized or even forbidden by the employer and regardless of whether the employer knew or should have known of their occurrence. The Commission will examine the circumstances of the particular employment relationship and the job junctions [sic] performed by the individual in determining whether an individual acts in either a supervisory or agency capacity.

(d) With respect to conduct between fellow employees, an employer is responsible for acts of sexual harassment in the workplace where the employer (or its agents or supervisory employees) knows or should have known of the conduct, unless it can show that it took immediate and appropriate corrective action.

(e) An employer may also be responsible for the acts of non-employees, with respect to sexual harassment of employees in the workplace, where the employer (or its agents or supervisory employees) knows or should have known of the conduct and fails to take immediate and appropriate corrective

1. The principles involved here continue to apply to race, color, religion or national origin.

action. In reviewing these cases the Commission will consider the extent of the employer's control and any other legal responsibility which the employer may have with respect to the conduct of such non-employees.

(f) Prevention is the best tool for the elimination of sexual harassment. An employer should take all steps necessary to prevent sexual harassment from occurring, such as affirmatively raising the subject, expressing strong disapproval, developing appropriate sanctions, informing employees of their right to raise and how to raise the issue of harassment under title VII, and developing methods to sensitize all concerned.

(g) Other related practices: Where employment opportunities or benefits are granted because of an individual's submission to the employer's sexual advances or requests for sexual favors, the employer may be held liable for unlawful sex discrimination against other persons who were qualified for but denied that employment opportunity or benefit.

Meritor Savings Bank, FSB v. Vinson,

477 U.S. 57 (1986)

Justice Rehnquist delivered the opinion of the Court. This case presents important questions concerning claims of workplace "sexual harassment" brought under Title VII of the Civil Rights Act of 1964 . . . .

In 1974, respondent Mechelle Vinson met Sidney Taylor, a vice president of what is now petitioner Meritor Savings Bank (bank) and manager of one of its branch offices. When respondent asked whether she might obtain employment at the bank, Taylor gave her an application, which she completed and returned the next day; later that same day Taylor called her to say that she had been hired. With Taylor as her supervisor, respondent started as a teller-trainee, and thereafter was promoted to teller, head teller, and assistant branch manager. She worked at the same branch for four years, and it is undisputed that her advancement there was based on merit alone. In September 1978, respondent notified Taylor that she was taking sick leave for an indefinite period. On November 1, 1978, the bank discharged her for excessive use of that leave.

Respondent brought this action against Taylor and the bank, claiming that during her four years at the bank she had "constantly been subjected to sexual harassment" by Taylor in violation of Title VII. She sought injunctive relief, compensatory and punitive damages against Taylor and the bank, and attorney's fees.

At the 11-day bench trial, the parties presented conflicting testimony about Taylor's behavior during respondent's employment.[2] Respondent testified that during her probationary period as a teller-trainee, Taylor treated her in a fatherly way and made no sexual advances. Shortly thereafter, however, he invited her out to dinner and, during the course of the meal, suggested that they go to a motel to have sexual relations. At first she refused, but out of what

---

2. Like the Court of Appeals, this Court was not provided a complete transcript of the trial. We therefore rely largely on the District Court's opinion for the summary of the relevant testimony.

she described as fear of losing her job she eventually agreed. According to respondent, Taylor thereafter made repeated demands upon her for sexual favors, usually at the branch, both during and after business hours; she estimated that over the next several years she had intercourse with him some 40 or 50 times. In addition, respondent testified that Taylor fondled her in front of other employees, followed her into the women's restroom when she went there alone, exposed himself to her, and even forcibly raped her on several occasions. These activities ceased after 1977, respondent stated, when she started going with a steady boyfriend.

Respondent also testified that Taylor touched and fondled other women employees of the bank, and she attempted to call witnesses to support this charge. But while some supporting testimony apparently was admitted without objection, the District Court did not allow her "to present wholesale evidence of a pattern and practice relating to sexual advances to other female employees in her case in chief, but advised her that she might well be able to present such evidence in rebuttal to the defendants' cases.". . .Respondent did not offer such evidence in rebuttal. Finally, respondent testified that because she was afraid of Taylor she never reported his harassment to any of his supervisors and never attempted to use the bank's complaint procedure.

Taylor denied respondent's allegations of sexual activity, testifying that he never fondled her, never made suggestive remarks to her, never engaged in sexual intercourse with her, and never asked her to do so. He contended instead that respondent made her accusations in response to a business-related dispute. The bank also denied respondent's allegations and asserted that any sexual harassment by Taylor was unknown to the bank and engaged in without its consent or approval.

The District Court denied relief, but did not resolve the conflicting testimony about the existence of a sexual relationship between respondent and Taylor. It found instead that

> "[i]f [respondent] and Taylor did engage in an intimate or sexual relationship during the time of [respondent's] employment with [the bank], that relationship was a voluntary one having nothing to do with her continued employment at [the bank] or her advancement or promotions at that institution.". . .

The court ultimately found that respondent "was not the victim of sexual harassment and was not the victim of sexual discrimination" while employed at the bank. . . .

The Court of Appeals for the District of Columbia Circuit reversed. . . .Relying on its earlier holding in *Bundy v. Jackson*, 205 U.S. App. D.C. 444, 641 F.2d 934 (1981), decided after the trial in this case, the court stated that a violation of Title VII may be predicated on either of two types of sexual harassment: harassment that involves the conditioning of concrete employment benefits on sexual favors, and harassment that, while not affecting economic benefits, creates a hostile or offensive working environment. The court drew additional support for this position from the Equal Employment Opportunity Commission's Guidelines on Discrimination Because of Sex, . . .which set out these two types of sexual harassment claims. Believing that "Vinson's grievance was clearly of the [hostile environment] type," . . .and that the

District Court had not considered whether a violation of this type had occurred, the court concluded that a remand was necessary.

The court further concluded that the District Court's finding that any sexual relationship between respondent and Taylor "was a voluntary one" did not obviate the need for a remand. "[U]ncertain as to precisely what the [district] court meant" by this finding, the Court of Appeals held that if the evidence otherwise showed that "Taylor made Vinson's toleration of sexual harassment a condition of her employment," her voluntariness "had no materiality whatsoever.". . .The court then surmised that the District Court's finding of voluntariness might have been based on "the voluminous testimony regarding respondent's dress and personal fantasies," testimony that the Court of Appeals believed "had no place in this litigation.". . .

As to the bank's liability, the Court of Appeals held that an employer is absolutely liable for sexual harassment practiced by supervisory personnel, whether or not the employer knew or should have known about the misconduct. The court relied chiefly on Title VII's definition of "employer" to include "any agent of such a person,". . . as well as on the EEOC Guidelines. The court held that a supervisor is an "agent" of his employer for Title VII purposes, even if he lacks authority to hire, fire, or promote, since "the mere existence—or even the appearance—of a significant degree of influence in vital job decisions gives any supervisor the opportunity to impose on employees.". . .

We granted certiorari. . .and now affirm but for different reasons. . . .

Title VII of the Civil Rights Act of 1964 makes it "an unlawful employment practice for an employer. . .to discriminate against any individual with respect to his compensation, terms, conditions, or privileges of employment, because of such individual's race, color, religion, sex, or national origin.". . .The prohibition against discrimination based on sex was added to Title VII at the last minute on the floor of the House of Representatives. . . .

Respondent argues, and the Court of Appeals held, that unwelcome sexual advances that create an offensive or hostile working environment violate Title VII. Without question, when a supervisor sexually harasses a subordinate because of the subordinate's sex, that supervisor "discriminate[s]" on the basis of sex. Petitioner apparently does not challenge this proposition. It contends instead that in prohibiting discrimination with respect to "compensation, terms, conditions, or privileges" of employment, Congress was concerned with what petitioner describes as "tangible loss" of "an economic character," not "purely psychological aspects of the workplace environment.". . .

We reject petitioner's view. First, the language of Title VII is not limited to "economic" or "tangible" discrimination. The phrase "terms, conditions, or privileges of employment" evinces a congressional intent " 'to strike at the entire spectrum of disparate treatment of men and women' " in employment. . . .Petitioner has pointed to nothing in the Act to suggest that Congress contemplated the limitation urged here.

Second, in 1980 the EEOC issued Guidelines specifying that "sexual harassment," as there defined, is a form of sex discrimination prohibited by Title VII. . . .The EEOC Guidelines fully support the view that harassment leading to noneconomic injury can violate Title VII.

In defining "sexual harassment," the Guidelines first describe the kinds of workplace conduct that may be actionable under Title VII. These include "[u]nwelcome sexual advances, requests for sexual favors, and other verbal or physical conduct of a sexual nature.". . .Relevant to the charges at issue in this case, the Guidelines provide that such sexual misconduct constitutes prohibited "sexual harassment," whether or not it is directly linked to the grant or denial of an economic *quid pro quo*, where "such conduct has the purpose or effect of unreasonably interfering with an individual's work performance or creating an intimidating, hostile, or offensive working environment.". . .

In concluding that so-called "hostile environment" (*i.e.*, non *quid pro quo*) harassment violates Title VII, the EEOC drew upon a substantial body of judicial decisions and EEOC precedent holding that Title VII affords employees the right to work in an environment free from discriminatory intimidation, ridicule, and insult. . . .

Since the Guidelines were issued, courts have uniformly held, and we agree, that a plaintiff may establish a violation of Title VII by proving that discrimination based on sex has created a hostile or abusive work environment. As the Court of Appeals for the Eleventh Circuit wrote in *Henson v. Dundee*, 682 F.2d 897, 902 (1982):

> "Sexual harassment which creates a hostile or offensive environment for members of one sex is every bit the arbitrary barrier to sexual equality at the workplace that racial harassment is to racial equality. Surely, a requirement that a man or woman run a gauntlet of sexual abuse in return for the privilege of being allowed to work and make a living can be as demeaning and disconcerting as the harshest of racial epithets."

. . .Of course,. . .not all workplace conduct that may be described as "harassment" affects a "term, condition, or privilege" of employment within the meaning of Title VII. . . .For sexual harassment to be actionable, it must be sufficiently severe or pervasive "to alter the conditions of [the victim's] employment and create an abusive working environment." *Id.* at 904. Respondent's allegations in this case—which include not only pervasive harassment but also criminal conduct of the most serious nature—are plainly sufficient to state a claim for "hostile environment" sexual harassment.

The question remains, however, whether the District Court's ultimate finding that respondent "was not the victim of sexual harassment,". . .effectively disposed of respondent's claim. The Court of Appeals recognized, we think correctly, that this ultimate finding was likely based on one or both of two erroneous views of the law. First, the District Court apparently believed that a claim for sexual harassment will not lie absent an *economic* effect on the complainant's employment. . . .Since it appears that the District Court made its findings without ever considering the "hostile environment" theory of sexual harassment, the Court of Appeals' decision to remand was correct.

Second, the District Court's conclusion that no actionable harassment occurred might have rested on its earlier "finding" that "[i]f [respondent] and Taylor did engage in an intimate or sexual relationship. . ., that relationship was a voluntary one.". . .But the fact that sex-related conduct was "voluntary," in the sense that the complainant was not forced to participate against her will, is not a defense to a sexual harassment suit brought under Title

VII. The gravamen of any sexual harassment claim is that the alleged sexual advances were "unwelcome.". . .While the question whether particular conduct was indeed unwelcome presents difficult problems of proof and turns largely on credibility determinations committed to the trier of fact, the District Court in this case erroneously focused on the "voluntariness" of respondent's participation in the claimed sexual episodes. The correct inquiry is whether respondent by her conduct indicated that the alleged sexual advances were unwelcome, not whether her actual participation in sexual intercourse was voluntary.

Petitioner contends that even if this case must be remanded to the District Court, the Court of Appeals erred in one of the terms of its remand. Specifically, the Court of Appeals stated that testimony about respondent's "dress and personal fantasies,". . .which the District Court apparently admitted into evidence, "had no place in this litigation.". . .The apparent ground for this conclusion was that respondent's voluntariness *vel non* in submitting to Taylor's advances was immaterial to her sexual harassment claim. While "voluntariness" in the sense of consent is not a defense to such a claim, it does not follow that a complainant's sexually provocative speech or dress is irrelevant as a matter of law in determining whether he or she found particular sexual advances unwelcome. To the contrary, such evidence is obviously relevant. The EEOC Guidelines emphasize that the trier of fact must determine the existence of sexual harassment in light of "the record as a whole" and "the totality of circumstances, such as the nature of the sexual advances and the context in which the alleged incidents occurred.". . .Respondent's claim that any marginal relevance of the evidence in question was outweighed by the potential for unfair prejudice is the sort of argument properly addressed to the District Court. . . .While the District Court must carefully weigh the applicable considerations in deciding whether to admit evidence of this kind, there is no *per se* rule against its admissibility. . . .

Although the District Court concluded that respondent had not proved a violation of Title VII, it nevertheless went on to consider the question of the bank's liability. Finding that "the bank was without notice" of Taylor's alleged conduct, and that notice to Taylor was not the equivalent of notice to the bank, the court concluded that the bank therefore could not be held liable for Taylor's alleged actions. The Court of Appeals took the opposite view, holding that an employer is strictly liable for a hostile environment created by a supervisor's sexual advances, even though the employer neither knew nor reasonably could have known of the alleged misconduct. The court held that a supervisor, whether or not he possesses the authority to hire, fire, or promote, is necessarily an "agent" of his employer for all Title VII purposes, since "even the appearance" of such authority may enable him to impose himself on his subordinates.

The parties and *amici* suggest several different standards for employer liability. Respondent, not surprisingly, defends the position of the Court of Appeals. Noting that Title VII's definition of "employer" includes any "agent" of the employer, she also argues that "so long as the circumstance is work-related, the supervisor is the employer and the employer is the supervisor.". . .Notice to Taylor that the advances were unwelcome, therefore, was notice to the bank.

Petitioner argues that respondent's failure to use its established grievance procedure, or to otherwise put it on notice of the alleged misconduct, insulates petitioner from liability for Taylor's wrongdoing. A contrary rule would be unfair, petitioner argues, since in a hostile environment harassment case the employer often will have no reason to know about, or opportunity to cure, the alleged wrongdoing.

The EEOC, in its brief as *amicus curiae*, contends that courts formulating employer liability rules should draw from traditional agency principles. Examination of those principles has led the EEOC to the view that where a supervisor exercises the authority actually delegated to him by his employer, by making or threatening to make decisions affecting the employment status of his subordinates, such actions are properly imputed to the employer whose delegation of authority empowered the supervisor to undertake them. . . .Thus, the courts have consistently held employers liable for the discriminatory discharges of employees by supervisory personnel, whether or not the employer knew, should have known, or approved of the supervisor's actions. . . .

The EEOC suggests that when a sexual harassment claim rests exclusively on a "hostile environment" theory, however, the usual basis for a finding of agency will often disappear. In that case, the EEOC believes, agency principles lead to

> "a rule that asks whether a victim of sexual harassment had reasonably available an avenue of complaint regarding such harassment, and, if available and utilized, whether that procedure was reasonably responsive to the employee's complaint. If the employer has an expressed policy against sexual harassment and has implemented a procedure specifically designed to resolve sexual harassment claims, and if the victim does not take advantage of that procedure, the employer should be shielded from liability absent actual knowledge of the sexually hostile environment (obtained, *e.g.*, by the filing of a charge with the EEOC or a comparable state agency). In all other cases, the employer will be liable if it has actual knowledge of the harassment or if, considering all the facts of the case, the victim in question had no reasonably available avenue for making his or her complaint known to appropriate management officials." Brief for United States and EEOC as *Amici Curiae* 26.

As respondent points out, this suggested rule is in some tension with the EEOC Guidelines, which hold an employer liable for the acts of its agents without regard to notice. . . .The Guidelines do require, however, an "examin[ation of] the circumstances of the particular employment relationship and the job [f]unctions performed by the individual in determining whether an individual acts in either a supervisory or agency capacity.". . .

This debate over the appropriate standard for employer liability has a rather abstract quality about it given the state of the record in this case. We do not know at this stage whether Taylor made any sexual advances toward respondent at all, let alone whether those advances were unwelcome, whether they were sufficiently pervasive to constitute a condition of employment, or whether they were "so pervasive and so long continuing. . .that the employer must have become conscious of [them],". . .

We therefore decline the parties' invitation to issue a definitive rule on employer liability, but we do agree with the EEOC that Congress wanted courts to look to agency principles for guidance in this area. While such common-law principles may not be transferable in all their particulars to Title VII, Congress' decision to define "employer" to include any "agent" of an employer,. . .surely evinces an intent to place some limits on the acts of employees for which employers under Title VII are to be held responsible. For this reason, we hold that the Court of Appeals erred in concluding that employers are always automatically liable for sexual harassment by their supervisors. See generally Restatement (Second) of Agency §§ 219–237 (1958). For the same reason, absence of notice to an employer does not necessarily insulate that employer from liability. *Id.*

Finally, we reject petitioner's view that the mere existence of a grievance procedure and a policy against discrimination, coupled with respondent's failure to invoke that procedure, must insulate petitioner from liability. While those facts are plainly relevant, the situation before us demonstrates why they are not necessarily dispositive. Petitioner's general nondiscrimination policy did not address sexual harassment in particular, and thus did not alert employees to their employer's interest in correcting that form of discrimination. . . .Moreover, the bank's grievance procedure apparently required an employee to complain first to her supervisor, in this case Taylor. Since Taylor was the alleged perpetrator, it is not altogether surprising that respondent failed to invoke the procedure and report her grievance to him. Petitioner's contention that respondent's failure should insulate it from liability might be substantially stronger if its procedures were better calculated to encourage victims of harassment to come forward. . . .

In sum, we hold that a claim of "hostile environment" sex discrimination is actionable under Title VII, that the District Court's findings were insufficient to dispose of respondent's hostile environment claim, and that the District Court did not err in admitting testimony about respondent's sexually provocative speech and dress. As to employer liability, we conclude that the Court of Appeals was wrong to entirely disregard agency principles and impose absolute liability on employers for the acts of their supervisors, regardless of the circumstances of a particular case.

Accordingly, the judgment of the Court of Appeals reversing the judgment of the District Court is affirmed, and the case is remanded for further proceedings consistent with this opinion.

It is so ordered.

[Justice Stevens joined both the Court's opinion and Justice Marshall's opinion.]

Justice Marshall, with whom Justice Brennan, Justice Blackmun, and Justice Stevens join, concurring in the judgment. I fully agree with the Court's conclusion that workplace sexual harassment is illegal, and violates Title VII. . . .[T]he Court's opinion, however, leaves open the circumstances in which an employer is responsible under Title VII for such conduct. . . .

The issue the Court declines to resolve is addressed in the EEOC Guidelines on Discrimination Because of Sex, which are entitled to great deference. . . .

The Commission, in issuing the Guidelines, explained that its rule was "in keeping with the general standard of employer liability with respect to agents and supervisory employees. . . .[T]he Commission and the courts have held for years that an employer is liable if a supervisor or an agent violates the Title VII, regardless of knowledge or any other mitigating factor.". . .I would adopt the standard set out by the Commission.

An employer can act only through individual supervisors and employees; discrimination is rarely carried out pursuant to a formal vote of a corporation's board of directors. Although an employer may sometimes adopt companywide discriminatory policies violative of Title VII, acts that may constitute Title VII violations are generally effected through the actions of individuals, and often an individual may take such a step even in defiance of company policy. Nonetheless, Title VII remedies, such as reinstatement and backpay, generally run against the employer as an entity. . . .The question thus arises as to the circumstances under which an employer will be held liable under Title VII for the acts of its employees.

The answer supplied by general Title VII law, like that supplied by federal labor law, is that the act of a supervisory employee or agent is imputed to the employer. . . .The courts do not stop to consider whether the employer otherwise had "notice" of the action, or even whether the supervisor had actual authority to act as he did. . . .Following that approach, every Court of Appeals that has considered the issue has held that sexual harassment by supervisory personnel is automatically imputed to the employer when the harassment results in tangible job detriment to the subordinate employee. . . .

The brief filed by the Solicitor General on behalf of the United States and the EEOC in this case suggests that a different rule should apply when a supervisor's harassment "merely" results in a discriminatory work environment. The Solicitor General concedes that sexual harassment that affects tangible job benefits is an exercise of authority delegated to the supervisor by the employer, and thus gives rise to employer liability. But, departing from the EEOC Guidelines, he argues that the case of a supervisor merely creating a discriminatory work environment is different because the supervisor "is not exercising, or threatening to exercise, actual or apparent authority to make personnel decisions affecting the victim.". . .In the latter situation, he concludes, some further notice requirement should therefore be necessary.

The Solicitor General's position is untenable. A supervisor's responsibilities do not begin and end with the power to hire, fire, and discipline employees, or with the power to recommend such actions. Rather, a supervisor is charged with the day-to-day supervision of the work environment and with ensuring a safe, productive workplace. There is no reason why abuse of the latter authority should have different consequences than abuse of the former. . . .There is therefore no justification for a special rule, to be applied *only* in "hostile environment" cases, that sexual harassment does not create employer liability until the employee suffering the discrimination notifies other supervisors. No such requirement appears in the statute, and no such requirement can coherently be drawn from the law of agency. . . .

I therefore reject the Solicitor General's position. I would apply in this case the same rules we apply in all other Title VII cases, and hold that sexual harassment by a supervisor of an employee under his supervision, leading to a discriminatory work environment, should be imputed to the employer for Title VII purposes regardless of whether the employee gave "notice" of the offense.

Notes and Questions

1. *The Intersection of Race and Gender.* The Respondent's Brief argued that Vinson's being African-American was relevant to the claim of sexual harassment.

> All too often, it is Black women like Ms. Vinson who have been specifically victimized by the invidious stereotype of being scandalous and lewd women, perhaps targeting them to would-be perpetrators. This is not to say that this is a case of race discrimination, but rather that minority race aggravates one's vulnerability as a woman by reducing one's options and undermining one's credibility and social worth. In the context of such beliefs, beliefs which animate this case, a picture can be painted which destroys the victim's ability to complain of sexual violation, such that sex acts can be inflicted upon her and nothing will be done about it.

Brief for Respondent at 45-46.

The *amicus curiae* brief of the Working Women's Institute made a similar argument.

> Black women and women who are members of other minority groups are especially vulnerable to sexual harassment, due largely to their inferior economic position. Black women may also be more vulnerable because of their unique place in American history. . . .
>
> Sociological research confirms that black and other minority women are more vulnerable to sexual harassment. The [August, 1985, study published by the Working Women's Institute, entitled "Results of a Survey on Gender Bias and Sexual Harassment in the FAA Eastern Region"] found that Black, Hispanic, and other minority women suffer more sexual harassment than white women. A study of sexual harassment in the automobile industry found that black women not only were harassed more frequently than white women, but also were harassed more severely.

Brief for Amicus Working Women's Institute at 24-26.

The Court, however, ignored these arguments and thereby failed to acknowledge that sexual harassment operates within race *and* gender stereotypes.

It should be additionally noted that the Respondent's Brief obliquely indicates that Taylor was also African-American. *See* Brief for Respondent at 45 n.18. Kimberlé Crenshaw demonstrates how racial specificity is essential to understanding the nature of the sexual harassing conduct.

> The racial specificity is grounded in the fact that there is a certain connection between black men and black women born from a common social history of racial exclusion. Often there is a sense of camaraderie between African Americans, a "we're in this together" sensibility. I call this a zone of familiarity, one that creates expectations of support and mutuality that are essential to survival in a work world that is in some ways alien. . . .However, this zone of familiarity can sometimes be seen as one of privileged sexual access as well. Consequently, one of the workplace dilemmas faced by black women is trying to negotiate between overlapping expectations in this zone, to maintain much-needed relationships but to avoid unwanted intimacy. This camaraderie and the notions of a shared fate make many black women reluctant

> to complain about or even to decisively reject the harasser. No doubt this silence contributes to some degree of confusion as to exactly where the boundaries between desired camaraderie and unwanted intimacy exist.

Kimberlé Crenshaw, Whose Story Is It, Anyway? Feminist and Antiracist Appropriations of Anita Hill, in Race-ing Justice, En-gendering Power: Essays on Anita Hill, Clarence Thomas, and the Construction of Social Reality 402, 426-27 (Toni Morrison ed., 1992). *See also* Maria L. Ontiveros, Three Perspectives on Workplace Harassment of Women of Color, 23 Golden Gate U. L. Rev. 817 (1993) (discussing how the issues of race and culture play a pivotal role in sexual harassment with specific analysis of harassment against African-American women, Asian-American women, and Latinas and of how a woman's immigrant or illegal status affects her reactions to the harassment).

2. *Importing Rape Law into Sexual Harassment Cases*. As we will see in Chapter 6, the last twenty years have produced legislative and procedural reforms designed to reduce the obstacles to the reporting and successful prosecution of rape. The central critique of traditional rape law has been its focus on the conduct of the victim rather than the perpetrator. The Respondent's brief made clear to the Supreme Court how the trial court's analysis of consent reflected a reversion to rape law's tradition of putting the victim's character on trial.

> The trial judge ruled that "if the plaintiff and Taylor did engage in an intimate or sexual relationship. . .[it] was a voluntary one by plaintiff". . .It amounts to an inference of consent although defendant Taylor did not plead consent and no one put on proof of consent. . . .
>
> How might one know that, if a sex act which may or may not have occurred, occurred, the woman did consent to it? This is a metaphysical riddle, not a factual finding. It is nothing other than a ruling that this is a woman who *would* have wanted it, whether it happened or not. As such it is not a finding of fact, it is an assassination of character. It is a reversion to an atavism from the law of rape that "a rape accusation. . .[is] the product of a woman's over-active fantasy life or. . .[the] consequence of a woman's communication of her sexual desires, subtly or otherwise, to a hapless male."

Brief for Respondent at 40-41.

Nevertheless, the *Vinson* Court adopted an analysis of unwelcomeness that was likely to recreate the obstacles for victims of sexual harassment that reform efforts intended to remove for victims of rape.

> [T]he Supreme Court's conclusion that the "gravamen" of a sexual harassment case is unwelcomeness seems all too painfully familiar. On its face, the standard presents at least three serious problems. First, as in rape cases, the focus is on the victim, not on the man: She may be less powerful, and economically dependent, but she still is expected to express unwelcomeness. Unless she does, no burden is placed on him to refrain from abusing his position of power. . . .
>
> The second problem. . .is that "conduct" is the yardstick by which we measure assent. The plain implication is that a polite "no" may not suffice. Though it is bad enough to presume consent in the absence of words, it is worse still to presume it notwithstanding a woman's words.

> Third, and most pernicious of all, since the focus of inquiry is on the plaintiff, and since the unwelcomeness test must be met by her conduct, should we be surprised if the trial focuses on what the plaintiff wears, how she talks, even who else she sleeps with? Whatever unwelcomeness means, the Court in *Vinson* squarely held that a "complainant's sexually provocative speech or dress" is "obviously relevant" in determining whether she found the particular sexual advances unwelcome. . . .
>
> The consequences of this approach are devastating for women. Women are invisible as anything other than potential sexual objects of men—invisible to the Court and, ultimately by its rules, invisible to themselves. And in making the determination of the harassment *of* women dependent upon the extent of "sexually provocative" behavior *by* women, the Court adopts a rule which holds women responsible for their own torment. Thus, the victim of harassment like the rape victim, suffers not only the direct injury of sexual abuse, but also the indignity of the Court's presumption that she is to blame.

Susan Estrich, Sex at Work, 43 Stan. L. Rev. 813, 828-29 (1991) (emphasis in original).

3. *"Welcoming" the Harassment*. The Seventh Circuit in *Reed v. Shepard*, 939 F.2d 484 (7th Cir. 1991) held that a woman employee's toleration and willing participation in "crude shenanigans" prevented her from prevailing on a sexual harassment claim. The plaintiff, who worked as a "civilian jailer" for a county sheriff's department in Indiana, explained her actions in this manner:

> Because it was real important to me to be accepted. It was important for me to be a police officer and if that was the only way that I could be accepted, I would just put up with it and kept [sic] my mouth shut. I had supervisors that would participate in this and you had a chain of command to go through in order to file a complaint. One thing you don't do as a police officer, you don't snitch out [sic] another police officer. You could get hurt. . . .

Id. at 492.

The court held:

> Although Reed suggests that tolerating and contributing to the crudeness of the jail was necessary for her career, other female employees testified that the male jail employees did not behave in this manner around women who asked them not to. . . .This showing that she welcomed the activity is fatal to her claim, particularly where Reed admits that the "harassment" did not adversely affect her ability to do her job.

Id.

Reed's message to women seems to be that, if they act "ladylike," they may obtain the protection of the law. Estrich, however, shows that the unwelcomeness requirement places women in a double bind.

> In practice, both traditional and nontraditional women may find that their own actions are used against them in the unwelcomeness analysis. A woman who behaves in the most stereotypical ways—complimenting men, straightening their ties. . .let alone eating dinner with the boss on a business trip, or remaining friendly even after rejecting his advances—may find that the sexual advances she rejects are, as a matter of law, not unwelcome. Sim-

> ilarly, women who act too much like men—who use "crude and vulgar language," or choose to eat with the men in the employee lunchroom—cannot be heard to complain of a worksite which is "permeated by an extensive amount of lewd and vulgar conversation and conduct." Their "unfeminine" behavior apparently deprives them of protection, whatever the statutory mandate. Like women in rape cases who have sexual pasts, their conduct makes them fair game.
>
> In short, the unwelcomeness requirement performs the doctrinal dirty work of the consent standard in rape law. At a minimum, it shifts the focus from the man to the woman. In too many cases, her conduct is evaluated in terms which see women only as the sexual objects of men. The standard of judgment is painfully male: Women who act like most women—who act "friendly," or dress stylishly, or keep silent—discredit themselves, but no more than do women who act too much like men—who use lewd language, or eat lunch with the boys. The apparent difficulty that many judges have finding the deserving victim raises the question whether, at least in some courts, the very point of the inquiry might be in effect to protect a broad category of sexual relations in the workplace, so long as these relations appear, at least to the men judging them, typical and acceptable.

Estrich, *supra*, at 830-31.

Although Estrich concludes that the unwelcomeness standard makes most women for one reason or another undeserving of protection, that does not mean it does not operate in disparate ways against women. How does the unwelcomeness standard permit the interjection of negative stereotypes into the adjudication of sexual harassment?

4. *"Why Didn't She Leave?"* One of the arguments used to attack the credibility of Anita Hill during the Thomas confirmation hearings was her decision to continue to work for him at the Department of Education and to move with him to the EEOC. Martha Mahoney, based on her study of separation assault (p. 247), considers the dangers of the view that resigning from a job is the appropriate response to sexual harassment.

> Once exit is defined as the appropriate response to abuse, then staying can be treated as evidence that abuse never happened. If abuse is asserted, "failure" to exit must then be explained. When that "failure" becomes the point of inquiry, explanation in law and popular culture tends to emphasize victimization and implicitly deny agency in the person who has been harmed. . . .
>
> In addition to indirectly promoting victimization, a focus on exit is directly opposed to the idea of resistance. In love and work, women build lives under conditions of inequality, and whatever we find of success, security, love and companionship is built on or against unequal ground. Exit proposes that one should leave, rather than hold on to what has been gained. In battering, this stigmatizes women's efforts to make viable families out of the raw material handed them by a profoundly sexist and violent society. In sexual harassment, the secrecy surrounding the abuse and the social expectation that women will react by departing create a "death before dishonor" mentality that denies respect to the stubborn determination to keep the job. . . .
>
> If agency among the oppressed is judged only by effectuated change, it is defined almost out of existence. The acting, aware self is often realized in love

> and in work through resistance against oppression, survival, and partial victories—like women who "just deal with" harassment, or women who seek to hold on to marriages without violence. Or—even closer to the experience of many women—the self is realized though a *combination* of accommodation and resistance, through private resistance chosen because oppression itself simultaneously makes exit difficult and open resistance impractical.

Martha Mahoney, Exit: Power and the Idea of Leaving in Love, Work, and the Confirmation Hearings, 65 S. Cal. L. Rev. 1283, 1285, 1311, 1313 (1992) (emphasis in original).

5. *Evidentiary Rules*. The Court of Appeals in *Vinson* found clear error in the trial court's exclusion of some evidence intended to show that Taylor sexually harassed other women at the bank. That ruling was not disputed before the Supreme Court. How might allowing evidence of the defendant's harassment of other employees lead to negative consequences for plaintiffs?

6. *Liability of Employer*. The *Vinson* Court essentially adopted the position put forward by the EEOC in its *amicus curiae* brief that an employer should be held strictly liable for a supervisor's behavior in cases of quid pro quo harassment but less than strictly liable in hostile environment situations. Does the distinction between quid pro quo and work environment harassment by supervisors make sense?

7. *Damages*. Until recently, Title VII provided prevailing plaintiff's with compensation for lost wages, but no compensatory or punitive damages. Employees who brought sexual harassment suits at great emotional and monetary costs, could obtain only injunctive relief and up to two years' back pay and attorneys fees.

Vinson is illustrative of the barriers faced by plaintiffs who bring sexual harassment suits. Mechelle Vinson filed her complaint in 1978 and it was not until 1986 that the Supreme Court remanded the case to the district court. After further proceedings in the district court over another half decade, a final stipulated order dismissing the action was filed on August 22, 1991. *See* Vinson v. Taylor, Civ. Docket for No. 78-CV-1793 (D. D.C.). In a telephone conversation on August 4, 1993, Eloise Kehler, law clerk for Joseph Sellers, one of the attorneys for Vinson, stated that the matter had been settled.

Congress found that additional remedies were needed to deter unlawful intentional discrimination. Under the Civil Rights Act of 1991, plaintiffs can recover compensatory damages. Punitive damages are also available if the defendant engaged in discriminatory practices with malice or with reckless indifference to the federally protected rights of the aggrieved individual. The total amount of recovery, however, is limited depending on the size of the employer. For employers of 14-100 employees, maximum damages are set at $50,000; employers of 101-200 employees, $100,000; employers of 201-500 employees, $200,000; and for employers of over 500 employees, maximum damages are set at $300,000. 42 U.S.C. § 1981a (b) (Supp. III 1992).

The tax treatment of recipients of employment discrimination awards and settlements has been heavily litigated recently under section 104(a)(2) of the Internal Revenue Code. For example the Supreme Court's 1992 decision in *U.S. v. Burke*, 112 S. Ct. 1867 (1992) held that amounts received in settlement of sex discrimination in employment claims under Title VII were not excludable from taxation. It reasoned that exclusion under the section is available only if the taxpayer satisfies the requirement in the Regulations that the amounts be received on account of tort or tort-type liabilities and that, because Title VII permitted only equitable relief and not compensatory or punitive damages, violation of Title VII did not impose a tort-type liability.

The amended Title VII would seem to meet the criterion established in *Burke* to exclude a damages award; the court's opinion in *Burke* suggests as much. A related development, however, is the amendment to section 104 in the Omnibus Budget Reconciliation Act of 1989 that precludes exclusion from taxation of punitive damages received in cases not involving physical injury or sickness. This development and the overarching controversy about taxation of discrimination awards undermine the validity of the harm caused by discrimination. They make it seem that compensation for discrimination is an undeserved windfall. The controversies reinforce the frequently disproved but tenaciously believed notion that physical injury is the only real proof of harm. Coincidental with the tax controversies was the emergence of an array of remedies for discrimination and courtroom successes, raising the question whether the Internal Revenue Service's [IRS] and Congress' position is good tax policy or bad discrimination policy.

To date, the IRS has not disputed the appropriateness of employers treating the payment of damages for discriminatory practices as a cost of doing business, thereby a deductible expense. An argument can be made, based on public policy grounds, for the nondeductibility of damages paid by employers for having discriminated. *See* Marvin A. Chirelstein, Federal Income Taxation 118-19 (6th ed., 1991).

8. *Other Legal Avenues*. Legal avenues other than a Title VII action are available to a complainant. As the facts in *Vinson* indicate, some conduct constituting sexual harassment under Title VII is also criminal, such as rape or assault. Civil actions under tort law also are available to an employee who has been sexually harassed. The basis of these suits will vary depending on the nature of the conduct, but the torts most likely to be applicable are battery, assault, and intentional infliction of emotional distress. The tort law, however, requires victims of sexual harassment to overcome significant obstacles.

> It was assumed that persons of ordinary sensibilities (that is, persons very much like the male decision-makers) would not be offended by conduct common in the workplace. Moreover, limitations on recovery of damages for emotional distress absent physical injury prevented sexually harassed women from recovering even though the barrage of offensive remarks and conduct they had to endure was obviously damaging to their mental health. In addition, the tort of battery can do little for those women who have not actually been touched, or for those who, out of fear of losing their jobs or their homes, engaged in intercourse in a way that appeared consensual and thus seemed to negate the required tort element of an "offensive" contact. The doctrinal requirements of tort law have been ill-suited to recognizing the kinds of harm women experience when they are sexually harassed.

Lucinda Finley, A Break in the Silence: Including Women's Issues in a Torts Course, 41 Yale J.L. & Feminism 41, 55-56 (1989).

How might the obstacles found in tort law affect each plaintiff differently depending on her abilities, class, race/ethnicity, and sexual orientation? What are the advantages and disadvantages of using tort law remedies rather than the public law remedy provided under Title VII?

9. *Sexual Harassment and the Trades.* Elvia Arriola argues that the law of sexual harassment has provided more protection for women in middle-class, white-collar work settings than for women who work in non-traditional, blue-collar fields. One significant reason for the differential impact is that the trades have remained almost exclusively male and white.

> Although all women experienced pervasive sexism, tradeswomen of color appeared most vulnerable. Plumber Carolyn Nowodzinski is white and from a working-class background. . . .Nowodzinski recalls that black tradeswomen and tradesmen were frequently assigned to the worst locations and the most difficult and dangerous jobs. Gladys Lopez, a Puerto Rican apprentice, says that in her nine years as an electrician she experienced both sexual and racial discrimination—"most of the time" because of her skin color. For example, her apprenticeship director once told her to "get a job as a cook like your father; you're not cut out for this business."
>
> Union officials frequently transferred a woman from one construction site to another, rather than deal with her complaints of harassment, intimidation and racial or sexual discrimination. The most vulnerable tradeswoman was the apprentice. Gladys Lopez remembers frequently being assigned to "coffee duty;" she also describes being laid-off during her six-month probation period on grounds that she was "not suited for this type of work." In fact, frequent layoffs kept many women, especially women of color, from fulfilling the requirements of their apprenticeships . . . .
>
> While in certain respects the experience of sexual harassment in the construction industry was no different from the experience of sexual harassment in white-collar settings, a study of sexual harassment in the construction industry reveals how deeply embedded masculine values were in blue-collar work culture. The mere presence of a woman in a hardhat threatened the masculine assumptions of male physical superiority on which the culture was based because masculine attitudes subordinated women to men. . . .Tradeswomen, who could do a "man's job" competently, were perceived as threats to the heterosexual social order. As a result, male workers viewed most of the early tradeswomen as "unfeminine"; they verbally attacked the women as "dykes." Those women who actually were lesbian had to hide their identities or endure expressions of intense male hostility. . . .
>
> By ignoring or penalizing women who complained of or reacted to extreme male sexual taunts, the construction industry became a "hostile work environment" for pioneer tradeswomen. By the early 1980s, while lawsuits brought by women in the white-collar sector were strengthening the jurisprudential trend that was started in the late 1970s, the frequently isolated tradeswomen had no public or private recourse for help. Consequently, out of fear or a sense of futility, many tradeswomen tolerated aggressive behavior aimed at displaying or preserving masculine superiority. One of Cyn-

> thia Long's transfers resulted from an incident involving a male co-worker who asked her for a date every day for two months. One day, as she stood on a ladder and he described a "wet dream" he had about her, Long finally "blew up" and threw a hammer at him. Long was off the job the next day. . . .Gladys Lopez does not remember ever being sexually touched or teased, but recalls that men were "constantly dropping their pants in front of [her]."

Elvia R. Arriola, "What's the Big Deal?" Women in the New York City Construction Industry and Sexual Harassment Law, 1970-1985, 22 Colum. Hum. Rts. L. Rev. 21, 58-59, 61-62 (1990).

The relationship of discrimination in hiring and discrimination through sexual harassment in the trades was explored in expert testimony in *Robinson v. Jacksonville Shipyards, Inc.*, 760 F. Supp. 1486 (M.D. Fla. 1991), *appeal docketed*, No. 91-3655 (11th Cir. July 12, 1991) (decision stayed pending action by Supreme Court), which held the employer liable for maintaining a hostile work environment. The plaintiff, Lois Robinson, had been a welder since 1977 and was one of a very small number of female skilled craftworkers employed by Jacksonville Shipyards. (In 1980, the employer reported employing 2 women and 958 men as skilled craftworkers. 760 F. Supp. at 1493.) She sued her employer under Title VII for creating and encouraging a hostile work environment. The race of the plaintiff and the racial makeup of the work force were not indicated in the court's opinion. The shipyard was tellingly described by male employees as a "boys club" and as "more or less a man's world." The "boys club" consisted of pictures of naked or partially naked women and pornographic photographs and plaques, including a picture of a woman's pubic area with a meat spatula pressed on it and a dart board depicting a woman's breast with the nipple as the bull's eye. After Robinson and other women complained, male employees retaliated by bringing in more pornography and by targeting Robinson with abusive graffiti and verbal abuse. Dr. Susan Fiske appeared as an expert witness on the plaintiff's behalf and testified that the

> sex stereotyping at JSI [w]as a situation of "sex role spillover," where the evaluation of women employees by their coworkers and supervisors takes place in terms of the sexuality of the women and their worth as sex objects rather than their merit as craft workers.

Id. at 1503.

Dr. Fiske described the necessary preconditions for the presence of stereotyping, one of which is "rarity."

> "Rarity" exists when an individual's group is small in number in relation to its contrasting group, so that each individual member is seen as one of a kind—a solo or near solo. Rarity or "solo" status exists when an individual's group comprises fifteen to twenty percent or less of the work force in the relevant work environment. . . .
>
> Solos capture the attention of the members of the majority group, providing fodder for their rumors and constantly receiving their scrutiny. . . .The solo is far more likely to become the victim of stereotyping than a member of the majority group, and the stereotype develops along the dimension that makes

the solos rare. . . .Solos typically elicit extreme responses from members of the majority group.

Id.

Another related precondition is the work environment structure.

This factor examines the group affiliation of the persons in the positions of power and the degree to which particular groups are given a sense of belonging. At JSI, this precondition arises because the people affected by the sexualized working conditions are women and the people deciding what to do about it are men. The in-group/out-group effect diminishes the impact of the women's concerns.

Id. at 1504.

The experience of women in the trades clearly demonstrates that heterosexism, racism, and sexual harassment function to preserve the dominance of white males in the workplace.

10. *The Bisexual Sexual Harasser.* Title VII liability for sexual harassment requires a showing of differential treatment—*i.e.*, a showing that women are treated differently from men. One rationale that was suggested in the past for why sexual harassment should not lead to Title VII liability is the possibility of sexual harassment of both women and men by a bisexual person.

Perhaps some of the doctrinal difficulty in this area is due to the awkwardness of classifying sexual advances as "discrimination.". . .It is "discrimination" if a man makes unwanted sexual overtures to a woman, a woman to a man, a man to another man, or a woman to another woman. But this court has twice stated that Title VII does *not* prohibit sexual harassment by a "bisexual superior [because] the insistence upon sexual favors would. . .apply to male and female employees alike." *Barnes v. Costle*, 561 F.2d 983, 990 n.55 (D.C. Cir. 1977); *Bundy v. Jackson*, 641 F.2d 934, 942 n.7 (D.C. Cir. 1981). Thus, this court holds that only the differentiating libido runs afoul of Title VII, and bisexual harassment, however blatant and however offensive and disturbing, is legally permissible. Had Congress been aiming at sexual harassment, it seems unlikely that a woman would be protected from unwelcome heterosexual or lesbian advances but left unprotected when a bisexual attacks. That bizarre result suggests that Congress was not thinking of individual harassment at all but of discrimination in conditions of employment because of gender.

Vinson v. Taylor, 760 F.2d 1330, 1330, 1333 n.7 (D.C. Cir. 1985), *denying reh'g en banc* 752 F.2d 141 (D.C. Cir. 1985), *aff'd Meritor Savings Bank, FSB v. Vinson*, 477 U.S. 57 (1986) (Bork, J., dissenting joined by Scalia and Starr, JJ.)(emphasis in original).

Catharine MacKinnon showed in her 1979 book *Sexual Harassment of Working Women: A Case of Sex Discrimination* that this argument takes seriously the sexual harassment of no one and fails to recognize that this type of harassment for both female and male victims is discrimination based on their sex.

[T]his argument. . .attempts to turn the possibility of gay (or bisexual) harassment into a reason that no likely victim, neither gays nor women, should be protected: because any prohibition would cover gays, women

> should not be covered from harassment by men. This attempt fails as a *reductio* the moment protecting both is recognized as not absurd.
>
> As a matter of law, no area of discrimination doctrine has ever required that because allegedly discriminatory treatment *could* be leveled equally against another group, when it is leveled against one, the reversed possibility destroys the group referent. Instead, the whole reason that discrimination can be "arbitrary" is that other groups could be, but are not, so treated. . . .
>
> In no case of alleged racial discrimination has the possibility that whites *could* be discriminated against in the same way prevented a finding of race discrimination when in fact only blacks were so treated. In fact, this possibility is what makes the treatment "arbitrary": it could be done to whites or men, but is done only to blacks or women. . . .
>
> By the logic of the differences argument, if a sexual condition of employment were imposed equally upon both women and men by the same employer, the practice would no longer constitute sex discrimination because it would not be properly based on the gender difference. Title VII, as interpreted, does not concern itself with abuses of human sexuality, only with impermissible differential consequences of the gender distinction in employment. Arguably, a sexual requirement placed on both a man and a woman would not have the same impact upon each.

Catharine A. MacKinnon, Sexual Harassment of Working Women: A Case of Sex Discrimination 201-03 (1979) (emphasis in original).

11. *Claims by Accused Harassers Against Employers.* Accused harassers have sued their employers after the employers have taken disciplinary action against them. Employees have sued claiming defamation, wrongful discharge, deprivation of due process, intentional infliction of mental distress, and breach of contract. *See*, *e.g.*, Scherer v. Rockwell Int'l Corp., 975 F.2d 356 (7th Cir. 1992).

The success of these claims is, of course, dependent on the specific facts of each individual case. Nonetheless, the bringing of these suits raises concerns about the willingness of employers adequately to discipline employees who are found to have engaged in sexual harassment. From the employer's point of view, if the employer's response to a sexual harassment claim was inadequate, equivocal, or dilatory, the complainant may bring a successful Title VII claim. If its response was too vigorous, however, the alleged harasser may bring a successful civil suit. The Civil Rights Act of 1991, which expands the monetary remedies available to the complainant, may encourage the employer to act in a manner to avoid Title VII liability notwithstanding the risk of civil suit by the alleged harasser. *See* Note 7, at p. 318.

Stephanie Riger, Gender Dilemmas in Sexual Harassment Policies and Procedures, 46 Am. Psychologist 497, 499-503 (1991)

Typically, procedures for resolving disputes about sexual harassment are written in gender-neutral terms so that they may apply to both women and men. However, men and women may react quite differently to the same procedures.

Analyzing this problem requires looking at specific policies and procedures. Educational institutions will serve as the context for this discussion for three reasons. First, they are the most frequent site of surveys about the problem, and the pervasive nature of harassment on campuses has been well documented. Second, although sexual harassment is harmful to women in all occupations, it can be particularly devastating to those in educational institutions, in which the goal of the organization is to nurture and promote development. The violation of relationships based on trust, such as those between faculty and students, can leave long-lasting and deep wounds, yet many surveys find that those in positions of authority in educational settings are often the source of the problem. Third, educational institutions have been leaders in the development of sexual harassment policies, in part because of concern about litigation. . . .

Although women may prefer informal mechanisms, they are problematic for several reasons. Because they do not result in punishment, offenders suffer few negative consequences of their actions and may not be deterred from harassing again. In institutions of higher learning, the most common form of punishment reported is a verbal warning by a supervisor, which is given only "sometimes." Dismissal and litigation are almost never used. It seems likely, then, that sexual harassment may be viewed by potential harassers as low-risk behavior, and that victims see few incentives for bringing official complaints.

The confidentiality usually required by informal procedures prevents other victims from knowing that a complaint has been lodged against a multiple offender. If a woman knows that another woman is bringing a complaint against a particular man who has harassed both of them, then she might be more willing to complain also. The secrecy surrounding informal complaint processes precludes this information from becoming public and makes it more difficult to identify repeat offenders. Also, complaints settled informally may not be included in reports of the frequency of sexual harassment claims, making these statistics underestimate the scope of the problem. Yet confidentiality is needed to protect the rights of the accused and may be preferred by those bringing complaints.

These problems in informal procedures could discourage male as well as female victims from bringing complaints. Most problematic for women, however, is the assumption in informal procedures that the complainant and accused have equal power in the process of resolving the dispute. This assumption is likely to put women at a disadvantage. Parties involved in sexual harassment disputes may not be equal either in the sense of formal position within the organization (e.g., student versus faculty) or status (e.g., female versus male students), and position and status characteristics that reflect levels of power do not disappear simply because they are irrelevant to the informal process. External status characteristics that indicate macrolevel social stratification (e.g., sex and age) help explain the patterns of distribution of sexual harassment in the workplace. It seems likely that these external statuses will influence the interpersonal dynamics within a dispute-resolution procedure as well. Because women are typically lower than men in both formal and informal status and power in organizations, they will have less power in the dispute resolution process.

When the accused has more power than the complainant (e.g., a male faculty member accused by a female student), the complainant is more vulnerable to retaliation. Complainants may be reluctant to use grievance procedures because they fear retaliation should the charge be made public. For example, students may fear that a faculty member will punish them for bringing a complaint by lowering their grades or withholding recommendations. The person appointed to act as a guide to the informal resolution process is usually expected to act as a neutral third party rather than advocate for the complainant, and may hold little formal power over faculty: "Relatively few institutions have persons empowered to be (nonlegal) advocates for the complainants; a student bringing a complaint has little assurance of stopping the harassment and avoiding retaliation." The victim then is left without an advocate to face an opponent whose formal position, age, and experience with verbal argument is often considerably beyond her own. The more vulnerable a woman's position is in her organization, the more likely it is that she will be harassed; therefore sexual harassment, like rape, involves dynamics of power and domination as well as sexuality. The lack of an advocate for the complainant who might equalize power between the disputing parties is particularly troubling. However, if an advocate is provided for the complainant in an informal process, fairness and due process require that the defendant have an advocate as well. The dilemma is that this seems likely to transform an informal, problem-solving process into a formal, adversarial one. . . .

In academic settings, harassment can adversely affect students' learning, and therefore their academic standing. It can deprive them of educational and career opportunities because they wish to avoid threatening situations. Students who have been harassed report that they consequently avoid taking a class from or working with a particular faculty member, change their major, or leave a threatening situation. Lowered self-esteem follows the conclusion that rewards, such as a high grade, may have been based on sexual attraction rather than one's abilities. Decreased feelings of competence and confidence and increased feelings of anger, frustration, depression, and anxiety all can result from harassment. The psychological stress produced by harassment is compounded when women are fired or quit their jobs in fear or frustration.

[Researchers have] proposed that victims of harassment typically go through several stages of reaction, at first questioning the offender's true intentions and then blaming themselves for the offender's behavior. Women with traditional sex-role beliefs are more likely to blame themselves for being harassed. Victims then worry about being believed by others and about possible retaliation if they take formal steps to protest the behavior. A victim may be too frightened or confused to assert herself or punish the offender. Psychologists who work with victims of harassment would do well to recognize that not only victims' emotional reactions but also the nature of the grievance process as discussed in this article may discourage women from bringing formal complaints. . . .

However, education alone is not sufficient. Sexual harassment is the product not only of individual attitudes and beliefs, but also of organizational practices. [Researchers have] described aspects of educational institutions that facilitate sexual harassment, including the autonomy afforded the faculty, the diffusion of authority that permits lack of accountability, and the shortage of women in positions of authority. Researchers are beginning to identify the practices in other work settings that facilitate or support sexual harassment, and suggest that sexual harassment may be part of a pattern of unprofessional and disrespectful attitudes and behaviors that characterizes some workplaces.

Perhaps the most important factor in reducing sexual harassment is an organizational culture that promotes equal opportunities for women. There is a strong negative relationship between the level of perceived equal employment opportunity for women in a company and the level of harassment reported: Workplaces low in perceived equality are the site of more frequent incidents of harassment. This finding suggests that sexual harassment both reflects and reinforces the underlying sexual inequality that produces a sex-segregated and sex-stratified occupational structure. The implementation of sexual harassment policies demonstrates the seriousness of those in authority; the language of the policies provides some measure of clarity about the types of behavior that are not acceptable; and grievance procedures may provide relief and legitimacy to those with complaints. But neither policies nor procedures do much to weaken the structural roots of gender inequalities in organizations.

Reforms intended to ameliorate women's position sometimes have unintended negative consequences. The presence of sexual harassment policies and the absence of formal complaints might promote the illusion that this problem has been solved. Assessment of whether organizational policies and practices promote or hinder equality for women is required to insure that this belief does not prevail. A long-range strategy for organizational reform in academia would thus attack the chilly climate for women in classrooms and laboratories, the inferior quality of athletic programs for women, differential treatment of women applicants, the acceptance of the masculine as normative, and a knowledge base uninfluenced by women's values or experience. In other work settings, such a long-range approach would attack both sex-segregation of occupations and sex-stratification within authority hierarchies. Sexual harassment grievance procedures alone are not sufficient to insure that sexual harassment will be eliminated. An end to this problem requires gender equity within organizations.

Ellison v. Brady,

924 F.2d 872 (9th Cir. 1991)

Beezer, C.J. Kerry Ellison appeals the district court's order granting summary judgment to the Secretary of the Treasury on her sexual harassment action brought under Title VII of the Civil Rights Act of 1964. . . .This appeal presents two important issues: (1) what test should be applied to determine whether conduct is sufficiently severe or pervasive to alter the conditions of employment and create a hostile working environment, and (2) what remedial actions can shield employers from liability for sexual harassment by co-workers. The district court held that Ellison did not state a prima facie case of hostile environment sexual harassment. We reverse and remand. . . .

Kerry Ellison worked as a revenue agent for the Internal Revenue Service in San Mateo, California. During her initial training in 1984 she met Sterling

Gray, another trainee, who was also assigned to the San Mateo office. The two co-workers never became friends, and they did not work closely together.

Gray's desk was twenty feet from Ellison's desk, two rows behind and one row over. Revenue agents in the San Mateo office often went to lunch in groups. In June of 1986 when no one else was in the office, Gray asked Ellison to lunch. She accepted. Gray had to pick up his son's forgotten lunch, so they stopped by Gray's house. He gave Ellison a tour of his house.

Ellison alleges that after the June lunch Gray started to pester her with unnecessary questions and hang around her desk. On October 9, 1986, Gray asked Ellison out for a drink after work. She declined, but she suggested that they have lunch the following week. She did not want to have lunch alone with him, and she tried to stay away from the office during lunch time. One day during the following week, Gray uncharacteristically dressed in a three-piece suit and asked Ellison out for lunch. Again, she did not accept.

On October 22, 1986 Gray handed Ellison a note he wrote on a telephone message slip which read:

> I cried over you last night and I'm totally drained today. I have never been in such constant term oil [sic]. Thank you for talking with me. I could not stand to feel your hatred for another day.

When Ellison realized that Gray wrote the note, she became shocked and frightened and left the room. Gray followed her into the hallway and demanded that she talk to him, but she left the building.

Ellison later showed the note to Bonnie Miller, who supervised both Ellison and Gray. Miller said "this is sexual harassment." Ellison asked Miller not to do anything about it. She wanted to try to handle it herself. Ellison asked a male co-worker to talk to Gray, to tell him that she was not interested in him and to leave her alone. The next day, Thursday, Gray called in sick.

Ellison did not work on Friday, and on the following Monday, she started four weeks of training in St. Louis, Missouri. Gray mailed her a card and a typed, single-spaced, three-page letter. She describes this letter as "twenty times, a hundred times weirder" than the prior note. Gray wrote, in part:

> I know that you are worth knowing with or without sex. . . .Leaving aside the hassles and disasters of recent weeks. I have enjoyed you so much over these past few months. Watching you. Experiencing you from O so far away. Admiring your style and elan. . . .Don't you think it odd that two people who have never even talked together, alone, are striking off such intense sparks. . .I will [write] another letter in the near future.[3]

Explaining her reaction, Ellison stated: "I just thought he was crazy. I thought he was nuts. I didn't know what he would do next. I was frightened."

She immediately telephoned Miller. Ellison told her supervisor that she was frightened and really upset. She requested that Miller transfer either her or Gray because she would not be comfortable working in the same office with him. Miller asked Ellison to send a copy of the card and letter to San Mateo.

Miller then telephoned her supervisor, Joe Benton, and discussed the prob-

3. In the middle of the long letter Gray did say "I am obligated to you so much that if you want me to leave you alone I will. . . .If you want me to forget you entirely, I can not do that."

lem. That same day she had a counseling session with Gray. She informed him that he was entitled to union representation. During this meeting, she told Gray to leave Ellison alone.

At Benton's request, Miller apprised the labor relations department of the situation. She also reminded Gray many times over the next few weeks that he must not contact Ellison in any way. Gray subsequently transferred to the San Francisco office on November 24, 1986. Ellison returned from St. Louis in late November and did not discuss the matter further with Miller.

After three weeks in San Francisco, Gray filed union grievances requesting a return to the San Mateo office. The IRS and the union settled the grievances in Gray's favor, agreeing to allow him to transfer back to the San Mateo office provided that he spend four more months in San Francisco and promise not to bother Ellison. On January 28, 1987, Ellison first learned of Gray's request in a letter from Miller explaining that Gray would return to the San Mateo office. The letter indicated that management decided to resolve Ellison's problem with a six-month separation, and that it would take additional action if the problem recurred.

After receiving the letter, Ellison was "frantic." She filed a formal complaint alleging sexual harassment on January 30, 1987 with the IRS. She also obtained permission to transfer to San Francisco temporarily when Gray returned.

Gray sought joint counseling. He wrote Ellison another letter which still sought to maintain the idea that he and Ellison had some type of relationship.[4]

The IRS employee investigating the allegation agreed with Ellison's supervisor that Gray's conduct constituted sexual harassment. In its final decision, however, the Treasury Department rejected Ellison's complaint because it believed that the complaint did not describe a pattern or practice of sexual harassment covered by the EEOC regulations. After an appeal, the EEOC affirmed the Treasury Department's decision on a different ground. It concluded that the agency took adequate action to prevent the repetition of Gray's conduct.

Ellison filed a complaint in September of 1987 in federal district court. The court granted the government's motion for summary judgment on the ground that Ellison had failed to state a prima facie case of sexual harassment due to a hostile working environment. Ellison appeals. . . .

The parties ask us to determine if Gray's conduct, as alleged by Ellison, was sufficiently severe or pervasive to alter the conditions of Ellison's employment and create an abusive working environment. The district court, with little Ninth Circuit case law to look to for guidance, held that Ellison did not state a prima facie case of sexual harassment due to a hostile working environment. It believed that Gray's conduct was "isolated and genuinely trivial." We disagree. . . .

The EEOC guidelines describe hostile environment harassment as "conduct [which] has the purpose or effect of unreasonably interfering with an individual's work performance or creating an intimidating, hostile, or offensive working environment.". . .The EEOC, in accord with a substantial body of judicial decisions, has concluded that "Title VII affords employees the right

---

4. It is unclear from the record on appeal whether Ellison received the third letter.

to work in an environment free from discriminatory intimidation, ridicule, and insult." *Meritor Savings Bank v. Vinson*, 477 U.S. 57, 65 (1986).

The Supreme Court cautioned, however, that not all harassment affects a "term, condition, or privilege" of employment within the meaning of Title VII. For example, the "mere utterance of an ethnic or racial epithet which engenders offensive feelings in an employee" is not, by itself, actionable under Title VII. *Id.* at 67. To state a claim under Title VII, sexual harassment "must be sufficiently severe or pervasive to alter the conditions of the victim's employment and create an abusive working environment." *Id.* . . .

Although *Meritor* and our previous cases establish the framework for the resolution of hostile environment cases, they do not dictate the outcome of this case. Gray's conduct falls somewhere between forcible rape and the mere utterance of an epithet. 477 U.S. at 60, 67. . . .

The government asks us to apply the reasoning of other courts which have declined to find Title VII violations on more egregious facts. In *Scott v. Sears, Roebuck & Co.*, 798 F.2d 210, 212 (7th Cir. 1986), the Seventh Circuit analyzed a female employee's working conditions for sexual harassment. It noted that she was repeatedly propositioned and winked at by her supervisor. When she asked for assistance, he asked "what will I get for it?" Co-workers slapped her buttocks and commented that she must moan and groan during sex. The court examined the evidence to see if "the demeaning conduct and sexual stereotyping cause[d] such anxiety and debilitation to the plaintiff that working conditions were 'poisoned' within the meaning of Title VII." *Id.* at 213. The court did not consider the environment sufficiently hostile. *Id.* at 214.

Similarly, in *Rabidue v. Osceola Refining Co.*, 805 F.2d 611 (6th Cir. 1986), *cert. denied*, 481 U.S. 1041 (1987), the Sixth Circuit refused to find a hostile environment where the workplace contained posters of naked and partially dressed women, and where a male employee customarily called women "whores," "cunt," "pussy," and "tits," referred to plaintiff as "fat ass," and specifically stated, "All that bitch needs is a good lay." Over a strong dissent, the majority held that the sexist remarks and the pin-up posters had only a de minimis effect and did not seriously affect the plaintiff's psychological well-being.

We do not agree with the standards set forth in *Scott* and *Rabidue*,. . .and we choose not to follow those decisions.[5] Neither *Scott*'s search for "anxiety and debilitation" sufficient to "poison" a working environment nor *Rabidue*'s requirement that a plaintiff's psychological well-being be "seriously affected" follows directly from language in *Meritor*.[6] It is the harasser's conduct which must be pervasive or severe, not the alteration in the conditions of employment. Surely, employees need not endure sexual harassment until their psychological well-being is seriously affected to the extent that they suffer anxiety and debilitation. . . .Although an isolated epithet by itself fails to support a cause

5. We note that unlike this case, the plaintiffs in *Scott* and *Rabidue* alleged that a hostile working environment contributed to their discharge. We need not and do not address how or whether a discharge would alter our analysis.

6. As we explained earlier, the Supreme Court in *Meritor* implicitly adopted the EEOC's position that sexual harassment which unreasonably interferes with work performance violates Title VII. 477 U.S. at 65. Conduct can unreasonably interfere with work performance without causing debilitation and without seriously affecting an employee's psychological well-being. . . .

of action for a hostile environment, Title VII's protection of employees from sex discrimination comes into play long before the point where victims of sexual harassment require psychiatric assistance.

We have closely examined *Meritor* and our previous cases, and we believe that Gray's conduct was sufficiently severe and pervasive to alter the conditions of Ellison's employment and create an abusive working environment. We first note that the required showing of severity or seriousness of the harassing conduct varies inversely with the pervasiveness or frequency of the conduct. *See King v. Board of Regents of University of Wisconsin System*, 898 F.2d 533, 537 (7th Cir. 1990) ("[a]lthough a single act can be enough,. . .generally, repeated incidents create a stronger claim of hostile environment, with the strength of the claim depending on the number of incidents and the intensity of each incident."). . .

Next, we believe that in evaluating the severity and pervasiveness of sexual harassment, we should focus on the perspective of the victim. . . .If we only examined whether a reasonable person would engage in allegedly harassing conduct, we would run the risk of reinforcing the prevailing level of discrimination. Harassers could continue to harass merely because a particular discriminatory practice was common, and victims of harassment would have no remedy.

We therefore prefer to analyze harassment from the victim's perspective. A complete understanding of the victim's view requires, among other things, an analysis of the different perspectives of men and women. Conduct that many men consider unobjectionable may offend many women. *See, e.g., Lipsett v. University of Puerto Rico*, 864 F.2d 881, 898 (1st Cir. 1988) ("A male supervisor might believe, for example, that it is legitimate for him to tell a female subordinate that she has a 'great figure' or 'nice legs.' The female subordinate, however, may find such comments offensive"). . .*See also* Ehrenreich, *Pluralist Myths and Powerless Men: The Ideology of Reasonableness in Sexual Harassment Law*, 99 Yale L.J. 1177, 1207-1208 (1990) (men tend to view some forms of sexual harassment as "harmless social interactions to which only overly-sensitive women would object"); Abrams, *Gender Discrimination and the Transformation of Workplace Norms*, 42 Vand. L. Rev. 1183, 1203 (1989) (the characteristically male view depicts sexual harassment as comparatively harmless amusement).

We realize that there is a broad range of viewpoints among women as a group, but we believe that many women share common concerns which men do not necessarily share.[7] For example, because women are disproportionately

---

7. One writer explains: "While many women hold positive attitudes about uncoerced sex, their greater physical and social vulnerability to sexual coercion can make women wary of sexual encounters. Moreover, American women have been raised in a society where rape and sex-related violence have reached unprecedented levels, and a vast pornography industry creates continuous images of sexual coercion, objectification and violence. Finally, women as a group tend to hold more restrictive views of both the situation and type of relationship in which sexual conduct is appropriate. Because of the inequality and coercion with which it is so frequently associated in the minds of women, the appearance of sexuality in an unexpected context or a setting of ostensible equality can be an anguishing experience." Abrams, Gender Discrimination and the Transformation of Workplace Norms, 42 Vand. L. Rev. 1183, 1205 (1989).

victims of rape and sexual assault, women have a stronger incentive to be concerned with sexual behavior. . . .Women who are victims of mild forms of sexual harassment may understandably worry whether a harasser's conduct is merely a prelude to violent sexual assault. Men, who are rarely victims of sexual assault, may view sexual conduct in a vacuum without a full appreciation of the social setting or the underlying threat of violence that a woman may perceive.

In order to shield employers from having to accommodate the idiosyncratic concerns of the rare hyper-sensitive employee, we hold that a female plaintiff states a prima facie case of hostile environment sexual harassment when she alleges conduct which a reasonable woman[8] would consider sufficiently severe or pervasive to alter the conditions of employment and create an abusive working environment.[9]. . .

We adopt the perspective of a reasonable woman primarily because we believe that a sex-blind reasonable person standard tends to be male-biased and tends to systematically ignore the experiences of women. The reasonable woman standard does not establish a higher level of protection for women than men. . . .Instead, a gender-conscious examination of sexual harassment enables women to participate in the workplace on an equal footing with men. By acknowledging and not trivializing the effects of sexual harassment on reasonable women, courts can work towards ensuring that neither men nor women will have to "run a gauntlet of sexual abuse in return for the privilege of being allowed to work and make a living." *Henson v. Dundee*, 682 F.2d 897, 902 (11th Cir. 1982).

We note that the reasonable victim standard we adopt today classifies conduct as unlawful sexual harassment even when harassers do not realize that their conduct creates a hostile working environment. Well-intentioned compliments by co-workers or supervisors can form the basis of a sexual harassment cause of action if a reasonable victim of the same sex as the plaintiff would consider the comments sufficiently severe or pervasive to alter a condition of employment and create an abusive working environment.[10] That is because Title VII is not a fault-based tort scheme. . . .To avoid liability under Title VII, employers may have to educate and sensitize their workforce to eliminate conduct which a reasonable victim would consider unlawful sexual harassment. . . .

The facts of this case illustrate the importance of considering the victim's perspective. Analyzing the facts from the alleged harasser's viewpoint, Gray could be portrayed as a modern-day Cyrano de Bergerac wishing no more than

8. Of course, where male employees allege that co-workers engage in conduct which creates a hostile environment, the appropriate victim's perspective would be that of a reasonable man.

9. We realize that the reasonable woman standard will not address conduct which some women find offensive. Conduct considered harmless by many today may be considered discriminatory in the future. . . .Fortunately, the reasonableness inquiry which we adopt today is not static. As the views of reasonable women change, so too does the Title VII standard of acceptable behavior.

10. If sexual comments or sexual advances are in fact welcomed by the recipient, they, of course, do not constitute sexual harassment. Title VII's prohibition of sex discrimination in employment does not require a totally desexualized work place.

to woo Ellison with his words.[11] There is no evidence that Gray harbored ill will toward Ellison. He even offered in his "love letter" to leave her alone if she wished. Examined in this light, it is not difficult to see why the district court characterized Gray's conduct as isolated and trivial.

Ellison, however, did not consider the acts to be trivial. Gray's first note shocked and frightened her. After receiving the three-page letter, she became really upset and frightened again. She immediately requested that she or Gray be transferred. Her supervisor's prompt response suggests that she too did not consider the conduct trivial. When Ellison learned that Gray arranged to return to San Mateo, she immediately asked to transfer, and she immediately filed an official complaint.

We cannot say as a matter of law that Ellison's reaction was idiosyncratic or hyper-sensitive. We believe that a reasonable woman could have had a similar reaction. After receiving the first bizarre note from Gray, a person she barely knew, Ellison asked a co-worker to tell Gray to leave her alone. Despite her request, Gray sent her a long, passionate, disturbing letter. He told her he had been "watching" and "experiencing" her; he made repeated references to sex; he said he would write again. Ellison had no way of knowing what Gray would do next. A reasonable woman could consider Gray's conduct, as alleged by Ellison, sufficiently severe and pervasive to alter a condition of employment and create an abusive working environment.

Sexual harassment is a major problem in the workplace. . . .Adopting the victim's perspective ensures that courts will not "sustain ingrained notions of reasonable behavior fashioned by the offenders." *Lipsett*, 864 F.2d at 898, *quoting*, *Rabidue*, 805 F.2d at 626 (Keith, J., dissenting). Congress did not enact Title VII to codify prevailing sexist prejudices. . . .We hope that over time both men and women will learn what conduct offends reasonable members of the other sex. When employers and employees internalize the standard of workplace conduct we establish today, the current gap in perception between the sexes will be bridged. . . .

[The court then considered the question of what remedial actions by employers would shield them from liability under Title VII for sexual harassment by co-workers.]

We reverse the district court's decision that Ellison did not allege a prima facie case of sexual harassment due to a hostile working environment, and we remand for further proceedings consistent with this opinion. Although we have considered the evidence in the light most favorable to Ellison because the district court granted the government's motion for summary judgment, we, of course, reserve for the district court the resolution of all factual issues.

Reversed and Remanded.

Stephens, D.J., dissenting. . . .I believe that [this]. . .is an inappropriate case with which to establish a new legal precedent which will be binding in all subsequent cases of like nature in the Ninth Circuit. I refer to the majority's use of the term "reasonable woman," a term I find ambiguous and therefore inadequate.

11. E. Rostand, Cyrano de Bergerac (B. Hooker trans., 1963).

Nowhere in. . .Title VII. . .is there any indication that Congress intended to provide for any other than equal treatment in the area of civil rights. The legislation is designed to achieve a balanced and generally gender neutral and harmonious workplace which would improve production and the quality of the employees' lives. In fact, the Supreme Court has shown a preference against systems that are not gender or race neutral, such as hiring quotas. . . .While women may be the most frequent targets of this type of conduct that is at issue in this case, they are not the only targets. I believe that it is incumbent upon the court in this case to use terminology that will meet the needs of all who seek recourse under this section of Title VII. Possible alternatives that are more in line with a gender neutral approach include "victim," "target" or "person."

The term "reasonable man" as it is used in the law of torts, traditionally refers to the average adult person, regardless of gender, and the conduct that can reasonably be expected of him or her. For the purposes of the legal issues that are being addressed, such a term assumes that it is applicable to all persons. Section 2000e of Title VII presupposes the use of a legal term that can apply to all persons and the impossibility of a more individually tailored standard. It is clear that the authors of the majority opinion intend a difference between the "reasonable woman" and the "reasonable man" in Title VII cases on the assumption that men do not have the same sensibilities as women. This is not necessarily true. A man's response to circumstances faced by women and their effect upon women can be and in given circumstances may be expected to be understood by men.

It takes no stretch of the imagination to envision two complaints emanating from the same workplace regarding the same conditions, one brought by a woman and the other by a man. Application of the "new standard" presents a puzzlement which is born of the assumption that men's eyes do not see what a woman sees through her eyes. I find it surprising that the majority finds no need for evidence on any of these subjects. I am not sure whether the majority also concludes that the woman and the man in question are also reasonable without evidence on this subject. . . .

The focus on the victim of the sexually discriminatory conduct has its parallel in rape trials in the focus put by the defense on the victim's conduct rather than on the unlawful conduct of the person accused. Modern feminists have pointed out that concentration by the defense upon evidence concerning the background, appearance and conduct of women claiming to have been raped must be carefully controlled by the court to avoid effectively shifting the burden of proof to the victim. It is the accused, not the victim who is on trial, and it is therefore the conduct of the accused, not that of the victim, that should be subjected to scrutiny. . . .Many state legislatures have responded to this viewpoint, and rules governing the presentation of evidence in rape cases have evolved accordingly. . . .

The circumstances existing in the work place [*sic*] where only men are employed are different than they are where there are both male and female employees. The existence of the differences is readily recognizable and the conduct of employees can be changed appropriately. This is what Title VII requires. Whether a man or a woman has sensibilities peculiar to the person and what they are is not necessarily known. Until they become known by manifesting themselves in an obvious way, they do not become part of the circumstances of the work place [*sic*]. Consequently, the governing element in the equation is the workplace itself, not concepts or viewpoints of individual employees. This does not conflict with existing legal concepts.

The creation of the proposed "new standard" which applies only to women will not necessarily come to the aid of all potential victims of the type of misconduct that is at issue in this case. I believe that a gender neutral standard would greatly contribute to the clarity of this and future cases in the same area. . . .

Harris v. Forklift Systems, Inc.,

62 U.S.L.W. 4004 (U.S. Nov. 9, 1993)

Justice O'Connor delivered the opinion of the Court. In this case we consider the definition of a discriminatorily "abusive work environment" (also known as a "hostile work environment") under Title VII of the Civil Rights Act of 1964 . . . .

Teresa Harris worked as a manager at Forklift Systems, Inc., an equipment rental company, from April 1985 until October 1987. Charles Hardy was Forklift's president.

The Magistrate found that, throughout Harris' time at Forklift, Hardy often insulted her because of her gender and often made her the target of unwanted sexual innuendos. Hardy told Harris on several occasions, in the presence of other employees, "You're a woman, what do you know" and "We need a man as the rental manager"; at least once, he told her she was "a dumb ass woman.". . .Again in front of others, he suggested that the two of them "go to the Holiday Inn to negotiate [Harris'] raise.". . .Hardy occasionally asked Harris and other female employees to get coins from his front pants pocket. . . . He threw objects on the ground in front of Harris and other women, and asked them to pick the objects up. . . . He made sexual innuendos about Harris' and other women's clothing. . . .

In mid-August 1987, Harris complained to Hardy about his conduct. Hardy said he was surprised that Harris was offended, claimed he was only joking, and apologized. . . .He also promised he would stop, and based on this assurance Harris stayed on the job. . . . But in early September, Hardy began anew: While Harris was arranging a deal with one of Forklift's customers, he asked her, again in front of other employees, "What did you do, promise the guy. . .some [sex] Saturday night?". . .On October 1, Harris collected her paycheck and quit.

Harris then sued Forklift, claiming that Hardy's conduct had created an abusive work environment for her because of her gender. The United States District Court for the Middle District of Tennessee, adopting the report and recommendation of the Magistrate, found this to be "a close case,". . .but held that Hardy's conduct did not create an abusive environment. The court found that some of Hardy's comments "offended [Harris], and would offend the reasonable woman,". . .but that they were not

> "so severe as to be expected to seriously affect [Harris'] psychological well-being. A reasonable woman manager under like circumstances would have

been offended by Hardy, but his conduct would not have risen to the level of interfering with that person's work performance.

"Neither do I believe that [Harris] was subjectively so offended that she suffered injury. . . . Although Hardy may at times have genuinely offended [Harris], I do not believe that he created a working environment so poisoned as to be intimidating or abusive to [Harris].". . .

In focusing on the employee's psychological well-being, the District Court was following Circuit precedent. See *Rabidue v. Osceola Refining Co.*, 805 F.2d 611, 620 (6th Cir. 1986), cert. denied, 481 U.S. 1041 (1987). The United States Court of Appeals for the Sixth Circuit affirmed in a brief unpublished decision.

We granted certiorari. . .to resolve a conflict among the Circuits on whether conduct, to be actionable as "abusive work environment" harassment. . .must "seriously affect [an employee's] psychological well-being" or lead the plaintiff to "suffe[r] injury." Compare *Rabidue* (requiring serious effect on psychological well-being). . ., with *Ellison v. Brady*, 924 F.2d 872, 877-78 (9th Cir. 1991) (rejecting such a requirement). . . .

Title VII. . .makes it "an unlawful employment practice for an employer. . .to discriminate against any individual with respect to his compensation, terms, conditions, or privileges of employment, because of such individual's race, color, religion, sex, or national origin.". . .As we made clear in *Meritor Savings Bank v. Vinson*, 477 U.S. 57 (1986), this language "is not limited to 'economic' or 'tangible' discrimination. The phrase 'terms, conditions, or privileges of employment' evinces a congressional intent 'to strike at the entire spectrum of disparate treatment of men and women' in employment," which includes requiring people to work in a discriminatorily hostile or abusive environment. . . . When the workplace is permeated with "discriminatory intimidation, ridicule, and insult," *id.* at 65, that is "sufficiently severe or pervasive to alter the conditions of the victim's employment and create an abusive working environment," *id.* at 67. . ., Title VII is violated.

This standard, which we reaffirm today, takes a middle path between making actionable any conduct that is merely offensive and requiring the conduct to cause a tangible psychological injury. As we pointed out in *Meritor*, "mere utterance of an. . .epithet which engenders offensive feelings in a employee,". . .does not sufficiently affect the conditions of employment to implicate Title VII. Conduct that is not severe or pervasive enough to create an objectively hostile or abusive work environment—an environment that a reasonable person would find hostile or abusive—is beyond Title VII's purview. Likewise, if the victim does not subjectively perceive the environment to be abusive, the conduct has not actually altered the conditions of the victim's employment, and there is no Title VII violation.

But Title VII comes into play before the harassing conduct leads to a nervous breakdown. A discriminatorily abusive work environment, even one that does not seriously affect employees' psychological well-being, can and often will detract from employees' job performance, discourage employees from remaining on the job, or keep them from advancing in their careers. Moreover, even without regard to these tangible effects, the very fact that the discriminatory conduct was so severe or pervasive that it created a work environment abusive to employees because of their race, gender, religion, or national origin offends Title VII's broad rule of workplace equality. The appalling conduct alleged in *Meritor*, and the reference in that case to environments " 'so heavily polluted with discrimination as to destroy completely the emotional and psychological stability of minority group workers,' " *supra*, at 66. . .merely present some especially egregious examples of harassment. They do not mark the boundary of what is actionable.

We therefore believe the District Court erred in relying on whether the conduct "seriously affect[ed] plaintiff's psychological well-being" or led her to "suffe[r] injury." Such an inquiry may needlessly focus the fact-finder's attention on concrete psychological harm, an element Title VII does not require. Certainly Title VII bars conduct that would seriously affect a reasonable person's psychological well-being, but the statute is not limited to such conduct. So long as the environment would reasonably be perceived, and is perceived, as hostile or abusive, *Meritor*, *supra*, at 67, there is no need for it also to be psychologically injurious.

This is not, and by its nature cannot be, a mathematically precise test. We need not answer today all the potential questions it raises, nor specifically address the EEOC's new regulations on this subject . . . .But we can say that whether an environment is "hostile" or "abusive" can be determined only by looking at all the circumstances. These may include the frequency of the discriminatory conduct; its severity; whether it is physically threatening or humiliating, or a mere offensive utterance; and whether it unreasonably interferes with an employee's work performance. The effect on the employee's psychological well-being is, of course, relevant to determining whether the plaintiff actually found the environment abusive. But while psychological harm, like any other relevant factor, may be taken into account, no single factor is required. . . .

Forklift, while conceding that a requirement that the conduct seriously affect psychological well-being is unfounded, argues that the District Court nonetheless correctly applied the *Meritor* standard. We disagree. Though the District Court did conclude that the work environment was not "intimidating or abusive to [Harris],". . .it did so only after finding that the conduct was not "so severe as to be expected to seriously affect plaintiff's psychological well-being,". . .and that Harris was not "subjectively so offended that she suffered injury,". . . . The District Court's application of these incorrect standards may well have influenced its ultimate conclusion, especially given that the court found this to be a "close case,". . . .

We therefore reverse the judgment of the Court of Appeals, and remand the case for further proceedings consistent with this opinion. *So ordered.*

Justice Scalia, concurring. *Meritor Savings Bank v. Vinson*. . .held that Title VII prohibits sexual harassment that takes the form of a hostile work environment. The Court stated that sexual harassment is actionable if it is "sufficiently severe or pervasive 'to alter the conditions of [the victim's] employment and create an abusive work environment.'" *Id.* at 67. . . .Today's opinion elaborates that the challenged conduct must be severe or pervasive enough "to create an objectively hostile or abusive work environment—an environment that a reasonable person would find hostile or abusive.". . .

"Abusive" (or "hostile," which in this context I take to mean the same thing) does not seem to me a very clear standard—and I do not think clarity is at all increased by adding the adverb "objectively" or by appealing to a "reasonable person's" notion of what the vague word means. Today's opinion does list a number of factors that contribute to abusiveness,. . .but since it neither says how much of each is necessary (an impossible task) nor identifies any single factor as determinative, it thereby adds little certitude. As a practical matter, today's holding lets virtually unguided juries decide whether sex-related conduct engaged in (or permitted by) an employer is egregious enough to warrant an award of damages. One might say that what constitutes "negligence" (a traditional jury question) is not much more clear and certain than what constitutes "abusiveness." Perhaps so. But the class of plaintiffs seeking to recover for negligence is limited to those who have suffered harm, whereas under this statute "abusiveness" is to be the test of whether legal harm has been suffered, opening more expansive vistas of litigation.

Be that as it may, I know of no alternative to the course the Court today has taken. One of the factors mentioned in the Court's nonexhaustive list—whether the conduct unreasonably interferes with an employee's work performance—would, if it were made an absolute test, provide greater guidance to juries and employers. But I see no basis for such a limitation in the language of the statute. Accepting *Meritor*'s interpretation of the term "conditions of employment" as the law, the test is not whether work has been impaired, but whether working conditions have been discriminatorily altered. I know of no test more faithful to the inherently vague statutory language than the one the Court today adopts. For these reasons, I join the opinion of the Court.

Justice Ginsburg, concurring. Today the Court reaffirms the holding of *Meritor Savings Bank v. Vinson* . . . .The critical issue, Title VII's text indicates, is whether members of one sex are exposed to disadvantageous terms or conditions of employment to which members of the other sex are not exposed. . . . As the Equal Employment Opportunity Commission emphasized . . .[in its *amici curiae* brief], the adjudicator's inquiry should center, dominantly, on whether the discriminatory conduct has unreasonably interfered with the plaintiff's work performance. To show such interference, "the plaintiff need not prove that his or her tangible productivity has declined as a result of the harassment." *Davis v. Monsanto Chemical Co.*, 858 F.2d 345, 349 (6th Cir. 1988). It suffices to prove that a reasonable person subjected to the discriminatory conduct would find, as the plaintiff did, that the harassment so altered working conditions as to "ma[k]e it more difficult to do the job." See *id*. Davis concerned race-based discrimination, but that difference does not alter the analysis; except in the rare case in which a bona fide occupational qualification is shown, . . .Title VII declares discriminatory practices based on race, gender, religion, or national origin equally unlawful.*

The Court's opinion, which I join, seems to me in harmony with the view expressed in this concurring statement.

---

* Indeed, even under the Court's equal protection jurisprudence, which requires "an exceedingly persuasive justification" for a gender-based classification, . . .it remains an open question whether "classifications based upon gender are inherently suspect." See Mississippi Univ. for Women v. Hogan, 458 U.S. 718, 724, and n.9 (1982).

Notes and Questions

1. *Reasonable Woman/Reasonable Person Standard. Ellison* was the leading case supporting the reasonable woman standard, *see also* Burns v. McGregor Elec. Inc., FEP Cases (BNA) 592 (8th Cir. 1993); Andrews v. City of Phila., 895 F.2d 1469 (3d Cir. 1990); Robinson v. Jacksonville Shipyards, Inc., 760 F. Supp. 1486 (M.D. Fla. 1991), *appeal docketed*, No. 91-3655 (11th Cir. July 12, 1991) (decision stayed pending action by the Supreme Court), and was viewed generally as reflecting a progressive development in the law of sexual harassment. *See* Susan Estrich, Sex at Work, at p. 342; B. Glenn George, The Back Door: Legitimizing Sexual Harassment Claims, at p. 345-46. The petitioner in *Harris* argued that "the severity or pervasiveness of offensive conduct can be viewed from a totality of the circumstances without resorting to any reasonableness standard." Brief for Petitioner at 29. In the alternative, the petitioner argued that the appropriate standard to apply is "the reasonable person in the position of the plaintiff" and not the "gender-neutral reasonable person standard." *Id.* at 34-35, 36. The respondent argued that the appropriate standard was the reasonable person, but that in any event the Court need not address the issue because the "magistrate in this case based his determination on the perspective of '[a] reasonable woman manager under like circumstances.'" Brief for Respondent at 29-30, 29 n.15. The Court did not specifically address the appropriateness of either standard but appeared to apply the reasonable person standard. What are the advantages and disadvantages of the *Harris* Court not adopting the reasonable woman standard?

2. *Effect on Job Performance.* How does Justice Ruth Bader Ginsburg's treatment of the effects on job performance as an element in proving a Title VII violation differ from Justice Sandra Day O'Connor's?

3. *The First Amendment Defense.* The respondent in *Harris* argued that the First Amendment requires that "Title VII [not]. . .be construed to prohibit all speech that may be sexually offensive . . . ." *Id.* at 32. Petitioner in her Reply Brief argued that First Amendment concerns did not need to be addressed because petitioner was not advocating an offensiveness standard and the facts of this case involved sex-based workplace conduct that was sufficiently severe and pervasive to alter the conditions of Teresa Harris' employment. The *Harris* Court apparently agreed with petitioner that the First Amendment was not implicated in this case. Although not addressed in *Harris*, First Amendment issues are likely to arise in future sexual harassment cases.

The court in *Robinson v. Jacksonville Shipyards, Inc.*, 760 F. Supp. 1486 (M.D. Fla. 1991), *appeal docketed*, No. 91-3655 (11th Cir. July 12, 1991) (decision stayed pending action by Supreme Court), described in Note 9, at p. 321, rejected the defendant's claim that the sexually explicit pictures and magazines and verbal comments were protected from regulation by the First Amendment. Other circuits have held that pornographic material in the workplace is evidence of a hostile work environment. *See, e.g., Andrews v. City of Phila.*, 895 F.2d 1469 (3d Cir. 1990); *Waltman v. Int'l Paper Co.*, 875 F.2d 468 (5th Cir. 1989).

Those who defend against a claim of a hostile work environment on the basis of the First Amendment rely on *R.A.V. v. City of St. Paul*, 112 S. Ct. 2538

(1992), which held that a city ordinance, which prohibited the display of a symbol which one knows or has reason to know arouses anger, alarm, or resentment in others on the basis of race, color, creed, religion, or gender, was unconstitutional. This "hate-speech" ordinance arguably prohibited some of the same type of expressions that Title VII, as interpreted by the courts, is designed to regulate. *See* Kingsley R. Browne, Title VII as Censorship: Hostile-Environment Harassment and the First Amendment, 52 Ohio St. L.J. 481 (1991). They also rely on *American Bookseller Ass'n v. Hudnut*, at p. 612, which held unconstitutional a municipal ordinance creating a civil cause of action for persons harmed by pornographic material.

Those who claim pornographic material contributes to a hostile work environment in violation of Title VII view the First Amendment's prohibition against regulation of speech as inapplicable to offensive expression in the workplace. Whatever the appropriate balance is in the general society between being free from the harm of pornography and having freedom of expression, the workplace is not an arena of nonregulated speech. Employers can and do limit workplace expression. In fact, in *Robinson* the employer required prior approval for posting any kind of material except calendars with pictures of naked women. *See* 760 F. Supp. at 1499. In addition, the workplace provides a captive audience not only because workers' ability to escape offensive expression may be limited by their economic needs but also because the design of workplaces typically do not permit a worker to avoid the offensive material. The workplace argument is essentially an argument for finding an accommodation between First Amendment rights of free expression and the right of equal employment opportunities.

Women's experiences in the workplace make clear the interconnections among sexual harassment, pornography, and subordination of women based on abilities, class, race/ethnicity, and sexual orientation. These interconnections will be further explored in Chapter 8.

Susan Estrich, Sex at Work, 43 Stan. L. Rev. 813, 831–34, 836, 838–47 (1991)

The strongest justification for the welcomeness doctrine is that the rule ensures that consensual workplace sex does not provide the basis for a civil action. The more radical response to this argument is that there is no such thing as truly "welcome" sex between a male boss and a female employee who needs her job. And if there is, then the women who welcome it will not be bringing lawsuits in any event. . . .

One need not adopt the more radical approach, however, to reject the welcomeness inquiry as unnecessary. The fact is that in both the quid pro quo and the hostile environment cases, additional requirements exist for proving that sex is harassment, making the unwelcomeness inquiry superfluous, and leaving no justification for the burden it imposes.

Consider, first, the case of quid pro quo harassment. In such a case, the woman is required to establish a direct connection between her acceptance or rejection of sexual advances and a job benefit or loss. The prototype fact pattern is simple: If you sleep with me, you'll be promoted; if you don't you'll be fired. The question of whether such a bargain is "welcomed" by the woman should startle even those who reject the more radical approach to workplace sex. Even if you believe that I might freely consent to sex with my supervisor in some other circumstances, can free will exist in the face of coercion?. . .

Nothing in Title VII requires one to afford protection to such an employer. When a boss threatens (or if you believe in welcomeness, "offers") to fire you if you don't sleep with him, or promote you if you do, we are not dealing simply with workplace sex, welcome or not. Sex in this context determines the conditions of employment. Title VII leaves the employer free to hire or fire for any reason he chooses other than sex; here, it is plainly sex—both the gender of the offeree, which renders her subject to such a bargain, and the very terms of the bargain—that functions as the basis for the employment decision. And this is so regardless of welcomeness. . . .

Thus, eliminating unwelcomeness as an element in quid pro quo cases would not, for better or worse, bar sex that many men and some women might consider welcome or consensual. Rather, doing so would prohibit only conditioning job benefits upon sex. The man who chooses to make the workplace his sexplace would in theory remain free to do so. He would simply be barred from using extortion—threats of harm and promises of benefit—to win his welcome.

Unwelcomeness is no more necessary in hostile environment cases, although for different reasons. The irony of the hostile environment case is that the subjective welcomeness inquiry, gravamen or not, is fundamentally at odds with all the other elements of the cause of action. A hostile environment, the courts have consistently held, must be based on objective criteria, evaluated from an "objective" viewpoint. The fact that a particular woman found the environment totally debilitating is beside the point; the question is what other persons, often mythic, would think. Thus the welcomeness inquiry is either utterly gratuitous or gratuitously punitive. It is gratuitous when the environment is not proven objectively to be hostile, because an unwelcome environment which is not objectively hostile does not give rise to liability in any event. It is gratuitously punitive if the environment is found objectively hostile, for in that case the employer can nonetheless escape the burden of addressing the issue, by portraying this particular woman as so base as to be unworthy of respect or decency, and by arguing that she thus welcomed, through her conduct, an environment which a "reasonable" woman would have perceived as hostile. In either case, welcomeness serves as a means to keep the focus on the woman rather than the supervisor; on what she, rather than he, has done wrong; and on whether *she* deserves to be treated with human decency, rather than whether *he* violated the standards of decency and humanity. . . .

The plaintiff in a quid pro quo case is not required, as a hostile environment claimant is, to prove that the harassment is pervasive and objectively intolerable. In practice, less harassment is necessary to satisfy the threshold requirement of a quid pro quo case.

There is, not surprisingly, a catch: While the quid pro quo plaintiff need not establish that harassment was pervasive, she faces two obstacles so substantial as to spell failure for many claimants. First, she must establish the existence of an actual threat. Second, she must prove that her reaction to the threat, rather than some other factor, resulted in her firing or demotion. In practice, these obstacles produce a working definition of quid pro quo harassment that may be so narrow as to make all but the most perfect plaintiffs unable to establish the requisite nexus, and all but the most perfectly stupid defendants able to rebut successfully a prima facie case. . . .

For a fired employee, the real question is not whether she is perfect, but whether her sexual rejection of her boss played a role in his concluding that she is not [a perfect employee]. Or, to frame the inquiry in a more telling way, *would she still have been fired if she had said yes?*. . .

What is troubling is. . .the judges' simplistic presumption that an employer can evaluate a woman's "qualifications" wholly apart from the sexual interactions that occurred, and that a court can and should do similarly. And what is so disappointing about these opinions in practice is that their embrace of this artificial meritocracy leaves all but the most ideal women without protection from sexual blackmail at work. Real women—women who are sometimes tardy, sometimes slow, and rarely perfect—are vulnerable women. . . .

Neither law nor policy commands such a result in sexual harassment cases. If the goal is to protect all women from sexual blackmail, and there is no basis to argue that it should be anything less, then the governing doctrines should be structured to serve that goal, and not to protect sexual access to everyone who might later be termed "unqualified." This means that we should find a prima facie case of sexual harassment whenever a woman can establish that she was subjected to an adverse employment action—whether she was fired, demoted, or not promoted—and that she rejected sexual advances of her superior. The law should impose on the employer the burden of showing not simply that she was "unqualified," but that the adverse action would have been taken even if she had said yes to sex.

Such a rule would be a significant advance for women in two respects. First, it would relieve them of the obligation of proving the elusive nexus between their responses to their bosses' propositions and the deprivation of an economic benefit. Instead it would place the burden of proving the absence of a nexus on the employer. Second, it would require the blackmailer or his employer to bear the responsibility for his blackmail: If an employer chooses to make sex a positive consideration in employment decisions, then all women should be entitled to the benefit, *regardless of whether they say yes or no*.

To be sure, an employer under this rule would be less free to fire than if he had never resorted to sexual extortion in the first place. So be it. No one forced him to engage in blackmail. Surely the law does not need to *encourage* sex in the workplace, let alone do so by affirmatively protecting sexual blackmail. . . .

At least two obstacles regularly complicate hostile environment lawsuits, in addition to the unwelcomeness gravamen. First, the woman must prove that the offensive conduct was "based upon sex." Second, she must show that the harassment was "sufficiently pervasive so as to alter the conditions of employment and create an abusive working environment.". . .

While the test is often stated, in legal terms, as whether the harassment is "equally offensive" to both sexes, it is often applied in practice as a question of whether the action is itself sexual. Presumably, nonsexual acts are directed at both men and women, and are equally offensive to both. Sexual acts, by contrast, are directed at women and are offensive only to them. Such a test might work for women if "sexual" acts were broadly defined, and viewed from a woman's perspective. The problem is that courts tend to define "sexual" very narrowly, based on a man's view of a man's acts. . . .

When criminal penalties are imposed, and mens rea required, one expects to hear the argument that the law should require a blameworthy choice by the man. Thus, it is said, his perspective, narrowly construed, should define the offense. Even that argument, however, is not necessarily irrefutable: If negligence is sufficient to give rise to criminal liability, as it is in some areas of the law, then the question should be not what the man thought was reasonable, but what we as a society decide is reasonable. And there is nothing inherently reasonable about a perspective which maximizes both sexual access of men and sexual injury to women.

If there are strong reasons for adopting a reasonableness standard in the criminal law, and I believe there are, these grounds are even more persuasive in the civil context, where the very purpose of the law is to protect women, and where the deprivation of liberty and the stigma inherent in criminal punishment are absent. Why, after all, should the courts protect a man's right to maul women? This is the only "right" to be lost if courts presume what most women would indeed assume: that being touched by a man is different than being touched by a woman, and that as a rule, men should keep their hands off. . . .

The second obstacle women complainants face is the requirement that they prove that the harassment is sufficiently severe or pervasive. . . .

Certainly the pervasiveness of the harassment should be relevant to the question of what relief is appropriate: For example, was the harassment sufficiently severe as to result in a constructive discharge of the plaintiff? But it does not inevitably follow that there is no harm in harassing, so long as it is sporadic.

One justification for the pervasiveness requirement seems, plainly, that every workplace insult should not be treated, quite literally, as a federal case. But in defining what counts as trivial or "de minimis," many courts have wrongly looked to social interaction outside the workplace as the standard, ignoring not only the "captive audience" nature of the employment context but also the fact that "society" hardly reflects a normative standard which women have had an equal role in shaping. . . .

A second and related justification for the pervasiveness requirement may be the recognition by federal courts that what even *they* would consider nontrivial harassment is itself pervasive in the workplace. . . .

The early federal courts recognized the highly sexualized atmosphere of many workplaces, and cited it as a reason not to afford protection under Title VII. More recent decisions that have reached the opposite result. . .have done so by stressing the limited application of Title VII action to only the most extreme cases of sexual harassment.

But the fact that a hazard is widespread should be a reason to ban it, not to tolerate it. The greater the number of women who are exposed to sexual harassment, the more of a reason strict standards are needed. . . .

Formally, the pervasiveness test is wholly objective: The harassment must be "so significant a factor that the average female employee finds that her overall work experience is substantially and adversely affected by the conduct."[12] . . .

[The] cases illustrate at least two problems . . . .First, for at least some of the courts, the objective standard of pervasiveness is defined by an idealized woman who simply may not exist. Such a woman is tough, not "hypersensitive"; she is aggressive, not passive. Such a woman complains in a way that effectively stops the harassment. Such a woman does not suffer in silence or confide only in other women. In short, the "reasonable woman" is very much a man. . . .

Moreover, even those courts that base their standard on the reactions of real women—of the particular plaintiff, or of others in the workplace—end up with a definition of pervasiveness that is often no broader than that of courts which cling to the idealized model. Few of these courts recognize that the extent to which women react to insults, propositions, and physical abuse may have far less to do with the severity of the harassment than with the need of women to keep their jobs. . . .

In truth, the "strongest" women may simply be the most needy, and the reality is that most working women are needy women.

Because courts fail to recognize this, or perhaps choose not to, many courts in hostile environment cases end up. . .translating the tolerance of powerless women for offensive conditions into a normative standard of acceptable workplace conduct. Thus, what the powerless must tolerate because of their need becomes what the law defines as acceptable conduct.

And yet, the very point of Title VII—indeed, the only point—should be to ensure that precisely this kind of "tolerance" by the powerless *not* define the prerogatives of the powerful. That women would be "willing" to work with hazardous chemicals, or for subminimum pay, or for fifty hours without overtime, is hardly a justification for those unlawful working conditions. Because the market does not protect women against these conditions, the law does. So, too, for discrimination—at least in theory. But the pervasiveness requirement, particularly as it has been most strictly interpreted, signals our (or at least judges') unwillingness to clearly state that sexual insults have no place on the worksite. Sexual harassment, unlike sweatshop conditions, remains an acceptable aspect of the American workplace.

It is one thing to believe that an isolated trivial comment should not give rise to a federal lawsuit; it is quite another to limit the hostile environment test so as to shield all but the most extremely offensive workplaces from even the possibility of liability. To be sure, the wrong should determine the remedy. But by holding that short of pervasiveness there is no wrong *at all*, courts have stripped the Title VII action of its teeth. And what is worse is that they have done so by taking women's neediness and turning it against them, mak-

---

12. Rabidue v. Osceola Ref. Co., 584 F. Supp. 419, 433 (E.D. Mich. 1984), *aff'd*, 805 F.2d 611 (6th Cir. 1986), *cert. denied*, 481 U.S. 1041 (1987).

ing women responsible under the law for the insults and abuse hurled at them.

B. Glenn George, The Back Door: Legitimizing Sexual Harassment Claims, 73 B.U.L. Rev. 1, 3, 19–24, 26, 28–33 (1993)

This Article proposes that courts elevate sexual harassment claims to the same front door status as other types of Title VII discrimination claims. If sexual harassment is indeed sex discrimination, then its prima facie case should be modeled closely after the prima facie case for other kinds of discrimination. . . .

To place hostile environment claims on a more equal footing with other kinds of Title VII claims, I propose a simpler framework. If a plaintiff proves that she is subjected to different working conditions than her male colleagues, she makes a prima facie case without regard to the triviality of the offense or the plaintiff's response to the behavior. As an affirmative defense, the employer may prevail by establishing that the plaintiff "welcomed" the behavior through specific words or gestures to which the supervisor responded *in kind*. . . .

By far the most difficult requirement for a hostile environment claimant to meet is establishing that the more elusive kinds of verbal and visual harassment are indeed "conditions of employment." The EEOC Guidelines require that "such conduct ha[ve] the purpose or effect of unreasonably interfering with an individual's work performance *or* creating an intimidating, hostile, or offensive working environment." [emphasis added] The courts, however, made a subtle but significant change to the Guidelines, which they purportedly adopted. They interpreted the EEOC standard to require proof that the harassment was severe enough "'to alter the conditions of [the victim's] employment *and* create an abusive working environment.'"[13] Furthermore, conduct must not only traumatize the victim so that it literally alters her working conditions, but her reaction must also be "reasonable." Finally, the victim must prove the absence of personal responsibility by establishing that the behavior was "unwelcome.". . .

Why is an "abusive work environment" *and* pervasiveness required? What kind of system protects the behavior of a male supervisor who refers to a female subordinate as "cunt," as long as he does not do it too often, or who regularly devalues women employees in some more subtle or "trivial" way? Such behavior is discriminatory, based on sex, and without legitimate justification or purpose. That should be enough. . . .

The courts' underlying assumption in hostile environment cases remains unchallenged: when men and women work in the same environment, some "flirting" or other comparable behavior is inevitable and appropriate. Our assumption should be just the opposite: sexually oriented conduct or discus-

---

13. Meritor Sav. Bank, FSB v. Vinson, 477 U.S. 57, 67 (emphasis added) (quoting Rogers v. EEOC, 454 F.2d 234, 238 (5th Cir. 1971)).

sions in the workplace are generally demeaning to women and, therefore, improper. Hence, if sexually oriented conduct occurs, the employer should assume all the risk. Even assuming that some sexually based conduct is inevitable, the issue of who is liable is separable from the issue of characterizing the behavior itself. If the conduct constitutes differential treatment, the employer should bear the risk that the supervisor's conduct disturbed the victim to the extent that she was willing to pursue a claim.

The proposed approach realigns the legal elements of sexual harassment doctrine more closely with other types of Title VII claims. Under disparate impact theory, for example, regardless of the employer's motive, a facially neutral policy with a discriminatory impact on a protected class may be successfully challenged, absent a business justification for the practice. The realignment of sexual harassment claims would follow much the same pattern. Even "trivial" sexually oriented behavior or conduct that systematically demeans women as a group discriminates by requiring women to work under more stigmatizing and stressful circumstances than men. The behavior lacks justification in the workplace and consequently should be banned if challenged, just as a court would enjoin a one cent pay discrepency [*sic*].

The seriousness of sexually oriented behavior then may be reflected in the remedial process . . . .The recently enacted Civil Rights Act of 1991 now permits the recovery of compensatory and punitive damages in appropriate Title VII cases. The ordinary standards for justifying this recovery should apply as well to hostile environment cases. The types of hostile environment claims that have been sustained under current standards—generally involving extreme and repeated incidents of abuse—should often qualify for compensatory and punitive damages. Less extreme cases established under the more lenient standard proposed here, involving what is now considered "trivial" behavior, would warrant no more than an injunction. Potential plaintiffs would, therefore, have no monetary incentive to pursue claims based on less egregious behavior. The absence of damages, along with the fear of employer retaliation and the unpleasantness of an investigation and litigation, should deter most trivial or meritless claims.

This approach is not without possible costs. An uncompromising judicial stance on sexual harassment may effectively dissuade some men from all warm, personal interaction with female subordinates or co-workers, for fear of being charged with sexual harassment. Arguably, the result for some women could be a colder, more impersonal working environment. For the hundreds of thousands of women who are subjected to sexual harassment, however, a more professional, albeit impersonal, workplace presumably would be a dramatic and welcomed improvement. . . .

Under current doctrine, the other element of the pervasiveness requirement that defeats many hostile environment claims is the consideration of perspective. Typically, a plaintiff must demonstrate not only that the alleged harassment seriously affected her working environment, but also that it would have affected a "reasonable person" equally. . . .

The controversy surrounding the proper scope of an objective standard ignores the more troubling issue of why a victim should be required to justify her response to sexually oriented behavior *at all*. Under my proposal, the issue would arise only in a limited set of cases. When the plaintiff or all women in the work environment are the targets of conduct to which male employees are not subjected, the behavior is discriminatory and the victim's reaction should be irrelevant, just as it is for other kinds of Title VII violations. If the complaint concerns generally offensive behavior that does not target one woman specifically or women in general, the "reasonable woman" standard would be relevant to determine if the behavior would likely be more offensive to women, creating a "discriminatory impact." Differential treatment for hostile environment claims should be no more troubling than the "inconsistency" of requiring proof of intent to discriminate for disparate treatment Title VII claims but not for disparate impact claims. . . .

Yet another obstacle faced by the unsuspecting plaintiff is that she must establish that her supervisor's behavior or suggestions were "unwelcome.". . .

Under my proposal, "unwelcomeness" is eliminated from the plaintiff's prima facie case. Instead, the defendant may raise the issue as an affirmative defense. Thus, the burden of persuasion, as opposed to production, shifts to the defendant. This evidentiary scheme parallels others in Title VII and employment law. . . .

Furthermore, the defendant should not be allowed to raise the defense of unwelcomeness at all unless he can present evidence of specific words or gestures that reasonably encouraged or solicited *in kind* behavior. Evidence of the victim's clothing or reputation would, therefore, not be admissible, and testimony that the victim told crude jokes would constitute a defense only to crude jokes being told to the plaintiff by others. Evidence of crude jokes told by the plaintiff would be irrelevant and inadmissible to justify sexual touching.

Although this proposal does not eliminate the victim focus problem entirely, the employer at least bears the burden of proving the issue so that doubts will be resolved in the plaintiff's favor. We start with the appropriate inference that any sexual conduct in the workplace is unwelcome. Furthermore, a victim's participation in sexually oriented behavior could be used against her only to the extent the alleged harassment involved comparable behavior. . . .

Title VII prohibits discrimination in the workplace that occurs "because of. . .sex.". . .

[P]articularly in the hostile environment arena, the "because of. . .sex" requirement has proven more problematic. When the "hostile environment" consists of generally offensive conditions that are not directed at identifiable individuals, some courts conclude that no discrimination has occurred because all employees are working in the same environment. . . .

The real problem is a pervasive cultural pattern that systematically demeans women by viewing them predominantly as sexual objects instead of competent and productive employees. A better solution would be to forego this absurd discussion of equal opportunity offensiveness and find all sexually oriented behavior actionable by recognizing its inherently differential impact on male and female employees. The conduct is out of place and serves no legitimate purpose in the working environment. If an employee is willing to jeopardize her job by complaining, the law should presume the requisite discrimination in recognition of women's general status in the workplace. . . .

In addition to the "because of. . .sex" requirement, some courts require that harassment involve conduct that is "sexual in nature." Some courts have taken the definition quite literally, expanding the "based on sex" requirement of Title VII to include two independent criteria: female employees must be treated differently than male employees and, moreover, they must be harassed in ways that were "clearly sexual."

The additional requirement that harassment be "sexual in nature" again illustrates the disfavored status of the claim. If harassment creates an abusive work environment, which would not have occurred but for an employee's gender, then sex discrimination is established even if the conduct is not overtly sexual in nature. . . .If the offensive conduct is directed solely at women, it is discriminatory and should be cognizable under Title VII, regardless of how we label the harassment.

Question

Sameness/Difference. B. Glenn George critiques sexual harassment law by comparing the legal elements for sexual harassment claims with the elements for other types of Title VII claims. Should her approach be categorized as a demand for equal treatment or for special treatment or neither?

Dillon v. Frank,

58 Empl. Prac. Dec. (CCH) ¶ 41,332 (6th Cir. 1992)

Boggs, C.J. Ernest Dillon is a middle-aged man and a former employee of the United States Postal Service. This case concerns his departure from that employment. During his tenure, Dillon was taunted, ostracized, and physically beaten by his co-workers because of their belief that he was a homosexual. Dillon contends that he left the employ of the Postal Service because of the cruel treatment he received from his co-workers. He asks the federal courts to redress that cruelty under the authority provided to us by Title VII of the 1964 Civil Rights Act and the Federal Tort Claims Act. While we sympathize with his plight, we are constrained to hold that he has not stated a cause of action under Title VII and that his FTCA claim was procedurally defective. We therefore affirm the district court's dismissal of his claims. . . .

Dillon worked as a mail handler at the Bulk Mail Center at Allen Park, Michigan. He started work in 1980, but his difficulties did not begin until late 1984. . . .A fellow employee, Kenneth Barrett, began calling Dillon "fag," and saying that "Dillon sucks dicks." Barrett also pushed materials into Dillon's work area, and turned off the bathroom lights when Dillon entered. This continued for five months, culminating in a physical assault by Barrett on Dillon in which Dillon suffered numerous injuries. The Postal Service fired Barrett as a result.

This did not end Dillon's travails. What had begun as a one-man band expanded into a full orchestral assault of verbal abuse. Other employees used similar epithets. Graffiti, the last refuge of the courageous, appeared on conveyor belts and Dillon's loading trucks informing the mail center that "Dillon sucks dicks" and "Dillon gives head." Dillon endured these circumstances for three years before he finally resigned in 1988 upon advice from his psychiatrist.

The Bulk Mail Center's management was well aware of these events. Dillon complained to eight different supervisors, and two union representatives. Management allegedly did nothing more than admonish the harassers, and hold meetings detailing the policy against sexual harassment in place at the center. Dillon alleges that management finally threw up their hands in despair, telling Dillon not to waste their time with his complaints and to fight back when taunted. . . .

This is a case of statutory interpretation. Title VII makes it illegal "to discriminate against any individual with respect to. . .compensation, terms, conditions, or privileges of employment, because of such individual's race, color, religion, sex, or national origin.". . .The Supreme Court has held that an employer who creates a hostile working environment for members of a class protected by Title VII, such as blacks or women, is discriminating "with respect to. . .terms [and] conditions" of employment. *Meritor Sav. Bank, FSB v. Vinson*, 477 U.S. 57 (1986). The question Dillon poses for us is whether such a hostile working environment involving sexual epithets and directed at a person because of perceived sexual behavior (homosexuality) is also proscribed by Title VII. In effect, Dillon asks us to define "because of sex" to mean "because of anything relating to being male or female,[14] sexual roles, or to sexual behavior." Because we believe that only discrimination based on being male or female is prohibited by Title VII, and that the cases proscribing hostile environment sexual harassment are not to the contrary, we affirm the district court. . . .

This would be an easy case if Dillon alleged that he was discriminated against because he was believed to be a homosexual. The circuits are unanimous in holding that Title VII does not proscribe discrimination based on sexual activities or orientation. . . ."It is a maxim of statutory construction that, unless otherwise defined, words should be given their ordinary common meaning. . . .The phrase in Title VII, prohibiting discrimination based on sex, in its plain meaning, implies that it is unlawful to discriminate against women because they are women and against men because they are men." *Ulane v. Eastern Airlines, Inc.*, 742 F.2d 1081, 1085 (7th Cir. 1984), *cert. denied*, 471 U.S. 1017 (1985). That such a "traditional" interpretation of the word "sex" was intended by Congress can be seen by the context in which it was placed, along with either immutable characteristics (race, color, national origin) and a characteristic so deeply rooted for most that it is almost immutable (religion). . . .[T]here is no indication that Congress intended to do anything more than prohibit discrimination against a person because that person is male or female. *See Vinson*, 477 U.S. at 63–64. . . .

This is not an easy case because Dillon does not allege that he is entitled to Title VII protection simply because he is alleged to be a homosexual. Rather, Dillon alleges that he was the victim of sexual harassment that was so pervasive that it rises to the level of a hostile work environment. He analogizes his circumstances to those under which it is clear plaintiffs can recover under Title VII. He directs us to cases where women who were subjected to demeaning

---

14. Because the very concept and definition of the word "sex" is at issue in this case, I will generally use terms such as "being male or female" to mean the genetic concept of the sex of a human as transmitted by the sex chromosome of the father.

and cruel verbal abuse (unaccompanied by demands for sexual favors) were able to secure a remedy through Title VII. . . .He further points to cases where plaintiffs subjected to demands by a boss for homosexual intercourse have been permitted to bring an action under Title VII. . . .These cases, he contends, hold that all extremely unpleasant working environments that arise because of verbal and other abuse regarding sex are proscribed, and that therefore the fact that the harassment in his case was predicated upon a belief that he is a homosexual, rather than specifically on his being male, is irrelevant. He contends that he was subjected to this abuse relating to homosexuality solely because he was a man, and therefore has stated a claim under Title VII.

Dillon also advanced a separate contention at oral argument. He pointed to the Supreme Court's decision in *Price Waterhouse v. Hopkins*, 490 U.S. 228 (1989), which considered a claim that a female plaintiff had been denied partnership at a prestigious accounting firm in part because she was not considered feminine enough. Dillon notes that the Court stated that evidence of such sex stereotyping[15] is admissible to prove sex discrimination. *Price Waterhouse*, 490 U.S. at 250-52. He contended that he was subjected to such stereotyping in that he was not deemed "macho" enough by his co-workers for a man, and that the verbal abuse resulted from this stereotyping.

It is clear that claims that the work environment was made hostile by animus against a person because that person was a man or a woman, even if the person was not subjected to demands for sexual favors, are cognizable under Title VII. *Vinson*, 477 U.S. at 64-67. The reason is simple: requiring a person to submit to abuse based on the fact that the person is male or female introduces sex as a factor in the workplace. *Vinson*, 477 U.S. at 67. It does so by forcing some persons, solely because they are male or female, to endure hostile working conditions, while permitting the other group to enjoy their workplace. Thus, a "condition" of employment includes whether the workplace is free from ridicule and other devices that stigmatize the recipient as inferior, and the refusal to provide that workplace because a person is male or female violates Title VII. . . .

Dillon's analogy is appealing because of the cruel treatment he was subjected to, and its similarity to the facts of many cases involving heterosexual hostile environment claims. The harassment that he was subjected to was clearly sexual in nature. It seriously affected Dillon's psychological well-being, to the point the [*sic*] Dillon felt compelled to resign. The Postal Service knew about the harassment, and yet it continued unabated, raising the strong possibility that there would be employer liability for the actions of Dillon's co-workers. It appears undeniable that Dillon was denied the "condition" of employment at issue in hostile environment cases, a workplace where each employee is treated with appropriate dignity and respect. . . .

We have searched for cases involving the type of claim Dillon makes here. We have found only one unreported district case that made a square holding

15. We define "sex stereotyping" to mean the assigning of certain behavioral characteristics as appropriate for women or for men, but not for the other sex. Sex stereotyping is illegal when it is the basis for discriminating against members of a protected class with respect to the terms and conditions of employment.

on Dillon's type of argument. *Carreno v. Local Union No. 226, Int'l Bhd. of Elec. Workers*, No. 89-4083-S, 1990 U.S. Dist. LEXIS 13817 (D. Kan. Sept. 27, 1990). *But see Fair v. Guiding Eyes for the Blind, Inc.*, 742 F. Supp. 151, 156 (S.D.N.Y. 1990) (contains dicta that "[c]omments of a homosexual nature directed at a man. . .might be considered to be based on sex.")[.] *Carreno* involved a man who divorced his wife and started to live with a man in a homosexual relationship. For this, plaintiff was subjected to verbal abuse, such as being called "Mary" and "faggot[.]" *Carreno*, 1990 U.S. Dist. LEXIS at *3-4. The court ruled that the plaintiff was arguing that he was harassed because he was a homosexual. . .[and precedent] holding that discrimination based on sexual preference or orientation is not discrimination "based on sex" with [sic] the meaning of Title VII compelled summary judgment for the defendants. *Id.* at *8-9.

Despite the compelling facts of Dillon's situation, we agree with the result in *Carreno*. Although the cases recognizing claims for hostile environment sexual harassment hold that employees have a right to a work environment free from denigrating comments, verbal abuse, and other tactics of marginalization, *see Vinson*, 477 U.S. at 65, that body of law does *not* hold that right to be absolute. Rather, Title VII only punishes those employers who withhold such environments from employees based on certain proscribed criteria: race, color, sex, religion, or national origin. . . .

In none of. . .[the leading sexual harassment] cases is the *content* of the harassment the deciding factor in determining if Title VII provides a remedy; it is whether the harassment was directed at the plaintiff for a statutorily impermissible reason. . . .

Thus, Dillon cannot escape our holding, and those of the other circuits, that homosexuality is not an impermissible criteria on which to discriminate with regard to terms and conditions of employment. Dillon's co-workers deprived him of a proper work environment *because* they believed him to be homosexual. Their comments, graffiti, and assaults were all directed at demeaning him solely because they disapproved vehemently of his alleged homosexuality. These actions, although cruel, are not made illegal by Title VII.

In a perfect world, the "right" to dignified treatment by one's employer and co-workers would be absolute: all workers of the world would unite in being "nice" toward one another. In our less than perfect world, both criminal and tort law may provide workers with protection against cruel harassment by their co-workers. Indeed, some of the actions Dillon complains of seem capable of remedy under both tort and criminal law, such as Barrett's beating (battery) and his co-workers taunting and graffiti-writing (intentional infliction of emotional distress). If Dillon can prove that the harassment ever caused him to be immediately apprehensive of another physical assault—and given the increase of the harassment after his recovery from Barrett's beating, this is not at all implausible—he can also sue for assault. . . .In fact, to the extent that his co-workers and employer wanted to see Dillon quit, he could even sue for tortious interference with contract or employment relationship. The base result, however, is undisturbed; our decision today does not leave those in Dillon's situation without legal remedy.

We interpret Title VII to prescribe only specified discriminatory actions.

What Title VII proscribes, although vitally important, is easily exceeded by what it does not. . . .

Dillon attempts to avoid this problem by alleging that he was discriminated against because he was male. His argument is that but for his being male, he would not have been abused. We find this argument unpersuasive, primarily because he has not shown that his co-workers would have treated a similarly situated woman any differently. Dillon's argument must presume that the abuse was either directed at his supposed homosexuality or at specific sexual practices (such as anal sex or fellatio). In two of its cases, the District of Columbia Circuit has raised the figure of the bisexual sexual harasser, preying equally on men and women, as a way to demonstrate that Title VII proscribes certain motives behind discrimination, not the practices used to implement those motives. *See Bundy v. Jackson*, 641 F.2d 934, 942 n.7 (D.C. Cir. 1981); *Barnes v. Costle*, 561 F.2d 983, 990 n.55 (D.C. Cir. 1977) (legal question to ask in sex harassment cases is whether a condition was imposed "which, but for his or her sex, the employee would not have faced"). Dillon has not shown such unisexual oppression: he has not argued that a lesbian would have been accepted at the Center,[16] nor has he argued that a woman known to engage in the disfavored sexual practices would have escaped abuse. . . .Without such a showing, his claim to have been discriminated against because he is male cannot succeed. . . .

Price Waterhouse v. Hopkins, 490 U.S. 228 (1989) does not direct a different result. *Price Waterhouse* was not a hostile environment case. It involved a specific management decision and the plaintiff's allegation "that gender played a part in a particular employment decision." Because. . .of this difference, we do not read the Court to mean that any treatment that *could* be based on sexual stereotypes would violate Title VII.

First, there is no specific evidence of "sex stereotyped remarks" in our case. In *Price Waterhouse*, the plaintiff's superiors had criticized her aggressiveness, advised her to use makeup, and suggested she go to "charm school.". . .In our case there is no evidence provided that Dillon's co-workers justified their outrageous behavior based on, or accompanied it with remarks indicating, a belief that his practices would be acceptable in a female but unacceptable in a male.

Further, the Court emphasized the "intolerable and impermissible Catch-22" in the stereotyping in that case. *Id.* A desirable trait (aggressiveness) was believed to be peculiar to males. If Hopkins lacked it, she would not be promoted; if she displayed it, it would not be acceptable. In our case, Dillon's supposed activities or characteristics simply had no relevance to the workplace, and did not place him in a "Catch-22."

Thus, the discussion of sexual stereotyping in *Price Waterhouse* does not support a holding that discrimination "on account of sex" was involved in this case. . . .

For the foregoing reasons, we Affirm the district court's judgment dismissing Dillon's claims.

---

16. Such proof might then show that Dillon's co-workers were not discriminating against him solely because he was a homosexual, but because he was a homosexual male.

Judges Brown and Gibbons concur in this opinion only to the extent that they agree that the district judge did not err in granting the defendant's motion to dismiss the complaint in this case.

Notes and Questions

1. *A Feminist Analysis of Dillon.* In *Goluszek v. Smith*, 694 F. Supp. 1452 (N.D. Ill. 1988), a case similar to *Dillon*, Judge Ann Williams granted summary judgment for the employer on a suit by a male worker against his employer for sexual harassment in the workplace. She found that

> the defendant's conduct was not the type of conduct Congress intended to sanction when it enacted Title VII. The goal of Title VII is equal employment opportunity. . . .That goal is accomplished in part by imposing an affirmative duty on employers to maintain a working environment free of discriminatory intimidation. . . .The discrimination Congress was concerned about when it enacted Title VII is one stemming from an imbalance of power and an abuse of that imbalance by the powerful which results in discrimination against a discrete and vulnerable group. . . .Title VII does not make all forms of harassment actionable, nor does it even make all forms of verbal harassment with sexual overtones actionable. The "sexual harassment" that is actionable under Title VII "is the exploitation of a powerful position to impose sexual demands or pressures on an unwilling but less powerful person." [Note, Sexual Harassment Claims of Abusive Work Environment Under Title VII, 97 Harv. L. Rev. 1449, 1451 (1984).]. . .In effect, the offender is saying by words or actions that the victim is inferior because of the victim's sex. . . .
>
> During the times relevant to his claim, Goluszek was a male in a male-dominated environment. . . .The argument that Goluszek worked in an environment that treated males as inferior consequently is not supported by the record. In fact, Goluszek may have been harassed "because" he is a male, but that harassment was not of a kind which created an anti-male environment in the workplace. . . .A wooden application of the verbal formulations created by the courts would salvage Goluszek's sexual-harassment claim. The court, however, chooses instead to adopt a reading of Title VII consistent with the underlying concerns of Congress . . . .

697 F. Supp. at 1456.

Is this a feminist reading of Title VII? Martha Chamallas provides an alternative feminist analysis to the facts of the case and argues that some types of harassment of a male worker by male co-workers should be actionable sexual harassment under Title VII.

> I disagree with the result in *Goluszek* and would interpret Title VII's prohibition against sex discrimination to cover cases like *Goluszek*. In my view, Goluszek was intimidated by aggressive male sexual behavior in much the same way that a woman would be intimidated. He was apparently singled out for harassment because he did not conform to the men's image of male heterosexuality. . . .
>
> Even if a man who has been harassed is spared a measure of the gender-specific injury associated with sexual harassment of women and is unable to

assume a woman's perspective, he may nevertheless be the victim of a system of gender domination whose principal effect is to subordinate women. I would read judicial adoption of a woman's perspective as a rhetorical strategy for attacking a gender ideology that finds its expression in sexual intimidation and exclusion. Goluszek, like other men ostracized for being effeminate or suspected of being gay, was punished for possessing attributes of the inferior sex, and his punishment reinforced women's inferiority by showing that men were willing to police gender boundaries. [Judge] William's observation that the workplace environment in *Goluszek* was not anti-male may have been accurate. However, she failed to investigate whether the environment was anti-female and whether this was the source of Goluszek's suffering. Like a man who earns a depressed wage in a predominantly female job, it makes sense to view Goluszek as a victim of sex discrimination. This is not the two-way street harassment as in the conservative vision, even though individual men can be victims. Instead, this analysis of *Goluszek* starts from an assumption of male domination, while at the same time recognizing that because sex is a social construct and difference is constructed through human relationships, sexism usually directed at women can be displaced onto men.

Additionally, I find it problematic to deploy the reasonable man standard to justify speech and conduct that demeans women and treats women as sexual objects. To the extent that *Ellison* and *Goluszek* suggest that it is reasonable for men to behave this way, gender oppression of women is legitimated. In my view, the value of the victim's perspective is that it dislodges socially suppressed views and challenges the status quo. The victim's perspective should not be used simply to refer to a point of view shared by the gender group to which plaintiff happens to belong. Instead, it should be reserved for designating the perspective of a cultural group that has experienced group oppression.

It may be that in a case involving a male plaintiff, it is too confusing and strained to apply the reasonable woman standard, particularly if the court must first determine whether the plaintiff was treated socially as if he were a woman. Perhaps the best way to address a case like *Goluszek* is to employ a non-gender-specific standard—for example, a reasonable target of harassment—that still focuses on the victim's perspective. Such an approach would avoid reinforcing male-centered views that are oppressive both to women and to men who fail to conform to socially dictated norms about gender. It would, however, also require the court to use a means other than plaintiff's gender to determine whether the conduct was sex-based. In these cases, the court could not avoid framing the inquiry in a direct substantive form, such as whether the sexual conduct had a tendency to reinforce male domination or to render the workplace inhospitable to women.

Allowing men to complain of sexually abusive environments could mean, of course, that even all-male workplaces would theoretically be required to maintain an environment that is not hostile to women. This seems appropriate if the message is that the source of the problem is the oppressive environment and not the "different" people. If diverse perspectives are valued for the positive impact they have on an institution, then totally segregated as well as predominantly segregated workplaces should be encouraged to change.

Martha Chamallas, Feminist Constructions of Objectivity: Multiple Perspectives in Sexual and Racial Harassment Litigation, 1 Tex. J. Women & L. 95, 127-30 (1992).

2. *The Intersection of Gender and Sexual Orientation.* The Dillon court held that the harassment was directed at the plaintiff's perceived sexual orientation and not based on the plaintiff's gender. Samuel Marcosson explains that the *Dillon* rationale would apply equally to heterosexual sexual harassment.

> [H]ad. . .Dillon's coworkers been homosexual, . . .Dillon would not have been the target[ ] of the harassment. . . .Dillon's coworkers harassed. . .Dillon, because of their. . .sexual orientation[ ]—heterosexual. But this is equally true in the classic quid pro quo sexual harassment situation where the male supervisor demands sexual relations with his female subordinate "because of" his heterosexual orientation (at least in the sense that if he were homosexual, he would not subject women to those demands).
>
> It follows. . .then, for the same reason, any harassment in the workplace can be said to be "not based upon the plaintiff's sex." What happened to. . .Dillon was as much because of [his]. . .gender as what happens to *any* victim of sexual harassment; had [he]. . .engaged in the same conduct but been of the opposite gender, [he]. . .would not have been harrassed [*sic*].
>
> The conclusion to be drawn from the analysis is that harassment on the basis of sexual orientation is a form of sexual harassment, rather than a different category altogether.

Samuel Marcosson, Harassment on the Basis of Sexual Orientation: A Claim of Sex Discrimination Under Title VII, 81 Geo. L.J. 1, 34 (1992) (emphasis in original).

3. *Sexual Orientation as Sex Discrimination and the Loving v. Virginia Analogy.* How might you use the reasoning in *Loving v. Virginia*, at p. 151, to argue that sexual harassment based on sexual orientation is sex discrimination under Title VII?

Chapter 6

Rape

The law and society draw sharp boundaries between rape and battering and between rape and sexual harassment. As we have seen in Chapters 4 and 5, however, the boundaries frequently prove to be artificial and misleading. By drawing these boundaries, the rapes that occur as part of domestic assault and as part of sexual harassment are hidden from public scrutiny. Moreover, the boundaries obscure the synergistic effects of the various forms of violence that are used by men to exercise control and power over women. While we will see these connections throughout this chapter, we also will see that the crime of rape raises specific issues about a woman's sexual autonomy that demand separate attention. One of the purposes of this chapter is to explore how rape, as defined by the law and by society, constructs gender and race.

Accurate data on the incidents of rape are essential for determining the proper allocation of governmental resources and for understanding rape as a widespread systemic problem in society as opposed to aberrational isolated events perpetrated by deviant men. In the United States, the two federal sources of rape incidence data are the Federal Bureau of Investigation's Unified Crime Reports [UCR] and the National Crime Survey [NCS] from the Bureau of Justice Statistics. The UCR collects only reported crimes of rape. Many experts who work in the area of sexual assault believe that reported rapes represent only a small percentage of the total incidents of rape. The NCS data also underreports rape; based on sample interviews, it fails to detect relevant incidents because of the methodology it uses. *See* Mary P. Koss, The Underdetection of Rape: Methodological Choices Influence Incidence Estimates, 48 J. Soc. Issues 61 (1992). Mary Koss concludes that "[a]n accumulation of independent data sources suggests that rape incidence may be 6-10 times higher than current NCS estimates and that women are up to 4 times more likely to be raped by someone they know than by a stranger." *Id.* at 73. A government-financed survey, released in April 1992, "estimated that 683,000 adult women were raped in 1990, a figure more than five times as high as the number of sexual assaults reported for the same year by the Justice Department." *See* David Johnston, Survey Shows Number of Rapes Far Higher Than Official Figures, N.Y. Times, Apr. 24, 1992, at A9. The study also "estimated that at least 12.1 million women have been the victims of forcible rape at least once in their life and found that 61 percent of the victims said they had been raped as minors." *Id.*

Part A of this chapter is designed to show how rape is an integral part of our social and cultural institutions and how it operates as an instrument for social control of women. The materials in this part make clear, however, that social control operates differently at different moments in history and that at all times its effects differ depending on a woman's abilities, class, and race/ethnicity.

In an excerpt from *Ain't I a Woman: Black Women and Feminism*, bell hooks describes the systems of gender and race oppression in the United States by situating rape in the historical context of African-American women's experiences under slavery. She shows how this history of sexual assault and exploitation is central to an understanding of rape today.

To help us understand the significance of the "myth of the African-American rapist" and how it is used to justify violence and terror against the African-American community, hooks' piece is followed by the 1953 Alabama case of *McQuirter v. State*, which represents the judicial embodiment of that myth. The excerpts from works by Arthur Raper and Jacquelyn Dowd Hall document and analyze the incidents of lynching that occurred from the latter part of the nineteenth century through 1930.

Hooks, *McQuirter*, and the lynching materials demonstrate that the practices of rape and lynching served to oppress and control, in differing ways, African-American women, African-American men, and white women. While all three groups were subordinated by white men, white women in certain circumstances aligned themselves with white men to garner some of their social and political advantages, becoming co-partners in racial oppression. Also, African-American men in certain circumstances imitated the oppressive attitudes and behavior of white men and practiced sexual violence against women.

Margo Nightingale examines the intersection of gender and race oppression by analyzing how the Canadian criminal justice system treats sexual assault cases involving Aboriginal defendants and victims/survivors. Nightingale believes that judicial sensitivity to Aboriginal values, community interests, and community treatment programs is essential, but demonstrates how ethnocentricism and sexism in the justice system obscure an aboriginal community's values, interests, or relevant cultural differences.

Catharine MacKinnon and Carol Smart each analyze rape by focusing exclusively on gender and the meaning of sexuality. They agree that what is taken to be sexuality is entirely constructed by men. Their work is important because it situates rape within a system of social control that defines sex for and on behalf of men. MacKinnon's purpose is to show the violence in sex and the sex in violence. Smart's purpose is to show how the "dominance of the male experience" turns female experience into pathology that in turn infects our understanding of the crime of rape.

Part B continues to analyze rape in terms of gender and race oppression by focusing on the specific elements of the crime of rape and the manner in which rape is prosecuted. It includes the Michigan statute on criminal sexual conduct, which was enacted in 1975 largely because of the work of the Michigan Women's Task Force on Rape. The marital rape section was enacted in its present form in 1988. This statute is an example of one state's attempt at reform of the common law's elements of the crime of rape. The Michigan statutory scheme can usefully be studied in conjunction with Susan Estrich's article, which critiques the commonly required elements of the crime of rape: *mens rea*, force, and consent. Complementing this examination of the elements of the crime of rape is an excerpt from Carol Smart's book *Feminism and the Power of Law*, which scrutinizes the gendered nature of the rape trial itself.

Part B ends by addressing specific issues that arise in the context of nonstranger rape. In recent years feminist activists and theorists have begun to question the conventional wisdom, practice, and judicial analytical assumptions that make nonstranger rapes more difficult to prosecute successfully than stranger rapes. Current law allows defendants to use a preexisting relationship to give credibility to a defense of consent or reasonable good faith belief of consent. We look here at two recent cases, *Commonwealth v. Berkowitz* and *State ex rel M.T.S.*. Both cases concentrate on the issues of force and consent but use very different approaches in analyzing the applicable statutes and reach very different results.

Finally, Part C examines, through the U.S. Supreme Court's decision in *Michael M. v. Superior Court*, the purpose and functioning of statutory rape laws, focusing on the question of whether differing ages of consent for men and women is constitutional and a benefit to underage women. The chapter ends with an excerpt from an article by MacKinnon in which she analyzes rape and the implications of *Michael M.*. She attempts to establish an equality framework that centers on questions of subordination rather than on sameness/difference.

A. Rape as an Instrument of Gender and Race Oppression

bell hooks, *Ain't I a Woman: Black Women and Feminism* 17–18, 25–30, 34–37, 53–62 (1981)

The African woman schooled in the art of obedience to a higher authority by the tradition of her society was probably seen by the white male slaver as an ideal subject for slavery. As much of the work to be done in the American colonies was in the area of hoe-agriculture, it undoubtedly occurred to slavers that the African female, accustomed to performing arduous work in the fields while also performing a wide variety of tasks in the domestic household, would be very useful on the American plantation. While only a few African women were aboard the first ships bringing slaves to the new world, as the slave trade gathered momentum, females made up one-third of the human cargo aboard most ships. Because they could not effectively resist capture at the hands of thieves and kidnappers, African women became frequent targets for white male slavers. Slavers also used the capture of women important to the tribe, like the daughter of a king, as a means of luring African men into situations where they could be easily captured. Other African women were sold into slavery as punishment for breaking tribal laws. A woman found guilty of committing an act of adultery might be sold into bondage.

White male slavers did not regard the African female as a threat, so often aboard slave ships black women were stored without being shackled while black men were chained to one another. The slavers believed their own safety to be threatened by enslaved African men, but they had no such fear of the African female. The placing of African men in chains was to prevent possible uprisings. As white slavers feared resistance and retaliation at the hands of African men, they placed as much distance between themselves and black male slaves as was possible on board. It was only in relationship to the black female slave that the white slaver could exercise freely absolute power, for he could brutalize and exploit her without fear of harmful retaliation. Black female slaves moving freely about the decks were a ready target for any white male who might choose to physically abuse and torment them. Initially every slave on board the ship was branded with a hot iron. A cat-o'-nine-tails was used by the slavers to lash those Africans that cried out in pain or resisted the torture. Women were lashed severely for crying. They were stripped of their clothing and beaten on all parts of their body. Ruth and Jacob Weldon, an African couple who experienced the horrors of the slave passage, saw "mothers with babes at their breasts basely branded and scarred, till it would seem as if the very heavens might smite the infernal tormentors with the doom they so richly merited." After the branding all slaves were stripped of any clothing. The nakedness of the African female served as a constant reminder of her sexual vulnerability. Rape was a common method of torture slavers used to subdue recalcitrant black women. The threat of rape or other physical brutalization inspired terror in the psyches of displaced African females. Robert Shufeldt, an observer of the slave trade, documented the prevalence of rape on slave ships. He asserts, "In those days many a negress was landed upon our shored already impregnated by someone of the demonic crew that brought her over.". . .

Black female slave narratives that provide information concerning the sexual education of girls suggest that they knew little about their bodies, where babies came from, or about sexual intercourse. Few slave parents warned their daughters about the possibility of rape or helped them to prepare for such situations. The slave parents' unwillingness to openly concern themselves with the reality of sexual exploitation reflects the general colonial American attitude regarding sexuality.

Sexual exploitation of young slave girls usually occurred after they left the hut or cabin of their parents to work in the white domestic household. It was a common practice for a young slave girl to be forced to sleep in the same bedroom with a master and mistress, a situation which provided a convenient setting for sexual assault. Linda Brent recorded in her autobiography a detailed account of her white master's obsessive desire to assert his power over her by constantly threatening rape. When Linda first entered the service of her owner Dr. Flint, she was thirteen years old. He did not rape her but began to constantly torment and persecute her by verbally announcing his intentions to take her sexually. At the onset of their encounter he informed her that if she would not willingly submit, he would use force. Describing herself at fifteen, Linda wrote:

> I was compelled to live under the same roof with him—where I saw a man forty years my senior daily violating the most sacred commandment of nature. He told me I was his property; that I must be subjected to his will in all things. . .

White male slaveowners usually tried to bribe black women as preparation for sexual overtures so as to place them in the role of prostitute. As long as the white slaveowner "paid" for the sexual services of his black female slave, he felt absolved of responsibility for such acts. Given the harsh conditions of slave life, any suggestion that enslaved black women had a choice as to their sexual partner is ludicrous. Since the white male could rape the black female who did not willingly respond to his demands, passive submission on the part of the enslaved black women cannot be seen as complicity. Those women who did not willingly respond to the sexual overture of masters and overseers were brutalized and punished. Any show of resistance on the part of enslaved females increased the determination of white owners eager to demonstrate their power. In an account of her slave experience, Ann, a young mulatto woman, documents the struggle for power enacted by white masters, overseers, whippers, and the female slave. In her case it was the paid whipper who planned to rape her. He demanded that she remove all her clothing prior to the whipping. When Ann realized that he intended to rape her, she struggled. Her resistance angered him and he responded, "Girl, you've got to yield to me. I'll have you now; if it's only to show you that I can. . .You've got to be mine. I'll give you a fine calico dress and a pretty pair of ear-bobs!" Ann tells readers:

> This was too much for further endurance. What! Must I give up the angel sealed honor of my life in traffic for trinkets. Where is the woman that would not have hotly resented such an insult. I turned upon him like a hungry lioness, and just as his wanton hand was about to be laid upon me, I dexterously aimed, and hurled the bottle against his left temple. With a low cry of pain he fell to the floor, and the blood oozed freely from the wound.

The paid whipper did not die from Ann's attack, so she was only punished by a prison sentence and daily floggings. Had he died she would have been tried for murder and sentenced to death.

Nineteenth century white female humanist Lydia Marie Child accurately summed up the social status of black women during slavery with the statement:

> The negro woman is unprotected either by law or public opinion. She is the property of her master, and her daughters are his property. They are allowed to have no conscientious scruples, no sense of shame, no regard for the feelings of husband, or parent: they must be entirely subservient to the will of their owner on pain of being whipped as near unto death as will comport with his interest or quite to death if it suits his pleasure.

White male slaveowners wanted enslaved black women to passively accept sexual exploitation as the right and privilege of those in power. The black female slave who willingly submitted to a master's sexual advance and who received presents of payments was rewarded for her acceptance of the existing social order. Those black women who resisted sexual exploitation directly challenged the system; their refusal to submit passively to rape was a denouncement of the slaveowner's right to their persons. They were brutally punished. The political aim of this categorical rape of black women by white males was to obtain absolute allegiance and obedience to the white imperialistic order. Black activist Angela Davis has convincingly argued that the rape of black female slaves was not, as other scholars have suggested, a case of white men satisfying their sexual lust, but was in fact an institutionalized method of terrorism which had as its goal the demoralization and dehumanization of black women. Davis contends:

> In confronting the black woman as adversary in a sexual contest, the master

> would be subjecting her to the most elemental form of terrorism distinctly suited for the female: rape. Given the already terroristic texture of plantation life, it would be as potential victim of rape that the slave woman would be most unguarded. Further, she might be most conveniently manipulated if the master contrived a random system of sorts, forcing her to pay with her body for foods, diminished severity of treatment, the safety of her children, etc.

In 1839, the book *American Slavery: As It Is* was published anonymously by white abolitionists who believed they could destroy the pro-slavery arguments by exposing in print the horrors of slave life. They relied on the accounts of white people who had observed slavery firsthand or had gained information from slaveholders and their friends. The work was compiled and collated primarily by Angelina and Sarah Grimke, two outspoken abolitionists. Because their brother had fathered children by a black female slave, they were particularly concerned about the sexual exploitation of black female slaves. For many other white female abolitionists the sole motivating force behind their anti-slavery efforts was the desire to bring an end to sexual contact between white men and black female slaves. They were not concerned about the plight of enslaved black women, but about saving the souls of white men whom they believed had sinned against God by their acts of moral depravity. Many pro-slavery white women ultimately denounced slavery because of their outrage at the sexual barbarity of white men. They felt personally shamed and humiliated by what they termed white male adultery (which was in actuality rape). Commenting on her mistress' attitude toward the sexual exploitation of black women, Linda Brent wrote:

> I was soon convinced that her emotions arose from anger and wounded pride. She felt that her marriage vows were desecrated, her dignity insulted; but she had no compassion for the poor victim of her husband's perfidy. She pitied herself as a martyr; but she was incapable of feeling for the condition of shame and misery in which her unfortunate, helpless slaves were placed.

The Grimke women sympathized with the plight of black females but Victorian social convention governing behavior did not allow them to graphically expose many of the cruel acts inflicted upon black slave women by white men. Proper decorum prevented them from speaking directly and honestly about the hidden evils of slavery. Angelina Grimke wrote:

> We forbear to lift the veil of private life any higher. Let these few hints suffice to give you some idea of what is daily passing behind the curtain which has been so carefully drawn before the scenes of domestic life in slave holding America.

Had Angelina and Sarah Grimke lifted the veil of private life any higher they would have exposed not only slaveowners siring children by black women, but sadistic misogynist acts of cruelty and brutality that went far beyond seduction—to rape, to torture, and even to orgiastic murder and necrophilia.

Modern historians tend to make light of the sexual exploitation of black women during slavery. In his *Daughters of the Promised Land* Page Smith writes:

> Most young Southern men doubtless had their initial sexual experience with

> a compliant slave girl. It was not unnatural that many of them should continue to indulge themselves after their marriages. In addition there was undoubtedly the attraction of the perverse, of the taboo, the association of darkness with pleasant wickedness, the absence of any danger to the sexual exploiter however unwelcome his attentions may have been. Moreover, there was the tradition of Negro sensuality which may well have worked to make the white wife a more restrained sexual partner. Thus when the Southern male looked to slave women for his basic sexual satisfaction, he increasingly found them there. Since there seems to be in masculine sexuality a measure of aggressiveness and even sadism, passivity and defenselessness seem often to enhance the desirability of the sexual object which was what the Negro woman was for her white masters.

The reader is encouraged by Smith to regard the brutality of white men as merely a case of "boys will be boys." Like many other historians, he paints a picture of slavery in which white men had "normal" male sexual desires that they indulged with submissive slave girls. While he acknowledges the sadism that often prompted sexual exploitation of the black female slave, he minimizes it by implying that it was an extension of "normal" male sexual expression.

The brutal treatment of enslaved black women by white men exposed the depths of male hatred of woman and woman's body. Such treatment was a direct consequence of misogynist attitudes toward women that prevailed in colonial American society. In fundamentalist Christian teaching woman was portrayed as an evil sexual temptress, the bringer of sin into the world. Sexual lust originated with her and men were merely the victims of her wanton power. Socialization of white men to regard women as their moral downfall led to the development of anti-woman sentiment. White male religious teachers taught that woman was an inherently sinful creature of the flesh whose wickedness could only be purged by the intercession of a more powerful being. Appointing themselves as the personal agents of God, they became the judges and overseers of woman's virtue. They instigated laws to govern the sexual behavior of white women, to ensure that they would not be tempted to stray from the straight and narrow path. Severe punishments were meted out to those women who overstepped the boundaries white men defined as woman's place. The Salem Witchcraft trials were an extreme expression of patriarchal society's persecution of women. They were a message to all women that unless they remained within passive, subordinate roles they would be punished, even put to death. . . .

It was difficult for abolitionists to discuss the rape of black women for fear of offending audiences, so they concentrated on the theme of prostitution. But the use of the word prostitution to describe mass sexual exploitation of enslaved black women by white men not only deflected attention away from the prevalence of forced sexual assault, it lent further credibility to the myth that black females were inherently wanton and therefore responsible for rape.

Contemporary sexist scholars minimize the impact of sexual exploitation of black women on the black female psyche and argue that white men used the rape of black women to further emasculate black men. Black sociologist Robert Staples asserts:

> The rape of the slave woman brought home to the slave man his inability to

> protect his woman. Once his masculinization was undermined in this respect, he would begin to experience profound doubts about his power even to break the chains of bondage.

Staples' argument is based on the assumption that enslaved black men felt responsible for all black women and were demoralized because of their inability to act as protectors—an assumption that has not been substantiated by historical evidence. An examination of many traditional African societies' attitudes toward women reveals that African men were not taught to see themselves as the protectors of all women. They were taught to assume responsibility for the particular women of their tribe or community. The socialization of African men to see themselves as the "owners" of all black women and to regard them as property they should protect occurred after the long years of slavery and as the result of bonding on the basis of color rather than shared tribal connection or language. Prior to their adoption of white American sexist attitudes toward women, there was no reason for enslaved African men to feel responsible for all enslaved African women. Assuredly, the sexual assault of black women had an impact on the psyches of black male slaves. It is likely that the black male slave did not feel demoralized or de-humanized because "his" women were being raped, but that he did feel terrorized by the knowledge that white men who were willing to brutalize and victimize black women and girls (who represented no great threat to their authority), might easily have no qualms about totally annihilating black men. Most black male slaves stood quietly by as white masters sexually assaulted and brutalized black women and were not compelled to act as protectors. Their first instincts were toward self-preservation. In her slave narrative, Linda Brent tells readers that black male slaves as a group did not see themselves as the protectors of black slave women. She comments:

> There are some who strive to protect wives and daughters from the insults of their master; but those who have such sentiments have advantages above the general mass of slaves. . .Some poor creatures have been so brutalized by the lash that they will sneak out of the house to give their masters free access to their wives and daughters.

Throughout the years of slavery, individual black men rallied to the defense of black women who were important to them. Their defense of these women was not motivated by a sense of themselves as the natural protectors of all black women.

Historian Eugene Genovese discusses the sexual exploitation of enslaved black females in *Roll, Jordan, Roll*, and contends:

> Rape meant, by definition, rape of white women, for no such crime as rape of a black woman existed at law. Even when a black man sexually attacked a black woman, he could only be punished by his master; no way existed to bring him to trial or to convict him if so brought.

The rape of black women by black male slaves is further indication that, rather than assuming the role of protector, black men imitated the white male's behavior. Genovese concludes:

> Some drivers forced the slave woman in much the same way as did some masters and overseers. It remains an open question which of those powerful

> white and black males forced the female slaves more often. Under the task system the driver set the day's work for each slave and had no trouble making a woman's lot miserable if she refused him. Under the more prevalent gang system, drivers could lay the whip on with impunity—if they had the power to whip at all—as many did—or they could find any number of other ways to reward and punish.

Given the barbaric nature of slave life, it is likely that black slave women allied with powerful black men who could protect them from the unwanted sexual advances of other slaves. Sexual jealousies and rivalries were a primary cause of most quarrels between black slave men.

The enslaved black woman could not look to any group of men, white or black, to protect her against sexual exploitation. Often in desperation, slave women attempted to enlist the aid of white mistresses, but these attempts usually failed. Some mistresses responded to the distress of female slaves by persecuting and tormenting them. Others encouraged the use of black women as sex objects because it allowed them respite from unwanted sexual advances. In rare cases, white mistresses who were reluctant to see sons marry and leave home purchased black maids to be sexual playmates for them. Those white women who deplored the sexual exploitation of slave women were usually reluctant to involve themselves with a slave's plight for fear of jeopardizing their own position in the domestic household. Most white women regarded black women who were the objects of their husbands' sexual assaults with hostility and rage. Having been taught by religious teachings that women were inherently sexual temptresses, mistresses often believed that the enslaved black woman was the culprit and their husbands the innocent victims. In *Once A Slave*, a book which contains a condensed body of information gleaned from slave narratives, the author Stanley Feldstein recounts an incident in which a white mistress returned home unexpectedly from an outing, opened the doors of her dressing room, and discovered her husband raping a thirteen year old slave girl. She responded by beating the girl and locking her in a smokehouse. The girl was whipped daily for several weeks. When older slaves pleaded on the child's behalf and dared to suggest that the white master was to blame, the mistress simply replied, "She'll know better in future. After I've done with her, she'll never do the like again through ignorance." White women held black slave women responsible for rape because they had been socialized by 19th century sexual morality to regard woman as sexual temptress. This same sexual morality was adopted by slaves. Fellow slaves often pitied the lot of sexually exploited females but did not see them as blameless victims. One female abolitionist states:

> Of all who drooped and withered under the inflictions of this horrible system, the greatest sufferer was defenseless women. For the male slave, however brutally treated, there was some recourse; but for the woman slave there was neither protection nor pity.

Rape was not the only method used to terrorize and de-humanize black women. Sadistic floggings of naked black women were another method employed to strip the female slave of dignity. In the Victorian world, where white women were religiously covering every body part, black women were daily stripped of their clothing and publicly whipped. Slaveowners were well aware that it added to the degradation and humiliation of female slaves for them to be forced to appear naked before male whippers and onlookers. A Kentucky slave recalled:

> The women are subjected to these punishments as rigorously as the men—not even pregnancy exempts them; in that case before binding them to the stake, a hole is made in the ground to accommodate the enlarged form of the victim.

Susan Boggs recalled:

> They would have a woman stripped and cobbed if she did anything they didn't like. Perhaps if the bread did not rise well, the mistress would tell the master when he came home; and she would be sent to the trader's jail to be cobbed. It is awful to think of women, of human beings, being exposed in this way.

. . .A devaluation of black womanhood occurred as a result of the sexual exploitation of black women during slavery that has not altered in the course of hundreds of years. I have previously mentioned that while many concerned citizens sympathized with the sexual exploitation of black women both during slavery and afterwards, like all rape victims in patriarchal society they were seen as having lost value and worth as a result of the humiliation they endured. Annals of slavery reveal that the same abolitionist public that condemned the rape of black women regarded them as accomplices rather than victims. In her diary, the southern white woman Mary Boykin Chesnut recorded:

> . . .(April 20, 1861.) Bad books are not allowed house room except in the library under lock and key, the key is in the Master's pocket; but bad women, if they are not white and serve in a menial capacity, may swarm the house unmolested. The ostrich game is thought a Christian act. These women are no more regarded as a dangerous contingent than canary birds would be.
>
> (Aug. 22, 1861.) I hate slavery. You say there are no more fallen women on a plantation than in London, in proportion to numbers; but what do you say to this? A magnate who runs a hideous black harem with its consequences under the same roof with his lovely white wife and his beautiful and accomplished daughters?

These diary entries indicate that Chesnut held enslaved black women responsible for their fate. Her wrath and anger is aimed at them and not at white men. Although stereotypical images of black womanhood during slavery were based on the myth that all black women were immoral and sexually loose, slave narratives and diaries of the 19th century present no evidence that they were in any way more sexually "liberated" than white women. The great majority of enslaved black women accepted the dominant culture's sexual morality and adapted it to their circumstances. Black slave girls were taught, like their white counterparts, that virtue was woman's ideal spiritual nature and virginity her ideal physical state, but knowledge of the acceptable sexual morality did not alter the reality that no social order existed to protect them from sexual exploitation.

When slavery ended, black women and men welcomed their newly acquired freedom to express their sexuality. Like the early white colonizers, newly manumitted black folks were without any social order to govern and restrain their sexual behavior and indulged themselves with proper abandon. It must have been a good feeling for the manumitted slaves to suddenly have the freedom to choose a sexual partner and to behave in whatever manner they so desired. Some manumitted black women exercised their new found sexual freedom by engaging freely in sexual relationships with black men. Whites saw the sexual activity of the manumitted female slave as further evidence to support their claim that black women were sexually loose and innately morally depraved. They chose to ignore the fact that the great majority of black women and men attempted to adapt the values and behavior patterns deemed acceptable by whites. During the years of Black Reconstruction, 1867-77, black women struggled to change negative images of black womanhood perpetuated by whites. Trying to dispel the myth that all black women were sexually loose, they emulated the conduct and mannerisms of white women. But as manumitted black women and men struggled to change stereotypical images of black female sexuality, white society resisted. Everywhere black women went, on public streets, in shops, or at their places of work, they were accosted and subjected to obscene comments and even physical abuse at the hands of white men and women. Those black women suffered most whose behavior best exemplified that of a "lady". A black woman dressed tidy and clean, carrying herself in a dignified manner, was usually the object of mudslinging by white men who ridiculed and mocked her self-improvement efforts. They reminded her that in the eyes of the white public she would never be seen as worthy of consideration or respect.

White journalists daily ridiculed the efforts of black people to improve their image in leading magazines and newspapers. They delighted in entertaining white readers with negative stereotypes of black people. Rayford Logan examines the extent to which leading newspapers and magazines deliberately perpetuated negative myths and stereotypes about black people in his study of the period from 1877 to 1918, *The Betrayal of the Negro*. Logan acknowledges that whites made a concerted effort to perpetuate the myth that all black women were sexually loose and immoral. He comments:

> The alleged unchastity of Negro women in general was analyzed in an article in the Atlantic. The practice was attributed to their lack of concern for sexual purity and to the free use that white men made of them. The author added that the sexual immorality of Negro women was a deterrent to loose morals between white men and white women.

Articles of this type were aimed at maintaining separation of the races. They convinced white readers that they would not want to live as social equals with black people by arguing that contact with the loose morals of blacks (and particularly those of black women) would lead to a breakdown of all moral values. The white public justified white male sexual assault of black females by arguing that the women invited sexual abuse by their lack of morals.

Sexual exploitation of black women undermined the morale of newly manumitted black people. For it seemed to them that if they could not change negative images of black womanhood they would never be able to uplift the race as a whole. Married or single, child or woman, the black female was a likely target for white male rapists. Young black girls were admonished by concerned parents to avoid walking down isolated streets and to avoid contact with white men whenever possible. While these practices curtailed sexual exploitation, it was not eliminated because most sexual assaults occurred on jobs. . . .Black women were often coerced into sexual liaisons with white employers who would threaten to fire them unless they capitulated to sexual demands. . . .

The sexual assault of black women was so prevalent in both the North and the South after slavery ended that outraged black women and men wrote articles in newspapers and magazines pleading with the American public to take action against white and black male offenders who assaulted black women. . . .When black people urged the white public to aid them in their struggles to protect black womanhood, their appeals fell on deaf ears. So pervasive was the tendency of whites to regard all black women as sexually loose and unworthy of respect that their achievements were ignored. Even if an individual black female became a lawyer, doctor, or teacher, she was likely to be labeled a whore or prostitute by whites. All black women, irrespective of their circumstances, were lumped into the category of available sex objects. As late at the 60s, black woman playwright Lorraine Hansberry in *To Be Young, Gifted, and Black* included scenes that dramatized the way in which all black women are perceived by whites (and in particular white men), as available sex objects, as prostitutes. In the play a young black domestic worker says:

> All right. So now you know something 'bout me you didn't know! In these streets out there, any little white boy from Long Island or Westchester sees me and leans out of his car and yells—"Hey there, hot chocolate! Say there Jezebel! Hey you—'Hundred Dollar Misunderstanding! YOU! Bet you know where there's a good time tonight. . . ."
>
> Follow me sometimes and see if I lie. I can be coming home from eight hours on an assembly line or fourteen hours in Mrs. Halsey's kitchen. I can be all filled up that day with three hundred years of rage so that my eyes are flashing and my flesh is trembling—and the white boys in the streets, they look at me and think of sex. They look at me and that's all they think. . .Baby, you could be Jesus in drag—but if you're brown they're sure you're selling!

Hansberry shows that this attitude toward black women transcended class boundaries. Later in the play a chic black professional woman of middle-age speaks:

> 'Hey there, hot chocolate! Say there, Jezebel! YOU. . .! The white boys in the streets, they look at me and think of sex. They look at me and that's all they think!

Like Susan Brownmiller, most people tend to see devaluation of black womanhood as occurring only in the context of slavery. In actuality, sexual exploitation of black women continued long after slavery ended and was institutionalized by other oppressive practices. Devaluation of black womanhood after slavery ended was a conscious, deliberate effort on the part of whites to sabotage mounting black female self-confidence and self-respect. In *Black Women in White America*, Gerda Lerner discusses the "complex system of supportive mechanisms and sustaining myths" white women and men established to encourage sexual exploitation of black women and to ensure no change would occur in their social status:

> One of these was the myth of the "bad" black woman. By assuming a different level of sexuality for all Blacks than that of whites and mythifying their greater sexual potency, the black woman could be made to personify sexual freedom and abandon. A myth was created that all black women were eager for sexual exploits, voluntarily "loose" in their morals and, therefore deserved none of the consideration and respect granted white women. Every black woman was, by definition, a slut according to this racist mythology; therefore, to assault her and exploit her sexually was not reprehensible and carried with it none of the normal communal sanctions against such behavior. A wide range of practices reinforced this myth: the laws against intermarriage; the denial of the title "Miss" or "Mrs." to any black woman; the taboos against respectable social mixing of the races; the refusal to let black women customers try on clothing in stores before making a purchase; the assigning of single toilet facilities to both sexes of Blacks; the different legal sanction against rape, abuse of minors and other sex crimes when committed against white or black women.

Systematic devaluation of black womanhood was not simply a direct consequence of race hatred, it was a calculated method of social control. During the reconstruction years, manumitted black people had demonstrated that given the same opportunities as whites they could excel in all areas. Their accomplishments were a direct challenge to racist notions about the inherent inferiority of dark races. In those glorious years, it seemed that black people would quickly and successfully assimilate and amalgamate into the mainstream of American culture. White people reacted to the progress of black people by attempting to return to the old social order. To maintain white supremacy they established a new social order based on apartheid. The period in American history is commonly known as the Jim Crow or "separate but equal" years, but both phrases shift attention away from the fact that separation of the races once slavery ended was a deliberate political move on the part of white supremacists. As miscegenation represented the greatest threat to white racial solidarity, a complex system of laws and social taboos was enacted to maintain separation of the races. In most states laws were enacted forbidding inter-racial marriage, but such laws did not prevent blacks and whites from uniting. Manumitted black men and white women in northern states were married in noticeable numbers. White men, who so desired, legalized relationships with ex-slave women. A report of a marriage between a white man and a black woman published in a New Orleans newspaper, the *Tribune*, carried the headlines, "The World Moves." In the article, the journalist advised other white men to "take a hint now that the law allows it legitimize their children." Inter-racial marriages between black women and white men evoked fear and rage in the white public. White male legalized sexual unions with black women and black male legalized sexual unions with white women threatened the entire foundation of apartheid. Since anti-amalgamation laws were not sufficient deterrents to inter-racial marriage, white men used psychological warfare to enforce the ideal of white supremacy. They employed two important myths to brainwash all whites against the newly manumitted blacks: the myth of the "bad," sexually loose black woman and the myth of the black male rapist. Neither myth was based on fact.

At no time in the early part of the 20th century were any large numbers of black men raping white women or seeking illicit relationships with them. Joseph Washington, Jr.'s study of inter-racial union, *Marriage in Black and White*, documents the fact that black men who sought relationships with white women were eager for marriage. White people were never reacting to any high incidence of inter-racial rape during reconstruction; they simply wanted to prevent inter-racial marriage. They used lynchings, castration, and other brutal punishments to prevent black men from initiating relationships with white women. They perpetuated the myth that all black men were eager to rape white women so that white females would not seek friendships with black men for fear of brutal assault. The horrific nature of violent attacks on black manhood has caused historiographers and sociologists to assume that whites feared unions between white women and black men most. In actuality, they feared legally sanctioned racial mixing on the part of the sexes of either group, but as black men were more likely to seek legal sanction through marriage of their relationships with white women, they received the brunt of attacks by white supremacists. By brainwashing white women to see black men as savage beasts, white supremacists were able to implant enough fear in the white female's psyche so that she would avoid any contact with black men.

In the case of black women and white men, inter-racial sex was both encouraged and condoned as long as it did not lead to marriage. By perpetuating the myth that all black women were incapable of fidelity and sexually loose, whites hoped to so devalue them that no white man would marry a black woman. After manumission, white men who treated black women with respect or sought to integrate a black female into respectable white society were persecuted and ostracized. During slavery, it had been a common occurrence for an upper class or middle class white man to take a black woman mistress and live openly with her without incurring much public disapproval. In *Roll, Jordan, Roll* Eugene Genovese comments:

> Some prominent planters flaunted their slave mistresses and mulatto children. David Dickson of Georgia, one of the most celebrated leaders in the movement to reform southern agriculture, lost his wife early in life, took a mistress, and accepted a measure of social disapproval to live openly with her and their children. Bennett H. Barrow of Louisiana exploded with rage over similar conduct on the part of his neighbors. His fellow planters of West Feliciana Parish were, he said, of course all opponents of the abolitionists. "Yet, the people submit to amalgamation in its worst form in this Parish. Josias Grey takes his mulatto children with him to public places, etc. and receives similar company from New Orleans. . ." The first mayor of Memphis, Marcus Winchester, had a beautiful quadroon mistress whom he married and took to Louisiana. His successor, Ike Rawlins, lived with a slave woman. He did not marry her but did provide handsomely for their sons. And the haughty nabobs of Natches had their own scandals. Other white observers report such relationships, displayed publicly and accepted by society with nothing worse than muttering and minor social ostracism. Several daughters of wealthy free Negroes married respectable white men.

Marriages between black women and white men could be tolerated during slavery because they were so few in number and represented no threat to the white supremacist regime. After manumission they were no longer tolerated. In the state of Kentucky, the Supreme Court was asked to judge insane a white man who desired to marry a female slave he had once owned. Once slavery ended and whites declared that no black woman regardless of her class status or skin color could ever be a "lady," it was no longer socially acceptable for a white man to have a black mistress. Instead, the institutionalized devaluation of black womanhood encouraged all white men to regard black females as whores or prostitutes. Lower class white men, who had had little sexual contact with black women during slavery, were encouraged to believe they were entitled to access to the bodies of black women. In large cities their lust for black female sex objects led to the formation of numerous houses of prostitution which supplied black bodies to meet the growing demands of white men. The myth perpetuated by whites that black women were the possessors of a heightened sexuality encouraged white male rapists and sexual exploiters.

Notes and Questions

1. *Resistance*. Bell hooks tells of the slave woman Ann, who was punished for defending herself against a rape by a whipper (p. 359). When enslaved African-American women resisted their white slave masters, the violence against them only escalated to ensure their continued subordination. The case of *State v. Celia, A Slave*, No. 4496 (Calloway County Ct., Mo. 1855), provides another example of enslaved African-American women resisting rape and also helps us to understand how and why such resistance was intolerable within the slave economy supported by political and legal institutions. Celia was bought by Robert Newsom, a Missouri farmer, in 1850 when she was fourteen years old. *See* Melton A. McLauin, Celia, A Slave 20 (1991). Newsom immediately established his power by raping her and he continued to sexually exploit her for the next five years. *See id.* at 20-22. During those five years, Celia gave birth to two children, who were probably fathered by Newsom. *See id.* at 24. As hooks describes as typical of slave owners (p. 358), Newsom provid ed Celia with "gifts," including a cabin of her own. *See id.* At some time before 1855, Celia established a romantic relationship with George, another of Newsom's slaves. In the winter of 1855, Celia was pregnant again and George was threatening to end their relationship unless she kept Newsom away from her. *See id.* at 24-25. Celia went to Newsom's daughters and asked them to intercede with their father on her behalf to keep him from coming to her cabin. *See id.* at 27. There is no evidence that the daughters attempted to intervene. *See id.* at 27-28. Sometime in late spring or early summer, Celia begged Newsom to leave her alone and even threatened to hurt him if he did not. *See id.* at 28-29. After this confrontation with Newsom, Celia obtained a large stick to protect herself. *See id.* at 29. Based on testimony at the trial, the following took place on the night of June 23.

> [Newsom] entered [Celia's] cabin. . . .Precisely what occurred in the few minutes after Newsom entered the cabin is unclear. It is reasonable to assume that Newsom, as was his custom, went to the cabin solely for the purpose of having sexual intercourse with Celia. Since Celia had warned her master

> not to come to her cabin again for that purpose, and had threatened to hurt him if he did so, it is also reasonable to assume that a confrontation occurred. We do know from testimony at Celia's trial that the two exchanged words. Whatever else was said, we know that Newsom demanded that Celia continue to have sex with him and that Celia refused.
>
> As Newsom approached her, Celia retreated before him into a corner of the house, with Newsom positioned between her and the fireplace. . . .Celia reached into the corner and retrieved the large stick. . . .As the old man continued to advance, with one hand she raised the stick. . .and brought it down against the head of her master. Dazed by the blow, Newsom "sunk down on a stool or towards the floor," groaning and throwing up his hands as if to catch Celia. Afraid that an angered Newsom would harm her, Celia raised the club with both hands and once again brought it crashing down on Newsom's skull. With the second blow the old man fell, dead, to the floor.

Id. at 29-30. Because Celia could not, as a slave, legally testify against a white person, the defense of self-defense was unavailable to her; the court could not obtain direct testimony from Celia that she feared for her life. *See id.* at 90. The defense argued that under Missouri law because it was a crime "to take any woman unlawfully against her will and by force. . .," Celia's action was justifiable if committed in resisting the commission of this crime. *See id.* at 91. The judge rejected this radical legal argument and refused to give the defense's requested jury instructions, making Celia's conviction inevitable.

> Acceptance of the defense's argument that slave women were protected by law from sexual exploitation by white men, including their masters, would have granted slave women legal equality with white women in an area of social activity that, more than any other, symbolized class relationships within the South's slaveholding society. In one sense it would have given more protection to slave than to free women, because it would have allowed slave women the right to resist the sexual advances of any man, including masters and husbands, since slave marriages were not afforded legal status. It would have checked the master's absolute power over female slaves to some degree, perhaps not so much as the fear of physical attack by a black mate, but certainly more than fear of social opprobrium. Since slaves could not testify against whites, it would have encouraged slave women, such as Celia, to seek aid from sympathetic whites, aid that could be provided within the law. It would have recognized the humanity of the slave, granted slaves not just a right to life, which the law recognized, but a right to human dignity. White southerners sought to deny slaves precisely this prerogative because of the moral dilemmas inherent within the system. Although the slaves' humanity could never be completely denied, it had to be minimized for the institution of slavery to function. It was in an effort to deny slaves dignity, to deny their humanity, that the law sought to categorize, to define slaves as something other than human, a separate category of being. To have done otherwise, to have recognized by law the basic humanity of slaves, would have created even greater tensions within the society and posed additional moral dilemmas.
>
> The arguments of the defense threatened not only the social assumptions

> under which slavery operated but the economics of slavery as well. . . .By granting slave women the legal right to use force to repel unwanted sexual advances, the defense's instructions would have interfered to some degree with what owners saw as a property right. . . .
>
> Perhaps most significant, the defense's instructions challenged the role of the white man as the protector of women within southern society. Indeed, it was the duty of the white man to protect all of those in his charge, especially white women. Another generally held expectation within the society was that the slaveholder be responsible for and behave morally toward his human property. . . .The defense's instructions challenged the southern concept of male honor, a crucial element of the South's social system. If slaves could not rely on the protection of their masters, could masters be trusted to protect others in their charge? Specifically, the requested instructions posed the question that if slave women could not be trusted to the protection of their white male masters, and in fact required the protection of the law against their masters, did not white women stand in essentially the same relationship to their husbands?

Id. at 99-101. Celia was executed on December 21, 1855, after the Supreme Court of Missouri refused the stay of execution. *See id.* at 113-14.

2. *"Raising the Curtain"/"Lifting the Veil."* One of the reasons why the law refused to protect female slaves from sexual violence by their masters was that a master's treatment of his female slaves was viewed as within the realm of domesticity and as therefore protected by the "veil of private life" (p. 360). How does the connection of privacy and domesticity to slavery in the United States affect your understanding of the North Carolina courts' invocation of the "curtain" of privacy in the nineteenth century to justify the law's failure to intervene in domestic assaults? *See State v. Rhodes*, at p. 196.

3. *Prostitution and Rape.* Hooks describes how white male slaveowners provided material goods to enslaved African-American women they raped ostensibly converting a rape into an economic exchange (p. 358). There is evidence that the slaveowner Newsom absolved his own behavior toward Celia in this way. *See* Note 1, at p. 352. As hooks also reports, the anti-slavery movement masked the rape of enslaved African-American women under the label of prostitution (p. 361). The relabeling of rape as prostitution contributed to the construction of African-American women as "available sex objects" (p. 366) and relieved white men of responsibility for raping African-American women. What beliefs of the white slaveowners, abolitionists, and the abolitionists' audiences underlie the relabeling of rape as prostitution?

4. *Sexual Harassment and Rape.* Hooks describes the sexual exploitation that African-American women experienced historically in their jobs (p. 365); this issue was also considered in Chapter 5. *See* p. 283, 300. Perhaps less well known is the role that sexual exploitation played in the migration of African-American women from the South to the North in the late nineteenth and early twentieth century. Darlene Clark Hine asks why African-American women migrated to the North given that discriminatory hiring policies meant that they would probably have to work in the same kinds of domestic service jobs that they were leaving in the South.

> There were some significant differences that help explain this phenomenon. A maid earning seven dollars a week in Cleveland perceived herself to be, and probably was, much better off than a counterpart receiving two dollars and fifty cents a week in Mobile, Alabama. A factory worker, even one whose work was dirty and low status, could and did imagine herself better off than domestic servants who endured the unrelenting scrutiny, interference, and complaints of household mistresses and the untoward advances of male family members.
>
> I believe that in order to understand this historical migratory trend we need to understand the noneconomic motives propelling Black female migration. I believe that many Black women quit the South out of a desire to achieve personal autonomy and to escape both from sexual exploitation from inside and outside of their families and from the rape and threat of rape by white as well as Black males. To focus on the sexual and the personal impetus for Black women's migration in the first several decades of the twentieth century neither dismisses nor diminishes the significance of economic motives.

Darlene Clark Hine, Rape and the Inner Lives of Black Women in the Middle West: Preliminary Thoughts on the Culture of Dissemblance, 14 Signs 912, 913-14 (1989). Paula Giddings provides further support for the prevalence of sexual exploitation as a factor motivating African-American women to migrate to the North and as a factor motivating African-American women to organize on their own behalf.

> [In 1896 African-American women formed the] National Association for Colored Women (NACW), with a membership that would reach 50,000 by 1916, it would act not only as a means to realize suffrage, education, and community development, but the vessel through which black women challenged, in public, the beliefs that were getting black men lynched and black women raped and exploited. Sexual exploitation was so pervasive that it drove black women north in search of safer climes. "It is a significant and shameful fact that I am constantly in receipt of letters from still unprotected women in the South," complained the nineteenth-century Chicago activist Fannie Barrier Williams, "begging me to find employment for their daughters. . .to save them from going into the homes of the South as servants as there is nothing to save them from dishonor and degradation." In 1893, before the predominantly white Congress of Representative Women, Williams challenged that black women shouldn't be disparaged but protected, adding that "I do not want to disturb the serenity of this conference by suggesting why this protection is needed and the kind of man against whom it is needed."

Paula Giddings, The Last Taboo, in Race-ing Justice, En-Gendering Power: Essays on Anita Hill, Clarence Thomas, and the Construction of Social Reality 441, 454 (Toni Morrison ed., 1992).

5. *Rape Constructed through Race.* Angela Davis explains the interconnection of racism and rape and how that interconnection socially constructs rape.

> Racism has always drawn strength from its ability to encourage sexual coercion. While Black women and their sisters of color have been the main targets of these racist-inspired attacks, white women have suffered as well.

> For once white men were persuaded that they could commit sexual assaults against Black women with impunity, their conduct toward women of their own race could not have remained unmarred. Racism has always served as a provocation to rape, and white women in the United States have necessarily suffered the ricochet fire of these attacks. This is one of the many ways in which racism nourishes sexism, causing white women to be indirectly victimized by the special oppression aimed at their sisters of color.
>
> The experience of the Vietnam War furnished a further example of the extent to which racism could function as a provocation to rape. Because it was drummed into the heads of U.S. soldiers that they were fighting an inferior race, they could be taught that raping Vietnamese women was a necessary military duty. They could even be instructed to "search" the women with their penises. It was the unwritten policy of the U.S. Military Command to systematically encourage rape, since it was an extremely effective weapon of mass terrorism. Where are the thousands upon thousands of Vietnam veterans who witnessed and participated in these horrors? To what extent did those brutal experiences affect their attitudes toward women in general? While it would be quite erroneous to single out Vietnam veterans as the main perpetrators of sexual crimes, there can be little doubt that the horrendous repercussions of the Vietnam experience are still being felt by all women in the United States today.

Angela Y. Davis, Women, Race, and Class 177 (1981).

Davis goes on to show how racism and capitalism, through the myth of the Black rapist, allow some white men's sexual exploitation not to be perceived as rape.

> The myth of the Black rapist continues to carry out the insidious work of racist ideology. It must bear a good portion of the responsibility for the failure of most anti-rape theorists to seek the identity of the enormous numbers of anonymous rapists who remain unreported, untried and unconvicted. As long as their analyses focus on accused rapists who are reported and arrested, thus on only a fraction of the rapes actually committed, Black men—and other men of color—will inevitably be viewed as the villains responsible for the current epidemic of sexual violence. The anonymity surrounding the vast majority of rapes is consequently treated as a statistical detail—or else as a mystery whose meaning is inaccessible.
>
> But why are there so many anonymous rapists in the first place? Might not this anonymity be a privilege enjoyed by men whose status protects them from prosecution? Although white men who are employers, executives, politicians, doctors, professors, etc., have been known to "take advantage" of women they consider their social inferiors, their sexual misdeeds seldom come to light in court. Is it not therefore quite probable that these men of the capitalist and middle classes account for a significant proportion of the unreported rapes? Many of these unreported rapes undoubtedly involve Black women as victims: their historical experience proves that racist ideology implies an open invitation to rape. As the basis of the license to rape Black women during slavery was the slaveholders' economic power, so the class structure of capitalist society also harbors an incentive to rape. It seems, in fact, that men of the capitalist class and their middle-class partners are

> immune to prosecution because they commit their sexual assaults with the same unchallenged authority that legitimizes their daily assaults on the labor and dignity of working people.

Id. at 199-200.

The analysis of the intersection of rape and race has primarily focused on the myth of the African-American male rapist. Kimberlé Crenshaw also makes clear, however, that the traditional treatment of rape in the justice system is a product of and results in discrimination against African-American women as victims of rape.

> Dominant narratives representing the intersections of racism and sexual violence continue to focus on the way that black men accused of raping white women are disproportionately punished relative to black-on-black or white-on-white rape. Within traditional antiracist formulations, this disproportionality has been characterized as racial discrimination against black men. Yet the pattern of punishing black men accused of raping white women more harshly than those accused of raping black women is just as surely an illustration of discrimination against black women. Indeed, some studies suggest that the race of the victim rather than the race of the defendant is the most salient factor determining the disposition of men convicted of rape. Clearly, black women are victims of a racial hierarchy that subordinates their experiences of sexual abuse to those of white women. Yet this intersectional oppression is rarely addressed in antiracist discourses in part because traditional readings of racism continue to center on power differentials between men. Consequently, there is relatively little emphasis on how racism contributes to the victimization of black women both inside and outside the criminal-justice system.

Kimberlé Crenshaw, Whose Story Is It, Anyway? Feminist and Antiracist Appropriations of Anita Hill, in Race-ing Justice, En-Gendering Power: Essays on Anita Hill, Clarence Thomas, and the Construction of Social Reality 402, 419 (Toni Morrison ed., 1992).

6. *Effects of Rape by Race.* Gail Elizabeth Wyatt undertook a study of women in Los Angeles to compare the effects of rape on white women and African-American women. Gail Elizabeth Wyatt, The Sociocultural Context of African-American and White American Women's Rape, 48 J. Soc. Issues 77 (1992). In this study 248 women were interviewed; 126 were African-American and 122 were white American women. *Id.* at 81. Of those women interviewed, 55 reported they had experienced 146 incidents of attempted or completed rape. *Id.* at 82. Twenty-five percent of African-American women and twenty percent of white American women experienced at least one such incident since age eighteen. *Id.* Wyatt's study concludes the following:

> African American women were significantly less likely to disclose incidents involving sexual assault. . . .
>
> Rape victims may not perceive the police as supportive because of their recollections of past racial incidents where race/ethnicity mediated police responses to other crimes or to rape incidents in the Black community. . . .
>
> In the present study, African American women were significantly more likely than White women to recognize the danger in their living environments that

> place them at risk of being victimized by men if the opportunity presented itself. . . .
>
> That more African American women had heard that they were more likely to be rape victims and believed this statement to be true suggests that rape is perceived as a likely rather than an unlikely occurrence in their lives. Such an assumption can complicate male-female relationships where feelings of trust and sexual vulnerability are at issue. . . .
>
> The immediate effects of incidents of rape were similar for both groups. Many of the symptoms that victims described in the areas of postassault physical, sexual, and psychological functioning were similar to descriptions of posttraumatic stress disorder.
>
> In addition to the immediate impact of abuse incidents, many women also indicated that they experienced lasting effects. Most of the 55 women who had experienced sexual assaults reported effects that had lasted, on average, 5 1/2 years. . . .
>
> It is possible that African-American women's awareness of rape stems not only from their personal experience, but also from membership in an ethnic group that lived through a period of American history where their incidents of sexual assault were not considered crimes. In the present study, some women recalled incidents that renewed memories of the historical treatment of Black women who were raped during the slavery era. For example, one African American woman recalled hearing about a relative who was abducted, beaten, raped, and killed while her family was living in the South. . . .Rape was described as something that could happen to you just because you were Black and female.

Id. at 86-88.

7. *Rape, Race, and Coalitions Between African-American and White Women.* Hooks describes the complicity of white women in the sexual exploitation of slave women (p. 363). Patricia Hill Collins believes that this historical legacy continues to affect the relationships between African-American and white women. *See* Patricia Hill Collins, Black Feminist Thought: Knowledge, Consciousness, and the Politics of Empowerment at Note 4, at p. 159.

Davis goes on to explain the conspicuous absence of African-American women in the beginnings of the contemporary anti-rape movement.

> [I]t may be due, in part, to that movement's indifferent posture toward the frame-up rape charge as an incitement to racist aggression. Too many innocents have been offered sacrificially to gas chambers and lifer's cells for Black women to join those who often seek relief from policemen and judges. Moreover, as rape victims themselves, they have found little if any sympathy from these men in uniforms and robes. And stories about police assaults on Black women—rape victims sometimes suffering a second rape—are heard too frequently to be dismissed as aberrations. . . .
>
> During the early stages of the contemporary anti-rape movement, few feminist theorists seriously analyzed the special circumstances surrounding the Black woman as rape victim. The historical knot binding Black women—systematically abused and violated by white men—to Black men—maimed and murdered because of the racist manipulation of the rape charge—has just begun to be acknowledged to any significant extent. . . .

It is a painful irony that some anti-rape theorists, who ignore the part played by racism in instigating rape, do not hesitate to argue that men of color are especially prone to commit sexual violence against women. In her very impressive study of rape, Susan Brownmiller claims that Black men's historical oppression has placed many of the "legitimate" expressions of male supremacy beyond their reach. They must resort, as a result, to acts of open sexual violence. . . .

When Brownmiller's book *Against Our Will: Men, Women and Rape* was published, it was effusively praised in some circles. . . .In other circles, however, the book has been severely criticized for its part in the resuscitation of the old racist myth of the Black rapist.

It cannot be denied that Brownmiller's book is a pioneering scholarly contribution to the contemporary literature on rape. Yet many of her arguments are unfortunately pervaded with racist ideas. Characteristic of that perspective is her reinterpretation of the 1953 lynching of fourteen-year-old Emmett Till. After this young boy had whistled at a white woman in Mississippi, his maimed body was found at the bottom of the Tallahatchie River. "Till's action," said Brownmiller, "was more than a kid's brash prank."

> Emmett Till was going to show his black buddies that he, and by inference, *they* could get a white woman . . . .The whistle was no small tweet of hubba-hubba or melodious approval for a well-turned ankle. . . .It was a deliberate insult just short of physical assault . . . .

While Brownmiller deplores the sadistic punishment inflicted on Emmett Till, the Black youth emerges, nonetheless, as a guilty sexist—almost as guilty as his white racist murderers. After all, she argues, both Till and his murderers were exclusively concerned about their rights of possession over women. . . .

Susan Brownmiller's discussion on rape and race evinces an unthinking partisanship which borders on racism. In pretending to defend the cause of all women, she sometimes boxes herself into the position of defending the particular cause of *white* women, regardless of its implications. . . .

In choosing to take sides with white women, regardless of the circumstances, Brownmiller herself capitulates to racism. Her failure to alert white women about the urgency of combining a fierce challenge to racism with the necessary battle against sexism is an important plus for the forces of racism today.

Davis, *supra*, 173, 177-79, 198-99.

McQuirter v. State,

63 So. 2d 388 (Ala. 1953)

Price, J. Appellant, a Negro man, was found guilty of an attempt to commit an assault with intent to rape, under an indictment charging an assault with intent to rape. The jury assessed a fine of $500.

About 8:00 o'clock on the night of June 29, 1951, Mrs. Ted Allen, a white woman, with her two children and a neighbor's little girl, were drinking Coca-Cola at the "Tiny Diner" in Atmore. When they started in the direction of Mrs.

Allen's home she noticed appellant sitting in the cab of a parked truck. As she passed the truck appellant said something unintelligible, opened the truck door and placed his foot on the running board.

Mrs. Allen testified appellant followed her down the street and when she reached Suell Lufkin's house she stopped. As she turned into the Lufkin house appellant was within two or three feet of her. She waited ten minutes for appellant to pass. When she proceeded on her way, appellant came toward her from behind a telephone pole. She told the children to run to Mr. Simmons' house and tell him to come and meet her. When appellant saw Mr. Simmons he turned and went back down the street to the intersection and leaned on a stop sign just across the street from Mrs. Allen's home. Mrs. Allen watched him at the sign from Mr. Simmons' porch for about thirty minutes, after which time he came back down the street and appellant went on home.

Mrs. Allen's testimony was corroborated by that of her young daughter. The daughter testified the appellant was within six feet of her mother as she approached the Lufkin house, and this witness said there was a while when she didn't see appellant at the intersection.

Mr. Lewis Simmons testified when the little girls ran up on his porch and said a Negro was after them, witness walked up the sidewalk to meet Mrs. Allen and saw appellant. Appellant went on down the street and stopped in front of Mrs. Allen's home and waited there approximately thirty minutes.

Mr. Clarence Bryars, a policeman in Atmore, testified that appellant stated after his arrest that he came to Atmore with the intention of getting him a white woman that night.

Mr. W. E. Strickland, Chief of Police of Atmore, testified that appellant stated in the Atmore jail he didn't know what was the matter with him; that he was drinking a little; that he and his partner had been to Pensacola; that his partner went to the "Front" to see a colored woman; that he didn't have any money and he sat in the truck and made up his mind he was going to get the first woman that came by and that this was the first woman that came by. He said he got out of the truck, came around the gas tank and watched the lady and when she started off he started off behind her; that he was going to carry her in the cotton patch and if she hollered he was going to kill her. He testified appellant made the same statement in the Brewton jail.

Mr. Norvelle Seals, Chief Deputy Sheriff, corroborated Mr. Strickland's testimony as to the statement by appellant at the Brewton jail.

Appellant, as a witness in his own behalf, testified he and Bill Page, another Negro, carried a load of junk-iron from Monroeville to Pensacola; on their way back to Monroeville they stopped in Atmore. They parked the truck near the "Tiny Diner" and rode to the "Front," the colored section, in a cab. Appellant came back to the truck around 8:00 o'clock and sat in the truck cab for about thirty minutes. He decided to go back to the "Front" to look for Bill Page. As he started up the street he saw prosecutrix and her children. He turned around and waited until he decided they had gone, then he walked up the street toward the "Front." When he reached the intersection at the telegraph pole he decided he didn't want to go to the "Front" and sat around there a few minutes, then went on to the "Front" and stayed about 25 or 30 minutes, and came back to the truck.

He denied that he followed Mrs. Allen or made any gesture toward molesting her or the children. He denied making the statements testified to by the officers.

He testified he had never been arrested before and introduced testimony by two residents of Monroeville as to his good reputation for peace and quiet and for truth and veracity.

Appellant insists the trial court erred in refusing the general affirmative charge and in denying the motion for a new trial on the ground the verdict was contrary to the evidence.

"'An attempt to commit an assault with intent to rape,'. . .means an attempt to rape which has not proceeded far enough to amount to an assault". *Burton v. State*, 8 Ala. App. 295, 62 So. 394, 396.

Under the authorities in this state, to justify a conviction for an attempt to commit an assault with intent to rape the jury must be satisfied beyond a reasonable doubt that defendant intended to have sexual intercourse with prosecutrix against her will, by force or by putting her in fear. . . .

Intent is a question to be determined by the jury from the facts and circumstances adduced on the trial, and if there is evidence from which it may be inferred that at the time of the attempt defendant intended to gratify his lustful desires against the resistance of the female a jury question is presented. . . .

In determining the question of intention the jury may consider social conditions and customs founded upon racial differences, such as that the prosecutrix was a white woman and defendant was a Negro man. . . .

We find no reversible error in the record and the judgment of the trial court is affirmed. Affirmed.

Arthur F. Raper, The Tragedy of Lynching 141–48, 150–53 (1969)

Lynched After An All-Night Man-Hunt Ocilla, Irwin County, Georgia

On the last day of January, 1930, in a rural community southeast of Ocilla, Irwin County, Georgia, the dead body of a sixteen-year-old local white girl was found in a puddle of water by the side of the road. Circumstantial evidence and suspicion pointed to James Irwin, a Negro of a nearby community. He was captured next morning and taken to the place of his alleged crime. There he was tortured and mutilated, and then burned. Great crowds rode out to see the body during the day.

Irwin County is of historical interest chiefly because at Irwinville, its earliest county seat, Jefferson Davis was captured. Some of the local people are hoping that a monument will be raised to mark the spot.

The Lynching

A Double Capital Felony. Shortly after noon on January 31, 1930, a sixteen-year-old white farm girl, living a few miles south of Ocilla, went down the road to another farm home with a letter, which, by mistake, had been left in her father's mail box. On her return, as she neared a stream about half way home,

James Irwin, seated on a load of corn, drove past her and stopped, pretending to be making repairs on the harness. When the girl came alongside the wagon he grabbed her. In her efforts to escape him a struggle ensued in which he stabbed her severely about the throat and breasts and knocked out one of her eyes with a dull knife. He raped her, threw her body in a puddle, got back on his wagon, and, laying the whip to the mules, hurried away.

The above story, according to the county sheriff, was the confession Irwin made when captured the next morning. While his reported confession agreed with the known facts about the crime, and while it is generally believed that Irwin was guilty, his guilt has never been conclusively established. The evidence against him was his reported confession, plus the fact that he had passed along the road shortly before the body was found.

When the crime was discovered, suspicion immediately fell upon Irwin. An automobile took up the chase and when it came close behind him, a little distance from the Lax community, Irwin left his wagon and ran down a small stream. The sheriff was notified and at once got in touch with officers in other counties for bloodhounds. The report spread rapidly, and by late afternoon several bloodhounds were on hand. In the meantime a host of armed and excited men had gathered. Automobiles rushed in from widely scattered communities. A man-hunt of huge proportions began.

An All-Night Man-Hunt. With more than a thousand men participating, the hunt lasted all night. Except for short intervals when the track was lost, the dogs trailed the Negro continuously. About three o'clock, he ran out of a cabin in the Lax community. The mob gave chase but a volley of shots failed to stop him. The dogs took up the trail again. Shortly afterwards the sheriff went home to get a little rest, returning to the chase about four-thirty in the morning.

Near daylight the dogs bayed before a farm cabin in the Mystic community. The Negro who lived there told the searching party that Irwin was not inside. The sheriff, however, found Irwin crouched in the kitchen safe. Members of the mob wanted to do violence to the Negro who had shielded Irwin, but the sheriff prevented them.

Several Ocilla business men who participated in the all-night hunt report that when the sheriff captured Irwin they returned home for breakfast and then went to work. Certainly law and order gained nothing when those who had work at offices and shops withdrew and left the situation in the control of those who had nothing to do.

Sheriff Fired on and Ordered About by Mob. No sooner had the sheriff captured Irwin than members of the searching party filled the cabin and took complete control of the situation. The sheriff no less than the suspect was subject to the mob's orders: Irwin was left in his hands only on condition that the sheriff follow their instructions. With the prisoner and two deputies, he was permitted to get in a car and follow close behind a truck carrying fifteen armed men. Behind the sheriff's car were seventy-five or a hundred cars.

Reaching the edge of Ocilla, the sheriff endeavored to get away from the mob by going straight ahead when the truck had made a right-hand turn. As soon as he veered from the route, however, his car was fired upon. A bullet pierced the gasoline tank, emptying it immediately; a second passed through the hood of the car and the radiator, and a third pierced the top. The sheriff got out of the car and with profuse profanity accused those who fired upon him of being the lowest kind of cowards, emphasizing the fact that his own life had been endangered. In commenting upon his narrow escape, the sheriff later stated that anybody was mistaken who thought he was going to jeopardize his life to save a "nigger brute"—that he wouldn't do it and he thought any other white man with good sense would feel the same way. It is evident that the mob meant to have Irwin regardless of what happened to the sheriff.

After this attempt to escape, the sheriff, so he stated, maintained as before the custody of the prisoner, but only within the will of the mob, which with suspect and sheriff passed by the county jail in Ocilla on its way to the place where the girl's body had been found the afternoon before.

Protracted Tortures, Followed by Fire and Bullets. Upon reaching the place where the body of the girl was found, Irwin was tied to a tree with chains. The tortures began. Approximately a thousand people were present, including some women and children on the edge of the crowd. Members of the mob cut off his fingers and toes, joint by joint. Mob leaders carried them off as souvenirs. Next, his teeth were pulled out with wire pliers. Whenever he expressed pain or tried to evade the approaches of his sadistic avengers, he was jabbed in the mouth with a pointed pole. Because of their nature, the remaining mutilations and tortures will not be described. Suffice it to say that they were indecent and brutal beyond belief.

After these mutilations, which lasted more than an hour, Irwin's mangled but living body was hung upon a tree by the arms. Logs and underbrush were piled beneath. Gasoline was poured on. A match was struck. As the flames engulfed the body, it was pierced with bullets.

James Irwin was dead. All day his body, burned past recognition, hung in the tree by the public road. Thousands of white people, including women and children, rode out to see the spectacle. At nightfall the county authorities took the body down and buried it.

The Mob's Victim. James Irwin was working as a wage hand for the uncle of the murdered girl. Until three years before, he had lived in Pulaski County, fifty miles north of Irwin County on the lower edge of the old Georgia Black Belt. The sheriff stated that Irwin had served a sentence in Pulaski County for raping a Negro woman, and that a few months before the lynching he found him prowling about a white home at Ocilla. The evidence in the latter case, however, warranted only a severe reprimand from the court. Following the lynching it was reported about town that Irwin had been treated for a venereal disease by an Ocilla physician in the fall of 1929.

The mob's victim, practically illiterate, had always worked as a farm wage hand. He was married and had one child. The majority of the white people who had known him referred to Irwin as a well-behaved Negro, and expressed surprise that he should have been accused of such crimes. Local Negroes reported that Irwin bore a good reputation, and was a hardworking field hand.

A Close-up on One Lyncher. One of the Commission's investigators, traveling by auto, happened upon one of the mob members, herein called "Sandy," and transported him from Irwin County to Atlanta, a distance of over two hundred miles. According to "Sandy's" statement, he was there from first to last; he cut off and now has a joint of one of Irwin's toes; he took part in the later tortures, and put three bullets through Irwin's suspended body just as the flames flared up from the gasoline-soaked rubbish. The details of the tortures described by him parallel those given by others, including a college professor who was in the vicinity. By several statements "Sandy" implied that the immediate kinsmen of the murdered girl took prominent parts in Irwin's slow death.

"Sandy" was 21 years old; he was recently married, and is a Primitive Baptist. He attended high school for two years. "Sandy stated that he drank some, but was never drunk beyond consciousness except one time, and that was when he was married. He told in detail how the morning after his marriage he awoke and demanded an explanation: "What are you doing here?" He could scarcely believe it when told by the girl that they were husband and wife.

The first year after his father moved to Irwin County, "Sandy" worked at Ocilla and Fitzgerald. The second year (1930) he share-cropped a farm, and hardly broke even. Without money he decided to hitch-hike to a Texas ranch, where he had worked for a few months two years before. He left his wife behind.

"Sandy" is about six feet tall, weighs near 175 pounds, and his posture is a bit slouched. His coarse blond hair curls a little, and occasional freckles emphasize the blueness of his eyes. When last seen he was dressed in soiled overalls and denim jacket; his right shoe sole was flapping; he had on no socks or hat. In his left hand he clutched a wad of clothes about the size of a ten-cent watermelon, while with his right hand he hailed approaching motorists for passage to Texas.

•

Reaction of the Community to the Lynching

Attention of State and Nation Focused on Lynching. The Ocilla lynching was the first in the United States in 1930;[1] it was first in the southeastern states, excepting Florida, since the triple lynching at Aiken, S.C., three years earlier; it was the first in Georgia since 1926, when Dave Wright, a white man, was taken from the jail in Douglas, county seat of Coffee County, which borders Irwin County on the southeast. In this last case sixteen members of the lynching party were indicted, tried, and given penitentiary sentences of from one to twenty years. A precedent had been set; Georgia lynchers had been punished, and in the three years following, there had been no lynching in the state.

The Ocilla lynching was spot news for all papers in Georgia, particularly the county weeklies. The nature of the reported double capital crime tended to inflame the weeklies and to dampen the ardor of most of the metropolitan papers which usually condemn lynching. The daily papers in Georgia and the southeast, excepting the Macon *Telegraph*, devoted but little space to it. The Northern Negro papers carried the report with box letter headlines.

Local Weekly Defends Mob Members. The Ocilla *Star*, Irwin County's weekly, comes from the press Thursday. The lynching occurred on Saturday;

1. In January a Negro, Jose Hernandez, had been lynched on the accusation of cannibalism at Yatepec, State of Morelos, Mexico.

and consequently, the first local report was nearly a week later. The news article of February 6th featured the horror of the crimes committed and the record of the Negro lynched. The lynching was dealt with in a matter of fact way, as though it was as it should have been:

> "Negro burned by Angry Mob for Brutal Crime. James Irwin gets swift justice for assault and murder of sixteen year old girl.
>
> "Swift punishment was meted out to James Irwin for the commission of the most dastardly crime ever committed in Irwin County, when a crowd of enraged citizens from this and surrounding counties, early Saturday morning, after binding him with chains to a tree where he had attacked and murdered a 16 year old white girl of the county the afternoon before, burned him to death and later hung him to a black gum tree near the public highway.
>
> "After being captured, Irwin confessed to the crime, giving the details substantially as has been related. He also stated that he was an escaped convict serving a ten year term in Pulaski County.
>
> "He lived for the last two years at the home of Mrs. J. M. Willis near Mystic, where he had worked about the house. He was caught last year prowling about a house at Ocilla and locked up, but the charge was not pressed against him.
>
> "Irwin was carried to the spot where he had committed the most heinous crime in the history of the county and soon a fire snuffed out his life."

The editorial in this number of the local paper was an open attack upon the "unfavorable publicity" given "Irwin County's own lynching" by the Macon *Telegraph*:

> "Some of those who have criticized us most severely for the lynching that occurred in our county last Saturday seem to have almost lost sight of the fact that a most heinous crime had been committed the afternoon before by the man who was lynched. They lose sight of the fact that one of our pure lovely young girls just budding into attractive young womanhood was attacked and slain by the wanton brute who was the victim of the mob's summary punishment. They write chiefly of the quivering flesh of the burning victim, and not at all of the grasp of the foul beast, or of the deep sorrow that has settled down in the stricken home from which she was no ruthlessly snatched.
>
> "It is one thing to sit behind a mahogany desk a hundred miles away when one knows none of the persons concerned and write scathing editorials on the abstract subject of lynching and its evils. It is quite another thing when it comes close home to us as did last Friday's crime. When it is some other man's daughter or wife, especially if she is far removed from the moralizer, it is easy to see what ought not to have been done. When it is one's own wife or daughter or the wife or daughter of one's neighbor, it is quite a different matter.
>
> "It is unfortunate that the law was not allowed to take its course. There was not a chance that the brute would escape prompt conviction and death at the hands of the law if the mob had permitted his trial.
>
> "But it is to be expected. When this kind of crime is committed, whether it be in Georgia or in Maine, men are going to see that the offender gets his punishment without waiting for the courts. Wrong, of course, but it will

nearly always be done. This paper does not condone lynching, but so long as this crime is committed, so long may criminals expect mob violence. . . .

"Let us all hope that there will never be another lynching in Irwin County and that there will be no crime like the one that caused this one."

In this same editorial the following comments on race relations appeared:

"And it is not a question of race. Had a white man been guilty of the crime that James Irwin committed last Friday afternoon, he would have been lynched just as surely as the Negro was. It is noteworthy that in the all night hunt for this criminal several negroes joined in the search, and many of them have expressed the conviction that Irwin got just what he deserved. While on the subject of race, it is to be noted that this crime was not committed by one of our Irwin County Negroes. He was an escaped convict from another section. Our Negroes are a much better class than was this man."

"The Macon Telegraph Flops," Says Local Editor. In the following number of the Ocilla *Star*, February 13, were two editorials, the first, "An Appreciation":

"The editor would be less than human if he did not appreciate the many kind things that have been said to him since the editorial on the lynching appeared last week. One commendation is especially appreciated, and that is the assurance that has come to him that the editorial played some part in reassuring the law abiding negroes of the county that no harm to them was meant. The relations between the negroes of Irwin County and the white people have always been agreeable. . . ."

Court Action Limited to Judge's Charge. The courts have done nothing. The coroner's inquest "found that the deceased came to his death by burning and gunshot wounds at the hands of parties unknown."

The judge of the Superior Court gave a lengthy charge to the grand jury in which he stressed the supremacy of the law as the only means of safety. . . .

[N]o indictments were brought, and nobody was surprised.

Governor's Request Amounts to Nothing. The part played by the state authorities is limited to Governor Hardman's request for a report on the lynching. In his request for the report from the local authorities the Governor virtually promised not to interfere with the matter when he said: "Any action of the state will depend upon what the sheriff and the solicitor general report to me." The solicitor general reported to the Governor that he found no information to warrant an indictment. Commenting upon the failure to indict, the Eastman *Times-Journal* remarked: "Foy said he reported to the governor he had talked with a score of persons about the incident, and that, as usual, those who knew anything would tell nothing, and those who would tell, knew nothing."

No Local Condemnation of Mob Death. No preacher, teacher, public official, or other individual—except the judge in his charge to the grand jury—voiced sentiment against the lynching. No organization made any protest. The ministers, while not proud of the mob's activities, have said nothing and plan to say nothing, reasoning that since there is so much pro-lynching feeling in the community it is best to leave the matter be. While a few white people apologize for the lynching, the masses of white people frankly justify it; and Negroes accept it—probably a condition of continued residence in Irwin County.

Not only is the public generally satisfied with the lynching, but little or no fault is found with those who during the man hunt fired into a car full of innocent Negroes, wounding some of them. The possemen claimed the Negroes would not stop when told to. The Negroes said nothing. The grand jury ignored the incident. The lynching was considered a local matter by the local people, and Editors W. T. Anderson, A. M. Pierce, and anybody else who found fault with it were damned.

In an adjoining judicial district, a Superior Court judge stated to one of the Commission's investigators that he knew personally many people of his own home town who were at Ocilla and participated in the lynching there; he stated further that no indictments had been brought or would be brought, and that if indictments were brought nobody would be convicted. The above statements were made in the presence of the district prosecuting attorney and the district court stenographer. This judge doubtless has not and will not communicate his evidence concerning the lynchers to the proper court officials of the adjoining judicial district.

And With What Results? The local people have given complete immunity to the lynchers, and are mightily pleased with the futile efforts of the press and the courts.

Jacquelyn Dowd Hall, *Revolt Against Chivalry: Jessie Daniel Ames and the Women's Campaign Against Lynching* 130–33, 136, 145–53, 155–56 (1979)

The American tradition of vigilante justice first emerged on the eighteenth-century frontier. The terms "lynch law" and "lynching" gained currency during the Revolutionary War when Charles Lynch of Bedford County, Virginia, formed a vigilante association to rid the area of plundering Tories. After the war, the Virginia legislature exonerated Lynch for his actions on the grounds that circumstances may arise under which "measures taken. . .may not be strictly warranted by law, although justifiable from the imminence of the danger."

Throughout the nineteenth century, frontier elites routinely banded together to impose social order in areas where population was sparse, officials few, and legal machinery rudimentary. Such "establishment violence" became a half-accepted aspect of American political life.

In the antebellum South, lynch law helped suppress both white dissidence and slave rebellion. The planter's self-interest and the ideology of pateralism [*sic*] gave a measure of protection to the slaves, and before the Civil War many victims of vigilante violence were white.[2] Nevertheless, the cycle of

2. Anti-abolitionist mobs, whose victims were primarily white men, increased markedly after 1830. . . .No statistics are available on the lynching of blacks in the antebellum period,

slave-insurrection panics, in which vigilance committees conducted mock trials, extracted confessions by torture, and staged public executions, set a bloody precedent for racial lynchings.

When the war began, lynching took on new significance as a systematic weapon of terror against blacks. As early as 1866, while white southerners still maintained political control, the head of the Freedmen's Bureau in Georgia reported that bands of vigilantes were committing the "most fiendish and diabolical outrages on the freedman." During the decade of Radical Reconstruction, the lynching of black men and the rape of black women became the most spectacular emblems of a counter-revolution that convulsed almost every former Confederate state. By the time federal troops withdrew in 1877, signaling the North's abandonment of the ex-slaves, private, collective violence in support of white supremacy was embedded in southern political culture.

Lynching, however, reached its height not during the pitched battles of Reconstruction but during the transition between 1877 and the establishment of a new caste system. Through the 1870s and '80s, southern farmers suffered a sustained decline in agricultural prices, capped by the severe recession of 1893. Bourbon regimes, anxious for a share of Gilded Age profits, sought to lure northern and British capital into the region with promises of cheap labor and natural resources. As the rigid adherence of a private banking system to the gold standard and a contracted currency, mediated through the furnishing merchant and the crop lien system, forced small farmers off the land, they fought back through the Farmers Alliances and the Populist Party. When white Populists pragmatically allied with blacks, their opponents responded with an extralegal campaign of physical and psychological intimidation that reawakened the passions of Reconstruction.

Lynching became a major issue in the movement, for blacks turned to the third party in part for protection against the whims of southern justice. Populist politicians, however, were tragically unable to shield their potential constituents from terrorism. In 1892, 255 persons were killed by lynch mobs, "the most staggering proportion ever reached in the history of that crime."[3] In some cases lynching was a specific mode of political repression. In others, it represented a diffuse reassertion of white solidarity. For example, a study of racial violence in 59 Louisiana parishes found a marked increase in lynching during election years at the height of Populist voting strength. Although the victims tended to be alleged criminals rather than Populist activists, mob violence undoubtedly served as a general warning to blacks of the dangers of political assertiveness. More significantly, lynching functioned as a means of uniting whites across class lines in the face of a common enemy, thus rekindling one of the major stumbling blocks to Populist success: the fear of "Negro domination" and the powerful pull of the notion of the Solid South.

Defeat in the election of 1896 spelled the end of the Populist challenge to

---

although several authors suggest that they composed approximately 10 percent of mob victims. . . .

3. The Negro Year Book: An Annual Encyclopedia of the Negro, 1912-1956, at 293 (Monroe Work ed., 1912-56). Of this number, 100 were white and 155 were black. In 1893, the total number of lynch victims declined to 201, but the number of black victims remained constant.

the emerging capitalist order. Formal disfranchisement eliminated the third party's constituency in the black community and restricted white political participation as well. By 1906, blacks had been excluded by law from primary elections in every southern state. Landowners replaced white tenants with more easily exploited blacks, and white farmers, who had once sought an interracial alliance, now, . . .competed with blacks . . . . The textile industry, harbinger of southern industrialization, became a whites-only enclave for an emerging southern proletariat, and mill owners systematically used racial fears to undercut the organizing efforts of their workers.

As the remnants of planter paternalism gave way to competition, a reinforcing system of debt peonage, disfranchisement, physical segregation, and terrorism replaced the "distant intimacy" and condescending tolerance of an earlier era. Industrialization increased class differences and sent landless workers. . .wandering across a once fixed agrarian landscape. A new generation of blacks, born in freedom and less willing to act out the etiquette of obsequiousness, seemed to many whites to betoken a society "whirling away into the unknown." The ideology of racism reached a virulent crescendo, as the dominant image of blacks in the white mind shifted from inferior child to aggressive and dangerous animal. Lynching, the ultimate weapon of social order in a society wracked by economic and racial tensions, seems to have become increasingly sadistic: emasculation, torture, and burning alive replaced the hangman's noose.

With the new caste system in place, lynching gradually declined from an average of 188 a year during the decade 1880-1899 to 93 a year during the first decade of the twentieth century. But from 1905 until World War I, little further change occurred. Throughout the period, the average number of lynchings never fell below two or three a week. After a resurgence during the "red summer" of 1919, mob violence dropped steadily, only to rise temporarily with the beginning of the Great Depression. Although twice as many threatened lynchings were prevented as were carried out during the decade of the twenties, the thwarted lynch mob frequently demanded that public officials impose the death sentence in a hasty mockery of a trial. If these "legal lynchings" were included in the statistics, the death toll would be much higher. Moreover, the proportion of lynchings taking place in the South increased from 82 percent of the total in the 1890s to 95 percent in the 1920s; over the same period the proportion of lynch victims who were white decreased from 32 percent to 9 percent. . . .

While these statistical changes lessened the chance that any one individual might lose his life to a lynch mob, they did little to undermine the psychological impact of mob violence. In the decades before World War I, the expansion of communications, the development of photography, and the popularity of yellow journalism gave reporting a vividness it had never had before. The rhetorical evocation of intimate human suffering implicated white readers in each act of aggression and drove home to blacks the consequences of powerlessness. . . .

The most relevant measure of the importance of lynching was never the percentage of blacks directly involved, for, like whipping under slavery, lynching was an instrument of social discipline intended to impress not only the immediate victim but all who saw or heard about the event. And the mass media, together with the late-Victorian relish in the details of death, spread the imagery of rope and faggot far beyond the community in which each lynching took place. Writing of his youth in the South of the 1920s, Richard Wright recalled:

> The things that influenced my conduct as a Negro did not have to happen to me directly; I needed but to hear of them to feel their full effects in the deepest layers of my consciousness. Indeed, the white brutality that I had not seen was a more effective control of my behavior than that which I knew. The actual experience would have let me see the realistic outlines of what was really happening, but as long as it remained something terrible and yet remote, something whose horror and blood might descend upon me at any moment, I was compelled to give my entire imagination over to it, an act which blocked the springs of thought and feeling in me, creating a sense of distance between me and the world in which I lived.[4]

. . .Of all aspects of racial etiquette, those governing sexual relations aroused the strongest emotions and carried with them the severest sanctions. Nowhere were the ethics of living Jim Crow more subtle and treacherous than when they touched on the proper conduct of black men toward white women. Any act of a black man, however innocent, that offended or frightened a white woman might cost him his life. Any transgression of the caste system was a step toward "social equality"; and social equality, with its connotations of personal intimacy, could end only in interracial sex. . . .

The main rationalization for lynching followed from this deeply felt taboo: only the threat of immediate and terrible retribution stood between the white women of the "lonely, isolated farmsteads of the South" and the overpowering desire of black men. Rape of a white woman was "THE MOST TERRIBLE CRIME ON THE FACE OF THIS EARTH" for which legal punishment was inadequate and too uncertain. Moreover, a woman who had already suffered, as the editor of the Conyers, Georgia, *Times* put it, a fate "many times more brutal than death itself," could not be "put on the stand in full view of a packed courtroom and then required to again look into the face of and publicly proclaim her assassin." As the anti-lynching reformer Ida B. Wells pointed out, "there could be framed no possible excuse more harmful to the Negro. . . .Humanity abhors the assailant of womanhood, and this charge upon the Negro at once placed him beyond the pale of human sympathy."

Southern moderates as well as racial extremists justified lynching for the one crime of sexual assault. The notion of black retrogression, which continued to influence both popular and academic thought into the 1930s, was closely bound up with the question of black sexual behavior. Freed from the restraints of slavery, the "new issue" Negro had supposedly reverted to African primitivism. The chief evidence was sexual immorality: family feeling, the cornerstone of social order, was unknown in the black community; black women were lapsing into prostitution and illegitimacy; above all, black men were acting upon the innate lasciviousness of the savage beast. . . .

This southern obsession with rape touched a responsive chord in the nation at large. It was rooted in the deepest of American communal preoccupations:

---

4. . . .Richard Wright, Black Boy: A Record of Childhood and Youth 190 (1966).

the conflict between "civilization" and "savagery," historically acted out in the destruction of the Indians and the subjugation of African slaves. In a culture that insisted upon work, instinctual repression, and acquisitive behavior, men struggled to separate themselves from nature; what James Madison called "the black race within our bosom [and] the red on our borders" became the repositories for those parts of the self which, in the process, had to be conquered and repressed. For nineteenth-century Americans, the association between "savagery" and sexual passion was central to the problem of social order. By setting white women apart as asexual guardians of morality, men could pursue acquisition and expansion secure in the knowledge that they were not abandoning the values of civilization. By projecting onto blacks the "animal within," the buried parts of themselves could be objectified and controlled. But this separation from spontaneous emotional life and heterosexual love generated longings, fantasies, and fears that could never be kept altogether at bay. The result was a society prey to "visions of violent, immoral possession." The image of black over white, of a world turned upside down, symbolized the ever present danger of the return of the repressed, of a regression to a primitive natural world of sexuality and violence. . . .

Despite its tenacity, this "Southern rape complex," was never founded on objective reality. Of the known victims of lynch mobs in the period 1882-1946, only 23 percent were accused of rape or of attempted rape. Every study of the crime has underlined the fact that despite the persistent mythology of black attacks on white women, rape has remained an overwhelmingly intraracial event, and the victims have been predominantly black women.

A major strategy of anti-lynching reformers, beginning with Ida B. Wells in the 1880s and carried on by the NAACP and the Association of Southern Women for the Prevention of Lynching, was to use facts and figures to undermine the rationalizations for mob violence. But the fear of rape, like the practice of lynching, was embedded far beyond the reach of factual refutation—in the heart not only of American racism, but of American attitudes toward women as well. . . .

For blacks, lynching reinforced social boundaries that became, quite literally, a matter of life and death. For the white women involved, the practice can be seen more accurately as a dramatization of cultural themes, a "story" white southerners told themselves about the social arrangements and psychological strivings that lay beneath the surface of everyday life. The archetypal lynching for rape thus served as a symbolic expression of sexual attitudes as well as a sanction against interracial sex. . . .

Rape and rumors of rape became a kind of acceptable folk pornography in the Bible Belt. As stories spread, the attacker became not just a black man but a ravenous brute, the victim a beautiful, frail, young virgin. The experience and condition of the woman (who could not be put on the witness stand to suffer the "glare and stare of public curiosity") were described in minute and progressively embellished detail: a public fantasy that implies a kind of group participation in the rape of the woman almost as cathartic as the subsequent lynching of the alleged attacker. . . .

The small percentage of lynchings that revolved around charges of sexual assault gripped the southern imagination far out of proportion to statistical reality. In such scenes, described in the popular press in strikingly conventionalized words and phrases, the themes of masculinity, rage, and sexual envy were woven into a ritual of death and desire. Participants might see in "lynch law" their ideal selves: the protectors of women, dispensers of justice, and guardians of communal values. But they must also have seen themselves in the victims of their acts. . . .

The story that such rituals told about the place of white women in southern society was subtle, contradictory, and demeaning. The frail victim, leaning on the arms of her male relatives, might be brought to the scene of the crime, there to identify her assailant and perhaps to witness his execution. Humiliation mingled with heightened worth as she played for a moment the role of the Fair Maiden violated and avenged. For this privilege—if the alleged assault had in fact taken place—she might pay with physical and psychological suffering in the extreme. In any case, she would pay with a lifetime of subjugation to the men gathered in her behalf.

The lynch mob in pursuit of the black rapist thus represented the trade-off implicit in the code of chivalry, for the right of the southern lady to protection presupposed her obligation to obey. The connotations of wealth and family background attached to the position of the lady in the antebellum South faded in the twentieth century, but the power of "ladyhood" as a value construct remained. The term denoted chastity, frailty, graciousness. "A lady," noted one social-psychologist, "is always in a state of becoming: one acts like a lady, one attempts to be a lady, but one never *is* a lady." Internalized by the individual, this ideal regulated behavior and restricted interaction with the world. If a woman passed the tests of ladyhood, she could tap into the reservoir of protectiveness and shelter known as southern chivalry. Women unable or unwilling to comply with such normative demands forfeited the claim to personal security. Together the practice of ladyhood and the etiquette of chivalry functioned as highly effective strategies of control over women's behavior as well as powerful safeguards of caste restrictions. . . .

Thus the threat of rape cannot be seen, as reform rhetoric claimed, simply as a rationalization used to obscure the real function of lynching. Rather, the two phenomena were intimately connected, for the fear of rape, like the threat of lynching, served to keep a subordinate group in a state of anxiety and fear. . . .

In the South, the double standard took on special and explosive force. White women were viewed *collectively* as the repositories of white racial legitimacy. Theodore Bilbo, for example, in a long treatise on "separation or mongrelization" advanced the perverse logic that even though miscegenation practiced by white men may have "poured a broad stream of white blood into black veins," white racial purity had been in no way impaired. "Southern white women have preserved the integrity of their race, and there is no one who can today point the finger of suspicion in any manner at the blood which flows in the veins of the white sons and daughters of the South." As absolutely inaccessible sexual property, white women became the most potent symbol of white male supremacy. . . .

The double standard had similarly pernicious effects on attitudes toward black women. The traditional American split image of women as Virgin and Whore, Fair Maiden and Dark Lady, was reified in the South. The association between darkness and eroticism cast white women *en masse* in the role of the "ice goddess"; upon black women were projected the fears and fascinations of female sexuality. . . .Recoiling with "horror and madness" from the image of sexual relations between white women and black men, white men regarded their own sexual crossing of the color line as "welcome attention" to black women.

Notes

1. *Women as Victims of Lynching.* The myth of the black rapist used to justify lynching and the widespread acceptance of that justification leads to the invisibility of the lynchings of African-American women. What follows are two of numerous reports of women who were lynched.

> Oklahoma, 1911
>
> At Okemah, Oklahoma, Laura Nelson, a colored woman, accused of murdering a deputy sheriff who had discovered stolen goods in her house, was lynched together with her son, a boy about fifteen. The woman and her son were taken from the jail, dragged about six miles to the Canadian River, and hanged from a bridge. The woman was raped by members of the mob before she was hanged.
>
> *The Crisis*, July, 1911.

Thirty Years of Lynching in the United States: 1889-1918, at 18 (NAACP 1919).

> Columbus, Miss. Dec. 17—Thursday a week ago Cordella Stevenson was found early in the morning hanging to the limb of a tree, without any clothing, dead. . . .She was hung there from the night before by a bloodthirsty mob who had gone to her home, snatched her from slumber, and dragged her through the streets without any resistance. They carried her to a far-off spot, did their dirt and then strung her up.

Chi. Defender, Dec. 18, 1915, quoted in Ralph Ginzburg, One Hundred Years of Lynchings 96 (1969). African-American women were particularly vulnerable to lynching if they reported being raped by white men.

> In 1918, a white Mississippi dentist sexually assaulted two teen-age black girls, one of whom became pregnant. The brothers of these girls visited the dentist, who died several days later. In response, a white mob lynched not only the two black men but also the two black women who had been victims of rape. Similarly, in Oklahoma, whites lynched a black woman because her brother had killed the white man who had raped her. Thus, if a black woman charged rape and named her assailant, she endangered the lives of black male kin who might seek revenge, and she herself became vulnerable to lynching.

Estelle B. Freedman, The Manipulation of History At the Clarence Thomas Hearings, 65 S. Cal. L. Rev. 1361, 1363 (1992).

2. *Women and the Anti-Lynching Movement.* The initiator of the anti-lynching movement and one of its primary leaders was Ida B. Wells. Her commitment to this issue began when three African-American men in Memphis, Tennessee were lynched in March 1892.

Wells knew all of the victims. A series of racist provocations by white businessmen in Memphis, trying to force the Black proprietors of a local grocery store out-of-business, had finally culminated in the triple slaying.

At the time of the lynching, Wells owned the only Black newspaper in town, the *Memphis Free Speech*. In the weeks following the lynching she wrote successive editorials demanding that the murderers be arrested and tried. When the white-owned newspapers responded by alleging that Black men were lynched because they raped white women, Ida B. Wells replied with an editorial that almost cost her her life:

> Nobody in this section of the country believes the old thread bare lie that Negro men rape white women. If the Southern white men are not careful, they will over-reach themselves and public sentiment will have a reaction; a conclusion will then be reached which will be very damaging to the moral reputation of their women.

Having intimated that white women could be sexually involved with Black men of their own accord, Ida Wells now faced the full fury of the white press, and the mob itself. Some of the more prominent white businessmen gathered at the Memphis Cotton Exchange Building six days later and openly discussed her lynching. Luckily, Wells was out-of-state attending a general conference of the African Methodist Church in Philadelphia.

With her life so threatened, Wells dared not return to Memphis. The offices of the *Free Speech* were sacked, creditors took possession of what was left, "and the *Free Speech* was as if it had never been," Ida Wells wrote from New York City five months later.

It was from New York that Wells launched what was to become an international crusade against lynching. Wells' experience in Memphis had convinced her that lynching had nothing to do with so-called Negro crime. Wells determined to reveal the exact details of all lynchings which came to her attention. . . .

Wells wrote scores of articles, and a half dozen pamphlets and books. Her writings shaped the political contours of the anti-lynching effort, and significantly influenced the direction of the Black woman's club movement.

Bettina Aptheker, Introduction to Lynching and Rape: An Exchange of Views 14-16 (Bettina Aptheker ed., 1977).

White women, through the Association of Southern Women for the Prevention of Lynching, founded in 1930, also played a role in the anti-lynching movement. Angela Davis, however, questions whether their efforts "were forty years late in coming." Angela Y. Davis, Women, Race and Class 195 (1981).

> Jessie Daniel Ames and her co-founders of the Association of Southern Women for the Prevention of Lynching resolved in 1930 to recruit the masses of Southern white women into the campaign to defeat the racist mobs bent on killing Black people. Eventually they obtained over forty thousand signatures to the Association's pledge [denouncing lynchings]. . . .
>
> These courageous white women encountered opposition, hostility and even physical threats on their lives. Their contributions were invaluable within the overall anti-lynching crusade. Without their relentless petition drives, their letter campaigns and their meetings and demonstrations, the

> tide of lynching would not have been reversed so swiftly. Yet the Association of Southern Women for the Prevention of Lynching was a movement that was forty years late in coming. For four decades or more, Black women had been leading the anti-lynching campaign, and for just about as long, they had appealed to their white sisters to join them. . . .
>
> While the Association of Southern Women for the Prevention of Lynching was a belated response to their Black sisters' appeals, these women's far-reaching achievements dramatically illustrate white women's special place in the struggle against racism.

Id. at 194-96.

3. *Executions of African-American Soldiers in World War II.* Preliminary research by J. Robert Lilly about military executions during World War II indicates that the distortions of the justice system fueled by the myth of the African-American-male rapist remain largely unacknowledged and invisible.

> The military data. . .show that blacks. . .made up 79 percent of the soldiers executed in Europe, as against 21 percent for whites. . . .
>
> The rate of execution for black soldiers was even higher for the rape of civilians, for which 25 blacks (87 percent) and 4 whites (13 percent) were put to death. . . .
>
> For less serious, less interracially explosive offenses, like barracks dishonesty and drunkenness, Mr. Lilly found the races represented proportionally. White soldiers were charged 9 times out of 10.
>
> But sex offenses registered differently, even apart from outright rape. Black soldiers made up more than 40 percent of the total accused of sex crimes, and they were convicted in two-thirds of the cases; white soldiers were convicted at a 40 percent rate.

Francis X. Clines, When Black Soldiers Were Hanged: A War's Footnote, N.Y. Times, Feb. 7, 1993, at 14.

Margo L. Nightingale, Judicial Attitudes and Differential Treatment: Native Women in Sexual Assault Cases, 23 Ottawa L. Rev. 71, 76, 81, 83–88, 90–98 (1991)

[T]his paper will focus upon judicial attitudes, and the differential *treatment* of Native women involved in cases of sexual assault [in Canada]. This will be done predominantly by an examination of judicial decisions in sexual assault cases involving Native people. . . .

As the basis for analysis, 69 cases involving Natives as offenders and/or victims were accumulated. The majority of the cases (47) arose in the Northwest Territories, and all but four cases involved sexual offenses. Of these four, two involved charges in some way related to a sexual offence, with two cases involving charges of simple assault.

Of the 67 cases involving or related to a sexual offence, 46 involved Native intra-racial sexual assault; two involved a Native offender and a non-Native complainant; five involved a non-Native offender and a Native complainant; and one involved non-Native intra-racial sexual assault. In nine cases the accused was a Native, but the race of the victim was unclear, and in four cases the race of both parties was unclear.

The cases found and reviewed are believed to be representative of cases reported and tried. However, it is not assumed that these cases represent all occurrences of sexual assault in Native communities, or all sexual assaults against Native women. It is also not assumed that sexual assault is generally perpetrated by Native men as the cases would tend to suggest. This element of the cases may result only from greater policing in Native communities, or from the fact that Native women are less likely to report a sexual assault committed by a White man if they fear their complaint would not be believed. . . .

In 45 of the 69 cases reviewed, the judge considered alcohol to be a factor in the commission of the offence. The judicial analysis of some degree of intoxication in a Native accused illustrates one of the most obvious ways in which an accused is adversely affected by judicial bias.

When the facts of a case disclosed that a Native accused had been drinking prior to the offence, a lengthy discussion of the level of intoxication and the presence, or absence, of alcohol abuse will often follow. . . .

Where Native offenders are sentenced, the judge will often blame alcohol as the "root cause" of the offence. In his reasons for sentence of two men charged with a violent assault against a woman, Judge Bourassa said:

> [I]t's no good to say that they wouldn't have done this if they were sober; I recognize that they wouldn't have done it if they were sober.

. . .Such a finding indicates a misunderstanding of the relationship between alcohol use and crime. If any connection can be established, alcohol use is more likely to be a *contributing* factor rather than a *causative* factor in criminal behaviour. . . .

[J]udges' and lawyers'. . .continued emphasis of the presence of intoxication in Native persons appearing before the court acts only to reinforce pre-existing stereotypes of the "drunken Indian". Courts, in fact, appear predisposed to finding and perpetuating this stereotype. Furthermore, judges often do not define drunkenness as a characteristic particular to an accused, but more generally and incorrectly, as constituting a cultural attribute of Native society. . . .

An examination of the judicial decisions collected reveals that the sexual assault of Native women is, as always, affected by disturbing judicial perceptions of sexual assault. Judges often fail to recognize any injury or harm, or will minimize that harm which cannot be avoided. . . .

In their discussion of the harm to women, judges appear to consider only that which is visible or physical, and which generally would constitute "short-term" harm. The true extent of the injury suffered by a woman who has been sexually assaulted is rarely addressed, or understood, particularly that injury which is psychological. . . .

Courts have also failed to recognize that Native women may suffer unique forms of injury. One example might be their ostracism from family or community after being sexually assaulted, or after reporting their assault. This may result if the victim is blamed for what transpires. The support of, and interconnection with one's family and community is of such importance in most

Native societies that ostracism can be particularly painful. In assessing the impact of an assault on a Native victim, a judge should also consider the relative isolation of most Native communities, especially in Northern Canada, and the lack of access to support or counselling services.

From conversations with 39 federally sentenced Native women it appears that their exposure to acts of violence, including their experiences of sexual assault, have affected them very profoundly:

> Our stories tell of all those self-destructive ways through which women who are victims seek escape. Suicide attempts are common. Thirty-one of 39 had abused alcohol, 10 coming from families with serious alcohol problems, and 10 considering their own abuse serious. Twenty-seven considered themselves severely addicted to narcotics, and many were addicted to prescription drugs. Twenty-three tell of addiction *in institutions* to prescription drugs provided by institutional psychiatrists or physicians. Ten of 39 describe slashing themselves: self-mutilations that are not suicide attempts, but the relief of tension and anger; physical pain self-inflicted as escape from what lies inside us.[5]

For some Native women, the exposure to violence is not limited to one experience of sexual assault, but has consisted of "long-term and systematic violence." Some of the violence occurred in birth families, while other instances arose in foster homes, juvenile institutions, or on city streets. In the report on federally sentenced Native women, a relationship has been established between the women's convictions for violent offenses and their histories as victims:

> As victims we carry the burden of memories: of pain inflicted on us, of violence done before our eyes to those we loved, of rape, of sexual assaults, of beatings, of death. For us violence has begotten violence: our contained hatred and rage has been concentrated in an explosion that has left us with yet more memories to scar and mark us.[6]

Judges and Crown counsel could learn much from these comments.

Another indication that judges misunderstand the nature of sexual assault is by placing blame for the assault upon the victim. . . .In one case, a nine-year-old girl walking home after dark was assaulted by a 30-year-old man. It was said that "her attempt to avoid him may have triggered his behaviour. . . .(but) it is impossible to tell what brought about this apparently senseless attack."

A more prevalent form of victim-blaming often results where the complainant was intoxicated at the time of the assault. In. . .[one case decided in 1988] the accused, once intoxicated, had a propensity to assault women sexually while they slept. His actions were characterized in the following manner:

> [I]t is clearly not only unfair and obnoxious, as well as potentially dangerous [due to the possibility of contracting sexually transmitted diseases], but also morally wrong and against the law designed to protect people such as the vic-

---

5. Fran Sugar & Lana Fox, Nistum Peyako Séht'wawin Iskwewak: Breaking Chains, 3 Can. J. Women & L. 465, 473 (1989). . . .

6. *Id.* at 473.

> tim in this case, *no matter how much such victims may regrettably and foolishly expose themselves to attack.* (emphasis added).

[In another case decided in 1986]. . .the accused sexually assaulted his former common law spouse while she slept; both had been drinking. The accused had a criminal record, including one conviction for assaulting the complainant to an extent that was "near-fatal". Despite the extent and severity of the accused's record, the trial judge saw alcohol abuse as the root cause of the offence. In offering his reasons for sentence, the trial judge said:

> This sexual assault is less severe than is often heard in this court, not just because no beating accompanied it, but also because the complainant's excessive drinking and drinking herself into a stupor exposed her, unnecessarily, to what occurred here, that is, exposed her to a risk that was unnecessary. That relates, however, to the question not of guilt or innocence, but of the sentence to now impose.

After considering these remarks, Appeal Court Justice Anderson said, "[i]n my view, the fact that the complainant may have exposed herself to risk is not a proper factor to take into account in imposing sentence." Despite this finding, the accused's sentence of two years less a day was not increased. . . .

Of the 69 sexual assault cases considered, 13 involved facts to the effect that the complainant was asleep or "passed out" when the sexual assault began. Of the 13, the facts disclosed that in three, the complainant had not consumed alcohol. The highest sentence ordered was two-and-a-half years, while six of the cases resulted in a sentence of two years less a day. Sentences in the remaining cases ranged from one month to 21 months. . . .

Two examples can be given that illustrate the impact of class upon a judge's sentence of a Native accused. The first involves a charge of sexual assault against a member of the Northwest Territories Legislative Assembly laid in July, 1989. The offence involved three occasions when the accused held his stepdaughter (a "pubescent" girl) next to him, putting his hands under her clothing and rubbing her breasts and vaginal area. These incidents were described as "inappropriate cuddling" in the pre-sentence report. The accused entered a guilty plea and was sentenced by Judge Michel Bourassa to five days in jail with nine months probation. In discussing this case with the media, Judge Bourassa said:

> He was stressed out; he wasn't liked by his peers; he was having trouble with his relationship with his wife and trouble with drink, and rightly or wrongly, he fondled his. . . .stepdaughter.

[A] Crown appeal was dismissed by Supreme Court Justice de Weerdt. . . .[The Justice] stated that the sentence, in combination with the accused's resignation from the Legislative Assembly, was adequate denunciation for this "relatively minor, or even minimal, sexual assault". . . .

[Another case decided in 1989] provides another example of the strong effect of class bias in sentencing. The complainant, who had suffered brain damage as a child, was sexually assaulted by the accused, then President of the local Métis association. Intercourse occurred while a friend of the accused held the victim's feet apart.

Although the crime was considered "cowardly and cruel deserving of public condemnation", sentence was imposed at two years less a day, with 200 hours community service and two years probation. Judge de Weerdt stated that the accused had kept himself out of trouble since the offence and was attempting to fix his alcohol problem:

> He's a person who could. . . .make a very good life for himself. He's obviously a capable person who's respected by his community. A long time has passed since the offence, relatively speaking, and I consider that in mitigation. . . .[as] time appears to heal most wounds.

Class bias is a factor that is likely to work against Native women far more often than the reverse. This is due to the general position of Native women within Canada. Review of the 1981 Census indicates that while Native women experience roughly twice the level of unemployment as non-Native women, they experience approximately the same level as Native men. Yet, employed Native women generally have substantially lower incomes than both non-Native women and Native men. While it should not be assumed that all Native peoples, or women, live in poverty, the bare statistics seem to indicate that in general, Native women are unlikely to be more economically or socially advantaged than most male offenders. . . .

When Gender and Culture Clash

Judicial sensitivity to Native values, community interests and community treatment programs is essential and has a number of advantages. Such an approach affords greater respect to Native peoples and their values. Reference to community standards is also preferable to subordinating a community's views regarding a federally based sentencing policy . . . .However, identifying a community's values, interests or relevant cultural differences is problematic. . . .

In [one controversial case decided in 1986] at the trial level, Judge Bourassa gave particular consideration to an existing community treatment program and its effect on the accused's sentence. The accused, a 21-year-old-resident of Arctic Bay, pled guilty to a charge of sexually assaulting his 14-year-old cousin. Within Arctic Bay, a council of elders known as the Inumarit provided traditional treatment and counselling to members of their community, including the accused. Judge Bourassa arranged a special sentencing hearing to receive evidence regarding the role of the Inumarit, and its treatment program for offenders.

The evidence presented suggested that the accused had responded well to the counselling provided by them to date, and that sending him to prison would not only be destructive to the accused, but would cause resentment within the community. Members of the Inumarit believed that a prison sentence would not be within the best interests of the community, the accused, or the victim.

Judge Bourassa was impressed by the Inumarit, stating:

> The very things that the Inumarit are trying to do is what the court is trying to do: rehabilitating an offender, reconciling the offender, the victim and the community so that there is unity in the community and a programme of education. Can any of us really say that jails do that? For the person that

> responds, the Inumarit, the Social Services Committee and the whole community together can obviously heal; they can unite; they can reconcile; and they can reform.

He then imposed a 90-day intermittent sentence, to be followed by two years probation and the completion of 100 hours of community service.

On appeal, an 18-month sentence was substituted, based on the belief that Judge Bourassa had erred in finding that this "counselling service" was adequate replacement for the longer sentence of imprisonment which would ordinarily be imposed. The Court noted the existence of electricity and other modern amenities and past exposure to Canadian laws, suggesting that Arctic Bay was like other Canadian towns and cities. Further, the Inumarit was said to resemble "the usual community counselling service rather than the traditional governing and counselling body of earlier times. I am unable to see. . . .that it is a remnant of ancient culture."

Through application of this ethnocentric reasoning, the recognition of any Inuit culture, ancient or otherwise, is made virtually impossible. This reasoning provides a prime example of judicial bias that has often arisen in land claim cases where traditional values are similarly dismissed or denigrated. This type of analysis has been criticized as indicating:

> . . . .a judicial view that the aboriginal peoples of Canada have rights so long as they remain in a fossilized or primitive state but their rights are progressively diminished to the extent that they avail themselves of the benefits and the burdens of the 20th [C]entury.[7]

While the trial decision shows a greater awareness of cultural diversity, neither it nor the appeal decision is acceptable as both fail to address, or consider the effect of the assault on the victim. The sexual assault occurred in the complainant's home. Once she resisted the accused's advances, the accused used an electrical cord to tie her hands behind her back. Although this violence was used, there was no significant consideration of the injury done to the complainant. There was also no emphasis on the fact that the complainant called the police following the assault, and not members of the Inumarit. In fact, without any discussion of her, both the Court and the community presumed to know the best interests of the complainant.

[In another case decided in 1984]. . .the three accused pled guilty to the offence of having intercourse with a female under the age of 14. The offences did not occur at the same time, and the Crown made no suggestion that these occurred without the girl's consent.

In considering appropriate sentence, Judge Bourassa stated that the "law and the morality it reflects [must] walk hand in hand with the people." He noted that Canadian law, which deems intercourse with a girl under 14 an offence, was in conflict with alleged Inuit values that a young woman was ready to engage in sexual intercourse once she began to menstruate. These values were ascertained from the pre-sentence report, and from "this court's experience in

---

7. Nigel D. Bankes, Judicial Attitudes to Aboriginal Resource Rights and Title, 13 Resources 3 (1985), cited in Joan Ryan & Bernard Ominayak, The Cultural Effects of Judicial Bias, in Equality and Judicial Neutrality 355 (Sheila L. Martin & Kathleen E. Mahoney eds., 1987).

the Eastern Arctic." Although the existence of Inuit tradition contrary to Canadian values is not synonymous with an ignorance of the law, Judge Bourassa reduced the case to these terms.

The accused had spent three weeks in custody prior to their hearing. Believing this time to be equal to two or three months in jail, Bourassa imposed a further term of imprisonment of one week, followed by eight months probation. It was believed this sentence would be sufficient to "educate" the community. The sentence incensed Native women's groups.

The case was appealed on the basis that the sentence was inadequate, and that the pre-sentence report's assertions of Inuit values were incorrect.[8] The Court of Appeal refused to entertain this latter submission on the basis that objection to the report should have been made at the initial sentence hearing. It then proceeded to consider the "cultural circumstances" raised by Judge Bourassa.

The Court assumed, as Judge Bourassa did, that different cultural values were behind the accused's ignorance of the law, suggesting that the mere presence of Canadian law is sufficient to show the inappropriate nature of Inuit values—regardless of what those values might actually be. . . .Such rigid enforcement of Canadian law does not negate Inuit values, it merely debases and suppresses them. The real impact of these judgments on Inuit or Native people is also questionable. In their 1989 Report, the Ontario Native Women's Association wrote that:

> . . .Canadian Judges and police officers are not the respected and revered members of the community. It means very little to us to have a non-Aboriginal person come into reserve communities to enforce laws which we did not develop and do not recognise as 'our' laws. This might be a powerful message for non-Aboriginal Canadians who see the *Criminal Code* as their law and their protection from wrongdoing, but the Canadian criminal law has served Aboriginal Peoples very tragically. Indeed, this non-Aboriginal interference is often viewed as a problem and not a solution.[9]

After assessing the trial judge's reasons, the Court of Appeal increased the sentence to four months imprisonment. This was deemed an appropriate sentence in consideration of the fact that this incident constituted "a simple matter of sex." No consideration was given to the fact that the 13-year-old complainant became pregnant as a result, nor was there an appreciation that she was particularly vulnerable to exploitation:

> [T]he young girl here was described as "slow", which I interpret as meaning not highly intelligent. She did not object to the intercourse, but I must temper that with the fact that she may not have completely understood what was going on. *Her silence, which was seen by these men as consent, may have in fact represented something else.* (emphasis added)

8. The Crown should have argued in the alternative that, presuming the report to be accurate, it was not correct to suggest that a young woman becomes available to all men once she has begun to menstruate.

9. Breaking Free: A Proposal for Change to Aboriginal Family Violence 50 (Thunder Bay: Ontario Native Women's Ass'n 1989).

With this in evidence, the Court of Appeal's assessment that this was "a simple matter of sex" is particularly disturbing. It appears from this statement that each of the three accused made no attempt to determine consent, and that, in fact, consent may have been absent. At the very least, it is easily argued that the girl may have been completely unable to consent.

Although it was the Crown's responsibility to recognize lack of consent as an issue, the trial and appeal decisions' failure to do this, and their refusal to consider what the true impact of Inuit values on sexual relations might be, are disappointing. They are also disappointing because the judges' ethnocentric bias is so highly visible and yet totally unacknowledged.

Both of these cases are indicative of several problems that Canadian courts experience when they attempt to recognize cultural difference in most cases. Often a consideration of cultural "differences" results in the perception or definition of these differences as inferiorities. . . .

Problems also arise from use of "an(other) language and conceptual apparatus (the Canadian legal system) to further an understanding of a different system of belief."[10]. . .

> [F]irst, cultural differences are also differences between ways of knowing, describing or understanding and that, second, cultural differences are differences among even the 'other' cultures. Consequently, a descriptive analysis of the differences between cultures, as contrasted with an analysis directed toward raising sensitivity or a sensibility of cultural differences, is an impossibility.[11]

Further, judicial reliance upon a system of law and order which may not be culturally relevant to Native or Inuit peoples is also problematic. Hence, the claims being made for the creation of a native justice system, or systems.

Another problem arises when the Inuit values or traditions outlined in the cases have been discussed from a predominantly male perspective, whether at trial or on appeal. As seen in [the cases]. . ., this is particularly problematic where sexual assault is at issue. The problems resulting from the lack of a female perspective are only compounded by the Court of Appeal's patronizing neo-colonial judgments that discount all Inuit perspectives, male or female.

While judicial attempts to assess and apply Inuit or Native values is to be commended, the deficiencies in these assessments must be recognized. Proper guidelines must be created to ensure that community programs or community values are used where possible, but judges—and more appropriately legislators—must be aware that they must proceed with caution. When undertaking any analysis of cultural difference, a judge must be particularly aware of his or her own bias(es), whether in the form of race, class or gender bias. The judge must also try to be aware of bias in the information collected and presented. . . .The cultural differences in evidence must also be evaluated to determine whether they are in fact relevant to the case before the court. While Native cultures are distinct from mainstream Canadian culture, it must be

10. Mary Ellen Turpel, Aboriginal Peoples and the Canadian Charter: Interpretative Monopolies, Cultural Differences, 6 Can. Hum. Rts. Y.B. 3, 17 (1989–90).
11. *Id.* at 30.

determined whether this affects what is particularly relevant in sexual assault cases: the definitions of acceptable and unacceptable sexual relations. . . .

Conclusion

The basic premise of this paper has been that race, gender and class bias are prevalent within Canadian society, and that judges, as members of this society, are not immune to their influence. . . .

Native women are particularly likely to experience differential treatment when they are perceived as being less advantaged (sympathetic) than the man who assaults them. Whether elements of race, gender or class are the cause of this difference will likely depend on the facts before the court. Clear articulation of the distinctions may, however, be impossible, especially when one considers the subtle manifestations of each of these elements. As Patricia Monture has said:

> I do not know, when something like this happens to me, when it is happening to me because I am a woman, when it is happening to me because I am an Indian, or when it is happening to me because I am an Indian woman.[12]

Finally, it must be emphasized that any discussion surrounding Native and Inuit women in Canadian sexual assault cases is incomplete without the inclusion of their experiences. It is hoped that in the future, Native and Inuit women will write about their experiences and their theories regarding sexual assault. Only then will it be possible to see the full extent of the impact of judicial attitudes on Native and Inuit victims of sexual assault.

Catharine A. MacKinnon, *Toward a Feminist Theory of the State* 127–30, 134–38, 145–47, 149–53 (1989)

Male dominance is sexual. Meaning: men in particular, if not men alone, sexualize hierarchy; gender is one. As much a sexual theory of gender as a gendered theory of sex, this is the theory of sexuality that has grown out of consciousness raising. Recent feminist work, both interpretive and empirical, on rape, battery, sexual harassment, sexual abuse of children, prostitution and pornography, support it. These practices, taken together, express and actualize the distinctive power of men over women in society; their effective permissibility confirms and extends it. If one believes women's accounts of sexual use and abuse by men;[13] if the pervasiveness of male sexual violence against women substantiated in these studies is not denied, minimized, or

12. Patricia A. Monture, Ka-Nin-Geh-Heh-Gah-E-Sa-Nonh-Yah-Gah, 2 Can. J. Women & L. 159, 167 (1986).

13. Freud's decision to disbelieve women's accounts of being sexually abused as children was apparently central in the construction of the theories of fantasy and possibly also of the unconscious. That is, to some degree, his belief that the sexual abuse in his patients' accounts did not occur created the need for a theory like fantasy, like unconscious, to explain the reports. . . . One can only speculate on the course of the modern psyche (not to mention modern history) had the women been believed.

excepted as deviant or episodic; if the fact that only 7.8 percent of women in the United States are not sexually assaulted or harassed in their lifetimes is considered not ignorable or inconsequential;[14] if the women to whom it happens are not considered expendable; if violation of women is understood as sexualized on some level—then sexuality itself can no longer be regarded as unimplicated. Nor can the meaning of practices of sexual violence be categorized away as violence not sex. The male sexual role, this information and analysis taken together suggest, centers on aggressive intrusion on those with less power. Such acts of dominance are experienced as sexually arousing, as sex itself. They therefore are. The new knowledge on the sexual violation of women by men thus frames an inquiry into the place of sexuality in gender and of gender in sexuality.

A feminist theory of sexuality based on these data locates sexuality within a theory of gender inequality, meaning the social hierarchy of men over women. To make a theory feminist, it is not enough that it be authored by a biological female, nor that it describe female sexuality as different from (if equal to) male sexuality, or as if sexuality in women ineluctably exists in some realm beyond, beneath, above, behind—in any event, fundamentally untouched and unmoved by—an unequal social order. A theory of sexuality becomes feminist methodologically, meaning feminist in the post-marxist sense, to the extent it treats sexuality as a social construct of male power: defined by men, forced on women, and constitutive of the meaning of gender. Such an approach centers feminism on the perspective of the subordination of women to men as it identifies sex—that is, the sexuality of dominance and submission—as crucial, as a fundamental, as on some level definitive, in that process. Feminist theory becomes a project of analyzing that situation in order to face it for what it is, in order to change it. . . .

Sexual meaning is not made only, or even primarily, by words and in texts. It is made in social relations of power in the world, through which process gender is also produced. In feminist terms, the fact that male power has power means that the interests of male sexuality construct what sexuality as such means, including the standard way it is allowed and recognized to be felt and expressed and experienced, in a way that determines women's biographies, including sexual ones. Existing theories, until they grasp this, will not only misattribute what they call female sexuality to women as such, as if it were not imposed on women daily; they will also participate in enforcing the hegemony of the social construct "desire," hence its product, "sexuality," hence its construct "woman," on the world.

The gender issue, in this analysis, becomes the issue of what is taken to be "sexuality"; what sex means and what is meant by sex, when, how, with whom, and with what consequences to whom. Such questions are almost

---

14. This figure was calculated at my request by Diana E. H. Russell on the random-sample data base of 930 San Francisco households discussed in *The Secret Trauma: Incestuous Abuse of Women and Girls* 20-37 (1986), and *Rape in Marriage* 27-41 (1982). The figure includes all the forms of rape or other sexual abuse or harassment surveyed, noncontact as well as contact, from gang rape by strangers and marital rape to obscene phone calls, unwanted sexual advances on the street, unwelcome requests to pose for pornography, and subjection to peeping toms and sexual exhibitionists (flashers).

never systematically confronted, even in discourses that purport feminist awareness. What sex is—how it comes to be attached and attributed to what it is, embodied and practiced as it is, contextualized in the ways it is, signifying and referring to what it does—is taken as a baseline, a given, except in explanations of what happened when it is thought to have gone wrong. It is as if "erotic," for example, can be taken as having an understood referent, although it is never defined, except to imply that it is universal yet individual, ultimately variable and plastic, essentially indefinable but overwhelmingly positive. "Desire," the vicissitudes of which are endlessly extolled and philosophized in culture high and low, is not seen as fundamentally problematic or as calling for explanation on the concrete, interpersonal operative level, unless (again) it is supposed to be there and is not. To list and analyze what seem to be the essential elements for male sexual arousal, what has to be there for the penis to work, seems faintly blasphemous, like a pornographer doing market research. Sex is supposed both too individual and too universally transcendent for that. To suggest that the sexual might be continuous with something other than sex itself—something like politics—is seldom done, is treated as detumescent, even by feminists. It is as if sexuality comes from the stork.

Sexuality, in feminist light, is not a discrete sphere of interaction or feeling or sensation or behavior in which preexisting social divisions may or may not be played out. It is a pervasive dimension of social life, one that permeates the whole, a dimension along which gender occurs and through which gender is socially constituted; it is a dimension along which other social divisions, like race and class, partly play themselves out. Dominance eroticized defines the imperatives of its masculinity, submission eroticized defines its femininity. So many distinctive features of women's status as second class—the restriction and constraint and contortion, the servility and the display, the self-mutilation and requisite presentation of self as a beautiful thing, the enforced passivity, the humiliation—are made into the content of sex for women. Being a thing for sexual use is fundamental to it. This approach identifies not just a sexuality that is shaped under conditions of gender inequality but reveals this sexuality itself to be the dynamic of the inequality of the sexes. It is to argue that the excitement at reduction of a person to a thing, to less than a human being, as socially defined, is its fundamental motive force. It is to argue that sexual difference is a function of sexual dominance. It is to argue a sexual theory of the distribution of social power by gender, in which this sexuality that is sexuality is substantially what makes the gender division be what it is, which is male dominant, wherever it is, which is nearly everywhere. . . .

[S]ome feminists. . .[conceive] rape as violence, not sex. While this approach gave needed emphasis to rape's previously effaced elements of power and dominance, it obscured its elements of sex. Aside from failing to answer the rather obvious question, if it is violence not sex, why didn't he just hit her? this approach made it impossible to see that violence is sex when it is practiced as sex. This is obvious once what sexuality is, is understood as a matter of what it means and how it is interpreted. To say rape is violence not sex preserves the "sex is good" norm by simply distinguishing forced sex as "not sex," whether it means sex to the perpetrator or even, later, to the victim, who has difficulty experiencing sex without reexperiencing the rape. Whatever is sex cannot be violent; whatever is violent cannot be sex. This analytic wish-fulfillment makes it possible for rape to be opposed by those who would save sexuality from the rapists while leaving the sexual fundamentals of male dominance intact. . . .

Force is sex, not just sexualized; force is the desire dynamic, not just a response to the desired object when desire's expression is frustrated. Pressure, gender socialization, withholding benefits, extending indulgences, the how-to books, the sex therapy are the soft end; the fuck, the fist, the street, the chains, the poverty are the hard end. Hostility and contempt, or arousal of master to slave, together with awe and vulnerability, or arousal of slave to master—these are the emotions of this sexuality's excitement. "Sadomasochism is to sex what war is to civil life: the magnificent experience," wrote Susan Sontag. "[I]t is hostility—the desire, overt or hidden, to harm another person—that generates and enhances sexual excitement," wrote Robert Stoller. Harriet Jacobs, a slave, speaking of sex with a white master, wrote, "It seems less demeaning to give one's self, than to submit to compulsion." It is clear from the data that the force in sex and the sex in force is a matter of simple empirical description—unless one accepts that force in sex is not force anymore, it is just sex; or, if whenever a woman is forced it is what she really wants, or it or she does not matter; or, unless prior aversion or sentimentality substitutes what one wants sex to be, or will condone or countenance as sex, for what is actually happening.

To be clear: what is sexual is what gives a man an erection. Whatever it takes to make a penis shudder and stiffen with the experience of its potency is what sexuality means culturally. Whatever else does this, fear does, hostility does, hatred does, the helplessness of a child or a student or an infantilized or restrained or vulnerable woman does, revulsion does, death does. Hierarchy, a constant creation of person/thing, top/bottom, dominance/subordination relations, does. What is understood as violation, conventionally penetration and intercourse, defines the paradigmatic sexual encounter. The scenario of sexual abuse is: you do what I say. These textualities and these relations, situated within as well as creating a context of power in which they can be lived out, become sexuality. All this suggests that what is called sexuality is the dynamic of control by which male dominance—in forms that range from intimate to institutional, from a look to a rape—eroticizes and thus defines man and woman, gender identity and sexual pleasure. It is also that which maintains and defines male supremacy as a political system. Male sexual desire is thereby simultaneously created and serviced, never satisfied once and for all, while male force is romanticized, even sacralized, potentiated and naturalized, by being submerged into sex itself. . . .

The reality of pervasive sexual abuse and its erotization does not shift relative to perspective, although whether or not one will see it or accord it significance may. Interpretation varies relative to place in sexual abuse, certainly; but the fact that women are sexually abused as women, located in a social matrix of sexualized subordination, does not go away because it is often ignored or authoritatively disbelieved or interpreted out of existence. Indeed, some ideological supports for its persistence rely precisely upon techniques of social indeterminacy: no language but the obscene to describe the unspeakable; denial by the powerful casting doubt on the facticity of the injuries; actually driving its victims insane. . . .The feminist point is simple. Men are women's material conditions. If it happens to women, it happens.

Women often find ways to resist male supremacy and to expand their spheres of action. But they are never free of it. Women also embrace the standards of women's place in this regime as "our own" to varying degrees and in varying voices—as affirmation of identity and right to pleasure, in order to be loved and approved and paid, in order just to make it through another day. This, not inert passivity, is the meaning of being a victim. The term is not moral: who is to blame or to be pitied or condemned or held responsible. It is not prescriptive: what we should do next. It is not strategic: how to construe the situation so it can be changed. It is not emotional: what one feels better thinking. It is descriptive: who does what to whom and gets away with it. . . .

Male sexuality is apparently activated by violence against women and expresses itself in violence against women to a significant extent. If violence is seen as occupying the most fully achieved end of a dehumanization continuum on which objectification occupies the least express end, one question that is raised is whether some form of hierarchy—the dynamic of the continuum—is currently essential for male sexuality to experience itself. If so, and if gender is understood to be a hierarchy, perhaps the sexes are unequal so that men can be sexually aroused. To put it another way, perhaps gender must be maintained as a social hierarchy so that men will be able to get erections; or, part of the male interest in keeping women down lies in the fact that it gets men up. Maybe feminists are considered castrating because equality is not sexy.

Recent inquiries into rape support such suspicions. Men often rape women, it turns out, because they want to and enjoy it. The act, including the dominance, is sexually arousing, sexually affirming, and supportive of the perpetrator's masculinity. Many unreported rapists report an increase in self-esteem as a result of the rape. Indications are that reported rapists perceive that getting caught accounts for most of the unpleasant effects of raping. About one-third of all men say they would rape a woman if they knew they would not get caught. That the low conviction rate may give them confidence is supported by the prevalence rate. Some convicted rapists see rape as an "exciting" form of interpersonal sex, a recreational activity or "adventure," or as a means of revenge or punishment on all women or some subgroup of women or an individual woman. Even some of those who did the act out of bad feelings make it clear that raping made them feel better. "Men rape because it is rewarding to do so." If rapists experience rape as sex, does that mean there can be nothing wrong with it?

Once an act is labeled rape there is an epistemological problem with seeing it as sex. Indeed, this is a major social function served by labeling acts rape. Rape becomes something a rapist does, as if he were a separate species. But no personality disorder distinguishes most rapists from normal men. Psychopaths do rape, but only about 5 percent of all known rapists are diagnosed psychopathic. In spite of the numbers of victims, the normalcy of rapists, and even given the fact that most women are raped by men they know (making it most unlikely that a few lunatics know around half of the women in the United States), rape remains considered psychopathological and therefore not about sexuality.

Add this to rape's pervasiveness and permissibility, together with the belief that it is both rare and impermissible. Combine this with the similarity between the patterns, rhythms, roles, and emotions, not to mention acts, which make up rape (and battery) on the one hand and intercourse on the other.

All this makes it difficult to sustain the customary distinctions between pathology and normalcy, parophilia and nomophilia, violence and sex, in this area. Some researchers have previously noticed the centrality of force to the excitement value of pornography but have tended to put it down to perversion. Robert Stoller, for example, observes that pornography today depends upon hostility, voyeurism, and sadomasochism and calls perversion "the erotic form of hatred." If the perverse in this context is seen not as the other side of a bright normal/abnormal line but as an undiluted expression of a norm that permeates many ordinary interactions, hatred of women—that is, misogyny—becomes a dynamic of sexual excitement itself.

Compare victims' reports of rape with women's reports of sex. They look a lot alike. Compare victims' reports of rape with what pornography says is sex. They look a lot alike. In this light, the major distinction between intercourse (normal) and rape (abnormal) is that the normal happens so often that one cannot get anyone to see anything wrong with it. Which also means that anything sexual that happens often and one cannot get anyone to consider wrong is intercourse, not rape, no matter what was done. The distinctions that purport to divide this territory look more like the ideological supports for normalizing the usual male use and abuse of women as "sexuality" through authoritatively pretending that whatever is exposed of it is deviant. This may have something to do with the conviction rate in rape cases (making all those unconvicted men into normal men, and all those acts into sex). It may have something to do with the fact that most convicted rapists, and many observers, find rape convictions incomprehensible. And with the fact that marital rape is considered by many to be a contradiction in terms ("But if you can't rape your wife, who can you rape?"). And with the fact that so many rape victims have trouble with sex afterward.

What effect does the pervasive reality of sexual abuse of women by men have on what are deemed the more ordinary forms of sexual interaction? How do these material experiences create interest and point of view? Consider women. Recall that more than one-third of all girls experience sex, perhaps are sexually initiated, under conditions that even this society recognizes are forced or at least unequal. Perhaps they learn this process of sexualized dominance as sex. Top-down relations feel sexual. Is sexuality throughout life then ever not on some level a reenactment of, a response to, that backdrop? Rape, adding more women to the list, can produce similar resonance. Sexually abused women—most women—seem to become either sexually disinclined or compulsively promiscuous or both in series, trying to avoid the painful events, or repeating them over and over almost addictively, or both, in an attempt to reacquire a sense of control or to make them come out right. Women also widely experience sexuality as a means to male approval; male approval translates into nearly all social goods. Violation can be sustained, even sought out, to this end. Sex can, then, be a means of trying to feel alive by redoing what has made one feel dead, of expressing a denigrated self-image seeking its own reflection in self-action in order to feel fulfilled, or of keeping up one's stock with the powerful.

Many women who have been sexually abused (like many survivors of concentration camps and ritual torture) report having distanced and split themselves as a conscious strategy for coping with the abuse. With women, this dissociation often becomes a part of their sexuality per se and of their experience of the world, especially their experience of men. Women widely report having this sensation during sex. . . .

All women live in sexual objectification the way fish live in water. Given the statistical realities, all women live all the time under the shadow of the threat of sexual abuse. The question is, what can life as a woman mean, what can sex mean, to targeted survivors in a rape culture? Given the statistical realities, much of women's sexual lives will occur under post-traumatic stress. Being surrounded by pornography—which is not only socially ubiquitous but often directly used as part of sex—makes this a relatively constant condition. Women cope with objectification through trying to meet the male standard, and measure their self-worth by the degree to which they succeed. Women seem to cope with sexual abuse principally by denial or fear. On the denial side, immense energy goes into defending sexuality as just fine and getting better all the time, and into trying to make sexuality feel all right, the way it is supposed to feel. Women who are compromised, cajoled, pressured, tricked, blackmailed, or outright forced into sex (or pornography) often respond to the unspeakable humiliation, coupled with the sense of having lost some irreplaceable integrity, by claiming that sexuality as their own. Faced with no alternatives, the strategy to acquire self-respect and pride is: I chose it.

Consider the conditions under which this is done. This is a culture in which women are socially expected—and themselves necessarily expect and want—to be able to distinguish the socially, epistemologically, indistinguishable. Rape and intercourse are not authoritatively separated by any difference between the physical acts or amount of force involved but only legally, by a standard that centers on the man's interpretation of the encounter. Thus, although raped women, that is, most women, are supposed to be able to feel every day and every night that they have some meaningful determining part in having their sex life—their life, period—not be a series of rapes, the most they provide is the raw data for the man to see as he sees it. And he has been seeing pornography. Similarly, "consent" is supposed to be the crucial line between rape and intercourse, but the legal standard for it is so passive, so acquiescent, that a woman can be dead and have consented under it. The mind fuck of all of this makes liberalism's complicitous collapse into "I chose it" feel like a strategy for sanity. It certainly makes a woman at one with the world.

On the fear side, if a woman has ever been beaten in a relationship, even if "only once," what does that do to her everyday interactions, or her sexual interactions, with that man? With other men? Does her body ever really forget that behind his restraint he can do that any time she pushes an issue, or for no reason at all? Does her vigilance ever really relax? If she tried to do something about it, as many women do, and if nothing was done, as it usually is not, does she ever forget that that is what can be done to her at any time and nothing will be done about it? Does she smile at men less—or more? If she writes at all, does she imitate men less—or more? If a woman has ever been raped, ever, does a penis ever enter her without some body memory, if not a flashback then the effort of keeping it back; or does she hurry up or keep trying, feeling something gaining on her, trying to make it come out right? If a woman has ever been raped, does she ever fully regain the feeling of physical integrity, of self-respect, of having what she wants count somewhere, of being able to make herself clear to those who have not gone through what she has gone through, of living in a fair society, of equality?

Given the effects of learning sexuality through force or pressure or imposition; given the constant roulette of sexual violence; given the daily sexualization of every aspect of a woman's presence—for a woman to be sexualized means constant humiliation or threat of it, being invisible as human being and center stage as sex object, low pay, and being a target for assault or being assaulted. Given that this is the situation of all women, that one never knows for sure that one is not next on the list of victims until the moment one dies (and then, who knows?), it does not seen exaggerated to say that women are sexual, meaning that women exist, in a context of terror. Yet most professionals in the area of sexuality persist in studying the inexplicabilities of what is termed female sexuality acontextually, outside the context of gender inequality and its sexual violence—navel gazing, only slightly further down.[15]

The general theory of sexuality emerging from this feminist critique does not consider sexuality to be an inborn force inherent in individuals, nor cultural in the Freudian sense, in which sexuality exists in a cultural context but in universally invariant stages and psychic representations. It appears instead to be culturally specific, even if so far largely invariant because male supremacy is largely universal, if always in specific forms. Although some of its abuses (like prostitution) are accentuated by poverty, it does not vary by class, although class is one hierarchy it sexualizes. Sexuality becomes, in this view, social and relational, constructing and constructed of power. Infants, though sensory, cannot be said to possess sexuality in this sense because they have not had the experiences (and do not speak the language) that give it social meaning. Since sexuality is its social meaning, infant erections, for example, are clearly sexual in the sense that this society centers its sexuality on them, but to relate to a child as though his erections mean what adult erections have been conditioned to mean is a form of child abuse. Such erections have the meaning they acquire in social life only to observing adults.

When Freud changed his mind and declared that women were not telling the truth about what had happened to them when they said they were abused as children, he attributed their accounts to "fantasy." This was regarded as a theoretical breakthrough. Under the aegis of Freud, it is often said that victims of sexual abuse imagine it, that it is fantasy, not real, and their sexuality caused it. The feminist theory of sexuality suggests that it is the doctors who, because of their sexuality, as constructed, imagine that sexual abuse is a fantasy when it is real—real both in the sense that the sex happened and in the sense that it was abuse. Pornography is also routinely defended as "fantasy," meaning

15. This is also true of Michel Foucault, *The History of Sexuality* (1976–84). Foucault understands that sexuality must be discussed with method, power, class, and the law. Gender, however, eludes him. So he cannot distinguish between the silence about sexuality that Victorianism has made into a noisy discourse and the silence that has *been* women's sexuality under conditions of subordination by and to men. Although he purports to grasp sexuality, including desire itself, as social, he does not see the content of its determination as a sexist social order that eroticizes potency as male and victimization as female. Women are simply beneath significant notice.

not real. But it is real: the sex that makes it is real and is often abuse, and the sex that it makes is sex and is often abuse. Both the psychoanalytic and the pornographic "fantasy" worlds are what men imagine women imagine and desire because they are what men, raised on pornography, imagine and desire about women. Thus is psychoanalysis used to legitimate pornography, calling it fantasy, and pornography used to legitimate psychoanalysis, to show what women really want. Psychoanalysis and pornography, seen as epistemic sites in the same ontology, are mirrors of each other, male supremacist sexuality looking at itself looking at itself.

Perhaps the Freudian process of theory-building occurred like this: men heard accounts of child abuse, felt aroused by the account, and attributed their arousal to the child who is now a woman. Perhaps men respond sexually when women give an account of sexual violation because sexual words are a sexual reality, in the same way that men respond to pornography, which is (among other things) an account of the sexual violation of a woman. Seen in this way, much therapy as well as court testimony in sexual abuse cases is live oral pornography. Classical psychoanalysis attributes the connection between the experience of abuse (hers) and the experience of arousal (his) to the fantasy of the girl child. When he does it, he likes it, so when she did it, she must have liked it, or she must have thought it happened because she as much enjoys thinking about it happening to her as he enjoys thinking about it happening to her. Thus it cannot be abusive to her. Because he wants to do it, she must want it done.

Feminism also doubts the mechanism of repression in the sense that unconscious urges are considered repressed by social restrictions. Male sexuality is expressed and expressed and expressed, with a righteousness driven by the notion that something is trying to keep it from expressing itself. Too, there is a lot of doubt both about biology and about drives. Women are less repressed than oppressed, so-called women's sexuality largely a construct of male sexuality searching for someplace to happen, repression providing the reason for women's inhibition, meaning unwillingness to be available on demand. In this view, one function of the Freudian theory of repression (a function furthered rather than qualified by neo-Freudian adaptations) is ideologically to support the freeing of male sexual aggression while delegitimating women's refusal to respond.

There may be a feminist unconscious, but it is not the Freudian one. Perhaps equality lives there. Its laws, rather than a priori, objective, or universal, might as well be a response to the historical regularities of sexual subordination, which under bourgeois ideological conditions require that the truth of male dominance be concealed in order to preserve the belief that women are sexually self-acting: that women want it. The feminist psychic universe certainly recognizes that people do not always know what they want, have hidden desires and inaccessible needs, lack awareness of motivation, have contorted and opaque interactions, and have an interest in obscuring what is really going on. But this does not essentially conceal that what women really want is more sex. It is true, as Freudians have persuasively observed, that many things are sexual that do not present themselves as such. But in ways Freud never dreamed.

Carol Smart, *Feminism and the Power of Law* 28–32 (1989)

Sexuality is comprehended as the pleasure of the Phallus, and by extension the pleasures of penetration and intercourse—for men. Although this does not disallow the possibility of homosexuality, it undeniably renders lesbianism incomprehensible and pathological. Female pleasure is assumed either to coincide with the male definition or to be beyond understanding. The former presumption is articulated in the remarkably constant belief that rape must be pleasurable for women because it involves penetration. The latter is demonstrated in the belief that when women deny the pleasure of penetration they are frigid or man-hating. The idea that what pleasures women might be different to men's pleasure presents a mystery in a phallocentric culture. I am not implying by this that all women have only the same pleasure, nor that intercourse may not be pleasurable at times, but that the focus on phallic pleasure does not inevitably coincide with the potential of female sexuality. It is this possibility that upsets the phallocentric applecart. . . .

It might be useful to consider some examples of this pathologization to which all women are vulnerable, most especially as this 'incomprehension' is imported wholesale into the rape trial. The following quotations come from a survey of men's 'sex lives' carried out by the magazine *Woman*. In this book the men are said to speak for themselves about aspects of their sexual relationships, their satisfactions and dissatisfactions. . . .In fact these men do not simply speak for themselves since the author of the book adds the necessary framework to ensure that these men's comments are understood 'correctly'. In case we fail to take the message from the men themselves [the author] informs us that women are too reserved and guilty to enjoy sex and satisfy their husbands. In other words the comments are contextualized into the phallocentric framework—as if this were really necessary. Unfortunately it does not occur to the author that there could be another interpretation of these men's comments.

> My wife is very conventional when it comes to sex. These days she will not let me give her oral sex. . .and she has never given oral sex to me. She tried it once but she didn't like the taste of it. I have offered to put some sort of different flavour on my penis but she still won't try.
>
> I have bought her sexy underwear and offered to buy some for me, but she is not interested. She will not wear suspender belt and stockings for sex as she thinks it is kinky.
>
> I would like my wife to be much keener on sex than she is now. Her lack of interest bothers us both but we are trying to adjust to it.
>
> I would like to try anything in bed but to have to persuade her a little at a time. This has to be a slow process as nothing destroys an intimate atmosphere quicker than realising she is 'closing her eyes and thinking of England.' She *must* enjoy it as well. (emphasis added)

These quotations are so familiar that they might be a script that is rehearsed over and over again. Basically the complaint is that wives do not 'come across' enough. What is implicit is the view that women possess something they are not prepared to share. This sharing is seen as a simple thing which could be easily achieved and which would make men very happy. This view is given substance by the often stated 'fact' that these wives used to provide the right kind of sex, either before marriage or during the early years. This recollection is presented as 'proof' that women can do it, can enjoy a particular form of sexual relationship, and confirms the belief that women are either selfish and unloving, or that their libido deteriorates, hence demonstrating the problematic nature of female sexuality (which contrasts with the virile straightforwardness of male sexuality).

The commonsense accounts provided by the men in the quotations are, of course, real experiences. The point is not to deny their reality, nor indeed the frustrations of these men, but to try to understand how male and female sexuality has been constructed and why this discourse, which pathologizes female sexuality, has so much currency. It must be stressed that there is no simple biological imperative underlying these understandings of sexual desire and frustration. The construction of sexuality and desire results from a complex interplay between culture (language), the psyche, and the body and it is precisely the deconstruction of sex-as-natural that feminists, historians, psychoanalysts, and philosophers have managed to achieve. [One writer,] for example, has challenged the conceptualization of sex-as-natural and has argued that the discourse of the insatiable male sex drive empowers men and constructs women as the passive objects of desire. She goes further, however, to reveal that part of this discourse entails the belief that women are potentially powerful and dangerous, and that they can 'swallow up' men who show weakness. Hence men's desire is constructed as omnipotent yet vulnerable to the wiles of women who, although appearing passive, will castrate them emotionally if they can. Men must therefore resist women on an emotional level, whilst exploiting them fully on a sexual level. The ideal therefore becomes the unemotional but highly proficient (hetero)sexual stud.

We need to consider how this widely disseminated discourse and its relationship to the everyday experiences of men (and women) relate to rape. It would follow that if all women are seen as having the thing that men most need, if they are also seen as grudging with it, or as so out of touch with their 'real' sexual feelings that they deny it to themselves and to men, then the problem for men is how to gain control of women's sexuality in spite of women themselves. This is as much a scenario for 'seduction' as for rape, but rape also serves to avoid the potential 'trap' of emotionality. As with prostitution, the raped woman cannot assert her 'misconceived' power by trapping the man into commitment or love.

In this formulation women's sexuality is constructed as separate from women themselves. Figuratively speaking women are seen as having charge of something which is of greater value to men than to women themselves. At the same time women can enjoy sex 'in spite of themselves'. So this sexuality of which they have charge is construed as an essence which can by-pass consciousness or which has a will of its own. This in turn allows for the construction of women's consciousness simply as a one-dimensional prudery, an inappropriate moral standard imposed by mothers on daughters. It is not regarded as an expression of a woman's will but rather the mouthing of a convention which defeats the woman's own potential for sexual satisfaction. In other words if women say 'no' they do not *really* mean it. This view is articulated clearly in *The Woman Report on Men*.

> Marriage may have made it officially OK for a woman to be sexual, but the parental prohibitions are still there in her head. . . .'Mother' is still in there, making her tense when her husband approaches her sexually, blocking her from making a pass when she feels sexy.

Not only do Mothers wreck things for their husbands, it seems they can spoil things for the next generation of men too.

It is these accounts which also form the basis of many accounts of rape. From the judge to the convicted rapist there is a common understanding that female sexuality is problematic and that women's sexual responsiveness is whimsical or capricious. As women do not know their own sexual responsiveness and enjoyment, it is held that it could occur in the most unlikely circumstances. It is held to occur even when a woman is in fear of her life or being gang raped. Yet by the same token it can simultaneously be maintained that it does not matter if she enjoys it or not. As men cannot 'really know' when they give pleasure to women, they can really only hope to please themselves. Men therefore do not have to trouble themselves with the mystery of women's pleasure. The following statements from convicted rapists reveal the continuity of this heterosexist discourse.

> Rape is a man's right. If a women [sic] doesn't want to give it, the man should take it. Women have no right to say no. Women are made to have sex. It's all they are good for. Some women would rather take a beating but they always give in; it's what they are for.
>
> I think I was really pissed off at her because it didn't go as planned. I could have been with someone else. She led me on but wouldn't deliver. . .I have a male ego that must be fed.
>
> Rape gave me the power to do what I wanted to do without feeling I had to please a partner or respond to a partner. I felt in control, dominant. Rape was the ability to have sex without caring about the woman's response. I was totally dominant.

Clearly there are themes here that resonate with the articulations of men who would not define themselves as rapists. For example, 'I feel my wife has the upper hand all the time. My sex life is what my wife will allow me to have and not what I would like'. The resentment felt by this man is clear, he would much rather be able to control his wife's sexual responsiveness and he sees her as too powerful because she can say 'no' and he does not want to risk taking other partners in case his wife divorces him. From where he stands she has failed to meet the contractual exchange of security and commitment for freely available sex. In his terms he has 'reason' to be angry and it is not hard to see that this resentment can extend to a generalized misogyny. The point is, however, that this contract represents the material and psychic oppression of women. Little wonder that so many women try to find a way out of such contracts. Yet women who do are the focus of abuse, and *all* women may be regarded as potential renegades and hence contemptible.

It is clear that in saying 'no' to sex, women are also challenging (even if unwittingly) the extensive power of men which goes beyond sex. The 'no' is understood as a challenge to manhood (or phallocentrism) which, in a way, it is. It is a form of resistance which goes beyond the site of individual relationships. It would be a mistake to see it as a form of unified guerrilla action on the part of women because this 'no' is really only overtly political in the case of political lesbianism or feminist celibacy. But the 'no' is very widespread—why else would there by so many jokes about wives having headaches or so many complaints from men that their wives are not responsive enough?

Notes and Question

1. *The Cultural Defense.* Margo Nightingale's analysis of criminal cases involving Aboriginal people examines the effects of class, gender, and racial stereotypes and their intersections on conviction and sentencing outcomes. Her analysis of the cases also demonstrates how cultural and gender biases in the criminal justice system produce a distorted view of Native culture when the system consciously acknowledges cultural differences. Given the ethnocentric attitude toward Native people displayed throughout the Canadian judicial system, it is worth asking the question: why is it in the interest of the judicial system to consider a cultural defense that mitigates the culpability of the defendant in sexual assault cases? See Note 2, at p. 218, for examples of when the courts in the United States have considered the cultural defense.

2. *Heterosexual Sex and Rape.* Both Catharine MacKinnon and Carol Smart analyze rape by showing how both heterosexuality and rape are male centered and defined and how both are inextricably connected to male dominance and female submission. Acknowledging the dangers of "any attempt to develop a positive account of heterosexuality for women in the context of compulsory heterosexuality and patriarchal society," Lynne Henderson believes "it is crucial to examine which heterosexual practices and attitudes hurt women and which heterosexual practices and attitudes give them pleasure." Lynne N. Henderson, Getting to Know: Honoring Women in Law and in Fact, 2 Tex. J. Women & L. 41, 55-56 (1993).

> [A] language of women's sexuality is not readily available, as sexuality remains described from a male point of view, using male words and metaphors. Nevertheless, this does not mean that female heterosexual experience cannot be described at all, or that women should continue to cede the description of heterosexuality to a masculine point of view. The challenge is to identify and express those elements of heterosexuality that are pleasurable, to separate those experiences from the ones that are painful, and to decide which of the painful experiences are rape and criminal.
>
> If one listens to women's experiences, it becomes apparent that heterosexual women do not always feel harmed by heterosexual penetration; they may indeed find it desirable and pleasurable in certain contexts. Many women also know that it is rape when they are ignored by a man who does not care about their wishes and forces his penis into them. It is painful, scary, degrading, and damaging. Thus, we see the beginnings of the continuum: at one end, pleasurable heterosexual sex, at the other end, rape. Between the two situations are encounters which are sometimes "rape" and sometimes "sex."

Id. at 58.

3. *Psychology and Rape*. MacKinnon notes that the Freudian theory that attributed child abuse to women's fantasy, which has come under substantial scrutiny, served the interest of men in constructing a sexuality based on what men desire (p. 407-08). Jenny Kitzinger analyzes contemporary psychological theory and practice to show how psychology continues to serve the dominant heterosexual, male-centered culture.

> There is a story about the role of psychology in combating sexual violence against girls. It is a story about progress. It goes something like this. Once upon a time, in the dim and distant past, psychologists, psychiatrists and psychoanalysts dismissed women's accounts of childhood sexual exploitation—they said it was just fantasy, or that it didn't do any harm, or they told women to forget what had happened and get on with their lives, or they locked them away in mental hospitals. But things are different now, *now* psychologists, psychiatrists and psychoanalysts recognize the widespread reality of abuse and they are at the forefront of acknowledging and documenting the full impact of such violence. *Now* they are really listening to women, taking their experiences seriously and responding to their needs. . . .
>
> However, this 'up the mountain' account of psychology's progress has been challenged by many feminists and survivors of abuse who tell the story in a different way. In this version, psychology is not part of the 'solution' to male violence. Rather, it is part of the problem. Psychology has not changed—it has merely dressed up old approaches in the new fashions of the time. Psychology has consistently operated as an instrument to police women's reactions to sexual assault—limiting and individualizing what we can learn from such experiences, and obscuring the political implications. . . .Psychology has devised a framework for processing our 'personal experiences' which erases feminist questions about the implications of sexual violence for relations between men and women, and which enforces conformity to heterosexual norms. . . .
>
> Scanning the more recent mainstream psychological literature on sexual violence reveals a proliferation of case studies, research findings and diagnoses which demonstrate women's failure to survive sexual assault unscathed. Now, instead of reassuring the public that most abused girls grow up to get married, research starts to reveal the worrying fact that around 40 percent of survivors remain without husbands. Now, instead of telling us that raped girls will grow up to be sexually 'normal', experts seem to vie with each other to diagnose 'poor sexual adjustment', 'disrupted sexual functioning' and various 'symptoms of feminine sexual incapacity'.
>
> Women who have been sexually assaulted are diagnosed as suffering from 'desire disorder', 'impaired sexual arousal' and 'sexual avoidance syndrome' (i.e. they may not want sex with men; they may not get excited by it; and sometimes they may even try to avoid it).
>
> We are warned that a woman who has been raped (whether during childhood or adulthood) may reject feminine clothing and display 'homosexual tendencies'. She may score poorly on the 'Female Sexual Arousability Scale'—for instance by expressing a distaste for pornography. She may only be capable of clitoral orgasms—not the mature, vaginal variety. She may be disgusted by the masculine body and perceive the penis as a weapon. She may

be incapable of having sex with her husband after an argument, and her 'clinical profile' may reveal a tendency to avoid virile, aggressive partners.

> Most troubling of all, according to these experts, is that many women display a profound distrust of men. This is clear evidence of a 'maladjusted reaction' which the psychologists variously explain as 'transference', 'projection' or 'displacement'. . . .
>
> The professionals who diagnose women's sexual maladjustments never question the politics of these 'problems'. They rarely address fundamental issues such as: Why *should* women get married? Why should we enjoy 'feminine' clothing? What is wrong with 'homosexual tendencies'? Why should we be turned on by pornography? Why shouldn't we fear and distrust men or feel anger about male sexual violence? What is wrong with choosing gentle, unaggressive partners. . .? Why shouldn't a woman reject having sex with a man while she feels angry or upset? What makes a 'vaginal orgasm' superior to a clitoral one, and what is so important about a woman not wanting a penis inside her anyway? Indeed, why should women want sex with men at all?. . .
>
> Women's naming of male violence and demands for change have been translated into a different language by the 'incest industry':
>
> > We spoke of male violence and deliberate socially accepted violation. They spoke of family dysfunction. . .We spoke of social change. They spoke of personal healing. We spoke of political battle. They spoke of our need to hug the child within.
>
> The ways in which psychology insists on sexual 'restoration' for survivors is only one part of this process of co-option, a process concerned with helping women to accommodate to living under heteropatriarchy and ensuring that male access to women's bodies continues unimpeded. Psychology is consolidating its monopoly of defining both the 'problem' and the 'solution' to sexual violence.

Jenny Kitzinger, Sexual Violence and Compulsory Heterosexuality, 2 Feminism & Psychol. 399, 399-402, 414 (1992) (emphasis in original).

4. *Gang Rape*. Gang rape, by which we mean the rape of a female by two or more males, has been the subject of a number of social science studies. *See*, *e.g.*, Peggy Reeves Sanday, Fraternity Gang Rape: Sex, Brotherhood, and Privilege on Campus (1990); Julie K. Ehrhart & Bernice R. Sandler, Campus Gang Rape: Party Games? (Project on the Status and Education of Women, Assoc. of Am. Coll. 1985). Sanday, an anthropologist, analyzed "certain group rituals of male bonding on a college campus." Sanday, *supra*, at 1. In particular she studied gang rape, which campus men also referred to as "pulling train" and "gang banging." *Id*. She found the following common pattern:

> A vulnerable young woman, one who is seeking acceptance or who is high on drugs or alcohol, is taken to a room. She may or may not agree to have sex with one man. She then passes out, or is too weak or scared to protest, and a train of men have sex with her. Sometimes the young woman's drinks are spiked without her knowledge, and when she is approached by several men in a locked room, she reacts with confusion and panic. Whether too weak to

> protest, frightened, or unconscious, as has been the case in quite a number of instances, anywhere from two to eleven or more men have sex with her.

Id. at 1-2. Sanday goes on to analyze the ritual as a manifestation of homophobia.

> Men entice one another into the act of "pulling train" by implying that those who do not participate are unmanly or homosexual. This behavior is full of contradictions because the homoeroticism of "pulling train" seems obvious. A group of men watch each other having sex with a woman who may be unconscious. One might well ask why the woman is even necessary for the sexual acts these men stage for one another. . . .
>
> In group sex, homoerotic desire is simultaneously indulged, degraded, and extruded from the group. The fact that the woman involved is often unconscious highlights her status as a surrogate victim in a drama where the main agents are males interacting with one another. The victim embodies the sexual urges of the brothers; she is defined as "wanting it"—even though she may be unconscious during the event—so that the men can satisfy their urges for one another at her expense.

Id. at 12-13. Sanday concludes that

> The sexual act is not concerned with sexual gratification but with the deployment of the penis as a concrete symbol of masculine social power and dominance. The male sexual bonding evident in "pulling train" is a sexual expression and display of the power of the brotherhood to control and dominate women. The discourse associated with acts of "pulling train" defines this form of control and domination as part of normal male sexual expression. Thus, this discourse operates as a strategy of knowledge that sanctions the deployment of male power in acts of sexual aggression. . . .
>
> Cross-cultural research demonstrates that whenever men build and give allegiance to a mystical, enduring, all-male social group, the disparagement of women is, invariably, an important ingredient of the mystical bond, and sexual aggression the means by which the bond is renewed. As long as exclusive male clubs exist in a society that privileges men as a social category, we must recognize that collective sexual aggression provides a ready stage on which some men represent their social privilege and introduce adolescent boys to their future place in the status hierarchy.

Id. at 10, 19-20.

Christine Gidycz and Mary Koss studied the effects of gang rape on its victims. They found:

> Group sexual assault victims indicated that they were more frightened during the assault, and they described the man/men as more aggressive than individual sexual assault victims. Group sexual assault victims were more likely to indicate that the offenders utilized severe forms of coercion such as hitting or slapping or the use of a weapon. . . .
>
> In this sample 39% of the group assaults were perpetrated by relatives (compared with 18% of the individual sexual assaults), and 39% of the group assaults were perpetrated by strangers (compared with 2% of the individual sexual assaults). . . .
>
> The results of this study further suggest that group sexual assault vic-

> tims may be particularly impacted by sexual assault. Group sexual assault victims were twice as likely as individual sexual victims to have experienced suicidal ideation after the assault. Although very few group sexual assault victims reported the assault to a crisis service or to the police, or sought therapy, they were more likely to do so than were individual sexual assault victims. . . .Finally, although individual and group *rape* victims did not differ in their label for the assault, it is noteworthy that approximately half of the women in both groups did not conceptualize their experience as rape.

Christine A. Gidycz & Mary P. Koss, A Comparison of Group and Individual Sexual Assault Victims, 14 Psychol. Women Q. 325, 338-40 (1990) (emphasis in original).

B. Rape Law as Man's Law

Mich. Comp. Laws Ann.

§ 750.520a-e, g-j, l (1991)

750.520a. Definitions

As used in sections 520a to 520l:

(a) "Actor" means a person accused of criminal sexual conduct.

(b) "Developmental disability" means an impairment of general intellectual functioning or adaptive behavior which meets the following criteria:

(i) It originated before the person became 18 years of age.

(ii) It has continued since its origination or can be expected to continue indefinitely.

(iii) It constitutes a substantial burden to the impaired person's ability to perform in society.

(iv) It is attributable to 1 or more of the following:

(A) Mental retardation, cerebral palsy, epilepsy, or autism.

(B) Any other condition of a person found to be closely related to mental retardation because it produces a similar impairment or requires treatment and services similar to those required for a person who is mentally retarded.

(c) "Intimate parts" includes the primary genital area, groin, inner thigh, buttock, or breast of a human being.

(d) "Mental illness" means a substantial disorder of thought or mood which significantly impairs judgment, behavior, capacity to recognize reality, or ability to cope with the ordinary demands of life.

(e) "Mentally disabled" means that a person has a mental illness, is mentally retarded, or has a developmental disability.

(f) "Mentally incapable" means that a person suffers from a mental disease or defect which renders that person temporarily or permanently incapable of appraising the nature of his or her conduct.

(g) "Mentally incapacitated" means that a person is rendered temporarily incapable of appraising or controlling his or her conduct due to

the influence of a narcotic, anesthetic, or other substance administered to that person without his or her consent, or due to any other act committed upon that person without his or her consent.
(h) "Mentally retarded" means significantly subaverage general intellectual functioning which originates during the developmental period and is associated with impairment in adaptive behavior.
(i) "Physically helpless" means that a person is unconscious, asleep, or for any other reason is physically unable to communicate unwillingness to an act.
(j) "Personal injury" means bodily injury, disfigurement, mental anguish, chronic pain, pregnancy, disease, or loss or impairment of a sexual or reproductive organ.
(k) "Sexual contact" includes the intentional touching of the victim's or actor's intimate parts or the intentional touching of the clothing covering the immediate area of the victim's or actor's intimate parts, if that intentional touching can reasonably be construed as being for the purpose of sexual arousal or gratification.
(l) "Sexual penetration" means sexual intercourse, cunnilingus, fellatio, anal intercourse, or any other intrusion, however slight, of any part of a person's body or of any object into the genital or anal openings of another person's body, but emission of semen is not required.
(m) "Victim" means the person alleging to have been subjected to criminal sexual conduct.

750.520b. First degree criminal sexual conduct

(1) A person is guilty of criminal sexual conduct in the first degree if he or she engages in sexual penetration with another person and if any of the following circumstances exists:

(a) That other person is under 13 years of age.
(b) That other person is at least 13 but less than 16 years of age and any of the following:
  (i) The actor is a member of the same household as the victim.
  (ii) The actor is related to the victim by blood or affinity to the fourth degree.
  (iii) The actor is in a position of authority over the victim and used this authority to coerce the victim to submit.
(c) Sexual penetration occurs under circumstances involving the commission of any other felony.
(d) The actor is aided or abetted by 1 or more other persons and either of the following circumstances exists:
  (i) The actor knows or has reason to know that the victim is mentally incapable, mentally incapacitated, or physically helpless.
  (ii) The actor uses force or coercion to accomplish the sexual penetration. Force or coercion includes but is not limited to any of the circumstances listed in subdivision (f)(i) to (v).
(e) The actor is armed with a weapon or any article used or fashioned in a manner to lead the victim to reasonably believe it to be a weapon.

(f) The actor causes personal injury to the victim and force or coercion is used to accomplish sexual penetration. Force or coercion includes but is not limited to any of the following circumstances:

(i) When the actor overcomes the victim through the actual application of physical force or physical violence.

(ii) When the actor coerces the victim to submit by threatening to use force or violence on the victim, and the victim believes that the actor has the present ability to execute these threats.

(iii) When the actor coerces the victim to submit by threatening to retaliate in the future against the victim, or any other person, and the victim believes that the actor has the ability to execute this threat. As used in this subdivision, "to retaliate" includes threats of physical punishment, kidnapping, or extortion.

(iv) When the actor engages in the medical treatment or examination of the victim in a manner or for purposes which are medically recognized as unethical or unacceptable.

(v) When the actor, through concealment or by the element of surprise, is able to overcome the victim.

(g) The actor causes personal injury to the victim, and the actor knows or has reason to know that the victim is mentally incapable, mentally incapacitated, or physically helpless.

(h) That other person is mentally incapable, mentally disabled, mentally incapacitated, or physically helpless, and any of the following:

(i) The actor is related to the victim by blood or affinity to the fourth degree.

(ii) The actor is in a position of authority over the victim and used this authority to coerce the victim to submit.

(2) Criminal sexual conduct in the first degree is a felony punishable by imprisonment in the state prison for life or for any term of years.

750.520c. Second degree criminal sexual conduct

(1) A person is guilty of criminal sexual conduct in the second degree if the person engages in sexual contact with another person and if any of the following circumstances exists:

(a) That other person is under 13 years of age.

(b) That other person is at least 13 but less than 16 years of age and any of the following:

(i) The actor is a member of the same household as the victim.

(ii) The actor is related by blood or affinity to the fourth degree to the victim.

(iii) The actor is in a position of authority over the victim and the actor used this authority to coerce the victim to submit.

(c) Sexual contact occurs under circumstances involving the commission of any other felony.

(d) The actor is aided or abetted by 1 or more other persons and either of the following circumstances exists:

(i) The actor knows or has reason to know that the victim is mentally incapable, mentally incapacitated, or physically helpless.

(ii) The actor uses force or coercion to accomplish the sexual contact. Force or coercion includes but is not limited to any of the circumstances listed in sections 520b(1)(f)(i) to (v).

(e) The actor is armed with a weapon or any article used or fashioned in a manner to lead a person to reasonably believe it to be a weapon.

(f) The actor causes personal injury to the victim and force or coercion is used to accomplish the sexual contact. Force or coercion includes but is not limited to any of the circumstances listed in section 520b(1)(f)(i) to (v).

(g) The actor causes personal injury to the victim and the actor knows or has reason to know that the victim is mentally incapable, mentally incapacitated, or physically helpless.

(h) That other person is mentally incapable, mentally disabled, mentally incapacitated, or physically helpless, and any of the following:

(i) The actor is related to the victim by blood or affinity to the fourth degree.

(ii) The actor is in a position of authority over the victim and used this authority to coerce the victim to submit.

(2) Criminal sexual conduct in the second degree is a felony punishable by imprisonment for not more than 15 years.

750.520d. Third degree criminal sexual conduct

(1) A person is guilty of criminal sexual conduct in the third degree if the person engages in sexual penetration with another person and if any of the following circumstances exists:

(a) That other person is at least 13 years of age and under 16 years of age.

(b) Force or coercion is used to accomplish the sexual penetration. Force or coercion includes but is not limited to any of the circumstances listed in section 520b(1)(f)(i) to (v).

(c) The actor knows or has reason to know that the victim is mentally incapable, mentally incapacitated, or physically helpless.

(2) Criminal sexual conduct in the third degree is a felony punishable by imprisonment for not more than 15 years.

750.520e. Fourth degree criminal sexual conduct

(1) A person is guilty of criminal sexual conduct in the fourth degree if he or she engages in sexual contact with another person and if any of the following circumstances exists:

(a) Force or coercion is used to accomplish the sexual contact. Force or coercion includes but is not limited to any of the circumstances listed in section 520b(1)(f)(i) to (iv).

(b) The actor knows or has reason to know that the victim is mentally incapable, mentally incapacitated, or physically helpless.

(c) That other person is under the jurisdiction of the department of corrections, and the actor is an employee or a contractual employee of, or a volunteer with, the department of corrections who has knowledge that the other person is under the jurisdiction of the department of corrections.

(2) Criminal sexual conduct in the fourth degree is a misdemeanor punishable by imprisonment for not more than 2 years, or by a fine of not more than $500.00, or both.

750.520g. Assault with intent to commit criminal sexual conduct

(1) Assault with intent to commit criminal sexual conduct involving sexual penetration shall be a felony punishable by imprisonment for not more than 10 years.
(2) Assault with intent to commit criminal sexual conduct in the second degree is a felony punishable by imprisonment for not more than 5 years.

750.520h. Corroboration of victim's testimony

The testimony of a victim need not be corroborated in prosecutions under sections 520b to 520g.

750.520i. Resistance

A victim need not resist the actor in prosecution under sections 520b to 520g.

750.520j. Admissibility of evidence; victim's sexual conduct

(1) Evidence of specific instances of the victim's sexual conduct, opinion evidence of the victim's sexual conduct, and reputation evidence of the victim's sexual conduct shall not be admitted under sections 520b to 520g unless and only to the extent that the judge finds that the following proposed evidence is material to a fact at issue in the case and that its inflammatory or prejudicial nature does not outweigh its probative value:

(a) Evidence of the victim's past sexual conduct with the actor.

(b) Evidence of specific instances of sexual activity showing the source or origin of semen, pregnancy, or disease.

(2) If the defendant proposes to offer evidence described in subsection (1)(a) or (b), the defendant within 10 days after the arraignment on the information shall file a written motion and offer of proof. The court may order an in camera hearing to determine whether the proposed evidence is admissible under subsection (1). If new information is discovered during the course of the trial that may make the evidence described in subsection (1)(a) or (b) admissible, the judge may order an in camera hearing to determine whether the proposed evidence is admissible under subsection (1).

750.520l. Married persons

A person may be charged and convicted under sections 520b to 520g even though the victim is his or her legal spouse. However, a person may not be charged or convicted solely because his or her legal spouse is under the age of 16, mentally incapable, or mentally incapacitated.

Susan Estrich, Rape, 95 Yale L.J. 1087, 1090–91, 1094–1108, 1115–22, 1125–27, 1129–32, 1182–83 (1986)

To examine rape within the criminal law tradition is to expose fully the sexism of the law. Much that is striking about the crime of rape—and revealing of the sexism of the system—emerges only when rape is examined relative to other crimes . . . .For example, rape is most assuredly not the only crime in which consent is a defense; but it is the only crime that has required the victim to resist physically in order to establish nonconsent. Nor is rape the only crime where prior relationship is taken into account by prosecutors in screening cases; yet we have not asked whether considering prior relationship in rape cases is different, and less justifiable, than considering it in cases of assault.

Sexism in the law of rape is no matter of mere historical interest; it endures, even where some of the most blatant testaments to that sexism have disappeared. Corroboration requirements unique to rape may have been repealed, but they continue to be enforced as a matter of practice in many jurisdictions. The victim of rape may not be required to resist to the utmost as a matter of statutory law in any jurisdiction, but the definitions accorded to force and consent may render "reasonable" resistance both a practical and a legal necessity. In the law of rape, supposedly dead horses continue to run. . . .

Most of the time, a criminal law that reflects male views and male standards imposes its judgment on men who have injured other men. It is "boys' rules" applied to a boys' fight. In rape, the male standard defines a crime committed against women, and male standards are used not only to judge men, but also to judge the conduct of women victims. Moreover, because the crime involves sex itself, the law of rape inevitably treads on the explosive ground of sex roles, of male aggression and female passivity, of our understandings of sexuality—areas where differences between a male and a female perspective may be most pronounced. . . .

The traditional way of defining a crime is by describing the prohibited act (*actus reus*) committed by the defendant and the prohibited mental state (*mens rea*) with which he must have done it. We ask: What did the defendant do? What did he know or intend when he did it?

The definition of rape stands in striking contrast to this tradition, because courts, in defining the crime, have focused almost incidentally on the defendant—and almost entirely on the victim. It has often been noted that, traditionally at least, the rules associated with the proof of a rape charge—the corroboration requirement, the requirement of cautionary instructions, and the fresh complaint rule—as well as the evidentiary rules relating to prior sexual conduct by the victim, placed the victim as much on trial as the defendant. Such a reversal also occurs in the course of defining the elements of the crime. *Mens rea*, where it might matter, is all but eliminated; prohibited force tends to be defined according to the response of the victim; and nonconsent—the *sine qua non* of the offense—turns entirely on the victim's response. . . .

But the problem is more fundamental than that. Apart from the woman's conduct, the law provides no clear, working definition of rape. This rather conspicuous gap in the law of rape presents substantial questions of fair warning for men, which the law not so handily resolves by imposing the burden of warning them on women.

At its simplest, the dilemma lies in this: If nonconsent is essential to rape (and no amount of force or physical struggle is inherently inconsistent with lawful sex), and if no sometimes means yes, and if men are supposed to be aggressive in any event, how is a man to know when he has crossed the line? And how are we to avoid unjust convictions?

This dilemma is hardly inevitable. Partly, it is a product of the way society (or a least a powerful part of it) views sex. Partly, it is a product of the lengths to which the law has gone to enforce and legitimize those views. We could prohibit the use of force and threats and coercion in sex, regardless of "consent." We could define consent in a way that respected the autonomy of women. Having chosen neither course, however, we have created a problem of fair warning, and force and consent have been defined in an effort to resolve this problem. . . .

Rape is not a unique crime in requiring nonconsent. But it is unique in the definition given to nonconsent. As it has been understood, the consent standard denies female autonomy; indeed, it even denies that women are capable of making decisions about sex, let alone articulating them. Yet consent, properly understood, has the potential to give women greater power in sexual relations and to expand our understanding of the crime of rape. That is, perhaps, why so many efforts have been made to cabin the concept. . . .

While the defendant's attitude toward consent may be considered either an issue of *mens rea* or a mistake of fact, the key question remains the same. In *mens rea* terms, the question is whether negligence suffices, that is, whether the defendant should be convicted who claims that he thought the woman was consenting, or didn't think about it, in situations where a "reasonable man" would have known that there was not consent. In mistake of fact terms, the question is whether a mistake as to consent must be reasonable in order to exculpate the defendant.[16]

In defining the crime of rape, most American courts have omitted *mens rea* altogether. . . .

To treat what the defendant intended or knew or even should have known about the victim's consent as irrelevant to his liability sounds like a result favorable to both prosecution and women as victims. But experience makes all too clear that it is not. To refuse to inquire into *mens rea* leaves two possibilities: turning rape into a strict liability offense where, in the absence of consent, the man is guilty of rape regardless of whether he (or anyone) would have recognized nonconsent in the circumstances; or defining the crime of rape in a fashion that is so limited that it would be virtually impossible for any man to be convicted where he was truly unaware or mistaken as to nonconsent. In fact, it is the latter approach which has characterized all of the older, and many of the newer, American cases. In practice, abandoning *mens rea* produces the worst of all possible worlds: The trial emerges not as an inquiry into the guilt

16. Arguably, viewing such situations as cases of a mistake "defense" rather than as cases where the required *mens rea* cannot be established invites a court or legislature to impose the burden of coming forward and of proving the defense on the defendant. But as long as nonconsent is spelled out as an affirmative element of the crime, such a shift at least in the burden of persuasion would raise serious constitutional questions. . . .

of the defendant (is he a rapist?) but of the victim (was she really raped? did she consent?). The perspective that governs is therefore not that of the woman, nor even of the particular man, but of a judicial system intent upon protecting against unjust conviction, regardless of the dangers of injustice to the woman in the particular case.

The requirement that sexual intercourse be accompanied by force or threat of force to constitute rape provides a man with some protection against mistakes as to consent. A man who uses a gun or knife against his victim is not likely to be in serious doubt as to her lack of consent, and the more narrowly force is defined, the more implausible the claim that he was unaware of nonconsent.

But the law's protection of men is not limited to a requirement of force. Rather than inquire whether the man believed (reasonably or unreasonably) that his victim was consenting, the courts have demanded that the victim demonstrate her nonconsent by engaging in resistance that will leave no doubt as to nonconsent. The definition of nonconsent as resistance—in the older cases, as utmost resistance, while in some more recent ones, as "reasonable" physical resistance—functions as a substitute for *mens rea* to ensure that the man has notice of the woman's nonconsent.

The choice between focusing on the man's intent or focusing on the woman's is not simply a doctrinal flip of the coin.

First, the inquiry into the victim's nonconsent puts the woman, not the man, on trial. Her intent, not his, is disputed; and because her state of mind is key, her sexual history may be considered relevant (even though utterly unknown to the man). Considering consent from *his* perspective, by contrast, substantially undermines the relevance of the woman's sexual history where it was unknown to the man.[17]

Second, the issue for determination shifts from whether the man is a rapist to whether the woman was raped. A verdict of acquittal thus does more than signal that the prosecution has failed to prove the defendant guilty beyond a reasonable doubt; it signals that the prosecution has failed to prove the woman's sexual violation—her innocence—beyond a reasonable doubt. . . .

Third, the resistance requirement is not only ill-conceived as a definition of nonconsent, but is an overbroad substitute for *mens rea* in any event. Both the resistance requirement and the *mens rea* requirement can be used to enforce a

---

17. A defendant enjoys no constitutional right to present irrelevant evidence; to the extent that the legal issue is framed in terms of his intent, rather than hers, facts about her reputation and history which were unknown to him are far less probative and far more prejudicial, especially in view of the strong public policy grounds favoring exclusion of such evidence. . . .

Explicitly recognizing the *mens rea* issue would, of course, allow defendants in states with shield laws to argue that their inability to present evidence of sexual history which they claim *was* known to them denied them their constitutional right to present exculpatory evidence. Certainly it would be reasonable to require such defendants to present persuasive evidence of the fact of their knowledge in the hearing provided for by most shield statutes. It is not clear why framing the issue in terms of the fact of consent—rather than the defendant's knowledge or intent with respect to consent—could constitutionally provide a woman victim with any more protection of her sexual history; to the extent that the key issue is her intent, a defendant would have an equally strong Sixth Amendment claim as to his right to present *all* evidence (whether known to him or not) that might be relevant to the fact of consent.

male perspective on the crime, but while *mens rea* might be justified as protecting the individual defendant who has not made a blameworthy choice, the resistance standard requires women to risk injury to themselves in cases where there may be no doubt as to the man's intent or blameworthiness. The application of the resistance requirement has not been limited to cases in which there was uncertainty as to what the man thought, knew or intended; it has been fully applied in cases where there can be no question that the man knew that intercourse was without consent. Indeed, most of the cases that have dismissed claims that *mens rea* ought to be required have been cases where both force and resistance were present, and where there was no danger of any unfairness.

Finally, by ignoring *mens rea*, American courts and legislators have imposed limits on the fair expansion of our understanding of rape. As long as the law holds that *mens rea* is not required, and that no instructions on intent need be given, pressure will exist to retain some form of resistance requirement and to insist on force as conventionally defined in order to protect men against conviction for "sex." Using resistance as a substitute for *mens rea* unnecessarily and unfairly immunizes those men whose victims are afraid enough, or intimidated enough, or, frankly, smart enough, not to take the risk of resisting physically. In doing so, the resistance test may declare the blameworthy man innocent and the raped woman guilty. . . .

In situations where a "reasonable man" would have known that the woman was not consenting, most defendants will face great difficulty in arguing that they were honestly mistaken or inadvertent as to consent. . . .

My view is that such a "negligent rapist" should be punished, albeit—as in murder—less severely than the man who acts with purpose or knowledge, or even knowledge of the risk.[18] First, he is sufficiently blameworthy for it to be just to punish him. Second, the injury he inflicts is sufficiently grave to deserve the law's prohibition.

The traditional argument against negligence liability is that punishment should be limited to cases of choice, because to punish a man for his stupidity is unjust and, in deterrence terms, ineffective. Under this view, a man should only be held responsible for what he does knowingly or purposely, or at least while aware of the risks involved. . . .

If inaccuracy or indifference to consent is "the best that this man can do" because he lacks the capacity to act reasonably, then it might well be unjust and ineffective to punish him for it. But such men will be rare . . . .More common is the case of the man who could have done better but didn't; could have paid attention, but didn't; heard her say no, or saw her tears, but decided to ignore them. Neither justice nor deterrence argues against punishing this man.

Certainly, if the "reasonable" attitude to which a male defendant is held is defined according to a "no means yes" philosophy that celebrates male aggressiveness and female passivity, there is little potential for unfairness in holding

18. I use the terms here in the sense they are used by the Model Penal Code, which distinguishes between recklessness and negligence not on the basis of the substantiality of the risk involved, but on the defendant's awareness of it. The notions of "advertence" and "foresight," which are the basis of the Code distinction, however, may not be wholly accurate as descriptions of the way people really act. . . .

men who fall below *that* standard criminally liable. Under such a low standard of reasonableness, only a very drunk man could honestly be mistaken as to a woman's consent, and a man who voluntarily sheds his capacity to act and perceive reasonably should not be heard to complain here—any more than with respect to other crimes—that he is being punished in the absence of choice.

But even if reasonableness is defined—as I argue it should be—according to a rule that "no means no," it is not unfair to hold those men who violate the rule criminally responsible, provided that there is fair warning of the rule. I understand that some men in our society have honestly believed in a different reality of sexual relations, and that many may honestly view such situations differently than women. But, it is precisely because men and women may perceive these situations differently, and because the injury to women stemming from the different male perception may be grave, that it is necessary and appropriate for the law to impose a duty upon men to act with reason, and to punish them when they violate that duty.

In holding a man to such a standard of reasonableness, the law signifies that it considers a woman's consent to sex to be significant enough to merit a man's reasoned attention. In effect, the law imposes a duty on men to open their eyes and use their heads before engaging in sex—not to read a woman's mind, but to give her credit for knowing her own mind when she speaks it. The man who has the inherent capacity to act reasonably, but fails to do so, has made the blameworthy choice to violate this duty. While the injury caused by purposeful conduct may be greater than that caused by negligent acts, being negligently sexually penetrated without one's consent remains a grave harm, and being treated like an object whose words or actions are not even worthy of consideration adds insult to injury. This dehumanization exacerbates the denial of dignity and autonomy which is so much a part of the injury or rape, and it is equally present in both the purposeful and negligent rape.

By holding out the prospect of punishment for negligence, the law provides an additional motive for men to "take care before acting, to use their faculties and draw on their experience in gauging the potentialities of contemplated conduct." We may not yet have reached the point where men are required to ask verbally. But if silence does not negate consent, at least the word "no" should, and those who ignore such an explicit sign of nonconsent should be subject to criminal liability.

Securing the protection of the criminal law is not, however, simply a matter of forcing courts or legislatures to focus on *mens rea* or mistake. First, it would require acknowledging an understanding of consent quite at odds with the "no means yes" philosophy which has characterized the common law tradition. Such a shift would require an awareness of the extent to which distrust of women has pervaded rape law. Second, criminal prohibition would require a move away from the traditionally narrow understanding of the force required, in addition to nonconsent, to define intercourse as rape. . . .

[There are] two views of force in human relations. The first understands force as most schoolboys do on the playground: Force is when he hits me; resistance is when I hit back. That is the definition of force traditionally enforced in rape cases. A second understanding of force, not acknowledged in the law of rape, recognizes that bodily integrity means more than freedom from the force of fists, that power can be exercised without violence, and that coercion is not limited to what boys do in schoolyards.

Virtually every jurisdiction has traditionally made "force" or "threat of force" an element of the crime of rape. Where a defendant threatens his victim with a deadly weapon, beats her, or threatens to hurt her, and then proceeds immediately to have sex, few courts have difficulty finding that force is present. These facts fit the schoolboy definition of force. But when some time elapses between the force and intercourse, when the force is more of the variety considered "incidental" to sex, or when the situation is threatening but no explicit threat of harm is communicated, "force" as defined and required by the criminal law may not be present at all. In such cases, the law fails to recognize, let alone protect, a woman's interest in bodily integrity. . . .

The requirement of force is not unique to the law of rape. But rape is different in two critical respects. First, unlike theft, if "force" is not inherent in noncriminal sex, at least physical contact is. Certainly, if a person stripped his victim, flattened that victim on the floor, lay down on top, and took the other person's wallet or jewelry, few would pause before the conclusion of a forcible robbery. Second, rape does not involve "one person" and "another person." It involves, in practice if not everywhere by definition, a male person using "force" against a female person. The question of whose definition of "force" should apply, whose understanding should govern, is therefore critical.

The distinction between the "force" incidental to the act of intercourse and the "force" required to convict a man of rape is one commonly drawn by courts. Once drawn, however, the distinction would seem to require the courts to define what additional acts are needed to constitute prohibited rather than incidental force. This is where the problems arise. For many courts and jurisdictions, "force" triggers an inquiry identical to that which informs the understanding of consent. Both serve as substitutes for a *mens rea* requirement. Force is required to constitute rape, but force—even force that goes far beyond the physical contact necessary to accomplish penetration—is not itself prohibited. Rather, what is required, and prohibited, is force used to overcome female nonconsent. The prohibition is defined in terms of a woman's resistance. Thus, "forcible compulsion" becomes the force necessary to overcome reasonable resistance. When the woman does not physically resist, the question becomes then whether the force was sufficient to overcome a reasonable woman's will to resist. Prohibited force turns on the judge's evaluation of a reasonable woman's response. . . .

In *Goldberg v. State*,[19] a high-school senior working as a sales clerk was "sold a story" by the defendant that he was a free-lance agent and thought she was an excellent prospect to become a successful model. She accompanied him to his "temporary studio" where she testified that she engaged in intercourse because she was afraid. Her reasons for being afraid, according to the appellate court which reversed the conviction, were: "1) she was alone with the appellant in a house with no buildings close by and no one to help her if she resisted, and 2) the appellant was much larger than she was." According to the appellate court, "[i]n the complete absence of any threatening words or actions

19. 41 Md. App. 58, 395 A.2d 1213 (Ct. Spec. App. 1979).

by the appellant, these two factors, as a matter of law, are simply not enough to have created a reasonable fear of harm so as to preclude resistance and be 'the equivalent of force.'"

The New York Supreme Court, sitting as the trier of fact in a rape case, reached a similar conclusion with respect to the threatening situation facing an "incredibly gullible, trusting, and naive" college sophomore. In *People v. Evans*,[20] the defendant posed as a psychologist conducting a sociological experiment, took the woman to a dating bar to "observe" her, and then induced her to come to an apartment he used as an "office." When she rejected his advances, he said to her: "'Look where you are. You are in the apartment of a strange man. How do you know that I am really who I say I am? How do you know that I am really a psychologist?. . .I could kill you. I could rape you. I could hurt you physically.' " The trial court found his conduct "reprehensible," describing it as "conquest by con job." But it was not criminal; the words were ambiguous, capable of communicating either a threat to use ultimate force or the chiding of a "foolish girl." While acknowledging that the victim might be terrified, the court was not persuaded beyond a reasonable doubt that the guilt of the defendant had been established.[21]

In both *Goldberg* and *Evans*, a woman finds herself alone and potentially stranded in a strange place with a man who is bigger than she. One need not be "incredibly gullible" to find oneself in this situation . . . .[22] There are at least four possible doctrinal approaches to these threatening situations, even accepting the courts' understanding that "force" can only be understood in relation to a woman's resistance.[23] It is noteworthy that all the decisions discussed above adopt the approach that not only makes conviction most difficult, but also operates to place guilt most squarely on the victim.

The simplest approach would be to ask whether this woman's will to resist was in fact overcome by this defendant's actions. Is she lying, or did she submit because she was truly frightened? If she is not lying—and none of the courts suggested that any of the women in these cases were actually lying—then affirm the conviction. But what about the poor man who didn't realize that the woman was overcome by fear of him, rather than desire for him? Properly regarded, such a man lacks *mens rea* as to force or consent.

A second approach resolves that problem without relying explicitly on

---

20. 85 Misc. 2d 1088, 379 N.Y.S.2d 912 (Sup. Ct. 1975), *aff'd*, 55 A.D. 2d 858, 390 N.Y.S.2d 768 (1976).

21. . . .Since the *Evans* decision, New York has amended its statute. . . .

Many states continue to follow New York's earlier definition of "forcible compulsion,". . .and the requirement of "actual physical force" or a threat which *the court* understands to place the victim in fear may continue to protect con-men like Mr. Evans, although it need not.

22. Had there been two or more men involved, rather than one, it seems likely that the defendants in *Goldberg* and *Evans* would have fared far less well in the courts. It is in such cases—and almost only in such cases—that courts consider the situations sufficiently threatening to not require that threats be verbally explicit. . . .

23. To abandon that understanding would suggest either that force itself is unlawful, regardless of whether it is used to coerce submission, or that consent is inconsistent with force. It would, in short, call into question the almost universal common law understanding that regardless of what the man does ("force"), consent remains a defense. . . .

mens rea. It asks instead: Were the defendant's acts and behavior intended to overcome this woman's will to resist?. . .

A third approach probes whether the defendant's acts and statements were calculated to overcome the will of a reasonable woman. This standard. . .obviously allows men greater freedom than the second approach. It tolerates their exploitation of naive and gullible women by claiming that, in their "reasonableness calculation," the tactics should not have been threatening enough. Even at its best, the "reasonably calculated" standard creates something of a paradox: If most women have a different understanding of force than most men, then the reasonable calculation standard is one that asks how a reasonable man understands the mind of a reasonable woman. But at least it focuses primarily on the defendant's actions and thoughts and makes his guilt or innocence the center of the trial.

The final approach doesn't even do that. It judges the woman, not the man. It asks—as did the court in each of these cases—whether the will of the reasonable woman would have been overcome given the circumstances. The focus is on women generally, and on the victim as she compares (poorly) to the court's assessment of the reasonable woman. The court then proceeds to conclude that a reasonable woman's will would not have been overcome in those circumstances, because there is no "force" as men understand it.

Such an approach accomplishes two things. First, it ensures broad male freedom to "seduce" women who feel powerless, vulnerable, and afraid; the force standard guarantees men freedom to intimidate women and exploit their weaknesses, as long as they don't "fight" with them. Second, it makes clear that the responsibility and blame for such seductions belong with the woman. Because the will of a reasonable woman by definition would not have been overcome, a particular woman's submission can only mean that she is sub-par as women go or that she was complicitous in the intercourse.

It is one thing to argue that none of the men in these cases should be considered in the same category (in terms of their blameworthiness, their dangerousness, or the harm caused by their actions), as the man who puts a gun to his victim's head and threatens to kill her if she refuses to have sex. It is quite another to argue that these men have committed no crime.

Most striking about these cases is the fact that had these men been seeking money instead of sex, their actions would plainly violate traditional state criminal prohibitions. Had Mr. Goldberg used his modeling agent story to secure money rather than sex, his would be a case of theft by deception or false pretenses. As for Mr. Evans, had he sought money rather than sex as part of his "sociological test," he too could have been found guilty of theft. Neither Goldberg nor Evans could have escaped liability on the ground that a "reasonable person" would not have been deceived, any more than a victim's leaving his front door unlocked or his keys in the automobile ignition serves as a defense to burglary or larceny. . . .

Lying to secure money is unlawful theft by deception or false pretenses, a lesser crime than robbery, but a crime nonetheless. Yet lying to secure sex is old-fashioned seduction—not first-degree rape, not even third-degree rape. A threat to expose sexual information has long been considered a classic case of extortion, if not robbery itself. But securing sex itself by means of a threat short of force has, in many jurisdictions, been considered no crime at all.

To the argument that it is either impossible or unwise for the law to regulate sexual "bargains" short of physical force, the law of extortion stands as a sharp rebuke: It has long listed prohibited threats in fairly inclusive terms. While extortion may be a lesser offense than robbery, it is nonetheless prohibited.

It is almost certainly impossible to expect that the law could address all of the techniques of power and coercion which men use against women in sexual relations. I am not suggesting that we try. Rather, I am suggesting that we do something that is actually quite easy—prohibit fraud to secure sex to the same extent we prohibit fraud to secure money, and prohibit extortion to secure sex to the same extent we prohibit extortion to secure money. Many states already have criminal coercion or fraud provisions that are worded with sufficient breadth (e.g., "engage in conduct") to be applied to prohibit such coerced sex. But cases enforcing such prohibitions are relatively rare, and the results have been divided. The broad reach of such statutes not only invites overbreadth challenges and claims of lack of warning, but fails to make clear that loss of bodily integrity is a different and greater injury than loss of money and thus merits greater punishment. Criminal coercion statutes are, at best, poor substitutes for an expanded understanding of the "force" that makes sex rape. . . .

Nonconsent has traditionally been a required element in the definition of a number of crimes, including theft, assault and battery.[24] Thus rape may be the most serious crime to encompass a consent defense,[25] but it is certainly not the only one.

Rape is unique, however, in the definition which has been accorded to consent. That definition makes all too plain that the purpose of the consent rule is not to protect female autonomy and freedom of choice, but to assure men the broadest sexual access to women. In matters of sex, the common law tradition views women ambivalently at best: Even when not intentionally dishonest, they simply cannot be trusted to know what they want or to mean what they say. While the cases that engendered this tradition date from the

---

24. . . .By contrast, sexual offenses are a classic and deservedly criticized example of a "morals" offense for which consent is no defense. *See* Sanford H. Kadish, The Crisis of Overcriminalization, 374 Annals 157, 159-60 (1967) (criticizing use of criminal law to enforce moral code prohibiting extramarital and abnormal sexual intercourse). "Deviant" sex punishable by law has included homosexual sex, sex with children, oral sex, sex for money, sex outside of marriage, and adultery. But in the long list of prohibited sexual relations, the absence of a separate category of "consensual," violent heterosexual sex is noteworthy; to the extent that such sex has traditionally been prohibited, it is because it has also been fornication or adultery, not because it is violent; in such cases, both man and woman are considered equally guilty.

25. Technically, nonconsent is an element of the offense or a required attendant circumstance. The difference between a defense and the absence of a required element or circumstance is not entirely technical, although it probably should be; the United States Supreme Court, in determining the constitutionality of requiring defendants to bear the burden of proof of "defenses," has drawn just such a line. *Compare* Patterson v. New York, 432 U.S. 197 (1977) (state may require defendant to prove defense of extreme emotional disturbance) *with* Mullaney v. Wilbur, 421 U.S. 684 (1975) (state's requirement that defendant prove actions occurred in "heat of passion" to reduce crime from homicide to manslaughter violates due process clause because requisite level of intent must be established by state), *overruled*, Patterson v. New York, 432 U.S. 197 (1977).

1870s and 1880s, the law reviews of the 1950s and 1960s, and the appellate cases of the 1970s and 1980s, have perpetuated it.

The justification for the central role of consent in the law of rape is that it protects women's choice and women's autonomy in sexual relations. Or, as one leading commentator put it: "In all cases the law of rape protects the woman's discretion by proscribing coitus contrary to her wishes." Not exactly. As discussed [previously]. . ., the law does not protect the woman from "coitus contrary to her wishes" when there is no "force." Secondly, the definition of nonconsent requires victims of rape, unlike victims of any other crime, to demonstrate their "wishes" through physical resistance. . . .

No similar effort is required of victims of other crimes for which consent is a defense. In trespass, for example, the posting of a sign or the offering of verbal warnings generally suffices to meet the victim's burden of nonconsent; indeed, under the Model Penal Code, the offense of trespass is aggravated where a defendant is verbally warned to desist and fails to do so. A defendant's claim that the signs and the warnings were not meant to exclude him normally goes to his *mens rea* in committing the act, not to the existence of consent.

In robbery, claims that the victim cooperated with the taking of the money or eased the way, and thus consented, have generally been unsuccessful. Only where the owner of the property actively participates in planning and committing the theft will consent be found. Mere "passive submission" or "passive assent" does not amount to consent—except in the law of rape.

That the law puts a special burden on the rape victim to prove through her actions her nonconsent (or at least to account for why her actions did not demonstrate "nonconsent"), while imposing no similar burden on the victim of trespass, battery, or robbery, cannot be explained by the oft-observed fact that consensual sex is part of everyday life. Visiting (trespass with consent) is equally everyday, as is philanthropy (robbery with consent), and surgery (battery with consent). Instinctively, we may think it is easier in those cases to tell the difference between consent and nonconsent. But if so, it is only because we are willing to presume that men are entitled to access to women's bodies (as opposed to their houses or their wallets), at least if they know them,[26] and to accept male force in potentially "consensual" sexual relations.

Were the purpose of the consent requirement really to afford autonomy to women, there is no reason why a simple but clearly stated "no" would not suffice to signify nonconsent. Viewing women as autonomous human beings would mean treating them as persons who know what they want and mean what they say. A woman who wanted sex would say yes; a woman who did not would say no, and those verbal signals would be respected.

---

26. That no such presumption is applied to property is evidenced in cases holding, for example, that leaving keys in the ignition does not exculpate a thief from prosecution for motor vehicle larceny, nor does leaving a front door unlocked eliminate the trespass. . . .In effect, conflicting presumptions are applied to bodily integrity (where a male right of access is presumed) and financial integrity (where a right to privacy and control is protected). Notwithstanding norms of charity, it is presumed that money is something which every individual is entitled to exclusive possession of until and unless he decides to share it. And notwithstanding the law's celebration of chastity and monogamy, a woman's body is presumed to be offered at least to any man whom she knows, drives home, or drinks coffee with, if not every man who desires it.

From a woman's point of view, the danger in this position is that many women who say "yes" are not in fact choosing freely, but are submitting because they feel a lack of power to say "no." From some men's point of view, the problem is that some women who say "no" would be willing to say "yes," or at least to "go along," if properly pressured. The "no means yes" philosophy, from this perspective, affords sexual enjoyment to those women who desire it but will not say so—at the cost of violating the integrity of all those women who say "no" and mean it.

A system of law that has traditionally celebrated female chastity and frowned upon sex outside of marriage might be expected to err on the side of less sex and to presume nonconsent in the absence of evidence to the contrary. But if ours has now become a society in which women have been "liberated" to say yes, that provides all the more reason—if more were needed—to respect a no. If the stigma attached to saying yes has been eliminated, then so have the grounds for claiming that no means yes. That we treat women in sexual encounters more like spectators at sporting events (where consent is presumed) than like owners of property (who are merely required to post a sign or verbally communicate nonassent) is only partly explained by the fact that rape is a more serious offense than trespass. It also reflects a view of women as lacking in autonomy, if not integrity, and secures the priority of men's sexual satisfaction. . . .

[I]nsisting that women do more than simply say no to sex is an essential means of protecting the man who exercises his judgment to ignore a woman's words of protestation.

Nonconsent, defined as physical resistance, serves this notice function in two ways. First, resistance defines the limits of force. The law avoids the task of inquiring into how much force in sex is too much by defining proscribed force according to victim resistance. Second, physical resistance means that this woman in fact means what she says; men are free to ignore words, but resistance signifies that no, in this case, means no. Resistance thus serves to give notice that sex is indeed unwelcome, that force is just that, and that the man has crossed the line.

Under this view, the "utmost resistance" standard could be understood by judges to reflect their view that a truly unwilling woman would fight nearly to the death to protect her virtue. If the judges believed this, then certainly a male defendant did not deserve the serious punishment of a rape conviction for acting on the same belief. Unless the woman offered utmost resistance, or had good reason (fear of death, unconsciousness, incompetence) for not doing so, the man presumably could not be held to be on notice that his advances were truly unwelcome.

In practice, the nonconsent standard has served a second important function as well. It has provided a convenient means for distinguishing between those victims deserving of the law's protection, characteristically the chaste, white victim, and those who were not. . . .

The consent standard, like the force standard, thus emerges as another means to protect men against unfair convictions by giving them full and fair warning that their (forceful) advances constitute an unwelcome rape rather than a welcome, or at least accepted, seduction. An alternative approach to this fair warning problem would be to spell out the crime or crimes of "rape" in detail, without regard to the response of the woman. In fact, most courts recognize the use of deadly weapons or a threat of imminent death as criminal without the need for too much reliance on the woman's response, at least most of the time. But to go further and prohibit all forms of physical force would inject the criminal law into what many conceive as private and appropriate choices: It is one thing to ban guns and deadly weapons, or even fraud and extortion, but quite another to say that "love bites" or vigorous thrashing or pushing is criminal regardless of consent.

Our inability or unwillingness to detail the sexual practices that we as a society will not tolerate, regardless of consent, creates the law's heavy reliance on the behavior of the woman. Because the law has provided that if the woman "consents"—regardless of the amount of force used—intercourse is not rape, men have a right to fair warning as to consent. But the consent standard does not necessarily lead to the denial of autonomy to women, or to the "no means yes" philosophy. Quite the contrary, the consent standard could be viewed as a means to afford women their deserved freedom to engage in sex however they choose—whether that is sex with women or sex with forcible penetration. The harm of rape, or part of it, is the denial of that freedom. Indeed, a consent standard that allowed the individual woman to say "yes" as well as "no," to define all of the limits of permissible sex for herself and then to have that definition incorporated and respected in law, would be a means of empowering women. It could also expand liability for criminal sex to any man who refuses to respect those limits.

Many feminists would argue that as long as women are powerless relative to men, viewing a "yes" as a sign of true consent is misguided. Yet if a "yes" might really mean "no," we might at least agree to respect the courage of a woman who dared to say "no." The insistence that men are entitled not only to presume consent from silence but actually to ignore a woman's explicit words makes all too clear the law's absolute determination not to empower women at all. The fear that women, acting from shame or spite or vengeance, will abuse any power they are afforded in sexual relations at the expense of "innocent" men is the most pervasive theme in the legal commentary on rape. A consent standard that further empowered women and potentially eased the burden of proving rape—limited sexual access—has been plainly unacceptable.

The refusal of the law (and the society it reflects) either to limit the scope of seduction regardless of consent or to empower women through the consent standard creates the fair warning problem that demands a resistance standard as its answer. We could seek to prohibit certain forms of seduction. We could seek to empower women, at least when they say no. Both alternatives would mean less freedom for men to coerce submission and secure sexual access. Both would eliminate the need for women to resist physically. Having chosen neither, we have created a fair warning problem whose only solution, at least to many courts and commentators, is to interpret force and consent in ways that punish women for "complicity" in sex, making their conduct the determinant of liability and the subject of our verdicts. There is nothing inevitable about either the problem or the solution. . . .

In short, I am arguing that "consent" should be defined so that "no means no." And the "force" or "coercion" that negates consent ought be defined to include extortionate threats and deceptions of material fact. As for *mens rea*, unreasonableness as to consent, understood to mean ignoring a woman's words, should be sufficient for liability: Reasonable men should be held to know that no means no, and unreasonable mistakes, no matter how honestly claimed, should not exculpate. Thus, the threshold of liability—whether phrased in terms of "consent," "force" or "coercion," or some combination of the three, should be understood to include at least those non-traditional rapes where the woman says no or submits only in response to lies or threats which would be prohibited were money sought instead. The crime I have described would be a lesser offense than the aggravated rape in which life is threatened or bodily injury inflicted, but it is, in my judgment, "rape." One could, I suppose, claim that as we move from such violent rapes to "just" coerced or nonconsensual sex, we are moving away from a crime of violence toward something else. But what makes the violent rape different—and more serious—than an aggravated assault is the injury to personal integrity involved in forced sex. That same injury is the reason that forced sex should be a crime even when there is no weapon or no beating. In a very real sense, what does make rape different from other crimes, at every level of the offense, is that rape is about sex and sexual violation. Were the essence of the crime the use of the gun or the knife or the threat, we wouldn't need—and wouldn't have—a separate crime.

•

Notes and Questions

1. *Gender Neutrality and the Renaming of Rape.* The Michigan statute is written in gender neutral terms and substitutes the term "criminal sexual conduct" for rape. What are the benefits and costs of this approach?

2. *Defining the Crime.* First-degree criminal sexual conduct under the Michigan statute is defined as sexual penetration, which is itself defined to include conduct other than sexual intercourse. Second-degree criminal sexual conduct under the Michigan statute is defined as sexual contact, which is defined as conduct that "can reasonably be construed as being for the purpose of sexual arousal or gratification." Does this approach appropriately respond to the criticism of traditional rape law that focused almost exclusively on sexual intercourse?

3. *"Force or Coercion"/The Consent Defense.* The Michigan statute relies on "force or coercion" to determine whether sexual conduct is criminal. Is the definition of "force or coercion" that is provided in the statute adequate? Does this mean that the defendant to a criminal sexual conduct charge cannot use consent as a defense?

4. *Gradations of Criminal Sexual Conduct.* One distinction in the Michigan statute between first-degree and third-degree criminal sexual conduct, both of which entail sexual penetration, is whether the defendant causes personal injury. The statute makes a similar distinction between second-and fourth-degree criminal sexual conduct, the provisions having to do with sexual contact. In view of the statutory definition of personal injury, which includes mental anguish, are these gradations meaningful and do they produce an appropriate scale for determining punishment?

5. *The Canadian Experience.* Carol Smart describes the problems that Canadian feminists have experienced after getting reforms enacted in the Canadian rape law that parallel those found in the Michigan statute.

> [T]he point about the Canadian legislation is that the apparent feminist victory (even marital rape was criminalized) brought with it disadvantages. The most apparent disadvantage was the increased penalties for sexual assaults (rape). Whilst the feminists wanted a more effective criminal justice system, they did not want to support the conservative law and order argument which demanded harsher punishments. It has to be recognized as well that, where juries are reluctant to convict men for doing 'natural' manly things, this reluctance may be increased if the penalties are seen as unreasonably high. . . .
>
> [T]his is not the only problem facing the Canadian feminists. As a general strategy they wanted to reduce the power of the state to regulate sexuality whilst increasing the autonomy of women by providing effective remedies against abuse. However, the feminist rape reform proposals became part of a package of greater regulation over sexual behaviors deemed undesirable, e.g. homosexuality or under-age sex (the age of consent in Canada being as high as 18 for 'consensual' sex with a person over 18). So the feminist reforms coincided with other demands for greater control over sexual behavior, but only those which gave more powers to the criminal justice system were adopted. What was achieved was a promise of easier conviction for rape (a promise which may not be honoured in practice) in exchange for a tightening of the net of regulation.

Carol Smart, Feminism and the Power of Law 45-46 (1989).

6. *Mens Rea.* Susan Estrich's article was revised and published as a book titled *Real Rape* in 1987. It was aimed at a general audience and was widely reviewed. In an extended review, Lynne Henderson criticizes Estrich's argument that the focus of reform should be on the *mens rea* requirement as to consent.

> Estrich's analysis has two flaws. First, her assertion that American courts ignore the issue of mens rea as to consent is wrong. Second, she is mistaken in thinking that shifting attention to the man's mental state about consent and reducing the mens rea requirement to negligence will relieve the victim of the burden of physical resistance and of having to "prove" she was raped. Estrich contends that absent a mens rea requirement for consent, the question becomes "was this woman raped?" rather than "is this man a rapist?". . . .In fact, focusing on whether or not the man believed he had consent is no solution at all. First, it returns us to the dangers of the focus on consent of the nineteenth century. Second, the methods of proving mens rea will continue to focus attention on the woman and her credibility. . . .
>
> It is likely that the victim would be scrutinized every bit as closely under Estrich's proposed standard as under prior standards. Thus, resistance once more becomes an issue. . . .Given the cultural context of rape cases, proving a defendant's intent inevitably reverts back to an examination of the victim, including. . .whether the victim physically resists.
>
> Concentrating on the defendant's mens rea as to consent may bring back another nightmare: the survivor's sexual history. As of this writing, forty-nine states have rape shield laws limiting the introduction and use of a rape survivor's sexual history in rape trials. These statutes do far more than pre-

vent "humiliating questions" in rape trials—they block the introduction of highly prejudicial evidence having little or no relevance to a victim's credibility. Traditionally, the premise underlying the use of this type of evidence has been that unchaste women are liars and should not be believed. A more recent premise is that if a woman previously consented to sex, she likely consented this time. Because the defendant in a criminal prosecution has the sixth amendment right to confront his accuser, inquiries focusing on a defendant's mens rea as to consent are likely to reopen the door to more extensive explorations of a victim's sexual past. . . .

Although verbal manifestations of non-consent certainly should be sufficient, concentrating on the rapist's mens rea is not necessary to accomplish this objective. If verbal non-consent is sufficient, Estrich's proposal for making negligence the culpable mens rea as to consent is unnecessary: a woman's "no" would put a man on notice and alert him to the risk of committing rape. For the man to continue his sexual advances would seem, at the very least, to constitute recklessness. Rather than get tied into mens rea knots that lead back to the consent-force-resistance conundrum, it might be better to define consent in unequivocal terms—"no means no"—and presume recklessness by imposing strict liability on men who continue. Of course, this approach raises problems under our culture's existing models of sexual interaction—it raises the questions did the victim really *mean* "no," and did she really *say* "no." This inevitably leads back to an examination of the victim's credibility.

Estrich dismisses strict liability as an answer to the consent issue. Her reluctance to impose strict liability on the element of consent, even after it is established that the woman did not consent, reflects the very male nightmare that she seeks to combat. Estrich states that strict liability regarding consent would result in punishment of men who engaged in intercourse when "no one would realize the woman was not consenting.". . .The question becomes whether, as a society, we wish to continue to allow aggressive unwanted male sexual advances.

Moreover, if the standard is "no means no," how can any man possibly claim not to have known of the woman's lack of consent? Such a belief can only be justified if one assumes that men need not accept a woman's "no," that male persistence pays off, and that such persistence is in fact what women desire. . . .

If Estrich's rejection of strict liability reflects a concern about women engaging in sexual relations who fail to outwardly manifest their non-consent, that is a different problem. Sexual intercourse with an adult woman who has not indicated her subjective opposition may be beyond the scope of what modern society can or should punish. That is, we must accept the notion that men should not be punished for engaging in sexual activity when the woman does not convey her subjective state in any tangible way. But, once the woman has managed *some* manifestation of that subjective state, whether by verbal, physical, or emotional behavior, imposing strict liability if the man proceeds seems justified.

Lynne N. Henderson, Review Essay: What Makes Rape a Crime?, 3 Berkeley Women's L.J. 193, 211-12, 214-16 (1987-88) (emphasis in original).

7. *"No Means No."* In general, the question of consent is most likely to be raised in nonstranger rape cases. This does not diminish its importance. Research suggests that the vast majority of rapes involve nonstrangers (p. 355). Moreover, some defense attorneys are constructing stranger rape cases as nonstranger rape cases so that the defendant can take advantage of the consent defense.

> Defense attorneys may go to great lengths to insist that the parties knew each other and to put the case in the category of acquaintance rape. For instance, since the complainant lived in the same general neighborhood as her attacker, the defense counsel tried to make the jury believe that they knew each other. A superior court judge related the case of an aerobics instructor who described a man who jumped out of the bushes and attacked her as she was going to a movie. The woman claimed that the man, whom she called a stranger, raped her in the parking lot, then kidnapped her, took her to her home, and raped her again. Most of the defense's case was built on the fact that these two people had worked at the same location several years previously. In his far different version, the alleged assailant stated that they were acquainted and that she was attracted to him and receptive to his advances.

Lee Madigan & Nancy C. Gamble, The Second Rape: Society's Continued Betrayal of the Victim 93 (1991).

Do you believe that the "no means no" rule proposed by Estrich is the appropriate standard by which to criminalize sexual behavior?

8. *Violence Against Women with Disabilities*. Although a definition of consent is not contained in the Michigan statute, the statute modifies the role of consent in determining criminal sexual conduct by taking into account the physical and mental capabilities of the victim/survivor. Data about rape and other forms of violence directed at disabled people show that they are "much more likely to be targeted for violence than their nondisabled cohorts." Barbara Faye Waxman, Hatred: The Unacknowledged Dimension in Violence Against Disabled People, 9 Sexuality & Disability 185, 188 (1991). These studies would seem to support the approach taken by the Michigan legislature. Although Barbara Waxman does not criticize the type of protections provided in the Michigan statute, she questions the underlying assumptions about disability inherent in the statutory scheme.

> The law does seek to protect disabled people, but only when they can be construed as vulnerable and lacking a choice about leaving the violent situation. . . .
>
> But while it is certainly true that society places disabled people in highly vulnerable situations, the contention that vulnerability is the primary explanation for disability-related violence is too superficial. Rather, hatred is the primary cause, and vulnerability only provides an opportunity for offenders to express their hatred. Indeed, people who are respected and considered an equal are not generally abused. . . .
>
> Where disability intersects with gender, the incidence of violence is startling. . . .
>
> [T]he sexual aspect of the violence directed at disabled women and children. . .has. . .become the focus of study.

Reasons for this attention to sexual violence can certainly be attributed in part to the women's movement raising the problem, to the outrage regarding sexual violence directed at children, and of course to humanitarian concern. However, there is a more profound premise to consider: the social dynamics of disabled people being seen as asexual. This captures interest and curiosity regarding why people believed to be asexual are targeted for sexual violence.

Society is threatened by the sexuality of children and disabled people. . . .[S]ociety relies on the notion of the asexuality of disabled people for safety, so that disabled people will not expect a sexual response from or stimulate sexual feelings in others. Society demands a safety zone of acceptable sexuality. When those perceived deviant violate that zone, society's inhibitions of expressing its hate can be mitigated. The expressed hatred comes from the threat one feels when a deviant group, such as disabled people, fails to comply with society's proscription. . . .The aim of violence against disabled women, then, is not merely to preserve male supremecy, [sic] but to preserve nondisabled superiority.

Id. 190-91, 194-96

Carol Smart, *Feminism and the Power of Law* 34–43, 48–49 (1989)

A great deal has been written about the rape trial. It must by now be well known that the trial, and even the pre-trial events in police stations are experienced as profoundly disturbing by many women who have been assaulted. The trial is truly Kafkaesque for the woman who has experienced terror and/or humiliation but who is treated like a bystander to the events she apparently willed upon herself and for which she is seen as seeking an unjustified and malevolent revenge. The Kafkaesque analogy is useful in that it can enable an appreciation of the woman's position. The experience she wishes to convey to the court is quite incomprehensible (except in those cases where her rape fits precisely with the legally acceptable notion of rape). The language she will use to explain her experience will be seen as flawed, and may introduce 'ambiguities' which immediately imply she is guilty of consent.

The whole rape trial is a process of disqualification (of women) and celebration (of phallocentrism). It is true that not all women are disqualified and some men are convicted and punished, but these instances never challenge the basic ritual which reaffirms the phallocentric view of sex. This is not a question of whether some judges are progressive enough to restrain the defence counsel's cross-examination of a raped woman, nor a question of the introduction of carpeted interview suites in police stations. Certainly it is possible to mitigate some of the worst horrors of the process of disqualification. But whether the disqualification is done nicely or not, it is still achieved. Equally, the rape trial may not celebrate random rape, but it does celebrate the deep-seated notions of natural male sexual need and female sexual capriciousness. . . .

Judges do not have to instruct juries to understand that a woman's no means yes; they are led to this conclusion by innuendo, 'common sense', and the very vulnerability of the woman that contributed to her rape in the first place. Adler has shown that in her study of rape trials at the Old Bailey that raped women can be found 'guilty' of consent by the skilful use of sexist and racist innuendo, for example, suggesting that a woman likes to have sex with 'coloured' men, or that she is 'unclean' or infected. But the problem is deeper than this still. A woman does not have to be tricked or led by skilful cross-examination to be found guilty of consent. . . .

Consent is recognized as the central pivot of the rape trial, but the question of pleasure is equally important even if it is less obvious. In practice this means that a woman must show, beyond all reasonable doubt, that she was unwilling to have intercourse *and* that she could not possibly have enjoyed it. The denial of enjoyment is vital because if there is any suggestion that she might have taken pleasure, then lack of consent becomes immaterial. No matter what violence might have been used to achieve submission, the slightest possibility of pleasure erases any responsibility for the preceding behaviour on the part of the man. This is summed up by a passage from a cross-examination noted by Adler in her study of the rape trials at the Old Bailey.

> Prosecution Counsel: And you say she consented?
> Defendant: I didn't say she consented, or that she didn't.
> Prosecution Counsel: Did she agree?
> Defendant: She didn't agree.
> Prosecution Counsel: Having said no at first, she just gave in?
> Defendant: She enjoyed it.
> Judge: The enjoyment wiped out her initial resistance—is that what you are saying?
> Defendant: Yes.

This focus on pleasure is something that Judith Rowland discusses in *Rape: the ultimate violation*. The following passage comes from her account of a rape case in which she was the prosecutor.

> Q: What positions were you in?
> A: The positions changed. We were side by side, and then I was on top of her.
> Q: Was she fondling your penis?
> A: Yes. She stroked it.
> Q: Did she put her mouth on your penis?
> A: I don't recall.
> Q: Did she help you put your penis in her vagina?
> A: She enjoyed it. I think it got inside by itself. She was wet, she definitely wasn't dry. She was enjoying it.
>
> Where had I heard that same language before? Or, I suppose, the question should be: when hadn't I heard it?

But how do juries know whether women enjoy particular sexual experiences? I have argued. . .that women's sexual pleasure remains opaque in a phallocentric culture. Men can never be sure, so it is deemed that women have no pleasure (are frigid) or take pleasure from acts defined as pleasurable by men. The latter can, in turn, become a double jeopardy for women. Not only is it asserted that women must enjoy penetration (because men do) but even where women may not enjoy the physical sensations of penetration, it is not infrequently argued that our pleasure is derived from being the vehicle of men's pleasure. So as long as men are enjoying themselves, women cannot deny pleasure; it is inevitably altruistic if it is not egoistic.

That women deny pleasure is unimportant in a legal forum. Their denials will usually carry weight only where class or racial difference is so great that the idea of pleasure is inconceivable. But even racial difference or social distance are no guarantee that a woman will be believed because they can be transformed into sexual preferences or perversions. Hence the racist presumption that a white woman would only have a sexual relationship with a black man if she was forced, becomes transformed into the equally racist idea that it is a kind of perversion that white women practice in choosing to have these sexual relationships. In both of these formulations the woman has no voice of her own. The black woman is also in this double bind. Racist stereotypes of black women as sexually voracious and constantly available fit black women much more readily than white women into the category of the woman who takes pleasure from promiscuous encounters or forced sexual contacts. In these circumstances, where all rapes can be deemed pleasurable, how can the jury ever be certain that a woman did not feel some pleasure? And if she felt pleasure can it be rape?

It is, of course, often argued that the fact that the legal system does convict some men and even imprisons them for rape, is proof that the system can work for women. Yet we know that the men who are ultimately convicted and imprisoned are a tiny minority of men who sexually abuse women. There is now a well-documented process by which women's complaints of rape are filtered out of the legal system long before they get to the trial stage. Informal processes, which are less visible than the trial, operate to deny women's account of rape in the same way that a legal hearing does. In addition we know that many women will not enter into the endurance test of the legal process in the first place. In view of how easy it is to disqualify her experience this should be no surprise. . . .

There are a number of levels on which women's experiences are disqualified in the process of the trial. Yet there is one further level—the level of women's bodies. Women's bodies are now sexualized terrain. Bits of female anatomy are heavily encoded with sexual messages and women are aware, whether consciously or not, of the sexual meaning of parts of their bodies or the movement of their bodies. In a rape trial she knows that she must name parts of her body, parts which in the very naming overtly reveal their sexual content. She must talk in public of her breasts, her vagina, her anus and, of course, what the accused did to these parts of her sexualized body, and with what parts of his body.

Catharine MacKinnon has argued that women do not want to go to court with cases of rape or sexual harassment precisely because 'in the flesh in court' women come to embody the standard fantasy of the pleasure of abuse and sexual power. It is not just that they must repeat the violation in words, nor that they may be judged to be lying, but that the woman's story *gives pleasure* in the way that pornography gives pleasure. The naming of parts becomes almost a sexual act, in that it draws attention to the sexualized body. But her account, distorted by the cross-questioning techniques of the defence counsel, does not only sexualize her, it becomes a pornographic vignette. Unfortunately for the woman in the dock she differs from the photograph because she is there in the flesh to feel her humiliation. The judge, the lawyers, the jury, and the public can gaze on her body and re-enact her violation in their imaginations. As MacKinnon argues, the statement that the trial is a second violation is more than metaphorical.

Take the following extract from a rape trial, reported by Adler, as an example of what I mean by the pornographic vignette.

> Defence Counsel: I suggest that you put a record on an [sic] started to dance around on your own. While you were doing that, the defendants sat down and opened three bottles of lager.
>
> Victim: I put no music on and didn't dance.
>
> DC: You were offered a lager with a glass—you just took the bottle. You continued dancing and drank it rather quickly.
>
> V: No.
>
> DC: You went on dancing and went up to one of the defendants and told him to get up and dance.
>
> V: This is all being made up.
>
> DC: He said he wasn't dancing. You grabbed him by the arm and pulled him to his feet. . . .You said you were a bad woman and ripped open your blouse. That's when various buttons fell off.
>
> V: It's all lies.
>
> DC: [Later] you told one of the defendants that you liked him and asked him where the bedroom was.
>
> V: It's all lies.
>
> DC: I suggest you said you were tired and wanted to relax.

In this exchange the woman is required to deny her part in a standard soft porn fantasy scenario. This account is common currency, not only in pornographic magazines, but in downmarket tabloid newspapers. Accounts of 'sexy housewives' and 'frustrated nymphettes' abound. In these accounts the women became lascivious and reveal, usually after the minimum of encouragement, that their sole enjoyment is sexual intercourse with total strangers, often in the most unlikely circumstances. These fantasies, like the standard window cleaner tale, or the man who picks up the hitch-hiker, reflect the notion of the lucky man (or group of men) who find(s) a real 'goer'. The problem is that the wide currency of such accounts adds to their plausibility. One might imagine that this is how many women lead their lives. More importantly for the rape trial, the jury only has to believe that this is how the woman in the dock leads her life. It is little wonder that the reporting of rape trials is little more than a pornographic form.

There is now historical evidence which traces the rise of the rape trial as a pornographic spectacle. Anna Clark has examined the treatment of rape in England in the eighteenth and nineteenth centuries. She has shown that as sexual mores changed in the Victorian era, the woman who was able to tell of her violation in open court was regarded as immoral. Modesty insisted that a pure woman could never speak of such acts in public, so the woman who complained of rape became lewd herself. The extreme of this was the tendency of magistrates to dismiss cases on the basis that a public airing of the case would corrupt public morals. So the woman who spoke of her violation would be deemed to have immoral effects, as well as providing proof of her sexual immorality. The twentieth-century rape trial may differ from this, but the consequences for a woman of openly talking about sexual abuse have not changed dramatically. Somehow it is still seen to reflect upon her own person rather than the rapist's.

Clark points to the dilemma for women arising from the growth in forensic medicine and a more efficient criminal justice system. It became imperative for women to give a very detailed account of every aspect of sexual abuse. In other words women were forced to become more and more of a sexual spectacle if they wished to prosecute rapists. The reporting of such cases in nineteenth-century newspapers became a pornographic genre. Yet whilst those women who could speak of their violation were disqualified, their sisters who did not have the words or who were too ashamed were equally disqualified. The law could not prosecute a man if the witness could not name his offence. This remains a major problem today, most especially where children are raped and they cannot use the discourse of the adult sex manual, combined with legal terminology.

Whilst there are continuities between the nineteenth-century and twentieth-century legal treatment of rape, it would be a mistake to give the impression that nothing has changed. Clark argues that consent was crucial in the nineteenth century, but the meaning of that consent was quite different to the meaning of consent now. She points out that consent was not a matter of a woman's will or whether she resisted or not. Rather consent was a matter of how she conducted herself, whether she—by her conduct—made it clear that she was the sexual property of her husband or father or the common property of all men. So if a woman was deemed to be unchaste, it did not matter that she clearly resisted the rape, she had consented at a general level. The legal concept of consent does not work in this way now. Although feminist writers have pointed out that certain categories of women find it almost impossible to establish that they have been raped (e.g. black women, prostitutes), the white, middle-class matron may also find it increasingly difficult to establish non-consent. This is because consent and non-consent are no longer the self-evident properties of certain categories of women. Consent is being psychologized, it is becoming a state of mind which can be attributed to all or any women. To this extent rape is being democratized.

It would seem that the law no longer simply exonerates certain classes of women whilst selecting others for particularly callous treatment. Rather, we can see that it is womanhood itself, the sexualization of *all* women and the removal of certain (limited) privileges in the field of sex, that almost equalizes the position of all women *vis-à-vis* rape. This is not to say that class and ethnicity have no relevance, but it is incorrect to assume that, in the UK at least, being white and middle class will protect a woman from the full rigours of the rape trial or will ensure a conviction.[27]

27. One example of this was an horrendous case of rape and murder which occurred in Sheffield in the north of England in 1985. In this case an escaped prisoner broke into the house of a wealthy white solicitor and murdered him and his wife. He then raped their daughter in sight of their bodies. Notwithstanding this, the defendant was able to argue in court that she had consented and she was put through the standard ordeal of cross-examination. One aspect of this was the argument that she was a 'rich bitch' who liked a 'bit of rough'. It was hoped that

This is a point which is possibly open to misinterpretation so I wish to make it clear that I am not arguing that class and ethnic differences between women are no longer important. Nor am I arguing that women are an undifferentiated category, united by their sexual anatomy. But the rape trial does precisely this. It constructs a category of Woman as if it was a unity. The individual woman who has been raped is subsumed into this single category of Woman which is known to be capricious and mendacious. This construction of Woman is confirmed by a common sense which is fed by routine phallocentric orthodoxy. Examples of this mythic category of Woman appear on a daily basis in tabloid newspapers with their stories about promiscuous women, women who say no when they mean yes, oversexed but hypocritical housewives and so on. The jury will recognize this Woman, they have been warned about her (whether they are men or women), it will be hard for them to be absolutely certain that the individual woman before the court is not this archetypal Woman. If she is black, or poor, or a prostitute it will just be easier to fit her into this category.

It is easier still to subsume the individual into the general category, when her account is manipulated into the standard pornographic vignette in the process of the trial. But even without this cross-examination the woman's story would still hang on the concepts of consent and pleasure. These are the core problems on which the rape trial is built, and they remain no matter how much we alter the form of the trial. They remain because they are the basic problem of heterosexual sex in a phallocentric culture.

Whilst the rape trial deals with the category of Woman in which differentiation embellishes rather than constructs the treatment of the victim, it can also be said that the trial deals with and celebrates the category of Man. This is not the same as saying that the trial celebrates the rapist, nor even condones those few men who are convicted of rape. But in the rape trial male sexuality and its satisfaction is always its own excuse or justification. Being a sexual predator is regarded as normal, even desirable for men. Sexualizing all women is equally regarded as natural. Pressing a woman until she submits is a natural, pleasurable phallocentric pastime. The rape trial will not allow for any criticism of this 'natural' activity. Even women share with men the view that this is natural, the only difference is that women may feel that men's pleasure is a cross for them to bear. If we find it difficult to attach responsibility to men in sexual matters, how much more difficult it is to attribute blame to him in a criminal trial. For the woman jurist who has been pressured into sex but who has not called this rape, how difficult is it for her to identify another woman's submission as rape? The jury must find a man guilty beyond all reasonable doubt, this means the woman's account must raise no doubts. This must be almost impossible in a culture in which Woman = sexual duplicity.

The restatement in court of the inevitable and natural sexual predatoriness of Man, which is condemned only if it oversteps certain boundaries, is equivalent to an unauthorized permission, a legal truth which confirms common sense. If our 'wise men' assert in solemn legal ritual that men are prey to specific sexual desires and that this in turn is the law of nature, those who chal-

---

through this the jury would believe that she had invited the man into the house. Her class position did not provide her with any protection.

lenge this received wisdom put themselves outside the Logos. Quite literally, they cannot be comprehended, they appear to be talking nonsense, they can be disqualified. . . .

It might be argued that rape remains an important area for feminist legal work, because even if the reforms that can be achieved are small, it provides an opportunity for confronting the problem of phallocentric sexuality. To a certain extent this is true, but there can be drawbacks. The first and paramount drawback is that we have no justification for using women who have been raped as horror stories in a kind of propaganda war. Rape Crisis Centres rightly refuse to do this because they are so clearly aware of the thin line between the woman's story and its use as a kind of pornography which is damaging to women. It is also a dubious practice that puts vulnerable women who have 'gone public' on their abuse in the vanguard of a struggle that concerns all women. The question that we must ask is whether it is a valid feminist policy to make the trial process tolerable enough to encourage women to use it, without any guarantee that the basic phallocentric assumptions of the trial have been altered. But here we have the horns of a dilemma. It is impossible not to object to what women must endure if they report a rape. For example, the requirement for the corroboration of a woman's evidence in English rape trials amounts to an overt disqualification of women's accounts on sexual matters. Yet it is clear that whilst its abolition would remove an objectionable practice, it would make little difference to whether a woman's account could be believed *beyond all reasonable doubt*. More worryingly, it could be presented as a major breakthrough for women, ironically strengthening the view that men acquitted of rape thereafter had most definitely been falsely accused. So a reform which is ineffectual in women's terms, may have the counter-effect of celebrating a system of justice which still tolerates the sexual abuse of women. It is precisely this irony which insists that, after the revelation and reform of a major abuse in the legal process, the English legal system is the best in the world. The more flaws we discover the more this proves the flawlessness of the basic system which allows us to articulate its flaws.

Of course to follow this argument to its logical conclusion would lead to total inactivity and political paralysis. I am not recommending that feminist policy should stop campaigning around rape and the law. Rape is already in the legal domain, therefore it must be addressed on that terrain. . . .It may be that we should tackle the law on rape in order to provide an alternative account rather than in the expectation that reforms as such will have a direct benefit for women. . . .[l]aw constitutes a discursive field. That is to say, it provides an important way of giving meaning to the world and of organizing social institutions and processes. Whilst law occupies this position, from which it can define women's sexuality in such an oppressive form, it cannot be ignored. It must be challenged most fundamentally, but we should not make the mistake that law can provide the solution to the oppression that it celebrates and sustains.

Notes and Question

1. *Rape Trauma Syndrome*. Carol Smart explains how the myths about rape and about victims of rape operate during a rape trial. One response to

these myths has been to introduce expert testimony about rape trauma syndrome. This is defined as "the acute phase and long-term reorganization process that occurs as a result of forcible rape or attempted forcible rape. This syndrome of behavioral, somatic, and psychological reactions is an acute stress reaction to a life-threatening situation." Ann Wolbert Burgess & Lynda Lytle Holmstrom, Rape Trauma Syndrome, 131 Am. J. Psychiatry 981, 982 (1974). A growing number of jurisdictions have admitted expert testimony on the rape trauma syndrome to explain a victim's post-rape behavior, such as delay in reporting an attack, which might be inconsistent with stereotypical expectations of victim responses to rape. *See* Morrison Torrey, When Will We Be Believed? Rape Myths and the Idea of a Fair Trial in Rape Prosecutions, 24 U.C. Davis L. Rev. 1013, 1064-65 n.252-53 (1991). What are the potential risks of responding to the myths with this kind of expert testimony? *See* Chapter 4, Part C regarding the use of the battered woman syndrome.

2. *Public Disclosure of the Victim's/Survivor's Identity.* In recent years there has been controversy over media disclosure of the identities of rape victims/survivors. Some legislatures have responded by requiring police, prosecutors, and court officials to keep the identities of victims/survivors confidential. *See, e.g.*, N.Y. Civ. Rights § 50-b to-c (McKinney 1992). Other legislatures have statutes that prohibit a news organization from revealing a rape victim's/survivor's identity. *See, e.g.*, S.C. Code Ann. § 16-3-730 (Law. Co-op. 1985). The constitutionality of a state's restriction to this information is unsettled.

3. *Mandatory HIV Testing.* Victims/survivors of rape have asserted a need to know the HIV (human immunodeficiency virus) status of their assailants. The constitutionality of mandatory testing has not yet been settled. The strongest argument against mandatory testing is that it fails to serve the needs of the victim/survivor given the inaccuracy of current testing and therefore that the utility of testing does not outweigh the assailant's Fourth Amendment right to be free of search. Whether the result is negative or positive, the victim/survivor will still have to continue self-testing because of the possibility that the result could be false because of testing inaccuracy or because of the latency period between infection and detection of the antibodies. *See* Bernadette Pratt Sadler, Note, When Rape Victims' Rights Meet Privacy Rights: Mandatory HIV Testing Striking the Fourth Amendment Balance, 67 Wash. L. Rev. 195 (1992).

Commonwealth v. Berkowitz,

415 Pa. Super. 505, 609 A.2d 1338, *allocatur granted*, 531 Pa. 650, 613 A.2d 556 (1992)

Per Curiam. Appellant appeals from judgment of sentence imposed following convictions of rape and indecent assault. We are called upon to determine the degree of physical force necessary to complete the act of rape in Pennsylvania. We find that under the totality of the circumstances, evidence of sufficient force was not adduced herein. We are also asked to decide whether the trial court improperly excluded evidence of the victim's motive to fabricate the charge of indecent assault. We find that it did. Accordingly, we discharge appellant on the rape conviction and reverse and remand for a new trial on the indecent assault conviction. . . .

In the spring of 1988, appellant and the victim were both college sophomores at East Stroudsburg State University, ages twenty and nineteen years old, respectively. They had mutual friends and acquaintances. On April nineteenth of that year, the victim went to appellant's dormitory room. What transpired in that dorm room between appellant and the victim thereafter is the subject of the instant appeal.

During a one day jury trial held on September 14, 1988, the victim gave the following account during direct examination by the Commonwealth. At roughly 2:00 on the afternoon of April 19, 1988, after attending two morning classes, the victim returned to her dormitory room. There, she drank a martini to "loosen up a little bit" before going to meet her boyfriend, with whom she had argued the night before. . . .Roughly ten minutes later she walked to her boyfriend's dormitory lounge to meet him. He had not yet arrived.

Having nothing else to do while she waited for her boyfriend, the victim walked up to appellant's room to look for Earl Hassel, appellant's roommate. She knocked on the door several times but received no answer. She therefore wrote a note to Mr. Hassel, which read, "Hi Earl, I'm drunk. That's not why I came to see you. I haven't seen you in a while. I'll talk to you later, [victim's name].". . .She did so, although she had not felt any intoxicating effects from the martini, "for a laugh.". . .

After the victim had knocked again, she tried the knob on the appellant's door. Finding it open, she walked in. She saw someone lying on the bed with a pillow over his head, whom she thought to be Earl Hassel. After lifting the pillow from his head, she realized it was appellant. She asked appellant which dresser was his roommate's. He told her, and the victim left the note.

Before the victim could leave appellant's room, however, appellant asked her to stay and "hang out for a while.". . .She complied because she "had time to kill" and because she didn't really know appellant and wanted to give him "a fair chance.". . .Appellant asked her to give him a back rub but she declined, explaining that she did not "trust" him. . . .Appellant then asked her to have a seat on his bed. Instead, she found a seat on the floor, and conversed for a while about a mutual friend.[28] No physical contact between the two had, to this point, taken place.

Thereafter, however, appellant moved off the bed and down on the floor, and "kind of pushed [the victim] back with his body. It wasn't a shove, it was just kind of a leaning-type of thing.". . .Next appellant "straddled" and started kissing the victim. The victim responded by saying, "Look, I gotta go. I'm going to meet [my boyfriend].". . .Then appellant lifted up her shirt and bra and began fondling her. The victim then said "no.". . .

After roughly thirty seconds of kissing and fondling, appellant "undid his pants and he kind of moved his body up a little bit.". . .The victim was still saying "no" but "really couldn't move because [appellant] was shifting at [her] body so he was over [her].". . .Appellant then tried to put his penis in her

---

28. On cross-examination, the victim testified that during this conversation she had explained she was having problems with her boyfriend. . . .

mouth. The victim did not physically resist, but rather continued to verbally protest, saying "No, I gotta go, let me go," in a "scolding" manner. . . .

Ten or fifteen more seconds passed before the two rose to their feet. Appellant disregarded the victim's continual complaints that she "had to go," and instead walked two feet away to the door and locked it so that no one from the outside could enter.[29]

Then, in the victim's words, "[appellant] put me down on the bed. It was kind of like—he didn't throw me on the bed. It's hard to explain. It was kind of like a push but no. . . .". . .She did not bounce off the bed. "It wasn't slow like a romantic kind of thing, but it wasn't a fast shove either. It was kind of in the middle.". . .

Once the victim was on the bed, appellant began "straddling" her again while he undid the knot in her sweatpants. . . .He then removed her sweatpants and underwear from one of her legs. The victim did not physically resist in any way while on the bed because appellant was on top of her, and she "couldn't like go anywhere.". . .She did not scream out at anytime because, "[i]t was like a dream was happening or something.". . .

Appellant then used one of his hands to "guide" his penis into her vagina. . . .At that point, after appellant was inside her, the victim began saying "no, no to him softly in a moaning kind of way. . .because it was just so scary.". . .After about thirty seconds, appellant pulled out his penis and ejaculated onto the victim's stomach. . . .

Immediately thereafter, appellant got off the victim and said, "Wow, I guess we just got carried away.". . .To this the victim retorted, "No, we didn't get carried away, you got carried away.". . .The victim then quickly dressed, grabbed her school books and raced downstairs to her boyfriend who was by then waiting for her in the lounge.

Once there, the victim began crying. Her boyfriend and she went up to his dorm room where, after watching the victim clean off appellant's semen from her stomach, he called the police.

Defense counsel's cross-examination elicited more details regarding the contact between appellant and the victim before the incident in question. The victim testified that roughly two weeks prior to the incident, she had attended a school seminar entitled, "Does 'no' sometimes means 'yes'?". . .Among other things, the lecturer at this seminar had discussed the average length and circumference of human penises. . . .After the seminar, the victim and several of her friends had discussed the subject matter of the seminar over a speaker-telephone with appellant and his roommate Earl Hassel. . . .The victim testified that during that telephone conversation, she had asked appellant the size of his penis. . . .According to the victim, appellant responded by suggesting that the victim "come over and find out.". . .She declined. . . .

When questioned further regarding her communications with appellant prior to the April 19, 1988 incident, the victim testified that on two other occasions, she had stopped by appellant's room while intoxicated. . . .During one of those times, she had laid down on his bed. . . .When asked whether she

29. The victim testified that she realized at the time that the lock was not of a type that could lock people inside the room. . . .

had asked appellant again at that time what his penis size was, the victim testified that she did not remember.[30]

Appellant took the stand in his own defense and offered an account of the incident and the events leading up to it which differed only as to the consent involved. According to appellant, the victim had begun communication with him after the school seminar by asking him of the size of his penis and of whether he would show it to her. . . .Appellant had suspected that the victim wanted to pursue a sexual relationship with him because she had stopped by his room twice after the phone call while intoxicated, laying down on his bed with her legs spread and again asking to see his penis. . . .He believed that his suspicions were confirmed when she initiated the April 19, 1988 encounter by stopping by his room (again after drinking), and waking him up. . . .

Appellant testified that, on the day in question, he did initiate the first physical contact, but added that the victim warmly responded to his advances by passionately returning his kisses. . . .He conceded that she was continually "whispering. . .no's,". . .but claimed that she did so while "amorously. . .passionately" moaning. . . .In effect, he took such protests to be thinly veiled acts of encouragement. When asked why he locked the door, he explained that "that's not something you want somebody to just walk in on you [doing.]". . .

According to appellant, the two then laid down on the bed, the victim helped him take her clothing off, and he entered her. He agreed that the victim continued to say "no" while on the bed, but carefully qualified his agreement, explaining that the statements were "moaned passionately.". . .According to appellant, when he saw a "blank look on her face," he immediately withdrew and asked "is anything wrong, is something the matter, is anything wrong.". . .He ejaculated on her stomach thereafter because he could no longer "control" himself. . . .Appellant testified that after this, the victim "saw that it was over and then she made her move. She gets right off the bed. . .she just swings her legs over and then she puts her clothes back on.". . .Then, in wholly corroborating an aspect of the victim's account, he testified that he remarked, "Well, I guess we got carried away," to which she rebuked, " 'No, we didn't get carried, you got carried away'.". . .

After hearing both accounts, the jury convicted appellant of rape and indecent assault. . . .Appellant was then sentenced to serve a term of imprisonment of one to four years for rape and a concurrent term of six to twelve months for indecent assault. Post-trial bail was granted pending this timely appeal.

On appeal, counsel for appellant has presented this Court with the following issues.

> 1. Did the trial court err in failing to define "forcible compulsion" as requested by counsel, in accordance with *Commonwealth v. Rhodes*, 510 Pa. 537, 510 A.2d 1217 (1986)?
> 2. Did the trial court err in its denial of defendant's pre-trial motion to explore complaint's [sic] sexual infidelity to her boyfriend, which was the basis for continued arguments between them and provided a clear motive to fabricate a rape and thus was exculpatory to the defendant?

---

30. The victim was unsure of exactly what date these events took place. . . .

> 3. Is there sufficient evidence of "forcible compulsion" to support a rape conviction where the uncontroverted facts established "reluctant submission"?
> 4. Was trial counsel ineffective in his failure to explore the use of character witnesses to be called on behalf of the defendant to testify as to his reputation for honesty and peacefulness?
> 5. Did the prosecutor's comment during her closing that the jury should "rest assured that somebody in his (the defendant's) position in a case like this is not treated the same as a brutal stranger", relieve the jury of its sense of responsibility for its verdict and thus deprive defendant of a fair trial?. . .

Since a finding of merit in the third issue would require the most encompassing relief for appellant, it is best addressed first. . . .

Appellant's argument in this regard was well summarized by appellant's counsel in his brief.

> The issues on appeal are real. At sentencing, they were recognized by the trial court as being on the cutting edge of the criminal jurisprudence of this Commonwealth:
>
> > The Court: Well, I'm comforted by the knowledge that whatever happens here today will certainly not end this case. This is going to go on and on for some time. . .[because] this case is on the cutting edge. . . .
>
> Mr. Berkowitz prays that this Court overturns his rape conviction. He asks that this Court define the parameters between what may have been unacceptable social conduct and the criminal conduct necessary to support the charge for forcible rape.
>
> We contend that upon review, the facts show no more than what legal scholars refer to as "reluctant submission". The complainant herself admits that she was neither hurt nor threatened at any time during the encounter. She admits she never screamed or attempted to summon help. The incident occurred in a college dormitory in the middle of the afternoon. There has never been an affirmed conviction for forcible rape under similar circumstances. Not one factor which this Court has considered significant in prior cases, exists here. The uncontroverted evidence fails to establish forcible compulsion. . . .

The Commonwealth counters:

> Viewing the evidence and its inferences in the light most favorable to the Commonwealth, the jury's conclusion that the Defendant's forcible conduct overcame [the victim's] will is reasonable. The assault was rapid and the victim was physically overcome. Because she was acquainted with the Defendant, [the victim] had no reason to be fearful or suspicious of him and her resorting to verbal resistance only is understandable. More importantly, perhaps, it is only her lack of consent that is truly relevant. It is entirely reasonable to believe that the Defendant sat on her, pushed her on the bed and penetrated her before she had time to fully realize her plight and raise a hue and cry. If the law required active resistance, rather the simple absence of consent, speedy penetration would immunize the most violent attacks and the goal-oriented rapist would reap an absurd reward. Certainly a victim must communicate her objections. But, contrary to the Defendant's arguments, Penn-

> sylvania law says she can "just say no." [The victim] said "no." She said it repeatedly, clearly and sternly. She was rapidly, forcibly raped and deserves the protection of the law.

. . .With the Commonwealth's position, the trial court agreed. We cannot.

In viewing the evidence, we remain mindful that credibility determinations were a matter solely for the fact finder below. . . .On appeal, we must examine the evidence in the light most favorable to the Commonwealth drawing all reasonable inferences therefrom. . . .If a jury could have reasonably determined from the evidence adduced that all of the necessary elements of the crime were established, then the evidence will be deemed sufficient to support the verdict.

In Pennsylvania, the crime of rape is defined by statute as follows:

> A person commits a felony of the first degree when he engages in sexual intercourse with another person not his spouse:
>
> (1) by forcible compulsion;
>
> (2) by threat of forcible compulsion that would prevent resistance by a person of reasonable resolution;
>
> (3) who is unconscious; or
>
> (4) who is so mentally deranged or deficient that such person is incapable of consent.

. . .A statutory caveat to this rule may be found in section 3107 of title 18.

> Resistance Not Required
>
> The alleged victim need not resist the actor in prosecution under this chapter: Provided, however, that nothing in this section shall be construed to prohibit a defendant from introducing evidence that the alleged victim consented to the conduct in question.

The contours of Pennsylvania's rape statute, however, are not immediately apparent. As our Supreme Court explained in the landmark case, *Commonwealth v. Rhodes*, 510 Pa. 537, 510 A.2d 1217 (1986):

> "[F]orcible compulsion". . .includes not only physical force or violence but also moral, psychological or intellectual force used to compel a person to engage in sexual intercourse against that person's will.
>
> Closely related. . .is [the] section. . .which applies to the situation where "forcible compulsion" is not actually used but is threatened. That section uses the phrase "by threat of forcible compulsion that would prevent resistance by a person of reasonable resolution." The Model Penal Code used the terminology "compels her to submit by any threat that would prevent resistance by a woman of ordinary resolution" and graded that offense as gross sexual imposition, a felony of the third degree. The Pennsylvania legislature rejected the concept that sexual intercourse compelled by "gross imposition" should be graded as a less serious offense . . . .By use of the phrase "person of reasonable resolution," the legislature introduced an objective standard regarding the use of *threats* of forcible compulsion to prevent resistance (as opposed to actual application of "forcible compulsion.")
>
> *The determination of whether there is sufficient evidence to demonstrate beyond a reasonable doubt that an accused engaged in sexual intercourse by*

> *forcible compulsion.* . . .or by the threat of such forcible compulsion that would prevent resistance by a person of reasonable resolution *is, of course, a determination that will be made in each case based upon the totality of the circumstances that have been presented to the fact finder.* Significant factors to be weighed in that determination would include the respective ages of the victim and the accused, the respective mental and physical conditions of the victim and the accused, the atmosphere and physical setting in which the incident was alleged to have taken place, the extent to which the accused may have been in a position of authority, domination or custodial control over the victim, and whether the victim was under duress. This list of possible factors is by no means exclusive.

Id. 510 Pa. at 557, 510 A.2d at 1226-27 n.15 (footnote 14 omitted) (emphasis added). . . .

Before us is not a case of mental coercion. There existed no significant disparity between the ages of appellant and the victim. They were both college sophomores at the time of the incident. Appellant was age twenty; the victim was nineteen. The record is devoid of any evidence suggesting that the physical or mental condition of one party differed from the other in any material way. Moreover, the atmosphere and physical setting in which the incident took place was in no way coercive. The victim walked freely into appellant's dorm room in the middle of the afternoon on a school day and stayed to talk of her own volition. There was no evidence to suggest that appellant was in any position of authority, domination or custodial control over the victim. Finally, no record evidence indicates that the victim was under duress. Indeed, nothing in the record manifests any intent of appellant to impose "moral, psychological or intellectual" coercion upon the victim. . . .

Nor is this a case of a threat of forcible compulsion. When asked by defense counsel at trial whether appellant had at any point threatened her in any manner, the victim responded, "No, he didn't.". . .Moreover, careful review of the record fails to reveal any express or even implied threat that could be viewed as one which, by the objective standard applicable herein, "would prevent resistance by a person of reasonable resolution.". . .

Rather, the Commonwealth contends that the instant rape conviction is supported by the evidence of actual physical force used to complete the act of intercourse. Essentially, the Commonwealth maintains that, viewed in the light most favorable to it, the record establishes that the victim did not consent to engage in the intercourse, and thus, any force used to complete the act of intercourse thereafter constituted "forcible compulsion."

In response, appellant urges that the victim's testimony itself precludes a finding of "forcible compulsion." Appellant essentially argues that the indisputable lack of physical injuries and physical resistance proves that the evidence was insufficient to establish rape.

In beginning our review of these arguments, it is clear that any reliance on the victim's absence of physical injuries or physical resistance is misplaced. Although it is true that the instant victim testified that she was not "physically hurt in any fashion,". . .and that it was "possible that [she] took no physical action to discourage [appellant],". . .such facts are insignificant in a sufficiency determination. As our Supreme Court has made clear, "'rape. . .is defined, not in terms of the physical injury to the victim, but in terms of the effect it has on the victim's volition.'" *Commonwealth v. Rhodes, supra*, 510 A.2d at 1226 (quoting *Commonwealth v. Irvin*, 260 Pa. Super. 122, 393 A.2d 1042, 1044 (1978)). . . .Similarly, our legislature has expressly commanded that the "victim *need not resist* the actor in prosecutions under" Chapter 31. . .(emphasis added). As the *Rhodes* Court observed, this legislative mandate was intended to make it clear that "lack of consent is not synonymous with lack of resistance." *Commonwealth v. Rhodes, supra*, 510 A.2d at 1227 n.14. Thus, while the *presence* of actual injury or physical resistance might well indicate "forcible compulsion," we are compelled to conclude that the absence of either or both is not fatal to the Commonwealth's case. . . .

What is comparatively uncertain, however, in the absence of either an injury or resistance requirement, is the precise degree of actual physical force necessary to prove "forcible compulsion." As the *Rhodes* Court has made clear, no precise definition of the term "forcible compulsion" may be found.

> The "force necessary to support convictions for rape and involuntary deviate sexual intercourse *need only be such as to establish lack of consent and to induce the woman to submit without additional resistance*. . .The degree of force required to constitute rape [or involuntary deviate sexual intercourse] is *relative* and *depends upon the facts and particular circumstances of the case*.". . .

Commonwealth v. Rhodes, supra, 510 A.2d at 1226. . . .The *Rhodes* Court specifically refused to "delineate all of the possible circumstances that might tend to demonstrate that sexual intercourse was engaged in by forcible compulsion or by threat of forcible compulsion . . . ." *Id.* at 1226. Rather, the Court left that delineation to evolve "in the best tradition of the common law—by development of a body of case law. . . .[W]hether there is sufficient evidence to demonstrate. . .that an accused engaged in sexual intercourse by forcible compulsion. . .is, of course, a determination that will be made in each case based on the *totality of the circumstances*. . . ." *Id.* at 1226 (emphasis added). . . .Thus, the ultimate task for the fact finder remains the question of whether, under the totality of circumstances, "the victim. . .was forced to. . .engage in sexual intercourse. . .*against his or her will*." *Id.* at 1227 (emphasis added).

Here, the victim testified that the physical aspects of the encounter began when appellant "kind of pushed me back with his body. It wasn't a shove, it was just kind of a leaning-type thing.". . .She did not testify that appellant "pinned" her to the floor with his hands thereafter; she testified that he "started kissing me. . .[and] lift[ing] my shirt [and] bra. . .straddling me kind of. . .shifting at my body so that he was over me.". . .When he attempted to have oral sex with her, appellant "knelt up straight. . .[and] tried to put his penis in my mouth. . .and after he obviously couldn't. . .he, we got up.". . .Although appellant then locked the door, his act cannot be seen as an attempt to imprison the victim since she knew and testified that the type of lock on the door of appellant's dorm room simply prevented those on the outside from entering but could be opened from the inside without hindrance. . . .Appellant did not push, shove or throw the victim to his bed; he "put" her on the bed, not in a "romantic" way, but not with a "fast shove either.". . .Once on the bed, appellant did not try to restrain the victim with his hands in any fashion. . . .Rather, while she was "just kind of laying there," he "straddled" her, "quick[ly] undid" the knot in her sweatpants, "took off" her sweatpants and underwear, placed the "weight of his body" on top of her and "guided" his penis inside her vagina. . . .

Even in the light most favorable to the Commonwealth, the victim's testimony as to the physical aspects of the encounter cannot serve as a basis to prove "forcible compulsion." The cold record is utterly devoid of any evidence regarding the respective sizes of either appellant or the victim. As such, we are left only to speculate as to the coercive effect of such acts as "leaning" against the victim or placing the "weight of his body" on top of her. This we may not do. . . .Moreover, even if the record indicated some disparity in the respective weights or strength of the parties, such acts are not themselves inconsistent with consensual relations. Except for the fact that appellant was on top of the victim before and during intercourse, there is no evidence that the victim, if she had wanted to do so, could not have removed herself from appellant's bed and walked out of the room without any risk of harm or danger to herself whatsoever. These circumstances simply cannot be bootstrapped into sexual intercourse by forcible compulsion.

Similarly inconclusive is the fact that the victim testified that the act occurred in a relatively brief period of time. The short time frame might, without more, indicate that the victim desired the sexual encounter as easily as it might that she didn't, given the fact that no threats or mental coercion were alleged. At most, therefore, the physical aspects of the encounter establishes that appellant's sexual advances may have been unusually rapid, persistent and virtually uninterrupted. However inappropriate, undesirable or unacceptable such conduct may be seen to be, it does not, standing alone, prove that the victim was "forced to engage in sexual intercourse against her will."

The only evidence which remains to be considered is the fact that both the victim and appellant testified that throughout the encounter, the victim repeatedly and continually said "no."[31] Unfortunately for the Commonwealth, under the existing statutes, this evidence alone cannot suffice to support a finding of "forcible compulsion."

Evidence of verbal resistance is unquestionably relevant in a determination of "forcible compulsion." At least twice previously this Court has given weight to the failure to heed the victim's oral admonitions. *See Commonwealth v. Meadows*, 381 Pa. Super. 354, 360, 553 A.2d 1006, 1009 (1989) (evidence sufficient to convict for rape where "appellant pinned [the victim] to the

31. The accounts differed in this respect only as to the tone in which the word was spoken. Appellant claimed it was whispered "passionately." . . . The victim testified that she voiced her objections *before* the intercourse in a "scolding" manner. . . . At trial, it was peculiarly for the jury to determine the credibility of the parties. . . . On appeal, we must view the record in the light most favorable to the Commonwealth. . . . Viewed in this way, we must consider the victim's admonitions *before* the intercourse to be sincere protests. Although the victim testified that *during* the intercourse she "moaned" the word "no," . . . the degree of the ambiguity of her protests at that point is inconsequential for a *sufficiency* determination. By that time, penetration had occurred and the crime, if any, was complete. . . . Such evidence merely went to the *weight* to attach to the victim's credibility. . . . Moreover, the victim carefully explained that her "moaning" during intercourse was in no way "passionate." . . .

ground and *knowingly disregarded her efforts to communicate the idea that she did not want to have intercourse.*") (emphasis added); *see also Commonwealth v. Dorman*, 377 Pa. Super. 419, 429, 547 A.2d 757, 761 (1988) (finding evidence of rape sufficient where "[d]espite the victim's protests, appellant. . .disrobed her, pushed her down on the seat of the car and had intercourse with her."). . .In each such case, however, evidence of verbal resistance was only found sufficient where coupled with a sufficient threat of forcible compulsion, mental coercion, or actual physical force of a type inherently inconsistent with consensual sexual intercourse. . . .Thus, although evidence of verbal protestations may be relevant to prove that the intercourse was against the victim's will, it is not dispositive or sufficient evidence of "forcible compulsion."

If the legislature had intended to define rape, a felony of the first degree, as nonconsensual intercourse, it could have done so. It did not do this. It defined rape as sexual intercourse by "forcible compulsion.". . .If the legislature means what it said, then where as here no evidence was adduced by the Commonwealth which established either that mental coercion, or a threat, or force inherently inconsistent with consensual intercourse was used to complete the act of intercourse, the evidence is insufficient to support a rape conviction.[32] Accordingly, we hold that the trial court erred in determining that the evidence adduced by the Commonwealth was sufficient to convict appellant of rape.

Having found appellant's rape conviction insufficient, we must determine whether any of appellant's allegations of trial error relating to the remaining conviction have merit. He argues, *inter alia*, that the trial court erred in applying the Rape Shield Law to exclude evidence that the victim may have denied consent to avoid the wrath of a jealous boyfriend. In light of the prosecution's emphasis upon the lack of any motive to fabricate and the possibility of permitting some evidence upon this subject without unduly encroaching upon the legislatively provided Rape Shield Law protections, we agree that reversible error occurred.

In determining whether the application of the Rape Shield Law violates a defendant's constitutional rights to confront and cross-examine witnesses against him, this Court has recently held,

> In Pennsylvania, we have come to resolve this question through a relatively elaborate procedure which is designed to ensure that no evidence of the vic-

32. It may be argued that our conclusion requires the victim, whose *verbal* resistance did not deter the sexual advances, to *physically* resist, in violation of the "no resistance requirement" . . . In this regard, we note the following. Although the "no resistance requirement" does not, on its face, in any way restrict the situations to which it may apply, it appears that the statute must have limits. [The statutory provision] . . . which describes the threat element of rape, states that rape occurs when a person "engages in sexual intercourse with another . . . by threat of forcible compulsion *that would prevent resistance* by a person of reasonable resolution" (emphasis added). If the "no resistance requirement" were applied in that setting, the description of the type of threat which is sufficient would be rendered wholly meaningless. To be consistent, therefore, the "no resistance requirement" must be applied only to prevent any *adverse inference* to be drawn against the person who, *while* being "forcibly compelled" to engage in intercourse, chooses not to physically resist. . . . Since there is no evidence that the instant victim was at any time "forcibly compelled" to engage in sexual intercourse, our conclusion is not a odds with the "no resistance requirement."

> tim's sexual history is introduced *unless* and *until* it can be established that to exclude such evidence would lay victim to the very raison d'etre of the trial itself: the pursuit of truth. The process begins with the defendant submitting a *specific* proffer to the court of exactly what evidence he or she seeks to admit and precisely why it is relevant to the defense. . . .This procedure forces the defendant to frame the precise issues and interests involved, and prevents him or her from embarking upon "fishing expedition style intrusions on Rape Shield law protections.". . .Where the proffer is but vague and conjectural, evidence of the victim's past sexual conduct will be excluded and no further inquiry need be entertained. . . .
>
> Where the proffer is sufficiently specific, the court must then undertake a three part analysis of the substance of the proffer. At the trial level, the court must conduct an *in camera* hearing at which they must determine: 1) whether the proffered evidence is *relevant* to the defense at trial; 2) whether the proffered evidence is *cumulative* of evidence otherwise admissible at trial; and 3) whether the proffered evidence is more probative than prejudicial. . . .On appeal, such evidentiary rulings must be offered due deference and overturned only where there has been an abuse of discretion. . . .Where, however, the proffered evidence excluded by the Rape Shield law is relevant, noncumulative, and more probative of the defense than prejudicial, it must be admitted. . . .

Commonwealth v. Wall, 413 Pa. Super. 599, 614-15, 606 A.2d 449, 457 (1992).

First we consider whether the proffer was sufficiently specific. . . .While it would be prudent to identify each proposed witness by name, and to summarize the anticipated testimony in terms of names, dates, locations, and events, we do not find that the proffer, taken as a whole in the context in which it arose, fails to meet a minimum standard of requisite specificity.[33] Essentially, appellant sought to establish that the victim might have lied because she had a jealous boyfriend.

Relevance would be problematic if we were to consider such evidence in a vacuum. Practically every rape case defendant could eviscerate the Rape Shield Law if the mere suggestion of a jealous boyfriend/fabrication theory was sufficient to open the floodgates to permit a wholesale review of the victim's social, interpersonal, and sexual relationships.

However, under the circumstances of this otherwise highly unusual case, the proffered testimony was unmistakably relevant. Appellant's defense theory was essentially that the victim consented to the sex with him but had decided *after* the incident that such consent had been unwise because it may have jeopardized her relationship with her boyfriend. Evidence that the victim had been arguing with her boyfriend over her fidelity might have given the jury cause to question whether the victim had chosen to claim that she had been raped rather than risk the consequences of her boyfriend's discovery that she had consented to sexual intercourse with someone else, *in her boyfriend's dorm*. Given the fact that the victim admitted that it was her boyfriend, not she, who

---

33. We note that it would have been entirely proper for the trial court to have required a more specific proffer.

first suggested that she had been raped and who called the police, evidence that the victim and her boyfriend had a history of arguing over her alleged infidelity may have played a significant role in the jury's determination of whether the claim had been fabricated. As such, the evidence was relevant to appellant's defense.

We note that our finding of relevance is not altered by the fact that the theory of defense involves not only the victim and the defendant, but also a third party. . . .

It matters not. . .the comparative sophistication or complexity of the fabrication scheme envisioned. . . .Where, as here,. . .the proffered evidence logically tends to show that the charges may have been fabricated, the evidence must be deemed relevant.

The evidence was not cumulative. No other evidence of its sort was available to the defense to impeach the victim. The defense was allowed only to establish that the victim and the defendant had "argued." As appellant points out, however, half a loaf was no better than none here. Without bringing to the jury's attention the fact that the victim and her boyfriend had previously argued *about her infidelity*, the jury was without reason to believe that she may have lied about consensual sex with appellant to avoid having her boyfriend hear that she had had sex with appellant.

Finally, while there exists a potential for prejudice, it does not outweigh the probative value of the excluded evidence. Here, the evidence was not that the victim had *actually* been unfaithful to her boyfriend; it was only that her boyfriend and she had argued over the question of her infidelity. The probative value of the excluded evidence, was sufficiently high herein to outweigh any potential for prejudice. . . .

However, the excluded evidence gained enhanced relevance and probative value. . .in light of two related developments at trial. First, the prosecution presented evidence that the victim had a steady boyfriend and, inferentially perhaps, that she had no reason to consent to intercourse with another. . . .Second, the Commonwealth took unfair advantage of the exclusion of the motive to fabricate evidence by repeatedly emphasizing the absence of a motive to fabricate in its closing argument:

> What you have to ask yourself at this point is this: Why? Why would she lie? You've got to examine her testimony and ask yourself if she's lying. Why ask yourself something like that? You got to have an answer and the real question is why?. . .
>
> What are the facts of the case? Girl tells you she was forcibly raped and *there's just really no reason to believe she would lie and go through this.* If he jilted her, if she was trying to go out with him and he wouldn't, if she stole money from him or he from her, if they had a fight, *if there was any reason; there's no reason here.*
>
> I suggest to you you have to have a reason.

. . .The combined effect of this conduct by the prosecution was to raise the issue of the victim's social, interpersonal, and sexual relationships and use it as a sword to promote an inference that a person in the victim's circumstances would not have consented to intercourse with the defendant. Once the prosecution raised the issue of motivation in terms of the victim's relationship with her boyfriend and that she had no reason to lie, it then became even more necessary to permit defendant to argue a contrary inference relating to that relationship. The Rape Shield Law was intended to be a shield, not a sword. Here, it was used improperly as a sword. . . .

This is not to say that the defendant should have been granted carte blanche to conduct a character assassination campaign under the guise of a fabrication motivation inquiry. Rather, it would have been sufficient to permit defendant to present evidence that the victim's boyfriend had engaged in a series of arguments with her regarding his jealousy and her alleged infidelity to the relationship. We *specifically reject* the suggestion that any evidence regarding the truth or falsity of any alleged instances of infidelity was probative or admissible. To the contrary, the fabrication motivation theory turns upon the *existence* of the boyfriend's jealousy, not its *validity*. Any prejudicial impact of the admission of such evidence could further have been reduced by a carefully constructed limiting instruction. . . .

For the foregoing reasons, we conclude that the evidence adduced by the Commonwealth was insufficient to convict appellant of rape, and that a new trial is warranted on the indecent assault charge. The remaining issues appellant raises need not be addressed in view of this disposition. Accordingly, we *discharge* appellant as to the rape conviction and *reverse* and *remand* for a new trial in accordance with this opinion.

Notes and Questions

1. *Rape Shield Laws.* Rape shield laws, which have been widely enacted, are designed to limit the admissibility of a rape complainant's prior sexual conduct with any person other than the defendant. The statutes vary widely in the degree to which they restrict the admissibility of evidence of the complainant's prior sexual conduct. *Berkowitz* demonstrates that "when rape shield laws are needed to protect women in hard cases, the statutes present a very mixed picture. Some are just plain poorly drafted and provide only illusory protections. And even some of the better ones contain loopholes which defense attorneys, in today's environment, may be able to use to swallow the rule." Susan Estrich, Palm Beach Stories, 11 Law & Phil. 5, 21 (1992). For an examination of how the rape shield laws fail to protect women used in prostitution, see *People v. Slovinski*, at p. 563; Margaret A. Baldwin, Split at the Root: Prostitution and Feminist Discourses of Law Reform, at p. 571-73.

The likelihood that rape shield laws will be interpreted in a manner that leaves the complainants unprotected may not be unrelated to the way that rape shield laws typically are taught in law school classrooms. Ann Althouse links the biblical story of the Judgment of Solomon, its frequent use in law school courses in evidence, and the testimony of the rape victim/survivor to demonstrate how the myth of the "Lying Woman" is perpetuated.

> I am fascinated by the presence of the Solomon problem at the beginning of a book that will lead us inexorably to the question of rape—for in evidence we have a rule particular to the crime of rape and so can avoid rape only by blatantly skipping over it. The Solomon problem juxtaposes male power and female behavior: man as the judge and woman as the judged. The female

behavior seen here sets up two distinct and familiar stereotypes of good and bad woman: the self-sacrificing, honest woman and the self-interested, lying woman. Later, when we encounter the rape shield rule in our casebook, we will find that the stereotypical Lying Woman plays a major role.

Though the rape shield rule was designed to protect women from abusive courtroom interrogation, the teaching of the rape shield rule, judging from many of the casebooks, centers on the following problem: How are we going to uncover the Lying Woman if we cannot subject her to prying interrogation? (How could Solomon have uncovered the Lying Woman if there had been a rule against threatening to cut babies in half?). . .

I took note of the stark contrast of good and bad women, the extreme highlighting of male power and male judgment, and the setting up of the archetypal Lying Woman, putting us on guard and preparing us to scrutinize the rape shield rule critically. When I reached the rape shield rule, I was struck by the ubiquity of the Lying Woman. The casebook I used unrelentingly presents the interests of the potentially innocent man victimized by an inexplicably evil woman.

Ann Althouse, Beyond King Solomon's Harlots: Women in Evidence, 65 S. Cal. L. Rev. 1265, 1274, 1276–77 (1992).

2. *"Thelma and Louise."*[34] Ann Althouse gains insights about nonstranger rape, the limitations and power of the rape shield laws, and the society's perceptions of nonstranger rape by examining the 1991 film "Thelma and Louise" and viewers' reactions to it.

In *Thelma and Louise*, Louise takes the law into her own hands and shoots Thelma's rapist.[35] She acts out of cynicism, despair and anger borne of personal experience: years ago, she was raped and, it is implied, she went through a painful and disillusioning trial.[36] They assume that the rapist would not have been convicted. But why not? Why doesn't the rape shield rule achieve its intended effect and encourage Thelma to report the rape (and Louise to forgo vigilantism)? The problem is not evidence of past sexual behavior. Thelma has been involved with only one man since she was fourteen years old. The problem in her case is the situation surrounding this event: she drank excessively, she smiled at her rapist and engaged in con-

34. Metro-Goldwyn-Mayer 1991, written by Callie Khouri; directed by Ridley Scott.

35. The moral and legal context of the film is muddied by the murder: it is not simply that Thelma cannot hope for a rape conviction anymore but that Louise quite justly faces a murder charge. (There is no valid claim of self-defense here, though Thelma suggests making such a claim, adding "It's almost the truth.") Thelma wants to go to the police at first, and Louise talks her out of it, on the ground that Thelma's story will not be believed. Thelma could, however, simply have declined to report the rape, as most rape victims do. She did not need to become an outlaw. It is only in following Louise, who *does* need to fear arrest, that Thelma becomes implicated in other crimes.

36. The film never more than alludes to this past event. The viewer is left to imagine Louise's past experience, which, in the absence of particularized information, tends to become a composite of all the stories of rape and rape trials one has ever heard. Interpretations of this film vary in part because each viewer must construct the story of Louise's rape and trial experience.

versation with him, she danced with him, she willingly accompanied him into the parking lot. As Thelma puts it, "They would have all made out like I'd asked for it.". . .

The way people think about the evidence they hear is more important than any rule. Consider how filmgoers saw and interpreted the events the camera allowed them to "witness" in *Thelma and Louise*. We see Thelma ordering a drink in a crowded roadside bar, engaging in conversation with a man (Harlan), agreeing to dance with him. We see Harlan, on hearing Louise say they were about to leave, aggressively spin the drunken Thelma, and then, when she predictably sickens, lead her into the parking lot purportedly for "air." We then witness Harlan's attack on Thelma.

Reading a large number of reviews of *Thelma and Louise*, I was struck by how consistently filmgoer-witnesses reached the conclusion that Harlan did not rape Thelma, but merely attempted it. Words like "would-be rapist" or "trying to rape" appear with disconcerting frequency. To my knowledge, not a single reviewer said unequivocally that Harlan raped Thelma, though two did say that he "was raping" Thelma when Louise stopped him at gunpoint. Given the sustained close-up of the sides of the two bodies and a good deal of suggestive manipulation of bodies and clothing and Thelma's explicit statement, "He was raping me," there is, I would think, no basis for downgrading the event to a mere rape attempt.[37] The movie reviewers were only purporting to describe what they saw and did not, like jurors, need to give Harlan the benefit of reasonable doubt. Indeed, since the movie takes Thelma and Louise's point of view one would think that reviewers would be more inclined to accept Thelma's characterization of the event than a juror would.

Many of the reviewers' other statements suggest the kind of thinking that leads jurors to construe evidence about the event in question against the alleged victim. John Simon wrote that Harlan "gets the somewhat drunk Thelma to dance with him in complete, newly emancipated abandon." This statement seems to imply that Thelma has opened herself up to sexual activity or at least has sent a strong message of availability. . . .

Rita Kempley places the blame squarely on the victim: "Thelma is the scatterbrain who gets them into trouble when she insists on stopping for a drink at a roadside honky-tonk. A drunken dance-floor flirtation turns suddenly ugly. . . ." Similarly, Janet Maslin acquits Harlan and astonishingly trivializes the event with the following statement: "Out for a weekend's fishing trip, mischievously stealing away from Thelma's husband and Louise's boyfriend, the two heroines first get into trouble in an Arkansas honky-

---

37. One never actually *sees* penetration, but one would probably not see it in real life. The visibility of penetration produced in hard-core pornography takes some doing. And reviewers could scarcely expect such a sight in an R-rated Hollywood film. It may be that the reviewers fail to find rape because they care about Thelma and wish a better outcome into existence. But that caring takes the form of disbelieving her. Another possibility should be considered. Perhaps the reviewers are not so bad at finding facts and they have merely transformed the law. Louise's interruption of Harlan's activity: her gun suddenly appears at the base of his skull, and he must pull away from Thelma to confront Louise. Perhaps the reviewers feel they have witnessed only an "attempt" because *his* goal was not fully attained.

tonk, where a man who makes a pass at Thelma mistakes her high spirits and alcoholic haze for sexual availability." . . .

To my eye, Harlan engages in egregiously predatory behavior: he buys the women a second round of drinks, he sits down with them uninvited and makes ingratiating conversation emphasizing their physical appearance, he deliberately spins Thelma and makes her dizzy, then takes advantage of her condition to lead her into isolation in the parking lot, and he slugs her with his full strength and pins her against the hood of a car. Thelma repeatedly says "no" and pleads with him ("I'm married."). Harlan scarcely is the victim of mistake.

Despite the apparent sympathy and admiration many of these reviewers express for Thelma, one can easily imagine them as jurors focusing on her behavior, finding it misguided, misleading and reckless, and acquitting Harlan, contemptible though they may have found him. Only in light of the hitting and bruising does conviction seem a real possibility. In adding this decisive violence, the film distinctly weights the evidence against Harlan. But one may rightly wonder what the reviewers would have written if they had witnessed a rape without the dramatic slugging or if they had merely heard a witness describe that sort of rape. . . .

Does the rape shield rule matter? Perhaps it matters the way a film or a famous rape case matters. It is a cultural phenomenon that shapes the minds of the judges and juries who decide the outcomes of trials. The rule represents an attempt to control the information a jury will hear and to rein in their tendencies to decide rape cases by judging the victim, but it cannot in one grand gesture change those tendencies. Judges who resist the conclusions that underlie the rule can find their way out from underneath even its strictly worded prescriptions. Juries who do not share the mindset of the rule's legislators can, even when the rule is used to bar evidence, find whatever way they can to judge the victim and not the defendant.

Ann Althouse, Thelma and Louise and the Law: Do Rape Shield Rules Matter?, 25 Loyola L.A. L. Rev. 757, 767-72 (1992) (emphasis in original).

What parallels do you find between how the court in *Berkowitz* analyzed the trial testimony and how the reviewers of "Thelma and Louise" understood the film's rape scene?

3. *Prior Sexual Misconduct by the Accused and the Rape Shield Laws.* The general rule is that a defendant's prior criminal history is not admissible for the purpose of showing she or he had a propensity to commit the crime for which she or he is standing trial. There are, however, exceptions to this general rule. *See, e.g.*, Fed. R. Evid. 404(b). Notwithstanding that the prior sexual misconduct by defendants charged with rape does not fall within the traditionally recognized exceptions, courts have, based on a variety of theories, admitted this evidence. *See, e.g.*, *People v. Salazar*, 144 Cal. App. 3d 799, 193 Cal. Rptr. 1 (1983). Other courts have held this type of evidence inadmissible. *See, e.g.*, *State v. Saltarelli*, 655 P.2d 697 (Wash. 1982). For further discussion of this issue, *see, e.g.*, Charles T. McCormick, McCormick on Evidence § 190, at 560-61 (Edward W. Cleary ed., 3d ed., 1984); Note, Other Crimes Evidence at Trial: Of Balancing and Other Matters, 70 Yale L.J. 762 (1961). The central concern about admitting this evidence is that the jury

will give too much weight to the prior sexual misconduct in deciding whether the defendant committed the rape for which he is being tried. How might the admissibility of prior sexual misconduct by the accused be used on behalf of the defense? How might the race of the complainant and the race of the defendant affect whether this type of evidence is more prejudicial than probative?

However this issue is ultimately resolved in the courts or by legislatures, what should be clear is that rape shield laws are not implicated. Rape shield laws should not provide a justification for excluding the prior sexual misconduct evidence because they were enacted to counter prevalent stereotypes regarding sexually active women. For the same reason, rape shield laws should not be made less restrictive in states that admit into evidence a defendant's prior sexual misconduct.

> Where both prosecution and defense seek to introduce evidence of past acts, of consensual sex by the woman and sexual abuse by the man, does symmetry demand that if hers are excluded, his must be as well?. . .
>
> [The] impact [of a rule of symmetry is]. . .not symmetrical: the rule hurt[s] the prosecution far more than the defense. That is because evidence of past acts of consensual sex by her are far less relevant and far less probative and yes, even less prejudicial, than the pattern of non-consensual sexual abuse by him that was similarly excluded.
>
> I do not believe that men should be convicted of rape because they are bad men, or because they have raped in the past. I recognize the danger that past acts evidence can carry too much weight with the jury. Still, it is a danger that we manage to live with, and deal with, in other criminal cases, where federal tax evaders may find past acts of state tax evasion, or Medicaid fraud, or mail fraud, introduced against them to establish willfulness. . . .
>
> The danger of the symmetry argument is that we are forced to choose between making acquaintance rape cases even harder to prove and making them even harder to endure. It is a phony symmetry that produces such an untenable choice. It is a reflection of our ambivalence about the crime, not a product of any careful analysis of the rules of evidence. Which is, ultimately, what the current credibility debate is also all about.

Estrich, *supra*, at 25, 27.

State ex rel. M.T.S.,

129 N.J. 422, 609 A.2d 1266 (1992)

Handler, J. Under New Jersey law a person who commits an act of sexual penetration using physical force or coercion is guilty of second-degree sexual assault. The sexual assault statute does not define the words "physical force." The question posed by this appeal is whether the element of "physical force" is met simply by an act of non-consensual penetration involving no more force than necessary to accomplish that result.

That issue is presented in the context of what is often referred to as "acquaintance rape." The record in the case discloses that the juvenile, a seventeen-year-old boy, engaged in consensual kissing and heavy petting with a fifteen-year-old girl and thereafter engaged in actual sexual penetration of the girl to which she had not consented. There was no evidence or suggestion that the juvenile used any unusual or extra force or threats to accomplish the act of penetration.

The trial court determined that the juvenile was delinquent for committing a sexual assault. The Appellate Division reversed the disposition of delinquency, concluding that non-consensual penetration does not constitute sexual assault unless it is accompanied by some level of force more than that necessary to accomplish the penetration. . . .We granted the State's petition for certification. . . .

On Monday, May 21, 1990, fifteen-year-old C.G. was living with her mother, her three siblings, and several other people, including M.T.S. and his girlfriend. A total of ten people resided in the three-bedroom town-home at the time of the incident. M.T.S., then age seventeen, was temporarily residing at the home with the permission of the [*sic*] C.G.'s mother; he slept downstairs on a couch. C.G. had her own room on the second floor. At approximately 11:30 p.m. on May 21, C.G. went upstairs to sleep after having watched television with her mother, M.T.S., and his girlfriend. When C.G. went to bed, she was wearing underpants, a bra, shorts, and a shirt. At trial, C.G. and M.T.S. offered very different accounts concerning the nature of their relationship and the events that occurred after C.G. had gone upstairs. The trial court did not credit fully either teenager's testimony.

C.G. stated that earlier in the day, M.T.S. had told her three or four times that he "was going to make a surprise visit up in [her] bedroom." She said that she had not taken M.T.S. seriously and considered his comments a joke because he frequently teased her. She testified that M.T.S. had attempted to kiss her on numerous other occasions and at least once had attempted to put his hands inside of her pants, but that she had rejected all of his previous advances.

C.G. testified that on May 22, at approximately 1:30 a.m., she awoke to use the bathroom. As she was getting out of bed, she said, she saw M.T.S., fully clothed, standing in her doorway. According to C.G., M.T.S. then said that "he was going to tease [her] a little bit." C.G. testified that she "didn't think anything of it"; she walked past him, used the bathroom, and then returned to bed, falling into a "heavy" sleep within fifteen minutes. The next event C.G. claimed to recall of that morning was waking up with M.T.S. on top of her, her underpants and shorts removed. She said "his penis was into [her] vagina." As soon as C.G. realized what had happened, she said, she immediately slapped M.T.S. once in the face, then "told him to get off [her], and get out." She did not scream or cry out. She testified that M.T.S. complied in less than one minute after being struck; according to C.G., "he jumped right off of [her]." She said she did not know how long M.T.S. had been inside of her before she awoke.

C.G. said that after M.T.S. left the room, she "fell asleep crying" because "[she] couldn't believe that he did what he did to [her]." She explained that she did not immediately tell her mother or anyone else in the house of the events of that morning because she was "scared and in shock." According to C.G., M.T.S. engaged in intercourse with her "without [her] wanting it or telling him to come up [to her bedroom]." By her own account, C.G. was not otherwise harmed by M.T.S.

At about 7:00 a.m., C.G. went downstairs and told her mother about her encounter with M.T.S. earlier in the morning and said that they would have to "get [him] out of the house." While M.T.S. was out on an errand, C.G.'s mother gathered his clothes and put them outside in his car; when he returned, he was told that "[he] better not even get near the house." C.G. and her mother then filed a complaint with the police.

According to M.T.S., he and C.G. had been good friends for a long time, and their relationship "kept leading on to more and more." He had been living at C.G.'s home for about five days before the incident occurred; he testified that during the three days preceding the incident they had been "kissing and necking" and had discussed having sexual intercourse. The first time M.T.S. kissed C.G., he said, she "didn't want him to, but she did after that." He said C.G. repeatedly had encouraged him to "make a surprise visit up in her room."

M.T.S. testified that at exactly 1:15 a.m. on May 22, he entered C.G.'s bedroom as she was walking to the bathroom. He said C.G. soon returned from the bathroom, and the two began "kissing and all," eventually moving to the bed. Once they were in bed, he said, they undressed each other and continued to kiss and touch for about five minutes. M.T.S. and C.G. proceeded to engage in sexual intercourse. According to M.T.S., who was on top of C.G., he "stuck it in" and "did it [thrust] three times, and then the fourth time [he] stuck it in, that's when [she] pulled [him] off of her." M.T.S. said that as C.G. pushed him off, she said "stop, get off," and he "hopped off right away."

According to M.T.S., after about one minute, he asked C.G. what was wrong; she replied with a back-hand to his face. He recalled asking C.G. what was wrong a second time, and her replying, "how can you take advantage of me or something like that." M.T.S. said that he proceeded to get dressed and told C.G. to calm down, but that she then told him to get away from her and began to cry. Before leaving the room, he told C.G., "I'm leaving. . .I'm going with my real girlfriend, don't talk to me. . .I don't want nothing to do with you or anything, stay out of my life. . .don't tell anybody about this. . .it would just screw everything up." He then walked downstairs and went to sleep.

On May 23, 1990, M.T.S. was charged with conduct that if engaged in by an adult would constitute second-degree sexual assault of the victim. . . .

Following a two-day trial on the sexual assault charge, M.T.S. was adjudicated delinquent. After reviewing the testimony, the court concluded that the victim had consented to a session of kissing and heavy petting with M.T.S. The trial court did not find that C.G. had been sleeping at the time of penetration, but nevertheless found that she had not consented to the actual sexual act. Accordingly, the court concluded that the State had proven second-degree sexual assault beyond a reasonable doubt. On appeal, following the imposition of suspended sentences on the sexual assault and the other remaining charges, the Appellate Division determined that the absence of force beyond that involved in the act of sexual penetration precluded a finding of second-degree sexual assault. It therefore reversed the juvenile's adjudication of delinquency for that offense. . . .

The New Jersey Code of Criminal Justice. . .defines "sexual assault" as the commission "of sexual penetration" "with another person" with the use of "physical force or coercion.". . .An unconstrained reading of the statutory language indicates that both the act of "sexual penetration" and the use of "physical force or coercion" are separate and distinct elements of the offense. . . .Neither the definitions section. . .nor the remainder of the Code of Criminal Justice provides assistance in interpreting the words "physical force." The initial inquiry is, therefore, whether the statutory words are unambiguous on their face and can be understood and applied in accordance with their plain meaning. The answer to that inquiry is revealed by the conflicting decisions of the lower courts and the arguments of the opposing parties. The trial court held that "physical force" had been established by the sexual penetration of the victim without her consent. The Appellate Division believed that the statute requires some amount of force more than that necessary to accomplish penetration.

The parties offer two alternative understandings of the concept of "physical force" as it is used in the statute. The State would read "physical force" to entail any amount of sexual touching brought about involuntarily. A showing of sexual penetration coupled with a lack of consent would satisfy the elements of the statute. The Public Defender urges an interpretation of "physical force" to mean force "used to overcome lack of consent." That definition equates force with violence and leads to the conclusion that sexual assault requires the application of some amount of force in addition to the act of penetration. . . .

Thus, as evidenced by the disagreements among the lower courts and the parties, and the variety of possible usages, the statutory words "physical force" do not evoke a single meaning that is obvious and plain. Hence, we must pursue avenues of construction in order to ascertain the meaning of that statutory language. . . .

The provisions proscribing sexual offenses found in the Code of Criminal Justice. . .became effective in 1979, and were written against almost two hundred years of rape law in New Jersey. The origin of the rape statute that the current statutory offense of sexual assault replaced can be traced to the English common law. . . .

Under traditional rape law, in order to prove that a rape had occurred, the state had to show both that force had been used and that the penetration had been against the woman's will. Force was identified and determined not as an independent factor but in relation to the response of the victim, which in turn implicated the victim's own state of mind. "Thus, the perpetrator's use of force became criminal only if the victim's state of mind met the statutory requirement. The perpetrator could use all the force imaginable and no crime would be committed if the state could not prove additionally that the victim did not consent." National Institute of Law Enforcement and Criminal Justice, *Forcible Rape—An Analysis of Legal Issues* 5 (March 1978) (*Forcible Rape*). Although the terms "non-consent" and "against her will" were often treated as equivalent,. . .under the traditional definition of rape, both formulations squarely placed on the victim the burden of proof and of action. Effectively, a woman who was above the age of consent had actively and affirmatively to withdraw that consent for the intercourse to be against her will. . . .

The presence or absence of consent often turned on credibility. To demonstrate that the victim had not consented to the intercourse, and also that sufficient force had been used to accomplish the rape, the state had to prove that the victim had resisted. . . .

The resistance requirement had a profound effect on the kind of conduct that could be deemed criminal and on the type of evidence needed to establish the crime. . . .Courts assumed that any woman who was forced to have intercourse against her will necessarily would resist to the extent of her ability. . . .

The judicial interpretation of the pre-reform rape law in New Jersey, with its insistence on resistance by the victim, greatly minimized the importance of the forcible and assaultive aspect of the defendant's conduct. Rape prosecutions turned then not so much on the forcible or assaultive character of the defendant's actions as on the nature of the victim's response. . . .

The resistance requirement had another untoward influence on traditional rape law. Resistance was necessary not only to prove non-consent but also to demonstrate that the force used by the defendant had been sufficient to overcome the victim's will. The amount of force used by the defendant was assessed in relation to the resistance of the victim. . . .Indeed, the significance of resistance as the proxy for force is illustrated by cases in which victims were unable to resist; in such cases the force incident to penetration was deemed sufficient to establish the "force" element of the offense. . . .

The importance of resistance as an evidentiary requirement set the law of rape apart from other common-law crimes, particularly in the eyes of those who advocated reform of rape law in the 1970s. . . .

Reformers criticized the conception of rape as a distinctly sexual crime rather than a crime of violence. They emphasized that rape had its legal origins in laws designed to protect the property rights of men to their wives and daughters. . . .Although the crime had evolved into an offense against women, reformers argued that vestiges of the old law remained, particularly in the understanding of rape as a crime against the purity or chastity of a woman. . . .The burden of protecting that chastity fell on the woman, with the state offering its protection only after the woman demonstrated that she had resisted sufficiently. . . .

Critics of rape law agreed that the focus of the crime should be shifted from the victim's behavior to the defendant's conduct, and particularly to its forceful and assaultive, rather than sexual, character. Reformers also shared the goals of facilitating rape prosecutions and of sparing victims much of the degradation involved in bringing and trying a charge of rape. There were, however, differences over the best way to redefine the crime. Some reformers advocated a standard that defined rape as unconsented-to sexual intercourse,. . .others urged the elimination of any reference to consent from the definition of rape. . . .Nonetheless, all proponents of reform shared a central premise: that the burden of showing non-consent should not fall on the victim of the crime. In dealing with the problem of consent the reform goal was not so much to purge the entire concept of consent from the law as to eliminate the burden that had been placed on victims to prove they had not consented. . . .

Similarly, with regard to force, rape law reform sought to give independent significance to the forceful or assaultive conduct of the defendant and to avoid a definition of force that depended on the reaction of the victim. Traditional interpretations of force were strongly criticized for failing to acknowledge that force may be understood simply as the invasion of "bodily integrity." Susan Estrich, *Rape*, 95 Yale L.J. 1087, 1105 (1986). In urging that the "resistance" requirement be abandoned, reformers sought to break the connection between force and resistance. . . .

The history of traditional rape law sheds clearer light on the factors that became most influential in the enactment of current law dealing with sexual offenses. The circumstances surrounding the actual passage of the current law reveal that it was conceived as a reform measure reconstituting the law to address a widely sensed evil and to effectuate an important public policy. Those circumstances are highly relevant in understanding legislative intent and in determining the objectives of the current law.

In October 1971, the New Jersey Criminal Law Revision Commission promulgated a Final Report and Commentary on its proposed New Jersey Penal Code. . . .The proposed Code substantially followed the American Law Institute's Model Penal Code (MPC) with respect to sexual offenses. . . .The proposed provisions did not present a break from traditional rape law. They would have established two principal sexual offenses: aggravated rape, a first-degree or second-degree crime involving egregious circumstances; and rape, a crime of the third-degree. . . .Rape was defined as sexual intercourse with a female to which she was compelled to submit by any threat that would prevent resistance by a woman of ordinary resolution. . . .The comments to the MPC, on which the proposed Code was based, state that "[c]ompulsion plainly implies non-consent," and that the words "compels to submit" require more than "a token initial resistance." . . .

The Legislature did not endorse the Model Penal Code approach to rape. Rather, it passed a fundamentally different proposal in 1978. . . .The new statutory provisions covering rape were formulated by a coalition of feminist groups assisted by the National Organization of Women (NOW) National Task Force on Rape. . . .Both houses of the Legislature adopted the NOW bill, as it was called, without major changes and Governor Byrne signed it into law on August 10, 1978. . . .The NOW bill had been modeled after the 1976 Philadelphia Center for Rape Concern Model Sex Offense Statute. . . .The Model Sex Offense Statute in turn had been based on selected provisions of the Michigan Criminal Sexual Conduct Statute. . .and on the reform statutes in New Mexico, Minnesota, and Wisconsin. . . .The stated intent of the drafters of the Philadelphia Center's Model Statute had been to remove all features found to be contrary to the interests of rape victims. . . .

The reform statute defines sexual assault as penetration accomplished by the use of "physical force" or "coercion," but it does not define either "physical force" or "coercion" or enumerate examples of evidence that would establish those elements. Some reformers had argued that defining "physical force" too specifically in the sexual offense statute might have the effect of limiting force to the enumerated examples. . . .The task of defining "physical force" therefore was left to the courts.

That definitional task runs the risk of undermining the basic legislative intent to reformulate rape law. . . .That risk was encountered by the Michigan Supreme Court in *People v. Patterson*, 428 Mich. 502, 410 N.W.2d 733 (1987). That court considered the sufficiency of the evidence of force or coercion in the prosecution of a sexual contact charge against a defendant who had placed his hands on the genital area of a seventeen-year-old girl while she was sleeping. A majority of the court concluded that the defendant had not used force as required by the statute because there was "no evidence of physical overpowering. . .[and] there was no submission." *Id.* 410 N.W.2d at 740. Justice Boyle, in dissent, soundly criticized the majority's position as a distortion of the legislature's intent to protect the sexual privacy of persons from the use of force, coercion, or other undue advantage. Concluding that the statute did not require a showing of any extra force, Justice Boyle pointed out that in "defin[ing] force by measuring the degree of resistance by the victim," the majority had effectively "reintroduc[ed] the resistance requirement, when the proper focus ought to be on whether the contact was unpermitted." *Id.* at 747-49.

Unlike the Michigan statute interpreted in *Patterson*, the New Jersey Code of Criminal Justice does not refer to force in relation to "overcoming the will" of the victim, or to the "physical overpowering" of the victim, or the "submission" of the victim. It does not require the demonstrated non-consent of the victim. As we have noted, in reforming the rape laws, the Legislature placed primary emphasis on the assaultive nature of the crime, altering its constituent elements so that they focus exclusively on the forceful or assaultive conduct of the defendant.

The Legislature's concept of sexual assault and the role of force was significantly colored by its understanding of the law of assault and battery. As a general matter, criminal battery is defined as "the unlawful application of force to the person of another.". . .The application of force is criminal when it results in either (a) a physical injury or (b) an offensive touching. . . .Any "unauthorized touching of another [is] a battery.". . .Thus, by eliminating all references to the victim's state of mind and conduct, and by broadening the definition of penetration to cover not only sexual intercourse between a man and a woman but a range of acts that invade another's body or compel intimate contact, the Legislature emphasized the affinity between sexual assault and other forms of assault and battery.

The intent of the Legislature to redefine rape consistent with the law of assault and battery is further evidenced by the legislative treatment of other sexual crimes less serious than and derivative of traditional rape. The Code redefined the offense of criminal sexual contact to emphasize the involuntary and personally offensive nature of the touching. . . .Sexual contact is criminal under the same circumstances that render an act of sexual penetration a sexual assault, namely, when "physical force" or "coercion" demonstrates that it is unauthorized and offensive. . . .Thus, just as any unauthorized touching is a crime under traditional laws of assault and battery, so is any unauthorized sexual contact a crime under the reformed law of criminal sexual contact, and so is any unauthorized sexual penetration a crime under the reformed law of sexual assault.

The understanding of sexual assault as a criminal battery, albeit one with especially serious consequences, follows necessarily from the Legislature's decision to eliminate non-consent and resistance from the substantive definition of the offense. Under the new law, the victim no longer is required to resist and therefore need not have said or done anything in order for the sexual penetration to be unlawful. The alleged victim is not put on trial, and his or her responsive or defensive behavior is rendered immaterial. We are thus satisfied that an interpretation of the statutory crime of sexual assault to require physical force in addition to that entailed in an act of involuntary or unwanted sexual penetration would be fundamentally inconsistent with the legislative purpose to eliminate any consideration of whether the victim resisted or expressed non-consent.

We note that the contrary interpretation of force—that the element of force need be extrinsic to the sexual act—would not only reintroduce a resistance requirement into the sexual assault law, but also would immunize many acts of criminal sexual *contact* short of penetration. The characteristics that make a sexual contact unlawful are the same as those that make a sexual penetration unlawful. An actor is guilty of criminal sexual contact if he or she commits an act of sexual contact with another using "physical force" or "coercion.". . .That the Legislature would have wanted to decriminalize unauthorized sexual intrusions on the bodily integrity of a victim by requiring a showing of force in addition to that entailed in the sexual contact itself is hardly possible.

Because the statute eschews any reference to the victim's will or resistance, the standard defining the role of force in sexual penetration must prevent the possibility that the establishment of the crime will turn on the alleged victim's state of mind or responsive behavior. We conclude, therefore, that any act of sexual penetration engaged in by the defendant without the affirmative and freely given permission of the victim to the specific act of penetration constitutes the offense of sexual assault. Therefore, physical force in excess of that inherent in the act of sexual penetration is not required for such penetration to be unlawful. The definition of "physical force" is satisfied. . .if the defendant applies any amount of force against another person in the absence of what a reasonable person would believe to be affirmative and freely given permission to the act of sexual penetration.

Under the reformed statute, permission to engage in sexual penetration must be affirmative and it must be given freely, but that permission may be inferred either from acts or statements reasonably viewed in light of the surrounding circumstances. . . .Persons need not, of course, expressly announce their consent to engage in intercourse for there to be affirmative permission. Permission to engage in an act of sexual penetration can be and indeed often is indicated through physical actions rather than words. Permission is demonstrated when the evidence, in whatever form, is sufficient to demonstrate that a reasonable person would have believed that the alleged victim had affirmatively and freely given authorization to the act.

Our understanding of the meaning and application of "physical force" under the sexual assault statute indicates that the term's inclusion was neither inadvertent nor redundant. The term "physical force," like its companion term "coercion," acts to qualify the nature and character of the "sexual penetration." Sexual penetration accomplished through the use of force is unauthorized sexual penetration. That functional understanding of "physical force" encompasses the notion of "unpermitted touching" derived from the Legislature's decision to redefine rape as a sexual assault. As already noted, under assault and battery doctrine, any amount of force that results in either physical injury or offensive touching is sufficient to establish a battery. Hence, as a description of the method of achieving "sexual penetration," the term "physical force" serves to define and explain the acts that are offensive, unauthorized, and unlawful.

That understanding of the crime of sexual assault fully comports with the public policy sought to be effectuated by the Legislature. In redefining rape law as sexual assault, the Legislature adopted the concept of sexual assault as a crime against the bodily integrity of the victim. Although it is possible to imagine a set of rules in which persons must demonstrate affirmatively that sexual contact is unwanted or not permitted, such a regime would be inconsistent with modern principles of personal autonomy. The Legislature recast the law of rape as sexual assault to bring that area of law in line with the expectation of privacy and bodily control that long has characterized most of our private and public law. . . .In interpreting "physical force" to include any touching that occurs without permission we seek to respect that goal.

Today the law of sexual assault is indispensable to the system of legal rules that assures each of us the right to decide who may touch our bodies, when, and under what circumstances. The decision to engage in sexual relations with another person is one of the most private and intimate decisions a person can make. Each person has the right not only to decide whether to engage in sexual contact with another, but also to control the circumstances and character of that contact. No one, neither a spouse, nor a friend, nor an acquaintance, nor a stranger, has the right or the privilege to force sexual contact. . . .

The insight into rape as an assaultive crime is consistent with our evolving understanding of the wrong inherent in forced sexual intimacy. It is one that was appreciated by the Legislature when it reformed the rape laws, reflecting an emerging awareness that the definition of rape should correspond fully with the experiences and perspectives of rape victims. Although reformers focused primarily on the problems associated with convicting defendants accused of violent rape, the recognition that forced sexual intercourse often takes place between persons who know each other and often involves little or no violence comports with the understanding of the sexual assault law that was embraced by the Legislature. Any other interpretation of the law, particularly one that defined force in relation to the resistance or protest of the victim, would directly undermine the goals sought to be achieved by its reform. . . .

In a case such as this one, in which the State does not allege violence or force extrinsic to the act of penetration, the factfinder must decide whether the defendant's act of penetration was undertaken in circumstances that led the defendant reasonably to believe that the alleged victim had freely given affirmative permission to the specific act of sexual penetration. Such permission can be indicated either through words or through actions that, when viewed in the light of all the surrounding circumstances, would demonstrate to a reasonable person affirmative and freely given authorization for the specific act of sexual penetration.

In applying that standard to the facts in these cases, the focus of attention must be on the nature of the defendant's actions. The role of the factfinder is not to decide whether reasonable people may engage in acts of penetration without the permission of others. The Legislature answered that question when it enacted the reformed sexual assault statute: reasonable people do not engage in acts of penetration without permission, and it is unlawful to do so. The role of the factfinder is to decide not whether engaging in an act of penetration without permission of another person is reasonable, but only whether the defendant's belief that the alleged victim had freely given affirmative permission was reasonable.

In these cases neither the alleged victim's subjective state of mind nor the reasonableness of the alleged victim's actions can be deemed relevant to the offense. The alleged victim may be questioned about what he or she did or said only to determine whether the defendant was reasonable in believing that affirmative permission had been freely given. To repeat, the law places no burden on the alleged victim to have expressed non-consent or to have denied permission, and no inquiry is made into what he or she thought or desired or why he or she did not resist or protest.

In short, in order to convict under the sexual assault statute in cases such as these, the State must prove beyond a reasonable doubt that there was sexual penetration and that it was accomplished without the affirmative and freely given permission of the alleged victim. As we have indicated, such proof can be based on evidence of conduct or words in light of surrounding circumstances and must demonstrate beyond a reasonable doubt that a reasonable person would not have believed that there was affirmative and freely given permission. If there is evidence to suggest that the defendant reasonably believed that such permission had been given, the State must demonstrate either that defendant did not actually believe that affirmative permission had been freely given or that such a belief was unreasonable under all of the circumstances. Thus, the State bears the burden of proof throughout the case.

In the context of a sexual penetration not involving unusual or added "physical force," the inclusion of "permission" as an aspect of "physical force" effectively subsumes and obviates any defense based on consent. . . .The definition of "permission" serves to define the "consent" that otherwise might allow a defendant to avoid criminal liability. Because "physical force" as an element of sexual assault in this context requires the *absence* of affirmative and freely given permission, the "consent" necessary to negate such "physical force" under a defense based on consent would require the *presence* of such affirmative and freely given permission. Any lesser form of consent would render the sexual penetration unlawful and cannot constitute a defense.

In this case, the Appellate Division concluded that non-consensual penetration accomplished with no additional physical force or coercion is not criminalized under the sexual assault statute. . . .It acknowledged that its conclusion was "anomalous" because it recognized that "a woman has every right to end [physically intimate] activity without sexual penetration.". . .Thus, it added to its holding that "[e]ven the force of penetration might. . .be sufficient if it is shown to be employed to overcome the victim's unequivocal expressed desire to limit the encounter.". . .

We acknowledge that cases such as this are inherently fact sensitive and depend on the reasoned judgment and common sense of judges and juries. The trial court concluded that the victim had not expressed consent to the act of intercourse, either through her words or actions. We conclude that the record provides reasonable support for the trial court's disposition.

Accordingly, we reverse the judgment of the Appellate Division and reinstate the disposition of juvenile delinquency for the commission of second-degree sexual assault.

For reversal and reinstatement—Chief Justice Wilentz, and Justices Clifford, Handler, Pollock, O'Hern, Garibaldi and Stein. *Opposed*—None.

Notes and Question

1. *Force and Consent*. In *M.T.S.*, the statutory language required "physical force." In *Berkowitz*, the statutory language required "forcible compulsion," which the court interpreted to mean physical force (p. 450-53). Notwithstanding the similarities in the statutory language, the two courts interpreted force in dramatically different ways. *Berkowitz* held that physical force means "force inherently inconsistent with consensual intercourse" (p. 453). *M.T.S.* held that "physical force in excess of that inherent in the act of sexual penetration is not required for such penetration to be unlawful. The definition of 'physical force' is satisfied. . .if the defendant applies any amount of force against another person in the absence of what a reasonable person would believe to be affirmative and freely-given permission. . ." (p. 467). The *M.T.S.* court's interpretation of physical force as the absence of affirmative permission arguably reintroduces the issue of consent back into the statute. In contrast, it may be argued the *Berkowitz* court viewed the question of consent (or perhaps more accurately, nonconsent) as irrelevant in the absence of physical force in excess of that which is required to accomplish penetration. Which approach is most likely to focus attention on the conduct of the defendant rather than on the conduct of the complainant?

2. *Credibility*. One question always to be asked in evaluating rape reform is whether it will make the criminal justice system more responsive to complainants. Reforms that initially might appear to make a difference may in fact be undermined because the criminal justice system will continue to target the complainant's credibility. Arguably, the *M.T.S.* standard of affirmative permission will not significantly change the prosecution of nonstranger rapes because defendants will challenge the complainant's testimony by arguing that the complainant did, through her words and actions, give permission. Prior to *M.T.S.*, the credibility issue was whether the complainant said no. After *M.T.S.*, the credibility issue will be whether the complainant said yes.

> Precisely because it is all but impossible these days to argue successfully that no means yes, or that men are privileged to have sex with crying women, or even that stupidity as to consent should serve as a defense, men charged with rape, and those who defend them, have few options but to argue the incredibility of the woman victim. And the argument has appeal, I think, because many people, including many prosecutors and judges, remain ambivalent about the expansion of rape liability: unwilling to continue to afford men the privilege of aggression, but also chary with their sympathy for women who should know better. So the old myths of the lying woman are reasserted, now that the rules of liability will no longer protect male defendants.
>
> Thus, we face a new stage in the changing realities of rape law—a final battle, one hopes, in the effort to expand liability to include date rape and acquaintance rape. The debate is less and less about what counts as force, or

> what is required to prove nonconsent. Today's debate. . .is about when women should be believed—and about what we need to know about the woman before we can decide whether to believe her.

Susan Estrich, Palm Beach Stories, 11 Law & Phil. 5, 14 (1992). If Estrich is right and credibility is the crucial issue in nonstranger rape, then to have any meaningful reform we must acknowledge that credibility is dependent upon the abilities, class, gender, race/ethnicity and sexual orientation of the complainant. Until we address the range of stereotypes that operates within the criminal justice system, achieving the goal of a criminal justice system that is responsive to complainants will remain illusive.

3. *Marital Rape.* The majority of states continue to treat marital rape differently than rape between persons who are not legally married. Robin West takes as a given the conclusion of feminist writers and progressive courts that the marital rape exemption unconstitutionally denies married women Fourteenth Amendment equal protection rights. She focuses on the question: "Why is it that this overwhelmingly obvious constitutional flaw in our criminal law has not, in the last ten years, attracted more attention, generated more outrage, and simply collapsed of its own unconstitutional weight?" Robin West, Equality Theory, Marital Rape, and the Promise of the Fourteenth Amendment, 42 Fla. L. Rev. 45, 49 (1990). She finds the answer to her question in part in the "inadequacy of the dominant or mainstream political theory of equality, which informs dominant legal understandings of the constitutional mandate of equal protection." She goes on to suggest that the marital rape exemption's tenacity is also caused in part by feminists' reliance on the judicial forum and urges feminists to construct their strategies with a congressional audience in mind. *Id.* at 50-51.

Rather than asking why the marital rape exemption continues to have vitality, Catharine MacKinnon asks what accounts for the erosion of the marital rape exemption and what the consequences are of that limited reform.

> As to adult women, to the extent an accused knows a woman and they have sex, her consent is inferred. The exemption for rape in marriage is consistent with the assumption underlying most adjudications of forcible rape: to the extent the parties relate, it was not really rape, it was personal. As marital exemptions erode, preclusions for cohabitants and voluntary social companions may expand. As a matter of fact, for this purpose one can be acquainted with an accused by friendship or by meeting him for the first time at a bar or a party or by hitchhiking. In this light, the partial erosion of the marital rape exemption looks less like a change in the equation between women's experience of sexual violation and men's experience of intimacy, and more like a legal adjustment to the social fact that acceptable heterosexual sex is increasingly not limited to the legal family. So although the rape law may not now always assume that the woman consented simply because the parties are legally one, indices of closeness, of relationship ranging from nodding acquaintance to living together, still contraindicate rape. In marital rape cases, courts look for even greater atrocities than usual to undermine their assumption that if sex happened, she wanted it.

Catharine A. MacKinnon, Toward a Feminist Theory of the State 176 (1989).

C. Statutory Rape

Michael M. v. Superior Court,

450 U.S. 464 (1981)

Justice Rehnquist with whom Chief Justice Burger, Justice Powell, and Justice Stewart join. The question presented in this case is whether California's "statutory rape" law. . .violates the Equal Protection Clause of the Fourteenth Amendment. Section 261.5 defines unlawful sexual intercourse as "an act of sexual intercourse accomplished with a female not the wife of the perpetrator, where the female is under the age of 18 years." The statute thus makes men alone criminally liable for the act of sexual intercourse.

In July 1978, a complaint was filed in the Municipal Court of Sonoma County, Cal., alleging that petitioner, then a 17½-year-old male, had had unlawful sexual intercourse with a female under the age of 18, in violation of § 261.5. The evidence, adduced at a preliminary hearing showed that at approximately midnight on June 3, 1978, petitioner and two friends approached Sharon, a 16½-year-old female, and her sister as they waited at a bus stop. Petitioner and Sharon, who had already been drinking, moved away from the others and began to kiss. After being struck in the face for rebuffing petitioner's initial advances, Sharon submitted to sexual intercourse with petitioner. Prior to trial, petitioner sought to set aside the information on both state and federal constitutional grounds, asserting that § 261.5 unlawfully discriminated on the basis of gender. The trial court and the California Court of Appeal denied petitioner's request for relief and petitioner sought review in the Supreme Court of California.

The Supreme Court held that "section 261.5 discriminates on the basis of sex because only females may be victims, and only males may violate the section.". . .The court then subjected the classification to "strict scrutiny," stating that it must be justified by a compelling state interest. It found that the classification was "supported not by mere social convention but by the immutable physiological fact that it is the female exclusively who can become pregnant.". . .Canvassing "the tragic human costs of illegitimate teenage pregnancies," including the large number of teenage abortions, the increased medical risk associated with teenage pregnancies, and the social consequences of teenage childbearing, the court concluded that the State has a compelling interest in preventing such pregnancies. Because males alone can "physiologically cause the result which the law properly seeks to avoid," the court further held that the gender classification was readily justified as a means of identifying offender and victim. For the reasons stated below, we affirm the judgment of the California Supreme Court. . . .

As is evident from our opinions, the Court has had some difficulty in agreeing upon the proper approach and analysis in cases involving challenges to gender-based classifications. . . .Unlike the California Supreme Court, we have not held that gender-based classifications are "inherently suspect" and thus we do not apply so-called "strict scrutiny" to those classifications. . . .Our cases have held, however, that the traditional minimum rationality test takes on a somewhat "sharper focus" when gender-based classifications are challenged. . . .

[T]his Court has consistently upheld statutes where the gender classification is not invidious, but rather realistically reflects the fact that the sexes are not similarly situated in certain circumstances. . . .As the Court has stated, a legislature may "provide for the special problems of women." *Weinberger v. Wiesenfeld*; 420 U.S. 636, 653 (1975).

Applying those principles to this case, the fact that the California Legislature criminalized the act of illicit sexual intercourse with a minor female is a sure indication of its intent or purpose to discourage that conduct. . . .Precisely why the legislature desired that result is of course somewhat less clear. . . .

The justification for the statute offered by the State, and accepted by the Supreme Court of California, is that the legislature sought to prevent illegitimate teenage pregnancies. That finding, of course, is entitled to great deference. . . .And although our cases establish that the State's asserted reason for the enactment of a statute may be rejected, if it "could not have been a goal of the legislation," *Weinberger v. Wiesenfeld*, *supra*, 420 U.S. at 648, n.16, this is not such a case.

We are satisfied not only that the prevention of illegitimate pregnancy is at least one of the "purposes" of the statute, but also that the State has a strong interest in preventing such pregnancy. At the risk of stating the obvious, teenage pregnancies, which have increased dramatically over the last two decades,. . .have significant social, medical, and economic consequences for both the mother and her child, and the State.[38] Of particular concern to the State is that approximately half of all teenage pregnancies end in abortion. . . .And of those children who are born, their illegitimacy makes them likely candidates to become wards of the State.[39]

We need not be medical doctors to discern that young men and young women are not similarly situated with respect to the problems and the risks of sexual intercourse. Only women may become pregnant, and they suffer disproportionately the profound physical, emotional, and psychological consequences of sexual activity. The statute at issue here protects women from sexual intercourse at an age when those consequences are particularly severe.[40]

---

38. The risk of maternal death is 60% higher for a teenager under the age of 15 than for a women [*sic*] in her early twenties. The risk is 13% higher for 15-to-19-year-olds. The statistics further show that most teenage mothers drop out of school and face a bleak economic future. . . .

39. The policy and intent of the California Legislature evinced in other legislation buttresses our view that the prevention of teenage pregnancy is a purpose of the statute. . . .

Subsequent to the decision below, the California Legislature considered and rejected proposals to render § 261.5 gender neutral, thereby ratifying the judgment of the California Supreme Court. That is enough to answer petitioner's contention that the statute was the " 'accidental by-product of a traditional way of thinking about females.' " Califano v. Webster, 430 U.S. 313, 320 (1977) (quoting Califano v. Goldfarb, 430 U.S. 199, 223 (1977) (Stevens, J., concurring in judgment)). Certainly this decision of the California Legislature is as good a source as is this Court in deciding what is "current" and what is "outmoded" in the perception of women.

40. Although petitioner concedes that the State has a "compelling" interest in preventing teenage pregnancy, he contends that the "true" purpose of § 261.5 is to protect the virtue and chastity of young women. As such, the statute is unjustifiable because it rests on archaic stereotypes. What we have said above is enough to dispose of that contention. The question for us—and the only question under the Federal Constitution—is whether the legislation violates the Equal Protection Clause of the Fourteenth Amendment, not whether its supporters may have

The question thus boils down to whether a State may attack the problem of sexual intercourse and teenage pregnancy directly by prohibiting a male from having sexual intercourse with a minor female. . . .We hold that such a statute is sufficiently related to the State's objectives to pass constitutional muster.

Because virtually all of the significant harmful and inescapably identifiable consequences of teenage pregnancy fall on the young female, a legislature acts well within its authority when it elects to punish only the participant who, by nature, suffers few of the consequences of his conduct. It is hardly unreasonable for a legislature acting to protect minor females to exclude them from punishment. Moreover, the risk of pregnancy itself constitutes a substantial deterrence to young females. No similar natural sanctions deter males. A criminal sanction imposed solely on males thus serves to roughly "equalize" the deterrents on the sexes.

We are unable to accept petitioner's contention that the statute is impermissibly underinclusive and must, in order to pass judicial scrutiny, be *broadened* so as to hold the female as criminally liable as the male. It is argued that this statute is not *necessary* to deter teenage pregnancy because a gender-neutral statute, where both male and female would be subject to prosecution, would serve that goal equally well. The relevant inquiry, however, is not whether the statute is drawn as precisely as it might have been, but whether the line chosen by the California Legislature is within constitutional limitations. . . .

In any event, we cannot say that a gender-neutral statute would be as effective as the statute California has chosen to enact. The State persuasively contends that a gender-neutral statute would frustrate its interest in effective enforcement. Its view is that a female is surely less likely to report violations of the statute if she herself would be subject to criminal prosecution. . . .In an area already fraught with prosecutorial difficulties, we decline to hold that the Equal Protection Clause requires a legislature to enact a statute so broad that it may well be incapable of enforcement. . . .

We similarly reject petitioner's argument that § 261.5 is impermissibly overbroad because it makes unlawful sexual intercourse with prepubescent females, who are, by definition, incapable of becoming pregnant. Quite apart from the fact that the statute could well be justified on the grounds that very young females are particularly susceptible to physical injury from sexual intercourse,. . .it is ludicrous to suggest that the Constitution requires the California Legislature to limit the scope of its rape statute to older teenagers and exclude young girls.

There remains only petitioner's contention that the statute is unconstitutional as it is applied to him because he, like Sharon, was under 18 at the time of sexual intercourse. Petitioner argues that the statute is flawed because it presumes that as between two persons under 18, the male is the culpable aggressor. We find petitioner's contentions unpersuasive. Contrary to his assertions,

---

endorsed it for reasons no longer generally accepted. Even if the preservation of female chastity were one of the motives of the statute, and even if that motive be impermissible, petitioner's argument must fail because "[i]t is a familiar practice of constitutional law that this court will not strike down an otherwise constitutional statute on the basis of an alleged illicit legislative motive." United States v. O'Brien, 391 U.S. 367, 383 (1968). . . .

the statute does not rest on the assumption that males are generally the aggressors. It is instead an attempt by a legislature to prevent illegitimate teenage pregnancy by providing an additional deterrent for men. The age of the man is irrelevant since young men are as capable as older men of inflicting the harm sought to be prevented.

In upholding the California statute we also recognize that this is not a case where a statute is being challenged on the grounds that it "invidiously discriminates" against females. To the contrary, the statute places a burden on males which is not shared by females. But we find nothing to suggest that men, because of past discrimination or peculiar disadvantages, are in need of the special solicitude of the courts. Nor is this a case where the gender classification is made "solely for. . .administrative convenience," as in *Frontiero v. Richardson*, 411 U.S. 677, 690 (1973) (emphasis omitted), or rests on "the baggage of sexual stereotypes" as in *Orr v. Orr*, 440 U.S. 268, 283 (1979). As we have held, the statute instead reasonably reflects the fact that the consequences of sexual intercourse and pregnancy fall more heavily on the female than on the male.

Accordingly the judgment of the California Supreme Court is *Affirmed.*

Justice Stewart, concurring. . . .At the outset, it should be noted that the statutory discrimination, when viewed as part of the wider scheme of California law, is not as clearcut as might at first appear. Females are not freed from criminal liability in California for engaging in sexual activity that may be harmful. It is unlawful, for example, for any person, of either sex, to molest, annoy, or contribute to the delinquency of anyone under 18 years of age. . . .All persons are prohibited from committing "any lewd or lascivious act," including consensual intercourse, with a child under 14. . . .And members of both sexes may be convicted for engaging in deviant sexual acts with anyone under 18. . . .Finally, females may be brought within the proscription of § 261.5 itself, since a female may be charged with aiding and abetting its violation.[41]

Section 261.5 is thus but one part of a broad statutory scheme that protects all minors from the problems and risks attendant upon adolescent sexual activity. To be sure, § 261.5 creates an additional measure of punishment for males who engage in sexual intercourse with females between the ages of 14 and 17.[42] The question then is whether the Constitution prohibits a state legislature from imposing this *additional* sanction on a gender-specific basis. . . .

The Constitution is violated when government, state or federal, invidiously classifies similarly situated people on the basis of the immutable characteristics with which they were born. Thus, detrimental racial classifications by government always violate the Constitution, for the simple reason that, so far as the Constitution is concerned, people of different races are always sim-

---

41. . . .According to statistics maintained by the California Department of Justice Bureau of Criminal Statistics, approximately 14% of the juveniles arrested for participation in acts made unlawful by § 261.5 between 1975 and 1979 were females. Moreover, an underage female who is as culpable as her male partner, or more culpable, may be prosecuted as a juvenile delinquent. . . .

42. Males and females are equally prohibited by § 288 from sexual intercourse with minors under 14. . . .

ilarly situated. . . .By contrast, while detrimental gender classifications by government often violate the Constitution, they do not always do so, for the reason that there are differences between males and females that the Constitution necessarily recognizes. In this case we deal with the most basic of these differences: females can become pregnant as the result of sexual intercourse; males cannot. . . .

[W]e have recognized that in certain narrow circumstances men and women are *not* similarly situated; in these circumstances a gender classification based on clear differences between the sexes is not invidious, and a legislative classification realistically based upon those differences is not unconstitutional. . . .

Applying these principles to the classification enacted by the California Legislature, it is readily apparent that § 261.5 does not violate the Equal Protection Clause. Young women and men are not similarly situated with respect to the problems and risk associated with intercourse and pregnancy, and the statute is realistically related to the legitimate state purpose of reducing those problems and risks. . . .[43]

The petitioner argues that the California Legislature could have drafted the statute differently, so that its purpose would be accomplished more precisely. . . .That other States may have decided to attack the same problems more broadly, with gender-neutral statutes, does not mean that every State is constitutionally compelled to do so.[44]. . .

Justice Blackmun, concurring in the judgment. It is gratifying that the plurality recognizes that "[a]t the risk of stating the obvious, teenage pregnancies. . .have increased dramatically over the last two decades" and "have significant social, medical, and economic consequences for both the mother and her child, and the State.". . .There have been times when I have wondered whether the Court was capable of this perception, particularly when it has struggled with the different but not unrelated problems that attend abortion issues. See, for example,. . .today's opinion in *H. L. v. Matheson*, 450 U.S. 398.

Some might conclude that the two uses of the criminal sanction—here flatly to forbid intercourse in order to forestall teenage pregnancies, and in *Matheson* to prohibit a physician's abortion procedure except upon notice to the parents of the pregnant minor—are vastly different proscriptions. But the basic social and privacy problems are much the same. Both Utah's statute in *Matheson* and California's statute in this case are legislatively created tools intended to achieve similar ends and addressed to the same societal concerns: the control and direction of young people's sexual activities. The plurality opinion impliedly concedes as much when it notes that "approximately half of all teenage pregnancies end in abortion," and that "those children who are born" are "likely candidates to become wards of the State". . . .

---

43. . . .The petitioner contends that the statute is overinclusive because it does not allow a defense that contraceptives were used, or that procreation was for some other reason impossible. The petitioner does not allege, however, that he used a contraceptive, or that pregnancy could not have resulted from the conduct with which he was charged. But even assuming the petitioner's standing to raise the claim of overbreadth, it is clear that a statute recognizing the defenses he suggests would encounter difficult if not impossible problems of proof.

44. The fact is that a gender-neutral statute would not necessarily lead to a closer fit with the aim of reducing the problems associated with teenage pregnancy. If both parties were equally liable to prosecution, a female would be far less likely to complain; the very complaint would be self-incriminating. Accordingly, it is possible that a gender-neutral statute would result in fewer prosecutions than the one before us. . . .

I, however, cannot vote to strike down the California statutory rape law, for I think it is a sufficiently reasoned and constitutional effort to control the problem at its inception. For me, there is an important difference between this state action and a State's adamant and rigid refusal to face, or even to recognize, the "significant. . .consequences"—to the woman—of a forced or unwanted conception. I have found it difficult to rule constitutional, for example, state efforts to block, at that later point, a woman's attempt to deal with the enormity of the problem confronting her, just as I have rejected state efforts to prevent women from rationally taking steps to prevent that problem from arising. . . .In contrast, I am persuaded that, although a minor has substantial privacy rights in intimate affairs connected with procreation, California's efforts to prevent teenage pregnancy are to be viewed differently from Utah's efforts to inhibit a woman from dealing with pregnancy once it has become an inevitability. . . .

I note, also, that § 261.5 of the California Penal Code is just one of several California statutes intended to protect the juvenile. . . .

I think, too, that it is only fair, with respect to this particular petitioner, to point out that his partner, Sharon, appears not to have been an unwilling participant in at least the initial stages of the intimacies that took place the night of June 3, 1978.* Petitioner's and Sharon's nonacquaintance with each other

---

*. Sharon at the preliminary hearing testified as follows:

"Q [by the Deputy District Attorney]. On June the 4th, at approximately midnight—midnight of June the 3rd, were you in Rohnert Park?

"A [by Sharon]. Yes.

"Q. Is that in Sonoma County?

"A. Yes.

"Q. Did anything unusual happen to you that night in Rohnert Park?

"A. Yes.

"Q. Would you briefly describe what happened that night? Did you see the defendant that night in Rohnert Park?

"A. Yes.

"Q. Where did you first meet him?

"A. At a bus stop.

"Q. Was anyone with you?

"A. My sister.

"Q. Was anyone with the defendant?

"A. Yes.

"Q. How many people were with the defendant?

"A. Two.

"Q. Now, after you met the defendant, what happened?

"A. We walked down to the railroad tracks.

"Q. What happened at the railroad tracks?

"A. We were drinking at the railroad tracks and we walked over to this bush and he started kissing me and stuff, and I was kissing him back, too, at first. Then, I was telling him to stop—

"Q. Yes.

"A.—and I was telling him to slow down and stop. He said, 'Okay, okay.' But then he just kept doing it. He just kept doing it and then my sister and two other guys came over to where we were and my sister said—told me to get up and come home. And then I didn't—

"Q. Yes.

"A.—and then my sister and—

"Q. All right.

"A.—David, one of the boys that were there, started walking home and we stayed there and then later—

"Q. All right.

"A.—Bruce left Michael, you know.

before the incident; their drinking; their withdrawal from the others of the group; their foreplay, in which she willingly participated and seems to have

---

"The Court: Michael being the defendant?

"The Witness: Yeah. We was laying there and we were kissing each other, and then he asked me if I wanted to walk him over to the park; so we walked over to the park and we sat down on a bench and then he started kissing me again and we were laying on the bench. And he told me to take my pants off.

"I said, 'No,' and I was trying to get up and he hit me back down on the bench and then I just said to myself, 'Forget it,' and I let him do what he wanted to do and he took my pants off and he was telling me to put my legs around him and stuff—

"Q. Did you have sexual intercourse with the defendant?

"A. Yeah.

"Q. He did put his penis into your vagina?

"A. Yes.

"Q. You said that he hit you?

"A. Yeah.

"Q. How did he hit you?

"A. He slugged me in the face.

"Q. With what did he slug you?

"A. His fist.

"Q. Where abouts in the face?

"A. On my chin.

"Q. As a result of that, did you have any bruises or any kind of an injury?

"A. Yeah.

"Q. What happened?

"A. I had bruises.

"The Court: Did he hit you one time or did he hit you more than once?

"The Witness: He hit me about two or three times.

* * *

"Q. Now, during the course of that evening, did the defendant ask you your age?

"A. Yeah.

"Q. And what did you tell him?

"A. Sixteen.

"Q. Did you tell him you were sixteen?

"A. Yes.

"Q. Now, you said you had been drinking, is that correct?

"A. Yes.

"Q. Would you describe your condition as a result of the drinking?

"A. I was a little drunk." App. 20-23.

CROSS-EXAMINATION

"Q. Did you go off with Mr. *M.* away from the others?

"A. Yeah.

"Q. Why did you do that?

"A. I don't know. I guess I wanted to.

"Q. Did you have any need to go to the bathroom when you were there[?]

"A. Yes.

"Q. And what did you do?

"A. Me and my sister walked down the railroad tracks to some bushes and went to the bathroom.

"Q. Now, you and Mr. *M.*, as I understand it, went off into the bushes, is that correct?

"A. Yes.

"Q. Okay. And what did you do when you and Mr. *M.* were there in the bushes?

"A. We were kissing and hugging.

"Q. Were you sitting up?

"A. We were laying down.

"Q. You were lying down. This was in the bushes?

"A. Yes.

"Q. How far away from the rest of them were you?

encouraged; and the closeness of their ages (a difference of only one year and 18 days) are factors that should make this case an unattractive one to prose-

---

"A. They were just bushes right next to the railroad tracks. We just walked off into the bushes; not very far.

* * *

"Q. So your sister and the other two boys came over to where you were, you and Michael were, is that right?
"A. Yeah.
"Q. What did they say to you, if you remember?
"A. My sister didn't say anything. She said, 'Come on, Sharon, let's go home.'
"Q. She asked you to go home with her?
"A. (Affirmative nod.)
"Q. Did you go home with her?
"A. No.
"Q. You wanted to stay with Mr. *M.*?
"A. I don't know.
"Q. Was this before or after he hit you?
"A. Before.

* * *

"Q. What happened in the five minutes that Bruce stayed there with you and Michael?
"A. I don't remember.
"Q. You don't remember at all?
"A. (Negative head shake.)
"Q. Did you have occasion at that time to kiss Bruce?
"A. Yeah.
"Q. You did? You were kissing Bruce at that time?
"A. (Affirmative nod.)
"Q. Was Bruce kissing you?
"A. Yes.
"Q. And were you standing up at this time?
"A. No, we were sitting down.

* * *

"Q. Okay. So at this point in time you had left Mr. *M.* and you were hugging and kissing with Bruce, is that right?
"A. Yeah.
"Q. And you were sitting up[?]
"A. Yes.
"Q. Was your sister still there then?
"A. No. Yeah, she was at first.
"Q. What was she doing?
"A. She was standing up with Michael and David.
"Q. Yes. Was she doing anything with Michael and David?
"A. No, I don't think so.
"Q. Whose idea was it for you and Bruce to kiss? Did you initiate that?
"A. Yes.
"Q. What happened after Bruce left?
"A. Michael asked me if I wanted to go walk to the park.
"Q. And what did you say?
"A. I said, 'Yes.'
"Q. And then what happened?
"A. We walked to the park.

* * *

"Q. How long did it take you to get to the park?
"A. About ten or fifteen minutes.
"Q. And did you walk there?
"A. Yes.
"Q. Did Mr. *M.* ever mention his name?
"A. Yes." *Id.*, at 27-32.

cute at all, and especially to prosecute as a felony, rather than as a misdemeanor chargeable under § 261.5. But the State has chosen to prosecute in that manner, and the facts, I reluctantly conclude, may fit the crime.

Justice Brennan, dissenting with whom Justice White and Justice Marshall join. . . .It is disturbing to find the Court so splintered on a case that presents such a straightforward issue . . . .Applying the analytical framework provided by our precedents, I am convinced that there is only one proper resolution of this issue: the classification must be declared unconstitutional. I fear that the plurality opinion and Justices Stewart and Blackmun reach the opposite result by placing too much emphasis on the desirability of achieving the State's asserted statutory goal—prevention of teenage pregnancy—and not enough emphasis on the fundamental question of whether the sex-based discrimination in the California statute is *substantially* related to the achievement of that goal.[45]. . .

The State of California vigorously asserts that the "important governmental objective" to be served by § 261.5 is the prevention of teenage pregnancy. It claims that its statute furthers this goal by deterring sexual activity by males—the class of persons it considers more responsible for causing those pregnancies.[46] But even assuming that prevention of teenage pregnancy is an important governmental objective and that it is in fact an objective of § 261.5. . .California still has the burden of proving that there are fewer teenage pregnancies under its gender-based statutory rape law than there would be if the law were gender neutral. To meet this burden, the State must show that because its statutory rape law punishes only males, and not females, it more effectively deters minor females from having sexual intercourse.[47]

---

45. None of the three opinions upholding the California statute fairly applies the equal protection analysis this Court has so carefully developed since *Craig v. Boren*, 429 U.S. 190 (1976). . . .

All three of these approaches have a common failing. They overlook the fact that the State has not met its burden of proving that the gender discrimination in § 261.5 is *substantially* related to the achievement of the State's asserted statutory goal. My Brethren seem not to recognize that California has the burden of proving that a gender-neutral statutory rape law would be less effective than § 261.5 in deterring sexual activity leading to teenage pregnancy. Because they fail to analyze the issue in these terms, I believe they reach an unsupportable result.

46. In a remarkable display of sexual stereotyping, the California Supreme Court stated: "The Legislature is well within its power in imposing criminal sanctions against males, alone, because they are the *only* persons who may physiologically cause the result which the law properly seeks to avoid." 25 Cal. 3d 608, 612, 601 P.2d 572, 575 (1979) (emphasis in original).

47. Petitioner has not questioned the State's constitutional power to achieve its asserted objective by criminalizing consensual sexual activity. However, I note that our cases would not foreclose such a privacy challenge.

The State is attempting to reduce the incidence of teenage pregnancy by imposing criminal sanctions on those who engage in consensual sexual activity with minor females. We have stressed, however, that "[i]f the right of privacy means anything, it is the right of the *individual*, married or single, to be free from unwarranted governmental intrusion into matters so fundamentally affecting a person as the decision whether to bear or beget a child." Eisenstadt v. Baird, 405 U.S. 438, 453 (1972) (footnote omitted). Minors, too, enjoy a right of privacy in connection with decisions affecting procreation. Carey v. Population Serv. Int'l, 431 U.S. 678, 693 (1977). Thus, despite the suggestion of the plurality to the contrary. . .it is not settled that a State may rely on a pregnancy-prevention justification to make consensual sexual intercourse among minors a criminal act.

The plurality assumes that a gender-neutral statute would be less effective than § 261.5 in deterring sexual activity because a gender-neutral statute would create significant enforcement problems. . . .However, a State's bare assertion that its gender-based statutory classification substantially furthers an important governmental interest is not enough to meet its burden of proof under *Craig v. Boren*. Rather, the State must produce evidence that will persuade the court that its assertion is true. . . .

The State has not produced such evidence in this case. Moreover, there are at least two serious flaws in the State's assertion that law enforcement problems created by a gender-neutral statutory rape law would make such a statute less effective than a gender-based statute in deterring sexual activity.

First, the experience of other jurisdictions, and California itself, belies the plurality's conclusion that a gender-neutral statutory rape law "may well be incapable of enforcement." There are now at least 37 States that have enacted gender-neutral statutory rape laws. Although most of these laws protect young persons (of either sex) from the sexual exploitation of older individuals, the laws of Arizona, Florida, and Illinois permit prosecution of both minor females and minor males for engaging in mutual sexual conduct. . . .California has introduced no evidence that those States have been handicapped by the enforcement problems the plurality finds so persuasive. . . .Surely, if those States could provide such evidence, we might expect that California would have introduced it. . . .

The second flaw in the State's assertion is that even assuming that a gender-neutral statute would be more difficult to enforce, the State has still not shown that those enforcement problems would make such a statute less effective than a gender-based statute in deterring minor females from engaging in sexual intercourse. . . .Common sense, however, suggests that a gender-neutral statutory rape law is potentially a *greater* deterrent of sexual activity than a gender-based law, for the simple reason that a gender-neutral law subjects both men and women to criminal sanctions and thus arguably has a deterrent effect on twice as many potential violators. Even if fewer persons were prosecuted under the gender-neutral law, as the State suggests, it would still be true that twice as many persons would be *subject* to arrest. The State's failure to prove that a gender-neutral law would be a less effective deterrent than a gender-based law, like the State's failure to prove that a gender-neutral law would be difficult to enforce, should have led this Court to invalidate § 261.5. . . .

Until very recently, no California court or commentator had suggested that the purpose of California's statutory rape law was to protect young women from the risk of pregnancy. Indeed, the historical development of § 261.5 demonstrates that the law was initially enacted on the premise that young women, in contrast to young men, were to be deemed legally incapable of consenting to an act of sexual intercourse. . . .Because their chastity was considered particularly precious, those young women were felt to be uniquely in need of the State's protection. . . .In contrast, young men were assumed to be capable of making such decisions for themselves; the law therefore did not offer them any special protection.

It is perhaps because the gender classification in California's statutory rape law was initially designed to further these outmoded sexual stereotypes, rather than to reduce the incidence of teenage pregnancies, that the State has been unable to demonstrate a substantial relationship between the classification and its newly asserted goal. . . .

I would hold that § 261.5 violates the Equal Protection Clause of the Fourteenth Amendment, and I would reverse the judgment of the California Supreme Court.

Justice Stevens, dissenting. Local custom and belief—rather than statutory laws of venerable but doubtful ancestry—will determine the volume of sexual activity among unmarried teenagers. . . .Nevertheless, as a matter of constitutional power, unlike my Brother Brennan,. . .I would have no doubt about the validity of a state law prohibiting all unmarried teenagers from engaging in sexual intercourse. The societal interests in reducing the incidence of venereal disease and teenage pregnancy are sufficient, in my judgment, to justify a prohibition of conduct that increases the risk of those harms. . . .

My conclusion that a nondiscriminatory prohibition would be constitutional does not help me answer the question whether a prohibition applicable to only half of the joint participants in the risk-creating conduct is also valid. It cannot be true that the validity of a total ban is an adequate justification for a selective prohibition; otherwise, the constitutional objection to discriminatory rules would be meaningless. The question in this case is whether the difference between males and females justifies this statutory discrimination based entirely on sex. . . .

The fact that the Court did not immediately acknowledge that the capacity to become pregnant is what primarily differentiates the female from the male. . .does not impeach the validity of the plurality's newly found wisdom. I think the plurality is quite correct in making the assumption that the joint act that this law seeks to prohibit creates a greater risk of harm for the female than for the male. But the plurality surely cannot believe that the risk of pregnancy confronted by the female—any more than the risk of venereal disease confronted by males as well as females—has provided an effective deterrent to voluntary female participation in the risk-creating conduct. Yet the plurality's decision seems to rest on the assumption that the California Legislature acted on the basis of that rather fanciful notion.

In my judgment, the fact that a class of persons is especially vulnerable to a risk that a statute is designed to avoid is a reason for making the statute applicable to that class. The argument that a special need for protection provides a rational explanation for an exemption is one I simply do not comprehend.[48]

In this case, the fact that a female confronts a greater risk of harm than a male is a reason for applying the prohibition to her—not a reason for granting her a license to use her own judgment on whether or not to assume the risk. Surely, if we examine the problem from the point of view of society's interest

---

48. A hypothetical racial classification will illustrate my point. Assume that skin pigmentation provides some measure of protection against cancer caused by exposure to certain chemicals in the atmosphere and, therefore, that white employees confront a greater risk than black employees in certain industrial settings. Would it be rational to require black employees to wear protective clothing but to exempt whites from that requirement? It seems to me that the greater risk of harm to white workers would be a reason for including them in the requirement—not for granting them an exemption.

in preventing the risk-creating conduct from occurring at all, it is irrational to exempt 50% of the potential violators. . . .And, if we view the government's interest as that of a *parens patriae* seeking to protect its subjects from harming themselves, the discrimination is actually perverse. Would a rational parent making rules for the conduct of twin children of opposite sex simultaneously forbid the son and authorize the daughter to engage in conduct that is especially harmful to the daughter? That is the effect of this statutory classification.

If pregnancy or some other special harm is suffered by one of the two participants in the prohibited act, that special harm no doubt would constitute a legitimate mitigating factor in deciding what, if any, punishment might be appropriate in a given case. But from the standpoint of fashioning a general preventive rule—or, indeed, in determining appropriate punishment when neither party in fact has suffered any special harm—I regard a total exemption for the members of the more endangered class as utterly irrational.

In my opinion, the only acceptable justification for a general rule requiring disparate treatment of the two participants in a joint act must be a legislative judgment that one is more guilty than the other. The risk-creating conduct that this statute is designed to prevent requires the participation of two persons—one male and one female. . . .In many situations it is probably true that one is the aggressor and the other is either an unwilling, or at least a less willing, participant in the joint act. If a statute authorized punishment of only one participant and required the prosecutor to prove that that participant had been the aggressor, I assume that the discrimination would be valid. Although the question is less clear, I also assume, for the purpose of deciding this case, that it would be permissible to punish only the male participant, if one element of the offense were proof that he had been the aggressor, or at least in some respects the more responsible participant in the joint act. The statute at issue in this case, however, requires no such proof. The question raised by this statute is whether the State, consistently with the Federal Constitution, may always punish the male and never the female when they are equally responsible or when the female is the more responsible of the two.

It would seem to me that an impartial lawmaker could give only one answer to that question. The fact that the California Legislature has decided to apply its prohibition only to the male may reflect a legislative judgment that in the typical case the male is actually the more guilty party. Any such judgment must, in turn, assume that the decision to engage in the risk-creating conduct is always—or at least typically—a male decision. If that assumption is valid, the statutory classification should also be valid. But what is the support for the assumption? It is not contained in the record of this case or in any legislative history or scholarly study that has been called to our attention. I think it is supported to some extent by traditional attitudes toward male-female relationships. But the possibility that such a habitual attitude may reflect nothing more than an irrational prejudice makes it an insufficient justification for discriminatory treatment that is otherwise blatantly unfair. For, as I read this statute, it requires that one, and only one, of two equally guilty wrongdoers be stigmatized by a criminal conviction.

I cannot accept the State's argument that the constitutionality of the discriminatory rule can be saved by an assumption that prosecutors will commonly invoke this statute only in cases that actually involve a forcible rape, but one that cannot be established by proof beyond a reasonable doubt. . . .That assumption implies that a State has a legitimate interest in convicting a defendant on evidence that is constitutionally insufficient. Of course, the State may create a lesser-included offense that would authorize punishment of the more guilty party, but surely the interest in obtaining convictions on inadequate proof cannot justify a statute that punishes one who is equally or less guilty than his partner.[49]

Nor do I find at all persuasive the suggestion that this discrimination is adequately justified by the desire to encourage females to inform against their male partners. Even if the concept of a wholesale informant's exemption were an acceptable enforcement device, what is the justification for defining the exempt class entirely by reference to sex rather than by reference to a more neutral criterion such as relative innocence? Indeed, if the exempt class is to be composed entirely of members of one sex, what is there to support the view that the statutory purpose will be better served by granting the informing license to females rather than to males? If a discarded male partner informs on a promiscuous female, a timely threat of prosecution might well prevent the precise harm the statute is intended to minimize.

Finally, even if my logic is faulty and there actually is some speculative basis for treating equally guilty males and females differently, I still believe that any such speculative justification would be outweighed by the paramount interest in evenhanded enforcement of the law. A rule that authorizes punishment of only one of two equally guilty wrongdoers violates the essence of the constitutional requirement that the sovereign must govern impartially.

I respectfully dissent.

Notes and Questions

1. *"Unattractive" Case.* What underlying class and gender stereotypes appear to have influenced Justice Blackmun's judgment that this case was "an unattractive one to prosecute" (p. 479-80)?

2. *Sameness/Difference.* The plurality opinion of the Court offers women "special treatment" by not treating their conduct as criminal under section 261.5. The dissent offers women "equal treatment" by arguing that underage women should be equally culpable as men for engaging in sex. How do these seemingly contradictory approaches limit the sexual freedom of underage women and reinforce negative stereotypes about women?

Michael M. demonstrates why the debate in feminism about sameness/difference may be the wrong issue. *See* Note 3 at p. 139. Frances Olsen goes further

49. Both Justice Rehnquist and Justice Blackmun apparently attach significance to the testimony at the preliminary hearing indicating that the petitioner struck his partner. . . .In light of the fact that the petitioner would be equally guilty of the crime charged in the complaint whether or not that testimony is true, it obviously has no bearing on the legal question presented by this case. The question is not whether "the facts. . .fit the crime,". . .—that is a question to be answered at trial—but rather, whether the statute defining the crime fits the constitutional requirement that justice be administered in an evenhanded fashion.

and argues that the debate between sameness/difference and domination/subordination presents false choices.

> One group of feminists focuses on women's ability to be independent sexual actors and to achieve a degree of autonomy; like other oppressed groups, women can and do make the best of what is available to them. Other feminists point out that women's sexuality exists as it does because it is created out of social conditions of oppression. It is wrong, these feminists argue, to interpret women's sexuality as self-expression or autonomy, as though sexism did not exist. What seems to be a split between feminist activists arises from the fact that in conditions of sexual inequality, women are oppressed by both sexual freedom and societal control of sexuality. Sexual freedom turns out to be freedom for men to exploit women; the burden of social control of sexuality falls primarily upon women. Of course, all culture is formed under conditions of various limitations and scarcity and much of culture is created under conditions of external domination. But this doesn't answer the question how to make the best of it and go on. Instead of arguing about which is worse—men's exploitation of women or the state's repression of women—let us devise strategies to overcome both.

Frances E. Olsen, Statutory Rape: A Feminist Critique of Rights Analysis, 63 Tex. L. Rev. 387, 429-30 (1984).

3. *Teenage Pregnancy.* The state of California and the U.S. Supreme Court linked sex by underage women, pregnancy, and welfare (p. 473). This linkage is not race neutral in the context of the last thirty years, in which policy and perceptions have been widely influenced by the publication of E. Franklin Frazier's book *The Negro Family in the United States* (1966) and by "The Moynihan Report", which was named after U.S. Senator Daniel P. Moynihan of New York. U.S. Dep't Labor, Office of Policy Planning and Research, The Negro Family: The Case for National Action (1965). The findings and conclusions of these studies were widely influential because they reflected the pervasive stereotypes of the African-American family structure as deviant and African-American women as matriarchs and welfare mothers. *See* Patricia Hill Collins, Black Feminist Thought: Knowledge, Consciousness and Political Empowerment 75-76 (1990). These studies also were well received because they relieved whites of some or all of their responsibility for the effects of slavery and discrimination. Their ultimate effect was that African-American women became the "scapegoats, responsible for the psychological emasculation of black men and for the failure of the black community to gain parity with the white community." Bonnie Thornton Dill, The Dialectics of Black Womanhood, 4 Signs 543, 548 (1979).

Had the Court recognized the connection between teenage pregnancy and African-American underage women, it would have found it harder to ignore the issues of sexual autonomy and male aggression in light of the historical legacy of slavery. *See* bell hooks, Ain't I a Woman: Black Women and Feminism, at p. 357.

> The post-World War II political economy has offered African-Americans rights not available in former historical periods. African-Americans have successfully acquired basic political and economic protections from a great-

ly expanded welfare state, particularly Social Security, Aid to Families with Dependent Children, unemployment compensation, affirmative action, voting rights, antidiscrimination legislation, and the minimum wage. . . .The large numbers of undereducated, unemployed African-Americans, most of whom are women and children, who inhabit inner cities cannot be forced to work. From the standpoint of the dominant group, they no longer represent cheap labor but instead signify a costly threat to political and economic stability. . . .

The image of the welfare mother provides ideological justifications for interlocking systems of race, gender, and class oppression. African-Americans can be racially stereotyped as being lazy by blaming Black welfare mothers for failing to pass on the work ethic. Moreover, the welfare mother has no male authority figure to assist her. Typically portrayed as an unwed mother, she violates one cardinal tenet of Eurocentric masculinist thought: she is a woman alone. As a result, her treatment reinforces the dominant gender ideology positing that a woman's true worth and financial security should occur through heterosexual marriage. . . .Creating the controlling image of the welfare mother and stigmatizing her as the cause of her own poverty and that of African-American communities shifts the angle of vision away from structural sources of poverty and blames the victims themselves. The image of the welfare mother thus provides ideological justification for the dominant group's interest in limiting the fertility of Black mothers who are seen as producing too many economically unproductive children.

Collins, *supra*, at 76-77.

4. *Women Divided*. Catharine MacKinnon analyzes statutory rape law by showing how it divides women between those who cannot say yes and those who cannot say no, with the effect that all women are left unprotected.

All women are divided into parallel provinces, their actual consent counting to the degree that they diverge from the paradigm case in their category. Virtuous women, like young girls, are unconsenting, virginal, rapable. Unvirtuous women, like wives and prostitutes, are consenting, whores, unrapable. The age line under which girls are presumed disabled from consenting to sex, whatever they say, rationalizes a condition of sexual coercion which women never outgrow. One day they cannot say yes, and the next day the cannot say no. The law takes the most aggravated case for female powerlessness based on gender and age combined and, by formally prohibiting all sex as rape, makes consent irrelevant on the basis of an assumption of powerlessness. This defines those above the age line as powerful, whether they actually have power to consent or not. The vulnerability girls share with boys—age—dissipates with time. The vulnerability girls share with women—gender—does not. As with protective labor laws for women only, dividing and protecting the most vulnerable becomes a device for not protecting everyone who needs it, and also may function to target those singled out for special protection for special abuse. Such protection has not prevented high rates of sexual abuse of children and may contribute to eroticizing young girls as forbidden.

Catharine A. MacKinnon, Toward a Feminist Theory of the State 175-76 (1989).

Catharine A. MacKinnon, Reflections on Sex Equality Under Law, 100 Yale L.J. 1281, 1296–97, 1300, 1304–07, 1324–26 (1991)

[L]egal sex equality theory has not been designed to address the substance of most lived sex inequality. . . .The worse the inequality is, the more like a difference it looks. . . .The more perfect the disparity, the more difficult the showing of discrimination, so long as the basis for disparity is not mythic but real. . . .

Because the "similarly situated" requirement continues to control access to equality claims, the laws of sexual assault and reproductive control—areas as crucial in the social construction of women's inferior status as they are laden with misogyny—have not been seen as amenable to constitutional sex equality attack. Comparatively few men are raped and no men are denied abortions; gender comparisons are therefore unavailable or strained. So sexuality and procreation become happy differences or unhappy differences but never imposed inequalities. The legal system's treatment of rape as illegal under law while overwhelmingly permitted in fact is thus not regarded as state action that discriminates on the basis of sex, nor is criminalizing or refusing to fund a medical procedure that only women need. First there must be similarly situated men with whom to compare. Men's comparative lack of sexual and reproductive violation is not visible as a lack because it is relatively unthinkable that men would be hurt in these ways. . . .

Much sex inequality is successfully accomplished in society without express legal enforcement and legitimation. Yet the law is deeply implicated in it. Law actively engages in sex inequality by apparently prohibiting abuses it largely permits, like rape, and by hiding the deprivations it imposes beneath ostensibly gender-neutral terms, like abortion. In the areas of sexual assault and reproductive control specifically, these legal concepts have been designed and applied from the point of view of the accused rapist and the outsider/impregnator respectively, and in the absence of the point of view of the sexually assaulted or pregnant woman. . . .

Women and men are not similarly situated with regard to sexual assault in the sense that they are not equally subject to it or equally subjected to it. But this is the inequality that indicts it, not the difference that exonerates it or exempts it from equality scrutiny. The one case in which the Supreme Court adjudicates the constitutionality of a sexual assault statute in the sex equality context misses this point entirely. *Michael M.* challenges the California statutory rape law as sex-discriminatory because it makes only males criminals for having sex with underage girls. The plurality upheld the statute on grounds that underage females could validly be protected from sex because they were likely to become pregnant. The dissent would have invalidated the statute, among other reasons, because it did not equally criminalize the two participants in the crime and because it embodied the invidious stereotype that men usually aggress in sex. The plurality opinion grasped the sex-differential reality at the cost of attributing it to biology. The dissent understood the reality of sexual assault of girls to be socially created rather than biological, at the cost of failing to understand it as nonetheless gender-based. The plurality saw a hierarchy but thought it was biologically fixed. The dissent saw the possibilities for change, but missed the hierarchy. The plurality allowed a sex difference—potential pregnancy—to render girls "not similarly situated" and to support a sex-differential statute that divides women by age. Never mind that many of those protected cannot become pregnant and more of those not protected can, that young boys are sexually assaulted too (usually by older males), and that girls do not lose their vulnerability to sexual coercion upon turning eighteen. The dissent revealed more concern with avoiding the stereotyping attendant to the ideological message the law communicated than with changing the facts that make the stereotype largely true. In the interest of opposing facial distinctions and debunking the supposed myth of male sexual aggression, the fact that it is overwhelmingly girls who are sexually victimized by older males for reasons wholly unrelated to their capacity to become pregnant was completely obscured. The facts of social inequality, of sex aggravated by age, that could have supported particular legislative attention to the sexual assault of girls were not even considered. Underage girls form a credible disadvantaged group for equal protection purposes when the social facts of sexual assault are faced, facts which prominently feature one-sided sexual aggression by older males. It seems that in order to imagine equality, one must first be blind to inequality, and to see inequality blinds one to seeing that equality is possible.

Perhaps this case reveals the reason that the law of sexual assault has never been held to sex equality standards, at the same time as providing clues to the reason equality is defined in terms of sameness and difference in the first place. Sexuality, hence sexual assault, is believed by many to be biological, a natural part of the so-called sex difference. We are dealing here with the assumption that rape is inevitable in gendered biology. If explicitly embodied in law, such an assumption ought to violate equal protection of the laws. In fact, in *Dothard v. Rawlinson*, it has been found to be a nondiscriminatory reason for excluding women from some employment, equating capacity to be raped with membership in the female gender.[50] What it comes down to is that the most extreme instances of sex inequality in society are considered sex differences, hence reasons equality law does not apply, as in *Michael M.*, or reasons discrimination can be openly justified, as in *Dothard*. Men can be raped, and sometimes are. That alone should suggest that the overwhelming numbers of women in the rape victim population expresses inequality, not biology. Will rape have to be comparably common in and definitive of men's status before women can be found deprived of equal protection of the laws when they are raped with legal impunity? How much legal impunity will it take before the law of sexual assault—its terms, enforcement, nonenforcement, and interpretation—is recognized as sex discrimination?

Sexual assault, in this argument, has a special place in women's social status and the law of sexual assault has a distinctive place in the history of women's oppression by government. There is no lack of atrocities disclosing

50. Dothard v. Rawlinson, 433 U.S. 321, 336 (1977) (women's capacity to be raped, termed their "very womanhood," justifies state regulation disqualifying female employees from contact positions in men's prison). Male gender, then, constituted a bona fide occupational qualification (BFOQ) for the job. Thus does sexual assault define gender as such.

judicial bias by courts in sexual assault adjudications. Condescending, demeaning, hostile, humiliating, and indifferent judicial treatment of female victims of sexual assault is not uncommon. Government commits this inequality and should rectify it. Law has a choice. It can inscribe this misogyny on society yet more authoritatively, promoting sex inequality, or it can move against it by promoting sex equality. Sexual assault cannot be treated as gender neutral because sexual assault is not gender neutral. The law of sexual assault cannot be treated as private action because it is government action. Women are not receiving equal protection of the laws. The equal protection clause is inconsistent with state law that promotes sex inequality. The law of sexual assault commands Fourteenth Amendment scrutiny.

Sexual assault is already seen as gendered in the Supreme Court's treatment of the statute in *Michael M.* as facial sex discrimination against men, apparently as a result of its use of the term "sexual intercourse." Sexual assault is squarely understood as a form of sex discrimination in the recognition that sexual harassment, which can include sexual assault, is actionable sex-based discrimination. Just as women are sexually harassed based on their sex, women are sexually assaulted based on their sex. Both forms of treatment (which overlap) are categorical and group-based. Men, usually heterosexual, harass and rape women. Any woman within the ambit of such a man is his potential victim and, when she is harassed, is disadvantaged because of her sex. But for her sex, she would not be so treated. Similar to the way Title VII governs the workplace, the criminal law of sexual assault, governed by the Fourteenth Amendment, would set sex equality standards for society at large. . . .

Inequality, as analyzed here, is not a bad attitude that floats in the sky but an embodied particular that walks on the ground. It is first concrete, historical, present, and material, only derivatively generic, and never abstract. Social inequality does not first exist in the abstract, in search of a basis or polarization or natural joint to carve or asymmetry to which to attach. It exists in the social reality of its particulars, such as the social dominance of men through which women are subjected. Sex equality as a norm comes into being through the resistance of women as a people to their subjection. The equality principle, in this approach, is properly comprised of the practical necessities for ending inequality in each of its real forms.

Such an analysis does not generate abstractly fungible categories. Inequality is not conceptually reversible, only concretely changeable. To be "similarly situated," a test which relies on and produces abstract counter-hierarchical comparisons as the essence of equality reasoning, thus cannot remain the threshold for access to equality guarantees. If inequality is concrete, no man is ever in the same position a woman is, because he is not in it as a woman. That does not mean a man cannot be recognized as discriminated against on the basis of sex. It does mean that it is no measure of virtue for an equality theory to accord the same solicitude to dominant groups as to subordinate ones, all the while ignoring who is who. If the point of equality law is to end group-based dominance and subordination, rather than to recognize sameness or accommodate difference, a greater priority is placed on rectifying the legal inequality of groups that are historically unequal in society, and less solicitude is accorded pure legal artifacts or reversals of social fortune. Although such a substantive interpretation is technically possible, indeed compelled, under existing law, the passage of an Equal Rights Amendment could help provide a political and textual basis for this rectification of constitutional emphasis.

Law furthering this equality norm would develop a new relation to society. In societies governed by the rule of law, law is typically a status quo instrument; it does not usually guarantee rights that society is predicated on denying. In this context equality law is unusual: social equality does not exist, yet a legal guarantee of equality does. If law requires equality, in a society that is structurally and pervasively unequal, and the social status quo were no longer to be maintained through the abstract equality model, then equality law could not even be applied without producing social change. For example, it is generally thought that nondiscrimination and affirmative action are two different things. Under the equality approach argued here, there is no difference between them. Equality law becomes a distinct species of law, in need of its own norms for its distinct relation to an unequal society.

One part of developing the jurisprudence of such law is creating new doctrine. Here, the laws of sexual assault and abortion are argued to constitute facially sex-discriminatory state action. While existing state action doctrine readily accommodates these obvious forms, and existing discrimination law provides a basis for this recognition, the larger implications of this exposed interface between the state and women's everyday lives suggests the need for more commodious notions of both discrimination and state action. On a continuum of examples, denial of access to abortion, the marital rape exclusion, failure to enforce laws against domestic violence, the mistaken belief in consent defense in rape, and state protection of pornography are all gendered acts of government. Are they facial discrimination? From the standpoint of a woman being injured by them, are they state action? If not, are the concepts gender biased?

These forms of discrimination look like much of it: perhaps less provably purposeful than the existing model for intentional, but far from facially neutral and massively disparate in impact, they show a supportive interaction between government permission or omission and male aggression. More explicitly invidious than the neutral, but less superficially intentional than existing requirements for motive, such discriminations have social markers of sex written all over them and would arguably happen very differently if the stance of the government were different. Such laws and practices are simply biased, their one-sidedness diagnosable from subordinate group disadvantage, provable from invidious social meaning and damaging material consequences. Failure to see the state's hand in these examples would miss much of the way law insinuates itself into social life, intruding on and structuring relations between the sexes, institutionalizing male dominance.

Equality approaches are often faulted as less powerful because inherently relative, while other approaches like liberty or security or privacy are thought more powerful because absolute. Existing absolutes have not proven particularly reliable; one suspects they are usually defined sub rosa in relative terms anyway. It is true that equality never entirely escapes the comparative, but substantive comparisons that recognize hierarchy and history pose few of the dangers that abstract Aristotelian comparisons do. Nor must the standard for comparison be conceded. Subordinate groups may challenge the dominant standard as a form of bias in itself. Equality allows critique of the social partiality of standards as well as opportunity to live up to existing ones. The contextual nature of the equality right seems to me a strength: what it seeks is always real, because it is real for someone. In one's zeal to make deeper change, it should not be overlooked that actually having the best any group currently has—for example, not being about to be raped at any moment—would be a big improvement for most of us.

LAW AND VIOLENCE AGAINST WOMEN

Chapter 7

Prostitution

Each of the chapters on battering, sexual harassment, and rape had as a starting point that the actions were harmful to women. This view reflects a growing societal consensus in the United States that these behaviors constitute acts of violence against women. Such a consensus does not exist with prostitution, however. Personal narratives and sociological studies documenting kidnappings, rapes, and beatings of women in prostitution are viewed by many people as byproducts of the business rather than as the business itself. Our social and legal cultures, which emphasize individual autonomy and freedom of contract, condition us to think that prostitution can take place without victimization. The dominant social and legal cultures, however, also foster an indifference toward the prostituted women. Notwithstanding statutory prohibitions, prostitution-related activities are tolerated as long as they do not interfere too greatly with nonprostitution activities. What we find, then, is a set of legal and social institutions that maintain a prostituted woman's right to sexual and contractual autonomy while also dehumanizing and demonizing her so that she is placed outside society's boundaries and viewed as unworthy of respect and protection.

The readings question dominant assumptions about prostitution and whether the act itself of a woman exchanging sex for money is anything other than a violent act.[1] Part A includes an article by Evelina Giobbe that shows how classism, heterosexism, racism, and sexism operate within prostitution and how the selling of sex for money is analogous to marital rape. Giobbe's piece is followed by narratives by Jean Johnston, Gloria Lockett, and Donna Marie Niles. Their stories are not meant to be representative of women who work or have worked in the sex industry, but they were included to ground our discussion of prostitution in the words of women who have lived it.

Part B includes historical and contemporary materials demonstrating how prostitution has been institutionalized in our society's political and economic structures. Judith Walkowitz examines how the interaction of the legal and medical establishments changed the nature of prostitution in late nineteenth-century England. Lucie Cheng describes the role that prostitution of Chinese women played in the economic development of California in the last half of the nineteenth century. Saundra Sturdevant and Brenda Stoltzfus address the U.S. military's complicity in the creation of a class of indigenous women

1. The chapter focuses almost exclusively on adult women used in prostitution. The issue of male prostitution is not addressed because it occurs in a different context and involves a different set of dynamics that would require a separate and distinct analysis.

to service the sexual demands of U.S. troops in Asia in the last half of the twentieth century.

Part C includes an excerpt from the "Report of the Florida Supreme Court Gender Bias Study Commission." Florida has been the only state to consider prostitution when examining gender bias in the justice system. This report is followed by Florida statutes that are either referred to in or part of the recommendations made by the study commission. We then look at *People v. Slovinski*, which considered the application of a rape shield statute when a defendant alleged that the complainant had been engaged in prostitution.

The chapter ends with Part D which consists of an excerpt from an article by Margaret Baldwin. After exploring the feminist discourses on violence against women, Baldwin concludes that feminist legal reform proposals and feminist discourse itself have a negative impact on women in prostitution because the reforms and the discourse place prostituted women into a separate and unprotected category.

A. Systems of Prostitution

Evelina Giobbe, Prostitution: Buying the Right to Rape, in *Rape and Sexual Assault III: A Research Handbook* 143 (Ann Wolbert Burgess ed., 1991)

Rape, or sexual assault, is commonly understood to mean the forced compliance or submission of an individual to unwanted or coerced sexual activity. Prostitution conversely is commonly believed to be an equal exchange of sex for money based on mutual consent. This paper presents a theory that the experience of being bought for sexual use is most like marital rape—even when women give mitigated consent. The framework of this analysis is an examination of the individual, institutional, and cultural factors that facilitate a woman's decision to engage in prostitution. . . .

Contrary to cultural mythology, the institution of prostitution most resembles the institution of marriage rather than a form of employment. In the marketplace the relationship of worker to proprietor (or the collective) is a legally binding contract that explicitly outlines the exchange of labor for compensation (cash and benefits). Unlike a labor contract, traditional marriage and prostitution are both predicated on ownership and unconditional sexual access to a woman's body. In fact, sexual harassment laws protect laborers from this presumption of sexual access.

Traditional marriage is premised on the long-term private ownership of a woman by an individual man, whereas the institution of prostitution is built upon the short-term public ownership of women by many men. Women are kept socially, sexually, and economically subordinate to individual men in marriage and to men as a class in prostitution. These systems allow males to exercise their prerogative to own and control women in both the private and public spheres. Based on the parallels between these two institutions, I argue that if the sexual act is predicated on ownership, as it was in traditional marriage, can be in modern marriage, and is vis-a-vis "rental" in prostitution, the act itself and its subsequent effects are that of rape. . . .

Prostitution is like rape. It's like when I was 15 years old and I was raped. I used to experience leaving my body. I mean that's what I did when that man raped me. I looked up at the ceiling and I went to the ceiling and I numbed myself. . .because I didn't want to feel what I was feeling. I was very frightened. And while I was a prostitute I used to do that all the time. I would numb my feelings. I wouldn't even feel like I was in my body. I would actually leave my body and go somewhere else with my thoughts and with my feelings until he got off and it was over with. I don't know how else to explain it except that it felt like rape. It was rape to me.

A hypothesis that equates prostitution with rape must provide a working definition of free choice and examine a woman's "choice" to engage in prostitution within the social context in which it occurs. Choice implies the chance, right, or power to choose, usually by the free exercise of one's judgment. To choose is to pick out by preference from what is available, to take as a choice, to select. In order for a choice to be made freely there must be an absence of coercion or violence. One must recognize that she has a choice, have a full range of comparable options to choose from, and have full mental capacities with which to make this choice. A freely made choice is an informed choice; one must know what she is choosing and realize the implications or consequences of the choice. Bribes, manipulation, or trickery are persuasive tactics that mitigate choice. Ideally, one would have personal or community support to actualize her choice. Minimally, one should have the right to change her mind should she realize that she has made a poor choice. . . .

The function of the institution of prostitution is to allow males unconditional sexual access to females, limited solely by their ability to pay. Culturally supported tactics of power and control facilitate the recruitment or coercion of women and children into prostitution and effectively impede their escape. The tactics are educational deprivation, job discrimination, and poverty; child sexual abuse, rape, and battery; and racism, classism, and heterosexism.

Economic necessity is one factor that facilitates the recruitment of women and girls into prostitution. In 1983, half of all poor families in the United States had a female head of household, and women comprised two-thirds of adults living below the poverty line. Although poor women may be eligible for welfare, this system maintains women at subsistence levels and punishes them if they secure employment by proportionately reducing subsidies. Eighty percent of American women work in sex-segregated, low paying jobs, most often without the benefit of health insurance or pension plans, and notwithstanding the rare exceptions, without subsidized child care. Discriminatory hiring practices have systematically barred women from jobs that have been traditionally defined as "men's work" and which are well-paid, secure, and include comprehensive benefit packages. In all of these ways women are kept economically subordinate to men. By maintaining a society in which women are kept economically marginalized, the system of male supremacy ensures that a pool of women will be vulnerable to recruitment and entrapment in prostitution. But this is only one factor.

Approximately 25 percent of women in the United States are sexually assaulted before the age of 13. One in three women are raped during their lifetime, and a rape occurs every three minutes. Additionally, it is estimated that some woman is battered by her husband or male partner every fifteen seconds.

Although child sexual abuse, rape, and battery are crimes committed by individual men, an argument can be made that they are institutionalized forms of social control because of their prevalence, the fact that they differentially target females, and the failure of male-controlled social institutions to prevent or redress the victims' injuries.

Prostitution creates an environment whereby crimes against women and children become a commercial enterprise. When a "john" uses a juvenile prostitute for his own sexual gratification he is committing the crime of child sexual abuse. When he demands that a prostitute allow him to use her in sadomasochistic sex scenes, he is battering her. When a john compels a woman to submit to his sexual demands as a condition of "employment," he is guilty of both sexual harassment and rape. He is committing rape by a feminist (if not legal) definition, which differentiates between compliance and consent. The fact that a john gives money to a woman or a child for submitting to these acts does not alter the fact that he is committing child sexual abuse, rape, and battery; it merely redefines these crimes as prostitution.

Racism and classism maximize oppressive conditions that make poor women, women of color, and white ethnic women particularly vulnerable to to [sic] prostitution. Limited educational and career opportunities foster dependence on an inadequate and punitive welfare system, creating economic vulnerability. Pornographic stereotypes of poor, black, and ethnic women as well as ordinances that zone sex oriented businesses and prostitution into poor and minority neighborhoods make the women who live there especially vulnerable to harassment from both pimps and johns. Additionally, the lack of community-based services in these areas leaves women with limited resources, increasing the probability that they will not receive effective advocacy to escape abuse.

Heterosexism defines heterosexuality as the only normal form of intimacy. This view supports the male sexual imperative: the belief that men have uncontrollable sexual urges that must be fulfilled or they will be driven to rape "innocent" females. Herein lies the ultimate justification for prostitution.

All of these factors are compounded by unequal application of laws prohibiting prostitution. Only a token number of johns and even fewer pimps are arrested or convicted. By allowing men to traffic in women and children with impunity while simultaneously prosecuting prostitutes, the legal system tacitly supports sexual exploitation and, through the collection of fines, profits from it. Over all, sexism, the values and beliefs used to justify the oppression of all women in a male supremacist system, overtly and covertly supports tactics of control and, by so doing, maintains systems of prostitution in the culture. . . .

In his book *Anatomy of Power*, Galbraith identifies three forms of power that allow groups or individuals to force the submission of others to their will: coercive power, compensatory or economic power, and conditioned power. Within the institution of prostitution johns use all three forms of power to compel prostitutes to engage in unwanted sex.

The most overt form of power used by men to ensure a prostitute's compliance is compensatory or economic power. Because an exchange of money occurs between the prostitute and the john, the john is given permission to use the woman's body in any manner that he chooses. Any refusal on the woman's part can result in the withdrawal of compensation, or the john may use another form of power to enforce his wishes. His ability to do so is enforced directly and indirectly by pimps and owners of prostitution businesses to maximize their profits. Jayme Ryan, a woman who had been used in the legal brothel system of Nevada, explained the house rules for prostitute/client interactions:

> *When you got a customer in your room you had to perform any sex act that he wanted. . . .S&M, "water sports,". . .Sometimes the men demanded that we wear costumes, other times we were filmed or photographed chained up, being whipped or being penetrated with various objects. . . .We were strictly forbidden to use condoms unless the customer asked for one as it took away from the customer's maximum pleasure.*

"House rules" were enforced by a system of fines levied against the women by the brothel. Reports of misconduct were directly relayed to pimps for disciplinary action. The compensatory power that johns use against prostitutes must also be viewed within the broader context of women's economic subordination to men generally and the specific educational and economic limitations that shape the lives of the majority of women used in prostitution.

A john can and often does use coercive power against a prostitute by threatening, battering, or raping a woman who refuses to meet his sexual demands. It is not unusual for police to find weapons (usually guns) in the possession of men arrested for soliciting undercover agents posing as prostitutes. Customer violence against prostitutes is quickly hidden by brothel owners whose primary concerns are happy customers and maximum profits. Ryan reported:

> *Once you were alone in your room with a customer you had no protection from him. There were many different occasions where a woman was brutally beaten or raped by a john, but as long as he paid the house it was kept quiet.*

Johns benefit indirectly from the coercive power that pimps wield over women under their control. A woman whose pimp uses violence or threats to force her to earn a certain amount of money daily (a quota) is unlikely to refuse to cooperate with the sexual demands placed on her by a customer. Furthermore, because of her stigmatized status, a prostitute is most often unable successfully to obtain legal redress for a crime of violence committed against her. In this way, society reinforces the ability of men to use violence against prostitutes. . . .

In spite of the relative advances of the second wave of feminism, women in western society are socialized to cultivate attractiveness, to be passive and nurturant, and to seek approval from and defer to men. Traditionally a woman's success has been measured by her relationships as opposed to her achievements. In a technological society, the media is one of the foremost transmitters of cultural norms. As such, television, films, and advertising have been especially pernicious in emphasizing women's primary value as sex objects.

The sexual objectification of women was exacerbated by Hugh Hefner's creation of the Playboy Bunny: half Barbie Doll, half geisha, with silicone-filled breasts and airbrushed waistlines, flatteringly photographed through greased lenses. Typically in their late teens and early twenties, these young women were used to set an impossible standard of attractiveness for adult women to emulate. With the explosion of "hard core" pornography onto the open market in the 1970s the definition of a woman's value as sex object expanded to include her willingness to engage in myriad "sexual acts," to which women were subjected in X-rated videos and magazines. Although pornographers claim to be sexual radicals, pornography presents the narrowest picture of the traditional female sex role. Women in pornography are passive; they are "nurturing" in their sexual ministrations to men; they appear to be seeking approval from the men for whom they are posed; they are depicted in a variety of stereotypical male fantasies; and because of pornography's implied promise of unconditional sexual availability, they are always in postures of deference to male consumers.

In a gender-stratified culture men exert conditional power over women when they use or manipulate sex role expectations in order to obtain their desires. This may happen overtly, as in the case of a husband who refuses to share child-care responsibilities because "that's a wife's job," or more subtly, as the man who shows disapproval or withholds affection from his partner because her career interferes with her attention to his self-defined needs. In both examples, female socialization that reinforces male expectations may constrain a woman from acting in her own best interest and contribute to her capitulation to his demands.

Women used in prostitution have not only been socialized in the traditional sense but may be further socialized in "hyperfeminine" roles after initial entry into prostitution. Sociologists describe this as an apprenticeship period during which the woman learns an occupational ideology that provides her with positive or neutralizing definitions that glorify prostitution and justify her participation. Positive definitions include the promise of financial success, the allegation that prostitutes contribute to the stability of marriage by performing sexual acts in which wives refuse to engage, and the myth that prostitution prevents rape. Neutralizing definitions include the justification that prostitutes are like other working women, that everyone is immoral or dishonest in some way but prostitutes are less hypocritical about it than "squares," and the idea that all male/female relationships (husband/wife, boyfriend/girlfriend) are a form of covert prostitution, that is, housewives and girlfriends get "paid" with dinners and gifts, prostitutes get their money "up-front."

Sociologists explain that a prostitute learns these rationales within the "deviant subculture" of prostitution, from a pimp or john, and to a lesser extent, from other prostitutes who have learned and accepted this vocabulary of motivation. Their focus, however, is on how she internalizes these messages rather than the beneficiaries of her socialization—the men who receive economic gain or sexual gratification from the sale of her body. When the teacher of an idea also benefits through its actualization, the lesson learned is suspect.

Johns exert conditioned power over prostitutes by using and manipulating traditional sex role expectations of women as well as the particular occupational ideology of prostitution. They rigidly define and control the conditions under which prostitution occurs and strictly proscribe prostitute/customer interactions. The role of prostitute is consistent with the traditional female sex role in that it requires that the woman make herself attractive to males, that she behave passively (prostitutes stand on street corners or line-up in brothels for men to "pick"), and that she nurture and defer to men's needs and desires by complying with their sexual demands. Johns also exert conditioned power over prostitutes by reinforcing positive and neutralizing definitions of prostitution. Last, johns indirectly benefit from positive and neutralizing definitions of prostitution that are instilled in women by pimps and perpetuated in the mainstream media and pornography.

In all of these ways a woman's "choice" to engage in unwanted sexual acts for financial consideration is shaped by individual men within a social context that promotes women's social, sexual, and economic subordination to males. From this perspective then, a woman's "choice" to engage in prostitution is mitigated to the point of meaninglessness. . . .

Studies of marital rape have revealed that women who are raped by their partners suffer many of the same physical and emotional effects as other rape victims: physical trauma, humiliation, guilt, and self-blame. In addition, they experience feelings of betrayal, isolation, and entrapment. Women describe feeling dirty and degraded, physically defiled, and used following such assaults. Furthermore, wives who are frequently sexually assaulted by their husbands suffer greater damage to their self-esteem, and are more likely to have psychosomatic symptoms and to attempt suicide.

Common long-term effects of marital rape include lingering fears, emotional pain, flashbacks and nightmares, and an aversion to intimacy and sex. Women who have been raped by their husbands have subsequent difficulty establishing intimate relationships with men; display extreme mistrust or caution; and may desire no contact with men. Their feelings about men range from disdain to hatred. In some cases it centers on "certain kinds of men," in others it generalizes to all men. . . .

Anecdotal information provided by women used in prostitution who have contacted WHISPER [Women Hurt in Systems of Prostitution Engaged in Revolt] for assistance, who have attended our weekly education groups, and who participated in the WHISPER Oral History Project, have revealed a pattern of responses to the sex demanded of them in prostitution that is shockingly similar to those expressed by women who have been sexually abused and raped by their husbands.

Interestingly, marital rape victims who also suffered verbal abuse typically were called "no-good tramp" and "whore" by their husbands. Recognizing on some level that that [sic] society set aside a certain group of women for that kind of verbal and sexual abuse, one woman said, "I felt like a prostitute afterwards," and another reported, "I felt like a two-bit French whore. What I was engaged in was nothing but prostitution.["]

Like victims of marital rape, women typically report feeling humiliated by the acts in which they were repeatedly required to engage with multiple customers daily. Most reported feelings of degradation, defilement, and dirtiness, sometimes for years after leaving prostitution . . . .

Not unlike women who have been raped by their husbands, women escaping prostitution had subsequent difficulty establishing intimate relationships with men. These difficulties resulted in wishes to have no contact with men and expressions of extreme mistrust or caution . . . .

Like victims of marital rape, survivors of prostitution typically express disdain for men and sometimes outright hatred. In some cases their anger focuses on specific groups of men, in others it generalizes to all men . . . .

As in the case of marital rape, prostitution has a profound impact on a woman's sexuality . . . .Some women have fears about the physical aspects of sexual intimacy . . . .Other women report that after years of sexual abuse and training themselves to disassociate their minds from their bodies during the sex act, it becomes difficult to reintegrate:

MD: *Well, sexually, I'm having a hard time. It's just something I'm going through, you know. It's hard for me to enjoy sex anymore.*

KJ: *Sex isn't something that I particularly enjoy. I think [prostitution] kind of like made me numb towards sex.*

MC: *I was pretty ruined. I don't think my sex life will ever be what it might have been, if I hadn't been totally sexually assaulted every fucking conceivable way possible in my life. For a long time after I got out of prostitution, it was very difficult for me, you know, intimacy. To turn myself back on, 'cause you turn yourself off when you turn tricks.*

. . .As in the case of marital rape, long term effects of prostitution include flashbacks (sometimes exacerbated by prolonged drug use) and nightmares. It's not unusual for adult women who have survived this kind of abuse to sleep with the lights on, or to take a small stuffed doll, a pet, or their infant children to bed with them at night . . . .

Survivors also typically suffer lingering fears. . .and deep emotional pain that often resembles grieving:

MD: *I feel like I imagine people who were in concentration camps feel when they get out. It will never go away. It's a real deep pain, an assault to my mind, my body, my dignity as a human being. I feel like what was taken away from me in prostitution is irretrievable. There's part of me that's dead, that's never gonna come back, that will never, ever be fixed, that can't be fixed, . . .like somebody cut off your arm, it can't grow back, like a hurt on this incredible deep, deep level. It's the pain that's not like any other pain that I can imagine. And the only way that I live is not to be in contact with that pain. Otherwise, I couldn't live.*

Women who have survived prostitution may also suffer from a unique, and quite irrational, fear that could be coined "the scarlet letter syndrome." They believe that people, especially men, can "tell" that they were prostitutes by merely looking at them. . . .This can cause great emotional stress and in extreme cases cause a woman to hurt herself . . . .In fact, public hospitals report 15 percent of all suicide victims are prostitutes. One survey of call girls revealed that 75 percent had attempted suicide.

The sexual abuse inherent in prostitution results in numerous health complications and lasting physical damage: trauma from beatings and rapes; complications from persistent bladder infections; and repeated exposure to venereal disease that often results in chronic pelvic inflammatory disease and infertility. However, it is the devastating emotional damage of prostitution that women label as the most profound impact on their lives.

DT: *I did have [a] broken nose, broken neck, stitches in my head. Those*

> *are health costs, those things healed, and they healed pretty fast. The mental, emotional part is still healing. Probably will for years, and years, and years, if ever. I don't know if that would ever be something that could be healed.*

When women's experiences in prostitution are incongruent with the culturally supported idea that prostitution is a victimless crime, women tend to blame themselves "for not doing it right" rather than acknowledging the abusive nature of the institution. This is not unlike the battered woman who believes that if she were more sexually forthcoming or inventive her husband wouldn't be reduced to forcing her to have sex. Both the prostitute and the sexually abused wife's realities are denied in the larger culture. Both are isolated within a closed system whose rules they have not designed, cannot control, and only minimally benefit them, if at all.

Finally, much has been hypothesized about the connection between a woman's "lack of self-esteem" and her victimization by her partner. Similar hypotheses have been advanced about "low self-esteem" as an antecedent to prostitution. Women used in prostitution have repeatedly expressed ideas and opinions of themselves that would lead an observer to comment on their poor self-image. However, like the woman who has been repeatedly sexually abused and/or battered by her partner, she has merely incorporated his definition of her valuelessness in an attempt to make sense of the abuse that she suffers. For a woman in prostitution, her valuelessness is reinforced on a daily basis by the numerous men who use her for their own sexual gratification without any regard for the physical, psychological, or emotional impact on her. Many women reported that during their first experiences in prostitution they openly cried while turning tricks, only to be shocked by the realization that their obvious emotional or physical distress did not affect nor diminish the customer's pleasure.

The parallel trauma responses that are found in victims of marital rape or prostitution are only replicated in victims of massive sexual abuse, rape, and battery. There is no other interpersonal, social, or work related type of situation or interaction that elicits these massive traumatic effects on its "participants," nor would we, as a society, condone or permit such an interaction to continue without intervention. . . .

In spite of the abusive conditions in their lives prostitutes are afforded neither the status of victim nor survivor, but are defined as fully consenting participants in an industry that, if viewed objectively, would be understood to be the commerce of sexual abuse and inequality. Prostitution is sexual abuse because prostitutes are subjected to any number of sexual acts that in any other context, acted against any other woman, would be labeled assaultive or, at the very least, unwanted and coerced. Yet because an exchange of money occurs, irrespective of whether the woman herself maintains control of or benefits from this exchange, the client is given permission to use the woman in a manner that would not be tolerated in any other business or social arrangement (including marriage in some states); and the woman's acceptance of the money is construed as her willingness to engage in such commerce.

If this construction were applied to other victims of sexual assault then one logically would have to assume that women raped by their husbands or teenagers molested by their fathers, for example, also choose abusive relationships because they accept monetary considerations from their assailants in the form of food, lodging, and sometimes actual cash. This analogy sounds strained only because we have learned to recognize the violence to which these particular women and youths are subjected. We have learned to distinguish the victim from the perpetrator. We do not assert that, because a victim is powerless at a particular moment in time to change the objective circumstances of her life, she has chosen those very circumstances, and in fact, is compensated handsomely for her acquiescence. On the contrary, we create alternatives for those so victimized.

As other victims of sexual assault and battering, women and girls used in prostitution need and deserve tangible assistance to escape and overcome the trauma of commercial sexual exploitation.

Less than a decade ago, marital rape was permitted by both church and state. The assumption of a male's ownership of his wife's body was so culturally entrenched that it was unthinkable for a woman to deny a husband sexual access. It was only by listening to women who had survived this ongoing sexual abuse in their homes that we, as a society, were willing to strike down the marital rape exemption in most states, thus sending a message to males that a $25 marriage license is not a license to rape their wives. We must send a similar message to males, through education and public policy, that that same $25 cannot buy them the right to rape any other woman.

Jean Johnston, Out in the Cold, in *Sex Work: Writings by Women in the Sex Industry* 29 (Frédérique Delacoste & Priscilla Alexander eds., 1988)

It is cold, a bare barren cold. The street is empty except for the fire and us "girls." We are the women waiting for work on the fringe of the park. Waiting near the fire which we built. Waiting for the warmth of a car, or maybe half an hour in a hotel room. Arctic air slices through my tight jeans and burns. I want to reach down and touch my legs so I can feel them, but it's too cold to take my gloved hands from my pockets.

Cherry is standing close by, staring at the fire. I put my arm in hers and pull her closer to the fire and to me. I don't have to worry that her man will see. He's sitting on the other side of the park in his green Cadillac. His car is probably turned on to keep him warm. Cherry once told me she met Tredwell when she was sixteen. "He had a yellow Cadillac then. And he had on a yellow suit with matching shoes." She comes from a small town in Ohio and when she looked out the window and saw Tredwell for the first time she said, "Mama, a movie star. There's a movie star downstairs!" Well, her mama knew all about Tredwell, but that didn't stop her baby from running off with him. Another time Cherry told me that she asked him what he was going to do when she got too old to work. He said he'd buy her a candy store or something like that. Maybe in Queens, that's where they live.

The fire starts to die down. Kim and Desi go into the park looking for some firewood. Cherry and I cross the street as winds whip into our flesh, through to the bone. On top of some garbage cans we find the Sunday News.

I hear a clanging sound and we grab the paper fast, running to the other side of the street. Behind us I hear rats scatter, but tell myself it's only the wind.

Desi runs down the street toward us, pavement hitting high heels. She has a table leg and throws it into the fire. I feel my face burning.

"Where's Kim?"

"She gotta date."

From under a brown suede cowboy hat Desi stares into the rising flames. Desi doesn't have a man. She's thinking about Lana, her woman. Desi doesn't want Lana working out here. One time Lana got stabbed by a trick on 12th Avenue. He stabbed her all over her arms and chest, then left her by the Hudson River to die. She almost did. So, now Desi works here to support Lana's kid who lives with her aunt in Brooklyn.

She throws more paper into the fire and I push it with a broomstick. The winds are blowing the fire toward her. She moves closer to Cherry and me.

A car turns the corner and Kim gets out of a tan Toyota. She's five months pregnant, but it doesn't show yet.

"How'd ya do?"

"Shit. There ain't no money out here tonight baby. It's too cold."

"Yeah, only ho's and fools out tonight."

Kim is nineteen. Her mother turned her out, five years ago, when she was fourteen. Her mother used to work out here, too, until she O.D.'ed on junk last year. They had the same man, Ronnie. He has an after hours club uptown. I go there sometimes after a good night, blow some coke and dance.

Another car is coming down the street. It slows up when it reaches the spot where we're standing.

"Wanna date honey?"

"You goin' out?"

Without even opening his window to answer, the guy in the black Impala nods and motions for me. I get in the car and he pulls off. He doesn't want to spring for a hotel, and parks under the Manhattan Bridge. The radio is playing. It's 4:00 a.m. The wind chill is 30 degrees below zero. This guy's going to get his money's worth because I'm not in any hurry to get back outside.

He comes.

Back on the street Cherry is alone crying by the spot where the fire has been.

"What's the matter, honey?"

"I'm freezing and Tredwell says I can't go home until I get a hundred dollars more."

"You wanna come home with me?" Wiping away her tears she shakes her head.

I took her home with me once, but Tredwell came looking for her. He told me, "You think you's a man, bitch. Running off with my ho like this." Then he took Cherry home and gave her a beating.

"Cherry, honey, I'm gonna go. You sure you won't come with me?" She shakes her head again.

Downstairs, the subway platform is as barren as the street above, but it's warmer. I think about Cherry, still out there in the cold. I feel helpless. The feeling fades as I count the money from under my wig. I put fifty dollars into my pocket and slip the rest back under my wig.

I ride the F train for two stops, reaching the street as dawn is breaking. I meet my man—the only man I really have—he's selling little cellophane bags of white powder fastened with red tape. I hand him fifty bucks for five bags, and tucking them into my glove, I walk away.

Gloria Lockett, What Happens When You Are Arrested, in *Sex Work: Writings by Women in the Sex Industry* 39 (Frédérique Delacoste & Priscilla Alexander eds., 1988)

When I was working on the street in Hollywood, the Los Angeles Police Department would round up a group of prostitutes. Before they would put is in the police car, they would take our purses, dump them on the ground, and make us pick the things out of the gutter. When they decided who was going to jail, looks were a big factor. The police would take the hands of the women who were not going to jail, and they would burn them on the hood of the engine. The women who were going to jail were piled in the back seat, usually six, seven or eight women. The police would drive us around for an hour or so, handcuffed, with people sitting on us. One time, the car was so crowded, one officer made me sit on his lap, handcuffed.

In Hollywood, the police arrested me for "obstructing justice" when I warned another prostitute of his presence. Both of my arms were almost broken when he picked me up by the handcuffs and threw me into the back of a pickup truck, which was the vehicle he and his partner used when trying to arrest prostitutes.

The first time Deborah got arrested, she was handcuffed behind. The officer was drunk and tried to kiss her and fondled her breast and body in the elevator of the hotel.

In San Jose, the police drive you around and leave you off in dark areas.

In Las Vegas, the police almost broke Deborah's arm when they arrested her.

In Berkeley, when the police used to drive us around in their cars for hours, one officer pulled into a very dark alley and demanded a blow job.

In Hollywood, a police officer who had responded to an ad in the paper (by that time we had stopped working on the street) came to our house in a car without a license plate. He pulled out his handcuffs so he could handcuff me to the bed and have intercourse with me. Luckily, I ran away.

I have been arrested thirty or forty times, who's keeping count? I've never done any time, but I have had to take cases all the way to jury trial at least nine times. In California, there is a mandatory thirty-day sentence for the second arrest, forty-five days for the third. The police make you think you will lose if you go to trial, so most women plead guilty and do the time.

Donna Marie Niles, Confessions of a Priestesstute, in *Sex Work: Writings by Women in the Sex Industry* 148 (Frédérique Delacoste & Priscilla Alexander eds., 1988)

When I was nineteen years old, I made what seemed like a conscious decision to become a prostitute. Having experienced sexual harassment on the job, in the streets, and in virtually every area of life, it was not a particularly fantastic leap to take. It was a very easy transition, raised as I was to be a female. I'm always surprised to find that more women don't choose to enter the life, especially those with extensive "dating" herstories. Any woman who has ever been on a date, who knows what it is to exchange affections or sex for dinner, or kindness, or survival, is quite prepared to be a hooker. Learning to serve, please and appease men is something that binds all women together. It's why secretaries, nurses, waitresses, wives, sales clerks, etc. are on the low paying end of the very same stick. To separate our experiences too much, or to believe that the ways we get by in this woman-hating world are so different, is a mistake. Women as either virgin or whore is one of the greatest lies that men ever created about us.

I took up working as profitably as I could within a structure that basically offered me either one man in marriage or many men for cash. As a white, educated, feminist hooker, I made more money than I ever expected to see again in life. Because I was an independent contractor, I had a lot of time left over to live my life in. These were two of the reasons why it was quite difficult to leave.

I'll never forget the depression I experienced in my first straight job out of the business. I was a secretary. As a prostitute, I had to keep moving, life was rarely predictable, and many people were interested in who and where I was: police, hotel security, tricks, cab drivers.

As a secretary, I was invisible, treated with either disregard or patronizing contempt. My credibility (i.e., getting heard or listened to) took a skydive as I changed from hooker to radical lesbian feminist. On top of this, I worked a regimented forty hour work week for ridiculously low pay. I was literally earning in two weeks what I had previously made in an evening, and paying taxes! It was a shocking welcome back to respectability.

But I have endured, and have not returned for many reasons. One of them is the exhaustion of the constant threat of arrest. It wears you out worrying about going to jail all the time. However, the major reason I left was I simply could no longer could [sic] justify working in an industry that profited from the sexual objectification of women. Since I felt I could no longer be in collusion with the men who make billions from our suffering, I had a lot of good-byes to work on. I said good-bye to the diet, fashion and the industries, and other institutions that tell me I am ugly and smelly and in need of alteration because I was born a woman.

When men sell women's bodies, or images of women's bodies, it is called pornography and it is legal, its right to exist vehemently defended with the first amendment. But when women sell their own bodies, it is called prostitution, and we can see what an imperative it's been to protect the rights of prostitutes in our society.

I began to get a glimmer of the magnitude, the enormity, behind the expression, "It's a man's world." I saw who was profiting from our blood, our loving, our bodies, and for whose profit and convenience every institution on planet earth was set up.

Ironically, I still expected them to give it all up. I can truly grasp the reformist feminist notion that by simply explaining, repeating the litany over and over, by holding enough demonstrations and writing enough letters, men will finally get it and abdicate. I spent years talking to men, trying to educate them as to the injustice of it all, explaining how feminism would save them, too. It was the only angle on feminism I was able to sustain their attention with.

Ultimately, I have come to realize that it is women who deserve that kind of loving, devoted patience, that passion and tenderness. We can't go around begging for their time, or attention, or power any longer. Men have no reason to surrender and no intention of handing over a system designed to nurture only themselves. We need to take back not just the night, but our lives if we are to have them.

Notes and Question

1. *Embedded Racism*. Evelina Giobbe identifies how racism contributes to the economic vulnerability of women of color and leads to and supports their sexual exploitation (p. 496). Giobbe's attack on the cultural mythology surrounding prostitution also provides a framework for analyzing white male supremacy and the racist stereotype of the African-American woman as sexually promiscuous. In *Ain't I A Woman: Black Women and Feminism* (p. 357), bell hooks describes how white slaveowners transformed rapes into prostitution by offering "a fine calico dress and a pretty pair of ear-bobs" (p. 359) and how abolitionists used the term *prostitution* to describe "mass sexual exploitation of enslaved black women" (p. 361). The myth that prostitution is a mutual economic exchange had the dual effect of making white men's rape of African-American women invisible and making African-American women "inherently wanton and therefore responsible for [their own] rape" (p. ^).

Vednita Nelson draws connections between the historical treatment of African-American women in the United States and the violence now perpetrated against African-American women used in prostitution.

> We are the silent majority, the invisible women. . .
>
> African American women used in prostitution never get heard, they are silenced by the myths that are attached to being Black and being used in the sex industry. These are "the bad girls, they get what they deserve, they like it, prostitution is a free choice.". . .
>
> There's a belief that prostitution is accepted in the black community. This is wrong. Prostitution is not accepted; it's been imposed on African Americans since the days of slavery when the master came out to the field and picked any Black women he chose to have sex with. Today middle-class White men from the suburbs drive through the ghettos of America to pick out any Black woman or girl he wants, as if our cities were his own private plantation. White men continue to assume free access to Black women. . . .
>
> Being Black and female in a White supremacist, male supremacist culture creates a very tight difficult space in which Black women struggle to survive. This place is where racism and sexism intersect. The mainstream feminist community must actively fight to end both systems.

Vednita Nelson, Black Women and Prostitution, 6 WHISPER, (WHISPER, St. Paul, Minn.), Summer/Fall 1992, at 1, 1.

2. *Unchastity*. Although the narratives by Jean Johnston, Gloria Lockett, and Donna Marie Niles reflect the differing experiences of women used in the

sex industry, they have as a common thread the sexual exploitation of the women by men. They raise the question of why the label "prostitute" or "whore" is used in our society to justify exploitation and abuse. Gail Pheterson theorizes about the social meaning of *unchastity* to explain the violence.

> As an adjective, "whore" is defined as "unchaste.". . .The whore stigma is specifically a female gender stigma which can be defined as "a mark of shame or disease on an unchaste woman.". . .
>
> One definition of unchaste is impure. Impure is defined as "dirty, mixed with foreign matter, adulterated, mixed with another colour." Unmistakably, such a definition activates associations of racial and ethnic diversity wherein only white, non-foreign people are chaste. . . .
>
> Women of color, Jewish women, and working-class women are vulnerable to the whore stigma as women *with a denigrated status*. . . .
>
> [U]nchastity is blamed for fatal corruption or pollution. In particular, the sexual unchastity assumed of prostitute women. . .is perceived as a choice wraught with shame and vulnerability. Violence, illness, and most extremely, death are considered the punitive consequences of self-imposed danger. . . .
>
> Disease, like violence, is often blamed on the unchaste. The whore stigma has been defined as *a mark of shame or disease on an unchaste woman.* Historically, even before sexual transmission of disease was understood, prostitution (the symbol of unchastity for women and men) was erroneously associated with epidemics such as the Plague. Also today, the attribution of disease to prostitution is often more based upon assumption than fact. Unchastity is assumed to begin with the whores and spread from them to chaste society via men. . . .
>
> Unchastity is used to justify oppression and abuse. Women in general. . .are especially subject to stigmatization as impure or defiled . . . .The task of recognizing unchastity as a normal human reality and not as a peculiar condition of inferior humans calls for a profound transformation of values and attitudes.

Gail Pheterson, The Consequences of Unchastity, in Sex Work: Writings by Women in the Sex Industry 215, 215-16, 225-27 (Frédérique Delacoste & Priscilla Alexander eds., 1988) (emphasis in original).

3. *Identifying Crimes Against Women.* Giobbe analogizes prostitution to marital rape and shows the similarities between these two forms of sexual violence. Kathleen Barry focuses on other sexual crimes and shows why prostitution should be included within the category of crimes against women.

> Crimes against women are defined as those acts of violence which are directed at women because of their female sexual definition. In committing a crime against a woman, sexual satisfaction, usually in the form of orgasm, is one of the intended outcomes of sexual violence for the aggressor who unites sex and violence to subdue, humiliate, degrade and terrorize his female victim. . . .
>
> The recognition of "crimes against women" as a special category of crime which is understood in the context of sex-structure of society and the social relations of power that men as a class hold over women as a class creating unequal gender identities, is the consequence of over a decade of ground-

breaking feminist research, analysis, action programs and legislative proposals. . . .

Yet, this analysis is incomplete without a consideration of the role of prostitution in the etiology of crimes against women. . . .[P]rostitution itself has not been considered a crime against women because the prostitute is recognized either as a willing participant or as a criminal herself. Recent research into female sexual slavery, the strategies that pimps use to procure women into prostitution and the subsequent conditions of the women working under pimps, documents coercion, torture and sometimes slavery of women in prostitution. Forced prostitution is a consequence of pimping strategies which include 1) the use of befriending or "love" to feign a relationship, create an emotional dependency and exploit a young woman's vulnerabilities until she can be "turned out" for prostitution; 2) fraudulent employment agencies procure young women and girls by promising them jobs in nightclubs as dancers or with modeling agencies which the victim finds after she has arrived are only covers for prostitution; 3) kidnapping, although less frequent in occurrence, continues to be a procuring strategy and in some countries where massive rural poverty can be exploited, young girls are purchased from their families and put into prostitution by procurers. . . .

To prepare new recruits for prostitution, pimps employ "seasoning" practices which are meant to break the will, change the legal identity, recreate the social psychological identity of the woman, and establish a dependency relationship. "Seasoning" often includes rape and systematic physical and verbal violence, humiliation and degradation until the victim's dependency upon the pimp is complete. . . .

Literal, abject conditions of slavery are now understood in the international human rights community to constitute a crime against women in prostitution. But under the influence of liberal ideology which guides the market economies of industrialized nations, when a woman is found to be in prostitution from economic necessity, she is understood to be engaged in a "profession," a form of work. She is seen to be acting from free choice and exercising her individual rights to engage in a "deviant" occupation in the sex industry which is viewed to be functioning according to the laws of supply and demand of a free market. . . .

To the prostitute, sex is the commodity that is sold. Prostitution is not a sexual experience for her, only for the customer. . . .The commodity exchange is reduced to woman's body parts separated from the self and the woman's sexual experience. For customers, this constitutes an essentially non-interactive, non-mutual sexual experience which establishes the basis for further demands of perversions and violence in the exchange. This is the same sex which is seized and forced in rape and other forms of sexual violence. Neither the prostitute nor the rape victim consider what they are subjected to as sex. But commoditized sex, purchased in prostitution, seized in rape is sex to the aggressor, for whom sexual satisfaction is usually achieved through orgasm. It is from this analysis of the intersection of prostitution through its sexual commoditization and rape that the etiology of crimes against women is traced back to the social construction of a deviant male sexuality which appears to be the same for the customers of prostitutes and for rapists.

Kathleen Barry, Social Etiology of Crimes Against Women, 10 Victimology 164, 164, 166-67, 169, 171-72 (1985).

Both Giobbe and Barry are using already identified forms of violence to reveal the violence in prostitution. Why is it so easy to hide the violence behind the curtain of market exchange?

B. Institutionalization of Prostitution

Judith Walkowitz, *Prostitution and Victorian Society: Women, Class, and the State.* 1–5, 196–213 (1980)

The Contagious Diseases Acts of 1864, 1866 and 1869 were introduced as exceptional legislation to control the spread of venereal disease among enlisted men in garrison towns and ports. By 1869, they were in operation in eighteen "subjected districts." Under the acts, a woman could be identified as a "common prostitute" by a special plainclothes policeman and then subjected to a fortnightly internal examination. If found suffering from gonorrhea or syphilis, she would be interned in a certified lock hospital (a hospital containing venereal wards) for a period not to exceed nine months. The definition of common prostitute was vague, and consequently the metropolitan police employed under the acts had broad discretionary powers. When accosted by the police, a woman was expected to submit voluntarily to the medical and police registration system or else be brought before the local magistrates. If brought to trial for refusing to comply, the woman bore the burden of proving that she was virtuous—that she did not go with men, whether for money or not.

The administration of the acts was extraordinarily complex, a testimony to the chaotic state of government expansion in the middle of the century. These were pieces of national legislation, officially overseen by the Admiralty and War Office, employing metropolitan police under the Home Office; yet they had to rely on provincial magistrates, doctors, and hospital authorities to enforce the sanitary and penal requirements. Not surprisingly, the opportunities for bureaucratic and jurisdictional conflicts were great.

Organized public agitation against the regulations first mounted in 1869, in response to the aggressive efforts of civilian doctors and authorities to extend the acts to the north. In December 1869 the National Association was formed, which excluded women from its first meeting, but soon opened its membership to them. This resulted in the formation of a parallel but separatist female organization, the Ladies' National Association (LNA).

Under the leadership of Josephine Butler, the LNA issued a sharply worded Ladies' Manifesto denouncing the acts as a blatant example of class and sex discrimination. The manifesto argued that the acts not only deprived poor women of their constitutional rights and forced them to submit to a degrading internal examination, but they officially sanctioned male vice. In the years to come, various repeal organizations proliferated, reflecting ideological, class, regional, and gender divisions within the repeal camp.

Between 1870 and 1886, when the acts were repealed, repealers sustained an impressive public campaign that sought both to educate public opinion about repeal and to influence elite political circles in Parliament. As part of their political agitation, repeal leaders and their paid agents descended upon the subjected districts, agitated among registered prostitutes, and encouraged them to resist the legal requirements of the acts. The subsequent controversy over the C.D. acts, as they were called in the nineteenth century, encouraged public discussion on a wide range of social, medical, and political questions. The double standard of sexual morality; the participation of women in political activity; the control of women by male doctors; and the role of the state in enforcing sexual and social discipline among the poor were all subjected to public scrutiny and debate.

Both the acts and the repeal campaign are familiar aspects of Victorian history that have never been adequately studied in their broad social context. Military historians and others have regarded the acts as a pragmatic response to a pressing social problem. From their perspective the acts were a realistic attempt to control prostitution and venereal disease in disorderly garrison towns and ports. However, the practical medical goals that underlay the C.D. acts were in fact fused with, and at the same time undermined by, a set of moral and ideological assumptions. In pressuring for the medical inspection of prostitutes without imposing periodic genital examination on the enlisted men who were their clients, architects of the acts obliterated from the start whatever effectiveness as sanitary measures the acts might have had. Just as important, regulationists reinforced a double standard of sexual morality, which justified male sexual access to a class of "fallen" women and penalized women for engaging in the same vice as men. Indeed, an earlier attempt to institute periodic examination among soldiers had failed because enlisted men violently objected and officers feared that compulsory examination would lead to the demoralization of their men. It was contended that such objections could not apply to prostitutes, who were presumably bereft of "self-respect" and more powerless to protest this intrusion.

This cultural interpretation, although important, does not explain, among other things, the timing of the acts. Why were they introduced in the 1860s, and why, from a European standpoint, so late? However blatant the sex prejudice, the acts were not simply a sign of the relative strength of the double standard in the mid-Victorian period. A casual acceptance of male sexual license was traditional among the British upper classes and continued to be upheld by aristocratic "reprobates" in parliamentary debates throughout the Victorian period. What may have changed was the increased official concern over prostitution as a dangerous form of sexual activity, whose boundaries had to be controlled and defined by the state.

The concern with prostitutes reflects another important ideological component of the regulationist position—a new enthusiasm for state intervention into the lives of the unrespectable poor. Both prostitutes and enlisted men were members of the social "residuum," the casual laboring poor who inhabited the "nether regions" of society. A source of cheap labor and illicit pleasures for middle-class Victorians, this social underworld was also the focus of deep-seated social fears and insecurities, most vividly expressed in the images of filth and contagion associated with the "Great Unwashed." Pollution became the governing metaphor for the perils of social intercourse between the "Two Nations"; it assumed heightened scatological significance in a society where the poor seemed to be living in their own excrement, and where the first programmatic attempt to deal with urban social problems was in the realm of sanitary engineering. Literally and figuratively, the prostitute was the conduit of infection to respectable society. She was nonetheless an object of class guilt as well as fear, a powerful symbol of sexual and economic exploitation under industrial capitalism.

The C.D. acts reflect this view of the social underclass as degraded and powerless, yet potentially threatening and disloyal. As military reforms, the acts were linked to a conscious policy to create a professional bachelor army and navy without family ties or local identities; military authorities additionally hoped that, by offering enlisted men controlled outlets for heterosexual activity, they could curb homosexuality in the ranks as well. For their part, local civilian officials warmly endorsed the acts as a means of curtailing street disorders and disciplining the unrespectable civilian poor in their community.

Through the control of sexuality, the acts reinforced existing patterns of class and gender domination. They illustrate the obsessive preoccupation with and codification of sex that, according to Michel Foucault, distinguished Victorian sexuality from the official sexual code of earlier epochs. The modern debate over sex, Foucault argues, was a strategy for exercising power in society. By ferreting out new areas of illicit sexual activity, a new "technology of power" and "science of sexuality" were created that facilitated control of an everwidening circle of human activity. The new "science of sexuality" identified sex as a public issue; rigidly differentiated male from female sexuality; focused attention on extramarital sexuality as the primary area of dangerous sexual activity; and "incorporated" perversions in individuals who, like the homosexual, were now accorded an exclusive and distinct sexual identity.

These shifts in focus and concern were embodied in and reinforced by the C.D. acts. Under the acts, extramarital sex became a question of state policy, a matter of vital national importance. A complicated "technology of power" was established to oversee and manipulate the social lives of the unrespectable poor. Special controls were placed on the female body in that prostitutes, not their male clients, were identified as the primary source of disease and pollution. This medical and police supervision in turn created an outcast class of "sexually deviant" females, forcing prostitutes to acknowledge their status as "public" women and destroying their private associations with the general community of the laboring poor. . . .

For most "public" women prostitution represented only a temporary stage in their life. The age concentration of registered women in their early twenties supports the likelihood that they had had prior work experience outside the home as well as noncommercial sexual activity. In addition, registered women appear to have stayed in prostitution for only a few years, leaving in their mid-twenties at a critical point in their lives—when most working-class women were settling into some domestic situation with a man. The timing here is important, for as long as prostitution represented a temporary stage in a woman's career, and as long as she could leave it at her discretion, she was not irrevocably scarred or limited in her future choices. . . .

Although prostitution represented a temporary stage in a woman's life, one would like to know whether she was rendered a social outcast during that transitional period. For prostitutes lived among the casual laboring poor, who were accustomed to hard times and who also had to make difficult, temporary accommodations to pressing social necessity. Poor neighbors were nonetheless of different minds about prostitutes. Some saw prostitution as a threatening and illegitimate form of social behavior. Others came to understand and tolerate prostitution as one of a series of strategies adopted by women to survive.

Plymouth and Southampton prostitutes resided in narrowly defined areas that were readily subject to police surveillance. In Plymouth, registered prostitutes inhabited the cramped streets and alleys radiating out of the Octagon, the pub and entertainment center of the Three Towns. The Octagon was centrally located on Union Street, Plymouth's major commercial thoroughfare. Here Plymouth prostitutes walked the streets in full view of respectable society, so much so that the wives of naval officers on their way to the penny bridge at East Stonehouse kept to the south side of Union Street, leaving the north side to public women and their customers. In contrast, Southampton prostitutes were mostly concentrated in the Simnel Street neighborhood, a closed-in area without good access to the new commercial district.

These disreputable "low" streets were repeatedly condemned in the local newspapers as infested with brothels and as sanitary abominations. The connection between the physical condition of the streets and the immoral behavior of the inhabitants was made clear in the town clerk's quip following the conviction of Maria Stevens, Granby Street, Plymouth, for brothel keeping in 1872: "The clerk jocosely remarked that the street was very unhealthy, its level being as low as the sea, and the inhabitants still lower."

Although these streets were notorious as brothel districts, in reality a more diverse social and economic life was present there. Residence on these streets was largely determined by economic necessity, although the general neighborhood tolerance of certain illegal or unrespectable behavior, as well as the availability of accommodations for transients, may have also attracted the large number of single men and women living outside their families. Although highly visible, these young people formed a distinct minority of the street population. Most people lived in families; even in brothels, prostitutes were outnumbered by members of the brothel keeper's family and by other lodgers living in families. The family operated as the main support system among people who existed just at or below subsistence level, where all adults and most children were required to contribute to the family income.

For most residents of these neighborhoods, the conditions of casual employment not only enforced economic cohesion within the family, but also required men and women to oscillate between casual work in large governmental and commercial establishments and odd forms of self-employment. Hence, fluctuations in income and occupation were experiences that neighbors shared in common with prostitutes. In addition, residents often found themselves on the wrong side of the law as well as physically constrained by institutions like the workhouse, prison, or in the case of prostitutes, the lock hospital, that were used interchangeably for the confinement of the social deviant.

The irregular pattern of these people's lives permitted and sometimes required a certain amount of geographic mobility. The movement of prostitutes and brothel keepers brought before the courts can be traced from one "furnished apartment" to another within a confined area. However, any "common" woman who ventured too far out of her neighborhood was highly suspect to the police, and the social isolation that existed among poor residents in different parts of town is striking. On the other hand, the summer exodus remained an established tradition among the Southampton and Plymouth poor. Although their migration into the towns was more or less permanent, this did not preclude an excursion during the summer to pick strawberries in Hampshire or to follow the fair circuit through Cornwall. Prostitutes also participated in the annual exodus: police noted that they regularly camped out in the summer and returned to town for the winter. . . .

Poor residents also adhered to standards of sexual and social behavior that were in sharp contrast to conventional Victorian mores. In 1882, the local clergyman of St. Peter's parish, Plymouth, asked his lady visitor to report on the moral condition of one of the streets in his parish. The street surveyed contained no lodging-house brothel but was adjacent to the notorious prostitute district. In her report, the lady visitor noted that many female residents who professed to be "respectable" were actually living with men out of wedlock. Most of the women had formerly been married, had been deserted or had exercised the traditional working-class option of self-divorce, and had subsequently established a new relationship with another man. To the shock and consternation of the lady visitor, the women defended the propriety of their action. "I," for example, had "three children by different fathers. Now living with a sailor, and passes for a married woman; says she is not ashamed of her baby—she never professed to be a Christian, and is not so bad as many that do make a profession." "W" was equally unrepentant. She was "married at registry office to a man whose wife is living, and argues that it is all right, as he [sic] first wife is remarried, and wrote a letter to give him leave to follow her example."

This flexible view of marriage and sexual respectability partially underlay the neighborhood toleration of prostitutes. The lady visitor also uncovered extensive financial connections between prostitutes and their more respectable neighbors. Some were "dressmakers to the girls," whereas others had relatives directly involved in the trade. "S," for example, "Seems to be living respectably now, but has her mother's likeness framed with the text round it 'Blessed are the dead that die in the Lord.' You remember the case. Mother kept a bad house."

The economy of prostitution on these streets hardly appears to have been highly formalized or rationalized: women were self-employed, paying only rent to lodging-house keepers, who nonetheless made larger profits off prostitutes than other lodgers, charging them anywhere from three shillings and sixpence a week for room only to thirteen shillings for room and board. Still, it would be incorrect to characterize the older women in charge of "disreputable" lodgings as the exploitative professionals generally associated with the term "brothel keepers." They were largely women with families, left to shift for themselves. Taking in lodgers represented one of the few ways that women could support their family. These women did not own the houses; they rented them from male landlords. And at least four Plymouth and Southampton women pleaded in court that they ran brothels to "keep the children off the parish."

Despite many shared experiences, prostitutes remained distinct from the social profile of their neighborhood in a number of ways. First, . . .their standard of living was perceptibly higher than that of other women. Second, their living arrangements also set them apart. Young women residing in lodgings appear strikingly cut off from the family system that was the organizing social and economic principle of these streets. Not only were they residing outside their families, but they were living independent of lovers and children as well. Prostitutes tended to form personal attachments with sailors who were not permanently in residence. As a consequence, sailors could not exercise the same kind of control over their women's lives as men who habitually lived off the wages of sin.

When not residing with their families, their lovers, or their own children, prostitutes did have female companions. Single women tended to live together in clusters of three or four in a few residences on Southampton streets and scattered throughout the notorious Plymouth streets. These groups formed the basis of an important and supportive female subculture. Most prostitutes were recruited into prostitution by other women—a process that is best understood as a system of access and initiation similar to that operating in other occupations. Prostitutes usually walked the streets together in twos and threes, both to protect themselves against physical abuse and to insulate themselves from the harassments of young boys. Repealers who visited their neighborhood made a special note of the "kindness and sympathy of those poor girls towards each other and their anxiety to aid and assist each other when in distress of any kind. . ."

Hence, prostitutes resided in special working-class districts as part of a distinct female subgroup. They lived among a very poor population that stood to benefit substantially from their commerce. It may be that many residents tolerated prostitutes more out of financial need than out of any strong sympathy and understanding of the women's plight. Yet this toleration easily wore thin if official pressure was brought to bear on neighbors and relatives who led very fragile social and economic lives. . . .

In their struggle for survival, the very poor maintained a delicate balance between private interest and public responsibility, between the toleration and the segregation of marginal social behavior. This fragile social equilibrium was upset by the enforcement of the Contagious Diseases Acts. On the one hand, the acts generated an extensive public resistance movement among the women and their community. On the other hand, by forcing prostitutes and their neighbors publicly to acknowledge what had been informally tolerated marginal behavior, they may well have forced a stricter redefinition of permissible behavior, thereby heightening the social isolation of prostitutes.

Among the prostitutes themselves one may observe a shift in attitudes and self-perception, forced upon them by the public exposure of the police registration and examination procedures. This is most plainly seen in the women's reaction to the periodical examination. Their vehement hostility to the internal examination may have partially been a reaction to the brutality of the doctors, as feminists alleged. No more than three minutes was spent on each examination; the instruments may have still been hot from immersion in boiling water (if they were sterilized at all). And of course, a tense, resistant woman could find the examination by speculum painful. Annie Clark found the examination "painful" and "disgraceful" and declared, "I would rather spend fourteen years in prison than submit to it." Elizabeth Hounsom, who held the record for multiple jailings—five—for refusing to attend examination, also maintained she preferred imprisonment to the "degradation" of the examination: "She tore the summons up when it was served upon her and did not appear at her fifth trial." Another woman who vowed to go to prison rather than to submit to examination told Josephine Butler, "We ought all to show the officers that we have some respect for our own persons.". . .

Nonetheless it would be misleading to dwell exclusively upon the brutal and sadistic character of the examination; more subtle means for humiliation were built into the whole procedure. In a society so profoundly class-bound as that of England, an examining physician would have had to do or say very little to make a registered woman feel worthless and degraded. The examination was demeaning because of its public character. Streetwalking at night was one thing; being forced to attend examination during the day, often taunted on the way by young boys who loudly questioned whether the woman were [sic] going up to the "Bougie Fair" or the "meat market," was another. One woman confided to a female missionary that "it was no use trying to reform now, she was registered as a prostitute and everybody would know what she had been doing, and what she was. Going up for examination, she said, was worse than going with 20 men. . ." The domiciliary visitation by the police and the central location of the examination house made it impossible for a subject woman to keep her private and public worlds apart. This is what destroyed her "self respect."

In this way the acts forced prostitutes to adjust their self-images. Repealers complained that the acts hardened the women by forcing many "who may not have made up their mind to continue as prostitutes" to acknowledge their outcast status. Although women appealing for legal aid to repealers made no attempt to hide the fact that they had been prostitutes, some certainly evidenced a strong ambivalence about their past and even expressed confusion as to what it meant to be a prostitute. Clearly the categories of acceptable social and sexual behavior were not that well defined. . . .

In fact, public shaming was one of the principal functions of police registration and surveillance. The "water police" made daily visits to known brothels; there they obtained the name of new arrivals and endeavored to place these women on the register. In many ways, they resembled both an occupying military force billeted on a subject population as well as a general morals police. Inspector Anniss actually lived above the examination house on Flora Street in Plymouth, around the corner from the most notorious Plymouth streets. Over the years, he was frequently called upon to testify at divorce cases, affiliation cases, and petty theft cases where a woman's character had to be ascertained. . . .

Through their surveillance and harassment the police made it impossible for a woman, once placed on the register, to have her name removed unless she left the district or married. Women complained bitterly of the "policemen a hunting you up. . .coming to your house, threatening you, and letting all the people around know what you are. If you wants to live quietly in your neighborhood, you can't do so. I've shifted more than once, but they were soon after you ordering you up to that beastly place." A Devonport magistrate, generally sympathetic to the acts but concerned about police intimidation, cited the case of Bessie Blewitt, who had abandoned prostitution and had gone to live with a man in a private house. In investigating the basis for her request to be removed from the register, the police went "several times to this house, where, in every probability. . .the persons she was lodging with would refuse to allow her to remain," forcing her back into a brothel. Indeed, according to the magistrate, Mr. Ryder, numerous women testified in court that they were remaining in brothels because they could not get any other place. This locked them into public registration as a prostitute. In the case of Elizabeth Bond, the justices said that "while she was lodging at a brothel the presumption was. . .that she was engaged in prostitution.". . .

The resistance of registered women and their community to the acts must be seen in the light of the economic and legal sanctions applied against those who tried to protect registered women. In the case of the Plymouth area, perhaps the police's greatest weapon was their power to inform against governmental employees and naval pensioners who let out rooms to prostitutes. If a pensioner proved uncooperative, his pension could be stopped, dock laborers and artisans could be dismissed, and pubs and beer shops harboring diseased prostitutes could be placed "out of bounds" for the men in service. The police also established a certain "discipline" among the unrespectable poor; brothel keepers brought to court on the complaints of moral reformers were sometimes exposed as police spies, reporting any new woman who took a room to the police in order to buy protection. . . .

The collective and individual support accorded prostitutes by their friends and neighbors underscores the role of women in those neighborhoods. Women seem to have been the organizing force behind public demonstrations in the defense of registered women. In their response to the Contagious Diseases Acts, they appear motivated by personal sympathy for the plight of a neighbor as well as by hostility toward the metropolitan police as interlopers in their community. Nonetheless the women of the community were clearly divided in their reaction toward registered women. Some bitterly opposed the presence of prostitutes on the streets. And even respectable women who aided prostitutes appeared ambivalent toward registered women; in some cases a deep resentment against the "water police" may well have overpowered a certain repugnance and distance they felt toward prostitutes. . . .

Women brought under the acts were often assisted by individual neighbors: hidden when police came, lent money, or permitted to pay their rent when they had the money. In 1883, at the trial of Mrs. Lang of 11 Central Street, Plymouth, for brothel keeping, Ellen de Courcy was asked how much she paid for her room: "She took a room from Mrs. Lang and paid her what she could." Although this may have perpetuated a system of indebtedness to brothel keepers, it also reflects the tradition of mutual aid among the poor, who understood much better than most middle-class reformers and philanthropists the character of seasonal and irregular employment and the hazards of poverty. . . .

In the face of glaring publicity, the women's support from neighbors, relatives, and friends inevitably crumbled. Many landladies experienced the same ambivalence toward subjected women as the latter's relatives. A basic concern over public respectability recurs in several cases. What bothered respectable neighbors was not the "immorality" of a young woman as much as the notoriety gained by police visits and the economic sanctions that could result. . . .

One can only speculate on the feelings of certain groups in these working-class communities who remained silent in the midst of the C.D. acts controversy. Young workingwomen who were not prostitutes articulated very little public response to the acts, although they may have participated in crowd activity on the streets and some may have signed the petitions against the acts that were circulated in these neighborhoods. . . .[Y]oung single women who chose to eke out a pitiful though respectable living may well have resented the flamboyant dress and easy spending habits of prostitutes. Part of their reticence may also have stemmed from motives of self-preservation, inasmuch as association with prostitutes rendered a woman's character suspect to the police and could lead to her name being placed on the registration list. One milliner who actually left Plymouth because of the system of police intimidation claimed that malicious neighbors contributed to this reign of terror by threatening "you with Water Police." She also noted that the general neighborhood response to subjected women was condemnatory: "When girls are arrested, all look on them with disdain; some perhaps with pity.". . .

By 1883, when the Contagious Diseases Acts were suspended, the character of prostitution in Plymouth and Southampton appears to have been distinctly altered. The women subjected to the acts were clearly getting older; much larger numbers were in the over-30 category. In the Devonport district, 106 out of 403 (26.3 percent) "known common women" were listed as thirty-one years and older for 1881, although there had been only 54 out of 557 (9.7 percent) in this age group in 1870. Southampton showed a similar trend: 4 out of 154 (2.6 percent) in 1870, as opposed to 20 out of 110 (18.2 percent) in 1881. Similarly, lock-hospital records document the increasing recidivist rate of registered women admitted to the lock wards throughout the 1870s. Hospital authorities acknowledged that their rehabilitation program only worked at all effectively with first-timers—women who had not yet entered upon a professional career of prostitution.

Contemporary reports confirm this trend toward professionalization. Both repealers and C.D. acts authorities noted that women were staying longer in prostitution, but predictably they disagreed on the reasons for this trend. Police officials tended to stress the improved health and increased longevity of prostitutes under the acts; repealers emphasized the stigma attached to being a registered woman. The latter also acknowledged that the women who remained in the districts profited from the system and bragged about being "Queen's women"—sanctioned by the government. What the change does suggest is that prostitution had become more profitable; because of police surveillance the amateur dollymops had been "deterred" and a streamlined, rationalized "work force" resulted. Also, as prostitutes became public figures through the registration process, it became increasingly difficult for them to gain respectable employment, and to move in and out of their other social identities. . . .

The history of the women of Southampton and Plymouth suggests the process by which working-class prostitutes were transformed into a specially identified professional class. But most of the accumulated evidence on subjected women presents a picture of poor women integrated rather than excluded from the community of the casual laboring poor. The eventual isolation of prostitutes from general lower-class life was largely imposed from above, although it received the passive acquiescence of the poor themselves.

It may well be that the experience of registered women was symptomatic of important and long-term changes in working-class life: a growing inflexibility in social norms and habits; a restriction in occupational identities and personal mobility. The isolation of a separate criminal class may have been a necessary corollary to the increasing social and legal pressures placed upon the poor to adhere to a more rigid standard of public respectability. Thus, it could be argued that the Contagious Diseases Acts, by establishing an unusually effective system of police surveillance and public stigmatization, simply accelerated a process occurring more slowly elsewhere. Criminal statistics for the late nineteenth century lend support to this thesis. The changing composition of registered women anticipates the national trend toward a general narrowing down of "antisocial" behavior among a smaller but more readily identifiable group of women—as indicated by declining arrest rates for women for both summary and indictable crimes, and by increased recidivism among women prisoners, who increasingly were to be found in older age categories.

Some indications of the changing character and dimensions of prostitution may be observed as well. If criminal statistics for the early twentieth century and the post-World War I periods are compared, in London, for instance, there was a notable decline in arrest rates for "known prostitutes," a change in the occupational background for those imprisoned, as well as increased recidivism among those imprisoned.

These changes were in part the result of new repressive public sanctions that stigmatized prostitutes and contributed to their social isolation as forcibly as the C.D. acts. The suspension of the acts in 1883 and their full repeal in 1886 extinguished any hope police might have cherished of using the acts to institute a national system of regulation, with formal brothels that would contain prostitution within carefully demarcated areas of cities. For some time the police in cities like Plymouth, Cardiff, and Liverpool tried to contain prostitutes in segregated districts. However, under pressure from social-purity groups in the last decades of the nineteenth century, police were forced to resort to an alternative policy of suppressing street solicitation and closing brothels. These repressive activities were facilitated by two new pieces of legislation—the Industrial Schools Amendment Act of 1880 and the Criminal Law Amendment Act of 1885. The Industrial School Amendment Act enabled police to remove children summarily from brothels and place them in industrial schools. Its intent was blackmail; working-class families were to be prevented from taking in prostitutes to supplement the family income, on pain of losing their children. Additionally, the Criminal Law Amendment Act of 1885 provided for easy summary proceedings against brothel keepers. Like the C.D. acts, these new measures helped to drive a wedge between prostitutes and their community. They were even more effective at destroying the brothel as a family industry, undermining the social and economic autonomy of prostitutes, and increasingly rendering them social outcasts.

Between 1890 and 1914, the systematic repression of lodging-house brothels was carried out in almost every major city in Great Britain. These clean-up campaigns were generally instigated in response to local pressure by social-purity groups. Purity crusades of this sort were conducted in Plymouth in 1904 and 1905, and the prostitute area in Southampton was deliberately cleared to make way for "civic improvements" in the 1890s. In many locales the legal repression dramatically affected the structure and organization of prostitution. Prostitutes were uprooted from their neighborhoods and had to find lodgings in other areas of the city and in the periphery. Their activity became more covert and furtive. Cut off from any other sustaining relationship, they increasingly were forced to rely on pimps for emotional security and for protection against legal authorities. This trend was noted with alarm by police and judicial authorities at the time. In 1895 one London magistrate waxed indignant at the self-righteous actions of vigilance committees, who were forcing prostitutes into the hands of pimps. The recent increase in the numbers of bullies, he maintained,

> has to a great extent been caused by those, who, in their excessive zeal, have made it impossible for a prostitute to live in apartments without a man living with her who appears to be her husband. The result of this has been that almost every prostitute is under the control of some bully who causes her to be a thief as well as a prostitute.

[T]he prevalence of pimps in the early twentieth century meant that prostitution had shifted from a female to a male-dominated trade and that there now existed third parties with a strong interest in prolonging women's stay on the streets.

Thus, by the outbreak of World War I, the organization of prostitution had undergone significant changes, mostly as the result of legal repression. Other long-term social and economic changes also helped to constrict the market for prostitution. Such trends began in the nineteenth century but culminated in the 1920s. The demand for commercial sex seems to have diminished by the postwar period, both because of the competition of "amateurs" and because of a decline in the unmarried transient male population. A similar decline in the "supply" seems to have taken place as well, a result of the economic transformation of the casual laboring-poor community. Historians have argued that decasualization in the late nineteenth century, and especially after World War I, transformed the life-style of the urban lower classes, affording the unskilled steadier incomes and higher real incomes. Despite high unemployment rates in postwar years, chronic casual poverty—which was the basic precondition for the kind of prostitution found in nineteenth-century cities like Plymouth and Southampton—had largely been eliminated by industrialization, a rise in real wages, and a decline in the birthrate and in overcrowding.

Nevertheless, it is unclear what the net effect of this improved living standard was for women. It may well have afforded women greater economic opportunity to support themselves, inasmuch as the real wages for women substantially exceeded prewar levels and increased mechanization expanded their employment opportunities. But it also may have made men more viable as supporters of the family, whether as husbands or fathers. The decline in mortality and birthrates and the easing of overcrowding may have helped strengthen the lower-class family unit, perhaps making it more possible for young women to remain at home longer. These developments may have further contributed to a privatized, home-centered culture and stimulated lower-class antagonism toward women who supported themselves as "public women."

More stringent public sanctions against unrespectable social behavior as well as economic access to the means of maintaining a respectable life-style seem to have had a decided impact on public prostitutes, poor workingwomen, and working-class culture in general. Decasualization may have meant higher real incomes and greater economic security, but also a significant loss of autonomy. As a result, the lower strata of the working class would be permanently enclosed within city walls, within the home, and within the bounds of respectable behavior, whereas the poverty and prostitution that persisted would be more invisible, isolated, and desperately anonymous. The history of Southampton and Plymouth prostitutes suggests the early outlines of this process, for their ultimate isolation from the community of the laboring poor marked an important formative stage in the making of an outcast group.

Notes and Question

1. *Josephine Butler*. Josephine Butler, who was born in 1828, was from a well-respected and wealthy family whose commitment to equality and social activism stemmed from their religious beliefs. Their views and activities greatly affected Butler's. *See* Nancy Boyd, Josephine Butler, Octavia Hill, Florence Nightingale: Three Victorian Women Who Changed Their World 23-30 (1982). In 1852 she married George Butler, a classicist, teacher, and Anglican priest, who had like-minded social views. *See id.* at 31-32. After losing one of her young children in an accident, she turned her attention to poor people.

> I only knew that my heart ached night and day, and that the only solace possible would seem to be to find other hearts which ached night and day; and with more reason than mine. I had no clear idea beyond that, no plan for helping others; my sole wish was to plunge into the heart of some human misery and to say (as I now knew I could) to afflicted people, 'I understand, I, too, have suffered'.

Id. at 37. It was in her work with poor people and her investigation into the causes of poverty that Butler became knowledgeable about prostitution. *See id.* at 38. She took young women into her home and ultimately established a home for women who, whether sick or healthy, had no prospect of employment. *See id.* at 38. In doing this, Butler came to believe that education for women was an imperative and devoted her energies to the movement for women's higher education. *See id.* at 39. In 1869, however, she redirected her energies to lead the campaign against the Contagious Diseases Acts. *See id.*

> It was, she well knew, a battle against formidable odds, pitting the poor and female against the rich and male. Victorian society would not look kindly on a wife who, with every possibility of domestic happiness, left the sanctuary of her home and the security of marriage to an Anglican priest to go to the aid of women of the gutter. She would be exposed to a double evil:

the viciousness of the life of the street and the equally dehumanizing anger of a male middle class that would turn on anyone who questioned its privileges and assumptions. The cause would consume all her energies and bring down scorn, hatred, and possibly even violence upon her family.

Id. at 39-40.

2. *AIDS.* Women in prostitution continue to be perceived as agents of disease, as in their contemporary identification with the spread of HIV (human immunodeficiency virus) and AIDS. Minouche Kandel examined the link between AIDS and prostitution as well as the law's response to that link in her 1990 study of the Boston Municipal Court's [BMC] treatment of prostitution.

In recent years, the outbreak of AIDS has created a new "justification" for enforcing prostitution laws. The concern that judges in the BMC reveal most frequently in the court papers I examined is that the AIDS epidemic has made prostitutes a public health threat, and that the judicial system should be mobilized to stem the spread of AIDS in this context. As one BMC judge put it, "There ought to be posters up in the Combat Zone that say "Prostitution = Death." Some judges in the BMC will use the knowledge that a prostitute has AIDS to deny her or him bail or make bail exceptionally high. . . .

[There] is. . .[a] current trend in some states requiring mandatory HIV testing of people arrested for or convicted of prostitution. At least nine states currently have such laws. Nevada has created a separate criminal offense for people who prostitute knowing they have AIDS. [*See also* Fla. Stat. § 796.08, at p. 555.]. . .

Admittedly, a significant number of street prostitutes test positive for the AIDS virus. However, several recent epidemiological studies question the extent to which heterosexual prostitution is responsible for the spread [of] AIDS in the United States.

While there is substantial data on HIV transmission from men to women, there are far fewer reported cases in the United States of women infecting men. One reason is that, as compared to men, fewer women in the general population have the virus. A second explanation is the lower efficiency of female-to-male AIDS transmission. . . .

Another factor which minimizes the risk of transmission is that the vast majority of street prostitutes provide oral sex rather than intercourse. The chance of contracting AIDS from receiving unprotected oral sex is quite small. Condom use further mitigates the risk of transmission. In short, recent data does not support the theory that prostitutes contribute significantly to the spread of AIDS in the United States.

Judges also see arrest/incarceration as a means of protecting prostitutes themselves from the risk of AIDS, a risk they view as inextricably tied to their work. Studies indicate, however, that in the United States prostitutes are at the greatest risk of contracting the HIV virus not from random intercourse with clients but through intravenous drug use. It is not surprising that a CDC study of prostitution in seven U.S. cities found that risk factors for AIDS in female prostitutes may be similar to those in other women living in the same geographic areas. . . .

> [E]ven among drug using prostitutes who may be HIV-positive, there is no conclusive evidence that prostitutes in the United States are responsible for spreading AIDS to their clients.

Minouche Kandel, Whores in Court: Judicial Processing of Prostitutes in the Boston Municipal Court in 1990, 4 Yale J.L. & Feminism 329, 340, 343-45 (1992).

For a further discussion of the connection between prostitution and disease, especially AIDS, see Saundra Sturdevant & Brenda Stoltzfus, Disparate Threads of the Whole: An Interpretive Essay, at p. 540.

3. *Heterosexism*. Judith Walkowitz suggests that authorities were interested in controlled heterosexual prostitution in part to curb homosexuality in the military ranks (p. 511). In what ways do the institutionalization of prostitution and heterosexism converge today?

4. *Boundaries*. Walkowitz describes the process by which the regulation of prostitution under the Contagious Diseases Acts rigidified the social category of prostitute. Neil Larry Shumsky explores in a parallel manner the creation of physical, legal, and moral boundaries in the late nineteenth-century and early twentieth-century United States.

> According to Kai Erikson, every group of people maintains boundaries. "Its members tend to confine themselves to a particular radius of activity and to regard any conduct which drifts outside that radius as somehow inappropriate or immoral." His theory also contains an implicit definition of a deviant—"a person whose activities have moved outside the margins of the group." Therefore, "deviant persons often supply an important service to society by patrolling the outer edges of group space and by providing a contrast which gives the rest of the community some sense of their own territorial identity." Erikson also argues that every society has its own way of deploying deviants and deviance; and he identifies three which appear frequently: special days on which rule violation is tolerated, special societies in which deviant behavior is considered normal for adolescents, and special clubs whose business it is to infringe ordinary group rules. Finally, Erikson posits a particular kind of deployment pattern characteristic of American society—"deviant behavior as the special property of a particular class of people who were more or less frozen into deviant attitudes." Americans have "generally thought it best to handle the problem by locking these people into fairly permanent deviant roles."
>
> In American cities between roughly 1870 and 1910, the segregated red light district served as another form of boundary maintenance—literally as well as figuratively. Nearly every advocate of segregation emphasized the need to avoid contaminating respectable neighborhoods and to separate moral from immoral behavior, just as traditional public health proponents had fought for the quarantine of biological plagues. The argument appeared repeatedly in New York City during the 1870s and 1880s. Letters and editorials in the *Times* questioned the desirability of police raids on disorderly houses and suggested that the major result would be to drive prostitutes into neighborhoods currently free from the nuisance. One study of Chicago's police department suggested that prostitution "be hammered and kept down" but not to the "extent of scattering it all over the city" and into the residential portions.

The foreman of San Francisco's grand jury of 1913 wrote Mayor Rolph that repression would not end prostitution, but simply scatter it into respectable neighborhoods. The district gave people a choice; they could either go there or avoid it.

And this was the point. The existence of the district allowed people to declare themselves openly—to accept or reject the new standard of morality. A New York City grand jury of 1876 advocated segregation because "patronage. . .would be limited to those who are not ashamed or afraid to be seen" in the district. After a police raid in 1883, a group of citizens protested. They preferred prostitutes to be confined to an area "known and avoided by all the respectable people" rather than be in places where one's presence was no sign of shame. One doctor summed it up most fittingly. If a cesspool existed, "let it remain a cesspool." Avoid spreading its contamination everywhere. "Isolate it." People who wanted prostitutes "would go to them. Those who wished to avoid them could do so. They were well known for what they were." The red light district clearly demonstrated the difference between acceptable and unacceptable behavior and thereby set boundaries for respectability.

The toleration of prostitution in a special, segregated district leads to yet another important question—where was this region to be located? The proponents never answered the question directly; they said only that it should be kept isolated from respectable neighborhoods. But even though they failed to definc the difference between respectable and unrespectable overtly, it is possible to understand the distinction from the actual locations of the districts. The red light district was universally restricted to poor or marginal neighborhoods of American cities. . . .

The comfortable classes believed that large numbers of less well-to-do people had different sexual standards and feared that without the segregated district these different mores would lead to attacks on "respectable" women. In this attitude, they reflected a general belief that the poor and the immigrants were vicious, licentious, and animalistic. Witnesses before Congressional committees throughout the 1870s, 1880s and 1890s made this point regularly and told lurid anecdotes—presumably illustrative of immigrant and working-class depravity. . . .

[A] major concern to respectable Americans in the latter half of the nineteenth century. . .[was w]hat should be done about what they perceived to be the rampant, uncontrolled, and uncontrollable sexuality of groups like workingmen and immigrants . . . .They could not afford to marry, but, it was feared, if some outlet was not provided for their sexual urges, they would run amuck and attack respectable women on the streets. Obviously, because of their animality, celibacy was not an option. Because of contemporary medical belief, masturbation could not be advocated. And because of social, sexual, and religious strictures, homosexuality was not even considered. The only remaining option, if the wives, mothers, daughters, and sisters of respectable Americans were to be protected, was to provide an arena for the deployment and control of other men's sexuality. . . .

Thus, accepting the existence of the red light district was part of the community politics of the era. American cities were becoming divided between the haves and the have-nots. There was a shifting balance of power with a dis-

> proportionate share of the resources—social, political, and economic—going to some segments of the population. Those who gained from the new distribution of resources wanted to entrench themselves further by controlling their adversaries. At the same time, they wanted to keep peace within the community and isolate themselves from the contagion of infection. One way of doing so was by providing their rivals with a separate space within which to act, a space within which to watch over, regulate, and subdue the lower, working, and immigrant classes.

Neil Larry Shumsky, Tacit Acceptance: Respectable Americans and Segregated Prostitution, 1870-1910, 19 J. Soc. Hist. 665, 671–74 (1985/1986).

Lucie C. Cheng, Free, Indentured, Enslaved: Chinese Prostitutes in Nineteenth-Century America, 5 Signs 3, 3–21, 29 (1979)

In societies undergoing rapid industrialization, prostitution serves a double economic function. It helps to maintain the labor force of single young men, which is in the interest of the capitalists who would otherwise have to pay higher wages to laborers with families to support. In addition, prostitution enables entrepreneurs to extract large profits from the work of women under their control and thus accumulate considerable capital for other investments. Further, in multiracial areas, prostitutes of minority or colonized groups can also provide cheap labor themselves. Chinese prostitutes in the nineteenth-century American West performed all three functions as free agents and as enslaved and indentured workers.

After the formal abolition of black slavery, the capitalist mode of production predominated in nineteenth-century America. However, aspects of slavery persisted in varying degrees among racial minorities, for example, in contract labor and in Chinese prostitution in California. White prostitution on the American frontier quickly moved from a precapitalist form of organization to one characterized by either a partnership between madam and prostitutes or a relationship of employer and wageworker. Chinese prostitution, in contrast, remained a semifeudal organization until the twentieth century. While sexual prejudice obscured the exploitative nature of prostitution as a business, a sense of racial superiority at first led whites to condone Chinese female slavery. In addition, the linkages between the emigrant societies in China and the Chinese community in California helped to perpetuate the precapitalist relations in prostitution. Chinese prostitution also provided Chinese entrepreneurs one of the few opportunities to accumulate capital in a hostile society. . . .

Victimized by population pressure, landlord oppression, and foreign imperialism, many peasant families in nineteenth-century China lived on the edge of subsistence. In a number of communities, particularly in Fujian and Guangdong, where emigration to distant lands was feasible, a large proportion of the male population left home in search of employment.

In times of natural disaster and war, families often resorted to infanticide, abandonment, mortgaging, or selling of children. Females, whose labor was less valuable than that of males, were frequently the first victims of extreme poverty. Furthermore, in patriarchal and patrilineal Chinese society, the family that raised a girl would not benefit from her labor and she could never carry on the ancestral line.

One remunerative solution for relieving the family of its female members was prostitution: the family did not have to provide for the girl's upkeep and her sale or part of her earnings could help support the family. The importance of this for the survival of the family is seen in the report of a Qing dynasty official, that ten family members were dependent for their sustenance upon every prostitute in Canton.

The discovery of gold in 1848 along the Sacramento River brought thousands of immigrants from many countries to California. Mining was an exclusively male activity; few of the men brought families with them because, among other reasons, mining involved moving from place to place seeking the most productive site. Among the first female arrivals were prostitutes of varying racial and national origins. In San Francisco, where miners from nearby sites congregated during the winter and where immigrants gathered before they went into the mining areas, prostitution became a lucrative business. It was not uncommon for successful prostitutes to use their earnings to finance the miners or to invest in other pursuits. The tremendous sexual imbalance. . .and the lack of alternative employment made prostitution a major occupation for women. . . .

Only a few women crossed the Pacific on their own in search of better compensation for their labor in prostitution. Usually the family, not the girl, arranged the sale. Girls often accepted their sale, however reluctantly, out of filial loyalty, and most of them were not in a position to oppose their families' decision. In addition, the sheltered and secluded lives that women were forced to live made them particularly vulnerable to manipulation, and many were tricked or lured into prostitution.

An important but unexplored facet of the relationship between patriarchy and prostitution in the Chinese case is its role in perpetuating Chinese sojourning abroad and in its support of the migrant labor system in America. The Chinese patriarchal family system discouraged or even forbade "decent" women from travelling abroad. In addition, the anti-Chinese sentiment and violence in California was often cited by immigrant Chinese merchants as a major reason for not bringing their families. These two factors discouraged the emigration of Chinese women, who would have made possible a stable Chinese community in America. The failure of the Chinese to form families that would reproduce the work force locally prolonged the use of the Chinese by American employers as a migrant labor force.

Further, the patriarchal system required the preservation of the relationship between the men who went abroad to seek work and the families they left behind. It was common practice for the emigrant male to marry before his departure to insure that a wife be at home to fulfill his filial duties and with luck to give him a male descendant. These married women in the emigrant communities of China and Hong Kong, as noted by Chen Ta and Watson, were under more watchful eyes than their counterparts in nonemigrant communities. The relatives were charged with the duty of keeping the women of the emigrants "pure," and in return the emigrants were obliged to send their earnings to support their families. This arrangement permitted the preservation of the Chinese family at home and the perpetuation of the Chinese emigrant laborer's sojourning role in America. The emigrants, whenever they could afford it, returned to China to sire a child. If the child was a boy, he eventually joined his father in America. This arrangement recirculated Chinese labor in the migrant labor system; and the home villages of China reproduced the labor force, in terms of procreation and child rearing, for work in America.

Chinese prostitution was an integral part of that arrangement. While patriarchy prohibited the emigration of "decent" women, it did not forbid the emigration of prostitutes. The emigration of Chinese prostitutes helped to stabilize and preserve the family because Chinese emigrant males could thereby avoid liaisons which might lead to permanent relationships with foreign women. On the other hand, the earnings of Chinese prostitutes in America helped to support their families in China. . . .

The phenomenon of Chinese sojourning and the use of Chinese as migrant labor could not be attributed to poverty, patriarchy, and prostitution alone. Equally, if not more important, was the racist hostility of white society. In addition, like the European colonists who often made sure that the African laborer's wife and children did not follow the man to his new workplace, American capitalists paid low wages to Chinese men to deter their women from crossing the Pacific. (The same phenomenon is observed in Western Europe today.) Some whites in California advocated the importation of more Chinese laborers and not their women so they would not establish a permanent population here; others advocated the importation of more Chinese prostitutes who could meet the sexual demands of Chinese men and thus lessen the threat they perceived to white womanhood. Similar arguments were later advanced by whites in Australia vis-à-vis Japanese prostitutes.

Despite these mutual economic and social advantages, profit was undoubtedly the major reason for the creation and maintenance of the traffic in prostitution. Two distinct periods of Chinese prostitution in California corresponded with two types of relations in profit making: (*a*) the initial period of free competition, during which the prostitute was also the owner of her body service; and (*b*) a period of organized trade, during which the prostitute was a semislave and other individuals shared the benefits of her exploitation. . . .

The brief period of free competition (ca. 1849-54) was characterized by individual initiative and enterprise. Like their white counterparts, a number of Chinese prostitutes during this period were able to accumulate sufficient capital to leave the profession. Some returned to China as relatively affluent members of the business community. Others remained in America and either continued in prostitution as brothel owners or invested in other businesses. . . .

This period of free competition among owner-prostitutes did not last long. Few Chinese prostitutes could afford the transportation expenses or had the business know-how to take advantage of the situation. Still, the affluence of the male residents and the extreme imbalance of the sexes suggested that a considerable sum of money could be made in the business. That prospect attracted Chinese entrepreneurs, who organized various aspects of the business; specialization occurred and a monopoly developed by 1854 under the control of the Chinese secret societies. . . .

In contrast to the first phase, the second period of Chinese prostitution in California (ca. 1854-1925) was characterized by a widespread organization of the trade with a network of specialized functions extending across the Pacific to Canton and Hong Kong. The persons chiefly responsible for this trade were the procurers who kidnapped, enticed, or bought Chinese women; the importers who brought them into America; the brothel owners who lived by their exploitation; the Chinese highbinders who collected fees for protecting them from other highbinders; the police who collected monies for keeping them from being arrested; and the white Chinatown property owners who leased their land and buildings for exorbitant rents.

The process by which brothels in San Francisco obtained their inmates was complex. The owner of a brothel recruited workers either by taking a trip to Canton or Hong Kong or by securing them through an agent or importer. A West Coast newspaper reported that agents of California brothels regularly went about China buying girls and young women. These agents received a regular circular or "price current" from San Francisco giving them information concerning the state of the market and the maximum prices which could be paid to derive an acceptable profit.

Luring and kidnapping were the most frequent methods of procurement, particularly after 1870. When the agents did not find enough females to fill their orders, they sent subagents into rural districts to lure or kidnap girls and young women and forward the victims to them at the shipping ports. Quite frequently those individuals who did the luring were returned emigrants from that community. The baits used included promises of gold, marriage, jobs, or education. Sometimes the victims were invited to see the big American steamer anchored at the docks, and while they were enjoying the tour, the boat would sail off to San Francisco. More often, kidnapping was carried out by force, and the victims were sometimes daughters of relatively well-to-do families.

A number of women came to San Francisco under a contractual arrangement similar to that described in the Chinese contract coolie system. The contract involved body service for a specified time, and if the prostitute succeeded in fulfilling the terms of service, she could, theoretically, get out of the business. Families, rather than women themselves, participated in these transactions. Most Chinese women, who could not read or write, could easily be duped into affixing their thumbprint to any document by the agent or party who was the beneficiary of the contract.

In the organization of the trade, importation was a separate activity from that of procurement. Importers received the women from the recruiting agents, arranged for their passage, and handed them over to the brothel owners upon arrival in the United States. Although other secret societies were known to have engaged in the traffic of women, the Hip-Yee Tong was clearly the predominant importer during the third quarter of the nineteenth century. It was estimated that between 1852 and 1873, the Hip-Yee Tong alone imported 6,000 women, or about 87 percent of the total number of Chinese women who arrived during that period. The Hip-Yee Tong charged a $40 fee to each buyer, $10 of which were said to have gone to white policemen. The Hip-Yee netted an estimated $200,000 between 1852 and 1873 from the import business.

The traffic in women became more difficult after the passage of the code which allowed the commissioner of immigration to prevent certain classes of people, including "lewd or debauched" women, from immigrating to California, and the enactment of the Page Act of 1875. The immediate effectiveness of these laws in reducing the number of female arrivals is unclear, but the statutes did subject women to close scrutiny both in Hong Kong and San Francisco and eventually made it more expensive to import women. These added expenses took the form of bribes which had to be paid to various U.S. consulate and customs officials.

The American consulate in Hong Kong was charged with the initial examination of Chinese women to determine if they were "lewd or debauched." If the consul's office was convinced of their good character, it would stamp the women's arms and send them to the harbor master, who would do the same. Only then would the women be allowed to purchase tickets and board the steamer. The certificate with the woman's photograph issued by the consulate was mailed to the collector of customs at San Francisco. Women without appropriate documentation were refused landing and often had to wait more than twenty-four hours before they were cleared. This procedure was subject to abuse by corrupt consular officials, who could be convinced of a woman's good character with money or could refuse to certify a woman's good character without money. It was discovered in 1879 that Consul Bailey's office received $10-$15 for every woman shipped to the United States during his tenure in Hong Kong.

Americans on this side of the Pacific also benefited materially from these new statues [sic]. As noted by the U.S. Supreme Court, the 1873 code was subject to a variety of abuses: "It is hardly possible to conceive a statute more skillfully framed, to place in the hands of a single man the power to prevent, entirely, the vessels engaged in a foreign trade, say with China, from carrying passengers, or to compel them to submit to systematic extortion of the grossest kind." The commissioner, noted the Court, could arbitrarily designate immigrants as paupers, idiots, convicted criminals, or prostitutes and deny them entrance on that basis.

These regulations benefited white lawyers as well as the customs inspector. Some lawyers colluded with the Chinese importers in obtaining habeas corpus decrees to allow the landing of Chinese women headed for the brothels. Although a number of these women were legal immigrants, some probably sought the help of American lawyers because U.S. customs officers were dissatisfied with their documentation.

The Chinese Exclusion Act of 1882 allowed only women who were native born, married, or born overseas to domiciled merchants to immigrate to the United States. Accordingly, enterprising Chinese developed elaborate arrangements to continue the traffic in women. Chinese agents in the United States instructed agents in China to coach the emigrant women in responding to questions by the immigration authorities. These coaching papers, circulated in Hong Kong and Canton, included eighty-one questions on subjects ranging from standard personal details to the geography of San Francisco. . . .

As importation became increasingly complex and expensive, the Hip-Yee Tong gradually lost its monopolistic control over the traffic. Because of the increasing complexity and costs of importing prostitutes, the price for their delivery skyrocketed. After 1870, for example, girls who originally sold for $50 in Canton now brought $1,000 in San Francisco. And in the 1890s it was reported that as much as $3,000 in gold was paid for a single Chinese female in San Francisco. . . .

Eventually, however, faced with the dwindling supply of females in China, the nearly prohibitive costs and difficulties of procurement and importation, and the loss of prostitutes from brothels in San Francisco to other cities and mining towns, the tongs were forced to look for their supply locally. Whereas local Chinese women were supplementary to overseas recruitment previously, after 1882 they became the major source of new supply. It was reported that, in just one week in February 1898, eight women were kidnapped for prostitution. . . .

After the women had been transported to Chinatown, they were housed in temporary quarters known as "barracoons" to await their distribution. One barracoon reputedly held up to 100 women. Those who had been imported for specific customers left when their owners paid the passage fare and the $40 fee. The others were carefully dressed and displayed before the bidding. Well-to-do Chinese in San Francisco purchased the cream of this lot as concubines or mistresses. The remainder fell into two categories: the best went into higher-class brothels reserved only for the Chinese, while the rest were sold to inferior dens of prostitution which served a racially mixed clientele.

The distinction between higher- and lower-grade brothels was one of both class and race. Chinese men generally felt that the most degrading thing a Chinese woman could do was to have sexual relations with a white man. However, because of their comparatively low fees of twenty-five to fifty cents, the lower-class prostitutes were visited by whites and Chinese alike, while higher-class prostitutes had an exclusively Chinese clientele. Thus, the lower-grade prostitutes tended to attract the poorest laborers, teenage boys, sailors, and drunkards. They were often mistreated by their owners as well as their customers. A few brothel owners, for example, occasionally even beat some of them to death, and white men often forced them to engage in aberrant sexual acts. Prostitutes in mining camps served both Chinese and white clients and were often more harshly treated than their counterparts in San Francisco.

The lower-grade prostitutes lived in rooms usually not larger than 4 x 6 feet, often facing a dimly lit alley. "Bright cotton hangings hung in the doorways leading off from the main room or were sometimes used to break a larger room up into smaller compartments." These rooms were sparsely furnished, usually with only a bamboo chair or two, a washbowl, and hard bunks of shelves covered with matting and set against the wall. The door, normally the only opening to the outside, was invariably covered with bars or a heavy screen behind which the woman would stand and call to passersby.

The prostitutes who only served Chinese generally lived in upstairs apartments and had more or less long-term, regular customers. Very often the prostitute's client was also her owner. It is not always accurate to characterize them as prostitutes, for some may have been concubines while others may have lived in polyandry. These higher-class prostitutes were often attractive and expensively adorned. Although they may have appeared to be well treated, they were nevertheless chattel, "one day loaded with jewels, the next day to be stripped and sold to the highest bidder, if it were the desire of their masters."

Neither lower- nor higher-class prostitutes received regular wages, but the latter were sometimes asked to entertain at parties given by tong leaders and Chinese merchants, and they were permitted to keep the jewelry, silk, and cash gifts given to them by their customers. This is perhaps how some prostitutes were able to send money to their parents in China.

The exploitative relations between the prostitute-worker and the procurer and brothel owner are clear. The capital outlay—kidnapper's fee, passage, bribes, legal fees—was minuscule compared with the profits from the woman's labor as a prostitute. For example, the cost of her passage would have been around \$50 if she traveled in the same manner as the Chinese male laborers, and at the most \$150 if she had comfortable accommodations, no doubt extremely rare. The kidnapper's fee was once reported at \$185. And although we do not have data on the exact amount of bribes and legal fees, it seems safe to say that these did not usually exceed \$100, though they became increasingly larger as restrictions on Chinese immigration grew.

The most profitable way of importing a woman, from the procurer's point of view, was to lure the woman to go with him or her voluntarily to America. In one such case, the procurer, after painting a glowing picture of life in California and paying \$98, obtained the consent of a girl's mother to permit her daughter to emigrate. Upon arrival, the procurer sold the girl for \$1,950, a net profit of at least \$1,700. This girl continued to bring in profits for her owner by laboring two years and averaging no less than \$290 per month. At the end of the two years she was resold for \$2,100. The brothel owner's gross income from her labor as a prostitute and from her resale was about \$9,060; even if she was kept at a higher standard of living and if we deduct the cost of her purchase, the brothel owner's net profit was no less than \$5,000 in two years.

Besides kidnapping and luring, Chinese women entered American brothels under a system of contract mentioned before. Although this was on the surface the least exploitative form of Chinese prostitution, it was in fact devised to mask those features which permitted the procurers, importers, and brothel owners to derive considerable profits without any real advantage to the prostitute or indentured worker. The contracts were drawn up in appealing terms: they offered the contractee free passage to America, an advance of over \$400, and a limited period of labor of about four and a half years. The contract system seemed all the more attractive considering that females were often sold for about \$400 at the time.

In reality, though, the contract system offered very little advantage over the outright sale or slave system and was, in a number of ways, more brutal because it raised false hopes. First, the length of a prostitute's career, as noted before, was about four or five years. Thus, as far as the brothel owner was concerned, a prostitute was useful only for about four years, the period of the contract. Second, the terms of the contract specified that the person must work a minimum of 320 days, failing which the contract period could be extended to one additional year. Third, the contract prostitute would have less incentive to run away because of her limited period of labor. Fourth, her family was discouraged from redeeming her because the repurchase price included an exorbitant interest. And finally, even after a woman had served out her contract, there were cases in which she continued in servitude and was not released. . . .

A fourth way in which Chinese women entered San Francisco brothels was through outright purchase; in this case the women were no more than slaves. Initially, the average capital outlay for a woman brought over in this way amounted to no more than $600: the purchase price, the cost of passage, and the expenses associated with importation. But as immigration restrictions became more severe and the complexity of the importation system grew, the cost of buying and importing a prostitute likewise increased. The purchase and importation of a seventeen-year-old prostitute named Tsoi Ye illustrates this process. Tsoi Ye was sold in Hong Kong in the 1880s for a little over $400. She was resold by the procuress to a tong man for $882, who in turn entrusted a Chinese sailor to bring her over. After she was landed successfully, she was resold to a brothel for $1,800 in gold. Despite the high cost, it is clear that brothel owners found it profitable to purchase women at such prices due to their potential earnings as computed above. . . .

White landlords, many of whom were prominent citizens of San Francisco, owned most of the real estate in Chinatown, and they extracted high rents from brothel owners, often double or treble the rent they received from whites. According to the Bureau of Labor Statistics, the average rental per month of a flat consisting of three to six rooms in San Francisco was $14. The Chinese brothel owners probably had to pay no less than $28 per month or $336 a year. . . .

The exploitation of Chinese prostitutes was not limited to sex alone but also included their labor as semiskilled workers. Many sources indicate that in the daytime, when business was slack, women in the brothels sewed buttonholes and pantaloons and worked on shirts, slippers, men's clothing, and women's underwear. The work was farmed out by sweatshops which subcontracted with the manufacturers. Since these female operatives probably did not receive payment for this extra work, the brothel owners and sweatshop owners reaped a handsome profit.

There were still other forms of exploitation. Besides the tax levied on brothel owners who were not tong members, the tongs imposed a weekly tax of twenty-five cents on every Chinese prostitute. If any woman refused to pay, they promised to use "harsh measures" to collect. These harsh measures included whipping, torture by fire, banishment to brothels in the mining regions, and finally, shooting and killing the victim. Blackmailing Chinese prostitutes was another method employed by the tongs to extort money. Members of a tong, noted one report, "went around among Chinese prostitutes and told them that a new chief of police had come in, and unless he received a handsome present, would shut up the houses. They collected from one and a half to five dollars from each one, and it was divided among the members of that society."

Owners of brothels sometimes also owned opium dens and gambling joints. A number of prostitutes were addicted to opium and/or gambled excessively. The owners often encouraged these addictions so that the loans needed to feed them would increase the prostitutes' debts. Desperate women committed suicide by swallowing raw opium or drowning themselves in the bay.

The best thing that could happen to these women was to be redeemed and married. Occasionally a white male fell in love with a brothel inmate and married her after having paid the owner. However, most of the men who married prostitutes were Chinese laborers. Chinese working people did not attach the same stigma to prostitution as whites did. One reason might have been that prostitutes in China were generally not seen as "fallen women" but as daughters who obeyed the wishes of the family. Although prostitution was not considered an honorable profession, particularly among the gentry, women who were able to get out of it were usually accepted in working-class society. Furthermore, the fact that there was such a shortage of Chinese women in San Francisco during this period would have tended to relax the sex mores that men might have held.

Apparently, quite a few women in San Francisco were able to leave the brothels, although not without struggle, and often at tremendous risk. Throughout the mid-nineteenth and the early twentieth centuries, reports of such instances abound. Typically, a woman ran away to a mission, the police station, or her lover, with the hired tong soldiers in pursuit. The lengths to which the tongs would go in recapturing a runaway prostitute indicated her value to her owner. The tongs often kidnapped the escaped woman or even used the American courts to get her back by filing a charge of theft, claiming the woman had absconded with some clothes or jewelry. After the police had located the woman, the tongs would hire white lawyers to arrange for her bail and then return her to the brothel. If that tactic failed, they placed public announcements on Chinatown walls, warning others who might assist her escape and offering rewards for her capture. . . .

As further insurance against the escape of a prostitute, tongs gave the local police a retainer fee. Until 1877, a Special Police Force was engaged in a quasi-official capacity as peace officers in Chinatown. They received no set wages but derived their income from the Chinese residents. Normally, the "Chinatown Specials" collected fifty cents a week from each prostitute, and they admitted that whenever there was a crackdown on prostitution, their income was reduced. Tongs also made payments to City Hall to secure its agreement not to interfere.

As mentioned before, a prostitute's work life in the brothels was normally four to five years, not surprising in the absence of sound medical care. The abundance of Chinese advertisements of "secret formulas" for curing syphilis and gonorrhea during the period testifies to the prevalence of such diseases. Although some doctors blamed the Chinese prostitutes for spreading the diseases to the white population, it was pointed out by other physicians that these illnesses were equally, if not more, prevalent among white prostitutes in San Francisco.

When a woman was no longer profitable as a prostitute, she might work as a cook or a laundry woman for the brothel. If she was hopelessly ill, she would be left to die by the brothel owners. Although, in general, the remains of the Chinese male laborers were shipped back to their place of nativity for burial, few cared about the remains of these working women. The *Alta* reported in 1870 that the bodies of Chinese women were discarded and left on the streets of Chinatown. . . .

The institution of Chinese prostitution was characterized by many layers of exploitative relations. Men and women, Chinese and white, reaped benefits from their oppression. The development of Chinese prostitution as a large enterprise in nineteenth-century California was related to both material and ideological conditions in the two countries; to the need for cheap labor in California and the economic underdevelopment of China; and to white racism and Chinese patriarchy.

Notes and Question

1. *More on Prostitution in San Francisco in the Nineteenth Century.* Lucie Cheng's study demonstrates both how racism and sexism can become the foundation of a system of economic profit-making and how prostitution is a basic component of the economic system itself. Jacqueline Baker Barnhart also studied prostitution in San Francisco during the last half of the nineteenth century and found that

> [t]here were only two non-American groups of professional prostitutes in San Francisco who did not significantly improve their social or economic condition by coming to California: Latin Americans and Chinese. Although individual Chinese or Latin American women might occasionally achieve both financial and social success, most were consistently on the lower steps of the institution's hierarchy. In both cases the cause seems to be that the majority of these women were, in effect, indentured into prostitution.
>
> In the first wave of forty thousand immigrants who came by ship in 1849, seven hundred were women, mostly Latin Americans. In some cases, the women themselves made arrangements with ship captains to carry them to San Francisco, where payment for the trip could be found. More often, however, cantina owners would contract with a captain to recruit women in his ports of call, or possibly send an agent to recruit them, guaranteeing the fare and a commission for the procurer. In the first few years of the gold rush, this was an extensive and lucrative speculative venture. Women, as an importable cargo, offered higher profits and less risk than other commodities. In return for passage, the women usually had to indenture themselves for six months to whoever paid their way. . . .
>
> The estimates of prices paid to the procurers for women range from twenty-five to two thousand dollars, according to the source, the period, and the condition of the sale. No definite fee is recorded for the ships' captains who brought Latin American women to San Francisco. Prices are equally obscure for Chinese prostitutes procured in the early years. Two Australian women sold on the docks in 1850, however, brought fifteen dollars apiece. . . .
>
> What is clear in looking at the many economic sectors of a nineteenth-century city like San Francisco is that prostitution was not a separate economic subculture. Some cities, such as Denver, tried to separate prostitution from the rest of the city by restricting it to a given area, but the institution was not simply a matter of individual prostitutes, their madams, or their cadets.

It was a large-scale and widely ramified business based, like all businesses, upon financial gain, and the profits from prostitution were woven intricately throughout society's business and social community. The multiplier effect applies to prostitution as well as to other businesses.

Jacqueline Baker Barnhart, The Fair But Frail: Prostitution in San Francisco 1849-1900, at 43, 79, 81 (1986).

Studies such as Cheng's and Barnhart's are important in understanding prostitution because they reveal contemporary society's legacy of violence, coercion, and exploitation. What is the role of prostitution in today's economy?

Desire has cash value; the market has no rules, possesses no scruples. From Eastern Europe to the Himalayas, from Tokyo to Tegucigalpa, transaction by sordid transaction has created a multibillion-dollar sex trade. It is encouraged by massive socioeconomic movements: the collapse of the Soviet empire, the increase in global mobility, the wrenching disparity of worldwide incomes. But its effect is most devastating on an individual level. Poor women and children are commodities traded on the street, products bartered, haggled over, smuggled and sold as hedges against hunger or as cruel but quick routes to profit. Souls do not count, only bodies, debased over and over, unmindful of social cost or disease.

Margot Hornblower, The Skin Trade, Time, June 21, 1993, at 45, 45.

2. *Mail-Order Brides*. The business of selling women to men in what is referred to as the "mail-order brides" industry is thriving, as Venny Villapando reports.

Selling Asian women is a thriving enterprise because the number of American men who seek Asian brides continues to grow. . . .In 1984 the Gannett News Service reported that seven thousand Filipino women married Australians, Europeans, and Americans. The *Wall Street Journal* noted that in 1970, only 34 Asians were issued fiancée-petitioned visas; while in 1983, the figure jumped dramatically to 3,428. . . .

[T]he mail-order brides business succeeds partly because it takes advantage of the economic deprivation faced by women in underdeveloped Asian countries. . . .

Added to economic exploitation, a major cornerstone of the mail-order bride business, is the prevalence of racial stereotypes. They have a widespread effect on the treatment of women and influence why so many men are attracted to mail-order romance. "These men believe the stereotypes that describe Oriental women as docile, compliant and submissive". . . .

Many of the Asian countries affected by the revived mail-order bride business have a history of U.S. military involvement. Troops have either fought battles or been stationed in Korea, the Philippines, and countries in Southeast Asia. During their stays, the soldiers have often developed strong perceptions of Asian women as prostitutes, bargirls, and geishas. Then they erroneously conclude that Asian American women must fit those images, too. Consequently the stereotype of women servicing and serving men is perpetuated. . . .

[T]he women's unfamiliarity with the U.S. immigration laws. . .[is] one of the most disturbing aspects of the business. "As a result [of the ignorance], they may miss an opportunity to become a naturalized citizen, forfeit rights as a legal spouse, or live under an unwarranted fear of deportation which may be fostered by their spouse as a means of control."

Venny Villapando, The Business of Selling Mail-Order Brides, in Making Waves, An Anthology of Writings By and About Asian American Women 318, 321-24, 326 (Asian Women United of California ed., 1989).

3. *A Human Rights Question and United Nations Action.* Trafficking in women for sexual exploitation has been an issue for international treaty making throughout the twentieth century. As Laura Reanda suggests in her study of the United Nations, international efforts to curb prostitution have been ineffective.

In the nineteenth century, early feminists considered state regulation of prostitution to be legalized slavery and fought against it in their countries and in the colonies, where mass prostitution was being organized to serve the needs of colonial troops. At the beginning of this century, however, trafficking in women became an issue for international treaty-making, primarily because of concern over the export of prostitutes from Europe to brothels in various parts of the colonial empires—hence the term "white slave traffic." Traffic within national borders was specifically excluded as a matter of domestic jurisdiction. . . .

When the League of Nations was established, the question of traffic in women was considered of such importance that it was included in the Covenant itself. Article 23(c) entrusts the League "with the general supervision over the execution of agreements with regard to the traffic in women and children. . . .". . .

[I]nternational efforts began to focus on ending the "regulationist" system (i.e., the licensing of houses of prostitution and the registration of prostitutes). In 1937 the League of Nations prepared a draft convention on the subject, which would have been concluded at an international conference in 1940, but for the outbreak of the Second World War. Eventually, the task of preparing a new international instrument was assumed by the Economic and Social Council of the United Nations. . . .

In 1946 the United Nations Economic and Social Council approved recommendations concerning the continuation of the activities of the League in the social field, including those involving the question of traffic in women and children. . . .

The text submitted by the Secretary-General eventually became the Convention for the Suppression of the Traffic in Persons and of the Exploitation of the Prostitution of Others [of 1949]. In accordance with the recommendations made earlier by the experts of the League of Nations, the main purpose of the Convention was to promote an end to the "regulationist" approach in favor of the "abolitionist" philosophy. Its primary intent was to punish trafficking, procurement, and exploitation, regardless of the victim's age or consent. It declared, for the first time in an international instrument, prostitution and the traffic in persons to be "incompatible with the dignity and worth of the human person and [to] endanger the welfare of the individual, the family and the community." The Convention did not distinguish between national and international traffic and made brothel-keeping and similar practices punishable. States parties to the Convention undertook to end systems of registration of prostitutes. . . .

[The] provisions would appear to establish at least the backbone of an international system for the suppression of trafficking in persons and for the reintegration into society of former prostitutes. The Convention, however, has a number of weaknesses. A fundamental problem is that it makes no provision for international supervision. It only requests that states parties annually communicate to the Secretary-General of the United Nations any laws, regulations, and other measures adopted by them to give effect to the Convention. The Secretary-General is directed to publish "periodically" the information received and to send it to all member and nonmember states of the United Nations (Article 21). A mechanism for receiving these reports and other information was established only in the mid-1970s, when the followup to this Convention was brought within the framework of the human rights program. However, procedural and other difficulties have so far continued to hamper efforts to supervise implementation . . . .A further drawback of the Convention has been the low level of international support: as of 1 March 1988, the Convention had been ratified or acceded to by only fifty-nine states. Even if an effective reporting system could be established, it would apply to only a minority of countries, and not necessarily those with the most problems in this area.

Perhaps not surprisingly, the Convention has come under increasing criticism in recent years. NGOs [nongovernmental organizations] have charged that its vague terminology and ineffective implementation machinery have allowed states to ignore its application. The Convention has also been faulted for being based on the traditional distinction between enforced and voluntary prostitution, and calls have been made for a new international instrument that would consider all prostitution as a form of gender-based discrimination rooted in sexual violence and violation of human rights. It has also been said that the Convention does not cover modern forms of prostitution, such as sex tourism and forms of traffic disguised as employment abroad, marriage markets, and the like. States parties themselves have expressed unhappiness with the terminology used in the Convention, stating that it lends itself to a variety of interpretations and therefore makes the Convention difficult to implement.

In 1987, in light of increasing dissatisfaction with existing measures, the Sub-Commission on Prevention of Discrimination and Protection of Minorities recommended that an additional protocol to the Convention be drafted covering modern forms of prostitution and providing for an implementation mechanism modelled after the Torture Convention. The proposal, however, was not accepted by the Commission on Human Rights. For the time being, therefore, this Convention remains the most complete international instrument available, despite its shortcomings. Attention likely will continue to concentrate on ways of making the existing machinery work more effectively.

Laura Reanda, Prostitution as a Human Rights Question: Problems and Prospects of United Nations Action, 13 Hum. Rts. Q. 202, 207-11 (1991).

In 1991, the United Nations Educational, Scientific, and Cultural Organization [UNESCO] and the Coalition Against Trafficking in Women (an NGO in Consultative Status with the Economic and Social Council [ECOSOC] of the U.N.) sponsored a series of meetings to develop a new Convention on the Elimination of All Forms of Sexual Exploitation of Women. The proposed convention, which addresses a broad range of sexually exploitative practices, includes the following Article:

> States Parties reject any policy or law that legitimates prostitution of any person, male or female, adult or child, western or third world; that distinguishes between forced and free prostitution including promotion of the "right prostitute" [sic]; or that legalizes or regulates prostitution in any way as a profession or occupation, and agree to adopt appropriate legislation that recognizes prostitution as an acute form of sexual exploitation, including the following,
>
> a) Punishment of any person who procures, entices, or leads away for the purposes of prostitution, another person, even with the consent of that person; exploits the prostitution of another person, even with the consent of that person; keeps or manages, or knowingly finances or takes part in the financing of a brothel; knowingly rents or lets a building or other place thereof for the purpose of the prostitution of others.
>
> b) Penalization of the customers, recognizing them as perpetrators to be criminalized while rejecting any form of penalization of the prostitute.
>
> c) Holding liable the producers and distributors of pornography, recognizing that the pornography industry enlarges the demand for, promotes, and is actively engaged in sexual exploitation.

Convention on The Elimination of All Forms of Sexual Exploitation of Women, Art. 6 (Revised Draft Mar. 1, 1993). In June 1993 this proposal was presented to the World Conference on Human Rights. *See* Hornblower, *supra*, at 51.

Saundra Sturdevant & Brenda Stoltzfus, Disparate Threads of the Whole: An Interpretive Essay, in *Let the Good Times Roll: Prostitution and the U.S. Military in Asia* 300, 303–09, 314–18, 321–26 (1992)

As early as 1902, toward the end of the three-year war between the Philippine Independence Movement and the United States, Governor-General William Howard reported that every military post in the Philippines had "houses of prostitution." At that time, the U.S. military sanctioned and facilitated the existence of brothels, due to the "physical necessities" of the troops, and the required weekly VD examinations by American physicians and surgeons of women working in houses of prostitution. This procedure did not result in lowering the disease rate . . . .

Within the United States, a similar procedure was followed. Among U.S. troops involved in the border war of 1916 with Mexico, about 30 percent [of the]. . .troops were infected. Again, it was military medical officers who inspected brothel women every two weeks and issued each a certificate validating the lack of disease. With World War I and the need for combat-ready troops, physicians within the military found that their primary focus was not treating the injured but keeping men fit for action through control of venereal disease. . . .

The situation was deemed critical, and policing of women selling their sexual labor was extended to the civilian sector. By March 1918, thirty-two states had passed laws requiring compulsory examinations of all women employed in this labor market. In practice, authorities sought to detain each infected woman until she tested negative. Legislation was also passed to place young women and girls convicted of prostitution in detention centers.

A notable antifemale rhetoric accompanied these official military and civilian efforts. It was the woman selling her sexual labor who was accused of "draining the virility" of the men. . . .Although the women selling their sexual labor near military installations in the United States were often ill-educated migrants from rural areas, the guys were clearly the ones who had to be protected, the ones to benefit from "draining the red-light district as one would drain a swamp.". . ."Bad and diseased women can do more harm than any German fleet of airplanes" was a popular slogan.

"Draining the swamps" would continue to be a tactic up through the end of World War II. . . .

The military began widely using penicillin in 1944. If the guys could not "say no," then they were instructed to take a prophylactic. Pro-kit stations were virtually everywhere, and condoms were distributed en masse. . . .

Since the end of World War II, the U.S. military has been involved in two large-scale wars in Asia. The need for "rest-and-recreation" (R&R) facilities has been and continues to be a major component of civilian and military policy formulated to ensure that support systems are in place for U.S. military personnel on duty outside the United States. Access to indigenous women's bodies has been recognized as a necessity. No longer is there disagreement between, on the one hand, those in the military and their civilian supporters who advocated and put into place R&R facilities and, on the other hand, those who cautioned against such practices or advised that they be located a reasonable distance from military bases.

It is important to note the paucity of information on the topic of the sale of women's sexual labor for either the Korean or Vietnam War periods. . . .

There are hundreds of works focusing on the devastating course of these wars and their impact on the lands, the peoples, and the fabric of society of those involved. But it is amazing that so little is known about the lives of the millions of prostituted women in these two countries. Nor is there any study of the nearby countries of the Philippines, Thailand, Taiwan, and Okinawa and Japan, which experienced a tremendous growth in the sale of women's sexual labor during these years. . . .

As we have stated, by 1944, the U.S. military no longer considered syphilis and gonorrhea deadly diseases. They did continue the policy of providing pro-kits, condoms, and educational warnings against the prostituted women that would necessitate the use of these items. This policy continues into the present. So, too, does the policy of U.S. military direction in policing, examining, treating, and certifying the women providing sexual labor to U.S. troops.

In both the southern part of Korea and the southern part of Vietnam, there were great numbers of women selling their sexual labor. . . .

The manner in which sexual labor was sold varied. At one end of the continuum, there was the woman who worked as the "wife" of a guy while he was in town or in country; she was called a "key woman," because the guy had a key to her place. . . .

These "key women" were few in number compared to those who worked in the approved/legal bars and brothels. A greater number worked on the streets and in off-limits areas. In order for a bar or brothel to be approved and licensed to provide entertainment and sex for U.S. military personnel, the women working there had to undergo periodic medical exams for VD, and, if found positive, undergo treatment. Bars and brothels not approved and licensed, or those with too many women testing positive, were off-limits. In Vietnam, there was a sign inside many of the bars saying that women who wore a certain badge were "clean" and thus could be purchased for their sexual labor.

Vietnam also had "recreational areas." At Lai Khe, there was a one-acre compound surrounded by barbed wire with American MPs on guard at the gate. . . .There were two barracks inside. Each had two bars, a bandstand, and sixty curtained cubicles in which Vietnamese women lived and worked. Many of these women were refugees; others had previously worked in Saigon. They were recruited by the province chief who took a payoff and channeled them into town where the mayor of Lai Khe also got a cut. The Americans "kept their hands clean" by leaving the procurement and price arrangement to Vietnamese. The Americans, however, regulated the health and security aspects. Army medics checked the women once a week for VD. . . .

Although during the Korean War the U.S. Air Force based squadrons on Okinawa that flew bombing missions over the territory of the northern part of Korea, it was during the Vietnam War that the Okinawan R&R industry experienced its greatest growth. . . .Army and Marines from Vietnam took R&R on Okinawa. The U.S. military used the "A" sign for "approved" to indicate which bars and brothels were legal. . . .

Yakuza, or gangs related to *yakuza*, controlled the sale of Okinawan women's sexual labor during this period. Control was exercised primarily through physical and psychological terror and intimidation. Once the women had been placed in a brothel, the brothel owner exercised another form of direct control over them through the "advance loan system." Under this system, the owner paid the gangs a certain amount of money for the woman. This purchase amount became the woman's debt, to be worked off through sale of her sexual labor. . . .

Although it is clearly U.S. policy to have women's bodies free of disease and available for men in the military, it is the economic, political, and social realities of the host country that determine how access to women's sexual labor is to be accomplished. If the host country is sufficiently disrupted by war and/or economically impoverished, there are women who will become prostituted. We have seen how this was the situation in Korea, Vietnam, and Okinawa during specific time periods. If local women are not available, or not available in sufficient numbers, or if the country is economically powerful and the women therefore too expensive, the occupying military must provide its own women. The French military in Vietnam had mobile brothel units of Algerian women. By the time the Americans replaced the French, the country was disrupted by war to the extent that sufficient numbers of Vietnamese women were available. In present-day Okinawa, Okinawan women are too expensive. Thus, women from the Philippines are brought to Okinawa to provide sexual labor for U.S. troops. Okinawan male leadership defends this commodity importation on the political and moral grounds that the U.S. military demands women for sexual labor. If Filipinas did not provide it, the military guys would use and threaten "respectable" women of Okinawa. The Filipinas provide a barrier that ensures the safety and well-being of Okinawan society. . . .

Today, in both Korea and the Philippines, the Social Hygiene Clinic (SHC) system is used to try to ensure "clean" women for U.S. servicemen. All bar areas outside a U.S. base have a SHC. All women selling their sexual labor in those areas must be part of the SHC system, with identification to prove their legitimacy and therefore "cleanliness." Women who do not have such an ID are subject to arrest. . . .The SHC is the avenue for doing business.

In both countries, the woman is given a medical check-up before receiving her ID passbook. Afterward, she is tested—once a week in Korea and every other week in the Philippines—for VD, gonorrhea, and syphilis. . . .In addition, the women are required to have a chest X-ray and blood test every six months and an AIDS blood test every three months in Korea and every six months in the Philippines. If a women tests HIV positive in the Philippines, she is given virtually no information about what that may mean. . . .

The U.S. "keeps its hands clean" to a greater or lesser extent in both countries. In Korea, the SHC receives no funding or assistance from the U.S., but the U.S. military does participate in spot checks of women's VD identification cards and conducts sanitary inspections of the bars. . . .In both countries, local women who are with American military men may be stopped on the street and asked to show an identification passbook and/or a night-off pass. Failure to show these forms of identification may mean time in prison for the woman.

This system of control is made possible only through a cooperative working relationship between the U.S. military and the local government and bar owners, who are members of an almost exclusively local male elite.[2] It is they who benefit—financially and politically—from the control and regulation of the prostitution industry. . . .

Prostitution around U.S. military installations in Asia has been effectively legalized regardless of the laws within each country. Like legalization elsewhere, it has enabled a high degree of regulation and control of the sale of women's sexual labor and of control over the distribution of profits from that sale. . . .

The sale of women's sexual labor has historically been at the base of economic systems of considerable proportions, though seldom to the benefit of the women themselves. This pattern continues today around the military bases in the three countries of our study, as well as in the areas of tourist prostitution that have become big business for the governments, elites, and businesspeople of the Philippines, Thailand, and Korea.

The tourist playgrounds and U.S. military base towns have considerable sim-

---

2. Bar owners in the Philippines may also be retired U.S. servicemen, particularly in Barrio Barretto and Subic City. A small number of bar owners are Filipinas.

ilarities, because the R&R centers developed by the U.S. military during the Vietnam War became the model for the development of the tourist prostitution industry in Asia. Some of the more famous tourist playgrounds are found in Manila, Chejudo, and Bangkok. The power relationship between industrialized countries and the Third World is integral to the sale of sexual labor in tourist areas and in base towns. Essentially, the rich buy and the poor sell. Those who play in the R&R playgrounds, whether tourist or military, are primarily men from Northern Europe, North America, Australia and Japan; those who work in the playgrounds are Third World women and children. The primary economic exchange is the sale of sexual labor, and the system ensures that the women receive a meager portion of the money earned in the business. . . .

But playgrounds are only one arena in which Third World women's sexual labor is the primary economic exchange. The international exchange of Third World women as prostitutes, domestic servants, and wives is another aspect of the power relationship between industrialized countries and the Third World. Women who work overseas as domestic servants often find that they are required, with or without their consent, to provide sexual labor to their bosses on a regular basis. They are raped. The mail-order bride system provides women for men from industrialized countries who cannot find or do not want women from their own country. These men are purchasing both sexual and domestic labor. Both the mail-order bride business and recruitment for overseas employment are sometimes used to trap women into selling their sexual labor in other countries.

When discussing potential marriage to an American, women in Olongapo often comment, "What he wants is a maid." This is not without a material base. A Navy guy will often pay a woman's steady bar fine while his ship is in Olongapo, usually for about five days. During that time he stays with her. She provides both sexual labor and the labor of a domestic servant—doing his laundry, cooking for him, and bathing him. . . .

Bathing is an instructive example of a complex situation. Although it is done in a way that makes the men feel they are being served and cared for, bathing is a precaution taken by the woman to make sure that the men are clean and to get rid of offensive odors. Bathing is one small aspect of the lives of the women whose sexual labor is being purchased, but it exemplifies how different something appears when seen from the perspective of the women. Their lives, however, have rarely been spoken about or photographed with much depth or sensitivity. . . .The silence exists both because prostituted women in the Third World are not considered important enough to take note of and because the U.S. does not want publicity about the GIs' off-duty hours.

When the silence is broken. . .two dominant and seemingly disparate images come into play. Photographs or cartoons depict a woman in the bikini worn by ago-go dancers. She is striking a seductive pose and has very large breasts. She appears to be enjoying herself immensely—the happy hooker. She is often shown happily chasing U.S. servicemen or waiting for them at the gate to the base. The contrasting image is that of the victim—the woman so desperately poor that she has no other alternative but to sell her sexual labor. Depending on the political slant of the article, she is either the symbol of imperialist oppression or she is being helped by the presence of the base through the job or money provided; if the base were not there, she would starve. . . .

The simplistic and superficial treatment of prostituted women constantly communicated to the public through the use of the ago-go and victim images is a continuation of the historical misogynist gaze that reduces all prostituted women to one stereotypical woman, thus doing injustice to the variety and complexity of the women's lives. . . .

The judgment of the women as hopelessly pro-bases that is implicit in the ago-go dancer image is also unjustly simplistic. This image is usually bolstered by accounts of pro-bases demonstrations in Olongapo or Angeles, where women from the bars participate in large numbers. In fact, in Olongapo, women will be fined a substantial sum by the bar owners if they don't participate. The fine will be deducted from their commission before it is given to them. In more extreme cases, women have lost their jobs for refusing to participate. It may be true that a majority of women in the clubs favor the retention of U.S. bases, but digging deeper one again sees complexity. The same women who favor retention of the bases also prefer not to be working in clubs. They would like other work. If the question is changed from "Do you want the U.S. bases to stay?" to "If you were able to have other work after the U.S. bases left, would you want them to stay?" [t]he result might be very different responses.

Most women from the clubs realize that with a low educational level, finding other work in the Philippines or Korea is very problematical. Not only are jobs scarce but the stigma of having worked in a club also makes it difficult to find other work. In Korea, the stigma is greater for those who have U.S. military personnel as customers. The existence of children also intensifies the difficulty of leaving the work. A child fathered by a U.S. serviceman is living evidence of what a woman's work is or has been. Amerasian children present more difficulties in the very homogeneous culture of Korea than in the Philippines with its variety of peoples and languages. . . .In the Philippines, if the child is Euro-American, acceptance is greater than if the child is African-American. Being lighter skinned in the Philippines is an indication of belonging to a higher class and/or being closely associated with the colonial power. . . .

A primary function that such images as victim, ago-go dancer, and diseased. . .serve is that of creating and maintaining distance. Whether she is morally reprehensible, politically hopeless, a victim of poverty, or diseased, she is Other. She is in a different class, the class of women required by the U.S. military for the morale of its boys. Such distance is important for the continuation of the bar areas and control over the women. Maintaining the distance is the reason that those in power do not want the silence broken or the images changed. They do not want anyone educating the public about the bar areas and they do not want anyone educating the women in the bars. The women must be kept in an isolated enclave. . . .

The ago-go-dancer image passes judgment on the women. They will therefore be left to their own devices. Distance is maintained. The victim image may provoke a social-work type of response which will take a few women out of the clubs but will not challenge the structure significantly. Distance is maintained. And there are plenty of fresh young women available to take the place of those removed by social workers. But if the empowerment process begins, if the women become educated and begin organizing, they may soon threaten the power structures. And if the distance is overcome, if other women are in solidarity with the women in the clubs, a crisis may occur in the power relationships. . . .

Who are the guys? They are the members of the all-volunteer military . . . .They are young—the vast majority ranging in age from seventeen to twenty-five. . . .

Wherever they are stationed, the guys train constantly. . . .It is hard, physical, work. All the guys report that they work harder than they ever did stateside.

When they get time off, it is party time. . . .

Party time means guys drinking together, talking it out . . . .And party time means purchasing the sexual labor of women. The bars, the strip, the brothels, hotels, and women's living space are right outside the gate of each base. So pervasive is this scene wherever the U.S. military is stationed, it is evident that it is the policy of the U.S. government to have it this way.

This arrangement provides the military with complete control over the guys: they are either busting ass while on duty, or drunk and/or in bed with a purchased sexual reward when off. There is little else. The guys do not know the local language . . . .In each of the countries they are quite uninformed about the value of local money, except how much it costs to purchase liquor, a pizza, a woman, or a night at a hotel. The use of local transportation is limited. . . .

Instilling a militarized masculine identity, where raw aggression is equated with the entire military mission and where the soldier's view of reality becomes that of the military, is the prescription for action under the extreme stress of contemporary warfare. . . .

One of our concerns with the military socialization process, and the reasons for its being as it is, is its potential impact upon gender relations. We know, for example, that feelings associated with being soft, with what is taken to be feminine, are meant to be crushed, eradicated during this socialization. This often has a homophobic or misogynistic component . . . .

Upon entering the bar areas around the bases, the guys enter a subculture where anything can be bought and the senses are bombarded with pornographic consumables. . . .In the bar areas the misogyny of militarized masculinity can be lived out to whatever degree and in whatever way the individual male chooses. . . .However it is expressed, this passing on of abuse and domination is a reflection of the male's public power coupled with a lack of private, authentic personal power.

For military men slated for combat, sex with prostituted women is the cap to the socialization process. It is after the unit's first experience of being on leave or liberty together that they gel. The key elements that bind them are getting drunk together and having sex with prostituted women. Through this ritual each guy becomes the "fuckin-hey-right" soldier ready to lay down his life for others in his unit.

This is sexual imperialism, worked out on the bodies of women selling their sexual labor. This imperialism has a strong racist component. In addition to the well-known epithets. . .the guys historically and commonly use racist terms to describe the women. . . .

Guys comment continuously on how brown the women are, how many they can have, or have had, how cheap they are, how they will do anything, and how young they are. . . .

The bar area is one place where the militarized masculinity of the guys may be taken to its logical conclusion. Central to U.S. military culture is a fundamental lack of responsibility that may extend to anything and anyone. This includes children the woman may bear. They are her responsibility alone. It is extremely difficult to find a guy who expresses any bonding emotion, let alone responsibility, for a child that he's the natural father of. The men see the women as vessels to be filled up. In social situations—the bars, the streets, the jeepneys, the restaurants—the guys are talking to one another, relating to one another. The women are props—they are for playtime, which is singularly defined by its sexual component.

Note

U.S. Obligations. In 1991, the Philippine government refused to renew U.S. leases on the naval base at Subic Bay. The United States had already decided to abandon Clark Air Base because of extensive volcano damage it had suffered. In March 1993, a class action suit was filed in the Federal Court of Claims contending that "the United States has a legal and moral responsibility to educate and provide medical care for an estimated 8,600 Amerasians in Olongapo." *See* Bruce Lambert, Abandoned Filipinas Sue U.S. Over Child Support, N.Y. Times, June 21, 1993, at A3. The suit goes on to argue "that the Navy effectively fostered and regulated an elaborate night-life and prostitution industry, live-in arrangements and marriages here in which servicemen fathered thousands of children." *Id.*

C. The Law and Prostitution

Report of the Florida Supreme Court Gender Bias Study Commission, March 1990, 42 Fla. L. Rev. 803, 892–908 (1990)

The justice system's present response to prostitution exhibits some of the most egregious gender bias to be found anywhere. Indeed, the Commission was disturbed to learn of the prevalence and uniformity of prostitution throughout a state as diverse as Florida. More disturbing still was the inability of law enforcement to deter prostitution or the human misery it creates. From everywhere—whether a small town, rural county, or major city—came grim stories of violence, coercion, murder, rape, "hunger, pain[,] disease[,] and desperation." The voices of those in the criminal justice system also echoed around the state. Everywhere the same complaints were heard: high recidivism, the "revolving door," connections with narcotics, and the tendency to punish women not men.

Some argued that prostitution is a victimless crime and should be decriminalized. But the Commission found that these advocates of decriminalization are wrong. Prostitution is not a victimless crime. Its victims are the girls who run away from abusive and incestuous relationships at home and are treated by the legal system, first as errant children, and then as hardened criminals. The Commission found that the dimensions of the problem are staggering, and by comparison, the legal system's efforts to combat prostitution have been futile at best and counterproductive at worst.

Just as with domestic violence and rape, an array of irrational and discredited cultural myths help to keep this ineffective system in place. . . .

At its first public hearing, the Commission heard persuasive testimony indicting the legal system for its failure to recognize the gender bias inherent in society's response to prostitution. Upon further inquiry, the Commission determined that no other gender bias task force in the nation had studied prostitution in the context of gender bias in the legal system.

The prostitution study (the Study) initiated by the Commission included interviews with law enforcement personnel; correctional officers; prosecutors; defense attorneys; private attorneys; juvenile, circuit, and county judges; rehabilitation and drug counselors; social workers; medical personnel; and women who engage in prostitution, and clients and pimps in nine Florida cities and rural areas around the state. The Study was distinctive in that the author[3] worked along with police during the research phase and participated in decoy operations aimed at apprehending "street" prostitutes and their clientele.[4] Her observations in conjunction with additional empirical research and public testimony form the basis for the findings and recommendations made in this section. . . .

Women who have become prostitutes overwhelmingly share a common trait: as children, they ran away from sexual and physical abuse at home. One study found that eighty-five percent of juvenile prostitutes were victims of incest. Other researchers found the same statistical correlation between incest and prostitution activities and explained the connection. Incestuous fathers take advantage of childrens' [*sic*] perceptions that no one will listen to them, or will accuse them of lying. This contributes to these children's susceptibility to prostitution later in life.

Not all incest victims become prostitutes but almost all prostitutes are the victims of incest. Although sexual abuse in the home is not the cause of prostitution, it is a precondition that lays the foundation for a life of prostitution.

Society's response to this problem usually only exacerbates the problem. For instance, the juvenile justice system inappropriately treats girls who run away from incest and sexual abuse in their homes as simple runaways. Juvenile authorities seem unaware of the direct link between sexual abuse in the home, runaway teenagers, and prostitution . . . .

The primary case investigator of Alternative Life Management for Streetwalkers (ALMS) program in Miami during the early 1980s testified about the impact of these practices:

> The thirteen and twelve year old begins on the street, but. . .what really

---

3. The author was Philippa Levine, who was then an assistant professor of history at Florida State University. Eds.

4. The term "street prostitute" is used here to distinguish the subject of the Commission's study from other less visible types of prostitution, such as call-girl operations. Because these other prostitutes are less visible, they have less risk of apprehension by police and are less accessible to researchers.

> happens to them is when they run away. . . .[T]hey are picked up on the street by the police, and the police know exactly what they are doing, the police know that they are prostituting, but if they are under the age of eighteen, okay, they go to juvenile court. And, how does our juvenile court deal with them? Juvenile court labels them as runaways, as incorrigibles, or as delinquent. If they are labeled as runaways or incorrigibles, they are returned to the family. Hey, that's where they just came from. That's where they are being abused and neglected. They are returned to the family. And I have sat in courts and watched judges say to these kids, ["N]ow your parents have the right to do anything they want to do to you to discipline you, and if you don't obey your parents, and if you run away again, I will declare you a delinquent.["] Now, we come back to juvenile court, and here we have the fourteen or fifteen year old now labeled delinquent. And, what happens to the delinquent the first or second time? The delinquent is given some sort of probation or supervision, or something like that. And, guess what? Where do they go? They go back to their family because we are going to have one big happy family no matter what the facts are. And what are the facts? The facts are that these kids on the whole are abused, [they suffer] longterm abuse and neglect [and are] the victims. That's really the reality. No assessment [is made]. . . .And so what happens is they go back to their families, they run away again, and pretty soon they are gone. They are out on the street.

By age eighteen, a runaway repeatedly may have been in and out of court and already may have been adjudicated a delinquent. Upon turning eighteen, however, she leaves the juvenile system and enters the adult criminal justice system, categorized as a "hardened prostitute." Testimony and research consistently indicated that judicial education was the key to successfully treating these children as the abuse victims they really are. . . .

Prostitutes are the victims of coercion and all who become prostitutes are coerced. While some forms of coercion may not appear as such, the coercion clearly is revealed when prostitution is stripped of its apologetic mythology. There are different forms. For some women, the coercion perhaps is economic in origin; for others it is psychological. More likely, it is a combination of the two. Whatever its form, it is coercion nonetheless. The societal myth that women choose a life of prostitution rests upon the premise that choice is possible and that an affirmative decision is made. This firmly entrenched belief allows society to blame the prostitute for the abusive treatment that inevitably comes from the life "they have chosen." But the realities are different. As runaways, these girls are led into prostitution by males offering the love and approval that they have been looking for all their lives. Usually a victim of incest, a prostitute finds violence familiar, and her submission results in male approval, care, a sandwich, and a place to sleep. "The pimp-prostitute relationship parallels in many respects the dynamic between rejection, guilt, and pain which is the psychological experience of abused children, fearing that noncompliance will lead to rejection, failing to understand why what is happening to them is happening, and experiencing pain both physically and psychologically."

Pimps control over ninety percent of street prostitutes, no matter what their ages. The pimp exerts control by offering the runaway the protection of isolation and anonymity from her past, her family, and her friends. She is given a new name, her thought processes are modified, and her will is broken.

Pornography is often the pimp's preferred route of introducing a "new girl" to prostitution. . . .

Because society does not understand, or acknowledge, the process of coercion that underlies prostitution, it often is presumed erroneously that women who prostitute are willing participants in pornography. In reality, these women more fairly are analogized to prisoners of war. However, the public's reaction to girls coerced into performing pornography is quite dissimilar to the public's reaction to coerced performances made by captive hostages . . . .

Adult prostitutes are "grown-up" juvenile prostitutes. While the legal system may treat them as distinct and different from juvenile prostitutes, they are merely in a different position on the same continuum. Adult prostitutes may have different problems than juvenile prostitutes, but the legal fiction that they are self-determining adults because of their age is counterproductive in eliminating prostitution. The entire continuum of prostitution practices must be dealt with in a coordinated campaign.

On their faces, the Florida prostitution statutes are gender-neutral. The definition of prostitution as "the giving or receiving of the body for sexual activity for hire" makes both the man and the woman subject to arrest. Other statutes outlaw coercing or offering another to commit prostitution. The Commission found that statewide enforcement practices primarily target women.[5] Thus, despite the seeming neutrality of the Florida Statutes, women primarily are held culpable for prostitution.

Given the gender-biased enforcement of the laws, decriminalization has gained advocates internationally. Decriminalization can occur in several forms. "Wholesale decriminalization" permits all prostitution activities but allows local municipalities to regulate the practice through licensing and zoning. The result most often is a two-tiered system: legal activities that are regulated, and illegal activities that are not. Another method is decriminalization for women only. Male customers and coercive agents such as "pimps" remain criminally liable, but women are not. This type of decriminalization focuses its attention on the male procurer and user, rather than on the prostitute. . . .

The standard profile of the man who pays for the services of the prostitute is white, middle class, and married. According to Florida police officers, the men they apprehended were likely to be "substantial citizens" such as lawyers and judges, politicians, priests and deacons, law enforcement officers, and high-ranking military personnel. They are the ordinary and often successful people of modern society, not misfits and psychopaths.

Despite engaging in criminal activity, these men are not regarded as crim-

---

5. . . .Nationwide, the overwhelming majority of those prosecuted for prostitution are also women. Prosecutions against male clients are close to nonexistent. In 1983, for example, 126,500 arrests were made for prostitution in the United States. Seventy-three percent of these were females and only 10% were males. The remainder of the arrests were of transvestites or transsexuals. U.S. Department of Justice, Sourcebook on Criminal Justice Statistics 179 (1985).

inals. The attorneys, judges, and police interviewed by the Commission justified this perception by explaining that these were "frequently respectable men who had much to lose by public exposure." They were "upstanding citizens. . .whose family and fortunes would suffer if too punitive an action were invoked." Law enforcement officials reported that one of two things would happen upon the arrest of a prominent man: either the state attorney quietly would drop the charge or, if the man was a celebrity, the case would become headline news. This reluctance to prosecute vigorously the criminal conduct of male customers encourages the coercion of young girls into prostitution, while shielding the motivating force of that coercion. Indeed, "[a]ny man picking up a twelve or thirteen year old. . .can hardly fail to notice that he is dealing with a pubescent child. [The children] looked their age despite the trappings of adulthood behind which they were so often attempting to hide."

This demand for young girls is the foundation of all prostitution activity. This demand for sexual experience with young girls does not occur only on the street, but starts in the home. The dynamic is the same, only the locale is different. Without demand from customers, there would be no prostitution. Yet our system currently gives clients the greatest legal and social protections of all, even though they are the *raison d'etre* of the entire institution. This means that prostitution will continue to flourish. It also strongly supports an inference that this gender-biased application of the law has the blessing, however tacit, of the state. . . .

Prostitution is one of the leading reasons for arresting women in Florida. Women constitute the substantial majority of prostitution arrests in Florida. Police uniformly focus on apprehending prostitutes rather than customers. On those occasions when customers actually are targeted, however, the number of arrests made are far greater and the burden on law enforcement resources is less. Even though the reverse decoy may be the most successful method of enforcing the prostitution laws, it is used only once a month at best, or only once every three months at worst, by most law enforcement agencies except the Florida Highway Patrol (FHP). FHP uses the reverse decoy operation with great success at rest stops throughout the state. The arrest operations, combined with prosecutions by the local state attorney's office, have demonstrated substantial decreases in prostitution activities where they have been initiated. . . .

Testimony and research indicated that many state attorneys' offices offer customers an opportunity to turn state's witness against the prostitute. As the Commission's Study concluded, "[I]n every case the predominantly female prostitution population is receiving more severe treatment, both in the courtroom and with regard to bail or jail, than is their more numerous but less beleaguered clientele." There are several apparent justifications for this unfair practice. The prostitute's testimony is considered unreliable and her crime more severe. This is because only the prostitute is thought to have deviated from the societal gender norms that the legal system protects and promotes. Whatever the rationale or rationalization, the practice allows customers to avoid arrest and prosecution. It affords them a degree of secrecy and lets them avoid being labeled as repeat offenders. . . .

The disparity in treatment of men and women continues at the sentencing stage. Consistently, the client is treated in a more lenient fashion. The common practice is to jail the woman and allow the client his freedom in exchange for an agreement to testify against the woman in court. In Orange County, for example, the state attorney's policy requires that clients be given the opportunity to turn state's witness against the prostitute. There were no reports of offering a similar opportunity to the prostitute. Other jurisdictions adhere to such policies as well. For example, in Jacksonville, women on the average spend over twenty days in jail for every six that customers spend. In 1987 adjudication was withheld for 212 male customers but only fourteen female prostitutes.

Recidivism was the most common argument given to justify the discrepancy in treatment. After all, criminal records usually disclose that prostitutes are repeat offenders while clients are not. Indeed, most women convicted of prostitution are repeat offenders. But as research and testimony indicated, the apparent low rate of recidivism among clients engaging street prostitutes is illusory:

> They know where to look for the women and men who hire their bodies. They know the language employed, the euphemisms, and the colloquialisms. They know the prices their potential consorts can command. They know the procedure, the preliminary conversational gambit and word game, the routine designed to find out if their target is an undercover detective. For the most part, I would conclude that men seeking the services of a prostitute are on familiar territory.

Judicial practices regarding the withholding of adjudications contribute to the illusion that male customers are not repeat offenders. Generally, the first-time offense of a customer yields a withholding of adjudication, whereas the first offense of a prostitute commonly yields more punitive treatment. In Duval County, for example, clients are issued a notice to appear while the prostitutes are jailed upon arrest. The clients receive a withholding of adjudication but the prostitutes usually enter a plea of nolo contendere at first appearance so they can receive a sentence of time served.

In Dade County, the standard practice and prosecutorial policy is to recommend a fifteen-day sentence for the women, with no plea bargain, even for a first offense; men, however, receive only a fine. In Fort Lauderdale, on first offense women go to jail with a recommended sentence of ten days, while the men are fined an average of $300 with adjudication withheld. The Hillsborough County state attorney's office routinely recommends adjudication even on first offense for prostitutes though not for customers. The most common practice for men charged as customers is for the court to withhold adjudication and impose a fine of around $300. Jail time rarely is used against this category of defendants. In Volusia County, clients customarily receive a withheld adjudication and a fine of about $250; prostitutes, on the other hand, receive ten to sixty days in jail. The policy of the state attorney's office in Orange County is to drop charges against out-of-state men arrested for prostitution.

Withholding adjudication is rare for rest-stop arrests in Alachua County for either of the accused parties; and bonds run as high as $5,000. In addition, the drivers' licenses of the arrested men are subject to revocation pursuant to section 322.26(7) of the Florida Statutes. Male rest-stop customers are issued a trespass warning that forbids them to reenter the rest stop where they were arrested. Moreover, they pay a towing fee, a fine of $500, and spend five days in jail. As a condition of release, they must provide verification of their employment or residence. . . .

At present, the criminal justice system is wasting enormous amounts of state funds on sanctions that fail appreciably to deter prostitution. During the Commission's Study, no one interviewed within the criminal justice system felt that existing practices or options were effective. However, there are alternatives.

One successful model program, the Miami Alternative Life Management for Streetwalkers (ALMS) project, found that prostitutes exhibited clear indications of psychological distress and were in urgent need of therapeutic treatment. The fifty women—ages eighteen to forty-four—who entered the two-year rehabilitation program were all victims of physical or sexual abuse as children, a phenomenon reported in similar findings nationwide. At least seventy-five percent of them had some form of drug habit. All the women had been arrested at least four times. The estimated cost of each arrest and overnight incarceration was $1,000, or some $4,000 per prostitute, while the cost of the ALMS project ran to only $2,000 per women per year. . . .

One successful treatment method used by the Miami ALMS project was a standardized legal protocol for arrested prostitutes: one courtroom with one judge, one public defender, and one state attorney. Counselors were present at all proceedings. Placement in a treatment program could result in having adjudication withheld for a first offense, or a suspended sentence. First offenders had access to a pretrial counseling program. Special mitigating circumstances were considered by the sentencing court. The project organizers discovered that by using the legal system to encourage women to participate in counseling and rehabilitation programs, women were able to escape from the pull of the pimps' "protection" and better take care of themselves.

There are other successful models. Covenant House in Fort Lauderdale is one of the busiest units in a chain of a nationwide juvenile treatment facilities, second only to its counterpart in New York City. Covenant House has been highly successful in serving the distressed and exploited juvenile population. . . .

Findings

1. Prostitution is not a victimless crime. Thus, legalization is not the appropriate way to confront or minimize the gender bias caused by the legal system's current response to the problem.
2. The legal system's efforts to combat prostitution have been futile at best and counterproductive at worst.
3. Almost all young prostitutes have run away from sexual and physical abuse in their homes. Upon being apprehended, they then are returned to these homes by juvenile courts that often are oblivious to the causal link between sexual abuse in the home, runaway teenagers, and prostitution.
4. Runaway teenagers often engage in prostitution. When they are picked up by law enforcement, they are identified as status offenders and not identified or treated as having been involved in prostitution. Upon

arrest and conviction after the age of eighteen, females then are categorized and criminalized as prostitutes by the legal system.

5. Prostitutes are most often the victims of coercion. Most women do not choose freely to prostitute themselves. Prostitution is an attempt to survive.
6. Ninety percent of street prostitution is controlled by "pimps" who use a variety of coercive methods to control the prostitute.
7. The Florida legislation on prostitution is gender-neutral in its language, but not in its application. Statewide enforcement practices hold women culpable for the offense. The overwhelming majority of those prosecuted for prostitution are women.
8. Prosecutions for male clients and pimps are nearly nonexistent. The male client generally is thought to be less culpable than the prostitute. However, the Commission finds that those who coerce prostitution, whether described as pimps or procurers, actually are more culpable because they are the ones who organize, maintain, and pay for the institution of prostitution.
9. Prostitutes, who largely are female, receive more severe treatment in the courts, in the jails, and in bail hearings than do their clients.
10. Many state attorneys' offices offer the client the opportunity to become a state's witness against the prostitute. In exchange, charges against the client usually are dropped.
11. Prostitution cases rarely go to trial. The prostitute usually waives the right to trial and to counsel in exchange for a sentence of time served.
12. Prostitute rape rarely is reported, investigated, prosecuted, or taken seriously.
13. Rape and prostitution are manifestations of violence against women.
14. The criminal justice system is spending enormous amounts of money on sanctions that fail to deter significantly prostitution.
15. There are successful models of treatment and rehabilitation that would require a smaller outlay of funds than the present enforcement efforts in Florida.
16. Proven programs such as the Miami Alternative Life Management for Streetwalkers (ALMS) project and the Fort Lauderdale Covenant House cost no more per person than incarceration. . . .

Recommendations

The jailing of prostitutes is a woefully inadequate response to the problem of prostitution. Rehabilitative and therapeutic options are needed to address the practical needs of prostitutes as well as the coercion they endure and the psychological factors that predispose them to this lifestyle. To begin the process, the Commission recommends the following:

1. Effective treatment programs must be established to offer prostitutes realistic alternatives to prostitution. The state should cease spending money on ineffective sanctions that will never make an impact on the situation. Accordingly, the Commission recommends the establishment of programs such as the Miami ALMS project and the Fort Lauderdale Covenant House.
2. Funding should be increased for outreach services in existing battered women's shelters and victims' services organizations. Special training should be instituted for shelter and organization workers who deal with young runaway girls. The goal would be to identify girls who are at risk of becoming victims of prostitution and to offer them realistic alternatives to street prostitution.
3. Florida law is gender-neutral as to criminalizing the prostitute and the client. In reality, the parties are not treated similarly. The least that should be expected is equal enforcement of the law. At a minimum, police agencies should establish procedures to ensure parity of enforcement against both prostitutes and clients. Such procedures would include greater and institutionalized use of decoy operations.
4. Judges should enforce section 322.26(7) of the Florida Statutes, under which a driver's license can be revoked for acts of prostitution or assignation accomplished through use of a motor vehicle.
5. State and local governments should enact new statutes and ordinances against "curb crawling," the practice of soliciting from a motor vehicle.
6. Judicial education should be mandated to inform and sensitize the judiciary about the true nature of prostitution and the causal link between juvenile and adult prostitution.
7. The Commission has found that those who coerce prostitution, whether described as pimps or procurers, are more culpable than the prostitutes themselves. Based on this finding, the Florida legislature should make three changes to current Florida law:

    (a) All present misdemeanor statutes prohibiting procurement and "pimping" should be raised to third-degree felonies. These statutes then should be consolidated under section 796.03 of the Florida Statutes, which currently deals only with the second-degree felony of procuring children under the age of sixteen. The crime of procuring persons under the age of sixteen should remain a second-degree felony, as under present law. Coercing or forcing someone to become a prostitute, a third degree [*sic*] felony, should remain a separate offense under section 796.04.

    (b) Section 796.05(1) of the Florida Statutes currently makes it unlawful only to derive support from a person the offender knows to be engaged in prostitution. The statute should be amended to read: "It shall be unlawful for any person, knowing or who should know another person is engaged in prostitution, to live or derive support or maintenance in whole or in part from the earnings or proceeds of such person's prostitution." The standard for guilty knowledge should be on par with that for other offenses such as theft or dealing in stolen property. This change thus would allow for increased prosecution of pimps.

(c) New legislation should be enacted to create a civil cause of action on behalf of women against their pimps, thus further discouraging trafficking in women.

8. The Commission recommends the establishment of a multi-agency task force to examine further the problems posed by prostitution and its relationship with substance abuse and the spread of acquired immune deficiency syndrome (AIDS) and other sexually transmitted diseases. The task force should include representatives of professions such as psychology, psychiatry, and law, as well as public health officials, academics, and social workers.

Fla. Stat.

§§ 322.26(7), 796.03-.05, .07-.09 (1991)

322.26. Mandatory revocation of license by department.

The department shall forthwith revoke the license or driving privilege of any person upon receiving a record of such person's conviction of any of the following offenses:

. . .

(7) Any violation of the law against lewdness, assignation, and prostitution where such violation has been effected through the use of a motor vehicle.

796.03. Procuring person under age of 16 for prostitution.

Whoever procures for prostitution, or causes to be prostituted, any person who is under the age of 16 years shall be guilty of a felony of the second degree . . . .

796.04. Forcing, compelling, or coercing another to become a prostitute.

(1) After May 1, 1943, it shall be unlawful for anyone to force, compel, or coerce another to become a prostitute.

(2) Anyone violating this section shall be guilty of a felony of the third degree . . . .

796.05. Deriving support from the proceeds of prostitution.

(1) It shall be unlawful for any person knowing another person is engaged

in prostitution to live or derive support or maintenance in whole or in part from the earnings or proceeds of such person's prostitution.

(2) Anyone violating this section shall be guilty of a felony of the third degree . . . .

796.07. Prohibiting prostitution, etc.; evidence; penalties; definitions.

(1) As used in this section:

(a) "Prostitution" means the giving or receiving of the body for sexual activity for hire.

(b) "Lewdness" means any indecent or obscene act.

(c) "Assignation" means the making of any appointment or engagement for prostitution or lewdness, or any act in furtherance of such appointment or engagement.

(d) "Prostitution" as used in paragraph (a) shall be construed to exclude sexual activity between a husband and his wife.

(e) "Sexual activity" means oral, anal, or vaginal penetration by, or union with, the sexual organ of another or the anal or vaginal penetration of another by any other object, or the handling or fondling of the sexual organ of another for the purpose of masturbation; however, the term does not include acts done for bona fide medical purposes.

(2) It is unlawful in the state:

(a) To keep, set up, maintain, or operate any place, structure, building, or conveyance for the purpose of lewdness, assignation, or prostitution.

(b) To offer, or to offer or agree to secure, another for the purpose of prostitution or for any other lewd or indecent act.

(c) To receive, or to offer or agree to receive, any person into any place, structure, building, or conveyance for the purpose of prostitution, lewdness, or assignation, or to permit any person to remain there for such purpose.

(d) To direct, take, or transport, or to offer or agree to take or transport, any person to any place, structure, or building, or to any other person, with knowledge or reasonable cause to believe that the purpose of such directing, taking, or transporting is prostitution, lewdness, or assignation.

(3) It is also unlawful in the state:

(a) To offer to commit, or to commit, or to engage in, prostitution, lewdness, or assignation.

(b) To solicit, induce, entice, or procure another to commit prostitution, lewdness, or assignation with himself or herself.

(c) To reside in, enter, or remain in, any place, structure, or building, or to enter or remain in any conveyance, for the purpose of prostitution, lewdness, or assignation.

(d) To aid, abet, or participate in the doing of any of the acts or things enumerated in subsections (2) and (3) of this section.

(e) To purchase the services of any person engaged in prostitution.

(4) In the trial of any persons charged with the violation of any of the provisions of this section, testimony concerning the reputation of any place, structure, building, or conveyance involved in said charge and of the person or persons who reside in, operate, or frequent the same and testimony con-

cerning the reputation of the defendant shall be admissible in evidence in support of the charge.

(5) Any person who violates any provision of this section is guilty of a misdemeanor of the second degree . . . .

796.08. Screening for sexually transmissible diseases; providing penalties.

. . .

(3) Any person convicted of prostitution or procuring another to commit prostitution with himself under the provisions of s. 796.07, shall be required to undergo screening for a sexually transmissible disease under direction of the Department of Health and Rehabilitative Services and, if infected, shall submit to treatment and counseling as a condition of release from probation, community control, or incarceration. Notwithstanding the provisions of s. 384.29, the results of any test conducted pursuant to this subsection shall be made available by the Department of Health and Rehabilitative Services to medical personnel, appropriate state agencies, or courts of appropriate jurisdiction to enforce the provisions of this chapter.

(4) Any person who commits prostitution and who, prior to the commission of such crime, had tested positive for a sexually transmissible disease and knew or had been informed that he had tested positive for a sexually transmissible disease and that he could possibly communicate such disease to another person through sexual activity is guilty of a misdemeanor of the first degree . . . .A person may be convicted and sentenced separately for a violation of this subsection and for the underlying crime of prostitution.

(5) Any person who commits prostitution by engaging in sexual activity in a manner likely to transmit the human immunodeficiency virus and who, prior to the commission of such crime, had tested positive for human immunodeficiency virus and knew or had been informed that he had tested positive for human immunodeficiency virus and that he could possibly communicate such disease to another person through sexual activity is guilty of a misdemeanor of the first degree . . . .A person may be convicted and sentenced separately for a violation of this subsection and for the underlying crime of prostitution.

(6) Any person convicted of procuring another to commit prostitution with himself in a manner likely to transmit the human immunodeficiency virus and who, prior to the commission of such crime, had tested positive for human immunodeficiency virus and knew or had been informed that he had tested positive for human immunodeficiency virus and that he could possibly communicate such disease to another person through sexual activity is guilty of a misdemeanor of the first degree . . . .

796.09. Coercion; civil cause of action; evidence; defenses; attorney's fees.

(1) A person has a cause of action for compensatory damages and punitive damages against:

(a) A person who coerced that person into prostitution;

(b) A person who coerces that person to remain in prostitution; or

(c) A person who uses coercion to collect or receive any part of that person's earnings derived from prostitution.

(2) As used in this section, the term "prostitution" has the same meaning as defined in s. 796.07.

(3) As used in this section, the term "coercion" means any practice of domination, restraint, or inducement for the purpose of or with the reasonably foreseeable effect of causing another person to engage in or remain in prostitution or to relinquish earnings derived from prostitution, and includes, but is not limited to:

(a) Physical force or threats of physical force.

(b) Physical or mental torture.

(c) Kidnapping.

(d) Blackmail.

(e) Extortion or claims of indebtedness.

(f) Threat of legal complaint or report of delinquency.

(g) Threat to interfere with parental rights or responsibilities, whether by judicial or administrative action or otherwise.

(h) Promise of legal benefit.

(i) Promise of greater financial rewards.

(j) Promise of marriage.

(k) Restraint of speech or communication with others.

(l) Exploitation of a condition of developmental disability, cognitive limitation, affective disorder, or substance dependency.

(m) Exploitation of victimization by sexual abuse.

(n) Exploitation of pornographic performance.

(o) Exploitation of human needs for food, shelter, safety, or affection.

(4) In the course of litigation under this section, any transaction about which a plaintiff testifies or produces evidence does not subject such plaintiff to criminal prosecution or any penalty or forfeiture. Further, any testimony or evidence, documentary or otherwise, or information directly or indirectly derived from such testimony or evidence which is given or produced by a plaintiff or a witness for a plaintiff shall not be used against these persons in any other investigation or proceeding. Such testimony or evidence, however, may be used against a plaintiff or a witness for a plaintiff upon any criminal investigation or proceeding for perjury committed while giving such testimony or producing such evidence.

(5) It does not constitute a defense to a complaint under this section that:

(a) The plaintiff was paid or otherwise compensated for acts of prostitution;

(b) The plaintiff engaged in acts of prostitution prior to any involvement with the defendant; or

(c) The plaintiff made no attempt to escape, flee, or otherwise terminate contact with the defendant.

(6) Evidence of convictions for prostitution or prostitution-related offenses are inadmissible in a proceeding brought under this section for purposes of attacking the plaintiff's credibility.

(7) In any action brought under this section, the court, in its discretion, may award prevailing plaintiffs reasonable attorney's fees and costs.

Notes and Questions

1. *Race Bias in the Criminal Justice System.* The study of prostitution in Florida by the Gender Bias Study Commission of the Supreme Court of Florida [hereinafter Commission] found that a disproportionate number of women and men of color are arrested on prostitution-related charges. In 1971, the percentage of nonwhite arrests on such charges was 56.6, while the nonwhite population in Florida was 15.4 percent. Although the proportional disparity declined over the next fifteen years, the numbers continued to show race bias. In 1986, the percentage of nonwhite arrests for prostitution-related charges was 37.8, while the state's African-American population in that year was 14.6 percent. *See* Philippa Levine, Prostitution in Florida, A Report Presented to the Gender Bias Study Commission of the Supreme Court of Florida 137-42 (1988).

2. *Prostituted Street Women.* A study consisting of "topical" histories obtained in 1986 from fourteen Milwaukee prostituted street women provides evidence to support the conclusions of the Commission about the coercion of women in prostitution by pimps.

> According to the women of this study, a prerequisite to working as a street hustler is that a woman must have a male sponsor, a "man," to act as a "keep-away" from other "men" who vie for a living on the street. She must turn her earnings over to this "man" in order to be considered "his woman" and to enjoy the "man's" protection. The "man," besides providing protection from other "men," gives his women material necessities and gifts and, most important, sex and love.
>
> The following, from an interview with a respondent whom we have named "Chris," illustrates why street women need "men" to work. When asked why she worked and turned her earnings over to a "man" instead of working for herself and keeping her money, she said:
>
>> Chris: You can't really work the streets for yourself unless you got a man—not for a long length of time. . .'cause the other pimps are not going to like it because you don't have anybody to represent you. They'll rob you, they'll hit you in the head if you don't have nobody to take up for you. Yea, it happens. They give you a hassle. . .[The men] will say, "Hey baby, what's your name? Where your man at? You got a man?"
>>
>> So you can't hustle on your own?
>>
>> Chris: Not really, no. You can, you know, but not for long.
>
> Women who do hustle on their own are called "outlaw" women, a term that clearly indicates that their solo activities are proscribed. Women who work as outlaws lose any protection that they had formerly been granted under the "law" of the street and are open targets for "men" who wish to harass them, take their money, or exploit them sexually.
>
> Street life is male dominated and so structured that "men" reap the prof-

its of women's labor. A "man" demands from his women not only money, but respect as well. Showing respect for "men" means total obedience and complete dedication to them. Mary reports that in the company of "men" she had to "talk mainly to the women—try not to look at the men if possible at all—try not to have conversation with them." Rita, when asked about the rules of the street, said, "Just basic, obey. Do what he wants to do. Don't disrespect him. . . .I could not disrespect him in any verbal or physical way. I never attempted to hit him back. Never." And, in the same vein, Tina said that when her "man" had others over to socialize, the women of the family were relegated to the role of servant. "We couldn't speak to them when we wasn't spoken to, and we could not foul up on their orders. And you cannot disrespect them.". . .

[Pimps] maintain a strong coalition among themselves allowing them to dominate women. As the number of women a "man" has working for him increases, the time he can spend supervising each female's activities decreases. It becomes very important that "men" be in contact with one another to assure the social and economic control of street women. With watchful "men" keeping tabs on their own and other "men's" women, women know that they must always work hard and follow the rules.

Rose gives an example, below, of one of the many ways in which "men" protect one another. Rose's sister, who is also involved in street life, was badly beaten by her "man" and decided to press charges against him. She decided to drop the charges because:

> Rose: She got scared 'cuz he kept threatening her. . . .His friends [were] callin' her and tellin' her if she didn't drop the charges they was gonna do somethin' to her. So she dropped the charges.

It is interesting to note that when working women are caught talking with "men" who are not their own, it is considered to be at the women's initiative and they are reprimanded. . . .Ann gives. . .[an] example of this element of the cohesiveness of "men": "If another pimp see you 'out of pocket' [breaking a rule] or bent over talkin' to another pimp or somethin' in their car, they will tell your man, 'Yea, she was talkin' to some dude in a Cadillac—he try and '"knock your bitch."' That the word they use."

> What does it mean?
>
> Ann: He tryin' to come up with her. He tryin' to have her for himself. That what they mean. That what they be sayin' all the time: "He tryin' to 'knock your bitch,' man. You better put her 'in check.' " In other words, you better, how should I say it? "In check" mean, tell her what's happenin', keep her under control.
>
> Or, if you be walkin' around on the stroll and stuff and somebody might see you sittin' down on the bench and they say, "Man your ho [whore] is lazy! All the cars were passin' by—that girl didn't even catch none of 'em." 'Cuz they [the "men"] know you and stuff.

. . .Once a woman becomes involved with a pimp, she unwittingly becomes involved in a self-perpetuating system from which escape is difficult. The "proper" way to leave one "man" is formally to "choose" another. A woman

> will pay her new "man" whatever price has been agreed upon and the new "man" and the old "man" meet to validate the exchange of the woman. . . .([T]he payment made to a new "man" is called a woman's "choosing money" and represents proof of her qualifications as a prostitute. In cases where a woman has been jailed, pimps symbolically transfer ownership rights to the woman by meeting at a bondsman office and formally withdrawing and redepositing—by the old pimp and the new—the bond money necessary to her release.) If a woman leaves without choosing a new "man," typically in a crisis situation (the occurrence of which is frequent), the "man" will pursue her; by street laws, he retains ownership rights to the woman. Women who leave "men" without first choosing a new "man" find themselves in a position where they must either hide out, leave the city, or find a new "man" fast to act as protector and, in effect, "owner" of record.

Kim Romenesko & Eleanor M. Miller, The Second Step in Double Jeopardy: Appropriating the Labor of Female Street Hustlers, 35 Crime & Delinq. 109, 116-18, 132-33 (1989).

3. *Marital Exception.* The Florida statute excludes sexual activity between a husband and wife from the definition of prostitution (p. 554). Why do you think the Florida legislature found it necessary to carve out this exception in the statute?

4. *Civil Cause of Action.* In 1991, the Florida legislature, following the Commission's recommendation, enacted section 796.09 to create a civil cause of action on behalf of women against their pimps. Could the statutory language be interpreted to allow for a civil cause of action against johns? Why is the creation of this civil cause of action significant?

5. *Discriminatory Enforcement.* The Commission concluded that gender bias permeated police practices, prosecutorial policies, and sentencing for prostitution-related charges. The majority of courts considering the issue of discriminatory enforcement have found the existing policies and practices to be constitutional. *See, e.g.*, People v. Superior Court of Alameda County, 19 Cal. 3d 338, 562 P.2d 1315, 138 Cal. Rptr. 66 (1977). In *Commonwealth v. An Unnamed Defendant*, 22 Mass. App. 230, 492 N.E.2d 1184 (1986), however, two criminal complaints for soliciting and for being "a common nightwalker" were dismissed because of discriminatory enforcement of the applicable statutes. The defense presented evidence including statistics showing an overwhelming number of female prostitutes arrested for a period of one year and testimony by a police officer that the police do not ordinarily arrest the male customer. No opposing evidence was presented by the state. The court found that the evidence "abundantly supplied the proof of intentional discrimination between the female prostitute and her male customers. . . ." *Id.* at 235, 492 N.E.2d at 1187.

6. *The Reform Debate.* The Commission raised the question of decriminalization in its report without specifying support for either partial or wholesale decriminalization (p. 547). It did, however, limit its recommendations to statutory reforms that focused on the activities of pimps and johns. As Jody Freeman describes, the debate surrounding reform of the prostitution laws has been part of a larger conflict within feminism.

> CORP [Canadian Organization for the Rights of Prostitutes] and COYOTE's [Cast Off Your Old Tired Ethics] essentially liberal argument is that women and men should be permitted to use their bodies and express their sexuality as they see fit. Underlying this position is an assumption that choice is possible and that prostitutes are entitled to determine for themselves whether selling sex is harmful. They encourage prostitution as sexual expression, even if it is considered "deviant," because it is private, freely chosen, and harmless to those not involved in the transaction. . . .
>
> CORP's leadership argues that decriminalizing and legitimizing prostitution promotes autonomy and is also the only effective way of minimizing the coercion present in "exceptional" cases. If prostitutes are permitted to organize, form support groups, and run self-help networks, they will then be able to exert some control over the coercive elements of the sex-trade. Putting power into the hands of the women in the industry will enable them to prevent the worst abuses of the system. . . .
>
> Radical feminists reject the notion that women are empowered by fulfilling male desire, and they see the desire for prostitution as male. . . .Radical feminists say that prostitution is not a harmless, "private" transaction but a powerful means of creating, reinforcing, and perpetuating the objectification of women through sexuality. They do not take the criminalization of prostitution to mean that society is committed to undoing the subordination of women. Rather, it serves as proof that female sexuality is not only manufactured by men, but also legally controlled through the exercise of authority in order to keep women isolated and powerless.

Jody Freeman, The Feminist Debate Over Prostitution Reform: Prostitutes' Rights Groups, Radical Feminists, and the (Im)possibility of Consent, 5 Berkeley Women's L.J. 75, 90-92 (1989-90).

Liberal prostitutes' rights groups support decriminalization.

> Decriminalization of prostitution and the regulation of pimping and pandering. . .offers the best chance for women who are involved in prostitution to gain some measure of control over their work. It would make it easier to prosecute those who abuse prostitutes, either physically or economically, because the voluntary, non-abusive situations would be left alone. . . .
>
> Legalization. . .has generally meant a system of control of the *prostitute*, with the state regulating, taxing, and/or licensing whatever form of prostitution is legalized, leaving all other forms illegal, without any concern for the prostitute herself. Traditional regulation has often involved the establishment of special government agencies to deal with prostitution.
>
> The brothels in Nevada, for example, are licensed and regulated by the government, and the women who work in them are registered as prostitutes with the sheriff. . . .[T]hey are severely restricted in their movements outside of the brothel. Independent prostitution is illegal, as is prostitution in massage parlors, for escort services, and of course, street prostitution. . . .
>
> The transaction between prostitute and client must be removed from the purview of the law, and the other laws dealing with prostitution must be reevaluated, and repealed or changed as necessary.

Priscilla Alexander, Prostitution: A Difficult Issue for Feminists, in Sex Work:

Writings by Women in the Sex Industry 184, 210-11 (Frédérique Delacoste & Priscilla Alexander eds., 1988) (emphasis in original).

In contrast, as reflected in the proposed Convention on the Elimination of All Forms of Sexual Exploitation of Women, radical feminists support partial decriminalization. *See* Note 3, at p. 536-37.

7. *Lesbians, Prostitutes, and State Control.* Joan Nestle has identified many parallels between the state's treatment of prostituted women and its treatment of lesbians; she concludes that the tactics used against prostituted women became a model for controlling lesbians.

> To make sure prostitutes did not pass into the population of true women, different states have set up regulations through the centuries controlling her self presentation and physical movements. . . .
>
> [P]rostitutes [were]. . .marked by the state, both in being forced to wear a certain kind of clothes or mark like a red shoulder knot, a white scarf or, in a chilling prefiguring of history, a yellow cord on their sleeves. They [were]. . .controlled in the places [where] they [were]. . .allowed to live and work. As I read of the demanded dress codes, I was reminded of the warning older lesbians gave me in the fifties as I prepared for a night out: *Always wear three pieces of women's clothing so the vice squad can't bust you for transvestism.* We dressed to answer two needs: to avoid the state's penalties for being women of difference and to announce our own cultural participation. . . .
>
> [In the early twentieth century] prostitutes were becoming the victims of anti-vice campaigns, campaigns that established practices of harassment, surveillance and arrest that were later to be used against clearly defined lesbians and their gathering places. "The growth of special courts, vice squads, social workers and prisons to deal with prostitution," became the lesbian legacy of the forties and fifties.

Joan Nestle, Lesbians and Prostitutes: A Historical Sisterhood, in Sex Work: Writings by Women in the Sex Industry 231, 234-35, 241 (Frédérique Delacoste & Priscilla Alexander eds., 1988) (emphasis in original).

8. *Mann Act.* Legislation on prostitution is primarily a matter of local and state control. The federal government has used its immigration laws to prevent the entry of women into the United States for the purpose of prostitution. *See* Ruth Rosen, The Lost Sisterhood: Prostitution in America, 1900-1918, at 19 (1982). In 1910, Congress also enacted the White Slave Traffic Act, ch. 395, 366 Stat. 825 (1910) (codified as amended at 18 U.S.C. §§ 2421-2424 (1988)). This act is also known as the "Mann Act" (after U.S. Representative Mann) and it is presently titled "Transportation for Illegal Sexual Activity and Related Crimes." Marlene Beckman traces "the transformation of the Mann Act from its original formulation as a weapon against commercial vice to its eventual use as a federal morals law" and discusses how it is used to prosecute "the women victims whom the Act was designed to protect." Marlene D. Beckman, Note, The White Slave Traffic Act: The Historical Impact of a Criminal Law Policy on Women, 72 Geo. L.J. 1111, 1111 (1984).

> [T]he historical development of the Mann Act reveals two themes. First, Congress intended the Act to apply only to commercial vice and those cases

where there was evidence of coercion. Second, the Act was not intended to apply to ordinary prostitution, control of which remained within the police powers of the states. Instead, Congress intended to supplement local authority by reaching interstate transportation for commercial purposes. . . .

Despite the clear congressional intent that the White Slave Traffic Act would apply only to those situations involving commercial vice, the Supreme Court in *Caminetti v. United States* [242 U.S. 470 (1917)]. . .held that the Mann Act applied to voluntary immoral acts even when no commercial intention or business profit was shown. . . .

The activity prohibited by the Mann Act was transportation of "any woman or girl" in interstate commerce. On a plain reading of the Act, it would seem that Congress intended the woman who was to engage in sexual conduct to be treated as the person "transported" and the persons who accompanied her or assisted in her transportation were to be prosecuted as "transporters." Only the latter were the obvious targets of the criminal sanctions of the Act. . . .

The Supreme Court in *United States v. Holte* [236 U.S. 140 (1915)]. . .held that a woman could not be liable as an accomplice to a Mann Act violation. The *Holte* Court went further, however, and held that the woman could be indicted for conspiracy. . . .

Holte stood for the limited proposition that a woman could under some circumstances, not yet precisely defined, be guilty of a conspiracy to violate the Mann Act. In *Gebardi v. United States* [287 U.S. 112 (1932)] the Court. . .indicated [its]. . .reluctance to find a conspiracy when the woman was an otherwise innocent person—that is, when she was not a prostitute or engaged in other illegal activities. This retreat from the broader implications of the earlier *Holte* decision may be explained on the ground that the *Gebardi* Court was confronted with a woman whose only "immoral" action was acquiescence to interstate transportation, as opposed to the situation in *Holte* in which the woman was actually a prostitute. . . .

In the 1960 case of *United States v. McClung* [187 F. Supp. 254 (E.D. La. 1960)] a federal district court held that an indictment which alleged that the defendant took a woman across a state line for the purpose of engaging in sexual intercourse and other sexual acts with her failed to charge a violation of the Mann Act. . . .[A]ccording to *McClung*, the phrase "any other immoral purpose" in the Mann Act does not include isolated acts of intercourse.

The *McClung* holding has not yet been adopted by the Supreme Court, but its philosophy is a modern one. . . .

Law enforcement authorities have become progressively less enthusiastic about enforcing a law that has grown increasingly unpopular as sexual mores have changed over the years. . . .

Nonetheless, men and women are still being sent to prison for Mann Act violations. According to Federal Prison System records, 439 defendants have been committed to federal prisons between 1970 and 1982 for violations of the Act, thirty-five of whom are women. . . .Although a review of the records of all thirty-five women most recently convicted is beyond the scope of this project, it is reasonable to assume from post-*Gebardi* trends that these women more closely resemble the violators whom Congress had in mind when the statute was enacted. While these women are more likely to be madams or procurers of other women for prostitution, however, they are not any more likely than their predecessors to be part of an organized white slave ring.

Id. at 1118-22, 1133-34.

People v. Slovinski,

166 Mich. App. 158, 420 N.W.2d 145 (1988)

Cynar, J. The people appeal by leave granted from an order granting defendant's motion allowing introduction of evidence alleging complainant to be a prostitute.

Defendant was charged with criminal sexual conduct in the first degree. . .and unarmed robbery . . . .At the preliminary examination, the complainant, testified that on March 17, 1986, she was standing on the corner of Division and Rose Streets in the City of Grand Rapids waiting for her girlfriend to pick her up. A white van, driven by defendant, pulled up and offered her a ride to the Lime Lite Bar.

However, rather than taking the complainant to the bar, defendant drove to a wooded area, parked, and threw her into the back of his van. She hit her head and passed out. When she awoke, defendant had partially removed her jeans and panties, and was engaged in sexual intercourse with the complainant.

After completing the sexual act, defendant allegedly began hitting the complainant about her face and right arm, while calling her a "bitch" and a "slut." This activity lasted approximately twenty minutes. Defendant then pushed her back into the front seat where he held her by her hair while he kicked her in the face. Defendant drove away from the area, stopped and threw the complainant out of the van. He followed her to the ground and continued to hit her until a truck pulled up. At that point, defendant fled. The truck driver summoned an ambulance and the complainant was hospitalized overnight.

On cross-examination, the complainant acknowledged that, at the time of the incident, she told police that she was forced into the van by defendant, while at the preliminary examination she testified that she willingly went with defendant. No explanation was offered regarding this discrepancy. The complainant denied that she was a prostitute. At the close of proofs, defendant was bound over.

After defendant was bound over, he filed a motion on October 6, 1986, seeking an in camera hearing to determine whether defendant could introduce evidence of the complainant's past sexual conduct. . . .

At the hearing, defendant testified that on March 17, 1986, he picked up the complainant on Division Street near Rose Street in Grand Rapids. At that time, he spoke with her about "sexual matters" in exchange for money. After their conversation, the complainant agreed to perform oral sex on defendant for money. The complainant went into defendant's vehicle and they drove to a "safe spot." She performed oral sex and defendant paid her. Afterwards, defendant offered more money for sexual intercourse and the complainant agreed.

On cross-examination, defendant stated that he offered the complainant twenty dollars for oral sex and five dollars additional for intercourse. During the oral sex act, defendant allegedly told her to stop and offered her five dollars more to "just let me penetrate you, because you ain't doing nothing for me." She agreed. After the sex acts were over, defendant refused to pay her "because she wasn't no good."

Thereafter, defendant called five witnesses who had positively identified photographs of the complaining witness as a prostitute working the Division and Rose Streets area. Under oath, three of the witnesses declined to positively say that the person in the photographs was known to them as a prostitute. One of the three witnesses had no knowledge of the reputation of the person as being a prostitute. It was revealed that these three witnesses had been interviewed at the Kent County Jail by the public defender's investigator, and at the time the witnesses identified the photographs they had been, or were being, represented by the same defender's office. . . .

[T]wo waitresses from the Acapulco Restaurant. . .positively stated that the complainant was a prostitute. One waitress testified to seeing the complainant in the restaurant once or twice a week during the summer of 1986 between 9 p.m. and 12 midnight. This waitress had not heard anything about the complainant's reputation as a prostitute. However, she saw her walking and standing on the streets quite a few times and she saw complainant associating in the restaurant with known prostitutes.

The other waitress stated that she served as a go-between for a restaurant customer and the complainant in that she questioned the complainant as to whether she was a prostitute. The complainant stated that she was. Her price was $50 for oral sex and $75 for other acts. The waitress also testified that during March, 1986, she saw the complainant every night in the restaurant. On cross-examination, the waitress stated that she has acted as a go-between for restaurant customers and prostitutes "at least a hundred times.". . .

[T]he trial judge ruled that he would not permit testimony from the three witnesses who hesitated about their identification. However, the judge stated that he would allow the two waitresses to testify for the purpose of impeaching the complainant's credibility. The court's bench ruling was incorporated into an April 24, 1987, order from which the people appeal by leave granted.

On appeal, the prosecution puts forth two arguments against the introduction of evidence that the complaining witness is allegedly a prostitute. First, such evidence is prohibited by the "rape shield" statute . . . .Second, if this Court permits the introduction of that evidence, defendant should be required to make a stronger objective showing that the complainant is a prostitute than has been shown.

Defendant, on the other hand, argues that the introduction of the aforesaid evidence is essential and critical in presenting a defense. He claims that this act of sexual intercourse was consensual arising from a verbally-assented-to agreement of sex for money. In addition, because the complainant denied being a prostitute, her credibility was placed in issue. Defendant should be allowed to impeach the complainant through extrinsic evidence. Finally, defendant maintains that the exclusion of this evidence would constitute a violation of his Sixth Amendment right of confrontation as guaranteed by the United States Constitution. . . .

In his first assertion for permitting evidence that the complainant is an alleged prostitute, defendant alleges that the complainant's past conduct is relevant on the issue of credibility because she denied being an alleged prostitute, thereby placing herself in a false light. Defendant claims that, through extrinsic evidence, he should be allowed to impeach the complainant. . . .

[T]o the extent that defendant sought to impeach the complainant's credibility as a witness by offering evidence that she was an alleged prostitute, it was an impermissible purpose and such evidence may not be introduced for that purpose.

Defendant also claims that while extrinsic evidence is normally inadmissible to prove collateral issues, a recognized exception does exist when a witness puts herself in a "false light." . . .

The federal courts have refused to recognize a "false light" exception . . . .The only time that specific instances of conduct may extrinsically be introduced is from the witness whose credibility is being attacked. We agree with the federal courts on this issue. Thus, defendant's purpose for this evidence, to impeach the complainant's veracity by extrinsic proof that she is an alleged prostitute, is improper and impermissible . . . .

While defendant is precluded from introducing evidence of alleged prostitution under a theory of impeachment, we conclude that this evidence is admissible on the issues of consent and right of confrontation. . . .

Defendant argues that this evidence is relevant to his theory of the case, namely, that the complainant consented to an act of prostitution. . . .

In this case then, the question is whether evidence of the existence of consent, a fact in issue, would have any tendency to make that fact more or less probable. We believe that it would. . . .

Evidence of the complainant's alleged status as a prostitute is being offered to show that the instant act of intercourse was consensual. This evidence is material. That is, it would help prove or disprove a matter in issue, consent.

Probative value refers to "the tendency of evidence to establish a proposition which it is offered to prove." McCormick, Evidence (2d ed), § 185, p. 435 . . . .

Thus, evidence of alleged prostitution is probative on the issue of consent if the fact that a complainant has engaged in intercourse for money has any tendency to make it more probable that the complainant consented to the sex act in issue. We conclude that, on the record made below, the proffered evidence of alleged specific acts of prostitution is probative on the issue of consent. It has a tendency to make it more probable that the complainant entered into a financial arrangement with defendant for sexual acts. . . .

The crux of defendant's claim is that because the complainant is an alleged prostitute, she consented to sex with him for money. Without such evidence, defendant would be unable to establish a defense. We recognize the prejudicial impact of such evidence. However, the jury would still be free to disregard the two waitresses' testimony that the complainant is a prostitute.

Although the evidence is more probative than prejudicial, it must nonetheless be admissible under MRE 404(a)(3). This rule prohibits character evidence to prove that a person acted in conformity therewith. In this case, at first blush, it appears that defendant's evidence is the type of character evidence prohibited by rule 404(a)(3). Introducing evidence of prostitution is tantamount to stating that because the complainant is an alleged prostitute, and because defendant offered her money for sex, she therefore engaged in sex for money in conformity with her character as a prostitute.

However, we do not find that the defendant seeks to introduce evidence of alleged prostitution to establish that the complainant acted in conformity therewith. Instead, the evidence is offered for the purpose of establishing the defense of financially induced consent. . . .

Defendant's final claim for admission of this evidence is based on his Sixth Amendment right of confrontation. Defendant alleges that without this evidence he has no defense and, thus, his right of due process would be violated. We agree. . . .

We recognize that the state has legitimate interests in prohibiting a defendant from inquiring into a victim's sexual past. The interests include the encouragement of victims to report sexual offenses and the recognition by courts and society in general that unchaste women are not especially prone to lying. . . .These interests need to be balanced against the defendant's right to present a defense and confront his accuser.

The Michigan cases dealing with this issue have not found undue infringement of a defendant's confrontation right by the exclusion of such evidence. Other jurisdictions, however, have addressed this issue. In *State ex rel. Pope v. Mohave Superior Court*, 113 Ariz. 22, 545 P.2d 946 (1976), the Supreme Court of Arizona noted that where the defendant alleges that the victim consented to an act of prostitution, the accused should be permitted to present evidence of her reputation as a prostitute and her prior acts of prostitution to support such a defense. . . .However, the *Pope* Court held that character evidence concerning unchastity is inadmissible for impeachment purposes.

In *State v. Quinn*, 121 Ariz. 582, 592 P.2d 778 (1978), the Arizona Court of Appeals held that a defendant may cross-examine a complainant on prior acts of prostitution where (1) the defendant alleges the victim actually consented to an act of prostitution, and (2) it is determined outside the jury's presence that the evidence is more probative than prejudicial. . . .

In *People v. Varona*, 143 Cal. App. 3d 566, 192 Cal. Rptr. 44 (1983), defendants claimed that the complainant solicited them for acts of prostitution, engaged in sex acts with them, and became enraged when she discovered that the defendants had no money. Defendants attempted to offer proof that the victim was then on probation for a plea-based conviction of prostitution. The evidence was excluded. The appellate court reversed, finding that on those facts evidence of prostitution should have been permitted since it would cast light on her story both in regard to why she was at the bus stop and whether she voluntarily engaged in the sex acts. The court specifically did not hold that prior evidence of prostitution to show consent would be admissible in every rape case. . . .

Finally in *Shaffer v. State*, 443 N.E.2d 838 (Ind. 1983), the defendant claimed that the complaining witness charged him with rape when he refused to pay her for an act of prostitution. He offered testimony of witnesses who claimed to have seen the victim in an area notorious for prostitutes, approaching cars and soliciting. . . .The trial court excluded such evidence under the state's rape shield law. The Indiana Supreme Court rejected the "more probative than prejudicial" standard as the one to be used in determining admissibility. Instead, the court explicitly relied on the rape shield law to uphold the trial court's ruling. . . .

The foregoing cases indicate a willingness on the part of some jurisdictions to allow evidence that a victim is a prostitute when the defense is consent and a proper showing thereof has been made. In our case, we conclude that evidence of the victim's prior sexual activity is absolutely critical in ensuring defendant a fair trial and in preserving his confrontation right. Without this evidence, defendant would be precluded from presenting his defense of consent.

The people further argue that the defendant has not made a strong objective showing that the complainant may be a prostitute. We disagree. . . .

Affirmed. Mies, J. concurs.

Danhof, C.J. (dissenting). I do not agree with the majority's holding that evidence of alleged prostitution is relevant to the issue of consent. The "rape shield" statute. . .and MRE 404(a)(3) reflect the general rule that "evidence of a complainant's prior sexual unchastity, in the form of reputation evidence or a specific instance of conduct, has little or no relevancy to the issue of complainant's consent with defendant." *People v. Hackett*, 421 Mich. 338, 354, 365 N.W.2d 120 (1984). Accordingly, our Supreme Court held that evidence of a complainant's reputation as a homosexual was irrelevant to show consent. . . .

Likewise, I do not think that complainant's reputation as a prostitute is relevant to show consent. The fact that financially induced consent is alleged does not make the evidence of alleged prostitution any more relevant than the reputation evidence in *Hackett* that was used to show consent to homosexual activity. I would not address the right to confrontation issue because defendant's right to confrontation only extends to relevant evidence. *Hackett*, *supra*, p. 354, 365 N.W. 2d. 120.

Notes and Question

1. *Consent*. The decision in *Slovinski* raises a number of concerns about the issue of consent in criminal prosecutions of rape. First, the court decided at the outset that evidence of the complainant's reputation as a prostitute was necessary for the defendant to mount any defense. This is clearly untrue. The defendant could argue consent without the reputational evidence. Although the defendant's claim of consent was weakened by the fact that the complainant was beaten and needed hospitalization, this does not mean that he had no defense. A second problem with the court's analysis is its assumption that evidence of sex for money in the complainant's past is relevant to the question of whether the complainant consented to sex in this instance. It was exactly this kind of reasoning that the rape shield statute was intended to prevent. The court's assertion that the "evidence is offered for the purpose of establishing the defense of financially induced consent" and not for the purpose of "establish[ing] that the complainant acted in conformity" with her character of being a prostitute (p. 566) appears to be little more than sophistry. It is also worth noting that the court found it necessary to rely on cases outside of Michigan to find support for its decision.

Even if we put aside the problematic reasoning of the *Slovinski* court, an underlying premise of the case is that sex for money is not rape. Based on the analysis of prostitution presented in Evelina Giobbe, Prostitution: Buying the Right to Rape, at p. 494, and Report of the Florida Supreme Court Gender

Bias Study Commission, March 1990, at p. 544, what arguments would you make to dispute that premise? In answering this question you might also consider Carol Pateman's response to the claim that prostitution is merely a contractual exchange.

> [A]s an examination of consent and rape makes graphically clear, throughout the whole of sexual life domination, subjection, and enforced submission are confused with consent, free association, and the reciprocal fulfillment of mutual desire. The assertion that prostitution is no more than an example of a free contract between equal individuals in the market is another illustration of the presentation of submission as freedom. Feminists have often argued that what is fundamentally at issue in relations between women and men is not sex but power. But, in the present circumstances of our sexual lives, it is not possible to separate power from sex. . . .
>
> Prostitution is the public recognition of men as sexual masters; it puts submission on sale as a commodity in the market.

Carol Pateman, Defending Prostitution: Charges Against Ericsson, 93 Ethics 561, 564 (1983).

2. *Defense Use of Bias*. Notwithstanding a rape shield statute, courts have admitted evidence of the complainants' past sexual behavior when defendants have alleged bias because of the complainants' involvement in prostitution. In *Commonwealth v. Joyce*, 382 Mass. 222, 415 N.E.2d 181 (1981), the defendant attempted to introduce evidence that the complainant had been charged with prostitution to show that her allegation of rape "may have been motivated by her desire to avoid further prosecution." *Id.* at 184. The trial judge ruled that this evidence was prohibited under the Massachusetts rape shield statute. The Supreme Judicial Court reversed, stating:

> We emphasize that we do not depart from the long held view that prostitution is not relevant to credibility. . . .Nor do we depart from the policy of the statute in viewing prostitution or the lack of chastity as inadmissible on the issue of consent. Where, however, such facts are relevant to a showing of bias or motive to lie, the general evidentiary rule of exclusion must give way to the constitutionally based right of effective cross-examination.

Id. at 187.

D. The Complaint: Feminist Theory

Margaret A. Baldwin, Split at the Root: Prostitution and Feminist Discourses of Law Reform, 5 Yale J.L. & Feminism 47, 47–48, 50–52, 58–78, 81, 93–95, 114–20 (1992)

. . .This article originated in some years of feminist activism, and a sustained effort to understand two sentences spoken by Evelina Giobbe, an anti-prostitution activist and educator, at a radical feminist conference in 1987. She said:

"Prostitution isn't like anything else. Rather, everything else is like prostitution because it is the model for women's condition."[6]. . .

This paper attempts to begin a response to Giobbe's insight. The fundamental inquiry I pursue is how the relationship between "prostitutes" and "other women" is given meaning in the sexual abuse of women and girls, in the legal response to that abuse, and in feminist reform strategies. In the design of existing law, in the behavior of individual men, and in the leading strategies of feminist law reform, the relationship is cast in oppositional terms: whoever a "prostitute" is, "other women" are not. In substance, the distinction provides a handy means of identifying appropriate female objects of punishment and contempt. To be deemed a "prostitute," whether by the state, by a john, or by any other man for that matter, immediately targets a girl or woman for arrest, for sexual assault, for murder, or, at the very least, dismissive scorn. Victims of rape, of incest, of domestic battery, of sexual harassment, are quite familiar with this difficulty. Declared to be "whores" and "sluts" by the men who abuse them, women then confront a legal system which puts the same issue in the form of a question: was she in fact a "slut" who deserved it, as the perpetrator claims, or not-a-slut, deserving of some redress? (The outcome of this interrogation is commonly referred to as "justice."). . .

Brutality, written about, is different from brutality, lived. Writing, especially theoretical writing, is a practice which requires and maintains a certain distance; perhaps roughly the same distance necessary for pain's infliction. . . .For me the attempt to render women's pain into words, cast to the kindness of strangers, has caused great anguish and frustration. . . .I finally came to understand that one cannot write objectively from the victim's point of view; she must be abandoned as one pulls chair to table. The urgent collaboration, rather, is between the author and the reader, a collaboration wherein the sufferings of the victims "are used to create something, works of art, that are thrown to the consumption of a world which destroyed them."

In a paper about prostitution, it is difficult to avoid the inference that this

---

6. . . .Evelina Giobbe has written and worked in the past under the name Sarah Wynter. In 1989, she took back her birth name. This is part of what she has said about that decision:

> I, quite frankly, am tired of having my name taken from me by the pimps who stole my youth or due to my fear of retaliation by the pornographers. This year I am taking my name back. I consider it as much a political act as a personal choice. I choose to give up the illusion of safety that a pseudonym gave me, understanding now that no woman is safe as long as the traffic of women and children is allowed to continue. I take this action in defiance of the pimps and pornographers who sell women's bodies and steal their souls, and the johns who think that they can turn child sexual abuse and rape into a job by throwing money at their victims. I hope that this public/private act will contribute to ending our silence, and I have one other personal reason. It's a fine name, my mother gave it to me because it was my grandmother's name. I reclaim it in memory of her struggles.

Evelina Giobbe, From the Editors, WHISPER 3 (Summer 1989). WHISPER is the newsletter of the prostitution activist organization of the same name. Giobbe is a founder and the executive director of the organization.

collaboration shares certain features with that between pimp and john, the "prostitute" shaped by the author into a representation suitable and desirable for the anonymous reader's temporary, fleeting engagement. Again, the "prostitute" is but a species of exchange in a transaction through which her value is debated, quarreled over, but to which she remains a stranger. This dilemma, the revictimization of the sufferer in the very act of the writing that renders her visible, can perhaps only finally, securely be overcome by the eradication of the suffering such writing seeks to disclose. That will require a new form of communication among us, one which does not depend on the exchange of represented "women," in words and by commerce and as sex, for the false communion of author and reader (false because I speak to you as not-a-prostitute but as an author who objectifies "them," false because you read as a member of a general audience and not as yourself until you become yourself an author in another place). . . .

One of feminism's stories, entrenched deeply in the history and political landscape of the contemporary movement, is that prostitution is indeed not "like anything else." The theme was often sounded in the early movement that prostitution is *only* a story, a representational overlay masking and justifying real abuse and sex-based inequality suffered by (other?) women. "Prostitution" was conceived as a symbol, a groundless stereotype, a cancerous, run-amok ideological construct; "the prostitute" was the embodied cultural sign representing the sum of depravations suffered by "all women" (real women?). . . .

At least for women who are not publicly identified as "prostitutes," this understanding of prostitution as a false and dangerous idea nevertheless seems well enough supported in the experience of many women . . . .Especially on occasions of sexually exploitative and violent episodes, the characterization of women as "sluts" by assaultive men runs like a sturdy thread through women's accounts of sexual victimization. The epithet is apparently intended to humiliate, to eroticize, and to satisfy an urge for self-justification. . . .

For example, investigators of wife beating commonly recite "jealousy" as an asserted motivation for men to beat and torture women with whom they are intimate. Submerged in this conclusion are the allegations of prostitution which repeatedly emerge as the stated origin of that jealousy. In one collection of thirty-three women's accounts of their experience of being battered, nearly one third had been accused of prostitution or labelled as "whores" during the course of beatings and rapes. . . .Similar recitations figure obsessively in prosecutions for men's murders of wives and girlfriends. As one defendant put the point, the victim was "just a slut" and he "had to kill her." The same theme arises repeatedly in divorce actions, commonly where the husband beat and tortured his wife during the course of the marriage, and explains his behavior by reference to her whorish behavior.

These claims of punitive entitlement may extend beyond the situational to the structural. As women gain increased economic importance within families, it appears to at least one sociological researcher that the dynamics of battery increasingly mirror the familiar violence and economic exploitation typical of pimping. Ann Jones explains:

> [I] meet more and more battered women—severely battered women and women who have struck back—who were not being supported by the men

> who were their abusers. Rather, the economic arrangement is often the other way around: the man lives off the woman, off her wages or her welfare check or off the proceeds of her prostitution. He dominates and exploits her economically, just as he does physically and sexually. The parties may be husband and wife or a cohabiting couple, but the arrangement is the classic one of pimp and prostitute.

Since, at the same time, contemporary analyses of pimping practices frequently discern parallels between those arrangements and those characteristic of the traditional family, it becomes increasingly difficult to discern who is mimicking whom. . . .

Similar patterns are discernible in less intimate relationships such as sexual harassment and rape. In substance, as Catharine A. MacKinnon points out, "a great many instances of sexual harassment in essence amount to solicitation for prostitution.". . .In hostile work environment claims, the presumption of a working woman's ardent sexual availability to her co-workers, inferred either from her presence in the "wrong" workplace (that is, in male dominated trades and professions, where she can make a living wage), or from the assumption that sexual availability *is* her work (that is, in female dominated jobs, where she cannot), echoes throughout the reported cases. The same presumption of a woman's exploitative "sluttish" sexual enticement of a rapist, summed up neatly by one defendant's view that "all women were whores and sluts and they all deserved what [the victim] was getting," persists *ad nauseum*. . . .

[M]uch feminist legal reform work against sexual violence has explicitly or implicitly advanced. . .strategies of lawyerly separation, distinguishing with great delicacy and equal urgency between "prostitutes" and "other women." The political rescue of "real womanhood" from conditions of prostitution, within the spheres of life believed occupied by "normal women," has been the mainstream feminist tactic advanced within many of our campaigns. These reform strategies have sought to displace these false beliefs by persuasion to counter-representations of our own devising, for example, "sexual harassment," "pornography victims," and "battered women." Each of these counter-stories constitutes an appeal to "more speech," the valid representation driving out the false. Each also promotes a predictable theme about prostitution: emphatically, that we are *not* prostitutes. A mistake has been made—a grievous failure to contour the proper distinctions between the prostitution with which we are charged and our own conduct, and a consequent failure to treat us with justice. This analysis initially notes the analogic relationship conventionally drawn between a woman's behavior and prostitution, usually to punish her, and proceeds, as a predicate for reform proposals, to criticize the appropriateness of the comparison. . . .

Each of our counter-representations, our "true" stories, seeks to disidentify any particular sexual violence victim from the status of "prostitute" by distinguishing her behavior from at least one of the legal elements of prostitution.

In rape law reform, for example, feminist lawyers have long labored to establish a victim's "discriminateness," both in articulating the injury rape entails and in the representation of the victim at trial. Our most significant work focuses on the habilitation of a woman's "no" as probative of her lack of consent. This commitment in turn locates the injury of rape in the disregard of a woman's sexual selectiveness. The enforcement of rape shield evidentiary rules and the articulation of women's injury through testimony of rape trauma syndrome continue this theme. Rape shield rules limit the admissibility of a woman's prior sexual history for the purpose of proving consent, at least when the defendant has not had sex with her before. This representational spin control seeks to sever in a jury's mind the inferential connection it might otherwise draw between a woman's sexual "promiscuity" and her conduct on a particular occasion. Less politely, these rules of exclusion are designed to defeat the whore status her prior activity would ascribe to her. The admissibility of evidence of rape trauma syndrome, cataloging the physical, psychological, and behavioral symptoms commonly consequent to sexual assault, has also been advocated by feminist reformers both to corroborate a woman's testimony that she did not consent to the act, and to dispel juror misunderstanding that women "ask for it," by rendering plain the profound, complex, and enduring suffering that unwanted sex causes.

Prostitutes, of course, say "yes" a great deal. Our threshold commitment to the dismissal of woman's "no" as the talismanic violation of rape both renders prostitution beyond the pale of our rape reforms and, praise be, prostitutes as the women we are not. The courts have also apparently aptly understood the intended limits of these reforms, consistently holding that the fictionalizing protections of rape shield rules should give way to the "plain truth" when the defendant can prove that the victim "really was" a prostitute or that financial arrangements were involved in the contested act. This conclusion is echoed in the avoidance of the question of whether prostitutes might likely endure some form, perhaps extreme, of rape trauma syndrome. It may seem to some the better part of discretion not to cheapen the significance of a woman's "no" by the potentially embarrassing display of women engaging in otherwise nonconsensual sex for twenty dollars, accepting what amounts to a pittance in liquidated damages for rape, while "other women" assert the deep and lasting trauma that difference twenty dollars makes. Our strategy of differentiating prostitutes from ourselves, begun by categorically distinguishing between "yes or no" sex, here seems elevated to an ontological divide between nice women who are hurt and not so nice women presumptively calloused or insensible to selling themselves for the equivalent of a parking fine.

Nor have we questioned deeply the exclusion of "non-stranger" assailants from the reach of the shield rules, even as we urge the prosecution of "voluntary social companions," husband-rapists, and incestuous fathers for sexual assault. . . .The. . .explanation for this acquiescence, because it is more closely linked with the perspectives of feminist activists (who, after all, identified the *injuries* of marital and date rape in the first place) lies in the proximity, both experientially and conceptually, of non-stranger sexual assault to the paradigm of domestic battery. As a tactical matter, argument for the expansion of the shield rules to exclude evidence of the sexual history of a relationship between victim and assailant runs head on into the principal strategy feminists have elaborated in behalf of battered women: the representation of battered women via battered women's syndrome testimony. Rather than placing restrictions in the factual context available to juries, we have in that domain sought the *expansion* of the representational frame to include the emotional history of the relationship, the psychological consequences of serial battery to victims, and the default in social recognition, support, and material alternatives women battered by cohabitant men commonly confront. The contrast in the scope of these explanations, with the freeze-frame, miniaturist portrait of the rape victim constructed under the shield rules, could not be more acute.

This strategic distinction in representational preference perhaps can be explained by the difference in the questions courts and juries typically have in mind for stranger rape victims and domestic battery victims. The question addressed to the stranger rape victim is some version of the "why were you *there*?" question (dressed as you were/drinking as you were/knowing what you did). The question the battery victim confronts is some version of the "why did you *stay*?" question (if you are telling the truth/if you didn't get something out of it). The presumption against the stranger rape victim is that she assumed the risk, against the domestic battery victim that she failed to exhaust her self-help remedies through separation or divorce. In the latter case, if the persistence of the relationship is the problem perceived by the law and by juries, we will explain it. The inference to be overcome is that she remained for her own motives, including a taste for pain or luxury, or that she was properly disciplined for real lapses in wifely devotion or fidelity.

Feminist explanations of "why she stayed" have been of two orders. The first describes women's *responses* to battery, detailing a woman's "socialization" *by* the relationship to hope for the man's eventual change, within a downward spiral of collapsing self-esteem extinguishing her feeling that she is entitled to better treatment. This emphasis stresses the complexities of love, intimacy, and commitment to a man over time as the crucial explanatory lens for comprehending women's decisions to remain in abusive relationships. . . .Christine Littleton expands. . .[on this] psychological explanation to one founded on broader normative commitments commonly held by women favoring the maintenance of ongoing relationships, independent of the measure of pain *or* pleasure the relationship yields. Women battered by men may "stay," on Littleton's account, regardless of whether any promised changes are likely to ensue, "because they are trying to rescue something beyond themselves"—the relationship itself. . . .On each of these accounts, the woman's "problem," if she has one, abides in an overcommitment to monogamous fidelity, even at the risk of her own life.

Self-defense strategies urge a similar framework for comprehending the reduction of a woman's options for survival to killing her abuser and for explaining the validity of her perception of imminent danger in circumstances which might be understood by a jury as less than immediate. . . .

This representation, like that drawn of rape victims under the rape shield laws, benefits women little in encounters with "real" johns, or toward explaining why a woman "stays" in prostitution; even if, like most women in the life, she is raped, assaulted, and threatened with murder on a regular basis. The ties and insights of persistent affection are not commonly present between a prostitute and a john. "Loving contrition" is not a common behavior pattern in men who buy women for sex. Nor does the prostitute enjoy the tidy legal status of an otherwise socially conforming "victim." The "good woman" sex role of loyalty to intimate monogamous fidelity, while perhaps of tactical assistance in garnering sympathy for women battered by husbands, is but a tool of punishment of women in prostitution. A prostitute who kills a john cannot argue a specialized understanding of a particular john's habits of violence, at least so long as johns are not understood as men who pose particular perils to prostituted women. Nor are these theoretical distancing strategies only of academic significance. The inapplicability, even structural hostility, of battered women defenses to women in prostitution contributed strongly to Aileen Carol Wuornos's recent first degree murder convictions for killing several johns, for which she has been sentenced to death.

This focus on women's responses to battery by an intimate partner is a relative latecomer to feminist analyses of wife beating, although now the dominant one in the legal arena. The originating critiques questioned more directly how men have come to enjoy the privilege, how male power is enacted in families, how the structure of the family reproduces that power, how law and other institutions of social control remain complicit in male torture of women in the home, and under what political conditions women continue to live with and marry men. The issue for these scholars and activists was not why some women "stayed," but how any woman escaped living in a violent household but by the grace of God or, less transcendentally, by a wholesale restructuring of her social options. These critiques bring to light the institutional controls rendering women targets for violence in marriage, including the social, sexual, and economic "channelling" of women into marital dependency to the near exclusion of other viable living arrangements. . . .

In the legal representation of women, these structural insights have largely been compressed to one line mention of women's common economic dependency on husbands in marriage, ordinarily in the context of a court's explication of the necessity of expert testimony on battered women's syndrome. . . .Nor have feminist legal critics much attended to this descriptive factor, even as the affinity of the heavily "psychologized" content of battered women's syndrome testimony with the stereotype of women as neurotic and helpless is critiqued. At most, we "maternalize" the economic dimension, attending to the "special" economic pressures on battered women with children to support to remain in abusive marriages. Further, the economic interest of *men* in the women they control by violence, in the time-honored tradition of pimping, remains wholly uninterrogated. Of course, avoidance of the economic question also serves to maintain the "good woman" distance from the inference of prostitution, which the emphasis on intimacy and love in the construction of battered women's syndrome testimony further severs. Whatever we are there for, it isn't for the money. If he is no trick, she is no whore.

"Legitimate" work is, after all, the place where women are supposed to make money, an assumption which has fueled anti-sexual harassment legal initiatives and education efforts. Here, our advocacy stresses the *distinction* between a woman's willingness to work and her willingness to have sex as part of the bargain, or to be sexualized in her status as worker: "real women" do not combine sex with money. . . .

[I]t would seem but a small step conceptually to hold all prostitution to be *per se* actionable as sexual harassment, as the demand for money in the transaction shows that a woman's sexual compliance in the acts were otherwise unwanted. Certainly, demand for payment, unequivocally delivered, might in most circumstances distinguish such transactions from the "romantic attractions" courts find so distressingly indistinguishable, at least in hypothethical [sic] contemplation, from unwanted workplace sexual attention. . . .Both in legal doctrine and in feminist theory, however, this coerced election is instead treated as if it instead defined one class of women who are injured by sexual harassment (the distant ones) and another, those who are not (the "welcoming" ones). . . .

Taken together, these boundary defenses form a solid wall against the imputation of prostitution to particular "other" women: she is not sexually promiscuous, does not subject herself to random treatment by strangers, and doesn't do it for cash. Beyond these defenses, is but silence. Domestic legal reform activity on prostitution is nearly nonexistent, both in feminist legislative projects and feminist legal scholarship. . . .

I have expressed a good deal of anger here, and mostly at the wrong people. In its legal expression, this feminist flight from prostitution seems largely reactive, driven by a tacit recognition that legal regulation of sexual violence and sex discrimination at bottom always functions as some form of judicial review of a man's conclusion that a complaining woman was, in fact, a whore, and therefore a permissible target of misogynist rage, contempt, and sexual use. The fate of a woman's claims on justice, we all seem to know somewhere, crucially depends on her success in proving that she is not, and never has been, a prostitute. As Andrea Dworkin puts the point, "The woman's effort to stay innocent, her efforts to prove innocence, her effort to prove that she was used against her will is always and unequivocally an effort to prove she is not a whore.". . .

If "other women" seek to split from prostitution by disidentifying from one element of it, prostitute advocates have sought to identify *as* "other women" by identifying *with* one of the "not a prostitute" stories. Prostitutes thereby can "become" other women; prostitution is but one variant of a condition shared in common with those others. If other women aren't prostitutes, neither are prostitutes. On *all* of the contending perspectives, prostitution *is* "like everything else." The dispute turns on what the "else" is characterized to be. The dignity abides in the simple claim that no woman is a "prostitute," no woman is deserving of the violence and contempt women in prostitution routinely suffer. The desperation comes in the cost of "proving" it. In this public discussion, that effort, already a brutal demand, seems to require that prostitutes' lives be *justified*, rather than empathetically understood.

In this compelled endeavor of justification, prostitute advocates have been assisted both by the contributions and the theoretical disputes of liberal feminism, socialist feminism, and radical feminism. In theoretical emphasis and strategic design, these tendencies in feminism identify discrete political "locales" as fundamental to women's oppression. Liberal feminism, with its stress on the conditions of women's individual consent, has had principal influence in rape law reform, foundationally in the sex-with-strangers variety. Radical feminism, with its stress on the conditions of women's coercion in "private" intimacy with men, has had principal influence in domestic violence intervention. Socialist feminism, with its stress on women's economic exploitation in the family and in the workplace, has had principal influence in altering monetary conditions of women's employment. Aside from some turf skirmishes (most vituperatively fought among academics), these tendencies co-exist relatively calmly, perhaps because the "sphere of influence" attended to by each conforms with what is viewed as a "natural" division of the street, from the home, and from the workplace, in women's lives.

This same tripartite division habilitates, if less serenely, the splits among prostitution advocates, providing political precedent for the contention by each that prostitutes are "other women," after all. In the liberal advocates' view, prostitution "is" non-monogamous, consensual sex, again taking up the selectiveness component as fundamental. In the socialist view, prostitution is work, attending to the matter of money. In the radical feminist view, the woman's circumstances of intimate coercion occupies the essential territory. Having distilled the crucial problem, we each notice that other women share it. Other women, too, are stigmatized for apparent sexual independence and nonconformity. Other women, too, are economically exploited, reviled for making money at all, the value of their labor cheapened if they do. Other women, too, are "invisibly" sexually coerced, the realities of lifelong sexual abuse masked and perpetuated under an erotic regime which rewards the compliance of the hopeless and thrives in the possibilities which proliferate when no questions are asked.

Each of these positions, in turn, is also argued from the representational framework commonly advanced by their "other woman" counterparts. Liberal advocates favor the "shielded" version, limiting their "story" of prostitution to the immediate sexual component of the transaction, while arguing to the irrelevance of any other feature of the exchange (often including the money), and of any other surrounding conditions of a woman's life. Socialist feminist advocates favor the categorical divide between "sex" and "work," familiar from sexual harassment campaigns, holding prostitution unambiguously to fall in the productive realm of "work." Radical feminist advocates urge an expanded version of the domestic violence story, stressing the effect of serial, sometimes life-long, suffering of sexual abuse in prostitutes' lives as the relevant interpretive context. Having set the terms, however divergent, on the correspondence of the oppression of women in prostitution with that suffered by "other women," the (feminist) debate on prostitution thus seeks to merge in theme and strategic focus with those familiar from other feminist campaigns without rupture. . . .

For the purpose of each of these positions is to destroy itself, and "prostitution" along with it. Each of us is more apt to savor this point in criticism of our opponents than reflect on its implications for ourselves, or for what it means toward advancing this debate. The measure of success we each set for our own accounts of prostitution is the ease with which our "other woman" story can swallow it whole. This same measure of success is, in turn, the measure of failure we use to castigate the failings of our opponents. The more persuasively we argue the continuity of our accounts of prostitution with our renditions of "other women's" life conditions, the more vulnerable we are to the charge that we have failed to grasp the specificity, the "reality" of "prostitution itself." Since each of us is bent on "de-specifying" prostitution in our own terms, the charge begins to ring rather falsely as a criticism.

If each of these positions is self-consuming in its own terms, the "debate" is as self-defeating.

The "real truth," I think, about this debate is its irreality *as* a debate, at least about *prostitution*, to all concerned. . . .The "true" question in contest in the prostitution debate is not really prostitution at all. Rather, the debate is the site of contest over the representational expansion and dominance of our "other women's" stories, beyond the zones of explanatory control each formerly more peaceably occupied. The struggle over prostitution, as it is presently argued, is a bid by each tendency in feminism for territory largely ceded to the others by each before prostitution entered the scene: a bid for a story of money by liberals, for a story of sex by socialists, and for a story of strange men by radicals. . . .

What is lost in the prostitution debate, as we are all asked to justify the lives of prostitutes as just like those of other women, is what other women need to learn and know and appreciate and politicize about the conditions of their own existence *from* women in prostitution. That is the fundamental condition of consciousness-raising that has been forfeited by the larger movement: that women in prostitution have insight and knowledge that other women need to make sense of their *own* lives. The continued silence, shame, the formalistic appeals, the elevation of theorizing over action stifling the participation of woman in prostitution in our movement is supported by a political climate that wants prostitutes only to ask permission to join, not authority to direct. "Other women" don't want to hear, perhaps, that our boyfriends and husbands are buying sex from women in prostitution. "Other women" don't want to hear, perhaps, that the "straight" jobs we have are sexualized top to bottom. "Other women" don't want to hear, perhaps, that we are each one man from the street. But if our stories are to gain in boldness and integrity, we all need to be able to hear all of that, and find the "point to it."

I am not about to say, as you may think I am about to say, that "all women are prostitutes." That is a glib and silly, nearly insulting, thing to say. (I mean, insulting to women in prostitution.) There is a theme, though, that obviously links all of these stories. That is the story that *no one is a prostitute*, recited with utmost conviction, or with the passion of a final plea for help and justice. And perhaps *that* is the story that is the prostitution story itself: a woman declaring, with equal parts conviction and resignation, that she is not a prostitute, to please somebody else upon whom her survival depends. . . .

[D]issociative strategies of distancing the act, herself, and the john are routine tactics practiced by women in prostitution, described by Kathleen Barry as constructing a "split-identity" between "that" woman performing an act of prostitution and her "other" self. . . .

"Disengagement" from her "real self" is the fundamental demand made of women in prostitution, the essential term of the transaction itself. What a john wants is for the woman to *act* like the woman he wants, and for the woman to maintain a credible performance as part of the bargain. . . .[T]he demand made of the woman is to demonstrate a happy complicity, to whatever role is demanded.

I would suggest that a similar demand, and similar strategy in the fact of it, drives the design of our feminist strategies in our public advocacy. The disengagement tactic step, has, I hope, been demonstrated throughout this paper: whatever we are, wherever we are, it is not prostitution. It is love, or freedom, or work, or force, or fear; anything but prostitution. We can prove it by our arguments, over and over, from every possible angle that might be mustered in opposition. It is all a great mistake, and if no else is convinced, we can at least convince ourselves. "I was never really into it." How many times a day do we turn this trick? How many years has feminism told this story, been "somewhere else" as a strategy of resisting what we are told we are?

And who are we talking to? Who is it, who cares so much, that we should care to convince? The men, it seems: the men who feel license to destroy us if we fail to convince them, the johns we hope at the risk of our lives will remember we are human beings. We are not prostitutes, and hope we can act well enough to fit the part of not being one. The law, too, we hope to convince. Our stories of "consent," of "work," of "intimacy," have been crafted with the law in mind, placating its demand that we not "really" be sluts. We deliver the goods, compliantly, now in the name of a self-determining, liberated feminism. "It was good for me, too, honest."

My further intuition is that this is a structural political requirement, not only a problem of bad men, silly laws, or short-sighted feminism. My belief, also my fear, is that within the existing political and legal order, and the possibilities for change afforded some women, is embedded a profound bargain: take what you can, but it will always be at the price of abandoning prostitutes, of gaining your advantage at her expense. There is a term for women who accept bargains like that. It's called being a pimp's "bottom woman," the one who treasures his highest regard, and sometimes gets off the street herself, but only if she helps run the less lucky girls. There is also a term for the arrangement which makes this bargain compelling. It's called pimping, period. If my intuition is correct, this is the arrangement women presently have with the state, motivating the "not a prostitute" content of our legal stories as a condition of our legal citizenship. My question for all of us, in love and struggle, is this: if I am right, in this intuition, do we love our pimp so much, after all? What stories would we tell, if not for him?

Notes and Questions

1. *Continuum of Violence.* Margaret Baldwin shows how the dynamics of prostitution are reflected in other forms of violence against women, including battering, rape, and sexual harassment. She also shows how all the forms of violence are interconnected and how feminist reforms that rigidify the legal boundaries among them may produce harmful consequences to some women. With Baldwin's themes in mind, reread *State v. Norman*, at p. 257, in which the violence included battering and prostitution.

2. *"Throwaway Women."* A crucial component of Baldwin's analysis of prostitution is society's indifference toward prostituted women, even when the violence they experience can be seen clearly. Jane Caputi demonstrates the extent of this indifference by looking at "sex murders."

> In the mid-1980s, at least 17 women, characterized by the police as prostitutes, were murdered within a 40-mile radius in South Central Los Angeles, a primarily African-American neighborhood; all but 3 of the victims

were African-Americans. The police waited until 10 women were killed before notifying the public that a serial murderer was operating and then waited until there were 4 more deaths before forming a task force. . . .[I]n many other instances of serial murder, the killer might begin with prostitute women, but then moves on to women of all types . . . .When the police or press describe the murdered women as prostitutes, it lulls nonprostitute women into a false feeling of safety. It plays upon sexist and frequently racist prejudices to mute the seriousness of the murders, and—most effectively—it diverts the blame to the victim.

In October 1888, Charles Warren, police chief in charge of the "Jack the Ripper" case, pontificated to the press: "The police can do nothing as long as the victims unwittingly connive at their own destruction. They take the murderer to some retired spot, and place themselves in such a position that they can be slaughtered without a sound being heard." That sentiment was echoed, one century later, in a piece in the *Los Angeles Times* titled, "Prostitutes: Easy Prey for Killers." It portrays "drug-dazed" women, good daughters gone bad, and contains a quote from Commander William Booth of the Los Angeles police department: "I think that's the highest-risk occupation there is. Mercenaries are way behind prostitutes. . . .There is nothing that carries the risk with it, in peacetime, as streetwalking prostitution."

Jane Caputi, The Sexual Politics of Murder, 3 Gender & Soc'y 437, 451-52 (1989).

The case of Aileen (Lee) Carol Wuornos, to which Baldwin refers (p. 574), presents another aspect of the "throwaway woman."

The media and social scientists have described Wuornos as the first "female serial killer"; the FBI has *classified* her as such. But is this true?. . .

Serial killers are mainly white male drifters, obsessed with pornography and woman-hatred, who sexually use their victims, either before or after killing them, and who were themselves *paternally* abused children. . . .

I don't think Wuornos fits this description. Wuornos was not a pornography addict, she did not eroticize her hatred of women (or of men); she did not stalk women, or male or female prostitutes; in fact, she *was* a prostituted woman. The men she killed all fit the profile of johns, those who frequent prostitutes.

In addition, most serial killers don't insist that they killed in self-defense—as Wuornos has. . . .

People say that Wuornos could not have killed *six times* in self-defense, that no one could—except of course men, in times of war. But Wuornos, a seriously abused child and a serially raped and beaten teenage and adult prostitute, has been under attack all her life, probably more than any soldier in any real war.

Phyllis Chesler, A Woman's Right to Self-Defense: The Case of Aileen Carol Wuornos, 66 St. John's L. Rev. 933, 946-47 (1993).

Further documentation of the repeated life-threatening violence that women in prostitution face is found in an interview conducted by the WHISPER oral history project.

Karen estimates that she was raped by a customer on approximately 15

> or 20 occasions. She defined rape as a situation in which a customer had sex with her and then refused to pay or took back their money after the act. These situations commonly entailed a customer driving her to a deserted area, forcing sex by knife point, and abandoning her there. Karen also described being literally forced to engage in sex acts by her customers that she defined as assaultive or abusive in spite of the fact that she was paid. On one occasion she was forcibly sodomized. On other occasions customers would ejaculate in her mouth against her expressed wishes, then force her to swallow their semen. Other times they would force intercourse a second time against her wishes. Karen expressed an extremely negative response to the sex she was compelled to engage in as a prostitute emphatically stating that she was "raped by all of them. Anytime someone did it and I didn't want to do it [which was] every time I turned a trick."
>
> Karen estimated that she was beaten up by a customer on approximately 30 separate occasions—usually within the context of a robbery or a sexual assault. After one such assault she required medical attention for a knife wound. She was also the victim of kidnapping by customers on three occasions where she was held against her will for "a couple hours" and sexually assaulted.

Evelina Giobbe, Juvenile Prostitution: Profile of Recruitment, in Child Trauma I: Issues & Research 117, 125-26 (Ann Wolbert Burgess ed., 1992).

3. *"Prostitution Isn't Like Anything Else."* Evelina Giobbe in "Prostitution: Buying the Right to Rape", at p. 494, argues that the institution of prostitution resembles the institution of marriage and that selling sex for money is like marital rape. As Baldwin states, however, Giobbe has also written that "[p]rostitution isn't like anything else. Rather, everything else is like prostitution because it is the model for women's condition." Evelina Giobbe, Confronting the Liberal Lies About Prostitution, in The Sexual Liberals and the Attack on Feminism 67, 76 (Dorchen Leidholdt & Janice G. Raymond eds., 1990). What is Giobbe's purpose in making each argument? How can the arguments be reconciled?

Chapter 8
Pornography

The materials in this chapter primarily take the position that pornography is violence and that the women's movement should press for legal and social reforms that respond to that violence. Like the chapters on battering, sexual harassment, rape, and prostitution, this chapter challenges legal and social distinctions between pornography and other forms of violence against women. Just as for prostitution, no consensus exists that pornography is violence against women. The focus of the debate changes from freedom of contract to freedom of speech, but the effect is the same—indifference toward women used in the pornography industry, women harmed by men mimicking the violence in pornography, and women harmed by their objectification and dehumanization in pornography. In recognition of the strength of the freedom of speech claim for many of us, the readings are designed to test the assumptions that make that claim compelling and to clarify that women bear the burden of the primacy of the First Amendment—a burden borne differently and differentially depending on the abilities, class, race, and sexual orientation of the woman.

Part A includes readings that identify the various harms caused by pornography and the interrelationship of pornography, battering, sexual harassment, rape, and prostitution. The first piece is excerpted from an interview by Laura Lederer of a former pornography model. It provides a glimpse into the conditions, for at least one woman, of working in the pornography industry and a framework for evaluating the theoretical discussions surrounding pornography. The interview is followed by a selection by Andrea Dworkin in which she explains the etymology of the word *pornography*. Patricia Hill Collins then demonstrates how race and gender intersect in the representations of women found in pornography and how our understanding of pornography changes when we place African-American women at the center of the analysis. This part concludes with a selection by Susan Griffin that analyzes pornography as a sadistic act.

Part B examines the tension among freedom of speech, equality, and legal recognition of harm to women. It begins with *American Booksellers Ass'n v. Hudnut*, in which the U.S. Court of Appeals for the Seventh Circuit held unconstitutional an anti-pornography ordinance enacted in Indianapolis that was modeled after an ordinance originated by Andrea Dworkin and Catharine MacKinnon. The ordinance provides a civil rights remedy for women harmed by pornography and includes a definition of pornography based on the subordination of women. *Hudnut* is followed by an article by MacKinnon in which she approaches the constitutionality question through the dual lenses of equality and free speech. This part ends with *Regina v. Butler*, in which the Supreme Court of Canada upheld the constitutionality of Canada's criminal obscenity law by recognizing the harm to women caused by pornography. An examination of *Hudnut* and *Butler* allows us to compare the two conflicting legal philosophies currently dominating the pornography debate.

A. Identifying the Violence

Laura Lederer, Then and Now: An Interview with a Former Pornography Model, in *Take Back the Night: Women on Pornography* 57 (Laura Lederer ed., 1980)

The question often arises, "Why do women star in pornographic films and model for pornographic magazines?" Many people suggest that feminists are aimed in the wrong direction: We should, they say, attack the women who pose for and act in such degrading films and photographs.

Presumably our society is set up so that women have a free choice as to what we want to do. If women can be convinced to stop modeling for pornographic magazines and films, goes the argument, then the industry will shut down. But the truth is, as long as we have a patriarchal culture which encourages women to use their bodies to get male approval and which rewards young girls for being sexy objects, we can expect to see many females turn to pornography, prostitution, and other forms of sexploitation to stay alive or even to earn prestige and social acceptance.

The following interview with Jane Jones (for purposes of anonymity her name has been changed) is one woman's story of how she got involved in the pornography industry and what it was like to be a pornography model. . . .

Jane Jones (JJ): My family life wasn't the greatest. I was the only female child. Both my parents were alcoholics and both were child abusers; though neither one admitted they were themselves, they used to accuse one another of mistreating us kids.

There were a lot of sexual imbalances in my family. For instance, I had my own room because I was the only girl, but I wasn't allowed to lock it, also because I was a girl. If I tried to lock it, my father or older brothers would use that as an excuse to burst in on me. One time I didn't have anything on and grabbed a sweater to cover myself. My brother ripped it off me. He had to pay for a new sweater, but no one said anything about how it was ripped off or why.

If I was in the shower, my father would come and turn off the hot water or throw ice cubes into the shower. Just a joke, of course, but I would have to jump out or yell. My father was sexually provocative. He was always touching me. My mother encouraged it in a strange way by not validating my experience when I would object. If my father fondled my butt and I protested to her, she would say, "But he's your father!" No one ever believed my problems. My father was my grandmother's only and precious son. There was a sense in my family that if I didn't put up with these jokes or antics, I was being paranoid, or a bad sport, or I had a dirty mind. It was always in *my* imagination.

My first experience with the camera was for high school graduation. My mother fixed me up to wear a low-cut black blouse which was deliberately suggestive. This was in the decade when females wore Peter Pan blouses and circle pins. I remember I felt extremely sexy. I had never liked my body, mostly because of the suggestive innuendoes of my father as I developed. I always thought I was plain-looking. But I photographed differently than I looked, and I found that out very quickly. I found out that I had a marketable commodity.

Laura Lederer (LL): How did you get started in the nude modeling business?

JJ: It was in 1967. I was just out of high school. I had run away from home. I was rebellious—"living in sin" with my boyfriend. We had a two-bedroom house, actually a little shack in the inner city, complete with rats and cockroaches, which we shared with a seven-and-a-half-month pregnant woman. I wasn't able to keep the jobs I had tried to get. I was fired from one job because of ill health. I remember feeling trapped. I had no real skills I could market in order to stay alive. That particular month was a hard one, and we ended up not having enough money to pay the rent. We needed a fairly large amount of money quickly. I looked in the want ads in the *L.A. Free Press*. There was an ad which read: "Models, $50.00/day, 18 and over." I called, and they asked me my height and weight and hired me that first day.

LL: Why do most women model for these agencies? Why do women come in the door in the first place?

JJ: A lot of women are hurt or crazy—women under stress. Yes, most women come in under a lot of stress. They're usually desperate when they first come in—maybe they need money for some emergency, like I did, or they've gone as long as they can doing odds and ends or working at shit jobs, and they finally just have to pay their bills. I met a woman whose kid was in the hospital, and I met lots of women who were financially strapped. There were also many illegal aliens there who couldn't work regular jobs even if they had the skills because they didn't have their green cards.

LL: Does the agency exploit this need?

JJ: I don't know. Well, they certainly know how to get you to do what they want. Some women are so bad off that they just go immediately into hardcore films.

Take the average woman who graduates from high school. Vast numbers of us are not skilled at anything but marketing our bodies, usually to get husbands, but sometimes to get money or fame. We spend all our time and money making ourselves pretty, being well made up. What I'm trying to say is that I don't see what is so unusual about a woman going to a modeling agency. It's just the logical extension of everything that is taught us at home and in school. The only difference is in the degree. Most of the women who came to the agency were poor, or in extreme times of crisis, or both. They were women from all walks of life. Runaways are a very big part of the business. This fed right into the 1960's hippie movement. I remember feeling nudity was okay and natural, so photos of it must be okay too—except that it didn't feel good.

LL: How did your agency work?

JJ: First, they took nude pictures of you. They had this huge book of photos of women. Most of the women were posed in high heels with no clothes on. There are a variety of poses—standing, sitting, back, front, side, and sometimes a closeup of the face. They had two books—one was of white women, one was of Black women and other women of color. Then they had a third portfolio, which was commonly known as the "Freaks" book—women who (in their eyes) were grotesquely overweight, or had some deformity or something abnormal like a tattoo. I remember feeling badly for them, not because they were overweight, but because they were treated much worse than the other women. It was almost as if they weren't human. . . .

LL: Could you talk more about the agency procedure?

JJ: There was a legal-size sheet of paper. It's actually your contract (at least it was in my agency). On the sheet there was a checklist of what types of modeling were available. There were boxes which you could check off—"hard core," "soft core," "pretty girl." "Pretty girl" was like the pin-up bathing suits, negligees, and "tasteful" nudity, always posed so the crotch was hidden. There were also boxes labeled "nude modeling" and "movies" and "hostessing." In another space on the contract, the agency checked off what age you could look. I could look as young as eleven, which was a benefit, since "young girls" were in big demand.

There was a place on the sheet to check off whether you were on the pill. The agency encouraged women to go on the pill because it made your breasts bigger. There was a large market for women with big breasts. They had a whole portfolio of these women which they called "Tit Rags" or "Mammary Reviews." If you got the job, photographers frequently asked you when your period was due and scheduled the photography session just before so your breasts were at their biggest. Photographers would come in and look at pictures in the portfolio and write down your code number and name. The agency had code numbers supposedly for your own protection, but also for their protection—so that the women wouldn't get jobs without giving the agency their cut. After the photographer had chosen a model, the agency would call you and you would appear for an audition. The audition usually consisted of you stripping and walking around the room. A lot of times you had to wear stockings, garters, and high heels without any underwear. I hated that part—it really made me feel creepy. Occasionally the photographer would take test shots before you were hired.

There was a lot of competitiveness between women at the agency. Most women were out to get the job, and women would cut one another down before the auditions. Almost every model was connected to a man. Contrary to popular belief that there are a lot of lesbians in the business, almost every woman I met there was hetero, as far as I knew.

It was a lonely sort of business in that you rarely worked with one another, but always in competition. Once in a while the agency would send two women on a job together, but that was the exception rather than the rule, and even then there was a competitive atmosphere. Sometimes they would have what's called a "cattle call," and all the women would line up. Cattle calls were very demeaning.

The photographers ranged from nice to real pricks. Some were old, grandfatherly types. Others were freelancers with no idea where they would sell their photographs. Some worked for specific magazines. Some men treated you okay, but most acted like you weren't even human and didn't give you lunch breaks or anything. There were some lecherous types who figured that once they had "paid" for you, you owed them more than just photographs.

LL: What were some of your first jobs?

JJ: On my first job there was a woman who had just had a baby two days prior to the assignment. She was bleeding. She was doing the movie to try to get the kid out of the hospital. She had this tampon—or two of them—in her to try to stop the bleeding, even though she wasn't supposed to use tampons right after birth. Our job was to simulate lesbian love. That was the first and last time I did that. I really disliked the woman-on-woman stuff. Most women asked for lesbian scenes. In fact, several women told me that I was crazy not to work with women because then I wouldn't get the clap. But I was very male-identified at that time and extremely homophobic, so I requested hetero scenes. In retrospect, it is easy for me to see that I was fighting my own sexuality.

The male image of lesbian love seems to dictate that it be violent and/or include a male voyeur. There is a very big demand for this sort of lesbian love scene in pornography.

It seems to me that it is important for male photographers to portray lesbian love in as repugnant a way as possible. They have very bizarre notions of women's sexuality. None of the gentle loving comes through. Male portrayal of lesbian sex is a real PR job for heterosexual sex.

I also had to do a simulated lesbian sadomasochism job. (At that time I was not a lesbian.) I was terrified. The woman who was playing the "S" was really into it (she wasn't a lesbian either), and that came out in the film. The photographer thought it was just great. . . .

LL: What other assignments did you have?

JJ: I did an album cover for an English group that was released here. Their music was terrible. I know the cover was what sold the album because of reviews I've read. It didn't sell well in the first issue, but they reissued it with the new cover and the album sold 50,000 copies in one day. It was written up in *Rolling Stone*—people were buying the album, tossing the record out, and taking the cover home to display. The picture on the cover was a crotch shot of me leaping high in the air to simulate flying. I had to go through hell to get that photo.

LL: What do you mean?

JJ: For the cover shot I jumped eighty-seven times off a coffee table onto a hard mat. I counted because it was such a nightmare. I had to resist my natural impulse to break my fall until the last possible moment. The photographer was underneath, taking pictures, straight up. Then he drove me out to the desert for the shot for the inside cover. I went alone with him.

LL: Wasn't that dangerous?

JJ: Yes—incredibly dangerous. But things like that happened all the time, and I never thought twice about them in those days. It was ridiculous. I put myself into all sorts of dangerous situations.

I rationalized it because I had been referred to the job by a photographer I knew, and because I was really impressed with the credentials of the guy taking the pictures—he had done several other album covers. Anyway, he said he wanted a photograph with no telephone poles on the horizon, but that also meant I was away from anyone else with a man in the desert, and I was nude. There was one point when I was very scared. He propositioned me, and I refused. I remember thinking, "I could easily get raped out here." After that I started leaving the license number of the photographer with my boyfriend so that if anything happened to me he could track me down.

LL: Why did you put up with situations like that?

JJ: At that time, it was just part of the job for me. Women are socialized to put up with a lot—to passively accept tremendous amounts of pain, indignity, and humiliation. They used to do the most ridiculous things to you—like paint your whole body or put glitter all over you.

LL: They still do. The cover of the Ohio Players album is called Honey, *and in the picture they have poured honey all over a woman—as if she were a thing to be consumed.*

JJ: That's it exactly. Women are portrayed, seen, and treated as "little treats." There aren't many other images to choose from when you're growing up. I was taught that I was a "sweet thing," and when I grew up, I found that I was a marketable commodity—which is exactly what a woman is in our society in one form or another. One of the porn series I was in used food names for the women, like Taffy, Candy, Cookie.

LL: What jobs did you like and dislike?

JJ: The jobs that were okay were the ones in which I could just sit there and get photographed. That allowed me to stay detached. As much as possible I tried to keep detached from the pictures, from how they were being taken, and where they would be going. I never thought about that. I never thought about the conditions under which I worked. I would try to think about what was going to happen later—what I would do when I got home or on the weekend, and how I would spend the money I had made.

The jobs I hated most were the ones where you had to "emote." Emote means the guy would say something like "Pretend you're really getting it," or "Make love to the camera."

LL: What was the pay like?

JJ: The average pay was very good. For one job I got $150 for twenty-five pictures. It took a half hour to take them. You could make forty-five dollars for a half hour of filming for a peep show. In those days (1968) that was quite a bit of money; but you couldn't count on regular work—it was very sporadic, and the agency took between 25 and 30 percent of everything I took in.

LL: And the photos were published here?

JJ: A lot of the photos were used in a magazine called *Jaybird*, which was supposed to be a magazine of nudists in nudist camps, but was really just a cover for legitimizing the pornography business. Their attitude was "the secret camera"—spying on the nudists. *Jaybird* photographed nudes swimming in a pool or hanging out in the sun. The interesting thing was that they were always pictures of naked *females*.

LL: What about your boyfriend? Did he approve?

JJ: He thought it was great. He was really turned on by the whole idea and came to watch me several times. He encouraged it a lot. He felt proud because my job was a sign that I was a "sexy chick," and that was a big reflection on him. I was "his." When his friends found out, they made weird sexual allusions and propositioned me. Once they knew I was doing the modeling, they thought I was free for the taking. There was this immediate assumption by men that I was turning tricks on the side. Men would ask me, "Did you get off on it?" or "Would you do it for your friends?" If a woman showed disapproval of what I was doing, my boyfriend would say, "She's just jealous that she can't do it."

The relationship between a man who is lovers with a woman who does nude modeling is just like the relationship of a pimp to a prostitute. In my household I bought the goodies and made the food and paid the rent. My boyfriend lived off me. It's ironic—when I look back now, I realize that I could have done much better without him and his drug habits. I could have supported myself, but back then I didn't believe I could do it alone.

LL: What would you say are the similarities and differences between the prostitute and the pornography model?

JJ: A prostitute is just being more honest about what she's doing. A pornography model can fool herself, and we did. We called what we were doing "modeling" or "acting." Pornography models have the illusion that they're not hooking. It's called acting instead of sex. Or it is labeled "simulated sex"—even sometimes when it's not simulated, it's called simulated. But it's all a form of rape because women who are involved in it don't know how to get out.

LL: When did the big money, the glamour, and the fun start to fade?

JJ: Fairly soon after I started modeling, the agency started to pressure me to do hard-core films. I would come in for a job, and they would say, "There's nothing available in the area you want, but I've got this other job—you really should think about it."

You would be furious and frustrated, but they would break you down little by little. You get more and more pressed to take what is available. And what is available becomes less and less attractive the longer you stay in the business.

I was always trying to get "softer" jobs and not stoop to doing films that were hard core. These standards might seem funny to people outside the modeling business, but it is a way for the model to maintain self-respect and some control over what is happening.

There is a real demand for women who haven't been photographed before. If you're a new person, everyone wants you because you're new. "Fresh meat" they call it. You think it is going to continue like that forever. When I first started modeling, I was offered several jobs every day, and I had my choice of anything I wanted to do. After I'd been around, they started to offer me less jobs, and things became tighter and tighter. The agency was always calling me and saying, "What about *this* job? It's really something you should take. And he doesn't even mind that you're not twenty-one." That was another thing: Many photographers didn't want you unless you were a legal adult, so that was one more thing the agency held over your head if you were younger.

LL: Why do women resist the pressure to do hard-core films?

JJ: Once you do hard core, you can't ever go back to the more "legitimate" modeling. There is this illusion of virginity lost when you do a hard-core pornography movie or magazine. Supposedly you are more "hard bitten." You have gone lower than the acceptable low. *Playboy* initiated that whole attitude back in the fifties. They were very picky about what flesh they exposed. They would never take any woman who had already been in a porn movie—especially a hard-core porn movie. When I was told that *Playboy* wouldn't take you if you'd ever had nude pictures published before, I was very angry because that meant I'd blown my chance! My great ambition in those days was to be a *Playboy* bunny—that was the direction I was headed in.

LL: Why do women do hard-core movies then?

JJ: A good analogy is to think of the pollution standard in Los Angeles. The air is dirty; the EPA measurement says it's beyond the acceptable level. But instead of cleaning up the air, pressure is just put on the EPA to lower its standards. That way Los Angeles air still falls within the acceptable category, and people go on living and thinking they have clean air when they really don't. The same thing happens in modeling. Your standards go down—they're forced down by circumstances. You become fearful that you'll never be able to work at anything else. You hook into the money, but that doesn't continue unless you'll do more and more things you don't want to do.

LL: Did you ever think about getting older—about what would happen then?

JJ: Yes. I was always aware of my body as a commodity. I couldn't have tan marks, so I never went out into the sun unless I could be nude. I worried about scars; I fussed over wrinkles. There was a woman at the front desk who was older. She was the wife of the man who owned the agency. She was also an ex-model. She had gargantuan silicone breasts. One of the first things I noticed when I came to the agency was a huge photo—a crotch shot of this woman when she was younger. Now she was sitting behind the desk encouraging other young women to go the same route.

There is no provision for aging in this business. She's lucky she's got the job behind the desk.

LL: Was there physical violence on your job?

JJ: There is a great deal of physical abuse on the job that is taken for granted. Most of these operations were low-budget cram-course films, and the men would work you to death. At the end of the day, I was often exhausted and sometimes in tears.

Sometimes I would show up on location and have to leave. I lost two jobs because I refused to wear the costumes. They were crusty with vaginal secretions and sperm. Women who work in the pornography business always have vaginal trichomoniasis or some infection from the working conditions, which run from bad to simply intolerable. At one point there was an epidemic of hepatitis and mononucleosis. The communicable diseases spread quickly.

Oftentimes women were put in physically dangerous positions. I knew a model who broke her leg trying to pose in a movie of a nude circus act. She fell off a trapeze because she just wasn't trained to do that sort of thing. Another example of this was a woman who received bad rope burns from a pose which required her to slide up and down a rope. There was also a woman who had an allergic reaction to paint. They sprayed her with paint (that was in the late sixties when psychedelic body painting was in). Her skin reacted, and the whole top layer peeled off. They weren't able to photograph her, so she never got paid for her trouble.

The most common kind of abuse was emotional abuse. There were suggestive sexual comments. You were treated like a piece of meat. Sexism is a given in that business. In those days I didn't understand the meaning of the word sexism and all its political ramifications, but I sure knew how the crap came down on a day-to-day basis. Many times there were hard sexual overtures at the end of a working day.

Another thing about pornographic films is that the men always referred to you in the third person. You would be standing right there, and they would talk about you or about your body. It was very degrading and humiliating. . . .

LL: Did you personally ever experience violence on the job?

JJ: Yes. One day I went on a modeling assignment with a photographer. We went on location to a very fancy Los Angeles home. It was an assignment for a typical fake, nudist magazine. He brought his assistant (a woman), his eight-year old daughter, and another female model. All four of us got into the swimming pool and swam nude while he took pictures. The setting was gorgeous, and I remember thinking that every assignment should be so good.

After the photographing he brought out this enormous strawberry pie and a glass of milk for each of us. I went in to make a phone call, and he followed me. A few seconds later my legs buckled out from under me, and I felt dizzy and out of control. I know now that he drugged me, but at the time I didn't understand what was happening. He carried me to a large bed and raped me. I was conscious but groggy and unable to move a muscle. After it was over he went to a picture on the wall and lifted it. Underneath it were [hatch marks]. . . .He added another one and put the picture back down. Afterward he drove me home. Later when I reported it to my agency, they brushed it off saying that they couldn't believe that I didn't know about his reputation as a "ladies' man." They also told me that he was a big client, and they weren't going to harass him over such a "little thing." That "Oh, it's nothing" attitude was pervasive—later I saw the same photographer at a nude-modeling contest. He couldn't understand why I became hysterical when he walked over to say hello.

LL: When did you stop modeling?

JJ: Around 1970. I was exhausted. I wasn't sleeping at night. I was having nightmares and throwing up. I was physically sick from the long hours of work, and I was getting bladder infections from the work conditions and the general uncleanliness. The last straw was when the agency tried to coerce me into signing a contract for a terrible hard-core pornography film without letting me see the script. In a rage I asked them for my contract, and when they gave it to me, I ripped it into shreds and walked out. I remember I felt absolutely exhilarated—I was free—but also absolutely terrified. I was asking myself, "How am I going to make a living?"

LL: And now?

JJ: Things won't ever be the same for me. My sex life has never been normal. I can't equate sex with affection. I have these images that never stop running in my head. They're fantasies of women as passive victims. All the scenes disgust me, but I can't stop them. I want to be able to be in a loving situation without having these scenarios going through my head. I hate myself if I have the fantasies, and if I don't have them I don't get off sexually. It seems to me that having masochistic fantasies is indicative of how I view myself as a woman. Even though I was socialized into it by a traumatic background, I can't forgive the part of me that is sexual in that way.

I've been in years of therapy. Some therapists say you can change; some say you just have to accept your fantasies. But I just feel damaged. I relate sexually to women now, and I feel that is a more loving and natural way for me. But the psychic damage has never really healed. Eventually I hope it will.

LL: How do you feel now about having been in the pornography business?

JJ: I have a very deep fear that my picture will show up somewhere, somehow, in the future. I was naïve. I used my real name. Most women change their names or use false names, but at that time I had no conception of a future that might be different for me.

Even when photographers give back the negatives, you can never be sure. They might have kept one or made new negatives or something. I am positive that my past is going to come back to me. It already has a couple of times. Once a man I knew (but not well) went into a camera store and saw a shot of me. He mentioned it to me the next time he saw me, and I felt raped—I really did. Suddenly he seemed to have this power over me. Another time a male friend in the army saw a picture of me pinned to some man's locker. I was obsessed to know what the picture looked like—not out of vanity but out of fear. Now that I am a feminist and active politically, there is all the more reason to be fearful. Photos like that can really be used. . . .

LL: Were there "snuff" films then?

JJ: I heard about "snuff" films right after I stopped modeling. Stories came down the grapevine. One agency in Los Angeles sent a woman out on an assignment with a man who killed her and took pictures of how he tortured her. The business just froze. Models went to work with their boyfriends, and some stopped coming in altogether. Everyone was terrified. That didn't last long though. People need money in order to live. My agency told me that that man had come to them, and that they had checked out his credentials and found that they were false. Obviously the murdered woman's agency didn't check. We valued ourselves so little.

LL: Have there been changes in the pornography industry since you modeled?

JJ: Yes, there's been a big change in pornography. The hating way in which women are portrayed has escalated so fast. They used to be afraid to portray it all, but now you see everything—women being skewered, women being killed. When I was modeling, I never saw any of what is now called hard core. It may have been around somewhere, but it was definitely underground.

There may have been allusions to struggle or antagonism between the sexes in the script, but there was never the out-and-out hatred that is seen in pornography today. Back then it was very "clean-cut" nudist, All-American, with photos of white underwear and tennis shoes. The sexuality was barely suggested. Back then hard core meant simply out-front sex. Now it means violence, brutality, sadomasochism. The people have harder-looking, subhuman faces.

LL: What do you think women can do to make the world a safer place for ourselves?

JJ: To tell you the truth, I'm not very optimistic. I've seen the worst of it. In order to change the industry, society and its view of women both have to change fundamentally. You can make an impact on some areas, but others are a lost cause. Damage is being done daily to young kids because at that age they are just forming an image of themselves, even though they don't know it. The media is marketing younger and younger girls.

I have a feeling of powerlessness. Women must get together and realize that it's not the women being photographed but the images they are forced to portray by the men in control that we must confront. The misogyny I see today is so blatant and so accepted as a matter of fact that when we challenge it, we're seen as irrational or bad sports, or lacking a sense of humor, much like my father viewed me when I objected to his incestuous advances. . . .To me the acceptability of pornography is the clearest statement about the acceptability of women-hating and of women's real status in society.

Notes and Questions

1. *Pornography's Victims.* The interview with the former pornography model was evidence of the harm caused to women used in the pornography industry. In describing her family history and reflecting on pornography in our culture, the former model also gave us insights into how pornography becomes a paradigm for women's treatment throughout society. We can find further support for the proposition that pornography is not victimless in an article by Robin West, in which women's testimony is excerpted from the 1986 report of the Attorney General's Commission on Pornography established by the Reagan Administration.

> It was clear to me that in the years I was in prostitution that all of the women I met were systematically coerced into prostitution and pornography in the same way a prisoner of war is systematically imprisoned, tortured and starved into compliance by his captors. The difference is that prisoners of war are not held responsible for coerced statements and acts but when a girl or woman is coerced in this very manner into prostitution and for use in pornography, she is held responsible.
>
> This pimp made pornography of all of us. He also made tape recordings of us having sex with him and recordings of our screams and pleading when he gave us brutal beatings. It was not unusual for him to threaten us with death. He would later use these recordings to humiliate us by playing them for his friends in our presence, for his own sexual arousal, and to terrorize us and other women he brought home.
>
> My father was my pimp in pornography. There were three occasions, from ages nine to sixteen, when he forced me to be a pornography model. This was in the 1950s and 1960s. . . .I don't know if the pictures and films are still being distributed.
>
> That night that I was filmed for a pornographic movie, my stepfather

> tortured me both physically and sexually because I did not perform adequately enough to be convincing. . . .
>
> [A]ccording to virtually all of the women who testified at the 1986 Commission, pornography. . .inspires a preference for and an interest in sexual *violence*, not sexual pleasure. If it is an aid to anything, it is an aid to rape, battery, assault, kidnapping, incest, and murder. Pornography, then, is not "victimless": pornography does indeed have victims, and the victims are women. Thus, one woman described her pornographically inspired marital rape:
>
>> When I first met my husband, it was in early 1975, and he was all the time talking about Ms. Marchiano's film, *Deep Throat*. After we were married, he on several occasions referred to her performances and suggested I try to imitate her actions. . . .Last January my husband raped me. . . .He made me strip and lie on our bed. He cut our clothesline up. . .and tied my hands and feet to the four corners of the bedframe. While he held a butcher knife on me threatening to kill me he fed me three strong tranquilizers. I started crying and because the baby got scared and also began crying, he beat my face and my body. I later had welts and bruises. He attempted to smother me with a pillow. . . .Then, he had sex with me vaginally, and then forced me to give oral sex to him.
>
> Another woman described her rape by strangers, also pornographically inspired:
>
>> The third man forced his penis into my mouth and told me to do it and I didn't know how to do it, I did not know what I was supposed to be doing. He started swearing at me and calling me a bitch and a slut and that I better do it right and that I wasn't even trying. Then he started getting very angry and one of the men pulled the trigger in his gun so I tried harder. Then when he had an erection, he raped me. . . .Then they started walking away and I put my clothes back on and it was not far from where they had set up their camp and I looked down and saw that they had been reading pornographic magazines. They were magazines with nude women on the covers. . . .
>
> Many more testified that pornography inspires sexual battery and assault. A former prostitute testified:
>
>> He stripped me, tied me up, spread-eagled on the bed so that I could not move and then began to caress me very gently. Then, when he thought that I was relaxed, he squeezed my nipple really hard. I did not react. He held up a porn magazine with a picture of a beaten woman and said, "I want you to look like that. I want you to hurt." He then began beating me, and when I didn't cry fast enough, he lit a cigarette and held it right above my breast for a long time before he burned me.

Robin L. West, The Feminist-Conservative Anti-Pornography Alliance and the 1986 Attorney General's Commission on Pornography Report, 4 Am. B. Found. Res. J. 681, 687-88 (1987).

Jane Caputi tells of her experience as an eleven-year-old with the effects of pornography to demonstrate the "intimate relationship of pornography and sexual violence." Jane Caputi, Advertising Femicide: Lethal Violence Against Women in Pornography and Gorenography, in Femicide: The Politics of Woman Killing 203, 203 (Jill Radford & Diana E.H. Russell eds., 1992).

> The neighborhood I grew up in had very few girls my age. When we were 12 and 11, my sister Margaret and I hung out with my cousin Billy, who lived one block over, and his boy friends. This was Long Island in the mid-1960s, and there were still some spots of undeveloped land. So we had a "fort" (the boys' word), a hollowed-out place among the vines and bushes on a hill, where we would all congregate. One day when Margaret and I walked into the fort, there was a new addition: large, glossy, colored pictures of naked women with their legs spread, hung on the vines and brambles. This itself was bad enough. But the boys also had burned out the vaginas and nipples with cigarettes. Sex and violence, all together, all at once. Very soon after, the boys started attacking us regularly, throwing us to the ground, calling us sluts and cunts and, as they put it, "depantsing" us. There never was any doubt in my mind that the attacks on us were connected to the pornography. That moment in the fort when I first faced those pictures precursed the boys' intentions and prepared me, as it had them, for my assigned role in this new ritual of patriarchal sexual initiation.

Id.

The multiple forms of harm caused by pornography will be further explored in the selections by Andrea Dworkin, Patricia Hill Collins, and Susan Griffin, which immediately follow.

2. *"Good Pornography."* While West acknowledges that pornography victimizes women, she also believes that a feminist analysis of pornography must consider that some women find some pornography liberating.

> [S]ome women experience some pornography as having value . . . .The value does not lie in its commodity or speech-like form, but in its content. Some pornography is valuable because it converges with, rather than conflicts with, a feminist and woman-centered conception of the good life, and even of virtue. Good pornography (and a lot of bad pornography as well)—like some forms of feminism—expresses a near-total hostility toward the patriarchal family (pornography *never*—by definition?—depicts "missionary style" penetration by a husband of a wife). Good pornography—like some forms of feminism—rejects the claim that women lack either the capacity or the need for sexual pleasure, and it rejects the claims that sex should be constrained within the institutions of family and marriage, or that only reproduction justifies the pleasure that sexuality confers. Some pornography—like at least some forms of feminism—affirms that non-instrumental pleasure, including hedonistic pleasure, is of moral value. . . .Some pornography—like some forms of feminism—celebrates men and women as natural animals, who can, should, and do pursue natural pleasures.
>
> Of course, these experiences of liberation contrast sharply with the experiences of women who have been victimized or oppressed by pornography. . . .It is simply not true that all women who have had experiences of pornography have been hurt by it, or that women who have recently spoken

> of their experiences with pornography have all told stories of injury and violation.

West, *supra*, at 694-95.

Sheila Jeffreys addresses the issue of some women's pleasurable experiences of pornography and their reactions to it.

> What I think happened is that as feminists started putting out slide shows analyzing pornography, and as women started having reactions to those slides—at times becoming turned on by those slides themselves—there were two choices that women could make. They could say: "I am turned on by these slides. Isn't it absolutely horrifying how my subordination as a woman has been eroticised [sic] and gotten into what is the most intimate and personal part of me—the middle of my heart and my body—and appears to be part of what is most personal and most mine?"
>
> They could say that, and become absolutely furious about the extent to which women's oppression can actually enter into our hearts and minds. That is the choice I have made and other feminists have made. And therefore it motivates us even more to fight pornography and male violence.
>
> Alternatively, women who are turned on by such slides could think: "I am aroused by this material. Therefore, I am angry with the feminists who are showing it to me. I am angry because they are making me feel guilty and ashamed. Therefore, I will fight them." I think this is why some feminists are fighting the antipornography activists, are fighting us.
>
> What I'm suggesting is that we all have the same problem: the way in which our subordination has been eroticized. . . .
>
> So it seems to me that the most important thing we have to do in order to move on is to talk together as women, consciousness-raise, about the construction of our sexuality. We've got to talk about those things that have been so hard to talk about, such as the fantasies we have had inside our heads, how we get turned on, what all of this is about. Then we can start discussing the difference between negative sexual feelings and positive sexual feelings. We can work out where we're going to draw the line for ourselves. . . .
>
> When we do that, when we are able to talk together about these things, we will be able to come to grips with the extent to which we have internalized our oppression, and how it has affected us. Then and only then will we be able to get together again, reconnect, unify, direct our anger out there at pornography and male sexual violence.

Sheila Jeffreys, Eroticizing Women's Subordination, in The Sexual Liberals and the Attack on Feminism 132, 133 (Dorchen Leidholdt & Janice G. Raymond eds., 1990).

Arguments similar to the ones made by West also have been made by Carl F. Stychin with regard to gay male pornography.

> [G]ay male pornography undermines rather than reinforces male supremacy because it questions the coherence of sexual subjectivity—a concept that the feminist pornography critique asserts is the foundation of hierarchy. If subjectivity or "personhood" is tied to masculinity, it must be tied to received constructs of gender. A person is a subject because *he* is *gendered*.
>
> Because gay men exhibit behavior that does not conform to the dominant

culture's understanding of gender, the concepts of gender and subjectivity begin to unravel . . . .

Gay male pornography, then, should not be understood to reinforce objectification. Rather, it redefines the sexual subject and reveals new possibilities . . . .

Gay male pornography and male homosexuality subvert the dominant culture because they represent a decision to shatter the boundaries of the self in an act of eroticism. . . .

The gay male identity emphasizes the oscillation between dominance and submission—power and powerlessness—and demonstrates the absurdity of equating human value with the arbitrariness of the sexual choice to be a "top" or a "bottom.". . .The flexibility of positions—of both fucking and being fucked—does not reinforce male power. Instead, it demonstrates the ridiculousness of suggesting that real value is coterminous with sexual position.

Gay male pornography uniquely exemplifies the explosion of the absurd boundaries of sexual individuality—graphically demonstrated by penetration. Sadomasochism further underscores the individual's willingness to entrust his sexual subjecthood to another and to allow the boundaries of his autonomy to be undermined, knowing that he will reappear no less a subject.

Carl F. Stychin, Exploring the Limits: Feminism and the Legal Regulation of Gay Male Pornography, 16 Vt. L. Rev. 857, 883, 884, 892-93 (1992) (emphasis in original).

Both West and Stychin claim that pornography can play a liberating and resisting role. What are the risks of relying on pornography to explore the construction of gender and sexual practices?

3. *The Contract.* Laura Lederer's interview with the former pornography model revealed how a legal contract and legal notions of consent distort the reality of how little control the pornography model has over her body and her sexuality. Ruth Colker, examining a set of cases in which women objected to the portrayal of themselves and sought legal relief for invasion of privacy or defamation, further explores the related issues of consent, choice, and injury raised in the interview.

The focus on consent in these privacy cases presumes that women who do consent are not injured. Because all women's work is sexualized, however, all women's choices result in injury. The fact that women must accept injury to survive should not preclude women from objecting to their injury. By focusing on consent, courts preclude women—regardless of what choices they make—from objecting to the norms of sexuality that are a part of invasions of privacy. . . .

A false presumption of political power also underlies the emphasis that courts place on the consent issue. Political power is an aspect of privilege. The focus on consent emphasizes the degree to which women may be privileged to avoid having only injurious options. More privileged women (for example, women who can afford to be unemployed) can choose to avoid sexual abuse through pornographic portrayals; however, they will still be subject to sexual abuse in other aspects of their lives . . . .

A woman's consent does not lessen her injury. In fact, evidence of consent

> is evidence of women's oppression as women—the injurious options to which women are limited. Control over women's sexuality exists regardless of whether women actually "consent" to it. Women's political powerlessness reflects their lack of control over their sexuality.
>
> The courts, when focusing on consent, presume that consent is an all or nothing concept. That false presumption contributes to the problems caused by the traditional formulation of consent. Courts fail to see that women may consent to sell some but not all of their sexuality. As a hat checker, model, actress, or dancer, a woman may make the choice to sell some of her sexuality. She has probably rationalized that she could sell some of her sexuality without entirely losing her sexual integrity. . . .Nevertheless. . .men fail[ ] to respect that choice and male jurisprudence. . .[upholds] their right to do so. Men rob[ ] these women of their last vestiges of control over their sexuality.

Ruth Colker, Pornography and Privacy: Towards the Development of a Group Based Theory for Sex Based Intrusions of Privacy, 1 Law & Ineq. J. 191, 218, 221-22 (1983).

How can we apply Colker's analysis of consent to prostitution?

Andrea Dworkin, *Pornography: Men Possessing Women* 199–202 (1979)

The word *pornography*, derived from the ancient Greek *porné* and *graphos*, means "writing about whores." *Porné* means "whore," specifically and exclusively the lowest class of whore, which in ancient Greece was the brothel slut available to all male citizens. The *porné* was the cheapest (in the literal sense), least regarded, least protected of all women, including slaves. She was, simply and clearly and absolutely, a sexual slave. *Graphos* means "writing, etching, or drawing."

The word *pornography* does not mean "writing about sex" or "depictions of the erotic" or "depictions of sexual acts" or "depictions of nude bodies" or "sexual representations" or any other such euphemism. It means the graphic depiction of women as vile whores. In ancient Greece, not all prostitutes were considered vile: only the *porneia*.

Contemporary pornography strictly and literally conforms to the word's root meaning: the graphic depiction of vile whores, or, in our language, sluts, cows (as in: sexual cattle, sexual chattel), cunts. The word has not changed its meaning and the genre is not misnamed. The only change in the meaning of the word is with respect to its second part, *graphos*: now there are cameras—there is still photography, film, video. The methods of graphic depiction have increased in number and in kind: the content is the same; the meaning is the same; the purpose is the same; the status of the women depicted is the same; the sexuality of the women depicted is the same; the value of the women depicted is the same. With the technologically advanced methods of graphic depiction, real women are required for the depiction as such to exist. . . .

In the United States, the pornography industry is larger than the record and film industries combined. In a time of widespread economic impoverishment, it is growing: more and more male consumers are eager to spend more and more money on pornography—on depictions of women as vile whores. Pornography is now carried by cable television; it is now being marketed for home use in video machines. The technology itself demands the creation of more and more *porneia* to meet the market opened up by the technology. Real women are tied up, stretched, hanged, fucked, gang-banged, whipped, beaten, and begging for more. In the photographs and films, real women are used as *porneia* and real women are depicted as *porneia*. To profit, the pimps must supply the *porneia* as the technology widens the market for the visual consumption of women being brutalized and loving it. One picture is worth a thousand words. The number of pictures required to meet the demands of the marketplace determines the number of *porneia* required to meet the demands of graphic depiction. The numbers grow as the technology and its accessibility grow. The technology by its very nature encourages more and more passive acquiescence to the graphic depictions. Passivity makes the already credulous consumer more credulous. He comes to the pornography a believer; he goes away from it a missionary. The technology itself legitimizes the uses of women conveyed by it.

Patricia Hill Collins, *Black Feminist Thought: Knowledge, Consciousness, and the Politics of Empowerment* 167–73 (1990)

> For centuries the black woman has served as the primary pornographic "outlet" for white men in Europe and America. We need only think of the black women used as breeders, raped for the pleasure and profit of their owners. We need only think of the license the "master" of the slave women enjoyed. But, most telling of all, we need only study the old slave societies of the South to note the sadistic treatment—at the hands of white "gentlemen"—of "beautiful young quadroons and octoroons" who became increasingly (and were deliberately bred to become) indistinguishable from white women, and were the more highly prized as slave mistresses because of this.

Alice Walker's description of the rape of enslaved African women for the "pleasure and profit of their owners" encapsulates several elements of contemporary pornography. First, Black women were used as sex objects for the pleasure of white men. This objectification of African-American women parallels the portrayal of women in pornography as sex objects whose sexuality is available for men. Exploiting Black women as breeders objectified them as less than human because only animals can be bred against their will. In contemporary pornography women are objectified through being portrayed as pieces of meat, as sexual animals awaiting conquest. Second, African-American women were raped, a form of sexual violence. Violence is typically an implicit or explicit theme in pornography. Moreover, the rape of Black women linked sexuality and violence, another characteristic feature of pornography. Third, rape and other forms of sexual violence act to strip victims of their will to resist and make them passive and submissive to the will of the rapist. Female passivity, the fact that women have things done to them, is a theme repeated over and over in contemporary pornography. Fourth, the profitability of Black women's sexual exploitation for white "gentlemen" parallels pornography's financially lucrative benefits for pornographers. Finally, the actual breeding of "quadroons and octoroons" not only reinforces the themes of Black women's passivity, objectification, and malleability to male control but reveals pornography's grounding in racism and sexism. The fates of both Black and white women were intertwined in this breeding process. The ideal African-American woman as a pornographic object was indistinguishable from white women and thus approximated the images of beauty, asexuality, and chastity forced on white women. But inside was a highly sexual whore, a "slave mistress" ready to cater to her owner's pleasure.

Contemporary pornography consists of a series of icons or representations that focus the viewer's attention on the relationship between the portrayed individual and the general qualities ascribed to that class of individuals. Pornographic images are iconographic in that they represent realities in a manner determined by the historical position of the observers, their relationship to their own time, and to the history of the conventions which they employ. The treatment of Black women's bodies in nineteenth-century Europe and the United States may be the foundation upon which contemporary pornography as the representation of women's objectification, domination, and control is based. Icons about the sexuality of Black women's bodies emerged in these contexts. Moreover, as race/gender-specific representations, these icons have implications for the treatment of both African-American and white women in contemporary pornography.

I suggest that African-American women were not included in pornography as an afterthought but instead form a key pillar on which contemporary pornography itself rests. As Alice Walker points out, "the more ancient roots of modern pornography are to be found in the almost always pornographic treatment of black women who, from the moment they entered slavery. . .were subjected to rape as the 'logical' convergence of sex and violence. Conquest, in short."

One key feature about the treatment of Black women in the nineteenth century was how their bodies were objects of display. In the antebellum American South white men did not have to look at pornographic pictures of women because they could become voyeurs of Black women on the auction block. A chilling example of this objectification of the Black female body is provided by the exhibition, in early nineteenth-century Europe, of Sarah Bartmann, the so-called Hottentot Venus. Her display formed one of the original icons for Black female sexuality. An African women [sic], Sarah Bartmann was often exhibited at fashionable parties in Paris, generally wearing little clothing, to provide entertainment. To her audience she represented deviant sexuality. At the time European audiences thought that Africans had deviant sexual practices and searched for physiological differences, such as enlarged penises and malformed female genitalia, as indications of this deviant sexuality. Sarah Bartmann's exhibition stimulated these racist and sexist beliefs. After her death in 1815, she was dissected. Her genitalia and buttocks remain on display in Paris. . . .

Bartmann was used as a pornographic object similar to how women are represented in contemporary pornography. She was reduced to her sexual parts, and these parts came to represent a dominant icon applied to Black women throughout the nineteenth century. Moreover, the fact that Sarah Bartmann was both African and a woman underscores the importance of gender in maintaining notions of racial purity. In this case Bartmann symbolized Blacks as a "race." Thus the creation of the icon applied to Black women demonstrates that notions of gender, race, and sexuality were linked in overarching structures of political domination and economic exploitation.

The process illustrated by the pornographic treatment of the bodies of enslaved African women and of women like Sarah Bartmann has developed into a full-scale industry encompassing all women objectified differently by racial/ethnic category. Contemporary portrayals of Black women in pornography represent the continuation of the historical treatment of their actual bodies. African-American women are usually depicted in a situation of bondage and slavery, typically in a submissive posture, and often with two white men. . . .White women and women of color have different pornographic images applied to them. The image of Black women in pornography is almost consistently one featuring them breaking from chains. The image of Asian women in pornography is almost consistently one of being tortured.

The pornographic treatment of Black women's bodies challenges the prevailing feminist assumption that since pornography primarily affects white women, racism has been grafted onto pornography. African-American women's experiences suggest that Black women were not added into a preexisting pornography, but rather that pornography itself must be reconceptualized as an example of the interlocking nature of race, gender, and class oppression. At the heart of both racism and sexism are notions of biological determinism claiming that people of African descent and women possess immutable biological characteristics marking their inferiority to elite white men. In pornography these racist and sexist beliefs are sexualized. Moreover, for African-American women pornography has not been timeless and universal but was tied to Black women's experiences with the European colonization of Africa and with American slavery. Pornography emerged within a specific system of social class relationships.

This linking of views of the body, social constructions of race and gender, and conceptualizations of sexuality that inform Black women's treatment as pornographic objects promises to have significant implications for how we assess contemporary pornography. Moreover, examining how pornography has been central to the race, gender, and class oppression of African-American women offers new routes for understanding the dynamics of power as domination.

Investigating racial patterns in pornography offers one route for such an analysis. Black women have often claimed that images of white women's sexuality were intertwined with the controlling image of the sexually denigrated Black woman: "In the United States, the fear and fascination of female sexuality was projected onto black women; the passionless lady arose in symbiosis with the primitively sexual slave." Comparable linkages exist in pornography. Alice Walker provides a fictional account of a Black man's growing awareness of the different ways that African-American and white women are objectified in pornography: "What he has refused to see—because to see it would reveal yet another area in which he is unable to protect or defend black women—is that where white women are depicted in pornography as 'objects,' black women are depicted as animals. Where white women are depicted as human bodies if not beings, black women are depicted as shit."

Walker's distinction between "objects" and "animals" is crucial in untangling gender, race, and class dynamics in pornography. Within the mind/body, culture/nature, male/female oppositional dichotomies in Western social thought, objects occupy an uncertain interim position. As objects white women become creations of culture—in this case, the mind of white men—using the materials of nature—in this case, uncontrolled female sexuality. In contrast, as animals Black women receive no such redeeming dose of culture and remain open to the type of exploitation visited on nature overall. Race becomes the distinguishing feature in determining the type of objectification women will encounter. Whiteness as symbolic of both civilization and culture is used to separate objects from animals.

The alleged superiority of men to women is not the only hierarchical relationship that has been linked to the putative superiority of the mind to the body. Certain "races" of people have been defined as being more bodylike, more animallike, and less godlike than others. Race and gender oppression may both revolve around the same axis of distain [sic] for the body; both portray the sexuality of subordinate groups as animalistic and therefore deviant. Biological notions of race and gender prevalent in the early nineteenth century which fostered the animalistic icon of Black female sexuality were joined by the appearance of a racist biology incorporating the concept of degeneracy. Africans and women were both perceived as embodied entities, and Blacks were seen as degenerate. Fear of and distain [sic] for the body thus formed a key element in both sexist and racist thinking.

While the sexual and racial dimensions of being treated like an animal are important, the economic foundation underlying this treatment is critical. Animals can be economically exploited, worked, sold, killed, and consumed. As "mules," African-American women become susceptible to such treatment. The political economy of pornography also merits careful attention. Pornography is pivotal in mediating contradictions in changing societies. It is no accident that racist biology, religious justifications for slavery and women's subordination, and other explanations for nineteenth-century racism and sexism arose during a period of profound political and economic change. Symbolic means of domination become particularly important in mediating contradictions in changing political economies. The exhibition of Sarah Bartmann and Black women on the auction block were not benign intellectual exercises—these practices defended real material and political interests. Current transformations in international capitalism require similar ideological justifications. Where does pornography fit in these current transformations? This question awaits a comprehensive Afrocentric feminist analysis. . . .

This linking of Black women and animals is evident in nineteenth-century scientific literature. The equation of women, Blacks, and animals is revealed in the following description of an African woman published in an 1878 anthropology text:

> She had a way of pouting her lips exactly like what we have observed in the

> orangutan. Her movements had something abrupt and fantastical about them, reminding one of those of the ape. Her ear was like that of many apes. . . .These are animal characters. I have never seen a human head more like an ape than that of this woman.

In a climate such as this, it is not surprising that one prominent European physician even stated that Black women's "animallike sexual appetite went so far as to lead black women to copulate with apes."

The treatment of all women in contemporary pornography has strong ties to the portrayal of Black women as animals. In pornography women become nonpeople and are often represented as the sum of their fragmented body parts. Scott McNall observes:

> This fragmentation of women relates to the predominance of rear-entry position photographs. . . .All of these kinds of photographs reduce the woman to her reproductive system, and, furthermore, make her open, willing, and available—not in control. . . .The other thing rear-entry position photographs tell us about women is that they are animals. They are animals because they are the same as dogs—bitches in heat who can't control themselves.

This linking of animals and white women within pornography becomes feasible when grounded in the earlier denigration of Black women as animals.

Developing a comprehensive analysis of the race, gender, and class dynamics of pornography offers possibilities for change. Those Black feminist intellectuals investigating sexual politics imply that the situation is much more complicated than that advanced by some prominent white feminists in which "men oppress women" because they are men. Such approaches implicitly assume biologically deterministic views of sex, gender, and sexuality and offer few possibilities for change. In contrast, Afrocentric feminist analyses routinely provide for human agency and its corresponding empowerment and for the responsiveness of social structures to human action.

Susan Griffin, *Pornography and Silence: Culture's Revenge Against Nature* 111–14 (1981)

[W]hether or not pornography causes sadistic acts to be performed against women, above all *pornography is in itself a sadistic act.*

Let us remember again that the central experience of sadomasochism is humiliation. The actual images of pornography degrade women. This degradation is the essential experience of pornography. It can be argued that for a woman to be disrobed in public at all, given the values of this culture, is a degradation. And yet such a nakedness could be a defiance. For instance, there is the posture of an Isadora Duncan, a woman who declares the body is beautiful, who refuses to hide herself; she reveals her body as part of a protest against the pornographic culture. But the model in a pornographic magazine is not defiant. She has been paid to take off her clothing. And she has about her posture the attitude of one who has been paid to move in a certain way. She is chattel. When she is chained, her chains are redundant, for we know she is not a free being. The whole value, the thrill of a "peep show" or a centerfold depends on a woman's degradation. In this way she plays the whore. For she is *literally* for sale. Her image, printed on a newspaper, is reproduced countless times, and lies flat under a plastic screen, to be had for twenty-five or fifty cents by any passing man.

And now, as her likeness shines out onto the public sidewalk, she has become all women: any woman walking by this image may feel the urge to turn her head away in shame. For this picture of the body of one woman has become a metaphor, in its anonymity (and in the general anonymity which belongs to women), for all women's bodies. Each sale of a pornographic image is a sadistic act which accomplishes the humiliation of all women.

One cannot overestimate the effect of this sadism in women's lives. Just as the image of cruelty can make a man become cruel, so the image of a degraded being can make a woman into a degraded being. Perhaps we can see this more clearly in the lives of those who produce pornography, whose lives are surrounded with these images every day and whose minds are involved in the making of these images. Indeed, the real lives of those who create pornography mimic the obsessional dramas they portray. . . .

This degradation does not remain on a conceptual level. The life of the pornographic actress would not change if she were to suddenly become socially "acceptable." For after her first birth as a human being, the pornographic actress suffers a second birth: she becomes a humiliated creature. In her autobiography, *The Ordeal*, the pornographic star Linda Lovelace[1] has documented this transformation. Even her entrance into this identity was a humiliation. For she was beaten and literally imprisoned by her lover [Chuck Traynor], and thus forced to act in pornographic films. . . .

In order to become a pornographic image, she had to erase her self. Frequently when she was forced into sexual acts she did not want or found shameful, she would cry. But whenever she cried, or even showed tears in her eyes, he would beat her. She learned to place a permanent fake smile over her face. She replaced her real feelings with a mask, and eventually became that mask. The people who met her remarked that she seemed hardly alive. . . .

When we hear the simple details of Linda Lovelace's life with Chuck Traynor (though we know that her life and the lives of those she loved were threatened), we wonder how she allowed this state of imprisonment to take place in the beginning. But to ask such a question is to be blind to pornographic culture. The society we consider to be "normal" helps to teach women acquiescence. It is the accepted feminine role to be submissive. A woman is taught that she is helpless, both physically and with regard to her ability to support herself. Many women have become pornographic models simply because they felt they could not find other employment. Here we see how a cultural idea works to reinforce a cultural event. Because of her cultural conditioning, a woman believes she is not capable. And at the same time, since culture also believes this, it is actually harder for women to find well-paying jobs in which we do not have to prostitute ourselves.

---

1. "Linda Lovelace" was the identity created by pornography. Linda Marchiano wrote of the violence she experienced in pornography in her autobiography, *Ordeal*. Eds.

Notes and Questions

1. *The Complaint.* Patricia Hill Collins criticizes the prevailing feminist analysis of pornography because it fails to interrelate issues of class, gender, and race. Her examination of objectification in pornography differs from that of Andrea Dworkin and Susan Griffin because she places African-American women at the center of her analysis. Her specificity is important not only because it demonstrates the interlocking nature of racism and sexism within pornography, but also because it destabilizes the conceptual boundaries of slavery, rape, prostitution, and pornography. *See also* bell hooks, Ain't I a Woman: Black Women and Feminism, at p. 357. Tracey Gardner approaches pornography, the anti-pornography movement, and race and gender from yet another perspective as she explores African-American women's reaction to the use of pornography by African-American men.

> So how does a Black woman feel when her Black man leaves *Playboy* on the coffee table?
>
> "It's a white folks' thing, and it's corrupting our men."
>
> That is what several Black women I have talked to think. Pornography speaks to the relationship *white* men and women have always had with each other. Because they have been forced to live under the values of white people, the identity of Afro-Americans has been distorted and belittled to the point where pornography also speaks in part to our relationships.
>
> The pornography I am reacting to is *soft-core* pornography, which objectifies but at least retains the woman's body in one piece. Most women in this country, white and Third World, are unaware of the nature of hard-core pornography and how widespread it is. I know that if any woman of color were to see some of the brutal and deadly hard-core pornography around, she would be outraged by it no matter what the color of the woman being exploited was.
>
> But when you talk about soft-core pornography, it's difficult for a Black woman to identify totally with what white women feel about it. Soft-core pornography is an extension of mass advertising and the beauty market; it is the Beauty Queen revealed. Until recently the Beauty Queen was by definition white: fair complexion, straight hair, keen features, and round eyes. Soft-core pornography was the objectification of white purity, white beauty, and white innocence. . . .
>
> Black women were allowed in *Playboy* in the last ten years as a result of the sixties riots, which also won a few Black men the right to wear business suits and carry briefcases and have wives who stayed at home. So, Black women have been elevated from the status of whore to "Playmate." Now white boys can put them in *Playboy* without damaging the magazine's respectability too much (though after the first appearance of Black women in *Playboy*, there were some angry letters to the editor saying "get them niggers out"). . . .
>
> The Black man, like the white man, is buying pornography. He is beating, raping, and murdering all kinds of women. Black women are going to have to deal with him on this. But when we do, we must deal with the Black man as a Black man, not as a white man. In this country it is the *white* man

> who is producing pornography, and it is the *white* man who is profiting from it.
>
> We need to hear from other races in this country, especially those, such as the Japanese, who have had their own highly developed tradition of violent pornography. We need to know how *all* women of *all* cultures are affected by violence within their communities and in the larger, white, male-dominated society.
>
> Unification of all women in the struggle to end violence against women can happen only if women of color share their experiences, hurts, and confusions with white women. Before this can happen though, white women must understand that while sexism might be the ultimate oppression for many of them, it is only *one* of the ways in which women of color are oppressed. White women must recognize the ways in which they have bought into the oppression and stereotyping of communities of color. . . .
>
> I believe white women have the resources to answer me and, for the most part, would like to, but you don't hear me because you never take the time to listen; so often you are afraid of me.

Tracey Gardner, Racism in Pornography in the Women's Movement, in Take Back the Night: Women on Pornography 105, 112-14 (Laura Lederer ed., 1980).

2. *Prostitution.* The etymology of the term *pornography* described by Dworkin shows the inextricable link between pornography and prostitution. That link is further explicated by Patricia Hill Collins (p. 598), Evelina Giobbe (p. 498), Laura Lederer (p. 587), Donna Marie Niles (p. 505), and the Report of the Florida Supreme Court Gender Bias Study Commission, p. 547. *See also* Convention on The Elimination of All Forms of Sexual Exploitation of Women, at p. 536-37.

Giobbe expands on the connections between prostitution and pornography when she reports some preliminary findings collected as part of the WHISPER Oral History Project.

> [The findings suggest] that pornography is an important factor in the seasoning of women and girls into prostitution. Fifty-two percent of the women interviewed revealed that pornography played a significant role in teaching them what was expected of them as prostitutes. Thirty percent reported that their pimps regularly exposed them to pornographic material in order to indoctrinate them into an acceptance of the practices depicted. One survivor explained:
>
>> He used pornography to give me role models to follow, you know, women to try and portray. He'd say, "This is what I want you to look like."
>
> This situation is compounded by the use of pornography by johns. Eighty percent of survivors reported that their customers showed them pornography to illustrate the kinds of sexual activities in which they wanted to engage, including sadomasochism, bondage, anal intercourse, urination and defecation, and the shaving of pubic hair to give an illusion of prepubescence. This information is consistent with testimony given by survivors of prostitution at public hearings and before fact-finding commissions:

> Porn was our text book. We learned the tricks of the trade by men exposing us to porn and us trying to mimic what we saw. I could not stress enough what a huge influence we feel this was.
>
> Fifty-three percent of the interviewees reported that their customers took pornographic photographs of them in addition to engaging in sexual activities.

Evelina Giobbe, Confronting the Liberal Lies About Prostitution, in The Sexual Liberals and the Attack on Feminism 67, 78-79 (Dorchen Leidholdt & Janice G. Raymond eds., 1990).

Mimi Silbert and Ayala Pines identified another aspect of the prostitution-pornography link when they studied 200 street prostituted women in the San Francisco Bay area. The study was designed to investigate sexual abuse of street prostituted women both before and after they entered into prostitution.

> Out of 193 cases of rape, 24% mentioned allusions to pornographic material on the part of the rapist. This figure is even more significant when it is understood that these comments were made by respondents without any solicitation, or reference to the issues of pornography by the interviewer. The comments followed the same pattern: the assailant referred to pornographic materials he had seen or read and then insisted that the victims not only enjoyed the rape but also the extreme violence. For example, the following is a typical comment reported by victims as one in which the assailant made reference to his prior use of pornography. "I know all about you bitches, you're no different; you're like all of them. I seen it in all the movies. You love being beaten" (He then began punching the victim violently). "I just seen it again in that flick. He beat the shit out of her while he raped her and she told him she loved it; you know you love it; tell me you love it." The assailant continued to beat and slap the woman while raping her, repeating his demand that she say that she loved it, just like the woman he saw in the movies. . . .
>
> In 19% of the rape cases, the victims tried to stop the violence of the rape by telling the assailant that they were prostitutes. For example, "Calm down. I'm a hooker. Relax, and I'll turn you a free trick without all this fighting." Rather than assuage the violence, this assertion only exacerbated the problem; the assailants *increased* the amount of violence in every single case. They became furious at hearing the woman say she was a prostitute. Most started screaming, demanding that she take back what she had said, insisting on taking her by force. In order to reassert their own control, assailants then became extremely violent. . . .
>
> In 12% of the 193 cases, the victims who told the rapists that they were prostitutes not only received more violent abuse than those who didn't tell, but also elicited overt comments from the assailants related to pornography. (In most of the other cases in which victims told the rapists they were prostitutes, indirect references were made to pornography.) An analysis of the 12% of the cases in which victims disclosed they were prostitutes reveals that there is a pattern of response among the assailants to the disclosure. In hearing that their victims were prostitutes, the assailants responded in a manner characterized by the following four elements: (1) their language became

more abusive, (2) they became significantly more violent, beating and punching the women excessively, often using weapons they had shown the women, (3) they mentioned having seen prostitutes in pornographic films, the majority of them mentioning specific pornographic literature, and (4) after completing the forced vaginal penetration, they continued to assault the women sexually in ways they claimed they had seen prostitutes enjoy in the pornographic literature they cited. For example, "After I told him I'd turn him a free trick if only he'd calm down and stop hurting me, then he just really blew his mind. He started calling me all kinds of names, and then started screaming and shrieking like nothing I'd ever heard. He sounded like a wailing animal. Instead of just slapping me to keep me quiet, he really went crazy and began punching me all over. Then he told me he had seen whores just like me in (three pornographic films mentioned by name), and told me he knew how to do it to whores like me. He knew what whores like me wanted. . .After he finished raping me, he started beating me with his gun all over. Then he said, 'You were in that movie. You were in that movie. You know you wanted to die after you were raped. That's what you want; you want me to kill you after this rape just like (specific pornography film) did.' " This particular woman suffered, in addition to forced vaginal penetration, forced anal penetration with a gun, excessive bodily injuries, including several broken bones; and a period of time in which the rapist held a loaded pistol at her vagina, threatening to shoot, insisting this was the way she had died in the film he had seen. He did not, in fact, shoot after all.

Similar results were found in regard to the subjects' experiences of juvenile sexual exploitation. Ten percent of the 200 respondents noted that they had been used as children in pornographic films and magazines. It is significant to note that these comments were made simply in open-ended descriptions of their lives . . . .

Again, in unsolicited comments, 22% of the 178 cases of juvenile sexual exploitation mentioned the use of pornographic materials by the adult prior to the sexual act. The particular manner in which the adult used the pornographic materials varied. For a few, they used the materials to try to persuade the children with comments such as, "Now doesn't that look like something that you and I would have a good time doing together?. . ." Others used pornographic materials to attempt to legitimize their actions. Several victims report that the abuser showed them pictures depicting children involved in sexual acts with adults to convince them that it was acceptable behavior and that it was something they wanted to do. . . .Others used the pornographic materials to arouse themselves prior to abusing the child. . . .

Thirty-eight percent of the 200 women prostitutes interviewed reported that they had been involved in the taking of sexually explicit photographs of themselves when they were children for commercial purposes, and/or the personal gratification of the photographer. The subjects were under the age of 16 years old. It should be noted that while many of the descriptions were open-ended comments included in their stories, some were responses given to questions of how they earned a living once they ran away from home and before they began prostituting.

Mimi H. Silbert & Ayala M. Pines, Pornography and Sexual Abuse of Women, 10 Sex Roles 857, 863-66 (1984) (emphasis in original).

The prostitution-pornography nexus not only has been recognized in the social science and feminist literature, but also has received legal acknowledgment. In the case of *People v. Zeihm*, 40 Cal. App. 3d 1085, 115 Cal. Rptr. 528 (1974) the court recognized that the making of pornographic films is a form of prostitution.

> Defendants Zeihm, Cichy and Rogers were charged in the information with [sex offenses in connection with the making of a pornographic movie]. . .and one count of violation of Penal Code section 261.5 (sexual intercourse with a female under the age of 18 years). . . .
>
> The charge of violating section 261.5 of the Penal Code had been dismissed following the preliminary hearing by the magistrate stating as follows: "With respect to Count VII, the Court finds from the facts as elicited by the testimony that the People have failed to show that the requisite intent was present on behalf of any of the defendants named in Count VII *because of the reasoning stated in* People v. Hernandez, 61 Cal. 2d 529 . . . .The Court, entertaining no strong suspicion as to the guilt of any of the defendants *because of that particular decision*, orders that count to be dismissed." (Emphasis added.). . .
>
> The case against the defendants as presented before the magistrate rested principally on the testimony of three young women, one of whom was 14 years of age. They testified essentially that they performed acts of sexual intercourse and oral copulation with various individuals during the course of a commercial movie-making venture in which the defendants participated variously as performers, camera operators and producers. . . .
>
> Concerning the charge of rape. . .the record discloses simply that as a result of defendants' activities a 14 year old girl engaged in sexual intercourse with defendant Zeihm before an operating motion picture camera. The record is devoid of testimony by anyone that any of the defendants believed the child to be over 18 years of age. In fact there was evidence that at least two of the defendants knew otherwise. The child herself testified that she was 5'4" tall and weighed about 107 lbs. Except for this testimony as to her having reached an average height and weight which might also be descriptive of an older female, we are left in the dark as to why the magistrate felt obliged to apply the doctrine of People v. Hernandez, *supra.*
>
> *Hernandez* held simply that in a *trial* of the charge of "statutory rape" a defendant may establish his lack of criminal intent and thus his lack of guilt by proof of a good faith belief that the victim was of the age of consent. . . .
>
> The heart of the *Hernandez* decision is contained in the. . .quote. . ."We hold only that, in the absence of a legislative direction otherwise, a charge of statutory rape is *defensible wherein a criminal intent is lacking.*" (Emphasis added.) The implication is clear that belief as to age is a matter of defense and is not part of the prosecution's burden of proof.
>
> In the case at bar the defendants have at this stage neither *defended nor shown any lack of criminal intent.* On the basis of the evidence presented to the magistrate it can only be concluded that defendants were engaged in illegal commercial exploitation of sex and perversion. There was no evidence upon which the magistrate or the superior court could have found that defendants entertained a belief that the child victim was over 18 years, and in any event since their conduct was otherwise illegal, "a mistake of

> fact relating only to the gravity of an offense will not shield a deliberate offender from the full consequences of the wrong actually committed. . . ."
> . . .In short, we do not believe that the shield of *Hernandez* is available to persons engaged in commercial vice activities. A defendant who exploits women in the field of prostitution and has women perform sex acts for money in making pornographic movies which is a form of prostitution, has the burden of making sure that his victims are of the age of consent.

Id. at 1087-89, 115 Cal. Rptr. at 529-31.

3. *Causative Role of Pornography in Violence Against Women.* Pornography harms women in four distinct ways: (1) women used in making pornography are injured by being coerced into pornography and by experiencing the violence portrayed; (2) the degradation and objectification of a woman in pornography reinforces the dehumanization and subordination of women in society and reinforces abilism, classism, heterosexism, and racism/ethnocentrism; (3) pornography itself is an act of violence against women because it humiliates by eroticizing subordination based on abilities, class, gender, race/ethnicity, and sexual orientation; and (4) pornography contributes to the perpetration of other forms of violence against women, including battering, sexual harassment, rape, and prostitution. The pieces by Dworkin, Collins, and Griffin focus on the first three types of harms. The causative role of pornography in violence against women is suggested in a number of the narratives found in the notes. *See* Note 1, at p. 591; Note 2, at p. 604.

The relationship between pornography and sexual assault has been the subject of social science investigation and Diana Russell summarizes the findings of some of the studies below:

> [Edward] Donnerstein has conducted a series of experiments on the effects of pornography on aggressive behavior in the laboratory. The delivery of a phony electric shock to a confederate of the experimenter constituted the measure of aggressive behavior. These experiments show that when male subjects are exposed to violent pornography in which a female is the victim, there is an increase in their aggression against females, but not against males. . . .
>
> Levels of aggression were higher when subjects were first angered by the confederate. In fact, when the victim in the pornographic movie remained distressed throughout, only subjects who had been first angered by the confederate showed higher levels of aggression than those subjects who had not. However, when the victim was portrayed as becoming sexually aroused at the end of the movie, there was a marked increase in aggressive behavior for both the angered and the nonangered male subjects. . . .
>
> [Neil] Malamuth undertook an experiment to test whether men's attitudes and sexual arousal by depictions of rape could predict aggression in the laboratory. . . .Malamuth concluded that "attitudes condoning aggression against women related to objectively observable behavior—laboratory aggression against women.". . .
>
> Both Donnerstein and Malamuth emphasize that their findings relate to violent and not to nonviolent pornography. . . .Donnerstein concludes that "nonaggressive materials only affect aggression when inhibitions to aggress are quite low, or with long-term and massive exposure. With a single exposure and normal aggressing conditions, there is little evidence that nonviolent

pornography has any negative effects." However, in the real world, inhibitions to aggress are often very low, and long-term and massive exposure to nonviolent material is also very common. . . .

Given the fact that even one brief exposure in an experimental situation increases subjects' acceptance of rape myths and interpersonal violence against women, and given the hypothesis that such increased acceptance would serve to lower viewers' inhibitions against acting out violent desires, one would expect pornography consumption to be related to rape rates. This is, indeed, what one ingenious study found.

Larry Baron and Murray Straus undertook a 50-state correlational analysis of rape rates and the circulation rates of eight pornographic magazines . . . .A highly significant correlation (+0.64) was found between rape rates and circulation rates. Baron and Straus attempted to ascertain what other factors might possibly explain this correlation. Their statistical analysis revealed that the proliferation of pornographic magazines and the level of urbanization explained more of the variance in rape rates than the other variables investigated (for example, social disorganization, economic inequality, unemployment, sexual inequality).

In another important study, Mary Koss conducted a large national survey of over 6000 college students from a probability sample of institutions of higher education. She found that college men who reported behavior that meets common legal definitions of rape were significantly more likely than college men who denied such behavior to be frequent readers of at least one of the following magazines: *Playboy*, *Penthouse*, *Chic*, *Club*, *Forum*, *Gallery*, *Genesis*, *Oui*, or *Hustler*. . . .

While correlation doesn't prove causation, and it therefore cannot be concluded that it was the consumption of the pornography that was responsible for the men's higher acceptance of violence against women, these findings are certainly consistent with a theory that a causal connection exists. . . .

[I]t is [also] significant that many sex offenders claim that viewing pornography affected their criminal behavior. . . .[T]hese studies. . .are relevant to the notion that a cause-and-effect relationship exists between pornography and sex offenses. . . .[I]n a. . .study of 89 nonincarcerated sex offenders. . ."slightly more than one-third of the child molesters and rapists reported at least occasionally being incited to commit an offense by exposure to forced or consenting pornography." Exactly a third of the rapists who reported being incited by pornography to commit an offense said their use of pornography in their preparation for committing the offense was deliberate, and 53% of the child molesters so reported. Although we do not know if pornography played a role in predisposing any of these sex offenders to desire rape or sex with children, these findings do indicate at least that pornography was used for arousal purposes. It may also have undermined the offenders' inhibitions against acting out their desires.

Diana E. H. Russell, Pornography and Rape: A Causal Model, 9 Pol. Psychol. 41, 64-67 (1988).

Whether one views these findings as persuasive evidence in showing the causative role of pornography in violence against women depends on one's theory of causation. Russell develops a causative theory that illuminates these findings.

> [I]n order for rape to occur, a man not only must be predisposed to rape, but his internal and social inhibitions against acting out his rape desires must be undermined. My theory, in a nutshell, is that pornography (1) predisposes some men to want to rape women or intensifies the predisposition in other men already so predisposed, (2) undermines some men's internal inhibitions against acting out their desire to rape, and (3) undermines some men's social inhibitions against acting out their desire to rape.
>
> Most discussions about the causative role of pornography in rape focus on whether or not pornography can create a desire to rape in someone who previously had no such desire. If a person is not convinced that this is possible, he or she frequently concludes that the causative role of pornography has not been established. I disagree with this very restricted interpretation of what the term cause means. . . .*[A]nything that transforms a desire to rape into rape behavior should be considered a cause of rape. . . .*
>
> I want to note. . .that I believe that the rich and varied data now available to us from all kinds of sources considered together strongly support this theory. A high percentage of nonincarcerated rapists and child molesters say that they have been incited by pornography to commit crimes; preselected normal healthy male students say they are more likely to rape a woman after one exposure to violent pornography; large percentages of male junior high school students, high school students, and adults in a nonlaboratory survey report imitating X-rated movies within a few days of exposure; hundreds of women have testified in public about how they have been victimized by pornography;. . .[and f]inally, experimental research has shown that the viewing of violent pornography results in higher rates of aggression against women by male subjects.

Id. at 49, 68-69 (emphasis in original).

Despite these studies, the relationship between pornography and violence continues to be disputed. *See*, *e.g.*, American Booksellers Ass'n v. Hudnut, at p. 616 n.3; George C. Thomas, III, A Critique of the Anti-Pornography Syllogism, 52 Md. L. Rev. 122 (1993). Why is there resistance to seeing pornography as causing harm to women?

4. *Continuum of Violence*. We have already seen the multi-faceted role that pornography plays in prostitution. *See* Note 2, at p. 604. To say that pornography is violence against women does not mean that it is a distinct category separate from other forms of violence against women. Within the making of pornography, battering, sexual harassment, and rape occur. Correspondingly, pornography interrelates with the other forms of violence. For example, pornography can affect the battering pattern that some women experience.

> With the invasion of the home by pornographic cable programs and video cassettes, the "good wife" has become equated with the "good whore," as more and more women are pressured into emulating the scenarios of pornography. In this context, the wife is pressured, seduced, and/or forced into the role of the prostitute while her husband adopts the role of "john.". . .The last barrier separating the roles of wife and prostitute is smashed when men engineer sexual encounters with prostitutes which include their wives.

Giobbe, *supra*, at 76-77.

Based on the readings in Chapters 5 and 6, how does pornography relate to sexual harassment and rape?

5. *Murder*. As the interview with the former pornography model indicated (p. 590), some women have been killed in the making of pornography. Beverly LaBelle examines this particular form of pornography, commonly referred to as "snuff" films.

> *Snuff* is the name of a highly publicized movie which purports to show the actual murder and dismemberment of a young woman. It achieved notoriety because of the carnage of its final five-minute sequence.
>
> The film first surfaced in 1975 shortly after the New York City Police Department announced that they had confiscated several "underground" South American pornographic films containing actual murder footage. These films were given the name "snuff" films because the actresses were murdered (snuffed out) in front of the cameras in order to excite the jaded sexual palates of a select pornography audience that requires death rather than mere sex as an aphrodisiac. The curiosity of the regular pornography market was whetted by this police discovery, and the idea of a commercialized "snuff" film was born. . . .
>
> *Snuff* was one of the very first pornographic films to elicit strong protest from the feminist sector of the population. It marked the turning point in our consciousness about the meaning behind the countless movies and magazines devoted to the naked female body. *Snuff* forced us to stop turning the other way each time we passed an X-rated movie house. It compelled us to take a long, hard look at the pornography industry. The graphic bloodletting in *Snuff* finally made the misogyny of pornography a major feminist concern.

Beverly LaBelle, *Snuff*—The Ultimate in Woman-Hating, in Take Back the Night: Women on Pornography 272, 272-74 (Laura Lederer ed., 1980).

Jane Caputi further theorizes the development of snuff films.

> [T]he essence of pornography consists in the conditioning of male arousal to female subordination, humiliation, objectification, pain, rape, mutilation, and even murder. It is largely because of pornography that members of contemporary culture can see the torture of women and think *sex*. It is in pornography that the basic meanings of sex crime are distilled—the female body fetishized, displayed, sacralized, only so that she can be hated, possessed, profaned, sacrificed. Moreover, although the entire range of sexual violations are nominally defined as despised and taboo acts, these very same acts, portrayed in pornography, are the very stuff of this massive "entertainment" industry. . . .
>
> Finally, it is in that quintessential pornographic product—the "snuff film"—that the wavering dividing line between patriarchal fantasy and patriarchal reality purely dissolves. In these films, an actress is told that she will appear in a scene of simulated murder, but then, with the camera running, the woman is actually tortured, murdered, dismembered. Here, clearly, the image not only potentially elicits the act, but is absolutely inseparable from the act.
>
> At the core of pornography is dissimulation—the lie that women are symbols, objects, possessions, dolls, i.e. that women are not real, and, cor-

respondingly, the pervasive assumption that pornography isn't real either, that it is "fantasy." Typically then, much of the debate aroused in patriarchal circles regarding snuff films is whether or not they are genuine or indeed whether any genuine snuff films can be proven to exist. . . .

Amidst the incomprehensibility of the horror itself, is yet another incomprehensible factor. There seems to be no sure way to discern on film what is a faked murder and what is a real one, which is a "symbolic annihilation" and which is an actual one. Here the characteristic messages of the unreality of sexual violence and the insignificance/unreality of women fuse purely with the properties of the medium as the camera itself works to confound the eye. This truly is phallic glamour.

Jane Caputi, The Age of Sex Crime 164, 168-69 (1987).

B. The Law and Pornography

American Booksellers Ass'n v. Hudnut,

771 F.2d 323 (7th Cir. 1985), *aff'd mem.*, 475 U.S. 1001 (1986)

Easterbrook, C.J. Indianapolis enacted an ordinance defining "pornography" as a practice that discriminates against women. "Pornography" is to be redressed through the administrative and judicial methods used for other discrimination. The City's definition of "pornography" is considerably different from "obscenity," which the Supreme Court has held is not protected by the First Amendment.

To be "obscene" under *Miller v. California*, 413 U.S. 15 (1973), "a publication must, taken as a whole, appeal to the prurient interest, must contain patently offensive depictions or descriptions of specified sexual conduct, and on the whole have no serious literary, artistic, political, or scientific value.". . .Offensiveness must be assessed under the standards of the community. Both offensiveness and an appeal to something other than "normal, healthy sexual desires". . .are essential elements of "obscenity."

"Pornography" under the ordinance is "the graphic sexually explicit subordination of women, whether in pictures or in words, that also includes one or more of the following:

(1) Women are presented as sexual objects who enjoy pain or humiliation; or

(2) Women are presented as sexual objects who experience sexual pleasure in being raped; or

(3) Women are presented as sexual objects tied up or cut up or mutilated or bruised or physically hurt, or as dismembered or truncated or fragmented or severed into body parts; or

(4) Women are presented as being penetrated by objects or animals; or

(5) Women are presented in scenarios of degradation, injury, abasement, torture, shown as filthy or inferior, bleeding, bruised, or hurt in a context that makes these conditions sexual; or

(6) Women are presented as sexual objects for domination, conquest, violation, exploitation, possession, or use, or through postures or positions of servility or submission or display."

Indianapolis Code § 16-3(q). The statute provides that the "use of men, children, or transsexuals in the place of women in paragraphs (1) through (6) above shall also constitute pornography under this section."...

The Indianapolis ordinance does not refer to the prurient interest, to offensiveness, or to the standards of the community. It demands attention to particular depictions, not to the work judged as a whole. It is irrelevant under the ordinance whether the work has literary, artistic, political, or scientific value. The City and many amici point to these omissions as virtues. They maintain that pornography influences attitudes, and the statute is a way to alter the socialization of men and women rather than to vindicate community standards of offensiveness. And as one of the principal drafters of the ordinance has asserted, "if a woman is subjected, why should it matter that the work has other value?" Catharine A. MacKinnon, *Pornography, Civil Rights, and Speech*, 20 Harv. Civ. Rts.-Civ. Lib. L. Rev. 1, 21 (1985).

Civil rights groups and feminists have entered this case as amici on both sides. Those supporting the ordinance say that it will play an important role in reducing the tendency of men to view women as sexual objects, a tendency that leads to both unacceptable attitudes and discrimination in the workplace and violence away from it. Those opposing the ordinance point out that much radical feminist literature is explicit and depicts women in ways forbidden by the ordinance and that the ordinance would reopen old battles. It is unclear how Indianapolis would treat works from James Joyce's *Ulysses* to Homer's *Iliad*; both depict women as submissive objects for conquest and domination.

We do not try to balance the arguments for and against an ordinance such as this. The ordinance discriminates on the ground of the content of the speech. Speech treating women in the approved way—in sexual encounters "premised on equality"...—is lawful no matter how sexually explicit. Speech treating women in the disapproved way—as submissive in matters sexual or as enjoying humiliation—is unlawful no matter how significant the literary, artistic, or political qualities of the work taken as a whole. The state may not ordain preferred viewpoints in this way. The Constitution forbids the state to declare one perspective right and silence opponents....

The ordinance contains four prohibitions. People may not "traffic" in pornography, "coerce" others into performing in pornographic works, or "force" pornography on anyone. Anyone injured by someone who has seen or read pornography has a right of action against the maker or seller.

Trafficking is defined in § 16-3(g)(4) as the "production, sale, exhibition, or distribution of pornography." The offense excludes exhibition in a public or educational library, but a "special display" in a library may be sex discrimination. Section 16-3(g)(4)(C) provides that the trafficking paragraph "shall not be construed to make isolated passages or isolated parts actionable."

"Coercion into pornographic performance" is defined in §16-3(g)(5) as "[c]oercing, intimidating or fraudulently inducing any person...into performing for pornography...." The ordinance specifies that proof of any of the following "shall not constitute a defense: I. That the person is a woman;. . .VI. That the person has previously posed for sexually explicit pictures. . .with anyone. . .;. . .VIII. That the person actually consented to a use of the performance that is changed into pornography;. . .IX. That the person knew that the purpose of the acts or events in question was to make pornography;. . .XI. That the person signed a contract, or made statements affirming a willingness to cooperate in the production of pornography; XII. That no physical force, threats, or weapons were used in the making of the pornography; or XIII. That the person was paid or otherwise compensated."

"Forcing pornography on a person," according to §16-3(g)(5), is the "forcing of pornography on any woman, man, child, or transsexual in any place of employment, in education, in a home, or in any public place." The statute does not define forcing, but one of its authors states that the definition reaches pornography shown to medical students as part of their education or given to language students for translation. . . .

Section 16-3(g)(7) defines as a prohibited practice the "assault, physical attack, or injury of any woman, man, child, or transsexual in a way that is directly caused by specific pornography."

For purposes of all four offenses, it is generally "not. . .a defense that the respondent did not know or intend that the materials were pornography. . . ." Section 16-3(g)(8). But the ordinance provides that damages are unavailable in trafficking cases unless the complainant proves "that the respondent knew or had reason to know that the materials were pornography." It is a complete defense to a trafficking case that all of the materials in question were pornography only by virtue of category (6) of the definition of pornography. In cases of assault caused by pornography, those who seek damages from "a seller, exhibitor or distributor" must show that the defendant knew or had reason to know of the material's status as pornography. By implication, those who seek damages from an author need not show this.

A woman aggrieved by trafficking in pornography may file a complaint "as a woman acting against the subordination of women" with the office of equal opportunity. Section 16-17(b). A man, child, or transsexual also may protest trafficking "but must prove injury in the same way that a woman is injured. . . ." *Id.* Subsection (a) also provides, however, that "any person claiming to be aggrieved" by trafficking, coercion, forcing, or assault may complain against the "perpetrators.". . .

The office investigates and within 30 days makes a recommendation to a panel of the equal opportunity advisory board. The panel then decides whether there is reasonable cause to proceed. . .and may refer the dispute to a conciliation conference or to a complaint adjudication committee for a hearing . . . .The committee uses the same procedures ordinarily associated with civil rights litigation. It may make findings and enter orders, including both orders to cease and desist and orders "to take further affirmative action. . .including but not limited to the power to restore complainant's losses. . . .". . .Either party may appeal the committee's decision to the board, which reviews the record before the committee and may modify its decision. . . .

The board's decisions are subject to review in the ordinary course. . . .Judicial review in pornography cases is to be de novo,. . .which provides a second complete hearing. When the board finds that a person has engaged in trafficking or that a seller, exhibitor, or distributor is responsible for an assault, it must initiate judicial review of its own decision, *id.*, and the statute prohibits injunctive relief in these cases in advance of the court's final decision. . . .

The district court held the ordinance unconstitutional. . . .The court concluded that the ordinance regulates speech rather than the conduct involved in making pornography. The regulation of speech could be justified, the court thought, only by a compelling interest in reducing sex discrimination, an interest Indianapolis had not established. The ordinance is also vague and overbroad, the court believed, and establishes a prior restraint of speech. . . .

The plaintiffs are a congeries of distributors and readers of books, magazines, and films. . . .Collectively the plaintiffs (or their members, whose interests they represent) make, sell, or read just about every kind of material that could be affected by the ordinance, from hard-core films to W.B. Yeats's poem "Leda and the Swan" (from the myth of Zeus in the form of a swan impregnating an apparently subordinate Leda), to the collected works of James Joyce, D.H. Lawrence, and John Cleland. . . .

Under the First Amendment the government must leave to the people the evaluation of ideas. Bald or subtle, an idea is as powerful as the audience allows it to be. A belief may be pernicious—the beliefs of Nazis led to the death of millions, those of the Klan to the repression of millions. A pernicious belief may prevail. Totalitarian governments today rule much of the planet, practicing suppression of billions and spreading dogma that may enslave others. One of the things that separates our society from theirs is our absolute right to propagate opinions that the government finds wrong or even hateful.

The ideas of the Klan may be propagated. . . .Communists may speak freely and run for office. . . .The Nazi Party may march through a city with a large Jewish population. . . .People may criticize the President by misrepresenting his positions, and they have a right to post their misrepresentations on public property. . . .People may teach religions that others despise. People may seek to repeal laws guaranteeing equal opportunity in employment or to revoke the constitutional amendments granting the vote to blacks and women. They may do this because "above all else, the First Amendment means that government has no power to restrict expression because of its message [or] its ideas. . . .". . .

Under the ordinance graphic sexually explicit speech is "pornography" or not depending on the perspective the author adopts. Speech that "subordinates" women and also, for example, presents women as enjoying pain, humiliation, or rape, or even simply presents women in "positions of servility or submission or display" is forbidden, no matter how great the literary or political value of the work taken as a whole. Speech that portrays women in positions of equality is lawful, no matter how graphic the sexual content. This is thought control. It establishes an "approved" view of women, of how they may react to sexual encounters, of how the sexes may relate to each other. Those who espouse the approved view may use sexual images; those who do not, may not.

Indianapolis justifies the ordinance on the ground that pornography affects thoughts. Men who see women depicted as subordinate are more likely to treat them so. Pornography is an aspect of dominance.[2] It does not persuade people so much as change them. It works by socializing, by establishing the expected and the permissible. In this view pornography is not an idea; pornography is the injury.

There is much to this perspective. Beliefs are also facts. People often act in accordance with the images and patterns they find around them. People raised in a religion tend to accept the tenets of that religion, often without independent examination. People taught from birth that black people are fit only for slavery rarely rebelled against that creed; beliefs coupled with the self-interest of the masters established a social structure that inflicted great harm while enduring for centuries. Words and images act at the level of the subconscious before they persuade at the level of the conscious. Even the truth has little chance unless a statement fits within the framework of beliefs that may never have been subjected to rational study.

Therefore we accept the premises of this legislation. Depictions of subordination tend to perpetuate subordination. The subordinate status of women in turn leads to affront and lower pay at work, insult and injury at home, battery and rape on the streets.[3] In the language of the legislature, "[p]ornography is central in creating and maintaining sex as a basis of discrimination. Pornography is a systematic practice of exploitation and subordination based on sex which differentially harms women. The bigotry and contempt it pro-

2. "Pornography constructs what a woman is in terms of its view of what men want sexually. . . .Pornography's world of equality is a harmonious and balanced place. Men and women are perfectly complementary and perfectly bipolar. . . .All the ways men love to take and violate women, women love to be taken and violated. . . .What pornography *does* goes beyond its content: It eroticizes hierarchy, it sexualizes inequality. It makes dominance and submission sex. Inequality is its central dynamic; the illusion of freedom coming together with the reality of force is central to its working. . . .[P]orgraphy [sic] is neither harmless fantasy nor a corrupt and confused misrepresentation of an otherwise neutral and healthy sexual situation. It institutionalizes the sexuality of male supremacy, fusing the erotization of dominance and submission with the social construction of male and female. . . .Men treat women as who they see women as being. Pornography constructs who that is. Men's power over women means that the way men see women defines who women can be. Pornography. . .is a sexual reality." Catharine A. MacKinnon, Pornography, Civil Rights, and Speech, 20 Harv. Civ. Rts.-Civ. Lib. L. Rev. 1, 17-18 (1985) (footnote omitted, emphasis in original). *See also* Andrea Dworkin, Pornography: Men Possessing Women (1981). A national commission in Canada recently adopted a similar rationale for controlling pornography. Special Commission on Pornography and Prostitution, 1 Pornography and Prostitution in Canada 49-59 (Canadian Government Publishing Centre 1985).

3. MacKinnon's article collects empirical work that supports this proposition. The social science studies are very difficult to interpret, however, and they conflict. Because much of the effect of speech comes through a process of socialization, it is difficult to measure incremental benefits and injuries caused by particular speech. Several psychologists have found, for example, that those who see violent, sexually explicit films tend to have more violent thoughts. But how often does this lead to actual violence? National commissions on obscenity here, in the United Kingdom, and in Canada have found that it is not possible to demonstrate a direct link between obscenity and rape or exhibitionism. The several opinions in *Miller v. California* discuss the U.S. commission. . . .In saying that we accept the finding that pornography as the ordinance defines it leads to unhappy consequences, we mean only that there is evidence to this effect, that this evidence is consistent with much human experience, and that as judges we must accept the legislative resolution of such disputed empirical questions. . . .

duces, with the acts of aggression it fosters, harm women's opportunities for equality and rights [of all kinds]." Indianapolis Code § 16-1(a)(2).

Yet this simply demonstrates the power of pornography as speech. All of these unhappy effects depend on mental intermediation. Pornography affects how people see the world, their fellows, and social relations. If pornography is what pornography does, so is other speech. Hitler's orations affected how some Germans saw Jews. Communism is a world view, not simply a *Manifesto* by Marx and Engels or a set of speeches. Efforts to suppress communist speech in the United States were based on the belief that the public acceptability of such ideas would increase the likelihood of totalitarian government. Religions affect socialization in the most pervasive way. . . .Many people believe that the existence of television, apart from the content of specific programs, leads to intellectual laziness, to a penchant for violence, to many other ills. The Alien and Sedition Acts passed during the administration of John Adams rested on a sincerely held belief that disrespect for the government leads to social collapse and revolution—a belief with support in the history of many nations. Most governments of the world act on this empirical regularity, suppressing critical speech. In the United States, however, the strength of the support for this belief is irrelevant. Seditious libel is protected speech unless the danger is not only grave but also imminent. . . .

Racial bigotry, anti-semitism, violence on television, reporters' biases—these and many more influence the culture and shape our socialization. None is directly answerable by more speech, unless that speech too finds its place in the popular culture. Yet all is protected as speech, however insidious. Any other answer leaves the government in control of all of the institutions of culture, the great censor and director of which thoughts are good for us.

Sexual responses often are unthinking responses, and the association of sexual arousal with the subordination of women therefore may have a substantial effect. But almost all cultural stimuli provoke unconscious responses. Religious ceremonies condition their participants. Teachers convey messages by selecting what not to cover; the implicit message about what is off limits or unthinkable may be more powerful than the messages for which they present rational argument. Television scripts contain unarticulated assumptions. People may be conditioned in subtle ways. If the fact that speech plays a role in a process of conditioning were enough to permit governmental regulation, that would be the end of freedom of speech.

It is possible to interpret the claim that the pornography is the harm in a different way. Indianapolis emphasizes the injury that models in pornographic films and pictures may suffer. The record contains materials depicting sexual torture, penetration of women by red-hot irons and the like. These concerns have nothing to do with written materials subject to the statute, and physical injury can occur with or without the "subordination" of women. As we discuss [later]. . ., a state may make injury in the course of producing a film unlawful independent of the viewpoint expressed in the film.

The more immediate point, however, is that the image of pain is not necessarily pain. In *Body Double*, a suspense film directed by Brian DePalma, a woman who has disrobed and presented a sexually explicit display is murdered by an intruder with a drill. The drill runs through the woman's body. The film is sexually explicit and a murder occurs—yet no one believes that the actress suffered pain or died. In *Barbarella* a character played by Jane Fonda is at times displayed in sexually explicit ways and at times shown "bleeding, bruised, [and] hurt in a context that makes these conditions sexual"—and again no one believes that Fonda was actually tortured to make the film. In *Carnal Knowledge* a woman grovels to please the sexual whims of a character played by Jack Nicholson; no one believes that there was a real sexual submission, and the Supreme Court held the film protected by the First Amendment. *Jenkins v. Georgia*, 418 U.S. 153 (1974). And this works both ways. The description of women's sexual domination of men in *Lysistrata* was not real dominance. Depictions may affect slavery, war, or sexual roles, but a book about slavery is not itself slavery, or a book about death by poison a murder.

Much of Indianapolis's argument rests on the belief that when speech is "unanswerable," and the metaphor that there is a "marketplace of ideas" does not apply, the First Amendment does not apply either. The metaphor is honored; Milton's *Aeropagitica* and John Stewart Mill's *On Liberty* defend freedom of speech on the ground that the truth will prevail, and many of the most important cases under the First Amendment recite this position. The Framers undoubtedly believed it. As a general matter it is true. But the Constitution does not make the dominance of truth a necessary condition of freedom of speech. To say that it does would be to confuse an outcome of free speech with a necessary condition for the application of the amendment. . . .

At any time, some speech is ahead in the game; the more numerous speakers prevail. Supporters of minority candidates may be forever "excluded" from the political process because their candidates never win, because few people believe their positions. This does not mean that freedom of speech has failed.

The Supreme Court has rejected the position that speech must be "effectively answerable" to be protected by the Constitution. . . .

We come, finally, to the argument that pornography is "low value" speech, that it is enough like obscenity that Indianapolis may prohibit it. Some cases hold that speech far removed from politics and other subjects at the core of the Framers' concerns may be subjected to special regulation. . . .These cases do not sustain statutes that select among viewpoints, however. . . .

At all events, "pornography" is not low value speech within the meaning of these cases. Indianapolis seeks to prohibit certain speech because it believes this speech influences social relations and politics on a grand scale, that it controls attitudes at home and in the legislature. This precludes a characterization of the speech as low value. True, pornography and obscenity have sex in common. But Indianapolis left out of its definition any reference to literary, artistic, political, or scientific value. The ordinance applies to graphic sexually explicit subordination in works great and small.[4] The Court sometimes bal-

4. Indianapolis briefly argues that *Beauharnais v. Illinois*, 343 U.S. 250 (1952), which allowed a state to penalize "group libel," supports the ordinance. In *Collin v. Smith*, [578 F.2d 1197, 1205 (1978)]. . .we concluded that cases such as *New York Times v. Sullivan* had so washed away the foundations of *Beauharnais* that it could not be considered authoritative. If we are wrong in this, however, the case still does not support the ordinance. It is not clear that depicting women as subordinate in sexually explicit ways, even combined with a depiction of pleasure in rape, would fit within the definition of a group libel. The well received film *Swept Away* used explicit sex, plus taking pleasure in rape, to make a political statement, not to

ances the value of speech against the costs of its restriction, but it does this by category of speech and not by the content of particular works. . . .Indianapolis has created an approved point of view and so loses the support of these cases.

Any rationale we could imagine in support of this ordinance could not be limited to sex discrimination. Free speech has been on balance an ally of those seeking change. Governments that want stasis start by restricting speech. Culture is a powerful force of continuity; Indianapolis paints pornography as part of the culture of power. Change in any complex system ultimately depends on the ability of outsiders to challenge accepted views and the reigning institutions. Without a strong guarantee of freedom of speech, there is no effective right to challenge what is. . . .

The definition of "pornography" is unconstitutional. No construction or excision of particular terms could save it. The offense of trafficking in pornography necessarily falls with the definition. . . .

The offense of coercion to engage in a pornographic performance,. . .has elements that might be constitutional. Without question a state may prohibit fraud, trickery, or the use of force to induce people to perform—in pornographic films or in any other films. Such a statute may be written without regard to the viewpoint depicted in the work. *New York v. Ferber*, 458 U.S. 747 (1982), suggests that when a state has a strong interest in forbidding the conduct that makes up a film (in *Ferber* sexual acts involving minors), it may restrict or forbid dissemination of the film in order to reinforce the prohibition of the conduct. A state may apply such a rule to non-sexual coercion (although it need not). We suppose that if someone forced a prominent political figure, at gunpoint, to endorse a candidate for office, a state could forbid the commercial sale of the film containing that coerced endorsement. The same principle allows a court to enjoin the publication of stolen trade secrets and award damages for the publication of copyrighted matter without permission. . . .

But the Indianapolis ordinance, unlike our hypothetical statute, is not neutral with respect to viewpoint. The ban on distribution of works containing coerced performances is limited to pornography; coercion is irrelevant if the work is not "pornography," and we have held the definition of "pornography" to be defective root and branch. A legislature might replace "pornography" in § 16-3(g)(4) with "any film containing explicit sex" or some similar expression, but even the broadest severability clause does not permit a federal court to rewrite as opposed to excise. . . .

The offense of forcing pornography on unwilling recipients is harder to assess. Many kinds of forcing (such as giving texts to students for translation) may themselves be protected speech. . . .Exposure to sex is not something the government may prevent . . . .We therefore could not save the offense of "forcing" by redefining "pornography" as all sexually offensive speech or some related category. The statute needs a definition of "forcing" that removes the government from the role of censor. . . .

The section creating remedies for injuries and assaults attributable to

---

defame. Work must be an insult or slur for its own sake to come within the ambit of *Beauharnais*, and a work need not be scurrilous at all to be "pornography" under the ordinance.

pornography also is salvageable in principle, although not by us. The First Amendment does not prohibit redress of all injuries caused by speech. Injury to reputation is redressed through the law of libel, which is constitutional subject to strict limitations. Cases. . .hold that a state may not penalize speech that does not cause immediate injury. . . .

The law of libel has the potential to muzzle the press . . . .A law awarding damages for assaults caused by speech also has the power to muzzle the press, and again courts would place careful limits on the scope of the right. Certainly no damages could be awarded unless the harm flowed directly from the speech and there was an element of intent on the part of the speaker . . . .

Much speech is dangerous. Chemists whose work might help someone build a bomb, political theorists whose papers might start political movements that lead to riots, speakers whose ideas attract violent protesters, all these and more leave loss in their wake. Unless the remedy is very closely confined, it could be more dangerous to speech than all the libel judgments in history. The constitutional requirements for a valid recovery for assault caused by speech might turn out to be too rigorous for any plaintiff to meet. . . .But the Indianapolis ordinance requires the complainant to show that the attack was "directly caused by specific pornography" (§ 16-3(g)(7)), and it is not beyond the realm of possibility that a state court could construe this limitation in a way that would make the statute constitutional. We are not authorized to prevent the state from trying.

Again, however, the assault statute is tied to "pornography," and we cannot find a sensible way to repair the defect without seizing power that belongs elsewhere. Indianapolis might choose to have no ordinance if it cannot be limited to viewpoint-specific harms, or it might choose to extend the scope to all speech, just as the law of libel applies to all speech. An attempt to repair this ordinance would be nothing but a blind guess.

No amount of struggle with particular words and phrases in this ordinance can leave anything in effect. The district court came to the same conclusion. Its judgment is therefore

Affirmed.

Catharine A. MacKinnon, Pornography as Defamation and Discrimination, 71 Bost. U.L. Rev. 793, 802–15 (1991)

[P]ornography, through its production, is revealed as a traffic in sexual slavery. Through its consumption, it further institutionalizes a subhuman, victimized, second class status for women by conditioning men's orgasm to sexual inequality. When men use pornography, they experience in their bodies, not just their minds, that one-sided sex—sex between a person (them) and a thing (it)—is sex, that sexual use is sex, sexual abuse is sex, sexual domination is sex. This is the sexuality that they then demand, practice, purchase, and live out in their everyday social relations with others. Pornography works by making sexism sexy. As a primal experience of gender hierarchy, pornography is a major way in which sexism is enjoyed and practiced, as well as learned. It is one way that male supremacy is spread and made socially real. Through the use of pornography for masturbation. . .power and powerlessness are experienced and inculcated as sexual excitement and release. Inequality between women and men is what is sexy about pornography—the more unequal the sexier. In other words, pornography makes sexuality into a key dynamic in gender inequality by viscerally defining gender through the experience of hierarchical sexuality. On the way, it exploits inequalities of race, class, age, religion, sexual identity, and disability by sexualizing them through gender.

Seen in this way, pornography is at once a concrete practice and an ideological statement. The concrete practices are discriminatory; the ideological statements are defamatory. Construed as defamation in the conventional sense, pornography says that women are a lower form of human life defined by their availability for sexual use. Women are dehumanized through the conditioning of male sexuality to their use and abuse, which sexualizes, hence lowers, women across the culture, not only in express sexual interactions. Pornography makes women a public sexual spectacle and common sexual property, works to lower the public standard of their perception and treatment, terrorizes and humiliates women, and also at times offends their sensibilities. Like group libel's historic atrocities, pornography's effects are known but denied or blinked at while being acted out. The abusive acts are presumptively illegal but pervasively permitted, decried in public and savored in private.

When pornography's reality is examined against the terms of group defamation as a legal theory, some of the theory fits, but much of it does not. Pornography does purvey an ideology about all women; too, pornography of women and men of color sexualizes racism. It is in this sense defamatory. But its ideological impact, the prejudice it engenders, while very real, is only one of its effects and is not the one on which the civil rights approach centrally focuses. The deepest injury of pornography is not what it says, but what it does.

It is possible to say what pornography says without doing what it does. For example, the paragraphs above say what it says but do not do what it does. Its damage neither begins nor ends in its mental content. Although all discriminatory damage says something as well as does something, coercion is not an idea; force is not an argument; assault is not advocacy, nor is trafficking in human beings a discourse. On a deeper level, pornography provides direct sexual stimulation, the experience of which is one of sex, not just the idea of sex. There is no adequate analogy to this, and no reply in kind exists. Its pleasure is a specific reinforcer for bigotry itself, not an argument about why bigotry is right, nor even a base appeal to bigoted interests. If you think an orgasm is an argument, try arguing with one some time.

The conditions of the production of pornography distinguish it further from the rest of group defamation. Nobody has to violate or use anybody to make most anti-Semitic propaganda. Nobody has to pose for a lynching, i.e. be lynched, to create most Klan hate literature. Most cities do not offer businesses where one can go and pay to abuse a Jew or a Black, unless she is a woman and the abuse is sex. When a live human being is not used, and the materials are not sex, it makes some sense to discuss the materials as representations or images and to focus on their consequences as the effects of ideas. Their idea content is a substantial vehicle for the harm they do. But, except in a realm of abstraction totally divorced from reality (where most academics seem to prefer to reside), it covers up reality to discuss pornography in these terms. Both pornography and hate literatures are hateful; both propagate invidious group stereotypes; both promote and often instigate violence; both dehumanize. But pornography, because it is also an industry, because its dynamic is sexual, and because the camera requires live fodder, not only springs from abuse and leads to abuse; it *is* abuse. It is not merely the groundwork or persuasive basis or impelling rationalization, however destructive or immediate, for consequent acts. It is an act.

This is the reason that pornography is most appropriately addressed as discrimination, not defamation. Defamation and discrimination emerge from distinct theoretical and political traditions. The idea of group defamation, like the idea of obscenity, is that group defamation *is* an idea about a group; discrimination, even when it expresses an attitude, as it always does, is always recognized as an act. Defamation is a tort addressing reputational harm to individuals; it is only derivatively applied to groups. Discrimination is first and always a group-based concept, even when applied to one person at a time. The law of defamation since *New York Times v. Sullivan* has been explicitly circumscribed by First Amendment safeguards because state laws against individual libel, and with it group libel, have been thought potentially to compromise freedom of expression. But discrimination that takes a verbal form has never—not until pornography was challenged as sex discrimination—been regarded as protected by the First Amendment.

Most common forms of discrimination are significantly accomplished through words: "you're fired," "it was essential that the understudy to my Administrative Assistant be a man," "whites only," "[m]ale help wanted," "did you get any over the weekend?" "sleep with me and I'll give you an 'A'," and "walk more femininely, talk more femininely, dress more femininely, wear makeup, have [your] hair styled, and wear jewelry." Nearly every time a refusal to hire or promote or accommodate is based on a prohibited group ground, some verbal act either constitutes the discrimination or proves it. When words are not the discriminatory act itself, like sexually harassing comments are, for example, they prove that the treatment is based on a prohibited group ground. In the discrimination context, verbal expressions are actionable per se or are evidence of actionable practices, not protected speech; they are smoking guns, not political opinion. . . .

The First Amendment frame on the issue, taken as exclusive, sees what is said but not what is done. When the traditions of defamation and discrimination confront each other, the First Amendment questions how equality can exist without free expression, and the Fourteenth Amendment questions how expression (or anything else) can ever be free without equality.

Defamation and discrimination imagine their harms differently. Defamation addresses harm to group reputation, discrimination to group status and treatment. But to the degree status is a matter of reputation, and reputation a matter of status, they overlap. Whether the treatment is verbal, symbolic, or physical, being treated as a second class citizen certainly furthers the second class reputation of the group of which one is a member. Segregated lunch counters or toilets or water fountains were not challenged as defamatory symbolic expression, nor defended because of what they said—that is, as symbolic speech or as expressions of political opinion—although they were arguably both expressive and political. Racial segregation in education was not regarded as protected speech to the extent it required verbal forms, such as laws and directives, to create and sustain it. Nor was it regarded as actionable defamation against African-Americans, although a substantial part of its harm was the message of inferiority it conveyed, as well as its negative impact on the self-concept of Black children. Yet the harm of segregation and other racist practices is at least as much what it says as what it does. Just as with cross burning, what it says is indistinguishable from what it does. Considered this way, it can be said that pornography does substantial reputational damage to women, but the harm does not end there. The civil rights approach to pornography does not center on its defamatory aspects any more than the civil rights approach to segregation centered on its defamatory aspects, although they are there in both cases.

Pornography is propaganda, an expression of male ideology, a hate literature, an argument for sexual fascism. It conveys ideas like any systematic social practice does. It is also, like most group defamation, often immoral, tasteless, ugly, and boring. But none of this is what pornography distinctively is, how it works, or what is most harmful about it. Was the evil of the Holocaust what it *said* about Jews? If the tortures at Dachau had been required to make anti-Semitic propaganda, would its harm be considered ideological? Would it be subject to varying interpretation? If lampshades made of women's skin were sold beside the road, would the law examine the impact of this practice on women's self-image or public reputation? Perhaps this traffic would offend people, but would we reduce its harm to its offensiveness, as if that were all it was about?

The theory of group defamation does not adequately encompass the reality of pornography. One has to wonder whether it adequately encompasses the reality of group defamation either. For instance, building on the individual libel model, some laws of group defamation require that the statements be proven false or permit truth as a defense. While much of what visual pornography says about women is a pack of lies, it actually has to happen to be made, and in that sense is empirically true. What it shows happened to the person it shows it happening to: what you see is what she got. Most group defamation contains a similar mix of lies with imposed realities. The stereotypes defamation presents begin false and remain largely false, but to the extent the stereotypes are imposed on a group, they will accurately describe at least some of its members sometimes. Success in forcing the world to correspond to a defamatory image, as in making the world a pornographic place, makes defamation both more true and arguably more damaging, not less, but it is, for that reason, legally regarded as *less* defamatory, or not illegal as defamation at all, where truth is a defense. Also, do we really want hearings on comparative African-American penis size or whether Jews bathe?

As another example, the law of group libel generally restricts the promotion of hatred, or hatred and contempt. Hatred is an extreme feeling of negative animus which can express itself verbally or physically. Discrimination begins with an assumption of human status and focuses on deviations in treatment from that standard. If a man chains his dog in his backyard, most people probably will not say that the dog's civil rights are violated. If a man chains a woman in his basement, maybe they will. It does not matter if he loves her or hates her. What matters is how he treats her and what that treatment and its permissibility say about what a woman socially is. Perhaps, in terms of human rights, such treatment can be considered hateful regardless of his subjectivity. But the bottom line of discrimination, I think, is less do they hate and more will they kill. Hatred rationalizes and impels genocide, certainly, but so do some things far colder, like self-interest, sense of superiority, or fun, and something far more banal, like indifference or system. In the case of women and men, love deals at least as much death, and so does something hotter, like pleasure. The fact that pornography so often presents itself as love, indeed resembles much of what passes for it under male dominance, makes its construction as hate literature a challenging exercise in demystification, to say the least. The concept of discrimination aims not at what is felt by perpetrator or victim or what is said as such, but at what is done, including through words.

A related issue in the contrast between defamation and discrimination is the mental element of "wilfulness" or a least knowledge of falsity required in many group defamation statutes. Sincere sex bigots, which the consumption of pornography creates, would presumably be exempt. Discrimination, on the other hand, need not always be intended or meant to be discriminatory. Indeed, after dealing with unconscious bigots, it can be an improvement to have one's humanity recognized enough to have it wilfully degraded. This is no less the case for the standard examples of group defamation than it is for pornography.

This analysis suggests that an equality theory may remedy some of the same inadequacies for group defamation that it has for pornography. A discrimination theory of defamation would center on its harm to subordinate groups.[5] Group libel is an equality issue when its promotion undermines the social equality of a target group that is traditionally and systematically disadvantaged. Group defamation promotes the disadvantage of disadvantaged groups. Group-based enmity, ill-will, intolerance, and prejudice are the attitudinal engines of the exclusion, denigration, and subordination that comprise social inequality. Without bigotry, social systems of enforced separation and apartheid would be unnecessary, impossible, and unthinkable. Stereotyping and stigmatization of historically disadvantaged groups through group hate propaganda shape their social image and reputation, arguably controlling the opportunities of individual members more powerfully than their individual abilities do. It is impossible for an individual to receive equality of opportunity when surrounded by an atmosphere of group hatred or contempt.

In this light, group defamation can be seen as a specific kind of discriminatory practice, a verbal form inequality takes. Anti-Semitism promotes the inequality of Jews on the basis of religion and ethnicity. White supremacy promotes inequality on the basis of race, color, and sometimes ethnic origin.

---

5. The Women's Legal Education and Action Fund (LEAF), with my participation, made the argument outlined in the following paragraphs of the text in defense of the constitutionality of the hate propaganda provision of the Criminal Code of Canada under which the defendant had been convicted in *R. v. Keegstra*, [1991] 2 W.W.R. (Supreme Court) 1, 6 (Can.). In response to the argument that criminalizing hatemongering violated the defendant's constitutionally protected freedom of expression, LEAF argued that the provisions were protected under the constitutional equality provisions. Although found to be violations of the freedom of expression, the provisions were upheld by the Supreme Court of Canada as justified in a free and democratic society largely on an equality rationale.

Group defamation in this sense is not the mere expression of anti-Semitic or white supremacist opinion but a practice of discrimination similar to sexual harassment and other discriminatory acts that take verbal form. It is arguably an integral link in systemic discrimination which keeps target groups in subordinated positions through the promotion of terror, intolerance, degradation, segregation, exclusion, vilification, violence, and genocide. The nature of the practice can be seen and proven from the damage it does, from immediate psychic wounding to consequent physical aggression. Where advocacy of genocide is part of group defamation, an equality approach to its regulation would observe that to be liquidated because of the group you belong to is the ultimate inequality.

Thus, any nation that has a constitutional guarantee of equality can potentially defend a group defamation statute that is challenged as a violation of freedom of expression on equality grounds. A law against group defamation promotes equality and opposes inequality. It would violate any constitutional equality provision in existence for a legislature to pass a law authorizing the promotion of hatred on the basis of sex, race, religion, and national origin. It follows that governmental action against promoting group hate is protected under constitutional equality provisions. Just as governmental action to promote group hatred would violate a constitutional equality provision, governmental action to prohibit group hatred promotes constitution-based equality.

Once laws against group defamation can be supported as well as challenged on a constitutional level, the tension between equality and speech would be resolved by whatever standards constitutional conflicts are accommodated. Typically, the courts would decide whether the group libel provision burdened expression significantly or at all, and whether its regulation promoted equality as unintrusively as possible, and in a way a legislature could have found effective.[6] The balancing would be done however balancing is done, but it would be two constitutional rights in the balance, not just one constitutional right against a nice idea or good manners or political sensitivity or standards of civility. Considered as defamation, the harms are comparatively trivialized, and the state interest is obscured, disabling the constitutional defense of such laws against First Amendment attack. When the equality interest is recognized, focusing on lived consequences rather than message content, practices like lynching, cross burning, and pornography are revealed as expressive forms inequality takes, and the constitutional balance shifts.

Analyzing group defamation in equality terms recasts many well-worn issues in free expression debate. Perhaps the most startling concerns the dogma that there is no such thing as a false idea for purposes of constitutional analysis of speech. When equality is recognized as a constitutional value and mandate, the idea that some people are inferior to others on the basis of group membership is authoritatively rejected as the basis for public policy. This does not mean that ideas to the contrary cannot be expressed. It should

---

6. This generally describes the respective tests in the United States and Canada. In the United States, the two steps are collapsed into one: does the provision violate freedom of expression?. . .In Canada, whether freedom of expression is violated is one step; whether it can be justified as a limit on expression in a free and democratic society is determined separately. . . .

mean, however, that social inferiority cannot be imposed through any means, including expression. Because society is made of language, distinguishing talk about inferiority from verbal imposition of inferiority may be complicated at the edges but is nonetheless very clear in most instances.[7] At the very least, such practices would not be constitutionally insulated from regulation on the ground that the ideas they express cannot be regarded as false. And attempts to address such practices should not be considered invalid because, in taking a position in favor of equality, they assume that the idea of human equality is true. There is no requirement that the state remain neutral when inequality is practiced—quite the contrary. Expressive means of practicing inequality have never been recognized as exceptions.

In the United States, the receptivity of the law of free speech to an equality theory of group defamation can be partially assessed from courts' responses to the sex discrimination ordinance against pornography. The U.S. Court of Appeals for the Seventh Circuit in *American Booksellers Association v. Hudnut* found that the ordinance violated the First Amendment guarantee of freedom of speech. The court reached this conclusion in spite of its agreement that pornography contributed materially to rape and other sexual violence, was a form of subordination in itself, and was partly responsible for second class citizenship in various forms, including economic ones. In some passages, the court conceded that pornography is a practice. Yet protecting the pornography was held to be more important than avoiding or remedying its harms. Indeed, the court held that pornography's importance as speech can be measured by its effectiveness in doing the harm that it does.

The civil rights law against pornography was held to be a form of discrimination on the basis of "viewpoint" because it was not neutral on the subject of sex-based exploitation and abuse. By this standard, every discriminatory practice and every anti-discriminatory law expresses a point of view. Acts express ideas, yet they are legally restricted and do not have to be proven expressionless first. Segregation expresses the view that Blacks are inferior to whites; rulings against segregation express the contrary view. Segregation is not therefore protected speech, nor are rulings against it considered "thought control." Affirmative action plans and anti-discrimination policies are not regarded as discrimination on the basis of viewpoint, although they prohibit the view that Blacks are inferior to whites from being expressed by discriminating against them, including by telling them "you're fired" for the wrong reasons. This remains true even though deinstitutionalizing segregation does a great deal to undermine the point of view it expresses, just as making pornography actionable as sex discrimination would delegitimize the ideas the practice advances. Under the ordinance, misogynist attitudes toward women

7. This seems to be what is at stake in the discussion about campus hate speech codes, most of which, in essence, extend sexual harassment prohibitions to racial and ethnic slurs and insults, and some to sexual orientation as well. . . .I do not think that the discrimination rationale on which sexual harassment law is based, and the sexual nature of the harassment which makes it so act-like, can be so simply transposed into the racial and ethnic defamation context. It is equally clear, however, that what is harassment in the gender context does not suddenly become pure idea in the racial context and that an equality theory can support such codes when properly drawn.

and sexuality can be expressed; they just cannot be practiced in certain ways, such as when verbal and visual subordination based on sex are trafficked. What the *Hudnut* court missed is both that acts speak and that speech acts. . . .

Actually, *Hudnut* does not rule on the Indianapolis ordinance at all, but on some imaginary group defamation ordinance directed toward what pornography says. By turning harmful practices into bad thoughts and acts into ideas about acts, *Hudnut* does rule on hate speech regulation, which, unlike the Indianapolis ordinance, *does* turn on point of view. Under anti-hate laws, love is not racially defamatory; hate is. After reducing discriminatory acts to defamatory ideas, the *Hudnut* court held that no amount of harm from group-based speech can justify legal action by its victims.[8] This is simply legally wrong. Courts are supposed to measure value against harm, not by harm. A doctrinally correct approach to the ordinance would have balanced the harms of such materials against their value, if any, or might even have considered the value of the materials irrelevant so long as they are proven to do injury which states can legitimately regulate. The harm of pornography as made actionable by the ordinance is not done through viewpoint, or even through content as such. Pornography is identified in part through its content, but regulated through its acts, the acts the ordinance makes actionable. But it must be faced that the *Hudnut* approach is fatal for regulating racial defamation, no matter how much harm it does.

Just as courts have often protected the group defamation of the past,[9] when the Supreme Court summarily affirmed *Hudnut*, protecting and defending pornography became the official state position in the United States. An entire class of women can be discriminated against so that others can have what they call freedom of speech: freedom meaning free access to women's bodies, free use of women's lives; speech meaning women's bodies as a medium for expression. As African-Americans, men as well as women, once were white men's property under the Constitution, all women are now men's "speech" because our pain, humiliation, torture, use, and second class status is some-

8. . . .On February 27, 1992, the Supreme Court of Canada explicitly held to the contrary in *Butler v. The Queen*, [[1992] 1 S.C.R. 452 (Can.)], adopting LEAF's argument that pornography damages social equality. The court ruled unanimously that pornography's harm to women justifies its criminal prohibition as obscenity. The court recognized the substantial body of opinion holding that pornography "results in harm, particularly to women and therefore to society as a whole," in concluding that harm to women violated community standards. In addition to applying to violent materials, the court's opinion found that "degrading and dehumanizing" materials can be prohibited because they "place women (and sometimes men) in positions of subordination, servile submission or humiliation. They run against the principles of equality and dignity of all human beings.". . .

9. David Riesman, in Democracy and Defamation: Control of Group Libel, 42 Colum. L. Rev. 727 (1942), explains how German courts espoused a general doctrine that only an individual could be defamed, thereby protecting favored groups. . . .Riesman recounts the use of defamation and manipulation of the law against defamation as a major weapon in the Nazi rise to power, making it possible systematically to defame Jews in a way calculated to lower their public esteem and to lure them into ruinous lawsuits. . . .Also important, members of the government were exempt from legal responsibility for defamation. . . .

The *Hudnut* court equates the role of Nazi propaganda in the Nazi rise to power with the role of pornography in the status of women as an argument for protecting pornography. . . .

thing they want to say. It does not matter that they cannot say it without doing it.

Now that the law has adopted the point of view of the pornographers on women's rights as its basis for state policy, holding that the pornography is more important than the women they know it harms, one might ask again the same questions that are asked of the classic experiences of group defamation. Why the silence? Why the complicity? How can "we" let this go on? How can it be officially permitted? How can the law be so twisted as to collaborate in it? What are people thinking? Don't they know? Don't they see? Don't they care? Perhaps the lack of explanation for the success of past campaigns of group defamation is connected with the lack of recognition of present ones. Why have most of you not heard all this before? Why have those who have seen the pornography not seen it in this way? Now that you know, why will most of you find satisfying reasons to do nothing about it?

Notes and Questions

1. *Viewpoint.* The *Hudnut* court held that the Indianapolis ordinance was unconstitutional because it established an "approved" view of women and an "approved" view of how men and women may relate to each other. Why did the court treat the ordinance as nonneutral, but treat the current law of obscenity as neutral?

2. *The Ordinance's Four Offenses.* The ordinance provides injunctive relief and damages for coercion into pornography, forcing pornography on a person, assault or physical attack due to pornography, and trafficking in pornography. The *Hudnut* court did not distinguish among the four offenses when finding the ordinance unconstitutional. Could the court have distinguished among the four provisions so that some parts of the ordinance would not have violated the First Amendment? Why, according to Catharine MacKinnon, would this analytical approach distort the underlying basis of the ordinance?

3. *FACT Brief.* An *amicus curiae* brief was filed on behalf of the Feminist Anti-Censorship Taskforce [FACT] and was co-signed by the Women's Legal Defense Fund and eighty individual feminists in opposition to the Indianapolis ordinance in *Hudnut*. The primary arguments made in the brief were as follows:

> The First Amendment prohibits any law regulating expression which would of necessity result in such unpredictable and arbitrary interpretations. This ordinance transgresses all three of the measures of impermissible vagueness. A person of ordinary intelligence would be at a loss to predict how any of a huge range of sexually explicit materials would be interpreted by a court. . . .
>
> [S]exually explicit expression, including much that is covered by the ordinance, carries many more messages than simply the misogyny described by Appellants. It may convey the message that sexuality need not be tied to reproduction, men, or domesticity. It may contain themes of sex for no reason other than pleasure, sex without commitment, and sexual adventure—all of which are surely ideas. . . .

Even pornography which is problematic for women can be experienced as affirming of women's desires and of women's equality . . . .

The ordinance presumes women as a class (and only women) are subordinated by virtually any sexually explicit image. It presumes women as a class (and only women) are incapable of making a binding agreement to participate in the creation of sexually explicit material. And it presumes men as a class (and only men) are conditioned by sexually explicit depictions to commit acts of aggression and to believe misogynist myths.

Such assumptions reinforce and perpetuate central sexist stereotypes; they weaken, rather than enhance, women's struggles to free themselves of archaic notions of gender roles. . . .

The ordinance damages individuals who do not fit the stereotypes it embodies. It delegitimates and makes socially invisible women who find sexually explicit images of women "in positions of display" or "penetrated by objects" to be erotic, liberating, or educational. These women are told that their perceptions are a product of "false consciousness" and that such images are so inherently degrading that they may be suppressed by the state. At the same time, it stamps the imprimatur of state approval on the belief that men are attack dogs triggered to violence by the sight of a sexually explicit image of a woman.

Brief Amici Curiae of Feminist Anti-Censorship Task Force, et al., in *American Booksellers Association v. Hudnut*, 21 J.L. Reform 69, 111, 121, 122, 129 (1988).

The filing of the brief brought into sharp contrast the divisions within the feminist movement.

To no one's surprise. . .[the ordinance] was opposed by many people. It was opposed by conservatives who discovered that they disliked sex equality a lot more than they disliked pornography. It was opposed by liberals, who discovered that they liked speech—i.e., sex, i.e., women being used—a great deal more than they liked sex equality. Then came the opposition from a quarter that labeled itself feminist: from FACT . . . .At this point, for me, the women's movement that I had known came to an end.

In an act of extraordinary horizontal hostility, FACT filed a brief against the ordinance in court as part of a media-based legal attack on it. They did what they could to prevent from existing, to keep out of women's hands, this law, written in women's blood, in women's tears, in women's pain, in women's experience, out of women's silence, this law to make acts against women actionable—acts like coercion, force, assault, trafficking in our flesh. Pornography, they said, *is* sex equality. . . .

Equality in the FACT brief means equal access to pornography by women. . . .[A]n entire population of women must continue to be treated in the ways the ordinance makes actionable so that this other population of women can experience its eroticism, liberation, or education at their expense.

Catharine A. MacKinnon, Liberalism and the Death of Feminism, in The Sexual Liberals and the Attack on Feminism 3, 9-10 (Dorchen Leidholdt & Janice G. Raymond eds., 1990) (emphasis in original).

4. *Hate Speech*. The Supreme Court in *R.A.V. v. City of St. Paul*, 112 S. Ct.

2538 (1992) held unconstitutional an ordinance that made it a misdemeanor to:

> place[ ] on public or private property a symbol, object, appellation, characterization or graffiti, including, but not limited to, a burning cross or Nazi swastika, which one knows or has reasonable grounds to know arouses anger, alarm or resentment in others on the basis of race, color, creed, religion or gender . . . .

Saint Paul, Minn. Legis. Code § 292.02 (1990).

Justice Antonin Scalia, writing for the majority, found that the ordinance discriminated on the basis of viewpoint. *R.A.V.* would seem to be consistent with the *Hudnut* court's rationale. Owen Fiss, however, analyzes *R.A.V.* in a manner that would allow an anti-pornography ordinance like the one reviewed in *Hudnut* to be upheld.

> It may seem that the Indianapolis trafficking provision runs afoul of Scalia's stricture since that provision is linked to the cause of equality: only those images or words that subordinate women or somehow promote their subordination, as opposed to their elevation or equal treatment, are proscribed. But Justice Scalia made clear that he is not proscribing all selective regulations, nor even those that embody a content discrimination, but only those in which. . .the content discrimination is unrelated to the "distinctively proscribable content" of the speech. He is complaining of extraneous content discrimination.
>
> Justice Scalia's hostility toward content discrimination is based on the fear that it tends to "drive certain ideas or viewpoints from the marketplace," but he does not see such a danger when the content discrimination that defines the selective regulation is related to the reasons why the state is allowed to regulate the category of speech in the first place. Accordingly, he acknowledged that the federal government could choose to criminalize only those threats of violence that are directed against the President, since, as he wrote, "[T]he reasons why threats of violence are outside the First Amendment (protecting individuals from the fear of violence, from the disruption that fear engenders, and from the possibility that the threatened violence will occur) have special force when applied to the person of the President." Similarly, while the trafficking ban does indeed single out certain sexually explicit images or material, specifically those that subordinate women, the reason for that selection is closely related to one of the reasons why obscenity is proscribable in the first place: to protect women from violence and sexual abuse.

Owen M. Fiss, Freedom and Feminism, 80 Geo. L.J. 2041, 2055-56 (1992).

5. *Hudnut's Aftermath*. Bellingham, Washington voted into law by initiative of the voters an ordinance similar to the one reviewed in *Hudnut*. A court granted summary judgment in favor of the plaintiffs, who were similar to the plaintiffs involved in *Hudnut*.

> [A] Supreme Court summary affirmance of a decision on the constitutionality of a statute may not be ignored by a court examining the same statute. . . .In this case, the Bellingham statute is virtually identical to the Indianapolis

statute previously ruled unconstitutional. Therefore, the Supreme Court's summary affirmance of that ruling is binding.

Village Books v. City of Bellingham, No. 88-1470 (W.D. Wash., Feb. 9, 1989), at 7-8.

Regina v. Butler,
[1992] 1 S.C.R. 452 (Can.)

Sopinka, Justice. This appeal calls into question the constitutionality of the obscenity provisions of the *Criminal Code*, R.S.C., 1985, c. C-46, s. 163. They are attacked on the ground that they contravene s. 2(*b*) of the *Canadian Charter of Rights and Freedoms*. The case requires the Court to address one of the most difficult and controversial of contemporary issues, that of determining whether, and to what extent, Parliament may legitimately criminalize obscenity. I propose to begin with a review of the facts which gave rise to this appeal, as well of the proceedings in the lower courts. . . .

In August 1987, the appellant, Donald Victor Butler, opened the Avenue Video Boutique located in Winnipeg, Manitoba. The shop sells and rents "hard core" videotapes and magazines as well as sexual paraphernalia. Outside the store is a sign which reads:

> Avenue Video Boutique; a private members only adult video/visual club.
>
> Notice: if sex oriented material offends you, please do not enter.
>
> No admittance to persons under 18 years.

On August 21, 1987, the City of Winnipeg Police entered the appellant's store with a search warrant and seized all the inventory. The appellant was charged with 173 counts in the first indictment: three counts of selling obscene material. . ., 41 counts of possessing obscene material for the purpose of distribution. . ., 128 counts of possessing obscene material for the purpose of sale. . .and one count of exposing obscene material to public view . . . .

On October 19, 1987, the appellant reopened the store at the same location. As a result of a police operation a search warrant was executed on October 29, 1987, resulting in the arrest of an employee, Norma McCord. The appellant was arrested at a later date.

A joint indictment was laid against the appellant doing business as Avenue Video Boutique and Norma McCord. The joint indictment contains 77 counts . . . .

The trial judge convicted the appellant on eight counts relating to eight films. Convictions were entered against the co-accused McCord with respect to two counts relating to two of the films. Fines of $1,000 per offence were imposed on the appellant. Acquittals were entered on the remaining charges.

The Crown appealed the 242 acquittals with respect to the appellant and the appellant cross-appealed the convictions. The majority of the Manitoba Court of Appeal allowed the appeal of the Crown and entered convictions for the appellant with respect to all of the counts . . . .

Relevant Legislation

Criminal Code, R.S.C., 1985, c. C-46

163. (1) Everyone commits an offence who

(*a*) makes, prints, publishes, distributes, circulates, or has in his possession for the purpose of publication, distribution or circulation any obscene written matter, picture, model, phonograph record or other thing whatever; or

(*b*) makes, prints, publishes, distributes, sells or has in his possession for the purpose of publication, distribution or circulation a crime comic.

(2) Every one commits an offence who knowingly, without lawful justification or excuse,

(*a*) sells, exposes to public view or has in his possession for such a purpose any obscene written matter, picture, model, phonograph record or other thing whatever;

(*b*) publicly exhibits a disgusting object or an indecent show;. . . .

(3) No person shall be convicted of an offence under this section if he establishes that the public good was served by the acts that are alleged to constitute the offence and that the acts alleged did not extend beyond what served the public good.

(4) For the purposes of this section, it is a question of law whether an act served the public good and whether there is evidence that the act alleged went beyond what served the public good, but it is a question of fact whether the acts did or did not extend beyond what served the public good.

(5) For the purposes of this section, the motives of an accused are irrelevant.

(6) Where an accused is charged with an offence under subsection (1), the fact that the accused was ignorant of the nature or presence of the matter, picture, model, phonograph record, crime comic or other thing by means of or in relation to which the offence was committed is not a defence to the charge.

(7) In this section, "crime comic" means a magazine, periodical or book that exclusively or substantially comprises matter depicting pictorially

(*a*) the commission of crimes, real or fictitious; or

(*b*) events connected with the commission of crimes, real or fictitious, whether occurring before or after the commission of the crime.

(8) For the purposes of this Act, any publication a dominant characteristic of which is the undue exploitation of sex, or of sex and any one or more of the following subjects, namely, crime, horror, cruelty and violence, shall be deemed to be obscene. . . .

Issues

The following constitutional questions are raised by this appeal:

1. Does s. 163. . .violate s. 2(*b*) of the *Canadian Charter of Rights and Freedoms*?

2. If s. 163. . .violates s. 2(*b*). . .can s. 163. . .be demonstrably justified under s. 1 of the *Canadian Charter of Rights and Freedoms* as a reasonable limit prescribed by law?. . .

The constitutional questions, as stated, bring under scrutiny the entirety of s. 163. However, both lower courts as well as the parties have focused almost exclusively on the definition of obscenity found in s. 163(8). . . .In my view, in the circumstances, this appeal should be confined to the examination of the constitutional validity of s. 163(8) only. . . .

In order for the work or material to qualify as "obscene", the exploitation of sex must not only be its dominant characteristic, but such exploitation must be "undue". In determining when the exploitation of sex will be considered "undue", the courts have attempted to formulate workable tests. The most important of these is the "community standard of tolerance" test. . . .

The community standards test has been the subject of extensive judicial analysis. It is the standards of the community as a whole which must be considered and not the standards of a small segment of that community such as the university community where a film was shown. . .or a city where a picture was exposed . . . .The standard to be applied is a national one . . . .With respect to expert evidence, it is not necessary and is not a fact which the Crown is obliged to prove as part of its case . . . .

Our Court was called upon to elaborate the community standards test in *Towne Cinema Theatres Ltd. v. The Queen*, [1985] 1 S.C.R. 494. Dickson C.J. reviewed the case law and found. . .:

> The cases all emphasize that it is standard of *tolerance*, not taste, that is relevant. What matters is not what Canadians think is right for themselves to see. What matters is what Canadians would not abide other Canadians seeing because it would be beyond the contemporary Canadian standard of tolerance to allow them to see it.
>
> Since the standard is tolerance, I think the audience to which the allegedly obscene material is targeted must be relevant. The operative standards are those of the Canadian community as a whole, but since what matters is what other people may see, it is quite conceivable that the Canadian community would tolerate varying degrees of explicitness depending upon the audience and the circumstances. [Emphasis in original.] [At pp. 508-09.]

Therefore, the community standards test is concerned not with what Canadians would not tolerate being exposed to themselves, but what they would not tolerate *other* Canadians being exposed to. . . .

There has been a growing recognition in recent cases that material which may be said to exploit sex in a "degrading or dehumanizing" manner will necessarily fail the community standards test. Borins Co. Ct. J. expressed this view in *R. v. Doug Rankine Co.* (1983), 9 C.C.C. (3d) 53 (Ont. Co. Ct.). . .:

> . . .films which consist substantially or partially of scenes which portray violence and cruelty in conjunction with sex, particularly where the performance of indignities degrade and dehumanize the people upon whom they are performed, exceed the level of community tolerance. [At p. 70.]

Subsequent decisions. . .held that material that "degraded" or "dehumanized" any of the participants would exceed community standards even in the absence of cruelty and violence. In *R. v. Ramsingh*, [(1984), 14 C.C.C. (3d) 230 (Man. Q.B.)], Ferg J. described in graphic terms the type of material that qualified for this label. He states on p. 239:

> They are exploited, portrayed as desiring pleasure from pain, by being humiliated and treated only as an object of male domination sexually, or in cruel or violent bondage. Women are portrayed in these films as pining away their lives waiting for a huge male penis to come along, on the person of a so-called sex therapist, or window washer, supposedly to transport them into complete sexual ecstasy. Or even more false and degrading one is led to believe their raison d'être is to savour semen as a life elixir, or that they secretly desire to be forcefully taken by a male.

Among other things, degrading or dehumanizing materials place women (and sometimes men) in positions of subordination, servile submission or humiliation. They run against the principles of equality and dignity of all human beings. In the appreciation of whether material is degrading or dehumanizing, the appearance of consent is not necessarily determinative. Consent cannot save materials that otherwise contain degrading or dehumanizing scenes. Sometimes the very appearance of consent makes the depicted acts even more degrading or dehumanizing.

This type of material would, apparently, fail the community standards test not because it offends against morals but because it is perceived by public opinion to be harmful to society, particularly to women. While the accuracy of this perception is not susceptible of exact proof, there is a substantial body of opinion that holds that the portrayal of persons being subjected to degrading or dehumanizing sexual treatment results in harm, particularly to women and therefore to society as a whole. . . .See. . .Attorney General's Commission on Pornography (the "Meese Commission"), *Final Report* (U.S., 1986), vol. 1, at pp. 938-1035; Metro Toronto Task Force on Public Violence Against Women and Children, *Final Report* (1984), at p. 66; *Report of the Joint Select Committee on Video Material* (Australia, 1988), vol. 1, at pp. 185-230; *Pornography: Report of the Ministerial Committee of Inquiry into Pornography* (New Zealand, 1988), at pp. 38-45. It would be reasonable to conclude that there is an appreciable risk of harm to society in the portrayal of such material. . . .

In *Towne Cinema*, Dickson C.J. considered the "degradation" or "dehumanization" test to be the principal indicator of "undueness" without specifying what role the community tolerance test plays in respect of this issue. He did observe, however, that the community might tolerate some forms of exploitation that caused harm that were nevertheless undue. The relevant passages appear at p. 505:

> There are other ways in which exploitation of sex might by "undue". Ours is not a perfect society and it is unfortunate but true that the community may tolerate publications that cause harm to members of society and therefore to society as a whole. Even if, at certain times, there is a coincidence between what is not tolerated and what is harmful to society, there is no necessary connection between these two concepts. Thus, a legal definition of

> "undue" must also encompass publications harmful to members of society and, therefore, to society as a whole.
>
> Sex related publications which portray persons in a degrading manner as objects of violence, cruelty or other forms of dehumanizing treatment, may be "undue" for the purpose of s. 159(8). No one should be subject to the degradation and humiliation inherent in publications which link sex with violence, cruelty, and other forms of dehumanizing treatment. It is not likely that at a given moment in a society's history, such publications will be tolerated. . . .
>
> However, as I have noted above, there is no *necessary* coincidence between the undueness of publications which degrade people by linking violence, cruelty or other forms of dehumanizing treatment with sex, and the community standard of tolerance. Even if certain sex related materials were found to be within the standard of tolerance of the community, it would still be necessary to ensure that they were not "undue" in some other sense, for example in the sense that they portray persons in a degrading manner as objects of violence, cruelty, or other forms of dehumanizing treatment. [Emphasis in original.]

In the reasons of Wilson J. concurring in the result, the line between the mere portrayal of sex and the dehumanization of people is drawn by the "undueness" concept. The community is the arbiter as to what is harmful to it. She states. . .:

> As I see it, the essential difficulty with the definition of obscenity is that "undueness" must presumably be assessed in relation to consequences. It is implicit in the definition that at some point the exploitation of sex becomes harmful to the public or at least the public believes that to be so. It is therefore necessary for the protection of the public to put limits on the degree of exploitation and, through the application of the community standard test, the public is made the arbiter of what is harmful to it and what is not. The problem is that we know so little of the consequences we are seeking to avoid. Do obscene movies spawn immoral conduct? Do they degrade women? Do they promote violence? The most that can be said, I think, is that the public has concluded that exposure to material which degrades the human dimensions of life to a subhuman or merely physical dimension and thereby contributes to a process of moral desensitization must be harmful in some way. It must therefore be controlled when it gets out of hand, when it becomes "undue". [At p. 524.]

. . .As counsel for the Crown pointed out in his oral submissions, the artistic defence is the last step in the analysis of whether the exploitation of sex is undue. Even material which by itself offends community standards will not be considered "undue", if it is required for the serious treatment of a theme. For example, in *R. v. Odeon Morton Theatres Ltd.* (1974), 16 C.C.C. (2d) 185, the majority of the Manitoba Court of Appeal held that the film *Last Tango in Paris* was not obscene within the meaning of the *Code*. To determine whether a dominant characteristic of the film is the undue exploitation of sex, Freedman C.J.M. noted that the courts must have regard to various things— the author's artistic purpose, the manner in which he or she has portrayed and developed the story, the depiction and interplay of character and the creation of visual effect through skilful camera techniques (at p. 194). Freedman C.J.M. stated that the issue of whether the film is obscene must be determined according to contemporary standards in Canada. Relevant to that determination were several factors: the testimony of experts, the classification of "Restricted" which made the film unavailable to persons under 18 years of age and the fact that the film had passed the scrutiny of the censor boards of several provinces.

Accordingly, the "internal necessities" test, or what has been referred to as the "artistic defence", has been interpreted to assess whether the exploitation of sex has a justifiable role in advancing the plot or the theme, and in considering the work as a whole, does not merely represent "dirt for dirt's sake" but has a legitimate role when measured by the internal necessities of the work itself. . . .

This review of jurisprudence shows that it fails to specify the relationship of the tests one to another. Failure to do so with respect to the community standards test and the degrading or dehumanizing test, for example, raises a serious question as to the basis on which the community acts in determining whether the impugned material will be tolerated. With both these tests being applied to the same material and apparently independently, we do not know whether the community found the material to be intolerable because it was degrading or dehumanizing, because it offended against morals or on some other basis. In some circumstances a finding that the material is tolerable can be overruled by the conclusion by the court that it causes harm and is therefore undue. Moreover, is the internal necessities test dominant so that it will redeem material that would otherwise be undue or is it just one factor? Is this test applied by the community or is it determined by the court without regard for the community? This hiatus in the jurisprudence has left the legislation open to attack on the ground of vagueness and uncertainty. That attack is made in this case. . . .

Pornography can be usefully divided into three categories: (1) explicit sex with violence, (2) explicit sex without violence but which subjects people to treatment that is degrading or dehumanizing, and (3) explicit sex without violence that is neither degrading nor dehumanizing. Violence in this context includes both actual physical violence and threats of physical violence. Relating these three categories to the terms of s. 163(8) of the *Code*, the first, explicit sex coupled with violence, is expressly mentioned. Sex coupled with crime, horror or cruelty will sometimes involve violence. Cruelty, for instance, will usually do so. But, even in the absence of violence, sex coupled with crime, horror or cruelty may fall within the second category. As for category (3), subject to the exception referred to below, it is not covered.

Some segments of society would consider that all three categories of pornography cause harm to society because they tend to undermine its moral fibre. Others would contend that none of the categories cause harm. Furthermore there is a range of opinion as to what is degrading or dehumanizing. See *Pornography and Prostitution in Canada: Report of the Special Committee on Pornography and Prostitution* (1985) (the Fraser Report), vol. 1, at p. 51. Because this is not a matter that is susceptible of proof in the traditional way and because we do not wish to leave it to the individual tastes of judges, we must have a norm that will serve as an arbiter in determining what amounts to an undue exploitation of sex. That arbiter is the community as a whole.

The courts must determine as best they can what the community would tolerate others being exposed to on the basis of the degree of harm that may flow from such exposure. Harm in this context means that it predisposes persons to act in an anti-social manner as, for example, the physical or mental mistreatment of women by men, or, what is perhaps debatable, the reverse. Anti-social conduct for this purpose is conduct which society formally recognizes as incompatible with its proper functioning. The stronger the inference of a risk of harm the lesser the likelihood of tolerance. The inference may be drawn from the material itself or from the material and other evidence. Similarly evidence as to the community standards is desirable but not essential.

In making this determination with respect to the three categories of pornography referred to above, the portrayal of sex coupled with violence will almost always constitute the undue exploitation of sex. Explicit sex which is degrading or dehumanizing may be undue if the risk of harm is substantial. Finally, explicit sex that is not violent and neither degrading nor dehumanizing is generally tolerated in our society and will not qualify as the undue exploitation of sex unless it employs children in its production.

If material is not obscene under this framework, it does not become so by reason of the person to whom it is or may be shown or exposed nor by reason of the place or manner in which it is shown. . . .

The foregoing deals with the interrelationship of the "community standards test" and "the degrading or dehumanizing" test. How does the "internal necessities" test fit into this scheme? The need to apply this test only arises if a work contains sexually explicit material that by itself would constitute the undue exploitation of sex. The portrayal of sex must then be viewed in context to determine whether that is the dominant theme of the work as a whole. Put another way, is undue exploitation of sex the main object of the work or is this portrayal of sex essential to a wider artistic, literary, or other similar purpose? Since the threshold determination must be made on the basis of community standards, that is, whether the sexually explicit aspect is undue, its impact when considered in context must be determined on the same basis. The court must determine whether the sexually explicit material when viewed in the context of the whole work would be tolerated by the community as a whole. Artistic expression rests at the heart of freedom of expression values and any doubt in this regard must be resolved in favour of freedom of expression. . . .

In light of our recent decision in *R. v. Keegstra*, [1990] 3 S.C.R. 697, the respondent, and most of the parties intervening in support of the respondent, do not take issue with the proposition that s. 163 of the *Criminal Code* violates s. 2(*b*) of the *Charter*. In *Keegstra*, we were unanimous in advocating a generous approach to the protection afforded by s. 2(*b*) of the *Charter*. Our Court confirmed the view expressed in *Reference re ss. 193 and 195.1(1)(c) of the Criminal Code (Man.)*, [1990] 1 S.C.R. 1123 (the "*Prostitution Reference*"), that activities cannot be excluded from the scope of the guaranteed freedom on the basis of the content or meaning being conveyed. . . .

In this case, both the purpose and effect of s. 163 are specifically to restrict the communication of certain types of materials based on their content. In my view, there is no doubt that s. 163 seeks to prohibit certain types of expressive activity and thereby infringes s. 2(*b*) of the *Charter*.

Before turning to consider whether this infringement is justified under s. 1 of the *Charter*, I wish to address the argument advanced by the Attorney General of British Columbia that in applying s. 2(*b*), a distinction should be made between films and written works. It is argued that by its very nature, the medium of the written word is such that it is, when used, inherently an attempt to convey meaning. In contrast, British Columbia argues that the medium of film can be used for a purpose "not significantly communicative". In its factum, British Columbia maintains that if the activity captured in hard core pornographic magazines and videotapes is itself not expression, the fact that they are reproduced by the technology of a camera does not magically transform them into "expression": the appellant cannot hide behind the label "film" to claim protection for the reproduction of activity the sole purpose of which is to arouse or shock.

In my view, this submission cannot be maintained. This position is not far from that taken by the majority of the Court of Appeal, that the depiction of purely physical activity does not convey meaning. First, I cannot agree with the premise that purely physical activity, such as sexual activity, cannot be expression. Second, in creating a film, regardless of its content, the maker of the film is consciously choosing the particular images which together constitute the film. In choosing his or her images, the creator of the film is attempting to convey some meaning. The meaning to be ascribed to the work cannot be measured by the reaction of the audience, which, in some cases, may amount to no more than physical arousal or shock. Rather, the meaning of the work derives from the fact that it has been intentionally created by its author. To use an example, it may very well be said that a blank wall in itself conveys no meaning. However, if one deliberately chooses to capture that image by the medium of film, the work necessarily has some meaning for its author and thereby constitutes expression. The same would apply to the depiction of persons engaged in purely sexual activity.

I would conclude that the first constitutional question should be answered in the affirmative. . . .

The appellant argues that the provision [s. 163] is so vague that it is impossible to apply it. Vagueness must be considered in relation to two issues in this appeal: (1) is the law so vague that it does not qualify as "a limit prescribed by law"; and (2) is it so imprecise that it is not a reasonable limit. Dealing with (1), the test is whether the law "is so obscure as to be incapable of interpretation with any degree of precision using the ordinary tools" . . . .

In assessing whether s. 163(8) prescribes an intelligible standard, consideration must be given to the manner in which the provision has been judicially interpreted. . . .

Standards which escape precise technical definition, such as "undue", are an inevitable part of the law. The *Criminal Code* contains other such standards. Without commenting on their constitutional validity, I note that the terms "indecent", "immoral" or "scurrilous", found in ss. 167, 168, 173 and 175, are nowhere defined in the *Code*. It is within the role of the judiciary to attempt to interpret these terms. If such interpretation yields an intelligible standard, the threshold test for the application of s. 1 is met. In my opinion, the interpretation of s. 163(8) in prior judgments which I have reviewed, as supplemented by these reasons, provides an intelligible standard. . . .

The respondent argues that there are several pressing and substantial objectives which justify overriding the freedom to distribute obscene materials. Essentially, these objectives are the avoidance of harm resulting from antisocial attitudinal changes that exposure to obscene material causes and the public interest in maintaining a "decent society". On the other hand, the appellant argues that the objective of s. 163 is to have the state act as "moral custodian" in sexual matters and to impose subjective standards of morality.

The obscenity legislation and jurisprudence prior to the enactment of s. 163 were evidently concerned with prohibiting the "immoral influences" of obscene publications and safeguarding the morals of individuals into whose hands such works could fall. . . .In this sense, its dominant, if not exclusive, purpose was to advance a particular conception of morality. Any deviation from such morality was considered to be inherently undesirable, independently of any harm to society. . . .[T]his particular objective is no longer defensible in view of the *Charter*. To impose a certain standard of public and sexual morality, solely because it reflects the conventions of a given community, is inimical to the exercise and enjoyment of individual freedoms, which form the basis of our social contract. . . .The prevention of "dirt for dirt's sake" is not a legitimate objective which would justify the violation of one of the most fundamental freedoms enshrined in the *Charter*.

On the other hand, I cannot agree with the suggestion of the appellant that Parliament does not have the right to legislate on the basis of some fundamental conception of morality for the purposes of safeguarding the values which are integral to a free and democratic society. . . .

As the respondent and many of the interveners have pointed out, much of the criminal law is based on moral conceptions of right and wrong and the mere fact that a law is grounded in morality does not automatically render it illegitimate. In this regard, criminalizing the proliferation of materials which undermine another basic *Charter* right may indeed be a legitimate objective.

In my view, however, the overriding objective of s. 163 is not moral disapprobation but the avoidance of harm to society. . . .

The harm was described in the following way in the *Report on Pornography* by the Standing Committee on Justice and Legal Affairs (MacGuigan Report) (1978). . .:

> The clear and unquestionable danger of this type of material is that it reinforces some unhealthy tendencies in Canadian society. The effect of this type of material is to reinforce male-female stereotypes to the detriment of both sexes. It attempts to make degradation, humiliation, victimization, and violence in human relationships appear normal and acceptable. A society which holds that egalitarianism, non-violence, consensualism, and mutuality are basic to any human interaction, whether sexual or other, is clearly justified in controlling and prohibiting any medium of depiction, description or advocacy which violates these principles. [At p. 18:4.]

The appellant argues that to accept the objective of the provision as being related to the harm associated with obscenity would be to adopt the "shifting purpose" doctrine explicitly rejected in *R. v. Big M Drug Mart Ltd.*, [1985] 1 S.C.R. 295. This Court concluded in that case that a finding that the *Lord's Day Act* has a secular purpose was not possible given that its religious purpose, in compelling sabbatical observance, has been long-established and consistently maintained by the courts. . . .

I do not agree that to identify the objective of the impugned legislation as the prevention of harm to society, one must resort to the "shifting purpose" doctrine. First, the notions of moral corruption and harm to society are not distinct, as the appellant suggests, but are inextricably linked. It is moral corruption of a certain kind which leads to the detrimental effect on society. Second, and more importantly, I am of the view that with the enactment of s. 163, Parliament explicitly sought to address the harms which are linked to certain types of obscene materials. The prohibition of such materials was based on a belief that they had a detrimental impact on individuals exposed to them and consequently on society as a whole. Our understanding of the harms caused by these materials has developed considerably since that time; however this does not detract from the fact that the purpose of this legislation remains, as it was in 1959, the protection of society from harms caused by the exposure to obscene materials. In this regard, I lend support to the analysis of Charron Dist. Ct. J. in *R. v. Fringe Product Inc.*,[(1990), 53 C.C.C. (3d) 422, 443]:

> Even though one can still find an emphasis on the enforcement of moral standards of decency in relation to expression in sexual matters in the jurisprudence subsequent to the enactment of s-s.(8), it is clear that, by the very words it has chosen, Parliament in 1959 moved beyond such narrow concern and expanded the scope of the legislation to include further concerns with respect to sex combined with crime, horror, cruelty and violence.
>
> It is the harm to society resulting from the undue exploitation of such matters which is aimed by the section. The "harm" conceived by Parliament in 1959 may not have been expressed in the same words as one would today. The court is not limited to a 1959 perspective in the determination of this matter. . . .

A permissible shift in emphasis was built into the legislation when, as interpreted by the courts, it adopted the community standards test. Community standards as to what is harmful have changed since 1959.

This being the objective, is it pressing and substantial? Does the prevention of the harm associated with the dissemination of certain obscene materials constitute a sufficiently pressing and substantial concern to warrant a restriction on the freedom of expression? In this regard, it should be recalled that in *Keegstra*, *supra*, this Court unanimously accepted that the prevention of the influence of hate propaganda on society at large was a legitimate objective. Dickson C.J. wrote with respect to the changes in attitudes which exposure to hate propaganda can bring about. . .:

> . . .the alteration of views held by the recipients of hate propaganda may occur subtly, and is not always attendant upon conscious acceptance of the communicated ideas. Even if the message of hate propaganda is outwardly rejected, there is evidence that its premise of racial or religious inferiority may per-

> sist in a recipient's mind as an idea that holds some truth, an incipient effect not to be entirely discounted. . . .
>
> The threat to the self-dignity of target group members is thus matched by the possibility that prejudiced messages will gain some credence, with the attendant result of discrimination, and perhaps even violence, against minority groups in Canadian society. [At pp. 747-48.]

This Court has thus recognized that the harm caused by the proliferation of materials which seriously offend the values fundamental to our society is a substantial concern which justifies restricting the otherwise full exercise of the freedom of expression. In my view, the harm sought to be avoided in the case of the dissemination of obscene materials is similar. In the words of Nemetz C.J.B.C. in *R. v. Red Hot Video Ltd.* (1985), 45 C.R. (3d) 36 (B.C.C.A.), there is a growing concern that the exploitation of women and children, depicted in publications and films, can, in certain circumstances, lead to "abject and servile victimization" (at pp. 43-44). As Anderson J.A. also noted in that same case, if true equality between male and female persons is to be achieved, we cannot ignore the threat to equality resulting from exposure to audiences of certain types of violent and degrading material. Materials portraying women as a class as objects for sexual exploitation and abuse have a negative impact on "the individual's sense of self-worth and acceptance".

In reaching the conclusion that legislation proscribing obscenity is a valid objective which justifies some encroachment on the right to freedom of expression, I am persuaded in part that such legislation may be found in most free and democratic societies. . . .

The advent of the *Charter* did not have the effect of dramatically depriving Parliament of a power which it has historically enjoyed. It is also noteworthy that the criminalization of obscenity was considered to be compatible with the *Canadian Bill of Rights*. As Dickson J.A. stated in *R. v. Prairie Schooner News Ltd.* [(1970), 75 W.W.R. 585, 604]. . .:

> Freedom of speech is not unfettered either in criminal law or civil law. The *Canadian Bill of Rights* was intended to protect, and does protect, basic freedoms of vital importance to all Canadians. It does not serve as a shield behind which obscene matter may be disseminated without concern for criminal consequences. The interdiction of the publications which are the subject of the present charges in no way trenches upon the freedom of expression which the *Canadian Bill of Rights* assures.

The enactment of the impugned provision is also consistent with Canada's international obligations (*Agreement for the Suppression of the Circulation of Obscene Publications* and the *Convention for the Suppression of the Circulation of and Traffic in Obscene Publications*).

Finally, it should be noted that the burgeoning pornography industry renders the concern even more pressing and substantial than when the impugned provisions were first enacted. I would therefore conclude that the objective of avoiding the harm associated with the dissemination of pornography in this case is sufficiently pressing and substantial to warrant some restriction on full exercise of the right to freedom of expression. The analysis of whether the measure is proportional to the objective must, in my view, be undertaken in light of the conclusion that the objective of the impugned section is valid only insofar as it relates to the harm to society associated with obscene materials. Indeed, the section as interpreted in previous decisions and in these reasons is fully consistent with that objective. The objective of maintaining conventional standards of propriety, independently of any harm to society, is no longer justified in light of the values of individual liberty which underlie the *Charter*. This, then, being the objective of s. 163, which I have found to be pressing and substantial, I must now determine whether the section is rationally connected and proportional to this objective. As outlined above, s. 163(8) criminalizes the exploitation of sex and sex and violence, when, on the basis of the community test, it is undue. The determination of when such exploitation is undue is directly related to the immediacy of a risk of harm to society which is reasonably perceived as arising from its dissemination. . . .

The proportionality requirement has three aspects:

(1) the existence of a rational connection between the impugned measures and the objective;

(2) minimal impairment of the right or freedom; and

(3) a proper balance between the effects of the limiting measures and the legislative objective.

In assessing whether the proportionality test is met, it is important to keep in mind the nature of expression which has been infringed. In the *Prostitution Reference*, *supra*, Dickson C.J. wrote. . .:

> When a *Charter* freedom has been infringed by state action that takes the form of criminalization, the Crown bears the heavy burden of justifying that infringement. Yet, the expressive activity, as with any infringed *Charter* right, should also be analysed in the particular context of the case. Here, the activity to which the impugned legislation is directed is expression with an economic purpose. It can hardly be said that communications regarding an economic transaction of sex for money lie at, or even near, the core of the guarantee of freedom of expression. [At. p. 1136.]

The values which underlie the protection of freedom of expression relate to the search for truth, participation in the political process, and individual self-fulfilment. The Attorney General for Ontario argues that of these, only "individual self-fulfilment", and only in its most base aspect, that of physical arousal, is engaged by pornography. On the other hand, the civil liberties groups argue that pornography forces us to question conventional notions of sexuality and thereby launches us into an inherently political discourse. In their factum, the British Columbia Civil Liberties Association adopts a passage from R. West, "The Feminist-Conservative Anti-Pornography Alliance and the 1986 Attorney General's Commission on Pornography Report" (1987), 4 *Am. Bar Found. Res. J.* 681, at p. 696:

> Good pornography has value because it validates women's will to pleasure. It celebrates female nature. It validates a range of female sexuality that is wider and truer than that legitimated by the non-pornographic culture. Pornography (when it is good) celebrates both female pleasure and male rationality.

A proper application of the test should not suppress what West refers to as "good pornography". The objective of the impugned provision is not to inhibit the celebration of human sexuality. However, it cannot be ignored that the realities of the pornography industry are far from the picture which the British Columbia Civil Liberties Association would have us paint. Shannon J., in *R. v. Wagner*, [(1985), 43 C.R. (3d) 318] described the materials more accurately when he observed. . .:

> Women, particularly, are deprived of unique human character or identity and are depicted as sexual playthings, hysterically and instantly responsive to male sexual demands. They worship male genitals and their own value depends upon the quality of their genitals and breasts. [At p. 331.]

In my view, the kind of expression which is sought to be advanced does not stand on equal footing with other kinds of expression which directly engage the "core" of the freedom of expression values.

This conclusion is further buttressed by the fact that the targeted material is expression which is motivated, in the overwhelming majority of cases, by economic profit. This Court held in *Rocket v. Royal College of Dental Surgeons of Ontario*, [1990] 2 S.C.R. 232, at p. 247, that an economic motive for expression means that restrictions on the expression might "be easier to justify than other infringements".

I will now turn to an examination of the three basic aspects of the proportionality test. . . .

The message of obscenity which degrades and dehumanizes is analogous to that of hate propaganda. As the Attorney General for Ontario has argued in its factum, obscenity wields the power to wreak social damage in that a significant portion of the population is humiliated by its gross misrepresentations.

Accordingly, the rational link between s. 163 and the objective of Parliament relates to the actual causal relationship between obscenity and the risk of harm to society at large. On this point, it is clear that the literature of the social sciences remains subject to controversy. In *Fringe Product Inc.*, *supra*, Charron Dist. Ct. J. considered numerous written reports and works and heard six days of testimony from experts who endeavoured to describe the status of the social sciences with respect to the study of the effects of pornography. Charron Dist. Ct. J. reached the conclusion that the relationship between pornography and harm was sufficient to justify Parliament's intervention. This conclusion is not supported unanimously.

The recent conclusions of the Fraser Report, *supra*, could not postulate any causal relationship between pornography and the commission of violent crimes, the sexual abuse of children, or the disintegration of communities and society. This is in contrast to the findings of the MacGuigan Report, *supra*.

While a direct link between obscenity and harm to society may be difficult, if not impossible, to establish, it is reasonable to presume that exposure to images bears a causal relationship to changes in attitudes and beliefs. The Meese Commission Report, *supra*, concluded in respect of sexually violent material. . .:

> . . .the available evidence strongly supports the hypothesis that substantial

> exposure to sexually violent materials as described here bears a causal relationship to antisocial acts of sexual violence and, for some subgroups, possibly to unlawful acts of sexual violence.
>
> Although we rely for this conclusion on significant scientific empirical evidence, we feel it worthwhile to note the underlying logic of the conclusion. The evidence says simply that the images that people are exposed to bear a causal relationship to their behavior. This is hardly surprising. What would be surprising would be to find otherwise, and we have not so found. We have not, of course, found that the images people are exposed to are a greater cause of sexual violence than all or even many other possible causes the investigation of which has been beyond our mandate. Nevertheless, it would be strange indeed if graphic representations of a form of behavior, especially in a form that almost exclusively portrays such behavior as desirable, did not have at least some effect on patterns of behavior. [vol. 1, at p. 326.]

[I]n *Keegstra*, *supra*, the absence of proof of a causative link between hate propaganda and hatred of an identifiable group was discounted as a determinative factor in assessing the constitutionality of the hate literature provisions of the *Criminal Code*. Dickson C.J. stated. . .:

> First, to predicate the limitation of free expression upon proof of actual hatred gives insufficient attention to the severe psychological trauma suffered by members of those identifiable groups targeted by hate propaganda. Second, it is clearly difficult to prove a causative link between a specific statement and hatred of an identifiable group. [At p. 776.]

McLachlin J. (dissenting) expressed it as follows. . .:

> To view hate propaganda as "victimless" in the absence of any proof that it moved its listeners to hatred is to discount the wrenching impact that it may have on members of the target group themselves. . . .Moreover, it is simply not possible to assess with any precision the effects that expression of a particular message will have on all those who are ultimately exposed to it. [At p. 857.]

The American approach on the necessity of a causal link between obscenity and harm to society was set out by Burger C.J. in *Paris Adult Theatre I v. Slaton*, 413 U.S. 49 (1972). . .:

> Although there is no conclusive proof of a connection between antisocial behavior and obscene material, the legislature. . .could quite reasonably determine that such a connection does or might exist. [At pp. 60-61.]

I am in agreement with Twaddle J.A. who expressed the view that Parliament was entitled to have a "reasoned apprehension of harm" resulting from the desensitization of individuals exposed to materials which depict violence, cruelty, and dehumanization in sexual relations.

Accordingly, I am of the view that there is a sufficiently rational link between the criminal sanction, which demonstrates our community's disapproval of the dissemination of materials which potentially victimize women and which restricts the negative influence which such materials have on changes in attitudes and behaviour, and the objective.

Finally, I wish to distinguish this case from *Keegstra*, in which the minority adopted the view that there was no rational connection between the criminalization of hate propaganda and its suppression. As McLachlin J. noted, prosecutions under the *Criminal Code* for racist expression have attracted extensive media coverage. The criminal process confers on the accused publicity for his or her causes and succeeds even in generating sympathy. The same cannot be said of the kinds of expression sought to be suppressed in the present case. The general availability of the subject materials and the rampant pornography industry are such that, in the words of Dickson C.J. in *Keegstra*, "pornography is not dignified by its suppression". In contrast to the hate-monger who may succeed, by the sudden media attention, in gaining an audience, the prohibition of obscene materials does nothing to promote the pornographer's cause. . . .

In determining whether less intrusive legislation may be imagined, this Court stressed in the *Prostitution Reference*, *supra*, that it is not necessary that the legislative scheme be the "perfect" scheme, but that it be appropriately tailored *in the context of the infringed right* (at p. 1138). . . .

There are several factors which contribute to the finding that the provision minimally impairs the freedom which is infringed.

First, the impugned provision does not proscribe sexually explicit erotica without violence that is not degrading or dehumanizing. It is designed to catch material that creates a risk of harm to society. It might be suggested that proof of actual harm should be required. It is apparent from what I have said above that it is sufficient in this regard for Parliament to have a reasonable basis for concluding that harm will result and this requirement does not demand actual proof of harm.

Second, materials which have scientific, artistic or literary merit are not captured by the provision. As discussed above, the court must be generous in its application of the "artistic defence". For example, in certain cases, materials such as photographs, prints, books and films which may undoubtedly be produced with some motive for economic profit, may nonetheless claim the protection of the *Charter* insofar as their defining characteristic is that of aesthetic expression, and thus represent the artist's attempt at individual fulfilment. The existence of an accompanying economic motive does not, of itself, deprive a work of significance as an example of individual artistic or self-fulfilment.

Third, in considering whether the provision minimally impairs the freedom in question, it is legitimate for the court to take into account Parliament's past abortive attempts to replace the definition with one that is more explicit. . . .The attempt to provide exhaustive instances of obscenity has been shown to be destined to fail . . . .It seems that the only practicable alternative is to strive towards a more abstract definition of obscenity which is contextually sensitive and responsive to progress in the knowledge and understanding of the phenomenon to which the legislation is directed. In my view, the standard of "undue exploitation" is therefore appropriate. The intractable nature of the problem and the impossibility of precisely defining a notion which is inherently elusive makes the possibility of a more explicit provision remote. In this light, it is appropriate to question whether, and at what cost, greater legislative precision can be demanded.

Fourth, while the discussion in this appeal has been limited to the definition portion of s. 163, I would note that the impugned section, with the possible exception of subs. 1, which is not in issue here, has been held by this Court not to extend its reach to the private use or viewing of obscene materials. . . .

Accordingly, it is only the public distribution and exhibition of obscene materials which is in issue here.

Finally, I wish to address the arguments of the interveners, Canadian Civil Liberties Association and Manitoba Association for Rights and Liberties, that the objectives of this kind of legislation may be met by alternative, less intrusive measures. First, it is submitted that reasonable time, manner and place restrictions would be preferable to outright prohibition. I am of the view that this argument should be rejected. Once it has been established that the objective is the avoidance of harm caused by the degradation which many women feel as "victims" of the message of obscenity, and of the negative impact exposure to such material has on perceptions and attitudes towards women, it is untenable to argue that these harms could be avoided by placing restrictions on access to such material. Making the materials more difficult to obtain by increasing their cost and reducing their availability does not achieve the same objective. Once Parliament has reasonably concluded that certain acts are harmful to certain groups in society and to society in general, it would be inconsistent, if not hypocritical, to argue that such acts could be committed in more restrictive conditions. The harm sought to be avoided would remain the same in either case.

It is also submitted that there are more effective techniques to promote the objectives of Parliament. For example, if pornography is seen as encouraging violence against women, there are certain activities which discourage it—counselling rape victims to charge their assailants, provision of shelter and assistance for battered women, campaigns for laws against discrimination on the grounds of sex, education to increase the sensitivity of law enforcement agencies and other governmental authorities. In addition, it is submitted that education is an under-used response.

It is noteworthy that many of the above suggested alternatives are in the form of *responses* to the harm engendered by negative attitudes against women. The role of the impugned provision is to control the dissemination of the very images that contribute to such attitudes. Moreover, it is true that there are additional measures which could alleviate the problem of violence against women. However, given the gravity of the harm, and the threat to the values at stake, I do not believe that the measure chosen by Parliament is equalled by the alternatives which have been suggested. Education, too, may offer a means of combating negative attitudes to women, just as it is currently used as a means of addressing other problems dealt with in the *Code*. However, there is no reason to rely on education alone. It should be emphasized that this is in no way intended to deny the value of other educational and counselling measures to deal with the roots and effects of negative attitudes. Rather, it is only to stress the arbitrariness and unacceptability of the claim that such measures represent the sole legitimate means of addressing the phenomenon. Serious social problems such as violence against women require multi-pronged approaches by government. Education and legislation are not alternatives but complements in addressing such problems. There is nothing in the *Char-*

ter which requires Parliament to choose between such complementary measures. . . .

The final question to be answered in the proportionality test is whether the effects of the law so severely trench on a protected right that the legislative objective is outweighed by the infringement. The infringement on freedom of expression is confined to a measure designed to prohibit the distribution of sexually explicit materials accompanied by violence, and those without violence that are degrading or dehumanizing. As I have already concluded, this kind of expression lies far from the core of the guarantee of freedom of expression. It appeals only to the most base aspect of individual fulfilment, and it is primarily economically motivated.

The objective of the legislation, on the other hand, is of fundamental importance in a free and democratic society. It is aimed at avoiding harm, which Parliament has reasonably concluded will be caused directly or indirectly, to individuals, groups such as women and children, and consequently to society as a whole, by the distribution of these materials. It thus seeks to enhance respect for all members of society, and non-violence and equality in their relations with each other.

I therefore conclude that the restriction on freedom of expression does not outweigh the importance of the legislative objective. . . .

I conclude that while s. 163(8) infringes s. 2(*b*) of the *Charter*, freedom of expression, it constitutes a reasonable limit and is saved by virtue of the provisions of s. 1. . . .

Gonthier, Justice. I have had the benefit of the reasons of Justice Sopinka and, while I agree both with his disposition of the case and with his reasons generally, I wish to add to them with respect to the judicial interpretation of s. 163. . .and to its constitutional validity. . . .

Section 163 of the *Code* offers a peculiar structure. Its subject matter, obscene materials, comprises the dual elements of representation and content. Representation here is understood in the sense of public suggestion. A representation is a portrayal, a description meant to evoke something to the mind and senses. Furthermore, in the context of s. 163 of the *Code*, one deals with representations to the public in general, without restriction, as will be explained below. Hence the *Oxford English Dictionary* (2nd ed.) defines "to represent" as "to bring clearly and distinctly before the mind" and "representation" as "the action or fact of exhibiting in some visible image or form". The element of representation in s. 163 of the *Code* is therefore a suggestion, a depiction to the public. By "content" I mean of course the content of the representation.

It is the combination of the two, the representation and its content, that attracts criminal liability. A representation as such is not enough, of course, to create the subject matter of s. 163, but neither is an act included in the content of s. 163 of the *Code*, without an element of representation.

It is indeed important to emphasize that the *Criminal Code* is grounded on the principles of sexual freedom between consenting adults, and of criminal liability for sexual relations between adults and minors (young persons between the age of 14 and 17 being in a special position). Offences such as sexual assault. . ., sexual interference. . ., sexual exploitation. . .or incest between an adult and a minor. . .are corollaries of these basic principles. Aside from them, few offences related to sexual practices exist: incest between adults. . ., anal intercourse when more than two persons are present. . ., bestiality. . .and necrophilia . . . .

Yet obscenity is not limited to the acts described above. Irrespective of the construction given to s. 163(8), a surface glance at its wording makes this obvious. The acts listed in the above paragraph might perhaps be included in the phrase "sex and. . .crime, horror, cruelty and violence" found in s. 163(8) of the *Code*. They certainly do not exhaust the meaning of this phrase, and s. 163(8) comprises in addition the phrase "undue exploitation of sex", which is central to this case. Hence the content of obscenity exceeds the acts prohibited in the *Code*.

This difference in content stems from the element of representation found in s. 163 of the *Code*. Parliament ascribed a broader content to obscenity because it involves a representation. In this combination of a given content and its representation lies the particular essence of obscenity, as was mentioned above. . . .

Without launching into a lengthy debate on the reasons why Parliament may have enacted s. 163 of the *Code*. . ., it can be seen that the combination of representation and content that constitutes obscenity leads to many ills. Obscene materials (I will not for reasons explained later differentiate between obscenity and pornography) convey a distorted image of human sexuality, by making public and open elements of the human nature which are usually hidden behind a veil of modesty and privacy. D.A. Downs, *The New Politics of Pornography* (1989), aptly describes how these materials do not reflect the richness of human sexuality, but rather turn it into pure animality, at p. 183:

> . . .the deeper objection to sheer pornography or obscenity. . .is that it represents a retreat from the human dilemma and the responsibility of acknowledging the tensions in our nature. Sheer pornography also reduces us to the lower aspects of our natures by stripping away the modesty that arises from our encounter with our animality.

This distorted image of human sexuality often comprises violence, cruelty, infliction of pain, humiliation, among other elements of the pornographic imagery. Not only are these materials often evidence of the commission of reprehensible actions in their making, but their representation conjures the possibility of behavioural influences. In a marketplace of ideas, to use that classic metaphor, pornographic imagery is there for the taking, and it finds without any doubt many takers. Attitudinal changes in these takers, because of exposure to pornographic materials, may lead to abuse and harm. As the Special Committee on Pornography and Prostitution concluded in its report entitled *Pornography and Prostitution in Canada* (1985) (the "Fraser Report"), at p. 103:

> . . .there are magazines, films and videos produced solely for the purpose of entertainment whose depiction of women in particular, but also, in some cases, men and young people, demeans them, perpetuates lies about aspects of their humanity and denies the validity of their aspirations to be treated as full and equal citizens within the community.

These conclusions echoed those of the Standing Committee on Justice and Legal Affairs, in its *Report on Pornography* (1978). . . .

Section 163(8) is the key to the identification of these materials. In the course of his reasons, Sopinka J. outlines the three tests that have been judicially developed for the application of s. 163(8), that is the "community standard of tolerance", "degradation or dehumanization" and "internal necessities" tests. . . .Sopinka J. essentially aligns the definition of obscenity in s. 163(8) of the *Code* with the definition of pornography nowadays. He introduces a three-part categorization that has surfaced in contemporary theory, and that had been adopted in some Canadian cases throughout the 80s:

(a) Explicit sex with violence, which generally constitutes "undue exploitation of sex" within the meaning of s. 163(8) of the *Code*, on the basis of demonstrable harm;

(b) Explicit sex that is degrading or dehumanizing, which will be "undue exploitation of sex" if it creates a substantial risk of harm; the risk of harm can be assessed with reference to the tolerance of the community, under the "community standard of tolerance" test; and

(c) Explicit sex that is neither violent nor degrading or dehumanizing, which will not generally fall under s. 163(8) of the *Code*, according to Sopinka J.

I must say at the outset that I differ only with respect to the third category of materials. I am not prepared to affirm as boldly as my colleague Sopinka J. does that it escapes the application of s. 163(8). . . .

The dual nature, as representation and content, of the subject matter of s. 163 comes into play here. Yet the classification proposed by my colleague Sopinka J. focuses only on content. The content of the first two categories of materials is so likely to harm that the characteristics of the representation do not really matter: if there is violence or degradation or dehumanization, as long as the element of representation is present, harm will probably ensue.

The content of the third category of materials is generally perceived as unlikely to cause harm, as Sopinka J. rightly points out. He mentions as an exception child pornography, i.e. materials in the production of which children were employed. This exception is important, since it obviously flows from the high likelihood of harm ensuing from the production and dissemination of child pornography.

In addition to this exception, it is quite conceivable that the representation may cause harm, even if its content as such may not be seen as harmful. . . .

The manner of representation, of public suggestion, can greatly contribute to the deformation of sexuality, through the loss of its humanity. Even if the content is not as such objectionable (and, I would say, even more so), the manner in which the material is presented may turn it from innocuous to socially harmful. After all, it is the element of representation that gives this material its power of suggestion, and it seems quite conceivable that this power may cause harm despite the apparent neutrality of the content. A host of factors could intervene in the manner of representation to affect the characterization of the material, among which are the medium, the type or the use.

The medium provides a good example. Indeed the differences between the various media are not acknowledged often enough in opinions dealing with s. 163 of the *Code*. This Court, in *Hawkshaw v. The Queen*, [1986] 1 S.C.R.

668, has decided that the definition of obscenity in s. 163(8) of the *Code* applies throughout the *Code*, whether the material is a publication or not, but that does not preclude s. 163(8) from taking into account the medium of representation. Statements are made regarding the law of obscenity where a movie is impugned, for instance, and it is often taken for granted that they will apply to all media.

Nevertheless it seems natural to me that the likelihood of harm, and the tolerance of the community, may vary according to the medium of representation, even if the content stays the same. Let me take, as an example, an explicit portrayal of "plain" sexual intercourse, where two individuals are making love. This falls within the third category of Sopinka J. If found in words in a book, it is unlikely to be of much concern (if found in a children's book, though, this may be different). If found depicted in a magazine or in a movie, the likelihood of harm increases but remains low. If found on a poster, it is already more troublesome. If found on a billboard sign, then I would venture that it may well be an undue exploitation of sex, because the community does not tolerate it, on the basis of its harmfulness.

The harmfulness, in the billboard sign example, would come from the immediacy of the representation, inasmuch as the sign stands all by itself (as opposed to a passage in a book, a film or a magazine). Its message is at once crude and inescapable. It distorts human sexuality by taking it out of any context whatsoever and projecting it to the public. This example goes to the extreme, of course, but it is meant to show that the element of representation may create a likelihood of harm that may lead to the application of s. 163 of the *Code*, even if the content of the representation as such is not objectionable.

As I mentioned, the medium of representation is but one variable pertaining to representation that may trigger the application of s. 163 to third-category materials. The overall type or use of the representation, be it education, art, advertising, sexual arousal or other, may also be relevant, among other factors. These factors tie in to the "internal necessities" test to some extent. This test, if it is to find a place within the interpretive framework of Sopinka J., must intervene at the representational level, to change the characterization that would ensue from a mere look at the content of the materials.

For these reasons, therefore, I would hold that materials falling within Sopinka J.'s third category (explicit sex with neither violence nor degradation or dehumanization), while generally less likely to cause harm than those of the first two categories, may nevertheless come within the definition of obscene at s. 163(8) of the *Code*, if their content (child pornography) or their representational element (the manner of representation) is found conducive of harm. . . .

The assessment of the risk of harm here depends on the tolerance of the community, as is the case with the second category of materials. This brings me to outline a certain shift in the meaning of "tolerance". . . .It seems that tolerance is for taste the conceptual equivalent of the reasonable person to the actual plaintiff: an abstraction, an average perhaps. Tolerance would be some form of enlightened, altruistic taste, which would factor in and sum up the tastes of the whole population. . . .

Sopinka J. uses the community standard of tolerance to gauge the risk of harm. In this context, tolerance must be related to the harm. It must mean not only tolerance of the materials, but also tolerance of the harm which they may bring about. It is a more complicated and more reflective form of tolerance . . . .Such a development is fully in accordance with the emphasis put by this Court on harm as the central element in the interpretation of s. 163(8).

In the context of the third category, the harm sought to be avoided is the same as in the first two categories, that is attitudinal changes. While this type of harm was clear in the case of the first category and was probable in the case of the second, it is perhaps more remote here, and will likely occur only in a limited number of cases. The main difference between the second and third categories lies in the presumed likelihood of harm: while degrading or dehumanizing materials are likely to cause harm regardless of whether the community may be ready to tolerate such harm, materials which show no violence, no degradation or dehumanization are less likely to cause harm, and the evidence with respect to the lack of tolerance of the community will be central. Still the risk of harm flowing from the content or the representational element of third-category materials is not always so slight as my colleague Sopinka J. pictures it. If the community cannot tolerate this risk of harm, then in my opinion these materials, even though they may offer a non-violent, non-degrading, non-dehumanizing content, will constitute undue exploitation of sex and will fall under the definition of obscenity at s. 163(8) of the *Code*. . . .

With respect to the constitutional aspects of this case, I am in agreement with Sopinka J., and I wish only to complement his reasons on the objective of s. 163 of the *Code*. . . .

Notes and Question

1. *Comparative Free Speech/Comparative Equality*. Before 1982, the Canadian Constitution did not contain a provision explicitly protecting freedom of speech. In 1982, the Constitution was amended to include a Charter of Rights and Freedoms, which expressly provides protection for "freedom of thought, belief, opinion, and expression, including freedom of the press and other media of communication." Can. Const. (Constitution Act, 1982), pt. I (Canadian Charter of Rights and Freedoms), § 2(*b*). Unlike the First Amendment to the U.S. Constitution, the Canadian protection is subject to another constitutional provision; section 1 of the Charter provides that:

> The *Canadian Charter of Rights and Freedoms* guarantees the rights and freedoms set out in it subject only to such reasonable limits prescribed by law as can be demonstrably justified in a free and democratic society.

Relevant to the question about governmental prohibition of pornography is how section 1 is interpreted in light of section 15 of the Charter, which provides

> (1) Every individual is equal before and under the law and has the right to the equal protection and equal benefit of the law without discrimination and, in particular, without discrimination based on race, national or ethnic origin, colour, religion, sex, age or mental or physical disability.

and section 28 of the Charter, which provides

> Notwithstanding anything in this Charter, the rights and freedoms referred to in it are guaranteed equally to male and female persons.

Kathleen Mahoney, who was counsel for the Women's Legal Education and Action Fund [LEAF] in its intervention at the Supreme Court of Canada in *Butler*, describes how the Canadian Constitutional provisions provide a different basis for analysis than that presently found in U.S. First Amendment jurisprudence. Kathleen Mahoney, The Canadian Constitutional Approach to Freedom of Expression in Hate Propaganda and Pornography, 55 Law & Contemp. Probs. 77, 77 n.* (Winter 1992).

> Section 1 of the Charter is the central, preeminent provision. . . .This is an unusual section if one compares it with other national or international rights-protecting instruments. . . .The presence of section 1 in the Charter requires the analysis to be split into two distinct stages. The first stage requires a court to determine the scope and content of the right and decide whether the right has been breached. In the second stage, the court determines whether any limitation on the right can be justified in the context of the free and democratic society of Canada. This double function embodies the idea that constitutional rights in the Charter are not absolute. . . .
>
> Canada's departure from American free speech doctrine is clear. Under the first amendment, social reality is not considered when legislation regulating extremist speech is challenged. This is a critical difference from the Canadian practice because, depending on the facts of the case, a contextual analysis can result in a right or freedom having a different value. . . .[The Canadian courts] demonstrate[ ] a firm acceptance of the view that equality is a positive right, that the Charter's equality provision has a large remedial component, and that legislatures should take positive measures to improve the status of disadvantaged groups. . . .
>
> [S]ection 15 read with section 28 guarantees women equal access to equality rights. Constitutional equality is concerned with eliminating the disadvantage of historically subordinated groups. This means that the Charter is not neutral on practices that promote inequality, but rather has a commitment to ending them.

Id. 78-79, 89, 94.

What is lacking in the *Butler* court's analysis of how pornography degrades and dehumanizes women? In answering this question, consider Patricia Hill Collins, *Black Feminist Thought: Knowledge, Consciousness, and the Politics of Empowerment*, at p. 597.

2. *Butler's Aftermath*. It is too early to evaluate the impact of the *Butler* decision on pornography in Canada. A recent article on legal developments concerning pornography reported that:

> In Canada. . .police raided Toronto's lesbian and gay bookstore Glad Day Bookshop on the heels of the *Butler* decision and confiscated the lesbian magazine *Bad Attitude*. The bookshop fought the confiscation in court, but lost in the end when one story in the magazine—a rape fantasy—was deemed illegal.
>
> [Kathleen] Mahoney maintains that discriminatory law enforcement, not *Butler*, is responsible for the confiscation of lesbian erotica. "There has been

> a homophobic response to this material since time immemorial," she says. The ACLU acknowledges that confiscation of sexually explicit materials by Canadian Customs without due process or judicial determinations of obscenity was commonplace long before the Supreme Court decision, yet notes an increase since *Butler*. Bruce Walsh, a member of Censorstop—a Canadian coalition which is fighting censorship and *Butler*—asserts that the incidence of Customs seizures "has increased a thousand-fold" since the ruling. Whereas in the past lesbians and gays were targeted as a vulnerable minority, now, according to Walsh "about half of Canada's bookstores have been harassed" as "Customs has gone after political dissidents" in general.

Ellen Levy, She Just Doesn't Understand: The Feminist Face-Off on Pornography Legislation, On the Issues, Fall 1993, at 17, 20.

3. *Federal Developments*. In 1992, the Senate Judiciary Committee referred to the full Senate the Pornography Victims' Compensation Act of 1992. S. 1521, 102d Cong., 2d Sess. (1991). It died on the Senate floor in 1992 without coming up for a vote. The act was similar to the Indianapolis ordinance in that it provided a civil cause of action to recover damages by victims of assault caused by pornography. Unlike the ordinance, however, it covered only child pornography and obscene materials, it allowed recovery by victims only against a pornographer who had been convicted of criminal obscenity or child pornography law violations for the material alleged to have been a substantial cause of the sexual offense, and it allowed recovery only by victims of sexual crimes for which the perpetrator had been convicted.

Index

References are to pages